THE DIPLOMACY

of

IMPERIALISM

1890-1902

WILLIAM L. LANGER

HARVARD UNIVERSITY

SECOND EDITION

WITH SUPPLEMENTARY BIBLIOGRAPHIES

NEW YORK: ALFRED·A·KNOPF

1951

To my Wife

Preface to the Second Edition

ℯ

THIS STUDY OF INTERNATIONAL DIPLOMACY IN THE PERIOD OF LATE Victorian imperialism was designed, as noted in the preface of the original edition, as a continuation of my earlier work on the *European Alliances and Alignments* of the Bismarckian period. Like its predecessor and companion. it is now being republished. without textual change, but with supplementary bibliographical notes covering the literature on the subject since 1935. Since I have explained, in the foreword of the new edition of the *European Alliances,* why I consider it not only impracticable but also unprofitable to undertake the vast labor of thoroughly revising these works, it is scarcely necessary to re-state my reasons here. A few remarks touching the different problems presented by the republication of the two books will suffice for the purposes of this new preface.

In point of recent historical scholarship the period here treated is hardly comparable to the earlier, Bismarckian period. Since 1935 no major collection of documents has been published, excepting only the volumes of the *Documents diplomatiques français* for the years 1890–1894; nor have any basic biographies, like Lady Cecil's *Life of Lord Salisbury* or J. L. Garvin's *Life of Joseph Chamberlain,* seen the light. Furthermore, the chief European archives have remained closed to scholars for the years after 1885, save only the Austrian (open to 1895) and to a slight extent the German. In short, but few additional sources of fundamental importance have become available to the historian during the past fifteen years. It is perfectly understandable, therefore, that for the last decade of the nineteenth century there has been nothing like the intensive research or the impressive outpouring of monographic literature so marked with respect to the preceding twenty years of history.

Of course I do not intend to imply that there has not been valuable historical work done on a number of problems treated in this study. For example, Soviet scholars have published a number of monographs, particularly on the Far East, of which several adduce evidence from the unpublished Russian archives. In the same connection it may be remarked that in recent years Chinese and to some extent Japanese sources of great interest to the student of diplomatic history have appeared in print. As yet another illustration it may be noted that the Italian-Ethiopian conflict of 1935–1936 led to extensive historical investigations by Italian scholars, many of whom were permitted to draw upon materials from the tightly closed Italian archives. And finally, full recognition is due various writers who, with or without the use of new materials, have re-examined special problems and have contributed materially to our knowledge and understanding of them. Arthur J. Marder's *The Anatomy of British Sea Power* is a case in point, being an exhaustive and profound analysis of a relatively neglected but all-important aspect of international relations at the turn of the century.

Considering that the present work is devoted to world politics rather than to merely European problems, the range of historical literature to be covered is naturally very extensive. On the other hand, much of this writing is looser in character and less technical than the literature of the preceding period. I have therefore often been at a loss as to what to select and what to omit. In general I have tended to be inclusive rather than exclusive. I have aimed to provide as generous a coverage as is humanly possible and I doubt if many items of importance have escaped me. I should say, however, that untranslated Chinese and Japanese works have not been individually listed. They are, I regret to say, beyond my linguistic capabilities and I suspect the same to be true of most of my readers. Those more particularly interested in Oriental materials will find most of them listed in Robert J. Kerner's excellent *Northeastern Asia: A Selected Bibliography* (Berkeley, 1939) and, in the case of Chinese sources and writings, analytically reviewed in John K. Fairbank's and Kwang-Ching Liu's forthcoming *Modern China: A Bibliographical Guide to Chinese Works, 1898–1937* (Cambridge, 1950).

In working on the Supplementary Bibliographical Notes I have been much troubled by the fact that the major problems covered by the book extend over several chapters and that relatively few of the writings analyzed fit snugly into my particular scheme. The only way to resolve the difficulty would have been to repeat a considerable number of titles many times. But this appeared to me a waste of time and effort. I have therefore held the repetition of titles to a minimum, and simply directed the reader to the other chapter bibliographies where kindred material may be found.

I believe I can honestly say that, since the original publication of this book, no other work has appeared in any language that covers the ground in the same manner or on the same scale. As a comprehensive treatment of international relations in this critical and crowded period, it still stands alone. It was widely reviewed and discussed when it first appeared and I can only conclude from its continued lively sale throughout the world that it has, over the years, served a useful purpose. I am therefore grateful to have it republished and have willingly undertaken the not insignificant task of providing the bibliographical data for the past fifteen years. The great majority of the books and articles listed are to be found in the Harvard College Library and I frankly do not see how this project could have been carried through without access to those rich collections. But at best much of such work is sheer drudgery and I gladly take this occasion to thank my wife for the unstinting help she has given me in carrying it through to completion.

Preface

❧

IN THE PRESENT STUDY I HAVE UNDERTAKEN TO CARRY FURTHER THE TREAT-
ment of European diplomacy which I began with my *European Alliances
and Alignments, 1871–1890* (New York: Alfred A. Knopf; 1931). There
are, however, important differences between the two works. During the Bismarckian period European international relations were predominantly continental in character. They centred very obviously upon the work of that great
master of statecraft, the German chancellor, and it would, therefore, be quite
correct to entitle the history of those years *The Bismarckian System,* or *The
Hegemony of Germany.* But with the great chancellor's fall in 1890 all that was
changed. The young Emperor's refusal to renew the famous Reinsurance Treaty
with Russia knocked the keystone from the European alliance structure. It restored to Russia a liberty of action which she did not want and paved the way
to the conclusion of the Franco-Russian Alliance. With the consummation of
that grouping in 1894 a new era in European diplomacy may be said to have
begun, for the new combination broke the preponderance of Germany and re-
established something like a balance of power on the Continent.

With two groups of powers fairly matched, the old European issues were
reduced to a deadlock. This fact, together with the growing economic pressure
and the increasing competition for markets, stimulated and facilitated that outburst of overseas expansion which we call *imperialism.* The interests and the
energies of most of the great powers were devoted to problems which touched
the ends of the earth. They carried with them into the colonial field their traditional European rivalries, but the exigencies of the situation often forced them
to modify time-honored policies. Had the focal point of international relations
continued to be the Continent, England might well have acted as the fulcrum
of the balance between the two rival combinations. As it was, she tended to become the object of attack for both groupings, for much of the globe was an
English preserve and the British were not backward in advancing claims to
such regions as were still unappropriated. I have therefore been obliged to make
a special study of late-Victorian imperialism as a movement, to examine in some
detail the maritime supremacy which made England and the Empire almost
unassailable, and to analyze the course of navalism in the other countries, the
more so as it was inextricably bound up with projects for a continental league
and with other hostile designs. Much of the history of these years hinges upon

British policy and so I have laid particular stress upon that aspect of the general problem. In a very real sense, then, this work is much broader in scope, much more a history of world policy than was the preceding study of the Alliances.

It stands to reason that the triumph of imperialism did not involve the complete neglect of the old European problems. I have gone over the history of the making of the Franco-Russian Alliance in rather cursory fashion, devoting only two chapters to it. In view of the very detailed study of the years 1890–1894 which I have published in my book *The Franco-Russian Alliance* (Cambridge: Harvard University Press; 1929), it seemed to me quite superfluous to go over the same ground in a microscopic way. I have therefore contented myself with giving an abstract of that earlier work, bringing the story up to date by drawing upon source material published in the last five years. The Lamsdorff diary is far more important than other sources of recent appearance, for it gives us, for the first time, an authentic and detailed account of Russian policy in those years. I am very happy to have been able to incorporate this material in the first two chapters. For the rest I have not neglected the history of the major European problems, of which the Near Eastern question was by far the most acute and the most dangerous. In the eighties Europe was kept on tenterhooks by the Bulgarian problem. In the following decade it was the Armenian question that threatened to precipitate a general conflagration. I find that few questions of recent history are more generally misunderstood than the so-called Armenian massacres. By the use of Armenian material I believe I have been able to give for the first time, in any language, a reasoned account of the Armenian revolutionary movement and thereby to place the whole Near Eastern question in a clearer light. To a lesser extent the same remarks apply to the Cretan and Macedonian movements, for the treatment of which I have had the use of Serbian and Bulgarian material hitherto not generally known. For the whole history of the Near Eastern crisis I have made extensive use of Russian materials recently published which, to my knowledge, have not been exploited by any Western writer.

The great imperial problems of these years were the Egyptian-Sudan question, the south African embroglio, and the Far Eastern crisis. All of these I have dealt with in detail, making very extensive use throughout of contemporary writings in newspapers and periodicals. I have exploited the English press in particular, not only because British policy was crucial in all these problems, but because the English journals were infinitely better informed and much more illuminating than those of any other country. Anyone who has worked with the periodical literature of the period will be ready to endorse this statement. It goes without saying that I have made the fullest use of contemporary Blue Books, Yellow Books, and other official publications, as well as of the great source collections published since the end of the World War. In the case of the south African problem I have been fortunate in having the *Milner Papers* and the third volume of Garvin's *Chamberlain* at my disposal, while my approach to the fascinating Nile problem has enabled me, I believe, to give a somewhat novel interpretation to the long-drawn antagonism which ended in the much-discussed and much-exploited Fashoda incident. My treatment of the Far Eastern affair is perhaps fuller than would seem to be justified after the publication of such special studies as Joseph's *Foreign Diplomacy in China, 1894–1900*. But Joseph and other recent writers have made little if any use of Russian materials, which are really very voluminous. Students of the subject will, I think, recognize the fact that the utilization of these sources changes the perspective decidedly and that there are not a few points which have been very generally missed. I should also point out that in my opinion the numerous monographic treatments of the Anglo-German negotiations of the years 1898–1901 sin, almost without exception, through the authors' ignorance of the Far Eastern situation. As I see it the two things were inextricably involved; no discussion of the Far Eastern problem can be worth while unless it is based upon intimate acquaintance with the European alignment, and the reverse holds equally true. When the two aspects are put together it will appear unmistakably that the real object of English policy, throughout these years and chiefly because of the critical developments in the Far East, was to reach an agreement with Russia. The details may be left to the narrative, but the bare fact reduces the Anglo-German negotiations to comparative insignificance. This interpretation, by the way, has a direct bearing also upon the history of the Anglo-Japanese Alliance. I hope to have shown that what the most eminent Japanese statesmen wanted was an agreement with Russia, and that it was the failure of both England and Japan to come to such an agreement that brought them rather reluctantly together. The use of Japanese documents bearing upon Prince Ito's mission to Europe in 1901 has proved most profitable and has served to give us, for the first time, irrefutable evidence of the complete reliability of our best Japanese source, *The Secret Memoirs of Count Hayashi*.

It has been no easy task to carry along the narrative of so many and such diverse problems. Naturally I have faced the historian's usual dilemma of having to choose between a topical and a chronological approach. I have chosen the latter without much hesitation, partly because I am convinced that it is almost impossible to convey the impression of the interplay of forces by any other method, and partly because each topic, though treated in separated chapters, can be easily enough followed by anyone interested in a certain problem and not in the others. In other words, I have followed the chronological development as closely as it seemed wise to do, but I have tried to make the chapters dealing with one and the same subject tie up in such a way as to make a unified whole.

Like most authors I have a good many obligations to recognize. Apart from my indebtedness to other students in the field, I owe real gratitude to my brother, Professor Rudolph E. Langer, who stole enough time from his mathematical pursuits to read most of the chapters and give me an unvarnished, non-professional criticism. My friend Dr. Philip E. Mosely was good enough, on more than one occasion, to put aside his own work to help me with some of the Slavic material. Mr. Shigeto Tsuru, though a stranger, did me an inestimable service in the translation and abstracting of Japanese documents. The Armenian sources were made available to me through the efforts of Mr. E. Chrakian. My assistant, Mrs. Elizabeth S. Fox, sacrificed much of her time in the drab work of preparing the manuscript for publication, and Dr. Donald C. McKay, my good friend and colleague, shouldered the great burden of proof-reading with me during the hottest months of the summer. I hope the efforts of all these collaborators has not been in vain and that the book is the better for their exertions. But I want also to make mention here of the seminars I have conducted both at Harvard and at Yale during the past years. With my students I have been over much of this ground, by no means without profit to myself. At any rate I think back with pleasure upon our researches in common.

A very special obligation I recognize toward the Bureau of International Research of Harvard University and Radcliffe College. The Bureau very generously voted me a grant which enabled me to devote a full year uninterruptedly to the investigations connected with this book, and more recently has come to my assistance most unstintingly to make possible the publication of so large and expensive a work. It is perfectly obvious, therefore, that the very existence of the book is due directly to the interest, encouragement, and support of the Bureau, and I am deeply grateful for all it has done.

WILLIAM L. LANGER

Harvard University
July 1935

Contents of Part I

The French and Russian Objections — Lobanov's Policy with regard to the Straits and the Suez Canal — The Tsar visits Balmoral
— Salisbury's Efforts to Reach an Agreement — Evasiveness of the
Russians — Nicholas visits Paris — The Franco-Russian Alliance
and the Tacit Renewal of the Triple Alliance — Interpenetration
of the Two Systems

Contents of Part II

List of Maps in Part I

List of Maps in Part II

THE DIPLOMACY
OF IMPERIALISM

∽

Part I

I

The Franco-Russian Entente

〜

BISMARCK'S FALL FROM POWER IN MARCH 1890 WAS THE GREAT DIVIDING point in the history of European diplomacy during the years that separated the Franco-German War from the great conflict of 1914. News of the event struck Europe like a thunder-bolt, and for some time the diplomatic world could hardly find its bearings. After all, the Iron Chancellor had served as the point of reference for European international relations for fully twenty years since the accomplishment of the great work of German unification. Rarely had one figure dominated diplomacy for so long a period, and it is therefore easy to understand that his enemies as well as his friends felt a certain emptiness, a certain dull apprehension regarding the future. Lord Salisbury declared Bismarck's fall to be " an enormous calamity, of which the effects will be felt in every part of Europe," and one of the leading English papers remarked that the great fly-wheel of the machine had been removed; if there was no crash, it would be due to Providence, not to the engineers.[1]

These opinions had reference chiefly to the " overhanging source of dread or reverence " which Bismarck personally had come to represent. Outsiders could not know at that time that the disappearance of the old statesman from the arena was accompanied by a fundamental departure from his policy. The young Emperor William II and his advisers made their debut in foreign policy by refusing to renew the famous Reinsurance Treaty with Russia, an agreement which was, in every sense of the term, the cornerstone of the Bismarckian alliance system. Pivoting upon the alliance between Germany and Austria-Hungary, the great chancellor had succeeded, during the last decade of his régime, in building up the Triple Alliance and at the same time in maintaining intact the wire to St. Petersburg. Through the Mediterranean Agreements of 1887 he had established the connexion with England by way of Rome and Vienna. The Bismarckian fold was a veritable menagerie; the Russian bear and the British lion lay down together with the imperial eagles. Only the Gallic cock was missing. France was completely isolated, and war between the great rivals on the opposite sides of the Rhine was, for the time being at least, a

---

[1] Lady Gwendolen Cecil: *Life of Lord Salisbury*, IV (London, 1932), p. 364; *Spectator*, March 29, 1890. See further Karl Lange: *Bismarcks Sturz und die Öffentliche Meinung in Deutschland und im Auslande* (Stuttgart, 1927), and my own book: *The Franco-Russian Alliance, 1890–1894* (Cambridge, 1929).

3

matter of small likelihood. If Bismarck had had his way France, too, would have been included in the organization of Europe. But it is always easier for the victor than for the vanquished to forget past conflicts. The experiment of the Franco-German entente had been tried and it had failed. In the end Bismarck was obliged to keep his right hand from knowing what the left was doing, in order that he might maintain the delicately adjusted balance between Russian aspirations on the one side and the opposing policies of England and Austria on the other.[2]

The non-renewal of the Reinsurance Treaty restored to Russia a freedom of action which, at the time, was not desired. In the last decade of the century the story of European diplomacy hinged largely upon the effects of this fatal move on Germany's part, and upon the working of certain general factors which made themselves more acutely felt as the dawn of the new century approached. For reasons which will be discussed presently, the Russian government felt impelled to conclude a political agreement and a military convention with France which completely upset the European system as it was in the time of Bismarck. The Franco-Russian Alliance radically altered the position of Germany and at the same time forced an entire reconsideration of the policy of Great Britain. For fully ten years European international relations were reduced to something like a state of flux. The old connexions began to dissolve and on all sides there was an uncertain groping for a new stability. We should look in vain for any trace, in these years, of the directness of policy and singleness of purpose of a Bismarck. In this volume the author must set himself the somewhat thankless task of unravelling the strands of an almost chaotic situation.

But the confusion of the period we are here dealing with was due only in part to the break-down of the Bismarckian system. Another *leit-motiv* of these years was the tremendous, almost epic outburst of European interest in affairs that lay beyond the frontiers of Europe. It was a decade of world policies, one that may conveniently be called by the vague name of imperialism. This impressive movement towards expansion, both in the territorial and non-territorial senses, was probably due in a measure to the dead-lock created in strictly European questions by the balance between the Triple Alliance and the new Franco-Russian accord. But there were in imperialism a great many other ingredients — psychological, economic and spiritual — which we shall have to consider in the proper place. Let it suffice here to point out that the rivalry and competition between the great powers in Africa, in the Far East and in the Near East were, during the last years of the dying century, every whit as important, and perhaps more important, than the shifting trends of purely European diplomacy. But it is useless to attempt comparisons. The fact was that the alignment of the powers with respect to European affairs reacted upon the conduct of these powers in the great crises of imperialism, and by the same sign the clashes of

---

[2] These matters I have dealt with in some detail in my book: *European Alliances and Alignments. 1871–1890* (New York, 1931).

interest in Africa and Asia to a large extent conditioned the history of the European system. First of all we must devote ourselves to the making of the Franco-Russian Alliance, which restored a balance of power on the Continent and made possible the devotion of attention and energy to extra-European problems.

It cannot be too often repeated that the Bismarckian system did not collapse because of any inherent weakness. William II and his new chancellor did not engineer the break with Russia because they had other plans in the field of foreign policy. On the contrary, the great events of March and April 1890 were due primarily to the restlessness, the impatience, the unreasoning dislikes and prejudices of the young ruler and to the dark machinations of Baron von Holstein, who, being the only person in the German foreign office with extensive experience, might well have succeeded in continuing the policies of Bismarck had he not been swayed by an almost frantic fear and hatred of his former chief and all that he stood for.[3] Holstein did not by any means lack ability, or, for that matter, a deep sense of devotion to his country, but the documentary evidence makes it quite clear that he was constantly influenced by fixed ideas and emotional attitudes rather than by the dictates of pure reason.[4]

Although the Emperor had come to dislike what he regarded as Bismarck's undue tenderness towards Russia, he certainly had no intention of embarking upon a policy hostile to the Tsar. He was, in fact, so alarmed by his own temerity and by the departure of the great chancellor that he kept repeating to the diplomats in Berlin that foreign policy had nothing to do with the dismissal of Bismarck and that German policy would remain unchanged. To foreign sovereigns he wrote that Bismarck's wretched health had made his retirement imperative and that physicians had declared that if the old Prince remained at work even for a few more weeks he would die of apoplexy.[5]

These assurances were gratefully received in the European capitals, though they did not by any means assuage the uncertainty, pessimism and even apprehension which was prevalent in both official and unofficial circles. Naturally enough the impression made by events in Berlin was deepest in St. Petersburg, because from the Russian standpoint the situation was aggravated by the refusal of the Germans to renew the Reinsurance Treaty. The Berlin government insisted that it meant to pursue a " simple and transparent " policy, and, in actual

---

[3] There is now an excellent biographical study of Holstein by George P. Gooch: " Baron von Holstein " (in Gooch: *Studies in Modern History,* London, 1931).

[4] Recent studies by Friedrich von Trotha: *Fritz von Holstein als Mensch und Politiker* (Berlin, 1931), Joachim Kürenberg: *Die Graue Eminenz* (Berlin, 1932), Helmuth Rogge: *Friedrich von Holstein, Lebensbekenntnis in Briefe an eine Frau* (Berlin, 1932) and Chang Kuei-Yung: *Friedrich von Holstein. Studien über den Charakter und die Methoden seiner Aussenpolitik* (Leipzig, 1934) have done much to correct the extremely unfavorable judgments passed on Holstein only a few years ago.

[5] G. E. Buckle: *The Letters of Queen Victoria,* Series III, vol. I (New York, 1930), pp. 581–2, 584 ff.; Alexandre Meyendorff: *Correspondance de M. de Staal* (Paris, 1929), II, pp. 75 ff.; Francesco Crispi: *Memoirs* (London, 1912), II, p. 431; and William's long letter to Francis Joseph (*Oesterreichische Rundschau,* February, 1919, pp. 100 ff.).

fact, neither the Emperor nor Caprivi had any idea of initiating a new departure. But it could not be expected that Giers, the Russian foreign minister, would accept these explanations without further question. After all, the facts looked suspicious. William had first declared himself in favor of renewing the treaty, and had then changed his mind. The German government insisted that it would stand by its former attitude, even with respect to Russian policy in Bulgaria, yet it firmly refused to give even the most informal written declaration to that effect. Giers was completely at sea, but for the time being there was nothing to be done. The Russian government decided on a policy of watchful waiting. Everything would depend upon the next turn in the situation.[6]

Now it so happened that just as the Reinsurance Treaty expired, on June 18, 1890, the German and English governments concluded an important colonial agreement under the terms of which the former made large concessions in east Africa in return for the cession of Heligoland, a small island in the North Sea of great strategic value for the defense of the German coast. At bottom there was nothing unusual about this arrangement excepting the cession of territory in Europe, for the occupation and partition of Africa was constantly giving rise to acrimonious disputes requiring adjustment. In this particular instance the rivalries of the English and Germans had become so acute that Bismarck had already taken up the question of a settlement.[7] By April 1890 the agitation on both sides had reached such dimensions that it threatened to impair the good relationship between the two countries. When negotiations were finally taken up in May neither side showed much disposition to give in. But Lord Salisbury felt that an agreement must be reached. " Any indefinite postponement of a settlement in Africa would render it very difficult to maintain terms of amity with Germany, and would force us to change our systems of alliance in Europe," he wrote to the Queen. For that reason he decided to offer the Germans the island of Heligoland in return for concessions in Africa. He spoke of the island as a mere sandbar which would eventually be washed away. The naval authorities were agreed that it could not be defended unless it were heavily fortified, and that would cost a great deal of money. The Queen and several members of the cabinet nevertheless objected to the proposal, but finally Salisbury induced them to agree.[8]

On the German side the English suggestion regarding Heligoland was received with great enthusiasm. The Emperor and Caprivi considered the possession of the island of great strategic importance, partly because of the danger of its serving as a convenient shelter and coaling station for a French fleet in time of war, partly because of its value as a protective outpost at the mouths of

---

[6] For details see my *European Alliances and Alignments*, pp. 500 ff.

[7] The African aspect of this treaty will be taken up in greater detail in a later chapter.

[8] Lady Gwendolen Cecil: *Life of Lord Salisbury*, IV (London, 1932), chap. x; *Letters of Queen Victoria*, I, pp. 610–5; *Die Grosse Politik der Europäischen Kabinette, 1871–1914*, VIII, nos. 1684–8; A. E. Gathorne-Hardy, *a Memoir* (London, 1910), p. 318; Lord George Hamilton: *Parliamentary Reminiscences and Reflections, 1886–1906* (London, 1922), pp. 140–2.

the German rivers and the Kiel Canal. In 1884 and in 1889 the question of its cession had been raised in the course of Anglo-German colonial negotiations, but the English had showed little enthusiasm for the idea and nothing had come of these earlier approaches. When Salisbury made the proposal in 1890 the Germans at once showed themselves ready to make far-reaching concessions in east Africa in order to prevent the scheme from falling through again. The result was that the negotiations were brought to a speedy end and the Treaty concluded.[9]

The agreement was well received in both countries; in England because of the extensive gains made in Africa, in Germany because of the sentimental interest in Heligoland, which was inhabited by Germans. In the political sense the treaty was of considerable importance because it checked the growing tension between the two nations. On the other hand its effects on German-Russian relations were bad. The Tsar had hoped that the island, if it were ever given up by the English, would be returned to the Danes, who had possessed it prior to 1815. But this was a minor point. What impressed the Tsar most was the fact that the Germans, having given up the Reinsurance Treaty, were now apparently angling for a closer connexion with England, even at the expense of far-reaching colonial sacrifices. The hearty reception given Emperor William when he visited England in August simply strengthened this feeling, the more so as the newspapers talked glibly about an " alliance " between the two countries. Count Shuvalov, the Russian ambassador at Berlin, was convinced that Bismarck's successors intended to replace the Russian connexion by an English one, and Staal, the ambassador at London, shared this view.

" The principal importance of this transaction," he wrote home, " seems to me to reside in the rapprochement effected between England and Germany, a rapprochement of which the present arrangement gives palpable witness. When one is united by numerous interests and positive engagements on one point of the globe, one is almost certain to proceed in concert in all the great questions that may arise in the international field. . . . Virtually the entente with Germany has been accomplished. It cannot help but react upon the relations of England with the other powers of the Triple Alliance. This accord does not need special clauses for signatures. It can stand alone." [10]

There could be no further doubt at St. Petersburg that Russia was isolated, completely isolated, and that she was exposed to the danger of a hostile coalition.

[9] See my *Franco-Russian Alliance*, pp. 76 ff.; Maximilian von Hagen: *Geschichte und Bedeutung des Helgolandvertrages* (Munich, 1916); Adolf Hasenclever: " Zur Geschichte des Helgolandvertrages " (*Archiv für Politik und Geschichte*, III, pp. 507–24, November, 1925); Manfred Sell: *Das Deutsch-Englische Abkommen von 1890* (Berlin, 1926); Raymond C. Beazley: " Das deutsche Kolonialreich, Grossbritannien, und die Verträge von 1890 " (*Berliner Monatshefte*, May, 1931, pp. 444–58); Reginald I. Lovell: *The Struggle for South Africa, 1875–1899* (New York, 1934), pp. 264 ff.

[10] Meyendorff, op. cit., II, pp. 89–90; Serge Goriainov: " The End of the Alliance of the Emperors " (*American Historical Review*, XXIII, pp. 324–50, January, 1918). For further details see my *Franco-Russian Alliance*, pp. 78–81.

After all, the great value of the Reinsurance Treaty derived from the fact that it guaranteed Russia against the complete identification of Germany with the Mediterranean coalition. It gave Russia the assurance that if she and England ever came to blows the Germans would not take advantage of the situation to attack on the Polish frontier. Now, however, there was every indication that Germany was joining the combination hostile to Russia. Indeed, during the spring and summer of 1890 the Germans gave up Bismarck's policy of abstention in the Bulgarian affair and showed a distinct tendency to take the lead in a question that concerned Austria and England more than Germany herself. Thus there was real cause for the uneasiness prevalent in the Russian capital.

The obvious remedy for this situation was for the Tsar to seek an ally, and the natural ally for Russia was France. Having already co-operated in the Egyptian question to check the activity of the English, the two powers might well extend their informal entente and conclude an agreement that would safeguard them against Germany too. But this solution was extremely distasteful to the Tsar and his foreign minister, Giers. They had fought against it in the time of Katkov and the great nationalist agitation of 1887, and had continued to make the alliance with Germany the " pivot " of Russian policy. Alexander disliked the " radical, atheistic French Republic " from the bottom of his heart, and had a very low opinion of the reliability and stability of French policy. At the same time he feared that the French, if they secured the alliance of Russia, would try to make use of it for aggressive purposes, that they might precipitate a conflict in the hope of reconquering Alsace-Lorraine. Furthermore, there was no knowing whether the French would really be willing to give up their traditional policy in the Near East, or whether they would be prepared to embark upon an out and out anti-English course. For these reasons the Tsar and his minister regarded the alliance with France as a last resort. They decided to reserve judgment until Emperor William and Caprivi came to Russia and there was some opportunity for open discussion of the international situation.

The Imperial visit took place from August 17-22. For five days the Emperors and their ministers were together at Narva. Viewed from the personal standpoint the intercourse of the rulers and statesmen was a complete success, but politically the journey had no important result. The Germans were very anxious to avoid embarrassing questions and had prepared in advance evasive replies to all possible queries. The conversation therefore turned chiefly on generalities, on the discussion of the danger of subversive movements and the necessity for monarchical solidarity in the face of these dangerous tendencies. Giers, to be sure, made an effort to secure from Caprivi a definite statement of Germany's intentions with regard to the Bulgarian question and the problem of the Straits, but Caprivi, while admitting that the presence of Ferdinand at Sofia was illegal and conceding that the Russian view of the Straits Convention was the correct interpretation, refused to go beyond this negative stand and, after the visit, flatly rejected the suggestion of Giers that he should give the Russians written confirmation of what he had said.[11]

The Germans insisted on underlining the break that had taken place in their relations with Russia. Whatever Giers suggested was rejected *a limine,* leaving no room for further discussion or explanation. On the other hand the new régime at Berlin seized upon every opportunity to strengthen the Triple Alliance and to reinforce the bonds uniting Germany and Austria. From Narva the Emperor and Caprivi proceeded to Rohnstock, where they met Francis Joseph and his foreign minister, Kálnoky. It was on this occasion that the Re-insurance Treaty was first communicated to the Austrians, the Germans hoping thereby to remove all suspicion of their policy. At the same time it was orally agreed between Caprivi and Kálnoky that a solution of the Straits question along lines desired by Russia should not be allowed and that no concessions should be made to Russia in the Near East without Austria's consent. In other words, the Germans reversed Bismarck's policy, and for the time being, at least, entered the service of Austrian policy in the Eastern question.[12]

The readiness of the Germans to make themselves agreeable and helpful to their Austrian allies was in part due to their fear lest Francis Joseph and the Tsar should come to an understanding in Balkan affairs. Alexander, deserted by the Germans, had made some efforts in this direction, and had hinted that he would accept any duly elected candidate for the Bulgarian throne, if only the usurper, Ferdinand, could be gotten rid of. The question, he insisted, was for him merely one of prestige. Nothing had come of these advances, for neither side was willing to make concrete proposals. But the relations between St. Petersburg and Vienna improved distinctly in the summer and autumn of 1890. The Tsarevich Nicholas was warmly received when he came to the Austrian capital in November, and the Archduke Francis Ferdinand was no less graciously treated when, in February 1891, he was sent to St. Petersburg to return the visit.[13]

The Austrian policy in this whole matter seems to have been to tease the Germans; that is, by flirting with the Russians to enhance their own value in the eyes of their ally and so make the latter more ready to lend support for Austrian interests in the Near East. The plan worked excellently, and should

11 *Die Grosse Politik,* VII, nos. 1609 ff.; Meyendorff, op. cit., II, pp. 100 ff.; Lothar von Schweinitz: *Denkwürdigkeiten* (Berlin, 1927), II, pp. 414 ff.; Alfred von Waldersee: *Denkwürdigkeiten* (Stuttgart, 1922), II, p. 141; Vladimir N. Lamsdorff: *Dnievnik, 1886–90* (Moscow, 1926), pp. 315 ff.; Goriainov, loc. cit.; and the material from the Austrian archives quoted in my *Franco-Russian Alliance,* pp. 101–4.

12 *Die Grosse Politik,* XXX (1), nos. 10987, 10989, 10998; Julius von Eckardt: *Aus den Tagen von Bismarcks Kampf gegen Caprivi* (Leipzig, 1920), p. 55; Waldersee: *Denkwürdigkeiten,* II, p. 146.

13 See my *Franco-Russian Alliance,* pp. 105–7; Wolfgang Herrmann: *Dreibund, Zweibund, England, 1890–1895* (Stuttgart, 1929), pp. 16 ff.; V. N. Lamsdorff: *Dnievnik, 1891–1892* (Moscow, 1934), pp. 5–10, 26–7.

have shown the Germans how much their position with respect to Austria had been weakened by the severance of the wire to St. Petersburg. But at bottom there was probably never real danger of Austrian defection from the Triple Alliance. It was on the Italian side that the situation was uncertain.

It will be recalled that Franco-Italian relations had become wretched in the years from 1887–1890. Crispi's fiery temperament and his incalculable alarms were no doubt in part responsible for this turn, but at the root of the matter lay the desire of the French to break the connexion of Italy with the Triple Alliance and England, and in this way to immobilize the Mediterranean coalition. The tariff war and the withdrawal of financial support from Italy were simply the economic aspects of this punitive policy, of which another side was the French activity in the dispute between the Pope and the Italian government.

As time passed the French government redoubled its efforts to force a decision in Italy, and in general to strengthen the French position by effecting an alliance with Russia. It may in fact be said that the French, once Bismarck had disappeared from the scene, passed from a static to a dynamic phase of foreign policy. The Boulangist troubles were practically over and the moderate elements were in control at Paris. The army had been reorganized and modernized and a strong fleet had been built up. France was in a better position than she had ever been since 1871 to play a part in international affairs commensurate with her past prestige and tradition. At the same time the obvious rapprochement of England and Germany as exemplified by the Heligoland Treaty represented a danger for France as it did for Russia. On both sides there was urgent need for some counter-action. The difference was merely this, that the French really went forward, while the Russians hung back, still waiting for further developments.

The double policy of bringing pressure to bear on Italy to force her out of the Triple Alliance and of attempting to inveigle the Russians into concluding an alliance can be well illustrated without going into all the details of what was a long, hard struggle. The keynote was struck when, on May 30, 1890, the French government suddenly departed from its former attitude and arrested a large group of Russian revolutionaries in Paris. This action was taken at the suggestion of the Russian ambassador, Baron Mohrenheim, and made so deep an impression at St. Petersburg that the Tsar ordered the Paris government to be thanked officially.[14] It was probably as a mark of gratitude, and as a silent warning to the Germans, that Alexander invited the French general, Boisdeffre, to attend the manoeuvres at Narva during the visit of the German Emperor. Boisdeffre did not fit very well into the general picture, but he had long talks with the Russian minister of war, Vannovski, and with the chief of staff, Obruchev, both men being well known advocates of a French alliance. What was

---

[14] Charles de Freycinet: *Souvenirs, 1878–1893* (Paris, 1913), pp. 442–3; Jules Hansen: *L'Ambassade du Baron de Mohrenheim* (Paris, 1907), pp. 113–5; Ernest Daudet: *Histoire Diplomatique de l'Alliance Franco-Russe, 1873–1893* (Paris, 1894), pp. 294 ff.

said in these conferences we do not know, but it is interesting to note that the French ambassador sent home a glowing account of the status of Franco-Russian relations.[15] In view of Giers's efforts to re-establish the connexion with Germany and in view of the Tsar's reputed remark to the Emperor that he would never make an alliance with a republic, it seems very doubtful whether Boisdeffre's mission was of much political consequence. France and Russia had perhaps drawn somewhat closer to each other, but there was still a very long way to go to a fixed agreement or alliance.

Meanwhile the interest of Europe became more and more focussed upon Italy. By 1890 French economic pressure had become so effective that the peninsula showed dangerous signs of unrest. Radical movements, both pro-French republican and anti-Austrian irredentist currents, were becoming ominously strong, and there was an increasing outcry against the Triple Alliance and the huge expenditures for armaments that it entailed. Even Crispi could not withstand the pressure and began to make some attempts to restore harmony. In his talks with the French ambassador he almost apologized for the Triple Alliance, while King Humbert dilated on the past Franco-Italian comradeship in arms at Magenta and Solferino.[16]

This exchange of courtesies was followed almost immediately by the opening of negotiations for the settlement of outstanding questions. The French were prepared to recognize the Italian claims to a protectorate over Abyssinia and to leave the Italians a free hand in Tripoli, provided the government at Rome agreed to give up all its claims in Tunis and leave the French free to annex this territory outright. Of course the abandonment of Italian claims in Tunis would have resulted in a great strengthening of the French position in the Mediterranean, and would for that reason have met with the disapproval of England, to say nothing of the Turks. Crispi therefore refused to entertain the suggestion and the pourparlers broke down in July. Perhaps they were never meant very seriously on the French side.[17]

This brief interlude was followed by a period of intense activity on the part of the French, who advanced to the attack not only upon Italy, but upon England. Together with the Russians they continued to make trouble for the English in Egypt. They protested loudly against the Anglo-German Treaty of June 1890 on the ground that the assumption by Britain of a protectorate over Zanzibar was a violation of an earlier treaty. They therefore demanded adequate compensation either in Egypt or in Tunis. The British cabinet was in a dilemma. The position in Egypt was too important to be tampered with, yet to yield in Tunis would be to estrange Italy. Crispi had already declared against

---

[15] L'Alliance Franco-Russe. Troisième Livre Jaune Français (Paris, 1918), no. 1; Schweinitz: Denkwürdigkeiten, II, pp. 415 ff.

[16] Crispi: Memoirs, III, pp. 181–3; Albert Billot: La France et l'Italie, 1881–1899 (Paris, 1905), I, pp. 183–4.

[17] Billot, op. cit., I, pp. 204–8; Gaetano Salvemini: La Politica Estera di Francesco Crispi (Rome, 1919), pp. 72 ff.; Italicus: Italiens Dreibundpolitik 1870–1896 (Munich, 1928), pp. 134 ff.

such a policy and had tried to mobilize both the Germans and the English in his efforts to stop the French harbor constructions at the strategic Tunisian port of Bizerta. He had found little encouragement in this matter, but Salisbury did promise not to make concessions to France in Tunis.

To complete the confusion the Italian premier came out with rumors that the French had concluded with the Bey of Tunis a secret treaty of devolution. He appealed to the Germans and to the English to oppose any attempt to change the existing status of the regency, suggesting at the same time that Italy would be satisfied if only she could get compensation in Tripoli. It was clearly the hope of getting this latter territory that lay behind Crispi's whole action, but his allies and friends did not want to sacrifice their position at Constantinople by approving designs on the Sultan's dominions. They therefore refused to recognize any obligation to take action under the terms of the Triple Alliance or the Mediterranean Agreements. They did, however, make inquiries at Paris, only to receive an emphatic denial from the French foreign minister of any intention of tampering with the situation in Tunis. Eventually, to put an end to Crispi's importunities, the German and English governments promised that no power other than Italy should be allowed to acquire Tripoli and assured Crispi of their support when the opportune moment for action should come. The French opposition to the Anglo-German Treaty was removed by England's recognition of the French claims to a protectorate over Madagascar.[18]

Although the outstanding immediate problems had been disposed of there was no let-down in Franco-Italian tension until Crispi's fall in January 1891. Now it was the French activity at Bizerta, now the French designs on the hinterland of Tripoli that stirred him to new efforts to enlist the aid of his allies. In the meanwhile nothing was done by the French to relieve the pressure. On the contrary, the Paris government was in close contact with the Vatican when the Pope decided on a spectacular action in the autumn of 1890. It will be remembered that Leo had been disappointed in his hopes of aid from Bismarck, and that, since 1887, the French influence at the Vatican had been steadily on the increase. This tendency continued even after the collapse of the Boulangist movement, for powerful French clerics succeeded in persuading the Pope that there was nothing to be hoped for from the outworn monarchist party. It would be better, they argued, to accept the Republic and attempt to mold it to the purposes of the church. One of the chief advocates of this change of front was Cardinal Lavigerie, Archbishop of Algiers and Primate of Africa. He had good connexions with the French government and evidently managed to convince the cabinet of the value of church influence not only in the struggle with the

---

[18] Crispi: *Memoirs*, II, pp. 438–76; III, pp. 30–67, 85–7; Cecil: *Life of Salisbury*, IV, pp. 372 ff.; *Die Grosse Politik*, VIII, nos. 1691 ff., 1701 ff., 1862–1893; details in Langer: *The Franco-Russian Alliance*, pp. 122–9; Italicus, op. cit., pp. 137–43; Rudolf Hoernigk: *Italien zwischen Frankreich und dem Dreibund* (Berlin, 1934), pp. 34 ff.

radical elements, but also in the policy of pressure upon Italy. After conferring with Freycinet, the prime minister, with Constans, the minister of the interior, and with Ribot, the minister of foreign affairs, Lavigerie secured the permission of the Pope to proclaim the new departure. On November 12, 1890, at a dinner to French naval officers visiting Algiers, he proposed a famous toast in which he declared it the duty of every individual to recognize the existing form of government once it had received popular approbation. In other words, he recognized the French Republic.

The Vatican made no attempt to disavow Lavigerie, though the Pope thought it expedient to keep himself in the background. Since the cardinal's pronunciamento went unchallenged by his superiors it caused a tremendous stir throughout Europe, particularly in Italy, where it was realized immediately that the Papacy had thrown in its lot with France and would co-operate in the attempt to undermine the Triple Alliance. The correspondence of Cardinal Lavigerie leaves no doubt that this idea actually motivated the Vatican. In one letter the cardinal says in so many words that " the Pope wishes to isolate Italy and fortify himself against the Triple Alliance, which has abandoned him and has subordinated him to the interests of Italy." [19] The reports of the Russian representative at the Holy See reflect the same distrust of the central powers and the desire to further the rapprochement between France and Russia.[20] Indeed we have the recorded words of the Holy Father himself on this subject. Speaking to a noted French journalist in November 1891, he remarked that France, if internally strong, would find in Europe the prestige which he, the Pope, so much desired her to have: " You have enemies. You must have friends too. See what a few months of wise policy have accomplished. . . . Russia. . . . But . . . if you change. . . . If the radicals . . . that will be the end." Or, a little later, " Russia cannot be the friend of a radical, revolutionary France." There was, he admitted, a sort of unsigned alliance between the Vatican, France and Russia.[21]

All this raises the very difficult question of the part played by the Curia in the consummation of the alliance between France and Russia. The subject is too elusive and technical a one to be treated at length here. Suffice it to say that the Pope, long at odds with the Russian government because of the position of the Catholics in Poland, seems to have accepted the aid of the French in making his peace with the Tsar. In return he legitimized the French Republic, so to speak, in the eyes of Alexander and thus undoubtedly made the idea of an alliance more palatable to the Russian autocrat. The Alliance, once it was made, was obviously in the interest of the Vatican, for it weakened the Triple Alliance by restoring something like a balance of power in Europe, and in consequence undermined the position of Italy. Of course the whole plan, if one can speak of

[19] E. Tournier: *Le Cardinal Lavigerie et son Action Politique* (Paris, 1913), pp. 277 ff.
[20] E. Adamow: *Die Diplomatie des Vatikans* (Berlin, n.d.), pp. 22 ff., 51, 119, 122.
[21] *Souvenirs de Charles Benoist* (Paris, 1932), I, pp. 185, 192.

a definite plan, did not work out just as it had been conceived. The relations between the Russian government and the Vatican were never all that could be desired, and the much-heralded *ralliement* of the French monarchists to the Republic proved more or less of a fiasco. Nevertheless there can be little doubt that in the years of the making of the Franco-Russian Alliance the Pope hovered over it like a guardian angel. It had his heart-felt blessings.[22]

It was probably because of the growing unrest in Italy and because of the general Mediterranean situation that Caprivi decided to pay a visit to Crispi. He arrived at Milan on November 7, just before the Italian elections. The discussions between the two statesmen turned almost entirely upon the problem of Italy's relations with France and her position in the Mediterranean. Crispi insisted that the French tariff was aimed primarily at Italy and urged the formation of a commercial league between the members of the Triple Alliance. This, he thought, might be developed later into a " monarchical league " to bolster up the tottering dynasties of Spain and Portugal. The necessity of strengthening the connexion with Spain evidently weighed heavily on Crispi's mind. Caprivi recognized the force of the argument, but pointed out again and again that Italy should lay chief emphasis on her relations with England. To this the Italian premier replied that he was absolutely sure of the British, even if the Salisbury cabinet were overthrown.[23]

It is not quite clear from the reports of Crispi and Caprivi just what was said at this meeting regarding the renewal of the Triple Alliance. Apparently Crispi suggested it, although the Treaty was not due to expire until 1892. Caprivi, on the other hand, was determined not to bind Germany in advance at a time when the international situation was so uncertain. It was, therefore, a great shock to the Germans to learn of Crispi's fall from power on January 31, 1891. A tactless remark had deprived him of the support of the conservative groups and left him without a parliamentary majority. He was obliged to resign and make way for the leader of the Right, Marquis di Rudini. The new premier had on numerous occasions declared his adhesion to the policy of the Triple Alliance, but he was known to favor the establishment of better relations with France and a policy of retrenchment which would involve less activity in colonial and foreign affairs, to say nothing of reduction in military expenditure.

The Emperor William hit upon a most extraordinary plan for meeting the dangers created by Crispi's fall. For some time he had been making efforts to

---

[22] I have discussed this question at some length in my *Franco-Russian Alliance*, pp. 113 ff., 131 ff., 235 ff., 320 ff., where numerous references are given. Among the most important treatments are Louis Baunard: *Léon XIII et le Toast d'Alger* (Paris, 1914), pp. 24–36; E. L. Woodward: " The Diplomacy of the Vatican under Popes Pius IX and Leo XIII " (*Journal of the British Institute of International Affairs*, May, 1924, pp. 113–39); Eduardo Soderini: *Il Pontificato di Leone XIII* (Milan, 1932), II, pp. 391 ff.; Josef Schmidlin: *Papstgeschichte der Neuesten Zeit* (Munich, 1934), II, pp. 428 ff.

[23] Crispi: *Memoirs*, III, pp. 6–16; *Die Grosse Politik*, VII, nos. 1393 ff.; Pribram: *The Secret Treaties of Austria-Hungary* (Cambridge, 1920–1921), II, pp. 89–90.

improve German relations with France, seizing every opportunity for small courtesies. Among thoughtful people on both sides of the frontier these advances were warmly welcomed. Eminent historians like Gabriel Monod and Hans Delbrück came out in favor of western European solidarity. Of course it was recognized that the Alsace-Lorraine problem was an almost insuperable barrier to the realization of an entente, but the acrimonious tone was at least beginning to disappear and there was greater readiness on both sides to appreciate the efforts of the other. When in January 1891 French artists were invited to participate in an exhibition at Berlin, many accepted and the French government informally lent its patronage. Such was the situation when news came of the overturn in Italy. The Emperor made a hasty decision. He arranged, or at least approved of his mother's visit to Paris. She had no specific mission and was to travel incognito. As a matter of fact, however, the visit was intended to sound out French sentiment and to pave the way for closer relations, first in the non-political, later in the political sphere.

The Empress remained in the French capital from February 18 until the 27, but her stay could hardly be described as a success. She lived at the German embassy, took part in receptions, visited the studios of noted painters, and even committed the incredible blunder of going to St. Cloud, the ruins of which were a standing reminder of the German invasion of 1870. This was too much for the Parisian populace. Déroulède called out the members of the former League of Patriots and organized vociferous protests. By the time the Empress was ready to leave Paris the uproar had become so great that it was necessary to take all sorts of precautions to ensure her safe departure.

This unfortunate incident led to an outburst of polemics in the press of both countries. The Emperor himself was disillusioned and enraged. He declared to the Austrian ambassador that " peace hung by a hair," and bitterly accused Freycinet of stirring up the dying chauvinism of the French with the idea of eventually conducting a war of revenge. To salve his feelings he issued an order to enforce the passport regulation in Alsace-Lorraine with full vigor. The unfortunate Alsace-Lorrainers were made to suffer for the mistakes of the Emperor and his mother.[24]

The French government hastened to disclaim all responsibility and sent an explanatory circular to the foreign governments. This note was undoubtedly intended primarily for Russia. At any rate it served its purpose in every way. At St. Petersburg the German efforts to conciliate France had been looked upon as another move designed to isolate Russia. The German ambassador at Paris

---

[24] *Die Grosse Politik*, VII, nos. 1543 ff.; Sir Frederick Ponsonby: *Letters of the Empress Frederick* (London, 1928), pp. 422 ff.; Waldersee: *Denkwürdigkeiten*, II, p. 197; Gaston Routier: *Un Point d'Histoire Contemporaine* (Paris, 1901); Pierre Albin: *L'Allemagne et la France en Europe* (Paris, 1913), pp. 212 ff., 282 ff.; Manfred Zapp: *Deutsch-Französische Annäherungsversuche und ihr Scheitern in den Jahren 1890–1898* (Weida, 1929), pp. 26 ff.; and the material from the Austrian archives in my *Franco-Russian Alliance*, pp. 140–4.

was even convinced that the protests against the Empress' visit were started by Russian agents and supported by Russian gold.[25]

However this may have been, news of the debacle was received with unmixed delight by the Russian government and public.

"I do not think, at bottom, that we have grounds to fear excessively misunderstandings which may arise between France and Germany," noted a high official of the Russian foreign office with some glee. "They do not in the least want an armed collision, and, if a collision should occur, what does it matter to us if 1870 is repeated? Russia has far more grounds to fear the possibility of a gradual rapprochement which might, little by little, smoothe out the hostility between Paris and Berlin. . . . Under present circumstances . . . we may, in case of a rupture, become the arbiter between them and realize to the full our national interests in the East, in return for complete neutrality, which would be extremely valuable to both. A sign of sympathy, expressed under present circumstances to the head of the French government, will merely force the Germans to be more cautious and will make the French less scared; it would also force Berlin not to neglect good relations with Russia, which no 'league of peace' can ever replace under any circumstances." [26]

So Giers hastened to assure the French government that it had acted correctly in every respect and that the Franco-Russian accord was " solid as granite." On March 26 this congratulatory message was followed up by the presentation of the Order of St. Andrew to President Carnot. At the same time it was decided that a French squadron should visit Russia in the coming summer. No doubt the visit of the Empress Frederick to Paris had given " a new impulse to the Franco-Russian rapprochement." [27]

Freycinet and his colleagues were anxious to turn these Platonic advances of the Russians into concrete obligations. Sometime late in March or early in April the French government instructed M. Laboulaye, the ambassador at St. Petersburg, to secure, if possible, some definite assurance for the future. The question he put to Giers was something like this: " What would be the attitude of the Russian government in case of war between France and Germany? " Just what the reply was we do not know, but it is certain that the move did not please the Tsar and the response did not satisfy the French. Curiously enough the French inquiries are not reported in the diary of Lamsdorff, but there is much material in this particular source to make clear the general attitude of the Russian foreign office. The St. Petersburg cabinet appears to have intercepted regularly the telegrams which passed between the Paris government and its ambassador at St. Petersburg. In this way the foreign office learned that the am-

[25] Die Grosse Politik, VII, nos. 1493, 1548, 1551, 1558; Lettres de la Princesse Radziwill au Général de Robilant (Bologna, 1933), I, pp. 68–9.

[26] Lamsdorff: Dnievnik, 1891–1892, p. 39.

[27] Die Grosse Politik, VII, nos. 1493–7; Livre Jaune Français, no. 2; Freycinet: Souvenirs, pp. 443–4, 464–5; Jules Hansen: L'Alliance Franco-Russe (Paris, 1897), pp. 59 ff.; Daudet: Histoire Diplomatique, pp. 297–301.

bassador at Paris, M. Mohrenheim, had read the despatch of congratulation to M. Ribot, thus giving it a certain official quality. Giers, who distrusted Mohrenheim, was enraged by this action and put no stock in the ambassador's explanations. Nothing much could be done because Mohrenheim enjoyed the protection of the Tsar, but the ambassador was warned that even if Russia needed France, France needed Russia even more. Therefore all excessive courtesy and all suggestion that Russia was making advances was to be carefully avoided. The incident is of some importance because it shows that despite the non-renewal of the Reinsurance Treaty the Russians were not yet prepared to bind themselves for the event of a Franco-German conflict. The policy of small courtesies, it was thought, would keep the French government in good humor.[28]

Meanwhile the question of the renewal of the Triple Alliance had become an urgent one for the central powers. On Crispi they had been able to rely without reservation, and they had therefore felt safe in taking a negative stand toward Italian efforts to secure further support in north African affairs. Rudini's advent to power placed the whole matter in jeopardy. His parliamentary position was not strong and the need for ending the Franco-Italian tension was great. Indeed, one of Rudini's first acts was to make advances to the French. But, as before, the Italians were told that they must first give assurances and explicit declarations calculated to dispel suspicion regarding the purpose and extent of the Triple Alliance. Such a declaration it was impossible for Rudini or any other Italian statesman to give at that time. For Italy to have turned her back on the Triple Alliance while it was still supported by England would have been nothing less than suicidal. The Italian premier recognized the hopelessness of his efforts and took the first step toward opening negotiations for the renewal of the Alliance. Further efforts made by the French to elicit from Rudini information regarding the terms of the pact were hotly rejected. Finally the French government, working through an agent of the Rothschilds, dangled before the Italians the prospect of financial aid if they would consent to observe a " hands off " policy in the event of a Franco-German conflict. The Italian premier burned with indignation at this suggestion of duplicity and was tempted to throw the bearer of the proposals out of doors. The French had gone the limit, but they had failed.[29]

The methods pursued by the French showed clearly enough that the tension between the two countries had been due not so much to Crispi's noisy bellicosity as to the desire of the Paris government to detach Italy from the Triple Alliance. The sole result was to hasten the premature renewal of the treaty, and

28 Lamsdorff: *Dnievnik, 1891–1892*, pp. 59–71; *Die Grosse Politik*, VII, nos. 1498–1501; Wilhelm Köhler: *Revanche-Idee und Panslawismus* (Berlin, 1919), pp. 280 ff.; Langer: *Franco-Russian Alliance*, pp. 146–8.

29 *Die Grosse Politik*, VII, nos. 402 ff.; Luigi Chiala: *Pagine di Storia Contemporanea* (Turin, 1898), pp. 542 ff.; G. Giacometti: " Cinq Mois de Politique Italien, février–juin 1891 " (*Revue des Deux Mondes*, September 15, 1891. pp. 388–452).

to redouble Italy's efforts to strengthen the connexion with England. In Rudini's mind the relation to Great Britain was more important than the Alliance with the central powers. But the latter was an essential stepping-stone to the former.[30]

The negotiations for the renewal of the Alliance were begun in April and went off with unusual smoothness and celerity. All three powers were anxious to clear up the situation. Rudini from the very start abandoned Crispi's idea of securing Austrian support for Italy's north African policy. Indeed, no further obligations were demanded of Austria. The negotiations were carried on at Berlin. It was finally decided to adopt the suggestion already made by Crispi that the three treaties of 1887 be merged in one document. The only real difficulty arose from Rudini's desire to increase Germany's obligation to support Italy in the western Mediterranean. After some discussion the Germans accepted an extension of Article III of the separate German-Italian Treaty of 1887. They agreed to work for the maintenance of the status quo, but only of the territorial status quo in Cyrenaica, Tripoli and Tunis. In case the existing situation could not be upheld and this fact were recognized by both parties after mature examination Germany promised, after a formal and previous accord, to support Italy in any action in the form of occupation or other taking of guarantee which the latter should undertake in those regions in the interest of the equilibrium or of legitimate compensation. In this form the treaty was signed on May 6th and ratified on May 17, 1891.[31]

The aid of Germany in support of Italian policy in north Africa could not in the nature of things be very extensive. The Germans could fight on the Rhine but they could play no rôle in the naval situation in the Mediterranean. Only England could protect the coasts of Italy and uphold the balance. It is quite clear that Rudini hoped to induce the British government to accept obligations more specific than those of the vague Mediterranean Agreement of 1887. Both Caprivi and Kálnoky were quite ready to assist in this attempt, for they knew that Italian military aid could never be expected unless England protected the sea coast of the peninsular. It was therefore provided in the new treaty that if the maintenance of the status quo in north Africa should prove to be impossible, the two powers (Germany and Italy) should seek to reach an agreement with England. A protocol was added providing that the parties to the treaty should exert themselves at the opportune moment and to the extent that circumstances might permit to bring about England's adhesion to those clauses which dealt with north Africa.[32]

The prospects for associating the British government more closely with the alliance of the central powers were not bad at this time. After all, the threatening combination of France and Russia concerned England as much as any

---

[30] See the interview with Rudini in the London *Times,* April 14, 1891.

[31] *Die Grosse Politik,* VII, chap. xlv; Pribram, op. cit., II, pp. 95 ff.; Italicus: *Italiens Dreibundpolitik* (Munich, 1928), pp. 149 ff.; Hoernigk, op. cit., pp. 24 ff.

[32] *Die Grosse Politik,* VII, nos. 1412, 1416, 1427; Pribram, op. cit., I, pp. 160–2.

state. In the Egyptian question the French and Russians were still co-operating to block the plans of the British administration. Even in Morocco there were indications of future action on the part of France. Salisbury was evidently prepared to do something to ensure the continuance of the connexion with Italy, and the German government was quite eager to act as mediator in the negotiations. But Rudini's hopes proved to be somewhat extravagant. He submitted for the approval of the German government the draft of an agreement which would have involved the formal adhesion of England to the Triple Alliance, on the basis of support in the Egyptian question in return for aid in maintaining the status quo in north Africa, including even Morocco. In fact Rudini envisaged eventual co-operation in case of French aggression against any one of the four powers even on the Continent. It was well known in Berlin that the British government would not consider anything so formidable as an actual alliance and for that reason Rudini was induced to substitute a proposal for a less extensive separate Italian-English pact. But before the matter could be taken up in London information regarding the negotiations leaked out and very embarrassing interpellations were made in the house of commons.[33]

The leakage just referred to was in part due to Rudini's own indiscretion. In order to make the renewal of the Triple Alliance more palatable to the Italians he repeatedly stressed the connexion between this problem and the question of an entente with England. In fact he arranged to have one of his friends insert articles in the newspapers indicating that England had entered the Triple Alliance, thereby making it quadruple. These overstatements in turn led to the interpellations in the British parliament. The government replied to a number of awkward questions very skilfully but evasively, so that the uncertainty in which the whole matter was shrouded was by no means dispelled. When the news of the renewal of the Triple Alliance was communicated to the Italian parliament on June 28, it created a great stir, chiefly because it was commonly supposed that England had actually become more closely associated with the central European bloc.[34]

The British government, while it warmly denied any connexion with the Triple Alliance, stated quite freely that there was an agreement with Italy dating back to 1887, and made it perfectly clear that England's sympathies were on the side of those powers which stood for peace and for the maintenance of the status quo. To emphasize the fact a British squadron was sent to visit Fiume and Venice during the last days of June and the first days of July. The squadron was honored by the visits of Emperor Francis Joseph and King Humbert. Then, on July 4, these minor demonstrations were followed by Emperor William's great state visit to London. The reception accorded him was almost unparalleled in its enthusiasm, cordiality and heartiness. It was quite in keeping with the spirit of the occasion that the Emperor in a famous Guildhall speech announced

---

[33] *Die Grosse Politik*, VIII, nos. 1707 ff.
[34] For details see my *Franco-Russian Alliance*, pp. 165–9, 176–8.

his determination to preserve the historic friendship between the two nations
At the same time Marschall, the German foreign minister, conferred with Lord
Salisbury regarding the danger of a possible Russian attack upon Constantinople. The conversation was of a general nature but the result was a complete
concurrence of views between the two governments.[35]

It may well be imagined what an impression these events and demonstrations made in Paris and St. Petersburg. Knowing nothing of the actual facts
the two governments feared for the worst. If England had really bound herself to the central powers the French position in the Mediterranean and the
Russian position in the Near East would be hopelessly weakened. " There is
something like a storm in the air; the political atmosphere is saturated with
electricity," wrote one French paper in a diagnosis of the situation. Clearly
the only remedy for this state of affairs was closer co-operation between France
and Russia. But since the premature inquiries of the French in April relations
between the two countries had cooled considerably. The Tsar had ignored the
opening of the French exposition at Moscow and the Rothschilds, acting evidently at the direction of the French foreign office, had refused to float a new
Russian loan for five hundred million rubles unless the Tsar altered his policy
towards the Jews.[36] This was a very effective blow at one of Russia's most sensitive spots. So also was the high-handed attitude assumed by the French government in connexion with a dispute which arose at this time between the Fran-
ciscans and the Greek monks in Bethlehem. Evidently Freycinet and his
colleagues were weary of the exchange of small courtesies, and were determined
to secure something tangible and concrete.

The effect of the French policy was instantaneous. The Tsar and his ministers felt indignant, but they could not afford to give their sentiments outward
expression; they needed money too badly to re-equip the army, to construct the
projected Transsiberian railway and to meet a threatening crop failure. If these
considerations were not in themselves sufficient to bring the Russians round to
the French view, the renewal of the Triple Alliance and the reputed adherence
of England served to force the decision. The events of May, June and July
1891 brought matters to a head and placed the Tsar before two alternatives:
isolation in the face of a hostile coalition; or an agreement with France. That
he chose the latter was the most natural thing in the world. It was really the
German policy that drove Russia into the arms of France. There is abundant
evidence to prove that it was the ill-fated *flirt anglo-triplicien* that led to the
conclusion of an entente between the two countries. Lamsdorff's diary is simply
packed with evidence on this point. Mohrenheim was reporting from Paris
that the French government was profoundly discouraged by the renewal of

---

[35] *Die Grosse Politik*, VIII, nos. 1724, 1727; IX, nos. 2111; XXII, nos. 7384; *Letters of Queen
Victoria*, II, pp. 48 ff.

[36] Daudet: *Histoire Diplomatique*, pp. 261–2; Langer: *Franco-Russian Alliance*, p. 179; Lamsdorff, op. cit., p. 107.

the Triple Alliance and that it was very apprehensive of the negotiations for a tariff treaty which were being initiated between Russia and Germany. At the same time Laboulaye, the French ambassador at the Russian court, informed Giers of the Anglo-Italian Agreement of 1887, of which the French had known for some time. From Constantinople came reports that were by no means reassuring. The ambassador, M. Nelidov, was convinced that England had joined the Triple Alliance. For some time he had been urging the conclusion of a Franco-Russian Alliance and common action between the two governments in all affairs of the Near East. All this uneasiness was, before long, reflected in the Russian press, where the influential journalist, Tatishchev, was demanding the solidification of Franco-Russian relations by the conclusion of a formal treaty.[37]

Giers became convinced that something must be done to allay the impatience and apprehension of the French. He invited the French ambassador to visit him, and, in a crucial conversation on July 17, took the initiative in suggesting that the renewal of the Triple Alliance and the indirect accession of England to it had created for France and Russia a new situation which might make it desirable to take a further step in the direction of an entente.[38] Laboulaye asked for instructions from his government for the event of Giers' returning to the subject. They were sent him on July 24, just as the French squadron arrived at Cronstadt on a visit.

There followed a two weeks' demonstration on an unprecedented scale. One festivity succeeded another in rapid succession, the French sailors were lionized wherever they went, the Marseillaise resounded in the streets, and to top it all the Tsar himself visited the squadron and stood bareheaded while the battle hymn of the Revolution was played by a Russian band. The Cronstadt days were of particular significance because in a country like Russia, which was autocratically ruled, the government could control even popular demonstration. By giving the people free rein the Tsar intended to manifest his determination to align himself with France. The visit came most conveniently for the Russian government and served as a starting point for serious negotiation.

The press of western Europe was disposed at first to take the whole affair light-heartedly. One influential German paper declared that the French squadron, instead of carrying an arsenal of bombs and grenades, was loaded with an inexhaustible supply of bottles and casks, with which it intended to open up such a cannonade of champagne corks against the walls of the Russian fortress that the hearts of the Muscovites would infallibly capitulate. This humorous vein was distinctly malapropos, for along with the popular manifestations went secret discussions between Giers and the French ambassador. Although the initiative had been taken by the Russians, the French had lost no time in following up the lead. A draft agreement had been sent to Laboulaye. The French

---

[37] Lamsdorff: *Dnievnik*, pp. 97, 102-5, 109, 140-1, 147-8, 151, 153; Langer: *Franco-Russian Alliance*, pp. 183-4.   [38] *Livre Jaune Français*, no. 3; Lamsdorff, op. cit., p. 151.

desires, so Ribot declared, were limited to two points: the two governments should agree to act in concert on all questions which might affect the maintenance of peace in Europe, and it should be understood that if peace were really menaced by one of the powers of the Triple Alliance France and Russia would, without delay, take the necessary measures to prevent surprise. In other words, France and Russia should come to an agreement to mobilize their forces simultaneously as soon as one of the nations of the Triple Alliance mobilized its forces.

This draft typified the views and aims of the French statesmen. For them Germany was the chief enemy and the most dangerous opponent. But the attitude of Giers showed at once how different was the Russian view. He desired to make the Entente as general as possible and to avoid specific military obligations. He objected to the attempt made by the French to confine the application of the accord to questions concerning only European peace. He therefore proposed that the second clause of Ribot's draft be recast to provide that, in case the maintenance of peace were threatened, and especially in case one of the two contracting powers were menaced by aggression, the two parties, should, if they thought necessary, take counsel to concert in advance measures to be taken immediately and simultaneously if the eventuality contemplated should actually materialize. It requires some effort to penetrate this maze of circumlocutions, but Giers' phrasing is interesting because it shows that he was anxious to lead the French on without assuming definite obligations or abandoning Russia's freedom of action.[39]

It could not be expected that the French would accept this counter-proposal without objection. They could not allow themselves to be bound without binding the Russians too, otherwise the new friendship would have been not only compromising, but dangerous. Ribot insisted on a more specific wording of the second clause. The text was to be made to read that, in case peace were threatened or one party menaced by aggression, the two contracting powers should *agree to concert measures,* and so forth. In other words, the preliminary negotiations were to be obligatory, not optional. The two powers were to discuss not *whether* measures should be taken, but rather *what* measures should be taken. Giers thought this version much too far-reaching, and the Tsar himself became a bit hesitant. So far as one can detect from the Russian sources, Alexander was much more favorable to the Entente than Giers. The surly autocrat appears in the diary of Lamsdorff as an almost immovable and wholly fearless giant. He did not like the Germans and was rather glad to see the Reinsurance Treaty go, despite the effects of its loss upon Russia's international position. All the dangers which Giers was repeatedly calling to his attention failed to impress him. He had no feeling for any nuance in diplomacy, but aimed at keeping himself popular in Russia and for the rest doing what he wished.

<hr />

[39] *Livre Jaune Français,* nos. 3, 5, 7, 9; Freycinet: *Souvenirs,* pp. 466, 467. See also the illuminating discussion by Eugen Fischer: " Der Sinn der Russisch-Französischen Militär-Konvention " (*Preussische Jahrbücher,* April, 1923, pp. 65–98).

Alexander decided to call home Baron Mohrenheim, in order to learn his views regarding the Entente with France. This decision gave Giers a headache, for he had no use whatever for Mohrenheim. The officials of the foreign ministry and of the ministry of war suspected the ambassador of being in the pay of French interests, especially of munitions interests, and there is every reason to believe that he was remunerated for his ardent support of a Franco-Russian alliance. As it happened, his talks with Giers went off better than the latter had expected. It was arranged that the Entente should be embodied in a letter from Giers to Mohrenheim, which the ambassador could then communicate to Ribot. Apparently Mohrenheim made no great effort to secure the acceptance of the whole French draft. That would have been hopeless. Giers' letter made no mention of any provision for mobilization and therefore did not fulfill the desires of the French. It was merely a compromise between the views of the two governments.[40]

Giers' letter to Mohrenheim was dated August 21 and was communicated to M. Ribot on August 27. The French government accepted it at once, but the foreign minister as well as M. Freycinet did not fail to urge the desirability of not postponing too long the discussion of technical matters of a military nature. The extraordinary rapidity, they said, with which a crisis might develop into a fateful conflict and the impossibility of discussing the situation in the event of a surprise made it essential to settle things in advance. Mohrenheim recognized in his covering letter that the development of the two points of the accord was a natural and necessary complement of the Entente and agreed that it should be proceeded with as soon as convenient. Thereby he again brought the imprecations of the Russian foreign office upon his head. " At bottom," noted Lamsdorff, " this whole rapprochement with France does not enjoy the sympathy of M. Giers." Once again the foreign minister did not dare take too strong a line with Mohrenheim, but he was evidently determined not to go beyond the two points of the accord for the time being. The ambassador, whom Lamsdorff continued to suspect of being well paid for his efforts by the French, tried to get around the obstacles presented by the Russian foreign office. In September 1891 Jules Hansen, a Dane naturalized in France who had for many years been one of the most notorious secret agents in Europe, was sent off to Copenhagen, where the Tsar was visiting his wife's relatives. Hansen was closely associated with Mohrenheim and apparently acted as a liaison officer between the French foreign office and the Russian embassy. Whether he was sent on this particular mission by the French or by Mohrenheim is a question of no importance. He carried a memorandum setting forth the French views and urging the need for an arrangement for both countries to mobilize simultaneously whenever news should arrive of the mobilization of the Triple

---

[40] *Livre Jaune Français*, nos. 4–17; Lamsdorff, op. cit., pp. 160–76; Hansen: *Mohrenheim*, p. 119.

Alliance. Nothing came of this demarche, for the Tsar would not go beyond a promise to consider the matter after his return to St. Petersburg.[41]

Alexander's reply was undoubtedly inspired by a long report which he received from Giers in the first days of September. The foreign minister wrote as follows:

"I make bold to think that in the present political situation the agreement arrived at on two points . . . may for the time being be looked upon as absolutely adequate, since it protects Russia against the danger of finding herself isolated in case of war, which, judging by the general feeling in Europe, no one looks for and no one desires. There is no doubt that this feeling is strengthened by our rapprochement with France, so obvious to all, which represents a powerful counterweight to the Triplice which is constantly increasing its military forces despite its chosen nickname, the 'league of peace.' In my opinion it would be very incautious for us to abandon this calm and advantageous position, but this might easily happen if, in accord with the presuppositions expressed in Baron Mohrenheim's correspondence with M. Ribot and in his conversation with Freycinet, we should *now* set about negotiations for adopting those measures which would prove necessary in the event of unforeseen occurrences. Without mentioning the fact that such negotiations, entrusted to *special delegates,* would scarcely be kept secret, and the fact that their noising abroad . . . can only hasten the fateful moment, it would seem to me very undesirable to bind ourselves *prematurely* by any positive engagements whatsoever in the military way, and thus embarrass our freedom of action. In consequence of these considerations it would seem to me necessary, while adhering strictly to the path laid down by Your Majesty, to be content for the time being with the agreement on the two points, as expressed in the instruction to Baron Mohrenheim, postponing all further explanations concerning them until Your Majesty's return to St. Petersburg. To depart from this program we could be induced only by some sudden, alarming circumstances, but, happily, they are not to be expected in the immediate future." [42]

There was nothing for the French to do but to exercise patience. For the time being they felt decidedly exposed, for there was nothing in the August Entente that would guarantee them immediate Russian aid in the event of their becoming embroiled with the Triple Alliance or with England. Fortunately arrangements had been made for the French squadron to visit Portsmouth on its return from Cronstadt. The invitation had come from England, and may be taken as evidence that Lord Salisbury, while convinced that it was to England's interest to stand well with the Triple Alliance, thought it well to disabuse France and Russia of any ideas of English hostility. The Paris government accepted the invitation with alacrity, for the obvious reason that the merest common sense dictated the avoidance of antagonism to England so long as Russia could not be certainly counted upon. As a matter of fact there was always a school of French political thought, of which Clemenceau may be taken as the outstanding ex-

---

41 Freycinet: *Souvenirs,* pp. 487 ff.; Hansen: *Mohrenheim,* pp. 132–6; *Livre Jaune Français,* nos. 16, 18, 19; Lamsdorff, op. cit., pp. 172–182.   42 Lamsdorff, op. cit., p. 183.

ample, which disliked and distrusted an alliance with " barbarous " and autocratic Russia, and sought an agreement with liberal England. On the very eve
of the Cronstadt visit Clemenceau had a long talk with Joseph Chamberlain
in which he asked for English support in effecting a settlement with Germany
in order that France might be spared the alliance with Russia. In return he was
prepared to give England a free hand in Egypt. Chamberlain reported all this
to Salisbury, but the prime minister insisted on the need for the time being of
maintaining a free hand while cultivating the friendship of the central powers.[43]

This did not, of course, preclude a friendly gesture towards France. " Though
in the present state of Europe our interests lie on the side of the Triple Alliance,"
wrote Salisbury to the Queen, " it is most important to persuade the French, if
we can, that England has no antipathy to France, or any partisanship against
her." [44] So every effort was made to assure the success of the Portsmouth visit
and the occasion proved in every way satisfactory.[45]

While the French statesmen were intent on avoiding anything like a provocative attitude, Baron Mohrenheim chattered all too freely about the new
Entente, much to the distress to the Russian foreign office, which was more than
ever convinced that he had gone off his head or that he was being richly rewarded.[46] Ribot, Freycinet and other members of the cabinet tried to counter-act
his baneful utterances by making a series of reassuring and pacific speeches in
the provinces, but there was nevertheless considerable uneasiness and apprehension in Berlin, Vienna and London. In September Emperor William and
Francis Joseph met at Schwarzenau. They discussed the general European scene
and decided to pursue a policy of calmness and conciliation. Soon afterward
Caprivi, Kálnoky and Rudini made public statements reflecting this policy.
But at bottom the cabinets of the central powers and of England were by no
means certain that the new Franco-Russian Entente would not lead to complications. For some time Europe had feared that the Russians were planning an
assault upon Constantinople or the Bosporus. In September there was something
of a scare when they began to threaten the Sultan because of his objection to
the passage of ships of the Russian volunteer fleet. At London the matter was
evidently considered to be a serious symptom, and a strong stand was decided
upon. By way of warning a British force was landed on the island of Sigri, near
the entrance to the Dardanelles (September 13), and the Sultan was obliged to
explain to the powers that his arrangement with Russia regarding the Straits involved no departure from the international regulations.[47]

---

[43] J. L. Garvin: *The Life of Joseph Chamberlain* (London, 1933), II, pp. 457 ff.

[44] *Letters of Queen Victoria*, II, p. 65; Cecil: *Life of Salisbury*, IV, p. 395.

[45] There is a rather amusing account in Lord George Hamilton: *Parliamentary Reminiscences
and Reflections, 1886–1906* (London, 1922), pp. 124–6; see also *Letters of Queen Victoria*, II, pp.
62 ff.; Langer: *Franco-Russian Alliance*, pp. 199 ff.

[46] Lamsdorff, op. cit., pp. 184, 187.

[47] H. S. Edwards: *Sir William White* (London, 1902), pp. 251 ff.; *Die Grosse Politik*, IX, nos.
2109 ff.; further details in my *Franco-Russian Alliance*, pp. 201 ff.; Martin Peters: *Die Meerengen
und die Europäischen Grossmächte, 1890–1895* (Erlangen, 1932), pp. 40–8.

During the winter of 1891–1892 the European situation was marked by an uneasy calm. Russia was entering upon one of the worst famines of her history. In some quarters it was feared that this disaster, far from paralyzing the government, might drive it into a desperate policy of foreign adventure. As a matter of fact, however, the Russians had no desire at all to embark upon a course of aggression. They were, on the contrary, literally sick with fear lest their neighbors take advantage of their plight. The minister of finance was already talking about the possibility of affecting some agreement for the reduction of armaments, an idea which rather intrigued the pacifically minded officials of the foreign office.[48] The scheme was somewhat phantastic at the time and was not followed up, but M. Giers, who had for some time been planning to pay a visit to the West, made good use of his leave to carry tidings of good will to the other powers. On October 13–14 he conferred with Rudini at Milan and Monza. The nature of these discussions has never become known, despite the deluge of rumors which filled the press at that time. It seems, however, that Giers gave assurances with regard to the new Entente with France, and promised to use his good offices to improve Franco-Italian relations. Rudini apparently agreed to do what he could to hasten the settlement of the Bulgarian difficulty.[49]

Although he had not originally planned to visit Paris, the Russian foreign minister decided that it would not be expedient to omit the French capital from his itinerary. He arrived there on November 20. On the following day there was an important conference at which Freycinet and Ribot, Giers and Mohrenheim were present. The Russian minister was intent on minimizing the dangers of the European situation in order to forestall the demands of his French colleague. He was convinced, he said, that the powers of the Triple Alliance were not willing to risk a war. Besides, he could do nothing about a military convention without consulting with the Tsar. In regard to the Near East Russia was anxious to prevent complications. She had no designs on Constantinople and had no intention of taking action unless the Austrians or Greeks attempted to gain possession of this important capital. With respect to Egypt, Russia would be willing to lend France moral support, but that was all. There was some talk of the desirability of establishing a Russian squadron in the Mediterranean and Russian ships were in fact sent on a series of demonstrative visits, but the only concrete result of the conference was the agreement that the two governments should send to their representatives at Constantinople instructions to co-operate in convincing the Sultan that the new Entente was not directed against Turkey, and to inform His Majesty that if he swerved too much to the side of the Triple Alliance and England, France and Russia would act accordingly. Taken by and large, Giers succeeded in evading awkward demands on the part of the

---

[48] Lamsdorff, op. cit., pp. 203, 205.
[49] The question is discussed in detail in my *Franco-Russian Alliance*, pp. 211–7; but some additional material from the Austrian archives is discussed in Wolfgang Herrmann: *Dreibund, Zweibund, England* (Stuttgart, 1929), pp. 29–31.

French. He had every reason to be satisfied. Freycinet, on the other hand, was disgusted with Giers' unwillingness to go beyond generalities or to discuss anything but the status quo.[50]

On his way back to St. Petersburg the Russian minister stopped at Berlin. He found the German statesmen very reserved and was therefore obliged to do most of the talking himself. He explained that the Entente with France was the result of the noisy renewal of the Triple Alliance and attempted to minimize the importance of the Cronstadt demonstration. Referring to his visit to Paris, he expatiated upon the desire for peace which he found among the French people. Neither Alsace nor Lorraine had even been mentioned in the conversations, he asserted. Apart from these generalities, Giers was anxious to bring up a very important question. Russia, which was badly in need of funds, had suffered a severe financial reverse in October when a loan for half a billion francs had been floated in Paris. The bankers had over-subscribed it seven times, but they had found it impossible to unload the bonds on the public, so that in the end the Russian ministry of finance was obliged to buy back many of the bonds in order to save itself from complete debacle. Giers hoped to be able to secure the approval of the German government for the participation of Berlin banks, and if possible to pave the way for a German-Russian tariff treaty. But he received little encouragement and left the German capital without accomplishing anything of note.[51]

As the year 1891 drew to a close, then, the relationship between Russia and France remained what it was when the exchange of notes took place in August. The Russians had taken the initiative through fear of their own isolation and through apprehension lest France be forced to make other arrangements. The Paris government had, from the outset, made no secret of its ultimate desires, but Giers and the foreign office had avoided definite commitments. During the months of uncertainty that followed the Cronstadt demonstration all efforts made by the French to initiate discussions looking to a military convention proved completely abortive. The Russians felt that they had done enough. The domestic crisis made a policy of watchful waiting more imperative than ever. Far from challenging the powers of the Triple Alliance, Giers, who was really a sick man, did not spare himself. His grand tour of the European capitals was a good will tour and he was pleased to think, when he arrived at home, that the danger of international complications was, for the time being, but slight.

---

[50] *Livre Jaune Français*, nos. 21, 22, 24, 25; Freycinet: *Souvenirs*, pp. 489–91; Hansen: *Mohrenheim*, pp. 137–8; Lamsdorff, op. cit., pp. 196, 205, 213; *Die Grosse Politik*, VII, nos. 1512, 1513.

[51] *Die Grosse Politik*, VII, nos. 1515, 1633, 1634; Daudet: *Histoire Diplomatique*, pp. 262–9; Lamsdorff, op. cit., pp. 196 ff.; some Austrian material is adduced in my *Franco-Russian Alliance*, pp. 221–4.

GENERAL TREATMENTS OF THE PERIOD

GOOCH, GEORGE P.: *History of Modern Europe, 1878–1919.* New York, 1923. Though now no longer up-to-date with regard to factual material, this stimulating account is still worth reading.

FAY, SIDNEY B.: *The Origins of the World War.* Two volumes. New York, 1928. Perhaps the best known and certainly one of the best general studies of the diplomatic background of the great war.

WILSON, H. W.: *The War Guilt.* London, 1928. A well-informed account, which tries to consider the more recently published material. The period covered by the present volume is given very slight treatment.

SPENDER, J. A.: *Fifty Years of Europe.* London, 1933. Another attempt to review the story of pre-war diplomacy in the light of the new material. The book, written by a well-known journalist, is interesting but does not cut very deep.

BEAZLEY, RAYMOND C.: *The Road to Ruin in Europe, 1890–1914.* London, 1932. A brief survey.

SONTAG, RAYMOND J.: *European Diplomatic History, 1871–1932.* New York, 1933. One of the best brief surveys, well-informed and impartial.

MOWAT, R. B.: *The Concert of Europe.* London, 1930. A general survey, with emphasis on the history of international co-operation. It adds very little.

WARD, SIR A. W., and GOOCH, G. P.: *The Cambridge History of British Foreign Policy, 1783–1919.* Three volumes. New York, 1923. Not very satisfactory for the period 1890–1902 and now generally superseded by the volumes mentioned above.

PRIBRAM, ALFRED F.: *England and the International Policy of the European Great Powers, 1871–1914.* Oxford, 1931. A series of lectures by a leading Austrian authority. It constitutes the best brief survey of the European policy of England in the pre-war period.

HAUSER, HENRI: *Histoire Diplomatique de l'Europe, 1871–1914.* Two volumes. Paris, 1929. This is a co-operative work and contains chapters by some of the leading French authorities. Though it is uneven in spots, it is, on the whole, the best French account.

BOURGEOIS, EMILE: *Manuel Historique de Politique Etrangère.* Volume IV. Paris, 1926. This final volume of a well-known manual covers the years 1878 to 1919. It is remarkably deficient on the factual side and is of relatively little value.

DEBIDOUR, A.: *Histoire Diplomatique de l'Europe.* Two volumes. Paris, 1916–1917. A well-known survey of the period from 1878 to the war. It never was as good as the author's earlier books and is of almost no value now.

SCHEFER, CHRISTIAN: *D'Une Guerre à l'Autre.* Paris, 1920. A general survey of the period from 1871 to 1914. On the whole the book is well-informed, but it is very drab in the presentation.

DESPAGNET, FRANTZ: *La Diplomatie de la Troisième République et le Droit des Gens.* Paris, 1904. An encyclopedic work, which emphasizes the juridical aspect of international problems. Still decidedly useful.

TARDIEU, ANDRÉ: *France and the Alliances.* New York, 1908. A series of lectures, now in many ways out of date, but still of considerable interest.

RECOULY, RAYMOND: *De Bismarck à Poincaré.* Paris, 1932. A lively journalistic survey, of little value to the scholar.

FRIEDJUNG, HEINRICH: *Das Zeitalter des Imperialismus, 1884–1914.* Three volumes. Berlin, 1919. One of the most extended treatments, written by a prominent Austrian historian. Unfortunately the first volume was written before most of the valuable documentary and other material had been published.

BRANDENBURG, ERICH: *From Bismarck to the World War.* New York, 1927. A very well-known systematic account of German policy from 1890–1914. The book is distinguished by its balance and by the absence of passion or partiality.

ONCKEN, HERMANN: *Das Deutsche Reich und die Vorgeschichte des Weltkrieges.* Two volumes. Leipzig, 1933. May well be read in connexion with Brandenburg. Oncken tries to treat German foreign policy in its connexion with German development in the larger sense. He has, of course, made use of much material published since the date of Brandenburg's book.

VALENTIN, VEIT: *Deutschlands Aussenpolitik von Bismarcks Abgang bis zum Ende des Weltkrieges.* Berlin, 1921. Treats the period from 1890–1902 in very cursory fashion, but is still interesting for the later period.

REVENTLOW, ERNST GRAF ZU: *Deutschlands Auswärtige Politik, 1888–1914.* 11th edition. Berlin, 1918. A pioneer work, marked by a strong nationalistic bias. The book was, however, based upon extensive reading, and need not be entirely discarded even now.

HAMMANN, OTTO: *The World Policy of Germany, 1890–1912.* New York, 1927. The writer of this book was for years the director of the press bureau of the German foreign office. His account is therefore of much interest, though it has been superseded by later and more scholarly accounts.

STIEVE, FRIEDRICH: *Deutschland und Europa, 1890–1914.* Berlin, 1926. Primarily an analysis of the German documents.

BARTSTRA, J. S.: *Twaalf Jaren " Vrije-Hands-Politiek," 1890–1902.* Leiden, n.d. A sound, scholarly study primarily of German policy in the period covered by the present work.

TARLE, E. V.: *Evropa v Epokhu Imperializma, 1871–1919 gg.* Moscow, 1927. Although this book purports to be a general survey of European history from 1871–1914, it is really devoted primarily to the history of diplomacy. It is interesting as a reflection of the Bolshevik interpretation, the more so as it is the work of a leading Russian historian.

SPECIAL LITERATURE ON THE PERIOD 1890–1894.

(See the bibliographical note at the end of Chapter II.)

LITERATURE SINCE 1935

GENERAL TREATMENTS OF THE PERIOD 1890–1902

RENOUVIN, PIERRE, PRECLIN, EDMOND, and HARDY, GEORGES: *L'Epoque contemporaine, 1871–1919.* Paris, 1939. 684 pp. A general text of world history, particularly strong on international affairs. Excellent bibliographies.

BAUMONT, MAURICE: *L'Essor industriel et l'impérialisme, 1878–1904.* Paris, 1937. 610 pp. A volume in the series *Peuples et Civilisations.* One of the best treatments of world history in this period.

GOOCH, GEORGE P.: *Recent Revelations of European Diplomacy.* Fourth edition. New York, 1940. 475 pp. A greatly enlarged and thoroughly revised edition of a work first published in 1927. Consists of a critical review of source materials dealing with the years 1888 to 1914. Highly interesting and instructive.

HALLGARTEN, WOLFGANG: *Vorkriegsimperialismus. Die soziologischen Grundlagen der Aussenpolitik.* Paris, 1935. 364 pp. A stimulating sociological and economic analysis of the major problems of the period after 1890.

ALBERTINI, LUIGI: *Le origine della guerra del 1914.* Milan, 1942. Three volumes. The most recent large-scale study of diplomacy before 1914. The author, former publisher of the *Corriere della Sera,* treats chiefly the relations of the European states. Of the first volume only about fifty-five pages deal with the years 1890–1902.

MANSERGH, NICHOLAS: *The Coming of the First World War. A Study in the European Balance, 1878–1914.* New York, 1949. 256 pp. A summary review, unfortunately by no means abreast of modern knowledge.

POTEMKIN, V. P.: *Istoriia Diplomatii.* Moscow, 1945. Volume II. This volume, part of the standard Soviet history of diplomacy, is written by V. M. Khvostov and I. I. Mints. It adds little beyond the Marxian interpretation.

ROUBAUD, A.: *Le paix armée et les relations internationales, 1871–1914.* Paris, 1945. 223 pp. A brief, popular review, of real merit.

SALVATORELLI, LUIGI: *La politica internazionale dal 1871 ad oggi.* Turin, 1946. 198 pp. Similar to the preceding; exceedingly brief.

POLETIKA, NIKOLAI: *Vozniknovenie Mirovoi Voini,* Moscow, 1935, 728 pp. A Marxist study of the origins of the First World War, running back to 1870. Notable chiefly for the stress on imperialism and militarism.

ROOSBROECK, ROBERT VAN: *Van Bismarck tot Poincaré.* Antwerp, 1935. 315 pp. An undocumented but entirely competent review of international affairs since 1870.

SETON-WATSON, R. W.: *Britain in Europe, 1789–1914. A Survey of Foreign Policy.* New York, 1937. 716 pp. A well-written and soundly critical review, though less detailed on the later nineteenth century than on the earlier period.

TEMPERLEY, HAROLD, and PENSON, LILLIAN M.: *Foundations of British Foreign Policy, 1792–1902*. Cambridge, 1938. 573 pp. A valuable collection of basic documents, including a number of thitherto unpublished materials.

DESCHANEL, L. P.: *Histoire de la politique extérieure de la France, 806–1936*. Paris, 1936. 284 pp. A comprehensive survey, with only one short chapter on the period from 1870 to 1904. Of no value.

CARROLL, E. MALCOLM: *Germany and the Great Powers, 1866–1914. A Study in Public Opinion and Foreign Policy*. New York, 1938. 852 pp. An exhaustive and valuable analysis of the German press and of the relation of opinion to foreign policy.

SCHWERTFEGER, BERNHARD: *Im Kampf um den Lebensraum*. Potsdam, 1940. 368 pp. Despite the title, this is a competent and well-written survey of German foreign policy.

EYCK, ERICH: *Das persönliche Regiment Wilhelms II; politische Geschichte des deutschen Kaiserreiches von 1890 bis 1914*. Zurich, 1948. 814 pp. Continues the author's important biography of Bismarck. An excellent, critical study of German history under William II.

MACOTTA, GIUSEPPE W.: *Guglielmo II, la Germania e l'Europa, 1888–1914*. Rome, 1934. 302 pp. A fairly well-informed revaluation of German foreign policy after 1888.

ESCHMANN, E. W.: *Der Aufstieg Italiens zur Grossmacht und zum Imperium von 1871 bis zum Kriegseintritt gegen die Westmächte*. Berlin, 1941. 104 pp. A brief but competent review of Italian foreign policy.

STÄHLIN, KARL: *Geschichte Russlands*. Volume IV, in two parts. Berlin, 1939. 1136 pp. A general history of Russia, noted here because of its unusually full and critical account of foreign relations.

GRUNVALD, C. DE: *Trois siècles de diplomatie russe*. Paris, 1945. 284 pp. An interesting and sympathetic summary account of Russian diplomacy, obviously based on wide reading.

TRAUTMANN, OSKAR P.: *Die Sängerbrücke*. Stuttgart, 1940. 220 pp. Written by a prominent German diplomat, this is reputed to be a masterly and non-academic treatment of Russian foreign policy from 1870 to 1914, based upon Russian as well as Western sources.

GOOCH, GEORGE P.: *Studies in Diplomacy and Statecraft*. London, 1942. 373 pp. Contains a revision, in the light of the recently published French documents, of the author's excellent essay on German-French relations from 1870–1914.

GOSSES, F.: *The Management of British Foreign Policy before the First World War, especially during the Period 1880–1914*. Leyden, 1948. 172 pp. An excellent, documented study of the mechanics of British foreign policy.

Benson, E. F.: *The Kaiser and English Relations*. New York, 1936. 304 pp. A systematic review, based on the obvious sources, of William II's relations with Britain.

Anderson, Pauline R.: *The Background of anti-English Feeling in Germany, 1890–1902*. Washington, 1939. 382 pp. An admirable dissertation, based on wide research and revealing a critical understanding of the forces behind Weltpolitik.

Hale, Oron J.: *Publicity and Diplomacy, with Special Reference to England and Germany, 1890–1914*. New York, 1940. 486 pp. An excellent study of the German and British press, its organization, operation, etc. Particularly valuable as an analysis of the process of imperialism.

Wollemborg, Leo: *Politica estera italiana: anteguerra e guerra, 1882–1917*. Rome, 1938. 358 pp. Actually deals very summarily and along Fascist lines with the period prior to 1915.

Silva, Pietro: *Il Mediterraneo dall'unità di Roma all'Impero Italiano*. Milan, 1941. Two volumes. The latest edition of a beautifully illustrated and generally well informed history of the Mediterranean problem. Full treatment of the period from 1890 to 1902.

Peteani, Luigi: *La questione libica nella diplomazia europea*. Florence, 1939. 254 pp. Actually a thorough, scholarly study of the whole Mediterranean problem and of the Mediterranean Agreements in the period after 1870.

Dietrich, Richard: " England und Italien, 1887–1902; ein Beitrag zur Vorgeschichte des Tripoliskrieges " (*Historische Vierteljahrschrift*, XXIX, May, 1935, pp. 768–800). A careful, well documented analysis of British-Italian relations, with special reference to agreements regarding Africa.

Kirchner, Ivan E.: *Der nahe Osten: der Kampf um Vorderasien und Ägypten vom Mittelalter bis zur Gegenwart*. Munich, 1941. 920 pp. A general text on Near Eastern history, particularly full on the late 19th century and stressing especially the clash of European economic interests.

Cognasso, Francesco: *Storia della questione d'Oriente*. Turin, 1945. 720 pp. A detailed, conventional survey of the Near Eastern question.

II

The Franco-Russian Alliance

∽

ESPITE THE EFFORTS OF THE RUSSIAN FOREIGN OFFICE TO REASSURE THE
other powers with respect to the Franco-Russian Entente, the situation
did not improve very much during the winter of 1891–1892. Relations
between Russia and Germany, for example, became more and more strained.
Emperor William was anxious about the new alignment and suspected that his
own allies were ready to make up to the Russians. The Tsar, on the other
hand, was tortured by fears lest England or the powers of the Triple Alliance
should attack Russia in her hour of tribulation. The unwillingness of the
Germans to lend money or to enter seriously upon the discussion of a tariff
treaty made the Russian autocrat even more suspicious of his German cousin's
ultimate plans. Finally, to crown it all, he was startled by the initiation of
a conciliatory policy toward the Poles on the part of the Berlin government.
It seemed almost as though the Germans were angling for the support of
the Poles in a coming war with Russia. These developments, taken together
with the continued unrest in Bulgaria and the constant friction between Russia
and Austria, convinced the Tsar that he was on the eve of a catastrophe, and
that his German neighbor was primarily responsible for Russia's difficulties.
When, in the autumn of 1891, Alexander twice passed through German territory without indicating a desire to see the Emperor, he was simply giving vent
to his personal feelings. It is not surprising, however, that William put a most
ominous interpretation upon this discourtesy.

In the meanwhile, Freycinet and his colleagues were as eager as ever to proceed
with the integration of the August Entente. They knew that if anything was to
be accomplished, the initiative must come from their side. The chief of staff,
General Miribel, was therefore instructed to draw up a preliminary draft for a
military convention. Nothing was done for the moment, because the Tsar's
aversion to any further action at that time was well known and even the Russian
press declaimed against the idea of a hard and fast alliance. Freycinet's fall from
power, which resulted directly from the new policies initiated by the Vatican,
made a very poor impression in St. Petersburg. The Russian ambassador at
Paris warned the French authorities that the Tsar did not like " new faces," and
it was probably for that reason that Freycinet was retained as minister of war
and Ribot as minister of foreign affairs in the new Loubet cabinet.

Finally, on March 8, 1892, the Miribel draft was submitted to the Tsar. The document was anything but welcome to the Russian foreign office, which simply resented all efforts of the French to capitalize the new relationship to Russia. Lamsdorff was much put out by the naval demonstrations in the Mediterranean: " Having entangled us in their nets, we shall be betrayed and sold at the first convenient opportunity," he moaned. The rapprochement with France, he argued, was perfectly proper as a reply to the renewal of the Triple Alliance: " We would not remain isolated and unprepared, we had to restore at least the appearance of a balance of forces in Europe, but why abuse good things? We need peace and tranquillity in view of the disasters of the famine, the incompleteness of our armaments, the desperate state of our railroads and finally the renewed agitation in the camp of the Nihilists." The best thing for Russia would be an arrangement with Germany.[1]

Giers shared this general view and felt convinced, after the fall of the Freycinet cabinet, that every precaution should be taken because of the instability of French affairs. He agreed with Lamsdorff that the Miribel draft, with its distinct point against Germany, was not in Russia's interest. Russia must avoid giving promises which would leave France a free hand to provoke a conflict. It would be a mistake to help the French crush Germany, when the French were unwilling to aid Russia against Austria or Turkey. The Tsar, however, showed little sympathy for the German proclivities of his minister. " We must indeed come to an agreement with the French," he noted, " and in case of war between France and Germany we must immediately hurl ourselves upon the Germans in order not to give them time to crush France first and then turn on us. We must correct the mistakes of the past and crush Germany at the first opportunity. When Germany breaks up, Austria will not dare do anything."

" The Tsar believes that once he has downed Germany he will be ruler of the world, have the Balkans in his pocket, etc.," remarked Giers bitterly to his assistant. " What," he asked the Tsar, " would Russia gain by helping France defeat Germany? " To which Alexander replied that Germany, once defeated, would fall to pieces. But the foreign minister argued that a struggle for independence would unite Germany more strongly than ever. And even if France were successful, she would then no longer require the support of Russia. Russia would, in fact, be left with an unprotected frontier on the side of a hostile Germany. Would not so compromising a document as a military convention be unsafe in the hands of an unstable government?

This material, taken from the Lamsdorff diaries, our first really authentic evidence from the Russian side, is most interesting because it reflects thus early in the negotiation the fundamental divergences in the aims of Russia and France, to say nothing of the proof it supplies of Giers' aversion to a hard and fast agreement with France. The remarkable thing is that the Tsar showed himself so open-minded on the subject. He was evidently more ready to swallow the French bait than was any one of his advisers. Whether this was due to the in-

---

[1] Lamsdorff: *Dnievnik, 1891–1892*, p. 262.

fluence of the shady Mohrenheim it is impossible to say. In any event Alexander, though not persuaded by the objections of Giers, yielded at least to the extent of promising to postpone serious consideration of the matter until his return from Denmark in July, when a high French officer was to be sent to St. Petersburg. In other words, the question of a military convention was allowed to hang fire.[2]

When the Tsar left for Denmark he finally gave in to the importunities of his ministers and agreed to pay a visit, already long overdue, to the German Emperor. On June 7 the two monarchs met at Kiel and spent the day together. Political discussion was scrupulously avoided, for it was felt on both sides that nothing could be gained by attempting explanations. As a result the visit was much more successful than either ruler had expected it to be. But in Paris this latest turn was viewed with considerable uneasiness, the more so as there had been some correspondence with Berlin regarding an international celebration of university students which was to be held at Nancy. The German students had not been invited to this affair. Indeed the difficulty arose from the fact that it was intended to make the whole demonstration anti-German and pro-Russian. The French government did everything in its power to throw cold water on the plans of the students, but President Carnot, who was visiting the eastern departments at that very time, was unable to avoid being present. Everything went well until, on June 6, the Grand Duke Constantine, a close relative of the Tsar, appeared at Nancy to pay his respects to Carnot. His presence was made the occasion for a huge Russophil demonstration which, coming as it did just before the meeting of the Tsar and the Emperor, looked very much like an affair pre-arranged by the Russian government to reassure the French and to overshadow the Kiel interview. As a matter of fact the French ministry was more alarmed than pleased by this unexpected incident, which was apparently staged by Mohrenheim as his own contribution to the good cause. The Tsar had nothing to do with it. In fact he was infuriated by the whole affair.[3]

Incidents of this sort, which might very well have led to serious consequences, made the French more anxious than ever to close the deal with Russia and thus make absolutely sure of her aid in case of eventual complications. But the Russians were less disposed than ever to yield to pressure. The fall of the Salisbury government in England in the summer and the advent of a new Gladstone ministry was everywhere expected to result in greater laxity in English policy. Gladstone was more interested in domestic than in foreign affairs, and was not nearly so suspicious of Russia as his predecessor. Lord Rosebery, the new foreign minister, was known to be an admirer of Salisbury's policies, but it was expected that he would not be able to secure the support of his colleagues for an active

[2] *Livre Jaune Français*, nos. 28–33, 38; Freycinet: *Souvenirs*, pp. 497–500; Lamsdorff, op. cit., pp. 270–1, 293, 298–9, 308.

[3] On the Kiel interview see: *Die Grosse Politik*, VII, no. 1636; Waldersee: *Denkwürdigkeiten*, II, pp. 241, 242. On the Nancy affair see: *Die Grosse Politik*, VII, nos. 1580 ff.; Hansen: *Mohrenheim*, pp. 138–42; Austrian material in my *Franco-Russian Alliance*, pp. 244–9.

course in international affairs. The enthusiasm of the Russians for the French had cooled considerably, and all the importunities of the Paris government went unheeded. The Tsar was abroad and Giers was sick in bed.

With no prospect of official action, M. Ribot finally decided to make use of the press to set forth the French view of the situation. On July 14, the French national holiday, the *Figaro* published a remarkable article entitled " Alliance or Flirtation? " The inspired writer of this article did not indulge in circumlocutions. It was high time, he argued, that the period of coquetting and of bagatelles should be brought to a close by an alliance contract. If the Russians did not approve of French conditions, neither did the French like the Russian situation with its economic and financial difficulties and its inadequate military establishment. France had the right to demand that something definite be done. These exchanges of vague promises and these manifestations of Platonic attachment were more dangerous than comforting. " We have been courting for the last year; let us resolutely raise the question of the marriage-contract as befits families that respect each other."

The Russians took the hint and, though they felt outraged by the temerity of the French, they saw the need for some concession. On August 1 Boisdeffre arrived at St. Petersburg according to previous arrangement. The French demands were roughly as follows: a) in case the Triple Alliance or Germany alone mobilized, Russia and France should do likewise without the need of previous agreement or notification; b) in case of war, Russia should place on her German frontier all the forces at her disposal excepting those necessary to hold Austria in check; c) the forces to be used against Germany should not confine themselves to observation, but should attack, in order to prevent the Germans from transporting their troops to the west and thus crushing France. It was a complete orderly program for which Ribot demanded the signature not only of the minister of war, but of the minister of foreign affairs.

Boisdeffre opened the discussion immediately with Vannovski and Obruchev, the Russian minister of war and chief of staff, but he discovered to his great disappointment that the situation was anything but auspicious. General Vannovski was favorable to an agreement with France, but wished to avoid specific obligations of a military nature. General Obruchev, the chief of staff, was prepared to go further than his colleague, but had to reckon with the specific needs of Russia and had to take into account the opposition of the foreign office. In a fundamental memorandum drawn up in May he had gone over the problem in detail. He recognized the tremendous importance of swift mobilization. " Beginning of mobilization," he pointed out, " cannot now be regarded as a peaceful act; on the contrary it is the most decisive act of war." Therefore it would be highly desirable for two allied powers to mobilize simultaneously, and with that move diplomatic action would cease. Furthermore, he remarked, the chances of a war remaining localized were very small. It would be a mistake to deal with the problem of mobilizing against any single enemy.

Russia and France would have to arrange to mobilize simultaneously against the Triple Alliance as a whole:

> " The French regard as their immediate enemy Germany almost exclusively; to Italy they attach secondary importance, while for Austria they cherish certain sympathies, continuing to regard her as the historic antagonist of Germany. Hence, the French would like, if possible, to conclude with us a convention solely for the event of war with Germany. To a certain extent this condition is mutually profitable. But one cannot help noticing that it is considerably more profitable for France than for us. Having secured a guarantee against her most dangerous enemy, France might, in case of war by Russia against Austria, even though it broke out at Germany's command, remain inactive and wait for developments, which might prove fatal to us. . . . Hence it is scarcely convenient for us to conclude a convention exclusively for the event of a war with Germany. We are faced by a Triple Alliance closely cemented in military matters; in no case can we imagine separate action against us by Germany or Austria; hence, in the convention it is necessary for us to base the simultaneous mobilization of the armies of France and Russia on the idea of an attack not by Germany, but by any power of the Triple Alliance."

As for the assignment of definite numbers of troops to any specific theatre of the war, Obruchev was resolutely opposed to such arrangements: " We must preserve absolute freedom of action, and hence in the question of joint operations with France the best thing will be to confine ourselves to a general obligation." [4]

At bottom this Obruchev memorandum was not far removed from the memorandum drawn up by General Miribel. But both Vannovski and Giers felt that written obligations were to be avoided, and they had secured the Tsar's approval of this standpoint. Therefore General Boisdeffre had a hard time during the first days he spent in St. Petersburg. The discussions were, at times, nothing less than acrimonious. Vannovski argued that there was no need for a formal agreement and that a gentlemen's understanding would suffice. He complained of the *Figaro* article, he dilated on the instability of the French ministries, he pointed out the unconstitutionality of agreements not approved by the French chamber, and he stressed the impossibility of submitting the Convention to the legislature because of the Tsar's insistence on absolute secrecy. Vannovski even hinted that the French people, once they had the Tsar's signature, would not really try to maintain peace. Regarding the specific French demands, the Russians raised serious objections. They rebelled against the idea of making the mobilization of Germany alone a *casus foederis*. For them Austria was the principal enemy. In the end, however, Vannovski agreed to submit a modification of the French draft to the Tsar, probably anticipating his disapproval. Obruchev and Boisdeffre drew up a new text based on the French draft but taking account of the Russian objections. It was this modified draft

---

[4] Lamsdorff, op. cit., pp. 336–40.

which was finally signed by the two governments and it is therefore necessary to say something of its variations from the French original.

The final draft shows that Article I of the French original, which dealt with mobilization, became Article II; Article II of the French draft, providing for common action in the event of actual hostilities, now became Article III. The last sentence of Article I of the original, which envisaged the speedy engagement of the forces to be used against Germany, was relegated to the end of Article III of the final text. From the definitive form it is clear that the French won their point providing for mobilization in case of mobilization by Germany alone (" In case the forces of the Triple Alliance, or of one of the powers composing it," etc.). But it must be noted that this same clause obliged France to mobilize in case Austria alone mobilized against Russia. To this the French objected, because they were no more willing to become embroiled in an Austrian-Russian quarrel than were the Russians to become involved in a Franco-German dispute. The French yielded in order not to wreck the negotiations, consoling themselves with the thought that an Austrian-Russian conflict would eventually bring in Germany or Italy anyway. The whole thing, then, was a compromise.

But why did the Russians consent to a compromise? It was not they but the French who were anxious to have the Convention. The explanation is that the changed sequence of the articles deprived the compromise of most of its value. In the original French draft the articles had followed logically one upon the other: 1. mobilization; 2. common action in case of actual hostilities; 3. division of forces, etc. In the final draft the cart was put before the horse, and there was a contradiction between Articles I and II. In the second, France bound herself to mobilize even if Austria alone mobilized, but according to the first she was obliged to lend active assistance only if Russia were attacked by Germany or by Austria supported by Germany. The same contradiction applied to Russia's obligations. There are indications that both sides agreed to the compromise with some mental reservations. The French, for example, could argue that they could not be expected to mobilize against Austria alone if they were not expected to fight against Austria alone. So far as one can detect, the Russians meant to take only Article I of the final draft seriously.

The remaining clauses of the agreement provided for co-operation of the two general staffs in time of peace, specified that France and Russia should not conclude a separate peace with the Triple Alliance, fixed the duration of the Convention at that of the Triple Alliance, and provided for rigorous secrecy.

After some hesitation Freycinet authorized Boisdeffre to sign this modified draft. The Tsar was inclined to approve it, but insisted that it be referred to Giers. This meant more trouble and objection, because of the foreign minister's absence in Finland and because of his known opposition. At bottom the draft convention was much more than a military arrangement. It was called that by common consent because it was important to have the agreement in a form other than a treaty, so that the French government would not have to submit it to the Chamber. The document was really something of a cross between a treaty of alliance and a military convention. Its political provisions will be obvious to anyone who consults the text. Now it was not the purely military arrangements between the general staffs that Giers objected to. Such arrangements were not considered to bind a government to any particular course of action, but simply laid down a course of procedure if war were actually embarked upon. It was the political aspect of the Boisdeffre-Obruchev draft that Giers could not stomach. He was appalled to learn that the Tsar seemed inclined to accept it. In a letter to Alexander he said: " I make bold to think that to accept premature obligations, not called for at the present moment by political conditions, would be . . . extremely dangerous, the more so as we do not know under what circumstances war will break out."

Thereupon the Tsar asked Obruchev to pay a hurried visit to Giers in the hope of persuading him. The chief of staff turned out to be more reasonable than Giers had expected to find him. Apparently both Vannovski and Obruchev had become somewhat irritated by the insistence of Boisdeffre. In any event it took but a short time for Obruchev and Giers to reach an agreement. Vannovski was to write Boisdeffre a letter embodying the revised draft, but with the clear understanding that it was merely a *draft,* that the Tsar's approval was *approval only in principle,* and that the political aspects of the draft (that is, the alliance aspect) should be further examined. On these terms the Tsar gave his approval on August 17. Boisdeffre left St. Petersburg discouraged and disgusted. Ribot and Freycinet shared his indignation. When Giers visited southern France in September they paid him a special visit and tried to reopen the question. They found him, as ever, full of general statements and benevolent assurances, but it was impossible to secure from him any definite promises.[5]

The French statesmen had had ample opportunity to become acquainted with the true disposition of the Russians. It was clearly quite futile to attempt further discussions, especially after the great Panama scandal began to throw its pall over the French political scene in the autumn of 1892. The Tsar, who had never had any sympathy with the republican form of government, was disgusted with the revelation of rottenness and corruption in French political life. When one of the French deputies made the assertion that Katkov, the great Russian journalist, had received half a million francs of Panama money to back the Franco-Russian Alliance, the press of St. Petersburg and Moscow rose in unison to defend the memory of its dead leader and to vilify the French. The relations between the two governments became even more strained when the

---

[5] *Livre Jaune Français,* nos. 35–82; Freycinet: *Souvenirs,* pp. 500 ff.; Lamsdorff, op. cit., pp. 343–57. For an excellent discussion and interpretation of the texts see Eugen Fischer: " Der Sinn der Russisch-Französischen Militärkonvention " (*Preussische Jahrbücher,* April, 1923, pp. 65–98) and Pierre Renouvin: " Les Engagements de l'Alliance Franco-Russe " (*Revue d'Histoire de la Guerre Mondiale,* October, 1934, pp. 297–310).

Russian ambassador, Baron Mohrenheim, was accused of having accepted some of the tainted funds.[6]

Worse than this estrangement was the unwillingness of the two powers to support each other in matters of real significance. The Russians and the English were drifting into a serious dispute on the borders of India, in the region of the Pamirs. For some time the Russians had been advancing over the high plateaus, their object being to discourage the English from an active support of the Bulgarian régime by bringing pressure to bear upon the British position in central Asia. In the autumn of 1891 a Russian detachment in the Pamirs had turned back Captain Younghusband, who had been sent from India to investigate its activities. The English had lodged a vigorous protest, and the Russian government had seen fit to apologize.[7]

During the spring and summer of 1892 there had been some talk of delimiting the claims of the two powers in these mountain fastnesses, but the Russians were evidently sparring for time and it seems from the official correspondence that the military men were in favor of taking a strong line. However that may have been, in the early autumn of 1892 Colonel Ianov, the very man who had expelled Younghusband, was sent out with a considerable force to assert the authority of Russia against the encroachments of China and Afghanistan. Before long there were serious clashes between the Russian and Afghan detachments, and there was some danger that the Amir would go over to the Russian side. The whole expedition was evidently engineered by the Russian war office, which wanted to secure control of the passes to India. The foreign office was anxious enough to come to an agreement, and attempted to carry on negotiations with the English. But it was quite impossible to come to any settlement, and the matter dragged on for many months.[8]

The continued danger of a conflict with England probably had something to do with the willingness of the Tsar to negotiate the Military Convention with the French. That is to say, the Russians, no longer assured of the neutrality of Germany, needed the French to hold the Germans in check. But the government at St. Petersburg was very anxious to avoid trouble, and for that reason flatly refused to support the French government in its protests when, in January 1893, the English interfered in Egypt and prevented the young Khedive from appointing an anti-English ministry.[9]

---

[6] Élie de Cyon: " L'Enquête sur le Panama et la Russie " (Nouvelle Revue, January 1, 1893); Hansen: Mohrenheim, pp. 143–54; C. Pobiedonostsev: Mémoires (Paris, 1927), pp. 637 ff.; Lettres de la Princesse Radziwill, I, p. 140.

[7] Sir Francis Younghusband: The Light of Experience (Boston, 1927), pp. 58 ff.; Baron A. Meyendorff: Correspondance de M. de Staal (Paris, 1929), II, pp. 157–64; Lamsdorff, op. cit., pp. 222–57.

[8] See especially Meyendorff, op. cit., pp. 178–213, passim; Letters of Queen Victoria, II, pp. 153–4.

[9] Earl of Cromer: Abbas II (London, 1915), chaps. ii, iii; Marquess of Zetland: Lord Cromer (London, 1932), chap. xvii; Marquess of Crewe: Lord Rosebery (New York, 1931), pp. 338 ff.;

For the time being European politics were in a fluid state. The Panama scandal turned France into a " wild sea of denunciation, suspicion and mutual recrimination," to quote Lord Dufferin. The Tsar was utterly disillusioned and disgusted, especially by the tactless efforts of French agitators to implicate Russian diplomats. Yet there was the constant threat of trouble with the English in central Asia, and the Bulgarian question was still an open sore. During the winter Stambulov had prepared the way for the marriage of Ferdinand with a Catholic princess of the house of Parma. This necessitated changes in the Bulgarian constitution, but the necessary measures were railroaded through the Assembly and the wedding actually took place in April 1893. The Russian government launched fiery protests and even hinted at the possible use of force, but no one took these threats very seriously, knowing full well that Russia was not prepared to act. This diagnosis of the situation was quite correct, for in actual fact efforts were being made by Russia to reach an agreement with Austria regarding the Bulgarian question. Nothing concrete resulted from these advances because the Austrians were quite unwilling to co-operate in the ejection of Ferdinand and his minister. Still, the relations between the two countries were decidedly improved, and in May Giers himself paid a visit to Vienna, where he was given a most cordial reception. After his departure Kálnoky declared in the Delegations that relations with Russia had improved and that they were now " very friendly." [10]

Of even greater importance than the efforts of the Russians to iron out their difficulties with Austria was the favorable development of Russian-German relations during the winter. In view of the possibilities of a conflict in central Asia, the Russians were more dependent than ever upon the good will of Germany. Furthermore, the series of tariff treaties concluded by Germany with her allies and with other continental states in the years 1891 and 1892 made the settlement of outstanding economic questions more imperative than ever for the Russians. It was hoped at St. Petersburg that the conclusion of a commercial treaty would lead also to the reopening of the German money market, a matter of great importance to Russia during these critical famine years. The negotiations for a tariff treaty were actually opened in August 1892 and were continued with numerous interruptions throughout the winter.[11]

Although these economic discussions made little progress, there was on the German side a distinct desire to re-establish connexions. The change of ministry in England had a good deal to do with this, for the Germans had far less confidence in the Gladstone cabinet than they had had in its predecessor. Whatever

Letters of Queen Victoria, II, pp. 203–20; Die Grosse Politik, VIII, nos. 1821 ff.; further details in Langer: Franco-Russian Alliance, pp. 271–4.

[10] A full account of this phase of the situation may be found in my Franco-Russian Alliance. pp. 275–84.

[11] Recent discussions may be found in Claus Grimm: Graf Witte und die Deutsche Politik (Freiburg, 1930), pp. 18 ff.; Alfred Klein: Der Einfluss des Grafen Witte auf die Deutsch-Russischen Beziehungen (Bielefeld, 1932), pp. 11 ff.

the personal attitude of Rosebery might be, Gladstone was known to be more favorably disposed toward Russia than Salisbury, and was thought to favor an agreement with France. He and his friends had declared time and again their desire to see Egypt evacuated and had left no doubt that England would not intervene on behalf of Italy if the latter came into conflict with France. Rosebery had finally been induced by the Germans to give a personal written declaration recognizing the validity of the Mediterranean Agreements, but he had found it impossible, because of the attitude of his colleagues, to make an official pronouncement.[12]

As viewed from Berlin, England was no longer a reliable factor in continental politics. The Germans now thought it unwise to estrange Russia in the hope of maintaining Anglo-German friendship. They did not, of course, intend to cut the wire to London, but they meant to reconnect the wire to St. Petersburg and, if possible, to maintain a sort of balance between the two great wing powers. This policy of having two irons in the fire had been successfully conducted by Bismarck and its resumption by his successors marked the end of the brief interlude during which everything had been staked on the Triple Alliance and the support of England.

A very instructive example of this change in the German policy may be found in the Egyptian question. The Germans had consistently supported the English in this matter, but in December 1892 it appeared that English interests at Constantinople were doing their utmost to oppose the award of a concession to a German syndicate for a railway to Konia. This concession, the second stage in the construction of what became known later as the Bagdad Railway, was of great interest to the Germans and particularly to the Emperor, who had frequently shown sympathy with the project. It was quite understandable therefore that the Germans should have resented English interference. The government decided upon a very significant action. In reply to the obstruction of the English, the Berlin foreign office wired its representative at Cairo to withhold the consent of the German government to an increase in the Egyptian army, which the English had very much at heart. This action was certainly effective. The London cabinet immediately retreated in the matter of the railway, and the Germans got their concession in February 1893. The upshot of the whole affair was that it showed clearly that Anglo-German relations were now on a business basis, and that the German foreign office was determined to take advantage of England's weakness in order to make gains for itself.[18]

With respect to Russia the German policy underwent a similar marked

---

[12] *Die Grosse Politik*, VIII, nos. 1732 ff. The officials of the British foreign office were never clear in their own minds whether the Mediterranean Agreements were terminated at this time, or not. As a matter of fact they were implicitly recognized for several more years. See on this point *British Documents on the Origins of the War, 1898–1914*, VIII, pp. 5–6, 13.

[18] *Die Grosse Politik*, VIII, nos. 1816 ff.; XIV, nos. 3958 ff.; *Letters of Queen Victoria*, II, pp. 203 ff.; Harold Nicolson: *Portrait of a Diplomatist* (Boston, 1930), pp. 68–72; Edward M. Earle: *Turkey, the Great Powers, and the Bagdad Railway* (New York, 1923), chap. iii.

change. In the Bulgarian question there was an open return to the Bismarckian attitude. The Germans would no longer support the Austrian and English policies in the Near East.[14] It stands to reason that Tsar Alexander appreciated this return of German policy to the old line, the more so as Russia's position during the winter was so uncertain. When General von Schweinitz retired from the post of German ambassador to St. Petersburg, the Tsar wrote directly to Emperor William asking for the appointment of General von Werder, a personal friend of the Imperial family, and a warm advocate of the Russian-German connexion.[15] At Berlin it was felt that this unusual procedure on the part of Alexander, taken together with the Panama crisis, should just about finish the Franco-Russian Alliance. In this belief the Germans were fortified by the Tsar's decision to send his son on a visit to Berlin. Nicholas arrived on January 24 and for six days was the object of flattering attentions on the part of the Emperor. Every effort was made to impress the Grand Duke with the arguments formerly used with such effect by Bismarck. The Emperor painted a lurid picture of the utter corruption and complete rottenness of the French government, and dilated upon the menace to the social order and to the monarchical system. At St. Petersburg and at Berlin it was believed that the whole scandal might end in the establishment of a military dictatorship and possibly war. The Emperor therefore pointed out that a crusade against France might become necessary. The Triple Alliance, he insisted, was based upon conservative principles, and was wholly defensive. It was in no sense an obstacle to the re-establishment of a Holy Alliance or a League of the Three Emperors to combat the revolution.

The Grand Duke raised no objections to this argumentation. On the contrary, he quite outdid the Emperor in the violence of his denunciations and his eagerness to resurrect the agreement between the three monarchies. He promised to discuss the situation with his father, and took along a memorandum which had been carefully worked out in the German foreign office.[16] Yet nothing substantial ever came of these discussions. The Emperor waited in vain for a report of their effect upon the Tsar. Alexander himself may have been sympathetic to the idea, but he obviously could not change the Russian policy overnight. First of all, he would have to see what attitude the Germans would take in the matter of the all-important commercial treaty. When, in March 1893, the German government presented its terms, they were pretty stiff and quite unacceptable to the Russians. After some further negotiation the whole matter was postponed until the autumn. In the meanwhile, in June, the Russian government announced a new and higher tariff schedule, to which the Germans replied. A

---

[14] *Die Grosse Politik,* IX, nos. 2126, 2128, 2129, 2131; Johannes Haller: *Aus dem Leben des Fürsten Philipp zu Eulenburg-Hertefeld* (Berlin, 1924), pp. 83–4.

[15] *Die Grosse Politik,* VII, nos. 1639–42; Schweinitz: *Denkwürdigkeiten,* II, pp. 442 ff.; Haller: *Eulenburg,* pp. 82–3.

[16] *Die Grosse Politik,* VII, nos. 1526, 1527; Haller: *Eulenburg,* pp. 83–4.

severe tariff war broke out between the two countries, which lasted for several months.

The unwillingness of the Germans to consider serious concessions in the economic field was an important obstacle in the way of the re-establishment of friendship with Russia. Another factor of great significance was the German military bill, which was introduced in parliament in November 1892. While it reduced the term of service in the infantry and artillery from three years to two, it involved an increase of the German forces by some 80,000 men. The bill led to a hotly contested parliamentary struggle and for a time became the centre of interest. In the course of the debates frequent reference was made by Caprivi and others to the danger of war on two fronts. Talk of war became all too prevalent as the government's chances of getting the bill passed steadily diminished. When the Reichstag rejected the bill on May 6, the news was hailed with delight in St. Petersburg, where it was hoped that the elections would return an even more recalcitrant assembly. As a matter of fact the elections proved disastrous for the Liberals who had opposed the bill, while the more conservative groups showed substantial gains. With the help of the Polish deputies, the military law was passed on July 15.[17] The worst fears of the Tsar were realized.

At the French foreign office the development of Russian-German relations had been watched with considerable uneasiness. To wipe out the bad impression made by the Panama affair, the government put through a bill providing for the protection of foreign ambassadors from vicious attacks in the press. M. Develle, who succeeded Ribot as foreign minister when the Freycinet cabinet was turned out in January, even induced President Carnot to apologize directly to the Tsar. Throughout the spring every effort was made by the French statesmen to avoid anything that might disturb the peace of the Continent. We know little of the correspondence between Paris and St. Petersburg at this time, but there is evidence that the French made full use of the German military law to urge upon Russia the necessity for precautionary measures. By way of contrast to the attitude of the Germans the French in June concluded a tariff treaty with Russia. After the passage of the German army bill the Paris government expected momentarily some suggestion from the Russians regarding further negotiations for a military convention.[18]

But so far as we know the Russians made no move. The Tsar's reply to the German military bill was to concentrate more and more troops in Poland until, in September, the French ambassador could speak of this region as a " vast entrenched camp " of more than 650,000 men. Russia was preparing for all eventualities, but Alexander was evidently not yet prepared to go all the way to meet

---

[17] Langer: *Franco-Russian Alliance*, pp. 306–10; Johannes Werdermann: *Die Heeresreform unter Caprivi* (Greifswald, 1928).

[18] *Livre Jaune Français*, nos. 82, 83; Hansen: *Mohrenheim*, pp. 153–4; Émile Bourgeois and Georges Pagès: *Les Origines et les Responsabilités de la Grande Guerre* (Paris, 1921), pp. 248–9.

the desire of the French. It will be remembered that negotiations with Germany for a tariff treaty were to be resumed in October. The Russians had an obvious interest in awaiting further developments. In the interval a very serious Anglo-French conflict changed the whole complexion of international affairs. In the time of Freycinet and Ribot the French foreign office had shown no disposition to take an out and out anti-English stand or to support Russia in a forward policy in Asia. These men had followed the traditional French course. They had caused the English considerable trouble by their constant nagging in Egyptian affairs, but the British could regard these activities with relative equanimity so long as England had the support of the Triple Alliance. The Russians, who had little direct interest in the Egyptian question, were much more concerned with securing French aid against England in Asiatic problems. The out and out protagonists of a Franco-Russian alliance in Paris, people like Madame Adam and the group that wrote in the *Nouvelle Revue,* had attacked the foreign minister time and again for his pusillanimous policy toward England and his indifference to Asiatic affairs.

Under Ribot's successor, M. Develle, the French government showed less hesitancy about antagonizing England, especially in Asia. Vigorous efforts were made to extend the frontier of the French possessions in Indo-China at the expense of the Kingdom of Siam. The English, who desired to maintain Siam as a buffer state between Burma and the French colonies to the east, opposed this forward policy in every way. In other words, they viewed the French encroachments upon Siamese territory as the counterpart of the Russian advance toward Afghanistan. Nevertheless, Lord Rosebery was anxious to avoid complications. He was willing to recognize the right of France to settle her accounts with Siam in any way she saw fit, though he refused to recognize the French claim to the left bank of the upper Mekong River. All this did not prevent the French from attacking the English and accusing them of underhandedly encouraging the resistance of the Siamese. On both sides the press became rabid and war seemed almost inevitable when news arrived that on July 13 two French gunboats had forced their way up to Bangkok and had submitted a very stiff ultimatum to the Siamese government. On the rejection of the note the French agent withdrew from the capital and a blockade was proclaimed. This blockade, incidentally, was a blow at the English more than at the Siamese, for fully ninety per cent of the trade was in British hands.[19]

The French action made a deep impression in London. The behavior of the French to Siam, wrote Lord Rosebery to the Queen, was " base, cruel and treacherous." There was probably nothing " so cynically vile " on record. But England could not afford to be " the Knight Errant of the World, careering about to redress grievances and help the weak." Her only interest was to main-

---

[19] *Correspondence Respecting the Affairs of Siam, 1887–1894,* pp. 189 ff.; Documents Diplomatiques: *Affaires de Siam (1893)*; A. de Pourvoirville: *L'Affaire de Siam 1886–1896* (Paris, 1897); further references in my *Franco-Russian Alliance,* pp. 324–6.

tain Siam as a buffer state. But, Rosebery thought, the cabinet and parliament would hardly approve a policy that might result in war, and he himself did not like the idea of appealing to the Triple Alliance. He did, however, sound out the Italians as to their attitude in the event of a crisis, and at the same time hinted to the German ambassador that if matters took a turn for the worse an opportunity might present itself of bringing about the quadruple alliance which had been so frequently discussed, but which had always been vetoed by Gladstone. The Italians were evidently tempted to take a strong stand, but they were warned by the Germans to hold off and wait until the English cannons had been fired or at least until there was a definite and specific treaty signed by Gladstone himself.[20]

It so happened that on July 27 the Emperor William himself arrived at Cowes to take part in the yacht races. On the 29th the Siamese accepted the French ultimatum, including the cession of the left bank of the Mekong, but before the English got over the excitement occasioned by this news a second the greater shock came on July 30 in the form of a telegram from Bangkok saying that the French commander had ordered the British gunboats to leave the river and remain outside the blockade limits. It was obvious that a power like England could not accept such dictation, the more so as withdrawal involved the abandonment of her nationals in the Siamese capital. The great crisis had arrived. When Rosebery sent a note to Paris stating that the British government could not withdraw the warships, he evidently expected the rejection of his note by the French.

As it turned out, the whole report from Bangkok was a false alarm based upon a misunderstanding. Its effect on international relations, however, was none the less great, because on the afternoon of July 30, before the first report was rectified, Rosebery and his colleagues decided on heroic measures. Expecting war to break out the next day, the foreign minister induced the Queen to send her secretary, Sir Arthur Ponsonby, to consult Emperor William at Cowes. When William was informed of the startling news from the east, he was entirely unnerved. He declared that the French had obviously chosen this moment to provoke war because the English fleet was not in the best condition and the German army had not yet reaped the advantage of the increase provided for in the military bill. His own inclination, on the spur of the moment, was to take the part of the English and assume the leadership in the whole action. But when his emissary arrived in London early on July 31, it was only to learn that the crisis had blown over and that the danger of war was past.[21]

In the meantime the Emperor's advisers had gone over the problem with

---

[20] Marquess of Crewe: *Lord Rosebery* (New York, 1931), pp. 346–8; *Letters of Queen Victoria*, II, p. 284; *Die Grosse Politik*, VIII, nos. 1749–51.

[21] Haller: *Eulenburg*, pp. 84–7; *Letters of Queen Victoria*, II, pp. 290 ff.; *Die Grosse Politik*, VIII, nos. 1752–4; Sir Sidney Lee: *Edward VII*, I, p. 707; Reinhold C. Muschler: *Philipp zu Eulenburg* (Leipzig, 1930), p. 312.

him. They persuaded him that it would be a mistaken policy to offer aid before the terms had been clearly laid down. It is very likely that if war had actually broken out, the Germans would have come to the assistance of the English, even without a definite agreement, for they realized that an initial English defeat would be almost fatal to the position of the central powers. But they were determined to conceal this fact and if possible to wait until England was irrevocably engaged before definitely committing themselves. Once an English warship had fired the first shot, wrote Caprivi on a report from the German ambassador, we can be certain that the Triple Alliance can be transformed into a quadruple alliance.[22] Of course the whole problem became academic as soon as the second telegram arrived from Bangkok on the evening of July 30. Rosebery knew that his colleagues would never consent to a war in behalf of the Siamese, and the road for a graceful retreat was paved by the readiness of the French government to recognize the principle of a buffer state on the upper reaches of the Mekong. But the whole incident made a wretched impression on the European governments. Not knowing the exciting developments of July 30 in London and at Cowes, they drew the conclusion that the English were afraid of the French and allowed them to do what they wished with the poor Siamese. Emperor William and his friends could never forget the dramatic scene at Cowes and the nervous excitement of Ponsonby when, his face ghastly white, he broke in upon the Imperial dinner party on the evening of the 30th. Rosebery, who had evidently been quite prepared to take a strong stand, and who fully understood all the implications of the situation, never heard the end of this unfortunate episode. Time and again he tried to explain away his conduct, but the Germans put no stock in his account. At Berlin it was thought that the English had actually been ordered by the French to withdraw their ships from Bangkok, and that they had meekly acquiesced.

The Siamese crisis was the most serious episode in Anglo-French relations before Fashoda. There was a widespread fear in England that the French on the Mekong and the Russians on the Pamirs were bent on attacking the British Empire at the most vulnerable point, in India, or at least on bringing sufficient pressure to bear upon the British position in Asia to compel England to yield in Balkan and Mediterranean questions. This idea was very eloquently expressed in a brilliant article by Lord Curzon, entitled " India between two Fires," which enjoyed an immense vogue in England.[23]

Under these conditions the balance of power obviously rested in the hands of Germany and her allies. If the English succeeded in securing the support of the Triple Alliance, both Russia and France would be so seriously threatened in Europe that they would be unable to act in Asia. It was therefore in the in-

---

[22] *Die Grosse Politik,* VIII, nos. 1752–7.

[23] G. N. Curzon: "India between two Fires " (*Nineteenth Century,* August, 1893); D. C. Boulger: " The Crisis in Indo-China " (ibid.); Sir Lepel Griffin: " England and France in Asia " (ibid., November, 1893); Meyendorff: *Correspondance de M. de Staal,* pp. 216–9.

terests of these powers to avoid all friction in their relations with Germany, and this they did. The English, on the other hand, tried repeatedly to draw the central powers to their side. Their efforts were directed particularly toward Italy, which had a very substantial navy and was therefore a factor to be reckoned with in Mediterranean affairs Italian relations with France were strained to the breaking-point at this particular time, because of the maltreatment of Italian workers in southern France. The government at Rome was therefore more or less disposed to throw in its lot with the British, but the Germans continued to exert themselves to prevent the Italians from making any move until the English had come into the open. It would be unpardonable on the part of the Italian government to take action first, and thus to assume the whole crushing burden of French hostility. It was essential that the English should first declare their stand. This, as we have seen, Rosebery was unable to do because of the opposition of Gladstone and other members of the cabinet.[24]

While the English were unable to secure support from the central powers, their position grew worse and worse. Within a week of the great Siamese crisis, the Russian government finally yielded to the importunities of the French and promised that a Russian squadron should visit Toulon in October.[25] The fact that the visit was to be paid to a Mediterranean port was in itself symptomatic, but its significance was enhanced by the decision to establish a Russian squadron permanently in the Mediterranean. This move threatened to upset the whole balance of sea-power and to checkmate England in all parts of the world. It should be particularly noted that England at this time possessed a navy only slightly larger than the navies of France and Russia combined. So far as the Mediterranean was concerned, the French force alone outnumbered the British squadron, and France had in addition the splendid naval base at Toulon, which was greatly superior to Gibraltar. It was quite clear that the establishment of a Russian squadron would put the British into a most precarious position. They would hardly be able to hold their own, and would certainly be unable to prevent the Russian Black Sea fleet, which was modern and powerful, from breaking through the Straits and entering the Mediterranean. The English were by no means blind to the danger of the situation, and in the autumn of 1893 a great agitation was begun for larger naval appropriations and especially for the construction of more ships. Gladstone and his chancellor of the exchequer, Sir William Harcourt, resisted to the utmost and denied the need for further armaments, but the responsible naval officers were almost unanimously of the opinion that the situation was fraught with danger.[26]

---

[24] *Die Grosse Politik*, VIII, nos. 1755–62; *The Private Diary of Sir Algernon West* (London, 1922), chaps. xv–xvii; A. G. Gardiner: *The Life of Sir William Harcourt* (London, 1923), II, pp. 245 ff., 252 ff.

[25] *Livre Jaune Français*, nos. 83, 86; Hansen: *Mohrenheim*, p. 157.

[26] *Brassey's Naval Annual* for 1894, chap. viii; Gardiner: *Sir William Harcourt*, II, pp. 201, 202, 230, 245 ff.; *The Memoirs of Admiral Lord Charles Beresford* (London, 1914), II, pp. 386 ff.; Nauticus: " The Official Estimates of Rival Navies " (*New Review*, March, 1894, pp. 385–99); for

On October 13 the Russian squadron of five ships under the command of Admiral Avellan arrived at Toulon. During a two weeks' stay the commander and a delegation visited Paris, Lyon and Marseilles. Everywhere the French populace was beside itself with joy. Demonstration followed demonstration, banquet followed banquet, and fête followed fête until disinterested observers expressed grave doubts whether the Russian sailors, who were after all human beings could stand the strain much longer. Admiral Avellan was lionized like a national hero, and took away presents worth half a million francs when he departed. Even the statue of Joan of Arc was decorated with Russian flags. The Toulon festivities completely outdid the Cronstadt days of two years before. Nothing of the kind had been seen in Europe within the memory of man. The French people, who knew nothing of the secrets of European diplomacy, were frantically enthusiastic at the idea of having found a friend. Compared with this unprecedented exhibition the Anglo-Italian naval fraternization, which had been arranged to take place at Taranto, was a very tame affair indeed. Nobody paid much attention to it, and even the English newspapers devoted as little space as they decently could to this unimpressive event. On the other hand, the Toulon episode made a tremendous impression on Europe. The German chancellor declared that no event of the preceding twenty years had so seriously threatened the peace of Europe, and one of the London newspapers asserted that the arrival of the Russian squadron in the Mediterranean marked the most serious day England had passed through since the battle of Trafalgar.

But the Toulon demonstration, for all its brilliance, was not entirely without danger for the French. The Franco-Russian Entente was a menace rather than a safeguard so long as the Military Convention had not been definitely accepted by the Tsar. With this idea in mind, the French foreign office had already provided the ambassador at St. Petersburg with a note to the Russian government in which the significance of the new German military law was clearly pointed out.[27] Giers, however, still evaded a definite commitment. From what little material we have on the Russian side, it is quite clear that the foreign office was as anxious as ever to avoid all complications. The diplomats wrote to each other in the most scathing terms of the military men who blocked an arrangement with England regarding the Pamirs, and of the minister for finance, that " crazy fool Witte," who had precipitated the tariff war with Germany.[28]

Giers had agreed to the Toulon visit only with reluctance. He saw to it that not only the Russian press but also the French press was instructed not to treat the affair in a bellicose spirit. The pacific nature of the Entente was constantly stressed. No doubt, if the Russian foreign minister had had his way, the Russians would have continued to hold off the French. But it had become quite

a detailed discussion see my *Franco-Russian Alliance*, pp. 336 ff., and Angela von Schönberg: *Um den Twopowerstandard* (Stuttgart, 1933).

27 *Livre Jaune Français*, nos. 85–8.
28 Meyendorff, op. cit., II, pp. 220–1.

clear that this policy could not be continued indefinitely, and the calm and composure exhibited by the German press indicated that there was nothing to be feared from the central powers. Indeed, the negotiations with Germany concerning a tariff treaty went along so smoothly that by January 1894 the text was finally ready. During the winter Russian-German relations, and even Franco-German relations had become more and more cordial. There was less prospect than ever that the Triple Alliance would allow itself to be harnessed to the British chariot. In other words, the situation on the Continent was quiet, and it was probably for that reason that the Tsar finally decided to go through with the Military Convention. On December 16, 1893, he opened his heart to the French ambassador and expressed his deep satisfaction with the arrangements of the Toulon visit. After stressing again the need for peace, Alexander made it clear that the French idea of revenge must be kept in the realm of sentiment and must not be translated into action. On December 30 the ambassador was able to forward to his government a letter from Giers, dated December 27, by which the Russian government formally adhered to the draft which had been worked out and signed by Boisdeffre and Obruchev fifteen months before. On January 4, 1894 the French replied with a note couched in almost identical terms. Therewith the Franco-Russian Alliance became a reality.[29]

The new alignment in European affairs was bound, sooner or later, to make itself felt in every phase of international relations, but it was England that was first affected. The Alliance did, to be sure, replace the Bismarckian system and did put an end to the hegemony of Germany. But the division of the Continent into two groups of powers, the re-establishment of a balance of power served at first only to create something of a dead-lock, because the Russians were quite unwilling to support any active or aggressive policy directed against Germany and her allies. On the other hand both France and Russia were at this time at daggers drawn in their relations with England. There they met on common ground, and it was to their mutual advantage to block the English in the Mediterranean, in Asia, in fact in almost every part of the world. The English had had their opportunity to identify themselves with the powers of the Triple Alliance. They had, for reasons of their own, eschewed this policy, therefore they could not, after the conclusion of the Franco-Russian Alliance, look for aid and comfort to the central powers.

The agreements between Russia and France were, like the treaties of the Triple Alliance, a dead secret. It was more than a year before any public reference was made by either side, even to the mere existence of a formal pact. But the demonstrations in Toulon and Paris were so extraordinary that they could not be misunderstood. The Franco-Russian rapprochement was clearly an accomplished fact, the evidence that these two powers could be reckoned on to support each other was irrefutable. The other powers were bound to take this into account, the English before all others. It was noticed at the time that the

---

[29] *Livre Jaune Français,* nos. 90–2.

Paris celebrations were carefully restrained with respect to all anti-German sentiment, but that no check whatever was put upon expressions of Anglophobia. " Englishmen hardly ventured to show themselves while the delirium lasted," wrote Thomas Barclay, a warm advocate of friendship between England and France. " It meant in the eyes of the Paris public, an entente against England with England's Asiatic enemy." [30] Lord Dufferin, one of the most gifted and experienced of British diplomats, who was at that time ambassador to Paris, reported home in like manner: " I am afraid I can only describe the sentiments of the French people of all classes toward us as that of unmitigated and bitter dislike. . . . I believe that, if war were inevitable, a war with England would be as popular, and would be considered less dangerous than a single-handed encounter with Germany." [31] Even *Punch,* which was not apt to take things too seriously, sounded a note of anxiety on November 11:

> " The Tzar, on peace and friendship all intent
> To France his Admiral Avellan has sent.
> 'Twere pity if this Russian olive-branch
> Portended merely General Avalanche."

As viewed in London, the Toulon-Paris love feast signified that the French had put their naval forces at the disposal of the Russians and that action against England in the Mediterranean was to be expected. Nothing could stop the Russian squadrons from coming out of the Black Sea and joining the French forces. In that event there would be no staying in the Mediterranean for the English. It would simply be a question of evacuating at once, or being locked up in some corner of the great sea. Under the circumstances a substantial increase in British naval power was urgently needed, and a systematic campaign was at once embarked upon by the leading organs of the press. Lord Rosebery and Earl Spencer, the first lord of the admiralty, were themselves convinced of the seriousness of the situation, but Gladstone and Sir William Harcourt, the chancellor of the exchequer, refused to listen to the " panic-mongers." The prime minister declared in parliament that the government was " perfectly satisfied as to the adequacy and capacity of the British navy to perform all the purposes for which it exists," and maintained that the country need not entertain " the smallest apprehension as to the maintenance of the distinct naval supremacy of Great Britain." [32]

The attitude of naval experts and of prominent leaders in the commercial world contrasted strongly with the equanimity of Gladstone and Harcourt. Reports and rumors were constantly creating apprehension. It was said that the

---

[30] Sir Thomas Barclay: *Thirty Years, Anglo-French Reminiscences, 1876–1906* (Boston, 1914). p. 111.

[31] *British Documents on the Origins of the War,* edited by G. P. Gooch and Harold Temperley (London, 1926–), II, no. 351. For further utterances of this sort, see my *Franco-Russian Alliance,* pp. 356–8.

[32] Statements of November 7, and 17, 1893 (Hansard: *Parliamentary Debates,* Series IV, vol. XVIII, pp. 349 and 1151); *Letters of Queen Victoria,* II, pp. 321, 329 ff.

French government had given the Russian squadron the use of Bizerta, that the Russians were arranging to lease an island in the eastern Mediterranean, that they were planning to establish themselves near Mount Athos, and that they were preparing to bring their whole Black Sea squadron through the Straits and into the Mediterranean.[33] Under the impression of these reports the agitation came to a head in December, when a great public meeting in London resolved that it viewed " with deep concern and anxiety " the state of the navy, and urgently pressed upon the government the need for providing additional means of defense. There was a great debate in parliament on December 19, in which Lord George Hamilton, Spencer's predecessor, described the dangers threatening the future naval supremacy of the country as of so insidious a character that neither the government nor the House could control or counteract it. It was becoming more and more apparent from the naval plans of foreign nations, he declared, that they had but one object and that was to act against England. Sir Charles Dilke insisted that there were " all the elements of a national catastrophe," and agreed with Chamberlain that if war were declared the British squadron in the Mediterranean would have to " cut and run — if it could run." [34]

The question of an increase in the naval appropriations led to a very sharp conflict within the cabinet. Gladstone refused to accept the demands of the naval authorities, and decided to resign. The final decision was not come to until March 1894, and even then the real reasons for the veteran statesman's retirement were not given out.[35] Lord Rosebery, who succeeded to the premiership, was in full sympathy with the naval chiefs, and an additional appropriation of £3,000,000 was arranged for. Provision was made for the construction of seven first-class battleships, and six second-class cruisers, this new building being part of a larger five year program, the details of which were not made public.

The naval situation was only one aspect of England's problem. Almost as serious was her relationship to her former friends of the Triple Alliance. Ever since the Siam crisis, when the prospect of England's joining the Alliance had loomed large on the horizon only to disappear with provoking suddenness, the Emperor William had made no secret of his disgust. Had it not been for Italy's difficulties he probably would have deserted the English without further ceremony, but Italy was as much menaced as England by the combination of France and Russia in the Mediterranean, and when Crispi became premier again on December 10 there was every prospect that the tension between France and

---

[33] For details see Langer: *Franco-Russian Alliance*, pp. 360–2.

[34] Hansard, Series IV, vol. XIX, pp. 1771–1886; Captain S. Eardley-Wilmot: " The Agitation in 1893 for the Increase of the Navy " (*Brassey's Naval Annual*, 1894, chap. viii). There is now a full discussion of the problem in Angela von Schönberg: *Um den Twopowerstandard* (Stuttgart, 1933).

[35] John Morley: *The Life of Gladstone* (London, 1903), III, chap. viii; *Letters of Queen Victoria*, II, pp. 369 ff.; A. G. Gardiner: *Life of Harcourt*, II, chap. xiv; Sir Algernon West: *Private Diary* (London, 1922), chaps. xiv–xvii.

Italy would soon reach the breaking-point. The economic crisis in the peninsula had come to a head, and the strikes and riots which broke out in Sicily
before the end of the year threatened to end in a genuine revolution. It was
thought by many people that the Italian government would have to patch up
its difficulties with the French or go to war with them.[36]

In view of the danger that Italy might take the initiative and thus save the
English from their dilemma, and because of the possibility that the Italians might
desert the Triple Alliance and patch up their difficulties with the French, the
Germans made some efforts to induce Lord Rosebery to enter upon a more
formal agreement with Italy. But these efforts were half-hearted and unconvincing. Emperor William felt certain that the English were not looking for allies,
but for lightning rods, and that nothing could be hoped for from them.[37]

The apathy of the Berlin foreign office was not at all shared by the Austrians.
Kálnoky considered the situation so grave that he hurried off to Italy in November and engaged in long conferences with the Italian statesmen. He found them
very discouraged and exceedingly anxious. They would not be comforted by his
assurances that in case of need the interests of England would force her to come
to the aid of the Italians. What they wanted was a concrete promise, nothing
less.[38] Kálnoky returned to Vienna filled with the conviction that something
would have to be done to prevent Italy from throwing herself into the arms of
France and Russia. On December 7 he forwarded to Count Deym, the ambassador at London, three long dispatches, in which he reviewed the course of
recent events and stressed the danger of Italy's defection. The time had come, he
argued, for England not only to increase her navy but also to decide whether
she intended to assert her traditional authority or whether she would allow herself to be crowded out of the Mediterranean. The need of assuring herself of
Italian support was especially emphasized.

Lord Rosebery, when the matter was taken up with him, asserted that England's sympathies were all on the side of Italy, and there could be no question
but that England would come to Italy's assistance if France launched an unprovoked attack; but, he added, it would be impossible for him to give assurances
for special cases. The cabinet would never approve such a policy. Kálnoky was
by no means pleased with the English stand. He pointed out in his further correspondence with Deym that these general assurances had not satisfied the Italians
in the past and so would hardly satisfy them in the future. The danger was not
so much that France would make war on Italy as that she would bring so great
pressure to bear upon the Italians that the latter would be forced to make an
agreement.

---

[36] Giovanni Giolitti: *Memorie della mia Vita* (Milan, 1922), I, pp. 82 ff.; Billot. op. cit., II,
pp. 30 ff.

[37] *Die Grosse Politik*, VIII, nos. 1757–64; further material from the Austrian archives in my
Franco-Russian Alliance, pp. 356–7, and in Wolfgang Herrmann: *Dreibund, Zweibund, England
1890–1895* (Stuttgart, 1929), pp. 87–9.

[38] Langer: *Franco-Russian Alliance*, p. 368; Herrmann, op. cit., p. 93.

The English foreign minister was really not in a position to fulfill the wishes of the Austrians and Italians. He was having a hard time with Gladstone in the matter of the naval appropriations and would certainly have failed to carry the cabinet with him in the question of further foreign commitments. He therefore minimized the danger of an agreement between France and Italy, while reiterating his statement " that the English cabinet could not regard with indifference the defeat of Italy by France." [39]

The new Franco-Russian Alliance was a menace to Austria's own position in the Near East. It was necessary for Kálnoky to find out what the Germans and the English meant to do if the Russians attempted to advance on Constantinople. The matter was taken up with the German Emperor when he visited Güns in September. His attitude was a very positive one: a Russian occupation of Constantinople would not be a *casus belli* for Germany, he said. In case of action by Russia, Austria could secure compensation by taking Saloniki. In other words, the Emperor was returning to the pro-Russian policy of Bismarck, and suggesting the old idea of a partition of the Near Eastern spoils between Russia and Austria.[40]

Kálnoky was no more ready than before to accept this solution. As the situation became more critical in the autumn, he returned to the charge. The correspondence between Vienna and London was communicated to Berlin. Caprivi expressed his approval of the efforts made to secure assurances for the Italians, but he was very sceptical regarding the possibility of early action by Russia. In any case, he argued, England would not adopt a more vigorous policy so long as Gladstone remained in power. It was quite clear to the Austrians that the statesmen of Berlin were much more interested in negotiating a tariff treaty with Russia than in helping the English out of their difficulty. Besides, they clearly resented the efforts which were being made by Kálnoky to assume the leadership in the Triple Alliance. In fact there was some suspicion that Kálnoky was contemplating a separate bargain of his own with the Russians.[41] At any rate, the Germans refused to be convinced that any obligation rested upon them to block Russian policy in the Near East. Kálnoky was thrown back upon the loose connexion with England. But before he was ready to take up the matter with London, Lord Rosebery himself took the initiative. The British foreign secretary was clearly uneasy about the astonishing decline of English influence at Constantinople and the triumph of the French and Russian ambassadors at the Porte. He decided to send a high official of the foreign office, Sir Philip Currie, as ambassador to Constantinople, and instructed Currie to talk the situation over with Kálnoky en route.

In his long discussions with the English diplomat during January, Kálnoky emphasized again and again the dangers of Russian action in the Straits and in

---

[39] Unpublished Austrian documents analyzed in my *Franco-Russian Alliance*, pp. 368–71.
[40] *Die Grosse Politik*, IX, nos. 2138, 2145.
[41] *Die Grosse Politik*, IX, nos. 2137 ff.

the Mediterranean. Italy, he said, is for the moment paralyzed; Germany is uninterested in the Near Eastern problem; Austria must defend the status quo on the land side. All depended upon whether the English would continue their traditional policy of defending Constantinople and the Straits against Russia. If not, Austria would have to abandon her former attitude and confine herself to the defense of her interests in the Balkans.

These arguments seem to have made a deep impression on Rosebery. After pondering the matter for some time, he made a personal statement which the Austrian ambassador reported on January 31, 1894. These were Rosebery's exact words:

" I assure you that I am absolutely determined to maintain the status quo in the Straits question, and that I would not recoil from the danger of involving England in a war with Russia; but I must tell you frankly that if France should take sides with Russia, it would be impossible for England to defend Constantinople against both powers; in any case we should be unable to allow our Mediterranean fleet to run the risk of a catastrophe by finding itself between the Russian and French fleets. In such a case, we should require the assistance of the Triple Alliance to hold France in check." [42]

This statement of Rosebery's was very astutely drawn. The English minister was really turning the tables on Kálnoky. The latter declared that Austria could maintain her traditional attitude in the Near East only if she were assured of English aid. The reply of the English minister was that England would maintain her British policy only if the Triple Alliance would lend its support. The question now was to find out just what Rosebery meant when he referred to " the assistance of the Triple Alliance to hold France in check."

In the course of the discussion it turned out that Rosebery was not thinking so much of the naval co-operation of Italy or Austria. In fact he believed the English fleet would be quite sufficient to defend the Straits. What he wished was that the Triple Alliance should exercise pressure on France and declare to her that she must remain neutral if she showed any disposition to go to the assistance of Russia. The Austrian ambassador was agreeably surprised by this renunciation of military or naval aid, but of course the formulation of the English viewpoint made it necessary for Kálnoky to approach the Germans. Count Hatzfeldt, the German ambassador at London, had been unofficially informed of the negotiations, so that the Berlin foreign office was, in a general way, posted. Kálnoky, in his instructions to the ambassador at Berlin, insisted that he desired merely a friendly discussion of the problem. How would the German cabinet regard the prospect of Russia's re-opening the Straits question? What reply would the German government make to Rosebery's appeal for the support of the Triple Alliance in the event of France's joining Russia in action in the Mediterranean? What did the German government think of the consequences

---

[42] Langer: *Franco-Russian Alliance*, pp. 376–9; *Die Grosse Politik*, IX, nos. 2141 ff.

likely to arise if England abandoned the Mediterranean? These were his questions.[43]

The German indifference to Russian policy in the Straits had been made perfectly clear to the Austrians in the autumn. It was only to be expected, therefore, that the Berlin foreign office should receive the Austrian inquiries with considerable coolness. Caprivi would go no further than to recognize that the Straits question was a European one, and that the existing regulations could not be altered without the consent of the powers. He was glad to note that England was determined to resist alone any move which Russia might make, but he would not entertain the suggestion that the Triple Alliance should hold France in check. Under such an arrangement England alone would decide when to act. In other words, she would reserve for herself the leadership. Furthermore, a mere warning to France to remain neutral would be of little effect. The Triple Alliance would have to be prepared to go to war, and then the brunt of the struggle would fall upon Germany. The game would not be worth the candle, and German public opinion would never approve a war which arose out of the Straits question. Besides, Rosebery was asking for the support of the Triple Alliance without in any way binding himself. If England were to join the " League of Peace " and assume definite permanent obligations, the situation would be very different. As it was, the only point to be considered by Germany was the question of her allies' interest. Efforts must be made to secure English support for Italy, and to induce England to maintain her traditional Near Eastern policy. But if Russia actually raised the Straits question, it would be better to settle the matter peacefully between Russia and the Triple Alliance on the basis of compensation.[44]

The Austrian ambassador reported that the German attitude was to be explained by the hope of concluding a tariff treaty with Russia, and of a general improvement in political relations. Both the Emperor and Caprivi, he wrote, distrusted England and feared that, as in the Siam crisis, the English government would take at first a vigorous stand but then yield, leaving the associated powers to their fate. This estimate of the situation was an accurate one. The very important Russian-German tariff treaty had been signed on February 10, and was accepted by the Reichstag on March 16. The Emperor and his advisors had done their very utmost to bring the negotiations to a successful conclusion, and they hoped that from this time on their relations with the Tsar's government would improve to such an extent that the vitality of the Franco-Russian Entente would gradually be sapped.[45]

---

[43] Kálnoky to Szögyény, February 27, 1894. See further, Langer: *Franco-Russian Alliance*, pp. 379–81, and *Die Grosse Politik*, IX, nos. 2147 ff.

[44] *Die Grosse Politik*, IX, no. 2152.

[45] Waldersee: *Denkwürdigkeiten*, II, pp. 306, 310; *Die Grosse Politik*, VII, nos. 1666–8; Count Sergius J. Witte: *Memoirs* (New York, 1921), pp. 70, and 403–4. There is an excellent discussion of the political importance of the Treaty in Rudolf Ibbeken: *Staat und Wirtschaft in der Deutschen Reichspolitik 1880–1914* (Schleswig, 1928), pp. 174 ff.

The desertion of England and the rapprochement with Russia was a complete reversal of the policy pursued by the Germans during the previous several years. It necessitated precautionary measures on the part of both Austria and Italy. The Emperor Francis Joseph, after staying some time on the French Riviera, conferred a high order upon President Carnot. At the same time the Vienna government did its utmost to avoid friction with Russia when the Serbian constitution was abolished in May, and when Stambulov was dismissed by Ferdinand of Bulgaria.[46] In Italy Crispi threatened to follow up the French offers of assistance if Italy gave up her support of England in Mediterranean questions. Negotiations were opened, and even though they did not result in a definite arrangement, the relations between the two countries were better than they had been for some years.[47]

Whatever may have been the significance of these démarches, it is quite clear that Kálnoky was anxious not only to maintain the Triple Alliance, but to uphold its connexion with England. Renewed efforts were made to induce the Germans to modify their stand, but without avail. The Emperor and his advisers continued to insist that England's own interests would oblige her to take an active part even without an agreement, and that it would be easier to induce the Russians to negotiate directly with the Triple Alliance if any concrete issue arose. When William paid a visit to Francis Joseph, early in April, attempts were made to revive the discussion, but the Emperor did not go beyond generalities. On April 20, Kálnoky made one last effort to secure a clear declaration from the German chancellor. Let Germany consider carefully what a rupture in the negotiations may involve, he wrote. Nothing would so effectively check Franco-Russian designs as the knowledge that in a crisis England would stand by the Triple Alliance. It would be a tremendous mistake not to take advantage of the moment when public opinion in England was favorable to closer co-operation with the Triple Alliance. Rosebery had not given any definite assurances, and could not expect any in return, but an agreement on general principles could and should be reached. Would Caprivi give a declaration similar to the one made by Rosebery? That alone would suffice to keep England by the side of the Triple Alliance, but if England were allowed to feel isolated, public opinion would undoubtedly veer about and demand a separate arrangement with Russia, which would be welcomed by the latter.[48]

Caprivi showed as little inclination as ever to follow the line of the Austrian argument. After going over the ground once more he stressed the fact that Germany's aim was to wean Russia from the Alliance with France, and that therefore Germany could not afford to make any statements which England might exploit in her eventual negotiations with Russia. So far as Austrian interests were concerned, he was willing to enter upon a discussion of principles, but he

---

[46] See Langer: *Franco-Russian Alliance*, pp. 385-6.
[47] Crispi: *Memoirs*, III, pp. 190-201.
[48] Kálnoky to Szögyény, April 20th (Langer: *Franco-Russian Alliance*, pp. 387-8).

thought it would be better to wait and see what demands the Russians made, if any. On one point, however, he was emphatic: the position of Austria-Hungary was absolutely and indisputably of vital interest to Germany, and therefore Germany must and would defend that position in all eventualities.[49]

The German reply was definitive, but Kálnoky delayed as long as he could before communicating it to London. It was not until June 8 that he sent to Berlin for approval the draft of a note to London. In this answer to Rosebery's inquiry it was stated that Austria regarded the English declaration as sufficient to warrant the maintenance of the traditional Austrian policy in the Near East; that Austria and Germany agreed that the Straits question was a European one which could not be altered without the consent of the powers; that this attitude would undoubtedly do much to deter Russia from opening the question; but that in view of the peaceful development of the international situation, the German government did not consider the time ripe for such assurances as Lord Rosebery desired, though the agreement of the powers as stated in the first point was sufficient guarantee to England that a diplomatic move by Russia, detrimental to English interests, would not be accepted in Berlin or Vienna. Kálnoky pointed out further that if Russia acted, France would not stand aloof, and if France interfered, the attitude of the German government would necessarily be influenced in a sense favorable to England.

There was nothing in this proposed reply to Rosebery that could in any way be interpreted as binding the German government to any specific course of action, and so no objection was raised to the Austrian draft. The note was sent on to London but was not actually handed to Rosebery until July 9. By this time the English prime minister had given up hope of a favorable outcome of the negotiations. He expressed his satisfaction and allowed the matter to drop.[50]

Thus ended a series of discussions which extended over more than six months, and which were of very great importance. They show how critical was the situation after Toulon, and how gravely menaced was the English position. For a time it seemed as though the whole European system were undergoing a profound transformation which threatened to end in the isolation of England and the return of Germany to the pro-Russian course marked out by Bismarck. Kálnoky, who put great store by the English connexion, had done his utmost to hold back the tide, but the German statesmen flatly refused to serve as shock absorbers. For years they had been courting England until the Siam crisis had shown them not only the weakness and danger of the English position, but also the pusillanimity of British policy. They had definitely returned to the Bismarckian idea, they denied any interest in Near Eastern affairs except as they affected Austria and Italy, they were ready to abandon the Straits and Constantinople to the Russians and they were intent on sapping the vitality of the Franco-

---

[49] Langer, op. cit., pp. 388–9; *Die Grosse Politik*, IX, no. 2155.
[50] Langer: *Franco-Russian Alliance*, pp. 389–90; *Die Grosse Politik*, IX, nos. 2157–60.

Russian Alliance by cultivating the friendship of the Tsar. Had England been willing to join the Triple Alliance out and out, the German attitude would have been different, for a real quadruple alliance would have been irresistible. But clearly there was no prospect of such an arrangement, so the Germans refused unconditionally to allow Austria to purchase English support in the Near East at the price of German engagements against France. The English would have kept their hands free but their back covered, and Germany would have been reduced to the position of a vassal obliged to furnish support without having any voice in making the decisions.[51]

In a sense the whole debate regarding England's relationship with the central powers was academic, for nothing happened in the Mediterranean even after the Toulon celebrations and the establishment of the Russian squadron in the south. The Franco-Russian Alliance turned out to be no less pacific than the Triple Alliance, at least so far as the old European issues were concerned. Indeed, it may be said that the four years from 1890 to 1894, outwardly quite unspectacular, were years during which the problems of the preceding period were gradually coming to rest and the transition to the new world policies was being made. The dickerings of the Italians and the French, the Roman question, the restless activity of Stambulov in Bulgaria, the pin-pricking and troublesomeness of the French in Egyptian affairs and even the Russian exploits in the Pamirs were irritating, but they were as nothing compared with the stirring incidents of the later Bismarckian period. The one really great event of the years we have been discussing was the conclusion of the Franco-Russian Alliance, which in the succeeding decade left its mark on every great development not only in Europe, but in the world at large.

We still have much to learn about this combination of powers, but certain points are reasonably clear and are worth stressing. In the first place, the Russians had no special love for the French, and they had no interest in helping the French reconquer Alsace-Lorraine. There would probably have been no Franco-Russian Alliance if the Germans had not committed the incredible blunder of snubbing the Russians by refusing to renew the Reinsurance Treaty and then demonstratively courting the English. Of course the St. Petersburg court had long had an interest in cultivating the friendship of France, and it had, since 1887, real need for the loans which were raised on the Paris market. One need not underestimate these factors, and yet it is clear that they were essentially secondary. The Tsar was impelled to approach France by his deeply-rooted dislike of the Germans, his distrust of Emperor William and his suspicions of German policy. After the noisy renewal of the Triple Alliance and all the loose talk of England's having joined it, even the Russian foreign office, which would have preferred, all the way through, a re-establishment of German-Russian friendship, recognized the need for taking another step.

On the Russian side there was no intention of going beyond an innocent

---

[51] *Die Grosse Politik*, IX, no. 2158. See also *Die Grosse Politik*, VIII, no. 1769.

flirtation. It was the French who insisted on having something with teeth in it. All this was perfectly natural. Just as the Russians valued more highly than anything else the assurance of German neutrality for the event of an attack on Russia in the Near East or in Asia, so the French felt that an entente with Russia without a definite assurance of military support would be more dangerous than comforting. Perhaps we exaggerate the desire of the French statesmen for the Russian connexion. In his heart of hearts the genuine French liberal or radical must have detested the Muscovite autocracy just as much as Alexander III abhorred the " godless republicans." There was certainly a strong current of opinion in France that would have preferred the old connexion with liberal England. Clemenceau always took that line and the rising Socialist leaders, like Jaurès, shared the preference. In fact one might say that all those groups that were later Dreyfusard and that later made the Entente with England already existed in 1890 and already leaned in the English direction. But Clemenceau's position, so strong in 1885, had been weakened by the Boulangist episode and was almost completely ruined by the Panama scandal. Furthermore, the English and the French had been so far estranged by the Egyptian question that no real co-operation was possible until that question was disposed of. This whole aspect of the Anglo-French relationship still requires illumination, but one is tempted to speculate on the proposition that if the British had evacuated Egypt at any time prior to 1893 there would have been no Franco-Russian Alliance.

It was perhaps the English position in Egypt as much as anything that made the French *patriotes* so very ardent in their worship of Russia. This may sound like an exaggeration, but anyone who has followed the writings of Madame Adam, who represented a strong group writing in the *Nouvelle Revue,* will find that there was little to choose between the hatred of these people for Germany and their detestation of England. These, incidentally, were the same groups that were constantly calling for a bigger and better navy. They were, in fact, roughly the groups that were later anti-Dreyfusard. The Franco-Russian Alliance on the French side was a triumph for the conservative, military, clerical elements. It is not hard to see why the Pope favored it.

The French statesmen who made the Alliance knew perfectly well what they wanted. It was a defensive pact directed against Germany. They had a hard enough time to get anything in the nature of definite commitments from the Russians, and in the end were obliged to accept an agreement which greatly extended French responsibilities and was in many respects a contradiction of the traditional French policy in the Near East. But in any case they knew that there was no chance of enlisting the Russians in an aggressive policy. The Alliance did not bring the day of revenge any closer. Indeed, it is more than questionable whether responsible statesmen at Paris regarded the reconquest of the lost provinces as anything but a consoling vision. Nevertheless they allowed the French people to believe that the day of retribution was at hand. Thereby they made the Alliance palatable.

We may learn something regarding this aspect of the problem from an exchange of opinions between Count Tolstoi and a well-known French journalist. After the delirious demonstrations in Toulon and Paris the great moralist published an essay entitled *Christianity and Patriotism,* in which he derided the theory that millions of Russians and Frenchmen had suddenly fallen in love with each other. The orgy of eating and drinking, of speech-making and hymn-singing simply nauseated him. He refused to believe that the endless harping upon the theme of European peace would help to secure the nations against war. "We all know," he declared, "that we have experienced no particular love for the French, neither before nor even now, even as we have not experienced any hostile feeling towards the Germans." [52] Tolstoi believed that the whole demonstration was the work of the French and Russian governments, who wished to lash the patriotic feelings of the masses into something like a mad frenzy, in order to make use of public opinion for their own ulterior ends.

This idea was hotly rejected by Étienne Lamy. Tolstoi, he maintained, could never have written these words if he had been present at the festivities. No doubt there had been a large number of ridiculous incidents, but they were ridiculous only when taken individually. Taken in the large the celebrations constituted an impressive spectacle. The ridiculous disappeared just as the homeliness of the individual soldier disappears or is transfigured by the beauty of the army. The demonstrations, he insisted, were genuinely popular, in fact the policy of the government was the result of popular pressure.[53]

In a sense they were both right. The French masses were genuinely enthusiastic, but not because they had suddenly discovered the loveliness of the Russians. They were enthusiastic rather because the Alliance meant for them the end of isolation, the end of the Cinderella days, and because they were given to understand that the Russians would help them regain the lost provinces. We know enough now about the systematic bribery of the French press by the Russians and the career of Mohrenheim is sufficiently illuminating to disabuse us of all exaggerated notions about the value of so-called public opinion. The Alliance was the work of a small group of politicians and soldiers who did not get exactly what they wanted, but who were determined to interpret the obligations of the Alliance to suit themselves, as we shall see later.

On the Russian side there are still many obscure points to be cleared up. We do not know even now what exactly decided Alexander to accept the Boisdeffre-Obruchev draft in December 1893. I myself labored at one time under the delusion that there must have been some definite, good and sufficient reason. But the evidence contained in the recently published Lamsdorff diaries reminds us once again of the hopeless divergences within the ranks of the Russian governing classes in the days of the autocracy. It is really misleading to speak of Russian

[52] *The Complete Works of Count Tolstoy,* translated by Leo Wiener (Boston, 1905), XX, pp. 381–459.

[53] Étienne Lamy: "À Propos d'Alliance Russe" (*Revue des Deux Mondes,* August 1, 1894).

policy. There were always several conflicting policies, with the ultimate decision resting with the Tsar. In the period we have been discussing the foreign office was sane. Giers was an experienced man who knew perfectly well what was good for Russia, but he was weak and timid. He was overruled by the military men and above all by the sovereign. He had no weapons with which to fight a Mohrenheim. In the end he had to give in against his better judgment. As for Alexander it may be permitted even the impartial historian to express a feeling of indignation at the heartless, irresponsible way in which this stolid, not to say stupid man directed the fortunes of millions according to the dictates of his personal dislikes and rancors.

BIBLIOGRAPHICAL NOTE

DOCUMENTARY SOURCES

L'Alliance Franco-Russe. Troisième Livre Jaune Français. Paris, 1918. The only official collection of documents bearing on the alliance. By no means complete.

Rapport sur le Livre Jaune relatif à l'Alliance Franco-Russe. By M. Margaine and others. (Annexe au procès-verbal de la Séance du 18 Avril, 1919. Chambre des Députés, 11ième législature, session de 1919, no. 6036. Paris, 1919). A valuable report on the French Yellow Book, drawn up by a committee of the Chamber. It deals primarily with the question of financial relations between France and Russia in this period.

Documents Diplomatiques. Affaires d'Égypte, 1884–1893. Paris, 1893.

Documents Diplomatiques. Affaires de Siam, 1893–1902. Paris, 1902.

Die Grosse Politik der Europäischen Kabinette, 1871–1914. Edited by Johannes Lepsius, Albrecht Mendelssohn-Bartholdy and Friedrich Thimme. Berlin, 1922–1927. Volume VII, chapter xlv: The renewal of the Triple Alliance; chapter xlvii: The Franco-Russian Alliance; chapter xlviii: Franco-German relations; chapters xlix and l: German-Russian relations. Volume VIII, chapters li and lii: The Anglo-German rapprochement; chapter liii: Mediterranean problems; chapter liv: Colonial problems. Volume IX, chapter lv: Near Eastern Problems from 1890–1895. The great German documentary collection is still by far the most important single source for this period.

Accounts and Papers. 1890–1891, Volume XCVI: *Turkey No. 2 and No. 3: Further Correspondence respecting Affairs in the East.* 1893, Volume CXI: *Egypt No. 1 and No. 2: Further Correspondence respecting the Affairs of Egypt.* 1894, Volume XCVI: *Siam No. 1: Correspondence respecting the Affairs of Siam.*

PRIBRAM, ALFRED F.: *The Secret Treaties of Austria-Hungary, 1879–1914.* Two volumes. Cambridge, 1920–1. Contains the most important texts, and in addition a detailed account of the renewal of the Alliance, based upon unpublished Austrian archive material.

MEMOIRS, AUTOBIOGRAPHIES, BIOGRAPHIES AND
   LETTERS

Letters of the Empress Frederick. Edited by Sir Frederick Ponsonby. London, 1928. Interesting in connexion with the Empress' visit to Paris, but otherwise of relatively little importance for this period.

The Letters of Queen Victoria. Edited by George E. Buckle. Series III, Volumes I and II. New York, 1930–1. One of the most illuminating English sources.

CECIL, LADY GWENDOLEN: *Life of Robert Marquis of Salisbury.* Volume IV. London, 1932. An important source, but contains relatively little on continental politics in this period.

CREWE, MARQUESS OF: *Lord Rosebery.* New York, 1931. Though based on the Rosebery papers this is an inadequate and rather disappointing biography.

GARDINER, A. G.: *The Life of Sir William Harcourt.* Two volumes. London, 1923. One of the best sources for the history of the last Gladstone administration.

HAMILTON, LORD GEORGE: *Parliamentary Reminiscences and Reflections, 1886–1906.* London, 1922. A candid account, by the first lord of the admiralty in the Salisbury cabinet.

FREYCINET, CHARLES DE: *Souvenirs, 1878–1893.* Paris, 1913. One of the most important sources for the study of the Franco-Russian Alliance.

FLOURENS, ÉMILE: *Alexandre III, sa Vie, son Oeuvre.* Paris, 1894. Contains an important chapter on Alexander's foreign policy, but is interesting chiefly as a reflection of French official views on the eve of the conclusion of the Alliance.

BILLOT, ALBERT: *La France et l'Italie. Histoire des Années Troublées, 1881–1899.* Two volumes. Paris, 1905. The account of the French ambassador to Rome. A detailed and useful study, though it contains almost nothing in the nature of revelations.

WILLIAM II: *The Kaiser's Memoirs.* New York, 1922. Slight and of little historical value.

Memoirs of Prince von Bülow. Volume IV. Boston, 1931. Entertaining, but of very little historical importance.

SCHWEINITZ, LOTHAR VON: *Denkwürdigkeiten.* Two volumes. Berlin, 1927. The diaries and records of the German ambassador to St. Petersburg. A valuable source.

WALDERSEE, ALFRED GRAF VON: *Denkwürdigkeiten.* Two volumes. Stuttgart, 1922. The memoirs of the German chief of staff, and an almost brutally frank commentary on the early years of William II.

EULENBURG-HERTEFELD, PHILIPP, FÜRST ZU: *Aus 50 Jahren*. Berlin, 1923. One of the most important sources for the history of the period, being the record of the Emperor's closest confidant.

ECKARDT, JULIUS VON: *Aus den Tagen von Bismarcks Kampf gegen Caprivi*. Leipzig, 1920. The reminiscences of a chief of the German press bureau, and an interesting contribution to the history of the first years after Bismarck's fall.

Lettres de la Princesse Radziwill au Général de Robilant, 1889–1914. Volume I. Bologna, 1933. An instructive correspondence which gives an intimate and well-informed picture of Berlin court life. The letters support other sources without adding much that is new.

GOOCH, GEORGE P.: " Baron von Holstein." (in G. P. GOOCH: *Studies in Modern History*, London, 1931). The best scholarly study of Holstein's career and influence.

CRISPI, FRANCESCO: *Memoirs*. Three volumes. New York, 1912–14. Easily one of the most useful sources for the period.

TOURNIER, J.: *Le Cardinal Lavigerie et son Action Politique*. Paris, 1913. Based upon the papers of Cardinal Lavigerie this study is a contribution of prime importance for the history of the Roman question in this period.

Souvenirs de Charles Benoist. Volumes I and II. Paris, 1923. An illuminating book by a well-known French journalist and diplomat. The reminiscences contain much that is of interest on the Roman question.

MEYENDORFF, BARON A.: *Correspondance Diplomatique de Baron de Staal, 1884–1900*. Two volumes. Paris, 1929. The correspondence of the Russian ambassador at London. Remarkably thin for this period.

LAMSDORFF, VLADIMIR N.: *Dnievnik, 1891–2*. Edited by F. A. Rotshtein. Moscow, 1934. The most important Russian source for the history of the making of the Franco-Russian Alliance. Lamsdorff was the assistant of Giers and was one of the few people who knew the secrets of the Russian foreign office. Unfortunately these diaries are by no means complete.

SPECIAL LITERATURE ON THE FRANCO–RUSSIAN ALLIANCE

DAUDET, ERNEST: *Histoire Diplomatique de l'Alliance Franco-Russe, 1873–1893*. Paris, 1894. One of the earliest but still one of the best books on the subject. The author, while writing uncritically, had an intimate knowledge of the course of French policy.

CYON, ÉLIE DE: *Histoire de l'Entente Franco-Russe, 1886–1894*. Third edition. Paris, 1895. Written by one of the most active proponents of the Alliance. Cyon was a collaborator of Katkov and a member of the *Nouvelle Revue* group. His account is distorted, but he was in a position to learn much, and his book is of value as source material.

BECKER, OTTO: *Das Französisch-Russische Bündnis*. Berlin, 1925. Easily one of the best treatments of the period, but the author approaches the subject chiefly from the angle of German policy.

LANGER, WILLIAM L.: *The Franco-Russian Alliance, 1890–1894*. Cambridge, 1929. A systematic study of the period and of the evolution of the Alliance. Based in part upon unpublished material from the Austrian archives. I have relied largely upon this monograph in the writing of the present chapter. The student is referred to it for further details.

HERMANN, WOLFGANG: *Dreibund, Zweibund, England, 1890–1895*. Stuttgart, 1929. This study is also based upon Austrian archive material. It deals chiefly with German policy, with special reference to Russia and England. The reasoning is not always sound.

HANSEN, JULES: *L'Alliance Franco-Russe*. Second edition. Paris, 1897.

—: *L'Ambassade à Paris du Baron de Mohrenheim, 1884–1898*. Paris, 1907. Hansen was one of the unofficial agents of the French foreign office and played a considerable rôle in the history of the Alliance. These two books are valuable as source material to supplement the Yellow Book.

DARMSTAEDTER, LUDWIG: " Die Vorgeschichte der Russisch-Französischen Allianz, 1891–1894." (*Preussische Jahrbücher*, CLXXVI, pp. 393–407, June, 1919). An analysis of the French Yellow Book.

FISCHER, EUGEN: " Der Sinn der Russische-Französischen Militärkonvention." (*Preussische Jahrbücher*, CXCII, pp. 65–99, April, 1923). A very keen and penetrating study of the text.

MICHON, GEORGES: *L'Alliance Franco-Russe, 1891–1917*. Paris, 1927. The only systematic history of the whole course of the Alliance. A scholarly, but rather prejudiced account.

PACKARD, LAURENCE B.: " Russia and the Dual Alliance." (*American Historical Review*, XXV, pp. 391–411, April, 1920). A careful study of the background, with a discussion of the contribution made by the French Yellow Book.

WELSCHINGER, HENRI: *L'Alliance Franco-Russe*. Paris, 1919. Chiefly a summary of the Yellow Book and the Margaine report.

PRELLER, HUGO: " Zur Entstehung und Struktur des Russisch-Französischen Zweibundes von 1890–1894." (*Archiv für Politik und Geschichte*, II, pp. 463–75, 1924); " Der Russisch-Französische Zweibund." (Ibid., III, pp. 65–77, 1925).

ROTHFELS, HANS: " Das Wesen des Russisch-Französischen Zweibundes." (*Archiv für Politik und Geschichte*, III, pp. 149–60, 1925). " Der Russische-Französische Zweibund." (Ibid., III, pp. 78–80, 1925). These articles of Preller and Rothfels are stimulating and suggestive contributions to the interpretation of the Treaty.

ANONYMOUS (ÉMILE FLOURENS): " M. Ribot au Quai d'Orsay et à la Présidence du Conseil." (*Nouvelle Revue*, LXXXV, pp. 225–50, November 15, 1893).

ANONYMOUS (ÉMILE FLOURENS): " M. Develle au Quai d'Orsay." (*Nouvelle Revue,* LXXXVII, pp. 449–68, April 1, 1894). These two articles, both evidently written by Flourens, are bitter attacks upon the policy of Ribot and Develle, who are accused of not having done enough to further the Alliance with Russia.

WROBLEWSKI, VIKTOR A.: "Zur Geschichte des Russisch-Französischen Bündnisses." (*Berliner Monatshefte,* September, 1934, pp. 750–6). A good abstract of the recently published Lamsdorff diaries.

RENOUVIN, PIERRE: "Les Engagements de l'Alliance Franco-Russe." (*Revue d'Histoire de la Guerre Mondiale,* October, 1934, pp. 297–310). An admirable review of the evolution of the Alliance, with full reference to recent material.

OTHER TOPICS

ALBIN, PIERRE: *La Paix Armée. L'Allemagne et la France en Europe, 1885–1894.* Paris, 1913. A splendid systematic study, unfortunately now out of date.

CHIALA, LUIGI: *Pagine di Storia Contemporanea.* Volume III: *La Triplice e la Duplice Alleanza, 1881–1897.* Second edition, Turin, 1898. Still the best general account of the period from the angle of Italian policy.

MEINECKE, FRIEDRICH: *Geschichte des Deutsch-Englishchen Bündniss-Problems, 1890–1901.* Munich, 1927. A brilliant monograph, but slight on the period treated in this chapter.

RACHFAHL, FELIX: *Die Deutsche Aussenpolitik in der Wilhelminischen Ära.* Berlin, 1924. The author argues that Bismarck's successors simply continued his policy of rapprochement with England.

RITTER, GERHARD: *Bismarcks Verhältniss zu England und die Politik des " Neuen Kurses."* Berlin, 1924. One of the keenest analyses of the Anglo-German problem.

BEAZLEY, RAYMOND: " Britain and Germany in the Salisbury-Caprivi Era, 1890–1892." (*Berliner Monatshefte,* October, 1934, pp. 839–52). Adds very little to an understanding of the problem.

SELL, MANFRED: *Das Deutsch-Englische Abkommen von 1890.* Berlin, 1926. A useful doctoral dissertation, stressing the factor of public opinion in connexion with the Heligoland Treaty.

FRANK, VICTOR and SCHULE, ERNST: "Graf Pavel Andreevic Suvalov." (*Zeitschrift für Osteuropäische Geschichte,* VII, 1933, pp. 525–59). A review of the diplomatic career of the Russian ambassador to Berlin. The monograph is based upon Russian materials, especially the Lamsdorff diaries for the years 1886–1890.

NOWAK, KARL F.: *Germany's Road to Ruin.* New York, 1932. A journalistic account of German policy in the years 1890–1895, reflecting chiefly the opinions of the Emperor William. Unreliable and of little value.

HOERNIGK, RUDOLF: *Italien zwischen Frankreich und dem Dreibund.* Berlin, 1931. A good systematic account of Italian policy with respect to the Alliance from 1890–1906.

PETERS, MARTIN: *Die Meerengen und die Europäischen Grossmächte, 1890–1895.* Erlangen, 1932. A doctoral dissertation of no great value. The author relies almost entirely upon a few obvious sources.

GIACOMETTI, G.: " Cinq Mois de Politique Italienne, février–juin, 1891." *Revue des Deux Mondes,* September 15, 1891, pp. 388–452). A most important account, clearly inspired. The author discusses in minute detail the renewal of the Triple Alliance, with special reference to Italy's relations with England.

BEAZLEY, RAYMOND C.: " Das Deutsche Kolonialreich, Grossbritannien, und die Verträge von 1890." (*Berliner Monatshefte,* May, 1931, pp. 444–58). A general discussion of Anglo-German colonial problem in 1890, which contributes little.

LITERATURE SINCE 1935

THE FRANCO-RUSSIAN ALLIANCE

Documents diplomatiques français. Series I. Volume VIII. Paris, 1938. Volume IX. Paris, 1939. Volume X. Paris, 1945. These three volumes of the great publication of the French Foreign Office documents cover the period from March 20, 1890 to December 31, 1893. They constitute the most important recent body of source material.

NOLDE, BARON BORIS: *L'alliance franco-russe; les origines du système diplomatique d'avant-guerre.* Paris, 1936. 704 pp. A well-informed, readable study, covering the years 1870 to 1893. Uses some unpublished Russian materials, but makes no significant contribution.

RIBOT, ALEXANDRE: " L'alliance franco-russe " (*Revue d'histoire de la guerre mondiale,* XV, July, 1937, pp. 202–228). Personal recollections of the French statesman, written in 1913 and dealing largely with the negotiation of the military convention.

LABOULAYE, ANDRÉ DE: " L'ambassade de Paul de Laboulaye à St. Pétersbourg " (*Revue de Paris,* XLV, April 15, 1938, pp. 735–747). An analysis of the Laboulaye mission and the development of the Franco-Russian Alliance between 1886 and 1891, by the diplomat's son.

LABOULAYE, PAUL DE: " L'Amiral Gervais à Cronstadt, aôut, 1891: Souvenirs " (*Revue de Paris,* XLV, April 15, 1938, pp. 748–772). Vivid and interesting notes on the Cronstadt visit, by the French Ambassador.

WROBLEWSKI, VIKTOR A.: " Lamsdorff über Deutschland und seine Zukunft " (*Berliner Monatshefte,* XIV, May, 1936, pp. 345–367). A translation of salient passages from the important Lamsdorf Diaries.

SCHWERTFEGER, BERNHARD: *Der neue franko-russische Zweibund im Lichte französischer Vorkriegsakten.* Potsdam, 1936. 70 pp. An analysis of the French documents together with a comparison of the Franco-Russian Alliances of 1893 and 1935.

SILVA, PIETRO: "Dalla duplice franco-zarista del 1893 alla duplice franco-sovietica del 1935" (*Rassegna di politica internazionale,* IV, 1937, pp. 763–780). Similar to the preceding; primarily a controversial tract.

ROLOFF, GUSTAV: "Die Entstehung der französisch-russischen Allianz von 1891" (*Gelbe Hefte,* XVI, October, 1939, pp. 9–23; November, 1939, pp. 33–43). A competent digest and analysis of the French documents.

GALTIER-BOISSIÈRE, JEAN: *Histoire de la Troisième République.* Volume II: Panama, the Franco-Russian Alliance, the Dreyfus Case. Paris, 1935. One of the most detailed and critical histories of the French Republic in this period.

DANSETTE, ADRIEN: *Les affaires de Panama.* Paris, 1934. 301 pp. The best general treatment of the difficulties of the Panama Company and of the political troubles to which they gave rise.

BUTHMAN, WILLIAM C.: *The Rise of Integral Nationalism in France, with special Reference to the Ideas and Activities of Charles Maurras.* New York, 1939. 355 pp. A valuable scholarly treatment, containing an excellent section on Déroulède and the revenge movement.

DEBORIN, G. A.: *Meshdunarodniye Otnosheniya v Period Skladyvayushchegosya Monopolistichekogo Kapitalizma, 1871–1893.* Moscow, 1940. 88 pp. Less formidable than the title: a popular survey of international affairs carrying the story through the conclusion of the Franco-Russian Alliance.

MANFRED, A.: "Iz prehistorii franko-russkago soiuza" (*Voprosy Istorii,* 1947, no. 1, pp. 24–52). A well-documented review of the origins of the Franco-Russian Alliance, making use of the French documents and other recent materials.

RENEWAL OF THE TRIPLE ALLIANCE

SALVATORELLI, LUIGI: *La triplice alleanza, 1877–1912.* Milan, 1939. 478 pp. The most recent and most extensive study of the Triple Alliance, with special reference to the Italian policy.

VOLPE, GIOACCHINO: *L'Italia nella triplice alleanza, 1882–1915.* Milan, 1939. 310 pp. A useful collection of key documents setting forth the history and problems of the alliance.

EBEL, ERNST: *Rumänien und die Mittelmächte von der russisch-türkischen Krise, 1877–1878 bis 1913.* Berlin, 1939. 244 pp. Though it adduces no new material, this is a sound study of Rumania's relation to the Triple Alliance.

SMEDOVSKI, ASSEN: "La Roumanie et la triple alliance, 1883–1913" (*Revue d'histoire diplomatique,* LI, January–March, 1937, pp. 39–56). A brief, undocumented survey, purporting to rest in part on new Bulgarian materials.

BRATIANU, G. I.: *La politique extérieure du Roi Charles I de Roumanie.* Bucharest, 1940. 40 pp. A competent, concise review.

BATAILLARD, P.: *Jean Bratianu et la politique extérieure de la Roumanie, 1891.* Bucharest, 1940. 49 pp. A previously unpublished memorandum by a Rumanian diplomat.

SPECIAL TOPICS

RASCHDAU, LUDWIG: *Unter Bismarck und Caprivi. Erinnerungen eines Diplomaten aus den Jahren 1885–1894.* Berlin, 1938. 381 pp. Valuable memoirs of a German Foreign Office official.

LERCHENFELD-KOEFERING, HUGO GRAF: *Erinnerungen und Denkwürdigkeiten, 1843–1925.* Berlin, 1935. 445 pp. Reminiscences of the Bavarian Minister in Berlin, containing interesting sidelights on German policy in this period.

DE CLERY, ROBINET: *La politique douanière de l'Allemagne depuis l'avénement de Caprivi jusqu'à nos jours, 1890–1925.* Paris, 1935. 400 pp. An exhaustive, scholarly study of the Caprivi tariff policy.

ENTHOVEN, H. E.: *Fritz von Holstein en de Problemen van zijn Tijd.* Utrecht, 1936. 178 pp. One of the best systematic studies of Holstein's role in the formulation of German policy.

KLOCKE, ERNST: *Der Einfluss Friedrich von Holsteins auf die deutsche Aussenpolitik während der Kanzlerzeit Caprivis.* Cologne, 1937. 88 pp. A dissertation which adds nothing in the way of facts or conclusions.

GOLTZ, HANS VON DER: " Holstein " (*Zeitschrift für Politik,* XXVII, April, 1937, pp. 217–225). A reappraisal of Holstein's career warning against the danger of exaggerating his influence.

GOOCH, GEORGE P.: " Holstein: the Oracle of the Wilhelmstrasse " (in the author's *Studies in German History,* New York, 1948). A completely revised version of an earlier essay. One of the soundest studies of the man's career.

FORNASCHON, WOLFGANG: *Die politischen Anschauungen des Grafen Waldersee und seine Stellungnahme zur deutschen Politik.* Berlin, 1935. 182 pp. An excellent treatment of the evolution of Waldersee's ideas, on foreign as well as domestic issues.

CAPRIVI, LEOPOLD VON: *Die ostafrikanische Frage und der Helgoland-Sansibar Vertrag.* Berlin, 1934. 55 pp. Uses unpublished German Foreign Office and Colonial Office archives to analyze the African aspects of the settlement.

SAVELLI, A.: " Francesco Crispi e la sua politica estera " (*Critica politica,* 1939, pp. 359–392).

GORRINI, GIACOMO: *Tunisi e Biserta. Memorie storiche di Giacomo Gorrini.* Milan, 1940. 198 pp. Gorrini was director of the Italian Foreign Office archives. His memorandum on Bizerta, written in 1891, is based on the unpublished Italian documents.

BERGER, ERNST: " Camille Barrère " (*Berliner Monatshefte,* XVIII, November, 1940, pp. 704–719). A well-informed review of the career of the French Ambassador at Rome.

ZAGHI, CARLO: " Italia e Francia nel 1890–1891 " (*Nuova Antologia,* CCCCVIII, April 16, 1940, pp. 324–333). Three new documents of July, 1890, revealing Crispi's efforts to arrive at a settlement of East African issues with France.

TORRE, AUGUSTO: " Un ' riavvicinamento ' italo-francese " (*Storia e politica internazionale,* 1940, pp. 230–256). Re-examines the French-Italian relationship in 1890–1891 in the light of the French documents and other recent materials.

SCHMIDLIN, JOSEPH: *Papstgeschichte der neuesten Zeit.* Volume II. Munich, 1934. One of the fullest and most scholarly treatments of the Roman question.

LUZIO, ALESSANDRO: " Il Cardinale Rampolla e il Marchese Di Rudini, con documenti inediti " (*Nuova Antologia,* CCCXCVII, May 1, 1938, pp. 16–43). Correspondence of Rudini's assistant, Count Arco, with a Vatican representative, looking to a settlement of the Roman issue, especially in 1891.

PENSON, LILLIAN M.: " The New Course in British Foreign Policy, 1892–1902 " (*Transactions of the Royal Historical Society,* Series IV, Volume XXV, 1943, pp. 121–139). A keen analysis of the process by which Britain drifted from the Triple Alliance to other combinations. Makes use of unpublished Austrian archive material.

KNAPLUND, PAUL: *Gladstone's Foreign Policy.* New York, 1935. 303 pp. A systematic review of the subject, apologetic in character.

TREVELYAN, GEORGE M.: *Grey of Fallodon.* New York, 1937. 393 pp. An excellent biography, which throws interesting light on British policy during the Gladstone ministry.

ISRAEL, LUDWIG: *England und der orientalische Dreibund, 1887–1896.* Stuttgart, 1938. 142 pp. A first rate study, based in part on unpublished German records, which analyzes all phases of the Mediterranean situation and Britain's relation to the Mediterranean Agreements.

MARDER, ARTHUR J.: *The Anatomy of British Sea Power.* New York, 1940. 580 pp. An exhaustive scholarly study of British naval policy in its political setting during the period 1880 to 1905. Makes use of much new material and is indispensable for the study of this period.

ANCHIERI, ETTORE: *Costantinopoli e gli stretti nella politica russa ed europea dal trattato di Qüciük Kainargi alla convenzione di Montreux.* Milan, 1948. 268 pp. The best, systematic account of the Straits Question, particularly during the last decade of the nineteenth century.

SYKES, SIR PERCY: *A History of Afghanistan.* New York, 1940. Two volumes. A standard history, which treats the various international issues in detail.

TAILLARDAT, F.: " La rivalité anglo-russe en Asie centrale. Les états tampons, 1860–1914 " (*Asie française,* August–September, 1935, pp. 214–220). A well-informed sketch of the Afghan-Tibetan-Persian questions.

HABBERTON, WILLIAM: *Anglo-Russian Relations concerning Afghanistan, 1837–1907.* Urbana, 1937. 102 pp. A strictly diplomatic monograph, with an extensive treatment of the Pamir problem.

TERENZIO, PIO C.: *La rivalité anglo-russe en Perse et en Afghanistan jusqu'aux accords de 1907.* Paris, 1947. 178 pp. Similar to the preceding title, which the author evidently did not know.

VAGTS, ALFRED: " William II and the Siam Episode " (*American Historical Review,* XLV, July, 1940, pp. 834–841). Prints a document of the year 1902, with the Emperor's comments. These make clear that Rosebery was genuinely afraid of war but never actually requested German aid.

III

The Triumph of Imperialism

✑

CENTURIES HENCE, WHEN INTERESTS IN THE DETAILS OF EUROPEAN DIPLO-
macy in the pre-war period will have faded completely, this period will
still stand out as the crucial epoch during which the nations of the western
world extended their political, economic and cultural influence over Africa and
over large parts of Asia. The tide of European control has already turned and
we are living now in an age of retreat and retirement. The tremendous outburst of expansion and the almost complete victory of Europe was, therefore,
crowded into a couple of generations, the peak of the movement being reached
in the last decade of the 19th and the first decade of the 20th centuries. During
that score of years the competition in the acquisition of territory and the struggle
for influence and control was the most important factor in the international
relations of Europe. We cannot avoid giving it some special attention.

Imperialism is a word which is now in bad repute, partly because of a psychological reaction to what it was supposed to stand for, partly because it is generally used in so loose a sense that it means nothing to the historian or the political
scientist. As everyone knows, the term was originally connected with the word
Imperator, and was frequently associated with the ideas of dictatorial power,
highly centralized government, arbitrary methods of administration, and in
general with the ideas of Caesarism and Bonapartism. In this sense it is now
almost obsolete. For our purposes it may be taken to mean simply the rule or
control, political or economic, direct or indirect, of one state, nation or people
over other similar groups, or perhaps one might better say the disposition, urge
or striving to establish such rule or control.

Taken in this sense, imperialism is probably as old as recorded history. One
writer has taken his discussion of it back to the Assyrians and the Egyptians,
and admirable studies have been made of both Greek and Roman imperialism.[1]
The medieval and earlier modern period has perhaps been somewhat neglected
by students, but there has been a wealth of critical writing on the imperialism
of recent times. Indeed, the socialists of the Neo-Marxian school have made a
specialty of the subject and have linked imperialism with capitalism as an object of condemnation. This is not the place to consider the purely theoretical

---

[1] Joseph Schumpeter: " Zur Soziologie der Imperialismen " (*Archiv für Sozialwissenschaft und
Sozialpolitik,* XLVI [1918–1919], pp. 1–39, 275–310); William S. Ferguson: *Greek Imperialism*
(Boston, 1913); Tenney Frank: *Roman Imperialism* (New York, 1914).

side of the problem. The historian, in fact, is apt to feel that the abstractions of the political scientist are of little help in reconstructing or understanding the past. Suffice it to say, then, that there is no agreement among those who have analyzed imperialism as to what the motives are that impel a state or people to expand its territory or control. The liberal-bourgeois writers, who generally deny that there is any natural or necessary connexion between capitalism and imperialism, are apt to stress considerations of prestige, the desire for security, the striving towards national self-sufficiency, the tendency towards the organization of ever larger social units, or the urge of deeply-rooted ethical sentiments as the impelling motives underlying the desire for expansion. Professor Schumpeter has advanced the ingenious and persuasive argument that imperialism is really nothing but an atavism, a belated outcropping of a primitive disposition towards aggression for the sake of aggression and of domination for the sake of domination, without any specific object or limit. Another recent student of the problem ends by rejecting all previous explanations and reduces imperialism to an expression of the honor motif which is so potent a force in the social group as in the individual.[2]

The Marxian interpretation, which makes practically all imperialism economic, does not go back to Marx himself, who appears to have had no definite theory on the subject. It was, as a matter of fact, first propounded by thoroughly bourgeois writers in the United States and England, starting perhaps with Charles A. Conant and going down to the remarkable book of J. A. Hobson.[3] It was then adopted and developed by socialist writers like Karl Kautsky, Otto Bauer, Rudolf Hilferding, Rosa Luxemburg and others, till now it has become enshrined in the works of Lenin and lesser communist prophets.[4] Writers of

[2] Schumpeter, op. cit., passim; Arthur Salz: *Das Wesen des Imperialismus* (Leipzig, 1931), passim. Among other good recent non-socialistic discussions might be mentioned Justus Hashagen: " Zur Ideengeschichte des englischen Imperialismus " (*Weltwirtschaftliches Archiv*, X, 1917, pp. 423–39); Idem: " Der Imperialismus als Begriff " (ibid., XV, 1919, pp. 157–91); Idem: " Zur Deutung des Imperialismus " (ibid., XXVI, 1927, pp. 134–51); Siegfried Marck: *Imperialismus und Pazifismus als Weltanschauungen* (Tübingen, 1918); Walter Sulzbach, *Nationales Gemeinschaftsgefühl und Wirtschaftliches Interesse* (Leipzig, 1929); Albert Lauterbach: " Zur Problemstellung des Imperialismus " (*Archiv für Sozialwissenschaft und Sozialpolitik*, LXV, 1931, pp. 580–99); Robert Michels: " Die Theorien des Kolonialismus " (ibid., LXVII, 1932, pp. 693–710). E. M. Winslow: " Marxian, Liberal and Sociological Theories of Imperialism " (*Journal of Political Economy*, XXXIX, 1931, pp. 713–58) seems to me to be weak on the liberal side.

[3] Charles A. Conant: " The Economic Basis of 'Imperialism'" (*North American Review*, September, 1898, pp. 326–40); Idem: " The Struggle for Commercial Supremacy " (*Forum*, June, 1899, pp. 427 ff.); Idem: " Can New Openings be Found for Capital? " (*Atlantic Monthly*, November, 1899, pp. 600 ff.); Idem: " Recent Economic Tendencies " (ibid., June, 1900, pp. 737 ff.); Ritortus: " The Imperialism of British Trade " (*Contemporary Review*, July, 1899, pp. 132–52; August, 1899, pp. 282–304); John A. Hobson: *Imperialism, a Study* (London, 1902).

[4] Kautsky barely indicated this viewpoint in his article: " Aeltere und Neuere Kolonialpolitik " (*Die Neue Zeit*, XVI, 1898, pp. 801–16), p. 812, but developed it fully in his *Nationalstaat, Imperialistischer Staat, und Staatenbund* (Nürnberg, 1915). It is broached by Otto Bauer: " Nationalitätenfrage und die Sozialdemokratie " (*Marx-Studien*, II, 1907), and developed by Rudolf Hilferding: " Das Finanzkapital " (*Marx-Studien*, III, 1910) and Rosa Luxemburg: *Die Akkumulation des Kapitals* (Berlin, 1913). See also N. Lenin: *Imperialism, the Last Stage of Capitalism* (New

this persuasion regard imperialism as the expression of a need for new markets for the surplus products of industrialism, as a search for raw materials and for cheap labor. Furthermore, they argue that it is an inevitable phase in the evolution of capitalism, a phase in which surplus capital, accumulated by the system of production, is obliged by the ever diminishing returns at home to find new outlets for investment abroad. Imperialism begins with the export of producers' goods and capital; when the last outlets for surplus capital have been taken up by capitalistic countries, the whole economic-social system is bound to die of congestion.

With all this mass of theoretical, not to say speculative writing, it is curious that almost no attempt has been made to analyze a concrete example of imperialist action in the period of high capitalism. Tenney Frank seems to have been driven to his study of Roman imperialism by his dissatisfaction with generalizations and formulas that drifted further and further from the ascertained facts. His conclusions are startling enough: the Roman Empire, in many ways the prototype of all later empires, appears to have grown up in spite of the Romans. "It is safe to say that the idea of universal power never occurred to any Roman before the Punic War." "Specific accidents . . . led the nation unwittingly from one contest to another until to her own surprise Rome was mistress of the Mediterranean world." "Pompey seems to be the first general frankly sent out for the purpose of extending Rome's boundaries," and Caesar was the first candid imperialist in Rome. These are some of the conclusions reached by a scholar working with the facts alone.[5] They seem to bear out the contention of Sir John Seeley that the British apparently "conquered and peopled half the world in a fit of absence of mind."[6] This was a reference to the growth of the Empire in the 17th and 18th centuries, but it might be that an examination of the imperialism of the late 19th century would bear out the conclusions of these writers who have analyzed the earlier manifestations of imperialism.

For practical reasons I shall more or less confine myself to a discussion of British imperialism in the late-Victorian period. This procedure is justifiable because Britain was at that time the imperial nation *par excellence,* because she quite naturally took the lead in the race for more territory, and because the whole imperial movement was more self-conscious and more widespread in England than in any continental country.

If you are willing to define the word imperialism loosely enough and to make it synonymous with love of country, patriotism, sense of nationality, etc.,

York, 1927); M. Pavlovitch: *The Foundations of Imperialist Policy* (London, 1922) and F. Sternberg: *Der Imperialismus* (Berlin, 1926); Henryk Grossmann, *Das Akkumulations und Zusammenbruchsgesetz des Kapitalistischen Systems* (Leipzig, 1929). A good general survey may be found in B. J. Hovde: "Socialistic Theories of Imperialism prior to the Great War" (*Journal of Political Economy,* XXXVI, 1928, pp. 569–91).

  [5] Tenney Frank: *Roman Imperialism,* pp. viii, 120–1, 325, 344.
  [6] John Seeley: *The Expansion of England* (London, 1883), p. 8.

you can trace it back to Shakespeare or even Chaucer. In the 19th century there was an unbroken line of literary men, from Carlyle and Kingsley through Ruskin to Tennyson, who sang the praises of Britain, gloried in her command of the sea and exulted in her imperial mission.[7] Since this literary strain was nothing new, we need not stop to discuss it in any detail. We may start by recalling the fact that in the period from 1840 to 1870 interest in the colonies reached its nadir in England. It was indeed the climax of anti-imperialism.[8]

It has been shown over and over again that this attitude was the direct reflection of England's industrial supremacy in the mid-century. England was in very fact, at that time, the workshop that clothed the world. She had something of a monopoly not only of the continental market but of the world market. Nothing more natural, then, than that she should have fallen under the sway of Manchester doctrine, that she should have become the great exponent of the principle of free trade, of laisser faire, of retrenchment and reform at home and good will and peace abroad. The Englishman at that time had no desire to expand the responsibilities of government — he did not want to rule, he wanted to trade. In this scheme of things there was no place for empire or expansion. Cobden, Gladstone and the other leaders of the school may not actually have worked for the dissolution of the Empire, but they expected the Empire to disintegrate, they were willing to aid the process by the extension of self-government, and they envisaged the ultimate dissolution of existing ties without misgiving and without regret.

With the year 1870 a distinct change becomes noticeable in the English attitude. Disraeli, in his famous Crystal Palace speech of 1872, sounded a new note of imperialism. With him, to be sure, the maintenance of the Empire was largely a question of prestige; the Empire was a proof of "the commanding spirit of these islands," a valuable make-weight in the councils of Europe. His policy in the years 1874-1880 was essentially concerned with questions of power and security, all pointed at the protection of the routes to India and the safe-guarding of the great Indian Empire itself. Disraeli never showed any genuine interest in Britain's self-governing colonies, and revealed no deep understanding of the needs of England in the economic sense. It is probably safe to say that his imperialist attitude was inspired directly by the changes that had taken place on the Continent. The triumph of the principle of nationality and the emergence of a powerful German Empire called forth a corresponding feeling of national pride among the English and resulted in a new appreciation of the Empire which was, at bottom, not at all in keeping with Manchester doctrine.[9]

[7] See especially Friedrich Brie: *Imperialistische Strömungen in der Englischen Literatur* (Second edition, Halle, 1928), passim; Edward Salmon: "The Literature of the Empire" (in *The British Empire*, XI, London, 1924).

[8] So well described by Robert L. Schuyler: "The Climax of Anti-Imperialism in England" (*Political Science Quarterly*, XXXVI, 1921, pp. 537-61), and thereafter in C. A. Bodelsen: *Studies in Mid-Victorian Imperialism* (New York, 1925).

[9] A contemporary pamphlet describes Disraeli's imperialism as a "policy of Bounce and Bluster'

The new pride in the Empire was reflected in the epoch-making books of Sir Charles Dilke (*Greater Britain*, 1870), Sir John Seeley (*The Expansion of England*, 1883) and J. A. Froude (*Oceana*, 1885). The writings of these men are so well known and their influence has been so generally recognized that there would be no point in reviewing them at length. It is important to note, though, that they were concerned with the Empire as it was, and not so much with the expansion of the Empire. Seeley, indeed, warned his audience that " when a State advances beyond the limits of the nationality, its power becomes precarious and artificial." G. P. Gooch, writing at the end of the century, remarked quite truly that if Seeley were still alive he would be classed as a Little Englander.[10]

Contemporaneous with this historical teaching was the activity of the Imperial Federation League, founded in 1884 for the purpose of furthering the integration of the Empire through constitutional and other devices. For a full decade the League was the chief embodiment of the imperial movement. It enjoyed the enthusiastic support of many prominent political and intellectual leaders and Lord Rosebery once declared that its object, imperial federation, was the " dominant passion " of his life.[11] But the agitation for imperial federation had only an indirect bearing upon international affairs, and we cannot, for that reason, afford the space required for a detailed analysis. Movements toward expansion of empire are often accompanied by a striving towards integration and concentration of forces within the existing state, and therefore the project for federation was not without its significance. It will suffice, however, to call attention to this aspect of it.[12]

The movement for imperial federation enjoyed the support of Liberals as well as Conservatives. The Liberals, in fact, had been responsible for the granting of self-government to the colonies and had thus made possible the idea of a free union of the white colonies and the mother-country.[13] But there was a further reason for their adoption of the new slogan. By the beginning of the last decades of the century the economic situation of England was no longer what it had been in the middle of the century. Dozens of books and hundreds

---

consisting " of a concerted series of political fireworks, a system of pyrotechnics designed to withdraw public attention from the necessity of domestic reform " (*Lord Beaconsfield's Imperialism*, London, n.d., p. 7); see further Edgar Herzog: *Benjamin Disraeli, Earl of Beaconsfield, als Imperialist* (Leipzig, 1922) and especially Boris Segalowitsch: *Benjamin Disraelis Orientalismus* (Berlin, 1930), part iv; H. Rühl, *Disraelis Imperialismus* (Leipzig, 1935).

[10] Seeley, op. cit., p. 46; G. P. Gooch: " Imperialism " (in *The Heart of the Empire*, second edition, London, 1902), p. 331.

[11] Lord Rosebery: *Speeches* (London, 1896), pp. 56–7.

[12] Sir George Parkin: *Imperial Federation* (London, 1892); Herman W. Marcus: " A Sketch of the Imperial Unity Movement " (in *The British Empire Series*, V, London, 1902); R. Thirlmere: *The Clash of Empires* (London, 1907); G. T. Denison: *The Struggle for Imperial Unity* (London, 1907), etc.

[13] This point is well made in L. T. Hobhouse: *Democracy and Reaction* (New York, 1905), p. 13, and in his *Liberalism* (New York, 1907), p. 239.

of articles, many of them loaded with a crushing burden of statistical matter, have been written on the theme of England's decline and approaching fall. We need not struggle through this welter of evidence, much of which was incomplete and distorted, and little of which was rightly understood. The main facts are fairly clear.

During the years of her economic ascendancy England had undoubtedly helped to equip the other nations of the Continent with the means of production which enabled them ultimately to set up on their own, take over their home markets for themselves and eventually to enter into competition in the world market. The temporary settlement of the great national questions in the years just before 1870 unquestionably released a good deal of energy for economic and especially industrial activity. The English themselves were surprised at the beneficial results for German business of the *Zollverein* and the political unification of the many German states. By the middle of the 1880's Germany was already becoming an important industrial power. Like most of the continental states she had thrown over the ideas of free trade, had adopted a protective tariff and had thrived under the new system. German goods had already begun to find their way into unprotected England, to say nothing of the British colonies, which, incidentally, were also erecting tariff barriers against the mother country. A parliamentary commission of 1886 had to listen to many complaints about German competition: in every quarter of the globe, said the final report of the commission, " the perseverance and enterprise of the Germans are making themselves felt. In actual production of commodities we have few, if any, advantages over them; and in a knowledge of the markets of the world, a desire to accommodate themselves to local tastes and idiosyncrasies, a determination to obtain a footing wherever they can, and a tenacity in maintaining it, they appear to be gaining upon us."[14]

Now the situation was aggravated, as the Englishman saw it, by the general depression during all but the closing years of the last quarter of the century. It was a period during which exports were declining while imports were rising in value; prices were generally falling, the population was steadily increasing, and unemployment, though not appalling when measured by present-day conditions, was felt to be a real problem. It is, to be sure, a relatively simple matter to show that the situation was not as black as contemporaries believed. The declining value of exports was at least in part to be explained by the steady fall in prices, while the growth of imports was due in no small measure to the increasing capital investment abroad, the interest on which had to be paid in goods.[15]

---

[14] There are good analyses of the Commission's report in Victor Bérard: *British Imperialism and Commercial Supremacy* (London, 1906), pp. 56 ff., 110 ff., 233 ff., and in Ross J. S. Hoffman: *Great Britain and the German Trade Rivalry, 1875–1914* (Philadelphia, 1933), chaps. ii and iii.

[15] Among the innumerable treatments of the problem I regard the following as particularly useful and illuminating: Ritortus: " The Imperialism of British Trade " (*Contemporary Review*, July, 1899, pp. 132–52, August, 1899, pp. 282–304); Michael G. Mulhall: " Forty Years of British

England's real economic difficulty in this period, though few contemporaries recognized the fact, arose not so much from the decrease of exports or from the growing disparity between exports and imports, as from the steady accumulation of capital and the ever more pressing need for opportunities for profitable investment. Throughout the early 19th century England's available capital had grown along with her productive powers. She was, prior to 1850, almost the only source for funds and in those times she poured money onto the Continent in the form of government loans, railway loans and to some extent industrial investments. After 1850 France and then Germany began to appear as lending countries, but England was still far in advance of any competitor. Despite the so-called depression and the prevalence of unemployment, which at times reached almost 10% of the trade unionists, there was a pretty steady and at times very striking rise in savings-bank deposits. The floating capital of Great Britain rose from about $7,300,000,000 in 1860 to $21,000,000,000 in 1896.[16] The discount rate, while fluctuating, tended to drop and reached its lowest point in the mid-nineties, when the bank rate was 2% and the market rate rarely much above 1%.[17]

Under the circumstances it was inevitable that capital should flow abroad in an ever stronger stream. Less money was being invested on the Continent, but tremendous sums went into railway loans to the United States, to Latin America and to Australia. The foreign investment of Great Britain has been put at nearly $6,000,000,000 in 1875 and at not much less than $10,000,000,000 in 1900. At the turn of the century the interest on the foreign investment was not far from $500,000,000 per annum, while the clear profit from foreign trade came to hardly a fifth of that figure. One half to two thirds of all new capital was going abroad.[18] "The necessity of sending capital abroad to obtain profitable returns is the salient economic lesson of the closing days of the 19th century," wrote an American economist. "England could not remain the workshop of the world; she is fast becoming its creditor, its mortgagee, its landlord," remarked

---

Trade " (*Contemporary Review*, March, 1900, pp. 382–96); Michael von Tugan-Baranowsky: *Studien zur Theorie und Geschichte der Handelskrisen in England* (Jena, 1901), chap. v; A. L. Bowley: *National Progress in Wealth and Trade since 1882* (London, 1904), pp. 20 ff., 57 ff.; W. J. Ashley: *The Tariff Problem* (London, 1903), especially chap. iii; Carl Fuchs: *The Trade Policy of Great Britain and her Colonies since 1860* (London, 1905), passim; Wesley C. Mitchell: *Business Cycles* (Berkeley, 1913), chap. iii; Alfred Marshall: *Industry and Trade* (London, 1920), Book I, chap. v; Lujo Brentano: *Eine Geschichte der Wirtschaftlichen Entwicklung Englands* (Jena, 1929), Vol. III, part II, chaps. lxvi and lxvii; G. D. H. Cole: *British Trade and Industry* (London, 1932), pp. 62–100; J. T. W. Newbold: "The Beginnings of the World Crisis, 1873–1896 " (*Economic Journal, Economic History Series*, II, 1932, pp. 425–42).

[16] Michael G. Mulhall: "British Capital Abroad " (*North American Review*, April, 1899, pp. 499–505), p. 503.

[17] Marshall: *Industry and Trade*, chap. v.

[18] Mulhall, loc. cit.; Charles A. Conant: "The Struggle for Commercial Supremacy " (*Forum*, June, 1899, pp. 427 ff.); J. A. Hobson: *Imperialism, a Study* (London, 1902), pp. 46 ff.; Sir George Paish: "Great Britain's Investment in other Lands " (*Journal of the Royal Statistical Society*, September, 1909, January, 1911); C. K. Hobson: *The Export of Capital* (London, 1914), chaps. v, vi, vii; Herbert Feis: *Europe the World's Banker* (New York, 1930), chap. i.

a contemporary British writer, who continued: " The fact is, the trade of the world, as well as its soil, if we do not foolishly disturb it, or meddle with it from unwarrantable jealousy, is becoming more and more one, and becoming more and more British, in whatever country it is going on and under whatever flag it sails." [19]

The Neo-Marxians, following the lead of these discerning bourgeois writers, have insisted on the close connexion between this accumulation of capital and the growth of imperialism. " The inexorable progress of economic tendencies has made expansion the inevitable policy of states which would survive in the future," declared Conant. " It is not too much to say that the modern foreign policy of Great Britain is primarily a struggle for profitable markets of investment. . . . Imperialism is the endeavour of the great controllers of industry to broaden the channel for the flow of their surplus wealth by seeking foreign markets and foreign investments to take off the goods and capital they cannot sell or use at home," according to J. A. Hobson.[20] But just what necessary connexion is there between these two phenomena?

It should be noted at the outset that the export of British capital developed at a remarkably rapid rate in the days when anti-imperialism reached its climax. In 1875 it was already more than half what it was in 1900. This would suggest that the accumulation of capital and the creation of a surplus have no necessary connexion with territorial expansion. In the hey-day of free trade and Manchester doctrine the British did not hesitate to export their surplus to continental countries and above all to the United States, where they could not possibly have had any political or territorial aspirations. Indeed, we know that such aspirations were unreservedly rejected by the Cobdenites.

It does not follow from this, however, that the movement for expansion in the last quarter of the century was not conditioned by the need for fields of investment, because in the interval new factors had been introduced into the situation. The continental nations had gradually become equipped with the means of production, they were no longer spending immense amounts of money on the conduct of expensive wars, they were frankly embarking upon a policy of industrial development and were scrapping the doctrine of free trade in order to secure the necessary protection. By the middle of the eighties France was already in a position to export large amounts of capital and Germany was invading the British preserves with her goods. Furthermore, French economists and statesmen, followed somewhat reluctantly by the Germans, decided that for future safety they must have colonies. On the Continent the advocates of colonial expansion were inspired in part, no doubt, by the British example. It was thought that the British had grown great through their foreign possessions. The French and Germans placed a much higher estimate upon the value of the

[19] Conant, loc. cit.; Ritortus: " The Imperialism of British Trade " (*Contemporary Review.* July, 1899, pp. 132–52), pp. 143, 151.
[20] Hobson: *Imperialism*, pp. 48, 75.

British Empire than did the British themselves. But for the rest it was generally held, following the teachings of the great French economist, Leroy-Beaulieu, that colonies were a *sine qua non* of national greatness. Jules Ferry, the founder of the second French Empire, never tired of stressing the need not only for new markets, but for new fields of investment: " Colonies are for rich countries one of the most lucrative methods of investing capital. . . . I say that France, which is glutted with capital and which has exported considerable quantities, has an interest in looking at this side of the colonial question. . . . It is the same question as that of outlets for our manufactures." [21]

What the French and Germans did, then, was to enter the colonial field and begin to take over territory in Africa and Asia, territories which they then surrounded by tariff walls. The impression this new departure made upon the English was as profound as it was natural. " There is nothing," says a well-known British historian of colonial policy, " which causes men to put so high a value on their own possessions as the observing that they are being coveted by their neighbours. The scramble for colonies among the continental nations has had the good effect at least of determining the English not to be left behind in the race for empire." [22] So what we observe in the eighties is not only a revaluation of the existing Empire, but a demand for a *Zollverein* between its component parts. There is a rising agitation for " fair trade " as opposed to free trade, an eagerness to build up some sort of wall of preferential treatment around the immense domains already under British rule.

It was but a natural step from imperial federation to a policy of expansion. As business men the English would undoubtedly have preferred to continue as before, with the whole world as a market and no very serious competitor. But now, with the setting aside of large parts of the unclaimed world as French and German colonies, there was an obvious danger that the British market would be steadily restricted. Hence the emergence and sudden flowering of the movement for expansion. The English felt that they had to take over large blocks of territory, if only to prevent them from falling into the hands of exclusive rivals. Economic control was no longer possible, it seemed, without political control.[23]

The English, being a commercially-minded people, thought almost exclusively in terms of markets and they discussed the situation primarily in terms of exports. It did little good to argue that trade does not follow the flag, but the price list; that the trade with the colonies was only a third of the total trade of England; that France, Germany, and the United States, all protectionist states and all rivals of Britain, were still England's best customers. It did no good either

[21] I have dealt with this aspect of the question at some length in my *European Alliances and Alignments, 1871–1890* (New York, 1931), pp. 283–9.
[22] Hugh E. Egerton: *A Short History of British Colonial Policy* (London, 1897), p. 6.
[23] William Cunningham: " English Imperialism " (*Atlantic Monthly*, July, 1899, pp. 1–7); similarly Charles A. Conant: " Can New Openings be found for Capital? " (ibid., November, 1899, pp. 600 ff.).

to point out to the Englishman his own short-comings, his easy-going business methods, his lack of interest in small orders, his unwillingness to adapt his goods to the peculiar needs of the customer, his inadequate technical training, etc. Frederick Greenwood accused his countrymen of positive levity. They pursued what he called a " skim-and-skip " system, taking the cream off a market, leaving the rest to competitors and then rushing off with a loud clamor in search of new markets.[24]

The fact remains, then, that during the eighties there was increasing alarm about the future. The economic situation brought with it a general revision of economic theory. In the last quarter of the century there was a pronounced decline in the popularity of the Manchester teaching. Cobdenism had lost its attractiveness for many. Economists and political writers began to point out the fundamental fallacy in the free trade doctrine. It had been assumed that the whole world would gradually adopt the free trade system, but in reality the reverse had proved to be the case. England had equipped other nations to be her competitors, and now, with the English market wide open, they were pouring their products into what ought to be a British preserve. Cobden, wrote H. E. Egerton, had preached that England's chief concern with foreign nations was to trade with them, but it had turned out that the chief concern of foreign nations was *not* to trade with England.[25] Cobden, said other critics, had looked forward to the spread of the new commercial spirit, which would make for general world prosperity and world peace. Yet what Europe had witnessed was a long series of wars. The keynote of the new Europe was not the development of internationalism, but the dominance of a spirit of militarism and bloated armaments. In short, Manchester doctrine had been belied by the facts. It was an outworn theory to be thrown into the discard. Birmingham and Manchester itself were said to have turned against it and at the London meeting of the Cobden Club in 1897 only thirteen members were present.[26]

Gladstone and many of the older leaders of the Liberal party repulsed all attempts to attack the teachings of Cobden. These men remained not only free traders, but Little Englanders — that is, anti-imperialists and anti-militarists — until the end of their careers. But among the younger members of the party there

---

[24] Frederick Greenwood: " The Cry for New Markets " (*Nineteenth Century*, April, 1899, pp. 538–47); see further such critiques as those of Lord Farrer: *Does Trade Follow the Flag?* (London, 1902), passim, and J. A. Hobson: *Imperialism*, especially chaps. ii, v.

[25] H. E. Egerton: *A Short History of British Colonial Policy*, p. 5.

[26] William Cunningham: *Growth of English Industry and Commerce* (London, 1882); Idem: *Rise and Decline of the Free Trade Movement* (London, 1904), especially pp. 85 ff.; Edward Salmon: " From Cobden to Chamberlain " (*Fortnightly Review*, June, 1896); Sidney Low: " The Decline of Cobdenism " (*Nineteenth Century*, August, 1896, pp. 173–86); John P. Young: " The Decay of Cobdenism in England " (*North American Review*, April, 1898, pp. 418–28); Fuchs: *The Trade Policy of Great Britain*, pp. 184 ff.; W. A. S. Hewins: *The Apologia of an Imperialist* (London, 1929), I, chaps. i and ii; Donald O. Wagner: " British Economists and the Empire," II (*Political Science Quarterly*, XLVII, 1932, pp. 57–74), pp. 64 ff.; Hoffman: *Great Britain and the German Trade Rivalry*, pp. 22 ff., 42 ff.

was much dissatisfaction. Joseph Chamberlain, who belonged to the radical wing, broke away in 1886 because of Gladstone's program for Irish home rule and took with him a not inconsiderable group which formed the Unionist party and ultimately joined the Conservatives in forming a government. Chamberlain was destined to be the most spectacular and probably the most influential imperialist among British statesmen. We need not here review his career or do more than to point out that he was, at an early date, an advocate of imperial federation and an ardent worker in the interests of trade. " True democracy," he said in a speech at Toronto in December 1887, " does not consist in the dismemberment and disintegration of the empire, but rather in the knitting together of kindred races for similar objects." The former policy of shirking in colonial affairs was a failure, he declared. England should keep what she had and should try to extend her influence in Africa. Trade follows the flag and the Empire is commerce, without which the home country could not exist:

> " Is there any man in his senses who believes that the crowded population of these islands could exist for a single day if we were to cut adrift from us the great dependencies which now look to us for protection and assistance, and which are the natural markets for our trade? . . . If tomorrow it were possible, as some people apparently desire, to reduce by a stroke of the pen the British Empire to the dimensions of the United Kingdom, half at least of our population would be starved." (May 14, 1888). " History teaches us that, no nation has ever achieved real greatness without the aid of commerce, and the greatness of no nation has survived the decay of its trade." (June 10, 1896).[27]

Lord Rosebery, who was less " pushful " than Chamberlain, has rarely been given all the credit he deserves as a leader of the new imperialism. He did not, like Chamberlain, part company with Gladstone on the Irish question, but he was, from an early date, an enthusiastic supporter of imperial federation. As foreign minister in 1886 he showed his determination to work for continuity in British foreign policy and to do whatever was possible for the protection and encouragement of British trade. British foreign policy, he declared in a speech at Leeds in 1888, was bound to become more and more a colonial policy, because " the other powers are beginning a career of colonial aggrandisement. We formerly did not have in our foreign affairs to trouble ourselves much with colonial questions, because we had a monopoly of colonies. That monopoly has ceased." In 1893 he delivered, before the Colonial Institute, what was one of the most eloquent and comprehensive addresses on imperialism, an address in which emphasis was put upon the need for the acquisition of more territory:

---

[27] *Foreign and Colonial Speeches* (London, 1897), pp. 13, 26, 102, 131, 197 ff., 235. The economic side of Chamberlain's imperialism has been so ably analysed that no good purpose would be served by going over the ground again. See especially Achille Viallate: *J. Chamberlain* (Paris, 1899); Victor Bérard: *British Imperialism and Commercial Supremacy* (London, 1906); G. von Schulze-Gaevernitz: *British Imperialismus und Englischer Freihandel* (Leipzig, 1906); J. L. Garvin: *The Life of Joseph Chamberlain*, II (New York, 1933), pp. 447 ff., 454 ff.

" It is said that our Empire is already large enough, and does not need exten
sion. That would be true enough if the world were elastic, but unfortunately
it is not elastic, and we are engaged at the present moment, in the language
of mining, 'in pegging out claims for the future.' We have to consider not
what we want now, but what we shall want in the future. We have to consider
what countries must be developed either by ourselves or some other nation, and
we have to remember that it is part of our responsibility and heritage to take
care that the world, so far as it can be moulded by us, shall receive an English-
speaking complexion, and not that of other nations. . . . We have to look forward beyond the chatter of platforms and the passions of party to the future of
the race of which we are at present the trustees, and we should, in my opinion,
grossly fail in the task that has been laid upon us did we shrink from responsibilities and decline to take our share in a partition of the world which we have not
forced on, but which has been forced upon us."

Rosebery was not very fortunate as a foreign minister, but he became very
important as the chief antagonist of the Little Englander viewpoint in the councils of the Liberal party. He had no use for what he called the " party of a small
England, of a shrunk England, of a degraded England, of a neutral England,
of a submissive England " (speech at Sheffield, October 25, 1894). It was largely
because of his insistence that Gladstone was obliged in 1892 to give up the idea
of evacuating Egypt. In the very next year Rosebery fought through the cabinet
a decisive issue of imperialism. Despite the opposition of the prime minister, of
Harcourt, of Morley and of others, the government decided to retain Uganda.
Therewith the division in the old Liberal party became a patent reality. Rosebery and the so-called Liberal Imperialists did not, to be sure, give up the ideas
of free trade, but they frankly believed in the maintenance and extension of the
Empire. By the end of the century the Liberal party was split wide open, the
great majority of its adherents, however, following the road marked out by
Rosebery.[28]

It would hardly do to discuss British imperialism of the late nineteenth century without some special mention of Cecil Rhodes, most picturesque and most
successful of all modern empire builders, a man who was personally responsible
for the annexation of a goodly share of the three and a half million square miles
of territory added to the British Empire between 1884 and 1900. We shall meet
Rhodes as well as Chamberlain and Rosebery a good many times in the course
of this study and there is no need here for more than a mention of the fact that
Rhodes' was essentially a single-track mind. He built up a tremendous fortune
with the idea of using the power which it brought for the aggrandisement and

---

[28] Anon: " The Disraeli of Liberalism " (*Fortnightly Review*, January, 1899, pp. 129–43);
Anon: " Democracy and Foreign Affairs " (*Quarterly Review*, January, 1899, pp. 241–65), especially
pp. 243–5; Anon: " A Lead for Liberalism " (*Fortnightly Review*, September, 1900, pp. 457–71);
Henry Newbolt: " The Paradox of Imperialism " (*Monthly Review*, October, 1900, pp. 1–14);
J. A. R. Marriott: " Lord Rosebery's Chance " (*Fortnightly Review*, December, 1900, pp. 935–46);
L. T. Hobhouse: *Liberalism* (New York, 1907), pp. 221–2.

glorification of the British Empire. He confessed that history had taught him "that expansion was everything, and that the world's surface being limited, the great object of present humanity should be to take as much of the world as it possibly could." Returning from a visit to England in 1899 he was delighted to report to his friends in south Africa that all thoughts of a Little England were gone:

> " They are tumbling over each other, Liberals and Conservatives, to show which side are the greatest and most enthusiastic Imperialists. . . . The people have found that England is small, and her trade is large, and they have also found out that other people are taking their share of the world, and enforcing hostile tariffs. The people of England are finding out that ' trade follows the flag ' and they have all become Imperialists. They are not going to part with any territory. . . . The English people intend to retain every inch of land they have got, and perhaps they intend to secure a few more inches." [29]

Chamberlain, Rosebery and Rhodes were only the most brilliant stars on the firmament of imperialism. There were, of course, innumerable lesser lights. Lord Salisbury, statesman of the old school, hardened diplomat and cynic, had but little use for extravagant verbiage and popular enthusiasms. Though he saw the humorous side of the break-neck race for territory, he nevertheless recognized the dangers of trade war and the need for expansion:

> " After all," he said in a speech at Hastings in 1892, " this little island lives as a trading island. We could not produce in foodstuffs enough to sustain the population that lives in this island, and it is only by the great industries which exist here and which find markets in foreign countries that we are able to maintain the vast population by which this island is inhabited. . . . We live in an age of war of tariffs. . . . In this great battle Great Britain has deliberately stripped herself of the armour and the weapons by which the battle has to be fought. . . . The weapon with which they (the nations) all fight is admission to their own markets. . . . I would impress upon you that if you intend, in this conflict of commercial treaties, to hold your own, you must be prepared, if need be, to inflict upon the nations which injure you the penalty which is in your hands, that of refusing them access to your markets."

This speech reveals a distinct leaning toward a policy of protection, but we must not stop to analyze the attitude of Salisbury or other individuals. Suffice it to recall the names of men like Cromer, Milner, Kitchener, Curzon, Johnston, Lugard, Goldie, MacKinnon and countless others who will appear in the narrative of this book. They all worked to increase the Empire by one third in the brief space of fifteen years, until, by 1900, it covered one fifth of the globe and

---

[29] Vindex: *Cecil Rhodes; His Political Life and Speeches* (London, 1900), pp. 7, 642. The literature on Rhodes is so extensive that it cannot be discussed here. Perhaps the best studies of his imperialism are those of William T. Stead: *The Last Will and Testament of C. J. Rhodes* (London, 1902); G. von Schulze-Gaevernitz: *Britischer Imperialismus und Englischer Freihandel*, pp. 123 ff.; and in the general biographies of Sir Lewis Michell: *The Life of Cecil J. Rhodes* (London, 1910); Basil Williams: *Cecil Rhodes* (London, 1921); Sarah G. Millin: *Rhodes* (London, 1933).

was four times the size of the Roman Empire or forty times the size of the contemporary German Empire.[30]

Perhaps the most remarkable feature of late Victorian imperialism was its
popularity with the lower classes. The political leaders of the movement never
tired of pointing out the advantages of expansion for the workingman. "You
must remember," said Chamberlain in a speech in 1895, "that, speaking generally, the great cure for this difficulty of want of employment is to find new
markets." Or again, in a somewhat earlier address (1894):

> "Give me the demand for more goods and then I will undertake to give plenty
> of employment in making the goods. . . . If the workingmen of this country
> understand, as I believe they do . . . their own interests, they will never lend
> any countenance to the doctrines of those politicians who never lose an oppor-
> tunity of pouring contempt and abuse upon the brave Englishmen, who, even
> at this moment, in all parts of the world are carving out new dominions for
> Britain, are opening up fresh markets for British commerce, and laying out fresh
> fields for British labour." [31]

Rhodes was, if anything, more outspoken:

> "The mechanic has woke up to the fact that unless he keeps the markets of the
> world he will be starved. The 'three acres and a cow' idea has been found to
> be humbug, and the workingman has found out that he must keep the world
> and the trade of the world if he is to live, and that if the world is shut to him
> he is done." [32]

Now it has frequently been asserted by opponents of imperialism that the
ignorant public was misled and deluded by false promises made by financiers,
industrialists, armaments manufacturers, stock speculators and politicians, into
supporting a movement which, in the last count, worked to its detriment by
halting the necessary work of social reform.[33] It is always difficult to determine
what is cause and what is effect in a case like this, but it does appear, from a
study of such imperial crises as the Kruger telegram episode, the Port Arthur
affair, the Fashoda crisis, etc., that the public was more excited than the government. There is surely some room for argument that popular pressure was more
important in the growth of imperialism than was the action of the ruling classes.
It must be recalled, for example, that the rise of imperialism was contemporaneous with the extension of the suffrage in 1867 and 1884 and that it fell in the

---

[30] Hobson: *Imperialism*, pp. 16 ff.; W. S. Lilly: "The Burden of Empire" (*Fortnightly Review*, October, 1900, pp. 533–43); L. T. Hobhouse: *Democracy and Reaction* (New York. 1905),
pp. 28 ff.

[31] Chamberlain: *Foreign and Colonial Speeches*, pp. 114–5, 131–3, 202. See also Anon: "Mr.
Chamberlain as Foreign Minister" (*Fortnightly Review*, August, 1898, pp. 317–25), pp. 321–2.

[32] Speech of April 21, 1898 (Vindex: *Cecil Rhodes*, pp. 701–2); similarly the speech of July 20,
1899 (Vindex, pp. 651–2).

[33] Hobson: *Imperialism*, chaps. iv and vi passim; Charles F. G. Masterman: "Realities at
Home" (in *The Heart of the Empire*, second edition, London, 1907, chap. i); John M. Robertson:
Patriotism and Empire (London, 1899), p. 189.

period when the effects of universal education were just beginning to make themselves felt. It was noted at the time that " power and dominion rather than freedom and independence are the ideas that appeal to the imagination of the masses." [34]

Both Masterman and Hobson, as well as other writers, recognized the danger. The workingmen, it was pointed out, had never had much use for Manchester liberalism with all its teaching of non-interference by the state in economic affairs. They expressed themselves as soon as the extended suffrage gave them a chance. Instead of working for peace and social reform they deserted the Liberal party, put the Conservatives in power, neglected reform and backed imperialism.[35] The new urban proletariat, says Masterman, was narrow-chested but voluble and excitable, and sought stimulus in drink, gambling and conflict at home and abroad. The half-literate slum-dweller demanded fiercer excitement: " more chops, bloody ones, with gristle." [36] The same conclusion was reached by an anonymous writer in the *Quarterly Review:*

> " The artisans and the peasantry, endowed with and conscious of constitutional power, have in no respect impeded, but on the contrary have facilitated the prosecution of a most complex and arduous imperial undertaking, necessarily protracted over many years. No limited electorate, not even any aristocracy, could conceivably have comported itself in such fashion as to create fewer hindrances to an enterprise such as that which we have been considering (Egypt). Nor could any other system of government than a popular one have afforded to those in command of the nation's resources the support and encouragement derived from the well-grounded conviction that the nation itself was at their back. . . . The tone of empire is to be heard everywhere now, strong, clear, and unmistakeable, and it has grown and spread and obtained its mastery during the reign of household suffrage." [37]

This popular thirst for excitement and pageantry was undoubtedly nourished by the great Jubilee celebrations of 1887 and 1897, with their tremendous display of pomp and power. The South African War at first was a wonderful outlet for the spirit of adventure and conflict. Mafeking Night of June 1900, with its unbridled rioting and its appalling vulgarity, shocked people who were not otherwise prudish or Victorian. But by that time the public had been nourished for fully a decade by a sensational newspaper press and by a literature of brutality which we cannot afford to leave out of account. In approaching the problem we are at once confronted by the question whether the press and literature of imperialism brutalized the people or whether the emergence of an unrefined,

---

[34] W. F. Monypenny: " The Imperial Ideal " (in *The Empire and the Century,* London, 1905), pp. 5–28).

[35] Edward Dicey: " The Downfall of Liberalism " (*Fortnightly Review,* November, 1900, pp. 803–14); L. T. Hobhouse: *Democracy and Reaction,* p. 50; Hobson: *Imperialism,* p. 89.

[36] Masterman, loc. cit.

[37] Anon: " Democracy and Foreign Affairs " (*Quarterly Review,* January, 1899, pp. 241–65), pp. 247, 249–50.

uncultured reading public called forth the type of literature which was so popu-lar in the last years of the century. Surely there was an interaction of the two, but in the last count it is, I think, fairly clear that it was the demand that created the supply. Walter Bagehot believed that ages as well as nations have a character, and held that this *Zeitgeist* ultimately finds expression through some writer, frequently not a genius, who produces something a bit more congenial to the minds about him. Thereupon other writers " catch the words that are in the air, and the rhythm which comes to them they do not know from whence." [38]

It was such a " tidal mood of mankind " which carried Kipling to unprece-dented literary success in the decade following 1890. Edmund Gosse, in one of his essays, has remarked upon the fact that in the early eighties there was still a pronounced dislike for any narrative literature which exalted the boisterous part of human nature. Literature was expected to be idyllic or reflective, and even historical writing was diverted to the unromantic, arid field of institu-tional study.[39] The success of Stevenson's *Treasure Island* in 1883 may be taken to mark the turn of the tide, which by 1886 had risen so high that Rider Hag-gard's *King Solomon's Mines* sold five thousand copies in the first two months.[40] His other African yarns, with their " colonial butcheries," were hardly less successful. Englishmen began to develop an interest in what Bismarck once called their " sporting wars," and in their colonial heroes. Mahan's glorifica-tion of British sea power and his warm appreciation of Nelson found a deep response. Books on the accomplishments of British rule in the far corners of the earth rivalled stories of adventure and war in popularity. Alfred Milner's *Eng-land in Egypt* (1892) made a deep impression, as did Sir Alfred Lyall's *Rise and Expansion of the British Dominion in India* (1894), Lord Roberts' *Forty-One Years in India* (1897) and William W. Hunter's *A History of British India* (1899). George Younghusband's *The Relief of Chitral* (1895) and espe-cially Sir George Robertson's *Chitral; the Story of a Minor Siege* (1898) were among the most widely read stories of British heroism. The tragedy of Gordon's death at Khartum struck the popular imagination more perhaps than any other event, and created a tremendous interest in the Sudan. Father Ohrwalder's *Ten Years Captivity in the Mahdi's Camp* (1892) ran through ten editions in a year, and Slatin Pasha's *Fire and Sword in the Sudan* (1896) at once became a classic. The public followed Kitchener's campaign of 1896–8 in a spirit of ex-citement, which accounts for the success of George W. Steevens' *With Kitchener to Khartum* (1898, thirteen editions in a few months) and Winston Churchill's *The River War* (1899). R. S. S. Baden-Powell's *The Matabele Campaign* (1897), Edmund Garrett's *Story of an African Crisis* (1897) and J. P. Fitzpatrick's *The Transvaal from Within* (1899) are three books that reflect the intense and wide-spread interest in all things south African.

---

[38] Walter Bagehot: *Physics and Politics* (New York, 1902), pp. 31–3.
[39] Edmund Gosse: " The Literature of Action " (*North American Review*, January, 1899, pp. 14–23).   [40] Sir H. Rider Haggard: *The Days of my Life* (London, 1926), I, p. 242.

Kipling fitted perfectly into this setting. From the time of the appearance of his first book in England (1890), his popularity increased so rapidly that by the end of the century it could be fairly said that no other writer of his time had so profoundly swayed the English mind. His influence, wrote Edmund Gosse, was " simply prodigious "; " his breath has stirred the veins not of hundreds of men, nor of thousands, but of a cluster of nations." Kipling stands revealed, wrote W. T. Stead at the time of Kipling's illness, " as the man who most of all has impressed the popular mind, fired the popular imagination, interpreted the popular consciousness." [41] More than any other writer he reflected the diverse ideas that went under the general term of imperialism. In his *Barrack-Room Ballads* and his army stories he stimulated interest in British activity over-seas and at the same time appealed to the fighting instincts of the race. Hostile critics accused him of exalting brutality and of giving a libelous picture of the British soldier. In his books, they said, he gave " a picture of unmitigated barbarism, drunken, swearing, coarse-minded, vulgar hooliganism, fit for low drinking-dens and gin-palaces." " The voice we hear is always the voice of the soldier whose God is a cockney ' Gawd ' and who is ignorant of the aspirate in either Heaven or Hell." There was, they said, in all his works the tacit assumption that the conquered natives were merely made to be fought with, conquered and ruled. They were viewed " merely as a huge mass of raw, brown, naked humanity to be manipulated by the civil and military officials for the arcane purposes of the great Indian Empire." They objected to his preaching contempt for individual rights, his glorifying of the soldier, his cult of the silent strong man and his idealizing of discipline and obedience.[42]

These criticisms, however justified, must not blind us to the fact that in the eyes of his admirers Kipling was the man who saved the Empire, that, more perhaps than any other one man, he roused " the sleeping nerve centres of Imperialism." In the larger sense his popularity merely reflects the impatience of the average Englishman with Ruskin and Browning Societies, with pre-Raphaelite poetry, to say nothing of the decadents, Wilde, Beardsley, Dowson and the rest. The young Englishman, it has been said, yawned and longed to go out and shoot something he could understand.[43] Hence the host of literary followers of Kipling, the " literary rough-riders " the exponents of a literature of energy and of action, the now forgotten writers of " blood-stained fiction." [44] We

---

[41] Gosse, loc. cit.; William T. Stead: "Mr. Rudyard Kipling: The Banjo-Bard of Empire " (*Review of Reviews*, April 15, 1899, pp. 317-27).

[42] Francis Adams: " Rudyard Kipling " (*Fortnightly Review*, November, 1891, pp. 686-700); Robert Buchanan: " The Voice of ' The Hooligan ' " (*Contemporary Review*, December, 1899, pp. 774-89); Richard Le Gallienne: *Rudyard Kipling* (New York, 1900), pp. 127-57; Esmé Wingfield-Stratford: *The History of British Civilization* (New York, 1928), II, pp. 1165 ff.; Victor Bérard: *British Imperialism and Commercial Supremacy*, p. 46.

[43] Le Gallienne, op. cit., p. 155; Cyril Falls: *Rudyard Kipling* (London, 1915), introduction.

[44] " Kipling as a Poet of Patriotism " (*Outlook*, January 6, 1900, pp. 18-9); Eugène Melchior de Vogüé: " La Littérature Impérialiste " (*Revue des Deux Mondes*, May, 1901, pp. 196-212); " The Literary Inspiration of Imperialism " (*Scottish Review*, April, 1900, pp. 262-78); André Chevrillon:

cannot and need not review the work of individual writers and must content ourselves with recalling the names of Alfred Austin, William Henley, William Watson, Henry Newbolt, Algernon Swinburne, Theodore Watts-Dunton. Most of these poets sang the glories of British sea-power and empire, but the cult of the sea is a manifestation of the imperial urge that had better be left for a later chapter.

The development of a cheap, popular newspaper press ran parallel to the rise of the literature of action. The attempt to give the rank and file of the population something more palatable than the dignified old newspapers of the ruling classes was made by William T. Stead and John Morley and the whole group gathered about the *Pall Mall Gazette* in the early eighties. But this " new " journalism was soon overshadowed by the " popular " journalism of which Alfred Harmsworth was the prophet. It was in 1894 that Harmsworth bought the *Evening News* and in May 1896 that he began the publication of the *Daily Mail,* the first halfpenny morning paper to attain larger success. He was convinced that the general public had no interest in the long and forbidding columns of parliamentary debates and court reports that were so characteristic of the older papers. His idea was to let people decide what they wanted and then give them just that, attractively presented in bold headlines and striking type.

It did not take Harmsworth and his collaborators long to realize that what the public wanted was general news of an exciting kind. " We realized," says one of his closest associates, " that one of the greatest forces, almost untapped, at the disposal of the Press was the depth and volume of public interest in Imperial questions." So Harmsworth, who was an admirer of Chamberlain, came out vigorously for imperialism. When the *Daily Mail* was founded the announcement was made that it would stand first and foremost

> " for the power, the supremacy and the greatness of the British Empire. . . . The *Daily Mail* is the embodiment and mouthpiece of the imperial idea. Those who launched this journal had one definite aim in view . . . to be the articulate voice of British progress and domination. We believe in England. We know that the advance of the Union Jack means protection for weaker races, justice for the oppressed, liberty for the down-trodden. Our Empire has not exhausted itself." [45]

The success of the Harmsworth papers literally startled thoughtful people. The *Daily Mail* had an average daily sale of over 200,000 copies in the first year. By 1901 it reached the unheard of figure of 1,000,000. So great in fact was the success of this type of journalism that even the best-established of the older

Three Studies in English Literature (New York, 1923), pp. 47 ff.; Friedrich Brie: *Imperialistische Strömungen in der Englischen Literatur* (second edition, Halle, 1928), pp. 221 ff.; Edward Salmon: " The Literature of the Empire " (in *The British Empire,* XI, London, 1924), pp. 154 ff.

45 Kennedy Jones: *Fleet Street and Downing Street* (London, 1920), pp. 84 ff., 141 ff.; R. Mac-Nair Wilson: *Lord Northcliffe* (Philadelphia, 1927), pp. 99 ff., 120; R. A. Scott-James: *The Influence of the Press* (London, n.d.), pp. 194-5; Hamilton Fyffe: *Northcliffe* (London, 1930), pp. 67-8.

papers were obliged to follow the same line, at least to a certain extent. The *Manchester Guardian* was a striking exception, but even the *Times* became vigorously imperialistic, until it could be said of it that it differed from the *Mail* only in price, quality of paper and volume of news.[46] It showed the same spread-eagleism, the same contempt for moral ideals, the same unquestioning confidence in the efficacy of force.

Journalists of the Harmsworth type created for themselves a tremendous personal power, and the fact could not remain hidden for very long. William T. Stead, himself a pioneer of modern journalism, wrote in 1898:

> "The fact is that the intervention of the Press in international disputes tends daily to become more and more hostile to peace and civilisation. If there is one thing more than another upon which I found that every one was agreed in my tour around Europe, it was that much of our modern journalism is the most potent weapon yet invented by the devil for banishing peace and goodwill from the earth. Sooner or later the nations will in self-defence have to provide some means of silencing newspaper comment when international questions are in debate, in the same way as English newspapers are promptly forbidden by law to express an opinion upon any case that is before the Courts."

Lord Salisbury, who began by saying that Harmsworth had invented a paper for those who could read but could not think, and another for those who could see but could not read, ended by becoming completely discouraged by the turn which had been given journalism:

> "The diplomacy of nations is now conducted quite as much in the letters of special correspondents, as in the despatches of the Foreign Office," he wrote to Canon MacColl in 1901. "The result is that there is a raw state of irritation between the upper classes in the two countries, which makes any advance on the part of either Government quite impracticable."[47]

The tone of realism, not to say ruthlessness and brutality, that was so striking a characteristic of imperialism was due in a measure to the general cast of sociological thought prevailing at that time. A large number of contemporary writers remarked upon the tremendous vogue of Darwinian theories of social evolution. The phrases *struggle for existence* and *survival of the fittest* carried everything before them in the nineties. One critic has asserted that the vogue of this doctrine was "the primary intellectual cause of the reaction."[48]

It has often been pointed out that Darwin himself made no effort to apply the principles of organic evolution to the study of the social structure, and that many of the ideas supposedly taken from his writings were ideas for which he could not justly be held responsible. That is, of course, the fate of every great

---

[46] G. P. Gooch: "Imperialism" (in *The Heart of the Empire*), pp. 339 ff.
[47] G. W. E. Russell: *Malcolm MacColl* (London, 1914), p. 283.
[48] L. T. Hobhouse: *Democracy and Reaction* (New York, 1905), pp. 84 ff. See also David G Ritchie: *Darwinism and Politics* (Second edition, London, 1891), pp. 2–3.

thinker. The historian, however, is obliged to study the impact of ideas, whatever their true origins or their scientific validity. In the matter of Darwinian influence it may be noted that before the publication of the *Descent of Man* in 1872 a theory of social evolution had been worked out by Spencer and the effort had been made by Walter Bagehot to apply the idea of organic evolution and natural selection to the study of social organization. In Bagehot's brilliant essay, *Physics and Politics,* may be found, at least in embryo, the argument as it was elaborated by others later on:

> "In every particular state of the world, those nations which are strongest tend to prevail over the others; and in certain marked peculiarities the strongest tend to be the best." "The strongest nation has always been conquering the weaker." "The majority of groups which win and conquer are better than the majority of those which fail and perish, and thus the first world grew better and was improved." [49]

Bagehot's book was only the first of a good many similar treatments published in Europe in the last fifteen years of the century. In 1883 the Austrian sociologist Gumplowicz brought out his book *The Struggle of Races,* expounding the theory of original heterogeneous forms which have been in conflict since the beginning of time. The tendency of history, he thought, was toward the formation of ever larger groups and toward greater, though rarer conflicts. The struggle of races, he concluded, is the eternal law of history.[50] A few years later, in 1886, a French scientist, Vacher de Lapouge, published a study of *Natural Selections,* in which he asserted that evolutionary teaching was probably more important for the social than for the biological sciences. Nations, like individual organisms, he argued, were born, lived and died. Race and race development are more significant than geography or history when it comes to explaining social evolution.[51]

The same year saw the publication of the first important work of the Russian sociologist, J. Novicow. Though Novicow later became one of the most active of European pacifists and a keen critic of what he called "social Darwinism," this first volume, entitled *International Policy,* was written along strictly biological lines. The gist of the argument may best be given in a few quotations:

> "Since societies are organisms, one can deduce *a priori* that they will conform to all the laws of biology."

---

[49] *Physics and Politics* (New York, 1902), pp. 43, 49, 218. See also George Nasmyth: *Social Progress and the Darwinian Theory* (New York, 1916), pp. 1–9; James P. Lichtenberger: *Development of Social Theory* (New York, 1923), p. 280; Raymond G. Gettell: *History of Political Thought* (New York, 1924), pp. 428 ff.

[50] Ludwig Gumplowicz: *Der Rassenkampf (Ausgewählte Werke,* III, Innsbruck, 1928), esp. p. 259. See especially Harry Elmer Barnes: "The Struggle of Races and Social Groups" (*Journal of Race Development,* IX, 1919, pp. 394–419), which is devoted largely to Gumplowicz. Idem: *Sociology and Political Theory* (New York, 1924), chap. xi; Lichtenberger, op. cit., p. 445.

[51] Georges Vacher de Lapouge: *Les Selections Sociales* (Paris, 1896), in which he reviews his work in the previous decade.

"Nature is a vast field of carnage. Between living creatures conflict takes place every second, every minute, without truce and without respite. It takes place first between separate individuals, then between collective organisms, tribe against tribe, state against state, nationality against nationality. No cessation is possible. Living means fighting."

"This subordination of the less fit individual and collective organisms to the more fit, this is justice in nature: an incorruptible but implacable justice which knows no pity, but which gives to each with absolute impartiality the place due to its merits. It is the struggle for existence which determines this place. If one animal is less perfect than another, he must serve as prey. If one society is less perfect than another, the first must work for the second."

"International policy is the art of conducting the struggle for existence between social organisms." [52]

In England the biological or "natural history" conception of social and international relations was, if anything, more in vogue than on the Continent. Much of the immense literature on Spencer and Darwin touched upon it and Huxley foresaw the indefinite continuance of the struggle.[53] Benjamin Kidd's book on *Social Evolution,* which first appeared in 1894, went through edition after edition and sold to the extent of some 250,000 copies. This is the more remarkable in view of the fact that the book was really very thin and unconvincing when critically appraised.[54] A much more forceful presentation of the whole biological approach was given in the *Saturday Review* for February 1896, by " A Biologist," reputed by some to have been Professor Mitchell. This " Biological View of our Foreign Policy " was clearly inspired by the Anglo-German crisis and the Kruger telegram: " The great nations of the earth," said the author, " are local varieties, species in the making, which are gathering themselves together, emphasizing their national characters, and unconsciously making for specific distinctness ":

"The foreign policies of the nations, so far as they are not the mere expressions of the individual ambitions of rulers, or the jog-trot opportunism of diplomatists, are anticipation of, and provision for, struggles for existence between incipient species. . . . The facts are patent. Feeble races are being wiped off the earth and the few great, incipient species arm themselves against each other. England, as the greatest of these — greatest in race-pride — has avoided for centuries the only dangerous kind of war. Now, with the whole earth occupied and the movements of expansion continuing, she will have to fight to the death against successive rivals."

---

[52] J. Novicow: *La Politique Internationale* (Paris, 1886), pp. 153, 231, 235–6, 242.

[53] E.g., in his essay " The Struggle for Existence " (*Nineteenth Century,* February, 1888, pp. 161–80).

[54] W. H. Mattock: " Physics and Sociology " (*Contemporary Review,* December, 1895, pp. 883–908; January, 1896, pp. 59–83) practically accused Kidd of plagiarizing his (Mattock's) book on *Social Equality,* which appeared in 1882. There is a good critical discussion of Kidd's work in David G. Ritchie: " Social Evolution " (*International Journal of Ethics,* January, 1896), and in Crane Brinton: *English Political Thought in the 19th Century* (London, 1933), pp. 282–92.

Perhaps the classic formulation of this entire viewpoint, however, was that given by Professor Karl Pearson in his essay of 1900 entitled *National Life from the Standpoint of Science*. In this he says:

"History shows me one way, and one way only, in which a state of civilisation has been produced, namely, the struggle of race with race, and the survival of the physically and mentally fitter race."

"This dependence of progress on the survival of the fitter race, terribly black as it may seem to some of you, gives the struggle for existence its redeeming features; it is the fiery crucible out of which comes the finer metal. You may hope for a time when the sword shall be turned into the ploughshare, when American and German and English traders shall no longer compete in the markets of the world for raw materials, for their food supply, when the white man and the dark shall share the soil between them, and each till it as he lists. But, believe me, when that day comes mankind will no longer progress; there will be nothing to check the fertility of inferior stock; the relentless law of heredity will not be controlled and guided by natural selection. Man will stagnate . . ."

"The path of progress is strewn with the wreck of nations; traces are everywhere to be seen of the hecatombs of inferior races, and of victims who found not the narrow way to the greater perfection. Yet these dead peoples are, in very truth, the stepping stones on which mankind has arisen to the higher intellectual and deeper emotional life of to-day." [55]

Many other writers of less importance could be quoted to the same effect. Indeed there was so much loose writing on this general theme that one critic was driven to cry out: "O Evolution, what crimes are committed in thy name!" while another spoke of the new beatitude: "Blessed are the strong, for they shall prey upon the weak." [56] We cannot stop here to examine the influence of this evolutionary conception in greater detail, but we must take time to note its two-fold effect, first in the growth of militarism, second in the cultivation of the idea of race-superiority and the divine national mission.

We have, in the years since the World War, heard so much about the prevention of war in the future, and we have watched with such solicitude the tender growth of internationalism that we are, I fear, apt to forget that in the years before the war, despite the peace movement and the Hague Conferences, military conflict was popularly regarded with less horror than now and the idea of universal peace was looked upon by many as little more than a pipe-dream. It may well be that the military successes of Prussia, and for that matter

---

[55] Karl Pearson: *National Life from the Standpoint of Science* (Second edition, London, 1905), pp. 21, 26-7, 64.

[56] C. O. Ovington: "War and Evolution" (*Westminster Review*, April, 1900, pp. 411-20); G. P. Gooch: "Imperialism" (in *The Heart of the Empire*), p. 312. Among the critical accounts it is worth mentioning further J. A. Hobson: "The Scientific Basis of Imperialism" (*Political Science Quarterly*, XVII, 1902, pp. 460-89); Idem: *Imperialism, a Study*, Book II, chap. ii; L. T. Hobhouse: *Democracy and Reaction* (London, 1905), chap. iv; Idem: *Social Evolution and Political Theory* (New York, 1913), chap. ii; J. Novicow: *La Critique du Darwinisme Social* (Paris, 1910), chap. ii; W. L. Blease: *A Short History of English Liberalism* (New York, 1913), pp. 305-15.

the obvious successes of Bismarck's " realistic " policy had much to do with the spread of this attitude. People liked to quote Moltke's famous dictum that perpetual peace was a dream and not even a pleasant dream. On the other hand it can be shown over and over again that the militaristic spirit was closely connected with the idea of the struggle for existence and the survival of the strongest. Had not Spencer himself written:

" Inconceivable as have been the horrors caused by the universal antagonism which, beginning with the chronic hostilities of small hordes tens of thousands of years ago, has ended in the occasional vast battles of immense nations, we must nevertheless admit that without it the world would still have been inhabited only by men of feeble types sheltering in caves and living on wild food."

And did not Renan maintain that

" War is in a way one of the conditions of progress, the cut of the whip which prevents a country from going to sleep, forcing satisfied mediocrity itself to leave its apathy." [57]

It is perfectly true that Spencer, while recognizing the achievement of war in the past, was unwilling to regard it as necessary in the future and hoped that the struggle for existence might be restricted to the intellectual and economic spheres.[58] But Spencer's argument was not at all convincing, and there were plenty of other writers to popularize the idea that progress depended on conflict and that conflict in international affairs has generally meant, sooner or later, military strife. William E. H. Lecky, the eminent historian, noted the steady spread of militarism and the growing popularity of the ideas of universal military service. It was claimed that universal service would carry the idea and sentiment of nationhood to multitudes whose thoughts would otherwise have never travelled beyond the narrow circle of daily wants or village interests. It would give the common man the tastes of the civilized man, and would make of him a brave, steady, energetic and patriotic citizen.[59] Lord Wolseley, commander in chief of the British forces, glorified the soldier's life:

" All other pleasures pale before the intense, the maddening delight of leading men into the midst of an enemy, or to the assault of some well-defended place. That rapturous enjoyment takes man out of himself to the forgetfulness of all earthly considerations."
" A sound, healthy, military spirit gives strength to a people. It is the guardian of the honour and interests of a nation, the safeguard of its freedom and liberties,

[57] Herbert Spencer: *Principles of Sociology*, Vol. II, part V, p. 241; Ernest Renan: *La Réforme Intellectuelle et Morale* (Paris, 1871), p. 111.

[58] *Principles of Sociology*, II, pp. 610, 664–5; on Spencer's dilemma see also C. O. Ovington: " War and Evolution " (*Westminster Review*, April, 1900, pp. 411–20), p. 412; George Nasmyth: *Social Progress and the Darwinian Theory*, pp. 1–14; Brinton: *English Political Thought*, pp. 233–4.

[59] William E. H. Lecky: *Democracy and Liberty* (New edition, London, 1899), I, pp. 307–14.

the purifier of its civilisation, its defence against enemies from without, and degeneracy from within." [60]

H. W. Wyatt, who was secretary of the Seeley Lecturers, declared that

" The only means, revealed to us by past experience, whereby the vigorous people has supplanted the weaker, has been war, without which change and movement must have ceased." [61]

Sidney Low, the well-known publicist, ridiculed the Hague Peace Conference and asserted that

" There is scarcely a nation in the world — certainly not in our high-strung, masterful, Caucasian world, — that does not value itself chiefly for its martial achievements. . . . There is no great nation that would think it worth while to read its own history if the wars were left out of it. . . . A righteous and neces-sary war is no more brutal than a surgical operation. Better give the patient some pain, and make your own fingers unpleasantly red, than allow the disease to grow upon him until he becomes an offence to himself and the world, and dies in lingering agony." [62]

And, if another quotation be permitted, one might add the words of J. A. Cramb:

" In the light of history, universal peace appears less as a dream than as a night-mare, which shall be realized only when the ice has crept to the heart of the sun, and the stars, left black and trackless, start from their orbits."

Cramb foresaw bigger and better wars as the result of universal striving for imperial ends.[63]

The biological conception of the struggle for existence and the survival of the fittest led not only to the glorification of the struggle but to the general acceptance of the ideas of race superiority, destiny and divine ordination. There was, in the last decade of the century, a widespread idea that the tendency of social development was toward larger and larger units and that ultimately the world would be divided between the three or four fittest nations. " It seems to me," said Chamberlain in 1897, " that the tendency of the time is to throw all power into the hands of the greater Empires, and the minor kingdoms — those which are non-progressive — seem to be destined to fall into a secondary and subordinate place." Or, to quote a speech of 1902: " The future is with the great Empires, and there is no greater Empire than the British Empire." [64]

---

[60] Lord Wolseley: " Is a Soldier's Life Worth Living? " (*Fortnightly Review*, May, 1889, pp. 597–610); " War and Preparations for War " (*United Service Magazine*, March, 1897).

[61] H. W. Wyatt: " War as the Supreme Test of National Value " (*Nineteenth Century*, Feb-ruary, 1899, pp. 216–25), p. 222.

[62] Sidney Low: " The Hypocrisies of the Peace Conference " (*Nineteenth Century*, May, 1899, pp. 689–98), pp. 690–2; Idem: " Should Europe Disarm? " (ibid., October, 1898, pp. 521–30).

[63] J. A. Cramb: *Origins and Destiny of Imperial Britain* (London, 1915), p. 146. This book consists of lectures delivered in 1900 and collected by his faithful students.

[64] The idea of a few great empires went back at least to Dilke and Seeley. It was much dis-cussed around the turn of the century. See, e.g., Henry Newbolt: " The Empire and Militarism " (*Monthly Review*, November, 1900, pp. 1–10); Ernest L. Bell: " The Mission of Empire " (*West-*

This last sentence will serve admirably to lead us to the all-important ideal-istic aspect of British imperialism. Not a few writers, of course, would deny that there was any such thing. For them the fine sentiments of the British are nothing but pure hypocrisy. Perhaps the classic formulation of this viewpoint is given by Bernard Shaw, in his *Man of Destiny*, from which a rather long quotation may not be amiss:

> "Every Englishman is born with a certain miraculous power that makes him master of the world. When he wants a thing he never tells himself that he wants it. He waits patiently till there comes into his head, no one knows how, the burn-ing conviction that it is his moral and religious duty to conquer those who have the thing he wants. Then he becomes irresistible. Like the aristocrat he does what pleases him and grabs what he wants; like the shopkeeper he pursues his purpose with the industry and steadfastness that come from strong religious conviction and deep sense of moral responsibility. He is never at a loss for an effective moral attitude. As the great champion of freedom and independence, he conquers half the world and calls it Colonization. When he wants a new market for his adul-terated Manchester goods, he sends a missionary to teach the natives the gospel of peace. The natives kill the missionary; he flies to arms in defense of Chris-tianity; fights for it, conquers for it; and takes the market as a reward from heaven. . . . There is nothing so bad or so good that you will not find an Eng-lishman doing it; but you will never find an Englishman in the wrong. He does everything on principle. He fights you on patriotic principles, he robs you on business principles, he enslaves you on imperialistic principles, he bullies you on manly principles, he supports his King on loyal principles, he cuts off his King's head on republican principles. His watchword is always duty; and he never for-gets that the nation which lets its duty get on the opposite side of its interest is lost."

Call the Englishman's faith in his mission rationalization of more sordid motives if you like, but I doubt if you can honestly speak of hypocrisy.[65] No one could deny the sincerity and high purpose of the missionary and aborigines protection societies which were so deeply interested in the spread of the gospel and the improvement of the " backward " races. No one could deny that the English, themselves the champions of the ideas of liberty and good govern-ment, had given their white colonies self-government and had maintained a sentimental bond with these colonies which was unprecedented in the history of modern expansion. So long as they kept to the policy of free trade they could argue with much force that they kept the territories under their rule open to the enterprise of the world and did not demand a monopolistic position for themselves. In short, they had been more successful than all others in making colonies profitable and contented. Their huge Empire was a standing proof

---

minster Review, October, 1900, pp. 446–50); C. S. Goldman, in *The Empire and the Century* (Lon-don, 1905), introduction, p. xix; W. F. Monypenny: *The Imperial Ideal* (ibid., pp. 5–28), pp. 17–8; W. J. Ashley: *The Tariff Problem* (London, 1903), pp. 198 ff.

[65] Even critics like Hobson: *Imperialism*, Book II, chap. iii warmly reject the idea of hypocrisy, which was, of course, lavishly used by foreigners when they discussed British policy.

of their fitness to rule, consequently the extension of the Empire would be a
boon to those peoples that were taken over, even if they were brought in by
force. They did not claim to be infallible, and they admitted that on occasion
they were brutal and rough, but they were convinced that it was all for the
best in the end.

In order to demonstrate this attitude a few of many of the utterances of the
leading imperialists may be quoted. First of all Chamberlain, who constantly
stressed this aspect of the problem:

" I believe that the British race is the greatest of governing races that the world
has ever seen." (November 11, 1895).

" I admit that we have made mistakes. I have no doubt that we are answerable
for sins of commission as well as for sins of omission; but, after all is said, this
remains — that we alone among the nations of the earth have been able to
establish and to maintain colonies under different conditions in all parts of the
world, that we have maintained them to their own advantage and to ours, and
that we have secured, not only the loyal attachment of all British subjects, but
the general goodwill of the races, whether they be native or whether they be
European, that have thus come under the British flag." (January 21, 1896).

" We, in our colonial policy, as fast as we acquire new territory and develop it,
develop it as trustees of civilisation for the commerce of the world. . . . In that
policy we stand alone, because all other nations, as fast as they acquire new territory . . . seek at once to secure the monopoly for their own products by preferential and artificial methods. . . . It is interesting to notice that we alone have
been successful, astonishingly successful, in making these acquisitions profitable."
(November 13, 1896).

" Let the Little Englanders say what they like, we are a great governing race,
predestined by our defects, as well as by our virtues, to spread over the habitable
globe, and to enter into relations with all the countries of the earth." (January
30, 1897).

" I do not say that our success has been perfect in every case, I do not say that
all our methods have been beyond reproach; but I do say that in almost every
instance in which the rule of the Queen has been established and the great *Pax
Britannica* has been enforced, there has come with it greater security to life and
property, and a material improvement in the condition of the bulk of the population." You cannot make omelettes without breaking eggs. " It is a gigantic
task that we have undertaken when we have determined to wield the sceptre of
empire. Great is the task, great is the responsibility, but great is the honour."
(March 31, 1897).

In similar fashion Lord Milner found that England was particularly fitted
to undertake and settle the Egyptian problem:

" Alike by the nature of our interests, by the nature of our power, and by certain
special qualities in our national character, we seem marked out for the discharge
of this particular duty." [66]

---

[66] Alfred Milner: *England in Egypt* (London, 1892), pp. 435–6.

Lord Curzon dedicated his book on the Far Eastern problem

" To those who believe that the British Empire is under Providence the greatest instrument for good that the world has seen, and who hold, with the writer, that its work in the Far East is not yet accomplished." [67]

William Watson sings, in *The Inexorable Law:*

> " We have reigned
> Augustly; let our part be so sustained
> That Time, far hence, shall hold our memory dear!
> Let it be said: ' This Mistress of the sword
> And conquering now, this Empire swoln with spoils,
> Yet served the human cause, yet strove for Man;
> Hers was the purest greatness we record.' "

Lord Rosebery, in turn, declared

" The Empire that is sacred to me is sacred for this reason, that I believe it to be the noblest example yet known to mankind of free adaptable just government. . . . When a community is in distress or under oppression it always looks first to Great Britain; while in cases which are quite unsuspected, I think, by Great Britain at large, and which are, as a rule, only known to Ministers, they constantly express the wish in some form or other to be united to our country, and to enjoy our government."

The British, then, were convinced that they were the patricians of the human race, and that they had been called upon to fulfil a certain duty, to carry the White Man's Burden, if we may borrow the name of Kipling's classic formulation of the idea. They are not, they think, imperialists because they want to be, but because they are called upon to be, because they must be:

" Why are we Imperialists? As well ask the owner of an estate why he is a landlord. We have inherited Empire and intend to do our duty by the many peoples included in it. . . . We are Imperialists in response to the compelling influences of our destiny. We are not grouped with nations ' vacant of our glorious gains.' We are the heirs of the ages, with all the great prerogatives and solemn obligations which attach to this high privilege. We are, and shall be, Imperialists because we cannot help it." [68]

" To us — to us, and not to others, — a certain definite duty has been assigned. To carry light and civilisation into the dark places of the world, to touch the mind of Asia and of Africa with the ethical ideas of Europe; to give to thronging millions, who would otherwise never know peace or security, these first conditions of human advance." [69]

---

[67] George Curzon: *Problems of the Far East* (London, 1894).

[68] J. Lawson Walton: " Imperialism " (*Contemporary Review*, March, 1899, pp. 305–10). p. 307.

[69] H. W. Wyatt: " The Ethics of Empire " (*Nineteenth Century*, April, 1897, pp. 516–30), p. 529; similarly Arnold White: *The Condition of Empire* (London, 1898); Anon.: " The Literary Inspiration of Imperialism " (*Scottish Review*, April, 1900, pp. 262–78), p. 265; William T. Stead: " The White Man's Burden " (*Review of Reviews*, February 15, 1899, pp. 107 ff.).

The whole conception of the mission and burden of empire presupposes
some sort of superhuman force intervening in the affairs of mankind. If England has been particularly fitted for empire there must be some divine purpose
in it all. In the eyes of some, evolution and the survival of the fittest was simply
the working of the divine will. Rhodes was a firm believer in this doctrine.
" The perfecting of the fittest species among the animals, or of races among
men, and then the conferring upon the perfected species or race the title-deeds
of the future; that seemed to Mr. Rhodes, through his Darwinian spectacles,
the way in which God is governing His world, has governed it and will continue to govern it, so far as we can foresee the future," says Rhodes' close friend
and admirer, William Stead.[70] The same idea of the divine nature of conflict
is brought out by J. A. Cramb, when he declares:

> "Empires are successive incarnations of the Divine ideas, and by a principle
> which, in its universality and omnipotence in the frame of Nature, seems itself
> an attribute of the Divine, the principle of conflict, these ideas realize their ends
> in and through conflict. The scientific form which it assumes in the hypothesis
> of evolution is but the pragmatic expression of this mystery."[71]

The mystical, religious note comes out time and again in the writings and
speeches of the period:

> " Behind the mistakes and failures of individuals and generations, there grows
> upon us, as we study the history, the sense of an unseen superintending Provi-
> dence controlling the development of the Anglo-Saxon race. Through the vistas
> of the ages the voice is heard: ' Be fruitful and multiply, and replenish the
> earth.' "[72]

Lord Rosebery was lost in adoration when he contemplated the handiwork of
God:

> " How marvellous it all is! Built not by saints and angels, but the work of men's
> hands; cemented with men's honest blood and with a world of tears, welded by
> the best brains of centuries past; not without the taint and reproach incidental to
> all human work, but constructed on the whole with pure and splendid purpose.
> Human, and yet not wholly human — for the most heedless and the most cynical
> must see the finger of the Divine. . . . Do we not hail in this less the energy and
> fortune of a race than the supreme direction of the Almighty? Shall we not,
> while we adore the blessing, acknowledge the responsibility? " (Inaugural ad-
> dress as rector of Glasgow University, November 16, 1900).

The logical conclusion from all this is that any interference with the progress
of British imperialism is an attempt to counteract the will of God. H. D. Traill
spoke of the complacent belief of the Englishman that he had a sort of roving

---

70 W. T. Stead: " Cecil Rhodes of Africa " (*Review of Reviews*, November 15, 1899, pp. 451-
62), pp. 460-1.
71 J. A. Cramb: *The Origins and Destiny of Imperial Britain*, pp. 218 ff.
72 Hugh E. Egerton: *A Short History of British Colonial Policy* (London. 1897), p. 476.

commission from above to carry the blessings of good government to all the races of the world which were either too undeveloped or too effete to provide it for themselves:

> "Any interference with him in the execution of this commission may be justly resented and resisted by him, not only on personal and self-interested grounds, but as a perverse attempt to obstruct the manifest designs of Providence." [73]
> "To sustain worthily the burden of empire is the task manifestly appointed to Britain, and therefore to fulfil that task is her duty, as it should also be her delight," says another writer. "But if that duty should be opposed, if her path should be traversed by some rival State, what then would be the necessity laid upon the British Government and people? Evidently . . . it then becomes strictly incumbent upon them to resist the assailant with the entire force which they can exert." [74]

This brings us back to the use of force and the inevitability of conflict. The circle is closed, and the line of argumentation is complete from the theory of evolution through the doctrine of the Divine mission back again to the struggle for existence and the survival of the fittest. There we may leave the discussion of British imperialism in the late-Victorian period. It is hard to theorize about it and of the many explanations that have been offered no single one is entirely satisfactory. At bottom the movement was probably as much economic as anything else. It resulted from the tremendously enhanced productive powers of European industry and the break-down of the monopolistic position of England through the appearance of competitors. The feeling that new markets must be secured was very widespread and the need for new fields of investment, though not much discussed at the time, was probably even more important. These needs, however, had been met in the past without any corresponding expansion of territory. It was the embarkation of France, Germany, and other countries on the course of empire that brought the British to the conviction that only political control could adequately safeguard markets.

But this economic side, whatever its importance, must not be allowed to obscure the other factors. Psychologically speaking, I imagine, the prevalence of evolutionary teaching was perhaps crucial. It not only justified competition and struggle but introduced an element of ruthlessness and immorality that was most characteristic of the whole movement. The rise of a popular electorate, quite without culture and only semi-literate, underlined the crudity of the expansionist movement. It called forth a cheap newspaper press and a raw literature of action. In the larger sense, I suppose, it is perfectly true that the industrial system, which was tending more and more toward the mechanization of humanity, made inevitable the yearning for escape and action. Just as, at this very time, people were beginning to seek an outlet for physical urges,

---

[73] H. D. Traill: "The Burden of Egypt" (*Nineteenth Century*, April, 1896, pp. 544–56), p. 549.

[74] H. W. Wyatt, loc. cit., pp. 529–30.

even if only vicariously by attendance at huge sporting events, so they tried to find some expression for the combative instincts of the race through the encouragement of aggressive action and adventure abroad. At the same time the religious strain was too strong in the English to be left out of account entirely. The profound conviction of their superiority as a governing race, of their divine mission to improve the world, was not only a rationalization of other motives, it was in itself a primary moving force.

Now this elaborate analysis of British imperialism must not be taken to imply that the British alone were imperialistic. I have examined their case in particular not only because they were, of all peoples, the most imperially minded, but because the political and economic structure of Britain of itself brought the imperial movement to its most perfect flower. The other nations also were imperialistic. Indeed, the main theme in the history of international relations in this period is the clash of imperialisms. These others, too, were convinced of their mission:

> " In every nation of Europe from England and France to Russia and Turkey, in almost every nation in the world from the Americans to the Chinese and the Finns, the same whisper from below the threshold sounds incessantly in men's ears. ' We are the pick and flower of nations; the only nation that is really generous and brave and just. We are above all things qualified for governing others; we know how to keep them exactly in their place without weakness and without cruelty. . . . The excellence of our rule abroad is proved in black and white by the books of our explorers, our missionaries, our administrators and our soldiers, who all agree that our yoke is a pure blessing to those who bear it.' " [75]

And so, if you have followed and analyzed the classic example of modern imperialism you are in a position to understand the others and to grasp the problems presented by the conflict between them. For in the larger sense the story is more than the story of rivalry between European imperialisms; it is the story of European aggression and advance in the non-European parts of the world.

BIBLIOGRAPHICAL NOTE

CRITICAL WORKS ON IMPERIALISM

ROBERTSON, JOHN M.: *Patriotism and Empire*. London, 1899. One of the earliest and one of the ablest indictments of imperialism as part of the capitalist ideology. Many later works draw on the arguments here presented.

HOBSON, JOHN A.: *Capitalism and Imperialism in South Africa*. New York, 1900.

—: *The Psychology of Jingoism*. London, 1901.

---

[75] Gilbert Murray: " National Ideals: Conscious and Unconscious " (*International Journal of Ethics*, XI, 1900, pp. 1–22), p. 21.

HOBSON, JOHN A.: " The Scientific Basis of Imperialism." (*Political Science Quarterly,* XVII, September, 1902, pp. 460–89).

—: *Imperialism, a Study.* London, 1902. These books by Hobson all belong together, the last named summarizing the arguments advanced in all. Hobson was the ablest critical writer on the subject in his time, and his *Imperialism* is perhaps the best book yet written on the subject. The most divergent theories can be traced back to his writings.

GOOCH, GEORGE P.: " Imperialism." (in *The Heart of the Empire,* London, 1901). Another keen and incisive critique of the movement, with special reference to the war in south Africa.

HOBHOUSE, LEONARD T.: *Democracy and Reaction.* New York, 1905. Contains a good discussion of British imperialism and its implications.

BÉRARD, VICTOR: *British Imperialism and Commercial Supremacy.* London, 1906. Easily one of the best foreign studies of the movement, with the emphasis on the economic side.

BARDOUX, JACQUES: *Essai d'une Psychologie de l'Angleterre Contemporaine.* Two volumes. Paris, 1906. Like Bérard, Bardoux gives a detailed, critical analysis.

SCHULZE-GAEVERNITZ, G. VON: *Britischer Imperialismus und Englischer Freihandel.* Leipzig, 1906. Should be read in conjunction with the preceding. Another unusually able study of the economic factors in British imperialism.

The Empire and the Century. London, 1905. A most important co-operative work, containing many articles on various aspects of imperialism, by writers thoroughly in favor of it.

IRELAND, ALLEYNE: " The Victorian Era of Expansion." (*North American Review,* April, 1901, pp. 560–72; May, 1901, pp. 734–50). A good general survey, with many facts and figures.

MARCKS, ERICH: *Die Imperialistische Idee in der Gegenwart.* Dresden, 1903. A stimulating essay by a leading German historian. It deals almost exclusively with the decline of Cobdenism.

WETZ, WILHELM: " Die Imperialistische Bewegung in England." (*Die Grenzboten,* 1899 (1), pp. 14–22, 81–8, 191–200). A remarkably good contemporary review of the intellectual forces of British imperialism.

BRIE, FRIEDRICH: *Imperialistische Strömungen in der Englischen Literatur.* Second edition, Halle, 1928. This is by far the most thorough and systematic study of the imperialistic current in English literature. A most excellent book.

REINSCH, PAUL S.: *World Politics.* New York, 1900. Contains one of the best contemporary accounts of imperialism, with stress on the American side.

WINGFIELD-STRATFORD, ESMÉ: *The History of British Civilization.* Two volumes. New York, 1928. Has a stimulating brief discussion of the imperialist movement, though it adds little.

VIALLATE, ACHILLE: *La Crise Anglaise. Impérialisme et Protection.* Paris, 1905. An excellent analysis of the imperialist wave, with emphasis on the economic side.

VIALLATE, ACHILLE: *Economic Imperialism and International Relations during the Last Fifty Years.* New York, 1923. A series of lectures, devoted chiefly to a critical discussion of international relations before the war.

MOON, PARKER T.: *Imperialism and World Politics.* New York, 1926. A study of the history of international relations in the age of imperialism, remarkably well-informed and sound.

SALOMON, FELIX: *Der Britische Imperialismus.* Leipzig, 1916. One of the best general accounts of British imperial policy and imperialism.

WOOLF, LEONARD S.: *Economic Imperialism.* London, 1920. A popular outline, by a very able and thoroughly informed writer.

—: *Imperialism and Civilization.* New York, 1928. Deals chiefly with the larger problem of international relations and the prospects of international co-operation.

EISENMANN, LOUIS: "The Imperial Idea in the History of Europe." (*Slavonic Review,* December, 1926, pp. 242–57). A very general essay not particularly relevant to the present problem.

BUKHARIN, NIKOLAI: *Imperialism and World Economy.* New York, 1929.

LENIN, NIKOLAI: *Imperialism, the Last Stage in the Development of Capitalism.* Detroit, 1924. These two works, by eminent Bolshevik leaders, may be taken as typical of a large body of Neo-Marxian writing on the subject.

HOVDE, B. J.: "Socialistic Theories of Imperialism prior to the Great War." (*Journal of Political Economy,* XXXVI, 1928, pp. 569–91). A good systematic survey of this body of theory.

HOVIKIAN, ARTAKI: *L'Impérialisme Économique, d'après les Doctrines Socialistes Contemporaines.* Paris, 1927. A useful analysis of recent socialistic writing on the subject.

STERNBERG, F.: *Der Imperialismus.* Berlin, 1926. One of the most exhaustive and scholarly presentations of the Marxian view.

WINSLOW, E. M.: "Marxian, Liberal and Sociological Theories of Imperialism." (*Journal of Political Economy,* XXXIX, December, 1931, pp. 713–58). Another convenient digest.

WAGNER, DONALD O.: "British Economists and the Empire." (*Political Science Quarterly,* XLVII, March, 1932, pp. 57–74). Deals primarily with the Manchester doctrine and its decline.

CRAVEN, WESLEY F.: "Historical Study of the British Empire." (*Journal of Modern History,* VI, March, 1934, pp. 40–69). Primarily a review of recent literature on the British Empire and its constituent parts.

SCHUMPETER, JOSEPH: "Zur Soziologie der Imperialismen." (*Archiv für Sozialwissenschaft und Sozialpolitik,* XLVII, 1918–19, pp. 1–39, 275–310). This is one of the most original and stimulating of all writings on imperialism. It has exercised much influence on other writers, though the conclusion has not been generally accepted.

HINTZE, OTTO: " Der Britische Imperialismus und seine Probleme." (*Zeitschrift für Politik*, I, 1908, pp. 297–345). A stimulating constitutional and sociological approach.

—: " Wirtschaft und Politik im Zeitalter des Modernen Kapitalismus." (*Zeitschrift für Die Gesamte Staatswissenschaft*, LXXXVII, 1929, pp. 1–28). An important discussion of the whole problem in its larger aspects, representing a compromise between the Marxian and non-Marxian viewpoints.

HASHAGEN, JUSTUS: " Zur Ideengeschichte des Englischen Imperialismus." (*Weltwirtschaftliches Archiv*, X, 1917, pp. 423–39).

—: " Der Imperialismus als Begriff." (*Weltwirtschaftliches Archiv*, XV, 1919, pp. 157–91).

—: " Zur Deutung des Imperialismus." (*Weltwirtschaftliches Archiv*, XXVI, 1927, pp. 134–51). All of these writings of Hashagen are of interest and importance. He is one of the most penetrating and best-informed writers of the non-Marxian school.

MARCK, SIEGFRIED: *Imperialismus und Pazifismus als Weltanschauungen*. Tübingen, 1918. A purely philosophical and psychological approach.

LAUTERBACH, ALBERT: " Zur Problemstellung des Imperialismus." (*Archiv für Sozialwissenschaft und Sozialpolitik*, LXV, 1931, pp. 580–99). A review of various interpretations, with stress on the multiplicity of aspects of modern imperialism.

SALZ, ARTHUR: *Das Wesen des Imperialismus*. Leipzig, 1931. One of the most effective critiques of the Marxian interpretation.

GRABOWSKY, ADOLF: " Das Wesen der Imperialistischen Epoche." (*Zeitschrift für Politik*, XII, 1923, pp. 30–66). Another first-rate critical essay analyzing the whole problem of imperialism. May well be read in connexion with Schumpeter and Hashagen.

LÖWE, ADOLF: " Zur Ökonomischen Theorie des Imperialismus." (*Festschrift für Franz Oppenheimer*, Frankfurt, 1924, pp. 189–228). A critique of Schumpeter and of the Marxian interpretations. An important contribution.

ERMS, K.: *Der Religiöse Britische Imperialismus*. Bochum, 1919.

KLEINSCHMITT VON LENGEFELD, FREIHERR: *Der Geistige Gehalt im Britischen Imperialismus*. Marburg, 1928. Deals almost entirely with the problem of federation of the Empire.

GERHARD, DIETRICH: " Hauptprobleme einer Geschichte des Britischen Empire." (*Historische Zeitschrift*, CXLIX, 1933, pp. 57–74). A stimulating review of the whole course of British expansion, with an effort at synthesis.

GROSSMANN, H.: *Das Akkumulations-und Zusammenbruchsgesetz des Kapitalistischen Systems*. Leipzig, 1929. An elaborate, keen presentation of the Marxian theory.

SULZBACH, WALTER: *Nationales Gemeinschaftsgefühl und Wirtschaftliches Interesse*. Leipzig, 1929. One of the best critical studies of nationalism and imperialism, being a devastating analysis of the socialist theory.

LITERATURE SINCE 1935

WINSLOW, E. M.: *The Pattern of Imperialism: a Study in the Theories of Power.* New York, 1948. 278 pp. A scholarly review of the various theories of imperialism, followed by a critical examination of the Marxian doctrine.

CLARK, GROVER: *The Balance Sheets of Imperialism.* New York, 1936. 136 pp. A strictly statistical appraisal of imperialist enterprises.

NAVA, SANTI: *Elementi di dommatica della colonizzazione.* Florence, 1937. 181 pp. The appendix of this work is a lengthy critical study of current theories of colonization.

SWEEZY, PAUL M.: *The Theory of Capitalist Development.* New York, 1942. 398 pp. This keen exposition of Marxian economics includes an extended treatment of the doctrine of imperialism.

HARDY, GEORGES: *La politique coloniale et le partage de la terre aux XIXe et XXe siècles.* Paris, 1937. 500 pp. A general factual survey.

TOWNSEND, MARY E., and PEAKE, CYRUS H.: *European Colonial Expansion since 1871.* Chicago, 1941. 629 pp. Perhaps the best general text of the subject.

DEBORIN, G. A.: *Meshdunarodniye Otnosheniya v Period Zaversheniya k Monopolisticheskomu Kapitalizmu, 1894–1903 gg.* Moscow, 1941. 104 pp. A general popular survey of international relations in the period indicated, based upon Marxian concepts.

KNAPLUND, PAUL: *The British Empire, 1815–1939.* New York, 1941. 850 pp. A competent historical survey, with good maps and extensive bibliographies.

SPENDER, JOHN A.: *Great Britain: Empire and Commonwealth, 1886–1936.* London, 1936. 906 pp. Another able review of the evolution of the Empire.

WINGFIELD-STRATFORD, ESMÉ: *The Foundations of British Patriotism.* London, 1939. 429 pp. A readable historical essay, containing a chapter on the imperialist fever.

KNORR, KLAUS E.: *British Colonial Theories, 1570–1850.* Toronto, 1944. 429 pp. An important, scholarly work, with an illuminating treatment of the White Man's Burden and a study of the relation of the Middle Classes to the Empire. Helpful for background.

SCHUYLER, ROBERT L.: *The Fall of the Old Colonial System: A Study in British Free Trade, 1770–1870.* New York, 1945. 344 pp. Contains a revision and amplification of the author's earlier excellent studies of mid-nineteenth century anti-imperialism.

TYLER, J. E.: *The Struggle for Imperial Unity, 1868–1895.* New York, 1938. 219 pp. One of the most important and illuminating studies, weaving together many issues and trends and taking full account of literature and thought as well as of trade and politics.

HARLOW, VINCENT: *The Character of British Imperialism*. London, 1939. 38 pp. An inaugural lecture which gives a broad synthesis of the subject.

WIEGNER, ERNST: *Der britische Imperialismus. Eine britische Betrachtung des Chamberlain-Programms*. Zurich, 1938. 258 pp.

LUFFT, HERMANN: *Der britische Imperialismus: Ideen und Träger*. Berlin, 1940. 288 pp. Covers the entire course of English history, with a rather inadequate treatment of the nineteenth century.

MARDER, ARTHUR J.: *The Anatomy of British Sea Power*. New York, 1940. 580 pp. Generally valuable for the study of British imperialism. Includes a chapter on the subject based upon extensive reading in contemporary materials.

STRAUSS, WILLIAM L.: *Joseph Chamberlain and the Theory of Imperialism*. Washington, 1942. 133 pp. A general review of Chamberlain's career and the evolution of his thought. Scholarly but not novel.

SHANKS, EDWARD: *Rudyard Kipling. A Study in Literature and Political Ideas*. London, 1940. 281 pp. A stimulating analysis of Kipling's political faith and especially of his role as prophet of empire.

BROWN, BENJAMIN H.: *The Tariff Reform Movement in Great Britain, 1881–1895*. New York, 1943. 170 pp. A sound monograph, based on much newspaper and pamphlet literature. Deals at some length with tariff reform and imperialism.

ZEBEL, SIDNEY H.: "Fair Trade: an English Reaction to the Breakdown of the Cobden Treaty System" (*Journal of Modern History*, XII, June, 1940, pp. 161–186). A careful re-examination of the international trade problem in the 1880's and 1890's.

ROBB, JANET H.: *The Primrose League, 1883–1906*. New York, 1942. 258 pp. A thorough study of the organization and operation of the League which did so much to popularize imperialism.

WINGENROTH, CARL G.: *Deutscher und englischer 'Imperialismus' vor dem Weltkrieg*. Bottrop, 1934. 139 pp. Compares and contrasts the British and German conceptions of imperialism and its effects on international trade and international relations.

PRIESTLEY, HERBERT I.: *France Overseas: a Study of Modern Imperialism*. New York, 1938. 463 pp. A comprehensive, factual account of French expansion, with extensive bibliographies.

IV

The Struggle for the Nile
1. The Congo Treaty

১

I F THERE WAS ONE EVENT MORE THAN ANOTHER THAT GAVE THE INITIAL
impetus to British imperialism in the last years of the century that event
was the occupation of Egypt in 1882, followed by the rising in the Sudan,
the mission of Gordon and his tragic death. There can be little or no doubt that
Gladstone intended to withdraw again from Egypt as soon as possible, and that
even Salisbury expected to make some adjustment. But after 1887, when France
and Russia ruined the projected convention between England and the Turkish
government, the chances of evacuation rapidly diminished, until in 1892 Rosebery and his imperialistically minded colleagues in the cabinet frustrated the
hopes of Gladstone and his friends that some agreement might be come to. It
was then clear to everyone that the English occupation would last for a long
time, and Lord Cromer, the British resident at Cairo, settled down with new
confidence to the great work of reconstruction which he had marked out.

By this time the Egyptian question had empoisoned not only the relations
between Great Britain and the Ottoman Porte, but also the relations between
Great Britain and France, where the nationalist and imperialist groups had
come to regard England with almost as much hate because of the Egyptian
question as they showed Germany on account of the lost provinces. Fortunately
for England she could count on German support against France in the Egyptian
question. With some exceptions Bismarck had always made the most of the
situation. He had used the Egyptian question as a bond to attach England to the
Triple Alliance. He lent German support in Egypt in return for British good
will in other questions.

This same policy had been followed, naturally enough, by Caprivi and Marschall, who were, if anything, more anxious for British friendship than Bismarck
had been. But, as we have seen in a previous chapter, the English and German
governments began to drift apart in 1893. The Germans were disillusioned and
disgusted by the unwillingness of the English to accept further obligations and
make further concessions, while the British, faced by the prospect of united
French and Russian action in the colonial field, played a shifty game. We need
not here repeat all that has been said on this subject in the preceding discussion;
it will suffice to remind the reader that Austrian efforts to bring the English and

Germans together in the spring of 1894 met with dismal failure. The Germans had begun to draw closer to Russia and indirectly to France. They were in no mood to court the British, especially when they found no disposition on the other side of the Channel to pay for German support by concessions in Samoa or elsewhere.[1]

The new drift in European alignments came out clearly when both the French and German governments protested against a treaty concluded by England and the Congo State on May 12, 1894. This treaty is of very great interest because of its place in the story of the struggle for the Nile which led ultimately to the Fashoda crisis. Article II of the agreement provided for the lease to King Leopold for the duration of his life of a considerable area along the west bank of the upper Nile, a region extending from the northern point of Lake Albert to Fashoda, and westward as far as the thirtieth meridian of longitude east from Greenwich. To the Independent State of the Congo the British leased a large area in the Bahr-el-Ghazal region lying between twenty-five degrees and thirty degrees east longitude, and between four degrees and ten degrees north latitude. In return for these concessions the Congo State agreed to lease to Great Britain a strip of territory sixteen miles (twenty-five kilometers) wide, running from the southern shore of Lake Albert Edward to the north tip of Lake Tanganyika. There were some other slight rectifications of the frontier at the southeastern end of the Congo State, but these need not concern us here.

In order to understand the purport of this agreement and the protests to which it gave rise, indeed, in order to comprehend the great and dramatic contest that ended in 1898 with the Fashoda crisis, it will be necessary to say something of British policy in this part of Africa. The Egyptian Sudan had been conquered in the early 19th century, while Egypt was ruled by that remarkable statesman, Mehemet Ali. But the Khedive Ismail, who had a veritable passion for territory, had extended the dominions of Egypt far beyond the frontiers as he found them on his accession. He sent expeditions which took possession of the Red Sea coast as far as Cape Guardafui, and conquered even the Abyssinian province of Harrar. In the 1860's and 1870's he sent out Sir Samuel Baker and later General Charles George (Chinese) Gordon. These men extended the authority of the Khedive to the upper reaches of the Nile, to Lake Albert and the so-called Victoria Nile, and established posts in the provinces of Bahr-el-Ghazal and Equatoria, as well as in Unyoro and up to the very frontiers of Uganda. Gordon realized clearly that, because of the blockade of vegetation (sudd) in the upper Nile, and because of the cataracts and rapids, communications would always be difficult, and strongly urged the Khedive to take possession of the east African coast, especially of the port of Mombasa, the gateway to Uganda. An expedition was actually sent out from Egypt and occupied Barawa and Kismayu, but the idea was given up, evidently because of the

---

[1] *Die Grosse Politik,* VIII, nos. 2024–9, 2035–9.

protests of the Sultan of Zanzibar and the objections of Sir John Kirk, the powerful British consul at the Sultan's court.[2]

In 1879 Gordon resigned from the Khedive's service. Two years later there broke out in the Sudan the extraordinary movement of religious fanaticism known as Mahdism, which led to Gordon's mission in 1884 to withdraw the Egyptian garrisons, and which ended, in January 1885, in the fall of Khartum and in Gordon's death. Egypt had been occupied by the British in 1882, and the Khedive's government now took its orders from London. Whatever the British government may have claimed later, there can be no question that in 1884 its intention was to abandon the Sudan completely and that it forced the Egyptian ministers to agree to this course. Gordon understood his instructions to reflect the " irrevocable decision " of the government not to incur " the very onerous duty of securing to the peoples of the Sudan a just future government. That, as a consequence, Her Majesty's Government have determined to restore to those peoples their independence, and will no longer suffer the Egyptian Government to interfere with their affairs." Gladstone, at that time prime minister, himself referred to the followers of the Mahdi as " a people struggling to be free, and rightly struggling to be free." [3]

Under the circumstances Gordon planned to hand back the whole area to the rule of the local chiefs, who were to form some sort of federation, while he himself expected to take over the administration of the provinces of Bahr-el-Ghazal and Equatoria, which would be ruled by Leopold of Belgium as sovereign of the Congo State.[4] All these schemes were blasted by the disastrous outcome of Gordon's mission. From 1885 onward the Mahdi and his successor, the Khalifa, were the undisputed masters of the whole region, excepting for Equatoria, where the famous adventurer, Eduard Schnitzer (Emin Pasha), held his own until " rescued " by Stanley in 1889.

In Egypt the loss of the Sudan was acutely felt. Not only was there fear of an attack by the victorious forces of the False Prophet, but there was serious apprehension lest the loss of control of the upper waters of the Nile should lead to attempts being made to interfere with Egypt's all-important water supply. In order to appreciate this state of mind one has to realize that for centuries it had been believed in Egypt that such interference was possible and that it was an ever-present threat. In the *Chronicles of the Saracenic Empire,* written by El Macin in the 13th century, the story is told how, in the last years of the 11th century, the King of Abyssinia actually turned aside the waters of the Blue Nile, until the Sultan of Egypt sent the Coptic patriarch with presents.[5]

---

[2] Frederick D. Lugard: *The Rise of our East African Empire* (London, 1893), II, p. 610; Sir Harry Johnston: *The Uganda Protectorate* (New York, 1902), I, chap. vii; and more recentiy the authoritative study by Bernard M. Allen: *Gordon and the Sudan* (London, 1931), pp. 37 ff., 67, 73 ff., 137–8.   [3] Allen, op. cit., pp. 204, 230, 337.

[4] Ibid., pp. 239, 272 ff., 446 ff. (Gordon's letter to Leopold of February 1, 1884).

[5] *Historia Saracenica a Georgio El-Macino,* 1625, Book III, chap. viii; the story is repeated by F. Vansleb (Wanzleben): *The Present State of Egypt* (London, 1678), pp. 37 ff.; by J. Ludolphus:

Even if this was a fable, as it probably was, it is significant that the tradition became firmly fixed in Egypt during the later Middle Ages. In the 14th and 15th centuries there are repeated references to it. Friar Jordanus reported in 1330 that the Sultan of Egypt paid the Abyssinians tribute, and at about the same time Marignolli bore out the statement, explaining that the Abyssinians " have it in their power to shut off the water, and then Egypt would perish." Simone Sigoli, writing in 1384, repeats the story and adds that " whenever this Prester John (i.e. the King of Abyssinia) chooses to open certain river sluices he can drown Cairo and Alexandria and all that country." [6] Guillebert de Lannoy wrote in 1422 that the Egyptian Sultan would let no Christian pass to India by the Red Sea or the Nile to visit Prester John, for fear that the Christians would induce the Abyssinian potentate to cut off the Nile water. Prester John, he adds, could give the river another direction if he chose, but he abstained from doing so because the Christians as well as the infidels in Egypt would starve. The same story is told by Bertrandon de la Broquière, who heard about Abyssinia in 1432 from Piettre de Naples. Piettre told him that the Nile came out of a cavern in the mountains. Prester John had erected two large towers and put a chain across so that no one could look in. It was not certain whether the cavern led to Heaven or to Hell, but it was said that Prester John could change the course of the river if he so desired.[7]

So much for the legend. There is, beyond this, certain evidence that the Abyssinians used the story, when convenient, to threaten the Egyptians. Jean de Lastic is reputed to have written from Rhodes to Charles VII of France in 1448 saying that Prester John had addressed an ultimatum to the Sultan saying that if he did not stop molesting the Christians a terrible war would be waged against him and that " a diversion of the Nile would starve out Egypt." In 1450 King Alphonse of Aragon sent messengers to Abyssinia asking for an attack on Egypt and a blocking of the Nile to support the Aragonese naval campaign in the Holy Land.[8] More interesting yet is what we read of Albuquerque's plans.

A New History of Ethiopia (London, 1682), pp. 40–4; by Renaudot: Historia Patriarcharum Alexandrinorum Jacobitarum (Paris, 1713), p. 480; and in more modern times by Charles T. Beke: The Sources of the Nile (London, 1860), pp. 90 ff., and by J. B. Coulbeaux: Histoire Politique et Religieuse d'Abyssinie (Paris, 1928), I, pp. 246–7.

[6] Henry Yule: The Wonders of the East by Friar Jordanus (London, 1863), p. 46; Simone Sigoli: Viaggi in Terra Santa (Florence, 1862), p. 202: see further Henry Yule: Cathay and the Way Thither (Second edition, London, 1914), III, pp. 222–4.

[7] Voyage et Ambassades de Messire Guillebert de Lannoy, p. 93; Charles Schefer: Le Voyage d'Outremer de Bertrandon de la Broquière (Paris, 1892), pp. 142–8.

[8] De Lastic: Chronique de la Maison de Lastic (Montpellier, 1919), I, p. 329; F. Cerone: " La Politica Orientale di Alfonso di Aragona " (Archivio Storico per le Province Napoletane, XVII. 1902, p. 64); on all this see further the excellent discussion in Charles de La Roncière: La Découverte de l'Afrique au Moyen Age (Cairo, 1925), II, pp. 111, 119; Albert Kammerer: La Mer Rouge, l'Abyssinie et l'Arabie depuis l'Antiquité (Cairo, 1929), Vol. I, part III, pp. 296, 303; Sir E. Denison Ross: " Prester John " (in Travel and Travellers of the Middle Ages, edited by A. P. Newton, New York, 1926), pp. 193–4, where the story of Bertrandon is given without reference. There is nothing on this matter in Prince Omar Tousson's: " Mémoire sur l'Histoire du Nil " (Mémoires de l'Institut d'Égypte, VIII–X, Cairo, 1925).

It is said in the *Commentaries* that in the Sudan, between Keneh and Kossair, "there live many Alarves . . . and when they were at variance with the Grand Sultan, they used sometimes to cut the bank of the Nile when the waters were rising, and let out the waters along some extensive valleys of their land, in order to be revenged upon him." Albuquerque therefore decided to do the same thing, and sent to King Manuel to forward him workmen from Madeira, men accustomed to cutting rock. "This undertaking could be carried out very easily, for the Preste João was very desirous of accomplishing it, but had no means of carrying it out; and if this had been done, the land of Cairo would have been entirely destroyed." [9]

And so the story is carried on through the records. Ariosto quotes it in his *Orlando:*

> "The Soldan, King of the Egyptian Land,
> Pays tribute to this sovereign, as his head,
> They say, since having Nile at his command
> He may divert the stream to other bed.
> Hence, with its district upon either hand,
> Forthwith might Cairo lack its daily bread." [10]

James Bruce tells of a letter written by the King of Abyssinia to the Pasha of Egypt in 1704, saying, "The Nile would be sufficient to punish you, since God has put into our power His fountain, His outlet, and His increase, and that we can dispose of to do you harm." [11] Apparently the threat continued to be used at suitable times right down to the 19th century. We are told that in 1840 the Egyptian commander tried to divert the Mareb River into the Atbara, using palm trees and straw mats to build the barrage. [12] Charles T. Beke, the eminent student of the Nile and of things Abyssinian, was deeply impressed with the possibility of such a diversion. In 1851 he sent to Lord Palmerston a "Memoir on the Possibility of Diverting the Waters of the Nile so as to Prevent the Irrigation of Egypt." In his books he expressed the firm conviction that the scheme was feasible. [13]

Of even greater importance were the views of Sir Samuel Baker, the most outstanding of all authorities in the later 19th century. Sir Samuel believed that the Biblical story of the seven years' famine in Egypt was probably to be explained by some diversion of the Nile water. He quoted passages from the Scriptures to bear out his opinion: "Behold, I am against thee, and against thy

---

[9] *The Commentaries of the Great Afonso Dalboquerque,* translated by Walter de Gray Birch (Hakluyt Society, London, 1884), IV, pp. 36, 39.

[10] *The Orlando Furioso,* translated by William S. Rose (New edition, London, 1858), Canto XXXIII, stanza cvi.

[11] James Bruce: *Travels to Discover the Sources of the Nile* (London, 1790), II, pp. 525–7.

[12] Ferdinand Werne: *Feldzug von Senaar nach Taka* (Quoted by Charles T. Beke: *The Sources of the Nile* [London, 1860], pp. 90 ff.).

[13] Emily Beke, letter to the *Times,* October 25, 1888; Charles T. Beke: *The Sources of the Nile,* pp. 90 ff.

rivers, and I will make the land of Egypt utterly waste and desolate; " " I will make the rivers dry, and sell the land into the hand of the wicked; and I will make the land waste, and all that is therein, by the hand of strangers; " " And they shall turn the rivers far away." [14] Baker therefore insisted from the very beginning on the terrible danger to which Egypt was exposed by the abandonment of the Sudan: " Should a civilised, or even a semi-civilised, enemy be in possession of that point (Khartum), the water of the Rahad, Dinder, Blue Nile and the Atbara Rivers could be diverted from their course and dispersed throughout the deserts, to the utter ruin and complete destruction of Egypt proper." Dams could be easily thrown across either the Blue Nile or the Atbara. The Atbara bed was dry for five or six months of the year and had along its banks forests of good material. There was a place about 230 miles up the river, near Gozerajup, where there was a great depression into which the water could be directed: " I can positively state that the plan is feasible, and that, should any European be in command at the rebellious centre of the Soudan, his first strategical operation would be to deprive Egypt of the water that is necessary for her existence. . . . If I were myself an enemy of Egypt I know the place where I should commence the fatal work upon the River Atbara." [15]

Baker's letters to the *Times* in October 1888 were occasioned by the abnormally low Nile of that year and the resulting shortage of water. Since the introduction of perennial cultivation for cotton, sugar and rice by Mehemet Ali, the water problem was something like this: practically all the flood water of high Nile comes down the Blue Nile and the less important Atbara and Sobat Rivers. This is the water which drenches the fields and makes winter cultivation possible. But the water that is used in summer for irrigation purposes comes almost entirely from the White Nile, which, flowing from the great lakes through the great marsh areas, is held back by the flood coming down the Blue Nile from Abyssinia, and then reaches Egypt in time to meet the needs of the spring and summer. In 1888 the Egyptian authorities were hampered by lack of information about the coming of the flood, for with the loss of Khartum the readings of the most important Nilometer on the upper river could no longer be obtained. An even more serious problem, however, was the almost chronic inadequacy of the summer water supply. Sir Samuel Baker had already proposed the construction of barrages in the region of the cataracts, and other engineers were working on schemes to construct a new Lake Meroe reservoir, or elaborating plans for what was later to be the great Aswan Dam. In any event it was clear that Egypt would have to store water somewhere and there was more and more talk of building barrages at the outlets of Lakes Albert and Victoria.[16]

---

[14] Ezekiel, xxix, 8; xxx, 12; Isaiah, xix, 4, quoted by Baker in the *Times*, October 17, 1888.

[15] Sir Samuel Baker: " Egypt's Proper Frontier " (*Nineteenth Century*, July, 1884, pp. 27-46); and his letters to the *Times*, October 9, 17, 25, 1888.

[16] Good accounts of the water problem may be found in William Willcocks: *Egyptian Irrigation* (London, 1889), chaps. i and xi (and in the second edition, London, 1899, chap. xiv); A. Chelu:

The very discussion of the possibility of damming the Nile at the exits from the lakes quite naturally raised the thought that some power hostile to Egypt might do the same thing. Fear of this had been in the minds of men like Baker from the very time of the abandonment of the Sudan. Sir Colin Scott-Moncrieff, who was chief of the irrigation works in Egypt at this time, tells us that in 1884 the British commander asked him if there were a possibility of the Mahdi's diverting the Nile water. The same apprehension is expressed in a memorandum handed to Sir Evelyn Baring by Riaz Pasha, the Egyptian statesman, in 1888. " No one will deny, so clear and evident a proposition is it, that the Nile is the life of Egypt. Now the Nile means the Soudan, and nobody will doubt that the bonds and connections which unite Egypt to the Soudan are as inseparable as those which unite the soul to the body." Suakin, he argued, must be held at all costs, " for no European power would occupy Suakin without wishing necessarily to extend its power into the interior, with a view to reaching richer districts. But if it attained its object, and took possession of the banks of the Nile, it would be all over with Egypt." Egypt could never consent " to such an attack on its existence." [17]

It was quite in keeping with this viewpoint that Lord Milner wrote in 1892 that the loss of the Khartum Nilometer was a serious handicap:

" But there is a graver anxiety behind. The savages of the Sudan may never themselves possess sufficient engineering skill to play tricks with the Nile, but for all that it is an uncomfortable thought that the regular supply of water by the great river, which is to Egypt not a question of convenience and prosperity but actually of life, must always be exposed to some risk, as long as the upper reaches of that river are not under Egyptian control. Who can say what might happen, if some day a civilized Power, or a Power commanding civilised skill, were to undertake great engineering works on the Upper Nile, and to divert for the artificial irrigation of that region the water which is essential for the artificial irrigation of Egypt? " [18]

" What the Mahdi could not do," wrote Scott-Moncrieff a few years later, " a civilised people could do. . . . I may be allowed to point out an evident enough fact, that the civilised possessor of the Upper Nile Valley holds Egypt in his grasp. . . . A civilised nation on the Upper Nile would surely build regulating sluices across the outlet of the Victoria Nyanza, and control that great sea as Manchester controls Thirlmere. This would probably be an easy operation. Once done, the Nile supply would be in their hands; and if poor little Egypt had the

---

Le Nil (Paris, 1891), pp. 160 ff., 448 ff.; Justin C. Ross: " Irrigation and Agriculture in Egypt " (Scottish Geographical Magazine, April, 1893, pp. 163–93); Sir Colin Scott-Moncrieff: " The Nile " (Proceedings of the Royal Institute of Great Britain, XIV, January 25, 1895, pp. 405–18); Egypt No. 2 (1904), Report of Sir William Garstin upon the Basin of the Upper Nile; Sir William Garstin: " Fifty Years of Nile Exploration " (Geographical Journal, February, 1909, pp. 117–47); Sir Murdoch MacDonald: Nile Control (Cairo, 1920), pp. 127 ff.; and the splendid recent book of H. E. Hurst and P. Phillips: The Nile Basin (Cairo, 1931) especially volume I.

[17] Memorandum of December 9, 1888, in Egypt No. 1 (1889), no. 35, inclosure.

[18] Alfred Milner: England in Egypt (London, 1892), pp. 197–8.

bad luck to be at war with this people on the upper waters, they might flood them, or cut off their water supply at their pleasure." [19]

The danger was there, and it was recognized. But if there was one thing the British authorities in Egypt would not consider in 1888–1889, it was the reconquest of the Sudan. Sir Evelyn Baring (later Lord Cromer), wrote at that time: "There is not now, and since the destruction of General Hicks' army there never has been, any serious idea of deliberately adopting a policy involving the reconquest of the Soudan by force of arms." [20] It was, for him, both a question of funds and of policy. At that time it was by no means certain that England would stay in Egypt, and even if she did, the available money was more urgently needed for problems of reconstruction. So long as the Mahdists controlled the Sudan there was no great danger of interference with the Nile water. It was rather the European powers which required watching. Since Egypt had abandoned the Sudan there was no reason why some other power should not attempt to conquer it. Sir Samuel Baker had prophesied in 1884 that it would become an easy prey to the first adventurer and had declared that if he were a Frenchman he would not neglect the opportunity. Other writers, like Sir Frederick Lugard, took the same view: "It would be preposterous that we, while abandoning in the face of Europe an administration already established in that country, should claim the right to restrain other European nations from developing it and suppressing the slave trade." [21]

It was therefore of the utmost moment that while Egypt was waiting for the funds needed to reconquer the Sudan and while England was unwilling to lend the money or undertake the conquest herself, all efforts should be made to deter other powers from the enterprise. Protection of the upper Nile — this became one of the keynotes of British policy in Africa, a policy which, from the very nature of the problem, had endless ramifications until it was brought to a successful solution by the Fashoda settlement.

The advance or the attack on the Nile could be made from various directions — from the Red Sea, from the east African coast, and from the Congo. We shall have to consider all these aspects, and may, for convenience' sake, begin with the Red Sea. The first step of the British government was to encourage the Italians to establish themselves on the Red Sea coast at Massowa. The purpose of this move was probably two-fold. Abyssinia had, since time immemorial, claimed the territory along the Blue Nile as far as Khartum and the main stream of the river. The Italians would divert them and prevent mere claims being translated into realities. And there were the French, who had a particular interest in causing

---

[19] Sir Colin Scott-Moncrieff: "The Nile" (*Proceedings of the Royal Institute of Great Britain*, January 25, 1895, pp. 405–18); see also A. Silva White: *The Expansion of Egypt* (London, 1899). p. 29.

[20] *Egypt No. 1 (1889)*, no. 22.

[21] Sir Samuel Baker: "Egypt's Proper Frontier" (*Nineteenth Century*, July, 1884, pp. 27–46), p. 41; Sir Frederick Lugard: *The Rise of our East African Empire* (London, 1893), II, p. 566.

the British difficulty in Egypt. In 1862 they had secured a station on the Red Sea coast at Obock, a move which had been answered by the British establishment at Zeila and on the Somali coast. In 1883, during the French war with China, the British had closed Aden to the French as a coaling port, causing them much embarrassment. The French government then began to take Obock more seriously, and in 1887 opened a better station at Jibuti, on the opposite side of the Gulf of Tajura, commanding the end of the caravan route from the province of Harrar and from Abyssinia proper. This move led to considerable friction between the two powers, until, in February 1888, they concluded an agreement delimiting their claims in this region. This whole area had been recognized as part of the Sudan in the period prior to 1884. A British report of 1883 defined the Sudan frontier at that time as running from Lake Victoria "north-east and including the Province of Harrar, and reaching the Indian Ocean about Cape Guardafui, and thence following the coast-line back to Berenice." [22] The agreement, which was not published until 1894, probably to save the susceptibilities of the Egyptian and Turkish governments, could not have been made had the British government at that time regarded these areas as subject in any way to Egyptian claims.[23]

The British government had tried to cut off French expansion into Abyssinia by the provision of Article IV of the agreement of 1888, which stated that "the two Governments engage not to endeavour to annex Harrar, nor to place it under their Protectorate. In taking this engagement the two Governments do not renounce the right of opposing attempts on the part of any other Power to acquire or assert any rights over Harrar." But this is exactly what the Italians seemed disposed to do. In 1889 they concluded with Menelik of Abyssinia the famous Treaty of Ucciali, by which, so they claimed, he recognized an Italian protectorate over the whole of Abyssinia. If this claim stood the Italians might take over the Abyssinian pretensions to all territory as far as the Nile. Abyssinia was a congeries of feudal principalities loosely held together by the King of Kings, when he was strong enough to impose his authority on the local chieftains, but the extent of the territory was not clearly defined. King John had defeated the Mahdists in battle in 1889, and his successor might well succeed in making good the claims to the Nile frontier. The Italians themselves were already demanding possession of Kassala, a most important town located roughly halfway between Massowa and Khartum. Lord Dufferin, the British ambassador at Rome, was complaining in February 1890, that the Italians were "a little too enterprising and may attempt to tap the Upper Nile and Sudan."

---

[22] *Egypt No. 11 (1883), Report on the Soudan by Lieutenant-Colonel Stewart.* The same point is brought out by numerous Turkish *firmans* issued to the Khedive of Egypt (see Sir Edward Hertslet: *The Map of Africa by Treaty* [Second edition, London, 1896], I, pp. 259 ff.).

[23] Hertslet, op. cit., III, pp. 976 ff., for the text; a good discussion in Jean Darcy: *France et Angleterre, Cent Années de Rivalité Coloniale* (Paris, 1904), pp. 364 ff.; Ernest Lavisse: "France et Angleterre" (*Revue de Paris,* February 1, 1899, pp. 453–82); Leonard Woolf: *Empire and Commerce in Africa* (New York, 1920), pp. 221 ff.

From Egypt Baring sounded a similar alarm, and urged the necessity for reoccupying Tokar.[24]

We are told by Lord Salisbury's daughter that from 1889 onward the reconquest of the Sudan became a dominating factor in her father's Egyptian policy.[25] He was indifferent to questions affecting the Red Sea coast, but anything touching the Nile basin was another matter. On March 28, 1890 he wrote to Baring: " The argument you have used with so much force in respect to Kassala, that it gives to the Power occupying it command over one of the main affluents of the Nile (the Atbara is meant), and therefore power of diverting a portion of the supply which is vital to Egypt, does not apply to any possessions on the East coast. Tokar has nothing to do with the Nile Valley." It would be better for the Egyptian Government to wait until it had funds to enable it to proceed to Berber or even Khartum. At the same time the prime minister opened negotiations with the Italian ambassador at London. He told him that Egypt had not given up her territorial claims, since England herself regarded the Nile valley as vitally necessary to Egypt. The discussions seem to have led to no result, and Baring himself had no better luck when he discussed matters with Crispi in the autumn of 1890. Salisbury had written the British negotiator: " we should insist on the command of all affluents of the Nile, so far as Egypt formerly possessed them." But Crispi argued that England had lost all prior claim to dominion in the Nile Valley when the Sudan was abandoned.[26]

Yet in the spring of 1891 a satisfactory agreement was arrived at. Crispi's successor, Marchese di Rudini, was not interested in African affairs. Furthermore, in September 1890 Menelik, whose attention had been called by the French to the Italian interpretation of the Treaty of Ucciali, had denounced this interpretation. It was therefore highly desirable from the Italian viewpoint to secure British recognition of their pretensions. Finally, the European situation was such at the time of the renewal of the Triple Alliance that the Italians were anxious not to estrange the London government. On the side of the English was the constant fear that the dervish power in the Sudan might collapse before Egypt had the money or the opportunity to take over her former territories. Two agreements were therefore signed, on March 24 and on April 15, 1891, defining the limits of the Italian sphere of influence. This sphere was to include all territory east of a line drawn from the mouth of the Juba River north to the sixth parallel of latitude and the thirty-fifth meridian east from Greenwich. From the point where this meridian intersects the course of the Blue Nile the boundary was to run northeast in a broken line to the Red Sea coast at Ras Kasar. The British and French possessions in Somaliland were, naturally, excluded. Kassala and the territory about it as far as the Atbara River Italy was

---

24 Lyall: *Lord Dufferin and Ava*, I, p. 231; Cecil: *Lord Salisbury*, IV (London, 1931), pp. 324 ff.

25 Cecil: *Salisbury*, IV, pp. 239-40.

26 Cecil: *Salisbury*, IV, pp. 327-32; Francesco Crispi: *La Prima Guerra d'Africa* (Milan, 1914), pp. 225-46; Francis Reginald Wingate: *Mahdiism and the Egyptian Sudan* (London, 1891), p. 489.

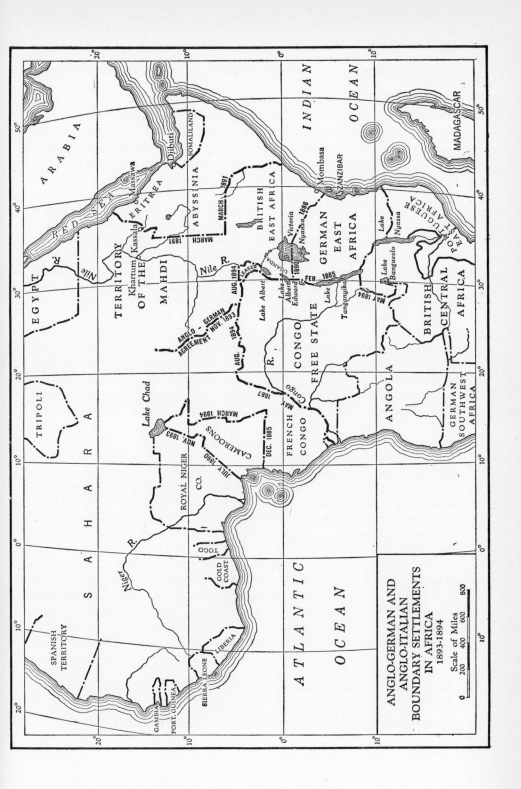

ANGLO-GERMAN AND
ANGLO-ITALIAN
BOUNDARY SETTLEMENTS
IN AFRICA
1893-1894

Scale of Miles
0   200 400 600 800

left free to occupy in case the military situation demanded it, but the rights of
the Egyptian government were reserved, and Egypt was to remain free to take
over this territory whenever ready to do so. Evidently this particular part of
the Sudan was to be given different treatment from the other Red Sea areas,
to which the Egyptian title was just as good. The reason, of course, was that
Kassala lay on an important confluent of the Atbara, and the British government was anxious to retain some control, through Egypt, of the water supply.
This follows clearly enough from the whole agreement with Italy, the upshot
of which was to keep her sphere of influence removed by one hundred miles
from the nearest approach to the Nile. It is even more clearly expressed in
Article III of the agreement of April 15, which reads: "The Italian Government engages not to construct on the Atbara, in view of irrigation, any work
which might sensibly modify its flow into the Nile." Thus Lord Salisbury ensured command of an important tributary of the Nile. The most extravagant
and ambitious demands of the Italians were met in order to safeguard this one
item in the British program.[27]

But Abyssinia and her would-be protector, Italy, were not the only powers
threatening the upper Nile and the Sudan. As Gordon had pointed out, the
best approach to the Lake region and Equatoria was from the East African
coast, from the vicinity of Mombasa. This region had been part of the dominions
of the Sultan of Zanzibar, and had for years been the scene of acute rivalry
between the British and the Germans. In an agreement signed October 29, 1886
the two governments had delimited their claims on the sea-coast between the
Rovuma River in the south and the Tana River in the north. The line of demarcation ran from the mouth of the Wanga or Umbe River inland to Lake
Jipe. Of course this arrangement settled nothing with regard to the great hinterland which stretched onward to the Lake country. In a supplementary agreement of July 1887 it was stated that, while no special geographical line had been
drawn, it was understood that in the interior Germany should have a free hand
in the territories south of the Victoria Nyanza, and England to the north.[28]
This in itself was vague enough, when one considers how little was known of
these areas.

While the British and the Germans were trying to settle their respective
claims on the coast and in the hinterland, an entirely new problem was raised
by the news which reached Europe in 1886 that Emin Pasha, Egyptian governor of the Equatorial province, was still holding his own on the upper Nile
against the attacks of the dervishes. Emin appealed for help and looked to
England particularly to aid him. He was not disappointed, for before the year
was out a relief committee had been formed, the funds had been raised, and

---

[27] Texts of these agreements in *Italy No. 1 (1891)* and in Hertslet, op. cit., II, pp. 665 ff. On
the negotiations see General Luchino dal Verme: "L'Italia nel Libro di Lord Cromer" (*Nuova
Antologia*, October 1, 1908, pp. 353–84), especially pp. 373 ff.; Lyall: *Life of Lord Dufferin*, II,
pp. 232–3. The French contention, made by Lavisse, loc. cit., and Darcy, op. cit., pp. 374 ff. that
these treaties were not revealed until 1894 is incorrect.   [28] Hertslet, op. cit., II, pp. 615–27.

Stanley had been chosen to lead an expedition into central Africa. It would be wholly out of place to repeat here the familiar story of Stanley's harrowing adventures in the tropical forests, of his meetings with Emin in May 1888 and of the final " rescue " and arrival of the party at Bagamoyo in December 1889. We have only to consider certain facts that are relevant to the present argument.

King Leopold's hope of securing the southern part of the Sudan through Gordon has already been remarked. The Khartum tragedy had put an end to the scheme in 1884, but the presence of Emin in Equatoria opened up a new possibility. Stanley, who had worked for years with Leopold, was a convenient instrument, and in the British East Africa Association the King found a ready collaborator. The Association was headed by Sir William MacKinnon, chairman of the British India Steam Navigation Company. MacKinnon had opened regular mail service to Zanzibar in 1872, and was a close friend of Sir John Kirk, the British agent in the island, as well as of the Sultan himself. His interest in Africa, which was at least in part philanthropic, had long since brought him into touch with Leopold. In 1876 he had been a delegate to the conference which met at Brussels to consider ways and means of opening up Africa. In 1878 he had been one of the few individuals to subscribe to Leopold's *Comité d'Études*.[29] By 1885 he was attempting to secure a lease of the mainland possessions of the Sultan of Zanzibar, and was planning to build a railway from Mombasa to Lake Victoria. The East Africa Association, of which he was chairman, hoped to develop the entire region from the coast to the great lakes and the Nile.[30]

The relief of Emin Pasha was almost exclusively the work of these three remarkable men: Leopold, Stanley and MacKinnon. MacKinnon and his " Clan," as Stanley calls them, raised £11,500 for the expedition, the Egyptian government adding another £10,000. Emin was known to have some seventy-five tons of ivory at Wadelai, estimated to be worth some £60,000, so that all expenses would ultimately be covered. The Relief Committee made it perfectly clear that it expected its share of the spoils.[31]

Despite all that has been written on the subject, it is even now impossible to unravel the tangled and diverse motives that lay behind Stanley's last great exploit. So much, however, is clear: that Emin had no intention of abandoning the region in which he had maintained himself for so long. In his letters to his friend Felkin he said in so many words that he would not leave and that all he wanted England to do was to bring him much needed supplies, especially of ammunition, to bring about a better understanding with the King of Uganda, and to open up a safe route to the coast.[32] Now the Egyptian government, re-

---

[29] Robert S. Thomson: *Fondation de l'État Indépendant du Congo* (Brussels, 1933), pp. 42, 66.

[30] *Africa No. 1 (1886)*, p. 17; P. L. McDermott: *British East Africa or Ibea* (Second edition, London, 1895), pp. 3–9.

[31] The subscriptions to the expedition are given by Henry M. Stanley: *In Darkest Africa* (New York, 1890), I, p. 35. On the ivory question see *Africa No. 8 (1888)*, nos. 4, 11, 32.

[32] H. R. Fox Bourne: *The Other Side of the Emin Pasha Relief Expedition* (London, 1891), pp. 11–2 conveniently collates this material.

flecting the views of Sir Evelyn Baring and the London foreign office, did want Emin to come out. His presence in central Africa involved responsibility which was no longer desired. It was this fact that aroused the interest of Leopold and his friend MacKinnon. Their original idea seems to have been that Emin, once he was reinforced, could make his province a terminus for the routes to be opened from the Congo State on the one hand and from the east coast on the other hand. After much debate the Relief Committee yielded to Leopold, who insisted that the expedition should go through the Congo to the relief of Emin, and thereafter return through east Africa to the coast. Both Stanley and Mac-Kinnon held long conferences with Leopold in Brussels before the start was made for Egypt and Zanzibar. When Stanley left for Cairo he went as the paid agent of Leopold as well as in the capacity of leader of the Relief Committee's (i.e. the East Africa Association's) expedition.[33]

At Cairo Stanley received from the Egyptian government letters for Emin making it clear to him that he was to come out with his men, and pointing out that if he insisted on remaining he would do so at his own risk. The road was open for the realization of the dual plan worked out in Brussels. Stanley went on to Zanzibar to collect his carriers and to execute some other " little commissions " for his supporters. He induced the Sultan to grant the lease which MacKinnon desired, so that in 1888 the East Africa Association secured from the British government a charter as the Imperial British East Africa Company (IBEA). He furthermore succeeded in enlisting in the service of Leopold Tippoo Tib, the most notorious slave trader of the upper Congo region. Tippoo was to furnish the carriers needed to bring out Emin's ivory.[34]

When Stanley, after untold harrowing experiences, finally met Emin on the shore of Lake Albert in May 1888 he had little relief to bring him. Most of the supplies had been left behind with the rear column. Stanley was more in need of relief than the Pasha, who, to tell the truth, looked disgustingly prosperous and contented. Stanley showed Emin the letters of the Egyptian government and says that he urged Emin to leave the country. If he did so urge him, the explanation can only be that the explorer had convinced himself that the route through the great forests of the upper Congo basin was impracticable, and that it would be difficult to keep the Pasha supplied. In any event Emin's rejoinder gave the situation another twist. He decided to come out if his people were willing, otherwise not. Thereupon Stanley made him two other offers: the first was the offer of Leopold that Emin remain in the province as administrator in the service of the Congo State. Stanley says this offer was conditional on Emin's making the province pay, but there is nothing in Emin's diary to bear this out. In any event the proposition did not appeal to the governor and

---

[33] Stanley, op. cit., I, pp. 43–5; Fritz Masoin: *Histoire de l'État Indépendant du Congo* (Namur, 1913), II, p. 234. The fact that Stanley was in Leopold's employ was notified to the British government only later; see the documents taken by the Germans from the Brussels archives during the war and published in the *Deutsches Kolonialblatt*, June 1, 1916, pp. 141 ff.

[34] Stanley, op. cit., I, pp. 60–9.

Stanley does not seem to have pressed it. His attitude at this time is very obscure, but one can hardly escape the impression that he was less ardent in the service of his Belgian master than in the service of the MacKinnon Clan. We know from Emin's correspondence that even Mr. Felkin, who was originally not at all favorable to the East Africa Association, was brought into line at this time. He kept writing Emin from Europe urging him to stay in the province and act as the representative of the British group. Indeed, he went so far as to assume the position of Emin's agent, and to conclude with the newly chartered company an agreement by which the Equatorial Province was to be handed over by Emin, who was to serve the Company as administrator.[35] This whole system of pressure by the company is revealed also in Stanley's alternative offer: that Emin take his men, go to the northwestern shore of Lake Victoria, build stations and wait for the company's forces to reach him from the coast.[36]

Stanley's second proposition made a greater appeal to Emin, though he had the feeling that the whole business was a " project of British tradesmen and British politicians." He did not make up his mind definitely at this time, having to return to Wadelai to consult his men. In the interval Stanley returned to bring up his rear column. The two men did not meet again until February 1889, and by that time the tables had been turned. Emin's forces had mutinied, and he had been, for some time, held captive. Stanley, on the other hand, had much more in the way of ammunition and supplies than he had had before. He was now in a position to offer some relief, but Emin was no longer in a position to benefit by it. Circumstances practically obliged the governor to accept Stanley's rather gruff invitation to leave for the coast. The whole plan had fallen flat. Emin could not stay and hold the province for either Leopold or MacKinnon. He could not even be established on Lake Victoria, where he might, under more favorable conditions, have prepared the way for the acquisition of Uganda and Unyoro by the Company. There was nothing Stanley could do but make the best of it. On his long trek to the coast he signed treaties with as many chiefs as possible in the area between Lakes Albert Edward and Victoria. Evidently it was hoped that Emin could yet be induced to take service with the Company. Offers were made to him by Mr. MacKay, the famous missionary, and these offers were repeated when finally the party reached Bagamoyo on the coast. If he could have gone back with adequate forces and supplies, he might yet have proved a valuable agent.[37]

But the important result of the fiasco of the relief expedition was that it left Equatoria a no-man's land. The MacKinnon Clan was profoundly disappointed

[35] Felkin's correspondence with Emin in 1888 and 1889 may be found in *Die Tagebücher von Dr. Emin Pascha,* edited by Franz Stuhlmann, IV (Berlin, 1927), pp. 440 ff.

[36] Stanley, op. cit., I, pp. 410 ff.; Emin: *Tagebücher,* IV, pp. 103 ff.; Georg Schweitzer: *Emin Pascha* (Berlin, 1898), pp. 401 ff.

[37] MacKay's letter was intercepted by Carl Peters, and is printed in Carl Peters: *Die Deutsche Emin-Pascha Expedition* (Munich, 1891), pp. 298 ff. MacKinnon's offers are mentioned by Stanley, op. cit., II, p. 472.

at the abandonment of the territory. Felkin wrote to Emin on November 1, 1889 saying that he hoped it was not true that he was coming out with Stanley: "However much we may wish to see you, and you can well understand how great that wish is, yet it seems to be the universal opinion that you should stop for another year or so before coming home, so that you might leave the province properly organized." [38]

If the province had simply fallen into the hands of the dervishes, its situation would have been no different from that of the rest of the Sudan. The danger arose from the fact that a European great power threatened to secure a foothold there. Felkin had warned the Pasha time and again against the machinations of the Germans, and with good cause, for Karl Peters and the German colonialists had from the outset viewed the British expedition with suspicion and distrust. In 1888 they had at last organized a relief expedition of their own, which, to be sure, received no support or approval from the German government, but might very well have created a situation like that of 1884–1885. In his books Peters makes no bones about revealing his objectives. Thinking that Emin was still in Equatoria he hoped to reach him before Stanley appeared on the scene, enlist him in the German service, induce him to extend his dominion to Lake Victoria and to the German colony farther south, and thus cut off the British from the interior while extending the German sphere to the Nile. "The German Emin-Pasha expedition," says Peters, "was no pleasure trip, but a large-scale colonial, political enterprise." [39]

Peters plan came very near to being realized. Emin, after recovering from a fall at Bagamoyo, entered the service of the German company, proclaimed Equatoria his province which he was about to turn over to Germany, and set out through German East Africa to regain his position. It is well known that he was killed by the Arabs while he was pushing through the Lake region in 1891. In the meanwhile Peters himself had gone northward along the coast to beyond the Tana River and, after evading the blockade, had struck inland. By March 1890 he had reached Uganda and concluded a treaty of protection with the King. An expedition sent out by the British East Africa Company arrived in Uganda only a month later.

This race for Uganda and the threat of Peters to cut the British off from the interior and from the Nile created a sensation in England. The *Times* on April 3 called attention to the danger of having the Germans on the Nile. The government itself was uneasy, and efforts were repeatedly made in the spring of 1890 to come to some agreement with the Berlin authorities. There were so many conflicting claims, however, that a compromise seemed almost hopeless. Salisbury therefore urged the British Association (which had been chartered in 1888 as the Imperial British East Africa Company, or IBEA) to send further troops to

[38] Emin: *Tagebücher*, IV, p. 445.
[39] Peters, op. cit., and especially his book: *Die Gründung von Deutsch-Ostafrika* (Berlin, 1906), pp. 236 ff., 254, 258 ff.

Uganda. According to Stanley the company was " egged on, urged on, advised, spurred and encouraged." [40] But it was given no material support, which led to bitter complaints at the time and even more bitter recriminations later.[41]

It seems fairly clear that Salisbury was unwilling to do much for the company, evidently because he thought the company would have to act in its own interest, as it actually did, thus saving the state money. But there was another important aspect to the problem. The prime minister was wrestling not only with the Mac-Kinnon Clan, but with another organized group, the British South Africa Company, which had been chartered in the autumn of 1889 to take over the territory in what is now Rhodesia. This group, of which Cecil Rhodes was the leading spirit, was wedded to the idea which later became familiar through the slogan *Cape-to-Cairo,* and which envisaged the ultimate connexion of British territory in south Africa with the new possessions in central Africa and Egypt.

It appears that this idea was first put forward in 1876 in a pamphlet written by Sir Edwin Arnold. In the very next year Gladstone recognized its implications when he decried any forward movement in Egypt:

> " Our first site in Egypt, be it by larceny or be it by emption, will be the almost certain egg of a North African Empire, that will grow and grow . . . until we finally join hands across the Equator with Natal and Cape Town, to say nothing of the Transvaal and the Orange River on the south, or of Abyssinia or Zanzibar to be swallowed by way of viaticum on our journey." [42]

In the later 1880's the idea became ever more popular. Sir Harry Johnston, the well-known African explorer, tells us how he expounded it to Lord Salisbury in 1888 and how the prime minister approved of an article which he published in the *Times* on August 22, 1888. In this essay Johnston stated that if the government granted some measure of support to British commercial and missionary enterprise in the Lake region, " our possessions in South Africa may be linked some day to our spheres of influence in Eastern Africa and the Egyptian Sudan by a continuous band of British dominions." At about the same time Sir James Siveright, a British engineer, advocated the construction of a telegraph line from south Africa to Khartum. In the spring of the next year Sir Charles Metcalfe, who was at that time building the railroad from Kimberley to Vryburg, published an article in the *Fortnightly Review* in which he referred to the " iron track that must ultimately join the Cape with Cairo and carry civilization through the heart of the Dark Continent." [43]

---

[40] Sir Henry M. Stanley: *Autobiography* (Boston, 1909), pp. 446 ff.

[41] This is the whole burden of P. L. McDermott's *British East Africa or Ibea* (Second edition, London, 1895), which is the authoritative presentation of the Company's case.

[42] William E. Gladstone: " Aggression on Egypt and Freedom in the East " (*Nineteenth Century,* August, 1877, pp. 149–66).

[43] Sir Harry Johnston: *Britain across the Seas, Africa* (London, 1910), p. 182; Idem: *The Story of my Life* (London, 1923), pp. 220–2; see also the illuminating accounts of Johnston, Metcalfe, Williams and Weinthal in the monumental story of *The Cape to Cairo Railway and River Route,* edited by Leo Weinthal (London, 1923), I, pp. 65–120, 211–7. Johnston's influence on Salisbury is discussed in Cecil: *Life of Lord Salisbury,* IV, pp. 242–3.

Rhodes seems to have been indoctrinated by Johnston in the course of a long discussion they had in London in May 1889. Thinking ever in the broadest terms the great imperialist was ready at once to take over anything in central Africa between the Zambezi and the White Nile. He began to subsidize the British African Lakes Company on Lake Nyasa, and gave Johnston £2,000 to hurry out to Nyasaland and set up posts between that lake and Lake Tanganyika, territory to which the Germans were also laying claim. By 1890 he was already engrossed in plans for a telegraph line from south to north.[44]

Now the British South Africa Company, in the spring of 1890, was interested chiefly in securing the territory between Lakes Nyasa and Tanganyika and between Tanganyika and Albert Edward. In this way there would have been established unbroken land and water communication between Rhodesia and Uganda. The British East Africa Company, on the other hand, was primarily interested in keeping the Germans south of the line running from the southern tip of Lake Victoria to the northern tip of Lake Tanganyika, and in excluding the Germans from the whole area along the coast north of the River Tana. Salisbury evidently saw from the outset that all these aims could not be realized. He was already thinking of the ultimate reconquest of the Sudan and was more interested in the Uganda problem than in anything else.[45] By this time (April 1890) Stanley had returned to Europe. He stopped for some time at Cannes, where he discussed the situation with MacKinnon. They then went on together to Paris and Brussels, where there were long conferences with King Leopold. Apparently at this time the King and MacKinnon came to a general agreement that they should divide the sphere of their activities along the line of the Semliki River.[46]

In the first week of May Stanley and MacKinnon were back in England. In a series of public addresses the great explorer raised the hue and cry about German aggressiveness and demanded that England press her claim to all the territory between Lake Victoria and the Congo State. Salisbury complained much to the German ambassador about the difficulties caused by this stirring up of public sentiment, but in reality he was not being attacked. From Queen Victoria's letters we know that the prime minister, Stanley and MacKinnon all dined together at Windsor on May 6.[47] We may assume that these gentlemen all knew what was the goal to be attained. It was only a question of how to go about the problem.

From his conversations with the German ambassador on May 14 and 17 the prime minister became convinced that the Germans would not agree to any arrangement which would drive a British wedge into the back of their posses-

---

[44] Edward Dicey: " Mr. Cecil Rhodes as Premier " (*Nineteenth Century*, August, 1890, pp. 176–85); Sir Harry H. Johnston: *The Story of my Life* (London, 1923), pp. 218 ff.; Sir Lewis Michell: *The Life and Times of Cecil John Rhodes* (New York, 1910), I, pp. 280, 288, 341; Weinthal, op. cit., I, pp. 67–83.

[45] *Die Grosse Politik*, VIII, nos. 1778, 1779.   [46] Stanley: *Autobiography*, pp. 412–3.

[47] *Letters of Queen Victoria*, Series III, vol. III, p. 601.

sions and cut them off from the Congo State. On May 22 Salisbury admitted that German territory should touch the Congo State in the region north of Lake Tanganyika.[48] This meant the end of the " All-Red Route " from the south to the north, at least so far as Germany was concerned. But another way out was found. Leopold had just arrived in London. He had talks with Salisbury, MacKinnon and Stanley, the result of which was the so-called MacKinnon Treaty, signed on May 24, 1890 by the Congo government and the British East Africa Company. By this arrangement the Company recognized the sovereign rights of the Congo State west of a line drawn from the southwest corner of Lake Albert northward along the Nile as far as Lado, while the Congo government recognized the sovereign rights of the Company over a strip of territory only five miles wide running from the southern shore of Lake Albert Edward to the northern point of Lake Tanganyika.

The agreement was communicated to Lord Salisbury, who raised no objection. He felt that the claim to a continuous strip had no international validity and pointed out that the German government " would view with considerable objection the concession of territory at the back of their own sphere without their knowledge and consent." Nevertheless he made every effort to secure such a strip from the Germans. But he found them adamant on this point and realized that to insist might lead to a rupture of the negotiations and a loss of everything. On June 2 the newspapers reported that the much-dreaded Peters had signed a treaty with the King of Uganda. Salisbury almost at once abandoned his efforts to secure the connecting strip. It was essential to save Uganda, and he therefore baited the Germans with the tempting offer of Heligoland, which they eagerly accepted. In the famous Agreement of July 1, 1890 the Germans gave up all claims to territory north and west of the British sphere provisionally marked out in 1886. They recognized as part of the British sphere all territory northward to the Italian sphere in Somaliland and to the confines of Egypt, and westward to the watershed between the Nile and the Congo and to the Congo State. The British got about everything that they wanted, excepting the much-coveted strip. Whether Salisbury cared much about this may well be doubted. He referred to the Cape-to-Cairo scheme in a speech delivered soon afterward as " a curious idea which has lately become prevalent," and pointed out that a strip removed by a three months' march from the sea would be a most " inconvenient possession." His correspondence with the Queen shows that his difficulties arose from the unwillingness of the two companies to accept his viewpoint. The really important thing — freedom of action between the ocean and the Nile — was secured. Under the settlement, he wrote the Queen, " the whole country outside the confines of Abyssinia and Gallaland will be under British influence up to Khartum, so far as any European competitor is concerned." [49]

---

[48] *Die Grosse Politik*, VIII, nos. 1676, 1677, 1678.
[49] *Letters of Queen Victoria*, I, p. 613. On the negotiations see ibid., pp. 606–10: *Die Grosse Politik*, VIII, nos. 1680–2; *Africa No. 5 (1890), Despatch to Sir E. Malet respecting the Affairs of*

Despite this optimistic utterance Salisbury was not content with the mere recognition of the British sphere by Germany. It was necessary to secure firm control of Uganda. Since 1885 there had been talk of constructing a railway from Mombasa over several hundred miles of barren territory to Lake Victoria. It was a project which Stanley advocated with great enthusiasm. Some people thought the scheme impracticable and too expensive to try, but Salisbury was a firm believer in it and the British East Africa Company was eager to go on with it, arguing that only through a railway could anything be done to abolish the caravans with their slave cargoes. In December 1890 the foreign office proposed to grant the Company a sum of money to embark on the enterprise, but it was finally decided to arrange first for a survey. The matter dragged on for some time, and it was only in December 1891 that a survey party set out under the command of Captain MacDonald.[50]

In the interval the East Africa Company had announced, in July 1891, that it would have to withdraw from Uganda. It was claimed by the directors that the company had been obliged to occupy the territory in 1890 because of the advance of the Germans and because of pressure from the British government. Had the government been willing to guarantee interest on the capital needed for a railway, Uganda might have been held. As it was, the company could not afford to continue an expense that amounted to some £40,000 to £50,000 per annum. So far as one can discover, Lord Salisbury was quite content to allow the Company to withdraw. He was staking everything on the railway, which Sir Harry Johnston described later as " the indispensable condition of the secure maintenance of British control over the regions about the sources of the Nile." Once the railway were built, it would be a simple matter for the government to restore control in Uganda itself.[51]

But the withdrawal from Uganda was not to be so easily effected. The *Times* came out openly against it on September 28, pointing out the danger to the Protestant Missions in a country where there had been civil war since 1889 between the Mohammedan, Catholic and Protestant elements, the first faction enjoying the support of the Arabs, the second following the leadership of the French Catholic missionaries. The agitation gained considerable momentum. The Church Missionary Society, the Anti-Slavery Society and other organizations

---

East Africa; Africa No. 6 (1890), Correspondence respecting the Anglo-German Agreement relative to Africa and Heligoland; Cecil: Life of Lord Salisbury, IV, pp. 277 ff. The text of the MacKinnon Treaty was first published in the Deutsches Kolonialblatt, June 1, 1916, pp. 142 ff. The facts soon leaked out; see the London Times, April 28, 1893; Anonymous (F. D. Lugard): " The New African Crisis with France and Germany " (Blackwood's Magazine, July, 1894, pp. 145–58); P. L. McDermott: British East Africa, pp. 314–7; Stanley: Autobiography, pp. 417 ff.

[50] Africa No. 2 (1892), Papers respecting the Proposed Railway from Mombasa to Lake Victoria Nyanza; McDermott, op. cit., pp. 181 ff., etc.

[51] Letters of Queen Victoria, II, p. 160; Africa No. 1 (1893), Further Papers relating to Uganda. Proposed Evacuation by the Company, especially no. 6; McDermott, op. cit., pp. 195 ff. On the Railway see also Hans Meyer: Die Eisenbahnen im Tropischen Afrika (Leipzig, 1902), pp. 140 ff., and E. de Renty: Les Chemins de Fer Coloniaux en Afrique (Paris, 1904), II, pp. 160 ff.

entered the lists. Eventually the missionary group lent the East Africa Company £40,000 and the Company agreed to continue the occupation until December 31, 1892. In the meanwhile Captain Lugard, who had been sent out by the Company in December 1890, had obliged the Uganda King to sign a treaty and had marched his force through the western areas between Lakes Albert Edward and Albert, establishing posts which he garrisoned with Emin Pasha's former Sudanese troops. When a new and more serious religious conflict broke out between the Catholic and Protestant converts in January 1892, he gave the French faction (Wa-Fransa) short shrift, suppressing the disturbances by methods which many people, especially the French, thought most questionable.[52]

In August 1892 Captain MacDonald reported on the railway survey. He estimated that the line to Lake Victoria would be seven hundred miles long, that construction would take roughly four years, and that the cost would be £2,240,000. But before anything further could be done in this matter the Salisbury government fell from power. Gladstone formed his last cabinet, with Lord Rosebery as foreign secretary. Rosebery himself was as much of an imperialist as Salisbury. He was convinced that Uganda must be retained. Something had to be done at once, because it would take months for orders to reach Uganda from England, and the Company was planning to withdraw on December 31. On September 20, therefore, Rosebery circulated to the cabinet a memorandum prepared by Sir Percy Anderson, the expert of the foreign office on African affairs. According to Sir William Harcourt this paper was one " in the highest jingo tune advocating the annexation of the whole country up to the Albert Lakes with a view to the 'reconquest' of the Sudan via the Upper Nile." [53]

With such proposals Rosebery was not likely to make a favorable impression on a cabinet which had Gladstone as premier and Harcourt controlling the purse strings. Harcourt had already done his utmost to wreck the Salisbury proposal for a railway survey, and he now wrote to Gladstone: " If we embark on this desperate business we shall have no end of trouble with the French and the Germans." There was, he went on to say, no trade to be gotten in the country, the religious factions were cutting each others' throats and there was no evidence of any slave-trade question in that area. Gladstone, Morley and Asquith supported him in these views. He thereupon wrote to Rosebery that the Company had gone to Uganda simply because of jealousy of the Germans and because of insatiable land hunger. Yet now England was to set out to reconquer the whole basin of the upper Nile. Why? For fear of the Germans, the French and the Belgians in the Congo. " This is Jingoism with a vengeance. We are to have a 'Wacht am Nile' and our drum and fife band is to play: 'Sie

---

[52] McDermott, op. cit., pp. 157, 165 ff., 204 ff.; Woolf: *Empire and Commerce in Africa,* pp. 277–89; Lugard: *The Rise of our East African Empire,* I, passim; *Africa No. 1 (1893), Africa No. 2 (1893),* containing Lugard's reports and the negotiations between the British and French governments about the maltreatment of Catholic converts.

[53] Gardiner: *Life of Sir William Harcourt,* II, p. 192; *Letters of Queen Victoria,* II, p. 159.

sollen ihn nicht haben, den freien britischen Nile.' The Nile is to be a freehold
from its source to its mouth, and Uganda is the point on which it turns." To
drive home his argument he referred to a memorandum drawn up in April 1892
by Sir Reginald Wingate, intelligence officer of the Egyptian army, in which
the effects of withdrawal upon Egypt were stressed and the reconquest of the
Sudan was strongly urged.[54]

This unbending attitude on the part of Harcourt led to many bitter scenes
in the cabinet as the question became more and more urgent. Sir Frederick
Lugard had returned to England and was carrying on an untiring campaign in
the newspapers, in the monthlies and on the platform. The country, and particularly the religious bodies demanded a decision. There was a "great outcry
from the heart of the Nation," and the Archbishop of Canterbury himself appealed for aid to enable the Company to remain.[55] Something had to be done,
and on September 30 Harcourt, in order to keep the cabinet together, agreed
that the government should bear the cost of the occupation until March 31, 1893,
in order to enable it to secure more information.[56]

On this very day a new possibility for a satisfactory solution presented itself.
King Leopold, sovereign of the Congo State, ever ready to step into the breach
when there was a chance of extending his territory, wrote to Gladstone suggesting that he take over the administration of Uganda and Unyoro, subject to
British authority. The idea struck Gladstone as one "of great novelty and
singularity," but Queen Victoria thought "it would be a great thing if we
could act with the King of the Belgians." The cabinet, while intrigued, decided, however, that no practical step could be taken for the moment, and
Gladstone wrote the King leaving the matter open for further discussion.[57]

Hardly had this letter been written when another and more palatable suggestion was put forward. In October 1892 Cecil Rhodes arrived in London. He
was now prime minister of the Cape, a man of influence and of excellent city
connexions. As the leading imperialist of his day he was, naturally, unalterably
opposed to British evacuation of Uganda. The territory had a particular value
for him because he was now deeply involved in the scheme for a telegraph line
from south Africa to Egypt. Even with Uganda British it would be necessary
to run the telegraph line through part of German territory. Rhodes therefore
wrote to the foreign office asking that it take steps to secure the sanction of the
German government as soon as possible, and expressing his hope that ultimately
the line could be extended to Wadi Halfa on the Egyptian frontier.[58] At the

[54] Gardiner: *Harcourt*, II, pp. 192–7.
[55] Woolf, op. cit., pp. 298 ff.; Lugard: *The Rise of our East African Empire*, II, pp. 547 ff.;
Joseph Thomsen: "The Uganda Problem" (*Contemporary Review*, December, 1892, pp. 786–96).
[56] Gardiner, op. cit., II, pp. 196–7; McDermott, op. cit., p. 207.
[57] *Letters of Queen Victoria*, II, pp. 161–2, 167.
[58] The letter is in *Africa No. 3 (1893)*, no. 33. See also Sir Lewis Michell: *The Life and Times
of Cecil Rhodes* (New York, 1910), II, p. 65, and the well-informed articles of W. T. Stead in the
Review of Reviews, May 14, 1892 and December 15, 1892.

same time Rhodes offered to take over Uganda itself from the British East
Africa Company, and to administer it with a subsidy of £20,000 per year. He
had long talks with Harcourt on the subject, and evidently made some impression upon this redoubtable Little Englander.[59]

Rhodes' suggestion with regard to Uganda was not followed any further
than King Leopold's. The scheme seemed rather impractical and the cabinet
was now taken up with a proposal that the territory be ruled through the Sultan
of Zanzibar, who was under British protection. This suggestion seems to have
been made by the East Africa Company as far back as July 1892.[60] It does not
appear to have satisfied Rosebery, for during November efforts were made by
the foreign office to induce the Company to continue in occupation for a time
with a subsidy from the government. The Company, however, was unwilling
to stay for less than three years and asked a subsidy of £50,000 a year, whereupon the negotiations were dropped.[61] Instead the government decided to send
out Sir Gerald Portal, the agent at Zanzibar, to investigate. His instructions were
to report on " the best means of dealing with the country, whether through
Zanzibar or otherwise." It is fairly clear that by this time even Harcourt had
seen that retention by Great Britain was inevitable, and that Portal's conclusions
were foregone. At any rate, when Portal reached Uganda, he promptly hauled
down the flag of the Company and hoisted the Union Jack.[62]

Throughout the spring of 1893 Portal sent home elaborate reports on conditions. The trade prospects were good: " I look upon East Africa as a mag-
nificent future market for European manufactures. The Waganda are clamour-
ing for shoes and stockings, opera-glasses, etc. and are daily developing fresh
wants," wrote Colonel Frank Rhodes in a letter sent home by Portal. As for
the religious situation, Portal found it bad. If the British withdrew, a war of
extermination would follow.[63] In his final report, dated from Zanzibar November 1, 1893, Portal summed up his impressions. He called attention to Uganda's
location and described it as " a strategical position of great natural importance
dominating the northern and western shores of Lake Victoria, holding almost
the only access to Lakes Albert and Albert Edward, and controlling the headwaters of the Nile." It was, he maintained, " the natural key to the whole of the
Nile Valley and the richest parts of Central Africa." If England withdrew, some
other power, probably the Germans, would take it over and Britain would lose
" the whole of that vast territory reserved by the Anglo-German Convention for
the sphere of British influence." Control by another power

---

[59] Gardiner: *Harcourt*, II, p. 199; Johnston: *Story of my Life*, p. 238; *Private Diaries of Sir
Algernon West*, p. 69.

[60] McDermott, op. cit., p. 276.

[61] McDermott, op. cit., pp. 279–83.

[62] Lugard: *Rise of our East African Empire*, II, pp. 564, 615 ff.; Johnston: *Uganda Protectorate*,
I, p. 234; West: *Diaries*, p. 82. The instructions to Portal in *Africa, No. 1 (1893)*, no. 40. His own
account in Sir Gerald Portal: *The British Mission to Uganda in 1893* (London, 1894).

[63] *Africa No. 2 (1894)*, nos. 1, 2.

"would inevitably extend, not only over Uganda and its immediate dependencies, but would embrace all the neighbouring countries, the great lakes, the Nile Valley, and the natural highways of the interior. The control of Uganda means, in the course of a few years, a preponderance of influence and of commerce in the richest and most populous section of Central Africa." [64]

This report, together with other considerations to be discussed presently, completed the conversion of Sir William Harcourt. The document was published on April 11, 1894. On the very next day the government announced its decision to proclaim a protectorate over Uganda. On June 18 the proclamation was officially made.[65] On the side of Uganda and east Africa the Nile was protected. Even a Liberal government that was constantly discussing the possibility of evacuating Egypt could not for long evade responsibility in this matter.

The Uganda issue was of very great importance in the development of British imperialism. It marked the beginning of the split in the Liberal party which was to prove so disastrous later. Rosebery and the Liberal imperialists won their first victory in the very first months of the last Gladstone administration. It is perfectly clear that both the prime minister and his faithful follower, John Morley, were desirous of evacuating Egypt. The French cherished fond hopes that something could be done. But the French ambassador, M. Waddington, knowing that Rosebery would be unsympathetic, made the fatal mistake of approaching Gladstone personally. When the foreign minister learned of this back-stairs manoeuvring he was naturally incensed. He made an issue of the Egyptian question and carried his point. The position of the French ambassador had, of course, become impossible, and he therefore resigned from his post.[66] The net result of the démarche was that the British decided, to all intents and purposes, to remain in Egypt for the time being. Before long the retention of Uganda was also settled. The one decision followed the other quite naturally. If Egypt was to be held, then the Nile had to be protected. Milner's famous book, *England in Egypt,* was published at this very time (1892). His glorification of the British achievement in Egypt undoubtedly influenced public opinion in favor of retention, and his warning of the danger of interference with Egypt's water supply in all probability had some bearing on the settlement of the Uganda problem. In a popular handbook of this latter question we read, as the first argument in favor of the government's taking over the country: "The relinquishment of Uganda to a civilised Power immediately imperils the safety of Egypt, as the diversion or blocking of the headwaters of the Nile could stop her water supply and starve her population." [67]

The settlement of the Uganda problem was not without its wider inter-

---

[64] *Africa No. 2 (1894),* no. 9.

[65] Gardiner: *Harcourt,* II, p. 312; McDermott, op. cit., pp. 304 ff.

[66] A long account of this episode was given by M. Ribot in a speech delivered in the Chamber on January 23, 1899.

[67] Ernest L. Bentley: *Handbook to the Uganda Question* (London, 1892), p. 8.

national aspects. In the basin of the Nile matters had been developing at a rapid tempo. Leopold was exhibiting an unwonted activity. He had in his pocket the MacKinnon Treaty of 1890, which left him free to extend his dominions to the Semliki River, Lake Albert, and the upper Nile. One of his ablest and most daring officers, Van Kerckhoven, urged him to take advantage of his opportunities, so Leopold sent him off in September 1890 with a considerable force. Van Kerckhoven's expedition pushed on through the country between the Congo watershed and the Nile, arming the local potentates with rifles with which to fight the dervishes. There seemed to be no obstacle in the way of the Belgian force, and part of it did, in fact, reach the Nile at Wadelai in October 1892.[68]

Lord Salisbury was keenly aware of the dangers to England of Leopold's activities. He lodged a protest at Brussels, and called attention to the agreements between England and Germany and Italy, by which this area was recognized as part of the British sphere. The King replied that the Congo State had not been officially informed of these transactions and had not recognized them. He stuck by the MacKinnon Treaty and ignored Salisbury's argument that this agreement had not been communicated to the British government or sanctioned by it.[69]

Leopold was less disturbed by the protests of the British than he was by the threatening attitude of France. Since Ferry's disastrous Tonkin adventure public opinion in France had undergone a considerable change with respect to colonial enterprise. The spectacular work of French explorers in Africa had aroused much interest and there had been for years a growing realization that France must not be left behind in the race for the acquisition of territory in the Black Continent. Chambers of commerce were agitating for greater activity and local enthusiasts everywhere were prepared at all times to organize receptions for returning adventurers. The *Société de Géographie de Paris*, the *Société de Géographie Commerciale*, the *Société Africaine de France*, the *Société Anti-Esclavagiste*, all these influential organizations and a great many others became centres of colonial propaganda. In 1890 there was founded the most energetic of all, the *Comité de l'Afrique Française*, which counted among its members editors, deputies, business men and writers. After 1889 the movement gained impetus so fast that the idea of acquiring a great block of territory running from the west to the east coast of Africa became very generally accepted. M. Hanotaux, one of the moving spirits of the new imperialism, tells us that all French ex-

---

[68] A. J. Wauters: *Souvenirs de Fashoda et de l'Expédition Dhanis* (Brussels, 1910), pp. 10–1; Masoin: *Histoire de l'État Indépendant du Congo*, II, pp. 259 ff.; Colonel Liebrechts: *Léopold II, Fondateur d'Empire* (Brussels, 1932), pp. 156–67; Pierre Daye: *Léopold II* (Paris, 1934), chap. x.

[69] Kimberley to Hardinge, May 23, 1894 (*Africa No. 4* [1894]); *Deutsches Kolonialblatt*, XXVII, pp. 144 ff. (1916); the long Belgian memorandum of 1899 quoted by Théophile Simar: "Léopold II et le Soudan" (*Congo*, V, pp. 506–28, November, 1924); Wauters: op. cit., p. 12; Anonymous (F. D. Lugard): "The New African Crisis" (*Blackwood's Magazine*, July, 1894, pp. 145–6). Lugard's view was that Salisbury's veto in 1890 was simply against the lease of a strip and that Leopold was justified in his advance.

plorations in Africa in the later nineteenth century were directed towards this end. From the international aspect of the situation the activities of the French were of importance because French aspirations, from the very outset, ran counter in every way to those of the British expansionists.[70]

De Brazza, the great French explorer, was at this time governor of the French Congo, which lay to the north of the Congo State, but had no clearly defined boundaries. In an agreement made with the Congo government in 1887 the French had defined the boundary as far as the Ubanghi River and the fourth parallel of latitude. The whole region lying north of this line was regarded as open to French enterprise and great efforts were being made to consolidate the French position about Lake Chad as well as further to the eastward. In 1890 De Brazza had sent out a very able administrator named Liotard to create " a French region with a door opening on the Nile." [71] Shortly afterward he had written to his lieutenant: " With regard to our action towards the northeast, the mere fact of our pushing our explorations in this direction as far as the affluents of the Upper Nile is of considerable importance." [72]

Liotard himself had only a small force of one hundred Senegalese troops and was as yet unable to accomplish much. The French were therefore much worried by the advance of the Van Kerckhoven expedition, a detachment of which reached Wadelai in 1892 and was sending out smaller groups to the north and even the northwest so that ultimately all French access to the upper Nile would be cut off. The whole procedure, according to the French, was contrary to the agreement of 1887, and negotiations were therefore opened with Leopold. The French began by insisting on the Ubanghi frontier, but the Belgians parried cleverly by asking whether this meant the Welle River or the M'Bomu, the two branches into which the Ubanghi divides in its upper reaches. In the end an agreement was drafted and signed which recognized as the frontier the Chinko River and the seventh parallel of latitude north. In return for this far-reaching concession Leopold seems to have agreed to divide with the French the region on the west side of the upper Nile, the Congo State taking the area as far north as Lado and leaving the rest to the French. M. Ribot, the French foreign minister, evidently acquiesced in this settlement at first, but later rejected it because of pressure brought to bear by the colonial group in the Chamber. Leopold, however, had a signed document and characteristically stood by it. In December 1892 the discussions came to an end.[73]

---

[70] Gabriel Hanotaux: *Fachoda* (Paris, 1909), p. 57; a good description of the colonialist outburst by Auguste Terrier, in Hanotaux: *Histoire des Colonies Françaises*, IV (Paris, 1931), pp. 435–9.
[71] Liotard's speech at Paris in October, 1898, in *Bulletin du Comité de l'Afrique Française*, 1898, p. 369.
[72] Auguste Terrier: " La Marche vers le Nord-Est et la Question du Haut Nil " (Hanotaux: *Histoire des Colonies Françaises*, IV, chap. vi, p. 507).
[73] *Bulletin du Comité de l'Afrique Française*, February, 1893; Hanotaux's speech in the Chamber, June 7, 1894; Cocheris: *La Situation Internationale de l'Égypte*, pp. 393–5; Wauters, op. cit., p. 12; Fritz Masoin: *Histoire de l'État Indépendant du Congo* (Namur, 1913), II, pp. 272 ff.

At this point a new factor was injected into French policy. On January 20, 1893 an eminent French engineer in the Egyptian service, M. Victor Prompt, gave an address to the Egyptian Institute on certain problems of the hydrography of the Nile. He had for years been occupied with the question of storing water for summer use, and had first suggested the construction of a dam at Aswan. In his lecture he went far beyond the question of a reservoir in Egypt. He discussed the feasibility of constructing great dams at the outlets of Lakes Victoria and Albert, or at the confluence of the Sobat and the White Nile. He estimated the flood discharge of the Nile at about seventy-five billion cubic meters over a period of five or six months, and argued that by building barrages as much or more water could be held back and stored for use during the summer. Thus far no objection could be raised to the speech. But M. Prompt went on to some rather indiscreet speculations. He noted that if the water in the great lake-reservoirs were not let out in time the summer supply of Egypt would be cut in half. If the reservoirs were thrown open suddenly and the whole flood sent down on Egypt, the civilization of the Nile could be drowned out by one great disaster. In conclusion he remarked that the dams he had in mind would not cost much to build. They could be constructed for about half a million francs apiece.[74]

The introduction of questions of Nile hydrography may seem out of place in a study of diplomacy, but it can be justified, because the address of M. Prompt had a real influence on French and probably on British policy. Sir Samuel Baker, who had long sensed the danger of interference with the flood water from Abyssinia, must have had Prompt's speech in mind when he wrote to an English friend on May 1, 1893: " If we settle down at the headwaters of the Nile, we command Egypt; and a barrage at a narrow pass, where the Nile cuts through a rocky defile only eighty yards in width, below the exit from the Albert Nyanza, would raise the level of the great reservoir of the Nile by fifty feet and entirely control the water supply of Egypt." [75] The addresses and writings of others, like Scott-Moncrieff, which were referred to earlier in this chapter, likewise bear the marks of the Prompt influence. From this time on the theory of the French engineer, which was sound in most respects, became a sort of nightmare to the English.

The influence of the speech upon French policy can be determined with even greater certainty. President Carnot happened to be an old school friend of M. Prompt, and evidently received a copy of the address at once. On May 5, 1893 he summoned to the Élysée Palace the undersecretary for the colonies, M. Delcassé, and the intrepid French explorer, Major Monteil, whom Delcassé had been urging for some time to embark on an expedition to the Nile. " I should

---

[74] Victor Prompt: " Le Soudan Nilotique " (*Bulletin de l'Institut Égyptien*, Series III, no. 4, pp. 71–116).

[75] Letter to Moberly Bell, in Thomas D. Murray and A. Silva White: *Sir Samuel Baker, a Memoir* (London, 1895), p. 373.

like to reopen the Egyptian question," said the president. " The Egyptian Sudan is *res nullius* and France needs an outlet on the Nile for her possessions on the Ubanghi." He then showed them a report of the Prompt address and outlined to them a plan for an advance upon Fashoda, which was not far from the confluence of the Sobat and the Nile. By occupying this position the French could forestall the Belgians and at the same time frighten the British out of Egypt by threatening the water supply. Monteil was to proceed at once to the upper Ubanghi with a considerable force, and was to advance to the Nile and occupy Fashoda. Liotard was placed under his orders. Preparations were pushed forward with great vigor. Lieutenant Decazes was despatched to the Congo at once, and Monteil was to follow in October 1893. But then, on the very eve of his departure, word was received from De Brazza that the Belgians were threatening to use force to stop the expedition. They had already acted rather high-handedly towards the French agents, and efforts had been made in Paris to come to some arrangement with them. But negotiations led to nothing. De Brazza himself counselled caution and advised that the expedition be postponed. At the moment there was great tension in the relations between France and Italy, so the Paris government, rather than become involved in further complications, suspended preparations for the advance to the Nile.[76]

During the winter of 1893-1894 negotiation and preparation alternated. The French foreign minister, M. Develle, discussed the situation with the secretary for foreign affairs of the Congo State in October. He was willing to concede the Congo a frontier running along the M'Bomu River and along parallel 5° 30′ north latitude. This was less than what the French had agreed to a year before, and so the Belgians rejected the offer.[77] The immediate result of the breakdown of conversations was that the plan of an expedition was gotten out again. For some unknown reason Monteil was no longer considered as the leader. In December he was sent off to Berlin to negotiate an agreement which will be discussed presently. But in October M. François Deloncle, one of the most active colonialists in the French chamber, approached Colonel Chaillé-Long, an Anglo-American who had been associated with Gordon and who was known for his aversion to British rule in Egypt. Deloncle suggested that he take charge of an expedition to the Nile by way of the Ubanghi, but Chaillé-Long thought this an absurd plan. Fully a decade before he had suggested to the French prime minister, Jules Ferry, that the French should induce the Abyssinians to attack and defeat the Mahdi, after which the King of Kings could be proclaimed Sultan of the Sudan " Under the protectorate of France." He now reiterated his opinion in speaking with Deloncle, who was evidently impressed. At any

[76] Jules Cocheris: *La Situation Internationale de l'Égypte* (Paris, 1903), pp. 393-4, 425-6, whose very interesting account is borne out by Monteil himself, in his *Souvenirs Vécus* (Paris, 1924), pp. 65-70, and by Auguste Terrier, in Hanotaux: *Histoire des Colonies Françaises*, IV, pp. 507-8. See also *Bulletin . . . de l'Afrique Française*, July, December, 1893.

[77] Cocheris, op. cit., pp. 429-31; J. L. Deloncle: " La Question de Fachoda " (*Revue Politique et Parlementaire*, November, 1898, pp. 277-300), p. 284.

rate, a conference was arranged with the French prime minister, M. Casimir-Périer. On January 17, 1894 the whole situation was gone over, but the prime minister finally decided that the scheme was too daring and would, in all probability, lead to conflict with Italy.[78]

On his return from Berlin in March Monteil began to urge upon the government the necessity for action. The expedition, he pointed out in a letter to the colonial office of March 7, had been decided on originally in view of British operations in Uganda and in view of Britain's obvious efforts to secure control of the Nile from the south: " Once masters of the upper and middle basins of the Nile they could, at their pleasure, fertilize or sterilize the countries of the lower Nile by building a few barrages." Fashoda, he concluded, was important because it controlled the Nile, the Bahr-el-Ghazal and the Sobat Rivers, and because it offered a possible connexion with Abyssinia. The only obstacle to the whole scheme was the opposition of the Congo government, and that should be removed by negotiation.[79]

Due to Monteil's prodding, the French government did reopen discussions with the Congo government. MM. Hanotaux and Haussman, two very able negotiators, were sent to Brussels on April 16. For ten days arguments were advanced *pro* and *con,* without much progress being made. Leopold insisted that he could take nothing less than what had been offered him in 1892, and *that* the French were no longer in a position to offer in 1894. There was talk about arbitrating conflicting claims, but no agreement could be reached on the terms of reference. On April 25 the negotiations were suspended and the French representatives returned to Paris.[80]

That the British were by no means oblivious to what was projected on the side of the Congo State and France is shown clearly enough by the concluding chapters of Lugard's book, published in the autumn of 1893. He there pointed out that " as regards France, there is no obligation which prevents that nation from encroaching in the Sudan." Egypt, he held, had abandoned all her claims, and France had never recognized the agreements between Britain on the one hand and Germany and Italy on the other. The Van Kerckhoven expedition showed what the Belgians were after, and it was to be feared that France and the Congo had made an agreement leaving Lado to the former. " If France held the Nile Basin, she would undoubtedly require and obtain an outlet towards the Red Sea, where she already holds a footing at Obok." She might do this through an arrangement with Italy or with Abyssinia. The Russians were already active in Abyssinia, exploiting their supposed religious affinities.

---

[78] Charles Chaillé-Long: " England in Egypt and the Soudan " (*North American Review,* May, 1899, pp. 570–80), pp. 578–9; Idem: *My Life in Four Continents* (London, 1912), II, pp. 447 ff.

[79] Monteil, op. cit., p. 103.

[80] Cocheris, op. cit., pp. 394–6; Monteil, op. cit., pp. 103–9; Robert de Caix: *Fachoda* (Paris, 1899), chap. v; A. J. Wauters: *Histoire Politique du Congo Belge* (Brussels, 1911), chap. xiv; *Bulletin . . . de l'Afrique Française,* April, May, 1894; *Mouvement Géographique,* April 1, April 29, 1894.

France once firmly established upon the upper Nile might easily construct dams at the Lakes that would cut off Egypt's summer water supply.[81]

Lugard advanced these arguments in favor of annexation of Uganda, which, he claimed, would fulfil the requirement of gradual establishment which the Berlin Act demanded as a basis for a claim to territory, and would force France and the Congo State " to acknowledge our sole influence in the Nile Valley." The British government did, after long hesitation, proclaim a protectorate over Uganda, but this was not regarded as sufficient. The threat to the Nile Valley was too great.

In Abyssinia the French and Russians were indeed active. It was the French who, in 1890, had called Menelik's attention to the Italian interpretation of the Ucciali Treaty and had provoked his protest to the powers, a protest which England calmly ignored in the agreements with Italy of 1891. It was probably also French influence that led to Menelik's circular of April 10, 1891, in which he reiterated the claim to all territory as far as the right bank of the Nile and expressed the intention of extending his kingdom to the " ancient frontiers " of Abyssinia, " to Khartum and Lake Nyanza." To emphasize his purpose Menelik, in February 1893, granted to Alfred Ilg, a Swiss engineer who acted as his confidential adviser, a permit to organize a company and study the problem of a railway line from the French port of Jibuti through the provinces of Harrar, Entotto and Kaffa to the White Nile.[82]

It was obviously necessary for the British to reinforce the Abyssinian front. Ilg's associate, M. Chefneux, a notorious figure in Abyssinian affairs, succeeded in securing a promise of funds in Paris and on March 9, 1894 the definitive concession was granted by Menelik for a railroad to Harrar, this to be the first stretch of the line to Adis Abeba and the White Nile! Whether or not this was known to the British and whether it influenced their action cannot be shown, but the earlier agreements with Italy had demonstrated beyond the shadow of a doubt how fully the British realized that " Egypt must always, as a matter of self-defence, be in a position to dominate Abyssinia, either directly or indirectly." [83] Since February Kitchener, at that time in the Egyptian service, had been suggesting negotiations with the Italians to bring about co-operation against the concentration of dervish forces around Kassala. The Italians were eager to participate, hoping always that an agreement of this sort would lead to comradeship in arms and a closer entente with Britain.[84] On May 5, 1894 a new treaty was signed. It was concerned chiefly with the delimitation of the frontier between British Somaliland and the areas claimed by the Italians. But there was a " Note Officieuse Annexée au Protocol " which, despite the

[81] Frederick D. Lugard: *The Rise of our East African Empire* (London, 1893), II, pp. 566, 569, 571, 583–4.

[82] Conrad Keller: *Alfred Ilg* (Leipzig, 1918), chap. ix; Darcy: *France et Angleterre*, pp. 368–70; A. Martineau: " La Côte Française des Somalis," in Hanotaux: *Histoire des Colonies Françaises*, IV, p. 587.   [83] A. Silva White: *The Expansion of Egypt* (London, 1899), p. 29.

[84] *Die Grosse Politik*, VII, nos. 1988–91, 1996.

Anglo-French Treaty of 1888 relating to the province of Harrar, abandoned this province to Italy, while at the same time a " Déclaration Sécrète " allowed England to act there and regard it as part of her sphere until Italy was prepared to take it over. Harrar formed the chief approach to Abyssinia. The new arrangement with Italy would effectively block any attempt by France to establish control over this strategic point.[85]

In the west as in the east the British government began to take precautions to safeguard the Nile Valley from encroachment. No secret had been made of the French expedition entrusted to Monteil and it was perfectly well known in London that by the end of 1893 Decazes with the vanguard had reached Abiras, at the junction of the Welle and M'Bomu Rivers. Lugard and other writers were continually warning the government of the design of the French to connect their possessions in the west and in the east, of their activities in Abyssinia and of the danger of an advance into the Nile Basin from the French Congo and from Obock. The rivalry of the English and the French in Nigeria had already developed to a high pitch of tension. For these reasons the British cabinet opened negotiations with Berlin, and in November 1893 concluded a treaty delimiting the western frontier of Cameroon and allowing German territory to extend as far north as Lake Chad. The southern frontier of the Cameroon had been settled by a German-French agreement in 1885, but to the eastward the frontier was open and could be extended as far as the limits of the Congo State. If the Germans had chosen to expand eastward, as the English probably hoped that they would, they could have cut off the eventual extension of French territory to the Nile. But they could never interfere with the British claims, for Article IV read: " The influence of Germany . . . shall not extend eastwards beyond the basin of the River Shari, and Darfur, Kordofan and Bahr-el-Ghazal . . . shall be excluded from her influence, even if affluents of the Shari shall be found to lie within them." [86]

The French saw the implications of this arrangement and protested against it. Their agents and those of the Germans had for some time been in fierce competition in the hinterland of Cameroon. A settlement was highly desirable, and Monteil, among others, strongly urged it. The German government, thor-

---

[85] There has been much confusion with regard to this agreement. Neither the *Note Officieuse* nor the *Déclaration Sécrète* appeared in the text as published in *Accounts and Papers*, 1894, *Treaty Series*, No. 15, nor do they appear in the Italian Foreign Office's *Trattati, Convenzioni, etc. relativi all' Africa, 1825–1906* (Rome, 1906), no. 153. But the *Note Officieuse* slipped into the first edition of Hertslet's *Map of Africa by Treaty* (London, 1894), II, p. 669. It was omitted from the second and third editions (this point is discussed in Leonard Woolf: *Empire and Commerce in Africa* [New York, 1920], pp. 221 ff. where the *Note* is reprinted). The French secured the document at once in some way, and it was included in a set of papers submitted to the Chamber on May 29, 1894 (*Documents Parlementaires, 1894*, annexe 653, p. 852). The existence of the *Déclaration Sécrète* was also known (see Ernest Lavisse: " France et Angleterre " [*Revue de Paris*, February 1, 1899, pp. 453–82], especially pp. 469 ff.) and is fully borne out by the statement of the Italian foreign minister to the German ambassador on May 20, 1894 (*Die Grosse Politik*, VIII, no. 1991).

[86] *Accounts and Papers*, 1893, *Treaty Series*, No. 17.

oughly sobered by the Toulon demonstration, was anxious to conciliate France as well as Russia. So in December 1893 Monteil and Haussman were sent to Berlin to negotiate. The pourparlers were carried on most cordially and early in February an agreement was reached which was signed on March 15, 1894. It constituted a great victory for France, for in return for minor concessions the Germans accepted a delimitation of the eastern frontier of Cameroon which left the French free to expand in the north as far as Lake Chad and in the east as far as they chose to go. More than that: The Emperor William and Caprivi tried hard to utilize this opportunity to establish an entente between France and Germany. If we may believe Monteil's account, Caprivi went so far as to mention Alsace and Lorraine, the annexation of which he described as " une acte impolitique." Of course, he added, the German Emperor could not give up even a bit of what he had inherited, at least not without compensation. " You find us the means by which we can return to you the lost provinces," he concluded. At Paris, of course, these suggestions were regarded with more than ordinary suspicion. Still, so far as Africa was concerned the French had secured about all that they cared about.[87]

That the outcome of the German-French negotiations did not please the British need hardly be indicated. What they had turned over to the Germans in November was passed on by the Germans to the French in February. To add to the tribulations of the Liberal cabinet there were the pretensions of the Congo government. Anxious questions were being asked in the House regarding the Belgian advance, but the government itself knew nothing definite.[88] Colonel Colvile, commissioner in Uganda, at that time carrying on an unexplained war with Kabarega, King of Unyoro, was directed to send out one of his subordinates, Major Owen, with the title " Assistant-Commissioner for the Nile Valley " and with instructions " to ascertain the truth of rumours . . . that an expedition, dispatched by the Government of the Congo Free State, under the command of the late Captain Van Kerckhoven, has established itself within the British sphere of influence, as settled by the Anglo-German Agreement of 1890." Owen did, indeed, make a " dash for Wadelai." On February 4 he reached the post, found it abandoned, planted the British flag on both sides of the Nile, made treaties with the native chiefs and left a provisional garrison.[89]

But these facts were not known in Europe until May, and before that time the British government had some inkling of Leopold's negotiations with France. Action had to be taken, and it was therefore decided to settle with the less formidable party, the Congo State. Towards the end of March Rennell Rodd, for-

---

[87] Monteil, op. cit., pp. 71 ff., 95 ff.; see also Darcy, op. cit., p. 267; Paul Darmstaedter: *Geschichte der Aufteilung und Kolonisation Afrikas*, II (Berlin, 1920), pp. 107–8.

[88] Hansard: *Parliamentary Debates*, Series IV, vol. xxii, p. 1576; vol. xxiv, pp. 756, 1274.

[89] *Africa No. 7 (1895)*, nos. 17, 23; Sir Henry Colvile: *The Land of the Nile Springs* (London, 1895), chap. xv; James R. MacDonald: *Soldiering and Surveying in British East Africa* (London, 1897), chap. xx.

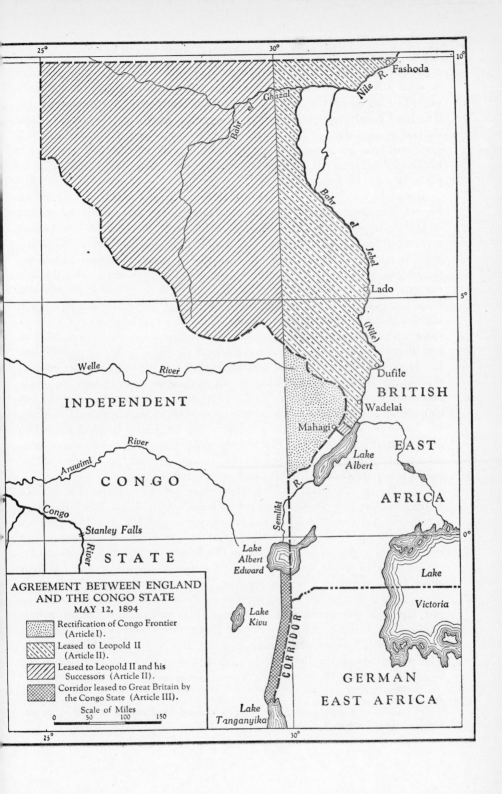

25°   30°   10°

                                                    R. Fashoda
                            Ghazal   Nile
                    Bahr el

                              Bahr
                                el
                                  Jebel

                                              Lado   5°

    Welle   River   (Nile)

INDEPENDENT   Dufile
                                              BRITISH
            River   Wadelai

        Aruwimi   Mahagi   EAST
                                    Lake
    C O N G O   Albert
Congo   AFRICA
    Stanley Falls   Semlikt
                              R.
    River
        S T A T E   Lake   0°
                        Albert
                        Edward   Lake

┌─────────────────────────────────┐
│ AGREEMENT BETWEEN ENGLAND   │   Victoria
│   AND THE CONGO STATE   │
│   MAY 12, 1894   │
│ ▦ Rectification of Congo Frontier│ Lake
│   (Article I).   │ Kivu
│ ▨ Leased to Leopold II   │
│   (Article II).   │ CORRIDOR
│ ▧ Leased to Leopold II and his │
│   Successors (Article II).   │ GERMAN
│ ▩ Corridor leased to Great Britain by│
│   the Congo State (Article III).│ EAST AFRICA
│   Scale of Miles   │
│ 0   50   100   150   │ Lake
└─────────────────────────────────┘ Tanganyika

25°   30°

merly British agent at Zanzibar, was hurried off to Brussels. To mask his mission he went first to Berlin. In a very short time he came to an agreement with Leopold. The essentials of the Treaty were evidently settled by April 12, for on that date Lord Kimberley telegraphed to the agent at Zanzibar: "Write to Colonel Colvile by mail that we have made a friendly arrangement under which Belgians will hold left bank of Nile from Lake Albert to Fashoda as leaseholders under Great Britain. If he comes in contact with them, he should maintain perfectly amicable relations." [90]

It will be seen from this document that the Treaty, which was signed on May 12, was simply a re-writing and acceptance of the MacKinnon Agreement of 1890, with some modifications. It gave Leopold just about all that he had ever hoped for from the British, and certainly more than the French were prepared to concede to him. There was evidently no trouble whatever in striking the bargain with Leopold for this very reason. The only hitch came through the opposition of one of the members of the British government, Sir William Harcourt, who was as uncompromising a Little Englander as Gladstone himself. He was not at first informed of the negotiations and perhaps did not know of them until the terms had been settled. Apparently it was then pointed out to him that the Treaty would relieve England of some of her responsibilities. But Harcourt was too clever to be taken in for long. When he saw the implications of the Treaty he protested loudly and made some effort to have the whole business rescinded. On April 23 Sir Percy Anderson, African expert of the foreign office, was sent to Brussels on special mission to see what could be done. We know nothing of the details, but it would seem that Leopold refused to draw back. It is worth noting that the wily old diplomat kept open the negotiations with the French until April 25, that is, until he could be sure that all obstacles to the treaty with England had been removed.[91]

The Treaty was signed on May 12, and was laid before parliament on May 21. Even before that time news of it had leaked out in Paris. When one stops to consider that the French had just been negotiating with Leopold themselves and that they had not given up all hope of an agreement one can understand the storm of indignation that broke in the French capital. Unfortunately for the French they found themselves at the moment in the midst of one of their all-too-frequent cabinet crises. Perhaps the Treaty was published at that moment in the hope that it would be lost sight of in Paris. Such was by no means the case, but there was an interlude of six days (May 22–27) during which a new ministry was being organized under M. Dupuy. In the interval the colonialist group of the Chamber was getting its stride and marshalling its arguments. The publication of the British-Italian agreement of May 5 added fuel to the

---

[90] *Africa No. 7 (1895)*, no. 5; Sir J. Rennell Rodd: *Social and Diplomatic Memories, 1884–1893* (London, 1922), pp. 345–8.

[91] Gardiner: *Life of Harcourt*, II, pp. 313 ff.; Marquess of Crewe: *Lord Rosebery*, p. 366; *Letters of Queen Victoria*, II, p. 396.

flames. Papers were laid upon the table of the Chamber setting forth France's earlier agreements with and claims against the Congo, rehearsing the Egyptian and Turkish rights to the Sudan, and exposing British " duplicity " in the matter of Harrar.[92]

On June 7 an important debate took place in the Chamber. M. Étienne, leader of the colonial group in the assembly, began with a long historical account of England's sharp practice in African affairs and violently condemned the British habit of making things hard for the French. Étienne was followed by another irreconcilable imperialist, M. François Deloncle. Deloncle brushed aside the details of the Congo Treaty and the British agreement with Italy and concentrated upon the essentials. British policy, he pointed out, had for years been devoted to the protection of the Nile Basin. Hence the long line of agreements which went back to 1890. Why was Britain so intent upon this policy? The reason was not far to seek. M. Deloncle entered upon a long discussion of the report of the French engineer, M. Prompt, an abstract of which he had inserted into the record. He referred to Prompt's plans for the construction of great dams at the mouth of the Sobat and at the Lakes. These, he said, were " grandiose projects, well worthy of French genius." But, he continued, M. Prompt was more frank than engineers should be. He had not concealed the fact that enough water could be stored in Lake Albert to wash out Egyptian civilization if it were released in time of high Nile. There was no doubt, said M. Deloncle, that since the Prompt revelations Britain had been more anxious than ever to secure control of the Nile Basin and hold Egypt at her mercy.

Deloncle's exposition makes it clear once again that the Prompt report was of the utmost importance in formulating French policy, and perhaps also British policy, as the speaker suggested. However that may be, M. Hanotaux, the new foreign minister, who had only six weeks before been negotiating in Brussels at a time when the Belgians had already closed with the British, had no hesitation about speaking out. He recalled the abortive efforts of the French to reach an understanding with King Leopold, he emphasized earlier agreements as to the boundaries of the Congo State, and finally he entered upon an extended discussion of the rights of Turkey and Egypt, which had been laid down as recently as 1892 in the *firman* of investiture of the new Khedive, a *firman* which had received the approval of all Europe. Britain was simply giving away territory to which she had no title. France could not allow sacred treaties to be torn to shreds in this way.[93]

---

[92] *Journal Officiel. Documents Parlementaires, Chambre, 1894.* Annexe no. 653. Séance du 28 mai, 1894.

[93] For the French objections see, in addition to Hanotaux' speech, the French memorandum of August 8, 1894 and the British reply, in *Egypt No. 2 (1898), Correspondence with the French Government respecting the Valley of the Upper Nile.* The detailed negotiations with France in 1894 have never been published. In *Accounts and Papers,* 1894, LVII the text of the Treaty is given (Treaty Series, No. 15), and the table of contents lists Command no. 7505: *Correspondence relating to the Independent State of the Congo.* But this last paper was never presented to parliament.

The words used by the French were bold and brave. In part, at least, their stiff attitude was due to the protests of the German government against the same treaty. By this there hangs an interesting and most unusual tale. The British government was, naturally, fully aware when it signed the Congo Treaty that the French would be enraged. For that reason efforts had been made, during the weeks preceding the signature of the document, to effect some sort of understanding with the Germans. The sad experience of the Franco-German Cameroon Treaty was forgotten and Lord Kimberley suggested the possibility of joint action to block the further advance of the French. But his soundings brought no result whatever. Had the English been prepared to fulfill the wishes of the German foreign office with regard to Samoa, something might have been accomplished, but since Kimberley made no move in that direction the Germans consoled themselves with the thought that the British were thoroughly worried by the spectre of a Franco-German entente in African affairs.[94]

It does not follow from this that the Germans would, *ipso facto,* have raised strong objections to the Congo Treaty. What gave them the most logical inducement was Article III of that Treaty itself. It will be recalled that under the terms of this article the Congo State was to lease to Great Britain a strip of territory sixteen miles wide, running from the southern shore of Lake Albert Edward to the northern tip of Lake Tanganyika, a distance of 188 miles. How this article came to be inserted in the Treaty is something of a mystery. The strip was wanted for a telegraph line and possibly, later, a railway. It would serve as the important connecting link in the famous Cape-to-Cairo scheme. By many it has been thought that Cecil Rhodes was responsible for the whole thing, and that was evidently the case. He was anxious to secure rights of way for his telegraph, and between 1892 and 1895 he negotiated with the German government in this matter on his own account. Nothing came of the discussions, evidently because the Germans feared that eventually they would be asked for permission to erect fortified posts or even cede territory. Rhodes, who had friendly connexions with the Rothschilds and with Rosebery, thereupon inspired the government to secure the necessary strip from the Congo.[95] Rosebery, forced to abandon the Bahr-el-Ghazal to Leopold, was glad to throw a sop to the Cape-to-Cairo enthusiasts. Sir Frederick Lugard might speak of the " ' Cape-to-Cairo ' claptrap " as " a mere sentimental jargon," but an authority like Sir Charles Dilke publicly regretted that in 1890 Salisbury had been unable to secure from the Germans the territory necessary for the " All-Red Route." [96] In any

---

[94] *Die Grosse Politik,* VIII, nos. 2022–5.

[95] The main source is Rhodes' interview with a representative of the *Kreuzzeitung,* and the reply of the *Kölnische Zeitung,* reported in the London *Times,* January 22, 1895, and in the *Bulletin du Comité de l'Afrique Française,* 1895, p. 94. See also Basil Williams: *Rhodes,* pp. 181, 200.

[96] Sir Frederick Lugard: " The New African Crisis with France and Germany " (*Blackwood's Magazine,* July, 1894, pp. 145–58); Sir Charles Dilke: " The Uganda Problem " (*Fortnightly Review,* February, 1893, pp. 145–61).

case it seems incredible that the British foreign office should have known nothing of Salisbury's abortive efforts in 1890 and of the unbending opposition of the Germans. Yet this was the argument advanced.[97]

Whatever the facts may have been, this Article III was to prove fatal to the British. The Germans were slow in finding their footing. When the agreement was published in the newspapers their minister at Brussels was instructed to secure from the Congo government a declaration that the leased strip should be not less than twenty kilometers from the frontier of German East Africa. To this arrangement Leopold offered no objection.[98] But on May 27 the German government lodged a vigorous protest against the whole of Article III. It was on the very same day that the French government made known its objections. As yet there was no concerted action between the two protesting powers, but we learn from a despatch to Hatzfeldt on May 28 that the German government thought it might use the Congo Treaty as a convenient stepping-stone to a further rapprochement with France, in the hope that such an entente might induce England to make concessions in Samoa.[99]

At Downing Street the German protests made but little impression. Opposition from the Germans was not expected and when it came was not taken too seriously. Under the circumstances the attitude of France, which had been fully expected, could be looked upon with equanimity. As M. Hanotaux pointed out to the Chamber on June 7, the British at first showed no inclination to enter upon a discussion. Their attitude was this: the territories leased to Leopold, to whomever they might belong, did not belong to the French and therefore the Paris government had no *locum standi*. As for the rights of Turkey and Egypt, a note annexed to the treaty stated that the contracting parties " do not ignore " these claims. When the effort was made in the house of commons to find out what the claims were that were not ignored, the undersecretary for foreign affairs evaded, but finally stated that whatever they were, they were reserved; a remark that caused natural amusement.

In any case, the British were not prepared to recognize a French right to interfere, and the Belgians too insisted that the Bahr-el-Ghazal had nothing to do with the Ubanghi-M'Bomu problem, which was the point at issue in earlier discussions.[100] We know nothing of the details of the Anglo-French negotiations in these days, since the Blue Book relating to them was never laid before parliament. But they were evidently acrimonious enough. M. Hanotaux has claimed that the British ambassador, Lord Dufferin, went so far as to speak of an ultimatum which, he said, he had in the pocket of his frock coat.[101]

[97] *Africa No. 5 (1894)*, nos. 3, 8; *Die Grosse Politik*, VIII, nos. 2042, 2043, 2047, 2071; *Das Staatsarchiv*, CVII, nos. 10581, 10590, 10591.

[98] *Die Grosse Politik*, VIII, nos. 2032, 2033; *Africa No. 5 (1894)*, no. 1 (enclosure) and no. 8.

[99] *Die Grosse Politik*, VIII, nos. 2034, 2035; the French protest has now been published in the *Deutsches Kolonialblatt*, XXVII, p. 148 (1916).

[100] See *Le Mouvement Géographique*, May 27, 1894.

[101] Gabriel Hanotaux: *Fachoda* (Paris, 1909), pp. 76–7.

But in the British cabinet this crisis in Anglo-French relations led to bitter criticism of the policy of the foreign office. Sir William Harcourt, who had been opposed to the Treaty from the start, objected resolutely to any provocation of France. Rosebery argued that the French were excited " because they had endeavoured to do the same thing and had failed," but this viewpoint was not convincing. To make matters worse the Germans were demanding, more and more insistently, the abrogation of Article III, and were bringing tremendous pressure to bear in Brussels. Their notes became so strong that Rosebery described them to the Austrian ambassador as " insufferable." At the same time the prime minister pointed out " that if Germany were going to side with France or appear to side with France in this and other African questions, we must consider our position as regards our general attitude in Europe, more particularly in the Mediterranean and the East." The German tone, he concluded, was appropriate for negotiation with Monaco, not with England. The Queen, indeed, considered writing the Emperor a remonstrance. But the ambassador at Berlin advised against it. The resentment of the Germans, he said, was natural. The Emperor was being carried along by a strong current of opinion. The strip in question would be very valuable if it were an integral part of British territory, but not if it were hampered by the obligations of the Congo State and its neutrality. He expressed strong anxiety lest Germany turn against England in the Egyptian question, " where the union of France and Germany would bring matters to a crisis." [102]

In the meanwhile Leopold was thoroughly frightened by the notes that rained in from Berlin. Finally he was authorized by the British foreign office to ask for the suppression of the objectionable third article, which was done by a declaration of June 22. Rosebery's idea was that the Germans, once satisfied, would be only too glad to co-operate in frustrating the action of France. In a memorandum of June 17 he stressed the fact

> " that the Nile is Egypt and Egypt is the Nile, and that as the occupying power our first interest was to obtain a recognition of this principle by the Great Powers. A conference should be proposed in which with the support of Germany we should get our sphere of influence defined. A protocol to be added that whenever Egypt is in a position to reoccupy it we should with pleasure hand over to her that part which is at present under our control."

Thus the real object of the Anglo-Congo Treaty would be attained.[108]

This was naive, to say the least. The co-operation between France and Germany was much more important than Rosebery realized. Some historians have spoken of it as a joint intervention, and others have accused the Germans of breaking down the entente and deserting France when once the abrogation of

[102] *Letters of Queen Victoria*, II, pp. 404–7; Gardiner: *Life of Harcourt*, II, pp. 317–9. *Die Grosse Politik*, VIII, nos. 2038–62.
[108] Crewe: *Lord Rosebery*, p. 367.

Article III was effected.[104] This accusation is not just. The Franco-German co-operation was well-planned and effective; what happened was this. On June 13 the German foreign minister spoke to the French ambassador of the efforts of the British to play off their two opponents against each other, and of the desirability of counter-acting this policy. He pointed out that French and German interests were not identical, but that the two countries did have a common interest in the central African situation as regulated by the treaties. The French government took up this suggestion and attempted to broaden the basis of co-operation. It was suggested that the two powers should adhere to a definite arrangement until they were prepared to recognize that they had each secured complete satisfaction. Marschall pointed out that this went too far. He proposed that each party should keep the other posted and that, before accepting a settlement, each should inform the other of its content and its forthcoming acceptance. This procedure was actually followed, and there is no evidence in the contemporary documents that the French government resented German action in accepting the abrogation of Article III. On the contrary, M. Hanotaux declared himself well satisfied and expressed the hope that relations between the two nations would become better and better.[105]

The abrogation still left the matter of French claims open. With the British the French government could make little headway, but Leopold was in a more exposed situation. The Paris government was determined to stop the Belgian advance, cost what it might. It was decided to send out Monteil immediately to drive the Belgians out of the territory north of latitude 4 and to push on to the Nile. Another expedition, coming from Abyssinia, was to bring down provisions from the direction of the Sobat. On June 9 the Chamber voted a credit of 1,800,000 francs " for the defence of French interests in Africa." Monteil was named commissioner for the upper Ubanghi and all other agents were placed under his command. On July 16 he set out from Marseilles.[106]

While these preparations were going forward every effort was made to induce Leopold to yield. It has been said, by a British diplomat, that the French government went so far as to intimate to Leopold that persistence in his policy might cost him his throne.[107] This is probably an exaggeration, but it is the fact that Leopold was " constrained and forced " into the agreement which he signed with the French on August 14. These are the very words used in a Belgian memorandum of later date, where there is much complaint that the British left the King in the lurch.[108] The agreement was, in fact, a compromise. Leo-

---

[104] Bourgeois and Pagès: *Les Origines et les Responsabilités de la Grande Guerre*, pp. 252–5; André Mévil: *De la Paix de Francfort à la Conférence d'Algéciras* (Paris, 1909), pp. 6–7.

[105] *Die Grosse Politik*, VIII, nos. 2049, 2061, 2069; Bourgeois and Pagès, op. cit., pp. 252–4; Manfred Sapp: *Deutsch-Französische Annäherungsversuche und ihr Scheitern, in den Jahren 1890–1898* (Weida, 1929), pp. 51–60.

[106] *Bulletin du Comité de l'Afrique Française*, July, August, 1894; Cocheris, op. cit., p. 410; Terrier, op. cit., pp. 509–10; Monteil, op. cit., pp. 111–4.

[107] Sir Arthur H. Hardinge: *A Diplomatist in the East* (London, 1928), p. 127.

[108] Théophile Simar: "Léopold II et le Soudan " (*Congo*, V, pp. 506–28, November, 1924).

pold was given the frontier of the M'Bomu and the Nile-Congo watershed eastward to 30° east longitude. On the other hand he bound himself " to renounce all occupation and to exercise in the future no political influence west or north of a line thus determined: Longitude 30° East of Greenwich, starting from its intersection of the watershed of the Congo and Nile basins, up to a point where it meets the parallel 5° 30', and then along that parallel to the Nile." In other words, he gave up the idea of occupying the Bahr-el-Ghazal region. The French road to the Nile remained open. On the other hand, France had left the Congo State the lease of the Lado area, had recognized her right to extend her frontiers, and had thus abandoned part of what was supposedly Egyptian territory, all of which was in contradiction to the French stand thus far.[109]

The British raised no objection to the settlement between France and the Congo. Rosebery felt that England could not oblige Leopold to occupy the territory leased to him. Besides, the King secured a better frontier than he could have hoped for. As the British prime minister looked back over the affair, he had to admit that the Congo Treaty had had a history that was neither auspicious nor fortunate. But Britain had at least obtained a recognition of her sphere of influence by the Congo State and had gotten rid of the MacKinnon Treaty.[110]

This was all true enough, but on the other side was the failure to secure the strip to complete the " All-Red Route " and the even more serious failure to block the advance of the French. Sir Thomas Barclay and many other writers have condemned the whole agreement as " one of the wildest pieces of diplomatic jugglery on record." [111] The Conservatives never ceased to remind Rosebery of his clumsy tactics. The analogy with the ill-fated treaty with Portugal in 1884 was too close to be missed. In both cases the carelessness of a Liberal government had led to nothing but closer co-operation between France and Germany. It is almost incredible that in 1894 the government should have been ignorant of what transpired in 1890. In any event Germany should have been consulted before the agreement was made. Failure to do so simply convinced the Emperor and his advisers that Rosebery was unfriendly to Germany, that he would not make concessions in colonial matters, and that he could be scared if the Germans joined the French in opposition to the British. The Germans at bottom had no intention of cutting the wire to London, but the whole episode stimulated the growth of distrust, resentment and suspicion. The Italian and Austrian governments were much exercised by these developments, but nothing they could do helped much to improve matters. The Emperor was half-hearted, and the British were cool. They were convinced that the Germans had strength-

---

109 Cocheris, op. cit., pp. 411 ff.; Arthur B. Keith: *The Belgian Congo and the Berlin Act* (Oxford, 1919), pp. 106 ff.

110 *Letters of Queen Victoria*, II, pp. 419–20.

111 Sir Thomas Barclay: *Thirty Years: Anglo-French Reminiscences* (Boston, 1914), p. 155.

ened the French and that at Cairo, Constantinople, Madrid, wherever the English and French were struggling for mastery, the Germans were co-operating with the opponents of Britain.[112] The first phase of the epic struggle for the Nile came to an end, but it left deep marks on the European alignment.

BIBLIOGRAPHICAL NOTE

DOCUMENTARY SOURCES

Accounts and Papers. 1892, vol. LVI. *Africa No. 2 (1892): Papers respecting Proposed Railway from Mombasa to Lake Victoria Nyanza; Africa No. 4 (1892): Papers relating to the Mombasa Railway Survey.* 1893, vol. LXII: *Africa No. 1 (1893): Further Papers relating to Uganda; Africa No. 2 (1893): Further Papers relating to Uganda; Africa No. 8 (1893): Further Papers relating to Uganda.* 1894, vol. LVII: *Africa No. 2 (1894): Reports relating to Uganda by Sir Gerald Portal.* 1895, vol. LXXI: *Africa No. 4 (1895): Correspondence respecting the retirement of the Imperial British East Africa Company; Africa No. 7 (1895): Papers relating to Uganda. Treaty Series,* 1894, No. 15: *Agreement between Great Britain and His Majesty King Leopold II, Sovereign of the Independent State of the Congo, etc. Africa No. 5 (1894): Further Papers relating to the Agreement between Great Britain and His Majesty the King of the Belgians. Treaty Series,* 1894, No. 20: *Declaration as to the Withdrawal of Article III of the Agreement of May 12, 1894.*

HERTSLET, SIR EDWARD: *Map of Africa by Treaty.* Second edition, London, 1896. This semi-official publication contains most of the agreements and exchanges of notes.

Die Grosse Politik der Europäischen Kabinette, 1871–1914. Vol. VIII, chap. liv: Samoa and the Congo question; vol. IX, chap. lix: German-French relations.

Deutsches Kolonialblatt. Vol. XXVII, no. 10/11, June 1, 1916, pp. 135–61: " Aus den Archiven des Belgischen Kolonialministeriums, Theil iii: Das Lado und Bahr-el-Ghazal Pachtgebiet des Kongostaates." A most valuable collection of materials taken by the Germans from the Brussels archives during the war.

MEMOIRS, AUTOBIOGRAPHIES, BIOGRAPHIES, AND LETTERS

GARDINER, A. G.: *The Life of Sir William Harcourt.* Two volumes. London, 1923. One of the few biographies that throw much light on the foreign policy of the Rosebery administration. Contains a wealth of material on the subject of this chapter.

CECIL, LADY GWENDOLEN: *The Life of Lord Salisbury.* Volume IV. London, 1931. This volume of the authoritative biography of Lord Salisbury reaches only to the end of his administration in 1892, but contains much new material on his African policy.

---

[112] *Die Grosse Politik,* VIII, nos. 1765–7, 2063; IX, nos. 2157–9; Deym to Kálnoky, July 12, November 1, November 30, December 13, 1894 (unpublished).

CREWE, MARQUESS OF: *Lord Rosebery*. New York, 1931. The standard life, based upon Rosebery's papers. On the whole adds very little and cannot be compared in importance with Gardiner's *Harcourt*.

Letters of Queen Victoria. Series III, volume II. New York, 1931. A source of prime value, containing a number of letters of great interest bearing on the subject of this chapter.

MONTEIL, P. L.: *Souvenirs Vécus. Quelques Feuillets de l'Histoire Coloniale*. Paris, 1924. The reminiscences of one of the leading French explorers and political agents. Contains much of importance on the intimate side of French policy.

BOULGER, DEMETRIUS: *The Reign of Leopold II*. Two volumes. London, 1925. A detailed and well-informed apology, dealing in detail with African questions.

LICTERVELDE, COMTE LOUIS DE: *Leopold of the Belgians*. New York, 1929. The best general biography of the King.

LIEBRECHTS, LIEUTENANT-COLONEL: *Léopold II, Fondateur d'Empire*. Brussels, 1932. An important account of Leopold's African policy, by one of his close associates.

DAYE, PIERRE: *Léopold II*. Paris, 1934. The latest biography, based in parts on the King's own papers. Unfortunately the book is not documented.

SCHWEITZER, GEORG: *Emin Pasha*. Berlin, 1898. The standard biography, based upon Emin's diaries, at that time still unpublished.

Die Tagebücher von Dr. Emin Pascha. Edited by Franz Stuhlmann. Six volumes. Berlin, 1917–1927. An all-important source for the history of Emin's career, and for his side of the relief expedition.

PETERS, CARL: *Die Gründing von Deutsch-Ostafrika*. Berlin, 1906. The most important account of German activities in the Uganda region.

STANLEY, HENRY M.: *Autobiography*. Boston, 1909. An interesting volume, though incomplete and not very revealing. An authoritative life of Stanley is still lacking.

SPECIAL STUDIES

ALLEN, BERNARD M.: *Gordon and the Sudan*. London, 1931. The latest and best history of Gordon's career in the Sudan, based in part on unpublished papers and materials in the British Record Office.

WOOLF, LEONARD: *Empire and Commerce in Africa*. New York, 1920. Strongly anti-imperialist, but unusually well-informed, critical and attractively written. One of the best books on the subject.

KELTIE, J. SCOTT: *The Partition of Africa*. Second edition. London, 1895. Though now in many respects out of date, this detailed study is still of interest.

LUGARD, FREDERICK D.: *The Rise of our East African Empire*. Two volumes. London, 1893. One of the most important accounts of the Ugandan situation, by the agent of the British East Africa Company.

McDermott, P. L.: *British East Africa*. Second edition. London, 1895. An authoritative presentation of the British East Africa Company's case. The author was secretary of the company, and uses much unpublished material.

Johnston, Sir Harry H.: *The Uganda Protectorate*. Two volumes. New York, 1902. Next to Lugard's book, this is the most illuminating study of the Uganda problem.

White, Arthur Silva: *The Expansion of Egypt*. London, 1899. Written by a well-informed publicist, this book brings together much useful material on the Egyptian and Sudan questions.

Cocheris, Jules: *La Situation Internationale de l'Égypte et du Sudan*. Paris, 1903. By all odds one of the most careful and thorough studies of the Egyptian question in the late nineteenth century. The author clearly received much information from some of the chief actors.

Terrier, Auguste: " La Marche vers le Nord-Est et la Question du Haut-Nil." Chapter vi of volume IV of G. Hanotaux: *Histoire des Colonies Françaises*. Paris, 1931. Written by a leading French authority on colonial history. Brief but reliable.

Darcy, Jean: *France et Angleterre. Cents Années de Rivalité Coloniale*. Paris, 1904. One of the best accounts from the French side, though not as well-informed or as well balanced as Cocheris.

Stanley, Henry M.: *In Darkest Africa*. Two volumes. New York, 1890. This famous narrative is still of value for political matters, if read in connexion with other material.

Peters, Carl: *Die Deutsche Emin-Pascha Expedition*. Munich, 1891. The German counterpart of the preceding. Requires supplementing by Peters' later account mentioned above.

Jantzen, Günther: *Ostafrika in der Deutsch-Englischen Politik, 1884–1890*. Hamburg, 1934. Goes over the Anglo-German relationship in detail, making use of some unpublished material, especially the papers of the German East African Association.

Bourne, H. R. Fox: *The Other Side of the Emin Pasha Relief Expedition*. London, 1891. A competent and valuable account of the side that does not appear in Stanley's narrative.

Gregory, J. W.: *The Foundation of British East Africa*. London, 1901. The work of an English geographer, this book is still one of the best systematic accounts of the subject.

Wauters, A. J.: *Souvenirs de Fashoda et de l'Expédition Dhanis*. Brussels, 1910. The work of the well-informed editor of the *Mouvement Géographique*. The most important " inside " account from the Belgian side.

—: *Histoire Politique du Congo Belge*. Brussels, 1911. Adds nothing to what is contained in the preceding title.

Keith, Arthur B.: *The Belgian Congo and the Berlin Act*. Oxford, 1919. The best general account in English, but conventional in approach and adducing little new information.

Masoin, Fritz: *Histoire de l'État Indépendant du Congo.* Two volumes. Namur, 1913. A detailed and on the whole well-informed study, but strongly biassed.

Deherain, Henri: " La Succession de l'Égypte dans la Province Equatoriale." (*Revue des Deux Mondes,* May 15, 1894, pp. 312–47). One of the best systematic reviews of the developments between 1890 and 1894, with special reference to the French policy of supporting the Turkish-Egyptian claims.

Simar, Théophile: " Léopold II et le Soudan." (*Congo,* V, November, 1924, pp. 506–28). A study of prime importance, by an expert in the field of Congo history. Based upon unpublished papers.

Hanotaux, Gabriel: *Fachoda.* Paris, 1909. Written by one of the French diplomats closely involved in African questions, but more important for the later period.

Lavisse, Ernest: " France et Angleterre." (*Revue de Paris,* February 1, 1899, pp. 453–82). A systematic review of the Anglo-French antagonism in Africa, with detailed treatment of the Harrar dispute and the treaties with Italy.

THE NILE PROBLEM

Ross, Justin C.: " Irrigation and Agriculture in Egypt." (*Scottish Geographical Magazine,* IX, April, 1893, pp. 169–93). The author was for some time inspector-general of irrigation in Egypt. His account of the system and his proposals for increasing the supply are of great interest.

Prompt, V.: *Le Soudan Nilotique.* Cairo, 1893. The crucial report on the problem of water storage. Reprinted from the Proceedings of the Egyptian Institute.

Scott-Moncrieff, Sir Colin: " The Nile." (*Proceedings of the Royal Institute of Great Britain,* XIV, pp. 405–18, January 25, 1895). Next to the Prompt report this is probably the best general study of the Nile problem as it was in the middle of the 1890's.

Egypt No. 2 (1904): Report of Sir William Garstin upon the Basin of the Upper Nile. The final report of a well-known British engineer. Absolutely essential for a study of the Nile problem since Fashoda, but also full of interesting information on the country and earlier developments.

Garstin, Sir William: " Fifty Years of Nile Exploration." (*Geographical Journal,* February, 1909, pp. 117–47). A masterly survey of geographical and hydrographical problems. The author pays a very high tribute to Sir Samuel Baker.

MacDonald, Sir Murdoch: *Nile Control.* Cairo, 1920. A technical study, which contains an admirable survey of the history of the reservoir projects and of recent plans for a dam at Lake Albert.

Hurst, H. E.: " Progress in the Study of Hydrology of the Nile in the Last Twenty Years." (*Geographical Journal,* November, 1927, pp. 440–64). Another technical study, very useful in the matter of Egyptian irrigation problems.

Hurst, H. E. and Phillips, P.: *The Nile Basin.* Two volumes. Cairo, 1931. The latest and finest descriptive work, lavishly illustrated with airplane photographs. Contains an immense amount of statistical material.

LITERATURE SINCE 1935

CIASCA, RAFFAELE: *Storia coloniale dell'Italia contemporanea.* Second edition. Milan, 1940. 775 pp. This is perhaps the best general history of Italian colonial policy.

DATTA DE ALBERTIS, GIULIA: *La formazione dell'impero coloniale italiano.* Volume I. Milan, 1938. 642 pp. The first part of an extremely detailed account.

SERTOLIS SALIS, RENZO: *Storia e politica coloniale italiana, 1869–1935.* Second edition. Messina, 1938. 346 pp. A competent general narrative.

SOMMARUGA, RODOLFO: *Le potenze europee in Africa dal Congresso di Berlino a Versailles.* Milan, 1938. 400 pp. A general review of the partition of Africa.

GIGLIO, VITTORIO, and RAVENNI, ANGELO: *Le guerre coloniali d'Italia.* Second edition. Milan, 1942. 631 pp. Contains a solid account of the background of the first Ethiopian War.

TRUFFI, RICCARDO: "La politica africana di Francesco Crispi durante il suo primo ministero, 1887–1890" (*Gerarchia,* XVIII, 1937, pp. 166–173). An apologetic account, dealing chiefly with the agreements of 1889 and 1891 with Britain.

MAGINI, MANLIO: *Variazione territoriali nell'A.O. dal 1880 al 1938.* Florence, 1939. 109 pp. A useful analysis, with maps, of the territorial changes effected by the many agreements concerning East Africa.

ANCHIERI, ETTORE: *Storia della politica inglese nel Sudan, 1882–1938.* Milan, 1939. 221 pp. A competent, popular survey, dealing largely with the period 1882–1899.

DIETRICH, RICHARD: "England und Italien, 1887–1902; ein Beitrag zur Vorgeschichte des Tripoliskrieges" (*Historische Vierteljahrschrift,* XXIX, May, 1935, pp. 768–800). Deals largely with the Italian claims in Africa, using the British documents and biographies. An excellent monograph.

SALATA, FRANCESCO: "Gibuti: documentazione diplomatica" (*Storia e politica internazionale,* 1939, pp. 15–78).

—: *Il nodo di Gibuti. Storia diplomatica su documenti inediti.* Milan, 1939. 342 pp. These two studies, based on extensive use of unpublished Italian records, review the entire East African problem in the 1890's, with reference to Italian relations with Britain and France.

ZAGHI, CARLO: "La conferenza di Napoli tra l'Italia e l'Inghilterra e la questione di Cassala" (*Rassegna di politica internazionale,* III, 1936, pp. 661–669).

—: "La missione Antonelli in Etiopia e il fallimento della politica scioana" (*Rassegna di politica internazionale,* III, 1936, pp. 473–485).

—: "I protocolli italo-britannici del 1891 e la guerra contro i Dervisci" (*Rassegna di politica internazionale,* IV, 1937, pp. 936–947).

—: " Le trattative coloniali italo-francesi del 1891 e il rinnovamento della Triplice " (*Rassegna di politica internazionale,* V, 1938, pp. 46–54).

—: " L'Italia e l'Etiopia nel 1891 in alcuni dispacci inediti dello Scarfoglio al ministro degli esteri Di Rudini " (*Storia e politica internazionale,* 1939 [2], pp. 507–531).

—: " Il problema di Cassala e l'Italia. Le trattative italo-britanniche del 1890 alla luce del carteggio Dal Verme-Crispi " (*Storia e politica internazionale,* 1940 [2], pp. 412–465).

—: " Zeila e la mancata occupazione dell'Harar " (*Storia e politica internazionale,* 1941 [1], pp. 67–137). All these articles, written by a leading Italian authority, are of importance for the subject, inasmuch as they are based on unpublished Italian records as well as upon a deep knowledge of all the other literature.

BRUHAT, J.: " Léopold II " (in *Les politiques d'expansion impérialiste,* Paris, 1949, pp. 73–122). An excellent, concise review of Leopold's policies, based on all recent materials.

HORNIK, M. P.: " The Anglo-Belgian Agreement of 12 May, 1894 " (*English Historical Review,* LVII, April, 1942, pp. 227–244). An interesting review of the whole problem, making use of unpublished Austrian archive materials.

VERGNIOL, CAMILLE: " Les origines de la mission Marchand " (*Revue de France,* August 1, 1936, pp. 420–434; August 15, 1936, pp. 630–645; September 1, 1936, pp. 112–129). One of the best studies of the Upper Nile problem. Covers the subject very thoroughly from 1885 to 1895.

STENGERS, JEAN: " La première tentative de reprise du Congo par la Belgique " (*Bulletin de la Société Royale Belge de Géographie,* LXIII, 1949, pp. 1–80). Based on Belgian and British archive material, this is a very important contribution to the study of the lease of 1894 and the entire complex of problems centering on the Upper Nile.

CHAVANNES, CHARLES DE: *Le Congo Français.* Paris, 1937. 406 pp. The memoirs of De Brazza's secretary; an important contribution covering the years 1886–1894.

CHEESMAN, R. E.: *Lake Tana and the Blue Nile.* London, 1936. 400 pp. A record of exploration, by a former British consul in the area.

DAINELLI, GIOTTO: *La regione del Lago Tana.* Milan, 1939. 117 pp. A lavishly illustrated, descriptive work.

WADDELL, W. G.: " On the Nile Rising " (*Bulletin of the Faculty of Arts of the University of Egypt,* IV, May, 1936, pp. 22–38). Discusses the knowledge of the ancients regarding the Nile flood.

V

The Armenian Question and the Near Eastern Triplice

⌇

THE UNFORTUNATE CONGO TREATY, LIKE THE AGREEMENT WITH POR-
tugal in 1884, left the London government somewhat discredited and
generally isolated in Europe. Rosebery, for one, did not relish this position. He was probably anxious to maintain the connexion with the Triple
Alliance despite all that had happened. During the autumn of 1894 he embarked
upon a policy which, to all appearances, was designed to frighten the Germans
into renewed friendship with England. An effective method of introducing this
policy was to make advances to the Dual Alliance. As a first step the British
abstained from antagonizing the French in Moroccan affairs, much to the despair of the Italians.[1] At the same time discussions were begun in Paris looking
toward the settlement of the difficult question of the upper Nile. To these
negotiations it will be necessary to return later. Suffice it to say that the transaction does not seem to have been very seriously meant on the part of the
British, which would indicate that Rosebery was more intent upon worrying
the Germans than in settling with the French.[2]

Since it was the new Dual Alliance which threatened the position of England, it was natural that the advances toward France should be supplemented
by efforts to pave the way for an understanding with Russia. The first steps in
this direction were taken in connexion with the difficulties between China
and Japan, which arose from the Korean question. These will have to be analyzed in greater detail later, but it may be said here that the Russians regarded
the British policy with suspicion. Still, the London government was not discouraged. The negotiations concerning the Pamirs were taken up with renewed
vigor, and finally led to the agreement of November 1894, in which almost all
the Russian demands were met. Just at this time death overtook Tsar Alexander. His last illness gave the Prince of Wales a golden opportunity to do
what he could in aid of the government policy. He hurried to Russia and stayed
there until after the funeral ceremonies. During these weeks he threw his whole
influence into the scales in favor of an entente. When he returned to England
early in December, the London *Times* referred to his visit as the mission of an

---

[1] *Die Grosse Politik*, VIII, nos. 1958 ff.   [2] Gardiner: *Life of Harcourt*, II, pp. 321-2.

ambassador extraordinary, which might be of considerable importance.[3] No secret was made of the hopes of the English. In fact Lord Rosebery, in a most remarkable speech at the Lord Mayor's banquet on November 9, seemingly laid his cards on the table. He pointed out that in the Far Eastern question England and Russia had proceeded hand in hand, and that the relations between the two countries had never been " more hearty." The recent Pamir settlement, he said, had removed almost the last obstacle to friendly co-operation. At the same time he recalled the Anglo-French friendship of Crimean War days, and expressed the hope that in the future the two nations would continue to compete, not in war, but in the works of peace.

While this flirtation was going on, the Germans, for whose benefit the whole thing was staged, were but little moved. It is quite true that so eminent a diplomat as Count Hatzfeldt viewed the situation with some misgiving, and feared that the English might make some concessions to the Russians in the Straits question if the St. Petersburg government would agree not to support the French in the Mediterranean. But the German foreign minister looked upon the whole business as a hoax, intended to intimidate Germany. He refused to believe in the possibility of an Anglo-Russian combination, and insisted on pursuing a policy of watchful waiting.[4]

There the matter would probably have rested had it not been for the interference of Kálnoky. Despite the fact that the Austrian ambassador at London reported quite correctly regarding the purposes of the British government, and transmitted to Vienna the admission of Kimberley and Rosebery that the whole policy was meant as a warning to Germany, Kálnoky scented the danger of a serious estrangement between England and Germany. He called the attention of the German ambassador to the Italian need of English friendship. In very sharp terms he castigated Germany's " systematic provocation " of England and demanded what the reason for it was. The ambassador insisted that Emperor William, though he was offended with England, had no intention of changing his policy. At the same time the English government, no doubt inspired by Kálnoky, notified the Germans that the British cabinet had no thought of deserting the Triple Alliance or of otherwise altering its course. The ambassador at Berlin carried out these instructions on December 14, and on this occasion a general peace was patched up between the two governments.[5]

It may be objected that Rosebery, in his efforts to bring about a rapprochement with France and Russia, was successful at least in so far as he established a course of common action between the three powers in the Armenian question. Some writers, indeed, go so far as to speak of an Armenian Triplice, and there was, for a moment, some prospect that the Armenian question might be made

---

[3] London *Times*, December 6, 1894; Sir Sidney Lee: *Edward VII*, I, pp. 689 ff.

[4] *Die Grosse Politik*, IX, nos. 2161–8.

[5] Deym to Kálnoky, November 15, 21, 30, 1894; Kálnoky to Szögyény, November 30; Kálnoky to Deym, December 4; Szögyény to Kálnoky, December 8, 15, 17, 22, 1894 (unpublished).

a stepping-stone to a broader entente.[6] But the German foreign minister, Marschall, once again declared his conviction that a combination of these three states was not to be anticipated, since it was out of the question that England should make the necessary concessions to both France and Russia.[7]

Marschall was right. The Armenian Triplice was of no permanent importance, and was, in actual fact, not so much a grouping designed for the attainment of a common aim as a combination in which two of the partners regarded it as their chief task to hold back the third. In order to make this perfectly clear it will be necessary to say something of the Armenian question and the problems which arose from the famous Sassun massacres of the autumn of 1894.

The Armenians were inhabiting the high mountainous areas and elevated plateaus of northeastern Asia Minor when Xenophon passed through those regions with his Ten Thousand. They had probably been there a long time even then. During the course of their checkered history they at times played a prominent rôle in world affairs, but generally they were under the rule of some great empire. In the 19th century they were divided between the Ottoman, Russian and Persian states, by far the greater number being under the rule of the Sultan. Though anything like reliable statistical matter is lacking, the best estimates of the later 19th century put the Armenian population of the Ottoman Empire at something like a million. There may have been as many as a million and a half, but in any event the Armenians were not, like the Greeks and Bulgarians, fairly concentrated in a certain area. In no vilayet (province) of Turkey were they in a majority in 1890, not even in the six provinces usually spoken of as *Armenia*.[8]

In the six vilayets of Greater Armenia (Erzerum, Bitlis, Van, Diarbekr, Mamuret and Sivas) the Armenian population was largely a peasant population living interspersed with the nomadic Kurdish tribesmen. Many writers have believed that at bottom Armenians and Kurds all belonged to the same race, and have pointed out that there are still Armenian herdsmen, just as there are still Kurdish peasants. However that may be, the symbiosis of settled agriculturalist and nomadic tribesman is a common phenomenon in that part of the world and has existed for many centuries. From the very nature of the case the nomad preys upon his more helpless neighbor, there is raiding and rapine and not infrequently massacre. But in the case of the Armenians the situation was aggravated by the religious difference. The Kurds were, at least officially, Moslems, who looked down upon the Christians and felt perfectly justified in ex-

---

[6] *Die Grosse Politik*, IX, no. 2188.   [7] Ibid., no. 2201.

[8] The best figures on population are those of L. Selenoy and N. von Seidlitz: " Die Verbreitung der Armenier in der Asiatischen Türkei und in Transkaukasien " (*Petermanns Geographische Mitteilungen*, XLII, 1896, pp. 1–9), which corrected the researches of Vital Cuinet: *La Turquie d'Asie* (Paris, 1891–1894). See further the detailed estimates in *Turkey No. 1 (1890–1891)*, no. 44; H. F. B. Lynch: " The Armenian Question " (*Contemporary Review*, September, 1894, pp. 433–56); Johannes Lepsius: *Armenia and Europe* (London, 1897), pp. 1 ff.; Marcel Léart: *La Question Arménienne à la Lumière des Documents* (Paris, 1913), p. 10.

ploiting them. They regarded them " as harmless, serviceable, comfortable in-fidels, whom one could not expect to meet in Heaven, but who were very useful here below." [9] The Assyrian Christians, to be sure, were able to hold their own against the Kurds, and the same was true of some Armenians, like those in the Zeitun and Sassun areas. But for the most part the Armenians did not try to fight back. One traveller after another was impressed with their cowardice and servility. To one of them an Armenian remarked: " We are not like Bulgars and other Christians. When the Turk robs us, we see nothing; when he thrashes us, we say nothing; and so we have peace." [10] The peace was, to be sure, a most precarious one, punctuated by all too frequent plunderings and massacres. So it had been for thousands of years and so it continued. The government was perfectly helpless. Nothing less than an army could have pacified the country. Under the circumstances the Porte got along as best it could with the powerful Kurdish chiefs and joined with them in the victimization of the peasantry. The travel literature of the later 19th century is full of complaints of the excesses of Kurds and government officials. Even those visitors who had no use whatever for the Armenians as a people were quite ready to testify to the horrors of their lot.[11]

From the angle of political and national development the large Armenian colonies in Constantinople, in Brussa, Smyrna and other cities of the west were much more important than the suffering peasantry in the mountain fastnesses of eastern Anatolia. For hundreds of years the Armenians had shown a strong tendency to emigrate to the larger cities, where they engaged in industry, trade, banking and government work. Fully half the Armenians in Turkey lived out-side the six vilayets. The Constantinople colony alone was said to number 150,-000, though this is probably an exaggeration. Like the Greek Orthodox Church, the Armenian Gregorian Church had been given practical self-government by Mohammed the Conqueror, so that the Patriarch of Constantinople was an im-portant and powerful official. In actual practice, however, he was, in the early 19th century, merely the agent of the wealthy Armenian officials and bankers of the capital (the *Amira*), who formed a sort of aristocracy, cringing before their Turkish masters but taking a high hand in all questions concerning the Armenian Church and the Armenian people.[12]

9 Odysseus (Sir Charles N. Eliot): *Turkey in Europe* (London, 1900), p. 442.

10 Henry C. Barkley: *A Ride through Asia Minor and Armenia* (London, 1891), p. 87.

11 Among many might be mentioned James Bryce: *Transcaucasia and Ararat* (London, 1877), p. 329; Frederick Milligen: *Wild Life among the Koords* (London, 1870), pp. 156–9; Humphrey Sandwith: " How the Turks Rule Armenia " (*Nineteenth Century,* February, 1878, pp. 314–29); Henry F. Tozer: *Turkish Armenia and Eastern Asia Minor* (London, 1881), pp. 232, 285, 415; J. Carlile McCoan: *Our New Protectorate* (London, 1879), pp. 137 ff.; Comte de Cholet: *Arménie, Kurdistan et Mésopotamie* (Paris, 1892), pp. 83 ff., 170 ff.; William M. Ramsay: *Impressions of Turkey* (New York, 1897), chap. viii; Richard Davey: *The Sultan and his Subjects* (London, 1897), II, pp. 167 ff. See also *Turkey No. 16 (1877),* nos. 13, 23, 86.

12 There is a splendid discussion of the situation in M. A. Ubicini: *Letters on Turkey* (London, 1856), II, letters iv–vii. See also M. B. Dadian: " La Société Arménienne Contemporaine "

The domination of the upper classes began to be broken in the time of Abdul Mejid. Factional strife between the official and banking groups gave an opening for popular intervention. In 1844 the representatives of the guilds were given fourteen of the thirty seats on the council advising the patriarch, and in 1847 the council was divided into ecclesiastical and lay branches.

By this time the Armenians, like so many of the peoples of the Balkans, were experiencing a cultural revival, in part, no doubt, inspired by the example of the Greeks. The movement was simply another aspect of the infiltration of European influence in Turkey, a result of the improved communications, the development of trade, the advent of missionaries, and so on. The first Armenian newspaper was published at Smyrna in 1839. At the end of twenty-five years there were no less than fourteen of them published in the Empire. Like other " backward " peoples the Armenians were seized with a veritable mania for education. One school after another was opened, until in 1866 there were thirty-two schools for boys and fourteen for girls in the capital alone. It was quite in keeping with this new spirit that the upper classes began to send their sons abroad to be educated. Since the 18th century there had been a haven of Armenian learning at Venice, where the Roman Catholic Mekhitarist Order had its monastery. In 1846 this order established the Collège de Samuel Moorat at Paris, which thenceforth became a centre for Armenian students. Many of these young men became infected with the ideas of democracy so prevalent in the period about 1848, and most of them returned to Constantinople as apostles of French ideas. They translated and carried back with them the works of Lamartine and Hugo, and before long the Armenian theatre in Pera was playing the French classical dramas as well.[18]

It was these young men who were largely responsible for the furtherance of the movement for reform within the government of the Armenian Church and nation as organized under the Turkish millet system. In 1860 they forced through a constitution which provided for universal suffrage in the election for the Assembly. Henceforth the Patriarchate was to be wholly under the control of the elected representatives of the people. Therewith, one might say, the Armenians, unmolested by the Ottoman government, succeeded in effecting a liberal or even democratic constitution. As a community they not only governed themselves, but governed themselves by a very advanced system.

But thus far there was no thought of breaking away from the Empire. It could still be said of the Armenians that the Turks had " almost unlimited con-

---

(*Revue des Deux Mondes,* June 15, 1867, pp. 903–28); Leon Arpee: *The Armenian Awakening* (Chicago, 1909), chap. ix; M. Varandian: *Haykakan Charjman Nakhapatmouthiun* (*Origins of the Armenian Movement,* Geneva, 1912–13) as abstracted by Frédéric Macler: *Autour de l'Arménie* (Paris, 1917), pp. 177–275.

[18] Dadian, loc. cit., gives one of the best accounts. See further Archag Tchobanian: *L'Arménie, son Histoire, sa Littérature* (Paris, 1897), pp. 62 ff.; J. Mathorez: " Les Arméniens en France de 1789 à nos Jours " (*Revue des Études Arméniennes,* II, 1922, pp. 293–313), pp. 297 ff.; Varandian, in Macler, op. cit., pp. 230 ff.; K. J. Basmadjian: *Histoire Moderne des Arméniens* (Paris, 1917), pp. 76 ff.

fidence " in them.[14] Indeed, if we may believe their own writers, there was at this time among the Armenians of Constantinople little knowledge of or interest in their fellow-countrymen in the isolated interior. The provinces themselves were untouched by all this ferment, excepting for the fact that in 1857 the abbot of the famous Varak Monastery at Van, Khrimian Hairig, started the publication of the first local journal, a monthly called *The Eagle of Vasburagan*. Khrimian, a self-taught man of the people, was one of the first and perhaps the greatest of the national leaders. Before any one else he began to preach resistance to the oppressor and to talk about national freedom. But his efforts were by no means appreciated by the Armenians in the capital, some of whom appear to have hired a Kurd to assassinate this unwelcome agitator. Nothing came of the plot and Khrimian soon became popular among the lower classes. In 1869 he was elected patriarch of Constantinople, thereby becoming the head of the whole Armenian community. Under his direction the church organization made its first systematic inquiries into conditions in the provinces and passed along to the government the first protests and demands for protection.[15]

While the ideas of resistance were beginning to take root among some elements in Constantinople, another factor came to play an important part in the situation. The Armenians who for centuries had been under the rule of the Persians seem to have been a more determined and vigorous group than those under Ottoman rule. In the 18th century they looked to Christian Russia to save them. They established contact with Peter the Great, who promised much and did little. They were encouraged by Catherine the Great to hope for the erection of a Kingdom of Ararat under Russian protection. Catherine deserted them as she deserted the Greeks, but a generation later, after the war between Russia and Persia, the larger part of Persian Armenia passed under Russian rule (1829).[16] The Armenians were well treated under Russian rule, and seem to have prospered greatly. But for almost fifty years more they had no contact with the Armenians of the Ottoman Empire. It was not until Russia began to embark upon a crusade to liberate the Christians under the Ottoman yoke that the Armenians of the Caucasus bethought them of their brothers across the frontier. Krikor Ardsrounie, editor of the important Armenian paper *Mushag* at Tiflis, in 1876 raised the question of aiding the Turkish Armenians. He called upon these people to revolt against the infidel and to rely upon Russia.[17]

---

[14] Dadian, loc. cit., p. 906.

[15] Tchobanian, op. cit., p. 73; M. Varandian: *Hairenikie Kaghapare* (*The Idea of Country*, Geneva, 1904), pp. 77 ff.; Idem: *Hai Heghapoghagan Dashnaghtzoutan Badmoutiun* (*History of the Armenian Revolutionary Federation*, Paris, 1932), I, pp. 13 ff.; E. B. Chrakian: " Notes on the Life and Work of Khrimian Hairig " (*The Armenian Mirror*, November 11, 18, 25, 1932). There is a good analysis of the patriarchal inquiries in M. G. Rolin-Jaequemyns: " L'Arménie, les Arméniens et les Traités " (*Revue de Droit International*, XIX, 1887, pp. 284–325), pp. 306 ff.

[16] Varandian, as quoted by Macler, op. cit.; Felix Valyi: *Spiritual and Political Revolutions in Islam* (London, 1925), p. 156.

[17] Leo: *Krikor Ardsrounie* (Tiflis, 1903), II, pp. 390 ff.

The appeal at first made little impression. As the Russian armies, commanded chiefly by Russian-Armenian generals, approached Erzerum in June 1877, the Christian population was enthusiastic and prepared to join the invaders, but when the Russians were obliged to fall back the Armenians hastily changed their minds. " A more selfish, narrow-minded, mean, cringing race I fancy does not exist," wrote an English correspondent on the spot.[18] At Constantinople the Armenian leaders at first repudiated any connexion with the Russians and protested loudly against all suggestions of revolt. But the insurrection in Bulgaria, followed by the active intervention of the western powers, brought about a change of mind. Armenians abroad were exerting themselves to enlist the sympathy and aid of the English, while the leaders at Constantinople appealed to Lord Salisbury during the meeting of the international conference in November and December 1876. The Turkish constitution of December 1876 opened up the prospect of better treatment and for a time appears to have satisfied the Armenians. But when the Russians crossed the Balkans and appeared in the environs of Constantinople in January 1878 the patriarch, Nerses Varjabedian, was sent out to the headquarters of the invaders to appeal for special consideration. The mission was well received by the Grand Duke Nicholas, but evidently did not secure as much as it had hoped for. Article XVI of the Treaty of San Stefano did not provide for self-government of the Armenian vilayets, but simply engaged the Porte to undertake without delay the ameliorations and reforms demanded by local needs and to guarantee the Armenians security against the Kurds and the Circassians.[19]

This article of the San Stefano Treaty, among others, aroused the apprehensions of the British, who had visions of a further Russian advance in Armenia which would threaten the road to the east. It was this fear that drove them to conclude with Turkey the famous Cyprus Convention of June 4, 1878. From the negotiations preceding the conclusion of the Convention it is perfectly clear that the English government was much less concerned with the Armenians than with the country they inhabited. They were interested in bolstering up the Turkish rule in northeastern Anatolia by reforming the Turkish governmental system. So it was provided, in the Convention, that the Sultan should undertake the reforms necessary for the good administration of the region and for the protection of the Christian and other subjects of the Porte in

---

[18] Charles B. Norman, in the London *Times*, October 1, 1877 (reprinted in G. Hagopian: *The Armenians and the Eastern Question*, London, 1878, pp. 45 ff.); see also his *Armenia and the Campaign of 1877* (London, 1878), pp. 329 ff.

[19] Arshag Tchobanian: " Badaskhanaduoutiunnere " (" Responsibilities," in *Anahid*, I, no. 3, January, 1899) claims that the Armenian colony did not approve of the patriarch's action. Varandian, in Macler, op. cit., takes the other view, and maintains that Nerses represented the general sentiment. Victor Bérard: *La Politique du Sultan* (Paris, 1897), p. 146 thinks the Turks encouraged the Armenians to appeal to Russia, in order to divert the Russians from more far-reaching schemes of annexation. See further Arshag O. Sarkissian: " The Beginning of the Armenian Question, 1870–1881 " (Abstract of a doctoral dissertation submitted at the University of Illinois, Urbana, 1934).

Asia Minor. It will be noted that not only the Armenians, but all the Sultan's subjects were envisaged by this provision.[20]

The Armenians were disappointed by the San Stefano Treaty but much encouraged by the attitude of the British. They therefore decided to send a delegation to the Berlin Congress. The group was headed by Khrimian and toured the European capitals before going to the Congress. But at Berlin nothing was accomplished and little attention was paid to the pleas of the Armenian delegation. Their program was reasonable enough in itself: it called for the appointment of a Christian governor-general, irremovable excepting with the consent of the powers, and for financial and judicial readjustments. A militia, from which nomad elements were to be excluded, and a gendarmerie were to preserve the peace. Nothing of this was embodied in the Treaty of Berlin. Article LXI of that famous document simply revived the provision of the San Stefano Treaty, adding, however, the important proviso that the Turkish government should report periodically to the powers what measures had been taken, while the powers should supervise their application.[21]

The Armenian delegation thought Article LXI quite inadequate and protested against it, though without result. On his return to Constantinople Khrimian told his people bitterly that the other small nations had come to the Congress with iron ladles, while the Armenians had only paper ones. There was already talk of following the Bulgarian example and revolting. But for the time being the Armenians still hoped for aid from England. Henry C. Barkley, who travelled through Armenia in the latter part of 1878, says that in many places the inhabitants thought he was the forerunner of the British, who were come to save the people. Everywhere he found the Armenians filled with hope of reform under English auspices.[22] This same feeling is reflected in the memoirs of one of the later revolutionists, who says, speaking of this period: " In each and every one of them (i.e. the Armenians) there was but one fixed idea, hammered in, as it were, like a nail: Bulgaria was freed by the intervention of Russia, why not Armenia with the help of England." [23]

There was at least some justification for this attitude, for the English took their obligations under the Cyprus Convention seriously enough. They sent military consuls into Anatolia and tried to bring sufficient pressure on the Sultan

---

[20] The English interest in Armenia (not the Armenians) and the fear of Russian advance in that region are admirably discussed by Dwight E. Lee: *Great Britain and the Cyprus Convention Policy of 1878* (Cambridge, 1934), pp. 39 ff., 61 ff.

[21] The essential documents are conveniently given in Léart: *La Question Arménienne à la Lumière des Documents* (Paris, 1913), pp. 27 ff. See also Frédéric Macler: *Autour de l'Arménie*, pp. 75 ff.; Rolin-Jaequemyns, loc. cit., pp. 318 ff.

[22] Henry C. Barkley: *A Ride through Asia Minor and Armenia* (London, 1891), pp. 137, 154, 244, 281.

[23] Khan-Azad: " Hai Heghapoghaganie Housheritz " (" Memoirs of an Armenian Revolutionary," in *Hairenik Amsakir*, V, June, 1927, pp. 60–72), p. 65. See further M. Varandian: *Hai Heghapoghagan Dashnaghtzoutan Badmoutiun* (*History of the Armenian Revolutionary Federation*), I, pp. 20 ff.

to introduce reform.[24] The Gladstone government, which came into office in 1880, was, if anything, more assiduous. Strong representations were made to the Porte and the other powers were persuaded to join in a collective note demanding reform. But the Sultan merely temporized and did nothing. Neither would the other powers go to the lengths envisaged by Gladstone. " The so-called Armenian reforms," wrote Bismarck in 1883, " are ideal and theoretical aspirations, which were given an appropriate place in the ornamental part of the transactions of the Congress, so that they could be used for parliamentary purposes. Their practical significance, whatever the final outcome, is very doubtful and cuts both ways so far as the Armenians are concerned." [25]

What Bismarck meant by this seemingly cynical remark was simply this: that the Turkish government could not be changed by a stroke of the pen, that none of the powers could afford to go to war to secure reforms for the Armenians, and that consequently the prodding of the Sultan would only result in arousing him to the point where he would take revenge on the Armenians. This is exactly what happened; but there was, by 1883, no turning back. The Armenians had been thoroughly stirred by the events of 1876-1878. Speaking of the colony in Constantinople James Bryce wrote in 1877: " They see that the time has come to make their voice heard in the world, and to claim (however little prospect there seems to be of their obtaining it) for their unhappy coreligionists in the Asiatic provinces of Turkey some share in Western sympathy." [26] There was no idea of leaving the Ottoman Empire or of setting up as a " Switzerland in Asia Minor," but in the writings of that time the same argument comes out over and over again: why should all the sympathy of Europe be lavished upon the Bulgarians? Why are not the Armenians just as much entitled to self-government or at least to far-reaching reform? The Armenians, so they claimed, did not love the Russians and would rather stay with the Ottoman Empire, but something would have to be done for them. Even Russian rule would be better than what they had at the time.[27]

As soon as it became clear that nothing much could be hoped for from English or international action the younger intellectuals began to talk of revolt. In June and July 1879 the English ambassador reported home that the Sultan, unless he took care, would some day have on his hands an Armenian question similar to the Bulgarian question: " The same intrigues are now being carried on in Asia Minor to establish an Armenian nationality and to bring about a state of things which may give rise to a Christian outcry and European interference." [28] Nothing much is known of the revolutionary activities to which

---

[24] See especially Lee, op. cit., pp. 155 ff.

[25] *Die Grosse Politik,* IX, no. 2183, footnote.

[26] Bryce: *Transcaucasia and Ararat,* p. 324.

[27] James Bryce, letter to the *Times,* March 20, 1878, reprinted in G. Hapogian: *The Armenians and the Eastern Question* (London, 1878), where there are many other documents to the same effect.

[28] *Turkey No. 10 (1879),* nos. 45, 62; *Turkey No. 7 (1880),* no. 3.

Layard referred. There appears to have been some sort of *Tugendbund* formed at that time at Erzerum, and there were not a few minor conspiracies, which were betrayed. Mugarditch Portoukalian, one of the most influential leaders of the national movement, was at that time already making his school at Van a centre for the propagation of revolutionary sentiment.[29]

But nothing much could be accomplished along these lines. Since the appeal of the Armenians to the Russians and to the Congress of Berlin the Turkish government had become very suspicious of them and had begun to class them with the Greeks and Bulgarians as dangerous elements. The lot of the Armenians became much harder than it had been. Every effort at organization failed, partly because there were always enough Armenians who would sell their fellow-countrymen for an adequate consideration, and partly because the authorities were on the *qui vive*. Men like Portoukalian were harried out of the land or thrown into prison. Portoukalian himself went to Marseilles, where there was a fairly large colony of Armenian traders, and there founded a paper, *Armenia*, in 1885. This organ was liberal rather than radical, but for years it was the rallying point of the revolutionary elements, who were organized in a Patriotic Union. One of Portoukalian's collaborators, Avedisian, returned to Van and is said to have started there an active revolutionary group, the *Armenakans*, of whom, however, little seems to be known.[30] Somewhat later a number of members of the Union who were resident in England began to publish *Haiastan*, in French. They succeeded in organizing, in 1888, an Anglo-Armenian Committee, which counted among its members a number of Liberal members of parliament and became a very influential centre of propaganda.

But these movements were fairly moderate. Portoukalian believed in the need for revolt, but thought that there should be long and careful preparation. This seems to have been the general attitude of the well-to-do Armenians, both in western Europe and in Constantinople. Very different was the viewpoint of a radical wing which began to emerge in the middle of the eighties. The short period from 1876 to 1883 was literally a golden age for the Armenians in Russia, a period of the most extraordinary cultural activity during which schools, theatres and newspapers sprang up like mushrooms. The whole Armenian population was fired with the idea of liberation. The great poet, Kamar-Katiba, called upon the Turkish Armenians to defend themselves, and not to rely upon Europe, which was too far, or upon God, who was too high. Raffi, greatest of modern Armenian novelists, denounced the resignation of the Armenians and decried the deadening influence of the clergy. Fortresses, he declared, would be of more use than convents, arms of more use than sacred vases, and the smoke

---

[29] Varandian, op, cit., I, pp. 20–35.

[30] Varandian, op. cit., I, pp. 35–6; Khan-Azad, loc. cit., pp. 68–72; Basmadjian: *Histoire Moderne des Arméniens*, p. 118, and especially M. Portoukalian: " *Armenia* " ie *Housharar* (*Anthology of " Armenia,"* Marseilles, 1890), which reprints the most important parts of the paper for 1885–1886 and contains an interesting preface.

of powder more agreeable than incense. No one man did more than Raffi to inflame the imagination of his people.[31]

Raffi's hostility to the Church was something new in Armenian affairs. So was the tendency of the younger generation to follow the lead of Russian nihilists and terrorists. In 1883 the Armenians of the Caucasus began to feel the effects of the new Russian policy marked out by Alexander III and Pobiedonostsev. Their schools were closed, their newspapers censored and their Church persecuted.[32] The effect of this was to drive the national and revolutionary movement under-ground. Student groups in St. Petersburg and Moscow came under the influence of the Russian socialists and terrorists. In Tiflis they organized secret groups, which read Darwin, Spencer, Lassalle and Marx.[33] In the summer of 1890 these groups, after many heated discussions and clashes, combined to form the Armenian Revolutionary Federation, or *Dashnagtzoutian,* which began to publish a paper, the *Droshag* (Standard). Its program was, from the outset, a mixture of socialistic and nationalistic teaching, but even its champions tell us that the socialistic element was regarded merely as a remote ideal, something for the intellectuals to think about. The essential plank in the platform was *action,* to secure the " political and economic freedom of Turkish Armenia." The purpose of the organization, says its leading apologist, was to bring about " a long drawn-out fight against the Ottoman tyranny, to create in the country a continuous revolutionary state, always having before our eyes the intervention of the third factor — the European factor." The Program of 1892 begins with a nebulous preamble of a purely socialistic nature, but then goes on suddenly to a discussion of the conditions of the Armenians in Turkey and declares that only " an armed revolution and the use of force " can put an end to an intolerable situation. The Federation therefore arranged to organize revolutionary bands which should fight the government incessantly and should terrorize government officials, traitors, usurers and all kinds of exploiters.[34]

The A. R. F. began its work with boundless enthusiasm. " The atmosphere was replete with the intoxicating odor of gunpowder, the roll of drums and the sound of speeches, songs and shibboleths." [35] Revolutionary groups were organized at Trebizond, Van, Constantinople and other places. But for all this coming and going little seems to have been accomplished. We are told that by 1892 the organization was already pretty much discouraged. The original plans

---

[31] Tchobanian: *L'Arménie, son Histoire, sa Littérature,* pp. 78 ff.; Leo: *Krikor Ardsrounie,* II, pp. 390 ff.; Khan-Azad, loc. cit., pp. 62–4.

[32] E. Aknounie: *Tebie Guriv (On to the Fight,* Geneva, 1904); Idem: *Les Plaies du Caucase* (Geneva, 1905); Arshag Tchobanian: " Russia ev Haiere " (" Russia and the Armenians," in *Anahid,* March, April, May, 1906, pp. 35 ff.); Valyi: *Spiritual and Political Revolutions in Islam,* pp. 165 ff.

[33] Varandian, op. cit., I, pp. 45 ff.

[34] *Dsrakir H. H. Dashnagtzoutian (Platform of the Armenian Revolutionary Federation,* 1892). Varandian, op. cit., I, pp. 80 ff., 302; M. Hovhannesian: *Dashnagtzoutiune ev nera Hageragortnere* (*The A.R.F. and its Opponents,* Tiflis, 1906), pp. 19–20, 151–2; K. S. Papazian: *Patriotism Perverted* (Boston, 1934), pp. 9–13.   [35] Varandian, op. cit., I, p. 84.

for *freedom* were given up and the leaders hardly dared hope even for autonomy, even if the program still spoke of "political and economic independence." [36] In any event it has never, to my knowledge, been claimed that the Federation played a leading rôle in the disturbances prior to 1895.

In these first years of the Armenian Revolution (and the Revolution is as important as the massacres) the direction was in the hands of a different group. In 1886 Avetis Nazarbek, an Armenian student at Paris who seems to have been financially well off, paid a visit to some fellow-students at Geneva. He had been a contributor to Portoukalian's *Armenia,* but found it too tame. His fiancée, Marian Vartanian, had taken an active part in the Russian revolutionary movement and had probably converted Nazarbek to the socialist, terrorist creed. Later critics maintained that Nazarbek was an incompetent who could not even pass his university examinations, and asserted that his fiancée was an hysterical woman who spoke only Russian and thought nothing of having the Turkish Armenians massacred in order to bring nearer the dawn of a new social era.[37] Whether this was true or not, Nazarbek seems to have had a persuasive tongue and a good pen, and Marian had all of the fire and passion of the woman revolutionary. As a result of the discussions in Geneva the students appealed to Portoukalian to head a new revolutionary society, which he refused to do. Thereupon Nazarbek and his friends arranged a *Caucasian Soirée* and raised enough money to buy type and start their own newspaper, *Hentchak* (The Bell), which is reminiscent of Herzen's *Kolokol.*

The first number of *Hentchak* was published in Geneva in November 1887. For the next two years all the articles were written by Nazarbek, who faked correspondence from Turkey and also contributions. The whole enterprise was really his, and his associates hardly numbered a half dozen. In the very first issue he announced the aim of his group to be the political independence of Turkish Armenia and ultimately its organization as a socialist state. Through propaganda, agitation and terrorization (the methods were borrowed in toto from the Russian *Will of the People*) it was hoped to start a great insurrectionary movement in Turkey. Nazarbek envisaged drawing the Assyrians, Yezidis and even the Kurds (!) into the movement and planned to co-operate with the Macedonian, Cretan and Albanian revolutionaries. It was confidently expected that when the whole Empire was aflame the European powers would step in and secure the rights of the small nations. Then, ultimately, it might be possible to unite Turkish, Russian and Persian Armenians in one socialist state.[38]

---

[36] Varandian, op. cit., I, pp. 83 ff., 106 ff. This seems much nearer the truth than the thesis of Darakir: "Angahkouthian Caghapare H. H. Dashnagtzouthian Hinnatirnere Medaynouthian metch" ("The Idea of Independence in the Minds of the Founders of the A.R.F.," in *Hairenik Amsakir*, September, 1932, pp. 87–103).

[37] Arshag Tchobanian: "Badaskhanaduoutiunnere" ("Responsibilities," in *Anahid*, I, January, 1899, pp. 85 ff.).

[38] *Hentchak*, I, no. 1 (November, 1887), nos. 11–2 (October–November, 1888), in which the Platform is for the first time outlined in full. The best source for the story is the memoirs of

The Hentchakian Revolutionary Party was, in 1890, invited to join the Armenian Revolutionary Federation, and did so, but the association of the two did not last long. Nazarbek was evidently not an easy person to get on with, and preferred to work on his own. At first he had trouble in finding followers, but his few collaborators worked hard. Khan-Azad, for example, went to Constantinople in July 1889 and began to spread propaganda. He consulted with Khrimian, but found the old man doubtful: "You are crazy," said the old patriot; "The Armenians are a very small nation, and how much blood will have to be shed." He could not see how anything substantial could be done without European help. But Khan-Azad was not discouraged. He went on to Tiflis, where he had no better luck. It was only in Trebizond that he found any real enthusiasm. There he established the central committee of the party, and from that centre agents were sent out who organized revolutionary cells in Erzerum, Kharput, Smyrna, Aleppo and many other places.[39] Nazarbek himself stayed discreetly in Geneva, but in a volume of stories published later he has given us vivid pictures of the agitators visiting the peasants, "talking the night through with them, speaking with them of their sufferings, unceasingly, impatiently, preaching the gospel of an eye for an eye, a tooth for a tooth, rousing their crushed spirits with high resolves and mighty aspirations."[40]

The ambassadors at Constantinople were not slow in following the development of this agitation. From 1888 onward the English representative reported the presence of revolutionaries and the seizure of seditious literature. Revolutionary placards were being posted in the cities and there were not a few cases of the blackmailing of wealthy Armenians, who were forced to contribute to the cause. Europeans in Turkey were agreed that the immediate aim of the agitators was to incite disorder, bring about inhuman reprisals, and so provoke the intervention of the powers. For that reason, it was said, they operated by preference in areas where the Armenians were in a hopeless minority, so that reprisals would be certain. One of the revolutionaries told Dr. Hamlin, the founder of Robert College, that the Hentchak bands would

"watch their opportunity to kill Turks and Koords, set fire to their villages, and then make their escape into the mountains. The enraged Moslems will then rise, and fall upon the defenceless Armenians and slaughter them with such barbarity that Russia will enter in the name of humanity and Christian civilization and take possession."

Nazarbek's close associate Khan-Azad: "Hai Heghapoghaganie Housheritz" ("Memoirs of an Armenian Revolutionary," in *Hairenik Amsakir*, V, 1927, no. 8, pp. 60–72, no. 9, pp. 52–63), but see also Nazarbek's own account in the article "Zeitun" (*Contemporary Review*, April, 1896, pp. 513–28) and in the introduction to his book *Through the Storm* (London, 1899). Further information and quotations from manifestoes, etc. may be found in Vicomte des Coursons: *La Rébellion Arménienne* (Paris, 1895), pp. 42 ff.; in Bérard: *La Politique du Sultan*, pp. 155–6, 166–70; and in the official Turkish publication: *Aspirations et Agissements Révolutionnaires des Comités Arméniens* (Constantinople, 1917), pp. 16 ff.

[39] Khan-Azad, loc. cit., V, no. 10, pp. 56 ff.; no. 11, pp. 127 ff.; no. 12, pp. 122 ff.; VI, no. 2, pp. 118 ff.   [40] Nazarbek: *Through the Storm*, p. 11.

When the horrified missionary denounced the scheme as atrocious and infernal beyond anything ever known, he received this reply:

> "It appears so to you, no doubt; but we Armenians have determined to be free. Europe listened to the Bulgarian horrors and made Bulgaria free. She will listen to our cry when it goes up in the shrieks and blood of millions of women and children. . . . We are desperate. We shall do it." [41]

Serious trouble began in 1890, when there were disturbances and some bloodshed at Erzerum. The outbreak had not been premeditated or planned, but the Hentchak hoped to capitalize it. The group was therefore much surprised that the powers made so little of it. To encourage interest it arranged to stage a great demonstration in Constantinople to impress both the Turkish and the European governments. The affair was carefully planned and the minimum demands of the revolutionaries (civil liberties) were sent in advance to the foreign ambassadors. A proclamation was read in the Armenian Church at Kum-Kapu, in which the Armenians were told in so many words: "You must be your own self-governing master." [42]

Even this demonstration had no favorable results. During the following months the efforts of the leaders seem to have gone into negotiations for an agreement with other revolutionary groups. There were long conferences at Athens, and in December 1891 the Hentchak officially joined the Oriental Federation of Macedonian, Albanian, Cretan and Greek revolutionists. The newspaper was transferred to Athens, where it remained until the end of 1894, at which time the Armenian organization moved to London. In the interval propaganda was being carried on in Armenia and efforts were being made to induce the Kurds to join forces with the insurgents. Agents were sent also to America, where branches were established in Boston, Worcester and other cities. Khan-Azad reports that he raised in America no less than $10,000 to support the cause. [43]

When the Gladstone cabinet came into power in the summer of 1892 the hopes of the Armenians ran high, for was not the Grand Old Man the savior of the oppressed? As a matter of fact the Liberal government began almost at once to send sharp notes to the Porte. The Anglo-Armenian Committee and the Evangelical Alliance made the most of the situation and raised the hue and cry of religious persecution. But English influence had sunk so low at Con-

---

[41] Letter in the *Boston Congregationalist*, December 23, 1893, reproduced in *Foreign Relations of the United States*, 1895, p. 1416, and in *Turkey No. 6 (1896)*, no. 214. Similar utterances were heard by Sir Edwin Pears (*Forty Years in Constantinople*, New York, 1916, p. 155). Further reports of revolutionary agitation may be found in *Turkey No. 1 (1889)*, nos. 8, 17, 95; *Turkey No. 1 (1890)*, no. 4; *Turkey No. 1 (1892)*, nos. 11, 63, 65, 78, 84; *Turkey No. 3 (1896)*, nos. 87 ff., 124 and especially nos. 131, 143, 195; *Turkey No. 6 (1896)*, nos. 12, 53, 68 and especially nos. 55, 95, 214; *Die Grosse Politik*, IX, nos. 2175, 2178; Edwin M. Bliss: *Turkey and the Armenian Atrocities* (Philadelphia, 1896), pp. 335 ff.

[42] *Hentchak*, III, no. 4 (August, 1890); Khan-Azad, loc. cit., VI, no. 1, pp. 123 ff.

[43] Khan-Azad, loc. cit., VI, no. 4, pp. 130 ff.; no. 5, pp. 107 ff.; no. 6, pp. 126 ff.

stantinople that no attention was paid to the protests from London. The Turkish government probably realized even then that the Russian government, just as hostile to the Hentchakian aspirations as the Turkish, would stand behind it. In 1890 the Russian officials had co-operated with the Turkish in breaking up an Armenian raiding party organized in the Caucasus.[44] Many writers have taken the stand that English intervention only made matters worse. " The Turk begins to repress because we sympathize," wrote David Hogarth; " and we sympathize the more because he represses, and so the vicious circle revolves." [45] England " is more responsible for the cold-blooded murders which have come near exterminating the Armenians than all other nations put together," remarked an American traveller.[46]

It requires no very vivid imagination to picture the reaction of the Turks to the agitation of the revolutionists. They had constantly in mind, if not the revolt of the Greeks, at least the insurrection in Bulgaria and the disastrous intervention of Russia and the powers. Whether Abdul Hamid deserves the black reputation that has been pinned to him is a matter for debate. If he was " the bloody assassin " and the " red Sultan " to most people, he was the hard-working, conscientious, much harassed but personally charming ruler to others. Those who have spoken for him have pointed out that the Sultan felt his Empire threatened by the Armenians, who, he knew or at least believed, were in league with the Young Turks, the Greeks, Macedonians, etc. They believe that Abdul Hamid was the victim of what we moderns call a persecution complex. He was terrified, and for that reason surrounded himself not only with high walls, but with all sorts of dubious characters, especially spies and delators who justified their existence by bringing ever more alarming reports.[47]

So much at least cannot be denied: that the revolutionists planned a great conflagration and that they gave the Sultan and his ministers ample fright. One of their proclamations read:

" The times are most critical and pregnant with ominous events. The cup is full. Prepare for the inevitable. Organize, arm, — arm with anything. If one place revolts or shows resistance, do the same in your locality. Spread the fight for liberation. Yes, in truth, it is better to live as a free man for a day, for an hour, and to die fighting, than to live a life of slavery for generations, nay for centuries." [48]

---

[44] Varandian, op. cit., I, pp. 69 ff.

[45] David G. Hogarth: A Wandering Scholar in the Levant (New York, 1896), pp. 147–8.

[46] George H. Hepworth: Through Armenia on Horseback (New York, 1898), p. 157; similarly Johannes Lepsius: Armenia and Europe (London, 1897), pp. 76–7, 103. Vicomte des Coursons: La Rébellion Arménienne is almost entirely devoted to denunciation of the Anglo-Armenian Committee and English " intrigue," and writers like Hans Barth: Türke, Wehre Dich (Second edition, Leipzig, 1898), chap. vii, were convinced that the Hentchak was supported by English money.

[47] See e.g. Sidney Whitman: Turkish Memories (London, 1914), p. 61; Hepworth, op. cit., pp. 6–13, 169 ff.; Die Grosse Politik, IX, nos. 2184, 2189; Colmar von der Goltz: Denkwürdigkeiten (Berlin, 1929), p. 157; and the article entitled " En Orient " (Revue de Paris, December 1, 1895, pp. 449–61), which has been attributed to Hanotaux. [48] Hentchak, V, no. 7 (July, 1892).

In the summer of 1894 the Revolutionary Committee wrote a letter to the Grand Vizier warning him that there would be a general rising in the Empire if the "very just demands of the Armenian people" were not met.[49] No one could blame the government for anticipating a tremendous upheaval and for taking precautions. Probably to counteract the efforts made to bring the Kurds into the movement, the Sultan had, in 1891, organized the tribesmen in the famous Hamidié regiments, which were modelled on the Russian cossack brigades and were supposedly meant to act as a frontier defense force. In 1877 and 1878, however, the Kurd troops had been more trouble than they were worth; it may therefore be assumed that the purpose of the new organizations was to satisfy the chiefs and keep them from joining forces with the Armenian revolutionaries. In fact they could and were, under the new system, used against the Armenians. Beginning in 1892 the Hamidié regiments, sometimes supported by regular troops, began to raid the Armenian settlements, burning the houses, destroying the crops and cutting down the inhabitants.

And so the revolutionaries began to get what they wanted — reprisals. It mattered not to them that perfectly innocent people were being made to suffer for the realization of a program drawn up by a group in Geneva or Athens, a group which had never been given any mandate whatever by the Armenian community. So far as one can make out the Hentchak agitators were ardently supported by the lower-class Armenians in Constantinople, with whose help they forced the election of the patriot Ismirlian as patriarch in 1894. But the upper classes appear to have been opposed to the whole program; indeed, they were victimized themselves by threatening letters and by blackmail into the financing of a scheme which they regarded as disastrous. As for the peasantry in the provinces, it is perfectly obvious that they did not know what it was all about. Isabella Bishop, who travelled through the country in 1891, makes the positive statement " that the Armenian peasant is as destitute of political aspirations as he is ignorant of political grievances . . . not on a single occasion did I hear a wish expressed for political or administrative reform, or for Armenian independence." Hogarth tells of Armenians in the provinces who said they wished the patriots would leave them alone. But these people were not consulted. Whether they liked it or not, they were marked out by others for the sacrifice; their lives were the price to be paid for the realization of the phantastic national-socialist state of the fanatics.[50]

After numerous minor exploits the Armenian revolutionaries arranged for a *grand coup*. They organized a really formidable rising among the Armenian

---

49 *Turkey No. 6 (1896),* no. 127.

50 Isabella Bishop: "The Shadow of the Kurd" (*Contemporary Review,* May, June, 1891, pp. 642–54, 819–35); David G. Hogarth: *A Wandering Scholar in the Levant,* p. 149. See further Lepsius, op. cit., pp. 70–3; Bérard, op. cit., pp. 175 ff.; Barth, op. cit., pp. 31–32 and chap. vii; *Turkey No. 6 (1896),* nos. 55, 282. No one could condemn the aims and methods of the Hentchak in stronger terms than did the eminent Armenian writer Tchobanian in his article on "Responsibilities" (*Anahid,* I, January, 1899).

mountaineers of the Sassun region, just to the southwest of Mush. There, and in the Zeitun district, the Armenians were, like the Kurds, a tough, warlike group of herdsmen who could be depended upon to put up a hard fight. The rising took place in the early autumn of 1894, but it was put down in a remarkably short time, for the simple reason that the government, probably forewarned, rushed in Hamidié regiments from other places and wiped out the insurrection by having some twenty-five villages destroyed and some ten to twenty thousand Armenians massacred.[51]

When news of these happenings reached England there was a repetition of the outcry that went up after the Bulgarian atrocities of 1876. Organizations like the Anglo-Armenian Committee and the Evangelical Alliance made the most of the religious aspect of the Armenian question and demanded immediate action by the government. At first it was proposed to send a British agent to investigate the situation, but finally, under pressure and amid loud protests, the Porte offered to despatch a commission of investigation. This satisfied public opinion until it was revealed that the commission was not to look into the massacre of the Armenians but was only " to inquire into the criminal conduct of Armenian brigands." The Turkish government flatly refused to admit that there had been *massacres*. There had been a *revolution,* it maintained, and that revolution had been put down. There was no reason for investigation and certainly no reason for foreign intervention. If, then, the government was prepared to send a commission, this was simply to show its readiness to meet the wishes of the British government. It need hardly be said that this attitude made a most unfavorable impression in England, where the Sultan and his government had long since become extremely unpopular, and where, it should be remembered, no one knew anything about the revolutionary movement, its aims or its methods. Speaking of the agitation in England, Sir Charles Eliot remarked quite aptly that the object of the Evangelical Alliance and other bodies was to ameliorate the lot of the Armenians, but that

> " this laudable project was hampered by their invincible ignorance of the spirit and methods of the East. They invoked public opinion, the rights of Armenia, religious equality, and other excellent principles, which were understood in Turkey about as well as a body of British electors would understand a proposal to cure agricultural depression by a Hatt-i-Sherif." [52]

Be that as it may, the London government had to take account of this attitude and therefore proposed to attach the consul at Erzerum to the Turkish commission.[53]

---

[51] *Turkey No. 1 (1895),* nos. 22, 28 indicate that the massacres were ordered. The statement has, of course, been made by countless writers, most of them not in a position to know anything about it. On the organization of the affair see Khan-Azad, loc. cit., VI, no. 6, pp. 126 ff. The most important account is the report of the Anglo-Franco-Russian consular investigation in *Turkey No. 1 (1895),* no. 252.   [52] Eliot: *Turkey in Europe,* pp. 442–3.

[53] *Turkey No. 1 (1895),* nos. 31, 37, 38, 49, 50, 54, 56; Documents Diplomatiques: *Affaires Arméniennes, 1893–1897,* nos. 12, 14, 15.

In the opinion of the German and Russian ambassadors at London, the British government itself was very anxious to avoid the serious complications in which public opinion threatened to involve it. No objection was raised therefore when the Sultan suggested that the French and Russian consuls should also take part in the work. After a good deal of delay, it was finally arranged that not even consuls but simply delegates were to accompany the Turkish commission. It is quite obvious that neither the Russian government nor the French government took much interest in this affair. The Russian government made it perfectly clear that it was averse to raising any political question. It is equally clear that it wished to avoid having too much done for the Armenians. It must be remembered that the Hentchak program had been published and that its realization would have endangered the Russian as well as the Ottoman Empire. The Tsar had as much interest as the Sultan in checking the Armenian revolutionary movement.

The French government, on the other hand, joined in the action in order not to be separated from its ally, and in order to keep the question international. In an article written some time afterward M. Hanotaux, who had had ten years' experience in Constantinople and probably knew a good deal more about conditions than the outraged humanitarians of the Evangelical Alliance, remarked that the matter could perhaps have been settled more easily if the powers had not intervened. " There is always somewhere in the British Empire," he said, " some committee, some sect, some club which in good faith and probably to while away the weary afternoons of foggy Sundays dreams of I know not what modification, amelioration, destruction or reconstruction of all or part of things past, present or future." " Modern science," he remarked in one of his first essays, " is compelled to recognise that social life is a struggle, and that this struggle may occasion moments of pitiless intoxication." [54]

The Commission proceeded with its labors during the entire spring of 1895, with the results that might have been expected. The Turks discovered what they wanted to discover, and the European delegates did likewise. The upshot of the whole affair was that in April 1895 the English, French and Russian ambassadors at Constantinople worked out a scheme of reform for the six vilayets. The terms of this reform scheme were so modest that one can not be far wrong in suspecting that the Russian and French ambassadors acted as a brake on their English colleague.[55] The British cabinet was by no means satisfied, but failed utterly in its efforts to get more extensive provisions. Prince Lobanov, who succeeded Giers as Russian minister of foreign affairs in March 1895, pointed out the difficulties of introducing reforms which would satisfy the Armenians unless the powers were prepared to undertake the reform of the administration of the

---

[54] " En Orient " (*Revue de Paris*, December 1, 1895, pp. 449–61); Gabriel Hanotaux: *Études Historiques sur le XVI et XVII Siècles en France* (Paris, 1880), pp. 42–3. On the negotiations, see *Die Grosse Politik*, IX, no. 2191; Meyendorff: *Correspondance de M. de Staal*, II, pp. 252 ff.; *Turkey No. 1 (1895)* passim; and *Affaires Arméniennes*.

[55] Lobanov admitted this later (*Die Grosse Politik*, X, no. 2446).

whole of Turkey in Asia. He objected to the inclusion of six vilayets in the term Armenia.[56] Somewhat later, when the Sultan temporized about accepting the proposals of the powers and the English ambassador began to talk of using pressure, Lobanov refused absolutely to associate his government with any measures of constraint. The Armenian committees in London and elsewhere aimed at the creation in Asia Minor of a district in which the Armenians should enjoy exceptional privileges, and which would form the nucleus of a future independent Armenian Kingdom, and to this Russia would not and could not agree.[57]

There we may leave the Armenian question for the time being. So far as international alignments were concerned it brought about a temporary association of England, Russia and France, a Near Eastern Triplice, which made it appear that Britain had finally broken away from the Triple Alliance and had succeeded in drawing closer to the new Dual Alliance. As a matter of fact the Near Eastern Triplice had no such significance. No effort was ever made to exclude the powers of the Triple Alliance from the action. Russia and France were originally invited to join England simply because they were the only other two powers having consuls at Erzerum. The Sultan was anxious to associate them in the action and they themselves thought it expedient not to allow England to act alone. The English government itself was forced by popular agitation to take a stronger line than it would have wished. It must have known, from the reports of its own representatives, what the nature of the Armenian revolutionary movement was and what a serious menace it might be to the whole situation in the Near East.

Enough has been said above to make unnecessary any further reference here to the Hentchak and its program and methods. The leaders were quite prepared to have thousands of their fellow-countrymen massacred in order to force intervention by the European powers and in order to raise from the ruins of the Ottoman Empire a new Armenian socialist state. Had they had only England to deal with they might very well have succeeded, for the English people are easily aroused in a religious or humanitarian cause, and have never shown themselves very critical when once they were excited. But the continental governments were not so easily deluded. After all, if the Turks were massacring the Armenians, so were the Russians massacring the Jews. If the Turks oppressed the Armenians, did not the Russians oppress them too? — did they not oppress the Poles and other nationalities as well? One might sympathize with these people, but one could not start a great European conflagration for their sake, and everyone understood that a reopening of the Turkish question might very well result in such a conflagration.

The Russians, of course, were in a special position, because the Armenian movement touched them as well as the Turks. It has often been remarked that

<hr>

[56] *Turkey No. 1 (1896)*, nos. 14 and 44.
[57] *Turkey No. 1 (1896)*, nos. 65, 66, 71, 76, 83.

the crime of the partition of Poland served as the strongest link binding the three criminals together for a hundred years. In the same way the Armenian agitation was a force that made for Russian support of the Turk, no matter what other forces tended to drive the Russians into aggression against him. And so the Russians from the outset opposed all far-reaching reform. France followed Russia in order to be of service to a new ally and in order to prevent the English from monopolizing the protection of the Christians in the Levant. But from such a combination nothing very constructive could be hoped. The revolutionaries had succeeded in provoking the intervention of the European powers, but the intervention was such that it was doomed to failure from the very beginning. The net result of this phase of the movement was that thousands of innocent Armenians lost their lives, and there was no real gain to be shown.

BIBLIOGRAPHICAL NOTE

DOCUMENTARY SOURCES

Accounts and Papers. 1895, vol. CIX. *Turkey No. 1 (1895): Correspondence relating to the Asiatic Provinces of Turkey.* 1896, vol. XCV. *Turkey No. 1 (1896): Correspondence respecting the Introduction of Reforms in the Armenian Provinces of Asiatic Turkey; Turkey No. 3 (1896): Correspondence relating to the Asiatic Provinces of Turkey, 1892–1893.* vol. XCVI. *Turkey No. 6 (1896): Correspondence relating to the Asiatic Provinces of Turkey, 1894–1895.* These voluminous Blue Books contain a mine of information on the state of affairs in Armenia, and still constitute the most important single source.

Documents Diplomatiques. Affaires Arméniennes. Projets de Réformes dans l'Empire Ottoman. 1893–1897. Paris, 1897. This French Yellow Book is far less full than the British papers, but contains some interesting supplementary material.

Foreign Relations of the United States, 1893, 1894, 1895. These volumes of American documents are of considerable value for the study of the Armenian question.

Die Grosse Politik der Europäischen Kabinette, 1871–1914. Volume IX, chapter lv: The Powers and the Near East, 1890–1894; chapter lvi: The Armenian Triplice; chapter lviii: German-Russian Relations, 1894–1895.

MEMOIRS, AUTOBIOGRAPHIES, BIOGRAPHIES, AND LETTERS

Letters of Queen Victoria. Series III. volume II. New York, 1931.

CREWE, MARQUESS OF: *Lord Rosebery.* New York, 1931. Of relatively little value.

GARDINER, A. G.: *The Life of Sir William Harcourt.* Two volumes. London, 1923. One of the best and most revealing contributions to the history of the Rosebery administration.

MEYENDORFF, BARON A.: *Correspondance Diplomatique de M. de Staal.* Two volumes. Paris, 1929. Not of great importance, though there are several revealing documents bearing on the Armenian crisis.

SPECIAL STUDIES

BÉRARD, VICTOR: *La Politique du Sultan.* Paris, 1897. One of the best general studies of the Armenian crisis, based in large part upon the British Blue Books.

PERRIS, G. H.: *The Eastern Crisis of 1897 and the British Policy in the Near East.* London, 1897. Contains a good journalistic account of the Armenian problem, based largely upon the Blue Books. Written very much in the Gladstonian spirit, anti-Turk and anti-Russian.

ROLIN-JAEQUEMYNS, M. G.: " L'Arménie, les Arméniens, et les Traités." (*Revue de Droit International et de Législation Comparée,* XIX, 1887, pp. 284–325; XXI, 1889, pp. 291–353). An expert analysis of the documents and especially the Blue Books for the period after 1876.

SURBÉZY, F.: *Les Affaires d'Arménie et l'Intervention des Puissances Européennes. 1894–1897.* Montpellier, 1911. A French dissertation which adds very little.

ODYSSEUS (ELIOT, CHARLES N.): *Turkey in Europe.* London, 1900. Still a useful book, well-informed and sane. Contains a good sketch of the Armenian national movement, especially of the literary revival.

BORIAN, B. A.: *Armenia Meshdunarodnaia Diplomatiia.* Moscow, 1928. A solid Russian study which unfortunately deals almost entirely with the later period.

MANDELSTAMM, A. N.: *Das Armenische Problem im Lichte des Völker- und Menschenrechts.* Berlin, 1931. Another scholarly monograph, but also devoted primarily to the later period.

LEPSIUS, JOHANNES: *Armenia and Europe.* London, 1897. The best-known German work, written by a missionary with an extreme anti-English bias.

BLISS, EDWIN M.: *Turkey and the Armenian Atrocities.* Philadelphia, 1896. The work of an American missionary, and one of the fairest accounts of what happened.

HEPWORTH, GEORGE H.: *Through Armenia on Horseback.* New York, 1898. The result of a careful personal examination carried out just after the massacres.

BASMADJIAN, K. J.: *Histoire Moderne des Arméniens.* Paris, 1917. The best general history, though far from what it might be.

VÁLYI, FELIX: *Spiritual and Political Revolutions in Islam.* London, 1925. The work of an eminent Orientalist. It contains a good sketch of the development of the Armenian question, but is marked throughout by a very pronounced anti-Russian bias.

COURSONS, VICOMTE R. DES: *La Rébellion Arménienne.* Paris, 1895. A well-informed though not wholly accurate account of the revolutionary movement, which reprints a good many Hentchak manifestoes, etc. The book is strongly anti-English.

MACLER, FRÉDÉRIC: *Autour de l'Arménie.* Paris, 1917. A collection of essays and reviews by one of the leading students of things Armenian. It contains good discussions of the Armenian constitutional development and of the Armenian renaissance.

VARANDIAN, M.: *Hairenike Kaghapare (The Idea of Country).* Geneva, 1904.
—: *Haykakan Charjman Nakhapatmouthiun (Origins of the Armenian Movement).* Two volumes. Geneva, 1912–1913.

—: *Hai Heghapoghagan Dashnagtzoutan Badmoutiun (History of the Armenian Revolutionary Federation).* Two volumes. Paris, 1932. The works of Varandian are among the most valuable treatments of the subject. They are written in a somewhat rhapsodical fashion and aim to defend the Federation from its critics, but they are well-informed and full of factual material which it is impossible to find elsewhere.

TCHOBANIAN, ARCHAG: *L'Arménie, son Histoire, sa Littérature.* Paris, 1897. An address, by one of the leading Armenian literary figures. It is instructive, sound and interesting.

KHAN-AZAD: "Hai Heghapoghaganie Housheritz" ("From the Memoirs of an Armenian Revolutionary"). In *Hairenik Amsakir,* volumes V and VI, 1927–1929. This is the only source that can compare with the books of Varandian. It tells the story of the Hentchak as he tells the story of the A. R. F., and is of absolutely first-rate importance.

LITERATURE SINCE 1935

CAMBON, PAUL: "Lettres de Turquie" (*Revue de Paris,* XLIII, June 15, 1936, pp. 757–785). Interesting personal letters from the French Ambassador at Constantinople during the years 1894–1897. These have been included in the following title.

CAMBON, HENRI, ed.: *Paul Cambon: correspondance, 1870–1924.* Paris, 1940. 461 pp.

(CAMBON, HENRI): *Paul Cambon, ambassadeur de France, 1843–1924, par un diplomate.* Paris, 1937, 323 pp. A general biography, based primarily on the family papers.

HANOTAUX, GABRIEL: "Carnets" (*Revue des deux mondes,* April 1, 15, 1949). Interesting and illuminating reminiscences of the French statesman, covering the years 1893–1895.

SARKISSIAN, A. O.: *History of the Armenian Question to 1885.* Urbana, 1938. 151 pp. An excellent monograph, based in part on Armenian materials. Indispensable as background.

VRATZIAN, SIMON: *Armenia and the Armenian Question*. Boston, 1943. 107 pp. An uncritical review, of no great importance.

RAAB, ALFONS: *Die Politik Deutschlands im Nahen Orient, 1878–1908*. Vienna, 1936. 168 pp. A well-documented, critical study.

PENSON, LILLIAN M.: "The Principles and Methods of Lord Salisbury's Foreign Policy" (*Cambridge Historical Journal*, 1935, no. 1, pp. 87–106). A first-rate interpretative synthesis, but deals more particularly with the period prior to 1892.

HEYMANN, EGON: *Balkankriege — Bündnisse — Revolutionen. 150 Jahre Politik und Schicksal*. Berlin, 1938.

VI

The Sino-Japanese War and the Far Eastern Triplice

✍

I F THE ARMENIAN TRIPLICE WAS AT BOTTOM A FARCE, A COMBINATION devoid of any sound basis of common interest, much the same can be said of the Russian-French-German coalition which was called into existence in the spring of 1895 by the acute crisis resulting from Japan's war with China. This conflict itself was of the utmost importance in the history of international relations, for it marked the transition of the Far Eastern question from a state of quiescence to one of extreme activity. From 1895 until 1905 the problems connected with China and her future demanded the untiring vigilance of the European powers. More and more they came to dominate the course of international relations.

During the 19th century the great Chinese Empire had been forced, by diplomacy and war, to open a large number of ports to European commerce; after the middle of the century Japan, too, had been obliged to give up her isolation and her policy of exclusion. England had taken the lead in forcing open the gates of China, and English traders lost no time in exploiting this immense new market of more than three hundred million people. In 1894 England controlled about 65% of the Chinese trade, and fully 85% of all imports and exports were carried in British bottoms. Germany, France and Russia, though they lagged far behind England, were rapidly developing their commercial position, and were finding China one of the most lucrative and promising of markets.[1]

Prior to 1894 the European interest in China was primarily commercial. The powers on the whole tended to act together against the Chinese government. But even before the war between China and Japan the policy of dismemberment had begun. England, France and Russia had all made attempts, some successful, some not, to lop off outlying territories that were tributary to the Chinese Emperor. In Burma, Indo-China, central Asia, and in the far north, along the Amur, this new policy had met with ominous success. It was in keeping with this hunger for territory that the Japanese began to turn covetous eyes upon Korea,

---

[1] George N. Curzon: *Problems of the Far East* (London, 1894), p. 302; R. S. McCordock: *British Far Eastern Policy, 1894–1900* (New York, 1931), pp. 71 ff.; B. A. Romanov: *Rossia v Manchzhurii, 1892–1906* (Leningrad, 1928), pp. 6–9.

another vassal state of China, but one which was far more important than the others because of its geographical position. Located at the entrance to the Gulf of Pechili it commanded the approaches to Tientsin and to Peking itself. The Japanese claims to Korea went back to the nebulous early ages of the Christian era, but since the famous expedition of Hideyoshi to Korea in the late 16th century the connexion had been allowed to fall more or less into desuetude. It was not until the re-establishment of the Mikado's power in 1867 that serious attempts were made to re-affirm Japanese overlordship. The first efforts were completely unsuccessful, and thereafter there was constant danger of Japan's resorting to the use of force. The warlike Samurai and their chiefs repeatedly pressed for action, and it was only with difficulty that the government succeeded in partially satisfying this belligerent element by expeditions to Formosa and to the Liu-Kiu Islands. Nevertheless, it was through the action of Japan that Korea was opened to foreign trade in 1876 and it was through the energetic policy of the government that an agreement was come to with China in 1885. Under the terms of this convention neither China nor Japan was to send troops into Korea without notifying the other. But the legal status of Korea in international law remained undefined. The Chinese, who had on several occasions repudiated responsibility for the transgressions of the Korean government and had allowed foreign powers to negotiate with the King of Korea as with an independent sovereign, made every effort, after 1885, to re-establish actual control over Korean affairs. Yuan Shih-k'ai, the Chinese resident of Seoul, acted almost like a mayor of the palace, and through him the Chinese government directed the course of Korean policy.[2]

But the Korean question was not one that concerned China and Japan alone. Korea, indeed, had by 1894 become a sort of focal point for great European rivalries, as well as for Asiatic antagonisms. A potential enemy was Russia, which, since the Crimean War, had become more and more interested in Pacific problems. The eminent Russian pro-consul, Count Muraviev-Amurski, had, in 1858 and 1860, taken advantage of China's conflict with France and England to secure Chinese recognition of Russia's title to Siberian territory south to the Amur River, as well as to the Maritime Province, at the southern tip of which, not far from the Korean border, he founded Vladivostok in 1860. But these considerable acquisitions satisfied neither Muraviev nor his government, for the harbor of Vladivostok was closed by ice for four months of the year. Russia needed an open harbor on the Pacific, if only as a base for naval operations. In 1861 the first efforts were made to secure such a base. A Russian force occupied

---

[2] Curzon, op. cit., p. 220; Nagao Ariga, in Alfred Stead: *Japan by the Japanese* (London, 1904), pp. 147-8, 165-6, 195; Seiji Hishida: *The International Position of Japan as a Great Power* (New York, 1905), pp. 169 ff.; and the excellent recent studies by Alfred Vagts: "Der Chinesisch-Japanische Krieg, 1894-1895" (*Europäische Gespräche*, IX, May, 1931, pp. 234-52; June, 1931, pp. 285-302); T. F. Tsiang: "Sino-Japanese Diplomatic Relations, 1870-1894" (*Chinese Social and Political Science Review*, XVII, April, 1933); and especially Payson J. Treat: "China and Korea, 1885-1894" (*Political Science Quarterly*, XLIX, December, 1934, pp. 506-43).

the island of Tsushima, a Japanese possession lying just off the southeast coast of Korea. But the attempt failed. The English were at once suspicious of the Russian advance and the commander of the British Far Eastern squadron obliged the Russians to leave.[3]

Thereafter the Russians began to concentrate their attention on Korea, which, with its broken coastline, had some of the finest harbors in the Far East. In the spring of 1885, during the acute tension in Anglo-Russian relations resulting from the Muscovite advance on the Afghan frontier, rumors got about that the Russians were about to seize Port Lazarev, which they had surveyed and named in 1854. Once again the British acted without hesitation. The admiral in command on the Far Eastern station was instructed to occupy Port Hamilton, an island off the south coast of Korea, without consulting either the Chinese or the Korean government. Though this action was an open violation of international law, the British remained in occupation until the spring of 1887, when the Chinese government succeeded in securing from the Russian government a promise that it would not seize any part of Korean territory. It appears that the British were induced to evacuate partly because the admiralty reported unfavorably on the possibilities of this particular port.[4]

During the next seven or eight years the Korean situation remained very unsettled. The Chinese were trying desperately to establish control over Korean affairs, thereby driving the King into the arms of Russia. He seems to have asked the Tsar to assume a protectorate over the Kingdom. Though the request was evaded by the authorities in St. Petersburg, the secret leaked out, the result being that the Chinese redoubled their efforts to make their influence paramount in Seoul. Naturally the Russians did not like this new turn. Neither, for that matter, did the Japanese or the Americans, though the English stood behind Li Hung-chang and probably encouraged him. There has recently been published an interesting Russian document — the record of a discussion which took place in May 1888 between the governor-general of the Cis-Amurian province and Zinoviev, head of the Asiatic department of the Russian foreign office. These gentlemen decided that though Korea was of great importance to Russia, it would be unwise to acquire the peninsula, because it was so exposed that it would be hard to defend and because action there would bring Russia into conflict with China, supported by England, and with Japan. On the other hand, Chinese control of Korea would be very detrimental for Russia. The best thing, therefore, would be to work with Japan and the United States in supporting the Korean government against the pretensions of the Chinese.[5]

[3] Curzon, op. cit., p. 224.

[4] William H. Dawson, in *The Cambridge History of British Foreign Policy*, III, p. 230; Curzon, op. cit., pp. 222 ff.; Tyler Dennett: *Americans in Eastern Asia* (New York, 1922), p. 480; H. B. Morse: *The International Relations of the Chinese Empire* (New York, 1918), III, pp. 12 ff.; Franke: *Die Grossmächte in Ostasien* (Hamburg, 1923), pp. 25–7; Vagts, loc. cit.

[5] A. Popov: "Pervyie Shagi Russkogo Imperializma na Dal'nem Vostoke" (*Krasnyi Arkhiv*, LII, 1932, pp. 34–124), pp. 54–61; the American reports bear out Russia's desire to avoid trouble (Vagts, loc. cit., IX, p. 288).

The Russians, then, were pursuing a decidedly cautious policy with regard to Korea, chiefly because they were afraid of becoming embroiled in war with England. For reasons that are not entirely obvious the British seemed determined to prevent the Russians from encroaching on Korea and from securing an ice-free port. " Permanent Russian squadrons at Port Lazareff and Fusan would convert her (Russia) into the greatest naval Power in the Pacific," declared Curzon in an interesting but perhaps somewhat alarmist volume published on the eve of the war between China and Japan. " Russia is the nightmare of all Chinese statesmen . . . and a burning, ineradicable sore in the breast of the Manchus," remarked another English publicist in 1885.[6] He advised the formation of an Anglo-Chinese alliance to meet this danger, and suggested that Japan too might be induced to join the combination. The same idea was put forward by Sir Charles Dilke and later by Curzon. Apparently some advances of this nature were made to China in 1885 and again in 1893. Nothing concrete resulted, but there was, in fact, a sort of unofficial Anglo-Chinese entente in the decade following 1885. England staunchly supported the Chinese policy in Korea.[7]

The Japanese, on their part, were pursuing a policy in Korea not so different from that of Russia. They too desired to see Korea independent and opened up to foreign enterprise. But, despite this community of policy, it was almost impossible for Japan to play an active rôle, for during these years the government was so taken up with domestic matters that an active foreign policy was almost out of the question. At the same time close co-operation with Russia was hardly feasible, for the Japanese were profoundly suspicious of the Russian designs. A mission sent to Korea as early as 1869 was instructed to inquire into the relations of that country with Russia as well as with China. During the ensuing years Count Ito and other Japanese statesmen firmly opposed military action in Korea on the plea that Russia was the enemy most to be feared and that, if Japan became involved in Korea, Russia would victimize them both. Of course the Tokyo government, and for that matter the Japanese people, continued to be deeply interested in the Korean problem. They had great economic as well as political and military interests in the peninsula. Ito is said to have told Li Hung-chang in 1885 that while China's claims were chiefly historical and sentimental, Japan's claims were based upon economic necessity: she needed Korea as an outlet for her surplus population and as a source of food supply.[8] The facts bear out this assertion. In 1894 fully ninety per cent of Korea's foreign trade was with Japan. There were considerable Japanese settlements in all the larger

---

[6] Archibald R. Colquhoun: *English Policy in the Far East* (London, 1885), pp. 24–6.

[7] Sir Charles Dilke: *Europe in 1887* (London, 1887), p. 175; Curzon, op. cit., p. 300; Chung Fu Chang: *The Anglo-Japanese Alliance* (Baltimore, 1931), pp. 11–2; André Chéradame: *Le Monde et la Guerre Russo-Japonaise* (Paris, 1906), p. 83; Baron Rosen: *Forty Years of Diplomacy* (New York, 1920), II, p. 134.

[8] Ariga, loc. cit., pp. 148–66, 197.

towns, and the Japanese were strengthening their economic hold on the country through the operation of banks, concessions and trading establishments.[9]

In the years preceding the outbreak of the war between China and Japan every effort was made by Li Hung-chang to bolster up the Chinese position in the north. Efforts were made to build up a modern fighting force, and, with the help of English instructors, to acquire a respectable modern navy. In Manchuria and especially at Port Arthur large arsenals and military and naval stores were established. Not content with these preparations, Li decided to provide the means of communication necessary to make these new forces effective. The railway from Tientsin to the Kaiping coal fields, the first serious attempt at railway construction in China, was completed in 1889. In 1891 its extension to the great wall at Shanhaikwan was undertaken. But the line was meant only as part of a much larger plan. In May 1890 Li sent the English engineer, Mr. C. W. Kinder, to plot a line from Shanhaikwan northeastward through Manchuria to Mukden and thence towards the Russian frontier. Kinder actually made the tour, travelling in great secrecy.[10]

Li's railway projects had very important consequences. Despite the secrecy of Kinder's movements the Russian intelligence service discovered his intentions. At Vladivostok and at St. Petersburg much alarm was felt, for the Manchurian railway scheme looked almost like a threat at Russia's territory on the Amur and the Ussuri. Ever since the time of Muraviev-Amurski there had been talk of connecting Russia's Siberian possessions with Europe by a transcontinental railroad. Muraviev himself was deeply interested in schemes advanced by English and American concession-hunters. During the 1870's and 1880's some attention was given to the matter, especially by the Russian minister of communications, Possiett, who repeatedly stressed the need of opening up the wealth of Siberia. But the war of 1877–1878 and the subsequent financial difficulties of the government, as well as the inability of experts to agree upon a route, prevented specific action being taken. Only after the acute crisis of 1885 was the strategic argument advanced persistently by the governors and military men in the Far East. It was clearly urgent that Vladivostok should be connected by rail with the hinterland. Tsar Alexander himself saw the need of the railway, and used his authority to push the project. But the minister of finance, Vishnegradski, continued to plead lack of funds and no substantial progress was made until news came of Li's projected Manchurian line. In February 1891 the decision was taken to construct the line, beginning at Vladivostok as well as at the European end. In September 1892, Count Sergius Witte became minister of finance. He believed firmly in the economic as well as in the strategic value of the road and became the most ardent supporter of the enterprise. Construction

---

[9] Curzon, op. cit., pp. 185, 204 ff.

[10] Hermann Schumacher: "Eisenbahnbau und Eisenbahnpläne in China " (*Archiv für Eisenbahnwesen*, XXIII, pp. 87 ff., 1900); Percy H. Kent: *Railway Enterprise in China* (London, 1907), pp. 27 ff., 36 ff., 41 ff.; Wuisin Siao: *Die Entwicklung des Eisenbahnwesens in China* (Berlin, 1927), pp. 9 ff.

was advanced as far as possible and there was every prospect that the line would be completed before scheduled time.[11]

The construction of the Transsiberian Railway was regarded throughout the world as a portentous departure in Russian policy; as an event bound to transform the whole Far Eastern question and at the same time to modify the whole framework of international relations. Japan as well as China watched the Russian plan with deep apprehension. In Tokyo it was feared that if the Russians once completed their system of communications it would no longer be possible to resist their advance with anything like even chances of success. Yet the independence of Korea or its ultimate control by Japan was looked upon by Japanese political circles as indispensable to the security of the Empire. No doubt the domestic situation in Japan also had a direct bearing on the government's policy. Since the election of the first parliament in 1890 there had been no end of trouble with the radical and militaristic elements. Time and again parliament had to be adjourned or dissolved. When, in 1893, a sharp crisis arose in the relations between Japan and Korea, growing out of the prohibition of the export of beans, the American minister at Tokyo reported that there was a strong war feeling among the Japanese ministers and that "an invasion of Korea would be popular." The military elements, he declared, would like "to transfer the spirit of strife and conflict from internal politics of Japan to foreign affairs." It is claimed by some that the Japanese government indirectly encouraged the revolutionary movement of the Tong-haks in Korea in 1893–1894. At any rate the affair created a tremendous degree of excitement in Japan, with violent attacks upon the government for the weakness of its policy.[12]

Under the terms of the Tientsin Convention both China and Japan had the right to send troops into Korea to preserve order. The Koreans invited the Chinese to come to their rescue, and Li Hung-chang, after some hesitation, despatched some three thousand men, duly notifying the Japanese of the fact. The Tokyo government followed suit by sending a force which before long amounted to eight or ten thousand. In the meanwhile the Korean government had itself put down the Tong-haks. The Chinese government was prepared to withdraw its forces, and invited the Japanese to do likewise. But the Tokyo government now came forward with a new program — it refused to evacuate until adequate reforms had been arranged for. The Peking government was invited to join in this reform action, but flatly refused to intervene in strictly

11 A. N. de Koulomzine: *Le Transsibérien* (Paris, 1904), Book I; B. B. Glinskii: *Prolog Russko-Iaponskoi Voini* (Petrograd, 1916), pp. 1 ff.; B. A. Romanov: *Rossia v Manchzhurii* (Leningrad, 1928), pp. 51 ff.

12 Vagts, loc. cit., IX, pp. 286, 289, 392; Payson J. Treat: *Diplomatic Relations between the United States and Japan, 1853–1895* (Stanford, 1932), II, pp. 449–50; A. M. Pooley: *The Secret Memoirs of Count Tadasu Hayashi* (New York, 1915), pp. 37 ff.; M. von Brandt: *Drei Jahre Ostasiatischer Politik, 1894–1897* (Stuttgart, 1897), pp. 9 ff.; Morse, op. cit., III, pp. 18 ff.; Franke. op. cit., pp. 31–4; Harold M. Vinacke: *A History of the Far East in Modern Times* (New York, 1928), pp. 126–9.

Korean concerns. The Japanese therefore decided to go on alone. They took over control of the Korean administration and declared war on China on August 1.

Whatever may have been the rights and wrongs of the Chinese claims to suzerainty (and these claims were indiscreetly stressed in the correspondence with Japan in June 1894), and whatever was the Japanese interest in the reform of Korea, it is almost impossible to evade the conclusion, which was widely held at the time, that Japan precipitated the war because of domestic considerations. This was the opinion of the *North China Daily News* at the time and it was shared by persons like Curzon, who denounced the " school-boy patriotism " of the Japanese and accused the Tokyo government of trying to escape from domestic tangles by embarking upon a spirited foreign policy. The American minister at Tokyo reported on June 14 that

> " the restless and aggressive spirit of her (Japan's) people will not now permit the government to draw back, even should it desire to do so. The nation is united to a man in its support of the government's Korean policy. . . . The Japanese government cannot now draw back. They have committed themselves to a task that the nation insists shall be accomplished."

Two weeks later the Japanese minister at Washington frankly confessed the correctness of this view when he told the secretary of state, Mr. Gresham:

> " Our situation at home is critical and war with China would improve it by arousing the patriotic sentiment of our people and more strongly attaching them to the Government."

He admitted that his government thought it would be easier to " whip " China than to overcome a revolution at home.[13]

Before declaring war the Japanese government took the precaution of sounding out the attitude of the two great powers most directly concerned, namely England and Russia. The English, being friends of China and being eager to preserve the status quo, declared pretty categorically that they would refuse to tolerate any actions which infringed upon their own interests in China or upon the integrity and independence of Korea; specifically, that they would not acquiesce in the annexation of Korean territory by Japan. They warned the Japanese representative that any attempt on the part of his government to control Korea would certainly lead to Russian intervention and possibly to the seizure of a Korean harbor by Russia.[14] As a matter of fact the Russian government too stood behind the Chinese in this whole dispute, evidently reckoning that Korea was safer under the tutelage of a weak China than under the

---

[13] Curzon, op. cit., pp. 204, 208; Vagts, loc. cit., IX, pp. 297–8, 302; Treat, op. cit., II, pp. 460, 463. Treat makes some effort to minimize these avowals and contends that at bottom the Chinese reassertion of suzerainty was the primary cause of the war. This view, I believe, is not very widely held.

[14] Pooley, op. cit., pp. 45–6, quoting the memoirs of the Japanese foreign minister.

control of an energetic and aggressive Japan. Taken by and large Japan's position was so unfavorable, diplomatically speaking, that the government thought it wise to give assurances that it had no designs on Korean territory, but was interested only in the realization of the necessary reforms.[15]

The powers had done their utmost to prevent the outbreak of hostilities, and they had failed. Their anxiety was somewhat mitigated, however, when trading interests were reassured by a Japanese promise not to attack Shanghai. Besides, it was generally believed that the Japanese, though they might score a few initial successes, were doomed to ultimate defeat. Lord Curzon and a few other observers insisted that " the Chinese army, under Chinese officers, even with muskets in its hands and cartridges in its pouches, is an undisciplined rabble of tramps," but the general opinion was that the immense resources of China would eventually make themselves felt, and that the navy and the powerful fortifications of Port Arthur, constructed under European supervision, would finally turn the scales.[16]

These hopes and expectations were very soon blasted by the first Japanese successes, in the battles of Pingyang and the Yalu, on September 16 and 17. These engagements showed beyond the possibility of further doubt that neither the Chinese army nor the navy was fit to cope on equal terms with the efficient Japanese forces. Almost at once English public opinion began to turn from China and to contemplate a revision of British policy in the Far East. " Great Britain and Japan have no interests which are obviously in conflict with each other," wrote the London *Times;*

" There are some interests which may prove of the highest importance that are common to both nations. . . . Despite her pledge to China not to occupy Korea, Russia still hankers after the possession of a secure and open harbour on the Pacific. . . . But neither Great Britain nor Japan could look upon its fulfillment without concern. To Japan's future development as a maritime state, no more dangerous blow could be inflicted. To ourselves it would be a cause of considerable cost and anxiety." [17]

This utterance is most revealing of the evolution of opinion in English business circles. Of course the government could not execute a *volte face* quite so easily. But on October 6 the British government invited Germany, France, Russia, and the United States to take part in a joint intervention on the basis of the independence of Korea, under a European guarantee, and an indemnity for Japan. Russia was willing to collaborate on this basis. In fact, the council of ministers had, on August 21, decided that the safest course to pursue would

---

[15] Pooley, op. cit.; Popov, loc. cit., pp. 62–7; there is some very valuable Russian material on the origins of the war and the efforts of the powers to prevent it in the *Krasny Arkhiv*, L, LI, pp. 3–63: " Ez Epokhi Iapono-Kitaiskoi Voini."

[16] Curzon, op. cit., pp. 347, 358 ff., 411.

[17] *Times*, September 24, 1894, quoted in Chung Fu Chang: *The Anglo-Japanese Alliance,* pp. 16–7.

be to work in company with England to stop hostilities and secure a peace based upon the *status quo ante* in Korea.[18] But the United States refused to take part in the projected action and Germany did likewise, arguing that Japan would probably refuse such suggestions and that the move would therefore be futile.[19] Somewhat later, on November 7, the Chinese government made another attempt to bring about a settlement on this basis, but this démarche had no more success than the previous one. The war was allowed to continue until, by the spring of 1895, the Chinese were completely routed. The Japanese had invaded Manchuria, they had captured Port Arthur and they had forced the surrender of Wei-hai-wei, on the south side of the Gulf of Pechili. Negotiations for peace were initiated in January 1895, and the great question of the day was what price the Japanese would place upon their success.

The victory of Japan was an epoch-making event in the history of the Far East, and its repercussions were hardly less pronounced in Europe than in the Pacific. The powers, having miscalculated with regard to the probable outcome of the conflict, were now confronted with an entirely new situation. In England public opinion had changed completely in the course of six months. Nothing but disgust was felt for the weakness and incompetence exhibited by the Chinese, and there was considerable apprehension lest her military defeat might lead to the fall of the dynasty, the break-up of the Empire, and general anarchy. In some quarters it was feared that Japan might ally herself to China and assume the leadership of the yellow race, to the detriment of European interests, but there was, on the whole, a good deal of admiration for the plucky little victors and a general feeling that the best policy for England would be to recognize frankly the appearance of a new great power upon the scene.

" Japan, for many years to come, will do us no harm," argued the *St. James Gazette* on March 18; " We need not object to her naval strength in the Pacific. No doubt she would menace and alarm Russia; but that is no affair of ours. Let Japan and Russia fight it out if they please. For ourselves, if Japan acts as a counterpoise to the formidable Empire which is stretching one of its long arms round Northern Asia, we are no losers, and if Japan throws open the gigantic territories of China to foreign trade, we of all peoples in the world have most to gain by it, in spite of the competition of Yokohama and Tokio. Instead of making attempts to maintain a status quo that exists no longer, let us see that when the situation is altered we do not lose by the alteration. We want a port and naval station far up the Chinese coast, a thousand miles north of Hong-Kong, and with the consent of Japan we can get it. With that secured and China really opened to trade, we might regard the state of affairs on the Pacific with some equanimity." [20]

---

[18] Romanov, op. cit., pp. 66–7; Popov, loc. cit., pp. 62–7; *Letters of Queen Victoria*, II, p. 428.

[19] *Die Grosse Politik*, IX, nos. 2215–7; Joseph, op. cit., p. 73; Treat, op. cit., II, pp. 492 ff.

[20] Franke, op. cit., pp. 64, 67; Joseph, op. cit., pp. 89–90; Meyendorff: *Correspondance de M. de Staal*, II, pp. 263–4; McCordock, op. cit., pp. 118–9.

Next to the British, the Russians were perhaps most concerned with the revolutionary changes wrought by the war. Russia, too, had failed to foresee the outcome of the conflict and had been unable to fix upon a definite policy. The whole question was thrashed out in a council of ministers held on February 1, 1895, but the discussions showed that there were very wide differences of opinion. The chief difficulty was that no one knew what peace terms Japan would put forward. If they were moderate, there would be no occasion for Russia to do anything. On the other hand, as the minister for foreign affairs *pro tem.* pointed out, if the Japanese established themselves at Port Arthur or in Manchuria, to say nothing of Korea, the interests of Russia would be directly affected. It might then become desirable to occupy some island, such as Kargodo, at the southern tip of Korea. Curiously enough the minister of marine thought that it would be better to take part of Manchuria, but the war minister reminded his colleagues that it would be difficult to do so until the Transsiberian Railway was completed. He agreed with Witte that it would be best, for the time being, to do nothing beyond strengthening the naval forces in the Far East. The general sense of the meeting was that it would be wise to work with England, in the hope that the two powers together could induce the Japanese to be moderate. Other powers could, of course, be drawn into the action, but the main thought seems to have been that Russia, by collaboration with England, could keep the latter power from making acquisitions herself. The point of chief interest to the Russians was to secure the independence of Korea.[21]

In accordance with the decision of the council the Russian government put itself in touch with the British and also the French. In the conversations which took place in February and March general agreement was established between these powers with regard to the independence and integrity of Korea.[22] The British were obviously glad to work with the Russians and there was every prospect that the two powers would be able to shape events in the Far East to suit themselves. From the Japanese standpoint an Anglo-Russian agreement would be fraught with danger. In order to frustrate it the foreign minister, Count Mutsu, spoke to the Russian minister at Tokyo on February 15. He gave the most positive assurances with respect to Japanese plans in Korea and promised that Japan would treat the interests of the other powers with due caution. Japan's demands, he said, would comprise an indemnity and a cession of territory, indicating that the territorial demand would refer to Formosa. He, Mutsu, would be glad to enter upon an exchange of thoughts with the Russian government in order to avoid all misunderstandings.[23]

But the Tokyo government was not the only one to be alarmed by the spectre

---

[21] Romanov, op. cit., pp. 67–9; Popov, loc. cit., pp. 67–74; Meyendorff, op. cit., II, pp. 260–4. The Russian circular of February 1, mentioned by Pooley, p. 51, is not to be found in the Russian sources and appears to me to be apocryphal.

[22] Meyendorff, op. cit., II, pp. 259–64.

[23] "Dnievnik V. N. Lamsdorff" (*Krasnyi Arkhiv*, XLVI, 1931, pp. 3–37), p. 32; Joseph, op. cit., p. 83; Treat, op. cit., II, p. 519.

of an Anglo-Russian entente. For different reasons the Germans were just as much upset.[24] Thus far they had played an inconspicuous part in the Far East. Their interests there, in 1894-1895, were still almost exclusively commercial, and for that reason they were, on principle, opposed to the break-up of the Celestial Empire. This did not imply, of course, that if dismemberment were begun by others, the Germans would stand aside. They already felt the need for a naval base in the Pacific, and were determined, if events took a bad turn, not to be left out of the reckoning. In November 1894 the Emperor had already written to the chancellor expressing the fear that England and Russia might enter a partnership in order that the one might get Shanghai and the other a cession elsewhere. In that case, he said, the Germans would have to demand something, possibly Formosa. The foreign office thought such speculations a little premature and still trusted that the partition of China could be avoided. There was some further discussion in government circles as to what should be done if the worst came to the worst, but during the winter the question was not acute. Now, in February, when the Berlin foreign office learned of the possibility of an Anglo-Russian entente, it was distinctly worried. Inquiries were made in London with regard to the chances of securing the Chusan Islands at the mouth of the Yangtze River, but the British showed themselves cool and evasive.[25]

Such being the situation there were two courses open to the Germans. In the first place they might use their influence to prevent the Japanese from putting forward demands that would lead to Anglo-Russian action, and in the second place they might try to wean Russia from the new Anglophil policy. Both these courses were, in fact, followed. German relations with Japan had always been very friendly. Many of the instructors of the Japanese army were Germans. The Krupps had had close dealings with the Tokyo government in the matter of munitions supply, and there were other healthier business relations between the two countries.[26] It was therefore easy enough for the Berlin government to give the Japanese friendly advice. On March 8 the German minister warned the Tokyo foreign office that a demand for the cession of territory on the mainland would probably provoke the intervention of the powers (i.e. of England, Russia and France).[27]

This friendly warning seems to have had no effect whatever. There is some doubt whether it was ever communicated to the prime minister, Ito, or to the foreign minister, both gentlemen being at the time at army headquarters. The German note was handed to Count Hayashi, the assistant foreign secretary, who expressed the thanks of his government for the kindly consideration of the

---

[24] *Die Grosse Politik*, IX, nos. 2223, 2224; Franke, op. cit., pp. 38, 41.

[25] *Die Grosse Politik*, IX, nos. 2219-24; see also Arthur J. Irmer: *Die Erwerbung von Kiautschou, 1894-1898* (Cologne, 1930), pp. 8 ff.

[26] See especially Ludwig Riess: " Deutschland und Japan " (*Preussische Jahrbücher*, May, 1917, pp. 202-29).

[27] *Die Grosse Politik*, IX, no. 2226.

Germans. But even if the note was communicated to Ito and Mutsu there were good reasons why it had no positive results. The chief reason was that there existed a strong cleavage of opinion regarding the peace terms between the civil government and the military men. In the last days of December the American minister reported from Tokyo that " the spirit of the Army and Navy is one of conquest; their ambition can be satisfied with nothing less than the occupation of Peking and the complete humiliation of China." [28] Marshal Yamagata, to be sure, was moderate in his views, and he was associated with the foreign minister in the peace negotiations in order that the terms might be made palatable to the army. But it must have been hard to reach a decision on the terms. Any infringement of the independence or integrity of Korea was out of the question, since that would have made English and Russian intervention a certainty. The annexation of Formosa and other islands would evidently not satisfy the army. Though we have no conclusive testimony, I think we may be certain that the attitude of the military men forced the government, despite the warning from Berlin, to write a demand for cessions on the mainland into the terms that were to be submitted to the Chinese. [29]

The negotiations with the Chinese had been carried on intermittently since November 1894, but no progress had been made for some time. The Chinese claimed that they wanted peace and they were all the time appealing to the other powers to help them get it, but the evidence would seem to show that they had no idea of paying the penalty of defeat. They were, throughout the winter and spring, hoping for foreign intervention, and played a very questionable game with the American minister, who tried to help them, as well as with the Japanese. When finally a peace mission was sent to Japan late in January it turned out that the negotiators did not possess full powers. The Tokyo government refused to have anything to do with the delegates. It took another six weeks to straighten matters out and open the way for serious negotiation. [30]

The negotiations for peace were opened at Shimonoseki on March 20, Li Hung-chang acting as the chief Chinese plenipotentiary. Nothing specific was known of the Japanese terms, however, until they were submitted to the Chinese delegation on April 1. The Tokyo government demanded, among other things, that China recognize the full and complete independence of Korea; that she cede to Japan Formosa, the Pescadores Islands, and the whole of the Liaotung Peninsula, including Port Arthur; that she pay an indemnity of three hundred million taels; that she conclude with Japan a new treaty of commerce and navigation and grant Japan most-favored-nation treatment; that she open seven new ports to commerce; that she accord Japanese the right to navigate the

28 Treat, op. cit., II, p. 509.
29 See *Die Grosse Politik*, IX, no. 2306; and especially Pooley: *The Secret Memoirs of Count Hayashi*, pp. 79 ff.; also Franke, op. cit., pp. 50 ff.
80 The story is well told in Treat, op. cit., II, chap. xliv, passim, where much American archive material is cited.

upper Yangtze River and some of its tributaries, to establish warehouses, to engage in all kinds of industry, etc. After some negotiation and a few slight modifications, the Chinese were obliged to accept these terms, and the Treaty of Shimonoseki was signed on April 17.

Li Hung-chang took good care, throughout the negotiations, to keep the representatives of the powers well informed. He had, in fact, done his utmost to arrange for European intervention before he left for Japan. A few days after the submission of the Japanese terms he communicated them to foreign diplomats. It now became urgently necessary for the European governments to define their attitude. The English had, from the very beginning, made known their opposition to any infringement of Korean independence and integrity, and their aversion to any annexations of Chinese territory on the mainland. When the Japanese demand for the cession of Liaotung became known in London, the foreign minister, Lord Kimberley, admitted to the Russian ambassador that Port Arthur in Japanese hands would disturb the balance of power in the Far East and threaten the security of Peking, to say nothing of Korea's independence. On the other hand, he was hesitant about interfering, especially when it became known that the commercial clauses of the Japanese peace terms were so full of promise for all the powers which enjoyed the advantage of the most-favored-nation agreement. Speaking to the Russian ambassador he pointed out that England's interests were primarily commercial and that she would benefit from the arrangements imposed by Japan upon China. If the powers were to intervene, Japan would almost certainly resist, and then force would have to be applied.[31]

The apparent satisfaction of the British was bound to react upon Russian policy, because it foreshadowed the break-down of the entente which had been in prospect. The St. Petersburg cabinet had been more or less on tenter hooks throughout the early months of the year. In an astonishingly discerning report of February 18 the American minister at St. Petersburg had pointed out to his government the sad dilemma in which the Russians found themselves:

". . . I conclude that what Russia most needs and wants at this time is outlets upon the Pacific Ocean. She would be glad to have with this a considerable population to help her make her railroads pay expenses. Mongolia is a desert, fit only to sustain cross ties or to act as a frontier. Manchuria is thinly populated and too far North to alone fully answer her purposes. Corea and the country about Pekin, one or both, coupled with the other, more nearly meet her requirements.

"This war has come too early for Russia. Her Siberian road is not completed, and the great increase of her navy is not finished. Both continue to be rapidly pushed, but some years are required for their completion. . . . In a few years she could pick a quarrel with China and take what she wanted. . . .

"I take it that Russia is in a state of extreme embarrassment. . . . If she cannot now get what I am sure she wants, she will at least leave nothing un-

---

[31] Meyendorff, op. cit., II, pp. 265–8; Die Grosse Politik, IX, nos. 2234, 2236, 2239.

done to prevent Japan from gaining a foothold upon the continent, and to prevent anything like a protectorate over Corea." [32]

When the long period of uncertainty was at last over and the peace terms became known in the first days of April, the Russian government had to decide at once what attitude to take. The press was calling loudly for a protectorate over Korea, and even for the annexation of part of Manchuria, but of course the cabinet did not and could not pay much attention to such extravagant demands.[33] A practicable policy had to be devised, and at short notice at that. According to Witte, the new foreign minister, Prince Lobanov, was utterly ignorant of Far Eastern affairs and played no part in reaching a decision.[34] This is evidently just one of the many exaggerations in Witte's vainglorious account of his own career. Lobanov was a diplomat of long and wide experience. He had views of his own, and the courage to express them. On April 6 he outlined his proposed policy in two long memoranda addressed to the Tsar. In the first he pointed out how undesirable was the occupation of Liaotung and Port Arthur by Japan. Russia should protest against this, but should she go so far as to use force? The English, he continued, had announced that in all probability they would not protest, and there was no knowing how far the French or the Germans would be prepared to go. Under the circumstances Russia could do little more than to point out to Japan in a friendly way that possession of Port Arthur would be an eternal obstacle to the restoration of good relations with China and the maintenance of peace in the Far East. But first of all Russia should find out if other powers would join in the expression of such apprehensions.

In the second memorandum Lobanov dealt with larger problems. In future should Russia aim to establish close relations with China or with Japan? If Russia is satisfied with her present position, he argued, China would be the best ally, for she will be, for a long time, weak and innocuous. But if Russia wants more, then she must proceed on another track. It may be her aim to secure a non-freezing port on the Pacific and to annex part of Manchuria in order to carry the Transsiberian railway straight to Vladivostok. Now China has no port suitable for Russia's purposes, and she cannot be expected to cede part of Manchuria voluntarily. It would therefore be far better to strive for the attainment of these aims with the aid of Japan, a power which, incidentally, might prove useful as a check to England. Russia should try, then, to secure the support of other powers, and especially England, to prevent Japan becoming too strong as a result of the war, but at the same time she should make sure not to act alone in such a way as to arouse the enmity of Japan. To all of which Nicholas noted: " Russia absolutely needs a free port, open the entire year.

---

[32] Treat, op. cit., II, pp. 532–3.

[33] Popov, loc. cit., pp. 46 ff.

[34] *The Memoirs of Count Witte* (New York, 1921), p. 82; Rosen: *Forty Years of Diplomacy,* II, pp. 134 ff.

That port must be on the continent (southeast Korea) and absolutely must be connected with our present possessions by a strip of land." [35]

There was much sense in this policy, and there is some reason to suppose that the Japanese government would have welcomed an entente if it had been offered by Russia. In Tokyo as elsewhere it was perfectly well understood that sooner or later Russia would want a suitable terminus for the Railway. Vladivostok, being closed by ice for several months of the year, was clearly inadequate. Surveys which were being made for the railway route between Sretensk and Khabarovsk had shown that there would be a stretch of over five hundred miles of difficult terrain, where high embankments would be necessary to protect the line against floods. Years before, toward the end of 1887, it had been suggested by Admiral Kopytov that this section of the line should be built through northern Manchuria, thus shortening the route by several hundred miles and taking it through flatter and more thickly populated country. The idea had been considered by the government, but it was not taken up seriously until the surveys showed the difficulties of an all-Russian route. About the end of February 1895, Witte suggested application to the Chinese government for permission to build the line through northern Manchuria, from the frontier post of Novo-Tsurukaitui through Mergen to Blagovestchensk, thus keeping it as close to the Russian frontier as possible. But this idea was given up as impracticable, and on May 24 the minister of communications asked permission to make a reconnaissance with a view to constructing the line from Chita straight through Manchuria to Vladivostok. Witte, however, was opposed to precipitate action, and hoped to secure what Russia wanted through an alliance with China.[36]

The Japanese government, as aforesaid, was by no means oblivious of Russian interests and desires. On April 2, 1895 the Japanese minister at Berlin, speaking to one of the officials of the German foreign office, remarked that Japan must demand part of southern Manchuria, and especially Liaotung with Port Arthur. He realized that Russia desired part of northern Manchuria in order to run her railway on a more southerly route and terminate it at Possiet Bay, south of Vladivostok. Japan had no objection to this scheme, and Russia could make her arrangements with China. Japan, he hinted, would be prepared to have England take the Chusan Islands, and to see the Germans take over a province in southeastern China.[37] In other words Japan was ready to proceed to the dismemberment of China, on the basis of *do ut des* among the powers. Obviously Lobanov could have struck a profitable bargain with the new power

---

[35] Romanov, op. cit., pp. 69–70; texts in Popov, loc. cit., pp. 74–6.

[36] Koulomzine, op. cit., p. 38 note, 133 ff.; Glinski: *Prolog*, pp. 30–3; and especially Romanov, op. cit., pp. 82 ff. The Russian newspaper, *Novoie Vremia*, probably inspired by Witte, openly demanded that the Railway should be run through Manchuria, in order to strengthen the Russian position and check the inordinate pretensions of Japan; see the quotations in Joseph, op. cit., p. 88.

[37] *Die Grosse Politik*, IX, no. 2231.

in the Far East. But another turn in the situation seemed to offer him a more acceptable solution.

The policy outlined on April 6 provided first of all for international protest to Japan. Therefore Lobanov suggested to the powers on April 8 that they join in expressing to Japan in a friendly way their opinion that the annexation of Port Arthur would be a lasting obstacle to good relations between China and Japan, and a constant menace to peace in the Far East. The German government, profoundly disturbed by the fear that the Japanese claims might lead to a general scramble for Chinese territory and ever dreading an Anglo-Russian collaboration, agreed immediately to this step. The French government appears to have followed suit.[38]

If the British had been as willing as the Germans and the French to join in a protest to Japan, the situation would have been simple for the Russians. But the English indicated that they saw no reason for interference, and therefore the whole question had to be reconsidered by the Russian cabinet. The discussion took place on April 11 and revealed once again the difficulty of reaching a decision. There was little sympathy for an agreement with Japan, for not even Lobanov trusted the Tokyo government. At the same time it was clear that Russia could not compensate herself for Japan's gains, because she had only 30,000 men in the Far East and communications were so poor that it would take months to get more men to the scene. Yet the presence of the Japanese at Port Arthur and in southern Manchuria was, they agreed, a serious threat to Russia's position. What was to be done? Should Russia, with Germany and France, eject the Japanese and risk the danger of war, possibly with England as well as Japan? Or should she accept the Japanese peace and bide her time until the Railway was completed? Witte's viewpoint finally prevailed over the general confusion. He advocated resistance to Japan at once, for, he argued, the occupation of Liaotung by the Japanese was clearly directed against the Russian railway and the presence of the Japanese at Port Arthur would entail the eventual acquisition of all Korea. Japan would then be strengthened to such an extent that she would attract all the warlike Mongols and Manchus; it was not unlikely that in a few years the Mikado would replace the Chinese Emperor. If Japan were allowed to stay in Manchuria, Russia would require thousands of men and a much stronger fleet to protect her Far Eastern possessions. Sooner or later a clash with Japan would be inevitable. The question was merely whether it would be easier to allow the Japanese to stay in Manchuria and to seek compensation for Russia after the completion of the Railway, or whether to dispute the Japanese position at once. He, Witte, was for immediate action, since Germany and France were ready to co-operate. It was not likely, he asserted, that war would result, for the Japanese would be impressed by the determination of the powers and by Russia's readiness for energetic measures.

---

[38] *Die Grosse Politik,* IX, nos. 2232 ff.; Erich Brandenburg: *Von Bismarck zum Weltkriege* (Second edition, Berlin, 1925), pp. 51 ff.

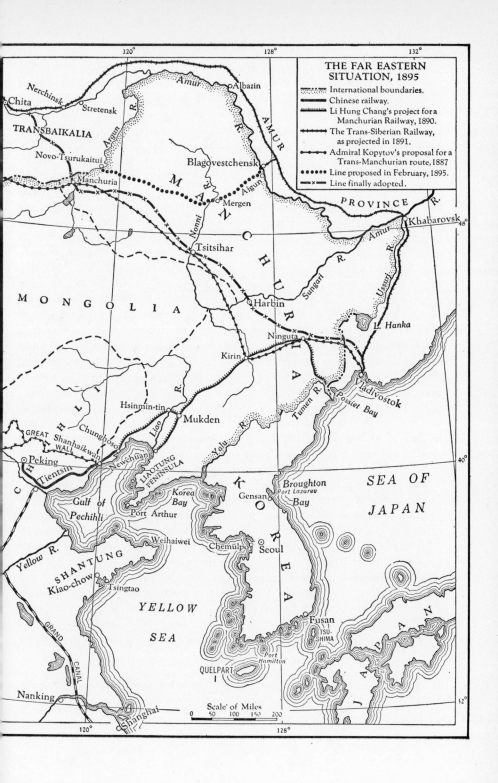

THE FAR EASTERN
SITUATION, 1895

International boundaries.
Chinese railway.
Li Hung Chang's project for a
  Manchurian Railway, 1890.
The Trans-Siberian Railway,
  as projected in 1891.
Admiral Kopytov's proposal for a
  Trans-Manchurian route, 1887
Line proposed in February, 1895.
Line finally adopted.

120°   128°   132°

Nerchinsk
Chita
Stretensk
TRANSBAIKALIA
Novo-Tsurukaitui
Manchuria
MANCHURIA
Amur R.
Albazin
Blagovestchensk
AMUR
Aigun
Mergen
PROVINCE
Khabarovsk   48°
Amur R.
Ussuri R.
Arun R.
Nonni
Tsitsihar
Sungari R.
MONGOLIA
Harbin
L. Hanka
Ninguta
Kirin
Vladivostok
Possiet Bay
Tumen R.
Hsinmin-tin
Chunghoso
Mukden
Liao R.
Yalu R.
GREAT
Shanhaikwan
WALL
Peking
Newchuang
Tientsin
LIAOTUNG
PENINSULA
Korea
Bay
Gensan
Broughton
Port Lazarev
Bay
SEA OF
JAPAN   40°
CHI-LI
Gulf of
Pechihli
Port Arthur
Weihaiwei
Chemulpo
Seoul
KOREA
Yellow R.
SHANTUNG
Kiao-chow
Tsingtao
YELLOW
SEA
Fusan
TSU-
SHIMA
JAPAN
Port
Hamilton
QUELPART
GRAND
CANAL
Nanking
Shanghai
Scale of Miles
0   50   100   150   200   32°

120°   128°

But if the Japanese should refuse to yield, the Russian fleet should take action and bombard the Japanese ports. Russia would then appear as the savior of China, and China, in gratitude, would peacefully agree to the extension of the Russian frontier.[39]

The report of the meeting was submitted to Nicholas only on April 15, apparently because Lobanov still hoped that a policy of non-resistance to the Japanese terms might be decided upon. The Tsar, however, approved Witte's stand, thereby ending the argument. On April 17 Lobanov officially approached the other powers and asked for support of Russia's protest.[40] The Germans showed no hesitation. They had offered their support and they stood by their offer. The reasons for their firmness are not hard to find. At bottom they were probably scared by the prospect of a Russian-French-English combination as much as by anything. These powers might help themselves to Chinese territory and shut Germany out from the feast. At the same time such a coalition might become extremely dangerous in European questions. So the German government, which at bottom favored the maintenance of Chinese integrity, decided that it would be the part of wisdom to be on hand if a partition took place. On this very April 17 the German admiralty reported that one station in the Far East would hardly suffice for German needs, and suggested various combinations of bases which might be put forward when the proper time came.[41] It is not impossible that Herr von Brandt, who had been for twenty years the German representative in the Far East and who became an official of the Berlin foreign office early in April, may have thrown his influence, which was considerable, into the scales in favor of action in behalf of China. He was in close touch with Li Hung-chang throughout the war, and it has been said that Li did not sign the peace treaty until he was assured by a code telegram from Brandt that there would be intervention on the part of the powers.[42]

But apart from the purely Far Eastern aspects of German policy, the Berlin foreign office was moved by considerations of a more general nature. The promise of support to Russia was simply another expression of the drift away from England and back to the Bismarckian tradition. The Emperor realized what the Iron Chancellor had realized long before, that it was to Germany's interest to divert Russian energies to the Far East in order to relieve pressure on the European frontiers. Furthermore, Baron Holstein, whose influence was all but decisive, was particularly anxious to prevent the new Franco-Russian combination from undergoing a " baptism of fire." In short, the Germans were

---

[39] Romanov, op. cit., pp. 71 ff.; the actual record is given in Popov, loc. cit., pp. 78–83; Witte's account, in his *Memoirs*, pp. 83–5, is very incomplete.

[40] Romanov, op. cit., pp. 75–6; *Die Grosse Politik*, IX, nos. 2243 ff.

[41] *Die Grosse Politik*, XIV, no. 3646; Irmer, op. cit., pp. 13–4.

[42] See the remarkable anonymous article " The Japanese Imbroglio " (*Blackwood's Magazine*, September, 1895, pp. 309–32) passim, and J. O. P. Bland: *Li Hung-Chang* (New York, 1917), pp. 175–80. The story was evidently told by the Chinese officials, for it was reported in full by the American minister on May 13, 1895 (Treat, op. cit., II, p. 538).

intent on avoiding any consecration of the Franco-Russian coalition, any encouragement of a larger English-Russian-French combination, and any antagonism between Germany and her continental neighbors.[43]

Little need be said of the French attitude. The Paris government supported
the Russians without much enthusiasm, because it would have preferred not
to oppose the Japanese demands. It feared that if Japan resisted, the English
might assist them and a general conflagration might result. Would it not be
better, said the French ambassador to Lobanov on April 14, to let things take
their course and put forward demands for compensation? France would be
satisfied with a small island in south Chinese waters, near Hainan, and Russia
could pick out a suitable port for herself.[44] But when the Russians decided on
another policy there was nothing to do but follow. France joined in the intervention, said M. Hanotaux later, from " considerations of general policy," in
other words for the sake of the alliance with Russia.[45]

Most important, of course, was the attitude of England. It is fairly clear that
up to the very end the Russians hoped that the London cabinet could be induced to take part in the action. The question was debated at some length and
with some heat in the cabinet meeting, but we know almost nothing of the
discussion or of the motives which kept the British standing aside. Curiously
enough no Blue Book was ever published dealing with the Far Eastern crisis of
1894–1895, and the memoir material is strangely silent on the matter. All we
know, from Queen Victoria's correspondence, is that Rosebery personally would
have liked to work with Russia, that he had great difficulties with his colleagues,
and that in the end he was unable to convince them. The Queen herself regretted
deeply that England could not join with the other powers, and wrote to the
Tsar to this effect.[46] It is difficult to pass any judgment on a policy when the
reasons behind it are not known. Certain it is that by this time the faith of the
English people had passed from the Chinese to the Japanese and that there was
opposition to the idea of interfering with Japan. Indeed, the public, having much
less use for Russia than the government, looked upon Japan as a valuable future
colleague in the work of blocking Russia. There was some criticism from well-
informed writers, who pointed out that England was making Russia a present
of her tremendous influence in China, that she was allowing the three powers
to weaken Japan, that in general she was abdicating her paramount position in
the Far East.[47] But the champions of the old connexion with China could no

[43] *Die Grosse Politik,* IX, chap. lvii, passim, but especially no. 2735; M. von Brandt, in
Deutsche Rundschau, June, 1895, p. 474; Otto Hammann: *Der Neue Kurs* (Berlin, 1918), p. 113;
Brandenburg, op. cit., pp. 50 ff.; Valentine Chirol: *Fifty Years in a Changing World* (London,
1927), p. 191.

[44] Popov, loc. cit., p. 77.

[45] Émile Bourgeois and Georges Pagès: *Les Origines . . . de la Grande Guerre,* pp. 251–3.

[46] *Letters of Queen Victoria,* II, pp. 496, 499, 507.

[47] Anon.: " The European Partners in Asia " (*Contemporary Review,* May, 1895, pp. 609–16);
Anon.: " The Japanese Imbroglio " (*Blackwood's Magazine,* September, 1895, pp. 309–32), to mention only two examples.

longer get a hearing. Before long the Chinese themselves would have nothing to do with the English. " One of the recommendations of any measure is that it will injure England," wrote the American minister at Peking in June 1895.[48]

The Treaty of Shimonoseki, concluding the war between China and Japan, was signed on April 17. On April 23 the representatives of the three powers at Tokyo handed in notes pointing out to the Japanese government that " the possession of the Peninsula of Liaotung, claimed by Japan, would be a constant menace to the capital of China, would at the same time render illusory the independence of Korea, and would henceforth be a perpetual obstacle to the peace of the Far East." Consequently they desired to give new proof of their friendship by advising the Japanese government to renounce the possession of the peninsula. The German minister, exceeding his instructions, supplemented his note with explanatory remarks couched in rather threatening and peremptory language, thus drawing upon his government, quite unnecessarily, the odium of the whole démarche.[49]

The Japanese foreign minister was seriously ill, and his assistant, Hayashi, asked for sufficient time to enable the government to reach a decision of such far-reaching importance. There followed several anxious days, during which it was impossible to predict whether Japan would accept the advice of the powers or not. If not, it would become necessary to use constraint, and in that case the great question would arise whether England would come to the assistance of the Japanese.[50] Since the beginning of the year the Russians had brought together a large naval force in Far Eastern waters. The commanders on the spot were anxious to act, and to settle the whole problem once and for all by putting the Japanese in their proper place.[51] But the French admiral deterred them.

Fully cognizant of the dangers of the situation the Japanese government consulted the military men, who were obliged to admit that resistance to the three powers was out of the question.[52] The government therefore offered, on May 1, to retrocede all of the Liaotung Peninsula, excepting the southernmost tip with Port Arthur. This solution was no solution, so far as the Russians were concerned, for Port Arthur was the most important part of the whole area. Supported by the Germans and the French, the Russian government rejected the offer, and finally, on May 5, the Japanese government yielded completely. It agreed to retrocede its acquisitions on the mainland, asking only that the Treaty of Shimonoseki be first ratified, and that a larger indemnity be allowed Japan. To this the powers assented. The Treaty was ratified at Chefoo on May 8,

---

48 Treat, op. cit., II, p. 543.

49 Hayashi: *Memoirs*, pp. 80 ff.; *Die Grosse Politik*, IX, nos. 2245 ff.

50 Meyendorff: *Correspondance de M. de Staal*, II, pp. 270–2.

51 Félix Martin: *Le Japon Vrai* (Paris, 1898), pp. 174 ff.; Chéradame, op. cit., pp. 323, 325; Comte de Guichen: "La Politique Extérieure du Japon" (*Revue d'Histoire Diplomatique*, XXIII, pp. 89–107, January, 1909); J. J. Matignon: "Li Hung Chang" (*Nouvelle Revue*, August 1, 1925), p. 217.

52 Treat, op. cit., II, p. 540.

while the Russian squadron lay at anchor in the harbor. " To make the demonstration more impressive," says Mr. Foster, the adviser of the Chinese delegation, " as each vessel came to anchor it immediately proceeded to don the war paint of dark gray and strip for action, using the shore just in front of the hotel in which the Japanese treaty commission was quartered for the storage of boats, sails and other superfluous paraphernalia." [53]

Thus far the three powers had acted together harmoniously, but it turned out before long that the Far Eastern Triplice suffered from the same weaknesses which characterized the Near Eastern Triplice in the Armenian question. None of the three powers was interested merely in checking the advance of Japan on the continent of Asia. All three, on the contrary, hoped, by securing the gratitude of the Chinese government, to obtain advantages for themselves.[54] Lobanov, while admitting that Russia was anxious to see the Chinese indemnity to Japan paid and the evacuation of Liaotung effected, wrote to the Russian ambassador at Paris that this was not the only motive behind Russian action: " It is no less important for our projects to bring China into a sort of dependence in relation to ourselves and not to let England extend her influence in China." [55] Negotiations with China to secure the right to run the Transsiberian Railway through Manchuria were begun only in the spring of 1896, but it is obvious from what has already been said that this object was behind Russian policy from the very beginning of the crisis. The German attitude, likewise, was determined by the hope that a grateful China would listen sympathetically to the argument that Germany needed a naval station in the Far East. The Chinese were told that it was Germany that initiated the action that resulted in the retrocession of Liaotung,[56] and only a few days after the submission of the warnings in Tokyo, Emperor William wrote to the Tsar saying:

" I shall certainly do all in my power to keep Europe quiet, and also to guard the rear of Russia so that nobody shall hamper your action towards the Far East. For that is clearly the great task of the future for Russia to cultivate the Asian continent and to defend Europe from the inroads of the Great Yellow race. In this you will always find me on your side, ready to help you as best I can. You have well understood that call of Providence and have quickly grasped the moment; it is of immense political and historical value and much good will come of it. I shall with interest await the further development of our action and hope that, just as I will gladly help you to settle the question of eventual annexations of portions of territory for Russia, you will kindly see that Germany may also be able to acquire a Port somewhere where it does not gêne you." [57]

---

[53] John W. Foster: *Diplomatic Memoirs* (Boston, 1909), II, p. 151; *Die Grosse Politik,* IX, nos. 2258 ff.; Auguste Gérard: *Ma Mission en Chine* (Paris, 1918), pp. 41 ff.; Nagao Ariga, in Alfred Stead: *Japan by the Japanese* (London, 1904), p. 204; K. Asakawa: *The Russo-Japanese Conflict* (Boston, 1904), p. 76.

[54] The American minister had warned the Chinese of this at the outset, and had argued in vain that nothing would hasten dismemberment as much as intervention (Treat, op. cit., II, p. 525).

[55] Meyendorff, op. cit., II, pp. 272, 274.   [56] Brandenburg, op. cit., pp. 56–7.
[57] *The Kaiser's Letters to the Tsar* (London, 1920), pp. 10–1.

Of the French motives less is known than of the Russian and German, but it appears clearly enough from the negotiations that the Paris government entertained desiderata not unlike those of its partners. For the time being all three powers were eager to impress the Chinese with their good will. An excellent occasion for this demonstration arose with the question of the Chinese indemnity, which amounted to about $150,000,000, apart from the additional indemnity to be paid in return for the retrocession of Liaotung, the exact amount of which had not yet been determined. It was generally assumed that the three powers would co-operate in supplying the necessary funds. All three were interested in excluding British capital and preventing the extension of British influence. But the outcome of the negotiations was quite different. All the details are not clear, but it seems that the Chinese government, anxious not to fall too much under the influence of its Russian savior, opened negotiations first with Berlin and London financial circles. The German government made no secret of its interest in the transaction, and itself communicated the details to the Russian chargé d'affaires, late in April. The Russian minister of finance, Witte, appears to have been but little perturbed, the more so as the whole affair was a purely financial one and the Russian government had no money to lend. But in the course of the discussions the proposal came up that an international commission be created to supervise the service of the Chinese debt. The French bankers, fearing that they would be in a minority in the composition of such a body, then invited the Russian government to join, offering at the same time to supply the necessary funds. Witte, however, was not satisfied; he felt that it would be better for Russia to guarantee the loan, thus freeing China of foreign financial supervision and leaving her at Russia's mercy. It was therefore decided to offer a Franco-Russian loan of 400,000,000 francs, and arrangements were completed with China on July 6. The terms of the contract are very interesting, as they illustrate clearly the motives behind the transaction. China was to receive 94% of the face value of the loan, and to pay only 4% interest. The Russian government undertook to guarantee the payments, but Article III provided that, in case of Chinese default, the Peking government should furnish the Russian government " additional security," the character of which was to be determined by a special agreement. It was further provided, in Article IV, that the Chinese government should not grant any foreign power any right or privilege concerning the supervision or administration of the revenues, and that, if it did grant such a right, it should be automatically extended to the Russian government also. In other words, the Russian government was taking precautions to prevent the control of Chinese revenues from falling into other hands, and was establishing for itself a privileged position.[58]

---

[58] The best account from the Russian side is in Romanov, op. cit., pp. 86–92, but see also Henri Cordier: *Histoire des Relations de la Chine avec les Puissances Occidentales* (Paris, 1902), III, pp. 304–6; Morse, op. cit., III, pp. 52–3; Gérard: *Ma Mission en Chine*, pp. 68–71; Joseph,

The Chinese indemnity loan was important not only because it marked the beginning of Russian preponderance in China, but also because of its international repercussions. The Germans felt that they had deserved better treatment at the hands of Russia, and were filled with righteous indignation. Later on Lobanov tried to excuse the Russian action by saying that the French bankers had been unwilling to collaborate with the Germans, a statement which Hanotaux disputed. The fact is that the Russians had a definite object in view and that, when Witte saw his opportunity, he seized it. It cannot be shown that he meant to circumvent the Germans, but it cannot be denied that his action was indiscreet and tactless. The result was that the Germans became cooler in their support of Russian policy during the long-drawn negotiations regarding the ways and means of Japan's withdrawal from Liaotung, and showed a greater disposition to take the side of the Japanese. It was not until November that the intervention episode was finally brought to a close.[59]

The question of the Chinese loan did much to illuminate the jealousies and rivalries of the three powers and to show up the fundamental weakness of the Far Eastern Triplice. Just as the Russians had co-operated with the English in the Armenian question to prevent the success of the English aims, so in the matter of the Japanese peace terms the Germans had acted with the Russians in order to prevent Russia and France from acting alone. But despite the misunderstandings that clouded the horizon, the relations between Germany on the one hand and France and Russia on the other remained fairly cordial. In June French ships took part in the great celebrations that marked the opening of the Kiel Canal. It was generally felt in Berlin that both President Faure and M. Hanotaux were sincerely anxious to cultivate friendly relations, and the French were given the benefit of the doubt whenever public opinion threatened to precipitate trouble. The fact was that the Germans did not feel that they could afford to estrange the French. The existence of a firm bond between Paris and St. Petersburg was hardly open to doubt, especially after M. Hanotaux stated in the Chamber on June 10 that France and Russia had joined hands, and Ribot said openly that France had " allied " her interests to those of another great power, and that this " alliance " must remain a guarantee of peace.[60]

But if Germany could not afford to estrange France, it was even more important for her to continue support of Russian policy in the Far East, not only because it was felt in Berlin that a station on the Pacific could best be obtained in this way, but also because Germany had a very great interest in preventing the Franco-Russian Alliance from becoming too close an association, and an even greater interest in diverting the attention of Russia from Europe to the

---

op. cit., chap. vi; and Arthur G. Coons: *The Foreign Public Debt of China* (Philadelphia, 1930), pp. 6–8.

[59] *Die Grosse Politik*, IX, nos. 2276 ff.; Joseph, op. cit., chap. vi, passim.

[60] *Die Grosse Politik*, IX, nos. 2343–58; Bourgeois and Pagès, op. cit., pp. 253–5; Raymond Poincaré: *Au Service de la France* (Paris, 1926), I, p. 286; E. M. Carroll: *French Public Opinion and Foreign Affairs, 1870–1914* (New York, 1931), pp. 162 ff.

Far East. This idea grew more and more in the mind of the Emperor during the summer of 1895, so that it overshadowed all other considerations and kept the German irritation at Russia's perfidy in the matter of the Chinese loan within very definite bounds.[61]

As one looks back over the years 1893 to 1895 it becomes very evident that during this period European international relations were in a state of complete flux. The statesmen of the old order disappeared. Caprivi was dismissed in November 1894, just as Alexander III departed from this life. Giers died soon after, and was succeeded by Lobanov. Then Kálnoky gave way to a new Austrian foreign minister, Count Goluchowski, and finally, in June 1895, the Liberal Rosebery cabinet in England was replaced by a Conservative-Unionist ministry under Lord Salisbury. In France cabinet changes were so rapid that they ceased to have much significance under ordinary circumstances. But these years were the years during which French foreign policy was controlled mainly by M. Hanotaux, as it was later by M. Delcassé. Hanotaux had a policy that was far different from that of his predecessors like Flourens, Ribot, Freycinet and Develle. In France, as in the other major countries, there was a distinct break in direction in the period following Toulon. Above all, European politics at this time underwent a pronounced transformation. African and Asian questions came to play a greater and greater part, and international relations came to mean world politics. This epoch-making change was due primarily to the marked economic development of the continental countries during the 1890's, but it was in a large measure due also to the evolution of the new alliance system. The creation of the Franco-Russian Alliance established a delicate balance of power on the Continent and brought about something like a deadlock. Neither the French nor the Russians were desirous of challenging Germany or the Triple Alliance. Two defensive systems stood opposed to each other. Nothing could be done, excepting at the cost of a great conflagration.

Under these circumstances the attention of the powers was necessarily diverted more and more to extra-European fields, and the natural consequence of this process was that England, the world power *par excellence,* felt the pressure of the new combinations more than any other power. The Franco-German action against the Anglo-Congolese Treaty is a striking illustration of this point. It showed that England was isolated and that the two great groups of continental powers, unwilling to drift into conflict with each other, might very well co-operate against the one great power which stood aloof from both groups. To remedy this situation Rosebery and Kimberley made real efforts to bring about an entente with Russia, but the experience of the Armenian Triplice made it all too evident that the interests of the two powers were too far apart. In the Far Eastern crisis, on the other hand, it was Germany that was haunted by the fear of exclusion from an English-Russian-French combination that would settle the affair to its own interests. While England gradually withdrew from

---

[61] *Die Grosse Politik,* IX, especially nos. 2313, 2318.

the operation and revised her attitude toward China and Japan, the Germans took care not to be left out. Their experience, however, was hardly less satisfactory than that of England in the Near Eastern Triplice. These new combinations were evidently ephemeral and weak in the foundations. In the summer of 1895 the situation at bottom was not far different from what it had been in 1893, at least so far as the European alignments were concerned. The Franco-Russian Alliance had shown itself to be a real factor, which had always to be taken into account. But the new grouping endangered England's position more than Germany's, for Germany, besides being a very strong power in her own right, had two allies on the Continent. England, on the other hand, had no real friends and no allies, yet at the same time her far-flung possessions exposed her particularly to attack. As Africa and Asia came to play an ever greater rôle in international relations, it was inevitable that England's position should become ever more precarious.

BIBLIOGRAPHICAL NOTE

DOCUMENTARY SOURCES

Documents Diplomatiques. Chine, 1894–1898. Paris, 1898. Contains very little on the period 1894–1895.

Die Grosse Politik der Europäischen Kabinette, 1871–1914. Volume IX, chapter lvii: The Far Eastern Triplice; chapter lviii: German-Russian Relations, 1894–1895.

Foreign Relations of the United States, 1894, 1895. These volumes of American documents are of great interest for the history of the Far Eastern question, though naturally they have little on the policies of European powers.

"Ez Epokhi Iapono-Kitaiskoi Voini, 1894–1895." (*Krasnyi Arkhiv,* L and LI, 1932, pp. 3–63). A valuable collection of Russian documents covering the period from February to August 1894. The documents are particularly important for the history of the efforts made by the powers to prevent the war. This material has been translated into English and published in the *Chinese Social and Political Science Review,* XVII, 1933, pp. 480–514, 632–70.

POPOV, A.: " Pervyie Shagi Russkogo Imperializma na Dal'nem Vostoke." (*Krasnyi Arkhiv,* LII, 1932, pp. 34–124). Another valuable collection of Russian documents, the first of which are the reports of meetings of the council of ministers in 1894 and 1895 to decide on the policy to be pursued in the Far East. The first part of this collection has been translated in the *Chinese Social and Political Science Review,* XVIII, 1934, pp. 236–81.

MEMOIRS, AUTOBIOGRAPHIES, BIOGRAPHIES, AND LETTERS

Letters of Queen Victoria. Edited by George E. Buckle. Series III, volume II. New York, 1931. Contains a few important scraps on British policy in the Far East.

CREWE, MARQUESS OF: *Lord Rosebery.* New York, 1931. Of very little help.

MEYENDORFF, BARON A.: *Correspondance Diplomatique de M. de Staal.* Two volumes. Paris, 1929. Not of first-rate importance, but contains some revealing documents from the Russian side.

The Memoirs of Count Witte. Edited by A. Yarmolinsky. New York, 1921. These memoirs are the best known source for the history of Russian policy, especially in the Far East. They are incomplete and often unreliable, and should be used with caution.

ROSEN, BARON: *Forty Years of Diplomacy.* Two volumes. New York, 1922. Interesting reminiscences of a level-headed diplomat. The discussion of Russia's Far Eastern policy is critical and of real value.

The Secret Memoirs of Count Tadasu Hayashi. Edited by A. M. Pooley. New York, 1915. The most important source for the history of Japanese foreign policy in this period.

BLAND, J. O. P.: *Li-Hung-Chang.* New York, 1917. A reasonably good biography of the Chinese statesman, though now somewhat out of date.

MUTSU, M.: *Hakushaku Mutsu Munemitsu iko.* Tokyo, 1929. The papers of the Japanese foreign minister. Evidently a rather important source, which unfortunately I have been unable to obtain.

SPECIAL STUDIES

CORDIER, HENRI: *Histoire des Relations de la Chine avec les Puissances Occidentales.* Three volumes. Paris, 1901–1902. Despite its age this is still one of the very best studies of China's foreign relations.

MORSE, HOSEA B.: *The International Relations of the Chinese Empire.* Three volumes. New York, 1918. A good systematic account, based chiefly upon American and British documents, but valuable because of the use it makes of periodical material.

FRANKE, OTTO: *Die Grossmächte in Ostasien von 1894 bis 1914.* Stuttgart, 1923. An excellent German account, by a well-known Orientalist. It is now somewhat out of date.

ZÜHLKE, HERBERT: *Die Rolle des Fernen Ostens in den Politischen Beziehungen der Mächte, 1895–1905.* Berlin, 1929. A sound, conventional study of the international aspects of the Far Eastern question.

DAVID, HEINRICH: *Zur Politik der Grossmächte im Fernen Osten, 1894-1902.* Zurich, 1932. A general essay, which adds little.

JOSEPH, PHILIP: *Foreign Diplomacy in China, 1894–1900*. London, 1928. The best single study, but deficient in the use of Russian material.

McCORDOCK, R. STANLEY: *British Far Eastern Policy, 1894–1900*. New York, 1931. A sound but in no way original dissertation.

ASAKAWA, K.: *The Russo-Japanese Conflict*. Boston, 1904. Still one of the best analyses of the problem from the Japanese side.

TREAT, PAYSON J.: *Diplomatic Relations between the United States and Japan, 1853–1895*. Two volumes. Stanford University, 1932. An extremely valuable book, which draws heavily upon unpublished American archive material.

" VLADIMIR ": *The China-Japan War*. New York, 1896. On the whole this is the best contemporary history of the war. It prints many oriental as well as western documents.

CLYDE, PAUL H.: *International Rivalries in Manchuria, 1689–1922*. Columbus, 1926. A general survey of the Manchurian problem, based upon the materials available in western languages.

KOULOMZINE, A. N. DE: *Le Transsibérien*. Paris, 1904. The French translation of the official Russian history of the Railroad, based upon unpublished material.

KENT, PERCY H.: *Railway Enterprise in China*. London, 1907. Still the best general account of the subject.

HSU, SHUHSI: *China and Her Political Entity*. New York, 1926. A study of the Korean and Manchurian problems, based in part upon Chinese sources, but adding little.

WEIGH, KEN SHEN: *Russo-Chinese Diplomacy*. Shanghai, 1928. Deals very cursorily with the earlier period and makes no contribution.

ARIGA, NAGAO: " Diplomacy." (In *Japan by the Japanese,* edited by Alfred Stead. London, 1904). One of the best studies of the subject, by an eminent Japanese expert on international law.

HISHIDA, SEIJI G.: *The International Position of Japan as a Great Power*. New York, 1905. Another good systematic study of Japanese diplomacy.

GLINSKII, B. B.: *Prolog Russko-Iaponskoi Voini*. Petrograd, 1916. A valuable book, based upon the Witte papers and an important supplement to the Witte memoirs. A large part of this book appeared in French translation under the pseudonym Pierre Marc: *Quelques Années de Politique Internationale; Antecédents de la Guerre Russo-Japonaise*. Leipzig, 1914.

ROMANOV, B. A.: *Rossia v Manchzhurii, 1892–1906*. Leningrad, 1928. Far and away the most important Russian treatment, based upon a large amount of unpublished material. An abstract of this work has appeared in English by J. J. Gapanovich, in the *Chinese Social and Political Science Review*, XVII, 1933, pp. 283–306, 457–79.

AVARIN, B.: *Imperializm i Manchzhuriia*. Moscow, 1931. An interesting and well-informed study of the economic aspect of the Manchurian question. Rather scant on the period prior to the Russian-Japanese War.

VAGTS, ALFRED: "Der Chinesisch-Japanische Krieg, 1894–1895." (*Europäische Gespräche,* IX, 1931, pp. 234–52, 285–302). The most recent and the best monographic treatment of the causes and background of the war. The author has made use of some unpublished American archive material.

TSIANG, T. F.: "Sino-Japanese Diplomatic Relations, 1870–1894." (*Chinese Social and Political Science Review,* XVII, 1933, pp. 3–107). Important if only because of the fact that it is based almost entirely upon Chinese materials. Unfortunately the treatment of the years 1885–1894 is rather slight.

TREAT, PAYSON J.: "China and Korea, 1885–1894." (*Political Science Quarterly,* XLIX, 1934, pp. 506–43). Based primarily upon unpublished material from the United States department of state. Should be read in conjunction with the preceding.

LITERATURE SINCE 1935

RENOUVIN, PIERRE: *La question d'Extrême-Orient, 1840–1940.* Paris, 1946. 435 pp. An excellent recent text.

CLYDE, PAUL H.: *The Far East: a History of the Impact of the West on Eastern Asia.* New York, 1948. 862 pp. Though this text covers the entire field, it is particularly strong on international relations of the nineteenth and twentieth centuries.

FRANKE, WOLFGANG: "Chinesische Quellen zur auswärtigen Politik des 19ten und frühen 20sten Jahrhunderts" (*Sinologica,* I, 1948, pp. 210–229). Discusses the important recently published Chinese sources on foreign policy and prints representative passages in German translation.

TREAT, PAYSON J.: "The Causes of the Sino-Japanese War" (*Pacific Historical Review,* VIII, June, 1939, pp. 149–158). Aims to prove that the basic cause of the war was the provocative Chinese policy in Korea.

SPINKS, CHARLES N.: "Origin of Japanese Interests in Manchuria" (*Far Eastern Quarterly,* II, May, 1943, pp. 259–272). Deals at some length with the origins of the Sino-Japanese War.

NAROCHNITSKII, A. L.: "Angliia, Kitaia i Iaponiia nakanune Iapono-Kitaiskoi Voini, 1894–1895 gg." (*Istoricheski Zapiski,* no. 19, 1946, pp. 189–214). Deals largely with economic aspects, using much contemporary writing and also to some extent Russian Foreign Office documents.

—: "Angliia, Rossiia i Koreiskii Vopros nakanune Napadeniia Iaponii na Kitai letom 1894 g." (*Istoricheski Zapiski,* no. 24, 1947, pp. 160–183). Similar to the preceding. A commendably solid job based on all available materials as well as Russian archival records.

NOZIKOV, N.: *Iapono-Kitaiskaia Voina, 1894–1895 gg.* Moscow, 1939.

GUBER, A. A.: "Mezhdunarodnye Otnosheniia na Dal'nem Vostoke, 1894–1904 gg." (*Ucheniye Zapiski Tikho-okeanskogo Instituta,* I, 1947).

TAKEUCHI, STERLING T.: *War and Diplomacy in the Japanese Empire*. New York, 1935. 524 pp. Though concerned chiefly with the problem of control of foreign policy in Japan, this volume contains an illuminating chapter on the Sino-Japanese War, based partly on Japanese sources.

AKAGI, ROY H.: *Japan's Foreign Relations, 1542–1936*. Tokyo, 1936. 560 pp. A convenient survey.

HISHIDA, SEIJI: *Japan among the Great Powers: a Survey of her International Relations*. New York, 1940. 405 pp. A general treatment, rather summary on the period before 1905, but making use of much Japanese material.

CRAMER, ANNELIESE: *Die Beziehungen zwischen England und Japan von 1894 bis 1902*. Zeulenroda, 1935. 78 pp. A doctoral dissertation.

POPOV, A.: " Ot Bosfora k Tikhomu Okeanu " (*Istorik Marksist*, no. 37, 1934, pp. 3–28). Based upon extensive use of Russian press and periodical material, this is a stimulating study of the shift of interest from the Balkans to the Far East after 1878.

SUMNER, B. H.: *Tsardom and Imperialism in the Far East and Middle East, 1880–1914*. New York, 1942. 43 pp. A learned lecture which, however, treats chiefly of the Manchurian and Persian questions.

POPOV, A.: " Dal'nevostochnaia Politika Tsarizma v 1894–1901 gg." (*Istorik Marksist*, XI, 1935, pp. 38–58). A valuable contribution, drawing heavily on contemporary Russian writing and on Russian archives. Deals chiefly with Russian economic expansion in China.

KRUPINSKI, KURT: *Die russisch-japanischen Beziehungen von ihren Anfängen bis zum Frieden von Portsmouth*. Königsberg, 1940. 126 pp. One of the best recent monographs, based upon Russian and Japanese as well as Western sources.

MINRATH, P.: " Frankreich-Russland und das englisch-japanische Bündnis von 1902 " (*Berliner Monatshefte*, XV, February, 1937, pp. 139–153). A supplement to an earlier book. Reviews the history of the Franco-Russian Alliance as it operated in the Far East between 1894 and 1902.

BEE, MINGE C.: " Origins of German Far Eastern Policy " (*Chinese Social and Political Science Review*, XXI, April, 1937, pp. 65–97). A scholarly review of German policy during the Sino-Japanese War and the period of the Shimonoseki Treaty. Adduces recently published Chinese materials.

EFIMOV, G. V.: " Germanskii Imperializm v Kitae, 1894–1902 gg." (*Uchenye Zapiski Tikho-okeanskogo Instituta*, I, 1947).

WOOD, CARLTON L.: *Die Beziehungen Deutschlands zu China*. Heidelberg, 1934. 110 pp. A dissertation covering the period 1894 to 1934, with slight treatment of the earlier part.

VII

Salisbury and the Near Eastern Problem

I N THE PRECEDING CHAPTER IT HAS BEEN SHOWN HOW THE CONSUMMATION of the Franco-Russian Alliance reduced the European states system to a condition of confusion. The British, whose far-flung interests were immediately threatened by the pooling of French and Russian power, executed a *volte face*. Having insisted on isolation for so long a time, they now tried to enlist the support of the Triple Alliance for their Near Eastern policy, only to meet with profound disappointment. The Germans, disillusioned in their efforts to establish a close connexion with Britain and disgusted by the weak-kneed policy of Rosebery in the Siamese question, made no move. On the contrary, to protect themselves they began to make up to the French as well as to the Russians. They took a strong stand against the English in the matter of the Congo Treaty, and threw such a fright into the British foreign office that Lord Rosebery began to cast about for ways to conciliate his combined antagonists. The Armenian Triplice was simply the most evident expression of his desire to establish contact with Russia and at the same time to focus her attention upon Near Eastern affairs, from which the powers of the Triple Alliance could not forever hold aloof. The reply of the Germans to this strategy was to support the Russians to the limit in the Far Eastern crisis, the basic idea of their policy being to divert Russia as much as possible from Europe and to prevent the Franco-Russian Alliance from operating on the German frontiers.

One of the most important results of these years of readjustment was the gradual estrangement of England and Germany and the steady growth of distrust and suspicion in the foreign offices of London and Berlin. When Lord Salisbury became prime minister and minister of foreign affairs in the last days of June 1895, it was generally believed by the diplomats of the central powers that he would make an effort to revise British policy, that he would devote himself to the resurrection of the old entente between England and the Triple Alliance. There is every indication that such was the case, but before the new cabinet was many months old the prime minister's hopes had been blasted; Germany and England were drifting more rapidly than ever toward a rupture.

Lord Rosebery left his successor the unwelcome legacy of the Armenian question. For weeks the ambassadors at Constantinople had been debating with the Sultan the exact measures of reform to be introduced in the Asiatic provinces, and the type of control to be established to guarantee their execution. Abdul Hamid, as usual, offered passive resistance and little progress could be made. In England public opinion was becoming more and more excited. " By the God Who made me," wrote one of the chief agitators to Gladstone in May, " I mean to do my level best to set the heather on fire on this question, cost what it may, and cost the Government what it may." [1] And he, together with kindred spirits, certainly did set the heather on fire. The government was exposed to sharp criticism, even from members of its own party. There was much dissatisfaction with the association of England with Russia and France, for it had long since become clear that Russia objected to coercive measures and that nothing could be accomplished without coercion. The " atrocitarians," as the *Saturday Review* once called them, were beginning to call for independent action: England owed a debt to humanity and she ought to pay it no matter what the cost. The Germans, evidently in the hope of breaking the Anglo-Russian entente, encouraged Rosebery to send the fleet to Besika Bay by way of demonstration, and there is some evidence that in June Rosebery and Kimberley were prepared to coerce the Sultan by sending the fleet through the Dardanelles. It is said that the move was frustrated by the opposition of Harcourt, but the information we have is so scanty that no definite conclusions can be reached.[2]

When Salisbury assumed office he was to a certain extent bound by the policy of the preceding ministry. It was obviously impossible to exclude Russia and France from the negotiations with the Sultan.[3] But there was no reason why the new premier should not try to put the entente on a broader basis or attempt to bring about a more heroic solution of the Eastern question. Liberal opinion was behind him in support of any radical measures he might take in the Armenian affair. He was, in fact, assured that the whole agitation was intended to strengthen his hand and show the unanimity of the country.[4] Salisbury personally had no use for the Turks and no confidence whatever in their ability to reform. This he had shown during the Eastern crisis of 1876–1878, and there are indications that the conviction had grown upon him during the years since the Berlin Congress. His view in 1895 seems to have been that the Ottoman Empire was beyond salvation, that its collapse was bound to come in the not very distant future, and that therefore it would be best to settle the whole problem by a friendly arrangement with the other powers. It is impossible to quote chapter and verse to support this view, for the English source material on the subject is unbelievably scant. But it will, I think, appear from what follows that this is a defensible thesis.

There is some evidence that in December 1894, when the Armenian ques-

---

[1] George W. E. Russell: *Malcolm MacColl* (London, 1914), p. 140.

[2] German encouragement, see *Die Grosse Politik*, IX, no. 2207; the rest of the statement depends upon what Morley told Dilke a year later (see Stephen Gwynn and G. M. Tuckwell: *Life of Sir Charles Dilke*, II, pp. 491–2).

[3] See Salisbury's letter to MacColl (Russell: *Malcolm MacColl*, p. 144).

[4] Russell: *MacColl*, pp. 141 ff.

tion first became acute, Lord Rosebery was disposed to allow the Russians to occupy the Armenian provinces of Turkey, in return for recognition of Britain's special position in Egypt and perhaps with some compensation for France in Syria. Apparently suggestions of this kind were made to the Russians, who rejected them, for reasons which are unknown, but which can be guessed.[5] Not only was the St. Petersburg government wrapped up in the Far Eastern crisis, but it must also have suspected that the British were aiming to involve Russia in European conflicts in order to be rid of her when the Chinese problem came to be settled. However that may have been, the Russians stuck by their original policy in the Near East. Prince Lobanov, the new foreign minister, was much more suspicious of the English than his predecessor, and was absolutely uncompromising in his opposition to the use of coercive measures against the Sultan.[6]

Under the circumstances Salisbury seems to have decided to try a far more ambitious program. He would offer the Russians a free hand to seize the Bosporus and Constantinople — an offer which they could hardly reject. But he would, at the same time, avoid the mistake of working only with Russia and France. If the Ottoman Empire was to be partitioned without a war, it could be done only by a general agreement between all the powers concerned. It was therefore imperative that the Triple Alliance should be brought into the scheme. In fact the powers of the Alliance, having thus far taken little part in the Armenian business, must be interested in the project first of all.

On July 9, 1895 Salisbury had a long talk with the German ambassador, Count Hatzfeldt, an old friend in whom he had complete confidence. He hinted to him that something would have to be done and that it might be necessary for England to make very extensive concessions to Russia in order to secure her co-operation in coercing the Sultan.[7] On the very next day he spoke to the Turkish ambassador in the most unequivocal language:

" I impressed upon His Excellency very strongly the perilous position in which it appeared to me that the Ottoman Empire was now placed. I was much struck on coming back to office to find how much ground it had lost in English opinion. It was not that there was any longer any strong excitement on the subject, but a settled conviction was growing that nothing was to be hoped from it in the way of improvement or reform, and that all that could be done was to finish with it. I pointed out that the danger was extreme, and if the Sultan did not take warning in time the blow would almost inevitably come upon him, and at a time when he least expected it." [8]

The next step in the development of this policy was taken when the Italians, whose Red Sea possessions were being seriously threatened by the Abyssinians, appealed to the German government for aid in getting support from England. What they wanted specifically was the seaport town of Zeila in British Somali-

[5] *Die Grosse Politik,* IX. nos. 2196–8.   [7] *Die Grosse Politik,* X, no. 2396.
[6] *Turkey No. 1 (1896),* nos. 89, 91, 92, 94, 110.   [8] *Turkey No. 1 (1896),* no. 112.

land, which they could use as a base for an attack upon the rear of the Abyssinians. Hatzfeldt was instructed to take the matter up with Salisbury, but he found that the prime minister was unwilling to make the concession. His reply lacked all logic unless taken in connexion with the Near Eastern crisis, for he suggested that the Italians might be compensated for their losses in Africa by certain concessions in Albania and Tripoli. This, said Salisbury, would bring about " une division des réclamations à Constantinople." This phrase might be interpreted in various ways, but Salisbury made his meaning fairly clear when he went on to say that even if the Armenian business were temporarily settled, the Ottoman Empire was " too rotten " to exist much longer. There were dangers and difficulties connected with partition, but they were simply unavoidable.[9]

When these conversations became known in Berlin they made a distinctly unfavorable impression. The German foreign office was well-disposed toward the new government at London and had been doing what it could to support the action of England, Russia and France at Constantinople.[10] But the veiled suggestions of Salisbury aroused all sorts of suspicions. The chancellor and the foreign minister happened to be off on vacation, and Baron von Holstein, the most distrustful of men, had practically complete charge of German policy. Writing to one of his friends just after Salisbury's first hints, he pointed out that the English foreign minister might be trying to postpone the ultimate conflict with Russia by making extensive concessions in Anatolia and the Far East: " In the meanwhile, he may think, the Franco-Russian storm may break on the Continent." Germany should, therefore, be very careful.[11]

The suggestion that Italy might receive compensation in Albania made an even worse impression on Holstein. Albania was a country in which Austria had a direct interest. Was it possible that Salisbury was trying to sow dissension between Austria and Italy and thus weaken the Triple Alliance? [12] Hatzfeldt was told to find out about this. He consulted the prime minister, who warmly denied harboring such sinister designs, but repeated what he had said before, that the break-up of Turkey, however regrettable, was decidedly probable and that therefore it should be considered in good season. If Austria was sensitive about Albania, it might be possible to compensate Italy in Morocco instead. But, he continued, he was not wedded to any specific scheme. Perhaps Hatzfeldt could outline a plan which would satisfy the Germans and which could then be discussed.[13]

The ambassador, reporting to his government, expressed the opinion that such a procedure might be very wise. If it had no other advantage it would at

---

[9] *Die Grosse Politik*, X, nos. 2369–72.

[10] *Die Grosse Politik*, X, nos. 2397, 2398, 2401, 2402.

[11] Letter of July 14, in *Erinnerungen und Gedanken des Botschafters Anton Graf Monts* (Berlin, 1932), p. 350.

[12] *Die Grosse Politik*, X, nos. 2373, 2374.   [13] *Die Grosse Politik*, X, no. 2375.

least serve to bring out what was in the mind of the British statesman. But Holstein refused to believe in the sincerity of Salisbury's suggestions. In his reply to Hatzfeldt, dated August 4, he forbade the ambassador's making any proposals touching the partition of Mediterranean territories. Germany, he said, had no aspirations there, and the powers which did, like England, Austria and Italy, should arrange matters between themselves. Then Germany could add her agreement. England and Austria, he went on, were interested in breaking down the connexion between Germany and Russia. They might be tempted to let the news leak out that Germany had made suggestions pointing to the partition of Turkey and Morocco. In that case Germany would lose her freedom of action, which she must retain, if only to secure something for herself (not necessarily in the Mediterranean) when the psychological moment arrived.[14]

It so happened that the Emperor was just then on his way to pay a visit to Cowes, where the yacht-racing season was at its height. It was expected that Lord Salisbury would come down for a couple of days to pay his respects, and it was feared that he would take up, with the Emperor, the question of partitioning Turkey. For that reason Holstein communicated his apprehensions and views to the foreign office official in the Emperor's entourage. William declared himself opposed to the whole scheme.[15] He received the British premier after dinner on August 5. Salisbury spoke in a general way of the growing crisis in Turkish affairs and the approaching danger of the Empire's dissolution, to which the Emperor, in accordance with instructions, said that things seemed to be getting better rather than worse and that the main thing was to induce the Sultan to get rid of bad officials and to replace them by competent people.[16]

There the matter might well have ended. Salisbury made no proposals for the partition of Turkey, and the Emperor gave him no opening for an introduction of the theme. But the episode had a peculiar and unfortunate aftermath. Hatzfeldt, having learned of Holstein's objections and the reasons for them, had telegraphed to Berlin on August 5, pointing out that Salisbury's "plan" obviously involved the most generous satisfaction for Russia in the Near East, that is, Constantinople "avec tout ce qui s'ensuit." Furthermore, that there was no doubt that if Germany participated in the agreement Salisbury would willingly accord her an appropriate share of the spoils. This put an entirely different aspect upon the matter, and Holstein hurriedly wired that if Salisbury were really prepared to satisfy Russia and thereby make her French connexion superfluous, it would certainly be wise to discuss the matter further. When this news reached Hatzfeldt at Cowes he reported to the Emperor and it was arranged that the latter should receive Salisbury again on the afternoon of August 6. The British premier, however, was at that time in conference with Queen Vic-

---

[14] *Die Grosse Politik*, X, no. 2379.
[15] *Die Grosse Politik*, X, nos. 2377, 2380.
[16] *Die Grosse Politik*, X, no. 2385; the Emperor's more embroidered account in K. F. Nowak: *Germany's Road to Ruin* (New York, 1932), pp. 141 ff. has no source value.

toria, and was detained until so late that, thinking the Emperor merely wished
to receive him in a formal way, and being already very late, he decided that the
invitation had lapsed and returned to London on urgent business. The Emperor
waited for a long time, and was naturally very much perplexed and angered by
the failure of the British statesman to keep his appointment.[17]

This account is based almost exclusively upon the German documents, because they are the only official papers that have ever been published, and the
non-documentary material at our disposal is either so sensational or so confused
that it does not help to elucidate the incident.[18] But this much can be said:
Hatzfeldt was to blame for the misunderstanding in as much as he failed to
inform the German foreign office definitely regarding Salisbury's ideas. To be
sure, the British premier never came out very clearly regarding what he planned
or proposed to do. But Hatzfeldt should never have allowed the impression to
arise at Berlin that Russia was to be excluded from a share in the spoils. In that
case, naturally, a great European war would have been inevitable. On the other
hand, Holstein made his decisions before he had properly informed himself in
regard to details. His suspicions were so great that he did not bother to verify
them. With respect to the interview between the Emperor and Salisbury, we
have no record by either of the two men.[19] Chirol says a memorandum drawn
up by William was shown him in the German foreign office in 1901, but this
record, if it ever existed, can no longer be found. Chirol says it told about Salisbury's disclosing " a scheme for the partition of Turkey between the European
Powers." From the documents we actually have it is clear that the conversation
never reached that stage. It is equally clear that Eckardstein's highly colored
story of a second meeting between the Emperor and Salisbury is entirely devoid
of foundation. There were no acrimonious debates and no sharp words. The
failure of Salisbury to appear for a second discussion was purely accidental, the
result of a misunderstanding. If it had taken place, matters might have taken a
very different turn and come to a very different end. But such is the irony of
history.[20]

One point, however, is beyond dispute. On both sides the episode resulted
in greater distrust and suspicion. The Germans felt that Salisbury had intended

---

[17] *Die Grosse Politik*, X, nos. 2381–6; *Letters of Queen Victoria*, II, pp. 544–8.

[18] The important accounts are those by Hermann, Freiherr von Eckardstein: *Lebenserinnerungen
und Politische Denkwürdigkeiten* (Leipzig, 1920), I, pp. 210 ff., II, p. 284; Idem: *Die Isolierung
Deutschlands* (Leipzig, 1921), pp. 11 ff.; Valentine Chirol: " The Ex-Kaiser and England," in the
London *Times*, September 11 and 13, 1920; his account in the *Cambridge History of British Foreign Policy*, III, p. 275; and in his *Fifty Years in a Changing World*, pp. 289–91. See also Holstein's
account of his interview with Chirol in 1901, in *Die Grosse Politik*, XVII, no. 5026.

[19] As aforesaid, the account in Nowak is of no value.

[20] For further discussion see Richard Fester: " Das angebliche Bündnisangebot Englands von
1895 " (*Die Grenzboten*, August 21, 1921, pp. 171–5); Raymond Sontag: " The Cowes Interview and
the Kruger Telegram " (*Political Science Quarterly*, XL, June, 1925, pp. 217–47); Friedrich Meinecke:
Geschichte des Deutsch-Englischen Bündnisproblems, 1890–1901 (Munich, 1927), pp. 37–49; and
above all Hugo Preller: *Salisbury und die Türkische Frage im Jahre 1895* (Stuttgart, 1930), passim.

to precipitate a conflict in which " perfidious Albion " could and would stand aloof, or at any rate that he hoped to play off the Triple Alliance against the new Franco-Russian combination.[21] Lord Salisbury, on the other hand, was personally through with the Emperor after the unfortunate Cowes interview. He had never had a high opinion of him and thought him an ill-bred and self-important young man. In 1888 he had written that " the Emperor William must be a little off his head." Three years later he doubted if the Emperor was " all there," and after William's visit in 1891 he told Lord George Hamilton " that he looked upon him (the Emperor) as the most dangerous enemy we had in Europe. He also added that he had never met a man with such a double tongue." For political reasons this distrust had been suppressed, but the Cowes incident brought it to a head. Writing to the Queen in December 1895 the prime minister remarked that the Emperor had " not yet recovered from the intoxication of his accession to power; it is rather growing worse." [22] In short, Salisbury resented the young ruler's attitude. From this time on both men tended to regard each other as enemies and to attribute to each other evil and sinister designs.

But for the time being there was no visible break. Salisbury evidently did not even give up his scheme entirely. On August 5, the very day of the Cowes interview, an inquiry was sent to Russia asking how far that power would be prepared to go in bringing pressure upon the Porte. The reply, as might have been expected, was decidedly discouraging. In fact it was more uncompromising than ever before. Both the Tsar and Lobanov " were strongly against force being used by any or all of the Powers." [23] That meant that Salisbury was helpless so far as the Armenian question was concerned. Speaking to the Russian chargé d'affaires he said bitterly that he himself was opposed to the idea of Armenian autonomy and had nothing more than reforms in view. But England, having called for reforms, could hardly give up because of the Sultan's obstinacy: " We cannot take our hats and depart, leaving the victory to recalcitrant Turkey." The employment of force was repugnant to him, he declared, but he thought that " big words spoken in a loud voice would be sufficient to intimidate Turkey." [24]

It was in pursuance of this idea that the premier made use of exceptionally strong language in his speech on the address from the throne, on August 15.

" If, generation after generation, cries of misery come up from various parts of the Turkish Empire, I am sure the Sultan cannot blind himself to the probability that Europe will at some time or other become weary of the appeals that are made to it, and the fictitious strength that is given to his Empire will fail it. . . . The Sultan will make a grave and calamitous mistake if, for the sake of maintaining a mere formal independence, for the sake of resisting a possible encroach-

---

[21] See especially *Die Grosse Politik,* X, no. 2388.

[22] Cecil: *Life of Salisbury,* IV, pp. 113, 367, 371; Lord George Hamilton: *Parliamentary Reminiscences and Reflections* (London, 1922), p. 137; *Letters of Queen Victoria,* II, pp. 583 ff.

[23] *Turkey No. 1 (1896),* nos. 129, 136.

[24] Meyendorff, op. cit., II, p. 256; *Die Grosse Politik,* X, no. 2391.

ment on his nominal prerogative, he refuses to accept the assistance and to listen to the advice of the European Powers in extirpating from his dominions an anarchy and a weakness which no treaties and no sympathy will prevent from being fatal in the long run to the Empire over which he rules."

Abdul Hamid, undoubtedly well-informed as to the attitude of Russia, did not take this resounding warning too seriously. The dreary negotiations at Constantinople continued, without leading to any satisfactory result. There are some vague indications that Salisbury, having found the Germans unwilling to talk about the future, made advances to France and Russia. There was discussion of Morocco and Egypt, perhaps also of the Dardanelles. To the German ambassador the prime minister spoke as though the eventual attainment of the Russian aims in the Straits was inevitable, and as though England would find such a solution quite acceptable. When asked what compensation England would demand for so portentous a change, Salisbury indicated that his aspirations were elsewhere, along the Euphrates. How much there was behind these hints it is impossible to say, but it appears that even the French ambassador could not make out just what Salisbury was after. In all probability he was sending out feelers, trying to bargain with Russia and France or at least trying to frighten the Germans with the spectre of an English-Russian-French understanding. This he had once attempted in 1887, and this he was to try again later.[25]

To a certain extent his tactics were successful. Hatzfeldt, in reply to Holstein's suspicious letters, defended the English statesman against the charge of wishing to embroil the continental powers in war, and insisted that it would be unsafe for Germany to rely too much on Russia. Germany's policy should be to keep her hands free and to be prepared to listen to proposals from either side. These arguments made an impression in Berlin. As matters in Turkey grew worse and worse the Emperor showed more and more sympathy for the partition scheme.[26] Even Holstein regretted past events, and complained, quite unjustly, that the Emperor had bungled the whole affair in his talk with Salisbury.[27] But the question was never again discussed between Salisbury and Hatzfeldt. The golden moment had passed.

In the meanwhile the Armenian revolutionary committees, convinced that there was no longer anything to be hoped from the action of the powers, decided to resume their activity. The Hentchak decided to organize a great demonstration in Constantinople. It has been claimed by one of the leaders that he and his friends received encouragement from the English, both from London and from the Constantinople embassy. They met and laid their plans in the offices of the Union Insurance Company in Galata.[28] If such encouragement was given

---

[25] *Die Grosse Politik*, X, nos. 2387, 2392.

[26] *Die Grosse Politik*, X, nos. 2391, 2416, marginal notes.

[27] Johannes Haller: *Philip Eulenburg* (New York, 1930), I, p. 309.

[28] Haverhilltzi Garo: " Bab Alii Tzoitze " (" The Bab Ali Demonstration," in *Hentchakian Darekirk*, II, 1932, pp. 35 ff.).

at all, it must have been unofficial. It is probably nearer the truth that Nazaɪbek was warned in London against a demonstration and that he kept these warnings from his agents in the Turkish capital. In any event the local leaders arranged that their followers should attend the " peaceful demonstration " heavily armed. It is hard to escape the conclusion that they wanted blood to flow.[29]

On September 28, 1895 the organizers notified the ambassadors at Constantinople that they were about to hold a peaceful meeting of protest. The manifestation was to have no aggressive character whatever and they therefore disclaimed in advance responsibility for any " regrettable consequences " which the intervention of the police or the troops might have.[30] All of which indicates that the leaders had a definite result in view. They wanted disorders and massacres, and they got them. For the first time in the Armenian crisis, blood was shed in the capital itself; in the provinces there were massacres at Trebizond and many other places. The winter of 1895–1896 was filled with horrible and lugubrious reports. It was perfectly obvious that the Sultan was determined to end the Armenian question by exterminating the Armenians.

The disorders and killings in the capital complicated matters, for they raised at once the question of the security of the large foreign colonies. To avoid trouble the three powers, supported by Germany, Austria and Italy, brought pressure to bear once more. The Sultan could not resist in the face of a united Europe. On October 17 he issued an *iradé* sanctioning the reforms which the three powers had been urging upon him for so many months. This did not, in itself, mean very much. For the moment there was a general feeling of relief among European statesmen, but in a short time more and greater massacres took place. It became increasingly plain that the outbreaks were part of a definite policy and that they were ordered and directed from above. The opinion was widespread in Europe that the Sultan was taking his revenge for having been forced by the powers to grant reforms.

The *iradé* marked the end of the Armenian Triplice, for England, Russia and France had attained the fulfillment of the demands for which that combination had been created. After the middle of October the so-called " concert of Europe " functioned in the Armenian question. The representatives of the powers together pressed for the execution of the reforms, protested against the outrages committed against the Armenians and took the measures necessary for the protection of the foreign colonies. It need hardly be added that the Sultan paid little attention even to the combined action of the powers so long as he was convinced that the employment of force was out of the question. He temporized as he had temporized before, and insisted that he needed time to carry through the measures of reform, that, above all, he would have to wait until the country was pacified.

---

[29] Arshag Tchobanian: " Badaskhanaduoutiunnere " (" Responsibilities," in *Anahid*, I, January, 1899, pp. 96–7).

[30] *Affaires Arméniennes, 1893–1897*, no. 91; *Turkey No. 2 (1896)*, no. 50; *Die Grosse Politik*, **X**, no. 2428; Bérard: *La Politique du Sultan*, p. 193.

And yet matters went from bad to worse. It seemed incredible that nothing could be done to stop the flow of blood. The question was, would England take the bull by the horns, and proceed on her own account, despite the opposition of Russia? or would the Russians invade Armenia and send a naval squadron to occupy Constantinople in order to prevent the English from precipitating the collapse of Turkey? It must be confessed that the final answer to this question cannot be given even now. The secret documents of the English government have not thus far been published, and from the German documents one can get but an imperfect picture of the situation. Towards the middle of October Prince Lobanov, returning from a visit to France, stopped to pay his respects to Emperor William and to his German colleague. He assured them of the desire of the French for peace and attempted to explain away the Franco-Russian Alliance. It was quite clear that he was anxious to do all he could to preserve close relations between St. Petersburg and Berlin. He was profoundly suspicious of the English policy, and expressed the fear that Lord Salisbury was planning to put an end to the Armenian question by executing a *coup,* that is, by occupying the Dardanelles or at least the islands near the entrance to the Straits. The French government had reason to suspect such designs and agreed with the Russian government that England could, under no circumstances, be permitted to score such a success. It was with immense satisfaction that Lobanov heard from the lips of the Germans that they would do nothing to help the English, but that they were, on the contrary, disposed to lend moral support to the Russians.[31]

Within a few days of Lobanov's departure Emperor William had a talk with his mother, the Empress Frederick, who was an English princess and spent much of her time on the other side of the Channel. The Empress spoke freely of the collapse of Turkey and the inevitability of a partition of the Sultan's dominions. These utterances were interpreted in Berlin as a reflection of the views of Queen Victoria and her advisers.[32] Filled with grave apprehensions, the Germans felt that it was imperative to avoid conflict with the Russian-French combination and to make sure that Germany and her allies were not made the cat's paws of England. On November 8 the Emperor telegraphed to the Tsar pointing out the great seriousness of the situation in the Near East and asking him what he proposed to do about it. The reply was cool and evasive, and was taken by the disappointed Emperor to be evidence that his Russian cousin did not appreciate the offer of German friendship.[33]

In actual fact the Russians found themselves in a great quandary. Having become involved in the Far East, they were above all anxious to avoid trouble in the Near East. Just as England, — the traditional champion of the Sultan against Muscovite aggression, — was becoming the advocate of the partition of

---

31 *Die Grosse Politik,* IX, nos. 2323, 2324; *The Kaiser's Letters to the Tsar,* p. 26.
32 *Die Grosse Politik,* X, nos. 2437, 2441, 2442, 2463, 2468, 2472.
33 *Die Grosse Politik,* X, nos. 2452, 2453, 2455, 2464.

the Ottoman dominions, the Russians, — since the time of Peter the Great the inveterate enemies of the Turk, — had come to pose as his protectors and saviors. Again and again Lobanov insisted that the encouragement given the Armenian revolutionaries in London was at the bottom of the whole trouble, and that it would be dangerous to use strong methods in dealing with the Sultan:

"It is presumably the object of every Power to get the Sultan to restore peace and order in his dominions," he told the British chargé d'affaires. " To do this in the present state of excitement among his subjects His Majesty must have time, and his moral authority must be unimpaired. Threats of intervention cannot but undermine that authority, and will therefore defeat the object the Powers have in view. . . . As things stand at present the Sultan has accepted all our demands and we should now give ample time to allow the excitement to subside, and await patiently the result of His Majesty's efforts to tranquillize the disturbed districts." [34]

But these appeals fell upon deaf ears. A large British squadron began to assemble at Lemnos and about the entrance to the Dardanelles. There was every indication that the English government was preparing to take action against the Sultan. Sir Frank Lascelles, the ambassador at Berlin, admitted later that Salisbury had brought before the cabinet the question whether the fleet should be sent up to Constantinople. In the course of the discussion, he said, the first lord of the admiralty, Goschen, inquired whether the prime minister knew what the French fleet would do in that case. Salisbury admitted that he could not say, whereupon Goschen pointed out that the fleet could not be sent up, for if it entered the Straits the French squadrons might assemble at the Dardanelles and the British would be in a trap. Thereupon, according to Lascelles, Salisbury lost his temper and declared that if the British ships were made of porcelain, he would, of course, have to pursue a different policy.[35]

Naturally nothing was known of these decisions in the European capitals, but the most sinister designs were generally attributed to the English. The St. Petersburg government was in something of a panic. Lobanov was not convinced that the English would actually enter the Straits, for, he argued, they would be able to count only on the support of Italy. Germany and England had more or less fallen out, and he had the assurances of the Emperor William that nothing would be done to support the London cabinet. Austria, he argued, would not dare move without German approval.

But this optimism was not shared by all Russian diplomats, or by the military men. For years M. Nelidov, the ambassador at Constantinople, had been urging his government to seize the forts of the Bosporus, in order to anticipate action by England. No serious attention had been paid to his arguments, if only

[34] *Turkey No. 2 (1896)*, nos. 241, 334; *Die Grosse Politik*, X, nos. 2436, 2446, 2515, 2518.

[35] *Die Grosse Politik*, XII, nos. 2918, 2934; Anon.: " Armenia and the Powers; from behind the Scenes " (*Contemporary Review*, May, 1896); MacColl thought it was Chamberlain who was holding back Salisbury (Russell: *MacColl*, p. 148).

out of consideration for the feelings of France, but in July 1895 a special council reported that Russia was prepared to seize control of the Straits: " We need the Bosporus and the entrance to the Black Sea. The rest, i.e. free passage through the Dardanelles, must be secured later by diplomatic means." Once Russia controlled the entrance to the Black Sea, she would be able to devote her attention to the Far East, being secure against attack in the south. It all seemed simpler to the military men than to the foreign office, where these schemes were thought to reveal a " nuance of poetic illusion." Nothing was done during the summer, though in September Nelidov once again urged his ideas upon Lobanov.[36]

But in November 1895 the situation became critical. The British squadrons were concentrated at Lemnos and the Italians sent four ships to the Levant. Only the strong protests of the Germans deterred them from openly joining the English.[37] Even the Austrians began to take an active part in the Near Eastern crisis. The new Austrian foreign minister, Count Goluchowski, was much less disposed than his predecessor to work for an agreement with Russia. His policy was based frankly upon the Alliance with Germany and the good understanding with England. With the aid of these two powers he hoped to be able to maintain Austrian interests in the Balkans, and this meant at Constantinople as well as in Bulgaria. The Germans, returning to the viewpoint of Bismarck, warned their ally that no support was to be had for a policy that might provoke or antagonize Russia,[38] but Goluchowski could not be held back. He not only had ships sent to the Near East, but actually offered his services to the English. Naturally Salisbury received this new ally with open arms. Very adroitly he led the Austrians on, promising them that England would stand by her traditional policy of opposing Russian designs in the Straits or at Constantinople, but at the same time avoiding any definite commitments. Time and again the Germans warned the Austrians not to allow themselves to be made the tools of British policy. There was no good reason, they argued, why the Austrians should oppose a Russian occupation of the Turkish capital, or the opening of the Straits to Russian warships. All Austria needed to do in such an event was to secure for herself adequate compensation along the road to Saloniki. Above all, they should avoid taking the lead and wait until the English themselves took action and thereby committed themselves.[39]

These were the arguments which the Austrians had heard so many times before. They made no impression. The Austrians never could accept the idea that a Russian occupation of Constantinople would do them no harm. They dreaded such a development, and were not interested in compensations for themselves. Speaking to the German ambassador Goluchowski said that he

[36] V. Khvostov: "Problemy Zakhvata Bosfora v 90 kh godakh XIX veka" (*Istorik Marksist*, XX, pp. 100–29), pp. 107–9.

[37] *Die Grosse Politik*, X, nos. 2502, 2504, 2508, 2509; *Turkey No. 2 (1896)*, nos. 91, 98, 179, 255, 269.

[38] *Die Grosse Politik*, X, nos. 2429, 2431, 2432, 2488, 2489.

[39] *Turkey No. 2 (1896)*, nos. 57, 58, 68; *Die Grosse Politik*, X, nos. 2490–5.

" simply abhorred " compensations. Austria, with her dangerous constitutional and racial problems, could not afford to acquire more territory. All he wanted was the status quo. He felt that he had to support the English in order to prevent the English from reaching an agreement with Russia by which the latter power would be allowed to establish herself at Constantinople.[40]

So Goluchowski went his own way. On November 11 he suggested to all the powers that they concentrate their squadrons, force the passage of the Dardanelles and oblige the Sultan to put an end to the bloodshed. The Russians at once rejected the idea and the French followed suit, so that Goluchowski got nothing for his trouble but a snubbing.[41] But the very proposal of combined fleet action was enough to cause something of a panic at St. Petersburg. It was hurriedly decided to mobilize the Black Sea fleet and to strengthen the Mediterranean squadron by the addition of three ships from the Baltic forces. It was hoped that if the British actually entered the Dardanelles, the Russian Black Sea fleet could promptly enter the Bosporus and arrive in the Golden Horn side by side with the British. In the opinion of Nelidov and others it would be wise to take advantage of the crisis to seize control of the Straits in any case. The Black Sea fleet, it was claimed, was in first class shape, and all arrangements had been made to transport 30,000 men to Constantinople. Lobanov himself viewed these optimistic assertions with some misgivings and scepticism, which, as it turned out, were entirely justified. Investigation showed that the naval officers at Sevastopol were worried .by the mere order to mobilize. They felt that the fleet was poorly equipped and supplied, and that it would be impossible to get ready more than 8,000 men. Under the circumstances Lobanov was obliged to concentrate his efforts on the prevention of action by other powers and on the enlistment of support for a possible crisis.[42]

In the hour of need the Russians bethought themselves of their French ally, who had a real interest in preserving the status quo in the Near East and had, therefore, been working in harmony with the Russians. In December Lobanov inquired of the French what help could be expected if, by the initiative of a third power, Russia should be obliged to intervene militarily in the Near East. Berthelot, the foreign minister, replied on December 20 that

" Only a great national interest like the regulation anew of the question which, since 1870, has so profoundly divided Germany and France, would be of sufficient importance (assez considérable) to justify in the eyes of the French people engagements implying military action in which the great powers might find

---

[40] *Die Grosse Politik*, X, nos. 2497, 2500; Haller: *Eulenburg*, I, pp. 237 ff.; Edmund Glaise-Horstenau: *Franz Josephs Weggefährte* (Vienna, 1930), pp. 380 ff.; Hohenlohe: *Denkwürdigkeiten der Reichskanzlerzeit* (Stuttgart, 1931), pp. 145–6.

[41] *Die Grosse Politik*, X, nos. 2505, 2515, 2518, 2527.

[42] V. Khvostov: " Blizhne-Vostochnyi Krizis, 1895–1897 gg." (*Istorik Marksist*, XIII, 1929, pp. 19–54), pp. 25–8, which is based upon unpublished Russian archive material; see also *Die Grosse Politik*, X, no. 2520; Meyendorff, op. cit., II, pp. 286–96.

themselves successively involved and which would, therefore, require the most
intense effort on our part." [43]

The French reply must have been a terrible blow to the Russians. It settled
once and for all the question of French support for Russian aspirations in the
Near East. Not even if Russia were the party provoked by the action of another
power would the French put their forces at the disposal of their ally. They stuck
by the strict interpretation of the Military Convention. It need hardly be said
that the honeymoon days of the Alliance were thereby ended, and that this first
divergence of interests was bound to reflect upon the future development of the
Franco-Russian relationship.

While the Russians were learning to their sorrow that they could not count
upon the French in all eventualities, the Austrians and the Italians were suffering a similar disappointment at the hands of the English. They both desired a
more specific agreement with England as to what should be done if the Russians
moved on Constantinople. The Berlin government was quite willing to lend
them support in procuring a more satisfactory definition of the Mediterranean
Agreement of 1887, though it insisted, now as ever, upon remaining in the background. When negotiations were opened with Salisbury it turned out that he
was quite prepared to recognize the continued existence of the Agreement of
1887, but that he had no desire for a re-definition of its terms. He argued that
the negotiations could not be kept secret, and that if they leaked out they would
cause distrust in Russia. In other words, he courteously evaded the advances of
the Italians and Austrians, going no further than to say that British feeling
against the Sultan did not necessarily extend to his dominions, and that the
British would not without concern see the control of the Bosporus and Dardanelles pass into the hands of Russia. Goluchowski declared himself satisfied
with these assurances, and even thought that the English were ready to join the
Triple Alliance. It need hardly be said that the Berlin cabinet did not share in
this optimism. [44]

Goluchowski, like Salisbury, had failed to accomplish anything in the Armenian affair. All efforts to bring pressure to bear upon the Sultan by the use
of force had ended in fiasco. By the end of December even the Austrian minister, whose temperament was sanguine, was obliged to admit that nothing further could be done and that the powers would have to wait until Abdul Hamid
introduced reforms of his own free will. [45] For the time being, at least, European

[43] *Documents Diplomatiques Françaises, 1871–1914,* Series III, vol. II, no. 202; see also Pierre
Renouvin: "Les Engagements de l'Alliance Franco-Russe " (*Revue d'Histoire de la Guerre Mondiale,* October, 1934, pp. 297–310), especially pp. 300–1. Hanotaux claimed that he had made the
French attitude clear even earlier in 1895. See his *Histoire Illustrée de la Guerre de 1914* (Paris,
1915), I, p. 203; Idem: "La Pretendue Conjuration Franco-Russe " (*Revue des Deux Mondes,* January 15, 1928). The German documents also reflect this attitude on the part of the French. See *Die
Grosse Politik,* XI, no. 2676; XII, no. 2916; XVIII, no. 5916.

[44] *Die Grosse Politik,* X, nos. 2538–69, passim; *British Documents on the Origins of the War,
1898–1914,* VIII, no. 1.   [45] *Turkey No. 2 (1896),* no. 458.

action in the Armenian question came to an end, and the Concert of the Powers could show no greater success than could the Armenian Triplice.

One is bound to be impressed with the deeper significance of Salisbury's policy in the Near East during the latter half of 1895. When he assumed office, he was convinced, firstly that reform in Turkey under the sultanate was practically hopeless, secondly that nothing was to be accomplished along the lines marked out by his predecessor, if only because of Russia's aversion to the use of force. He therefore envisaged a grand *coup,* a partition of the Ottoman Empire, leaving to the Turks, perhaps, Anatolia; giving Russia what she wanted, the Straits and Constantinople; according Austria a free hand in the western Balkans; compensating Italy in Tripoli or Morocco; satisfying the French either in Morocco or Syria and taking for England both Egypt and Mesopotamia. Just what Germany would have gotten out of such a division of the spoils is not entirely obvious. In any event one may rightly reflect upon the future course of European affairs if such an ambitious scheme could have been carried through. It would have effected the great changes in the Near East which in our day were brought about only through the World War.

What, then, were the reasons for failure? Was it that the Russians would not agree? I doubt it. They were, to be sure, deeply involved in the Far East, but they were never so deeply involved in China as to forget their traditional aspirations. If they could have been convinced that all the powers would join, they might have been brought to accept this solution. The difficulty arose from the fact that the other continental powers did not welcome the scheme. The French were squarely for the maintenance of the Ottoman Empire, where they had a tremendous financial investment. The Austrians " abhorred " the idea of compensation and were equally devoted to the status quo. The Germans had more to gain from keeping things quiet than from starting a huge scramble. Add to this the fact that the Germans, whose position was decisive and who were, for that reason, approached first by Salisbury, distrusted British policy and took a thoroughly unstatesmanlike view of the situation. Later on they themselves came to see the advantages of the British proposal. But it was then too late. While the iron was hot, they could not bring themselves to strike. Holstein felt convinced that there must be some ulterior motive. Salisbury, he believed, was trying to set the Austrians off against the Italians and so weaken the Triple Alliance. This idea was absurd. What was there to be gained by it? So long as England failed to reach an agreement with Russia and France, it was highly desirable for her to have the Triple Alliance in existence as a check on the Franco-Russian combination. Then there was Holstein's further suspicion that Salisbury was simply trying to undermine the revived friendship between Russia and Germany, that he was aiming to engage the continental powers in the Near East in order that England might have a free hand in the Far East and in Africa. Of course one cannot prove that these thoughts were not in the mind of the veteran statesman, who was not very communicative. But the impression one gets from the rather deficient material is that Salisbury was perfectly straightforward in his proposals. Hatzfeldt thought so and whatever other material there is seems to bear out his opinion. There was no adequate reason for giving the prime minister the snub which he received at the hands of the Emperor during the Cowes interview. On that disastrous day a personal enmity was born that was to influence the course of Anglo-German relations during the next half dozen years. The solution of the Eastern question was, for the time being, an impossibility, for the powers would not act together and no one, or two, or even three of them dared act while the others were in opposition. Even more important was the fact that all the cordiality was gone from Anglo-German relations. It needed only the famous Kruger telegram to bring to the surface all the jealousy, distrust and ill-feeling that had been gradually accumulated.

*

BIBLIOGRAPHICAL NOTE

DOCUMENTARY SOURCES

Accounts and Papers. 1896, vol. XCV. *Turkey No. 1 (1896): Correspondence respecting the Introduction of Reforms in the Armenian Provinces of Asiatic Turkey; Turkey No. 2 (1896): Correspondence Relative to the Armenian Question.* These two Blue Books cover the periods from May to October and from October 1895 to February 1896.

Documents Diplomatiques. Affaires Arméniennes. Projets de Réformes dans l'Empire Ottoman, 1893–1897. Paris, 1897.

Die Grosse Politik der Europäischen Kabinette, 1871–1914. Volume X, chapter lx: Salisbury's Partition Plans; chapter lxi: Salisbury and the Armenian Question, July-December, 1895; chapter lxii: Efforts at new Groupings of the Powers. These are the fundamental sources for the subject. In this matter the German materials are far more important than any others now available.

MEMOIRS, AUTOBIOGRAPHIES, BIOGRAPHIES, AND LETTERS

MEYENDORFF, BARON A.: *Correspondance Diplomatique de M. de Staal.* Two volumes. Paris, 1929. Of some use, though pretty disappointing.

ECKARDSTEIN, HERMANN FREIHERR VON: *Lebenserinnerungen und Politische Denkwürdigkeiten.* Two volumes. Leipzig, 1919. Contains a well-known account of the Cowes episode, which can be definitely shown to be unreliable.

HALLER, JOHANNES: *Philip Eulenburg: The Kaiser's Friend.* Two volumes. New York, 1930. A valuable source, throwing much light not only on the Emperor, but upon Holstein.

The Letters of Queen Victoria. Series III, volume II. New York, 1931. Has some material, though not much, on the Cowes interview and the Near Eastern crisis.

RUSSELL, GEORGE W. E.: *Malcolm MacColl.* London, 1914. The biography of one of the leading "atrocitarians," containing a good deal of correspondence with Gladstone and Salisbury.

CHIROL, VALENTINE: *Fifty Years in a Changing World.* London, 1927. Interesting recollections of a former *Times* correspondent at Berlin. Contains some valuable material on the Cowes incident.

SPECIAL STUDIES

FESTER, RICHARD: "Das Angebliche Bündnisangebot Englands von 1895." (*Die Grenzboten,* August 21, 1921, pp. 171–5). An early and very suggestive study of the Salisbury plan, written before the publication of the German documents.

SONTAG, RAYMOND: "The Cowes Interview and the Kruger Telegram." (*Political Science Quarterly,* XL, June, 1925, pp. 217–47). An admirable analysis of the documentary material.

MEINECKE, FRIEDRICH: *Geschichte des Deutsch-Englischen Bündnisproblems, 1890–1901.* Munich, 1927. One of the best studies of the Cowes episode.

PRELLER, HUGO: *Salisbury und die Türkische Frage im Jahre 1895.* Stuttgart, 1930. The most detailed analysis of the problem, keen and provocative but also somewhat provoking. It is intended to refute the thesis of Meinecke, but is only partially successful. One should read with it Meinecke's reply (*Historische Zeitschrift,* CXLII, 1930, pp. 587–92).

NOWAK, KARL F.: *Germany's Road to Ruin.* New York, 1932. Contains a phantastic account of the Cowes episode, based upon evidence furnished by the Emperor and by a "distinguished British statesman."

KHVOSTOV, V.: "Blizhne-Vostochnyi Krizis, 1895–1897 gg." (*Istorik Marksist,* XIII, 1929, pp. 19–54). A rather confused study of the Turkish problem in these years, but invaluable because of the use it makes of unpublished Russian material.

PETERS, MARTIN: *Die Meerengen und die Europäischen Grossmächte 1890–1895.* Erlangen, 1932. Based almost exclusively upon the German documents, this dissertation adds nothing.

LITERATURE SINCE 1935

(See also the Supplementary Bibliographical Note to Chapter V.)

TEMPERLEY, HAROLD: "British Policy towards Parliamentary Rule and Constitutionalism in Turkey, 1830–1914" (*Cambridge Historical Journal,* IV, 1933, pp. 156–191). A brilliant review of the changes in British policy and the conditions underlying them.

YERUSALIMSKII, A.: "Borba Derzhav za Balkany i Prolivy v Kontse XIX veka" (*Voprosy Istorii*, 1947, no. 9, pp. 83–105). This article has since been incorporated in the next title.

—: *Vneshniaia Politika i Diplomatiia Germanskogo Imperializma v Kontse XIX veka.* Moscow, 1948. 767 pp. A most detailed and heavily documented study of German foreign policy from 1895 to 1900, utilizing to some extent unpublished Russian documents.

ISRAEL, LUDWIG: *England und der orientalische Dreibund, 1887–1896.* Stuttgart, 1938. 142 pp. The best single treatment of the Mediterranean and Straits problems in these years. Makes use of unpublished German documents.

PETEANI, LUIGI: *La questione libica nella diplomazia europea.* Florence, 1939. 254 pp. Another excellent monograph, ranging over the entire Mediterranean question.

FRAUENDIENST, WERNER: "Zur orientalischen Frage. Eine diplomatischer Schriftwechsel" (*Berliner Monatshefte*, XX, August, 1942, pp. 368–381). Prints a long report of the German Ambassador at Constantinople, dated December 28, 1896 and appraising the Near Eastern situation.

ZUG, JOSEF: *Versuche der Widerannäherung an Russland unter Reichskanzler Fürst Chlodwig zu Hohenlohe-Schillingsfürst.* Rottenburg, 1934. 184 pp. Based on obvious materials, this dissertation supplies a useful analysis of the German-Russian relationship in the years 1895–1898.

ANCHIERI, ETTORE: *Costantinopoli e gli stretti nella politica russa ed europea dal trattato di Qüciük Kainargi alla convenzione di Montreux.* Milan, 1948. 268 pp. The best single treatment of the Straits Question, especially during the 1890's.

WOBST, PAUL G.: *Die Dardanellen Frage bis zum Lösungsversuch des Abkommens von Montreux.* Leipzig, 1941. 107 pp.

STADTMÜLLER, GEORG: "Die Dardanellenfrage in Geschichte und Gegenwart" (*Zeitschrift für die gesamte Staatswissenschaft*, CI, 1941, pp. 448–470).

VIII

The South African Crisis

༺༻

I N THE YEARS 1895 AND 1896 THE GOOD OLD-FASHIONED NEAR EASTERN crisis probably brought the European nations nearer to war than did any other dispute. But much of the tension between the various chancelleries was concealed from the public. It is not generally known, even now, how close both the British and the Russian governments came to taking action which might have precipitated a cataclysm. As we look back on these years we can easily see that in spite of the acuteness of the crisis the question was really less important than the Far Eastern problem of the same period, a problem which concerned the fate of a tremendous region and of a large fraction of the world's population, to say nothing of valuable trading interests. And yet even the Far Eastern question was overshadowed at the time by the popular interest in what was happening in south Africa. There an impressive drama was being played, largely in the open. There the issues were more obvious, the action more understandable, the personalities more fascinating. It was the south African affair which became the touchstone of British imperialism and which called forth among the European powers a veritable storm of indignation and jealousy.

We have to deal, in this chapter, with Jameson's famous raid into the Transvaal and with the repercussions of this spectacular incident upon the international relations of the European governments. Like all such events, it had a long and complicated history, stemming from the fundamental antagonism of the English and Dutch in south Africa, from the conflict of British imperialist ideas and republican aspirations, from the peculiar economic problems of the four south African states, from the revolution brought about by the discovery of great gold fields in the Transvaal, and lastly from the growing pressure of German competition in the colonial and commercial fields. Something must, of course, be said of this historical background in order to make the culmination of the story comprehensible, but I shall restrict myself rigorously to the main lines of the development. Recent books have covered the ground so thoroughly in many respects that another detailed treatment, even if it were possible, would be quite superfluous.[1]

---

[1] I have in mind three books in particular: Eric A. Walker: *A History of South Africa* (New York, 1928), in every way admirable; Raymond W. Bixler: *Anglo-German Imperialism in South Africa, 1880–1900* (Columbus, 1932), conscientious but uninspired; Reginald I. Lovell: *The Struggle for South Africa, 1875–1899* (New York, 1934), which goes over the ground with great thoroughness,

We need go no further back than the year 1884, which is, for several reasons, a significant turning point. At that time the Boers of the Transvaal, having defeated the English troops in the battle of Majuba Hill in 1881, secured from the Gladstone government a recognition of their independence, subject to the reservation that they should not conclude any treaties with foreign powers without submitting them to the British government for approval. The English government gave up the suzerainty which it had exercised under the terms of the convention of 1881. Nothing more was heard of suzerainty for fully a decade, and then even the lawyers of the crown were of the opinion that the British claim was hardly defensible.[2] It should be noted, however, that quite apart from the technical question of suzerainty, the London government undoubtedly enjoyed a special position with regard to the Transvaal. In fact it is impossible to deny that the Transvaal, being limited in the conduct of its foreign relations, was not really an independent state. Suzerainty existed in fact if not in law.

It was in this same year 1884 that Germany appeared as a colonial power in south Africa and took over a large dominion on the southwest coast. This event caused a good deal of uneasiness among the politicians at the Cape, who feared that Germany might ally herself with the Transvaal, establish a great belt of territory across south Africa, and thus block forever the expansion of the English colonies to the north. How much justification there was for such fears it is hard to say, but what evidence we have would indicate that they were exaggerated. During the seventies there had been some talk in Germany of securing a protectorate over the Transvaal, and President Bürgers of the Republic was prepared to conclude a protective alliance in 1875. An influential German writer on colonial affairs, Ernst von Weber, constantly stressed Germany's need for a port in that area (preferably Delagoa Bay) and the desirability of acquiring influence in the Transvaal. His writings were widely read, and Cecil Rhodes himself is said to have known and annotated them.[3] Even though the home government was not disturbed by the spectre of German designs, men like Rhodes were. As a member of the Cape ministry in 1884 he did his utmost to impress upon his colleagues the need for taking over the hinterland of Walfisch Bay, that is, the region which became German Southwest Africa. The ministry was too slow and the Germans were too fast, so the damage was done. But Rhodes had better luck in bringing about the establishment of a British protectorate over Bechuanaland, the territory lying between the Transvaal and the new German colony. Thus the road to trade and territorial expansion towards the north was kept open.[4]

---

[2] Lucien Wolf: *Life of the First Marquess of Ripon* (London, 1921), II, p. 228; *Letters of Queen Victoria,* III, p. 18; the matter is discussed at length by Lovell, op. cit., pp. 58 ff.

[3] Johannes Wüd: *Die Rolle der Burenrepubliken in der Auswärtigen und Kolonialen Politik des Deutschen Reiches in den Jahren 1883–1900* (Nürnberg, 1927), pp. 7–9; Basil Williams: *Cecil Rhodes* (London, 1921), p. 79; Lovell, op. cit., pp. 109–10.

[4] Imperialist: *Cecil Rhodes* (London, 1897), pp. 27 ff.; Sir Lewis Michell: *The Life and Times of Cecil John Rhodes* (New York, 1910), I, pp. 217 ff.; II, p. 137; Williams, op. cit., chap. viii; Lovell, op. cit., pp. 51 ff.

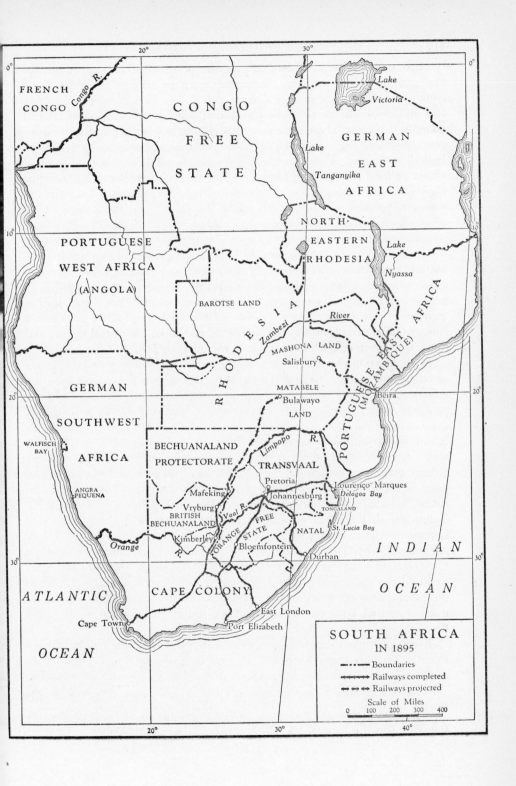

FRENCH
CONGO

CONGO *R.*

CONGO

FREE

STATE

Lake
Victoria

GERMAN

EAST

AFRICA

Lake

Tanganyika

PORTUGUESE

WEST AFRICA

(ANGOLA)

NORTH-

EASTERN

RHODESIA

Lake
Nyassa

BAROTSE LAND

R   H   O   D   E   S   I   A

River

Zambezi

MASHONA LAND

Salisbury

MATABELE

Bulawayo

LAND

PORTUGUESE EAST AFRICA
(MOZAMBIQUE)

Beira

GERMAN

SOUTHWEST

AFRICA

WALFISCH
BAY

ANGRA
PEQUENA

BECHUANALAND

PROTECTORATE

Limpopo   *R.*

TRANSVAAL

Pretoria

Mafeking

Johannesburg

Lourenço Marques
Delagoa Bay

Vryburg
BRITISH
BECHUANALAND

Vaal R.

ORANGE   FREE

STATE

TONGALAND

St. Lucia Bay

NATAL

Kimberley

Orange   *R.*

Bloemfontein

Durban

30°

INDIAN

OCEAN

ATLANTIC

CAPE   COLONY

OCEAN

Cape Town

East London

Port Elizabeth

SOUTH AFRICA
IN 1895

–·–·–· Boundaries
+–+–+– Railways completed
+–+–+– Railways projected

Scale of Miles

0   100   200   300   400

After this settlement of the relations between England and the Transvaal and after this first flare-up of the south African problem as an international issue, the various states — Cape Colony, Natal, The Orange River Free State and the South African Republic (Transvaal), returned to their own difficult domestic problems. These were primarily economic in nature and were so urgent that before 1895 they had come to overshadow even the racial antagonism. Indeed, at the time of the Jameson raid Rhodes, as prime minister of the Cape, was in political alliance with Hofmeyer and the Dutch Afrikander Bond. The Cape government was, at the same time, united with the Dutch Free State in a customs agreement, while the other English colony, Natal, maintained a close connexion with the Dutch Transvaal as a counterweight to the Cape-Free State combination. The reason for this strange alignment is to be found in the relative natural poverty of the region. Both the Cape and Natal were dependent in large measure upon trade with the interior. Fully half their revenue came from customs dues and railway receipts. The two English colonies were therefore of necessity rivals for the favors of the two Dutch republics. " They were," says an authoritative writer, " determined to take all they could get, to gain an exclusive entrance to as many markets as possible, to filch from each other's ports and railways as much of the interior trade as could be lured away." [5]

Many efforts were made, at various times, to bring about a general *Zollverein* among all the south African states, but these efforts were frustrated by the unwillingness of any one state to make concessions in the interest of general prosperity. It was only in keeping with this selfish spirit that President Kruger of the Transvaal did all that he could to buttress the political independence of his country by strengthening its economic independence. While the Cape and Natal were eager to push their railways up into the Free State and the Transvaal, Kruger was intent on opening up connexions of his own with the coast. For years he tried to secure a corridor through Swaziland and Tongaland to St. Lucia Bay or Kosi Bay, until the British finally blocked his efforts by annexing Tongaland in 1894. The only other non-British port on the east coast was Lorenzo Marques, situated on Delagoa Bay, the finest harbor on the whole east African seaboard. The place had for years been a bone of contention between England and Portugal until in 1875 an arbitral award had assigned it to Portugal.[6] From Kruger's standpoint, then, it had the double advantage of being closer to the Transvaal by 150 miles than the nearest Natal port and by almost 400 miles than the nearest Cape port (East London), and of giving access to the ocean through non-British territory.

Ever since 1860 there had been discussion about building a railway from Lorenzo Marques to the Transvaal. In 1872 an Englishman had secured from the Portuguese government a concession to build to the Transvaal border. But

[5] Jean van der Poel: *Railway and Customs Policies in South Africa, 1885–1910* (London, 1933), p. 14.

[6] See Raymond W. Bixler: " Anglo-Portuguese Rivalry for Delagoa Bay " (*Journal of Modern History*, VI, December, 1934, pp. 425–40), which is based upon unpublished British material.

there had been much confusion and little money. It was not until 1889 that the line to the Transvaal frontier was opened and not until a decade later that an arbitral award settled the claims of the concessionaires against the Lisbon government.[7] Kruger was very anxious to secure railway communication with Delagoa Bay, but he was suspicious of the Portuguese project. The concessionaire who built the line was an American named MacMurdo, but his financial support came almost entirely from English sources. His agreement with the Portuguese government gave him certain rate-fixing rights which Kruger feared might be used by English interests to the detriment of the Transvaal. For these reasons he hesitated about building the section of the line to Pretoria that lay within the Transvaal territory, though a syndicate had been formed to undertake the project. This was the Netherlands South African Railway Company, which was chartered in 1887. It was really an agent of the Transvaal government, which owned a large number of the shares and dictated the policies.

By 1889 an entirely new factor had been introduced into the already complicated situation. Gold had been discovered in the vicinity of Johannesburg in 1884. Two years later it had been shown that these deposits on the Witwatersrand were among the richest that had ever been struck. The gold rush began at once, and in the short space of a few months Johannesburg was a busy mining center, filled with foreign adventurers of all types. It was to be but a few years before the foreigners in the Transvaal greatly outnumbered the adult Boers in the state.[8] It goes without saying that the phenomenal growth of the gold mining industry very soon made Johannesburg the most important market in south Africa. The Cape government and the Natal government began a race to push their railway connexions to the Transvaal frontier, while Kruger himself hastened to begin the construction of the line to the Portuguese border.

We may safely omit the details of the long-drawn negotiations through which it was hoped, though in vain, that some sort of satisfactory agreement might be reached between the Cape, Natal and the Transvaal. Suffice it to say that the railroad from the Cape, passing through the Orange River Free State, reached the Vaal River in December 1890; only fifty miles beyond the river lay the gold city — Johannesburg. By this time Cecil Rhodes had become prime minister of the Cape Colony. He had already made an immense fortune through manipulation and amalgamation in the Kimberley diamond industry and he already controlled a large part of the Rand gold industry through the Consolidated Goldfields, which was one of the leading companies. Rhodes was perhaps the greatest of all apostles of British expansion and meant to use his tremendous

---

[7] These were the famous MacMurdo claims. The dreary story of this relatively short line may be read in Montague G. Jessett: *The Key to South Africa* (London, 1899), chap. v; Malcolm McIlwraith: "The Delagoa Bay Arbitration" (*Fortnightly Review,* September, 1900, pp. 410–29); *Manual of Portuguese East Africa* (London, 1920), chap. x; Van der Poel, op. cit., pp. 18 ff.

[8] On the discovery of gold on the Rand see now William MacDonald: *The Romance of the Golden Rand* (London, 1933). A good picture of the boom days of Johannesburg may be found in Hedley Chilvers: *Out of the Crucible* (London, 1929).

financial resources for the greater glory of the British Empire. Having helped to keep open the " Suez Canal " of south Africa — i.e., Bechuanaland — in 1884, he had organized the British South Africa Company, which was granted a charter in the autumn of 1889. The charter gave the company almost unlimited rights and powers of government in the huge area north of the Transvaal and west of the Portuguese possessions, without fixing any northern limit. As we have seen in an earlier chapter, Rhodes was even at this time swayed by visions of an un- interrupted British belt from the Cape to Cairo. But the first step was to organize and exploit what was to become Rhodesia, thus hemming in the Transvaal in the hope of forcing that state into an economic if not political union with the English colonies.[9]

Rhodes could not regard the Delagoa Bay Railway as anything but a menace to his schemes with respect to the Transvaal. In a speech delivered in 1886 he had pointed out that " if the Delagoa Bay Railway is carried out, the real union of South Africa will be indefinitely deferred." [10] Fortunately for him, Kruger found it very difficult to raise the funds necessary to carry through the project and for a time there seemed to be a fair prospect that the whole thing would fall through. The Portuguese government was in dire financial straits and Rhodes seized the opportunity to offer to buy the Portuguese end of the line to the Transvaal, as well as the Delagoa Bay region or even the whole of the Portuguese territory south of the Zambezi. He planned to have his friends, the Rothschilds, act as agents, but evidently the famous bankers, to say nothing of the English government, thought these plans too ambitious and did not sup- port them. The full story is not known, but nothing came of the project.[11]

In the interval Kruger had been forced by hard necessity to make an agree- ment with the Cape. Under the terms of this arrangement, concluded in De- cember 1891, the Cape was to lend the Netherlands South African Railway Company not less than £300,000 and not more than £900,000 in return for debentures of the Company. The Company agreed to build a railway bridge over the Vaal and to construct the fifty miles of railroad from the Vaal to Johannesburg within a specified time. The Cape government was given the right, till December 1894, to fix the rates for through traffic from its ports to the Transvaal.[12] A few months later the Rothschilds lent the Transvaal govern- ment £2,500,000, to be used to construct the Delagoa line; that is, to liberate themselves from the dependence upon the Cape route which it was Rhodes' great ambition to establish.

   9 See W. J. Leyds: *The Transvaal Surrounded* (London, 1919), part iv; the highly critical account of John H. Harris: *The Chartered Millions* (London, 1920), part ii; and the well-documented study of Hugh M. Hole: *The Making of Rhodesia* (London, 1926), passim. The subject is, of course, discussed in all the biographies of Rhodes and in books like Walker: *History of South Africa,* pp. 415 ff.; Lovell, op. cit., pp. 134 ff.

   10 Ian Colvin: *The Life of Jameson* (London, 1922), II, p. 25.

   11 Walker, op. cit., pp. 445 ff.; Jessett, op. cit., pp. 171 ff.; Van der Poel, op. cit., pp. 61-2.

   12 J. H. Hofmeyer and F. W. Reitz: *The Life of Jan Hendrik Hofmeyer* (Cape Town, 1913), pp. 394-403; Van der Poel, op. cit., pp. 59-60.

The first trains from the Cape reached Johannesburg in September 1892. For a couple of years the Cape enjoyed practically a monopoly of trade with the gold city and the Transvaal. But it was perfectly obvious that the situation was a purely temporary one. Natal would soon be bringing in lines from Durban, which would be much shorter than the line to East London or Port Elizabeth. Above all, the Delagoa line would soon be completed and thereby the lines to the south would be driven to ruin. When one stops to consider that the economic welfare of the Cape and Natal depended very largely on this trade to the interior, one can understand the feverish state of mind created by Kruger's policy.

Rhodes and his associates viewed the situation with greater anxiety because they were convinced that the Germans were deeply involved with Kruger and had designs on Delagoa Bay and the Portuguese end of the railway. These suspicions were shared even in London. Chamberlain remarked in a speech delivered in 1888 that " sooner or later (the Dutch in the Cape Colony), with the sympathy of the Dutch in the Transvaal and of the Orange Free State, would stretch out their hands to the kindred nation (Germany), which is already established on the west coast of Africa." Lord Rosebery too referred to the affair as " a grave and pregnant matter," and called attention to the danger of having the railroad fall into hands which, if not hostile, were at any rate unfriendly.[13] It was known that the Germans were heavily interested in the Netherlands Railway Company, and that they were making very successful efforts to increase their trade with the Transvaal by way of Delagoa Bay. In fact, Germans had been streaming into the Transvaal since the opening of the gold fields in 1886. There were thousands of them in Johannesburg; in Pretoria, out of a population of 6,000, it is said that there were 400 Germans. They were enterprising and successful, not only in mining, but also in other industries. Kruger showed them preference in making appointments to administrative positions and in awarding concessions. They controlled the National Bank and secured the all-important dynamite monopoly, which made tremendous profits at the expense of the mining companies. They also held a whiskey monopoly, which netted them 20%, and they built waterworks, collieries, etc. Imports of iron and steel, chemicals, machines and utensils came in large quantity from Hamburg, so that German exports to the Transvaal increased five-fold between 1889 and 1894. Krupp, Siemens and Halske, Goerz, Eduard Lippert and other large interests were established in Johannesburg. In October 1895 the Dresdener Bank opened a branch at Pretoria, with a capital of £1,000,000. It has been estimated that fully one fifth of all foreign capital invested in the country was German.[14]

---

[13] See J. L. Garvin: *The Life of Joseph Chamberlain* (London, 1933), II, pp. 464 ff.; Ross J. S. Hoffman: *Great Britain and the German Trade Rivalry, 1875–1914* (Philadelphia, 1933), p. 203. Similar arguments are advanced in Charles Marvin: *Boer-German Republic or English Dominion?* (London, 1887), p. 18.

[14] The best statistics may be found in the anonymous article: " Deutschlands Beziehungen zu Transvaal " (*Die Grenzboten*, 1896, I, pp. 305–10); and in Wüd, op. cit., p. 76. See also W. H.

These interests were purely private in nature, but there was also some evidence of German political activity. It was believed that the Germans stood behind Kruger in his efforts to secure control of Delagoa Bay in 1891 and again in 1893. In September 1894 a native insurrection broke out in the region. The British consul landed twenty blue-jackets to protect English nationals, whereupon the Germans protested and sent two men-of-war to the scene. How deep an impression this German interest made in London may be gathered from the remark of the biographer of Lord Ripon, who was at that time colonial secretary, to the effect that " during the whole of his tenure of office, Ripon's eyes were anxiously glued on this part of the east coast. Not a disturbance occurred in the Portuguese possessions which might give an opportunity for Boer intervention but he at once trotted round to the Foreign Office and worried Kimberley to send gunboats to Delagoa Bay." [15] He favored a strong warning to the Germans that the Transvaal was within the sphere of British influence and that they must keep their hands off. But relations with France were, at the time, so strained that Rosebery was anxious to avoid friction with Berlin. Ripon kept insisting that the Germans planned to take the Transvaal under their protection and that it would be fatal to the British position and influence to have them meddling at Pretoria, but the foreign office could not be induced to make a definite statement to the German ambassador. Hatzfeldt was warned about interfering at Delagoa Bay and was reminded that England was deeply concerned with the question of the Portuguese colonies, but nothing specific was said regarding the Transvaal.[16]

Lord Sanderson, who was permanent undersecretary at the foreign office from 1894 to 1905, asserted later that in the spring of 1895 the Germans tried to open negotiations regarding the eventual disposition of the Portuguese colony on the east coast of Africa. They claimed, he said, everything south of the mouth of the Zambezi, and insisted that Delagoa Bay be neutralized. Kimberley was " hot with indignation " and the discussions ended abruptly, but from then on the Germans came out more and more openly on the side of the Boers. It is hard to say how much weight should be attached to this story, since there is no reference to it in the German documents or in the other sources and there appears to be no record of it even in the British foreign office archives.[17] This much, however, is clear, that in the early months of 1895 there was already considerable tension between the London and Berlin chancelleries with regard to the

Lawson: " German Intrigues in the Transvaal " (*Contemporary Review*, February, 1896, pp. 292–304); and the analysis of the material brought out in the British parliamentary investigations in Bixler: *Anglo-German Imperialism*, pp. 61 ff. Hoffman, op. cit., pp. 202 ff. has an excellent analysis of German interests in south Africa.

[15] Lucien Wolf: *Life of Ripon*, II, p. 230.

[16] Wolf, op. cit., II, pp. 230–4; *British Documents on the Origins of the War*, I, pp. 323 ff.; Michell: *Life of Rhodes*, II, pp. 95–8; Walker, op. cit., p. 449; J. F. van Oordt: *Paul Kruger en de Opkomst der Zuid-Afrikaansche Republiek* (Amsterdam, 1898), pp. 607 ff.

[17] *British Documents on the Origins of the War*, III, p. 425 (Sanderson's comments on the famous Crowe memorandum of January, 1907).

south African problem. The British, from Rhodes down, were suspicious of German designs and machinations. Much of this no doubt went back to the unfortunate speech which Kruger made to the Germans at Pretoria on the occasion of the Emperor William's birthday (January 27). After extolling the virtues of the German element in the Transvaal, he said:

"When the convention with Her Majesty's Government was signed (in 1884) I regarded this Republic as a little child, and a little child has to wear small clothing. But as the child grows up it requires bigger clothes — the old ones will burst, and that is our position to-day. We are growing up and although we are young we feel that if one nation tries to kick us the other will try to stop it. When we asked Her Majesty's Government for bigger clothes they said, 'Eh? Eh? What is this?' and could not see that we were growing up. I am pleased to see you Germans here . . . and I feel certain that when the time comes for the Republic to wear still larger clothes, you will have done much to bring it about. It is my wish to continue those peaceful relations, and I wish also to give Germany all the support a little child can give to a grown-up man. The time is coming for our friendship to be more firmly established than ever." [18]

This address was too much even for the London foreign office. The British ambassador at Berlin was at once instructed to warn the Germans against "coquetting" with the Transvaal and to emphasize the fact that Kruger was not in a position to conclude treaties with foreign powers without British approval. Germany's policy was strengthening the Boers in their hostility to England. To which Marschall replied that the Germans desired only the status quo and the safeguarding of their economic interests. If the Boers were becoming more and more hostile to the English, the explanation was to be found not in what the Germans did, but in the policies and utterances of Rhodes.[19]

To the Rhodesian policies we must now return. It will be recalled that the problem of the Transvaal had become largely a problem of communications. The Cape railways were running to Johannesburg, but the Delagoa Bay line was to be ready for service in January 1895 and the right of the Cape government to fix the rates to the Rand was to expire on December 31, 1894. The Netherlands Railway Company had given due notice of the termination of the agreement and during the autumn of 1894 great efforts had been made by Rhodes to reach some satisfactory *modus vivendi*. The question was, for the Cape, nothing less than crucial, for its railway system was bound to fail if it could not reckon on at least a substantial part of the Transvaal trade, and that railway system represented an investment of £17,000,000. Rhodes himself visited Kruger in November 1894 and tried to make some arrangement, but his efforts, like those of his agents, failed. The Cape wanted more than the Transvaal could

---

[18] Report of the speech in the Johannesburg *Star*, as quoted in Hugh M. Hole: *The Jameson Raid* (London, 1930), pp. 39–40.

[19] *Die Grosse Politik*, XI, no. 2577; *British Documents on the Origins of the War*, I, p. 326. See also *Letters of Queen Victoria*, II, pp. 454–5, 483.

accord, and the old president was not in a very conciliatory frame of mind. Rhodes came away disgusted and hopeless. " I am sometimes told," he said in the Cape parliament, " that the question of South Africa at the present moment is the question of a united South Africa . . . but I think it is the settlement of tariffs between Delagoa Bay, Durban and the ports of Cape Colony, because if we do not settle these tariffs it will be ruinous for us all." [20]

After his conference with Kruger, Rhodes paid a visit to England, where, among other things, he arranged to have his friend Sir Hercules Robinson appointed as high commissioner in the place of Sir Henry Loch. He was just about to return to the Cape when the news of Kruger's famous speech reached him. Evidently it made a deep impression upon him, as it did upon the foreign office. His biographers are generally agreed that it convinced him that nothing was to be hoped for from Kruger and that it persuaded him of the existence of an actual understanding between the Germans and the Pretoria government. Referring later to the events which led up to the Jameson raid he himself declared:

" I must admit that in all my actions I was greatly influenced by my belief that the policy of the present Government of the South African Republic was to introduce the influence of another foreign power into the already complicated system of South Africa, and thereby render more difficult in the future the closer union of the different states." [21]

This brings us to the story of the conspiracy which led to the famous Raid, to the revolutionary movement which aimed at the overthrow of Kruger and so at the settlement of the whole customs and transportation problem of south Africa. In this movement the foreigners in Johannesburg played a leading part, and the tales of their grievances still fill many pages of all books on the subject. Johannesburg, the centre of the mining area, had a population of about 100,000, of whom half were whites. At this time no accurate census of the population of the Transvaal at large had been taken, so that it is impossible to say what the proportion of Uitlanders (Outlanders) to Boers really was. The most conflicting statements were made at the time and have been repeated since. Lord Salisbury claimed that the foreigners were in a large majority, and Rhodes once stated that there were 100,000 British subjects as against only 14,000 Boers. Even so careful a writer as James Bryce reported that there were more than 100,000 English-speaking Uitlanders and only 65,000 Boers.[22] On the other hand Dr. Leyds, foreign secretary of the Republic, maintained in a speech in January 1896 that the total white population was 226,000, of whom 75,720 were Uit-

[20] Williams: *Cecil Rhodes*, p. 249. The negotiations of the autumn are very well treated by Van der Poel, op. cit., pp. 79 ff.

[21] *Report of the Select Committee on British South Africa (1897)*, questions 19, 1067, 1086; Williams: *Cecil Rhodes*. p. 254; G. Seymour Fort: " The True Motive and Reason of Dr. Jameson's Raid " (*Nineteenth Century*, June, 1896, pp. 873–80).

[22] James Bryce: *Impressions of South Africa* (New York, 1897), p. 435.

landers, and of these 41,445 were British.[23] For some unknown reason the figures collected by the British representative in Pretoria in October 1894 seem to
have been neglected. He put the numbers of the Uitlanders at 78,000, claiming
that 62,500 of them were British, and estimated the Boer population at about
71,000.[24] These figures are probably nearer the truth, possibly a little low with
respect to the Boer population if we are to judge by the astonishing numbers
which they put into the field during the war of 1899–1902. Apparently the Boer
population and the Uitlander residents were roughly equal in number, though
of course the foreigners were almost all adult males, while only a fraction of the
Boer population was politically of age. In any case, the absurd stories of the
Uitlanders outnumbering the Boers ten to one, or even three to one, as put
about by unscrupulous agitators and the reporters of sensational newspapers,
are wholly misleading.

The tremendous influx of foreigners, many of them of a disreputable type,
had created a serious problem in the Transvaal. The conservative, agrarian or
pastoral Boers felt themselves threatened in their position by the outsiders.
Under the leadership of Kruger they took the necessary steps to protect themselves. A long residence was required before an alien could become a burgher.
No support was given to schools for foreigners, and the needs of the Rand population were generally ignored. It is quite impossible and in fact it is unnecessary
to go over this whole subject in detail or to re-examine minutely the great mass
of conflicting evidence.[25] Whatever may have been the reality and the extent of
the Uitlander grievances, the fact is that many of the newcomers felt that they
were being wronged and so in 1892 they founded a National Union for the
purpose of reform agitation. On several occasions this organization petitioned
the legislature for an extension of the franchise, without making any impression upon the burghers.[26] The National Union was not supported by the influential mine owners and capitalists, who feared that agitation might react
unfavorably upon their relations with the government. It was only in 1895 that
Rhodes, Beit, Phillips and other capitalists of the Rhodes group changed their
policy and began to work with and for the National Union. Need it be said that
their interest was less in the removal of grievances than in making trouble for
Kruger? A part of the mine-owning group, which was opposed to Rhodes and
his friends, stayed out of the movement entirely. But Rhodes saw here an opportunity to overthrow the obstinate old president and reshape the Transvaal
government for his own purposes.

---

[23] *Saturday Review*, February 1, 1896.

[24] *Accounts and Papers*, 1895, LXXI: *Correspondence Respecting the Number of British Subjects Resident in the South African Republic* (C-7633).

[25] See Bryce, op. cit., chap. xxv; J. P. Fitzpatrick: *The Transvaal from Within* (London, 1899),
passim; Walker: *History of South Africa*, pp. 440 ff.; Lovell: *The Struggle for South Africa*, pp.
290 ff., etc.

[26] There was, to be sure, a reform party among the Boers, led by Joubert, but this was of
little account after the re-election of Kruger to the presidency in 1894.

From the spring of 1895 onward preparations were made to precipitate a revolution in Johannesburg. A force of armed men was to be stationed on the frontier to invade the country as soon as necessary. Rhodes, who was not only prime minister of the Cape Colony but chairman of the boards of both the South African Company and the Consolidated Goldfields, did not allow himself to be hampered by his divided responsibilities. He and his associates paid for the large stores of ammunition and arms that were smuggled into Johannesburg, and his agents arranged for the establishment of remount and provision stations along the route to be followed by the invading force. It was arranged that the police of the Chartered Company, under the command of the administrator, Dr. Leander Starr Jameson, should be used for the expedition. But in order that the shortest route, from Mafeking (temporary terminus of the railway being built northwards as part of the Cape-to-Cairo scheme), might be followed, it was necessary to secure a suitable " jumping-off place " in Bechuanaland. Arrangements to this end were completed in a general way before the Rosebery government resigned in June 1895. The fact is that the whole Rhodes plan derived from that worked out by the high commissioner, Sir Henry Loch, a year before, when the Uitlanders threatened to revolt rather than serve in the Transvaal army during a native insurrection. The British government was at that time convinced that if serious trouble broke out in Johannesburg intervention would be unavoidable, and that it would be wise to have a force ready at Mafeking. Rhodes and his associates were still entirely out of sympathy with the Uitlander agitation, but by the middle of 1895 they had not only opened their eyes to the grievances of the Johannesburgers, they had even taken over the encouragement of the revolutionary movement and had adopted a plan which before they had vetoed.[27]

Rhodes had no reason to welcome the fall of the Rosebery ministry, for Rosebery was his friend and the Liberal government had shown much sympathy for what he was trying to do. On the other hand the English elections of July 1895, which gave the Conservative-Unionist cabinet a huge majority, represented a disastrous defeat for the old Gladstonian liberalism and a resounding victory for the imperialists. It has often been pointed out, quite correctly I think, that the hero of these elections was not Lord Salisbury but Joseph Chamberlain, already known at this time as a fervent exponent of imperial federation and of imperialism. Chamberlain's position was so strong that he was, to all intents and purposes, co-premier with Salisbury during the next half dozen years.[28] Yet he took the astonishing step of choosing the position of secretary for the colonies, a post which had thus far always been regarded as being of secondary importance. His choice was, of course, merely a reflection of his interest in the Empire and his belief in the significance of imperial relations.

---

[27] Walker, op. cit., pp. 445–6; Lovell, op. cit., pp. 300–1; and now especially J. L. Garvin: *Life of Joseph Chamberlain* (London, 1934), III, p. 58.

[28] Garvin, op. cit., III, pp. 7–8.

As secretary for the colonies Chamberlain was brought at once into contact with the south African embroglio. He did not care much for Rhodes personally and evidently distrusted his methods of doing things. When Rutherfoord Harris, an agent of Rhodes, approached him with the request that Bechuanaland be turned over to the South African Company, objections were raised. The colonial secretary was quite prepared to turn over British Bechuanaland to the Cape, but he would not agree to assign the much larger Bechuanaland Protectorate to the Company. It was not until October 1895 that he finally consented to turn over a strip of territory along the Transvaal frontier, with the understanding that it was to be used for the railway northwards to Buluwayo, the railroad project being one with which Chamberlain sympathized in every way.[29]

Harris claimed later that it was during his talks with Chamberlain that he initiated him into Rhodes' plan for an insurrection at Johannesburg and for an invasion of the country from the west. Upon this assertion much of the case against Chamberlain has been made to rest. Not a few people who stood high in the political life of England were convinced that the colonial secretary knew what Rhodes was up to, and that he was therefore an accessory to the conspiracy.[30] No irrefutable documentary evidence has ever been adduced to prove the charge and we may accept the conclusions of the authoritative biographer of Chamberlain, which admit much, even if they exonerate him from actual complicity. Mr. Garvin concedes that Chamberlain knew of the revolution that was brewing in Johannesburg, though he did not know of Rhodes' activity and support. As a matter of fact no secret was made of the preparations. Everyone at all in the know realized that the crash was not far off.[31] Chamberlain must have been aware of the Loch plan as outlined in the summer of 1894; in any event he was told by his friend Lord Grey that it would be highly desirable to have a force on the frontier, ready to go in, if needed. When the " jumping-off place " was turned over to the South African Company, Chamberlain realized that a police force was going to be concentrated there, ostensibly to protect the railroad. He himself thought that it would be convenient to have it where it might be used in the Transvaal if the occasion required, but he did not know that Rhodes was planning to use it for that purpose on his own hook. The government's idea all through seems to have been that if the insurrection broke out the high commissioner would hasten to Johannesburg to arbitrate. He would call in the force from the frontier if it were needed.[32]

If you accept this version of Chamberlain's connexion with the plot, there still remains the fact that the colonial secretary knew of the revolution that was brewing and that he did nothing whatever either to discourage it or to warn

---

[29] Garvin, op. cit., III, pp. 33–4, 36, 49.

[30] Gardiner: *Life of Harcourt*, II, pp. 429–30; J. A. Spender: *The Life of Campbell-Bannerman*, I, pp. 193 ff.; *The Personal Papers of Lord Rendel* (London, 1931), p. 163. See also the sane and moderate statement in Hole: *The Jameson Raid*, p. 61; Lovell, op. cit., pp. 320–6.

[31] See Bryce, op. cit., p. 425; Garvin, op. cit., III, pp. 45–6.

[32] Garvin, op. cit., III, pp. 36 ff., 52–3, 59–63, 110 ff.

the Transvaal authorities. On the contrary, he was prepared to make full use of it when it was successful and had a full plan of action ready. Sir Hercules Robinson, the high commissioner, was the key man in the scheme. He was to take charge as soon as Johannesburg rose, in order to prevent the Uitlanders from setting up a republic of their own. We know that Robinson feared such a development and that Rhodes did too. There is no reason to suppose that Robinson, the friend of Rhodes, was not fully initiated into the whole scheme, even though he never consented to tell what he knew about it. If he was, that might explain the lack of energy he showed in dealing with Kruger after the Raid.[33]

After this rather lengthy digression we must take up again the narrative of happenings in south Africa. The worst expectations of Rhodes were fulfilled when the Netherlands Railway, in order to divert the traffic from the Cape lines to the newly opened Delagoa Bay Railroad, raised the rates on the fifty mile stretch from Johannesburg to the Vaal River from 2.4 pence to 8 pence per ton per mile. Everything possible was done to make transportation from the Cape difficult as well as expensive. And yet at Lorenzo Marques there were no facilities for taking care of large shipments. In September 1895 the Delagoa line was carrying only about 60 tons a day, while at Johannesburg 20,000 to 30,000 tons were awaiting transportation. At the other end matters were even worse. There were no adequate wharves or piers, to say nothing of warehouses. From October 1895 to February 1896 ships landed over 100,000 tons of goods at the port, most of it assigned to the Transvaal. Yet the Railroad was taking away less than 10,000 tons a month. The rest lay about in the open, exposed to the terrific sun.[34] " Lorenzo Marques appeared to have sustained either a bombardment or an earthquake," reported an American journalist:

> " It was difficult to discover where the customs-house ended and the town commenced; for bales, boxes and general wreckage were scattered up and down the streets leading in any direction from the government landing-place, offering every temptation to thieves; and, indeed, there are thieves in plenty, wearing the Portuguese uniform." [35]

Shippers from the Cape decided to circumvent the high rates imposed by the Transvaal by reverting to the use of ox-carts to carry goods from the Vaal River to the Rand. Freight was unloaded at the river, taken over the ford (drifts) and then carted the remaining fifty miles. Kruger's reply to this move was to order the drifts closed to all goods coming from over-seas, as from October 1, 1895. The Cape government regarded this measure as a violation of

---

33 Viscountess Milner: " Footnotes to Chamberlain's Life " (National Review, December, 1934, pp. 796–801).

34 Foreign Office. Miscellaneous Series, 1896, no. 398: Report on the Port and Railway of Lorenzo Marques.

35 Poultney Bigelow: " The White Man's Africa " (Harper's Magazine, January, 1897); similarly M. G. Jessett· The Key to South Africa: Delagoa Bay (London, 1899), chaps. ii, iii; London Economist, September 28, 1895.

the Transvaal's treaty obligations to Britain and appealed to the colonial office for aid. Chamberlain took a strong stand, sent what amounted to an ultimatum and made it clear that England was prepared to resort to the use of force, if necessary. Thereupon Kruger backed down. The drifts were re-opened early in November.[36]

By this time the situation had become very acute and even the English public was much excited. In any discussion of the south African problem it must be remembered that great numbers of people were financially interested in what went on in the Transvaal. The picturesque figure of Rhodes had a sort of glamour and the story of his extraordinary career undoubtedly did much to encourage popular hopes of getting rich quickly. At any rate the like of the stock-jobbing that took place in connexion with the Rand mines had never been seen before. Since 1890 the English people had lost interest in foreign investments to a considerable extent, and capital had been accumulating. When, therefore, the " Kaffir millionaires " decided in 1894 to promote the south African market, they found a gullible public. In the spring of 1895 there seemed to be an insatiable hunger for gold shares. Bogus companies sprang up like mushrooms to meet the demand. Newspapers were full of attractive prospectuses, and shares, in small one pound units, were unloaded upon the public without difficulty. Brokers had to double their office forces and the police had to be called out to control the crowds that surged around the exchange. The " Kaffir Boom " or " Kaffir Circus " was much more widespread than any since the days of the railway mania. " Within the recollection of the oldest member of the Stock Exchange," wrote the London *Economist*, " there has been no speculative movement at all comparable, in point either of duration or of volume, to the existing ' Kaffir Boom,' which has gone on practically without interruption for fully twelve months, and shows as little sign of abatement as ever." [37]

The common man made no effort to determine the economic strength of the enterprises into which he sank his money. Names like Rhodes, Beit and Barnato were enough for him. He did not ask whether the firms in question paid dividends or not. They would make fortunes in the future, and it was frankly a gambling proposition. Anything was paid for shares of the Rand mining companies. While the large, established firms declared dividends running in some cases to more than 100%, the new enterprises which had no profits to show benefitted from the investment craze. With a declared capitalization of about £28,000,000, their market valuation in the summer was no less than £113,000,000. Finance and holding companies, with a capital of £16,000,000, enjoyed a market value of £63,500,000.[38] Naturally these halcyon days could not

---

[36] *Accounts and Papers,* 1897, LXII: *Correspondence Relative to the Closing of the Vaal River Drifts;* Lovell, op. cit.. pp. 325 ff.; Garvin, op. cit., III, pp. 40 ff.; Van der Poel, op. cit., pp. 81 ff.

[37] *Economist,* August 17, 1895.

[38] *Economist,* August 17. September 14, 1895; S. T. Van Oss: " The Gold-Mining Madness in the City " (*Nineteenth Century,* October, 1895, pp. 537-47); W. R. Lawson: " Kaffir Finance " (*National Review,* May, 1896, pp. 412-23).

last forever. The values of Rand shares had been forced up to preposterous levels and when the manipulators had unloaded their shares the slump was bound to come. The collapse, which began early in October, took but little time to run its course. By the middle of November the bottom was touched. Thousands of innocents had lost all or almost all they had.[39] As usual in such cases, they did not blame those who had fleeced them. Most of them did not realize that they had been fleeced. Rhodes and the rest were as popular as ever, but there was a dull, sore feeling that Old Man Kruger and his Dopper crowd were at the bottom of it all. It must be remembered that the collapse coincided with the drifts crisis. Taking it all in all, it was but natural that for the time being popular interest should be focussed upon the next moves in the south African game.

Even after the re-opening of the drifts there was no prospect of coming to an agreement with Kruger. Conferences were held, but no one really hoped for success. In government circles there seems to have been a growing feeling that the Germans were squarely behind Kruger and that for that reason, if for no other, progress would be impossible. A group of capitalists, opposed to Rhodes and represented by Eduard Lippert, were regarded as the agents of the Germans. There was general dissatisfaction·with the prominent part taken by the German warships in the formal opening of the Delagoa Bay Railway in June 1895.[40] All this suspicion led to a rather sharp passage between Sir Edward Malet, the ambassador at Berlin, and von Marschall in the middle of October. What the special occasion for the incident was we do not know. Malet was about to leave his post, and, while discussing the general situation with the German foreign minister, remarked that the Transvaal was the " black point " in Anglo-German relations. Germany, he said, was encouraging the Boers, a policy which might eventually become intolerable to the British. It might lead to " serious complications." Marschall at once challenged him to produce the evidence for his charges, and at the same time reiterated the German position. Germany desired only the status quo, but she could not allow the Transvaal to become the victim of Rhodes' schemes. Neither could she allow the Pretoria-Delagoa Bay Railway to fall into his hands.[41]

This conversation brought the mutual irritation to a head. The Emperor William took Malet's utterances to be the equivalent of an ultimatum and spoke bitterly of the English " threats " to Colonel Swaine, the military attaché. England, he said, was estranging her only real friend, the German Emperor. By her policy in Armenia she had already aroused the distrust of all the continental powers. England must not think that she could go on making capital of the antagonism between the two continental alliance groups. It would be rela-

[39] *Economist*, October 12, 19, November 16, 1895.

[40] See, e.g., Sir J. Percy Fitzpatrick: *South African Memories* (London, 1932), pp. 66 ff.; Garvin, op. cit., III, pp. 64 ff., 69 ff. Morley Roberts: " The War Game in South Africa " (*Fortnightly Review*, February, 1899) may be taken as reflecting the most exaggerated fears.

[41] *Die Grosse Politik*, XI, no. 2578.

tively easy for Germany to make up with Russia and France, perhaps at England's expense. England should make up her mind either to join the Triple Alliance, formally and definitely, or else join the ranks of Germany's enemies.[42]

Swaine's report of this conversation was taken very seriously in London. It was printed and distributed to the cabinet. In conversation with the German ambassador Lord Salisbury warmly denied having instructed Malet to speak as he did to Marschall. Eventually Malet was induced to send a letter explaining away his remarks.[43] Whether he actually had instructions or not is a question we need not try to answer. The episode is interesting because it illumines the attitude of the English toward the south African problem. There is nothing in the German archives that would in any way indicate that the German government or its agents encouraged Kruger to oppose the English or that they had anything to do with the dispute that had developed. It is clear from the German documents that in Berlin they were anxious not to arouse the distrust of the Transvaalers by taking too active a part. If Kruger reckoned on German support, that was his business.[44] But the suspicions of the English remained as strong as ever. Toward the end of November 1895, the English agent at Pretoria reported to the governor at the Cape that German intrigues were rife and that he thought the Germans were aiding and abetting the Transvaal authorities in their endeavor to get possession of the Delagoa Bay Railway. Germans were trying to buy up all the land they could at Delagoa Bay in order to strengthen their claims and pretensions.[45]

In south Africa the preparations for revolution had reached the final stage. December 27 was the date tentatively set for the rising in Johannesburg. Jameson was supplied with an appeal, drawn up weeks in advance, urging him to come to the rescue of the helpless women and children. He was to be ready to start as soon as word came to him from Johannesburg. But at the last moment things began to go wrong. Jameson had only about 600 men, instead of the 1,500 arranged for. The leaders at Johannesburg, though they had smuggled in large supplies of ammunition and rifles, considered their equipment inadequate. Above all, there was serious misunderstanding in regard to the flag. Several of the leading spirits desired the movement to take place under the Transvaal flag, and Rhodes was supposed to have agreed to this. But in the last days before the rising he changed his mind or at any rate failed to make himself clear. Emissaries had to be sent to Capetown. In view of the general uncertainty the leaders of the National Union decided to postpone action until January 6. But they did issue, on December 26, a manifesto in which the grievances of the Uitlanders were rehearsed and their demands set forth. Having stated what they

---

[42] *Die Grosse Politik*, XI, no. 2579.

[43] *Die Grosse Politik*, XI, nos. 2580–4; Garvin, op. cit., III, pp. 64 ff.

[44] Friedrich Thimme: " Die Krüger-Depesche " (*Europäische Gespräche*, May-June, 1924, pp. 201–44).

[45] *British Documents on the Origins of the War*, I, p. 326; see also *The Letters and Friendships of Sir Cecil Spring Rice* (London, 1929), I, pp. 182–3.

wanted, they still had before them the problem of getting it. That problem they arranged to take up on January 6.[46]

Jameson, who was on the frontier, at Pitsani Potlugo, with his 600 men, was instructed by Rhodes' agents and by the leaders at Johannesburg to defer action. But he was convinced that the Johannesburg people had lost heart and that they would never move unless forced to do so by outside action. So, ignoring the urgent warnings that came to him, he crossed the frontier on the afternoon of Sunday, December 29, and started out on the long ride of 140 miles to Johannesburg, cutting the telegraph wires so that no further instructions could reach him. His mission was hopeless from the very start. Kruger, who detested the Uitlanders and made no secret of it, had no fear of anything the " gold-grubbers " might do. He had a well-stocked arsenal at Pretoria and some 10,000 burghers in the militia, ready to move at short notice. Kruger had known for some time that something was brewing, for on December 24 the German agent at Pretoria wired home that there was likelihood of trouble in the next days.[47] But he regarded the situation with equanimity. Returning from a short trip on December 26 he said to the burghers of the capital: " I was often asked about the threatened risings, and I said, wait until the time comes. Take a tortoise; if you want to kill it, you must wait until it puts out its head, then you cut it off." [48]

While the leaders of the National Union had not yet unpacked the rifles (which had been smuggled into Johannesburg in oil-drums) and while they were panic-stricken by the news that Jameson was on his way, the Transvaal government quietly took precautions. As the raiders proceeded they noticed more and more parties of Boers on all sides of them. The enemy gradually closed in, until on Thursday, January 2, 1896, Jameson's force was surrounded and obliged to surrender at Doorn Kop, near Krugersdorp and hardly twenty miles from Johannesburg. The leaders of the Raid, as well as the more prominent members of the National Union, were taken and put on trial at Pretoria in the spring. Several of the Johannesburgers were condemned to death, but the sentence was suspended on the promise of the British government to try the accused in London. There followed investigations of the affair by the Cape government, and in 1897 by a committee of the British parliament. Rhodes was obliged to resign as prime minister, Jameson and some of the other leaders

---

[46] The literature on the subject is very extensive; see especially the accounts of the chiefs, such as J. P. Fitzpatrick: *The Transvaal from Within* (London. 1899); Lionel Phillips: *Some Reminiscences* (London, n.d.); John Hays Hammond: *The Truth about the Jameson Raid* (Boston, 1918); Edmund Garrett: *The Story of an African Crisis* (Westminster, 1897); see also Ian Colvin: *The Life of Jameson* (London, 1922), II. chaps. xxiv–xxvi; Garvin: *Life of Chamberlain*, III, pp. 73 ff.; and the detailed recent studies of Hugh Marshall Hole: *The Jameson Raid* (London, 1930), and Lovell: *The Struggle for South Africa*, chap. viii. On the Boer side consult N. J. Hofmeyr: *De Afrikaner-Boer en de Jameson-Inval* (Capetown, 1896), and Philip R. Botha: *Die Staatkundige Ontwikkeling van die Suidafrikaanse Republiek onder Krüger en Leyds* (Amsterdam, 1925), chaps. xxx–i.   [47] *Die Grosse Politik*, XI. no. 2585.

[48] *Correspondence on the Subject of the Recent Disturbances in the South African Republic* (C-7933, London, 1896), no. 179, enclosure.

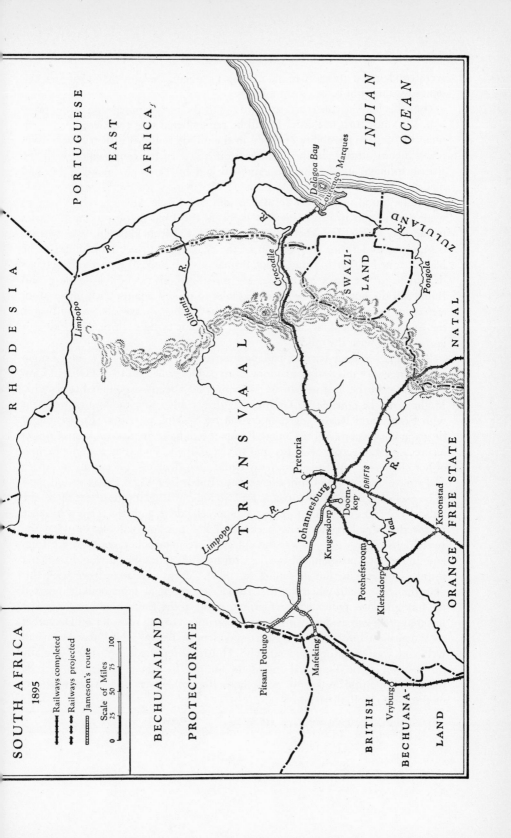

SOUTH AFRICA
1895

Railways completed
Railways projected
Jameson's route

Scale of Miles
0   25   50   75   100

RHODESIA

PORTUGUESE EAST AFRICA

INDIAN OCEAN

Delagoa Bay
Lourenço Marques

ZULULAND

SWAZI-LAND

Pongola

Crocodile R.

Olifants R.

Limpopo R.

TRANSVAAL

NATAL

Pretoria

Johannesburg

Krugersdorp

Doorn-kop

DRIFTS

Vaal R.

Kroonstad

Potchefstroom

Klerksdorp

ORANGE FREE STATE

Pisani Potlugo

Mafeking

Vryburg

BECHUANALAND PROTECTORATE

BRITISH BECHUANA-LAND

were condemned to short terms of imprisonment, and much unedifying evidence was brought before the public.

But this book is concerned primarily with the international side of the problem. We must turn to Berlin. It will be remembered that the German government had left no possibility of doubt in the minds of the British representatives regarding its attitude in the Transvaal difficulty. In his conversation with the British military attaché the Emperor had laid his cards on the table. He had made it only too clear that the ultimate explanation for the German attitude was to be found in Britain's refusal to join the Triple Alliance. The Germans were determined to drive this fact home to the English by putting obstacles in the way of Rhodes' schemes in south Africa. Baron Holstein, who was intriguing to undermine the position of the chancellor, Prince Hohenlohe, as he had intrigued earlier to bring about Bismarck's fall, seized upon the Emperor's démarche to stir up a great fuss. He mobilized his friends, Eulenburg and Bülow, in the hope of inducing Hohenlohe to protest against such imperial interference in matters of foreign policy. In the Wilhelmstrasse all was confusion, the Emperor, Hohenlohe, Marschall and Holstein being each of them more or less incensed with the others.[49]

But this personal friction had nothing to do with the course of German policy. In a very interesting memorandum of December 30, 1895, Holstein himself developed the idea which the Emperor had already expounded to Swaine: Might it not be possible for Germany with her allies to come to an agreement with France and Russia for co-operation for specific purposes? France might be given concessions in the Congo, Russia a free hand in Korea. Austria might secure a guarantee of the status quo in the Balkans, and Italy a strengthening of her claims in Abyssinia. Germany could then demand concessions in Africa and a naval base on the Chinese coast. But India, Egypt and Persia would have to be excluded from the discussion, for " so long as England possesses these, she will be obliged eventually to effect a rapprochement with the Triple Alliance unless she is willing to draw back from her position without drawing the sword." In other words, it was the object of German policy not to strike England in any vital position, but to create for her difficulties which would force her to turn to Germany and her allies for relief.[50] It was in accordance with this plan that Marschall, when the first rumors of unrest at Johannesburg reached the foreign office, reiterated the German stand to the English ambassador. The inspired press was evidently instructed to assume a strong tone, for on December 26 Valentine Chirol, the *Times* correspondent at Berlin, who knew Marschall well and was on intimate terms with Holstein, reported: " Of late especially the position of the Transvaal and of the Orange Free State appears to exercise the German mind as keenly as if those Republics were the direct offshoots of the German Fatherland." [51]

[49] Haller: *Philip Eulenburg*, I, pp. 315–33.   [50] *Die Grosse Politik*, XI, no. 2640.
[51] London *Times*, December 27, 1895; *Die Grosse Politik*, XI, nos. 2586–7.

News of the Jameson raid reached Berlin early on the afternoon of December 31. In his diary Marschall noted: "Now we must act." He immediately informed Lascelles, the new English ambassador, and once more restated the German position: Germany must insist on the independence of the Transvaal; her commercial interests and her public opinion demand it. He went on to give another warning to the English: they must not rely too much on the antagonism between the two continental alliance groups. Germany, he said, could make an agreement with Russia and France at England's expense. Having thus unburdened himself, Marschall went to Potsdam to report to the Emperor the news from Pretoria. The German consul had telegraphed that Kruger reckoned on the intervention of Germany and France, and had asked permission to land German marines from the warship *Seeadler,* which lay at Lorenzo Marques. The Emperor agreed that marines should be landed to protect German nationals in case of trouble in the Transvaal. An inquiry was sent to the governor of German East Africa, asking whether he would be able to send 400 to 600 men to Delagoa Bay and the Transvaal without jeopardizing the safety of the colony, and, presumably with the Emperor's approval, a telegram was sent to London before the day was over. Count Hatzfeldt, the ambassador, was to inquire whether the British government approved the Raid, and if so, to demand his passports.[52]

On the following day, January 1, reports came in from Pretoria and from London which left no further doubt that both the British commissioner at the Cape and the home government disavowed the Raid and that every effort was being made to recall Jameson. Marschall nevertheless approached the French ambassador and suggested that England, relying on the enmities of the continental powers, thought she could permit herself anything. Could not the two continental groups reach an understanding for concrete purposes, leaving aside all questions which might lead to a European war, such as the questions of the Near East, of Egypt and of the Mediterranean? The main thing was to " check the insatiable appetite of the English," and to show them that they could no longer reckon on Franco-German antagonism to secure a free hand for themselves. Writing to the ambassador at Paris, Marschall added that other powers would probably join the Franco-German combination, and that by such pressure England might be forced into association with the Triple Alliance. But the French were too clever not to see through this ruse, which, it must be confessed, was rather naive. Herbette pointed out immediately to Marschall that by excluding the Egyptian question he was excluding the one matter which might tempt France to take part.[53]

---

[52] *Die Grosse Politik,* XI, nos. 2588–91; Friedrich Thimme: "Di: Krüger-Depesche " (*Europäische Gespräche,* May-June, 1924, pp. 201–44), p. 210, where extracts from the unpublished diary of Marschall are quoted.

[53] *Die Grosse Politik,* XI, no. 2641; Thimme, loc. cit.; Bourgeois and Pagès: *Les Origines et les Responsabilités de la Grande Guerre,* pp. 256–7.

In the meanwhile there was nothing to do but await the outcome of the Raid. German opinion was very excited; Chirol reported that conservative and liberal papers were united in their hatred of England. In the public mind Germany had a sort of " moral protectorate " over the Transvaal, and the government might be forced to interfere.[54] Marschall talked the situation over with Chirol on the morning of January 2, and the correspondent then reported: " I am not speaking without authority when I state that as far as Germany is concerned the issue of this question may determine her whole policy towards England, whether it shall continue to be, as during the last six years at least, one of friendship and goodwill, or whether it shall be one of calculated hostility." The Germans, he continued, suspected the English of reckoning on continental antagonisms, but the English might be surprised to find a continental coalition directed against them.[55]

It was only late on the afternoon of January 2 that a telegram arrived from Pretoria reporting that Kruger had asked that the landing of German marines be deferred pending the negotiations between the Transvaal government and the British commissioner at the Cape. This telegram decided Marschall. Evidently fearing that the English would score a success, he made himself the exponent of an alarmist policy. To the Emperor he wrote that the consular report showed that the raiders had not obeyed the orders of the British government and that they were advancing, led by British officers. The English, through the commissioner at the Cape, were obviously preparing to reap the benefits from a long-laid plan. It was now time to warn the British government officially against any change of the status quo. With the consent of the Emperor and of the chancellor a strong note of protest was forwarded to London. But before the day was over news arrived that Jameson had been forced to surrender. The ambassador at London was then hurriedly instructed to withhold the note. He had already sent it to the foreign office, but fortunately it had not yet been opened and could be returned to him unread.[56]

Contemporary records of what happened in Berlin in these days are unusually scant and contradictory. In 1924 Professor Thimme, one of the editors of the German documents, published extracts from Marschall's diary which are more valuable than perhaps any other source. But since that time some additional evidence has appeared that must be taken into account. Prince Radolin, the ambassador at St. Petersburg, was at that time in Berlin. One of his close friends has testified that on the evening of January 1 or 2 the Prince was summoned to attend the Emperor at the opera. He came back and reported that William was beside himself and in a very bellicose mood. He had read the ambassador the draft of a despatch to Kruger, which Hohenlohe had refused to approve. In fact, the chancellor had threatened to resign if the telegram were

---

[54] *Times*, January 2 (Berlin, January 1).
[55] *Times*, January 3 (Berlin, January 2).
[56] *Die Grosse Politik*, XI, nos. 2599–2606; Thimme, op. cit.

sent.[57] Now Marschall says nothing in his diary of an imperial draft for a telegram to Kruger. At the time he evidently did not know anything about it. But he and Holstein told Chirol afterwards, and repeated the assertion to Bülow and Bethmann-Hollweg later, that the Kruger telegram, as we know it, was a much milder document than the original draft of the Emperor. Bülow says that Marschall told him that it had been the Emperor's wish and intention to "localise" the conflict between the Boer Republic and the English Cape Colony. "In 1896 His Majesty had harboured the fantastic idea of concluding a Defensive and Offensive Alliance with the Boers and to fight on their side against the English in Africa. In Europe, on the other hand, he wanted to preserve peace with England." The Jameson raid he attributed to his uncle, the Prince of Wales, and to the latter's two capitalist friends, Alfred Beit and Sir Ernest Cassell.[58]

These remarks may seem at first blush unworthy of serious notice. But the contemporary evidence shows that the Emperor was suffering at the time from something very close to hysteria. On New Year's Day he had an argument with the war minister and created a terrific scene. The minister told Hohenlohe afterward that if it had been anyone but His Majesty he would have drawn his sword upon him. Bronsart had grave doubts whether the Emperor was in his normal mind.[59] Radolin, after a two-hour discussion with William, came back with his head awhirl and nervously a complete wreck.[60] Alexander von Hohenlohe reports his father as having said that at Potsdam, on the afternoon of January 2, he found His Majesty very much agitated and talking of declaring war on England.[61]

Bearing these considerations in mind the situation becomes more understandable. Despite Thimme's conclusions, competent scholars no longer doubt that the Emperor actually had a draft telegram which he meant to send to Kruger. Since this draft was drawn up before the fate of Jameson was known, it could not have been a telegram of congratulation. Just what was in it we do not know, but something can be deduced from the entry in Marschall's diary for January 3. He says there that the Emperor came to a conference that morning with "somewhat wondrous plans. Protectorate over the Transvaal, which I immediately talk him out of. Mobilization of the marine infantry. Sending of troops to the Transvaal. And when the chancellor objects: 'That would mean war with England,' His Majesty replies: 'Yes, but only on land.'"[62] Just what was meant by "protectorate over the Transvaal"? Professor Thimme was of

---

[57] Arnold O. Meyer: "Fürst Hohenlohe und die Krügerdepesche" (*Archiv für Politik und Geschichte*, II, pp. 591–6, 1924).

[58] *Memoirs of Prince von Bülow* (Boston, 1931), I, p. 546; see also Holstein's account to Chirol (*British Documents on the Origins of the War*, VI, no. 101).

[59] Hohenlohe: *Denkwürdigkeiten der Reichskanzlerzeit* (Stuttgart, 1931), p. 151.

[60] Meyer, loc. cit.

[61] Hohenlohe, op. cit., pp. 612–4.

[62] Thimme, op. cit., p. 212.

the opinion that the Emperor's idea, which it was attempted to carry into execution later, was to bring about an international conference at which Germany should take the lead in ameliorating the position of the Transvaal. Thus indirectly the Germans would strengthen their own hold on the Republic. But there is no proof that this was the plan. It may very well be that the Emperor intended, in his telegram to Kruger, to offer to proclaim outright that the Transvaal was under German protection.[63] In any case the Emperor's desire to mobilize the marine infantry and to send troops to the Transvaal, as well as his reply to Hohenlohe that this would mean war only on land, supports Marschall's later statement to Bülow and shows that William actually harbored the phantastic notion that the Germans could fight in south Africa by the side of the Boers against the troops of the Chartered Company, without becoming involved in war with England. Indeed, he appears to have had some harebrained idea of fighting England without involving the fleets. In 1897 Holstein referred to this as one of the Emperor's " pet ideas." [64] His Majesty's extraordinary ideas on the Raid are brought out further by his remarks to the British ambassador, Sir Frank Lascelles, in March 1896: " The whole matter had been fictitious — the expedition was got up by three German Jews who have bought the Times, 'he knows it.' 'I know the men and the money they gave.' " [65]

On the morning of January 3, at ten o'clock, the Emperor appeared at the chancellor's palace for a conference with his advisers. According to Holstein's account he arrived with Admiral von Senden, chief of his naval cabinet, Admiral von Hollmann, the secretary of state for the navy, and Admiral von Knorr, chief of the naval high command. These gentlemen had primed him beforehand, if that was necessary. Marschall arrived with Holstein, but the latter did not take part in the conference. He stayed in a neighboring room, with von Kayser of the colonial office. Hohenlohe arrived last. The discussion opened with the presentation of the Emperor's plans, which have already been referred to. There is no mention in Marschall's notes or in Hohenlohe's diary of any further reference to the imperial draft of a telegram to Kruger, but such reference may have been omitted for reasons of discretion. Marschall and Hohenlohe devoted their efforts to dissuading the Emperor from trying to establish a protectorate over the Transvaal, and from sending troops from east Africa to Delagoa Bay. There followed, so it seems, some inconclusive argument as to what could be done to support the Boers.

[63] This is the opinion of Konrad Lehmann: " Die Vorgeschichte der Krügerdepesche " (*Archiv für Politik und Geschichte*, V, August, 1925, pp. 159–177). Paul Haake: " Das Krügertelegram " (*Velhagen und Klasings Monatshefte*, July, 1925, pp. 507–12) does not go so far.

[64] Hohenlohe, op. cit., p. 328; see Konrad Lehmann: " Zu Kaiser Wilhelms England-Politik " (*Historische Zeitschrift*, CXLVII, 1933, pp. 553–8).

[65] *The Letters and Friendships of Sir Cecil Spring Rice* (London, 1929), I, p. 200; similarly his remarks to Princess Radziwill (*Lettres de la Princesse de Radziwill au Général de Robilant*, II, pp. 10–1). The idea that the Prince of Wales and his capitalist friends were implicated probably derived from the fact that Prince Edward was in close contact with Beit and others, and that the Duke of Fyffe, a member of the British royal family, was a high official of the Chartered Company.

During a brief intermission Marschall went into the adjoining room to consult Holstein and Kayser. The former would not hear of any rash action, and apparently left the building. Kayser, however, suggested that the imperial desire for action might be satisfied by a telegram of congratulation to Kruger, which would, in the very nature of the case, be very much milder than the telegram offering support which William had in mind. Marschall took up the idea. A telegram was drafted which, according to the memoirs of the former Emperor, pleased Marschall immensely. William was less delighted with it. The evidence indicates that it was not strong enough to suit him. The fact is that the Kayser draft, while it had its defects, was fairly innocuous. Kruger was congratulated on having " maintained the dignity " of his government. The Emperor insisted that this be changed to read " in maintaining the independence of the country against attacks from without." This wording was most unfortunate, for the independence of the Transvaal was not absolute, and Marschall himself, in speaking to the British ambassador, had always been careful to refer only to the " independence of the Transvaal according to the Convention of 1884." Marschall knew better than to say what was said in the Telegram, but, as he reiterated again and again to Holstein, Chirol and others, he did the best he could. Some sop had to be thrown to the Emperor, and the famous Telegram went out at 11.20 A.M. in the following version:

> I express to you my sincere congratulations that you and your people, without appealing to the help of friendly powers, have succeeded, by your own energetic action against the armed bands which invaded your country as disturbers of the peace, in restoring peace and in maintaining the independence of the country against attacks from without.[66]

Apparently the Emperor was not satisfied even with this compromising telegram. He insisted that one of his adjutants be sent to the Transvaal to see what could be done to help Kruger. Fortunately Hohenlohe was able to dissuade him from this decision before the officer left Berlin.[67] But steps were actually taken to assist the Transvaal government in freeing itself of its treaty obligations, and perhaps to pave the way for the establishment of a special position for Germany. The consul at Pretoria was instructed to say to Kruger that the London Convention of 1884 did not prevent him from appealing to

---

[66] *Die Grosse Politik,* XI, no. 2610; Thimme, op. cit.; Hohenlohe, op. cit.; William II: *Ereignisse und Gestalten* (Leipzig, 1922), pp. 68 ff. Otto Hammann: " Die Entstehung der Krüger-depesche " (*Archiv für Politik und Geschichte,* II, 1924, pp. 203-8) says Holstein told him of the Kaiser's draft on January 4, 1896, and Spring Rice mentions it in a letter of January 11 (*Letters and Friendships,* I, p. 188). Hollmann's account to Eckardstein (*Lebenserinnerungen und Politische Denkwürdigkeiten,* I, pp. 271 ff.) is unreliable as Eckardstein gives it; the story as given in Nowak: *Germany's Road to Ruin,* pp. 152 ff. is worthless.

[67] Hohenlohe, op. cit., p. 151. According to the entry in Marschall's diary (Thimme, op. cit., pp. 231, 241-2) the mission of the adjutant was discussed and settled before the matter of the Telegram was taken up. Hohenlohe seems more reliable on this point. He indicates that the adjutant was called in after everything else was settled.

the powers for an international conference to discuss the legal position of the Transvaal and possibly to secure its neutralization. Germany would support such an appeal, though she could not take the initiative. Apparently it was intended that Germany, at a conference, should take the lead in a general international assault upon the British position.[68]

The genesis of the Kruger telegram has been discussed at some length in order to show that Marschall, though he was opposed to the dangerous measures advocated by the Emperor, was not at all averse to dealing England a severe blow. He made the idea of the telegram of congratulation his own and agreed to the introduction of an offensive and questionable phrase. No effort was made to mitigate the possible effects of the Telegram. Quite the contrary, the Germans were working for an effect. Hatzfeldt was specifically instructed to tell Salisbury that only the failure of the Raid had spared him a painful note from the German government.[69] Marschall himself expounded the purpose of the Telegram to Chirol, stressing the fact that it was not the expression of "a mere generous impulse" on the part of the Emperor, but that it had been drawn up at a conference of ministers and therefore had the character of a state action. "One is reluctantly driven to the conclusion that in more responsible quarters than the editorial offices of Chauvinist newspapers the occasion has been gladly seized 'to subject England to the well-deserved humiliation of a bitterly severe lesson,'" Chirol wrote to his newspaper.[70]

The German statesmen aimed at making a deep impression upon the English government. In order to evaluate their efforts we must turn to a consideration of the situation in London. It will be recalled that Chamberlain and the colonial office were quite fully informed of the progress of the revolutionary movement in Johannesburg. They knew that the rising was scheduled to take place on the day after Christmas and they had agreed to a plan of procedure. In order to prevent the movement from turning into a republican victory, the high commissioner at the Cape was to hurry to the scene, mediate between the parties, and, if necessary, call in the forces of the South African Company to support him. But in mid-December it appeared for a time that England might have other and more serious difficulties to cope with. On the 17th President Cleveland brought to a head a long-standing dispute regarding the boundary between Venezuela and British Guiana. The matter had been treated dilatorily by the British government, so the President asked congress for an appropriation to

---

[68] *Die Grosse Politik*, XI, no. 2609; Thimme, op. cit., pp. 229–30.

[69] *Die Grosse Politik*, XI, no. 2607.

[70] *Times*, January 4 (Berlin, January 3); Chirol later told the story many times: in an article on "The Origins of the Present War" (*Quarterly Review*, October, 1914, pp. 415–49); in the *Times*, May 14, 1918, September 11, 1920, November 14, 1922; in the *Cambridge History of British Foreign Policy*, III, pp. 263–4; and in his *Fifty Years in a Changing World* (London, 1927), pp. 279–80. He says the interview took place on the morning of the publication of the telegram, but Marschall's diary records a conversation with him on January 4. There may, of course, have been two interviews, but see Thimme, loc. cit., pp. 216–8.

enable him to send a commission to determine the boundary. This having been done, he said in his message to congress, it would, under the Monroe Doctrine, " be the duty of the United States to resist by every means in its power as a wilful aggression upon its rights and interests, the appropriation by Great Britain of any lands or the exercise of governmental jurisdiction over any territory which, after investigation, we have determined of right belongs to Venezuela." This was unbelievably strong language and might very well have been regarded as tantamount to an ultimatum or declaration of war. American opinion was wild with excitement and eager to take up the cudgels in behalf of Latin America. The American, like the German diplomats believed that it was necessary to give England " a distinct shock." [71]

The English, however, refused to be challenged. Both the government and the country were opposed to a " fratricidal " war and every effort was made to avoid a crisis. But for the moment the Cleveland message created something of a panic. Officials of the colonial office suggested to Chamberlain that it might be well to have the south African insurrection stopped, but the secretary felt that the Venezuelan crisis, whatever its outcome, would take several months to develop and that therefore it would be better for the Johannesburgers to go ahead at once or to postpone action for a couple of years. The word was therefore passed on to the leaders not to delay.[72] But on the evening of December 27 Chamberlain learned of the collapse of the Johannesburg movement. For a couple of days it was thought that the whole business had fizzled out, but then Chamberlain was informed by one of his subordinates, who had it from an agent of Rhodes, that there was a possibility of Jameson's setting out on a filibustering expedition into the Transvaal. Thereupon the colonial secretary at once warned the high commissioner and instructed him to warn Rhodes. Such action would be a violation of the South Africa Company's charter and might lead to its cancellation.

The cable to Robinson was sent out on December 29, the day on which Jameson started from the border. On the very next day the news of this fatal move was received in England. Chamberlain, who had been at Birmingham for some time, hurried up to London. As his biographer quite rightly says, he was in a serious quandary. If the Raid were to prove successful, much might be gained from it. But Chamberlain withstood temptation, cabled the high commissioner to denounce the Raid to Rhodes and himself repudiated it in a message to Kruger. In the instructions to Robinson he remarked significantly: " If the Government of the South African Republic had been overthrown, or had there been anarchy in Johannesburg, there might have been some shadow of excuse for this unprecedented act." To Salisbury he wrote his condemnation of Jameson's action, but again showed himself quite realistic about the situation:

---

[71] Allan Nevins: *Henry White* (New York. 1930), p. 109. On the incident generally see Alfred L. P. Dennis: *Adventures in American Diplomacy, 1896–1906* (New York, 1928), chap. ii; Garvin, op, cit., III, pp. 65 ff.   [72] Garvin, op. cit., III, pp. 71–4.

the Raid, if not repudiated by the government, would justify the accusations which were constantly being brought against England by other powers. Besides, he doubted if Jameson had enough men to get the better of the Boers.[73]

The undisputed fact, then, is that Chamberlain, whatever his reasons, denounced and repudiated the action of Jameson long before it was known whether the Raid would be successful or not. Thereby he protected himself and his government, but for the moment he got nothing but popular criticism for his decision. Though it was impossible to defend Jameson's action from the legal standpoint, the *Times* and all the lesser papers, especially the more popular ones, championed his Raid as a gallant effort to rescue the poor women and children in Johannesburg, who were at the mercy of the Boers. Alfred Austin, the newly appointed poet laureate, published a poem called *Jameson's Ride* in the *Times* of January 11, which put into Jameson's mouth words that may well have been on many English lips:

> " ' Let lawyers and statesmen addle
>   Their pates over points of law:
> If sound be our sword, and saddle,
>   And gun-gear, who cares one straw?
> When men of our own blood pray us
>   To ride to their kinsfolk's aid,
> Not Heaven itself shall stay us
>   From the rescue they call a raid.

> " ' There are girls in the gold-reef city,
>   There are mothers and children too!
> And they cry, ' Hurry up! for pity! '
>   So what can a brave man do?
> If even we win, they'll blame us:
>   If we fail, they will howl and hiss.
> But there's many a man lives famous
>   For daring a wrong like this! ' "

" It is impossible to help condemning him," wrote the *Times* itself on January 4, " but the masses of people will remember that, though he has used wrongful means, he was actuated by generous motives."

For days the British public followed the news of Jameson's advance with the tense excitement of spectators at a race-track. Dr. Jim's surrender was a very severe blow to English pride and caused general dejection. It was at this crucial moment that the Kruger telegram was published. With rare unanimity the English press broke out in passionate denunciation. The *Times* described the Emperor's message as " distinctly unfriendly to this country," and pointed out

---

[73] Garvin, op. cit., III, pp. 79–82, 90. The instructions to Robinson and other documents may be found in *Accounts and Papers*, 1896, LIX: *Correspondence on the Subject of the Recent Disturbances in the South African Republic.*

that the reference to the " help of friendly powers " plainly implied that Kruger had a right to invoke such aid when he thought proper, and that it contained " a tolerably direct intimation that, had he chosen to exercise that right in the present instance, his appeal would have been entertained." The reference to the " independence " of the Transvaal was a challenge to the British view that the Convention of 1884 secured for England the position of suzerain over the Republic. The *Morning Post* declared that it was hard to speak of the Telegram with coolness. The English nation would never forget it and would always think of it in the future when deciding on its foreign policy. According to the *Daily Telegraph* the Telegram exceeded the bounds of diplomacy and came near to being an international insult.

The *Saturday Review* wrote on January 4:

" Even if it be true that the Drill-Sergeant Autocrat would be supported in his remonstrance by the Governments of France and Russia, we still say that their interference is impertinent and not to be tolerated. Great Britain should resent such unprovoked insolence. . . . We are no Jingoes, and we have no wish to provoke war even with Germany; we say ' even with Germany ' for Germany is today our trade rival, and we stand to win much and lose nothing by a war with her. But between the dislike of war and the degradation of tamely submitting to undeserved insult, only one choice is possible. Lord Salisbury must remember that we hold the command of the seas. . . . We allowed the Germans to bluff us out of East Africa, and bluff us but the other day out of the Convention which Lord Kimberley had entered into with the Congo State. Lord Salisbury should now tell Germany and her allies to mind their own business. We do not propose to endure their interference in the affairs of the Transvaal."

A week later the same paper wrote that the Telegram was " the most complete and ingeniously worded insult which can be imagined. . . . Bonaparte himself could not have devised a more comprehensive affront to a people he meant to overrun and subjugate." The staid and dispassionate *Economist* used very similar language. Rarely, perhaps never since Napoleon was sent to St. Helena, it wrote on January 11, had the indignation of the British public been so profoundly aroused. The Telegram was " a deliberate affront " to the nation, and German interference in south Africa was " a piece of gratuitous insolence, a pure and intended affront which they (the English) are bound to resist, even if resistance costs them a great war."

In letters to the newspapers the Emperor's Telegram was declared to be " as deadly and unprovoked an insult as was ever offered by the head of a European nation to one of equal rank," and to be " in letter and in spirit a deliberate and premeditated insult to the Queen and the British nation of so gross and wanton a nature as to call for an immediate and decisive reply." [74] Among the dock workers of eastern London there were outbreaks against the German workers and sailors. The windows of German shops were broken, and Germans were

[74] *Times*, January 6.

boycotted in the clubs. It was almost impossible for them to do business with Englishmen in the City; even the ambassador received numerous scurrilous and threatening letters.[75]

On January 5 Chirol reported from Berlin that orders had been sent out to land men from the *Seeadler* and that the German ship *Condor* had been instructed to leave Dar-es-Salaam for Lorenzo Marques. In view of the fact that Lorenzo Marques was Portuguese territory, Chirol pointed out two days later, arrangements must have been made between the German, Portuguese and Transvaal governments some time before. Then it was reported from Capetown that Dr. Leyds, the Transvaal state secretary, who was in Berlin, was setting on foot a scheme to settle five thousand retired German soldiers in the Republic. All this served to increase the tumult. Here at last was the evidence of a deep-laid German plot. The plan to land marines, wrote the *Times,* showed that German interference

> " was not the result of sudden indignation at the action of Dr. Jameson, but, on the contrary, had been meditated, discussed, and presumably concerted with the Boers. . . . There is grave reason to suspect that hostile designs against this country have been in contemplation for a long time; and that the Transvaal was deliberately selected as the spot at which a blow might advantageously be struck." [76]

The theme was taken up everywhere. Magazines were filled with articles on German intrigues in the past, and the Telegram was declared to be " the climax of a conspiracy carried on for years by official Germany against British rule." [77] Even in diplomatic circles the idea found acceptance: " That Germany has for years had the design of annexing the Transvaal is perfectly natural, and I believe can be proved," noted Spring Rice in his diary.[78] Years afterward a high official of the British foreign office could still write: " It is certain that Germany believed she might by some fortuitous circumstances hope some day to establish her political dominion over the Boers, and realize her dream of occupying a belt of territory running from east to west right across Africa. . . . Opposition to British interests was deliberately encouraged in the most demonstrative fashion at Pretoria. . . ." [79]

English opinion was so thoroughly aroused that when Chirol reported, quite rightly, that one of the chief purposes of the Telegram had been to serve as " a

---

[75] Schulthess: *Europäischer Geschichtskalender,* 1896, pp. 185 ff.; *Die Grosse Politik,* XI, no. 2636.

[76] *Times,* January 8, 1896.

[77] William H. P. Greswell: " The Germans in South Africa " (*Fortnightly Review,* LXV, pp. 209-15, February, 1896).

[78] *The Letters and Friendships of Sir Cecil Spring Rice* (London, 1929), I, pp. 186-7.

[79] *Crowe Memorandum, 1907 (British Documents on the Origins of the War,* III, p. **410).** See further William T. Stead's comments in the *Review of Reviews,* February, 1896; G. W. Steevens: " The Indiscretion of the Kaiser " (*New Review,* February, 1896); Scrutator: " German Diplomacy " (*United Service Magazine,* February, 1896).

warning to England that she could only find salvation in closer contact with Germany and her allies," the idea was received with bitter cynicism. " The paramount necessity of the moment," wrote the *Times* on January 7, " is to bring home to the German mind the fact that England will concede nothing to menaces and will not lie down under insult." The *Spectator* (January 11) thought the idea of " plaguing " Great Britain into joining the Triple Alliance was too foolish: " Kicking a Briton into submission is a possible expenditure of energy; but even a man like the German Emperor, who seldom judges men aright, would hardly dream of kicking him into friendship." " No Englishman will trust him again while he lives," wrote the same paper a week later, " or believe that he entertains any feeling towards this country except the one expressed in Blücher's celebrated saying about London: — ' Lord, what a place to plunder.' "

The reaction of the English people to the Kruger telegram will always remain something of a mystery. Of course the text of the message was unfortunate and provocative. But even Bismarck, though he objected to the phrase " friendly powers," approved of the congratulations sent to Kruger and thought that the British had gotten their deserts. The Telegram, he remarked, might very well have been sent to Kruger by the British government itself, since Jameson and his band had no standing in international law and were merely filibusters and marauders.[80] This interpretation rather overshoots the mark, for the British, it will be remembered, refused to acknowledge the unqualified independence of the Transvaal. But it is a fact that the Telegram was not as bad as the English press made it out to be. The *National Review* pointed out quite rightly that it was an " infinitely less offensive document " than the Cleveland message. Why, then, all the indignation? Partly, no doubt, it was an expression of the irritation resulting from the American affront. Much was forgiven the erring sons on the other side of the Atlantic — elegance and finesse were not expected of them. But many of the pent-up feelings of the people needed an outlet, which they found in the action of the German Emperor. One must consider, too, that the public was much more interested in south Africa than in British Guiana. The Transvaal situation was a sore spot, and the meddling of outsiders was resented on principle.

But there were other factors that help to explain the outburst that followed the publication of the Kruger telegram. Despite many disagreements the English still looked upon the Germans as friends upon whom they could rely if it came to a conflict with Russia or France.

" Many Englishmen," says one contemporary writer, " have been accustomed to regard the difficult position of Germany between a hostile France and a hostile Russia as a guarantee that in a war between England and either of those powers, Germany would take part on the side of England. In this way the German army was annexed by many English imaginations, which thought that we were to have the benefit of German compulsory service without its burdens. A friendly

---

[80] Thimme, loc. cit., p. 222.

Germany was supposed to be a Germany able and willing to fight England's battles. The recent discovery that Germany has her own business to mind, and that in attending to it in her own way she may come into disagreeable opposition to England, has produced a resentment against Germany almost as unreasonable and as much exaggerated as the previous unfounded confidence which it has replaced." [81]

Now suddenly the English found themselves all alone in the midst of many enemies. It made them bellicose and they turned upon that country which, with a small fleet, seemed least able to take up a challenge. Chamberlain understood this perfectly well. On January 4 he wrote to Salisbury that some act of vigor would be needed to soothe the wounded vanity of the nation: " It does not much matter which of our numerous foes we defy, but we ought to defy someone." [82]

Germany was a suitable object for defiance for yet another reason: for years there had been felt the pinch of commercial competition, which had been made the explanation of many of the common man's woes. The Telegram brought to the surface a surprising " amount of solid hate towards Germany," wrote someone to the *Times,* — hate because " in Germany we have the one power who is doggedly, slowly but surely working away at the undermining of our whole national supremacy." [83] " With France and Russia," wrote a well-known publicist,

" we may have more immediate causes of friction, but among European Powers Germany is our true enemy. We are commercial rivals, engaged at this very moment in a life and death struggle for the markets of the world. This kind of enmity makes little show at ordinary times on the surface, but it goes very deep. Moreover, it comes home to everyone, be he politician or not. You cannot go into the City without seeing before your own eyes, hearing in your own ears, evidences of the commercial war and what is worse, the successful war, which Germany is waging against us." [84]

The importance of this aspect of the Anglo-German problem was brought out only too clearly by the deluge of writings on German competition which poured from the press in 1896. Ever since the publication of Williamson's *British Industries and Foreign Competition* in 1894, efforts had been made to arouse the country to the realization of the German trade menace, the invasion of the home-country by German goods and the loss of foreign markets. These efforts had met with only indifferent success, but they had created a certain amount of ill-feeling and distrust. The Kruger telegram episode therefore served as a match to set off the explosion of popular feeling. In January 1896 E. E. Williams began the publication in the *New Review* of the series of articles which were printed later in the year in pamphlet form with the significant

---

[81] Spenser Wilkinson: *The Nation's Awakening* (London, 1897), pp. v-vi.

[82] Garvin, op. cit., III, p. 95.   [83] J. K. C.: letter to the *Times,* January 11, 1896.

[84] George W. Steevens: *Naval Policy* (London, 1896), p. 184.

title *Made in Germany*. The articles were rather sensational, but they were factually well supported and much to the point. " A gigantic commercial state is arising to menace our prosperity and to contend with us for the trade of the world," wrote Williams. " On all hands England's industrial supremacy is tottering to its fall, and this result is largely German work. . . . Germany has entered into a deliberate and deadly rivalry with her (England) and is battling with might and main for the extinction of her supremacy."

Williams' campaign was supported at once by a host of other writers. The *Saturday Review,* the newly founded *Daily Mail* and even the liberal *Chronicle* entered the lists. Public men took part in the discussion and Lord Rosebery in a speech at Epsom on July 24, 1896 identified himself with the movement. He spoke of " one very formidable rival . . . who . . . is encroaching on us as the sea encroaches on the weak parts of the coast — I mean Germany." In the summer of 1896 the panic called forth by the German menace was at its height. No doubt it was exaggerated, but that does not alter the fact that it was important. The idea of a German conspiracy against British trade was in a considerable measure responsible for the outburst that followed the Kruger telegram, and that episode again fanned the flames of jealousy and hate. Reputable writers have discounted the importance of this commercial rivalry and have taken the view that it was not decisive in shaping the relations between England and Germany. In a sense this is true, but after wide reading in the contemporary material it is hard to escape the conclusion, reached also by the best student of the problem, that trade rivalry had much to do with creating the popular feeling that decided the government in the formulation of its policy.[85]

It has been pointed out in a previous chapter how closely the imperialist movement was bound up not only with economic problems, but also with the general atmosphere of conflict nurtured by current ideas of evolution. It was only natural then that the antagonism between England and Germany should have been interpreted in this way. The Kruger telegram incident brought forth the first of the well-known *Saturday Review* articles: " A Biological View of our Foreign Policy," by a Biologist.[86] " Of European nations," said the author,

" Germany is most alike to England. In racial characters, in religious and scientific thought, in sentiments and aptitudes, the Germans, by their resemblances to the English, are marked out as our natural rivals. In all parts of the earth, in every pursuit, in commerce, in manufacturing, in exploiting other races, the

[85] E. E. Williams: *Made in Germany* (London, 1896), went through three editions in that year. An effective reply to it was George W. Medley: *The German Bogey* (London, 1896). The substance of Williams' book, together with the speeches of leading men on the subject, was republished as a penny pamphlet called " Wake up, John Bull " and issued by the *Review of Reviews*. The whole subject of the Anglo-German trade rivalry has been gone over so thoroughly and with such a wealth of illustrative material by Ross J. S. Hoffman: *Great Britain and the German Trade Rivalry, 1875–1914* (Philadelphia, 1933) that there seems to be no point in dilating on the subject. For the panic of 1896 see especially chapter vi of Hoffman's book.

[86] *Saturday Review*, February 1, 1896. This article is much less known than the later one of September, 1897.

English and Germans jostle each other. . . . Were every German to be wiped out tomorrow, there is no English trade, no English pursuit that would not immediately expand. Were every Englishman to be wiped out tomorrow, the Germans would gain in proportion. Here is the first great racial struggle of the future: here are two growing nations pressing against each other, man to man all over the world. One or the other has to go; one or the other will go."

The article ended on the ominous note, much used later, " Germania est delenda."

As we leave the subject of the January storm of 1896, we can perhaps do no better than to quote a passage from the *Spectator,* which called attention repeatedly to the profound discontent so widespread in Europe as a result of economic pressure, tension between capital and labor, revolt against the drudgery of the machine age, etc.:

" The civilised world, in truth, which for nearly a century has advanced so rapidly on the path of material progress, is at this point of its strenuous labours seething with discontent, ready to risk all it has attained in an outburst of furious wars, intended to secure objects which it only half perceives in the distance, and is by no means certain that it really at heart desires. . . . There is a certain fear of war everywhere, due to a perception of the vast scale on which it must be fought, and the terrible reduction in the chances of escape which the new weapons will ensure, but nevertheless there is hardly a nation which is without the feeling that if war came life would be brighter, more vivid, more like the dreams which fill the brains of youth." [87]

Of course these feelings were not confined to the English. The German people, taken in the large, was no less bellicose in the beginning of 1896. One reason for the despatch of the Telegram to Kruger was indubitably the hope of making a hit with the German public and restoring the popularity of the Emperor. In any event the Telegram served that purpose. It was received in the country with an orgy of delight. " Certainly no act of the present regime has been acclaimed with such universal enthusiasm," wrote Chirol on January 6.[88] The German Colonial Society and the Pan-German League sent resolutions to the government, thanking it for its vigorous stand.[89] Beyond question the Emperor was, for the moment, extremely popular. German public opinion was delighted to think that its sentiments had found adequate expression. The press did not quail even when news of the English reaction was received. The indignation on the other side of the Channel was simply taken as irrefutable proof that the British government had really been behind the Raid and had hoped to profit by it. It was their own intervention, thought the Germans, that had forced the London government to repudiate the whole thing.

---

[87] " The Restlessness of Nations " (*Spectator,* January 25, 1896); " The Appetite for War " (ibid., February 15, 1896).

[88] *Times,* January 7, 1896; see also Thimme, loc. cit., p. 232.

[89] Wippermann: *Deutscher Geschichtskalender,* 1896 (I), pp. 5 ff.

All this did not help the government to strengthen its position with relation to the Transvaal. Kruger replied rather coolly and evasively to the Emperor's telegram, though for a moment he appears to have planned to take
advantage of the Raid to denounce the clauses of the London Convention and
proclaim the full independence of his country. Emperor William still talked
bravely to the Boer state secretary, Dr. Leyds, and declared that under no circumstances could the English be allowed to seize Delagoa Bay. If it changed
hands at all it would have to pass to the Germans or the Boers. But his advisers
were clearly impressed with the force of British defiance, and kept stressing the
fact that Germany must not take the initiative or go too far. In correspondence
with the English they still stood by their interpretation of the London Convention of 1884; they even saw to it that the semi-official press should expound this
interpretation in detail. But they made no effort to press the point. Chamberlain
openly refused to consider any change in the existing agreements with the
Transvaal, and by January 11 Marschall was himself urging Leyds to stay within
the treaties. Holstein, who had never approved of the Telegram, wrote to Hatzfeldt that the German foreign office was glad to have the thing end with a little
success for the Germans and a little lecture for the English. In short, the Germans got nothing for their pains, and neither did the Boers. The English made
their peace with the Transvaal and from that time onward no further efforts
were made from Berlin to influence the course of events.[90]

Now it must be remembered that the chief purpose of the German action was
not to improve the position of the Transvaal or even to strengthen the German
hold on the Boer Republic. The main objective was to frighten the English into
closer relations with the Triple Alliance, and in the pursuit of this end the
Emperor and his advisers had reckoned on the friendly support of France and
Russia. The French press had, in fact, come out quite as violently as the German. The *Temps,* regarded as the mouthpiece of the French foreign office,
called the Raid " land piracy " and " deliberate brigandage." " To allow such
a precedent to be established would be to sanction the gravest blow dealt at
national rights since modern Europe abandoned the system of letters of marque.
Joint stock wars, limited liability invasions, cannot possibly be tolerated in Africa
any more than elsewhere." [91] When the Kruger telegram was published it was
acclaimed in Paris as in Berlin. " All Europe is bound by the force of events to
intervene in favor of the Boers," declared the *République Française.*

But what did all this mean? Would the French really side with the Germans
against England? The English press did not think so: " The nations of the
world are quite malicious enough to stand by and exult while England and
Germany pummel each other and so grow gradually weaker; but they are not
so foolish as to join in the fray merely for the sake of gratifying a jealousy which
would be appeased, without fighting, by the mere spectacle of the conflict." [92]

---

[90] *Die Grosse Politik,* XI, nos. 2613–33, passim.   [91] *Temps,* January 2, 1896.
[92] *Spectator,* January 11, 1896.

In other words, the French, it was thought in London, were glad to see the Germans spank the English, but they wished to be excused from the spanking themselves. This view was the correct one. Marschall's advances to Herbette came to nothing, and on January 6 the *Temps* came out strongly in opposition to " unnatural alliances." The Germans had been unwilling to attack the British position in so crucial a matter as Egypt and the route to the east. Anything less than that, on the other hand, failed to interest the French. On January 8 Holstein still spoke in strong terms to Chirol, and solemnly warned him " that Germany could count in this matter on the support of other powers, and that, in fact, England stood in more imminent peril of a great European coalition against her than at any time since the days of Napoleon the First." [93] But the German foreign office knew better, and had to admit to itself that the enthusiasm of the French had lasted only twenty-four hours. Co-operation with France against England was clearly impossible.[94]

With Russia the Germans had no more success. On January 2 the Emperor wrote to the Tsar, apparently without consulting the foreign office:

" I have used very severe language in London and have opened communications with Paris for common defence of our endangered interests. . . . I hope you will also kindly consider the question, as it is one of principle of upholding treaties once concluded. I hope that all will come right, but come what may, I never shall allow the British to stamp out the Transvaal."

To this Nicholas replied non-committally, strongly condemning the British policy in south Africa and subscribing to all that the Emperor had said, but not offering to do anything. The Russian foreign minister, Prince Lobanov, was no more encouraging.[95] In the last count the Germans by no means fortified their position by their stand in the Transvaal question. Neither France nor Russia showed any disposition to come to their support, while both the Austrians and the Italians were profoundly dismayed by the growing antagonism between Germany and England. There was, in fact, real danger that Italy might break away from the " league of peace " and throw in her lot with France and Russia. The German ambassador at Rome had to use fairly strong language to prevent the defection of the Italians.[96]

Quite in contrast to the amateurish jockeying of the German Emperor and his advisers was the attitude of the British government. At no time did it lose its head. The Telegram itself created a natural indignation. The Queen thought it " outrageous and very unfriendly," and the Prince of Wales con-

---

[93] Chirol, in the *Quarterly Review*, October, 1914, p. 424; see also Holstein's account of the interview in *Die Grosse Politik*, XI, no. 2621.

[94] *Die Grosse Politik*, XI, nos. 2618, 2625, 2651, 2735. E. M. Carroll: *French Public Opinion and Foreign Affairs* (New York, 1931), pp. 168–9, and Manfred Zapp: *Deutsch-Französische Annäherungsversuche und ihr Scheitern in den Jahren 1890–1898* (Weida, 1929), pp. 81 ff. add little on this question.

[95] *The Kaiser's Letters to the Tsar*, p. 30; *Die Grosse Politik*, XI, nos. 2622–4.

[96] *Die Grosse Politik*, XI, nos. 2642, 2645, 2649, 2656, etc.

sidered it "a most gratuitous act of unfriendliness." [97] Chamberlain, as we have seen, thought some "act of vigour" was necessary and suggested a strong despatch to Berlin or the commissioning of more men and ships. But Lord Salisbury remained cool. Several ships were at once sent to south Africa, but chiefly in order to impress Kruger and to warn him against abusing his victory.[98] But the most striking move was the commissioning of a "flying squadron" consisting of two battleships and two first-class cruisers, to be used wherever needed. The announcement to this effect on January 8 called forth great enthusiasm in England. At home and abroad it was interpreted as a threat against Germany, and the government was quite content to let it go at that. As it happens, the idea originated before the Kruger telegram was even thought of, and had reference to the Venezuelan crisis as well as to the south African affair. "It might be wise to organise a 'flying squadron,'" wrote the first lord of the admiralty to Salisbury on December 31, "not directed to any particular point, but kept in hand in the Channel, or at all events not far off, ready for any service. . . . The outlook seems to me very bad in many directions, not the least in that of Germany, who now seems inclined to protect the Boers, as the Americans protect Venezuela." [99]

The Queen was not informed about these measures until they had been taken, probably because she was known to be opposed to making things worse than they were. Looking at the Telegram as a personal act of the Emperor she wrote to him on January 5 remonstrating. William was still in a fighting mood and had no mind to "knuckle down." On the contrary, he hoped to make use of the surge of German opinion to float through the Reichstag a large loan for naval construction. His advisers ultimately dissuaded him, arguing that naval activity would appear as a provocation of England.[100] But the Emperor, despite his brave front, was at bottom a good deal chastened by the attitude of Russia and France. He wrote his grandmother an amusing though inaccurate letter on January 8, saying that the Telegram had been sent in the name of peace and in the interest of German investors. Furthermore,

"as your Government and Ambassador had both made clear that the men were acting in open disobedience to your orders, they were rebels. I, of course, thought that they were a mixed mob of gold-diggers quickly summoned together, who are generally known to be strongly mixed with the scum of all nations, never suspecting there were real Englishmen or Officers among them. Now to me

---

[97] *Letters of Queen Victoria*, III, p. 7.

[98] Garvin, op. cit., III, pp. 95–9.

[99] Arthur D. Elliot: *The Life of George J. Goschen* (London, 1911), II, pp. 204–5; see also Goschen's letter to the Queen, in the *Letters of Queen Victoria*, III, pp. 16–7, and also Fred T. Jane: " The Problem in the Far East " (*Contemporary Review*, March, 1898, pp. 387–93).

[100] Thimme, loc. cit., pp. 220 ff. makes too much of the Emperor's naval aspirations at this time, and has been corrected by Hans Hallmann: *Krügerdepesche und Flottenfrage* (Stuttgart, 1927), especially pp. 34 ff.; Raimund Foerster: *Politische Geschichte der Preussischen und Deutschen Flotte bis zum Ersten Flottengesetz* (Dresden, 1928), pp. 71 ff.; and Eckart Kehr: *Schlachtflottenbau und Parteipolitik, 1894–1901* (Berlin, 1930), pp. 51 ff.

Rebels against the will of the most gracious Majesty the Queen, are to me [*sic*] the most execrable beings in the world, and I was so incensed at the idea of your orders having been disobeyed, and thereby Peace and the security also of my Fellow-Countrymen endangered, that I thought it necessary to show that publicly. It has, I am sorry to say, been totally misunderstood by the British press. I was standing up for law, order, and obedience to a Sovereign whom I revere and adore, and whom to obey I thought paramount for her subjects. Those were my motives, and I challenge anybody who is a Gentleman to point out where there is anything hostile to England in this." [101]

Victoria was not convinced by this explanation. She thought it " lame and illogical," but she was willing to let the matter rest. Rejecting the suggestion of the Prince of Wales that the Emperor be given " a good snub " she excused William on the score of his impetuosity and conceit, and noted that the best weapons against these traits were calmness and firmness. Salisbury, too, considered it best to accept the explanation without examining its truth.[102] After all, the prime minister knew by this time that the real purpose behind the German policy was to frighten Britain into closer relations with Germany. Count Hatzfeldt told him so in just so many words on January 11. Indeed, there are some veiled passages in Salisbury's letters to the Queen that would indicate that, at the very height of the popular excitement, the diplomats were calmly discussing the *pros* and *cons* of an alliance. " Count Hatzfeldt now wants a secret engagement signed by Lord Salisbury and three or four of his colleagues," wrote Salisbury; " he enforced this view yesterday in many warnings of the danger of isolation. But the demand is inadmissible. Isolation is a much less danger than the danger of being dragged into wars which do not concern us."

The Queen was not wholly persuaded. She reminded the prime minister of the Mediterranean Agreements, which might serve as a precedent, and admitted that isolation seemed to her dangerous. But Salisbury stood firm: " The secret alliance of which Count Hatzfeldt spoke was an alliance binding England to go to war under certain conditions." [103] This England could not do. There the matter seems to have been dropped. We know nothing more about Hatzfeldt's suggestions or proposals, but even these vague references suffice to show not only the bent of German policy, but the coolness with which the situation was examined in London in the midst of all the popular furor.

Even if Salisbury had been willing, it is quite clear that public opinion at that time would have made any agreement with Germany impossible. There was, it is true, a loud demand at the time that England should give up her friendless isolation and seek support among the other powers. " We frankly can go no further alone, in the face of the obstacles which it is now within the power of Germany, Russia and France to pile up in our path," wrote the *Satur-*

---

[101] Lee: *Edward VII*, I, p. 726; *Letters of Queen Victoria*, III, pp. 17–8; Thimme, loc. cit., p. 243.
[102] *Letters of Queen Victoria*, III, pp. 19–21.   [103] *Letters of Queen Victoria*, III, pp. 20–2.

day Review on January 25. The British government had come to an agreement with France regarding Siam on January 15. The buffer state on the upper Mekong, on which so much eloquence had been expended in 1893, was abandoned. In fact the whole agreement was strikingly favorable to the French claims. England even promised to proceed to the delimitation of the British and French possessions on the west side of the lower Niger River and to negotiate a new convention with Tunis to replace the old one which was so distasteful to the Paris government.[104]

Despite the concessions it made to France, this agreement was hailed with enthusiasm in England and was talked about as the first step to a larger entente. " The English people as a whole would much rather have a cordial and sympathetic understanding with France than anything else that the Continent has to offer," wrote the *Saturday Review* on January 18 and again on January 25. In view of the unfriendliness of Germany, said the *Spectator* on January 18, " the friendship of France is the most valuable we could possibly obtain." Despite the friction over Egypt, an agreement should be possible, for England could promise neutrality in a Franco-German war, and could withdraw her opposition to French aspirations in the Congo and in Morocco. Furthermore, she might be able to smoothe out the difficulties between France and Italy, and bring Italy into the new combination.

Even more pronounced was the demand in England that a rapprochement with Russia be attempted. It was felt that Russia held the upper hand in the Franco-Russian Alliance, and that an agreement with France would be impossible unless Russia too were satisfied. To quote the *Spectator* of January 18 once again:

" It is nothing to us who holds Constantinople if it is held by a friend, and if Russia can turn Sibiria into a Canada, so much the better for us and for the world. We do not believe there is an Englishman alive who, but for his suspicion of ulterior designs, would object to Russia owning Port Arthur and Manchuria, or exercising a predominant influence over Northern China and Japan. We seek nothing up there except trade and dread nothing except the rise of an unfriendly Power, who might practically deprive us of our markets, or even compel us to abandon the North Pacific."

Russia could set England at ease with regard to India and help her secure herself in southern China, as well as to arrange for the " transformation " of the Turkish Empire. Russia and England could command peace from Constantinople to Canton.

Similar ideas were developed by St. Loe Strachey in an article in the *National Review* much commented upon at the time. Strachey insisted that the events

---

[104] *France No. 2 (1896): Despatch to Her Majesty's Ambassador at Paris, inclosing a copy of the Declaration between Great Britain and France of January 15, 1896 for the Settlement of the Siamese and other Questions;* Documents Diplomatiques: *Affaires du Siam et du Haut-Mékong* (Paris, 1896); Albert de Pourvoirville: *L'Affaire de Siam, 1886–1896* (Paris, 1897), chap. vi; W.: " The Partition of Indo-China " (*Fortnightly Review*, March, 1896).

of the past weeks had shown that "England's attempt to maintain a certain friendly understanding with Germany as the head of the Triple Alliance has proved a complete, and very nearly a disastrous, failure." It was necessary to find a new key-note for England's foreign policy, and that should be an agreement with Russia. There were no fundamental causes of antagonism between the two, and England had objected to Russia's taking Constantinople only because Germany and Austria were opposed to it. Let Russia occupy Armenia and take Constantinople and the sting of the Franco-Russian Alliance so far as England was concerned would disappear. France could be brought into the agreement too, by being given a free hand in Syria, and in Morocco, excepting for Tangier. Italy might find it profitable to join, by being assured of French friendship and English support, and by the bait of Tripoli. It would be too bad to wound the feelings of the faithful Austrians, but they could be given Macedonia and Saloniki as a balm. Only Germany would be injured by this combination, but England could not be troubled on that score. "Germany has shown us that she is utterly careless of wounding us when she thinks her own ambitions and interests may be served. She has taught us the way, and she has no right to complain. Indeed, a counterstroke to Germany's blow should by itself produce an excellent effect." [105]

Space limitations forbid the quotation of further writings of this tenor, but there were many of them.[106] Did the government pay any attention to them? This we cannot discuss in detail, for we have few official papers dealing with this period of British policy. All we can say is that the German foreign office was disturbed by reports of the activities of the French ambassador at London, and feared that negotiations regarding Egypt might be under way.[107] The utterances of British ministers, too, seemed to indicate that advances were being made to Russia. On February 3 Mr. Balfour, a nephew of Lord Salisbury, said at Bristol:

> "So far from regarding with fear and jealousy a commercial outlet for Russia in the Pacific Ocean which should not be ice-bound half the year, I should welcome such a result as a distinct advance in this far-reaching region, and I am convinced, not merely that Russia would gain by it — that the world generally would gain by it — but that British commerce and enterprise would be the gainers."

A few weeks later Mr. Goschen, the first lord of the admiralty, declared in a public address, with reference to England's international position: "If there be isolation, it is at all events self-imposed. I say that which I know when I

---

[105] St. Loe Strachey: "The Key-Note of our Foreign Policy" (*National Review*, XXVI, pp. 741–57, February, 1896).
[106] W.: "Two Eastern Questions" (*Fortnightly Review*, February, 1896); Arnold Foster: "Our True Foreign Policy" (*Nineteenth Century*, February, 1896); Canon M. MacColl: "Armenia and the Transvaal" (*Fortnightly*, February, 1896). All these advocated the abandonment of Constantinople to Russia.
[107] *Die Grosse Politik*, XI, nos. 2636, 2637, 2649, 2650, 2681, 2682, 2687.

say that we have but to hold up our hand and our isolation will terminate, and we shall receive a welcome into several groups of other Powers."

The Russian ambassador at London was, in actual fact, approached by members of the government. On February 19 he reported home that Chamberlain had said to him with some warmth that the more he reflected upon the matter the more persuaded he was that the two countries were not divided by any irreconcilable interests, that Russia was so vast that she would not tend in the direction of colonial expansion, and that, consequently, no serious rivalry could arise between them. An entente between the two countries would be a guarantee of peace and civilization. A few days later Balfour spoke to Staal in the same vein, though less unreservedly.[108]

The Russian ambassador was pretty sceptical about these soundings. The Blue Books on the Armenian question had just been published, and there was a good deal of feeling aroused on both sides by the exposures that they contained. But in any event so much can be determined with certainty: that there was a real demand for some continental connexion in the early months of 1896; that the public would have welcomed an understanding with either France or Russia or both; and that the government was prepared to go a long way to patch up differences. It would have made some concessions in the Egyptian question and might have abandoned to the Russians the Straits and Constantinople, always on condition that England should be duly compensated. The scheme, which went back at least to the days of Lord Rosebery, was wrecked not by Salisbury, but by the Russians, who were more suspicious of the English than the English had ever been of them.

The Germans got just enough information about these English-French-Russian conversations to give them the sort of scare which they had planned for the English. The effect was decidedly sobering. " They have been kicking us for years, on the assumption that they were kicking a dead ass. It is a great surprise to see starting up a live lion," wrote Cecil Spring Rice.[109] He was convinced that " the fear that led to the knuckle-down of Germany was the rumour of the abandonment of Egypt and the rapprochement to France." " Knuckle-down " was perhaps too strong a term, but the impression of Spring Rice was in general correct. It was not to be long before even the Emperor was putting himself out to regain the good will of the British. The hoary Egyptian question was again to be made the basis for Anglo-German co-operation.

Yet if you regard the fundamental policy of the Germans at this time, you will be struck not only by its clumsiness, but by its complete failure. It was psychologically mistaken and utterly hopeless to try to kick the English into friendship with Germany. When Bismarck bludgeoned them in 1884 the situation was quite different, for his alliance with Russia was secure, and the co-operation

---

[108] Meyendorff: *Correspondance de M. de Staal*, II, p. 309; V. Khvostov: " Blizhne-Vostochnyi Krizis, 1895–1897 " (*Istorik Marksist*, XIII, 1929, pp. 19–54), p. 35.

[109] *Letters and Friendships*, I, p. 189.

of France was assured. With the Continent behind him, he forced the British to grant Germany a place in the colonial sun. But in 1895–1896 the Germans threatened first and sought support afterward. Their case in the Transvaal question was none too good to begin with, and it was therefore a mistake to make that affair the test. The responsibility evidently rests with Marschall, the chief advocate of a strong stand. As for the larger plan of forcing Britain into the Triple Alliance by the use of pressure, that was unquestionably the product of Holstein's fertile if somewhat unusual mind. But there is at least this to be said for Holstein, that he would never have gone about it as William II did. The evidence that he had nothing to do with the Kruger telegram and that he was opposed to it is irrefutable. It was altogether contrary to the finesse with which he ordinarily operated. But the fools rushed in where the angels feared to tread. The elephantine procedure of Marschall and the Emperor was the negation of all diplomacy.

The Telegram must stand, then, as one of the greatest blunders in the history of modern diplomacy. Not that it disturbed Salisbury particularly or had any direct effect upon Anglo-German relations in the official sense. But it outraged public opinion in England and gave an opportunity for the crystallization of all the jealousy and distrust of the Germans which had gradually been accumulating. When an eminent German historian like Friedrich Thimme argues that the policy of the German foreign office was not wholly mistaken because it obliged the British to approach the Germans with suggestions for an alliance in the years 1898–1901, he not only misunderstands Anglo-German relations in those years, but fails to take into account the fact that popular dislike of the Germans made it almost impossible for the English government to consider an alliance seriously. Furthermore, as England and Germany drifted apart, the diplomats of the younger generation found a perennial excuse for their prejudices in the Kruger telegram. It was a trump card for all those who tried to make out a case against Germany. But the main thing was the effect on the popular mind. Nothing illustrates that better than the story told by Prince Bülow: During the great Jubilee celebrations in London in June 1897, the crowds continually shouted, as Prince Albrecht of Prussia passed by: " If you want to send a telegram to Oom Kruger, you'll find a post-office round the corner on the right." [110]

---

[110] *Memoirs of Prince von Bülow* (Boston, 1931), I, pp. 21, 476.

DOCUMENTARY SOURCES

Accounts and Papers. 1896, volume LIX: *South African Republic. Correspondence on the Subject of the Recent Disturbances in the South African Republic.* 1897, volume LXII: *Report of the Select Committee of the Cape of Good Hope House of Assembly on the Jameson Raid into the Territory of the South African Republic;* volume LX: *Second Report of the Select Committee on British South Africa.*

Correspondentie van de Zuid-Afrikaansche Republiek met Betrekking tot de Beroeringen in den Aanvang van 1896. Pretoria, 1896. The Boer documents on the Raid.

Aktenstücke, betreffend die jüngsten Vorfälle in der Südafrikanischen Republik. Berlin, 1896.

Die Grosse Politik der Europäischen Kabinette, 1871–1914. Volume XI, chapter lxiii: The Kruger Despatch and Anglo-German Relations; chapter lxiv: The Projected Continental League.

MEMOIRS, AUTOBIOGRAPHIES, BIOGRAPHIES, AND LETTERS

GARVIN, J. L.: *The Life of Joseph Chamberlain.* Three volumes to date. London, 1932–4. Volume three of this new biography is one of the most important sources for the period. Garvin, it seems to me, finally clears up the vexed question of Chamberlain's knowledge of the Raid.

The Letters of Queen Victoria. Edited by George E. Buckle. Series III, volumes II and III. These letters are most interesting for the entire period, and not infrequently contain information not to be found elsewhere.

LEE, SIR SIDNEY: *Edward VII, a Biography.* Two volumes. London and New York, 1925. Discusses at length the reaction of the royal family to the Kruger telegram. The whole work is so biassed as to be of little historical value.

The Letters and Friendships of Sir Cecil Spring Rice. Edited by Stephen Gwynn. Two volumes. London, 1929. Spring Rice was at this time secretary of the British embassy at Berlin. His letters and notes are sometimes of real value.

MICHELL, SIR LEWIS: *The Life and Times of the Right Honourable Cecil John Rhodes.* Two volumes. New York, 1910. Though by no means a wholly satisfactory biography, this is one of the most useful books on Rhodes, since it quotes many letters.

WILLIAMS, BASIL: *Cecil Rhodes.* London, 1921. Still one of the best, if not the best, biography of Rhodes. It is very well-informed and perfectly detached in its treatment.

MILLIN, GERTRUDE G.: *Rhodes*. London, 1933. An excellent, critical character study.

WOLF, LUCIEN: *Life of the First Marquess of Ripon*. Two volumes. London, 1921. Of first-rate importance for the history of the south African problem in the time of the Rosebery ministry.

COLVIN, IAN: *The Life of Jameson*. Two volumes. London, 1922. The standard life of Jameson. Important for the whole story of the south African difficulties at this time.

HOFMEYER, J. H., and REITZ, F. W.: *The Life of Jan Hendrik Hofmeyer*. Cape Town, 1913.

WALKER, ERIC A.: *Lord de Villiers and his Times*. London, 1925.

FITZPATRICK, SIR J. PERCY: *South African Memories*. London, 1932. These three titles are among the most important contributions to the history of the south African problem itself.

MEYENDORFF, BARON A.: *Correspondance Diplomatique de M. de Staal*. Two volumes. Paris, 1929. Disappointing, but has a few valuable bits of information on this period.

HOHENLOHE-SCHILLINGSFÜRST, FÜRST CHLODWIG ZU: *Denkwürdigkeiten der Reichskanzlerzeit*. Stuttgart, 1931. New material from the Hohenlohe papers. The book is devoted chiefly to German domestic policy, but has some very interesting notes and letters on foreign policy too.

ECKARDSTEIN, HERMANN FREIHERR VON: *Lebenserinnerungen und Politische Denkwürdigkeiten*. Two volumes. Leipzig, 1919. Contains a story of the Kruger telegram which is not to be trusted.

HALLER, JOHANNES: *Philip Eulenburg: The Kaiser's Friend*. Two volumes. New York, 1930. A very valuable source, especially for the study of the situation at the German court and in the foreign office.

SECONDARY WORKS AND SPECIAL STUDIES

WALKER, ERIC A.: *A History of South Africa*. New York, 1928. An altogether admirable, scholarly work.

BIXLER, RAYMOND W.: *Anglo-German Imperialism in South Africa, 1880–1900*. Columbus, Ohio, 1932. A careful digest of the more obvious material.

LOVELL, REGINALD I.: *The Struggle for South Africa, 1875–1899*. New York, 1934. By far the best single treatment, covering the subject in a much broader and much more understanding way than the Bixler volume.

VAN OORDT, J. F.: *Paul Kruger en de Opkomst der Zuid-Afrikaansche Republiek*. Amsterdam, 1898. One of the most detailed and reliable Dutch histories of the period.

BOTHA, PHILIP R.: *Die Staatkundige Ontwikkeling van die Suid-Afrikaanse Republiek onder Kruger en Leyds.* Amsterdam, 1925. A history of the Transvaal from 1844 to 1899. The most recent study from the Boer side, written with the use of the German documents and other official papers.

VALTER, M.: *Duitschland en de Hallandsche Republieken in Zuidafrika.* Amsterdam, 1918.

WÜD, JOHANNES: *Die Rolle der Burenrepubliken in der Auswärtigen und Kolonialen Politik des Deutschen Reiches in den Jahren 1883–1900.* Nürnberg, 1927. A painstaking dissertation, based primarily upon the German documents, but making use of some unpublished material.

VAN DER POEL, JEAN: *Railway and Customs Policies in South Africa, 1885–1910.* London, 1933. One of the most illuminating monographs, dealing with the crucial aspect of the whole problem.

HOFFMAN, ROSS J. S.: *Great Britain and the German Trade Rivalry, 1875–1914.* Philadelphia, 1933. An excellent piece of work, which pretty nearly disposes of this problem. The author gives a wealth of statistical material, but also studies the movement of opinion.

HOFMEYR, N. J.: *De Afrikaner-Boer en de Jameson-Inval.* Amsterdam, 1896. The best contemporary Boer account of the raid.

FITZPATRICK, J. PERCY: *The Transvaal from Within.* London, 1899. Still one of the best accounts of the Outlander problem and the revolutionary movement, by a man who played a prominent part in it.

GARRETT, F. E., and EDWARDS, E. J.: *The Story of an African Crisis.* London, 1897. The best contemporary journalistic account, written, however, before the results of the investigations were known.

HOLE, HUGH M.: *The Jameson Raid.* London, 1930. The latest and also the best general monograph, based upon careful study of the sources, though of course lacking the material since published in the Chamberlain biography.

THIMME, FRIEDRICH: " Die Krüger-Depesche; Genesis und Historische Bedeutung." (*Europäische Gespräche,* May–June, 1924, pp. 201–44). The most important single study, written by a leading German historian who was able to use the diaries of Marschall and other material.

MEYER, ARNOLD O.: "Fürst Hohenlohe und die Krügerdepesche." (*Archiv für Politik und Geschichte,* II, 1924, pp. 591–6). Adds a highly interesting account derived from Prince Radolin.

HAMMANN, OTTO: "Die Entstehung der Krügerdepesche." (*Archiv für Politik und Geschichte,* II, 1924, pp. 203–13). Written by the former director of the press bureau of the foreign office and based upon information received from Marschall and Holstein.

HAAKE, PAUL: " Das Krügertelegramm." (*Velhagen und Klasings Monatshefte,* July, 1925, pp. 507–12). A minute study of the episode with special reference to the writings of Thimme and Meyer.

SONTAG, RAYMOND: "The Cowes Interview and the Kruger Telegram." (*Political Science Quarterly*, XL, 1925, pp. 217–47). An excellent reconsideration of the problem in the light of the available source material.

HALLMANN, HANS: *Krügerdepesche und Flottenfrage*. Stuttgart, 1927. With the use of material from the German marine archives the author corrects Thimme's account of the influence of the Transvaal crisis on the development of German naval policy.

LEHMANN, KONRAD: "Die Vorgeschichte der Krügerdepesche." (*Archiv für Politik und Geschichte*, V, 1925, pp. 159–77). A microscopic study of much interest, dealing chiefly with the vexed question of the Emperor's original draft.

—: "Zu Kaiser Wilhelms II England-Politik." (*Historische Zeitschrift*, CXLVII, 1933, pp. 553–8). Revises somewhat his earlier opinion, in the light of the Hohenlohe Memoirs.

NOWAK, KARL F.: *Germany's Road to Ruin*. New York, 1932. Mentioned only in order to be repudiated. Contains a phantastic account of the Jameson raid and a wholly incorrect and misleading account of the Kruger telegram.

LITERATURE SINCE 1935

DUGDALE, BLANCHE E. C.: *Arthur James Balfour, First Earl of Balfour*. Two volumes. New York, 1937. Contains some interesting material on the South African crisis and on Anglo-American relations.

The Cambridge History of the British Empire. Volume VIII: South Africa. New York, 1936. Treats the Jameson Raid and its background at length, using all the recent materials.

WALKER, ERIC A.: *Britain and South Africa*. New York, 1941. 64 pp. A popular pamphlet, by a leading South African historian.

YERUSALIMSKII, A. S.: *Vneshniaia Politika i Diplomatiia Germanskogo Imperializma v Kontse XIX veka*. Moscow, 1948. 767 pp. Deals with the South African crisis at length, making the most of the clash of economic interests.

STRAUSS, WILLIAM L.: *Joseph Chamberlain and the Theory of Imperialism*. Washington, 1942. 133 pp. A scholarly review of Chamberlain's life and thought, with considerable discussion of his relation to Rhodes's plans.

CROUZET, M.: "Joseph Chamberlain" (in *Les politiques d'expansion impérialiste*, Paris, 1949, pp. 157–205). A compact, scholarly review of Chamberlain's policy, fully abreast of the recent literature.

HALPERIN, V.: *Joseph Chamberlain*. Zurich, 1942.

COUDURIER DE CHASSAIGNE, JOSEPH: *Les trois Chamberlain*. Paris, 1939. 236 pp. A sympathetic, well-informed sketch of Joseph Chamberlain and his two statesmen sons.

WINKLER, HENRY R.: "Joseph Chamberlain and the Jameson Raid" (*American Historical Review*, LIV, July, 1949, pp. 841–849). A review of the question of Chamberlain's complicity, which the author regards as almost certain.

EMDEN, PAUL H.: *Randlords*. London, 1935. A lively analysis of the financial maneuverings of the goldmine interests.

CLOETE, STUART: *Against these Three*. Boston, 1945. 472 pp. Biographies of Kruger, Rhodes and Lobengula, based on obvious sources but interesting for the handling of their relationship.

CROUZET, M.: "Cecil Rhodes" (in *Les techniciens de la colonisation*, Paris, 1946, pp. 232–254). Like the author's study of Chamberlain, this is an able résumé of Rhodes's career and work.

OUDARD, GEORGES: *Cecil Rhodes*. Paris, 1939. 254 pp. Popular and breezy, but adds nothing.

RAPHAEL, LOIS A. C.: *The Cape to Cairo Dream: a Study in British Imperialism*. New York, 1937. 514 pp. An excellent, scholarly treatment of a grand design.

AGAR-HAMILTON, J. A. I.: *The Road to the North: South Africa, 1852–1886*. New York, 1937. An admirable background study.

HARDING, COLIN: *Frontier Patrols: a History of the British South Africa Police*. London, 1939. 272 pp. Of considerable interest in connection with the Jameson Raid.

WALKER, ERIC A.: "The Jameson Raid" (*Cambridge Historical Journal*, VI, no. 3, pp. 283–306). A searching review of the whole problem by a leading historian of South Africa.

HALLGARTEN, WOLFGANG: "L'essor et l'échec de la politique Boer de l'Allemagne, 1890–1898" (*Revue historique*, CLXXVII, 1936, pp. 505–529). A thorough analysis of German economic interests and activities, based in part on unpublished German records.

PENNER, C. D.: "Germany and the Transvaal before 1896" (*Journal of Modern History*, XII, March, 1940, pp. 31–59). A careful re-examination of the same problem, drawing heavily on contemporary materials.

LEHMANN, KONRAD: "Zu Kaiser Wilhelms II England-Politik (Krüger-telegramm und Bündnisfrage)" (*Historische Zeitschrift*, CXLVII, 1933, pp. 553–558). A revision of an earlier study, adducing the more recent evidence.

HALE, ORON J.: *Publicity and Diplomacy, with special reference to England and Germany, 1890–1914*. New York, 1940. 486 pp. Fundamental for the impact of the crisis on public opinion.

FRANKE, BRUNO W.: "Handelsneid und grosse Politik in den englisch-deutschen Beziehungen, 1871–1914" (*Zeitschrift für Politik*, XXIX, 1938, pp. 455–475). Chiefly a critique of the Hoffman book, which the author thinks exaggerates the importance of the trade rivalry.

BANZE, ANGELIKA: *Die deutsch-englische Wirtschaftsrivalität. Ein Beitrag zur Geschichte der deutsch-englischen Beziehungen, 1897–1907.* Berlin, 1935. 105 pp. A thorough, scholarly analysis which, like the preceding title, tends to minimize the importance of trade rivalry.

PERKINS, DEXTER: *The Monroe Doctrine, 1867–1907.* Baltimore, 1937. 489 pp. Contains a thorough treatment of the Venezuela Crisis.

SLOAN, JENNIE A.: " Anglo-American Relations and the Venezuelan Boundary Dispute " (*Hispanic-American Historical Review,* November, 1938, pp. 486–506). A well-documented review of the incident as a conflict of Pan-Americanism and British Imperial Federationism.

BLAKE, NELSON M.: " Background of Cleveland's Venezuelan Policy " (*American Historical Review,* XLVII, January, 1942, pp. 259–277). An interesting analysis of the forces that prodded Cleveland into an aggressive nationalist stand.

CALLCOTT, WILFRED H.: *The Caribbean Policy of the United States, 1890–1920.* Baltimore, 1942. 524 pp. Uses some new materials for a systematic account of the entire development.

TANSILL, CHARLES C.: *The Foreign Policy of Thomas F. Bayard, 1885–1897.* New York, 1940. 800 pp. Based on the unpublished American records and on the Bayard Papers, this study is valuable for the treatment of the Venezuelan issue and the Anglo-American relationship.

SCHOENRICH, OTTO: " The Venezuela-British Guiana Boundary Dispute " (*American Journal of International Law,* XLIII, July, 1949, pp. 523–530). Quotes information from one of the legal counsel for the Venezuelan Government as to how the decision of the Tribunal was arrived at.

IX

The Struggle for the Nile
11 Reconquest of the Sudan

∽

URING THE MOST CRITICAL DAYS OF JANUARY 1896 BOTH GERMANY
and England tried to fortify their positions by sounding out the prospects of support from France and Russia. In these conversations the
Egyptian question played a very important part. Had the Germans been willing
to identify themselves with the French policy in the Egyptian question, it is
by no means improbable that some sort of entente might have been arranged.
The trouble was that the Berlin foreign office was unwilling to strike at England in any vital matter, for the simple reason that the whole German policy
aimed, ultimately, not at a struggle with England, but at an alliance with her.
Naturally the French, on their side, could not be interested in a combination
which from the outset excluded the question which they had most at heart. Of
the British advances to France, which necessarily hinged upon the Egyptian-
Sudan problem, we know very little. The evidence on this subject will have to
be reviewed a little further on, and the matter is touched on here merely to show
that the Anglo-French as well as the German-French relationship at the time
depended almost entirely upon this Nile question.

Nothing came of either the German or the English approaches to France.
The crisis passed, leaving the British practically where they were before. But
the Germans did not come off so easily, because the antagonism between Berlin
and London reacted so very unfavorably upon the relationship of the powers
of the Triple Alliance to each other. The Austrians and the Italians were so put
out by the Kruger telegram episode that, for a time, there was real danger that
the Triple Alliance might go to pieces. It seemed fairly unlikely that this famous
coalition, designed primarily to meet the needs of the European situation, would
be able to withstand the strain put upon it by the new colonial conflicts and the
requirements of world policy.

The threatened break-up of the central European bloc was postponed by an
important event in African history. On March 1, 1896 the Italian army was completely defeated by the Abyssinians in the great battle of Adua (Abba Garima).
The battle was one of world importance, for it marked the first substantial
success of a backward people against the armies of the invading European and
thereby stimulated resistance to the encroachments of modern imperialism. But
its immediate effects were hardly less important, for the Italian adventure in
Abyssinia was part and parcel of a delicately constructed policy and treaty

system which centred upon the Nile problem and the Egyptian question. The collapse of the Italian position was likely to upset all the arrangements and to precipitate a conflict between the great powers. It is therefore essential that we study the repercussions of the Adua disaster. But in order to gauge them accurately we must recur to the story of the struggle for the Nile as it developed from 1894 to 1896.

It will be recalled that the treaty made by the British with King Leopold in May 1894 had been wrecked by the action of France and Germany. The co-operation of these two countries had caused a sensation in London, and had led to efforts to reach an understanding with France or Russia. The Little Eng-landers in the cabinet had been definitely opposed to the policy of Rosebery and Kimberley from the very start. They strongly objected to any course that would lead to further friction with France, and probably brought pressure to bear in behalf of friendly negotiations with Paris. Discussions of this kind had, in fact, become imperative, for, the scheme of a Belgian buffer state on the left bank of the upper Nile having failed, some other means had to be found to check the French advance from the west.

Of the negotiations which ensued in Paris we know almost nothing. A few veiled references are all that can be found in the sources. It appears, however, that the discussions were initiated at the suggestion of Lord Dufferin, the British ambassador at Paris, and that the plan was to effect a general settlement of colonial difficulties, not excluding Egypt itself. Hanotaux accepted the sug-gestion with alacrity, and took an active part in the conversations, which, on the British side, were carried on by Sir Constantine Phipps, secretary of the embassy. Apparently the British asked frankly for recognition of the British sphere as defined in the agreement with Germany in 1890. Thereupon Hanotaux asked the pertinent question: What is the British sphere? It had a southern, eastern and western limit, but what was its northern limit? Furthermore, where did Egypt stop and the British sphere begin? In reply to these queries Phipps apparently answered, without instructions, that the line of the British sphere was the line drawn in the Anglo-Belgian lease, that is, latitude 10° north. In return for recognition of this sphere England would be willing to make com-pensation, perhaps by the cession of islands in the Pacific or territory in the Gambia region. However this may have been, it seems that a draft agreement was made in January 1895, in which, so it is said, the possessions of Egypt were delimited at Khartum. In other words, the English were willing to leave for the Egyptians only the territory south as far as the junction of the White and the Blue Niles. They wanted to reserve to themselves not only Uganda, but everything northward along the Nile as far as Fashoda (latitude 10° N.), which meant that the region between Fashoda and Khartum would be left open for competition.[1]

---

[1] What information we have on these negotiations may be found in Gardiner: *Life of Harcourt*, II, pp. 321-2; Sir Thomas Barclay: *Thirty Years*, pp. 123-4; J. L. Deloncle: "La Question de

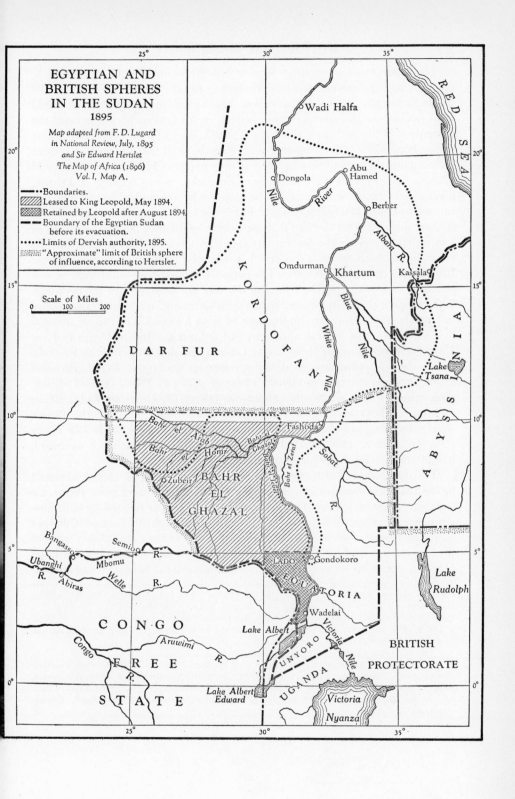

EGYPTIAN AND
BRITISH SPHERES
IN THE SUDAN
1895

Map adapted from F. D. Lugard
in National Review, July, 1895
and Sir Edward Hertslet
The Map of Africa (1896)
Vol. I, Map A.

···· Boundaries.
░░ Leased to King Leopold, May 1894.
▨▨ Retained by Leopold after August 1894.
— — Boundary of the Egyptian Sudan
before its evacuation.
•••• Limits of Dervish authority, 1895.
░░░ "Approximate" limit of British sphere
of influence, according to Hertslet.

Scale of Miles
0   100   200

RED SEA

Wadi Halfa

Dongola   Abu
                 Hamed

                        Berber

Nile   Albara R.

River

KORDOFAN

Omdurman   Khartum   Kassala

DAR FUR   White Nile

                    Blue Nile

                              Lake
                              Tsana

Bahr el A   ob   Fashoda

Bahr el Homr   Bahr el Ghasal

Zubeir   Sobat

BAHR   Bahr el Zeraf   R.

EL   Bahr el Jebel

GHAZAL

ABYSSINIA

Bangasso   Semio R.

Ubanghi   Mbomu   Gondokoro

R.   Abiras   Welle   R.   LADO

CONGO   EQUATORIA

                              Wadelai

            Aruwimi   R.

FREE   Lake Albert   Victoria Nile

Congo   UNYORO

R.   UGANDA

STATE   Lake Albert
                        Edward

Lake
Rudolph

BRITISH

PROTECTORATE

Victoria

Nyanza

The terms of this arrangement seem at first almost unbelievable, for they indicate that at one time the British were willing to take something less than the whole Sudan for Egypt and themselves. Yet the contemporary material would seem to bear out this interpretation. Milner, in his famous book, discussed the reconquest of the Sudan only as far as Fashoda on the White Nile and Senaar on the Blue Nile: " This, together with Kassala, is all that we need at present contemplate, perhaps all that Egypt may ever require." He doubted if it would be wise for Egypt to try to reconquer Kordofan, to say nothing of Darfur, the Bahr-el-Ghazal or Equatoria. The reason why the Sudan was formerly so ruinous to Egypt, he argued, was that Egypt tried to hold too much of it.[2] There is, then, some basis for the idea that the British, when they thought or talked of Egypt's reconquering the Sudan, envisaged an advance only to Khartum. So far as the southern Sudan is concerned, it is beyond all doubt that, whatever the British may have said later, they felt perfectly free, at least until 1896, in disposing of former Egyptian territory in the area not controlled by the dervishes. This came out clearly in the agreements with Germany, in England's own policy in Uganda and Unyoro, and in the lease to King Leopold. The British assumed that their own east African sphere extended from the Indian Ocean to Lake Victoria, thence through Uganda and Unyoro and down the Nile to Fashoda. So it is shown, beyond any possibility of misunderstanding, in Keltie's *Partition of Africa* (1893) and even in Hertslet's *Map of Africa by Treaty* (second edition, 1896, volume I, map A). Stieler's *Handatlas* (1893), the *Deutsches Kolonialblatt* (VI, no. 4, 1895) and Debes' *Neuer Handatlas* (1895) all show the British sphere extending as far north as 12° and westward to the Nile, while *The Times Atlas* (editions of 1895, 1896) draws the line at 10° but extends it westward, like Hertslet, to the Nile-Congo watershed.[3]

The question is of importance only in connexion with the claims advanced by the British at various times. In 1894–1895 it had no bearing upon events, for the draft treaty of January 1895 came to nothing. It was rejected by both governments for reasons unknown, on the French side probably because it did not touch the question of the evacuation of Egypt and because the cabinet was not much interested in the Nile problem, on the English side perhaps because Rosebery did not want to face the question of evacuation. Harcourt had the im-

---

Fachoda " (*Revue Politique et Parlementaire*, November, 1898, pp. 277–300); Christian Schéfer: *D'Une Guerre à l'Autre* (Paris, 1920), p. 190; Auguste Terrier: " La Marche vers le Nord-Est et la Question du Haut-Nil " (in Gabriel Hanotaux: *Histoire des Colonies Françaises*, IV, chap. vi, Paris, 1931), p. 515; and especially Hanotaux' speech in the French senate on April 5, 1895; see also Louis Gillet: *Gabriel Hanotaux* (Paris, 1933), p. 78.

[2] Alfred Milner: *England in Egypt* (London, 1892), p. 201.

[3] Similar maps may be found much later, e.g., in Sir Harry Johnston: *A History of the Colonization of Africa* (Cambridge, 1899), pl. viii; Arthur S. White: *The Expansion of Egypt* (London, 1899); Frederic W. Fuller: *Egypt and the Hinterland* (London, 1901); Carl Graf Kinsky: *Vade Mecum für Diplomatische Arbeit auf dem Afrikanischen Continent* (Third edition, Leipzig, 1900), etc.

pression that the discussions were a farce from the beginning, so far as the English government was concerned. Whether this was the fact it is impossible to say. In the *Letters of Queen Victoria* we get veiled references to negotiations which were carried on with the Sultan in the autumn of 1894. Apparently the Turks suggested a convention, as they did periodically. We do not know the terms but we do know that Rosebery was unenthusiastic about them.[4] If he considered the matter at all, and if he agreed to negotiate with the French, it may have been partly because of the pressure brought to bear by Harcourt, partly because of uneasiness aroused by the co-operation of Germany and France. But by the early months of 1895 this latter danger, at least, had passed. The Germans had returned to their traditional policy of supporting the British policy in Egypt.[5] The elaborate and much heralded French expedition sent out under Monteil had evidently fallen through. After the conclusion of the French treaty with the Congo in August 1894, the famous explorer had been ordered to direct his energies to the suppression of the revolt of Samory on the Ivory Coast. It seemed that, for the time being, at any rate, the aspirations of the French had been forgotten.

But this proved not to be the case. Hanotaux, it seems, was genuinely interested in an agreement, and the failure of the draft convention, whatever may have been the reasons for that failure, led to a new campaign on the part of the French colonialists. On February 12, 1895 De Brazza, governor of the French Congo, said in an interview that the agreement with the Congo State on August 14 assured France access to the Nile Valley, and that France should take advantage of this opening. " Access to the Nile Valley from the South is the only means which will enable us some day to settle the Egyptian Question according to our interests." Shortly afterward, on February 28, M. Deloncle made an even more startling speech in the French chamber. He pointed out that the French policy in advancing to Lake Chad, the upper Ubanghi and the upper Nile was not based on the supposition that permanent colonies could be established in these unhealthy regions. The aim of French policy was to bring pressure on the British to make them respect their promises to evacuate Egypt. Now that France had a real access to the upper Nile, she could " take Britain in the rear." French diplomacy had now been supplied with new arguments for use in negotiation; France had taken guarantees.

These utterances made more than a passing impression in London, the more so as news began to leak through that the French were not inactive on the upper Ubanghi. Monteil had been sent to the west, but Decazes had received half of the forces assigned to his expedition. In September M. Liotard, whom Sir Frederick Lugard described as " a notably ' pushing ' officer," was made commissioner of the upper Ubanghi and was instructed to extend the French sphere

---

[4] *Letters of Queen Victoria*, II, pp. 422–3; *Die Grosse Politik*, VIII, nos. 1856–8.
[5] *Die Grosse Politik*, VIII, nos. 1859–61.

of influence to the Nile. He did, in fact, set about systematically occupying the country in the direction of the Nile-Congo watershed.[6]

On March 5, 1895 the London *Times* sounded the alarm. It was perfectly evident from Deloncle's speech, said this influential newspaper, that the French colonial party would not rest until the tricolor had been planted on the upper Nile. What did the British government propose to do? A French force had secretly started eight months before and might now be within hail of the Nile. France and King Leopold were evidently on the best of terms, and the Congo State had ordered the establishment of training camps for forty thousand men with a view to operations on the upper Nile. Even in Abyssinia the French and Russians were active. Britain's position was being threatened on all sides.

This article in the *Times* led directly to the famous and all-important Grey statement of March 28, 1895. On March 11 Sir Ellis Ashmead-Bartlett interpellated the government with respect to the De Brazza and Deloncle utterances. Would the government " now clearly state that the whole Nile water-way is within the British sphere, and that no Foreign occupation of the Nile will be permitted by Great Britain? " In reply the under-secretary for foreign affairs, Sir Edward Grey, said that the " extent of the British sphere of influence in the Nile Valley is defined by the agreements made with Germany and Italy in 1890," and that he could not add to the definition there given. When pressed to state whether this definition included within the British sphere the whole Nile water-way, he answered: " No; but the Egyptian and British spheres together do cover the whole Nile water-way." [7]

This questioning was simply the skirmishing preliminary to a direct assault on the government. On March 28 Sir Ellis made a detailed statement of the situation. He stressed the fact that the security of the upper Nile was one of the principal questions of foreign policy, and he emphasized the threat involved in the ambition of the French to extend their influence from west Africa to the Red Sea. If realized, this would make all of north Africa, including Egypt, a French possession, and the Mediterranean would be bound to become a French lake. It would be a matter of great gravity if France were to be allowed to establish herself on the upper Nile. Sir Samuel Baker had said that any European power holding the upper Nile would hold Egypt at its mercy, and a distinguished military man had told the speaker that if he were the Mahdi he would make Egypt pay for every quart of water that ran down the Nile. Only a few months ago Sir Colin Scott-Moncrieff, the great expert on Egyptian water problems, had stated " that the civilised possessor of the Upper Nile Valley holds Egypt in his grasp. . . . A civilised nation on the Upper Nile would surely build regulating sluices across the outlet of the Victoria Nyanza. . . . This would be an easy operation. Once done, the Nile supply would be in their hands, and if poor little Egypt had the bad luck to be at war with this people

---

[6] P. L. Monteil: *Souvenirs Vécus* (Paris, 1924), pp. 113, 119–21; Jean Darcy: *France et Angleterre*. pp. 390–2.   [7] Hansard: *Parliamentary Debates*, Series IV, vol. XXXI, p. 782.

in the upper waters, they might flood Egypt or cut off the water supply at their pleasure." Now there were rumors of French advances in that area and the British government might find itself confronted with a *fait accompli*. The statements of De Brazza and Deloncle left no doubt as to the objectives of the French colonialists.

Sir Edward Grey's reply to this speech has become famous. He discussed first the general situation and the accusation brought against the government of having shown pusillanimity in the matter of the Congo Treaty. He then proceeded to say that the foreign office had

> " no reason to suppose that any French Expedition has instructions to enter, or the intention of entering, the Nile Valley." " I cannot think that these rumours deserve credence, because the advance of a French Expedition under secret instructions right from the other side of Africa, into a territory over which our claims have been known for so long, would be not merely an inconsistent and unexpected act, but it must be perfectly well known to the French Government that it would be an unfriendly act, and would be so viewed by England." [8]

This statement, with the use of the strong term *unfriendly act,* created a considerable stir. Henry Labouchere, a violent anti-imperialist, described it as " a quasi-declaration of war against France." Historians have found it difficult to explain the use of such strong language when there was no obvious need for it. In his memoirs Sir Edward Grey gives an explanation of the incident that might be called amusing if the subject were not so serious. Sir Edward says that one morning news came of very unwarranted and provocative encroachments by the French in *west* Africa. He thereupon asked Lord Kimberley what he should say in parliament if questions were asked. " You must do the best you can, but I think you should use pretty firm language," replied the foreign secretary. In the House no question was asked about *west* Africa but Grey was pressed on the matter of French designs on the Nile Valley. There were vague rumors of a French expedition. " We felt sure no French expedition was on the way to the Nile, in which belief we were quite justified, for the Marchand expedition, as was ascertained later on, did not start while we were in office." There was, then, ample time to give France full warning. Grey " transferred to the subject of the Nile " the firmness he had been authorized to show about competing claims in west Africa.[9]

The historian must find it difficult to accept this story without reservation. In the first place it may be conceded that Kimberley, as he himself admitted, had given Grey only " some general instructions." But the draft of the statement on the Niger difficulties had been shown to Harcourt, who had stricken out all words apt to be offensive to France.[10] In the House on March 28 Sir Ellis Ashmead-Bartlett, before discussing the situation with respect to the Nile, did

[8] Hansard, Series IV, vol. XXXII, pp. 388–406.
[9] Grey of Fallodon: *Twenty-Five Years* (New York, 1925), I, pp. 17 ff.
[10] Gardiner: *Life of Harcourt*, II, pp. 335–6.

ask questions about the Niger. There was no reason why Grey should not have given the reply as modified by Harcourt. As for the French expedition, if the foreign office was really ignorant of it, the fact may be taken as evidence of woeful neglect. No secret was made of it in the French press. Grey's assertion that his disbelief was later borne out, and that the Marchand mission did not set out until later, is wholly misleading. There was no question here of the Marchand expedition, but of the activities of Monteil's successor, Liotard. When all is said and done, it would be hard to find justification for the Grey statement. What is one to think of a statesman who prepares a declaration on one subject and then simply transfers it to another topic, ending with a threatening utterance and warning against what he himself considers a mere possibility? It is no wonder that the episode resulted in a storm in the cabinet. Harcourt saw no excuse whatever for the " deliberate tirade." Rosebery, however, was less ignorant than the foreign office. From his correspondence with the Queen it appears that he was quite anxious about French activity in the direction of the Nile. This, he wrote, would be very awkward, " as an expedition to dislodge them would be a very serious and costly affair." The French, he pointed out, had never recognized the British sphere: " We should not be on very strong ground if we had to rely on diplomatic action only." He admitted that the Grey declaration was " rather too strong to please some members of the cabinet," but finally he carried his colleagues with him, with one exception, evidently Harcourt.[11]

Apart from the discussion raised by the Grey declaration in English circles, there was, of course, distinct consternation in Paris. Imagine the surprise of Hanotaux and the Paris government when, in the midst of negotiations still pending with London, this bomb was suddenly touched off. Baron de Courcel, the ambassador in London, remonstrated. He pointed out that the Grey statement amounted to a declaration that the British would not admit any question of their rights in the very territory which was the subject of the negotiation with France. It was practically a " prise de possession " of the whole basin of the upper Nile. To this Kimberley replied that the reiteration of a claim could not be regarded as a " prise de possession." According to the French version he even went so far as to admit that the question of the upper Nile " remained open to debate." [12]

This modified version of the British view gave some satisfaction in Paris. But the incident practically meant the end of the long and futile negotiations which had been going on, and left the situation more confused than ever. The French had begun the discussions in the autumn of 1894 by inquiring what the British sphere was. In the draft agreement of January 1895, as in the maps of the time, the British claimed the Nile banks as far north as Fashoda and claimed for Egypt the territory as far south as Khartum, leaving a considerable stretch

[11] *Letters of Queen Victoria*, II, pp. 488–92.

[12] Kimberley to Dufferin, April 1, 1895 (*Egypt No. 2, 1898*, appendix iv); André Lebon: *La Politique de la France en Afrique, 1896–1898* (Paris, 1901), p. 7; Gabriel Hanotaux: *Fachoda* (Paris, 1909), pp. 91–4. See also Marquess of Zetland: *Lord Cromer* (London, 1932), pp. 254 ff.

open for the first comer. The treaty had not been signed, but the French evidently felt that they had secured a definite idea of the limits of the British-Egyptian claims. Yet now, quite abruptly, Grey made his threatening statement, declaring at the same time that the British and Egyptian spheres together covered the whole of the Nile water-way. What did that mean? No one could make out. Now there was talk of the Nile *Valley,* now of the *Water-way,* now of the *Basin.* When asked what was meant by *Water-way* Grey replied that he had used the word to mean " the River Nile generally," but added that it could, of course, not be taken " as a special definition of territory." You may form your own conclusion, but it is hard to escape the fact that the British had suddenly changed their previous stand and were now setting aside the whole Nile Basin as the sphere of Egypt and England, without, however, saying what part was to go to which partner. All this was pointed out by Hanotaux in his speech of April 5, 1895, which he ended by expressing the hope that when the destinies of these distant countries came to be definitely decided, the two nations, while assuring respect for the rights of the Sultan and the Khedive and while reserving each for itself the share that belonged to it by right of accomplishment, would find it possible to reach a satisfactory arrangement as to the rest. This may be taken as a veiled return to the situation before the Grey declaration. The French government could take no account officially of what was said in parliament. Hanotaux was suggesting that when the time came, Egypt should get her share, England should have hers (i.e., north to Fashoda), and others (e.g., France) should have the part they deserved by right of exploration and occupation (probably from Fashoda to Khartum).

In the interval both sides prepared to establish more than verbal claims. On April 10 the London Chamber of Commerce passed a resolution calling for measures to " assure control of the Nile Valley from Uganda to Fashoda," and immediate action in the construction of the Mombasa Railway. At the same time Colonel Colvile, commissioner in Uganda, was reported to have said that nothing could stop the British advance in the Nile Valley. It was merely a question of government orders. If England wanted the Valley all she had to do was to take it. Treaties, however numerous, would not matter.[18] Simultaneously Lord Rosebery wrote directly to Cairo to ask Cromer whether the Egyptian government was at all disquieted by the French advance, whether it had shown any recent desire to push up the Nile to Dongola, and whether it would be difficult for the French to get into the Bahr-el-Ghazal. Cromer replied that the Cairo government was " a good deal agitated " by the activities of the French. The military advisers of the government thought the French would have little trouble in capturing the Bahr-el-Ghazal, and Egyptian opinion generally was in favor of the reconquest of the Sudan. Cromer himself had always opposed such a policy, for he did not believe that the Sudan was worth Egyptian

---

[18] *Bulletin du Comité de l'Afrique Française,* 1895, p. 157.

bankruptcy and extremely oppressive taxation. But he admitted that the presence of the French changed the situation and that it might force the issue. War, he thought, was " a not improbable solution of the whole mess." " It is obvious that if any civilised Power holds the waters of the Upper Nile, it may in the end be in a position to exercise a predominating influence on the future of Egypt." To prepare for all eventualities he had already arranged to extend the railway south to Aswan and the telegraph line half way across the desert from Korosko to Abu Hamed.[14]

One important part of the British program had all along been the construction of the railway from Mombasa to Lake Victoria. Sir Gerald Portal had warmly urged prompt action in this matter, but the opposition of Harcourt had obliged Rosebery to confine the British protectorate to Uganda proper and had prevented any further steps being taken with respect to the railway. A bullock road had been constructed from Mombasa to Lake Victoria, however, and on May 27, 1895 Rosebery was finally able to report to the Queen that the cabinet had decided on the building of the Uganda Railway immediately.[15] Rosebery's ministry resigned in June before anything could be done, but Lord Salisbury, one of the warmest protagonists of the Railway, was not apt to let the matter rest. On August 30 parliament voted £20,000 for the construction of the Railway to the Lake.

On the French side the preparations for action were, if anything, more extensive. It will be recalled that in June 1894 the government had been voted 1,800,000 francs to finance the Monteil mission and a similar expedition to approach the Nile from Abyssinia. Monteil had been diverted to the Ivory Coast after the signature of the agreement with the Congo. Liotard had taken his place, but the idea of an immediate advance to the Nile had been temporarily shelved pending the negotiations with England. In the same way the projected expedition from Abyssinia had been allowed to slumber.[16] But now, in the spring of 1895, the chances of an understanding with England were gradually fading away. In May Monteil and some of his lieutenants appeared in Paris. One of them, Captain Marchand, had been particularly impressed with the plans which his chief had revealed to him. He began to carry on an extensive propaganda among politicians and to bombard the government with memoranda. Possessing great personal charm and considerable persuasive power, he soon won over the foreign minister, M. Hanotaux. But it seems that the colonial office for some time refused to proceed with the daring scheme which had been outlined so many times.[17]

---

[14] Marquess of Zetland: *Lord Cromer* (London, 1932), pp. 213–5, 221.

[15] *Letters of Queen Victoria*, II, pp. 515–6; Gardiner: *Harcourt*, II, p. 334.

[16] Cocheris: *La Situation Internationale de l'Égypte*, pp. 430–1; Charles Michel: *Vers Fachoda* (Paris, 1901); Monteil: *Souvenirs Vécus*, pp. 110 ff.

[17] Cocheris, op. cit., pp. 488–9; Monteil, op. cit., p. 121; Schéfer, op. cit., p. 195; Terrier, op. cit., p. 518; J. L. Deloncle: " La Question de Fachoda " (*Revue Politique et Parlementaire*, November, 1898, pp. 277–300), p. 292.

In the meanwhile another factor had entered into the situation. Leopold II, having been frustrated in his plans for advance into the Sudan, was not the man to allow the question to rest. Deserted by the British, he now began to re-establish contact with the French, who had made it clear that they were a force to be reckoned with. In January 1895 Félix Faure, an old friend of Leopold, became president of the French Republic in succession to Casimir-Périer, who apparently had little understanding for colonial adventure. Leopold was eager to go to Paris, and as soon as Faure was warm in his position the Belgian King arrived. In September 1895 he spent eleven days visiting the theatres and the galleries, but also conferring at great length with Faure, Hanotaux, Ribot, Lebon and other French statesmen. It is not clear what the outcome of these discussions was, but it is fairly obvious that a course of common action was de-cided upon. Leopold had already begun preparations for a huge expedition under Baron Dhanis, which was to march to the Nile and occupy the so-called Lado Enclave, the one part of the British lease which had not been discarded in the Franco-Congo Agreement of August 1894. This expedition was evidently to co-operate as closely as possible with the Marchand mission advancing farther to the north. Nothing was said in the instructions to Dhanis about the frontier fixed in August 1894. He was told to go as far north as possible, and was given sealed instructions to be opened when he reached Fashoda! Just when the Mar-chand mission was definitely decided upon it is hard to say. The instructions were dated February 24, 1896, but it is quite clear that by the beginning of November 1895 it was a settled matter in all essentials.[18]

Evidently the Marchand mission was regarded in Paris as a last resort, and there was still a strong current of feeling in government circles in favor of an agreement with England. At any rate Leopold seems to have taken it upon himself to act as mediator. In October 1895 he appeared in London and con-ferred with Salisbury. He tried to get the prime minister to induce the Khedive of Egypt " to make over to him on lease the whole of the Valley of the Nile from Khartoum up towards the Nyanza Lake, up to the point where our own claims commence." To this extraordinary proposal Salisbury gave no encourage-ment, fearing that any action in the matter would stir up France and possibly other powers to try to establish themselves in the Nile Valley. But in the first days of December 1895 Leopold was back again in the British capital. This time he kept harping on his close relations with the French, who, he asserted, dealt with him without reserve. In mystical language he referred to a " unique crisis " and an opportunity that never would return. What he wanted was that England should throw herself into the arms of France, fix a date for the evacuation of

---

[18] See Mangin's letter of November 2, 1895 (General Mangin: "Lettres de la Mission Mar-chand," in *Revue des Deux Mondes,* September 15, 1931, pp. 241–83, especially p. 241). On Leopold's activities the main source is A. J. Wauters: *Souvenirs de Fachoda et de l'Expédition Dhanis* (Brus-sels, 1910), pp. 18–9, 28, and the same author's *Histoire Politique du Congo Belge* (Brussels, 1911), pp. 131 ff., 143; see also Col. Liebrechts: *Léopold II* (Brussels, 1932), pp. 171 ff.; Pierre Daye: *Léopold II* (Paris, 1934), pp. 410 ff.

Egypt and persuade the Khedive to make a concession of the Sudan above Khartum " to some person who was *au courant* of the affairs of Africa." In return for all this Britain should have a free hand for annexations in China, and if the Ottoman Empire should fall to pieces, England might have Egypt back again.

Salisbury, listening to these phantastic schemes, could not believe that they were all meant to be taken seriously. He did feel, however, that Leopold was anxious to raise some discussion about the Valley of the Nile, to which France should be a party. More than ever the prime minister felt the need of keeping things quiet until England was properly prepared. To the Queen he wrote: " Our only chance is to keep the thing quiet until our railway to Uganda is sufficiently far advanced to enable us to send troops by it." [19]

The great question was whether Britain's rivals would leave her so much time. Something was evidently in the wind. In mid-January Leopold appeared for the third time, pressing once again his suggestion for a lease of the Sudan above Khartum. When he had subdued the Sudanese he would put them at England's disposal, he said. They could be used to invade and occupy Armenia. This was too much for the British lord. Writing to the Queen he remarked that the idea struck him as being so quaint that he " hastened to give the conversation another turn " lest he should be betrayed " into some disrespectful commentary." The Queen agreed that the account of the King's visit was " quite preposterous," and added: " It really seems as if he had taken leave of his senses." [20]

Perhaps so, but Europe had had too much experience of Leopold's wily manoeuvres to take his activities lightly. The moment was an uncomfortable one for England, when the Cleveland message and the Kruger telegram followed rapidly upon each other. It has been pointed in the preceding chapter that in the early part of January 1896 some advances were made to France by the English government. Unfortunately these advances are shrouded in almost as deep mystery as the negotiations of the Rosebery period. The French have maintained that in the last days of December 1895 Salisbury approached Baron de Courcel, saying that the Egyptians were planning an advance up the Nile to Dongola. The expedition, he said, would not go beyond that point without arrangements having been previously made with the French. Courcel had all along been working for an agreement with England and the radical Bourgeois-Berthelot cabinet, which had come into power in October 1895, was also well-disposed to the idea. But, says the French version, the French cabinet objected on the plea that an agreement would involve recognition of the British position in Egypt.

This account seems most improbable. In the first place, even if the advance up the Nile was being discussed at that time, it was not decided upon. There-

---

[19] *Letters of Queen Victoria*, II, pp. 577–9, the only source for these remarkable advances.
[20] *Letters of Queen Victoria*, III, pp. 24–5.

fore Courcel could not have been informed of it. Furthermore, it would be hard
to understand how Salisbury could have bound himself to limit the advance to
Dongola and to obligate himself to secure the agreement of France before the
campaign was resumed. The fact probably is that Courcel was very anxious and
that Salisbury, whose interest it was to keep the French in good humor at the
time, discussed the Egyptian-Sudan question in general terms. We learn from
Marquess Zetland's biography of Cromer that early in January 1896 Courcel
made advances to Salisbury. He declared that the French had no desire to see
an international government or condominium established in Egypt. In fact he
doubted if the Paris government really wished to have the British leave Egypt,
on account of the great French investment there. In a vague way he suggested
that all France desired was that her *amour propre* should be satisfied, that England should withdraw the army of occupation, appoint more Frenchmen to
administrative positions and in general consult France more frequently on
Egyptian affairs. Hanotaux, too, though he was at that time not in office, informed Salisbury, through a friend, that France asked for very little. Salisbury
was interested but sceptical. Cromer was even more sceptical and dreaded both
evacuation and consultation. He opposed any concessions to France unless the
French were prepared to give England full financial liberty, he wrote Salisbury
in a letter of February 29, 1896.[21]

It is impossible to form an estimate of the importance of these conversations,
but the probability is that Salisbury allowed Courcel to hope. He was glad to
have the negotiations drag on over the most critical weeks of January and
February 1896 in order to discourage the French from joining in any hostile
action. It is more than doubtful whether he was ready to make any real concessions in the Egyptian question. His object appears to have been to shelve
the whole business until England was fully prepared to act with vigor.

As matters turned out, the British were not to choose their own time for the
advance into the Sudan. Events in Abyssinia were fast coming to a crisis, and
when the bubble of Italian colonial enterprise burst, the London government
had to come to a decision.

Ever since 1890 the Italians had been getting into more and more trouble
with Menelik, King of Kings of Abyssinia since the death of King John in
1889. Menelik, who had originally been King of Shoa in southern Abyssinia, had
been on the worst of terms with John, and their relations had come to a crisis
when an attack of the dervishes distracted John. The Emperor lost his life in
battle and the road was open for Menelik to succeed him. The Italians, who
had also been at daggers drawn with John, supported Menelik with arms and

---

[21] Zetland: *Cromer*, pp. 256-7; see further *Bulletin du Comité de l'Afrique Française*, 1896,
pp. 130 ff.; Darcy: *France et Angleterre*, pp. 400-2; Charles Giraudeau: " Après Adoua — avant
Dongola " (*Revue Politique et Littéraire*, March 21, 1896, pp. 362-4); Hanotaux: *Fachoda*, pp.
101-2; *Die Grosse Politik*, XI, nos. 2681-708 passim, 2733, 2739. There is a rather inconclusive
discussion of this whole episode, based chiefly on the German documents, in Heinz Kossatz: *Untersuchungen über den Französisch-Englischen Weltgegensatz im Fashodajahr* (Breslau, 1934), pp. 5 ff.

munitions and in other ways. Menelik was not unappreciative, and, being an astute statesman, he realized that Abyssinia, if it was to avoid the fate of the rest of Africa, would have to establish close relations with one of the great European powers. Among the Europeans the Italians were the least dangerous. In May 1889 he therefore concluded with the Italian agent, Count Antonelli, the famous Treaty of Uccialli, by which he abandoned to the Italians part of northeastern Abyssinia, thus enabling them to extend their possessions from the insalubrious coast area to the attractive inland plateau. But the most important article of the Treaty was the much disputed Article XVII, which, according to the Italians, provided that Menelik and his successors agreed to make use of the Italian government in all their dealings with foreign powers. In other words, this article gave the Italians what amounted to a protectorate over the entire possessions of the King of Kings.

The government at Rome was not slow to take advantage of this great gain. Crispi was a firm believer in modern imperialism. " Colonies are a necessity of modern life," he had said in the Chamber in May 1888. " We cannot remain inactive and allow other powers to occupy all the unexplored parts of the world." Time and again he spoke of Abyssinia as a splendid area for Italian colonization, a place where Italian emigrants could find a living without being lost to the mother country.[22] He therefore notified the other powers of Italy's new position in northeast Africa. It was not long before Menelik's attention was called to the pretensions of his allies. Now it appears that in the Amharic text the famous Article XVII read that the King of Abyssinia " might make use " of the Italian government in all relations with other powers, not that he consented to make use of it. It happened further that only the Amharic text had been actually signed, so that it alone was valid. How this curious and important difference in the texts had come about it is hard to say. The Italians always claimed that it was due to the malevolence of the Abyssinian translator, who had behind him the influence of men hostile to the Italian advance. Others, especially French writers, have insisted that the whole thing was a clumsy ruse on the part of Antonelli, who had more than a little of the adventurer in him, and Crispi, who thought that Menelik would never know the difference. The Italians assert that the Abyssinian ruler's attention was called to the discrepancy by French intriguers, who translated for him the Italian Green Book on the subject and supplied him with ample abstracts from the French newspaper comment. In reality Menelik noted what was going on from the replies he received from Emperor William and Queen Victoria after he had notified those sovereigns of his accession to the throne.[23]

22 G. Palumbo-Cardella: " Crispi e la Politica Coloniale " (*Politica*, XXIX, pp. 150–79, 387–431; XXX, pp. 350–80, 1929); Francesco Geraci: " La Politica Coloniale di Francesco Crispi " (*Rivista delle Colonie Italiani*, November, 1930).

23 The details make a long story, often discussed. See Palumbo-Cardella, pp. 399 ff.: Francesco Crispi: *La Prima Guerra d'Africa* (Milan, 1914), chap. vi; T. Palamenghi-Crispi: *L'Italia Coloniale e Francesco Crispi* (Milan, 1928), pp. 118 ff.; Gennaro Mondaini: *Manuale di Storia e*

Menelik lost no time in trying to straighten out the misunderstanding. Antonelli was sent again to the Abyssinian capital. There were months of discussion, with numerous proposals for obviating the difficulty. But Antonelli made it quite clear that the Italian government was unwilling in any case to give up the substance of the protectorate. The conversations became more and more discordant, and in February 1891 Antonelli, uttering dire threats and throwing to the wind all considerations of form, left Adis Abeba, having accomplished nothing.

The Italians still stood by their interpretation of the Treaty. The English approved, and in the agreements of 1891 recognized the whole of Abyssinia as part of the Italian sphere of influence. But the government at Rome now had to reckon with the hostility rather than the friendship of Menelik. They therefore began to establish contact with Menelik's rivals, especially with Ras Mangasha, the King of Tigré, who was a son of King John and a pretender to the throne of the King of Kings. It was evidently hoped in Italian government circles that some sort of a balance could be established between the Abyssinian rulers, and that under such conditions the position of the Italians could be gradually strengthened.

But Menelik, to quote a well-known British anti-imperialist, " made it clear that Italy would never win an empire by mistranslating Amharic." [24] At the advice of his able Swiss counsellor, Alfred Ilg, he began preparations for war and started to seek the support of France. In February 1893 he formally denounced the Treaty of Uccialli, and it became clear that hostilities were not far in the future. Roads were quietly built from Shoa to the north, and magazines were established at key places. Nothing pleased Menelik so much as a present of a few thousand rifles or a dozen modern mountain guns. A European who took him an old fowling piece and explained to him that it went " bum-bum " was positively staggered when Menelik took him on a visit to the arsenal at Adis Abeba. By 1895 Menelik must have had a hundred thousand rifles with the appropriate amount of ammunition.

Most of these munitions reached Abyssinia through the French ports of Obock and Jibuti. It cannot be proved that the French government was responsible for this traffic, forbidden under the terms of the Brussels Act of 1890. But there is no satisfactory evidence either that the French government made any great effort to stop shipments by speculators and adventurers. The Italian sources are simply filled with complaints of French duplicity and of the utter failure of the Italian government to secure satisfaction from Paris. It is fairly obvious that the French authorities were not sorry to see the Italians in difficulties, and that they looked with pleasure upon the weakening of Britain's

Legislazione Coloniale (Rome, 1927), part I, pp. 89 ff.; J. L. Morié: *Histoire de l'Éthiopie* (Paris, 1904), II, p. 425; Sir E. A. Wallis Budge: *A History of Ethiopia* (London, 1928), II, pp. 528 ff.; and especially the intimate account in Conrad Keller: *Alfred Ilg* (Leipzig, 1918), pp. 66 ff.

[24] Leonard Woolf: *Empire and Commerce in Africa*, p. 172.

client in east Africa. The same was true of the Russians, who began to develop an extraordinary activity in Abyssinia, cloaked by geographical and religious interests. In January 1895 a Russian adventurer of the worst sort, named Leontiev, appeared in Adis Abeba with extravagant gifts. In July 1895 Menelik himself sent a huge mission to pay his respects to the Tsar, and by the end of the year Leontiev was back on the scene. It is said that he commanded the artillery at the Battle of Adua. In any event, he was active in the Franco-Russian cause and was made full use of by the wily Abyssinian ruler.[25]

By this time an undeclared war had already broken out. Attempts at negotiation having failed, the Italian commander, General Baratieri, began the advance into Tigré, and defeated Ras Mangasha in three engagements. The Italians occupied the capital of the province, Adigrat, and pushed on to Adua. At the same time efforts were made to undermine the position of Menelik in southern Abyssinia. Appeals were made to England to permit the landing of troops at Zeila, in British Somaliland, so that an attack could be made on Harrar. But the British refused to help. They were just then engaged in discussion with the French and did not want to expose themselves to the accusation of having violated the Harrar agreement of 1888. The Italian requests for the publication of the secret declaration of May 1894, which was hardly in consonance with the agreement of 1888, was steadfastly refused.[26]

After the advance to Adua, Baratieri was instructed to halt and to establish a strong defensive position at Adigrat. There was a strong current in Italy opposed to further colonial adventure, and Sonnino, the secretary of the treasury, was constantly objecting to the huge expenditure.[27] But Baratieri had his own ideas on the subject and advanced the classic argument of the need of security. Crispi, himself an ardent exponent of expansion, did not put insurmountable obstacles in his way. The whole subject of responsibility has been thrashed over so frequently and so thoroughly by Italian writers that the disinterested reader is apt to find himself lost in a thick fog of pros and cons. All one can say is that the instructions to Baratieri were usually so sibylline in their nature that they left ample room for interpretation by the recipient. In the late summer Baratieri himself spent some time at home. What was said during his conferences with Crispi and Blanc we do not know.

It was perfectly obvious to all concerned that Menelik was preparing for war on the largest scale, and that the conflict would break out in the autumn.[28] In

[25] Crispi: *Memoirs*, III, pp. 205–6; Crispi: *Prima Guerra d'Africa*, pp. 328 ff., 347 ff., 352 ff., 362 ff.; Palamenghi-Crispi, op. cit., pp. 155 ff.; Leopoldo Traversi: *Let-Marefià* (Milan, 1931), pp. 407 ff.; Woolf, op. cit., pp. 172–3; Mondaini, op. cit., p. 91; *Die Grosse Politik*, VII, no. 1463; VIII, no. 1999; IX, no. 2754, etc.

[26] *Die Grosse Politik*, VIII, nos. 1999–2012; Italicus: *Italiens Bündnispolitik* (Munich, 1928), pp. 195 ff.; Crispi: *Prima Guerra d'Africa*, pp. 282 ff.

[27] *Italian Green Book: Avvenimenti d'Africa, Gennaio 1895–Marzo 1896*, nos. 3, 9, 10; Mondaini, op. cit., pp. 104 ff.; Crispi: *Prima Guerra, etc.*, pp. 300 ff.; Palumbo-Cardella, loc. cit. XXX, pp. 367–8.

[28] *Avvenimenti d'Africa*, nos. 19, 21.

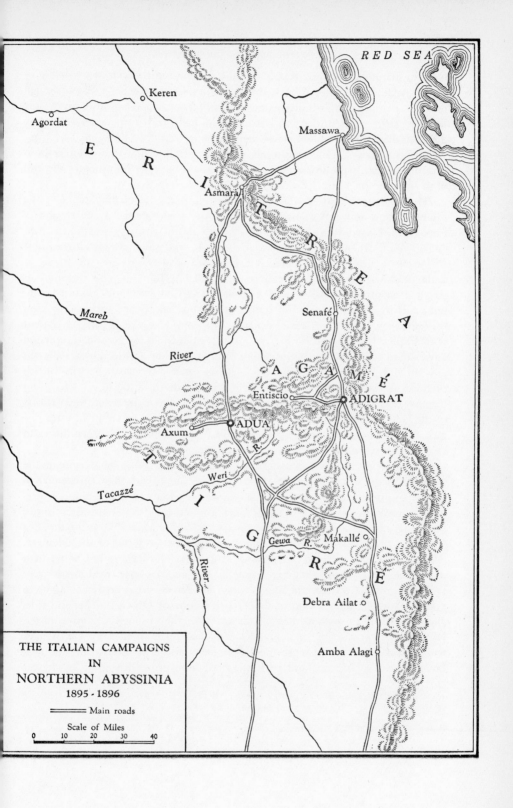

RED SEA

Keren

Agordat

E

R

Massawa

Asmara

I

T

Mareb

R

River

Senafé

E

A

G

A

M

É

Entiscio

ADIGRAT

Axum

ADUA

R

T

Weri

I

R

Tacazzé

G

Gewa

R.

Makallé

R

E

Debra Ailat

Amba Alagi

THE ITALIAN CAMPAIGNS
IN
NORTHERN ABYSSINIA
1895 · 1896

━━━ Main roads

Scale of Miles
0   10   20   30   40

October Baratieri defeated Ras Mangasha for the fourth time in the battle of Dabra-Ailat. It was to be the last Italian victory. On December 7 Ras Makonen of Harrar attacked the Italians under Toselli at Amba Alagi and completely defeated them. The important fortress at Makallé was immediately besieged. The tide had turned and the Italians were now seriously threatened by over-whelming forces. Baratieri promptly withdrew from Adua to a stronger posi-tion in the rear.[29] Reinforcements were hurried out from Italy before the end of the month.

The defeat at Amba Alagi was in many respects the turning point in the drama. Crispi now felt that withdrawal before a victory would be absolutely impossible. The most urgent thing was to prepare for certain success in the next engagement. An attack upon Menelik's flank, upon Harrar, would be most efficacious, but in order to execute it, it would be necessary to land troops at Zeila, the British port. Application was made in London, and negotiations dragged on through a large part of January 1896. Lord Salibury declared him-self ready to allow the transit of Italian troops, but he objected to an occupation of Zeila even for a short time, stressing the point that the British agreement with France with respect to Harrar made it impossible for Britain to sanction any change in the status of Harrar that did not have the approval of the French government. It is perfectly clear from the documents we have that the British premier, at that time above all anxious not to irritate the French, was unwilling to make any substantial concession to the Italians. Even the determined efforts of the German ambassador availed nothing. The Italians gave up in utter dis-gust. " The British do nothing but kick us," remarked the foreign minister to the German representative at the end of the negotiations.[30]

In the course of the discussions with the Italians, Lord Sanderson of the British foreign office made the statement that the French had threatened to oppose by force of arms any Italian expedition against Harrar, unless a pre-vious agreement were arrived at between France and Italy.[31] In other words, action depended on French consent. Crispi certainly had no liking for the idea of asking French permission, but there was no other way out of the dilemma. About January 12 a special agent was sent to Paris. We have only Crispi's own statements as to what went on. From these it appears that the Italians were willing to make very far-reaching concessions. They were prepared to agree to a very favorable delimitation of the French colony of Obock on the land side, and were ready to give up their claims in Tunis. The French foreign minister, who had been discussing these matters with the Italian ambassador for the past weeks, was eager for an agreement and negotiations seemed to be taking a favorable course. Yet on January 23 the French government drew back. It was

---

[29] Oreste Baratieri: *Memorie d'Africa, 1892–1896* (Turin, 1898), chaps. xix–xx; and the detailed scholarly study of Emilio Bellavita: *Adua* (Genoa, 1931), chaps. xviii–xix.

[30] *Avvenimenti d'Africa*, nos. 76–8; Crispi: *Prima Guerra d'Africa*, pp. 331 ff.; *Die Grosse Politik*, XI, nos. 2748–61; Mondaini, op. cit., pp. 114–5.   [31] *Die Grosse Politik*, XI, no. 2758.

said to be impossible to confront the French parliament with an agreement at that time, and the prime minister, M. Bourgeois, told the Italian agent, Signor Bodio, that the thoughts of France were fixed on Alsace-Lorraine. " An understanding between the two countries is impossible so long as Italy remains a party to the Triple Alliance," he added.[32]

Crispi, frustrated on all sides, became mad with desperation. He blamed the Kruger telegram and the Anglo-German estrangement for Britain's unwillingness to do something for the Italians, and blamed the Triple Alliance for France's refusal to come to some satisfactory arrangement. " Our position is intolerable. I repeat that this state of affairs is worse than war." In fact, France was practically waging war on Italy already. What good was the Triple Alliance if it did not safeguard the interests of its members in times of peace. It seemed very doubtful whether the Alliance could be renewed: " The Italian people are not yet disillusioned with regard to the alliance with Germany, but who can guarantee that they may not be so tomorrow, if things continue as they are? "[33]

But these complaints and threats made relatively little impression in Berlin. The Germans simply warned the Italians against defection from the Alliance. As Bülow put it, the Italians in the company of France, Russia and the Pope would be comparable to Little Red Riding Hood, alone in the woods with the wolf, the fox and the bear. Again and again the German chancellor advised against a further advance in Abyssinia, and warned the Italian government that a naval war with France and Russia would not be a *casus foederis*.[34] All this did Crispi little good. In Africa things were going from bad to worse. On January 20, 1896 the important fortress at Makallé fell into the hands of the Abyssinians. More than ever the Italian premier felt the need for a decisive victory. His dictatorial policy at home had brought upon him the uncompromising enmity of the radical groups, which were, at the same time, the chief opponents of the colonial adventure. Baratieri, who was once again attempting to negotiate separately with Menelik's vassals, Mangasha and Makonen, was empowered to negotiate with Menelik himself. The basis for these discussions, as outlined to Baratieri on January 18, shows that the government was determined to uphold its interpretation of the Treaty of Uccialli to the utmost, that it demanded Menelik's recognition of it, and that it expected further concessions of a far-reaching nature.[35]

The negotiations were probably only a blind. From the correspondence it is clear that Crispi felt that a victory must precede any satisfactory settlement. He pressed this view on the commander, called for " un' azione resolutiva," and

[32] Crispi: *Memoirs*, III, p. 336; Crispi: *Prima Guerra d'Africa*, pp. 330–46; Gaetano Salvemini: *La Politica Estera di Francesco Crispi* (Rome, 1919), p. 87; *Die Grosse Politik*, XI, nos. 2657, 2762, 2816, 2817.

[33] Crispi: *Memoirs*, III, pp. 337 ff., 342–3, 347; *Die Grosse Politik*, XI, no. 2649; Pribram: *Secret Treaties of Austria-Hungary*, II, p. 107.

[34] *Die Grosse Politik*, XI, nos. 2655–8, 2765, 2766.

[35] *Avvenimenti d'Africa*, no. 49.

spurred him on to more vigorous action.[36] Baratieri had no illusions about the situation. He had written home that the Italian terms would not be accepted by Menelik even if he were defeated, and that, to realize the aspirations of the government it would be necessary to occupy Adis Abeba itself.[37] The Italian commander had entrenched himself strongly at Adigrat and was ready for all eventualities. The reasons for his advance and the questions of responsibility for the great defeat at Adua are matters that have been and still are hotly debated by the protagonists of Crispi and Baratieri. Into the details we need not enter here, excepting to say that recent researches have been favorable to Baratieri rather than to the prime minister. It seems not unlikely that the commander on the spot was goaded into action by the impatient and sarcastic telegrams that reached him from Rome. He had, furthermore, to consider questions of food and supply. Sooner or later he would have to withdraw unless a victory were won. On February 28 he held a war council with his brigadiers. They were all of the opinion that an effort must be made to gain some success, and so the decision was made to advance in the direction of Adua. Baratieri's plan appears to have been to compensate for his numerical inferiority by taking up a strong position some ten miles from Adua, resting on the mountains Eshasho, Rebbi Arienni and Raio, which rose to heights of 7500 to 8500 feet and were steep and rocky. Entrenched in this position the Italians would have been able to withstand an attack by greatly superior numbers. If the Abyssinians did not feel strong enough to attack they would have to withdraw from the whole area around Adua in about a week, for they would be unable to find supplies. In any event the chances seemed to lie with the Italians. Baratieri was a good strategist and his plan seems, to the layman at least, sound in its fundamentals.

Just before midnight on February 29 the Italians began the forward movement, marching in four brigades under Generals Dabormida, Arimondi, Albertone and Ellena (reserve). There was some confusion on the march, due evidently to the very imperfect map at the disposal of the commanders. But Dabormida and Arimondi, followed by Ellena, came into Rebbi Arienni early in the morning of March 1. Only Albertone, for some reason mistaking the place of rendezvous, continued the march and found himself several miles in advance of the others. Baratieri, discovering this fact through his glasses and seeing that Albertone was already hotly engaged by the enemy, sent Dabormida to support him. To make matters worse Dabormida, following a road marked on the map, found before long that this road led in quite another direction. Instead of taking him southwest in the direction of Albertone it took him far to the north where he ran into the Abyssinian forces under Ras Makonen. Dabormida fought hard in the afternoon but his brigade was finally overwhelmed and almost annihilated in what was practically a separate engagement. Long before that Albertone, isolated and unsupported, was surrounded by the Abyssinians who swarmed down from the encircling mountains. A large part of his force was

---

[36] *Avvenimenti d'Africa*, nos. 52, 78.   [37] Baratieri, op. cit., pp. 322-3.

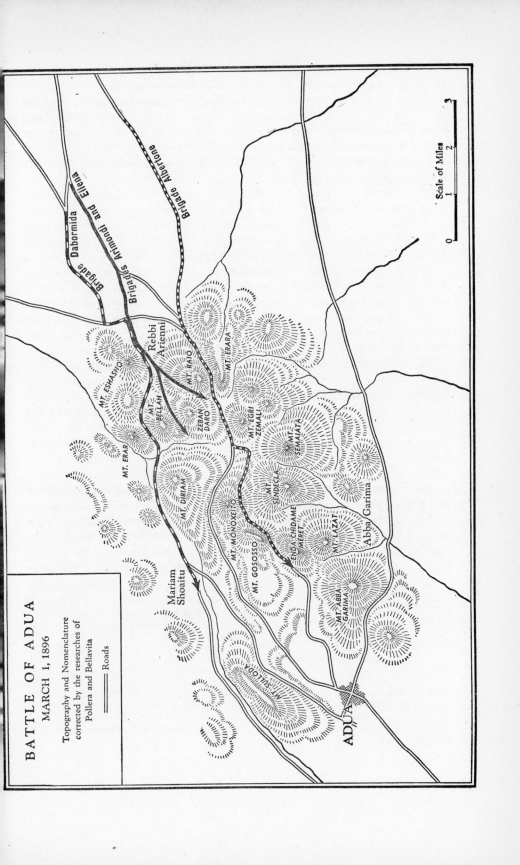

BATTLE OF ADUA
MARCH 1, 1896

Topography and Nomenclature
corrected by the researches of
Pollera and Bellavita

——— Roads

Scale of Miles

0   1   2   3

Brigade Albertone

Brigades Arimondi and Ellena

Brigade Dabormida

Rebbi Arienni

MT. ESHASHO

MT. ERAR

MT. RAIO

MT. ERARA

ZEBAN DARO

MT. BELLAH

MT. DIRIAM

MT. EGRI

ZEMAL

MT. SEMAIATA

MT. SENDECIA

ENDA CHIDAME

MERET

MT. AZAT

Abba Garima

MT. MONOXEITO

MT. GOSOSSO

Mariam Shoaitu

MT. SPIDDOO

MT. ABBA GARIMA

ADUA

captured. The Abyssinians, having given short shrift to Albertone's brigade, then turned upon Arimondi's. The Italians were violently attacked upon all sides and, being in the mountain passes, they hardly had room to deploy. Only parts of Ellena's reserve were able to get away without being captured. By the middle of the afternoon only a few shattered fragments of the Italian forces were in flight to the rear. Generals Dabormida and Arimondi were dead, Albertone was a prisoner.

The disaster was one of great magnitude. At the time the Italians did not know how numerous and how well armed their adversaries were. Of course the Abyssinian forces can only be estimated even at the present time. Menelik himself could not have said how many men he had. It is fairly certain, however, that he had not less than 80,000 and not more than 120,000 troops, of whom some four fifths were equipped with good rifles and the necessary ammunition. The Abyssinians had fewer mountain guns than the Italians, but their guns are said to have been superior to those of their opponents. Under the direction of Leontiev and other European officers they did deadly work throughout the battle. As against these formidable forces the Italians had only about 20,000 men, of whom roughly half were native troops. Hopelessly outnumbered and caught separated in the defiles of the mountains they never had a chance of victory. They fought valiantly and doggedly and the battle was in no sense a disgrace to them. In fact they inflicted heavier losses upon the Abyssinians than they themselves received. They lost about 6000 men killed, 2000 wounded and about 2000 captured, in addition to 11,000 rifles and all their artillery. The Abyssinians seem to have had about 15,000 killed and wounded. Taken in the large the battle was pretty much of a slaughter and the percentage of casualties was very high.[38]

The first incomplete news of the disaster in Africa reached Rome on March 2 and was released in a communiqué at 2 A.M. on March 3. The cabinet assembled at once and Crispi decided to resign rather than expose himself to the attacks of the Radicals in the Chamber, which he knew to be unavoidable. Parliament met on March 5. The government's announcement of its decision to withdraw was met with cheers. Crispi and most of the ministers had gone

---

[38] Of the very extensive literature on the battle may be mentioned the following, mostly recent, titles: Baratieri's own account (*Memorie d'Africa*), part iii; the excellent study in Augustus B. Wylde: *Modern Abyssinia* (London, 1901), chap. ix, based on contemporary investigations and discussions with Menelik, Ras Mangasha, Ras Makonen and other Abyssinian leaders; G. F. Berkeley: *The Campaign of Adowa and the Rise of Menelik* (London, 1902); Cesare G. Pini: *Adua* (Turin, 1926); Alberto Pollera: *La Battaglia di Adua* (Florence, 1928), with beautiful panoramic views and interesting topographical information; Field-Marshal E. Caviglia: "La Battaglia di Adua" (*Echi e Commenti*, February 25, 1928); A. Gaibi: *La Guerra d'Africa, 1895–1896* (Rome, 1930); Igino Pinci: *Francesco Crispi e la Campagna d'Africa* (Rome, 1931); General R. Corselli: "La Battaglia di Adua secondo gli ultimi accertamenti" (*Rivista Militare Italiana*, IV, March, 1930, pp. 327–74); Guglielmo Ferrero: "La Bataille d'Adoua" (*Europe*, June 15, 1930, pp. 163–210), and above all the exhaustive, heavily documented account of Emilio Bellavita: *Adua* (Genoa, 1931), and the critical review of Gennaro Mondaini: "La Battaglia di Adua" (*Nuova Rivista Storica*, XVI, 1932, pp. 575–92).

to the meeting by circuitous routes to avoid the huge crowds that thronged the streets shouting "Abbasso Crispi" "Via dall'Africa" and occasionally even "Viva Menelik." The Quirinal and the foreign embassies as well as the government buildings were guarded by troops and shops closed down, because the restless mob was in an ominous frame of mind. Despite the pouring rain the police were unable to clear the most important squares and thoroughfares. Not only in Rome, but in Naples and especially in the Lombard towns serious disturbances broke out. Ministerial newspapers were burned in great bonfires, railroad tracks were torn up to prevent the departure of troops for Africa, stones were thrown at the police and in some instances it became necessary for the cavalry to charge the mob. Italy had clearly entered upon a great and serious crisis. All the pent-up discontent with the government, with the dictatorial methods of Crispi, with the policy of colonial adventure found an outlet in the hour of national grief. It was to be years before the situation in Italy became stabilized, years before Italy was prepared once more to play a really independent rôle in international affairs.[39]

We are less concerned here with the repercussions of the Abyssinian catastrophe upon the domestic situation in Italy than with its reaction upon international affairs. The new cabinet, constituted by the Marchese di Rudini on March 10, immediately took up the negotiations for peace with Menelik which had already been opened at Crispi's behest. Rudini had always been an opponent of the Abyssinian enterprise. Looking back years later he confessed that the Italians had, in his opinion, gone to Massowa with no serious purpose and without realizing the difficulties. They had simply gone in order to keep up with the expansion of the other powers, "in a spirit of imitation, a desire for sport, and for pure *snobism*." He doubted whether even the government at the time knew what it was aiming at.[40] Had he had his own way in 1896 he would probably have withdrawn even from Eritrea. But, just as there were rabid anti-colonialists in Italy, so there was a strong group composed largely of military men who would never listen to such a proposal. The King himself was anxious to make good the Italian defeat by a new campaign against Menelik. That was out of the question, but the government decided to hold Eritrea, while offering to Menelik the abandonment of all claims to Tigré and the abrogation of the whole Uccialli Treaty. Negotiations to this end were carried on through the spring and summer and ultimately led to the conclusion of peace in October 1896.

So far as the Triple Alliance was concerned the Adua disaster was a staggering blow. It has already been pointed out how the Kruger telegram and the Anglo-German estrangement affected Germany's allies. The Italians had made no secret of their disapprobation, and the Austrian foreign minister, Count

---

[39] London *Times*, March 4 to 15, inclusive; Saverio Cilibrizzi: *Storia Parlamentare, Politica. e Diplomatica d'Italia* (Milan, 1929), III, pp. 2 ff.
[40] A. di Rudini: "L'Egitto Moderno" (*Nuova Antologia*, May 16, 1908, pp. 193–224).

Goluchowski, was more than a little irritated when his efforts to enlist English support in the Near East proved entirely futile. In the spring the Treaty of the Triple Alliance had to be denounced if it was not to run for a second period of years, as provided for in 1891. The Italians were demanding that the obligations of Austria should be extended in the eastern Mediterranean and that Germany should agree to give Italy greater support in the western part of that sea. At the same time the Austrians were disgruntled by the pronounced German tendency to effect a rapprochement with Russia. There was rather acrimonious debate about the *casus foederis* of the Austro-German Alliance, and thinly veiled references to the futility of all these agreements.[41]

It does not appear that the German chancellor or foreign minister took this discontent too seriously. They had their own explanation of the Anglo-German antagonism, and felt smug enough in their cordial relations with Russia. The Emperor, on the other hand, was quite unhappy. He had evidently repented of the Kruger telegram, and had come to realize that, in a crisis like that of January 1896, his advances to Russia and France did not amount to much. When the dreadful news from Africa reached him on March 3, he took advantage of the arrival of the new British military attaché, Colonel Grierson, to transmit to London his own views of the situation. He discussed the position of Great Britain as opposed to a combination of continental powers and repudiated the idea that the Triple Alliance was in any way hostile. Again and again he stressed the fact that Russia was England's worst enemy and that France " had prostituted herself into the arms of Russia." The French army was now merely a tool for Russian purposes and one with which Russia played " as one does with a terrier on a chain, hounding him on to bite someone." The policy of Germany was to keep on friendly terms with both these wing powers. But Germany could not afford to see Europe swamped by the Slavs. Hence he wished to maintain friendly relations with Britain, as she and Germany were the two great Protestant powers standing in the forefront of civilization and united by ties of blood, religion and mutual interest. He then tried to explain away the south African difficulty, and proceeded to discuss the position in the Mediterranean and the disaster in Abyssinia. When Grierson left the imperial presence he was convinced " that, in spite of appearances, his [the Emperor's] friendship for Great Britain and his desire for a British alliance had never wavered and that his great wish now was to replace matters upon the friendly footing upon which they were before the present regrettable estrangement took place." [42]

William was not content with his démarche. After a conference with the Italian ambassador he decided upon more vigorous and spectacular action. Late on the evening of March 3 he appeared at the British embassy. It was 1.30 A.M. before he departed. During the time of his stay he conferred with Sir Frank

[41] Pribram: *Secret Treaties of Austria-Hungary*, II, pp. 105 ff.; *Die Grosse Politik*, XI, chaps. lxv and lxvi, passim.

[42] D. S. Macdiarmid: *The Life of Lieutenant-General Sir James Moncrieff Grierson* (London, 1923), pp. 117–9.

Lascelles for at least two hours. The burden of his argument was that the international situation was critical. France was practically waging war against Italy in Abyssinia. France and Russia were united, at least by a military alliance, and the French forces were at Russia's disposal. Russia, on the other hand, was determined to annihilate her two enemies, England and Austria, by fair means or foul. The Tsarist aim was to annex Bulgaria and the Balkan states as well as the Slavic provinces of Austria, offering Germany the German provinces of the Hapsburg Empire as compensation. After the expulsion of the Italians the Russians would establish themselves at Massowa and other places and secure control of the sea route to India. The Egyptian question would be raised again, and, to make matters worse, the French were trying to buy from Spain the Canary Islands. If these fell into French hands even the Cape route to India would be endangered. The English press and some English statesmen, concluded the Emperor, had treated him badly, but he considered it his duty to warn the British. He was glad that they were increasing their naval power and expected " that England would join the Triple Alliance or at any rate come to the assistance of the Italians in their difficult situation." [43]

The Emperor's picture of the world situation was lurid enough and more than a little tinged with alarmism. It is no wonder that the Italian and British ambassadors were a trifle upset by " tant de désinvolture " and a bit puzzled to know what he was driving at.[44] The German foreign office was by no means pleased with His Majesty's independent action. Neither Marschall nor Holstein was prepared to repent and crawl on his knees to secure British assistance. The appeal, they argued, was undignified and would be misunderstood in England as a sign of weakness. Hohenlohe was urged to protest to the Emperor against his independent conversations with ambassadors. The chancellor refused to interfere. He evidently felt that the foreign office was more than a little to blame for estranging Britain by the policy pursued in south Africa and was quite prepared to mend matters as much as possible. In the meanwhile the foreign office went its own way. Weeks later Marschall was still trying to persuade the French ambassador that France and Germany had an identical interest in preserving the status quo in south Africa and insisted that willy-nilly France and Germany, excepting in the Egyptian affair, must march together against England, which was everywhere the invader.[45]

Something of the divergent aims of the Germans must have been known in London. In any event it was not likely that Lord Salisbury would be carried away by the somewhat hysterical utterances of the Emperor. The idea that William's talk with Lascelles induced the British government to take action is almost certainly erroneous, even though the Emperor credited himself with it.

---

[43] *Die Grosse Politik,* XI, nos. 2770, 2771 (the Emperor's account to Hohenlohe and Lascelles' telegram home); Hohenlohe: *Denkwürdigkeiten der Reichskanzlerzeit,* pp. 185, 187; *The Letters and Friendships of Sir Cecil Spring Rice,* I, p. 200; Bourgeois and Pagès: *Les Origines et les Responsabilités de la Grande Guerre,* p. 259.　　　[44] Bourgeois and Pagès, op. cit., pp. 259, 262.

[45] Hohenlohe, op. cit., pp. 192–3; Bourgeois and Pagès, op. cit., p. 271.

Count Hatzfeldt was obliged to report that Lord Salisbury could not see his way clear to afford the Italians assistance. As late as March 8 the Italian ambassador at London had to admit that he had accomplished nothing. Salisbury refused the repeated offer even of Kassala, which the Italians feared would have to be evacuated. All of which elicited from Marschall the opinion that England would join no other power, but was working hard to precipitate a conflict on the Continent and thus extricate herself from a host of difficulties.[46]

And yet, on March 12, Salisbury was able to tell Count Hatzfeldt that the cabinet had decided to allow the Egyptian government to begin a military advance up the Nile to Dongola, about two hundred miles distant from the frontier at Wadi Halfa. What had happened in the interval? This is a question difficult to answer with complete assurance. Some writers, like Winston Churchill, would have us believe that the government was carried away by public opinion. There was the feeling that Gordon must be avenged: " There was an earnest desire on the part of a pious nation to dissociate his name from failure." And the moving accounts of dervish rule brought back by Father Ohrwalder and Slatin Pasha horrified the nation. The misery of the Sudan aroused " that great volume of generous humanitarian feeling which sways our civilized state." [47] Other writers believe that Lord Salisbury's hand was forced by Chamberlain, who disapproved of the prime minister's attempts to reach an agreement with France on matters touching Egypt and the Nile. When the Italians appealed for help Chamberlain is supposed to have won over the cabinet with the suggestion: " Let's go to Dongola." [48]

The explanation of the British decision, fraught as it was with serious consequences, should, in all probability, be sought in other directions. Lord Salisbury, it has been already pointed out, appreciated the fact that ultimately the Nile Valley must be reconquered, but he hoped that action could be postponed until the Uganda Railway was finished and an advance from Egypt could be supplemented by an advance from the south. Lord Cromer also felt strongly about the eventual reconquest of the Sudan, but he did not want to see the attempt made until Egypt was financially and militarily prepared, and this, he believed, would not be the fact for many years to come. There was a growing agitation for action in England, due to the obvious plans of France and the Congo State. Influential people like Sir Samuel Baker and Sir Frederick Lugard were constantly stressing the dangers of delay. " It is imperative to make an advance from Uganda and occupy the Nile Valley as far as Fashoda, together with the whole of the Bahr-el-Ghazal province . . ." wrote the latter. " Simultaneously with the advance from the south it would be advisable to make a forward movement from Egypt." [49]

[46] *Die Grosse Politik*, XI, nos. 2772–6.
[47] Winston Churchill: *The River War* (London, 1899), pp. 167–9.
[48] Charles à Court Repington: *Vestigia* (Boston, 1919), p. 105.
[49] Sir Frederick Lugard: " England and France in the Nile Valley " (*National Review*, July,

And yet the government did not act. As late as November 1895 Cromer was told " that there was not any present prospect of the government consenting to the despatch of a military expedition into the Soudan." [50] It was only the critical condition of the Italians in Abyssinia that forced the reconsideration of the decision in January 1896. The British, for reasons already explained, were not prepared to allow the Italians to occupy Zeila and launch an attack upon Harrar. They were probably not too much worried by the Italian-Abyssinian situation in any case. What troubled them was rather the renewed activity of the dervishes. On January 5 the Italian ambassador at St. Petersburg reported that there was an agreement between Menelik and the Khalifa to launch a simultaneous attack upon the Italian position. Menelik's adviser, Alfred Ilg, in an interview later, hinted that there was actually an understanding of this sort.[51] At all events the dervishes began to concentrate in great numbers near Kassala, the farthest Italian outpost in the Sudan, a most important commercial and strategic position half-way between Khartum and Massowa, which had been occupied by the Italians in July 1894 in pursuance of the Anglo-Italian agreements of 1891.

The fall of Kassala would have been a very serious matter for the British, as for the Italian government. Lord Cromer happened to be in London and the matter was debated at length. The British military authorities evidently favored an advance up the Nile in order to create a diversion, while Cromer argued that it would be cheaper and more effective to start out from Suakim and make for Kassala itself. In the end it was decided to wait and see whether the dervishes would actually begin operations. The Italians kept appealing for aid and even offered to turn over Kassala to the British, but Salisbury rejected these proposals and matters took their course.[52] It was not until the very last days of February 1896 that authentic information arrived concerning the concentration of the dervish forces in front of Kassala. The Adua disaster followed almost immediately. The Italian appeals for help became more and more insistent. But, as we have seen, Lord Salisbury paid little attention to them. In the meanwhile discussions were going on at Cairo between Cromer, Kitchener and the British military attaché at Rome, who had been sent off to Egypt on special mission. These gentlemen agreed that something had to be done, and decided to send a force from Tokar to Kassala to take over the place from the Italians.[53] The decision was telegraphed to Lord Salisbury without much hope that the London government would approve. Nothing more was heard until, at 3 A.M. on March 13, Kitchener received a telegram telling him of the decision to advance from Wadi Halfa to Akasheh and Dongola. No doubt this decision

---

1895, pp. 609–22); see also Thomas D. Murray and A. Silva White: *Sir Samuel Baker, a Memoir* (London, 1895), chap. xxvii, passim.　　[50] Cromer: *Modern Egypt* (New York, 1908), II, p. 82.

[51] Crispi: *La Prima Guerra d'Africa*, p. 369; London *Times*, March 9, 1896.

[52] Cromer, op. cit., II, p. 83; Rennell Rodd: *Social and Diplomatic Memoirs*, pp. 85–6; Sir George Arthur: *Life of Lord Kitchener* (London, 1920), I. p. 187; *Die Grosse Politik*, XI, no. 2776.

[53] *Die Grosse Politik*, XI, no. 2709; Wilfrid S. Blunt: *My Diaries* (New York, 1919), I, p. 273: London *Times*, March 12 (Cairo, March 11), 1896.

caused some surprise and excitement in the inner circles of the British residency, but it can hardly have been the bolt from the blue as described by English writers.[54]

How the British cabinet came to its decision it is hard to say. All we know is that the cabinet met several times, and that Lord Wolseley and General Grenfell attended some of these meetings. Both Salisbury and Chamberlain were convinced that some sort of advance had become necessary, but they both favored a moderate program and were against any operations that would cost more than the Egyptian government could afford. Chamberlain's distrust of Kitchener and the officials at Cairo was shared by Salisbury, who wrote on March 12: " I earnestly pressed on Lansdowne that he must be prepared to sit heavily on Kitchener and on his own military advisers." [55] But a decision had to be arrived at when an Italian telegram of March 10 reported that there were 10,000 dervishes before Kassala, that they had attacked on the morning of March 8 and that communications were interrupted.[56] The question was simply this: Should the advance be made from Suakim or Tokar, as Cromer and Kitchener wished, or from Wadi Halfa? It seems likely that both Wolseley and Grenfell favored the Nile route, though the Suakim route would have brought aid to Kassala more promptly. But the main thing was that Salisbury himself favored an advance toward Dongola. He explained this himself in a letter to Cromer of March 13, in which he declared that the cabinet's action " was inspired specially by a desire to help the Italians at Kassala, and to prevent the dervishes from winning a conspicuous success which might have far-reaching results. In addition, we desired to kill two birds with one stone, and to use the same military effort to plant the foot of Egypt farther up the Nile. For this reason we preferred it to any movement from Suakim or in the direction of Kassala, because there would be no ulterior profit in these movements." [57]

Salisbury's letter would indicate that at bottom it was anxiety for the Sudan that determined him. Whether he had gotten wind of the Marchand mission we do not know, but by this time the French designs, whatever the French plans, had become only too much advertised. In short, then, the prime minister was intent on protection of the great River. One of the best-informed writers on Egyptian affairs, H. D. Traill, put this side of the matter succinctly in a contemporary article when he said:

[Egypt's] " very lifeblood is drawn from sources which, now for the first time in the long ages of her history, are being brought within the reach of powerful European states, and might pass under the control of some great Power which

[54] Cromer, op. cit., II, pp. 83–4; Rodd, op. cit., III, pp. 86–7; Arthur, op. cit., I, pp. 187–8; Blunt, op. cit., I, pp. 271, 280.

[55] Garvin: Life of Chamberlain, III, pp. 169 ff.; Memoirs of Field-Marshal Lord Grenfell (London, n.d.), pp. 124–5.

[56] See statements of Salisbury and Curzon in parliament, March 17 and March 20 (Hansard, Series IV, vol. XXXVIII, pp. 1113 ff., 1174, 1458–9).

[57] Marquess of Zetland: Lord Cromer, p. 223; Letters of Queen Victoria, III, pp. 33, 37.

could lay an arresting finger on its pulse at will. It would not take much effort on the part of modern engineering science in the hands of an enemy to spread famine and death along the whole Nile Valley. . . . Egypt cannot afford to dispense with the protection of a great Power on the North, when another such Power might any day approach her from the southward and obtain command of the very seat of her life." [58]

The government had some difficulty in explaining to parliament the reasons for the sudden advance up the Nile. As fate would have it, Cromer's annual report for 1895, with the statement that the dervishes had maintained " a strictly defensive attitude," was published on March 13, the very day on which the news of the advance was given out. That made it hard to argue the case for the government, especially when it was proposed to remove the dervish menace at Kassala by advancing from Wadi Halfa. Curzon therefore spoke feelingly of the Italians as " a nation of gallant soldiers and staunch allies," and made the most of the fact that " the cause of civilization in Africa was at stake." The opposition refused to be convinced. Labouchere ridiculed the story of the dervish menace and told the government to its face that the real reason for action was the desire to secure the Sudan and thus have a further excuse for retaining Egypt. Sir Charles Dilke pointed out that the advance to Dongola could hardly be expected to help the Italians at Kassala, which was five hundred miles away. [59]

This doubt as to the efficacy of British aid was shared in Rome, but the Italians were grateful for even a show of friendship. The British " alliance " was very valuable to them and so, when the garrison at Kassala succeeded in turning back a dervish attack on April 2, it was decided to hold the place at least until autumn, despite the fact that the foreign minister and the new governor of Eritrea were opposed. [60] Emperor William had used all his influence to assure this decision. He was immensely pleased with recent developments, which he ascribed to the happy inspiration of the talk with Lascelles. There was no doubt in his mind that the Egyptian troops would be thoroughly trounced by the dervishes and that the English themselves would have to interfere. " My purpose has been attained," he noted; " England has proceeded to take action and has compromised herself; the flirtation with Gallo-Russia is ended, and that is all I wanted." Or again: " The English will yet come to us crawling on their knees if only we let them struggle long enough." [61]

The situation as it presented itself in the middle of March elicited from Sir Cecil Spring Rice, at that time connected with the Berlin embassy, the sad remark: " Germany has, through Egypt, our tail between her teeth and can give it a bite whenever we don't do what she wants." There was much truth in this, as

[58] H. D. Traill: " The Burden of Egypt " (*Nineteenth Century*, April, 1896, pp. 544–56). p. 556; see also his book *England, Egypt and the Sudan* (London, 1900), p. 149.

[59] *Hansard*, Series IV, vol. XXXVIII, pp. 1027–60.

[60] *Die Grosse Politik*, XI, nos. 2780, 2782, 2783, 2784, 2785.

[61] Hohenlohe, op. cit., p. 199; *Die Grosse Politik*, XI, no. 2713; *Letters of Cecil Spring Rice* I, pp. 201–2.

Bismarck had demonstrated on many an occasion. No doubt realization of the fact had had something to do with Salisbury's hesitancy and with his attempts to come to an agreement with France in the days after the Kruger telegram. But now he had committed himself. German good will was absolutely indispensable, for it was planned to pay for the Dongola expedition from Egyptian funds. The only funds available were those in the control of the International Debt Commission, and these funds could be used only with the consent of the powers. It could be safely assumed that Italy would support the British demand and that France and Russia would oppose it. Austria's attitude would in all probability depend somewhat on Germany's. To assure a majority vote, therefore, the support of Germany was essential. The British premier made the necessary advances. On March 13 he replied to the points raised by the Emperor in his talk with Lascelles. " He desired," so he said, " to remain on a footing of friendship with Germany as in times past. England would ' lean ' to the Triple Alliance, but without ever promising or obligating herself to making war in some future eventuality." [62]

Two days later the British government appealed to the powers for their consent to the appropriation of £500,000 from the Egyptian reserve fund. A few days later, after a special request from the Italian government, the German government gave its consent, while the Russian government at the same time refused its approval. Prince Lobanov, the foreign minister, disillusioned by the Armenian entente and now become deeply suspicious of British designs against the Turkish Empire, was clearly determined to frustrate British policy in Egypt in every conceivable way. With France matters were somewhat more complicated. The announcement of the Dongola expedition was, naturally, a terrific shock, especially to Baron Courcel, who had been carrying on discussions with Salisbury looking to a settlement of the whole Egyptian question. At first it was announced that he would go on prolonged leave of absence, but in a few days he was back in London. So far as one can deduce from the very meagre source material it seems that Courcel was a convinced and ardent advocate of an agreement with England and that the foreign minister, Berthelot, had been converted to this viewpoint. But the same was evidently not true of President Faure and M. Bourgeois, the prime minister. It was the latter, according to the German ambassador, who caused a communiqué to be inserted in the *Temps* on March 18 saying that Berthelot, in conversation with Lord Dufferin, had called the ambassador's attention " to the gravity of the consequences " of the Dongola expedition. Berthelot in private denied that such minatory language had been used. It seems that he had nothing to do with the communiqué. Bourgeois wanted to arouse public feeling in order to gain support for his policy in Madagascar and for his domestic program. Clearly pressure was being brought upon him by the Russian ambassador, and he in turn was bringing pressure upon Berthelot. In the Chamber on March 19 the foreign minister

---

[62] *Die Grosse Politik,* XI, no. 2779.

spoke of the Dongola project as " essentially offensive and poorly defined," and indicated that France would probably refuse to sanction the financing of it from the reserve fund, the more so as it might eventually consume all the available money and would in any case prolong the British occupation of Egypt. And yet Courcel appears to have had some further conversation with Salisbury and to have tried to extract concessions in the matter of the evacuation of Egypt in return for French sanction to the use of the reserve fund. Nothing came of this. On March 31 Berthelot was forced to resign, it is said at the insistence of the Russian ambassador.[63]

It was not until March 26 that the French government definitely refused its sanction to the use of the reserve fund for the financing of the Dongola expedition. Of course, with the support of the German, Austrian and Italian representatives the British still had a majority vote, which sufficed them. But, according to the French and Russian view, this was not adequate; a *unanimous* vote was necessary. The matter was carried before the mixed tribunals, which on June 8 decided in favor of the French and Russian view. The British appealed, but on December 2, 1896 judgment was again passed against them. By that time, however, the British government was prepared. It advanced the money to the Egyptian government and thereby established a certain claim upon the Egyptian conquests, as the Emperor William had long before anticipated.[64]

Pending litigation the French and Russians, especially the former, were not idle. At the end of April 1896 the Bourgeois cabinet fell from power and was succeeded by a ministry under the leadership of Méline, with Hanotaux once more at the foreign office. Hanotaux was generally regarded as a strong protagonist of the alliance with Russia, but the evidence would indicate that he set very distinct limits to the agreement and France's obligations under its terms. It seems that some efforts were made in April and May to induce the Turkish government to reopen the question of the evacuation of Egypt and to take a more active part by sending Turkish troops to Suakim. Nothing came of these efforts to embarrass the British.[65]

More forceful and dangerous was the policy followed by Prince Lobanov, the Russian foreign minister. Lobanov was a firm believer in Russia's mission in the Far East, and was completely engrossed by the prospects of expansion in China. His aim was, as the Armenian crisis had shown, to do nothing in the

---

[63] *Die Grosse Politik*, XI, nos. 2697–2708, 2717–22; *Bulletin du Comité de l'Afrique Française*, April, 1896, p. 133; Gabriel Hanotaux: *Fachoda*, pp. 101–3; Kossatz, op. cit., pp. 5–6.

[64] Cromer: *Modern Egypt*, II, pp. 85 ff.; Charles de Freycinet: *La Question d'Égypte* (Paris, 1905), pp. 383–8; Pierre Crabitès: *The Winning of the Sudan* (London, 1934), chap. x; the technicalities and the law of the problem are well dealt with by Nicolas Politis: " La Caisse de la Dette Égyptienne, ses Pouvoirs et sa Responsabilité " (*Revue Générale de Droit International Public*, III, 1896, pp. 245–53), and by H. Babled: " Le Procès de la Caisse de la Dette Égyptienne devant la Cour Mixte d'Alexandrie " (ibid., pp. 537–57); the documents were published in *Egypt No. 1* (*1897*).

[65] Rodd, op. cit., p. 92; *Die Grosse Politik*, XI, no. 2734; Georges Lachapelle: *Le Ministère Méline* (Paris, 1928), pp. 56–7.

Near East beyond watching and guarding against British designs against the Sultan. Now the problem of Russian expansion in the Far East was largely a problem of communications. The Transsiberian Railway was under construction, but it would take years before even a single-track system was in running order. Until then everything would depend upon the long sea route, through the Baltic and North Seas, across the Mediterranean, through Suez and the Red Sea into the Indian Ocean. A very long journey indeed, which could be materially shortened if Russia could open the Bosporus and the Dardanelles for her warships and transports and if she could be guaranteed unobstructed passage through the Suez Canal at all times.

These few words will explain the basis of Lobanov's policy in 1896. With regard to the Straits there was a good prospect of attaining the Russian wishes so long as Russia and Turkey were on such good terms, and provided always that the other powers could be brought to sanction the Russian program. The trouble, however, had always been that the Russians wanted the Straits opened only to their own warships, while they remained closed to the ships of Russia's enemies. It is clear from the contemporary documents that an arrangement might have been made not only with Germany but with England on the basis of complete opening to the warships of *all* nations in times of peace, and Lobanov, just before his death in August 1896, seems to have toyed with this as a possible solution. But in the eyes of most Russian statesmen any such plan, involving as it did the abandonment of the principle of the Black Sea as a *mare clausum,* meant merely exposing Russia to attack. The real aim should be to open for Russia alone, but that implied almost certain opposition on the part of the other powers, even of Russia's ally, France. Lobanov discussed the matter on several occasions with M. Hanotaux, but always found him ill disposed toward the raising of the troublesome question. France was not eager to have the Russians in the Mediterranean, which she liked to think of as a French lake.[66]

With the Suez Canal the situation was somewhat different. Its status in international law had been often discussed but was still very uncertain. All the powers were interested in the guarantee of free passage for the merchant ships and warships of all nations in time of war as in time of peace. Great Britain was, if anything, more concerned in the enforcement of these principles than any other power, in view of the importance of the Canal for her communications with Asia. Her interest was, in fact, so great that she hardly trusted any other power with the execution of such regulations. The occupation of Egypt in 1882 was unquestionably due in part to anxiety for control of the Canal. The other governments, however, looked upon British command of the passage as an unwarranted and unsatisfactory arrangement. They constantly pressed for inter-

---

[66] Gabriel Hanotaux: *Histoire Illustrée de la Guerre de 1914* (Paris, 1915), I, p. 203; Idem: " La Prétendue Conjuration Franco-Russe " (*Revue des Deux Mondes,* January 15, 1896); *Die Grosse Politik,* XI, no. 2676; XII, nos. 2916–22; XVIII, no. 5916.

national control of the passage to insure its freedom. In 1885 a conference had been held on the subject at Paris, and the essential difference of view had immediately become evident. A draft convention was finally worked out, but the British delegate, Sir Julian Pauncefote, practically nullified its value for the other powers by adding a reservation to the effect that the convention did not limit the freedom of action of England so long as she was in occupation of Egypt. This reservation was formally notified to the powers by Lord Salisbury in 1887. By it the question of the Canal became part and parcel of the problem of the evacuation of Egypt. After the failure of the Drummond Wolff Convention in 1887 negotiations were reopened and another agreement was come to in October 1888. This new document represented some concession to France, for it recognized a very mild form of international supervision. All the consular agents at Cairo were to meet on the request of any three of them in case the Canal was threatened, and were to inform the Egyptian government of the danger; but in any case they were to convene once a year to "take note of the due execution of the treaty." The new convention was signed and ratified by all the great powers, but its importance was reduced to almost nothing by the British reservation of 1885. In practice it was in abeyance so long as the British continued in occupation. Ten years later an expert of the British foreign office could not find that it had ever been distinctly stated whether the Suez Canal Treaty was or was not in operation. In other words, from the standpoint of the other powers the Canal was in Egyptian, that is, in British control — a thoroughly unsatisfactory situation.[67]

Lobanov, intent on securing communications with the Far East, was determined to put an end to this anomalous condition of affairs. He exploited the Russian religious interest in Abyssinia to the full, and it was thought by many that he envisaged the establishment of a Russian base on the Red Sea. With respect to the Suez Canal he contemplated the convocation of an international conference that would replace British guarantee of free passage by control by all the interested powers. He could count upon the support of France, hitherto the power chiefly concerned. But the support of France alone was of little value. It was necessary to win over Germany to assure success. The greatest efforts were made in this direction throughout the spring and summer of 1896. To overcome German suspicions of France the Russians gave the most explicit assurances: "Rest assured that so long as you follow a policy of peace in Europe you can count on us and through us upon France, which will not again risk isolation," said the Russian ambassador at Berlin. "We will guarantee France's attitude." On other occasions it was pointed out to the Germans that they too had a great interest in Suez and that they ought to be prepared to co-operate against England in Egyptian affairs. Even the French made advances. Baron

---

[67] *British Documents on the Origins of the War,* I, no. 380; Sir James Headlam-Morley: *Studies in Diplomatic History* (London, 1930), pp. 75–81; and the very convenient summary in Charles W. Hallberg: *The Suez Canal* (New York, 1931), chap. xvii, passim.

Courcel continually pressed upon Hatzfeldt the desirability of an entente on special questions, and Hanotaux himself seems to have carried on serious negotiations through the medium of prominent French and German journalists. But the German attitude was unpromising. The reply of the foreign office to the sounding of the Russians and the French was always the same: It had been shown by the Transvaal incident that France was still dominated by the thought of revenge and that she was, therefore, untrustworthy. The situation was not such that the Germans would feel justified in making a radical change in their policy.[68]

Emperor William made full use of the Russian designs in his communications with British representatives in Berlin, and the evidence would indicate that the situation was viewed with anything but equanimity in London. Salisbury hoped that the Russians would not go so far as to convene a conference, but said to the German ambassador that he felt sure Austria and Italy, and he hoped Germany too would be on the British side. Nevertheless he made systematic efforts to come to some sort of understanding with the French and the Russians. In June the Prince of Battenberg was sent to St. Petersburg, apparently to call the Tsar's attention to the policy of Lobanov and the dangers which it involved. He accomplished nothing, but was told by Lobanov himself that Russia's interests required free navigation in the Suez Canal and the Red Sea. Thereupon Salisbury approached the French ambassador, indicating that modification or withdrawal of the British reservation regarding the Canal Convention of 1888 might be possible: " It was never originally intended by us and certainly would not now be used for the purpose of jeopardising the neutrality of the Canal." But nothing seems to have come of these suggestions and advances. It was fortunate for the English that Lobanov, leader of the anti-British campaign, died suddenly late in August. It had already been arranged that the Tsar should pay a family visit to the Queen at Balmoral in the last days of September. All possible efforts were made to magnify the event and to enlist the Tsar in the cause of better Anglo-Russian relations. Lord Salisbury himself went to Balmoral and had a long talk with the young Tsar. But Nicholas kept his counsel and refused to go beyond general expressions of good will. Efforts were made by Queen Victoria to tempt him with some prospect of concessions in the matter of the Straits, but the Tsar evaded discussion even of this all-important matter. In the meanwhile Salisbury began conversations with M. de Staal, the Russian ambassador. He thought he could deduce from his talks with the Tsar, he said, that Russia's interest centered upon the Straits question. The existing régime was ambiguous and not durable. No doubt a solution of the problem according to the wishes of Russia would meet with the opposition of Europe. But England would not oppose it. The British government would be ready to negotiate. A month later, in the middle of November, he returned to

---

[68] *Die Grosse Politik,* XI, nos. 2728–46, 2837–44; Meyendorff: *Correspondance de M. de Staal,* II, pp. 315–8; Nicolas Notovich: *L'Europe et l'Égypte* (Paris, 1898), chap. x.

the charge. England, he declared, would be prepared to annul the reservation to the Suez Canal Treaty and would be willing to consider a Russian request for guarantees of the free passage of the Canal at all times, if only the evacuation of Egypt were left out of the discussion.[69]

Nothing came of Salisbury's advances to Russia, far-reaching and important though they were. The explanation seems to be that the Russians feared British plans in the Near East and distrusted the offers made. Furthermore, they had to remember their alliance with France and the possible effects of an arrangement regarding Egypt. Besides, the interest of the Russian government had turned to the Far East, and the main thought in St. Petersburg was to uphold the status quo in the Ottoman Empire. But all this does not detract from the significance of these little-known negotiations. They show beyond the possibility of doubt that Salisbury, had he been able, would have made an agreement with Russia even in 1896.

The great disaster at Adua and the hurried announcement of the Dongola expedition came as a great shock to Europe and profoundly affected the international alignments. In their own interest the British felt obliged to come to the assistance of the Italians. This involved a rupture of conversations with the French and gave the Russians an excellent opportunity to press the Paris government into a more anti-English policy than either Hanotaux or Courcel would have liked. It seems fairly clear that the French were rather disappointed by the Franco-Russian Alliance, which promised them little good and involved France in the danger of being dragged into war with Britain. Still, they were more than ever dependent on the connexion with Russia as the prospect of an arrangement with England faded. The Tsar's coronation at Moscow in May 1896 was celebrated with great enthusiasm in Paris, and prompted the German ambassador to remark that the French acted as though France were joined to Russia in a personal union under one Emperor.[70] The Tsar's first visit to Paris in October of the same year was made the occasion for the most rhapsodical outbursts. Madame Adam, one of the oldest protagonists of the Alliance, declared it to be " a mystical union transcending ordinary human associations." To some it seemed as though the French authorities actually blushed " at the thought of France being a Republic." The extremists of course seized the opportunity to remind the Tsar that the French hoped for aid in the recovery of the lost provinces. Clemenceau complained that " the peace of the *status quo* on which the alliance is reputed to be based is for us a peace of dismemberment, a German peace." But the Russians had no thought of encouraging a French war of revenge. Inspired articles in the press urged moderation and caution, and the

---

[69] Reports of Staal, October 3 and November 11, quoted by V. Khvostov: " Blishni-Vostochnyi Krizis, 1895-1897 " (*Istorik Marksist*, XIII, 1929, pp. 19-54), pp. 35-8. See also *Die Grosse Politik*, XI, nos. 2733, 2737, XII, no. 3078; *British Documents on the Origins of the War*, I, no. 380; Lee: *Edward VII*, I, pp. 695 ff.; *Letters of Queen Victoria*, III, pp. 68-75, 82-6, 102; Meyendorff: *Correspondance de M. de Staal*, II, pp. 321-2.

[70] *Die Grosse Politik*, XI, no. 2853. See also nos. 2846, 2848, 2854.

more balanced writers admitted that the alliance, far from signifying war, obliged France to maintain better relations with Germany. According to M. Leroy-Beaulieu the Tsar's visit was a promise of peace based upon a tacit acquiescence in the treaties, whether France liked them or not.[71] There was no gainsaying the fact that France had enlisted in the service of the Tsar, that she was required to shelve all thoughts of revenge, that she was prevented from cultivating to the full the opportunities for an agreement with England, and that she was obliged to make at least some show of effort in behalf of better relations with Germany.

While the developments of March drove France further into the arms of Russia, they served to fortify the tottering Triple Alliance. The Kruger telegram episode had called forth pretty acrimonious words between the capitals of the central powers. It is certain that the Alliance would not have long withstood a permanent estrangement between England and Germany. The announcement of the Dongola expedition, even if it meant only ostensible aid to the stricken Italians, was at least a word of comfort. Emperor William hastened to Italy and persuaded King Humbert to give up all ideas of seeking revenge for the Adua catastrophe. Count Goluchowski came to Berlin and expressed his satisfaction that England and Germany had again made up, at least after a fashion. There was no longer serious danger that the Triple Alliance would be denounced. Rudini made known his determination to continue the connexion. He made some effort to renew the clause stating that the agreement was not directed against England. This the Germans refused to consider, on the plea that the clause was neither necessary nor desirable. The *casus foederis* would arise only if England attacked together with another power, and an Anglo-French or Anglo-Russian combination was out of the question. Besides, if the clause were included it would give the Alliance entirely too anti-French and anti-Russian an aspect. Rudini finally accepted the argument, but he took care in public to announce that the agreement with England was " the cornerstone of Italy's other alliances," and that " friendly relations with England were the natural complement of the Triple Alliance." [72]

But even though the Triple Alliance was allowed to run on for six more years this did not imply that the Alliance was what it had been in the days of Bismarck and Crispi. The German foreign office, if not the Emperor, was still filled with suspicion of the British and of British designs, and was the more intent, therefore, on the cultivation of good relations with Russia. The Germans did not, it is true, follow the Russian suggestions of action against England in the Suez and Egyptian questions, but relations were cordial nevertheless. In

---

[71] See the extracts from the press in Chiala: *Pagine di Storia Contemporanea*, III, pp. 647 ff., and in Georges Michon: *The Franco-Russian Alliance*, pp. 82 ff.

[72] *Die Grosse Politik*, XI, nos. 2680, 2784, 2801–7; Pribram: *Secret Treaties of Austria-Hungary*, II, pp. 107–12; Hohenlohe, op. cit., pp. 208 ff.; Chiala, op. cit., III, pp. 621 ff.; Gaetano Salvemini: " La Triple Alliance " (*Revue des Nations Latines*, 1916, I, pp. 481–510).

September, before going to Balmoral and Paris, Tsar Nicholas and his ministers conferred with Emperor William and Hohenlohe in Silesia, and Lobanov went on to Vienna. The result of the discussions was very satisfactory. The Tsar went so far as to promise to take up with the French government the idea of a continental combination to resist the increasing invasion of American foodstuffs. On his return from Paris he stopped for some time with his relatives in Darmstadt, where Emperor William visited him again. The Tsar made it fairly evident that he could have dispensed with this meeting, but the discussion, which did not go beyond innocuous generalities, in no wise compromised the friendly relations between the two rulers and their governments. The Germans, while avoiding all commitments and continuing their support of the British in Egyptian affairs, were keeping intact the wire to St. Petersburg, weak though it was.[78]

The Italians were no more prepared than were the Germans to stake everything on the Triple Alliance. The pressure of the French and the Russians in the Abyssinian affair had been very marked and very painful. Britain's good will was uncertain, and depended to a large extent upon Anglo-German relations, which were unaccountable. Rudini saw clearly enough, as he had in 1891, that Italy could not afford to keep up the antagonism to France. The tariff war that had been going on for years was simply causing havoc and ruin. A tariff arrangement, he told the German ambassador on March 17, was a question of life and death. For the time being the liquidation of the Abyssinian adventure took up all of the minister's time, but in addressing the Chamber on May 25 he made it clear that the Triple Alliance did not preclude the establishment of friendly relations with France and Russia, and that he meant to devote himself to this end.[74]

Rudini's statement was the prelude to the opening of negotiations in Paris, in the early days of June. The French government, which in 1891 had rejected Rudini's advances until Italy should have left the Triple Alliance, had thought better of it, and was quite prepared to consider proposals in a conciliatory spirit. The Italian ambassador, Count Tornielli, was told frankly that the time had not yet come for a tariff agreement. The high wave of protectionism, on which the Méline cabinet had been carried into power, made an arrangement impracticable for the time being. But the French were anxious for an agreement with regard to Italian rights in Tunis, and they were willing to combine with such an agreement certain concessions in the matter of navigation. The Italians had concluded a commercial treaty with the Bey of Tunis in 1868 which gave them a privileged position in the regency. This treaty had a term of twenty-four years, and was to continue unless denounced one year in advance. The date for denunciation was September 29, 1895 and the date for expiration one year later.

[78] Die Grosse Politik, XI, nos. 2861, 2862, 2868; Hohenlohe, op. cit., pp. 258, 261, 268; Waldersee: Denkwürdigkeiten, II, pp. 373-4.

[74] Die Grosse Politik, XI, no. 2819; Chiala, op. cit., pp. 622 ff., 629-30; Albert Billot: La France et l'Italie (Paris, 1905), II, pp. 333-4.

In August 1895 the French government had served due notice, acting as the representative of the Tunisian government. Crispi had taken the attitude that this action was in itself inadmissible and that in any case, if the Treaty lapsed, Italy could resurrect her rights under the capitulations and under previous agreements.

The legality of this view was open to question. Politically it was futile to put it forward, for Italy could not hope to find support from other powers. England, which had a perpetual treaty with Tunis and was therefore in a much stronger position, had in January 1896 indicated readiness to make new arrangements with France. The Germans were but little interested and refused to subscribe to the Italian argumentation. The Austrians, always anxious to maintain at least cordial relations with France, were beginning to negotiate secretly, and in August 1896 concluded an agreement by which, first of all the great powers, Austria recognized the French protectorate over Tunis. Under these circumstances Rudini was wise in giving up the extreme standpoint of Crispi and making the best of a rather poor position. Negotiations were opened, as aforesaid, early in June. They made little headway, even when, in July, the Marchese Visconti-Venosta, old Cavourian and friend of France, succeeded the Duke di Sermoneta at the Italian foreign office. It is hardly necessary to follow the discussions in detail here, the more so as the official papers on the subject have never been published. Suffice it to say that at the last minute, just before the expiration of the Treaty on September 29, an agreement was reached, the substance of which was that Italy tacitly recognized the French protectorate and accepted for herself the status of a most favored nation in Tunis. The new agreement on navigation granted some alleviation of the restrictions that had been placed by the two powers on commerce between the ports of their respective states, and the whole Treaty was regarded by the Italians, evidently with good right, as the prelude to a more far-reaching arrangement on tariff matters.[75]

While France and Italy were gradually giving up the old hostility, efforts were being made to effect a rapprochement between Russia and Italy also. The details of this policy are unknown. So far as one can deduce from the very scant material it seems that after the failure of the first Italian efforts to conclude peace with Menelik, the Abyssinian King of Kings sent the notorious Russian agent, Leontiev, to St. Petersburg with the request that Russia offer her mediation. What the Italian reply was we do not know. But Leontiev himself came to Italy in the summer, and was received by Rudini. He accompanied Lobanov when the latter visited Vienna in August, and had several conversations with the Italian ambassador, Count Nigra. It appears that Visconti-Venosta hoped and desired that Tsar Nicholas would visit Italy as well as the other European capitals on his autumn journey and that, even after this scheme fell through, he hoped for a visit in the spring. The new contact be-

---

[75] Billot, op. cit., II, Book III, chap. ii; *Die Grosse Politik,* XI, nos. 2820–3; Chiala, op. cit., III, pp. 641 ff.

tween Russia and Italy was evidently not of a far-reaching nature, but it was symptomatic, and as such is worth mentioning.[76]

Professor Salvemini, the eminent Italian historian, speaking of this period, refers to the " interpenetration of alliances." The phrase is a very descriptive and entirely accurate one. The new extra-European interests of the powers had led to the undermining of the old alliance system as it had been raised by Bismarck. It troubled even the new Franco-Russian combination. European alignments no longer sufficed for the broader needs of world policy. The members of both groups attempted to avoid sharp antagonisms in Europe and to secure aid for their African schemes. Under the circumstances it was natural that England should feel the brunt of the attack, for her world interests were as wide as those of all the others put together. And so it was that the second phase of the struggle for the Nile, the Dongola phase, opened wider the rift between England on the one hand and France and Russia on the other. Despite the Kruger episode the British were driven into closer relationship with the Triple Alliance. But the old cordiality was gone. On all sides it was understood that there should be no sentiment. It was a case of everyone for himself and the devil take the hindmost. But in the fog of uncertainty the Germans were in the most favorable position. Through no brilliant accomplishment of their own, but through chance, they were able to follow a policy of having two irons in the fire. Britain needed them in order to frustrate the action of the Franco-Russian Alliance in the Egyptian and Suez questions. Russia needed them in order to turn the scales against England. Britain's favor helped to keep the Italians and the Austrians loyal. Russia's courtship brought with it better relations with France. Underneath all was suspicion, even in Anglo-German relations. But on the surface Germany was still, as in the days of Bismarck and before the conclusion of the Franco-Russian Alliance, the arbiter of Europe.

BIBLIOGRAPHICAL NOTE

DOCUMENTARY SOURCES

Die Grosse Politik der Europäischen Kabinette, 1871–1914. Volume XI. chapter lxv: England's refusal to integrate the Mediterranean Agreement; chapter lxvi: Germany, Austria and the Triple Alliance; chapter lxvii: The Egyptian Question and the Anglo-French relationship; chapter lxviii: Italy and Abyssinia; chapter lxix: The renewal of the Triple Alliance; chapter lxx: Franco-German relations; chapter lxxi: The Franco-Russian Alliance. Volume XII. chapter lxxiv: The Straits Question. The German documents are the most important single source for this period, the more so as other documentary material is very meagre indeed.

---

[76] *Die Grosse Politik*, XI, nos. 2785, 2786, 2788, 2791, 2793, 2813; Carlo Richelmy: " Lettere inedite di Costantino Nigra " (*Nuova Antologia*, November 16, 1928, pp. 155–61).

Ministero degli Affari Esteri. Avvenimenti d'Africa, Gennaio 1895–Marzo, 1896.
A most interesting and valuable Italian Green Book, published by the Rudini
government in April 1896, it is said without consultation with the British government. The documents here given are much less selective than those in most
official publications, and throw much light not only on Crispi's policy, but upon
Italian relations with England.

PRIBRAM, ALFRED F.: *The Secret Treaties of Austria-Hungary, 1879–1914.* Two
volumes. Cambridge, 1920–1921. Based upon the documents in the Austrian
archives, Pribram's second volume contains a good succinct account of the renewal of the Triple Alliance in 1896.

MEMOIRS, AUTOBIOGRAPHIES, BIOGRAPHIES, AND LETTERS

The Letters of Queen Victoria. Edited by George E. Buckle. Third Series, volumes II and III. New York, 1931–1932. The concluding volumes of the Victoria
correspondence, covering the years 1891–1901. Not particularly full, but of great
value on certain points.

GARVIN, J. L.: *Life of Joseph Chamberlain.* Volume III. London, 1934. Adds
very little on this subject.

LEE, SIR SIDNEY: *Edward VII.* Two volumes. New York, 1925–1927. Of no
great interest for the period discussed in this chapter, though there is some
material on Anglo-Russian relations.

GARDINER, A. G.: *The Life of Sir William Harcourt.* Two volumes. London,
1923. One of the best studies of the Rosebery period, very full on matters of
foreign policy.

ZETLAND, MARQUESS OF: *Lord Cromer.* London, 1932. Based upon the Cromer
papers, an excellent and informing biography with some new material.

RODD, SIR JAMES RENNELL: *Social and Diplomatic Memoirs.* Three volumes.
London, 1922. Rodd was one of the chief assistants of Lord Cromer, and his
memoirs are an important source for the history of the Egyptian question in
these years.

The Letters and Friendships of Sir Cecil Spring Rice. Edited by Stephen Gwynn.
Two volumes. London, 1929. Spring Rice was secretary of the British embassy
at Berlin. His letters and notes reflect a man of keen insight and considerable
humor.

GREY OF FALLODON, VISCOUNT: *Twenty-Five Years.* Two volumes. New York,
1925. In 1894–1895 Grey was undersecretary for foreign affairs. His memoirs
reveal little, though there is an important account of the famous Grey statement
of March 1895.

MACDIARMID, D. S.: *The Life of Lieutenant-General Sir James Moncrieff Grierson.* London, 1923. Grierson was British military attaché at Berlin. This book is carelessly written and tells chiefly of the lighter side of Grierson's life. Nevertheless it records a number of important conversations.

BLUNT, WILFRID S.: *My Diaries.* Two volumes. New York, 1919. Blunt was immensely interested in Egyptian affairs and had excellent contacts in Cairo. His day by day entries are therefore of very considerable interest.

ARTHUR, SIR GEORGE: *Life of Lord Kitchener.* Three volumes. London, 1920. The authorized biography of Kitchener, who in 1896 was Sirdar of the Egyptian army. Contains some interesting side lights.

Memoirs of Francesco Crispi. Edited by T. Palamenghi-Crispi. Three volumes. New York, 1912–1914. The third volume of Crispi's memoirs contains some material, but for this period his book on the African war is far more important.

CRISPI, FRANCESCO: *La Prima Guerra d'Africa.* Milan, 1914. Primarily a collection of letters and documents. A book of the highest value for the study of the Italian policy in Abyssinia.

BARATIERI, ORESTE: *Memorie d'Africa, 1892–1896.* Turin, 1898. A sane and well-balanced account of the Italian campaigns by the general in command at the battle of Adua.

KELLER, CONRAD: *Alfred Ilg.* Leipzig, 1918. A valuable biography of Menelik's Swiss adviser. Contains many interesting side lights on the Abyssinian side of the Italian policy.

BILLOT, ALBERT: *La France et l'Italie, 1881–1899.* Two volumes. Paris, 1905. The memoirs of the French ambassador at Rome. One of the best systematic accounts of Franco-Italian relations from the French side, but very weak on the discussion of policy and the intimate side of French diplomacy.

HOHENLOHE-SCHILLINGSFÜRST, PRINCE CHLODWIG ZU: *Denkwürdigkeiten der Reichskanzlerzeit.* Edited by Karl A. von Müller. Stuttgart, 1931. An important German source, which serves as a useful supplement to the German documents.

SPECIAL STUDIES

CROMER, LORD: *Modern Egypt.* Two volumes. New York, 1908. Cromer discusses in detail the Sudan problem, but with great caution. A book that must be corrected in the light of other material.

WOOLF, LEONARD: *Empire and Commerce in Africa.* New York, 1920. One of the best critical accounts of African problems.

CHIALA, LUIGI: *Pagine di Storia Contemporanea.* Three volumes. New edition. Turin, 1898. Contains much valuable press comment, texts of speeches, extracts from Italian documents, etc.

CILIBRIZZI, SAVERIO: *Storia Parlamentare, Politica e Diplomatica d'Italia.* Three volumes. Milan, 1929. A useful detailed account primarily of the domestic sides of Italian policy.

MONDAINI, GENNARO: *Manuale di Storia e Legislazione Coloniale del Regno d'Italia.* Volume I. Rome, 1927. The best general history of Italian colonial policy, well-documented and sound.

MASI, CORRADO: " L'Eritrea e la Somalia nella Storia Politica e Diplomatica della Nazione Italiana." (in Tomaso Sillani: *L'Africa Orientale Italiana,* Rome, 1933, pp. 11–70). The most recent and one of the best systematic accounts of the diplomacy of the Abyssinian crisis.

PALAMENGHI-CRISPI, TOMMASO: *L'Italia Coloniale e Francesco Crispi.* Milan, 1928. Written by Crispi's nephew. A very partisan account based largely on Crispi's *Prima Guerra d'Africa* and upon Crispi's *Memoirs.*

PALUMBO-CARDELLA, G.: " Crispi e la Politica Coloniale." (*Politica,* Volume XXIX, 1929, pp. 150–179, 387–431; Volume XXX, 1929, pp. 350–380). Written by one of Crispi's collaborators. A detailed, undocumented and one-sided account.

BELLAVITA, EMILIO: *Adua.* Genoa, 1931. By far the most detailed scholarly study of the battle of Adua and the Italian policy in Abyssinia from the beginning to the catastrophe. The author was a participant in the battle, and comes to conclusions favorable to Baratieri.

WYLDE, AUGUSTUS B.: *Modern Abyssinia.* London, 1901. The author was a British consular agent. His account is very full and interesting, especially for the native side. Critical of the policies of the great powers.

ITALICUS: *Italiens Dreibundpolitik, 1870–1896.* Munich, 1928. A good, scholarly study of Italian foreign policy before Adua. Based largely upon the German documents, Crispi *Memoirs,* etc.

HOERNIGK, RUDOLF: *Italien zwischen Frankreich und dem Dreibund.* Berlin, 1931. A dissertation covering the years 1890 to 1906. Based primarily upon the German documents. Not a contribution of great significance.

MORIÉ, J. L.: *Histoire de l'Éthiopie.* Two volumes. Paris, 1904. A detailed and very biassed account of modern Abyssinian history. Valuable as reflecting the French view of Italian aspirations.

ELETZ, U.: *Imperator Menelik i Voina ego s Italiei.* St. Petersburg, 1898. The most important Russian account, based upon Leontiev's papers. Beautifully illustrated, but rather anecdotal.

WAUTERS, A. J.: *Histoire Politique du Congo Belge.* Brussels, 1911. The best general history of the foreign policy of the Congo State, by the former editor of the well-informed *Mouvement Géographique.*

HANOTAUX, GABRIEL: *Fachoda.* Paris, 1909. Not as revealing as it might be, but an indispensable source for the study of French policy.

DARCY, JEAN: *France et Angleterre.* Paris, 1904. One of the most complete and best-informed accounts of French policy, but distinctly biassed.

COCHERIS, JULES: *La Situation Internationale de l'Égypte et du Soudan.* Paris, 1903. On the whole the best scholarly monograph on French policy in the Egyptian and Sudan questions.

CRABITÈS, PIERRE: *The Winning of the Sudan.* London, 1934. A readable popular account which adds little, though there is a good chapter on the financial side of the Dongola expedition.

KOSSATZ, HEINZ: *Untersuchungen über den Französisch-Englischen Weltgegensatz im Fashodajahr.* Breslau, 1934. An interesting study of the bearing of French domestic affairs on foreign policy. One of the few studies that considers the negotiations between England and France on the eve of the Dongola advance.

GLANVILLE, JAMES L.: *Italy's Relations with England, 1896–1905.* Baltimore, 1934. The treatment of the period before the Adua disaster is very scant and adds little.

DIETRICH, R.: "England und Italien, 1887–1902." (*Historische Vierteljahrschrift,* XXIX, 1935, pp. 768–800). A useful review of Anglo-Italian relations, based upon German, English and French documents.

LITERATURE SINCE 1935

(See also the Supplementary Bibliographical Note to Chapter IV.)

VOSSLER, OTTO: "Die italienische Expansion, 1881–1935" (*Historische Zeitschrift,* CLVI, 1937, pp. 284–306). A competent analysis of Italian imperialism within the framework of European international relations.

BOURGIN, GEORGES: "Francesco Crispi" (in *Les politiques d'expansion impérialiste,* Paris, 1949, pp. 123–156). An admirable, up-to-date review of Crispi's colonial policy.

TRUFFI, RICCARDO: *Precursori dell'Impero Africano.* Rome, 1936. One of the more solid Fascist writings on the earlier phase of Italian expansion.

DÉHERAIN, HENRI: "Le Soudan perdu et reconquis" (in Volume VII of Hanotaux, G.: *Histoire de la nation égyptienne,* Paris, 1940). An excellent general account of the Mahdist movement and its overthrow.

HOFE, H. VON: *Der Sudanfeldzug. Die diplomatischen Hintergründe des Sudanfeldzuges.* Bleicherode, 1939. 58 pp. A rather conventional German dissertation.

CONTI-ROSSINI, CARLO: *Italia ed Etiopia del trattato di Uccialli alla battaglia di Adua.* Rome, 1935. 494 pp. Written by an eminent authority and based on unpublished Italian colonial and war department archives as well as on Ethiopian records, this is the most important single recent book.

WORK, ERNEST: *Ethiopia, a Pawn in European Diplomacy.* New Concord, Ohio, 1935. 354 pp. A solid, systematic review, based on the published British, Italian, German and French materials.

SCHWARZ, HERBERT: *Die Entwicklung der völkerrechtlichen Beziehungen Aethiopiens zu den Mächten seit 1885.* Berlin, 1937. 76 pp. A serious, well-documented study, but rather slight on the period prior to 1896.

REICHIES, SIEGFRIED: *Abessinien als Kampfobjekt der grossen Mächte, 1880–1916.* Breslau, 1937. 107 pp. A superior dissertation which exploits all the recent materials.

DEL BONO, GIULIO: *Da Assab ad Adua.* Rome, n.d. 246 pp. A general review, with emphasis on the military side.

PIGLI, MARIO: *Etiopia l'incognita africana.* Padua, 1935. 189 pp. A new edition of a brief but competent review, first published in 1932.

SABELLI, LUCA DEI: *Storia di Abissinia.* Volume III. Rome, 1938, 439 pp. A standard history, containing a detailed treatment of the later nineteenth century.

JONES, ARNOLD H. M., and MONROE, ELIZABETH: *A History of Abyssinia.* New York, 1935. 188 pp. A good though very brief book, which devotes only one short chapter to the events treated here.

FALCONE, E.: *Menelik II. L'Etiopia e le relazioni con l'Italia in base allo studio essenzialmente delle fonti abissine.* Udine, 1941. 171 pp.

KHVOSTOV, V.: "Nachalo Italianskoi Kolonialnoi Ekspansii i Pervaia Italo-Abissinskaiia Voina, 1895–1896 gg." (*Istorik Marksist,* XII, 1935, pp. 58–75). Scholarly but Marxian interpretation of Italian imperialism in Africa.

PIAZZA, GIUSEPPE: "L'Inghilterra e il protettorato italiano sull'Etiopia" (*Nuova Antologia,* CCCLXXXII, December 1, 1935, pp. 254–261). Adds nothing.

SCARFOGLIO, EDOARDO: *Abissinia, 1888–1896.* Two volumes. Rome, 1936. A reprint of interesting contemporary articles by a prominent Italian journalist.

BERKELEY, GEORGE F. H.: *The Campaign of Adowa and the Rise of Menelik.* London, 1935. 403 pp. Unrevised reprint of a good book first published in 1902.

RIZZI, B.: *Il carteggio di Oreste Baratieri, 1887–1901.* Trent, 1936. Correspondence of the Italian commander. An important source.

ZAGHI, CARLO: "La conquista di Cassala" (*Nuova Antologia,* October 16, 1934, pp. 601–612). An interesting monograph, by a leading authority on the period.

—: "La missione Antonelli in Etiopia e il fallimento della politica scioana" (*Rassegna di politica internazionale,* III, 1936, pp. 473–485). A thorough re-examination of this important mission.

CURATO, FEDERICO: "Il rifiuto inglese di cedere Zeila all'Italia nel 1894–1896" (*Gerarchia,* November, 1935, pp. 948–950). Though part of the Fascist campaign literature, this is a concise, documented review of the episode.

CONTI-ROSSINI, CARLO: *La battaglia di Adua.* Rome, 1939. 68 pp. A popular but authoritative account, with excellent photographs.

VELTZE, ALOIS: *Die Schlacht bei Adua.* Berlin, 1935.

ANONYMOUS: "Une négociation sécrète de Léopold II; ses efforts pour acquérir l'accès du Congo au Nil. Les pourparlers avec l'Italie au sujet de l'Erythrée" (*Le XXe siècle politique,* January 6, 1933).

X

The Near East
Macedonia, Crete, Armenia

∽

ESPITE THE FACT THAT DURING THE MID-NINETIES THE GOVERNMENTS of Europe were engrossed by problems of over-seas expansion, and that public interest was focussed upon the exploits of the new imperialism, it was impossible for either the governments or the peoples to shake themselves free from the traditional questions of European policy. In the west the agitation of Boulangist days had died away and Franco-German relations were tolerable, to say the least. But the other great sore of Europe, the familiar Near Eastern question, continued to be as troublesome as ever and filled the statesmen of the great powers with varied fears and forebodings. In the years 1896 and 1897 affairs in the Balkans once more came to a head. They actually led to war between Greece and Turkey. No account of the oscillations of the European pendulum could be complete without adequate treatment of this time-honored and always dangerous problem.

The efforts of the so-called Armenian Triplice to secure for the Armenians better administration had resulted in nothing but the well-known Turkish promises. Throughout the winter and spring of 1895–1896 sporadic massacring of the Armenians was reported from various localities of Asia Minor. Foreign offices were deluged with consular reports and ambassadors were wearied with endless and futile protesting. Sultan Abdul Hamid, than whom no one knew better how to play off one power against the other, had long since recognized the rifts in the ranks of the powers. He was only too well aware that his most formidable opponent, England, was the subject of the gravest suspicion on the part of the other powers, and that Turkey's traditional enemy, Russia, would now protect him against all British schemes for interference or for disruption of the Empire.

But the Armenian question could not be isolated from the whole complex of problems presented by the Near East. From the very beginning of the massacres it was realized in the government chancelleries that the " disturbances " might spread to other parts of the Sultan's dominions and that, thereby, questions more serious by far than the fate of the Armenians might be forced upon the attention of the powers. The greatest danger spot was in Macedonia, that ill-defined area around and behind Saloniki, roughly the three Turkish vilayets or provinces of Saloniki, Monastir and Kossovo. This territory was the meeting place of the Balkan races, a region where Slavs, Greeks, Vlachs and Jews lived more or less intermingled, exposed alike to the oppression of Turkish landlords, the extortion of Ottoman officials and the depredations of Albanian tribesmen. In a book of this kind it is hardly necessary to analyze the mass of controversial material on the subject of Macedonia, or to venture upon the volcanic subject of Macedonian ethnology. The all-important fact is that the majority of the inhabitants were racially Slavic — according to some writers a branch of the Serb race, according to others merely a part of the Bulgarian population of the Balkans, and according to yet others a transitional type between Serbs and Bulgars, which might be described as Macedonian or Macedonian Slav.[1]

Bulgarians from Macedonia had taken a prominent part in the struggle that led to the establishment of the Bulgarian principality in 1878, and the Treaty of San Stefano, it will be remembered, had incorporated most of Macedonia in the great new Bulgaria. The opposition of England and Austria to the erection of a strong " Russian outpost " in the Balkans had resulted in the revision of the Russian-Turkish Treaty and the return of Macedonia to the Sultan under the terms of the Treaty of Berlin. To be sure, it had been provided in the Treaty (Article XXIII) that organs of self-government should be established by the Sultan with the aid of commissions chosen from the population, but to all appearances this provision was not very seriously intended and the Ottoman government made no move to fulfil the obligation.

The decisions of the Berlin Congress came as a " thundering blow " to the Bulgarians. There were at first some insurrectional outbreaks, but after an impassioned meeting of protest at Tirnovo it was decided that it would be best to accept, at least for the time being, the decision of the powers, while the Bulgarians of all parts " should look upon the young principality as an organ for the whole of the nation." [2] In other words, the new state, still a vassal of Turkey, was to serve as headquarters for the work of redeeming the Bulgarians still under the Turkish yoke in Macedonia. For the Bulgarian patriots Macedonia was everything. Unlike the Roumanians and Serbs they had nothing to hope from the ultimate breakup of the Hapsburg Empire, unlike the Greeks they had no aspirations to other parts of the Sultan's dominions. They were convinced, as were most contemporary and later travellers, that by far the larger part of the Slavic population of Macedonia was truly Bulgarian, and they were not prepared to rest until this territory was securely joined to Bulgaria proper.

In the old Ottoman Empire the government recognized no differences of race or nationality. The only accepted distinction between populations was made

---

[1] Among the best of recent studies may be mentioned Gustav Weigand: *Ethnographie von Makedonien* (Leipzig, 1924); Jacques Ancel: *La Macédoine* (Paris, 1930); Walter Jacob: *Die Makedonische Frage* (Berlin, 1931).

[2] *La Macédoine et le Vilayet d'Andrinople, 1893–1903* (Sofia, 1904), pp. 1–3; Bulgarian Ministry of Foreign Affairs: *The Bulgarian Question and the Balkan States* (Sofia, 1919), p. 10.

on the basis of religion. All adherents of the Greek patriarchate were classed as Greek, all followers of the Armenian patriarch as Armenian. At an early date the Bulgarian leaders had seen that the realization of their aims would be possible only if they succeeded in establishing their own church as distinct from the Greek patriarchate. After long struggles they succeeded, and the recognition of the Bulgarian exarchate by the Porte in 1870 is therefore one of the great landmarks in the rise of Balkan nationalities. Under the terms of the Turkish *firman* the territories which later became the new Bulgarian principality were turned over to the jurisdiction of the new exarch, but it was provided further that in Macedonia any district might adhere to the new church if two thirds of the population so voted. The result was that a large part of Macedonia, probably most of the Slavic parts, abandoned the Greek patriarchate and joined the Bulgarian church, not always because the people were Bulgarian, but because they were Slavs and therefore disliked the Greek clergy and the incomprehensible Greek service.[3] Be that as it may, the Exarchate was, for the Bulgarians, as potent an engine of propaganda as the Greek patriarchate had been for the Greeks. Everywhere in Macedonia Bulgarian schools were opened, until by 1895 there were, according to Bulgarian statistics, some six to seven hundred schools with between twenty-five and thirty thousand pupils. This educational work, it was estimated, cost the Bulgarian government between one and two million francs annually, but it was worth it, for by the middle of the nineties the Slav population of Macedonia had to a large extent been Bulgarized in its sympathies.[4]

At first the Bulgarian activities in Macedonia met with little competition. The Greeks were still concerned with their aspirations in Thessaly and Epirus, while the eyes of the Serbs were riveted at first upon Bosnia and Herzegovina, and then upon the regions of western Bulgaria. Prior to 1878 the Serbs had, in fact, been very favorably disposed towards the Bulgarian claims in Macedonia. It was felt that there was little real difference between Serbs and Bulgars and it was confidently expected that before long the various branches of the southern Slavs would be united in one large state. Prince Michael of Serbia, who was assassinated in 1868 after having made all preparations for a concerted attack upon Turkey, was one of the outstanding exponents of this idea.[5] It was not until the beginning of operations of the Bulgarian exarch that some Serbian leaders began to realize that the new church, which they

---

[3] See Émile Haumant: "Les Origines de la Lutte pour la Macédoine, 1855–1872" (*Le Monde Slave*, III, October, 1926, pp. 52–66).

[4] A Diplomatist: *Nationalism and War in the Near East* (Oxford, 1915), p. 89; detailed figures on schools in *The Bulgarian Question and the Balkan States*, pp. 225 ff.; Richard von Mach: *Die Macedonische Frage* (Vienna, 1895), pp. 67 ff.; Cléanthes Nicolaides: *La Macédoine* (Berlin, 1899), pp. 121, 138 ff.

[5] William L. Langer: *European Alliances and Alignments, 1871–1890* (New York, 1931), pp. 61 ff.; Édouard Engelhardt: "La Confédération Balkanique" (*Revue d'Histoire Diplomatique*, VI, 1892, pp. 29–55); M. R. Ivanovitch: "The Future of the Balkans" (*Fortnightly Review*, June, 1909, pp. 1040–59), pp. 1046 ff.

had thought of as a Bulgarian-Serbian or generally southern-Slav institution, was really an organ for the furtherance of purely Bulgarian interests. The eminent Serbian statesman, Jovan Ristič, then tried to open Serbian schools in Old Serbia and Macedonia. But the movement was frowned upon by the Russians, and the interest of the Serbs themselves still ran too strongly in the direction of Bosnia. Nothing much came of these early efforts.[6]

At the Congress of Berlin the Serbs were abandoned by the Russians and were forced to look to Austria for the realization of even very modest claims. The Austrian government, in fact, encouraged the Belgrade cabinet to concentrate its attention on Bulgaria and Macedonia, in order to distract the Serbs from activity in Bosnia. During the negotiations for the Austrian-Serbian Treaty of 1881 Baron Haymerlé, the Austrian foreign minister, is reported to have said to the Serbian envoy: " We are ready to bind ourselves by a formal convention to recognize the Serbian pretensions to the Vilayet of Kossovo and in Macedonia (up to a certain point) and to use all our influence in the next European congress to bring the great powers to recognize the annexation of these territories to Serbia." Article VII of the actual treaty of alliance made this obligation binding, though the terms were somewhat vague.[7] But when in 1885 the revolution at Philippopolis was successfully carried through and Serbia went to war with Bulgaria in order to obtain compensation for the enlargement of the principality, the Serbs were overwhelmingly defeated at Slivnitsa and all their hopes of annexations in western Bulgaria were completely blasted. From that time on suspicion and enmity ruled Serbian-Bulgarian relations. The Belgrade government suddenly became aware of the great success of Bulgarian propaganda in Macedonia and realized the fact that very soon this territory, like eastern Rumelia, would be joined to the principality unless heroic efforts were made to rescue at least a part for Serbia. In 1888 there appeared at Vienna a book by Spiridion Gopčevič entitled: *Makedonien und Alt-Serbien*. The book may be taken as the first counter-blast to the Bulgarian propaganda. It put forward in detail the Serbian claims, in such extravagant and phantastic terms that no serious student, not even a Serbian, would now pay much attention to it.

Gopčevič's book was probably meant as an announcement to western Europe. Behind it the Serbs were laying preparations for extensive activity in Macedonia itself. In 1886 there was founded the Society of Saint Sava, which aimed at awakening national consciousness in all Serb lands, but especially in Macedonia. It printed books and trained teachers for schools in the Turkish Empire, it issued proclamations and kept the matter of propaganda before the attention of the public. In a few years, however, its activities were curtailed by the government because it was thought to be too noisy and therefore more

---

[6] Haumant, loc. cit.; and the same author's *La Formation de la Yougoslavie* (Paris, 1930), chap. xxxix.

[7] Chédomille Mijatovich: *The Memoirs of a Balkan Diplomatist* (London, 1917), pp. 38-40; Pribram: *The Secret Treaties of Austria-Hungary*, I, p. 55.

harmful than useful. The work of propaganda was taken over first by the ministry of education and in 1889 by the ministry for foreign affairs.[8]

But the Serbs found not a few difficulties in the way of the realization of their hopes. Since 1885 the wave of anti-Austrian feeling had been mounting higher and higher in Serbia, and the Radical party, led by vigorous men like Nikola Pasič, was growing stronger and stronger. King Milan, thoroughly discredited, could hold out no longer. In March 1889 he abdicated in favor of his thirteen-year-old son, Alexander, for whom he appointed a regency headed by Ristič. But before taking this momentous step Milan took care to extend the treaty of alliance with Austria, which was due to expire in 1891. Until January 13, 1895, it remained in force, for before abdicating Milan obliged the regents to declare in writing that they would observe it exactly and faithfully.[9] Knowledge of this treaty kept Ristič from following his own Russian proclivities, but none of the ministers were informed of Serbia's obligations to Austria. Once the restraining hand of Milan was removed the Russophil current was allowed to run unchecked. The press, given greater freedom under the terms of the new Constitution of 1888, spoke wildly of Serbia's " brothers under the yoke," of Slav solidarity and of the popular determination to shake off the Hapsburg influence. Relations became more and more strained as one " incident " followed another. The Hungarian government began to retaliate by putting obstacles in the way of the importation of Serbian pork until something like a little " pig war " ensued. The Serbs then tried to break the bond of economic dependence by shipping their pigs over the newly opened railway to Saloniki and thence by sea to Marseilles, but this proved unprofitable. There was no circumventing the plain facts of geography. Economically Serbia was at the mercy of Austria-Hungary, from which she took sixty per cent of her imports and to which she sent eighty per cent of her exports. Finally, in 1892, the Serbian government concluded a new tariff treaty with the Hapsburg monarchy, an agreement in which the terms of the 1881 treaty were repeated in all essentials, though a few concessions were made to the Serbs by the Vienna government.[10]

While relations with Austria were distinctly strained in the first years after 1889, the Radical government then in power made every effort to enlist the sympathy and support of Russia. Pasič was in close touch with Pan-Slav circles and was thought by many to be an enemy of the Obrenovič dynasty. In 1890 he went to St. Petersburg, where he was received and decorated by the Tsar. The Slavic Welfare Society elected him a life member. When he returned to Belgrade, he brought with him a Russian present in the shape of seventy-five thousand rifles and almost two million cartridges, to say nothing of a very substantial

---

[8] I am following here chiefly the excellent, documented account of Slobodan Yovanovič: *Vlada Aleksandra Obrenovića* (Belgrade, 1929), I, pp. 88 ff., 98 ff.

[9] Stojan Protitch: " The Secret Treaty between Servia and Austria-Hungary " (*Fortnightly Review*, May, 1909, pp. 838–49), p. 840; Yovanovič, op. cit., pp. 75–6.

[10] Yovanovič, op. cit., pp. 76–80, 219–22; Karl Grünberg: *Die Handelspolitischen Beziehungen Osterreich-Ungarns zu den Ländern an der Unteren Donau* (Leipzig, 1902), pp. 194–201.

loan. In the following year the Radical leader, having become prime minister, returned to Russia in the company of the young King Alexander. The veering of Serbia in the Russian direction was clear, and the Russians therefore promised to support the Serbian activities in Macedonia. This support was what the Belgrade statesmen wanted more than anything else.[11]

But Russian support, though valuable, was not enough. If the Russians stood behind the Serbs, the Austrians made themselves the champions of the Bulgarians and even the Turks were sympathetic. The great Bulgarian statesman, Stambulov, had, ever since 1887, based his policy upon friendship with Turkey, so that he could count upon the Porte's acquiescence in the work of peaceful cultural penetration in Macedonia. Now the Serbian Radicals had always given a prominent place in their program to the idea of southern Slav unity as the necessary basis for the formation of a Balkan league. They wanted good relations and a friendly understanding with Bulgaria. So in the autumn of 1889 Pasič went to Sofia to conclude an entente. But Stambulov, seeing that such an arrangement would of necessity turn against Turkey, rejected the idea and even betrayed it to the Porte, receiving by way of reward the right to appoint several Bulgarian bishops to Macedonian dioceses. Clearly nothing could be done with the Bulgarian minister. Serbia's relations with her neighbor became more and more strained as Stambulov's enemies made Belgrade their headquarters and their base of operations against the régime of the Bulgarian dictator.[12]

Failing an understanding with Bulgaria the Serbians were forced to look to the Greek patriarchate for permission to open schools and for the appointment of Serbs to the Macedonian priesthood. But the Greek clergy had no liking for the idea. It was already suffering enough from the Roumanian propaganda among the Macedonian Vlachs. Instead of making concessions to the Serbs the Greek clergy started something like a campaign against the reading of the service in Slavic and against all priests who insisted on continuing the practice. The plain fact of the matter was that the question was not a religious one, but a strictly political one. If the Serbs desired an adjustment with the Patriarchate they had first to come to an agreement with the Greek government about Macedonia. The Belgrade government took the hint. In June 1890 discussions were started with the Greek envoy in Belgrade. But, so far as one can see in these obscure questions, the Greek government was not as anxious as the Serbian. It wanted, if possible, to include Bulgaria in the arrangement. In June 1891 the eminent Greek statesman, Charilaos Tricoupis, paid a visit to Belgrade and Sofia, in the hope of constructing a Balkan league directed against Turkey and based upon the principle of the partition of Macedonia between the three powers. The

[11] Yovanovič, op. cit., pp. 82–6, 96–8; Walter M. Markov: *Serbien zwischen Oesterreich und Russland* (Stuttgart, 1934), chap. i.

[12] Yovanovič, op. cit., pp. 86 ff.; K. Kratchounov: *La Politique Extérieure de la Bulgarie, 1880–1920* (Sofia, 1932), pp. 25–7.

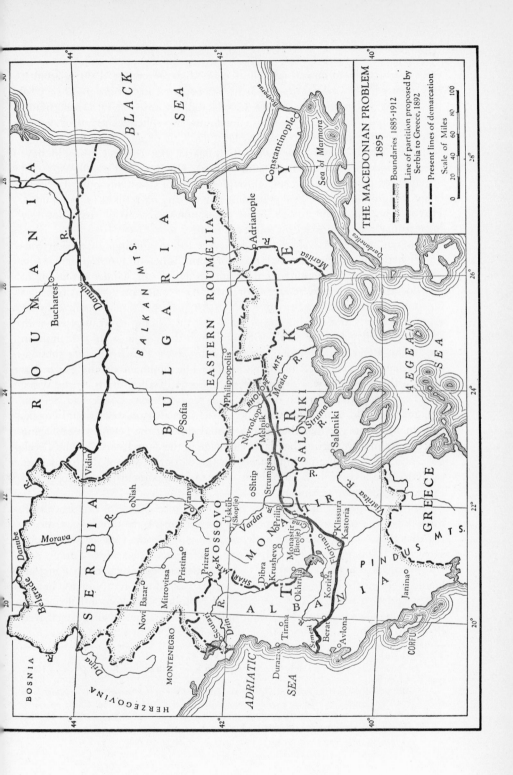

THE MACEDONIAN PROBLEM
1895

.... Boundaries 1885-1912
———— Line of partition proposed by
        Serbia to Greece, 1892
—·—·— Present lines of demarcation

Scale of Miles
0 20 40 60 80 100

BLACK

SEA

ROUMANIA

Bucharest

Danube R.

BOSNIA

HERZEGOVINA

Belgrade

Danube

Morava

SERBIA

Nish

Vranya

Novi Bazar

Mitrovitsa

Pristina

Prizren

MONTENEGRO

Drina R.

Scutari

Drin R.

ADRIATIC

SEA

Durazzo

Tirana

ALBANIA

SHAR MTS.

KOSSOVO

Üskül
(Skoplje)

Dibra

Krushevo

Okhrida

Berat

Semeni R.

Avlona

CORFU

BALKAN MTS.

BULGARIA

Sofia

Vidin

EASTERN ROUMELIA

Philippopolis

Nevrokopo

Melnik

RHODOPE MTS.

Vardar

Ship

Strumitsa

NoPrilip

Monastir
(Bitolje)

Florina

Klissura

Kastoria

Koritza

PINDUS

MTS.

Janina

GREECE

TURKEY

Adrianople

Maritsa R.

Mesta R.

Struma R.

Vardar R.

SALONIKI

Saloniki

Vistritsa R.

AEGEAN

SEA

Constantinople

Bosporus

Sea of Marmora

Dardanelles

Serbs were ready to enter upon the scheme, but Stambulov flatly rejected it and reported it to Constantinople, as he had betrayed Pasič's proposals in 1889. It is said by a contemporary writer, usually well informed about Greek affairs, that Tricoupis offered to divide Macedonia into two spheres, the line of demarcation to be the forty-first parallel of latitude. This parallel runs just south of Monastir, which would have fallen to Bulgaria. But to Greece would have fallen Saloniki and the entire Aegean seacoast. The forty-first parallel, it might be remarked parenthetically, runs through the city of Constantinople. To Stambulov the proposal seemed preposterous, that is why he refused to entertain it. He could not know that in less than a generation Greece would have not only the territory she then asked for, but even more.[13]

Though the Greek-Bulgarian *pourparlers* led to nothing, discussion continued between Athens and Belgrade for some time. In December 1892 the Serbian government submitted a draft for an agreement. Under the terms of this document the Serbs reserved for themselves Macedonia and Albania as far south as Berat and the Semeni River in Albania, the Monastir vilayet as far south as Kastoria and Florina and as far east as the Cherna River, together with the Saloniki vilayet as far south as Strumitsa in the Vardar Valley, Melnik on the Struma River, and Nevrokop on the Mesta River. This left Greece substantially what she had asked of Bulgaria. The line proposed by the Serbs was roughly the line as it was drawn after the Second Balkan and World Wars. Various other articles in the draft of 1892 provided that Greek and Serbian diplomacy should propagate everywhere " the idea that only Serbs and Greeks exist in Macedonia "; that the Greeks should support the Serbs in establishing schools and in introducing the Slavic language in the church service. The Greek government was to use its influence with the patriarch, whom the Serbs were ready to give a pension. Serb bishops were to be appointed to the dioceses of Prizren and Skoplye (Uskub).[14]

Nothing came of this interesting Serbian advance. So far as one can determine the Greek patriarch was opposed to the agreement, the Greek government felt that there was no need for haste, and there was some fear in Athens that such an agreement would end in a yet closer entente between Turkey and Bulgaria. The Greek government therefore demanded much more generous boundaries, insisting not only upon the award of Monastir (Bitolye), but of Prilep and Krushevo, and to the eastward Melnik, Nevrokop and Strumitsa. These demands were probably meant only as a subterfuge. If so they achieved their purpose. In January 1893 the negotiations broke down.[15]

[13] The details in Henry Norman: " The Wreck of Greece " (*Scribner's Magazine*, October, 1897, pp. 399–426), p. 410; see also J. D. Bourchier, in Luigi Villari: *The Balkan Question* (London, 1905), p. 88.

[14] Abstract of the text in Édouard Driault and Michel Lhéritier: *Histoire Diplomatique de la Grèce*, IV (Paris, 1926), pp. 291–2; according to the summary in Yovanovič, op. cit., I, pp. 94–5, the Serbs were willing to leave Melnik and Nevrokop to the Greeks.

[15] Driault and Lhéritier, op. cit., p. 292; Yovanovič, loc. cit.

Thus far the Radical government in Serbia had been unable to accomplish much. Austria was estranged, the Russians hardly got beyond kind promises, the Bulgarians had rejected Serbian advances, and the Greeks had refused to come to an agreement for dividing Macedonia into spheres of influence. And yet in Belgrade the Macedonian problem was looked upon as a matter of life and death. Having no separate Church and therefore no method of putting its priests and school-teachers into Macedonia, there was no other course left open to the Serbians than to follow the example set by Stambulov in Bulgaria, that is, to establish close relations with Turkey and to secure from the Porte the right to open schools apart from the Patriarchate. This policy had long been urged by Vladimir Karič, the Serbian consul in Skoplye (Uskub), who was one of the leading Serb experts on things Macedonian. In 1893, after the failure of negotiations with Greece, it was taken up seriously and pursued systematically. The Porte showed some appreciation, and before long granted permission for the establishment of Serb schools in the vilayet of Kossovo. The Sultan even expressed the desire to have King Alexander visit Constantinople. At Belgrade it was hoped that such a visit might help secure permission for the Serbs to open schools in the vilayets of Monastir and Saloniki, and that it might be possible to bring Turkish pressure to bear upon the patriarch to appoint Serbian bishops in the dioceses of Prizren and Skoplye. Alexander therefore went to the Turkish capital in June 1894. The reception accorded him was brilliant and the Sultan friendly. Alexander left in high hopes that the Serbian desires would be realized. But nothing came of his efforts. At Belgrade it was said, probably with good reason, that the Sultan had helped the former King Milan meet his gambling debts to the tune of half a million francs, and had secured for him a collection of very compromising letters written to one of his many mistresses. Abdul Hamid, it was believed, had been repaid by the visit of young Alexander. There was nothing in the visit for the Serbian people.[16]

The Turkophil policy of the Belgrade government seemed to be as futile as the other policies it had tried. From Constantinople the Serbian minister, Vladan Georgevič, urged a stronger policy and if necessary the use of threats to secure concessions from the Porte. But King Alexander felt, quite rightly, that Serbia was not strong enough to embark upon so dangerous a course. In 1893 the young King had proclaimed his majority and had gotten rid of the regency. In 1894 he had abrogated the liberal Constitution of 1888 and had temporarily restored the system initiated in 1869. His father, King Milan, the great proponent of the connexion with Austria, was behind the scenes again, while the pro-Russian Radical party was out of power. Serbian politics were in a perfectly chaotic state. It was in truth no time for an heroic foreign policy.

Though the Serbs had by no means attained the realization of even their most modest wishes, they had, by 1894, become a factor in the Macedonian situa-

---

[16] Yovanovič, op. cit., pp. 276–80; Felix Kanitz: *Das Königreich Serbien und das Serbenvolk* (Leipzig, 1914), III, p. 279; Nicholas Iorga: *Histoire des États Balkaniques* (Paris, 1925), pp. 428 ff.

tion. By that time they had over a hundred schools in the Kossovo vilayet, and their pupils numbered over five thousand.[17] The Bulgarians, it will be recalled, claimed to have over six hundred schools with more than twenty-five thousand pupils, while the Greek schools of the Patriarchate in 1895 numbered, according to Greek statistics, over fourteen hundred, with eighty thousand pupils.[18] In addition the Roumanians, who had been carrying on an active propaganda for some time and were spending some four hundred thousand francs annually on Macedonian schools, put the number of their institutions at over thirty and the number of their pupils at some two thousand.[19] Of course these figures are all exaggerated. Still, Europe had rarely seen such an all-consuming passion for education as seized the Balkan peoples in behalf of their Macedonian brothers during the last decade of the 19th century. The whole thing had a distinctly ludicrous side, for the natives found themselves torn this way and that. A contemporary observer tells us that the Christians in Macedonia were " utterly broken down in spirit: their manhood melted into pathetic servility, their enterprise turned to stolid endurance, their hopes weak, and their fears overwhelmingly strong." They looked with grave suspicion upon the missionaries and crusaders from the neighboring states and " shunned them like the pest." In the meanwhile, he continued, these agents " openly or in disguise employ every means they consider lawful to attain the end which they profess to believe desirable, bribing infidel Turks, buying the consent of parents to have their children educated in this school or in that, distributing gratis books, pamphlets and leaflets in which they virtually abuse each other and eulogize the cause — delighted at the conversion or apostasy of a child or a family, as if the political problem could be solved, at this hour of the day, on the basis of ' cooked ' or even genuine statistics." [20]

The pressure of Serbian and Greek propaganda and the dissatisfaction of Bulgarians at home with the Turkophil policy of Stambulov led, in 1893, to a new development in the Macedonian problem. At Ressen (Resna) a number of Bulgarian Macedonians, under the leadership of Damian Gruev, founded the secret revolutionary committee usually referred to as the " Internal Organization." The object of this group was to prepare, morally and physically, for a great rising of the Bulgarians against Turkish rule, in the hope of securing self-government. The Committee was exceptionally well led and efficiently organized. In a few years it had its branches all over Macedonia, had begun the training of bands in the villages and had amassed considerable stores of munitions.[21]

[17] Émile Haumant: *La Formation de la Yougoslavie*, p. 443; William Miller: *Travels and Politics in the Near East* (London, 1898), p. 379; T. R. Georgevitch: *Macedonia* (New York, 1918), p. 175.   [18] Cléanthes Nicolaides: *La Macédoine* (Berlin, 1899), pp. 138 ff.

[19] Gustav Weigand: *Die Aromunen* (Leipzig, 1894–1895); Carlo de Stefani: " La Lotta dei Popoli nella Peninsola Balcanica" (*Nuova Antologia*, January 15, 1895, pp. 304–21), p. 307; Victor Bérard: *La Turquie et l'Hellénisme Contemporain* (Paris, 1896), p. 255.

[20] Anonymous: " Macedonia and the Macedonians " (*Contemporary Review*, September, 1895, pp. 305–25), pp. 317–8.

[21] *La Macédoine et le Vilayet d'Andrinople, 1893–1903. Mémoire de l'Organisation Intérieure*

The situation now developed rapidly. In March 1894 the Turkish government, probably acting under Russian pressure, announced that thenceforth the right of the Bulgarian exarchate to found and control schools would be withdrawn. This news caused consternation. In Bulgaria there was a very large number of Macedonian emigrés, variously estimated at between sixty and one hundred thousand. From one third to one half of the population of Sofia was composed of Macedonians.[22] These people now organized great meetings of protest and forced the government to take up the question. The excitement subsided only when Stambulov had persuaded the Porte to rescind its order and grant the Bulgarians two more bishoprics in Macedonia.[23]

But Stambulov, with his modest and patient policy in Macedonia, his highhanded and dictatorial rule at home and his hatred and hostility toward Russia, had long since ceased to be popular among Bulgarian politicians, from the Prince downward. As soon as Ferdinand dared assert his authority, he dismissed his great minister (May 1894) and appointed an out-and-out Russophil cabinet headed by Stoilov. An amnesty was granted to all the persecuted leaders of the Russian faction and the government set its course toward reconciliation. As for the Macedonian element, there was now no further obstacle to the full expression of its desires. Stimulated by the organization of a revolutionary committee in Macedonia and keyed up by hope of European action after the intervention of the powers in behalf of the Armenians, the Macedonians in Sofia arranged a great meeting in November 1894. It was resolved to petition the powers for the enforcement of Article XXIII of the Treaty of Berlin, and to work for the establishment of self-government in Macedonia. Branch committees were started and all sorts of entertainments arranged in order to collect the necessary money. During the first days of April 1895 another secret meeting was held in Sofia, and at that time there was established the Supreme Macedonian Committee, generally referred to as the " External Organization." Its president was a man named Kitanchev, and its vice-president a certain Tufekchiev, who appears to have been the moving spirit in the great conspiracy which ended in July with the unspeakably brutal murder of Stambulov. The former minister, who had no sympathy for the methods advocated by the Macedonian patriots, had been engaged in a bitter feud with the government ever since his dismissal. He knew of the plots against him and he knew that the government would not protect him. He was probably the least surprised when, as he returned from his club one evening, the assassins fell upon him, opened immense gashes in his head and

(Sofia, 1904), pp. 5–7; *The Bulgarian Question and the Balkan States* (Sofia, 1919), p. 18; *Mémorandum Presenté par l'Organisation Révolutionnaire Intérieure de Macédoine à la V ième Assemblée de la Société des Nations et aux Gouvernements de Tous les Pays* (1924); Simeon Radeff: *La Macédoine et la Renaissance Bulgare* (Sofia, 1918), p. 297; Iordan Ivanoff: *La Question Macédoine* (Paris, 1920), p. 111; H. N. Brailsford: *Macedonia* (London, 1906), pp. 115 ff.; Karl Strupp: *La Situation Juridique des Macédoniens en Yougoslavie* (Paris, 1931), pp. 69–70.

[22] *Die Grosse Politik*, XII, no. 2961; Miller: *Travels and Politics in the Near East*, p. 458; *The Bulgarian Question and the Balkan States*, p. 18.

[23] *Annual Register*, 1894, pp. 296–7.

all but amputated his hands with their yatagans, all on the streets of Sofia, with the police evidently uninterested.[24]

Even before the assassination of Stambulov the hot-heads in the Macedonian party, ignoring the disapproval of Ferdinand, had set out to revolutionize Macedonia. The Armenian situation offered a chance that was not to be missed. In June 1895 a number of extremists, several of them former officers of the Bulgarian army, organized raiding parties and crossed the frontier into Macedonia. The most ruthless and the most able of them, Boris Sarafov, who later became president of the External Organization, managed to seize the town of Melnik and hold it for some time against the Turks before he was obliged to flee across the border. The whole episode was simply a foretaste of what was to come later. At the time it was premature, but the raiders undoubtedly hoped for action by the powers, under the leadership of Russia. In this they were mistaken. Prince Ferdinand, to be sure, was conciliating the Russians. On the very day of Stambulov's death, July 17, the Tsar and Lobanov received a Bulgarian deputation, and later in the year the Russians were delighted when Prince Ferdinand announced his intention of allowing the crown prince Boris to be rebaptized in the Orthodox faith. For the grand occasion, in February 1896, the Tsar sent a special envoy. More than that he took the initiative in procuring for Ferdinand the recognition of the Porte and the other powers. The reconciliation between Russia and Bulgaria was complete.[25]

But this did not mean that the Russian government was prepared to support a violent action by Bulgaria in Macedonia. The one thing the Russians were anxious for was the preservation of the status quo in the Balkans. Russia, like the other powers, gladly followed the lead of Austria in warning the Bulgarian government against precipitating a crisis. Lobanov was even prepared to make an agreement with Goluchowski to safeguard the peace in the southeast.[26] Goluchowski was suspicious and tried to bring about an international arrangement, but in any case the action of the powers quashed the efforts of the Macedonian patriots. Serbia and Greece, too, came out strongly in opposition to the Bulgarian program, and gave the Turks a free hand in repressing the rising.[27]

The Macedonian unrest was only the first incident in an involved concatenation of disturbances in the Near East called forth by the Armenian massacres and the action of the powers. From the first serious outbreak in Con-

---

[24] Nikola Stanev: *Istoriia na Nova B"lgaria, 1878–1928* (Sofia, 1929), pp. 156 ff.; Frederick Moore, in Luigi Villari: *The Balkan Question*, pp. 186–7; *The Bulgarian Question and the Balkan States*, pp. 18–9; Richard von Mach: *Die Macedonische Frage*, p. 52; Idem: *Aus Bewegter Balkanzeit, 1879–1918* (Berlin, 1928), pp. 99 ff. (one of the very best accounts); A. Kutschbach: *Der Brandherd Europas* (Leipzig, 1929), pp. 312–20; Harold Nicolson: *Portrait of a Diplomatist* (Boston, 1930), pp. 77–9.

[25] *Die Grosse Politik*, XII, nos. 2943 ff.; Stanev, op. cit., pp. 112–7; Hans von Madol: *Ferdinand von Bulgarien* (Berlin, 1931), p. 87; Anna Stancioff: *Recollections of a Bulgarian Diplomatist's Wife* (London, 1930), pp. 110 ff.; Kratchounov, op. cit., pp. 27–9.

[26] *Die Grosse Politik*, XII, nos. 2962 ff.

[27] Yovanovič, op. cit., pp. 329 ff.

stantinople in August 1895 the Armenian affair passed rapidly to a phase of acute international tension that extended through October and November and did not subside until February 1896. At that time the European diplomats confidently expected another Macedonian rising in the spring. But instead of that they were faced with an insurrection in Crete, the eighth that had taken place within the century.

The island of Crete more or less closes the Aegean Sea. It is about one hundred and seventy miles long, generally mountainous and inaccessible, with a population long noted for its bellicosity. For several centuries the island was ruled by the Venetians with a harshness not exceeded by the later Turk masters. It is said, in fact, that the Cretans themselves called in the Turk in 1645, when the memorable siege that ended in Ottoman conquest in 1669 was begun. But the transfer of ownership meant no gain for the inhabitants. It simply meant that the Venetian dukes were replaced by a new exploiting class, the Moslem landlords. The larger part of the ruling caste was not even Turk, but consisted chiefly of native Cretans " converted " to Mohammedanism for practical reasons. The population of Crete was almost entirely Greek by race, but in the first century of Turkish rule apostasy was very widespread, and in 1760 it was estimated that of a total population of about two hundred and seventy-five thousand, only sixty thousand were Christian.[28]

In 1770 the first of a long series of revolts against Turkish rule took place. In the War of Greek Independence the Cretans took an active and effective part. It was a great and serious mistake on the part of the British government that in 1830 and for a generation thereafter it rejected all suggestions from the Russian government that Crete should be incorporated with Greece. Even in 1830 Lord Palmerston, then in opposition, declared: " No man who had turned his attention to the subject could doubt that the political existence and the defence of Greece would depend on the possession of that island." [29]

From 1824 to 1840 Crete was ruled with a strong hand by Mehemet Ali of Egypt. After its return to the direct rule of the Sultan conditions rapidly became critical. So much of the population had returned to Christianity that in 1895 the proportions were about the reverse of what they had been in 1760. The peasants resented the oppressive rule of the Moslem beys who occupied the most desirable, low-lying land at the mouths of the streams, the more so as these " upper classes " were nothing more than religious renegades. One revolt broke out after another until in 1858 the Porte was induced to initiate a policy of reform. Following the insurrection of that year a famous *firman* granted the Cretans greater religious freedom, liberation from the system of forced labor and control over the distribution of taxes. An even greater revolt in the years 1866–1868

---

[28] Victor Bérard: *Les Affaires de Crète* (Paris, 1898), pp. 47–63.

[29] G. H. Perris: *The Eastern Crisis and British Policy in the Near East* (London, 1897), pp. 116–7. An excellent documented study of the evolution of the Cretan question in its diplomatic aspects in Georges Streit: " La Question Crétoise au Point de Vue International " (*Revue de Droit International Public*, IV, 1897, pp. 61–104).

resulted in the issuance of the Organic Statute, which freed the inhabitants from contributions for exemption from military service and introduced a complete system of administration. The governor, or Vali, was to have associated with him a Christian assessor and a mixed council. Greek was recognized as an official language and a general assembly, elected by the inhabitants, was provided for, to meet annually. This Organic Statute was, in October 1878, greatly expanded by the so-called Pact of Halepa, which provided that the general assembly should be composed of forty-nine Christians and thirty-one Moslems, that natives should have the preference for official posts, and that, after the cost of administration had been deducted from the revenue, one half of the remainder should be devoted to local needs.[30]

By the Halepa Pact the Porte practically abandoned the Cretans to their own devices. For seven years the island was ruled by a governor of Greek race, Photiades Pasha. Outwardly things were quiet, but in the Cretan assembly the Christians had formed parties which fought with each other lustily in the time-honored struggle for the spoils of office. In 1889 the overwhelming victory of the Liberals precipitated a crisis and a new movement for liberation and union with Greece. This agitation rekindled the antagonism between Christians and Moslems; murders took place and everything pointed to a new outbreak on a large scale. The Greek government was for a time inclined to exploit the situation and appealed to the powers. But even England refused to encourage a new movement for liberation. Greece was obliged to keep the peace, while the Sultan, strengthened by the attitude of the powers, sent a large force to the island, put down the incipient insurrection, and in December 1889 issued a new *firman* which rescinded many of the concessions embodied in the Halepa Pact. The governor was to hold office for an indefinite term, the number of deputies was reduced and the assembly's powers curtailed. Preference in the award of office was given to those who spoke Turkish, and the recruiting of the gendarmerie from other parts of the Empire was declared permissible.[31]

For the next five years Crete was ruled by a succession of Moslem governors, none of whom even summoned the general assembly. The Cretans began to look back with regret on the days of the Halepa Pact. Just as soon as the Armenian massacres promised a chance for success and for the intervention of the powers, the agitation was resumed. The Sultan, having trouble enough on his hands, yielded to the representations of the powers and in March 1895 appointed a Greek Christian, Karatheodori Pasha, as governor of the island. When the general assembly met in June there was an astonishing degree of harmony between the Christian and Moslem deputies. Affairs seemed to have taken a

---

[30] These documents are conveniently printed in the French Yellow Book: *Affaire de Crète, juin 1894–février 1897*, no. 1.

[31] *Turkey No. 2 (1889);* William Miller: *The Ottoman Empire and its Successors, 1801–1927* (Cambridge, 1927), pp. 431 ff.; Max Choublier: *La Question d'Orient depuis le Traité de Berlin* (Paris, 1899), pp. 316 ff.; Bérard, op. cit., pp. 76 ff.; Driault and Lhéritier: *Histoire Diplomatique de la Grèce*, IV, pp. 275–80.

favorable turn. But appearances proved deceptive. The Cretan leaders in Greece, organized in an influential Cretan Committee, were determined not to let the opportunity presented by the Armenian massacres pass by unutilized. They started a large-scale agitation and sent agents to Crete who organized armed bands (Epitropi) and prepared for action. The British consul at Canea, Sir A. Biliotti, spoke with great bitterness of the " self-constituted Committee of Reform . . . acting against the wish of the whole Christian population " of three out of the five provinces and against law-abiding Christians everywhere. The reply of the Moslems to the agitators was to establish a Mussulman Committee, the object of which was to secure aid from Constantinople and to make trouble for the Christian governor. Small detachments of troops were in fact sent, and during the winter of 1895 to 1896 the situation, though charged with danger, was relatively quiet.[82]

On February 14, 1896 the British consul at Canea reported the beginning of racial murders, the initiative evidently having come from the Christians. Matters quickly took a turn for the worse; the Sultan appointed a new Moslem governor and began to send troops to the island. The consuls on the spot tried to mediate between the governor and the rebels, but without success. On May 24 there was a violent outbreak at Canea, in which a considerable number of Christians were killed. England, France, Russia and Italy despatched warships to the spot. In Greece the excitement reached a high pitch. The government thus far had withstood the pressure of the Cretan Committee and was evidently anxious to avoid complications in Crete at a time when affairs in Macedonia were hanging in the balance. But now public opinion demanded that ships be sent to rescue the Christians of the island. The King himself declared that he could not assume responsibility for the future unless something were done. The government was already powerless to prevent the shipment of arms and ammunition to the insurgents.[33]

The prospect of further difficulties in the Near East thoroughly alarmed the powers. Working at first individually, they urged the Greek government not to send ships and to do all that was possible to stop the despatch of volunteers and munitions. At the same time they pressed upon the Porte the need for care in the suppression of the rising and used strong language to the Sultan in pointing out the need for reforms. The British and French ambassadors at Constantinople took the lead in the action, but they had little success. The Sultan insisted that the insurrection must be put down before reforms could be introduced. If the rebels would make submission, he would consider their " admissible and legitimate demands." Rumors were going the rounds that the British government was working for a protectorate over Crete. The report

[82] *Turkey No. 7 (1896)*, nos. 3, 9, 21, 42, 44, 47, 79; *Affaire de Crète, juin 1894–février 1897*, nos. 11, 16, 17, 29; S. B. Chester: *Life of Venizelos* (New York, 1921), pp. 20–2.

[33] *Turkey No. 7 (1896)*, nos. 83, 85, 90, 114, 121, 128, 143, 157, 174, 208; *Affaire de Crète*, nos. 36, 54, 70; *Die Grosse Politik*, XII, no. 2994; Driault and Lhéritier, op. cit., IV, pp. 312 ff.

caused something of a panic in the Turkish capital and frightened the Greek government too. Though there is no satisfactory evidence to substantiate the charge, it is interesting as another reflection of the profound distrust of British policy at the time. Even in serious modern books the report of England's ulterior motives is credited.[34]

The ambassadors at Constantinople were agreed that the vague promises of the Sultan settled nothing. Only substantial concessions would stifle the revolt and prevent intervention by Greece. An amnesty, a Christian governor, the convocation of the general assembly and the restoration of the Halepa Pact were steps which they regarded as indispensable. Under the leadership of Russia these demands were presented to the Porte on June 25. For a time the Sultan tried to evade and to put off the ambassadors with half-measures. But on June 28 he appointed the Christian governor of Samos, George Berovič, to be governor of Crete, and on July 3 he accepted the program of the powers in full. On the following day the Pact of Halepa was proclaimed anew.[35]

The Turks having given in on all essentials, there remained the problem of inducing the insurgents to accept the terms offered. So long as Greece stood behind them there was little prospect of this. The Cretan leaders in Greece declared that they would not accept autonomy but would work for annexation to Greece. The insurgents themselves announced that they would accept no reforms unless guaranteed by the powers.[36] The key to the situation clearly lay in Athens. Ever since the time of the Canea massacre in May the German government had been stressing the need for pressure upon the Greek government. The rising in Crete would never die down, wrote the ambassador at London, until the powers had made it clear that Greek support would not be allowed.[37] Now that the Sultan had been brought around, the powers accepted a suggestion put forward by Goluchowski. On July 3 representations were made to the Greek government. The powers urged that shipments to Crete be stopped and that the Greek government use its influence to induce the rebels to accept the Turkish terms. But they received only an evasive reply. The powers had hoped that the government would find it easier to yield to outside pressure, but at Athens the King and his ministers were not in a position to yield to anyone. On July 16 the Cretans mobbed the office of the Central Committee and mauled the chairman because he had not been doing enough for the cause. The government was practically helpless.[38]

The European powers were now in a serious dilemma. Stronger action at

[34] *Turkey No. 7*, nos. 197, 198, 200, 209, 213, 238; *Affaire de Crète*, nos. 73, 113, 117, 118, 120; *Die Grosse Politik*, XII, nos. 2998–3001; Choublier, op. cit., pp. 319 ff.; Driault and Lhéritier, op. cit., IV, pp. 312–7.

[35] *Turkey No. 7 (1896)*, nos. 214, 229, 249, 250, 255, 276, 280, 286, 319; *Affaire de Crète*, nos. 118, 120, 134–136, 143, 146, 148, 158, 174 ff.; *Die Grosse Politik*, XII, nos. 3003, 3007, 3015.

[36] *Turkey No. 7 (1896)*, nos. 266, 273.   [37] *Die Grosse Politik*, XII, nos. 2995, 3013.

[38] *Die Grosse Politik*, XII, nos. 3022 ff.; Driault and Lhéritier, op. cit., pp. 319–20; *Turkey No. 7 (1896)*, no. 370.

Athens was imperative if the Cretan affair was to be hushed up. At first it had been feared that united action would be frustrated by England, where public opinion was strongly hostile to the Turks and favorably disposed towards the Greeks. But Salisbury had declared over and over again that he was anxious to co-operate and not to separate himself from the other powers. On July 7 Count Hatzfeldt reported the British premier as saying that he would not abstain from further action by the powers, even if they thought a new blockade necessary.[39] The road was evidently clear for the proposal that the rebels be cut off from supplies by a blockade of the island and that Greece be brought to heel by a blockade of Greece itself if necessary. Prince Hohenlohe talked the matter over with Count Goluchowski when the two men met on July 21. The Austrian minister declared roundly that he cared nothing whatever about Crete, but that he feared very much the possible repercussion of events upon the situation in Macedonia. The Cretan affair, he agreed, must be adjusted at all costs. On July 25 the Austrian government came forward with the proposal that, if Greek support of the insurrection did not stop, the powers should leave Crete to be reconquered by the Turks. They should, in fact, join Turkey in a blockade of the Cretan coast, if drastic action should become necessary.[40]

On the very day that this proposal was put forward the German ambassador at London reported Salisbury as saying that he was ready for any steps at Athens or in Crete. The British minister thought a blockade by one power with a European mandate would be most effective. But this power could not be England, because public opinion would never tolerate such action. Yet a few days later, on July 29, Hatzfeldt reported to his government that the British government had definitely refused to join in a blockade, on the theory that such action would "place Great Britain in the position of an ally of the Sultan, in the task of repressing the insurrection of his Christian subjects." The whole cabinet, as well as the Queen, was opposed to the policy suggested by Goluchowski.[41]

Though Salisbury insisted, in his conversation with the German ambassador, that he had no objection to other powers blockading Greece, the defection of England really sounded the death-knell of the project. Goluchowski put forward the idea that during the blockade the consuls might renew their attempts to mediate, and the Russian foreign office seems to have proposed that the other governments go forward with the blockade even without England. But nothing came of the scheme. The German Emperor was not at all certain that an end of Turkish rule in Crete would be a bad thing. Germany could not give more than moral support to the blockading powers in any event, as she had no ship available for service. Sooner or later, he noted, Crete would have to come to Greece,

---

[39] *Die Grosse Politik*, XII, nos. 3026, 3027.

[40] *Die Grosse Politik*, XII, nos. 3033, 3034; *Turkey No. 7 (1896)*, nos. 389, 403; *Affaire de Crète*, nos. 250–5.

[41] *Turkey No. 7 (1896)*, nos. 416, 419, 433, 438, 453, 471–4; *Affaire de Crète*, nos. 283, 307; *Die Grosse Politik*, XII, nos. 3040, 3042, 3046; *Letters of Queen Victoria*, III, p. 57.

and if the insurgents were cut off, the Turks would massacre them all. Germany could not take the initiative in putting forward suggestions of annexation to Greece, but the Emperor's lukewarmness probably had something to do with the shelving of the blockade idea.[42]

Meanwhile the Sultan appeared anxious to settle the Cretan problem, even at the expense of further concessions. The ambassadors at Constantinople had been working for some time on another scheme of reforms. When the Sultan appealed to them for help on August 23 they were able to send him detailed proposals, based on the demands of the insurgents, almost immediately. Contrary to custom the Porte occasioned no further delay. On August 25 the ambassadorial program was accepted. The Sultan agreed to name a Christian governor for five years and to secure the approval of the powers for the choice made. The Christians in Crete were to have two thirds of the government offices, and the general assembly was to be given wide powers. A European commission was to be established to reorganize the gendarmerie system, the finances and the courts. On September 4 the Cretan leaders formally accepted these terms, and on September 12 they issued a proclamation stating that " Anyone will deserve to be considered a real enemy of his country who, contrary to the wish of the whole community, shall dare to continue to disturb public order or to ill-treat anyone, especially Mussulmans, who must henceforth be considered as our brothers." [43]

In the Macedonian and Cretan affairs the powers were united in their desire to prevent any disturbance of the peace. They acted together to bring pressure upon Bulgaria and together they worked out the scheme of reforms for Crete which the Sultan accepted in August. But the " concert " of Europe was at best a very precarious association. Far from being characterized by mutual trust as between the members, it was based rather upon deep suspicion of motives. Each power, anxious to avoid trouble, clung to the principle of unity of action. " In the European concert," said a noted French historian, " each power feared to speak; each declared itself ready to follow the advice of the majority; but how could a majority be formed, when no one had an opinion? " [44] Under such circumstances the program followed by the powers was bound to be the minimum program; Europe did what the most unwilling and reluctant power was willing to do, nothing more. That explains why no effort was made to find a definite solution for the Macedonian question, why no effective pressure could be brought to bear upon Greece, and why the powers had to rely upon the good will of the Sultan to bring about a half-way satisfactory reform program for Crete.

---

[42] *Die Grosse Politik*, XII, nos. 3021, 3043, 3044, 3048, 3052; *Turkey No. 7 (1896)*, no. 412.

[43] *Turkey No. 7 (1896)*, nos. 538, 552, 565, 578, 582, 597, 623; *Turkey No. 8 (1897)*, no. 16; *Affaire de Crète*, nos. 336, 343, 349, 383; *Die Grosse Politik*, XII, nos. 3057–63; Driault and Lhéritier, op. cit., IV, pp. 327–8.

[44] Ernest Lavisse: " Notre Politique Orientale " (*Revue de Paris*, May 15, 1897, pp. 274–311), p. 299.

But both the Macedonian and the Cretan problems were still minor issues when compared with the Armenian question. It was the massacre at Sassun in 1894 that had brought the whole Eastern question into a critical state, that had led to the formation of the short-lived Armenian Triplice, that had revealed to the world the fundamental difference of view between England on the one hand and Russia, generally supported by the continental countries, on the other. The Russians had uncompromisingly opposed all measures of coercion. The utmost that could be extracted from Abdul Hamid, therefore, was the establishment of a commission of reform, which was to consider the whole position of the Armenians in the Empire. The commission was composed of able and well-intentioned men, but lacked authority. Though it was in session during the spring and summer of 1896, nothing substantial resulted from its deliberations.[45]

The reform program put forward by the powers had never satisfied the revolutionary Hentchak, which had set out to attract the attention of Europe through the wholesale massacre of the Armenians. There was much criticism within the organization. Nazarbek, the leader, was accused of spending too much money on socialist propaganda and of making too much sensation about small accomplishments. A general meeting was held despite his objections. He was ousted from the party and the socialist plank in the platform was thrown out. This break in the ranks of the party occurred in September 1896 and may be taken as marking the end of the effective action of the Hentchak for some years.[46] But just as the Hentchak ceased to play an active rôle, the Armenian Revolutionary Federation (Dashnagtzoutiun) began to open operations. This Federation was essentially a Russian-Armenian organization, but it had committees in Geneva and Constantinople as well as in various towns of Anatolia. Its headquarters seem to have been at Van, where it practically commanded the situation. Early in March 1896 Mr. Williams, the English vice-consul at Van, reported to his government a manifesto issued by this group. Denouncing " that beast, the Sultan," the revolutionaries declared:

" There can be no reconciliation; we will not put down our arms. We have a holy war, and it will be continued with greater savageness. Therefore let the Commission of the tyrant go to Hell. Let there be no yielding. We are revolutionists and this is our last word."

Williams reported further that the Federation had about four hundred members in Van, hiding in the maze of narrow streets and blind alleys known as the Garden Town:

[45] *Turkey No. 8 (1896)*, nos. 53, 67, 78, 188; *Turkey No. 3 (1897)*, no. 86; *Turkey No. 7 (1897)*, no. 135.
[46] Khan-Azad: " Hai Heghapoghaganie Housheritz " (" Memoirs of an Armenian Revolutionary," in *Hairenik Amsakir*, VI, February, 1929, no. 7); M. K. Jismedjian: *Badmoutiun Ameriga-hai Kaghakagan Gousagtstoutiantz, 1890–1925 (History of American-Armenian Political Parties*, Fresno, 1930), pp. 53 ff. See also the very interesting report of one of the Armenian patriarch's agents in western Europe, dated March 17, 1897 (in *Turkey No. 1 (1898)*, no. 142); Bérard: *La Politique du Sultan* (Paris, 1897), pp. 166 ff.

" They terrorize over their countrymen," he wrote, " and, by their outrages and folly, excite the Mohammedan population and render nugatory all efforts to carry out reforms. I am firmly convinced that if they could be put down, or even kept quiet, one of the greatest obstacles to security in this district, as probably all over Anatolia, would be removed." The Armenian population, he believed, disapproved of the agitation. " The more I learn of past events and the present state of this province, the more clearly I see that the criminal actions of these societies have been largely responsible for the terrible scenes enacted here and all over Anatolia during the last autumn, much as the Turks are to blame. It must be remembered that this and many other provinces of Anatolia are barely civilised. With a weak and corrupt government and different religious creeds, of which one, and that the stronger, thought itself threatened with extinction, the wonder to me is, not that we have had these terrible massacres, but that they have not been still worse." [47]

Very similar was the impression of Lord Warkworth after paying a visit to Van:

" Those who in England are loudest in their sympathy with the aspirations of a people ' rightly struggling to be free' can hardly have realised the atrocious methods of terrorism and blackmail by which a handful of desperadoes, as careful of their own safety as they are reckless of the lives of others, have too successfully coerced their unwilling compatriots into complicity with an utterly hopeless conspiracy." [48]

That the members of the Federation meant business was shown by the outbreak it organized in Van in mid-June 1896. The Armenians fell upon the Kurds and killed a goodly number, with the usual result — the massacre of the innocent population.[49] The outbreak was evidently meant as the first move in the new campaign of frightfulness which was to attract the attention of the powers, for in rapid succession similar " disturbances " took place in many other centres. Eastern Anatolia, from the Black Sea to Syria, was once more in uproar and panic. The ambassadors at Constantinople began to receive a whole series of communications from the revolutionaries, threatening extreme action unless their demands were fulfilled. On August 25 they received from " The Armenian People " a protest against the deposition of the patriarch, who was sympathetic to national aims. " The Powers," said this declaration, " by their attitude, make themselves accomplices of the Porte. In Crete, as in Armenia, they receive the demands of the Christians with the same disdain as our executioners. But the patience of down-trodden nations has its limits." On the next day came another letter, this time signed by the Armenian Revolutionary Federation: " ' Might gets the better of right,' Europe has said to us in her murderous indifference, and we, the weak, deprived of our rights as men, find ourselves compelled to have recourse to science in seeking every means to break the abominable yoke

[47] *Turkey No. 8 (1896)*, no. 117.

[48] Lord Warkworth: *Notes from a Diary in Asiatic Turkey* (London, 1898), pp. 122 ff.

[49] *Turkey No. 8 (1896)*, nos. 246 ff., 273 and especially no. 337; *Affaires Arméniennes, 1893–1897*, no. 220.

of the Sultan; we can no longer bear it. The time of diplomatic play is passed." [50]

The " recourse to science" took the form of a daring coup on Wednesday, August 26. Shortly after one o'clock several men, dressed as porters, entered the Ottoman Bank at Galata. On their shoulders they carried sacks ordinarily used for transporting money, but now filled with bombs and dynamite. Once they were safely inside, a whistle was blown, some twenty of their accomplices rushed from the street, shot down some of the bank guards and started a regular fusillade inside the Bank and through the windows. All doors were shut and barricaded with sacks of coin, while more than a hundred employees, petrified with fear, found themselves trapped in the company of the desperadoes. Sir Edgar Vincent, now Lord D'Abernon, the director of the Bank, barely succeeded in escaping from his office on the top story over the roof to an adjoining building. His assistant, M. Auboyneau, was less fortunate.

At first the police attempted to retake the place by assault, but the building was well designed to stand a siege, and after two hours of heavy firing at and from the Bank, the police withdrew. In the meanwhile the employees began to negotiate with their captors. They were told that the conspirators intended to attract the attention of Europe and that they meant to stay for forty-eight hours. If by that time the ambassadors did not guarantee their demands for reforms they would blow up the Bank and everyone in it. In order to establish contact they allowed M. Auboyneau to leave, on promise that he would return. The assistant director went to Sir Edgar and the latter proceeded to the council of ministers. It was agreed that the only way to save the Bank was to treat with the revolutionaries. M. Maximov, dragoman of the Russian embassy, consented to assume the difficult task of mediation. He argued with the desperadoes for three hours from the street, and evidently won them over through his remarkable eloquence. At two o'clock in the morning they left the Bank under safe conduct and were taken to Sir Edgar's yacht. There they awaited the visit of the foreign representatives who were to discuss with them the demands they had made. Why they gave up their original plan was never revealed, but it appears that the most prominent leader was killed at the outset and that the others, worn down by long hours of tension and suspense, lacked the courage to go through with the scheme. They left in the Bank forty-five unused gunpowder bombs, twenty-five dynamite cartridges and some twenty pounds of dynamite.

On the yacht with the conspirators was Mr. F. A. Barker, one of Sir Edgar's secretaries. The plotters made no attempt to conceal from him their plans and hopes. The whole thing had been planned several months before and had been very carefully organized. They had chosen the Bank for attack because it contained people of so many nationalities that the representatives of the powers would have to act to save their nationals. Two of the three chiefs had come from Van, and the coup was clearly the work of the Revolutionary Federation, though

---

[50] *Turkey No. 1 (1897): Correspondence Respecting the Disturbances at Constantinople in August 1896*, no. 25, enclosures.

the men said they did not belong to any one society. They had planned other attacks in Stambul, Galata and Pera, including assaults upon the Sublime Porte and the Armenian patriarchate. When Barker pointed out to them that the whole thing would probably end in massacre of the Armenians and alienation of the sympathies of the powers, they replied: " Those who die will do so as true patriots and martyrs, and as to the sympathy of the Powers, if we had thought we would lose it, we would have forced their hands by remaining in the Bank." To which Barker added in his report: " Their hatred of the Turks was beyond all description, and the gloating of the rank and file over the Turks they had killed was truly horrible and savage. . . . They also told me that it had been their intention to kill all the Turks in the employ of the Bank before blowing the latter up, but that they had not had time, as things finished sooner than they had expected." [51]

The statements of the desperadoes were substantially correct. There were minor outbreaks in various parts of the city and for weeks afterward bomb outrages and shooting at the troops by Armenian revolutionaries took place sporadically. No one had any sympathy for this mode of action, or for the self-appointed committees that felt called upon to make Armenian martyrs of the innocent population. Mr. Herbert, the British chargé d'affaires, described them as " criminals, who cannot be condemned too strongly." " It cannot be denied," he reported, " that this repeated bomb throwing on the part of the Armenians is a cause of great provocation to the Turks." [52] Revenge had not been slow in coming. On the afternoon of the attack on the Bank, bands of Turks of the lower classes began to appear in the streets and attack Armenians with clubs and iron bars. It is fairly certain that the government had learned of the revolutionaries' plans some days before they were put into execution, and that these Turk bands had been organized and armed. The clubs were mostly of one design and the men who wielded them were rarely residents of the neighborhood in which they operated. The troops conducted themselves well and took little if any part in the proceedings. They merely looked on while the carnage took place. For fully thirty-six hours, till the evening of the 27th, the mob was in control of the city. No foreigners, not even Greeks or Jews, were injured. The attack was levelled at the Armenians only, and chiefly at the lower classes in Stambul, the *hamals* or porters. These were ruthlessly cut down and hunted through the houses, " like rabbits," said eyewitnesses. In all it was estimated that five to six thousand of the two hundred thousand Armenians in Constantinople lost their lives.

[51] The fundamental accounts in M. Varandian: *Hai Heghapoghagan Dashnaghtzoutan Badmoutiun* (*History of the Armenian Revolutionary Federation*, Paris, 1932), I, pp. 158 ff., and in *Turkey No. 1 (1897)*. nos. 25, 26; but see also *Affaires Arméniennes*, nos. 236 ff., 254; *Die Grosse Politik*, XII, nos. 2894 ff.; and the very well-informed anonymous article " The Constantinople Massacre " (*Contemporary Review*, October, 1896, pp. 457–65).

[52] *Turkey No. 1 (1897)*, nos. 3, 14; see also the scathing remarks in the anonymous article referred to in the preceding note.

Carts were in readiness to truck them off to the Armenian cemeteries, where they were indiscriminately dumped in any convenient spot.[53]

Nothing is further removed from my intention than to condone the Constantinople massacre or any other. At the same time it is the duty of the historian to look at the facts from all possible angles, and to avoid being carried away by the tidal wave of uncritical emotionalism. The British and the Americans were, from the start, the most gullible and the most thirsty for stories of blood-curdling atrocities. The greater credit, therefore, to those among them who managed to keep some sense of perspective. Mr. Herbert, the British chargé, appreciated the provocation to the Turks. Mr. Hume-Beaman, an expert on things oriental, roundly declared that every member of the Armenian committees should be hanged, and that the responsibilities for the massacres rested divided between these cowardly committees and " the braggart and ineffectual intervention of Europe." Speaking of the Sultan he continued: " It is all very well to call him the ' Great Assassin,' but from the Moslem point of view he was very fairly justified in killing any number of rebellious infidels who were being supported by combined Europe in what he and every Turk considered as a plot against the realm. The Turks retorted on England especially, that we used to blow Moslems from the muzzles of our guns and burn whole villages and mosques in India for an insult offered to one of our officials, and were they not to make an example of these Armenian dogs? "[54] Sir Charles Eliot, one of the best-informed and most conscientious writers about modern Turkey, thought it pretty certain that the Armenian community knew what was on foot. Many of the wealthy families, he says, left the city on the morning of the assault on the Bank. The Turks were aware of this " national conspiracy." The authorities prepared the mob for all eventualities, probably not so much with the idea that they should slaughter Armenians as with the idea that they should protect the city. " In fact, the Turks thought that the whole Armenian people were combining against them, and they combined against the Armenians."[55]

At the time, of course, there was no chance of calm reflection. During the massacres and for weeks afterward Constantinople was first panic-stricken, then still in awe and apprehension. While bombings took place periodically the Turkish police uncovered large caches of explosives in Armenian churches and schools. In the cupboard of the mistress of the girls' school in the Psamatia district the police found thirty-six bombs, some boxes of revolver cartridges and a parcel of dynamite capsules. And to top it all the revolutionary committees

---

[53] *Turkey No. 1 (1897)* passim, but especially no. 26; *Affaires Arméniennes,* nos. 236 ff.; *Die Grosse Politik,* XII, nos. 2894 ff. Among unofficial eye-witness accounts may be mentioned the anonymous one in the *Contemporary Review*; Sidney Whitman: *Turkish Memories* (London, 1914), chap. ii; Baron Wladimir Giesl: *Zwei Jahrzehnte im Nahen Orient* (Berlin, 1927), pp. 116–21; Louis Rambert: *Notes et Impressions de Turquie* (Paris, 1926), pp. 15 ff.

[54] Ardern G. Hume-Beaman: *Twenty Years in the Near East* (London, 1898), pp. 304–5.

[55] "Odysseus" (Sir Charles N. E. Eliot): *Turkey in Europe* (London, 1900), p. 456.

kept threatening further action. On September 10 they warned the ambassadors: "A fresh movement is in preparation by which our nation will display its vitality. If the present notice is followed by no effective step on your part, you will see that we will once again make death a feature of the struggle." By some Europeans this was taken as a threat of violence against the foreign colonies. Constantinople was on edge day and night, awaiting in terror some new catastrophe.[56]

The foreign diplomats were more or less affected by the panic. They hastily chartered ships in the harbor to serve as refuges for the terror-stricken Europeans. Acting with rare unanimity and determination they did not wait for instructions, but on the afternoon of August 28 sent a message directly to the Sultan, calling his attention to what was going on, even in the summer colonies on the Bosporus: "In view of these occurrences," they concluded, "the Representatives of the Great Powers, in the name of their Governments, address themselves directly to Your Majesty, as Head of the State, and urgently request that you will forthwith issue such precise and categorical orders as will put an immediate end to this unheard-of state of things, which is calculated to bring about the most disastrous consequences for Your Majesty's Empire." Thereupon the massacres promptly stopped. When the Sultan inquired of Baron Calice, the dean of the diplomatic corps, what was the meaning of the menace in the message, the like of which he had never before received, the ambassador stood to his guns, pointing out that it was now clear that the government was unable to maintain order even in the capital. The nature of the remedy would have to be considered.[57]

This preliminary exchange was followed by a prolonged debate between the embassies and the palace regarding the responsibility for the massacre. Into this argument there is no need to enter, in as much as the matter of the government's responsibility has already been touched upon. What interests us here is rather the impression made upon Europe by the events in Constantinople, and the policies and actions of the European governments in the ensuing crisis.

The news from the Turkish capital sent shivers of horror through western Europe. For the moment humane and religious sentiments crowded out all political considerations. The Emperor William, who was so often accused of cherishing a particular affection for the "Great Assassin" expressed his immediate reaction in the words: "The Sultan must be deposed."[58] The strong language in which the German ambassador warned the Sultan of the consequences of his action was not nearly strong enough for the Emperor. Lavisse is, in all probability, right when he expresses an opinion widely held at the time, namely that if, immediately after the massacre, any European power had sent its ships through the Dardanelles to make a demonstration at Yildiz Kiosk, the

---

[56] *Turkey No. 1 (1897),* nos. 11, 14, 19, 24, 43, 44.
[57] *Turkey No. 1 (1897),* nos. 10, 12, 26.
[58] *Die Grosse Politik,* XII, nos. 2898, 2901, footnote.

Sultan would have been overthrown by a revolution, and Europe, far from opposing such single action, would have loudly applauded.[59]

In England the furor caused by the new massacres reached the highest pitch and lasted longest. The newspapers, led by the Liberal *Daily News* and *Daily Chronicle,* published the most lurid accounts, full of hair-raising details, illustrated with almost incredible imaginary pictures which were accepted without question as gospel truth. All through September and October the agitation was at its height and sought expression in a veritable frenzy of meetings and protests. " All England is blazing with rhetorical pyrotechnics, and even the craven crew of ambassadors are waxing insolent," wrote William T. Stead in the *Review of Reviews.* "If good, round, hard swearing from high and low in every key of profanity or of prayer could have settled the Eastern Question, then assuredly it had been settled this week." [60] Everywhere could be heard the demand for immediate action, either with Russia and France, or alone. Abdul Hamid, it was said, must be deposed, even though the British fleet would have to bombard him in his palace. At St. James Hall a meeting attended by more than a hundred mayors called loudly for a policy of extreme measures. " The roof would have gone off with the roar of exultation which would have greeted an announcement by the Chairman that a declaration of war against Turkey had been launched by Lord Salisbury," wrote Stead.[61]

In the earlier stages of the Armenian question the great obstacle to action had been the reluctance of Russia. This was attributed by some writers to Russian suspicion of Britain's ulterior motives, as they had been revealed in 1878. The guilt really lay at England's door, wrote Stead, for having protected Abdul Hamid in 1878 and for having perpetrated the larceny of Cyprus, "a crime almost unparalleled in history for its combination of Pharisaism and theft." " The indelible infamy of that performance clings to us like the shirt of Nessus. . . . A standing reminder to all Europe of the trickiness and dishonesty of ' perfide Albion,'" continued the able and influential journalist. The only remedy would be to give up Cyprus in order to reassure the Russians of the purity of British motives.[62]

Lord Salisbury could not justly be called a Turcophil. Had he had his own way the Sultan would certainly have been deposed, and possibly some effort might have been made to dissolve the Ottoman Empire. But Salisbury had no faith in the remedy so eloquently expounded on all sides and so vehemently demanded by Gladstone in a speech at Liverpool on September 24. He simply did not believe that Britain could intervene alone, or that the other powers would

---

[59] Ernest Lavisse, loc. cit., pp. 302–3; this was also Gladstone's opinion (George W. E. Russell: *Malcolm MacColl,* London, 1914, pp. 261 ff.); see also the anonymous author in the *Contemporary Review,* October, 1896; and Major General Maurice: "Ought we to Shell Yildiz?" (*United Service Magazine,* October, 1896).

[60] *Review of Reviews,* October 15, 1896, p. 291.

[61] *Review of Reviews,* November 15, 1896, p. 391; the most revealing account of the agitation is in Russell: *MacColl,* pp. 149 ff.   [62] *Review of Reviews,* October 15, 1896, pp. 355–61.

it idly by while the British fleet sailed through the Dardanelles and anchored off the Turkish capital. It was all right for the poets and poetasters, like William Allan, to brush aside the considerations of diplomats and sing:

> We fear not Frank nor Muscovite
>   When Liberty is calling,
> With British pluck for those we'll fight,
>   'Neath Moslem vengeance falling;
>   Cease your preaching! Load your guns!
>   Their roar our mission tells,
>   The day is come for Britain's sons
>   To seize the Dardanelles.

Such fanfaronades showed more passion than literary taste or common sense. The only possible mode of action, as Salisbury saw it, was to effect an understanding with England's chief opponent, Russia, and, if possible, to revive the Armenian Triplice with a program of action. When the Emperor William hurried to the British embassy on the day after the Constantinople coup, to find out what Britain proposed to do, Sir Frank Lascelles made no secret of the fact that Lord Salisbury was prepared to abandon Constantinople to the Russians and Syria to the French, if only they could be induced to act with Britain.[63]

That this was not mere conjecture on Sir Frank's part is borne out by other testimony. On the last day of August Salisbury wrote a letter in which he reviewed the whole past policy of England with respect to Russia and France. He thought it was a mistake on Palmerston's part to shape his foreign policy according to political proclivities, thus courting France and estranging Russia and Austria. " Politics is a matter of business: our allies should be those who are most likely to help and not to hinder the interests of which we, as the Government, are the trustees." What were the results of Palmerston's policy?

"We have not kept France, — she is more our enemy than ever. But the feud with Russia remains. Austria has become of less importance, because out of the fragments of her dominions or her followings Germany and Italy have been created; and we have to find in the nominal alliance of these two last what consolation we can for the necessity of coping, practically alone, with the alliance of France and Russia. If we had only listened to the Emperor Nicholas when he spoke to Sir Hamilton Seymour, what a pleasanter outlook would meet us when we contemplate the continent of Europe. It is much easier to lament than to repair. It may not be possible for England and Russia to return to their old relations. But it is an object to be wished for and approached as opportunity offers. At all events efforts should be made to avoid needless aggravation of the feud between them which the Governments and not the nations have made. The French and German *people* both hate us; the Russian people do not. It is not possible to stop the impulse which past mistakes have given. . . . All we can do is to try to narrow the chasm that separates us. It is the best chance for some-

---

[63] *Die Grosse Politik*, XII, no. 2918; similar indications in *Affaires Arméniennes*, no. 263.

thing like an equilibrium of Europe. There is no reason why Germany, under steady guidance, should not go with us, but steadiness is not the note of its Government just now." [64]

This letter leaves no doubt whatever that Salisbury desired an entente with Russia touching the Near East. He wanted to proceed against the Sultan, but he did not believe, with Gladstone and the " atrocitarians," that England could afford to act alone in coercing the " Assassin." Chamberlain had, since December 1895, been pressing upon him the idea of making large concessions to the Americans in the Venezuela affair and then enlisting the aid of the great republic for a move against the Sultan. Parenthetically it may be remarked that Chamberlain took the matter up with Olney in September 1896 and that the American secretary of state gave a sympathetic if inconclusive reply:

" If England should now seriously set about putting the Armenian charnel-house in order there can be little doubt that the United States would consider the moment opportune for vigorous exertion on behalf of American citizens and interests in Turkey. It would feel itself entitled to demand full indemnity for past injuries to them as well as adequate security against the like injuries in the future. It would support such demands by all the physical force at its disposal — with the necessary result, I think, that its attitude would both morally and materially strengthen the hands of England. . . ." [65]

Chamberlain's biographer tells us nothing about the fate of this singular proposal, though he indicates that it made little impression upon the unromantic and hard-headed prime minister. Salisbury still had some hope of establishing contact with Russia. Acting no doubt on instructions, Sir Philip Currie, returning to his Constantinople post just after the massacres, hurried to his Russian colleague and assured him that Salisbury as well as the country were strongly in favor of an understanding with Russia. But Nelidov had his suspicions of the English and nothing seems to have come of Currie's advances. Salisbury, indeed, received information saying that Russia, Austria and Germany had made an agreement to work together on the Armenian problem:

" *Since* the recent massacres," he wrote MacColl on September 12, " Austria, Russia and Germany have agreed to do their utmost to maintain the status quo as long as they can. As far as I know France has not spoken; but she would undoubtedly have taken the same side. . . . You might turn this Government out, and ten other Governments after it, but you would not be able to accomplish a result which Austria, Russia, Germany, France and Turkey are determined to prevent." [66]

---

[64] Salisbury to Iwan-Muller, August 31, 1896 (*British Documents on the Origins of the War,* VI, London, 1930, p. 780).

[65] J. L. Garvin: *Life of Chamberlain*, III, pp. 68–9, 96, 166 ff. The American claims are discussed in Leland J. Gordon: *American Relations with Turkey, 1830–1930* (Philadelphia, 1932), pp. 240 ff.

[66] Russell: *Malcolm MacColl,* pp. 153–4.

In other words, Salisbury regarded the situation as being hopeless. There could be no thought of action so long as the continental powers stood together and protected the Sultan. But the young Tsar was expected to visit Queen Victoria at Balmoral in the last days of September. Prince Lobanov, the soul of the anti-British party at court, had died suddenly on August 30 and no successor had been appointed. Nicholas was deeply attached to the old Queen, and there was, consequently, some prospect that he might be brought to see the light. During the Balmoral visit both the Queen and Lord Salisbury pressed upon Nicholas the idea of an entente. They tried to convince him that the Sultan should be deposed. They even dangled before him the prospect of concessions in the Straits question.[67]

But Nicholas, though he may have been weak-willed, was not unintelligent. The teachings of Lobanov were still fresh in his mind, and Lobanov positively hated the British. Furthermore, what had Russia to gain by deposing the Sultan? Her interest was to keep things as they were while she pursued her policy of expansion in the Far East. The situation really could not be improved upon. Never since the days of Ignatiev in the early 1870's had Russian influence at Constantinople been so all-powerful. It would have been the purest folly to abandon Abdul Hamid and set on the throne a monarch who suited the British.

But there were other considerations. M. Nelidov, the able if somewhat high-strung ambassador at Constantinople, was absolutely convinced that the danger from the British fleet was a real one. When, just after the massacres, it was suggested to him that the fleet might come up, he exclaimed excitedly: " We shall never give up the key to our house! " [68] He had, almost immediately, opened negotiations with the Porte to arrange for the eventual protection of the Straits. He inspected the Turkish fleet that lay at anchor in the Golden Horn, and arranged that General Chickhachev, chief of staff of the Odessa military district, should come and examine the fortifications at the Dardanelles. In the meanwhile he bombarded his government with alarming reports. Further disorders in the capital were inevitable, and when they took place the British fleet would certainly be ordered up, thus settling the Straits question without argument. The only salvation for Russia lay in firm action. If the British fleet entered the Dardanelles the Russian fleet should at once occupy the upper part of the Bosporus, land a force and fortify itself. Furthermore, Russian and French ships should join the British in entering the Dardanelles. Then Russia would be in a position to negotiate. If England insisted on remaining within the Straits, Russia would at least be in possession of the upper Bosporus.[69]

---

[67] *Letters of Queen Victoria*, III, pp. 82–6.

[68] Sidney Whitman: *Turkish Memories*, p. 19.

[69] V. Khvostov: " Proekt Zakhvata Bosfora v 1896 g." (*Krasnyi Arkhiv*, XLVII, 1931, pp. 50–70), pp. 55–60; idem: " Blizhne Vostochnyi Krizis, 1895–1897 gg." (*Istorik Marksist*, XIII, 1929, pp. 19–54), pp. 23–5, 35, 36; *Die Grosse Politik*, XII, nos. 2926, 2927, 2928; Siegmund Münz:

The Russian foreign office was deeply impressed with this report. M. Shishkin, temporarily in charge of the foreign office, told the French chargé that the Russian Black Sea fleet was ready for all eventualities.[70] The Tsar, too, was put on his guard. On Nelidov's report he noted: " I am against an agreement with England. That would in fact be the first step on the way to the gradual partition of Turkey." [71] It was natural, therefore, that when he came to England he should have listened to the British suggestions with some mental reservations. When the freedom of the Straits was held out to him as an inducement he evaded by saying that Russia desired some such solution " in due time." For the rest he would not consider the deposition of the Sultan, on the plea that Russia did not want to interfere in Turkey's domestic affairs. The utmost that he would concede was that, if the Sultan rejected the proposals for reform to be put forward by the powers, he should be overruled by force.[72]

Before going to Scotland the Tsar had been reinforced in his determination to work for the status quo and the maintenance of the Sultan's authority by his conversation with the German Emperor at Breslau.[73] When he reached Paris after his visit to Balmoral he heard even stronger arguments in the same sense. It is true that the French ambassador at Constantinople, M. Paul Cambon, was one of the most vehement advocates of action. He was simply " boiling with rage against the Sultan," according to his German colleague, and certainly frightened Abdul Hamid with his very outspoken warnings. It was Cambon's conviction that France could successfully mediate between the British and the Russian views and thus reconstitute the Armenian Triplice of 1894-1895.[74] But in Paris government circles there was little sympathy for such a forward policy. Ernest Lavisse, himself a critic of Hanotaux' course, at least agreed with the foreign minister on the principles. France, he said, should avoid sentimental considerations, but should stick to her traditional Near Eastern policy, " which is to prevent, or at least to postpone as long as possible a dismemberment (of the Empire) in which several powers would get their share and in which France could not find hers. We know perfectly well that the government of the Turks is brutal, barbarous and vicious, and that their domination will come to an end some day, breaking down bit by bit; but we desire that this dissolution should be slow and that it should profit, not the great powers whose aggrandizement will diminish our own position, but the Christian populations." Hanotaux subscribed whole-heartedly to this view. He stood for the defense and integrity of the Ottoman Empire.[75]

" Graf Nigra über Fragen der internationalen Politik " (*Deutsche Revue*, December, 1911, pp. 307-20), pp. 315-20.   [70] *Affaires Arméniennes*, no. 266.

[71] Khvostov: " Proekt Zakhvata Bosfora," p. 55.

[72] *Letters of Queen Victoria*, III, pp. 85-6; Khvostov: " Blizhne Vostochnyi Krizis," p. 36; *Die Grosse Politik*, XII, no. 3078.   [73] *Die Grosse Politik*, XII, no. 2925.

[74] *Die Grosse Politik*, XII, no. 2908; *Affaires Arméniennes*, nos. 269, 287; Rambert: *Notes et Impressions de Turquie*, pp. 31, 33.

[75] Lavisse, loc. cit., p. 282; Georges Lachapelle: *Le Ministère Méline* (Paris, 1928), pp. 65-8.

Apart from these political aspects of the situation there were yet other factors to be taken into consideration by the French. Paris banks were heavily interested in the financial side of the Turkish situation, for nine per cent of the French foreign investment, coming to something like five hundred million dollars, was in the Ottoman Empire. In fact, France held sixty per cent of the Turkish government bonds. Now Turkey was in serious financial straits, and it was perfectly obvious to everyone that there could be no thoroughgoing reform of the administration until money could be made available. Financial breakdown, it was feared, would inevitably precipitate the political collapse, just as the dissolution of the Empire would place the whole foreign investment in question. M. Hanotaux therefore proposed to the Tsar and his advisers that Turkish finance should be reorganized on the basis of European control. By means of the conversion of existing loans, the extension of time for redemption, and the introduction of monopolies, favorable conditions could be established for a huge new loan, to be guaranteed by the European powers. But all this was to be conditional on important changes in the administration of the Ottoman debt as organized by the decree of Mouharrem of 1881. The council of the Ottoman Public Debt Administration was composed of representatives of the bondholders of all the great powers but Russia. The French proposal was that this Council should be reorganized and transformed into a representation of the powers themselves, and furthermore, that it should in future exercise control over the entire financial system of the Ottoman Empire.[76]

During the Paris conversations M. Hanotaux was able to persuade the Tsar to accept a far-reaching French program. An agreement with England was to be sought on the basis of an Egyptian settlement. So far as one can make out from the meagre and somewhat defective material at hand, Hanotaux was prepared to recognize the British occupation, in return for guarantees of French financial interests, the neutralization of the Suez Canal, and also, it seems, territorial compensation elsewhere in Africa, probably on the upper Nile and in Nigeria. Russia was, of course, greatly interested in the Suez matter, and in any arrangements which would protect her against the supposed British efforts to break up the Ottoman Empire. In any case, the Tsar agreed to have a Russian representative upon the Council, and to adopt the French scheme for international control of Turkish finance.[77]

If the French program had been carried through it might have resulted in a

[76] *Annual Register,* 1896, p. 296; Donald C. Blaisdell: *European Financial Control in the Ottoman Empire* (New York, 1929), pp. 100-2; and especially V. Khvostov: " Problemy Zakhvata Bosfora v 90-kh godakh XIX veka " (*Istorik Marksist,* XX, 1930, pp. 100-9), pp. 120-2; R. G. Lévy: " Les Capitaux Français à l'Étranger " (*Revue des Deux Mondes,* March 15, 1897).

[77] The documents are only summarized by Khvostov (" Problemy Zakhvata Bosfora," etc. p. 123), whose account is not very clear. In Hanotaux' communication to Cambon (October 22, in *Affaires Arméniennes,* no. 279) the decisions concerning Ottoman finance are given, but the projected negotiations with England are very carefully veiled: France and Russia " reconnaissent l'opportunité d'échanger avec l'Angleterre des explications précises et conciliantes." See finally Lavisse, loc. cit., p. 306.

fundamental recasting of the European alignments and possibly in the formation of an English-French-Russian entente like that effected in 1907. At the end
of the last chapter it has been pointed out that Salisbury was, at this time, eager
for an arrangement with France and Russia, on any terms short of the evacuation of Egypt. Concessions in the Straits question and in the matter of the Suez
Canal he was prepared to make, and it was clearly in the hope that some compromise could be reached that the British premier on October 20 sent to the
governments of the great powers a famous circular outlining a plan of action.
After reviewing the many earlier provisions for reforms in the Ottoman Empire
and the failure to realize them, Salisbury pointed out that the massacres, while
they had for their nominal purpose the maintenance of the Sultan's government,
had had the effect of bringing that government into greater peril than it had
yet encountered:

" Financial collapse threatens the military strength by which the Empire is supported, while the atrocious cruelty of many of those by whom the Government
is administered has roused among Christian nations a sympathy and an indignation of unexampled intensity; and there is little probability that the Christian subjects of the Porte will submit again quietly to the oppression under which
they have hitherto suffered. It necessarily follows that the causes which threaten
the stability of the Empire are constantly gaining in force, while the forces which
sustain it are melting away." " It is the common object of the European Powers
that the Turkish Empire should be sustained, because no arrangement to replace it can be suggested which would not carry with it a serious risk of European conflict. The predominant importance of this consideration has led the
European Powers to protect the Turkish Empire from dissolution, under the
hope that the many evils by which the Ottoman rule was accompanied would
be removed or mitigated by the reforming efforts of the Government. Not only
has this hope been entirely disappointed, but it has become evident that unless
these great evils can be abated, the forbearance of the Powers of Europe will
be unable to protract the existence of a dominion which by its own vices is
crumbling into ruin." " All the Powers of Europe are at one in desiring to maintain the territorial status quo of the Turkish Empire, and those Powers whose
territories lie nearest to that Empire are most strongly impressed with this necessity. Their convictions upon this point may be sufficient to guarantee the Empire
from any possible shock arising from external aggression, but they will not save
it from the effect of misgovernment and internal decay." " I propose that the Six
Powers should instruct their Representatives (at Constantinople) to consider and
report to their Governments what changes in the Government and administration of the Turkish Empire are, in their judgement, likely to be most effective
in maintaining the stability of the Empire, and preventing the recurrence of the
frightful cruelties by which the last two years have been lamentably distinguished.
But before those instructions are given, Her Majesty's Government are of opinion that provision ought to be made that any resolution to which the Powers
may, in consequence, unanimously come should be carried into operation. It is an
object of primary importance that the concert of Europe should be maintained;

and as long as any of the Powers, or any one Power, is not satisfied with the expediency of the recommendations that are put forward, no action in respect to them can be taken. But if any recommendations made by the Ambassadors should approve themselves to all the Powers as measures suitable for adoption, it must not be admitted, at the point we have at present reached, that the objections of the Turkish Government can be an obstacle to their being carried into effect. I trust that the Powers will, in the first instance, come to a definite understanding, that their unanimous decision in these matters is to be final, and will be executed up to the measure of such force as the Powers have at their command." [78]

Extended extracts from this long document have been quoted because the discussions of the powers during the following months hinged upon it. The striking thing about the Salisbury proposal was that the powers should agree in advance to impose by force if necessary any decision to which they came unanimously. At bottom the suggestion was so innocuous that any power might have agreed to it with an easy mind, for it left a *liberum veto* — any single power could prevent action by simply disagreeing. Furthermore, Salisbury made a special point of subscribing to the principle of the status quo territorially. It is not surprising, then, that the Austrian and Italian governments almost immediately promised support, and that the German government announced that it would join in any steps to which the powers unanimously agreed. [79]

Yet Salisbury's proposals met with obstruction from other quarters. M. Hanotaux was evidently well disposed, for on November 3 he made a speech in the Chamber in which he declared that the powers were striving to put aside all that could divide them and to find the elements of an agreement. All idea of isolated action should be discarded and any action by the concert should avoid aiming a blow at the integrity of the Ottoman Empire. But Hanotaux, despite these words, was unwilling to give a reply to the British proposals before he had heard from his Russian ally. [80] Shishkin, who was in charge of the Russian foreign office, saw no serious objections to the British program, but he could give no definite answer until the Tsar had returned to Russia. On November 4 he was rather evasive, and urged upon the English ambassador as the best remedy for the ills of Turkey the scheme that had been accepted at Paris, namely that the powers, through the Ottoman Public Debt Administration, should take over control of Turkish finances and see that the money was spent in such a way as to strengthen the government and enable it to carry out reforms. What he did not like about the Salisbury program was the idea of coercion implied in the last paragraph of the circular. " The idea of having to resort to coercive measures was extremely repugnant to His Majesty the Emperor." [81]

[78] *Turkey No. 2 (1897)*, no. 2.
[79] *Turkey No. 2 (1897)*, nos. 4, 5, 6; *Die Grosse Politik*, XII, nos. 3068 ff.
[80] *Affaires Arméniennes*, nos. 278, 284.
[81] *Turkey No. 2 (1897)*, nos. 11, 12; *Correspondance de M. de Staal*, II, p. 324.

This was not very encouraging, but it did not shut the door on Salisbury's proposal. In the Guild Hall speech on November 9 the premier still spoke hopefully. The idea of isolated action, he said, had been pretty generally given up. People had come to realize that a fleet demonstration might serve to punish the Sultan, but it would not help the Armenians. " No fleet in the world can get over the mountains of Taurus to protect the Armenians," and the suggestion of one lady that the fleet should sail up the Euphrates to Lake Van was no more ridiculous than some other suggestions made by people who ought to have known better. The only possible course of action was through the Concert of Europe. Other powers had means of bringing military pressure which Britain did not possess. But it should be remembered that the Concert of Europe did not mean " that the armies of all the nations of the Continent are directed according to the will of the minister who sits in Downing Street." A war in the Near East might not trouble England much, but it would be a catastrophe for many of the other powers, and they could not be blamed for trying to avoid it. To redress the wrongs of thousands of Armenians was one thing; to plunge millions of men into a deadly conflict was another. Still, he had hope that the concert would do something:

> " The Concert of Europe seems to be in a more favourable position for achieving the purpose of extirpating this terrible disease from the South-East of Europe than it has ever been in before. . . . I see no prospect of any difference on the part of France that should baffle the action of the Concert of Europe. With the Triple Alliance we have always been in sympathy with respect to the Eastern Question; our doctrines have always been the same as theirs. I see no ground for believing that they will not co-operate heartily in the same sense."

As for Russia, Salisbury rejected entirely the idea of Bismarck, that there was an insuperable antagonism between Briton and Muscovite:

> " It is a superstition of an antiquated diplomacy that there is any necessary antagonism between Russia and Great Britain. . . . I may say that I have good ground for believing that the Russian Government pursues the same object and entertains the same view as we do concerning these terrible events in the East. Of course there may be difference of opinion, and possibly there will be, as to the means to be pursued. I do not see any difficulty in concurring in any proposition to exercise force in which the five other Powers may concur, but whether they will do so I do not know."

It was to be some time before the prime minister received a definite reply from either Russia or France, for in St. Petersburg affairs were taking an extraordinary turn. The Russian officials had returned from Paris full of enthusiasm for the program arranged with Hanotaux. " We have done a great thing in Paris," one of them noted. But their enthusiasm was short-lived. Witte, the powerful finance minister, opposed the project. From Vienna the ambassador, Count Kapnist, wrote scathing condemnations of it, and from Constantinople

Nelidov sent threats of resignation if the instructions he had received were adhered to. For months he had been lecturing his government: Russia must prevent two things, foreign intervention which might end in foreign control of the Straits, and any efforts to "internationalize" the Ottoman Empire, and thereby reduce Russian influence to one sixth of the whole. "The transfer of Turkey's economic resources to European hands would be equivalent to the neutralization of the Ottoman Empire and to the substitution, by international arrangement, of a strong government hostile to us for a weak but still independent one." The Tsar at first resisted this pressure and promised the French ambassador to try to win over Witte and Nelidov. But before long he gave in, noting on Nelidov's report: "The more I think about this matter, the more strongly I feel that we made a great blunder and must renounce these ideas of Hanotaux." So Nicholas, who had already misled Salisbury by his original assent to the principle of using force, and who had formally agreed to the Hanotaux program, went back on his word. Nelidov was so far successful that he secured permission to come to St. Petersburg himself.[82]

Nelidov arrived in the Russian capital on November 15 and immediately set himself to the task of reversing Russian policy. On November 18 a statement was issued from "well-informed quarters," evidently designed to reassure foreign chancelleries with regard to Nelidov's visit:

"The Russian Government still adheres resolutely to the position which it has taken up on the strength of existing treaties, in the first rank of which is the clause relating to the Black Sea. This clause, far from being disadvantageous, is a valuable guarantee for the Muscovite Empire, for though it is an obstacle to the egress of Russian men-of-war from the Euxine, it constitutes an equivalent obstacle to the entrance of foreign ships into the sea, and consequently an indirect safeguard for Russia's southern coast, as well as for her weak and newly created Black Sea Fleet. On the other hand, it has to be borne in mind that in time of peace vessels bound for or from the Far East with Russian soldiers or munitions of war are at perfect liberty to pass the Dardanelles, and in time of war Russian ironclads would, probably, have little difficulty in forcing the passage of these Straits if the interest of the Empire required that such an extreme course should be resorted to. The Russian Government no more desires the abrogation of the clause relating to ingress and egress from the Black Sea than it does the occurrence of such events as the deposition of the Sultan, or the fall and partition of the Ottoman Empire, which would give rise to serious international complications, in harmony neither with Russia's aspirations nor with her interests at the present time; and, far from pursuing a policy calculated to give rise to such eventualities, the Government is determined to shape its diplomatic action in such a way as to prevent, or at any rate delay, their occurrence." [83]

---

[82] Khvostov: "Problemy Zakhvata Bosfora," pp. 121–5.
[83] London *Times*, November 20, 1896; *Annual Register*, 1896, p. 293.

A few days later there appeared a second announcement, clearly inspired by the ministry of finance: Russia, it said, would not appoint a candidate to the council of the Ottoman Public Debt Administration:

" The whole policy of Russia since the last war has been to set aside the interference of Europe in the affairs and fate of Turkey. . . . We have succeeded in isolating Turkey from England, which has now lost all prestige in the eyes of the Ottoman Government, and Russia stands face to face with Turkey alone. Finding no support from any one of the European Powers and feeling completely dependent upon Russia, there is no doubt that Turkey will fulfill every demand that we make upon her and probably in a comparatively short space of time will place herself entirely at Russia's disposition." [84]

The British ambassador had already been told definitely that " His Majesty (the Tsar) was not willing to agree to any undertaking which implied measures of coercion against the Sultan." But the idea of active measures, it will be shown presently, was essential for Nelidov's plan. Salisbury's proposal was most convenient. On November 25, the Russian government reversed its position and stated that, if the Sultan resisted the demands of the powers, Russia " would not refuse to take into consideration " the British proposal for the application of coercive measures.[85] The stage was now set. The Russians had put away the tempting bait of concessions in the Straits question, and they had gone back on their promises to the French. The debris of old policies having been cleared away the road now lay open for the introduction of Nelidov's own policy. His ideas, already outlined in his report of September 18, were further developed in a long memorandum dated November 30. The argument, briefly, was as follows: The situation in the Ottoman Empire is a very ominous one. The capital is in ferment, the provinces in anarchy. Another insurrection is pending, and there may well be a revolution, with excesses by the troops and ending possibly with the deposition of the Sultan. Intervention by the powers will become inevitable. Whether this takes the peaceful form of international control of the Ottoman administration or the belligerent form of a fleet demonstration, Russia's interests will in any case be sacrificed to Europe. Russia will forfeit her security in the Black Sea and her free communication with the Mediterranean. Her influence in Turkey will be reduced to one sixth. She must, therefore, assure herself of her safety by establishing herself on the upper Bosporus. The first condition of such action is suddenness and swiftness. The Russian fleet and landing-force must arrive before the British ships, for even if the powers, acting together, could not stop the appearance of the Russians in the Bosporus, they might be able to prevent a landing. Nelidov, then, should send a telegram from Constantinople to Sevastopol as soon as disorders in the capital made intervention inevitable. A few hours before the fleet was to enter the Bosporus the Sultan

[84] London *Times*, November 24, 1896, quoting from the *Petersburgskaiia Vedomosti; Affaires Arméniennes*, nos. 310, 311.

[85] *Turkey No. 2 (1897)*, nos. 17, 21, 22.

should be informed of the fact. Russia would promise the integrity of his personal and sovereign power in return for assistance or at least non-resistance. In case he should resist, he would have to take the consequences. At the same time the other powers should be invited to enter the Dardanelles. Russian ships should go with them and if they landed troops Russia should do the same. The whole affair would probably have to be settled by an international conference. No one would dare dispute Russia's occupation of the upper Bosporus, and Russia, having made a second Gibraltar of it, could calmly agree to the neutralization of the Dardanelles and the razing of their fortifications. Russia could with equanimity participate in the further disposition of the Sultan's territories. She would have the key to her house, and free access to the Mediterranean.[86]

This memorandum was discussed in detail by a crown council held on December 5 with the Tsar himself in the chair. The ministers present were Vannovski (War), Tyrtov (Navy), and Witte (Finance). Shishkin (in charge of foreign affairs), Obruchev (chief of staff) and Nelidov himself also attended. From most of the ministers and officials there was no objection to the Nelidov scheme, which, after all, had been discussed on and off for a long time, notably in the autumn of 1895. Admiral Tyrtov merely objected to giving Nelidov authority to summon the fleet. Orders for the beginning of operations, he thought, should come from St. Petersburg. But this was a minor point. A more serious matter was the positive stand taken by Witte against the whole project. The finance minister insisted that the action contemplated by Nelidov would almost certainly lead to a great European war, which Russia could not afford and which would be contrary to her interests. Yet, despite his opposition, the Tsar sided with the ambassador. It was finally voted, Witte dissenting, that, on his return to his post, Nelidov, together with the other ambassadors, should seek means of restoring order to the Ottoman Empire, while guaranteeing the safety of the Christians and avoiding the substitution of international control for Turkish organs. The ambassadors were to use advice and remonstrances, but if the Sultan resisted, Nelidov was to find out what methods of coercion the other governments proposed to use. If they decided on a naval demonstration in the Sea of Marmora then, even if the Russian squadrons took part, Russia should not agree to the entrance of a considerable number of foreign ships into the Dardanelles without occupying at the same time (or earlier) the upper Bosporus, in order to ensure the closure of the Black Sea, as provided for in the treaties. Nelidov was therefore to inform his government in good time, remembering that from the moment of the decision of the powers to make a naval demonstration, the ships in the Mediterranean would require less time to enter the Dardanelles than would the Russian ships coming from Odessa and

---

[86] The memorandum in Khvostov: "Proekt Zakhvata Bosfora," pp. 59–64. The anonymous account of E. J. Dillon: "A Diplomatic Reminiscence" (*National Review*, February 1909, pp. 908–18) is so accurate that he must have seen the memorandum. He repeats the story in his *Eclipse of Russia* (London, 1918), pp. 231 ff.

Sevastopol to the Bosporus. The ambassadors might summon the fleets without previous agreement if serious disorders broke out in Constantinople. In that case Nelidov should immediately warn the commander in chief of the Black Sea fleet of the need for the immediate despatch of the squadrons. In any event, as soon as the fleet left Sevastopol and Odessa, Nelidov should inform the Sultan of the decision made and offer him Russia's guarantee of his personal safety if he agreed to co-operate or at least not to obstruct a landing on the Bosporus, which would protect the passage into the Black Sea forever (*forever* added in blue pencil by the Tsar).[87]

Witte's great argument against the plan was that, without previous agreement with the powers, the operation would certainly lead to war. He and his apologists take the attitude that the whole scheme was nefarious and immoral. Now that is certainly a distorted view of the situation. In discussing the Nelidov plan it must be remembered that it was not the sudden inspiration of a fevered brain, but a scheme that had been considered and discussed for many years, and that the steady development of the Black Sea fleet and the volunteer fleet during the 1880's was merely one phase of the preparation. That the Turks could defend the entrance to the Black Sea with their ancient forts and antiquated fleet was out of the question. Russia had to be prepared to take the protection of the entrance to her house in hand herself. It was characteristic of Bismarck's breadth of view that he realized and appreciated this fact. More than that, he had a clear idea of what the Russians would do when the time came. In an inspired article in the *Hamburger Nachrichten* on April 10, 1891 he expressed his doubts of Russian plans for a land campaign. It would be more likely, he thought, that Russia, when the international situation was favorable, would land thirty to fifty thousand men on the Bosporus, occupy Constantinople and then simply wait to see whether any European power would declare war or whether the powers would prefer a peaceful arrangement, to which Russia could agree the more readily as the other powers could be satisfied with compensations at the expense of others (i.e. the Turks). The Sultan could be offered a treaty of guarantee which would permit him to live as Grandseigneur without his previous anxieties.[88]

Militarily speaking it is quite clear that the Russian *coup de main* on the Bosporus would in all probability have been successful. The Russians had a small but powerful modern squadron in the Black Sea, and could get together the necessary vessels to ship about thirty thousand men and one hundred guns from Odessa and Sevastopol in the first transport, and follow this contingent with another twenty-five thousand men in ten days.[89] The northern part of the

---

[87] Khvostov: "Proekt Zakhvata Bosfora," pp. 64–7; *Memoirs of Count Witte* (New York, 1921), pp. 186 ff.; *Die Grosse Politik,* XII, no. 2930.

[88] Johannes Penzler: *Fürst Bismarck nach seiner Entlassung* (Leipzig, 1897), II, p. 83; similarly Bismarck's conversation with Maximilian Harden in October 1892 (Ibid., IV, p. 186).

[89] "Proekt Zakhvata Bosfora v 1897 godu" (*Krasnyi Arkhiv*, I, 1922, pp. 152–61), letter of Vannovski to Muraviev, April 20, 1897.

Bosporus, it is true, " bristled with batteries," but military writers at the time were generally agreed that they could not hold out against the Russians. Most of the forts were old and poorly equipped. On the European side only Rumili Fener, Rumili Kavak, Kirich Burnu and the batteries near Therapia, on the Asiatic side only Anadoli Fener, Anadoli Kavak, Majar Kalessi, Yucha and the batteries at Fil Burnu were of importance. These were equipped with modern Krupp guns (calibre 15–28 cm.), but all in all the artillery numbered only about sixty-five or seventy pieces. The forts were most of them pretty low, near the water, and dominated by elevated land in the rear. The Russians, having landed a force of men on the beach west of Kilia, could easily have rushed these forts from the rear and held them. With a torpedo flotilla they could have surprised and taken Constantinople with considerable ease. The Constantinople garrison immediately available numbered only some seventeen to twenty thousand men. Even though some hundred thousand could be assembled in the region of the Bosporus during the first week, the Russians would by that time have been in possession of the forts and probably the capital. It would have been too late for the Turks to do much. Even a writer like Spenser Wilkinson, who was much opposed to the abandonment of Constantinople to the Russians, was obliged to admit that it was doubtful whether any or all of the powers could prevent Russia from seizing the capital by a *coup de main*.[90]

Leaving aside the military aspects of the problem, what foundation was there for the argument advanced by Witte that the operation advocated by Nelidov would lead to a general war? Very little indeed. The ambassador obviously relied upon the abstention of the other powers, and he was probably right. Austria's opposition, to be sure, was almost certain. In the very days when the project was discussed at St. Petersburg the inspired journals of Vienna and Budapest reiterated the Austrian stand in unmistakable terms.[91] But Austrian opposition would mean very little if the other powers refused to move. The Germans were determined, as they had been in Bismarck's time, not to stake their future on Austrian policy. Emperor William was anxious to conciliate the Russians and was quite prepared to abandon the Straits to them, especially if compensation could be obtained. The Russians were told this quite frankly. In fact, they had a little the feeling that the Germans were trying to force the issue, and that the Germans were trying to embroil them with other powers. But the Berlin government was quite sincere. When the Nelidov plan and Witte's opposition were reported to the Emperor William he expressed profound surprise at the finance minister's objections: " Why war? Who is to make

---

[90] Spenser Wilkinson: " The Value of Constantinople " (*National Review*, November, 1896, pp. 315–24). For the rest see Carl Didelot: *La Défense des Côtes d'Europe* (Paris, 1894), pp. 501–3, and atlas, plate 200; Léon Lamouche: *L'Organisation Militaire de l'Empire Ottoman* (Paris, 1895), pp. 177 ff.; and especially the minute technical study of the whole problem by F(itzau): *Darf Russland einen Angriff auf den Bosporus wagen?* (Vienna, 1892).

[91] London *Times*, December 4 and 7, 1896.

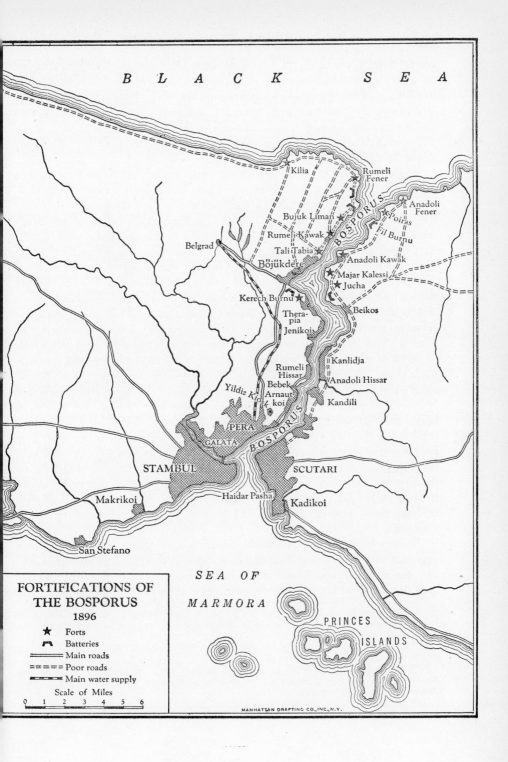

FORTIFICATIONS OF
THE BOSPORUS
1896

★ Forts
⌐ Batteries
═══ Main roads
═ ═ ═ Poor roads
▰ ▰ ▰ Main water supply

Scale of Miles
0 1 2 3 4 5 6

MANHATTAN DRAFTING CO., INC., N.Y.

war? " [92] Italy was quite in sympathy with her German ally. The Russians for some time had been trying to get on better terms with the Italians, and there had been a distinct rapprochement since the disaster at Adua. According to the ambassador at Vienna, Count Nigra, it was generally agreed in diplomatic circles that Constantinople could pass only to the Russians. Italy, he said, would rather welcome the establishment of a Russian counterweight to French power in the Mediterranean.[93]

There remained England and France to be considered. With Germany on the Russian side France, already bound by her alliance with Russia, could hardly have taken a hostile stand once the Russians were in possession of the prize. England then would have been helpless, for her naval position in the Mediterranean was a precarious one at best, and the British squadrons could hardly have dared enter the Dardanelles with a Russian squadron before them and a French fleet behind them. But apart from this line of argument, the fact was that Lord Salisbury was prepared to bargain with the Russians about the Straits. British opinion was, in general, favorable to such a course. England, it was said, could not keep the Russians from Constantinople. Therefore it would be better to invite them to take the Turkish capital and indemnify oneself elsewhere.[94] Salisbury, while he may not have been prepared to go so far, made no secret of the fact that England could not and would not defend Constantinople if the " others " would not help, and he would not even promise British aid if Austria resisted an advance by Russia. There are some indications that Nelidov had gone over the situation with Currie before he left for St. Petersburg, and that some general scheme had been worked out for the eventual breakup of the Ottoman Empire. From veiled references it seems that England was reserving for herself the Euphrates Valley. Curiously enough a British warship appeared in the Shatt-el-Arab in the last days of October and went up the river to Basra, causing a considerable stir in Berlin. It would be ridiculous to draw far-reaching conclusions from the meagre material we have, but what evidence there is would indicate that Nelidov planned and hoped to square England.[95]

Nelidov hoped that Russia could first occupy the upper Bosporus and then negotiate with England. He feared that if discussions with London were started first, the terms offered Russia would be too unfavorable. In this he may have been right, and yet it was probably a mistake to leave the matter open. If he had

---

[92] *Die Grosse Politik*, XII, no. 2930 marginalia; on the German attitude see also *Die Grosse Politik*, XII, nos. 2914, 2933 etc.; Hohenlohe: *Denkwürdigkeiten der Reichskanzlerzeit*, pp. 258, 294; Khvostov: " Problemy Zakhvata Bosfora," p. 118.

[93] Siegmund Münz: " Graf Nigra über Fragen der Internationalen Politik " (*Deutsche Revue*, December, 1911, pp. 307–20), pp. 319–20.

[94] Roland K. Wilson: " Shall we Invite the Russians to Constantinople? " (*Contemporary Review*, February, 1897, pp. 265–75); J. W. Gambier: " Russia on the Bosporus " (*Fortnightly Review*, May, 1897, pp. 757–9).

[95] *Die Grosse Politik*, XII, nos. 2929, 2931, 2932, 3083, note, 3086; XIII, nos. 3396, 3397; Khvostov: " Problemy Zakhvata Bosfora," pp. 115–6.

had Britain's consent and Germany's moral support, his position would have
been unassailable. France could not have dreamed of opposing her ally. But
as it was, Hanotaux was in a good position to raise objections. The French
minister was " extremely discouraged " and " displeased " by the news that the
Russians had gone back on the Paris program for international control of
Turkish finance. He felt that it was a " turning point " in Russian policy, and
insisted that his own position had been shaken by it. To the Russian ambassador
he spoke in the most unvarnished terms:

> " Your new policy aims to secure a monopoly of influence in Turkey for Russia.
> Are your people striving for a protectorate like that which exists in Egypt or
> even in Tunis? And have you weighed all the difficulties? If this matter affected
> only us, only France, I would understand and would not cause too many diffi-
> culties. But do not forget that we are not alone, do not forget that you have to
> deal with too strong an opponent. You may be absolutely certain that even if you
> are allowed to enter Constantinople, that will be done only in order not to let
> you get out, for that same day the English with the aid of the Italians will create
> in the Dardanelles a Gibraltar which will close up any way out for you." [96]

To reinforce his remarks Hanotaux, having waited since the end of October
to learn the Russian attitude on the Salisbury circular, notified the Russian government on December 12 that France intended to make any action by the
powers conditional on the previous acceptance of the following three points:
1) maintenance of the integrity of Turkey; 2) no condominium; 3) no isolated
action in any way.[97]

The French attitude was not known in St. Petersburg at the time of the
conference on December 5, or at any rate it was not considered. Nelidov left for
his post on December 12, and it must have been after that date that Witte, in
all probability relying on the additional arguments supplied him by the news
from Paris, took steps to rescind the vote of the council. He appealed to the
powerful procurator of the Holy Synod, M. Pobedonostsev: " At this rate we
may meet the New Year on the battlefield," he remarked. Pobedonostsev, it
seems, agreed entirely with the minister, and used all his great influence with the
Tsar. Probably at Nelidov's suggestion, the government had already, on November 25, reversed its policy with regard to the Salisbury circular. The British
ambassador was told that " should the Sultan resort to his customary tergiversa-
tion in regard to the reforms which were recommended by the Ambassadors
at Constantinople, the Imperial Government would not refuse to take into
consideration your Lordship's proposal for the application of coercive measures,
provided that there were unanimity among the Powers." [98] Nelidov's scheme
presupposed that there should be some foreign intervention to precipitate matters. Therefore Salisbury's proposal was very convenient. But now, under the

---

[96] Mohrenheim's reports, November 26, December 10, 1896, quoted by Khvostov: " Problemy
Zakhvata Bosfora," p. 125.

[97] *Affaires Arméniennes*, nos. 322, 323.   [98] *Turkey No. 2 (1897)*, no. 22.

influence of Witte and Pobedonostsev, the Tsar accepted the three French reservations. Russia could not refuse without revealing her plans for seizing the Straits. Hanotaux' move had been a very clever one indeed.[99]

It is not true, however, that the Nelidov project was dropped as the result of Witte's action. What really happened was this: Nelidov returned to the Turkish capital, evidently with the intention of precipitating intervention that would make possible the realization of his scheme. His instructions, probably written by himself, were to use strong language to the Sultan and to warn him that resistance to the recommendations of the powers would mean intervention, the consequences of which might be disastrous for the Empire. Everywhere he spoke in the gloomiest terms of the prospects for the Ottoman state. On December 19 he was received by the Sultan, who, it was reported, was " greatly impressed " with what he heard. But by that time Nelidov had already learned of Russia's approval of Hanotaux' three points. In alarm he telegraphed home, pointing out that the second point in particular, directed against isolated action by any one power, would completely nullify the plan already agreed upon. The foreign office was hard put to it for an answer, but Nelidov was told that it would have been impossible to come to an agreement with the other powers for joint action if they had been allowed to suspect that Russia would act separately. The decisions taken on December 5, it was pointed out, bore no relation to the current phase of the negotiations. They envisaged only the eventuality that measures of coercion might become necessary or that unforeseen developments might take place. Furthermore, Russia had not accepted a definite obligation with regard to these three points, but had simply told the French that these points " correspond to His Majesty's views." Rumors had gotten around that Russia meant to take action and would hasten the collapse of Turkey in order to take advantage of the crisis. It was therefore impossible to avoid recognition of the three points. " If we are forced to act, we shall always have time to point out to the Powers the exceptional circumstances which oblige us to take advantage of our geographical position, of existing treaties, etc. Premature explanations concerning this question would cause opposition on their part, would be fruitless and therefore all the more dangerous." [100]

For the moment there was nothing to be done but to go on with the ambassadorial conference according to the program outlined in the Salisbury circular of October 20. The Sultan had attempted to anticipate such action by promulgating reforms for the whole Empire on November 18, but these concessions were universally condemned as quite inadequate and unsatisfactory. The ambassadors had to begin at the beginning, and they had a large problem

---

[99] Khvostov: " Problemy Zakhvata Bosfora," p. 127; Affaires Arméniennes, nos. 323, 332.

[100] Nelidov's telegram of December 18; Shishkin's replies of December 20 and 30, 1896 (Khvostov: " Proekt Zakhvata Bosfora," pp. 68–70). On Nelidov's instructions see also Affaires Arméniennes, nos. 319, 325; Correspondance de M. de Staal, II, 328–30; Die Grosse Politik, XII, no. 3080.

before them, the more so as every point required the unanimous consent of all six ambassadors. It was expected that the reform scheme would take a long time to work out. In fact, Lord Salisbury thought the German ambassador could take not only a little vacation trip, but a leisurely jaunt around the world before anything definite was decided on. Emperor William was afraid he would be an old man before the ambassadors had even completed their catalog of grievances.[101] Besides, toward the end of December news of Nelidov's schemes leaked out in diplomatic circles and acted like a cool douche on the whole proceedings. The situation was then simply this: if a reform scheme were worked out and the Sultan refused to accept it, the powers would be obliged to use coercion. If they did that it would give Nelidov his opening and the catastrophe would break over Europe. What was known of Russia's ulterior plans placed a premium on inaction.[102]

But Nelidov did not give up the ship. From the few documents we possess on the subject it appears that on January 11, 1897 the Tsar approved the detailed measures which were to be taken in an emergency. Nelidov was to notify the commander at Odessa and the chief of the Black Sea fleet by telegram. Then all telegrams were to be stopped and all ships detained twenty-four hours. The fleet was to sail on receipt of orders from the Tsar, and the occupation of the upper Bosporus was to extend to Beikos on the Asiatic and to Keretch-Burnu on the European side.[103] At the same time efforts seem to have been made to overcome the opposition of France. But Hanotaux remained unbending. This was not merely a question of pleasing Russia, it was a question of fundamental French interests. To the ambassador at St. Petersburg he wrote on January 12:

> " The risk is too great, our interest too uncertain and the chances of seeing the most serious of international questions settled according to justice are too doubtful for us to do anything but desire above all things the maintenance of the *status quo*. . . . I told him (the Russian ambassador at Paris) that, if a conflict arose concerning the Black Sea and the Straits, our country seemed by no means disposed to take an active part in the military events which might ensue, in view of the fact that the risks would be so great and the advantages for France so little apparent."

When Count Muraviev came to Paris at the end of the month, after taking over the direction of the Russian foreign office, Hanotaux impressed upon him the need for a defensive policy and the avoidance of all separate initiative. This was the prelude to a new attempt on the part of the French minister to induce his Russian colleague to appoint a Russian delegate to the Ottoman Debt commission, an attempt which Muraviev evaded. The conversation then drifted to the prob-

---

101 *Die Grosse Politik*, XII, nos. 3086, 3098.

102 The rumors in *Die Grosse Politik*, XII, nos. 2930, 2936, 3090; *Correspondance de M. de Staal*, II, p. 330.

103 " Proekt Zakhvata Bosfora v 1897 godu " (*Krasnyi Arkhiv*, I, 1922, pp. 152–61), translated in part in the *Kriegsschuldfrage*, IV, March, 1926, pp. 175–81.

lem of action in the event of new disorders at Constantinople. Muraviev pointed out that if the united fleets of the powers entered the Dardanelles, Russia would have to take material guarantees for self-protection, namely the occupation of the heights of the upper Bosporus and the key to the Black Sea. To this Hanotaux responded that he appreciated the needs of his ally and would offer his services for sounding out the other powers. This idea struck Muraviev with horror and he rejected it categorically, pointing out that such a discussion with the powers might lead to the partition of Turkey. It was pointed out to him that if Russia attempted to seize the Bosporus, England might anticipate the coup. Furthermore, such action would certainly lead to a general war that neither Russia nor France desired. Nevertheless, if war were inevitable Russia could count on the fullest co-operation and assistance of France, said Hanotaux, according to Muraviev's report to the Tsar.[104] The French correspondence, however, would indicate that the assurance given was not so inclusive. Hanotaux, in a letter to the ambassador at St. Petersburg, claimed that he had warned Muraviev against the temptations of Germany, and had added: " You will have the support of our diplomacy, but I do not think that you can have any illusions respecting our military assistance. The true service that we can render Russia will be the observation of a neutrality that will oblige Germany to remain neutral too, and prevent her from taking part in the conflict." [105]

It is evident, even from Muraviev's report to the Tsar, in which he was not apt to minimize his own accomplishments, that the discussions in Paris were not marked by extraordinary warmth or confidence. The Russian minister was apparently anxious to draw the French into closer co-operation with Russia and Germany. But he found little encouragement: " We can go along with Germany," said Hanotaux, " only if we can thus secure the fulfilment of our vital and most important interests or similar interests of yours, as in the Chinese question. In secondary questions such a course of action is unthinkable and impossible, since no government in France would last half an hour before it would be overthrown by the feeling of complete and unanimous indignation of the entire French people." Evidently the only real tie that bound the two allies was their mutual distrust and dislike of England.[106]

The Russian minister's reception in Berlin was marked by much greater cordiality. Late in October 1896 Bismarck had startled the world by revealing, in an inspired newspaper article, the fact of the former existence of the Reinsurance Treaty and its non-renewal by his successor. The old chancellor's purpose, it was said, was to throw cold water on the Franco-Russian celebrations in Paris, but it is just as likely that he wanted to take his revenge on the Emperor, for he argued that since 1890 Russian-German relations had been steadily

---

[104] F. V. Kelyin, editor: " Zagranichnoe Puteshestvie M. N. Muravieva v 1897 g." (*Krasnyi Arkhiv*, XLVI, 1931, pp. 71–89).

[105] Ernest Judet: *Georges Louis* (Paris, 1925), pp. 145–7.

[106] Kelyin, loc. cit., p. 84.

cooling. The whole affair caused a furor in Germany. The Emperor even talked of having the old statesman tried on a charge of high treason. But there is no need for discussing here the details of the episode, for it had no serious effect upon international relations. Whatever resentment the Russians and the Austrians may have felt was explained away or gradually blew over. Sufficient for the day were the troubles thereof. In actual fact Emperor William had taken his stand squarely by the rapprochement with Russia, and the relations between the two countries were distinctly friendly, despite the Russian Alliance with France.[107]

Muraviev found the German ministers at one with the Emperor in their profound distrust of British designs in the east. They urged co-operation between the continental powers to prevent a partition of Turkey and a general war. The Russian minister replied that what he feared above all things was the possibility of the British fleet being summoned to the Dardanelles by the British ambassador. Emperor William reassured him:

" According to my secret information Lord Salisbury, at a meeting of the Privy Council a week ago, asked the First Lord of the Admiralty if the British fleet, at the first summons of the ambassador, could enter the Dardanelles and take its stand before Constantinople, in the event of an attack upon a British subject or subjects. To this the First Lord replied by asking whether Lord Salisbury knew what orders would be given to the French squadron in such a case. On Lord Salisbury's negative reply the First Lord said that he would never allow such a summons of the English squadron into the Dardanelles, for at the present time it might find itself between two fires, that is between your fleet of the Black Sea and the French Mediterranean squadron."

Besides, added the Emperor, the British could do little since they had no landing-force. Yet despite Britain's weakness William urged upon Muraviev the need for meeting the growing friendship between England and the United States with a continental combination for political as well as economic ends. It was a favorite idea of the Emperor which he had already expounded to the Tsar in the autumn of 1896. Muraviev avoided committing himself. It would be unwise, he thought, to drive England to extreme measures by forming a *bloc*. It would be better to co-operate in separate instances. Furthermore, he pointed out the limitations of French co-operation with Germany, which the German ministers had already stressed in their discussions with the Emperor. A continental grouping, they argued, was useful for defensive purposes, but a close or permanent understanding with France would be possible only after a revision of the Treaty of Frankfurt. The best course for the moment would be to support Russia's policy of the status quo in the Near East. In as much as this was the most urgent

[107] On the Bismarck revelations see especially *Die Grosse Politik*, VII, nos. 1384–92; Johannes Penzler: *Fürst Bismarck nach seiner Entlassung* (Leipzig, 1898), VII, pp. 106–91; Hermann Hofmann: *Fürst Bismarck, 1890–1898* (Berlin, 1914), I, pp. 90–115; II, pp. 370–87; Hohenlohe: *Denkwürdigkeiten der Reichskanzlerzeit*, pp. 270 ff.

problem, Muraviev left the German capital completely at rest in his mind with respect to the German attitude.[108]

The opposition of Hanotaux and the assurances of the Germans helped to put the quietus on the whole Nelidov project. The military and naval men, to be sure, continued to plan and to prepare. More and more ships were concentrated in the Mediterranean, until in February 1897 the Russians had four battleships and six other war vessels in the Aegean, to say nothing of the powerful Black Sea fleet, composed of six new battleships and several cruisers together with six ships of the convertible volunteer fleet.[109] But all the preparations went for naught. On February 19 the important Russian newspaper, *Novoie Vremiia,* probably inspired, published an article entitled " Russia and Europe on the Bosporus," in which the writer stressed the fact that before any move could be made against Constantinople, the Bosporus would have to be occupied. To seize the Bosporus without the consent of Turkey would produce immediate anarchy and incite the Turks to deeds of horror. To take the Bosporus by agreement with England would necessitate separate compensation for England, and this would be beyond the power of Russia.[110]

We may, I think, assume that this article was published at the instigation of Witte or his associates. It was intended to ruin the Nelidov scheme by arousing the suspicions of the other powers. The *Times* correspondent began to make inquiries and was soon in a position to send home a pretty accurate account of the whole development of Russian naval policy in the Black Sea since 1882, duly emphasizing the plan to seize the Bosporus. Forty thousand men, he reported, could be sent off from the Black Sea ports. Not long afterward he reported that the Russian squadrons were keeping up steam and that they were prepared to proceed on their mission on receipt of a telegram. So the whole business was out and the London government knew what to expect. Of course the news from Russia was not the first information which the foreign office had. Salisbury must have known for some time what the true situation was, for we have an interesting instruction of his dated January 20, 1897 in which be goes over the problem. It seems that the Austrian government had suggested, at that time, that the English and Austrians co-operate in resisting an attack on the Straits by Russia. Salisbury's reply, as usual, was that England could not make such engagements in advance. Besides, he pointed out, it was no longer sure that the Sultan would sanction or support action in his behalf. He had fortified the Dardanelles but had neglected the Bosporus. Evidently he preferred the probability of being invaded by Russia to that of being assisted by the Powers: " I knew of no declaration of English policy which had ever pointed in the direction of assisting the Sultan to an independence which he did not desire, against an

---

108 *Die Grosse Politik,* XIII, nos. 3424–9; Kelyin, loc. cit., pp. 86–9; Hohenlohe, op. cit., pp. 295–8.

109 London *Times,* February 22, 1897; T. A. Brassey: *The Naval Annual,* 1897, pp. 58–9.

110 London *Times,* February 22, 1897 (St. Petersburg, February 20).

invader whom he himself welcomed." Forcing the Dardanelles would now be a more arduous task than it would have been ten years ago. Naval experts were opposed even to making the attempt, without corresponding operations on the land side. But there was, to be sure, the possibility that England's hand might be forced by disturbances in Constantinople which would endanger the lives of British nationals.[111]

In view of the general uncertainty all that could be done was to take precautions. The British fleet in the Mediterranean was hardly a match for the Russian squadrons in that sea and in the Black Sea, especially if they were supported by the French. The British Channel fleet was therefore sent on a " visit " to Gibraltar. During the latter part of February and the early part of March the ships of that fleet were available for use in the Mediterranean. Under the circumstances Nelidov himself lost hope of realizing his plan. The famous project was gradually lost from sight.[112]

A few words remain to be said about the reform program of the powers. By the beginning of February 1897 the ambassadors, by dint of hard and steady labor, had completed a scheme of reform running to sixty-four pages. The scheme was based frankly upon the measures already introduced by the Sultan, in the hope that it might be made palatable to the Turks. But the program was never even submitted to the Porte, because the Armenian question was soon lost sight of in the new Cretan crisis. As a matter of fact the plan would probably have been no more successful than those previously put forward. So long as the " idiotically criminal conduct " of the Armenian revolutionaries continued, it was unlikely that the " disturbances " would end. " I cannot see how the state of the Christians is to be improved while this agitation continues," wrote vice-consul Williams from Van on January 24. No scheme of reforms, he added, would be likely to satisfy them. They had gathered in large numbers in Persia, just over the Turkish frontier, and were making every effort to organize a general revolt, if possible in conjunction with Greeks, Macedonians and other Christian groups, provoke a fresh effusion of blood and thus force the powers to intervene further. Mr. Elliot, one of the British consuls who visited the Persian camp in May 1897, found that there were about fifteen hundred of the Armenians living on the inhabitants. " It is clear," he reported, " that the leaders of these men, at any rate, are no patriots, but reckless and dissolute ruffians." In August two large parties crossed the Turkish frontier, surprised a Kurdish camp and killed or barbarously mutilated men, women and children. At the same time there were

---

111 Salisbury to Rumbold, January 20, 1897 (British Documents on the Origins of the War, 1898–1914, vol. IX, p. 775).

112 Krasnyi Arkhiv, I, pp. 152–61; Die Grosse Politik, XII, no. 2940. British knowledge of the plan is revealed further in the Times of February 24, 25, 1897, and in the following writings: Henry Norman: " The Globe and the Island " (Cosmopolis, March, 1897, pp. 702–11), p. 707; Sir Ellis Ashmead-Bartlett: The Battlefields of Thessaly (London, 1897), p. 40; see also the detailed article on " The Naval Situation in the Mediterranean " (Times, February 22, 1897) and the discussion in Brassey's Naval Annual, 1897, pp. 58–9.

new bomb outrages in Constantinople, and the ambassadors were warned that if the powers refused to act, the revolutionaries would carry out a project " which is far more terrible than that of the great assassin, a project the idea of which fills even us with terror." But the powers did not move. Perhaps they had come to realize that the revolutionaries, who were so free in sacrificing others, were simply exploiting the interest of the Christian nations, and perhaps they had learned that the more vigorously they interfered the worse the Turkish massacres and reprisals became. Since the reform question had been shelved the Turks had behaved well. The vali of Van had successfully frustrated all efforts on the part of the Moslems to take revenge for the massacre of the Kurds in August. Gradually the revolutionaries themselves realized that Europe was through with them. Of the Armenian question less and less was heard until, by the end of 1897, it may be said that the storm had blown over.[113]

BIBLIOGRAPHICAL NOTE

DOCUMENTARY SOURCES

Accounts and Papers. 1896, Volume XCVI: *Turkey No. 7, Correspondence respecting the Affairs of Crete.* 1897, Volume CI: *Turkey No. 2, Correspondence respecting the introduction of reforms in the administration of the Ottoman Empire; Turkey No. 1, Correspondence respecting the Disturbances at Constantinople in August 1896; Turkey No. 3, Further Correspondence respecting the Asiatic Provinces of Turkey and Events in Constantinople; Turkey No. 7, Further Correspondence respecting the Asiatic Provinces of Turkey and Events in Constantinople.* 1898, Volume CVI: *Turkey No. 1, Further Correspondence respecting the Asiatic Provinces of Turkey.* The British Blue Books on the Armenian and Cretan affairs are extraordinarily full and detailed. They offer a mass of contemporary material of high value and of necessity form the basis for any study of the problems concerned.

Documents Diplomatiques. Affaires Arméniennes. Project de Réformes dans l'Empire Ottoman, 1893–1897. The French Yellow Book, not nearly as detailed as the British publication, but containing some valuable supplementary material.

Documents Diplomatiques. Affaires d'Orient. Affaire de Crète, juin 1894–février, 1897. The French Yellow Book on Crete.

---

[113] On the reform project see *Die Grosse Politik,* XII, nos. 3100–12; on the later phases of the Armenian activities see Varandian, op. cit., I, pp. 172 ff.; Lord Warkworth: *Notes from a Diary in Asiatic Turkey* (London, 1898), pp. 124 ff.; and *Turkey No. 1 (1898),* especially nos. 55, 142, 240, 256, 290, 301, 306, 316, 317, 323, 332, 340, 354, 358.

Die Grosse Politik der Europäischen Kabinette, 1871–1914. Volume XII. The whole of this volume of the German documents is devoted to Balkan affairs in the years 1896–1899. There is considerable material on the Armenian, Cretan, Macedonian and Straits problems, as well as documents dealing with general international relations. An indispensable source.

MEMOIRS, AUTOBIOGRAPHIES, BIOGRAPHIES, AND LETTERS

Letters of Queen Victoria. Edited by George E. Buckle. Third series, Volume III. New York, 1932. The concluding volume of an important collection. The most important single source for the inner history of British policy in these years.

MEYENDORFF, BARON A.: *Correspondance de M. de Staal.* Two volumes. Paris, 1929. Contains almost nothing that is not to be found in the British Blue Books. Not of great importance for the subject of this chapter.

GARDINER, A. G.: *The Life of Sir William Harcourt.* Two volumes. London, 1923. Important only for the account of the split in the Liberal Party through disagreement on matters of foreign policy.

CREWE, MARQUESS OF: *Lord Rosebery.* New York, 1931. Gives the other side of the Rosebery-Harcourt conflict.

RUSSELL, GEORGE W. E.: *Malcolm MacColl.* London, 1914. A most important account of the agitation in England, with a number of letters from Gladstone and Salisbury.

RONALDSHAY, EARL OF: *The Life of Lord Curzon.* Three volumes. London, 1928. Curzon was at the time undersecretary in the foreign office. This biography has an interesting account of his activity, but reveals little that is new.

HOHENLOHE, FÜRST CHLODWIG ZU: *Denkwürdigkeiten der Reichskanzlerzeit.* Berlin, 1931. A most valuable supplement to the German documents. Though it contains relatively little on foreign affairs, what there is, is usually of great interest.

MACH, RICHARD VON: *Aus Bewegter Balkanzeit.* Berlin, 1928. The recollections of an able German journalist. Contains a very full account of the Stambulov régime in Bulgaria and of the dictator's assassination.

KUTSCHBACH, A.: *Der Brandherd Europas.* Leipzig, 1929. Also reminiscences of a German journalist in Bulgaria. Not as interesting or valuable as Mach's.

MADOL, HANS R.: *Ferdinand von Bulgarien.* Berlin, 1931. An apologetic biography, well-written but not very revealing.

GIESL, BARON WLADIMIR: *Zwei Jahrzehnte im Nahen Orient.* Berlin, 1927. An Austrian diplomat's recollections. Contains a good account of the events in Constantinople in August 1896.

RAMBERT, LOUIS: *Notes et Impressions de Turquie.* Paris, 1926. The recollections of a French business man. Interesting on the disturbances in Constantinople and the policy of Cambon.

The Memoirs of Count Witte. Edited by A. Yarmolinsky. New York, 1921. Contains an important account of the Nelidov scheme and how it was quashed. Must be read with caution and in conjunction with other material.

Rosen, Baron: *Forty Years of Diplomacy.* New York, 1922. The author also discusses the Nelidov plan, but adds nothing to what was known from other sources.

Chester, S. B.: *Life of Venizelos.* New York, 1921. Contains a very detailed account of the Cretan insurrection. Well informed and generally reliable. One of the best accounts in English.

Whitman, Sidney: *Turkish Memories.* London, 1914. A journalist's story of the troubles in Armenia and in Crete.

SPECIAL STUDIES

Macedonia

Haumant, Émile: " Les Origines de la Lutte pour la Macédoine, 1855–1872." (*Le Monde Slave,* III, October, 1926, pp. 52–66). An excellent scholarly treatment of the earlier phase of the Macedonian question. Most of this article has been incorporated in the author's book: *La Formation de la Yougoslavie* (Paris, 1930).

Mach, Richard von: *Die Macedonische Frage.* Vienna, 1895. One of the best contemporary studies.

Bérard, Victor: *La Macédoine.* Paris, 1897. Another excellent contemporary study, based on extensive travel.

Radeff, Simeon: *La Macédoine et la Renaissance Bulgare.* Sofia, 1918. Deals primarily with the earlier period, but has a good chapter on the organization of the revolutionary groups.

Nicolaides, Cléanthes: *La Macédoine.* Berlin, 1899. One of the best presentations of the Greek view.

Georgevich, T. R.: *Macedonia.* London, 1918. Perhaps the best exposition of the Serbian claims.

Miller, William: *Travels and Politics in the Near East.* London, 1898. A most instructive travel book, containing a full discussion of the Macedonian question.

Brailsford, H. N.: *Macedonia.* London, 1906. Though somewhat partial to the Bulgarians, this is, on the whole, the best one-volume book on the Macedonian question. Very interestingly written.

La Macédoine et le Vilayet d'Andrinople. Mémoire de l'Organisation Intérieure. Sofia, 1904. The report of the Macedonian revolutionary organization. A fundamental contribution, dealing with the first decade of Bulgarian revolutionary activity.

The Bulgarian Question and the Balkan States. Sofia, 1919. Published by the Bulgarian ministry for foreign affairs. A well-documented and important presentation of the Bulgarian views and aims.

Ivanov, Iordan: *La Question Macédoine*. Paris, 1920. Perhaps the best one-volume historical and analytical study from the Bulgarian standpoint.

Yovanovič, Slobodan: *Vlada Aleksandra Obrenovica*. Two volumes. Belgrade, 1929–1931. An absolutely indispensable account, based upon all the Serbian memoir material and upon unpublished documents. The account is fair and well-balanced and adds greatly to our knowledge of Balkan affairs in the period of the 1890's.

Strupp, Karl: *La Situation Juridique des Macédoniens en Yougoslavie*. Paris, n. d. This monograph, written by an eminent German jurist, is more than the title implies. It gives a good documented account of the whole evolution of the Macedonian problem.

Schacht, Horand H.: *Die Entwicklung der Mazedonischen Frage um die Jahrhundertwende zum Mürzsteger Programm*. Halle, 1929. A German dissertation concerned chiefly with the background of the Mürzsteg program. Adds nothing on the earlier period.

Kratchounov, K.: *La Politique Extérieure de la Bulgarie, 1880–1920*. Sofia, 1932. A thoroughly competent study, based on Bulgarian as well as western materials. The monograph suffers chiefly from its brevity.

Crete

Driault, Édouard, and Lhéritier, Michel: *Histoire Diplomatique de la Grèce*. Five volumes. Paris, 1925–6. By far the most detailed and authoritative account, based in large part upon unpublished material. Unfortunately the material is not always well presented.

Passadis, Augustin: *La Question d'Orient et la Grèce*. Paris, 1929. A doctoral dissertation, giving a straightforward, conventional account. Undocumented and adds nothing.

Softazade, Ahmed: *La Crète sous la Domination Ottomane*. Paris, 1902. A dissertation based chiefly upon Blue Book and other obvious material. Of no great importance.

Bérard, Victor: *Les Affaires de Crète*. Paris, 1898. Like the writer's other books, this is brilliantly and suggestively written. One of the most vivid pictures of the rising.

Streit, Georges: "La Question Crétoise au Point de Vue International." (*Revue de Droit International Public*, IV, 1897, pp. 61–104, 446–83; VII, 1900, pp. 5–52, 301–69; X, 1903, pp. 222–82, 345–418). On the whole this is still the best detailed, documented, scholarly treatment of the Cretan problem. It is based upon the British Blue Books and French Yellow Books as well as upon Greek documents. The tone is Grecophil, but moderate.

Perris, G. H.: *The Eastern Crisis and British Policy in the Near East*. London, 1897. A rather violent attack upon the policy of the conservative government in the Cretan and Armenian affairs.

L<small>AVISSE</small>, E<small>RNEST</small>: "Notre Politique Orientale." (*Revue de Paris,* May 15, 1897, pp. 274–311). The first part of an able but moderate criticism of the Hanotaux policy, by a prominent French historian.

Armenia and the Nelidov Plan.

A<small>MATEUR</small> (D<small>ILLON</small>, E. J.): "A Diplomatic Reminiscence." (*National Review,* February, 1909, pp. 908–18). The first revelation of the inner history of the Nelidov project. The story as told here is repeated by Dillon in his book: *The Eclipse of Russia* (New York, 1918).

"Proekt Zakhvata Bosfora v 1897 godu." (*Krasnyi Arkhiv,* I, 1922, pp. 152–61). A collection of documents from the Russian archives dealing with the last phase of the project. The essential parts have been translated in the German periodical *Kriegsschuldfrage,* IV, March, 1926, pp. 175–81.

J<small>UDET</small>, E<small>RNEST</small>: *Georges Louis.* Paris, 1925. Contains some interesting material on Hanotaux's attitude towards the scheme and his talks with the Russian ambassador.

K<small>HVOSTOV</small>, V.: "Blishne Vostochnyi Krizis, 1895–1897 gg." (*Istorik Marksist,* XIII, 1929, pp. 19–54).

—: "Problemy Zakhvata Bosfora v 90-kh godakh XIX veka." (*Istorik Marksist,* XX, 1930, pp. 100–29).

—: "Proekt Zakhvata Bosfora v 1896 g." (*Krasnyi Arkhiv,* XLVII–XLVIII, 1931, pp. 50–70).

These articles, recently published by a Russian historian on the basis of the materials in the Russian archives, are fundamental for the study of the Nelidov scheme and for the study of the whole Russian policy in the Near East in the years 1895–1897. Unfortunately the material is very poorly presented. The articles are confused and repetitious and make it very difficult, from the lack of systematic presentation, to get a complete picture of developments.

LITERATURE SINCE 1935

(See also the Supplementary Bibliographical Notes to Chapters V and VII.)

G<small>ESHKOFF</small>, T<small>HEODORE</small> I.: *Balkan Union: A Road to Peace in Southeastern Europe.* New York, 1940. 345 pp. Though it deals chiefly with the period after 1919, this study contains a well-informed review of the earlier projects for Balkan cooperation.

S<small>TAVRIANOS</small>, L. S.: *Balkan Federation: A History of the Movement toward Balkan Unity in Modern Times.* (Smith College Studies in History, volume XXVII). Northampton, 1944. 338 pp. The best general treatment of the subject, based on extensive use of Balkan sources.

ANASTASOFF, CHRIST: *The Tragic Peninsula: A History of the Macedonian Movement for Independence since 1878*. St. Louis, 1938. 384 pp.

KRAINIKOWSKY, ASSEN: *La question de Macédoine et la diplomatie européenne*. Paris, 1938. 344 pp. A scholarly study, devoted chiefly to an account of the reform problem at the turn of the century.

FRANÇOIS-DAINVILLE DE LA TOURNELLE, JEAN: *Le "Drang nach Osten" du Congrès de Berlin aux guerres balkaniques*. Paris, 1938. 180 pp. A rather superficial analysis of the German, Austrian and Italian interests in the Balkans, together with a study of the British reaction thereto.

MALZKORN, RICHARD: *Die deutsche Balkanpolitik in den neunziger Jahren des vorigen Jahrhunderts*. Cologne, 1934. 156 pp. A doctoral dissertation.

SCHINNER, WALTER: *Der oesterreichisch-italienische Gegensatz auf dem Balkan und an der Adria von seinen Anfängen bis zur Dreibundkrise, 1875–1896*. Stuttgart, 1936. 204 pp. An excellent, scholarly monograph, the best on the subject.

CLAAR, MAXIMILIAN: "Zwanzig Jahre habsburgischer Diplomatie in Rom, 1895–1915" (*Berliner Monatshefte*, XV, July, 1937, pp. 539–568). Personal recollections of an Austrian journalist, of no great importance.

MARKOV, WALTER M.: *Serbien zwischen Oesterreich und Russland, 1897–1908*. Stuttgart, 1934. 88 pp.

YERUSALIMSKII, A. S.: *Vneshniaia Politika i Diplomatiia Germanskogo Imperializma v Kontse XIX veka*. Moscow, 1948. 767 pp. Allowing for its Marxist bias, this is one of the most thorough analyses of German policy in this period.

XI

The Greek-Turkish War

◡◠

EUROPE LOST INTEREST IN THE ARMENIAN QUESTION IN THE SPRING OF
1897 because by that time the storm centre in the Near East had passed
again to Macedonia and Crete. The action of the powers in behalf of the
Armenians quite naturally revived the hopes of the Macedonian revolutionaries.
Throughout the summer and autumn of 1896 there were sporadic outbreaks
and raids in the more inaccessible regions. Visits were exchanged between the
rulers of Serbia, Bulgaria and Montenegro. There was much talk of the organization of a Balkan League to partition Macedonia between the three Slav states.
The Greeks had already become alarmed by the activity of the Bulgarians in
Macedonia and by the more aggressive program of the Serbs. In November 1894
there had been founded at Athens a secret organization designed to consolidate
the national forces and to stimulate the government to defend the rights of
Hellenism abroad. Its program was to carry on the propaganda of the Greek
idea and to work for the gradual liberation of all Greeks still under Turkish
domination. This committee, which was joined by many influential and wealthy
Greeks, took the name *Ethniké Hetairia,* and was to play a large part in the
events of 1896–1897. Its immediate object, so contemporary writers tell us, was
to counteract the Bulgarian organization in Macedonia. It has even been said
that the Greek government was prevented, by pressure from the members of
the committee, from taking a stronger line in the Cretan question in 1896 because the Ethniké Hetairia looked upon Macedonia as the proper sphere for
immediate action.[1]

While the Ethniké Hetairia was making preparation for a concerted drive
in Macedonia, the Cretan leaders were not idle. As month after month passed
in discussion of the details of the reform program without producing any concrete results, the Christian elements began to have doubts whether the whole
thing was seriously meant. It was said that the military commander in Crete
was frustrating the efforts of the Christian governor, and that the latter was a
mere figurehead. Moslem committees in Constantinople, who took their *mot*

---

[1] S. G.: "La Guerre de 1897" (*Revue de Droit International et de Législation Comparée,*
XXX, 1898, pp. 25–87), pp. 32–3; Georges Streit: "La Question Crétoise au Point de Vue Inter-
national" (*Revue de Droit International Public,* VII, 1900, pp. 5–52), p. 15; Nicolas Politis: *La
Guerre Gréco-Turque* (Paris, 1898), pp. 3–4. On the visits of the Balkan rulers see especially
Slobodan Jovanović: *Vlada Aleksandra Obrenovića,* I, pp. 331–4.

d'ordre from Yildiz, were reported to be fomenting opposition to reform in the island, and to be doing everything to show that the program could not be worked. The charge was often repeated, but its truth can hardly be established. Observers on the spot gave a somewhat divergent explanation of the trouble. Sir A. Biliotti, the British consul at Canea, reported that the Christians spoke with such exaggeration of the concessions that had been made to them that the Moslems became convinced that all their interests had been sacrificed. The French consul, M. Blanc, thought the root of the difficulty lay in the fact that the Cretans wanted the powers to show the same interest in them that they showed in the Armenians. Colonel Chermside, who had a very wide experience in Turkish administrative work, declared roundly that the Christians were afraid that the new charter would actually work and thus serve to postpone indefinitely the annexation of the island to Greece.[2]

Sir Charles Eliot compared the perpetual quarrel between the Christians and Moslems in Crete to a vendetta, similar to the Albanian blood-feuds.[3] Resumption of the feud was always marked by a few murders on one side or the other. On January 4, 1897 the consuls reported outrages of this sort, which rapidly spread over the island. The Moslem population quickly sought refuge in the coast towns, the wretched columns forming a convenient target for the insurgents as they wound their way through the narrow river valleys. While the foreign representatives were desperately trying to organize the gendarmerie provided for by the reforms of August 1896 and while they were using their best efforts to restore order, two of the leading members of the Ethniké Hetairia arrived in Crete towards the end of January. Though nothing definite is known of their objects and activities, it would appear that the organization was prepared to use the Cretan question as an opening wedge for the furtherance of its schemes with respect to Macedonia. It is stated, even by very Grecophil writers, that the house of the Greek consul at Canea, M. Gennadis, was the very centre of insurrectionary activity, the outcome of which was the establishment of a new Insurrectionary Assembly aiming at union of the island with Greece.[4]

The situation developed rapidly. On February 2 fighting began around Canea, and on February 4 the town went up in flames, much firing and massacring making the confusion worse confounded. On February 5 the Greek consul, Gennadis, sent to Athens a fateful telegram, in the following terms: " The Turkish soldiers have given the signal for massacre by shooting from the ram-

[2] *Turkey No. 8 (1897)*, nos. 21, 50; *Turkey No. 10 (1897)*, no. 250; *Turkey No. 11 (1897)*, nos. i, 13, 59; *Affaire de Crète; Conflit Gréco-Turc, février-mai, 1897*, nos. 27, 47; Henri Turot: *L'Insurrection Crétoise et la Guerre Gréco-Turque* (Paris, 1898), p. 11; London *Times*, February 9, 1897.

[3] Sir Charles Eliot: *Turkey in Europe*, p. 338.

[4] Driault and Lhéritier: *Histoire Diplomatique de la Grèce*, IV, pp. 335, 337; *Turkey No. 10 (1897)*, nos. 1, 36; *Turkey No. 11 (1897)*, no. 5; *Affaire de Crète*, no. 17; S. B. Chester: *Life of Venizelos*, p. 32; Baron Wladimir Giesl: *Zwei Jahrzehnte im Nahen Orient* (Berlin, 1927), chap. iii.

parts into the town. I have asked the consuls to debark marines to save what is possible; the consuls have refused. No hope. The Christians of the town will all be massacred." [5]

The consuls later denied with some warmth that they had been asked to land troops and that they had refused. Whatever the truth may be, it is fairly clear that Gennadis painted in very dark colors, probably with a definite purpose. His telegram proved decisive in Athens. The foreign minister, M. Skouses, had from the first insisted that the Moslems were systematically undermining the work of reform, and that they were responsible for all the trouble. The news from Crete spread like wildfire through the Greek capital. Sensational telegrams followed one another. The press o'erleapt all bounds in its demands for action. Huge mobs surged about the Chamber. The steady and widespread propaganda of the Cretan Committee and the Ethniké Hetairia had been well done. The public was thoroughly aroused. For the moment, it is clear, no government in Greece (where all governments were weak) could have resisted the popular pressure. Greek warships and transports were immediately despatched to Canea to protect Greek nationals and take off refugees. To the warnings of the foreign ministers the Greek government simply replied that, since the powers would not protect the Greeks, the Athens government would have to do so. [6]

On February 6 the Ethniké Hetairia issued a fervent and flowery appeal to the Cretans:

" Fortune is favorable. The time has come! After long ages of suffering and tears the blindness of the conqueror has rendered all dealings with tyranny impossible, and impossible all toleration, all attempt at life in common with an implacable foe. The last endeavour of civilized Europe, which desired to save the wreck of the established order, and to gild over a false peace, has failed. Many a time have you given up in vain the laurels of victory which crowned the arms of Crete, the priceless fruit of so much bloodshed, and of so many sacrifices, to the interests of Europe. . . . Barbarism cannot be changed to civilization by the expedients of diplomacy. There is but one solution, the solution for which the Cretan people has for centuries prayed, and which they have pursued through the blood of countless martyrs. The prayer of the living and the voice of the dead unite in one overpowering desire, in one sole determination inevitable and sweet. Proclaim the union with your Hellenic motherland. In her bosom you will find the calm of tender affection, in her countenance a mother's smile. In union with her you will find relief from unbearable ills, the joy of liberty, the support of your prosperity."

Two days later the Cretan Central Committee issued a similar appeal, though in somewhat less emotional terms. One can hardly escape the impression that

---

[5] *Affaire de Crète*, no. 11.

[6] *Turkey No. 10 (1897)*, nos. 43 ff., 69, 71; *Turkey No. 11 (1897)*, nos. 15, 35; *Affaire de Crète*, nos. 2 ff., 8, 20, 43; Driault and Lhéritier, op. cit., IV, pp. 337-9; and the detailed, documented studies of S. G.: *La Guerre de 1897*, loc. cit., and Georges Streit, loc. cit.

affairs had been pretty carefully planned in advance when one learns that simultaneously with the first proclamation, on February 6, the insurgent leaders in Crete decreed the union with Greece and appealed to the King of the Hellenes to assume possession of the island.[7]

The Greek government was not slow in following up the demands of the rebels. On February 10 Prince George, the second son of the King, left the Piraeus for Crete with four torpedoboats. The foreign minister insisted that the warships were necessary to prevent the landing of large Turkish contingents that were being despatched. According to the British ambassador at Constantinople the Turkish government had no intention of sending troops. It is perfectly bootless to weigh the *pros* and *cons* in this matter. The plain facts were that the Greek people, by nature excitable, had been thoroughly roused by the propaganda of the revolutionary organizations and driven into a frenzy by the lurid reports from Crete and the sensational stories of the thousands of refugees who were being landed daily at the Piraeus. They demanded action, and the government was quite unable to resist the demand. To tell the truth the Greek foreign minister made little enough effort to resist. Talking like a member of the Hetairia to the Austrian chargé d'affaires he forgot himself to such an extent as to say " that Greece would sooner raise a general conflagration by means of her large communities at Constantinople and all over the East than yield in the matter of Crete." The three hundred thousand Greeks in the Turkish capital would set fire to the place.[8] Prince George's filibustering expedition was simply the culmination of a general movement. The Greeks, who were already shipping volunteers and munitions to Crete in large numbers, were preparing for a bombardment and attack upon Canea as a preliminary to taking possession of the island.[9]

Prince George arrived off Canea on February 12, but left again on the next day. Why? No one knows. It may be that the whole expedition was intended simply as a demonstration of the dynasty's patriotism, which was seriously questioned by the Hetairia. It has also been thought that King George of Greece had received assurances from the Tsar, and possibly from Austrian circles, that Crete should go to his son. Prince George left, it is said, because he discovered on his arrival that the situation was quite different from what had been pictured to him.[10] The whole episode did not mean much, for on February 13 Colonel Vassos left the Piraeus with fifteen hundred men, landed soon after near Canea and joined the insurrectionary forces. At the same time the rebels began the

---

[7] *Turkey No. 10 (1897)*, nos. 75, 89; *Turkey No. 11 (1897)*, nos. 64, 114.

[8] *Turkey No. 11 (1897)*, no. 68; *Die Grosse Politik*, XII, no. 3153; Driault and Lhéritier, op. cit., IV, p. 344.

[9] *Turkey No. 10 (1897)*, nos. 94, 104, 105; *Turkey No. 11 (1897)*, nos. 39, 59, 60; *Affaire de Crète*, nos. 36, 46, 64.

[10] The Tsar's assurances in *Die Grosse Politik*, XII, nos. 3014, 3030; Austrian encouragement, see Driault and Lhéritier, op. cit., IV, p. 332. See also Victor Bérard: *Les Affaires de Crète* (Paris, 1898), pp. 188 ff.

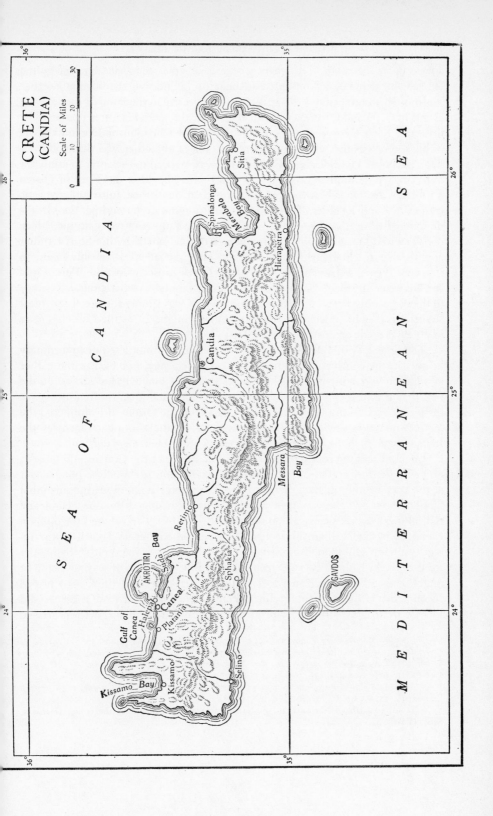

CRETE
(CANDIA)

Scale of Miles
0   10   20   30

SEA OF CANDIA

MEDITERRANEAN SEA

Sitia

Spinalonga

Mirabelo Bay

Hierapetra

Candia

Messara Bay

Retimo

AKROTIRI Bay

Suda Bay

Canea

Halepa

Platania

Selino

Kissamo Bay

Kissamo

Gulf of Canea

Sphakia

GAVDOS

attack upon the town. The governor, realizing that the situation had gotten entirely out of hand, fled on board a Russian ship and sought refuge at Corfu.[11]

In order to understand the attitude of the great powers towards the exciting events in Crete and Greece, one must remember the special features presented by this case. King George of Greece was the son of Christian of Denmark. One of his sisters was the wife of the Prince of Wales, the other was the mother of Tsar Nicholas. His eldest son Constantine was married to the sister of Emperor William, whose mother was the Empress Frederick, eldest daughter of Queen Victoria. The Danish royal family more than any other cultivated dynastic connexions and loyalties. Through the King's family relationships the Greeks undoubtedly hoped to gain much. The Tsar, the Empress Frederick, the Prince of Wales and Queen Victoria were, indeed, deeply moved by the heart-rending appeals that reached them from Athens. They did all they possibly could to influence their governments to support the Greek cause against the Turk. Only the German Emperor was unmoved by these family considerations. His reply to the beseeching letters of his sister and mother was simply the novel if cynical suggestion that his uncle, the Prince of Wales, might act as the *Cœur de Lion* of a new crusade against the infidel Turk.[12]

The tide of Phil-Hellenism, while considerable, did not rise to extraordinary heights in the continental countries. In both Germany and France the earlier admiration and sympathy for the Greeks had been somewhat tempered by the fact that the little state was in financial default, and that the realization of the Greek aspirations might mean the collapse of the Ottoman Empire and the loss of an impressively large investment. Of all the continental peoples the Italians were perhaps most whole-heartedly on the Hellenic side.[13]

England was the centre of the agitation in behalf of the Cretans and Greeks, as it was the focal point of the Armenian movement. It should be pointed out at the very beginning that there was not the almost unanimous outburst that had characterized the action in behalf of the Armenians. But the liberal and radical groups were nearly all on the side of the Greeks, and shared the opinion expressed by Sir William Harcourt when he said that every breach in the integrity of the Ottoman Empire was so much gain for mankind.[14] Sympathy for the Greeks had always run strong among British liberals. It was, in fact, part of the classical tradition and part of the political credo of those who prided themselves on their championship of enlightened ideas. Byron Societies did their share to keep alive the Phil-Hellenic sentiment. William Watson greeted

---

[11] *Turkey No. 10 (1897)*, nos. 113, 114, 118; *Turkey No. 11 (1897)*, nos. 70, 71; *Affaire de Crète*, nos. 83, 103; Driault and Lhéritier, op. cit., IV, pp. 344–5.

[12] Hohenlohe: *Denkwürdigkeiten der Reichskanzlerzeit*, pp. 299–303; *Letters of Queen Victoria*, III, pp. 121–39, passim.

[13] A good digest of European opinion may be found in *Questions Diplomatiques et Coloniales*, I, pp. 35 ff., 104 ff., 236 ff., 294 ff. (March 1, 15, April 15, May 1, 1897).

[14] Gardiner: *Life of Harcourt*, II, pp. 441–2; similarly his remarks in the House (Hansard, Series IV, vol. XLVI, p. 529).

the news of the Greek expedition to Greece with a poem which reflected very well the psychology of these circles:

> Hellas Hail!
> Little land so great of heart,
>   'Midst a world so abject grown,
> Must thou play thy glorious part,
>   Hellas, gloriously alone?
> Shame on Europe's arms, if she
> Leave her noblest work to thee!
>
> . . . .
>
> Not since first thy wine-dark wave
>   Laughed in multitudinous mirth,
> Hath a deed more pure and brave
>   Flushed the wintry cheek of Earth,
> There is heard no melody
> Like thy footsteps on the sea.

While dynastic influence and a considerable amount of public pressure was being thrown into the scales in favor of the Greek claims, the governments were, one and all, exceedingly cautious from the very beginning. Diplomacy as a rule has little liking for filibustering expeditions and *coups de main,* which are the very negation of the principle of negotiation. Greece was violating international law, an offense which, when committed by a small state, is a serious matter. Furthermore, European statesmen had just passed through months of acute crisis in Near Eastern affairs. It must be remembered that by February 1897 Nelidov's plans were pretty generally known in inner circles. In the European chancelleries, therefore, it was felt to be necessary above all things to prevent another crisis that might lead to serious conflict. As M. Lavisse so aptly put it, the powers were riveted together by mutual suspicion.[15] They were so terrified by the prospect of a general European war that they took refuge in united action. The essential thing, as they saw it, was to avoid any isolated action. To be sure, it had been shown in the Armenian affair that the Concert of Europe could operate only on a minimum program, and minimum programs were usually worthless. Even so, better to do nothing than to get involved in a great war. It is more important to be French than to be Armenian or Cretan or Greek, said M. Francis Charmes, a leading French political writer. The sentiment was no doubt widely shared in governmental circles.

Speaking in the house of lords on February 15 Lord Salisbury, referring to the Greek expedition to Crete, said that " all the Powers, without exception, were of the opinion that this was a most ill-advised act." They retained their opinion of its " utter unwisdom " and were not disposed to sanction it. Britain intended, under the circumstances, to continue her efforts to work in concert with

---

[15] Ernest Lavisse: " Notre Politique Orientale " II (*Revue de Paris,* III, June 15, 1897, pp. 872–914). p. 888.

the other powers.[16] The prime minister took a perfectly realistic view of the situation. From the reports that reached him he was convinced that the Christians in Crete were as much to blame for the trouble as were the Moslems. To the Queen, who bombarded him with letters from her Greek relatives, he wrote that even though England could not take vigorous action in any movement in favor of the Sultan, it would be out of the question to unite Crete with Greece. There was no use in bringing up the much-quoted precedent of the East Rumelian rising in 1885. The fact was that in 1897 the abandonment of Crete to Greece would mean the beginning of the partition of the Ottoman Empire, with insurrections in Macedonia and elsewhere. To support the Cretans would result in conflict with the other powers.[17]

This was a fairly accurate statement of the situation. Whatever may have been the personal feeling of Tsar Nicholas, his ministers were absolutely opposed to the Greek claims from the very start. Muraviev, the foreign minister, was a man of no great ability or consequence, but Witte and other powerful influences were determined to have peace at almost any price while Russia was busy in the Far East. Muraviev therefore announced that Russia would take part in any concerted action against the " intolerable aspirations " of Greece.[18] He suggested representations at Athens and put forward the proposal that the powers should land troops from their ships at Canea to help the Turkish authorities restore order. Crete, he suggested, should be held in trust (" dans une sorte de dépôt ") by the powers until its fate could be settled. It has been said that the Russians offered to let the Greeks have Crete if they would turn over Suda Bay to the Russian government for a naval base, but we have no way of checking the story. Anyway, Russia at the outset declared her strong opposition to the idea of union of the island with Greece.[19]

The Russian suggestions were warmly supported by the German government, which in Near Eastern affairs had come to accept the Russian view *sans phrase*. Germany, it was said in Berlin, cared nothing about the matter in hand and was interested solely in the principle of the thing. The idea of a third-rate power like Greece acting against the will of the great powers was simply intolerable. Germany would support any suggestion for action, provided it was understood that Crete should not be joined to Greece.[20] England also agreed to follow the Russian suggestions. On February 15 the admirals in command at Canea each landed about one hundred marines, the French, Austrians and Italians following the lead of Russia, Germany and England.[21]

---

[16] Hansard, XLVI, p. 369; similarly Balfour in the house of commons, February 16 (ibid., p. 526).   [17] *Letters of Queen Victoria*, III, pp. 122–3, 130.

[18] *Correspondance de M. de Staal*, II, p. 338; *Die Grosse Politik*, XII, no. 2941.

[19] *Turkey No. 11 (1897)*, nos. 76, 86; *Affaire de Crète*, nos. 81, 85; *Die Grosse Politik*, XII, no. 3142; Driault and Lhéritier, op. cit., IV, pp. 347–8. MacColl claimed he had seen in Athens " evidence in black & white " of the Russian offer (Russell: *Malcolm MacColl*, pp. 198 ff., 205).

[20] *Turkey No. 11 (1897)*, nos. 61, 90; *Die Grosse Politik*, XII, nos. 3132, 3138, 3140, 3142, 3144.   [21] *Turkey No. 11 (1897)*, nos. 83, 86, 96; *Affaire de Crète*, nos. 108, 120.

The action of the powers could not, of course, settle the question. Five or six hundred men in ruined Canea might restore and preserve order there, but they could not affect the insurgents in the mountains, or the forces of Vassos, who were co-operating with them. The great question was how to induce the Greek government to withdraw its troops. The Russian ambassador at Berlin, Count Osten-Sacken, had on February 10 already mooted the suggestion made by Goluchowski in the summer of 1896, namely, to blockade the Piraeus. The German foreign office was ready to go the limit, but in the opinion of the Emperor higher leadership was necessary. On February 14 he went over the heads of his ministers and took the whole matter in hand personally. From this time on German policy in this question was the Emperor's policy. He himself claimed credit for what was done. Now what was the policy? The Emperor visited the ambassadors of England, France, Austria and Russia. Declarations of disapprobation were of no use, he said. What was needed was vigorous action against the Greek fleet, and if necessary a blockade of the Piraeus.[22]

The Austrians could not do otherwise than accept the proposal they had themselves originally made. The Russians were perfectly willing to join in a blockade of Greece. Hanotaux, while not enthusiastic, thought it would be the only sensible procedure if coercion was to be used at all. The Italians were cool, but certainly would have joined if the other powers had been in agreement. All depended upon England, just as in the previous summer. On February 17 the cabinet met. Whatever Salisbury's own ideas may have been, it turned out that the Unionist element in the cabinet, and others like Goschen and Hicks Beach, would not listen to a blockade. The least they would accept for Crete was a position of complete autonomy within the Ottoman Empire. Until this had been secured they would oppose all measures of coercion against Greece. Salisbury, who was clearly anxious lest too great concessions to the Cretans might start trouble in the Balkans, was helpless against Chamberlain and his followers in the cabinet. His hands were tied.[23]

The Germans at first refused to consider the British suggestion. The Cretan question, they argued, could not even be discussed until the Greeks had withdrawn their forces. Otherwise Europe would be acting under pressure from Athens. Furthermore, the appetite of the Balkan states would be whetted. There would be no stopping further outbreaks in southeastern Europe. For a week the powers wrangled about the course to be pursued, until on February 24 the Russian government brought forward a program intended to be a compromise between the British and the German views: there was to be no annexation of Crete by Greece, but the island was to be given autonomy. An ultimatum was to be sent to Greece requiring the government to withdraw the troops, failing

[22] *Turkey No. 11 (1897)*, nos. 61, 82, 90, 151; *Affaire de Crète*, nos. 66, 112; *Die Grosse Politik*, XII, nos. 3133, 3148, 3152.

[23] *Turkey No. 11 (1897)*, nos. 104, 109, 125, 135; *Die Grosse Politik*, XII, nos. 3153, 3156 ff.; *Letters of Queen Victoria*, III, pp. 133-7.

which " suitable rigorous measures " were to be used, in the form of a blockade of the Piraeus or direct action against the Greek forces in Crete.

This proposal was accepted by all the powers, including England, the British government insisting, however, on a toning down of the language of the Russian note. There is no need for entering upon all the details of the discussion. The documents in the British Blue Books and French Yellow Books on this Cretan affair alone number more than three thousand, the equivalent of about twelve ordinary volumes. It would take a whole book to analyze them in detail. Suffice it to say that on March 2 identic notes were handed to the Greek and Turkish governments. These notes expressed the determination of the powers to endow Crete with " an absolutely effective autonomy " under the suzerainty of the Sultan. The Greek government was therefore called upon to withdraw its ships and forces within six days. In case of refusal the powers were " irrevocably determined not to hesitate at any measures of constraint." The Porte made no difficulty, and accepted the principle of autonomy. But the Greeks were obdurate. Affairs in Crete had been going from bad to worse. The insurgents had attempted an attack upon Canea, ignoring the warnings of the admirals. As a result the foreign warships, on February 21, had fired upon the insurgent forces. The incident caused a tremendous outbreak of indignation, especially in England, where many people regarded the action as open partisanship for the Turk. In Greece the excitement reached unheard-of proportions. Mobs surged about on the square before the palace, snatching up the newspapers, of which new editions were being sold every few minutes. The demand for war was so strong that no one could think of resisting it. The King himself was obliged to humor the crowds with brave utterances in order to avoid being swept away by the tide.[24]

Under the circumstances the Greek reply could be nothing but a rejection of the terms of the powers. The Athens government refused the offer of autonomy and demanded annexation on the basis of a plebiscite. While willing to recall its ships, it insisted that the troops stay in Crete until the island was pacified. The reply was clearly unsatisfactory, and the next step, equally clearly, was to apply measures of constraint. The admirals of all the powers were unanimously in favor of blockading the Piraeus and other Greek ports, and the continental governments were one and all in favor of following their advice. But the British government refused to do the logical thing. It was not that he had any sympathy with the Greeks, said Lord Salisbury to the German ambassador, but that public opinion forced the government to adopt a slower pace. It would be better to start with the blockade of Crete and possibly of the Gulf of Volo,

---

[24] *Turkey No. 11 (1897)*, nos. 156, 158; *Affaire de Crète*, nos. 179, 201; Politis: *La Guerre Gréco-Turque*, pp. 8–9; Streit: *La Question Crétoise*, loc. cit., pp. 341 ff.; S. G.: *La Guerre de 1897*, loc. cit., pp. 324–74, 345–7. For events in Crete see *Turkey No. 9 (1897)*, the reports of the admirals. The notes of March 2 in *Turkey No. 4 (1897)*. For the negotiations see *Turkey No. 11 (1897)*; *Affaire de Crète*; *Die Grosse Politik*, XII, nos. 3167 ff.; *Letters of Queen Victoria*, III, pp. 138 ff.; Driault and Lhéritier, op. cit., IV, pp. 358 ff.

a method " at once more effective and less exasperating." The British premier even went so far as to suggest that the Greek troops in Crete might be used as a gendarmerie force, under the divided command of the powers, a suggestion which the Germans thought would turn the powers into a laughingstock, and which Muraviev flatly rejected. The Russian minister proposed that Crete be occupied by some ten thousand troops furnished by any two powers with a European mandate, for example, France and Italy. This suited England, but did not suit France and Italy. In the end the British sent a further six hundred men to the island and the other powers, excepting Germany and Austria, did likewise. On March 18 the admirals proclaimed the blockade, to take effect March 21, and on March 19 they announced the granting of autonomy, but neither of these developments had much effect on the situation. The insurgents wanted union with Greece, not autonomy. They paid no attention to the blockade, and it was not thought advisable to cut off their food supply. In Crete a regular war took place between the rebels and the forces of the powers. The former were in the mountains, the latter in the coast towns. Whatever may be said of the action of the admirals, their position was a most difficult one. They could hardly get at their opponents. No decision could be reached in this way.[25]

The course of European diplomacy with regard to the Near Eastern question was simply repeating itself. Once again the British government refused to act in accord with the other powers. It was a question of breaking up the Concert or breaking up the cabinet, and under such circumstances English statesmen always prefer to sacrifice the Concert. All this did not disturb the German Emperor very much. His distrust of British policy in the Near East was as profound as that of the Russians, and he had therefore striven from the start to invoke action by the three Empires, followed by France and Italy, even without England: "We can do without England. The Continent must for once show the British that it cannot be made a fool of," he noted on one report. To the Tsar he telegraphed, when the note to Greece had finally been agreed upon:

"You see by the result that your *démarche* has rallied all the Powers, willing or not, to a common demonstration, which will, I hope, make the Peace of Europe an undisturbed one. You have shown the world once more that if the 3 great Empires *marchent d'accord* and are joined by the other great Continental Powers, i.e. if the whole Continent keeps together in an unbroken front, the rest of the world must follow us, even the strongest! The King of Greece must be clean mad if he does not stop in his mad attempt to set the world on fire ' pour y allumer sa pipe.' "[26]

But the Emperor's elation at the prospective consummation of the continental " combine " was soon tempered when he realized that a naval action

[25] *Turkey No. 10 (1897)*, nos. 291, 300; *Turkey No. 11 (1897)*, nos. 245, 252, 253 ff., 259, 267, 276, 303–7, 311; *Affaire de Crète*, nos. 243, 251, 275, 291, 294, 335; *Die Grosse Politik*, XII, nos. 3175 ff.; *Letters of Queen Victoria*, III, pp. 144 ff.; Driault and Lhéritier, op. cit., IV, pp. 370–7.
[26] *The Kaiser's Letters to the Tsar* (London, 1920), pp. 41–2; *Die Grosse Politik*, XII, nos. 3167, 3168.

without England was bound to be futile.[27] The Greeks felt encouraged by the attitude of the English and had no faith whatever in the punitive measures threatened by the other powers. But it is doubtful whether the English were doing the King of Greece and his cabinet a good turn. King George used some strong and threatening language on occasion. He is reported to have declared that he would take Crete and, if the powers tried to stop him, that he would put himself at the head of the nation with 300,000 Greeks and put the match to the insurrection in Macedonia and elsewhere. To an English visitor he remarked that within an hour of the declaration of a blockade of Greece he would send his troops across the frontier of Thessaly. There would then be a general rising of the Greeks throughout the Ottoman Empire, and probably insurrections in Macedonia, Arabia and Syria.[28] But these threats need not be taken too seriously. The King had to put on a brave front to maintain his prestige and to scare the European powers, if he could. Other evidence would seem to show that at bottom he and his ministers would have welcomed a blockade of the Piraeus, which would have enabled them to draw back with dignity under *force majeure*, and so to have saved their faces before the Greek public. The government clearly would have accepted an autonomous régime for Crete, had it dared. Throughout March the ministers were in negotiation with the Porte, evidently trying to reach an agreement on this basis. But they needed more to satisfy the country than the Porte felt able to offer, and it may be that Russia or some other power warned the Turks against giving up Crete.[29]

By some writers it has been claimed that the efforts at a settlement between Turkey and Greece were wrecked by nefarious German and Russian influences. The Emperor William, it is said, wanted war and wanted it badly.[30] But there is no evidence of German instigation beyond the hearsay that passed into the reports of journalists. On February 28 Waldersee noted in his diary that the Emperor's brother, Prince Henry, reported William as having asked the Turkish ambassador why the Sultan did not proceed against the Greeks, and telling him that the Sultan should act with the greatest vigor if he valued German friendship.[31] But even if this indirect evidence is accepted, it will be noted that the Emperor's remark was made with reference to the Cretan question. As soon as the danger of conflict spread from Crete to Macedonia the

---

[27] *Die Grosse Politik*, XII, no. 3215, marginal note.

[28] Georges N. Philarétos: "La Localisation de la Lutte Gréco-Turque aidée par le Roi des Hellènes" (*Questions Diplomatiques et Coloniales*, March 15, 1898, pp. 337–49); Russell: *Malcolm MacColl*, pp. 195 ff.

[29] *Turkey No. 11 (1897)*, nos. 303 ff.; *Die Grosse Politik*, XII, no. 3215; S. G.: "La Guerre de 1897," pp. 362–4, 374; Politis, op. cit., pp. 8–10; Driault and Lhéritier, op. cit., IV, p. 385; Turot: *L'Insurrection Crétoise*, pp. 95–6; Sir Vincent Corbett: *Reminiscences* (London, 1927), p. 257; Vindex (Malcolm MacColl): "A Plot against British Interests in the Levant" (*Fortnightly Review*, June, 1897, pp. 811–24), p. 822.

[30] See especially the article by Vindex which is referred to in the preceding note.

[31] Waldersee: *Denkwürdigkeiten*, II, pp. 392–3.

Emperor was as much worried by the prospect of European war as was anyone.[32]

It will be recalled that the Greek organization, Ethniké Hetairia, was designed to further Greek interests in Macedonia by revolutionary means. For this group the Cretan affair was a secondary sphere of action. The chief theatre of operations was to be Thessaly and Epirus and then Macedonia. The society had practically complete control of the army, since three quarters of the officers were members, and the King was helpless against it. The organization was in some ways anti-dynastic and did not even hesitate to send the ruler threatening letters.[33] For some time the members of the society had been assembling volunteers on the border. It was claimed that there were twelve thousand armed men available for duty. On March 19 the Greek commander on the frontier received orders from the war minister to deliver five hundred thousand cartridges to the Hetairists, and to help them get over the border, but to do it secretly.[34] While all this was going on, the government, under pressure, was concentrating the regular troops in Thessaly. On February 15 there were only five thousand troops in the north. By February 27 there were about twenty-five thousand. Complete mobilization was ordered on March 15. On March 21 the French minister at Athens reported that almost all the troops had been sent to the north, about forty-five thousand to Thessaly and about twenty-five thousand to Epirus. The excitement in Greece was tremendous, and the demand for war was rapidly becoming irresistible.[35]

In view of the Greek preparations, the Turks began to take precautionary measures. They too concentrated their forces on the frontier. At the same time the Sultan attempted to make an agreement, that is a military convention, with Serbia, and to establish closer contact with Roumania. Neither of these feelers bore fruit.[36] Both the Bulgarians and the Serbs were very much excited by the prospect that Greece might secure Crete while the other Balkan states obtained nothing. They were in favor of the status quo, reported the French minister at Belgrade, but the status quo for all. Prince Ferdinand of Bulgaria, probably stimulated by the Macedonian organizations, was ready to take steps to prepare for all eventualities. In January 1897 there appeared at Athens a Bulgarian representative who proposed that Bulgaria and Greece together lay before the ambassadors of the powers at Constantinople their demand for reforms in Macedonia according to the provisions of Article XXIII of the Treaty of Berlin. A similar démarche was made at Belgrade. The Greek government, it is said, took the view that no reliance was to be placed upon Turkish promises of re-

---

[32] Die Grosse Politik, XII, nos. 3183, 3185, 3193 ff.; The Kaiser's Letters to the Tsar, p. 42.

[33] Politis: La Guerre Gréco-Turque, pp. 3–8; Turot: L'Insurrection Crétoise, etc., p. 97; William Miller: Travels and Politics in the Near East (London, 1898), p. 282.

[34] The revelations of General Macris, and of Delyannis, quoted by Chester: Life of Venizelos, pp. 50–1; Turot, op. cit., p. 112; Affaire de Crète, nos. 257, 324, 347.

[35] Affaire de Crète, nos. 142, 157, 216, 251.

[36] Vladan Georgevich: Das Ende der Obrenovitch (Leipzig, 1905), pp. 60, 64; Idem: Die Jungtürkische Revolution (Leipzig, 1908); Tranafir G. Djuvara: Mes Missions Diplomatiques (Paris, 1930), pp. 42–3.

form. What was needed was a definition of spheres of influence in Macedonia. The suggestion was one which the Bulgarians were always loath to accept, because their claims in Macedonia were quite incompatible with the aspirations of the Greeks and Serbs. They did, we are told, agree to leave Greece the littoral, with Saloniki, but insisted on a corridor to the Aegean for Bulgaria. The Greeks, incredible though it may seem, evidently rejected the proposal. The negotiations therefore came to naught so far as Bulgaria and Greece were concerned. At Belgrade, however, the proposals from Sofia were more favorably received. The Serbian public was anxious for action, but the government knew that the army was unprepared and that it would be impossible to mobilize the forces even for a few months. Under the circumstances co-operation with Bulgaria seemed the wiser course. In the last days of February King Alexander paid a visit to Sofia which resulted in a gentlemen's understanding on March 1. This provided that every question touching the interests of the Bulgarians and Serbs in the Ottoman Empire should be settled by agreement; that neither party should undertake single-handedly anything that might disturb the status quo, either politically or militarily; that, so long as spheres of interest had not been defined by mutual agreement, neither party should put obstacles in the way of the other but should aid in all national, ecclesiastical and educational questions. Montenegro was to be invited to join in this agreement.[37]

The Russian government was evidently informed of these proceedings and gave them its blessing. Muraviev was greatly exercised by the threat of trouble in Macedonia and was anxious to prevent a possible clash between Serbia and Bulgaria or between either of these states and the Turks. Indeed, the Russian government was throwing all its influence into the scales to effect a reconciliation between the Bulgarian and Greek churches, and was by no means favorably disposed towards Serb plans for the erection of a Serbian patriarchate. It was with the same general purpose in mind that Muraviev exerted himself to stop possible aggression by Greece in Macedonia. The Greeks were shipping all their men and supplies by sea from the Piraeus to Volo, the railroad to Thessaly being still incomplete. The Russian minister therefore urged upon the powers the blockade of Volo as the most effective way of putting a stop to preparations. Speaking to the British ambassador he used very strong language: " If England abstained at this juncture, the concert of the Powers would be broken up; it would lead probably to war breaking out between Turkey and Greece, and to a general conflagration in Macedonia. The responsibility of this would fall on Her Majesty's Government." [38] But not even this warning

[37] Yovanovič: *Vlada Aleksandra Obrenoviča*, I, pp. 366–7; *Affaire de Crète*, nos. 67, 150, 193, 260; Vladan Georgevich: *Das Ende der Obrenovitch*, pp. 67–8; *Die Grosse Politik*, XII, nos. 2982–5; for the Bulgar-Greek negotiations see Vindex, loc. cit., especially pp. 811–2, and Russell: *Malcolm MacColl*, pp. 198 ff. MacColl had his information from the Bulgarian representative at Athens. See, further, Henry Norman: " The Wreck of Greece " (*Scribner's Magazine*, October, 1897, pp. 399–426), pp. 411–2; J. D. Bourchier, in Luigi Villari: *The Balkan Question* (London, 1905), p. 87.

[38] *Turkey No. 11 (1897)*, nos 330, 335; *Affaire de Crète*, nos. 351, 373.

sufficed to unite the British cabinet. Salisbury was obliged to announce that England would join in a blockade of Volo only if the Greeks and Turks refused to withdraw their troops fifty kilometers from the border. The admirals, however, were pressing continuously for a blockade of the Piraeus, which all the powers urgently recommended. Reluctantly the British, on March 31, promised to join if all the powers approved. At last all were prepared to act, but there followed several days of discussion as to the ways and means of the blockade, and finally the whole project was allowed to drop. Events had made the blockade utterly futile.[39]

April 6 was the anniversary of Greek independence, and it was generally feared that, in the enthusiasm of the moment, the Greeks might take irrevocable steps. On the suggestion of Russia both the Greek and Turkish governments were warned on that day that the powers would hold the aggressor responsible for all the consequences of a clash, and that " whatever the issue of the struggle might be, they would in no case allow the aggressor to derive the least benefit from it." The Greeks ignored all these warnings. On April 3 the foreign minister admitted that war had been decided upon. A week later some two thousand Greek irregulars crossed the frontier and attacked the Turkish outposts. The Turks were mobilized and ready, yet for more than ten days they maintained a strict defensive. The Sultan, no doubt, was anxious to avoid war, though the military party in Constantinople was pressing for it. When on April 17 the Greek regulars attacked, there was no further holding back. The Ottoman government broke off relations and declared war.[40]

The German Emperor has been accused of having forced the war and of having encouraged the military party in the Turkish capital.[41] Whether this was the fact or not one cannot definitely say. The reports of the Greek diplomats show that they firmly believed it.[42] The German documents, significantly enough, have a considerable lacuna between April 3 and April 11, but they make it clear that the Austrians and the Germans had become convinced that the only way out of the Cretan embroglio was through war. The Russians evidently shared this view.[43] Of the victory of the Turks there could be no serious question. Apart from their greater manpower (ultimately they could put over a million men into the field), their preparations were better than they had been on the eve of any war they had fought in modern times. Under the direction of General von der Goltz Pasha the whole system had been overhauled in the preceding dozen years. The mobilization and campaign plans had been care-

---

[39] *Turkey No. 11 (1897)*, nos. 341, 376–7, 385, 392; *Affaire de Crète*, nos. 370, 395, 396, 453; *Die Grosse Politik*, XII, nos. 3203 ff., 3211 ff.

[40] *Turkey No. 11 (1897)*, nos. 395, 401, 412, 415, 417, 434, 438; *Affaire de Crète*, nos. 474, 485, 503, 535, 537, 544; Driault and Lhéritier, op. cit., IV, pp. 384, 389–92.

[41] Notably by Georges Gaulis: " Les Allemands à Constantinople " (*Revue de Paris*, March 15, 1898, pp. 326–52), p. 351.

[42] Driault and Lhéritier, op. cit., IV, pp. 386–7.

[43] *Die Grosse Politik*, XII, no. 3222; Driault and Lhéritier, op. cit., IV, p. 387.

fully worked out, and the frontiers had been exhaustively studied. Excellent military schools had been established, and many of the younger staff officers were German trained. In 1893 the government had rearmed the infantry. The artillery was equipped with Krupp guns. The only great weakness of the government was its desperate need for funds. This problem was solved with noteworthy ease: the government simply took over the pension funds and the Caisses Agricoles and raised a " voluntary " loan. Everything was ready and the military men were more than eager to try out the new system.[44]

The Greeks were in no way ready to meet such an adversary, and the government knew it. At best they could put into the field about one hundred thousand men. But the army was not a trained fighting force, it was part of the political machine. Anyone could buy himself off and evade the conscription system. The officers were almost all political appointees, the men in the ranks were unequipped and untrained. Of discipline there was hardly a trace. Artillery was inadequate, and the supply of small arms was not sufficient until the end of the war. The government then secured a large number of Gras rifles, much inferior to the Martini-Henris of the Turkish troops, and not to be compared to the new Mausers of which the Turks had several hundred thousand on hand. The supply system was pathetic. Of plans of campaign there was nothing worth mention. No one in his right mind could hope for victory under these cirumstances. The government, indeed, seems to have hoped, with Micawber, that something " would turn up " to save it from its folly. Once the war had started, efforts were made to secure the aid of Bulgaria. The Bulgarians had a considerable force mobilized upon the frontier, but even if they had been willing to throw in their lot with the Greeks, they were prevented from doing so by strong warnings from Russia: " We received an order which we could not disobey without compromising our very existence," said Karavelov soon after. The Bulgarians, like the Serbs, had to confine their activity to demands for bishoprics in Macedonia, and were obliged to content themselves with promises from the Porte. It was only after many months of waiting that they secured what they wanted. By that time the Greeks had been thoroughly beaten and the Near Eastern question had passed from the critical phase.[45]

There is no need in a book of this sort for a full discussion of the campaigns in Thessaly and Epirus. The Turks held the advantageous side of the frontier

---

[44] Colmar Freiherr von der Goltz: *Der Thessalische Krieg* (Berlin, 1898), pp. 5-15; Generalfeldmarschall Colmar Freiherr von der Goltz: *Denkwürdigkeiten* (Berlin, 1929), pp. 135-63.

[45] Karavelov's remarks to Franklin-Bouillon, in the *Figaro,* July 25, 1897 (in Politis: *La Guerre Gréco-Turque,* p. 62); on the policy of Bulgaria and Serbia see especially Henry Norman: " The Wreck of Greece " (*Scribner's Magazine,* October, 1897, pp. 399-426), p. 412; Yovanovič, op. cit., I, pp. 368 ff.; Politis, op. cit., pp. 63-4; Driault and Lhéritier, op. cit., IV, p. 388. On the Greek army see, among other contributions, H. W. Wilson: " The Downfall of Greece " (*National Review,* June, 1897, pp. 525-35); E. J. Dillon: " The Fate of Greece " (*Contemporary Review,* July, 1897, pp. 1-34); Bennet Burleigh: " The Greek War, as I saw it " (*Fortnightly Review,* July, 1897, pp. 134-51); Charles Williams: " The Thessalian War of 1897 " (ibid., June, 1897, pp 959-72).

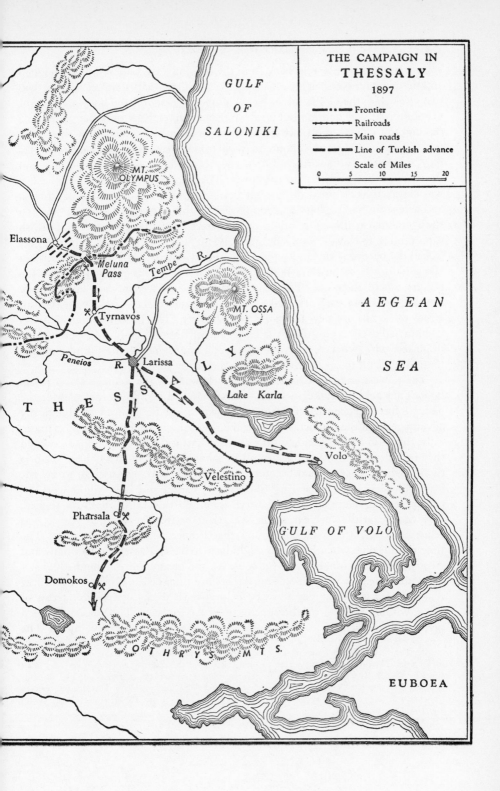

THE CAMPAIGN IN
THESSALY
1897

Frontier
Railroads
Main roads
Line of Turkish advance

Scale of Miles
0   5   10   15   20

GULF

OF

SALONIKI

MT.
OLYMPUS

Elassona

Meluna
Pass

Tempe R.

Tyrnavos

MT. OSSA

AEGEAN

Peneios R.   Larissa

SEA

T H E S S A L Y

Lake Karla

T H E S S A L Y

Volo

Velestino

Pharsala

GULF OF VOLO

Domokos

O T H R Y S   M T S.

EUBOEA

and soon pushed the Greeks back from the Meluna Pass. Larissa was abandoned and the army retreated upon Pharsalos. By that time, that is, before the war was two weeks old, the Greek forces were completely demoralized and in a state of dissolution. It was nothing but a rabble that streamed back over the plains. Excepting the valiant resistance of General Smolensky at Velestino there was nothing the Greeks could point to with pride. According to many observers they showed only cowardice. Often they could have held, in Thessaly and Epirus, but they preferred to run away. The fleet, which commanded the sea, was expected to do great things, but beyond a futile bombardment of Prevesa and a few similar exploits it accomplished nothing. Even if Saloniki was too strong to attack, the effort might at least have been made to cut the Turkish supply lines at Kavalla or Dedeagach. But it was said by some that the fleet lacked the necessary fuel to keep the sea, and by others that the King would not allow it to act, because he hoped that when the Turks reached Larissa the powers would intervene. The whole war, says one writer, was " une guerre simulée, fictive, fausse." To make a long story short, the Greeks were, within a few weeks, completely and hopelessly defeated. The Italian volunteers, who had hurried to the scene under the leadership of Ricciotti Garibaldi, were utterly disgusted with what they saw and experienced. The warmest Phil-Hellenes found it difficult to say much in favor of their protégé.[46]

The powers, says Sir Charles Eliot, " behaved like the managers of a prize-fight. They held the stakes — Crete — en dépôt, and laid down the rules for the game — for instance, that the aggressor would not be allowed to obtain any advantage from the conflict, whatever the result might be." [47] As umpires, naturally, they also had to decide on the terms of victory. The question was: would they be able to find common ground in solving the problem? Queen Victoria thought the " concert " had become " contemptible and very useless, to say the least." She had hoped that England, France, Russia and Italy might work together, leaving Germany and Austria aside. To this Lord Salisbury replied, very wisely, on the very eve of the war, that the trouble was that Russia was reluctant to part from Germany and that France would follow Russia. The time would come when England would have to break away from Germany and Austria, but that time had not yet come. In the meanwhile England could not allow the defeat of Greece. Salisbury therefore proposed to Russia on April 23 that a conference of ambassadors be held at Paris to discuss possible terms of peace, without waiting for the conclusion of an armistice. The Queen appealed personally to Nicholas to join England and France in this new move. The

---

[46] The best critical account of the campaign is Colmar Freiherr von der Goltz: Der Thessa- lische Krieg (Berlin, 1898), but see also Colonel Robert Weber: Aus dem Feldzug in Thessalien (Zurich, 1898); Baron Wladimir Giesl: Zwei Jahrzehnte im Nahen Orient, chap. iii; Sir Ellis Ashmead-Bartlett: The Battlefields of Thessaly (London, 1897), passim; Henri Turot: L'Insurrection Crétoise et la Guerre Gréco-Turque (Paris, 1898), passim; Hans Barth: Türke, Wehre Dich! (Leip- zig, 1898), chaps. xiii. xiv.
[47] Sir Charles Eliot: Turkey in Europe, pp. 342–3.

Tsar agreed, but nothing came of the suggestion, in as much as Hanotaux, on whom Salisbury counted, insisted that it would be useless, at the time, to think of anything but an armistice. Germany and Austria also regarded a conference as premature.[48]

In reality Count Muraviev was not much taken with the British suggestion, and was not at all prepared to abandon Germany and Austria for the sake of England. At this very time, that is on April 27, Francis Joseph and Goluchowski arrived at St. Petersburg to return the Tsar's visit to Vienna in 1896. Goluchowski, like most Poles, was no friend of the Russians. His ideal was still the connexion of the Triple Alliance with England, a combination which would be able to obstruct the Russian designs in the Near East and especially in the Straits. He was put out by the estrangement of Germany and England, and distrusted the new rapprochement between Germany and Russia. But in Berlin no attention was paid to his likes and dislikes. Holstein spoke of the Austrian minister as a " mutton-head," and Goluchowski on his part positively detested both Marschall and Holstein. In March 1897 the German ambassador could write to Prince Hohenlohe that things had reached the pass where the only supporters of the Austro-German Alliance were the Emperor William, Prince Hohenlohe and he (Eulenburg) himself.[49]

Unable to rely upon British help or German sympathy the Austrian government had no choice but to take the advice of Berlin and seek an arrangement with Russia. Military circles in Vienna were always prone to urge this course. In April 1897 General von Beck, the chief of staff, worked out a memorandum to guide the Emperor on his forthcoming visit to St. Petersburg. In it he discussed the event of a forced partition of Turkey. Russia, he argued, would be entitled to the coast of the Black Sea and to control of the Straits. But Austria would have to control the Straits of Otranto as against Italy, and Austria could not tolerate Russian expansion in the western Balkans. Russia's advance to Constantinople might be delayed by wars, but ultimately it could not be prevented. It would be better therefore for Austria to declare her disinterestedness in the Balkans east of the Morava and Vardar valleys. In the western Balkans she should demand nothing but Bosnia and Herzegovina and the necessary parts of Novibazar. A close connexion with Serbia, Montenegro and an Albanian state, to be created, must be striven for, and Austria should also work for an independent Macedonia.

This program, which was really only a revival of the idea of dividing the Balkans into Russian and Austrian spheres of influence as Bismarck had so often recommended, was too far-reaching for Francis Joseph and his foreign minister. Goluchowski even doubted if Russia wanted an agreement. But when

---

[48] *Letters of Queen Victoria*, III, pp. 148–55; *Turkey No. 11 (1897)*, nos. 469, 474, 479; Driault and Lhéritier, op. cit., IV, pp. 397–8.

[49] Hohenlohe: *Denkwürdigkeiten der Reichskanzlerzeit*, p. 317; Johannes Haller: *Philip Eulenburg* (New York, 1930), I, pp. 374 ff.; *Die Grosse Politik*, XII, nos. 3114–6.

the Austrian party arrived at St. Petersburg, its members, from the Emperor down, were surprised by the warmth and brilliance of the reception tendered them. They found the Russians quite willing to discuss the situation and an agreement was reached with very little difficulty. It was not a formal alliance or even a hard and fast written agreement, but rather a gentlemen's understanding. The basis of it was the idea of maintaining the status quo in the Balkans as long as circumstances would permit. It was in accordance with this fundamental principle that the two governments telegraphed to their representatives at the Balkan capitals on April 30 that they would not allow " even the least movement in the Balkans." [50]

The principle of the status quo was a purely negative one. There was no knowing that it could be maintained. Certainly it could not last forever. The two governments therefore discussed the future arrangement of the Balkans. Both parties agreed to discard in advance all idea of conquest and decided to make this principle respected by every other power that might manifest designs on Balkan territory. Constantinople and the adjacent territory as well as the Straits, having an eminently European character, were not of a nature to be made the object of a separate understanding between the two powers, but Muraviev declared that Russia, far from striving for any modification of the existing state of affairs as laid down in the treaties, held to the complete maintenance of the provisions relating to the Straits which gave Russia " full and entire satisfaction " in prohibiting access to the Black Sea to foreign warships. As for the territory of the Balkans apart from Constantinople and the Straits, this was to be the subject of a special stipulation between the two parties, on the following bases: " The territorial advantages, accorded to Austria-Hungary by the Treaty of Berlin, are and remain acquired by her. In consequence, the possession of Bosnia, of Herzegovina, and of the Sanjak of Novibazar may not be made the object of any discussion whatsoever, the Government of His Imperial and Royal Apostolic Majesty reserving to itself the right of substituting, when the moment arrives, for the present status of occupation and of right of garrisoning that of annexation." That part between Janina in the south and Lake Scutari on the north should form an independent state under the name of Albania. The rest of the territory should be equitably partitioned between the small Balkan states. While inclined to take into consideration as far as possible the legitimate interest of the participants, Austria and Russia were resolved " to safeguard the principle of the present equilibrium, and, if need be by the means of rectifications of frontiers, to exclude every combination which would favor the establishment of a marked preponderance of any particular Balkan principality to the detriment of the others." And finally the two powers,

---

[50] *Affaire de Crète*, no. 631; *Die Grosse Politik*, XII, no. 3121; for the visit and the Beck memorandum see Edmund von Glaise-Horstenau: *Franz Josephs Weggefährte* (Vienna, 1930), pp. 383 ff.; Roderich Gooss: *Das Oesterreichisch-Serbische Problem bis zur Kriegserklärung an Serbien* (Berlin, 1930), pp. 68–70.

having recorded the fact that their only objective in the Balkans was " the maintenance, the consolidation, and the pacific development " of the small states established there, agreed " to pursue in future in this field a policy of perfect
harmony," and to avoid in consequence everything which might engender between them the " elements of conflict or of mistrust."

These were the lines of the agreement as noted by Goluchowski after his
return to Vienna and submitted to Muraviev for his approval. In his reply the
Russian minister took exception only to the passage relating to Bosnia, Herzegovina and the Sanjak of Novibazar. He pointed out that the Treaty of Berlin
accorded Austria the right of military occupation. " The annexation of these
two provinces would raise a more extensive question, which would require
special scrutiny at the proper times and places. As to the Sanjak of Novibazar,
there would also be the necessity to specify its boundaries, which, indeed, have
never been sufficiently defined." He even made a veiled reservation to the partition of Ottoman territory among the Balkan states: " It seems to us that points
b and c, having regard to the eventual formation of a principality of Albania
and to the equitable partition of all the territory to be disposed of between the
different small Balkan States, touch upon questions of the future which it would
be premature and very difficult to decide at present." [51]

The Austro-Russian agreement of May 1897 was of more than ordinary importance in the general alignment of the European powers. But the larger significance of the understanding may best be discussed a little later. So far as the
Greek situation was concerned it involved not only renewed warnings to the
Balkan states to keep the peace, but implied co-operation between the two
powers in whatever action was to be taken. The German Emperor warmly
welcomed the new combination. France would not be able to hang back without compromising the Alliance with Russia. Italy was of no great importance.
Even if Italy sided with England these two powers would be in a helpless
minority. Salisbury's hopes that Russia could soon be pried loose from Germany
and that England, France and Russia could solve the Near Eastern question to
their own satisfaction were now entirely blasted. The prime minister was grieved
to learn that the Tsar, who had agreed to the British proposal for a conference
of ambassadors at Paris, had gone back on his promise: " Nicky having evidently yielded to Mouravieff and pressure from Germany. France would not
act without Russia." [52]

By May 1 it had become urgently necessary to do something to bring the
war to a close. Violent anti-dynastic demonstrations were taking place at Athens
and for a moment it seemed that the King, who had before been faced with the
alternatives " lead or leave," would have no other choice than to leave. " The
Greeks are a contemptible race," wrote Lord Salisbury, " and I have no doubt

[51] Alfred F. Pribram: *The Secret Treaties of Austria-Hungary*, I, pp. 185–95; *Die Grosse Politik*, XII, no. 3126; Glaise-Horstenau: *Franz Josephs Weggefährte*, pp. 383–5; Gooss, loc. cit.
[52] *Letters of Queen Victoria*, III, p. 156.

turn upon the King and blame him for the policy which they themselves, the Greek mobs, forced upon him. I hope they will be too much cowed to proceed to extremities." But for emergencies the British gunboat *Nile* was sent to the Piraeus. in the end the dynasty was saved by the intervention of the vigorous opposition leader, M. Rhallis, who harangued the crowds from the box of a cab and somehow managed to tide over the crisis. On April 29 Rhallis took over the government from Delyannis.[53]

On May 3 the Greek government recalled Colonel Vassos from Crete. The Greeks were very eager for an armistice, but it was felt that the dynasty could not afford to ask for it. Queen Victoria was prepared to do all she could. She appealed to Emperor William. But the Emperor replied that Greece would have to " beg " for an armistice and promise to submit in advance to the decisions of the powers. Greece must immediately recall all her troops from Crete and accept the autonomy which the powers had agreed to. The Queen thought this " a rude answer " but there was nothing whatever to be done: " Intervention without the consent of Germany and Austria is not difficult, it is quite *impossible*," wrote Salisbury. The Queen therefore urged King George of Greece to give in. On May 8 the rest of the troops were recalled from Crete and on May 10 the Greek government accepted the rest of the German terms.[54]

The ambassadors at Constantinople now took steps to secure an armistice. They found, however, that the Turkish terms were inacceptable. The Sultan demanded the retrocession of Thessaly and the payment of a considerable indemnity. This was too much even for the German Emperor, who had advised the Sultan at the very beginning of the war to offer peace after the first victories and to content himself with the withdrawal of Vassos and the recognition of autonomy for Crete, without an indemnity.[55] So negotiations between the ambassadors and the Porte began to drag. On May 17 the Greeks were once more overwhelmingly defeated at Domokos. The Turks were at the gates of Attica. At this critical moment the Tsar wrote a personal appeal to the Sultan, who decided to yield. On May 19 the armistice was signed.

The actual peace negotiations were drawn out through the whole summer and the final settlement was not reached until September 18, 1897. The Sultan insisted on a considerable part of Thessaly and the payment of an indemnity. The powers would agree only to a slight rectification of the frontier. How was Greece to pay an indemnity when she was bankrupt? Germany favored a loan and the institution of international control of Greek finances, a proposal which the Greeks hotly rejected. The British government was prepared to use strong methods in forcing the Turks to accept the terms submitted to them and for a

[53] *Turkey No. 11 (1897)*, nos. 492, 508; William Miller: *Travels and Politics in the Near East*, pp. 261 ff., 291–2; Driault and Lhéritier, op. cit., IV, pp. 298 ff.

[54] *Turkey No. 10 (1897)*, nos. 456, 459, 468; *Turkey No. 11 (1897)*, nos. 517, 525, 527, 564, 565, 578; *Affaire de Crète*, nos. 639, 640, 651, 676, 681; *Die Grosse Politik*, XII, nos. 3227 ff.; Driault and Lhéritier, op. cit., IV, pp. 401–3; *Letters of Queen Victoria*, III, pp. 157–62.

[55] *Die Grosse Politik*, XII, no. 3226.

time there was danger lest the "concert" break up. But finally the Germans and Russians induced the Sultan to yield and the British gave in on the matter of financial control. Rarely has a victorious power been put off with so little of the fruits of victory; even more rarely has a state so completely defeated as Greece emerged from a war of aggression so lightly penalized. The principle that territory once taken from the infidel Turk and assigned to a Christian power could never be returned to Moslem rule was sanctified by the proceedings of the great states in 1897.[56]

Something must yet be said about the further development of the Cretan question. Thus far nothing had been decided upon excepting that the island should be endowed with an autonomous régime which the inhabitants did not want. The admirals were in command and Crete was still blockaded. All through the summer and autumn of 1897 the powers discussed the choice of a governor to organize the new autonomous régime. There was talk of appointing the Italian admiral, Canevaro, or a former president of the Swiss Confederation, M. Droz. A former Luxemburger, M. Schaefer, was seriously mentioned, but finally the powers agreed upon a member of the Montenegrin ruling family, Bojedar Petrovich. Unfortunately the latter refused the position and everything remained as before until in November 1897 the Russian government put forward the candidacy of Prince George of Greece, leader of the torpedo flotilla in February 1897. Prince George was a cousin of the Tsar, and had saved Nicholas from the hand of an assassin during their visit to Japan in 1891. His name had been mentioned in February and March 1897, but had not been pressed. Now, however, the Russian government put it forward with great insistency. The Sultan, who always maintained that the governor should be an Ottoman subject chosen by the Ottoman government with the approval of the powers, flatly refused to consider the Russian proposition. The Germans, who in the meanwhile had fallen out with the Russians over Far Eastern affairs, likewise refused to sanction the Russian choice. Eventually, in March 1898, the Germans withdrew their troops and their ship from Crete and refused to have anything more to do with the question. As Count Bülow, the new German foreign minister, said: Germany, having played the flute in the European Concert, laid down her instrument and withdrew rather than play the tune called by the others. Austria, rather reluctantly, followed suit, leaving the Cretan affair in the hands of Russia, France, England and Italy. There was further debate as to the choice of a governor or commissioner until in September 1898 a serious outbreak occurred at Candia. Several hundred Christians and fourteen British soldiers were killed. The powers, under British lead, now insisted upon the complete withdrawal of the Turkish forces from the island, and finally Prince George was named, in

---

[56] For the peace negotiations see *Turkey No. 11 (1897)*, nos. 602 ff.; Documents Diplomatiques: *Affaires d'Orient: Négociations pour la Paix; Traité Gréco-Turc, mai-décembre, 1897;* Documents Diplomatiques: *Arrangement Financier avec la Grèce; Die Grosse Politik,* XII, nos. 3239-53; Driault and Lhéritier, op. cit., IV, pp. 409 ff.

November 1898, commissioner of Crete with a mandate from the four powers to organize a proper system of government.[57]

Everyone understood that the appointment of Prince George was only the first step on the road to the union of Crete with Greece. The Turkish troops had been withdrawn, and nothing remained to indicate Ottoman sovereignty except the Sultan's flag waving on the ramparts of one of the fortresses. But while the Sultan had his flag, the King of Greece had his son. The Greek cause had triumphed, to all intents and purposes. After the exchange of thousands of despatches and notes between the powers, after the most flagrant breach of international law by the Greeks, after the intervention of Europe and a crisis that threatened a general conflagration in the Balkans and possibly a European war, the Greeks, totally defeated on the field of battle, secured what they had started out to get. It made no difference whether the Turk was the aggressor or whether he was the victim of aggression. His domain was dismembered nevertheless. There was no logic in all this. It was simply the victory of force. Christian Europe had marked out the Sultan's dominions for partition, and in the end he had to submit because he could not resist.[58]

And yet the Cretan crisis and the defeat of Greece marked an important turning-point in Near Eastern history. The preparation, equipment and organization of the Turkish armies, their bravery and their discipline (which were testified to by the British correspondents in the field) made a considerable impression upon Europe. The Balkan states, which had been on the verge of military action and the seizure of Macedonia, saw that the Ottoman Empire would be a formidable opponent. Europe realized that the Empire, even if it could not reform, could at least resist. It was not so near the point of dissolution as had been generally supposed. The final collapse was evidently still pretty far off. As on many previous occasions the talk of partition died away. For the next ten years the Near East played a distinctly secondary rôle in European international relations.

From the larger standpoint of European alignments the Near Eastern crisis of 1896-1897 was of very great significance. It completed the " interpenetration " of the alliances, so that, to quote an Italian historian, " Allies acted as though they were adversaries, while members of opposing diplomatic systems acted as though they were more than friends." [59] At the root of this process lay the

---

[57] See the reams of correspondence on this later phase of the question: *Turkey No. 12 (1897); Turkey No. 3 (1898); Turkey No. 5 (1898); Turkey No. 6 (1898); Turkey No. 7 (1898); Turkey No. 1 (1899);* Documents Diplomatiques: *Affaires d'Orient; Autonomie Crétoise, mai-décembre, 1897; Die Grosse Politik,* XII, chap. lxxxi. Among the best secondary studies are those by Georges Streit: " La Question Crétoise au Point de Vue International " (*Revue de Droit International Public,* X, 1903, pp. 222-82, 345-418), and Driault and Lhéritier: *Histoire Diplomatique de la Grèce,* IV, pp. 438-68.

[58] Driault and Lhéritier, op. cit., IV, p. 467, for all their Phil-Hellenism, have some good things to say on this point. See also the summing up in the report of the German ambassador at Constantinople in *Die Grosse Politik,* XII, no. 3309.

[59] Gaetano Salvemini: " La Triple Alliance " (*Revue des Nations Latines,* II, 1916, pp. 226-57), p. 228.

estrangement and antagonism between England and Germany, which had reached its climax in the Kruger telegram. It is true that the German government in 1896 toned down its hostility and supported the British policy in Egypt and the Sudan in order to save Italy, preserve the Triple Alliance, and prevent an understanding between England and France. But the hostility and suspicion were there nevertheless, and they were shared by the other continental powers, with the possible exception of Italy and Austria. In France and in Russia, as in Germany, it was devoutly believed that England, with her advocacy of strong methods and her policy of coercing the Sultan in the Armenian and Cretan questions, was simply working for a conflict in the Near East. Such a struggle would completely occupy the continental powers and give Britain a free hand to settle in her own interest questions in south Africa, Egypt and the Far East, questions in which France, Germany and Russia felt that they had much at stake. It is hard to believe that even the statesmen of " perfidious Albion " should have harbored such nefarious plans, and it is certain that no judge and no jury would convict on the scrappy hearsay evidence that is available. Of course British sympathies varied with British interests. In 1877 and 1878, when England was the champion of the Sultan against the wicked Russians, the government went so far as to withhold from the Blue Books material favorable to the Bulgarians, as Professor Temperley has shown.[60] In 1896 and 1897 the British were without all influence at the Porte. Russia was the defender of the Sultan, who straightway became the "Red Assassin."

But for all this revolution in sentiment it would be going too far to accuse the British government of trying to precipitate a war between the other powers. A more accurate exposition of the situation would probably be something like this: Isolated action against the Sultan, which was widely called for in England at the beginning of the crisis, was entirely out of the question. Thoughtful Englishmen realized that British policy in the past (especially the Cyprus Convention) had ingrained suspicion of British designs so deeply among the peoples and governments of other nations that any effort to act single-handedly would almost certainly have resulted in war. But war with France and Russia would have distracted British power to such an extent that other states might easily have done what England was accused of wishing to do, namely settle African and Asiatic questions to their own liking. The British hated Abdul Hamid and wanted to see him deposed. But they did not hate him enough to want to take the chance of steaming into the Sea of Marmora when they knew full well that they would find a strong Russian squadron before them and an even stronger French fleet behind them.

What, then, could Lord Salisbury do? The obvious solution for the dilemma was to strike a bargain with England's leading opponents, France and Russia. Russia was more important than France, firstly because of her great influence

---

[60] Harold Temperley: "The Bulgarian Horrors and other Atrocities" (*Proceedings of the British Academy*, XVII, 1931, pp. 105–47).

and interest in the Near East, secondly because France was clearly in a position where she had to follow the Russian lead. Nothing is more interesting and striking, and nothing has been more generally overlooked than the repeated and strenuous efforts made by Lord Salisbury and Queen Victoria to reach an agreement with Russia at this time. From the material we now have it is perfectly safe to conclude that the British prime minister, estranged from Germany and faced with the opposition of the new Dual Alliance, would have paid a high price to secure the support of Russia and France. The Constantinople area was no longer as important for England as it had been. British opinion was prepared to sacrifice it. Salisbury at bottom was honestly trying to buy off the Russians with the dominions of the Sultan of Turkey. His readiness to partition the Ottoman Empire seems to be fairly well proved. He would have abandoned the Straits and possibly Constantinople to the Russians and Syria to France. Italy could have helped herself to Albania. For Austria there was always the road to Saloniki. Germany claimed to have no aspirations in that part of the world. Britain herself might have established herself in Mesopotamia, to preserve something of a balance. But for England the great gain would have been in the recognition and guarantee of her position in Egypt. That was the crux of the situation. That was where England was most threatened, that was where the jugular vein of the Empire lay.

It appears to me fairly clear that M. Hanotaux would have been only too glad to strike a bargain with the British. The French ambassador at London, Baron de Courcel, was an ardent advocate of such a policy. Nothing would have pleased the French more than to supplement the Alliance with Russia by an agreement with England. It would have made France less dependent on Russia, it would have increased French security, it would have meant concrete gains somewhere. The difficulty was not with the French, it was with the Russians. They distrusted the British policy even more than the Germans did. Prince Lobanov was the ablest opponent England had had to face for a long time. He was " a great misfortune," as Queen Victoria put it. His policy was to maintain friendly relations with Germany, strengthen Russian influence at Constantinople, put the Balkans "on ice" (his own phrase), and shift the centre of Russian activity to the Far East. Witte, the powerful finance minister, subscribed entirely to this policy, and beside him a nonentity like Muraviev was of no account. The young Tsar was well enough disposed, but so weak-willed that no one could rely upon him. The last person who talked to him convinced him. Time and again he promised the British and French this or that, only to go back on his promise after his ministers had argued with him. For a moment it seemed that Nelidov would carry the day with his scheme for a *coup de main* on the Bosporus and an agreement with the powers, but even though Lobanov was dead and only a bureaucrat like Shishkin was at the foreign office, the powerful ambassador was unable to carry the day. Witte, capitalizing the opposition of Hanotaux, quashed the whole project.

The British government, unwilling to take the risk of isolated action and unable to come to an agreement with Russia and France, had no other course open to it but to work with the other powers, in other words to fall back on the so-called Concert of Europe. The phrase made a great appeal to the liberals and radicals and to all those who take the sentimental view of international relations. After all, it meant co-operation of the powers, harmonious action for the attainment of a common end. But, just as a chain is no stronger than its weakest link, so the Concert of Europe, in which action could only be taken by unanimous vote, could not be more effective than its most unwilling and reluctant member. What happened was that Russia blocked British plans for action in the Armenian question, and Britain blocked the German-Russian plan for action in the Cretan-Greek question. The British ministers continued to extol the Concert. Salisbury called it the " Federation of Europe " and Curzon, at that time undersecretary of the foreign office, spoke of it as " the Cause of Peace, the Privy Council of Europe, and the Cabinet of the Nations," in fact, " the greatest advance in international law and international ethics the century had seen." But the members of the government must have spoken with a lump of regret in their throats. They were furious at the obstructive tactics of their associates in the Concert. Had they been able to settle accounts with Russia and France they would have thrown overboard the Concert and all the paraphernalia that went with it. When the liberals began to criticize the Concert for its inability to do anything, the government lost patience. In the debate on supply on May 7 Sir Robert Reid spoke of the Concert as " nothing better than a group of greedy, selfish, pitiless, heartless Powers." To which Curzon replied with unusual bitterness: " It is very easy to denounce the Concert of Europe. Any platform spouter can do that. . . . If you had an alternative I could understand it. Denounce the Concert if you have something to set up in its place, but you come here barren of any policy — with your mouths full of denunciation and your brains empty of suggestion." [61] That was the sum and substance of the situation. If England was tied to the apron strings of two young despots, as Gladstone called the German Emperor and the Russian Tsar, there was no help for it. It was the only course open. There was no choice. But it was silly to be deluded. When the crisis was finally ended, Lord Salisbury wrote: " I am afraid the upshot of our experience . . . is that the Concert of Europe is too ponderous a machine for daily use." [62]

In both the Armenian and the Cretan crises England was, to all intents and purposes, isolated within the Concert. Italy was sympathetic and Austria lukewarm, but the three leading powers of the Continent were against Britain. The idea of the continental coalition was in the air, and particularly in the mind of Emperor William. The combination did not materialize. In fact the German statesmen were themselves more than dubious of its practicability. Neverthe-

---

[61] Hansard: *Parliamentary Debates*, Series IV, vol. XLIX, pp. 30, 45–6.
[62] Russell: *Malcolm MacColl*, p. 282.

less the trend of events was away from the old alignments. Italy had already be-gun to make her peace with France. Austria was laughed at and snubbed by Ber-lin. The Hapsburg dominions were passing through an intense constitutional crisis and the conflict of nationalities had reached such a pass that graver and graver doubts were being expressed for the future of the Empire. Germany was throwing in her lot more and more completely with Russia. At Vienna the diplo-mats still clung desperately to the hope of maintaining the connexion with the English and securing British aid against Russian designs in the Balkans. When that hope faded in the spring of 1897 the Austrians were driven into the agree-ment with Russia. They were surprised by the liberal terms the Russians offered. A new spirit came into Austro-Russian relations, and the new combination, flanked by Germany, suggested the possibility of a revival of the old Three Emperors' League. At the same time the agreement involved disloyalty to Italy. The Italian government was informed only in the most general terms of what had taken place. There was no mention of the project for an independent Al-bania, to which the Italians would never have subscribed. In short, the Austro-Russian arrangement was " a moral violation " of the Triple Alliance. The famous coalition still existed on paper, but for practical purposes the new com-bination of the three Empires was much more potent and important.

The Dual Alliance between Russia and France suffered hardly less than the Triple Alliance in the course of the Eastern crisis. To be sure, it was during these very months that the existence of the Alliance was openly acknowledged on both sides. But what M. Michon has called the " honeymoon stage " of the agreement was already passing. The divergent interests of France and Rus-sia in the Ottoman Empire and elsewhere were demanding recognition, and when the Nelidov plan was brought forward Hanotaux felt obliged to lay his cards upon the table. French aid was not to be counted upon. France asserted her independence, but naturally this did not strengthen the connexion with Russia. By the spring of 1897 the cooling of Franco-Russian relations was evi-dent to everyone. There was a growing feeling in France that the Republic could not afford to tie herself to the chariot wheels of the Russian autocracy. In intellectual circles there was, in fact, increasing discussion of an ultimate settlement with Germany.[63]

The Near Eastern crisis, then, marked the progressive disintegration of the old system of alliances. The powers could no longer act with this one problem in mind. Their policies were determined by considerations arising from numer-ous and complicated colonial problems. The European system no longer fitted the needs of world policy. England, the power that stood in the way of every nation which dreamed of expansion overseas, was the object of suspicion and distrust. The wire from London to Berlin was snapped and Britain no longer could rely upon the Triple Alliance. Neither could she establish a new con-nexion with France and Russia. The continental powers hung together, more

---

[63] *Die Grosse Politik*, XIII, no. 3432.

or less willingly, more or less loosely. But the Triple Alliance hardly existed in more than name and the Dual Alliance was losing its pristine attractiveness. It was the new combination of the three Empires that called the tune, and the tune was: integrity of the Ottoman Empire, peace and the status quo in the Near East, imperialism abroad. It was in the Far East that the new combination was to make itself most effectively felt, and to the problem of the Chinese Empire we must now devote more detailed discussion.

BIBLIOGRAPHICAL NOTE
(SUPPLEMENTARY TO THE BIBLIOGRAPHY OF CHAPTER VII)

DOCUMENTARY SOURCES

Accounts and Papers. 1897, Volume CII: *Turkey No. 4 (1897), Notes addressed by the Representatives of Great Britain, Austria-Hungary, France, Germany, Italy, and Russia to the Turkish and Greek Governments in regard to Crete; Turkey No. 5 (1897), Replies of the Turkish and Greek Governments to the Notes addressed to them on March 2, 1897; Turkey No. 8 (1897), Further Correspondence respecting the Affairs of Crete; Turkey No. 9 (1897), Reports on the Situation in Crete; Turkey No. 10 (1897), Further Correspondence respecting the Affairs of Crete.* 1898, Volume CVI: *Turkey No. 11 (1897), Correspondence respecting the Affairs of Crete and the War between Turkey and Greece; Turkey No. 12 (1897), Further Correspondence respecting the Affairs of Crete.* Volume CVII: *Turkey No. 3 (1898), Further Correspondence respecting the Affairs of Crete; Turkey No. 2 (1898), Correspondence respecting the Negotiations for the Conclusion of Peace between Turkey and Greece.* 1899, Volume CX: *Turkey No. 5 (1898); Turkey No. 6 (1898), Further Correspondence respecting the Affairs of Crete.* Volume CXI: *Turkey No. 1 (1899), Further Correspondence respecting the Affairs of Crete.*

Documents Diplomatiques. Affaires d'Orient. Affaire de Crète — Conflit Gréco-Turc, février–mai, 1897.

Documents Diplomatiques. Affaires d'Orient. Autonomie Crétoise, mai–décembre, 1897.

Documents Diplomatiques. Affaires d'Orient. Négociations pour la Paix — Traité Gréco-turc, mai–décembre, 1897.

Documents Diplomatiques. Arrangement Financier avec la Grèce.

Documenti Diplomatici. Creta e Conflitto Turco-Ellenico. Rome, 1897.

MEMOIRS, AUTOBIOGRAPHIES, BIOGRAPHIES, AND LETTERS

CORBETT, SIR VINCENT: *Reminiscences.* London, 1927. The author was in 1897 secretary of the British legation in Athens. He gives a vivid picture of the exciting war period.

GLAISE-HORSTENAU, EDMUND VON: *Franz Josephs Weggefährte. Das Leben des Generalstabschefs Grafen Beck*. Vienna, 1930. Contains important material on the Austro-Russian agreement of May 1897.

RUSSELL, GEORGE W. E.: *Malcolm MacColl*. London, 1914. MacColl was a friend of King George and was in Athens during the war.

STUDIES ON THE GREEK–TURKISH WAR

MILLER, WILLIAM: *Travels and Politics in the Near East*. London, 1898. The best single contemporary account of events in Greece before and during the war.

TUROT, HENRI: *L'Insurrection Crétoise et la Guerre Gréco-Turque*. Paris, 1898. The observations of a French journalist in Crete and in the Balkans in the spring of 1897.

NORMAN, HENRY: " The Wreck of Greece." (*Scribner's Magazine*, October, 1897, pp. 399–426). One of the most important periodical articles. Norman was in Greece in the spring of 1897 and was in close touch with the palace. His article is very revealing.

S. G.: " La Guerre de 1897." (*Revue de Droit International et de Législation Comparée*, XXX, 1898, pp. 25–87, 324–74, 546–605). The best contemporary documented study of the war and its diplomacy, making extensive use of Greek newspaper and other material. Not so moderate or well-balanced as the articles of Georges Streit mentioned in the bibliography of Chapter VI.

POLITIS, NICHOLAS: *La Guerre Gréco-Turque*. Paris, 1898. Primarily a study of the international law of the war, but contains an admirable account of the origins of the conflict.

GOLTZ, COLMAR FREIHERR VON DER: *Der Thessalische Krieg*. Berlin, 1898. By far the best scientific study of the conduct of the war on the military side. The work of the famous German general who organized the Turkish forces.

WEBER, ROBERT: *Aus dem Feldzug in Thessalien*. Zurich, 1898. One of the best studies of the campaign by a neutral military observer.

BARTLETT, SIR ELLIS ASHMEAD: *The Battlefields of Thessaly*. London, 1897. The experiences of a British parliamentarian and war correspondent. Very partial to the Turks.

GIESL, BARON WLADIMIR: *Zwei Jahrzehnte im Nahen Orient*. Berlin, 1927. Giesl accompanied the Turkish armies as observer for the Austrian government. His account is one of the best-balanced and most honest of all.

PHILARÉTOS, GEORGES N.: " La Localisation de la Lutte Gréco-Turque Aidée par le Roi des Hellènes." (*Questions Diplomatiques et Coloniales*, March 15, 1898, pp. 337–49). A well-informed indictment of the King and his policy. Draws heavily on Greek materials.

LITERATURE SINCE 1935

(See also the Supplementary Bibliographical Notes to Chapters V, VII, X.)

XII

The Far Eastern Situation, 1895-1897

W E HAVE HITHERTO BEEN FAVOURED WITH ONE EASTERN QUESTION, which we have always endeavoured to lull as something too portentous for our imagination, but of late a Far Eastern Question has been superadded, which, I confess, to my apprehension is, in the dim vistas of futurity, infinitely graver than even that question of which we have hitherto known. . . ."

This quotation is taken from an address delivered by Lord Rosebery at the Royal Academy Banquet on May 4, 1895, that is, just after the end of the Chino-Japanese War and the intervention of Russia, Germany and France against Japan. It will serve very well as the introduction to this chapter, in which we must take up again the Far Eastern problem — a problem of such magnitude that it soon came to overshadow all other issues and became the touchstone for European international relations.

Lord Rosebery's remarks show clearly enough that he appreciated the gravity of events in the Far East, but they also make it apparent that he had little conception of the urgency of the problem. British policy throughout the war had betrayed this same lack of understanding. When British writers criticized the government for having failed to prevent the war, for having deserted China, or for having abandoned Japan in her hour of need, they were all, in a sense, right. It was not so much a question of *which* policy as a question of *a* policy. There was no denying that the British, those in China as well as those in London, had completely miscalculated the situation. They had " put their money on the wrong horse " in the Far East as well as in the Near East. The policy of supporting China as a bulwark against Russia was proved to be as mistaken as the older policy of bolstering up Turkey. The big difference was that the invalid in the Far East was sicker than his colleague in the Near East, and that his heritage was far more valuable. China was four times as large as the Ottoman Empire, was twelve to fifteen times as populous, and had incomparably greater natural resources. " There we have a sick man worth many Turkeys, of more value to us as a people than all the Armenians that ever walked the earth; as a commercial inheritance priceless, beyond all the ivory and peacocks that ever came out of Africa." [1]

It was bad enough to have miscalculated and to have been taken unawares

---

[1] Alexander Michie: " Our Interest in China " (*Asiatic Quarterly Review*, January, 1896, pp. 41–54), p. 43; Pierre Leroy-Beaulieu: *The Awakening of the East* (New York, 1900), p. 183.

by the Japanese victories. It was worse to do nothing to rectify a past error. The British government had far and away the greatest foreign stake in China, controlling almost three quarters of the trade and shipping. She was entitled to take the lead in the settlement of the conflict which she had failed to prevent. She should, clearly, either have defended China from the exorbitant demands of Japan and thrown her whole influence in the direction of reforming and strengthening the Celestial Empire, or else she should have frankly welcomed the rising star of Japan and have intervened to prevent the other powers from interfering. Neither policy was followed. The British deserted China as soon as they learned that Japan's terms included demands for the opening of more Chinese ports. But they refused to stand by Japan when the pressure of the other powers began to make itself felt.

It was only natural, then, that British traders and writers should find themselves on the morning after with aching heads and confused brains. Some there were who still hoped for China. The experiences of the war, they said, would show even the Chinese mandarins the need for reform and modernization. There was, in fact, some talk of building railways, of constructing arsenals, of reorganizing the army and navy. But after a few feeble moves all the good resolutions were forgotten. The unbelievable inefficiency and the indescribable system of extortion and corruption continued as of yore. Anti-foreign outbreaks and attacks upon missionaries became more frequent than ever, and the government seemed powerless to check them. In the south, about Canton, where the dynasty was anything but popular, the unrest was already crystallizing. It was in the autumn of 1895 that Sun Yat-sen first appeared upon the stage of history as the leader of an anti-dynastic reforming movement which was discovered and broken up before it had time to materialize.[2] Everything went on as before in the familiar channels. The most eminent authorities on things Chinese had to admit that the situation was hopeless: " Of the existing Chinese Government it is impossible to say a good word, or even to entertain a hope," wrote D. C. Boulger. " The whole system of administration is rotten to the core, and there is no sign or symptom of any effort towards progressive reforms. Ninety-nine out of every hundred mandarins are wedded by long habit and personal interest to the existing system," remarked Robert K. Douglas. Henry Norman went further yet, and declared roundly that " every Chinese official, with the possible exception of one in a thousand, is a liar, a thief and a tyrant." Valentine Chirol summed it up when he wrote: " A more hopeless spectacle of fatuous imbecility, made up in equal parts of arrogance and helplessness, than the central government of the Chinese Empire presented after the actual pressure of war had been removed, it is impossible to conceive." [3]

---

[2] Henry B. Restarick: *Sun Yat Sen* (New Haven, 1931), chaps. iv and v; Holt S. Hallett: " The Partition of China " (*Nineteenth Century*, January, 1898, pp. 154–64); George N. Steiger: *China and the Occident* (New Haven, 1927), pp. 58–9.

[3] Demetrius C. Boulger: " The New Situation in the Far East " (*Contemporary Review*, December, 1895, pp. 815–25); Robert K. Douglas: " Some Peking Politicians " (*Nineteenth Century*,

Over against helpless China lay victorious Japan, progressive and efficient, confident and ambitious. What would be her next move? By many it was thought that the Japanese abstained from revolutionizing China and dethroning the dynasty only in order to secure a strangle hold where resistance was impossible. Japanese statesmen, it was said, were at bottom aiming at an " Asia for the Asiatics " and were envisaging the day when they could take the place of the European powers in the Far East. Had not Count Okuma said in a speech: " The European Powers are already showing symptoms of decay, and the next century will see their constitutions shattered and their empires in ruin. Even if this should not quite happen, their resources will become exhausted in unsuccessful attempts at colonization. Therefore who is fit to be their proper successor if not ourselves? " [4] In that case the Japanese would have at their disposal the great masses of the Chinese population. If properly trained they would make an army which would be positively irresistible. What could Europe do against a " yellow peril " that had behind it some four hundred million people?

The military danger from the yellow race was at the worst still in the far future. It would take decades for Japan to establish her position in China and to put China in shape to suit her purposes. Much more immediate, in the eyes of some writers, was the threat of Asiatic emigration, and the menace of Oriental labor. Ferdinand von Richthofen, geographer and greatest of European authorities on China in his day, had called attention to this aspect of the problem in the great book which he wrote in 1870 and published in 1882. He repeated his warnings later, pointing out that the Europeans, by forcing the Chinese to make available their natural wealth and their tremendous supply of labor, were cutting their own throats: " Every coal mine that is opened, every factory which is financed for the Chinese, every railroad that is forced upon them, is a part of this suicidal process." [5] In a noteworthy and much discussed book published in 1893 Professor Charles H. Pearson drew for the European world a gloomy picture of Chinese and other Orientals gradually flowing over southern Asia and the Pacific area: " We were struggling among ourselves for supremacy in a world which we thought of as destined to belong to the Aryan races and to the Christian faith. . . . We shall wake to find ourselves elbowed and hustled, and perhaps even thrust aside by peoples whom we looked down upon as servile, and thought of as bound always to minister to our needs." [6] And the same thought pervades the closing pages of Brooks Adams' astonishing essay, *The Law of Civilization and Decay* (1895):

December, 1896, pp. 896–906); Henry Norman: *The Peoples and Politics of the Far East* (New York, 1895), p. 282; Valentine Chirol: *The Far Eastern Question* (London, 1896), p. 9; see also the unsparing comments of the American minister, in Payson J. Treat: *Diplomatic Relations between the United States and Japan, 1853–1895* (Stanford, 1932), II, pp. 499–500.

[4] Quoted by Norman, op. cit., p. 392; see further chap. xxv.

[5] F. von Richthofen: " Kiautschou, seine Weltstellung und Voraussichtliche Bedeutung " (*Preussische Jahrbücher*, January, 1898, pp. 167–91), p. 190.

[6] Charles H. Pearson: *National Life and Character: A Forecast* (London, 1893), p. 85.

" By their inventive genius the western races have attained a velocity of movement so unprecedented that, for more than a century, they have defied the cheap
labour of the East. But apparently, like other qualities which at the outset are a
source of strength, the inventive faculty carries with it the seeds of its own decay; for as, by means of electricity and steam, all peoples are welded into a compact mass, competition brings all down to a common level." European agriculture
had already been ruined by overseas competition, and before long industry would
go the same way: " As successive races are seized and whirled into the vortex,
as labour and capital become fluid, it must press equally on industry. Even now
factories can be equipped almost as easily in India, Japan and China, as in Lancashire or Massachusetts, and the products of the cheapest labour can be sold
more advantageously in European capitals, than those of Tyre and Alexandria
were in Rome under the Antonines." [7]

That these prognostications were not the mere products of an unbridled
phantasy is convincingly proved by the reports of the British consuls in the Far
East, and by the writings of earnest and well-informed observers. Since the
general introduction of the gold standard in western Europe in 1873 the yellow
metal had appreciated very considerably, thus giving the silver-using countries
of the east a distinct advantage in the sale of their products in world markets.
Take cotton, for example. Cotton and cotton goods were the chief articles in
British export trade to the Far East. But since about 1880 England had lost
heavily in the supply of cotton to India. The export of this commodity had
fallen by one half, while the Indian factories, taking advantage of the monetary
situation and the cheapness of labor, were shooting ahead. The export of cotton
yarn from India was fifteen times as great in 1893 as in 1877, and the export of
piece goods almost six times as great. Between 1881 and 1891 the export of cotton
goods from England to the Far East fell from £47,500,000 to £28,000,000, while
the export from India rose from £28,000,000 to £165,000,000. While the mills
of Lancashire were closing down or running at a loss, those in Bombay were
paying fifteen to twenty-five per cent dividend.

To make matters yet worse Japan had entered the field. Leaving aside the
Japanese coal trade, the expansion of shipping and the production of novelties,
let us take cotton once more. In 1883 Japan imported less than three million
pounds of cotton. In 1893 she imported one hundred and fifty-four million
pounds. Her factories worked in twelve-hour shifts with the cheapest labor
in the world. Men were paid eight to ten cents a day, while the women earned
little more than half that. How could England hope to compete under such
conditions? In the markets of the Far East, at Singapore, for example, Japanese
products were selling at one half the price of the British. Add to all this the
danger of Chinese labor entering the competition. Von Richthofen had pointed
out in the 1870's that " the slumbering factors of an immense industrial production all exist in China." At Shanghai Chinese capitalists were opening up cotton

[7] Op. cit., p. 291.

and silk factories, which could easily outdistance their European competitors. No wonder that keen observers and authorities on Chinese affairs joined in a loud note of warning: " So far from the opening of China . . . being a benefit to British manufactures," said Mr. T. H. Whitehead, one of the leading figures in the business world of Hongkong, " unless some change is made, and that soon, in our monetary standard, the Celestial Empire, which has been the scene of so many of our industrial victories, will only be the field of our greatest defeat." " With or without the participation of European capital," wrote Max von Brandt, for twenty years German minister to China, " an industrial struggle will develop between Europe and Eastern Asia, which will be the more violent and the more detrimental to the former according to the financial aid which Europe puts at the disposal of Asia for its campaign against European industry." The European powers, he said, should unite, for only in united action was there the possibility of fighting off the common danger.[8]

These general considerations may appear to the reader to be rather far removed from the story of diplomacy. It is, indeed, remarkable how little attention was paid in government circles to the broader aspects of the problems confronting the nation. Lord Rosebery foresaw difficulties, but only " in the dim vistas of futurity." Lord Salisbury was equally unperturbed by the discussion of the menace to British trade. Speaking before the Associated Chambers of Commerce on March 10, 1897, he remarked that history taught " that, left alone, British industry, British enterprise, British resource is competent, and more than competent, to beat down every rivalry, under any circumstances, in any part of the globe, that might arise." The trouble was, and Lord Salisbury must have realized this, that British industry, enterprise and resource were not being left alone; on the contrary, they were being assailed by competition unlike anything that had been experienced before.

The charitable explanation of governmental optimism would be that the foreign office regarded the problem as first and foremost a political one, and hoped to solve it by political methods. In other words it was concerned with keeping the great Chinese market intact, keeping the door open for British trade, or, in the last count, with securing for Britain the major part of the spoils if the Celestial Empire finally went to pieces.

Reduced to its lowest terms the question the British government was called upon to answer was how the action of the Franco-Russian Alliance could be neutralized in the Far East. From the very birth of this combination there had been not a few French writers who had emphasized the possibility of joint action in the Far East against England. This would be the cement that would

---

[8] On this whole subject see Norman, op. cit., pp. 14, 311, 380 ff.; and especially T. H. Whitehead: " The Critical Position of British Trade with Oriental Countries " (*Proceedings of the Royal Colonial Institute*, XXVI, pp. 106–63, February 12, 1895); Max von Brandt: *Die Zukunft Ostasiens* (Stuttgart, 1895), pp. 44–80, passim; B. d'Estournelles de Constant: " Le Péril Prochain " (*Revue des Deux Mondes*, April 1, 1896, pp. 651–86), passim; George Briscoe: " Eastern Competition and Western Trade " (*Westminster Review*, January, 1897, pp. 47–56).

hold the two powers together and would put England "between two fires." [9] The Russian advance in the Pamirs and the French forward thrust in the direction of Siam supplied ample proof of the feasibility of such a plan. In 1895 it was again the Russian-French combination that threatened the British position in China.

In a previous chapter the story has been told of how the Russian and French governments, ignoring the hopes and claims of their recent German collaborators, had practically forced upon the Chinese government the loan with which the first installment of the indemnity was paid to Japan. It was the golden bait that was eventually to catch the monstrous fish. But neither Russia nor France was content with merely indirect influence over the fate of China. Both powers had more immediate desiderata, for the fulfilment of which the aid given in the spring of 1895 seemed to offer more than sufficient claim. Curiously enough the French scored the first success, due, no doubt, to the vigor of M. Hanotaux and to the energy, firmness and general ability of the French minister at Peking, M. Gérard.

Ever since the exploration of the Red River by Jean Dupuis and Francis Garnier in the years 1871-1872 the French had had their eyes on this important approach to China from the south. Admiral Dupré, writing in 1873, declared that French domination in Tongking, "the natural outlet for the rich southwestern provinces," was a question of life and death for French domination in the Far East. It was an open secret that the French aim in acquiring Tongking in 1885 was primarily to get control of this thoroughfare to China, which Baron von Richthofen himself had declared to be the best route.[10] But the French operations in Tongking were so unpopular in France that they led to the downfall of Jules Ferry in 1885. Nothing much could be done with the colony. A commission in 1887 recommended the construction of railroads into southern China and into the province of Yunnan, and M. Lanessan, for a time governor-general of Indo-China and one of the most vigorous colonialists of his day, expatiated in his book *La Colonisation Française en Indo-Chine* upon the urgency of this program, yet no progress was made to speak of. Tongking remained a preserve for French officialdom. Henry Norman estimated in 1895 that the colony had cost France over five hundred and thirty-five million francs, or one hundred and twenty-two thousand francs a day for every day since the occupation. The total trade of France with Tongking in the first ten years came to only sixty-three million francs and, apart from the region of the Red River delta, the country was still ravaged by bandit gangs.[11]

With the year 1890 a certain change in French opinion became noticeable. The French consul, M. Rocher, wrote a most sanguine report on the commercial

---

[9] See the extended discussion and the references in my book: *The Franco-Russian Alliance* (Cambridge, 1929), pp. 324-36.

[10] Jean Dupuis: *Origines de la Question du Tonkin* (Paris, 1896); Idem: *Le Tonkin de 1872 à 1886* (Paris, 1910); Jules Ferry: *Le Tonkin et la Mère-Patrie* (Paris, 1890), pp. 80-96.

[11] Norman, op. cit., pp. 106, 133-5.

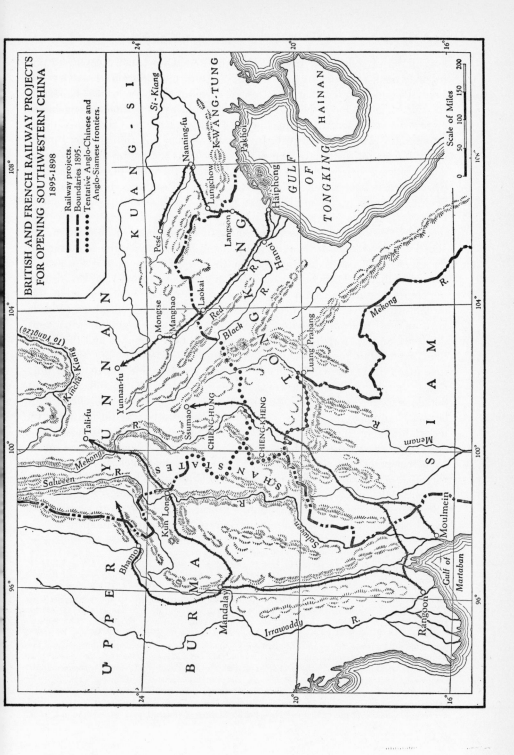

BRITISH AND FRENCH RAILWAY PROJECTS
FOR OPENING SOUTHWESTERN CHINA
1895-1898

Railway projects.
Boundaries 1895.
Tentative Anglo-Chinese and
Anglo-Siamese frontiers.

Scale of Miles
0   50   100   150   200

possibilities of southwestern China and the Red River route. Jules Ferry published a book on Tongking that made a distinct impression. Travellers like Louis Pichon reported that the Chinese, millions of them, were "famished" for European products, that the Red River could easily be made navigable for a great distance, etc.[12] In the meanwhile French interest was stimulated by the activity and plans of the British. In 1886 the Indian government had annexed upper Burma to frustrate French designs. For years the British had been eyeing with suspicion their rival's advance, and for years there had been a demand for the construction of a railroad from Rangoon or Moulmein through northern Siam to Yunnan, or, failing that, from Mandalay or Bhamo by way of Kunlong Ferry to Tali-fu or Yunnan-sen. Archibald Colquhoun and Holt Hallett were the special protagonists of the Siam route. In a long series of publications and addresses they repeatedly impressed upon the British public the seriousness of the threat to British trade presented by the French advance and the Franco-Russian Alliance. Their propaganda did, in fact, leave its mark on British trading circles, and in the later 1880's there were repeated demands for action. The trouble was that the government was more interested in the northern (Mandalay-Kunlong) route while both Colquhoun and Hallett advocated the southern direction. Surveys for the Mandalay route were begun in 1892 and the line to Kunlong was authorized in 1895. The French successes in Siam had by that time made the Moulmein-Ssumao line appear less desirable, but the determination to build some sort of a railroad into the reputed Yunnan-Szechuan Eldorado was greater than ever. Speaking to a delegation of the Associated Chambers of Commerce on June 30, 1896 Lord Salisbury said: "I do not value the mere addition of so many square miles of territory; what I value is the addition of so many free markets to the commerce of the country. Looking at the matter from that point of view, of course there is nothing that interests us more than this attempt to obtain access to the markets of China from behind." All of which shows that Henry Norman was not exaggerating when he wrote in 1895 that "the political rivalries of England and France in Indo-China during the last two decades may be summed up in one phrase as a race for Yunnan."[13]

---

12 Louis Pichon: *Un Voyage au Yunnan* (Paris, 1893), chaps. xi–xiii.

13 Norman, op. cit., p. 503. The British scheme goes back really to R. H. F. and C. H. F. Sprye: *The British and China Railway from H. M. Port of Rangoon . . . through Pegue and Burmah to the Yunnan Province of China, with Loop-lines to Siam and Cambogia, Tonquin and Cochin China* (London, 1858); it was put forth and discussed by Archibald R. Colquhoun in his book *Through Chryse* (London, 1883), II, chaps. xvii, xviii, and in the same author's *Report on the Railway Connection of Burmah and China* (London, 1884); see also his article "The Railway Connection of Burmah and China" (*Journal of the Manchester Geographical Society*, III, 1887, pp. 141–53); his book *China in Transformation* (London, 1898), chap. v; and his article "The Railway Connection of India and China" (*Asiatic Quarterly Review*, July, 1898, pp. 35–61); see further the writings of Holt Hallett: "Exploration Survey for a Railway Connection between India, Siam and China" (*Journal of the Manchester Geographical Society*, I, 1885, pp. 162–4); "The Burmah-Siam-China Railway" (*Blackwood's Magazine*, 1889, pp. 647–59); "The Remedy for Lancashire" (ibid., 1892, pp. 348–63); "Western Nations and Eastern Markets" (*Nineteenth Century*, March, 1894, pp. 378–96); "New British Markets: Western China" (ibid., August, 1895,

While the British were surveying a line from Mandalay to Yunnan, and while their goods were penetrating into Szechuan by way of the Yangtze (opened for foreign trade as far as Chungking in 1890), the French redoubled their efforts. In 1893 they took over a large part of eastern Siam, despite British protests. Prince Henri of Orleans, famous and popular traveller in Asia, urged upon his countrymen yet greater activity:

"It is in Asia . . . that will be decided the destinies of the world. In Asia will be founded and will increase great empires, and whoever succeeds in making his voice heeded in the Far East will be able also to speak in dominating accents to Europe. Far-seeing men understood the interest France had in planting herself upon the flanks of China. They seized, at the extremity of the old continent, a strip of land on which they might set up a box for the French sentinel at the gates of the Celestial Empire. . . . It was at the head of the line leading directly to the most populous and one of the most productive empires in the world. . . . We held all the trumps. We still hold them, and we may win the game with the products of our national industry in the great markets of China." [14]

The French writers unquestionably had the arguments on their side. The Red River route was certainly the shortest route to Yunnan, and it was also the easiest and the cheapest. It took less than half as much time as the route from Bhamo in upper Burma, or the route from Canton up the Si Kiang (West River), or the Yangtze route, which required a long and arduous portage. Consequently freight was relatively cheap. It was estimated that a ton of goods could be transported to Yunnan by way of Bhamo for nine hundred and sixty francs; by way of Canton for nine hundred and fifty; by way of the Yangtze for eight hundred and eighty; and by way of the Red River for four hundred and fifty.[15] The British routes from Burma were practically hopeless so far as railroad transportation was concerned. The Rangoon-Ssumao project had to be given up at an early date, partly because of territorial changes that made it undesirable. The Bhamo route, which the Indian government particularly favored, had to be abandoned because of difficulties of terrain. All efforts were then centered upon the Mandalay-Kunlong-Tali-fu scheme. Over two hundred miles of it were built by 1898, but it is not completed even at the present day. The tremendous "mass of heaving, ragged mountains" which runs through this whole area is an effective bar. To tunnel them would cost millions of pounds, which no one was willing to invest, the more so as it soon became apparent that the resources of Yunnan were not all that had been imagined and reported

---

pp. 236–46); "France and Russia in China" (ibid., March, 1897, pp. 487–502). The whole question is admirably discussed in John Nisbet: *Burma under British Rule — and Before* (London, 1901), II, chaps. i, ii; and by Hermann Schumacher: "Eisenbahnbau und Eisenbahnpläne in China" (*Archiv für Eisenbahnwesen*, XXII, 1899, pp. 901–78), pp. 955 ff.

[14] Prince Henri d'Orleans: *Around Tonkin and Siam* (London, 1894), p. 425; but see the whole of chapter ix.

[15] Ferry, op. cit., p. 234.

by over-optimistic travellers, who, finding little of note above ground, brought back glowing accounts of what they thought must be underground.[16]

M. Hanotaux was a man upon whom the arguments of the imperialists made a deep impression. As a pupil of Ferry he had a particular interest in Indo-China. When the war broke out between China and Japan he did not wait to see what would happen, but immediately instructed Gérard at Peking to press upon the Tsungli Yamen, or board for foreign affairs, the necessity for settling the Chinese-Tongking frontier and extending the trade privileges already accorded to France. The discussions dragged, as was usual in Peking, but when China's collapse was complete and France joined Russia and Germany in rescuing the vanquished, the prospects for M. Gérard became better. On June 20, 1895 he and Prince King signed two conventions, one of which delimited the Chinese-Tongking boundary between the Red River and the Mekong in a way most favorable to France, while the other provided for the opening of three new trade stations on the frontier, secured for the Tongking trade a reduction of four fifths in the customary tariff, and specified that China should apply first of all to French manufacturers and engineers for the exploitation of mines in the provinces of Yunnan, Kuangsi and Kuangtung. China furthermore agreed that the railroads in French territory, both the existing and the projected, might be continued into Chinese territory after mutual agreement, and that there should be further telegraph connexion. M. Gérard soon showed that he did not mean to stop at paper promises. On the basis of the June Convention he brought forward a demand for a concession to a French Company to extend the railroad from Langson across the frontier to the town of Lungchow. The Chinese saw the implications of the proposal and resisted as long as possible. But in March 1896 they had to yield. The French company secured the concession for thirty-six years, subject to renewal or prolongation. M. Gérard described this victory as " a date in the history of the opening of China," and he was right. It was the first time that a foreign company was given a concession to construct a railroad on Chinese territory. No attempt was made to conceal the fact that this short line was simply meant as the opening wedge for the realization of a much larger program.[17]

It stands to reason that the British opposed these concessions in all possible ways. On June 20, 1895, while M. Gérard was trying to induce Prince King to sign the territorial convention, Sir Nicolas O'Conor, the British minister, sat in a neighboring room, pointing out that the agreement was contrary to former

---

[16] Archibald R. Colquhoun: *China in Transformation,* chap. v; Anonymous: " Political and Commercial Affairs in Asia " (*Edinburgh Review,* January, 1896, pp. 237–66), pp. 251–9; and especially John F. Fraser: " Our Trade with Western China " (*Contemporary Review,* February, 1898, pp. 235–40), passim.

[17] The essential sources are Documents Diplomatiques: *Chine, 1894–1898,* nos. 1–22, 27; Auguste Gérard: *Ma Mission en Chine 1894–1897* (Paris, 1918), pp. 196 ff., 226 ff.; Idem: *Mémoires* (Paris, 1928), chap. xiv; excellent accounts will be found in Henri Cordier: *Histoire des Relations de la Chine avec les Puissances Occidentales* (Paris, 1901), III, pp. 161 ff.; and in Philip Joseph: *Foreign Diplomacy in China 1894–1900* (London, 1928), chap. vii.

engagements between Britain and China and threatening all sorts of retribution. Poor Prince King hurried from one to the other, not knowing what to do, until Gérard finally won his point by threatening to withhold payment of the indemnity loan unless the Chinese gave in. Soon afterward the British government recalled O'Conor, whose language had been so strong as to offend the Chinese government. But the English did not allow the matter to rest. In January 1896, at the height of the excitement in Anglo-German relations resulting from the Kruger telegram, the British concluded with the French an agreement with respect to the area under dispute. The French received most of what they had claimed, but in return they agreed that both powers or their nationals should share whatever commercial or other privileges had been or might be accorded to them in the provinces of Yunnan or Szechuan. The British then proceeded to claim compensation for the violation of the Anglo-Chinese convention of 1894 by the Franco-Chinese agreement of 1895. In February 1897 they secured from the Chinese government a rectification of the Burmese frontier as well as the right to extend the Burmese railroads into Yunnan when the time came. M. Gérard admitted that there was nothing in this agreement to which France needed object, but since it was concluded in retaliation for the Franco-Chinese agreement it was necessary for France to get satisfaction — at the expense of China, of course. Prince King felt outraged. When, he asked, was there to be an end of this game which the British and the French were playing at China's expense? For a time he would not listen to any suggestion, but in the last count all he could do was to yield. In June 1897 the French obtained the right to extend the Lungchow railroad to Nanning-fu and Pesé, and beyond; the right to priority in the exploitation of the mines of the provinces of Kuangtung, Kuangsi and Yunnan; and the right to connect Indo-China and Yunnan by rail.[18]

It would be unfair to accuse the French of having set the example for the dismemberment of China. That process had been going on for some time, and the territorial gains made by the French through the agreements of 1895 lay wholly in an area where the frontier had never been definitely delimited. On the other hand it is the indisputable fact that the French took the initiative in wresting from the Chinese concessions for railways and mines, and that they were in the lead when it came to setting aside large parts of China as a special preserve, " sphere of influence " or " sphere of interest " or whatever else it may be called. At the time the French undoubtedly meant to realize on their gains. In July 1895 the Chamber of Commerce of Lyons organized a committee of investigation, to which the chambers of Bordeaux, Lille, Marseilles, Roubaix and Roanne sent delegates. A commission was sent out to study " the best routes for penetrating China commercially from the south," to determine the capacity for production and consumption in the southern provinces, and in general to

---

[18] Gérard: *Ma Mission en Chine*, pp. 199 ff.; *Mémoires*, pp. 281–2; Joseph, op. cit., pp. 181 ff.; R. Stanley McCordock: *British Far Eastern Policy, 1894–1900* (New York, 1931), pp. 152 ff.

study ways and means for diverting to Tongking the trade that was going down
the Si Kiang through Canton. The Commission arrived in the Far East in October 1895, went to Yunnan, broke up into sections and explored Szechuan,
Kuangsi and Kuantung, the whole Yangtze Valley, the treaty ports, the Si
Kiang Valley, and even Burma. Its labors were not completed until it had
travelled some ten thousand miles. Among its chief findings were those dealing with the Red River route and the urgent need for a railroad. Yunnan, it
reported, had great mineral wealth, but Szechuan was much more populous
(it was said to have forty million inhabitants) and much richer. All it needed
was communications. It was highly desirable that it should be attached to the
French commercial and political sphere.[19]

The British were unable to offer effective resistance to the French program
because the whole French policy enjoyed the vigorous support of the Russians.
M. Gérard dilates on his close connexions with Count Cassini, the Russian minister at Peking, and points out how irresistible was the combination of Cassini's
knowledge and maturity and his own youth and vigor. Valentine Chirol spoke
of these two gentlemen as " the Siamese twins of Peking diplomacy." [20] That
the Russians received equally cordial and whole-hearted support from their
allies need hardly be remarked upon. Neither is it surprising that the Russians
cherished hopes and laid plans even more extensive than those of the French.
If France had a thousand miles of frontier with China, Russia had over three
thousand. Compared with the grand and imposing project of the Transsiberian
Railway the French railway schemes were almost trivial. It must be remembered
that the decisive move in Russian policy in the Far East was the order to commence the construction of the Transsiberian. It was perfectly clear from that
day on to many well-informed observers that Russia would never allow so important a road to end in a harbor which, like Vladivostok, was frozen for four
or five months in the year. Writers like Norman and Hallett continually drew
attention to this point even before the Chinese-Japanese conflict. It was logical
to assume, as these writers did, that Russia would attempt to acquire a suitable
port in Korea. Gensan and Port Lazarev on Broughton Bay (east coast of
Korea) were located on " one of the finest harbours in the world." Either one
would serve as an ideal terminus for the Railway. There can be little doubt
that fear of Russia's establishing herself in Korea had much to do with hastening
the outbreak of war over the Korean question.[21]

The Russian plans for ending the great railway at some Korean port necessarily implied the transit of northern Manchuria, and it was primarily to this

---

[19] Gérard: *Ma Mission en Chine,* pp. 233 ff.; Ulysse Pila: " La Mission Lyonnaise en Chine "
(*Questions Diplomatiques et Coloniales,* September 1, 1897, pp. 130–43); Henri Brenier: " Rapport
Générale de la Mission Lyonnaise d'Exploration en Chine " (ibid., December 1, 1897, pp. 513–35;
December 15, 1897, pp. 585–612).

[20] Chirol: *The Far Eastern Question,* p. 69.

[21] See especially Henry Norman: *Peoples and Politics of the Far East,* pp. 165–6, 325–6; and
this volume, supra, chap. vi.

problem that the Russian statesmen devoted themselves in the period immediately following the conclusion of peace between China and Japan. For the time being there was little hope of opposing Japan in Korea. The Japanese had forced the King into an alliance at the beginning of the war and their troops were still in occupation of many strategic points. At the court the Japanese resident was all-powerful. His policy was to reform and strengthen Korea as quickly as possible, in order to make the peninsula an effective barrier to the Russian advance. There is some evidence that the Japanese hoped eventually to have the Korean government use the proceeds of a Japanese loan to build a railway system from Fusan (at the southern tip of Korea) to Wichu at the mouth of the Yalu River. At the same time the Japanese were to build a road from Newchuang and Kinchow on the Manchurian coast northward to Mukden, and were to allow the Chinese government to make use of the indemnity due Japan to construct a line connecting the Korean and Japanese lines with Peking.[22] It is impossible to say how seriously these extensive plans were meant. What we do know is that the Japanese showed themselves too optimistic and too energetic in their Korean program. Their reform ordinances regulated even the length of the Korean pipe and the top-knot of the Korean men. The natives had no desire for reform to begin with and engaged in what Lord Curzon described aptly as " an obdurate conspiracy of resistance." In October 1895 matters came to a crisis when the Queen, an able opponent of the Japanese party, was murdered by Japanese *soshi* or strong-arm men, with the connivance of the Japanese resident. For a few months the King was practically a prisoner in his palace. Then, in February 1896, he succeeded in smuggling himself out of the palace and took refuge in the Russian legation. The Russians suddenly found themselves on the crest of the wave. The Japanese, by their indefensible policy, had done the work of the Russians more effectively than the Russians themselves could have done it.[23]

Even in Manchurian matters the Russians did not seem anxious to attain their ends. Together with their French allies, they had secured the first indemnity loan to China, but after that they made haste slowly. The reason was that Witte wished to lay his plans carefully and to eliminate all chance of failure. One of the most urgent necessities, as he saw it, was the establishment of a Russian bank in China, so that the Russians would no longer be dependent on British, German and French establishments for the conduct of their now extensive financial relations with China. Throughout the summer the details of such an institution were carefully worked out in St. Petersburg. The important

---

[22] This scheme was put forward by the Railway League of Japan and received the approval of Count Kawamura and prominent government officials (*Japan Daily Advertiser*, quoted by the *North China Herald*, April 19, 1895, p. 579).

[23] Among the many accounts the best are those of George Curzon: *Problems of the Far East* (Revised edition, London, 1896), pp. 376 ff.; Max von Brandt: *Drei Jahre Ostasiatischer Politik* (Stuttgart, 1897), chap. v; R. Villetard de Laguérie: *La Corée* (Paris, 1898), part iv; Isabella Bishop: *Korea and her Neighbours* (London, 1898), II, chaps. xxii, xxiii; William F. Sands: *Undiplomatic Memories* (New York, 1930), pp. 64 ff.

thing was to get the necessary capital in Paris. This was not easy, for the collapse of the south African gold speculations had made money very tight. Furthermore, the French bankers seem to have disapproved of Russian methods of spending French money. It was felt that in the matter of the Chinese loan it would have been just as easy to get 5% interest as 4%, and considerable dissatisfaction was aroused by rumors that the Russian agents, especially M. Rotshtein, Witte's right hand man, had cleaned up about twenty-six million francs in commissions.[24] Still, the French government threw its weight on the side of the Russian, and urged the need of accommodation in the interests of the Alliance. The seven French banks (Hottinguer, Banque Ottomane, Banque de Paris, Comptoir Nationale d'Escompte, Société Générale, Credit Lyonnais and Credit Industriel), having already supplied the money for the loan to China which Russia guaranteed, now produced the funds necessary for the foundation of the Russo-Chinese Bank, the charter of which was granted in December 1895 to the Committee of the Siberian Railway. Apart from the right to engage in regular banking operations the new institution was empowered to collect taxes, handle local government business, coin money, act as commission merchant, secure concessions for railways, etc. When Baron Rosen described it as " a hybrid political-financial institution which in reality was but a slightly disguised branch of the Russian treasury," he was not far from the truth.[25]

For Witte the new Bank was primarily part of the Transsiberian Railway scheme. In a report to the Tsar he said that " it may prove to be a very positive weapon in the hands of the Russian government in the latter's carrying out of measures most closely connected with the completion of the construction of the Siberian Railroad." One of the first tasks imposed upon the Bank was to receive and distribute as the Russian minister at Peking saw fit " the proper sum " that might be required to induce high Chinese officials to see the value of concessions to Russia. As a matter of fact Count Cassini at Peking was already alarmed lest, if the Russians did not soon bring forward their demands, the Chinese might grow cool: " The feeling of gratitude felt by China," he wrote in December 1895, " is beginning to weaken and to make way for an undefined feeling of fear and mistrust, caused by a foreboding that in the near future exceptional demands, the significance and extent of which are still hidden, may be presented on our part." Cassini himself was unable to understand the hesitancy of the Russians, but strongly urged upon the government the need for avoiding exorbitant demands.[26]

The delay in the formulation of Russian desires may have been due, in part at least, to the opposition in government circles to Witte's scheme of running

---

[24] Élie de Cyon: Où la Dictature de M. Witte conduit la Russie (Paris, 1897), p. 48.

[25] The fundamental accounts are those of B. B. Glinskii: Prolog Russko-Iaponskoi Voiny (Petrograd, 1916), pp. 25 ff., based upon the Witte papers; and B. A. Romanov: Rossia v Manchzhurii 1892–1906 (Leningrad, 1928), pp. 88 ff., based on all the Russian archive material. The Memoirs of Witte are incomplete.

[26] Romanov, op. cit., pp. 92, 95.

the Railroad deep into Manchuria and direct to Vladivostok. Count Kapnist, chief of the Asiatic department of the foreign office, pointed out that to run a railroad so far from one's territory would be without precedent, that it would involve taking over the entire internal administration of the country, which would mean military occupation, protests from other powers and the eventual partition of China — exactly what Witte maintained was to be avoided. According to Kapnist all these difficulties could be obviated if the line were run through the northernmost tip of Manchuria, say from Tsurukhaitui to Blagoveshchensk, a matter that could be easily arranged with China. Much the same viewpoint was expressed by General Dukhovskii, governor of the Amur province, who thought the Witte scheme a " great historical mistake," and stressed the military aspects of the problem. Witte, however, replied to these objections by pointing out that the construction of the road direct to Vladivostok would make that port the chief gateway for the greater part of Manchuria. Russia would, furthermore, be able to penetrate economically into other parts of China, because, as he put it, " the very force of things will oblige us shortly to carry through branches from this line into the depths of China." It was essential that Russia should strive in every way " to transfer into her own hands the network of railroads in Northern China." Once she had the line to Vladivostok no other line would be built in northern China without Russian consent.[27]

Witte had no trouble in securing his own way, in as much as the Tsar, the foreign minister and the minister of war were his strong supporters. During the autumn and winter of 1895-1896 the ministry of communications had a rapid survey of northern Manchuria made. The route could be shortened by some three hundred and fifty miles, the difficult country along the Shilka and the Amur could be avoided, and the new line through Manchuria would obviate competition with the steamboat traffic on the Amur. No serious opposition was to be reckoned with from China, and it seemed that even the British would become reconciled to the new scheme. In October the Hongkong correspondent of the London *Times* had sent home a report that Russia and China had concluded an agreement which would secure to Russia the right to construct and work certain railways from Vladivostok to Port Arthur by way of Tsitsihar, and that Russia was to have the right of anchorage at Port Arthur. This report, the accuracy of which was denied by the Russian embassy in London, led the *Times* to employ some very strong language: Russia " cannot possibly imagine that the other Great Powers having interests in the Far East can view with indifference an enterprise which would constitute a destruction of the existing balance of power almost unparalleled in its audacity." But this outburst in no way reflected the attitude of the government. Speaking to the German am-

---

[27] The texts of the Dukhovskii and Witte memoranda of January 23 and April 12, 1896 respectively are printed by A. Popov: " Pervyie Shagi Russkogo Imperializma na Dal'nem Vostoke" (*Krasnyi Arkhiv*, LII, 1932, pp. 34-124), pp. 83 ff., 91 ff. See also Romanov, op. cit., pp. 97-100; *Zapiski Generala Kuropatkina o Russko-Iaponskoi Voinie* (Berlin, 1909), p. 149.

bassador Lord Salisbury made it clear that his interest was, for the moment, focussed upon the Near East. If Russia, he said, became further involved in the Far
East she would tie up more and more of her forces there and be less and less likely
to attempt an advance in the Near East. Only if Russia demanded exclusive
rights for her ships at Port Arthur would England protest.[28] These were much
the same thoughts which he expressed shortly afterward in his Guild Hall speech
of November 9: he deprecated " unnecessary disturbance and alarm." " I think
we foreshorten time and distance. Depend upon it, whatever may happen in
that region, be it in the way of war or in the way of commerce, we are equal
to any competition which may be proposed to us. . . . I cannot forget the great
words of Lord Beaconsfield — ' in Asia there is room for us all.' " Speaking at
Bristol on February 3, 1896 Mr. Balfour reiterated the government view: " I for
my part frankly state that so far, for example, from regarding with fear and
jealousy a commercial outlet for Russia in the Pacific Ocean which should not
be ice-bound half the year, I should welcome such a result as a distinct advance
in this far distant region, and I am convinced not merely that Russia would
gain by it, that the world generally would gain by it, but that British commerce
and enterprise would be the gainers. Let us lay to heart this doctrine that what
is good for one is not necessarily bad for the other — surely Asia and Africa are
large enough for all of us." " A vast landlocked empire," said an anonymous
writer in the Edinburgh Review for January 1896, " with only two issues to the
open sea, upon waters that are for many months frozen, may be pardoned for
vigorous, if not violent, efforts to break through her barriers." If England, continued this writer, again blocked the Russian advance, the only result would be
renewed pressure on the Indian frontier. " The main object to be kept steadily
in view is some permanent understanding between Russia and England." [29]

These astonishing statements, which represented nothing less than an invitation to the Russians to take a Chinese port, provided they left it free for the
commerce of all nations, can be explained only by lack of understanding of
Chinese affairs in London, by Salisbury's desperate efforts to secure Russian
co-operation in the Armenian question, and by the desire, so widespread after
the Kruger telegram episode, to obtain a general understanding with Russia.
Be that as it may, it requires no great exercise of the imagination to picture the
effect of the British utterances upon Russian statesmen. They now felt quite
free to pursue their plans as they saw fit.

Yet the Chinese proved to be less amenable than Witte had hoped. The
Chinese minister at St. Petersburg would have nothing to do with the project,
and at Peking Count Cassini had no more luck. Li Hung-chang, with whom
Russia had co-operated in arranging the intervention in 1895 and with whom
the loan agreement had been signed, was in disgrace. The Emperor hated him,

---

[28] *Die Grosse Politik,* X, nos. 2393, 2493.
[29] Anonymous: " Political and Commercial Affairs in Asia " (*Edinburgh Review,* January,
1896, pp. 237–66), pp. 248–9; for the rest see Joseph, op. cit., pp. 156–8.

and his enemies at court demanded that he be removed either by assassination or by trial for treachery. Only the protection of the powerful Empress Dowager, and the distribution of bribes to the tune of five million dollars, saved the famous viceroy.[30] His successors, most of them staunch conservatives, were, in the meanwhile, negotiating for a second indemnity loan with a syndicate of British and German banks. French interests did their utmost to secure the juicy plum (it is said that their commission was thirteen million francs on the first loan), but Witte refused to give more than " moral support." He evidently did not wish to overdo the Franco-Russian influence or to estrange England and Germany at a time when he was reckoning on their benevolent neutrality in the matter of the Transmanchurian Railroad. The loan actually went to the Anglo-German syndicate.[31]

Count Cassini had held his hand until the loan negotiations were completed, late in March. For reasons unknown he did not bring his proposals before the Chinese ministers until the beginning of April. It was high time, for the Chinese were seriously discussing the continuation of their own line from Shanhaikwan to Chinchow, and the representative of an American syndicate was trying hard to secure a concession for the construction of a great trunk line from Canton by way of Hankow to Peking, which was to be connected in the north at Shanhaikwan with new lines running to Mukden, Kirin, Tsitsihar and thence to the Russian and Korean frontiers. Cassini, when he went to the Tsungli Yamen on April 6, found it necessary to use strong language. He argued the need of the Transmanchurian road from both the Russian and the Chinese angles. If granted, the new railroad would make it easy for Russia to defend China " from the danger of fresh collisions with Japan and in general with any power whatsoever." The Chinese ministers were, or pretended to be " smitten with stupor " by the Russian suggestion. For twelve days they thought it over and then declared that they had " once and forever taken the firmest and most resolute decision not to grant such concessions to any one of the foreign powers or to any foreign company." They themselves would build the Manchurian line as soon as possible. They were willing to make use of Russian engineers and Russian materials. Cassini argued for three hours, iterating and reiterating that the Chinese stand would make the " most painful " impression in St. Petersburg. There was nothing to be done. The Russian minister therefore reported home that if the government had to have the concession, the only thing to do was to " make the Chinese government understand that its refusal will immediately bring after it the most disastrous consequences for China." This was the method of Gérard. Would it be equally successful when used by Cassini? [32]

The method was not to be put to the test, for the Chinese government had

---

[30] A. Michie: " Li Hung Chang " (Nineteenth Century, August, 1896, pp. 226–39); Robert K. Douglas: " Some Peking Politicians " (ibid., December, 1896, pp. 896–906); Colquhoun: China in Transformation, pp. 189 ff.; J. O. P. Bland: Li Hung Chang (New York, 1917), pp. 180–1.

[31] Gérard: Ma Mission en Chine, pp. 126 ff.; Romanov, op. cit., p. 96; Joseph, op. cit., pp. 152–3.

[32] Romanov, op. cit., pp. 101–5; Gérard: Ma Mission en Chine, pp. 136–7.

decided, some months before, to send Li Hung-chang to Russia to represent the Emperor at the coronation of the Tsar. It was generally supposed at the time that this decision was the result of pressure brought to bear by Cassini, but the truth of the matter seems to be that the Peking court realized that the Russians were going to demand permission to run the Transsiberian through Manchuria sooner or later and that presumably they would ask also for an ice-free port. Li was to try to settle these outstanding questions. He was on good terms with the Russians, and it was probably hoped that he could secure better terms than any-one else. Li left China late in March, aboard a French ship bound for Marseilles. Cassini had, however, persuaded him to leave the ship at Port Said and there board a Russian ship for Odessa. In the viceroy's suite were his son, Li Chinfan, and a financial expert, Victor Grot, a Russian subject who was in the Chinese customs service.

Witte had realized immediately the possibilities of Li's visit. One trouble with negotiating at Peking was that discussions could never be kept secret. High Chinese officials habitually sold information to the legations or to journalists. In St. Petersburg it would be much simpler. Witte therefore decided to send one of his lieutenants, Prince Esper Ukhtomskii, to meet Li at Port Said and prepare his mind for what was coming. Ukhtomskii was an interesting figure. In 1890–1891 he had accompanied Nicholas on his journey through the Far East, a journey which he described in a set of beautiful volumes of narrative and philosophical reflection. In this work and in other writings he set forth the idea of Pan-Asia, under Russian leadership. In poetical and emotional language he stressed the fundamental community of Russians and other Asiatics: " Asia! We have been part of it from the beginning, we have lived its life and shared its interests; our position has destined us to be at the head of the rudimentary forces of the Orient. Only through us has the Orient been able to arrive gradually at consciousness of its being, at a higher life." [33]

As a close friend of the Tsar, as editor of the influential newspaper *Petersburgskaia Viedemosti,* and as president of the new Russo-Chinese Bank, Ukhtomskii was a valuable ally of Witte. If the finance minister advocated the strengthening of economic bonds between China and Russia, Ukhtomskii set forth the doctrine of Russia's cultural and religious mission. The Prince went off to meet the Chinese viceroy armed with instructions and empowered " not to skimp on certain promises to the most influential persons of the ambassadorial suite or through them to their friends and allies at Peking." He evidently made some impression, for from that time on he acted as go-between in the financial negotiations between Witte and Li. On April 30 the party reached St. Petersburg, where the discussions were resumed between Rotshtein, Witte's chief

[33] Prince Esper E. Ukhtomskii: *Travels in the East of Nicholas II* (London, 1896–1900; Russian edition 1893–1897). See also Ukhtomskii's book *K Sobitiiam v Kitaie. Ob Otnosheniiakh Zapada i Rossii k Vostoku* (St. Petersburg, 1900), and J. R. Rees: " The Tsar's Friend " (*Fortnightly Review,* April, 1901, pp. 612–22). Louis Leger: *Russes et Slaves* (Third series, Paris, 1899), chap. iii has a good discussion of Ukhtomskii and his teaching.

financial aide, and Grot, who acted as Li's adviser. Then the matters at issue were taken up by the two principals.

Li was not easy to persuade. The Russian demand was for a concession to run the railroad through Manchuria, the concession to have no time limit, and the Chinese to have the right to buy the road only after eighty years. Witte demanded also a branch from the main line " to one of the ports of the Yellow Sea." Whether there was any talk of the cession of a port is not clear. The Chinese expected such a demand, but Witte may have shelved it for the time being so as not to compromise the success of the negotiations for the Railroad. He secured by no means all that he wanted. Li definitely refused a concession to the Russian government and stood firmly by the plan of constructing the Transmanchurian with Chinese funds. Witte replied with the argument that China did not possess the requisite money and that the building of the Road would take her ten years. He pointed out that if the Road were built it would lessen the danger to China from Japan. But Li remained obdurate. The Tsar had to be drafted in the busy days of the coronation to use his influence. He received Li in a second audience and repeated the Russian arguments: " Russia owns vast territories which are but thinly populated. Therefore she will not trespass upon a foot of soil which is the property of others. Moreover, the ties which bind her to China are very intimate. Hence her only motive in desiring the junction of the railways through Manchuria is the quick conveyance of troops for the purpose of affording effectual help to China whenever the latter country is hard set. Consequently it is not for Russia's advantage alone that the line would serve. On the other hand, China's resources are not sufficient to enable her to build the Railway. If she hands over the building concession to the Russo-Chinese Bank at Shanghai, safeguarding her right of control by means of suitable stipulations, no difficulties need be anticipated. Such things are done in every country." And, he added, China could not be sure that England and Japan would not brew trouble for her very soon, but she could at least enable Russia to come to her assistance.[34]

Li was offered a bribe of about one and a half million dollars if he would agree to the Russian proposals and get them accepted in Peking. It was perfectly well known that " corruption on the hugest and most unblushing scale " prevailed amongst Li's friends and supporters, and Li himself had a private fortune reputed by some to be the largest in the world. It was fairly clear that he was corruptible, and yet his biographer, Mr. Bland, is probably right in thinking that in the case of the Moscow Treaty the bribery was not decisive.[35] We know that Li was disgusted with England's " desertion " of China in 1895, and that he had come to regard the British policy as " selfish, shortsighted and

[34] Quoted from Li's telegrams to the Tsungli Yamen. These are printed only in E. J. Dillon's *The Eclipse of Russia* (London, 1918), pp. 260–3, but they seem to be authentic enough, and Dillon was a man with unusual ability to get secret material.

[35] J. O. P. Bland: *Li Hung Chang*, pp. 199–200; Valentine Chirol: *The Far Eastern Question*, pp. 25–7.

weak." [36] It seems likely that he really wanted a defensive alliance with Russia, and that he feared Russian hostility if the demands of Witte were refused. This conjecture is strengthened by consideration of the fact that Li pared down the Russian program almost to the bone. He flatly refused a railroad concession to the Russian government. The road was to be built under a concession to the Russo-Chinese Bank, the time limit being eighty years, with China retaining the right to buy it from the Bank at the end of thirty-six years. The terms for repurchase were, to be sure, very hard. With respect to the construction of a branch road to a port on the Yellow Sea nothing definite was decided. Li agreed to the construction only on condition that this road should have the regulation European gauge rather than the wider Russian one. This suggestion was turned down flatly by Witte and the matter had to be left open.

In return for these concessions, which after all were pretty extensive, Li secured a defensive alliance for fifteen years which provided that in the event of " any aggression directed by Japan against the Russian territory in Eastern Asia, or the territory of China or that of Korea," the two contracting parties should " support each other reciprocally with all the land and sea forces they may be able to dispose of at the moment," and that neither one should make peace with the enemy without the consent of the other. Chinese ports were to be open to Russian warships during hostilities. The Railroad was represented as a necessary means for Russia's bringing aid to China. In times of peace, troops were to be transported over the line only on condition that they make no stops other than " those justified by the necessity of transportation." Li secured the approval of the Chinese government for this treaty on May 30, and it was duly signed by Lobanov, Witte and Li at Moscow on June 3, 1896 (May 22, the date frequently given, is old style). [37]

One striking fact about the Russian-Chinese Treaty was that it extended to Korea as well as to the Russian and Chinese possessions. This peculiarity can be understood only in connexion with the broader aspects of Russian policy. It will be recalled that in February 1896 the King of Korea, outraged by the murder of his queen and terrified by the high-handed action of the Japanese repre-

---

[36] Chirol: *Fifty Years in a Changing World*, p. 185; *Die Grosse Politik*, XIV, no. 3663.

[37] The basic accounts are those of Glinskii, op, cit., pp. 33–8; *The Memoirs of Count Witte* (New York, 1921), pp. 87 ff.; Romanov, op. cit., pp. 105–17. The account of Joseph, op. cit., pp. 160 ff. requires rectification, as he used no Russian materials. The substance of the treaty was first revealed in an obviously inspired anonymous article entitled: " Origines Exactes de la Guerre Russo-Japonaise " (*Revue de Paris*, July 15, 1905, pp. 225–38). Li's son revealed the main facts of the negotiation and supplied the French text of the Treaty, without preamble, to the *London Daily Telegraph* on February 15, 1910 (reprinted by John V. A. MacMurray: *Treaties and Agreements with and Concerning China*, New York, 1921, I, pp. 81–2). The Chinese delegation to the Washington Conference also supplied an official summary (*Conference on the Limitation of Armaments, 1921–1922*, twenty-fifth meeting of the Committee on Pacific and Far Eastern Questions, p. 1414). On the Russian side the text was first published by Romanov in *Bor'ba Klassov*, nos. 1–2, 1924, pp. 101 ff.; the French text is given in the same author's *Rossia v Manchzhurii*, pp. 111–3; an English translation of the French text in the Moscow archives has been published in Victor A. Yakhontoff's *Russia and the Soviet Union in the Far East* (New York, 1931), pp. 365–6.

sentatives, had secretly fled, disguised as a woman, to the Russian legation. A new conservative ministry, friendly to Russia, was appointed in the place of the reforming pro-Japanese cabinet. Russia's position in Korea seemed unassailable, and there was nothing very remarkable in the fact that the King of Korea sent the brother of the murdered queen to Moscow in May 1896 to ask the Tsar to assume a protectorate of Korea. So well-informed a person as Baron Rosen felt certain that Nicholas, without consulting his ministers, actually gave some personal assurance to that effect.[38] Whether or not this was so, it is perfectly clear that both Lobanov and Witte saw the situation in a somewhat different light. Korea, it was fully realized in St. Petersburg, was of the utmost importance to Japan. There were no less than ten thousand Japanese engaged in trade in the country, and another ten thousand exploiting the coast fisheries. Next to China, and not very far behind, Japan had the largest economic stake in the country, to say nothing of the vital interest of Japan in keeping Korea out of the hands of any large power, be it China or Russia. Japan, said Count Okuma, had to get over her condescending attitude towards the Koreans if she was to increase her trade; but in any case she " must strongly oppose any obstruction of the independence of Korea. . . . Japan should be like a father dealing with the Korean son, or an elder brother dealing with a younger." [39]

That Japan would fight for her position in Korea was practically a foregone conclusion. Colonel Vogak, the Russian military observer in the Sino-Japanese War, warned his government again and again: Not China or England, he argued, was the real enemy of Russia in the Far East. " Japan is the most important and is an extremely grave factor. Japan represents a new power, which will have a tremendous influence on the further fortunes of the Far East." [40] The new Japanese military and naval programs showed that the government was in grim earnest. By the law of 1895 the Japanese army was to be trebled in numbers. The peace strength was to be one hundred and seventy thousand men and the war strength six hundred thousand. The total military expenditure was to increase from roughly eleven million yen in 1895 to about sixty million in 1900. Under the terms of the naval program of 1896 Japan was to construct by 1904 four battleships of the largest kind (fifteen thousand tons), as well as a number of cruisers and destroyers, so that the strength of the Japanese navy would be four times as great as it had been. The Japanese planned to spend almost four hundred million yen on the navy in this one decade.[41]

---

[38] Baron Rosen: *Forty Years of Diplomacy* (New York, 1922), II, p. 125.

[39] Speech of November 6, 1896 to the Japanese and Korean Commercial Society (*Korean Repository*, December, 1896, pp. 493-4); for Korean trade see report of the Japanese Chamber of Commerce at Chemulpo, and the report of the British consul-general W. C. Hillier, both in *Korean Repository*, August, 1896, p. 341; October, 1896, pp. 411 ff. When Norman (op. cit., p. 367) speaks of Japanese trade being twice as large as Chinese he must be referring to the abnormal situation during the war.

[40] Quoted by Prince G. Trubetzkoi: *Russland als Grossmacht* (Stuttgart, 1917), pp. 47-8.

[41] Giichi Ono: *War and Armament Expenditures of Japan* (New York, 1922), pp. 61-8; C. von Zepelin: *Der Ferne Osten* (Berlin, 1907), pp. 49 ff.

The Russians could not hope to compete with the Japanese forces in the Far East until the Transsiberian Railway was finished. It was therefore essential that they come to some sort of temporary agreement with Japan about Korea. In Japan the leading civil and military figures like Count Ito and Marshal Yamagata were in favor of compromise until the military and naval programs should have been carried into effect. So Yamagata was sent to the coronation ceremonies at Moscow with the handsomest offer the Japanese ever made. He proposed to the Russians that they divide Korea at the thirty-eighth parallel of latitude, the northern part to be a Russian sphere, the southern part (with the capital Seoul) a Japanese sphere. Those who like to speculate may ruminate on what might have happened had the Russians accepted this offer. But Yamagata's suggestion was rejected on the ground that Russia had recognized the independence and integrity of Korea. The real reasons for this decision were probably three: In the first place Lobanov may have feared complications with England and the United States. In both countries there was a strong sentimental and religious interest in Korea, " The Land of the Morning Calm," to say nothing of trading enterprises. Secondly, southern Korea, which was to be abandoned to the Japanese, was the most developed and richest part of the country, and from the strategical and naval viewpoint was of very great importance. Russian naval men had for some time been trying to decide upon the port in Korea that would best meet their needs. Curiously enough there seems to have been little mention of Gensan, the best harbor on the Korean seaboard. Naval men were rather partial to Masampo at the southern tip of the peninsula, and for that reason would have opposed the relinquishment of all influence in the south. Thirdly, there was respect for Korean independence. When Lobanov brought out this argument he was, in a sense, sincere. The Russians, for the time being, desired the independence of Korea for the same reason that they desired the independence of Turkey. They hoped eventually to be able to lay their hands on the whole country and therefore objected to a premature division of the inheritance. As Count Lamsdorf said in a later memorandum: " The fate of Korea, as a future integral part of the Russian Empire by force of geographical and political conditions, had been determined upon by us." [42]

Under the circumstances Lobanov and Yamagata made a general agreement of a thoroughly unsatisfactory kind. On May 26 the representatives of the two powers at Seoul had drawn up a memorandum specifying that the King's return to the palace should be left to his discretion but that they should both advise him to do so just as soon as there was no further danger of disturbance. Japan was to be allowed to keep two hundred men to guard the telegraph line, and eight hundred more to protect the Japanese settlements at Seoul, Fusan and Gensan. All other Japanese troops were to be withdrawn. Russia was to keep as

---

[42] Romanov, op. cit., pp. 141 ff.; the only other account of the Yamagata offer is in the Russian official history of the war with Japan (Der Russisch-Japanische Krieg. Amtliche Darstellung des Russischen Generalstabes, Berlin, 1911–1912), I, p. 6. On the Russian naval plans see Rosen, op. cit., II, p. 141; Die Grosse Politik, XIV, nos. 3648, 3664.

many men as the Japanese, and both sides were to withdraw their forces as soon as order was restored. This general protocol was expanded by the Lobanov-Yamagata Agreement (Moscow Protocol) of June 9, 1896. Both parties were to support the King of Korea in his efforts to restore order and build up a military and police force, as well as to straighten out the finances. They declared themselves prepared to guarantee foreign loans if necessary, so that the police force could be reorganized and order preserved without intervention by other powers. In short, then, both powers tacitly recognized the principle of Korean independence, and renounced separate action. Secret articles of the protocol provided that if the tranquillity of the country became disturbed and Russia and Japan decided that it was necessary to send troops, the two powers should consult and determine beforehand their particular spheres of action, with the object of demarcating a neutral zone between the fields of operation. What they established was something in the nature of a condominium, a joint protectorate.[43]

The Russian historian Romanov is of the opinion that this agreement was concluded by the Russians in bad faith. The evidence he adduces would seem to leave little doubt on this point. It will be remembered that there was a Korean delegation in Moscow at the time of the coronation. This delegation asked that Russia supply counsellors to the Korean King and also furnish a loan with which the debt to Japan might be paid. In reply Prince Lobanov promised that the Russian legation and legation guard should watch over the King's safety even after he returned to his palace. An experienced officer should be sent to assist in the formation of the royal bodyguard, and a financial expert should also be put at the disposal of the Korean government. A loan should be furnished as soon as the needs of the Korean government had been made clear. In other words, Lobanov committed himself to a program of separate action which was in no sense consonant with the agreement concluded with Japan.[44]

The military part of the Russian program was immediately put into effect. Colonel Putiata was sent out with three officers and ten drill instructors. An army of over four thousand men was organized, with a royal bodyguard of eight hundred men. The drill and words of command were Russian, and the new troops were equipped with three thousand Berdan rifles presented by the Russian government.[45] But Witte, who had had little to do with the Lobanov-Yamagata negotiations, showed little interest in the economic aspects of the Korean problem. He sent out a financial expert in the summer of 1896 to investigate the situation. Soon afterward M. Pokotilov of the Russian legation in Peking was sent to Seoul. He reported the need for immediate action. There-

---

[43] Glinskii, op. cit., pp. 63 ff.; Witte: *Memoirs*, p. 97; Romanov, op. cit., pp. 139 ff.; the texts of these agreements as published by the Japanese in March, 1897 are reprinted in German translation by Brandt: *Drei Jahre Ostasiatischer Politik*, pp. 251–3. English texts in Isabella Bishop: *Korea and her Neighbours* (London, 1898), II, pp. 307–10.

[44] Glinskii, op. cit., pp. 63 ff.; Romanov, op. cit., pp. 144–5.

[45] Bishop: *Korea and her Neighbours*, II, pp. 263, 290.

upon Witte agreed that the Russo-Chinese Bank should make a loan, but only on condition that the Korean customs, at that time in charge of Mr. M'Leavy Brown, should be put in the control of a Russian adviser. Yet the appointment of such an adviser was not recommended by Witte until May 1897, and it was not until August of that year that M. Alexeiev appeared in Korea to take over these functions. In short, Witte was by no means eager to proceed in Korea. He allowed the French company which had secured the railway concessions in southern China to obtain a concession for a railroad from Seoul to Wichu on the Manchurian border, and a Russian speculator, Brinner, to arrange for the exploitation of the timber in northern Korea (this was the origin of the famous Yalu Concession of a later period), but he hesitated about sending out a financial adviser and did little towards founding the Russo-Korean Bank which many Russian expansionists had at heart. To contemporary observers Russia seemed to be neglecting her opportunities. M. Waeber, who had been Russian representative at Seoul for twelve years, was a kind and gentlemanly person, moderate and dependable. After the stormy period of the Japanese reform experiment the years of Russian predominance seemed almost above reproach.[46]

The reason for Witte's lack of interest in the Korean situation was a very simple one. He wished first of all to dispose of the Manchurian problem, and that problem continued to cause difficulty. The Treaty signed by Li in Moscow had, to be sure, been approved by the Chinese government, but when it came to the details and to the concrete specifications for the Railroad, the Chinese ministers baulked. " Take it away, we will not look at it," Prince Kung, chairman of the Tsungli Yamen, is reported to have exclaimed.[47] The court was no more favorably disposed. According to Valentine Chirol even the Empress refused to receive Li on his return from Europe and America until he had handed over eight hundred thousand pounds sterling out of his swag.[48] In the meanwhile long and tedious negotiations had been carried on in St. Petersburg between the Russian officials and Grot (Li's financial expert who had stayed to discuss details) and later with Hsü Ching-ch'eng, Chinese minister to Berlin and St. Petersburg. At Peking Li finally persuaded the Empress to appoint a special committee to consider the Russian proposals. The viceroy argued that China was exposed to the danger of British-Japanese action and that the alliance with Russia was absolutely indispensable. From Russia warning was received that if the concession were not granted, the Russians " would resort to other

---

[46] Romanov, op. cit., pp. 146–59; Bishop, op. cit., II, p. 291; on the French concession see *Korean Repository*, July, 1896, pp. 297–8; Gérard: *Ma Mission en Chine*, pp. 171–2; Homer B. Hulbert: *The History of Korea* (Seoul, 1905), II, p. 309; on the Brinner concession *Korean Repository*, September, 1896, p. 380; the important anonymous article: " Why Russia went to War with Japan " (*Fortnightly Review*, May, 1910, pp. 816–31); the fundamental article of B. A. Romanov: " Konzessia na Yalu " (*Russkoye Proshloye*, I, 1923, pp. 87–108); and now Friedrich von Steinmann: *Russlands Politik im Fernen Osten und der Staatssekretär Bezobrazov* (Leipzig, 1931), chap. ii.

[47] Anonymous: " Secret History of the Russo-Chinese Treaty " (*Contemporary Review*, February, 1897, pp. 172–83), p. 176.   [48] Chirol: *Fifty Years in a Changing World*, p. 186.

combinations and the alliance with China would remain a dead letter." Finally, in September, the Emperor was won over, and on September 8, 1896 (new style) the contract was made between the Chinese government and the Russo-Chinese Bank. The main terms were that the Bank should organize a Chinese Eastern Railway Company, of which a Chinese should be president: the railroad to be constructed should have the Russian wide gauge; the Chinese government should aid the company to obtain materials and labor at current prices; lands actually necessary for the construction, operation and protection of the line, as also such lands as were needed for procuring sand, stone, lime, etc., should be turned over to the company gratis if they were state lands, and for a payment or for rental if they were private; " the Company shall have the absolute and exclusive right of administration of its lands," and should also have the right to construct upon them buildings of all sorts, telegraphs, etc.; the road was to be free of all taxes and imposts; goods carried on the line in either direction were to pay the Chinese customs duties less one third; the Company was to be free to fix its own rates and to have the " complete and exclusive right to operate the line on its own account and risk " for eighty years; the Chinese government, however, reserved the right to repurchase the road at the end of thirty-six years by paying in full the capital and also all the debts of the company, plus accrued interest.[49]

The concession having been at last secured, there remained only the organization of the Chinese Eastern Railway Company. In May 1896 the Russian government had made an agreement with the Russo-Chinese Bank " which would guarantee the fullest influence of the government on the construction and operation of the railroad "; which would, in fact, " transfer the concession to the disposal of the Russian government." [50] This agreement specified that the Russo-Chinese Bank should subscribe the entire capital (one thousand shares at five thousand rubles each). Of the thousand shares, seven hundred were to be reserved for the Russian government. The other three hundred shares, it was thought, might be taken by French interests. This, as it turned out, was not the case, so the whole thousand shares were reserved for the government. There was an ostensible public sale of the three hundred shares on December 29, 1896, but this was a prearranged deception. No shares were held by the public. Neither had the Chinese government any financial interest in the Company. It is quite unnecessary to examine here the details of the complicated financial relationships which existed between the Russian government, the Russo-Chinese Bank and the Chinese Eastern Railway Company. Suffice it to say that the statutes of the company received the approval of the Tsar on December 16, 1896. With this the preparation for the great Russian enterprise was complete; the

---

[49] Text in MacMurray, op. cit., I, pp. 74–7; see also Glinskii, op. cit., pp. 38 ff.; Romanov, op. cit., pp. 117, 126 ff.; the article of Li's son, Li Chang-mai, in the *Daily Telegraph*, February 15, 1910; Joseph, op. cit., pp. 164 ff.

[50] Witte's report to the Tsar May 30, 1896 (Romanov, op. cit., p. 119).

Russian government had succeeded in cloaking its action by using the fiction of a private company, and everything was regulated to meet the needs of the government as Witte saw them.[51]

Despite the preliminary reconnaissance of the country that had been made in the summer of 1896, the Russian engineers had no adequate maps or topographical material bearing on Manchuria, and so most of the year 1897 had to be devoted to preparatory exploration and surveying. In the meanwhile Witte and his assistants resumed their efforts to secure from the Chinese government a concession for a line to be built south from the Transmanchurian either to the Yellow Sea, or to the Chinese railway running north from Shanhaikwan. There can be no doubt whatever that Witte's idea was to connect with this line and thus establish contact with Peking. In fact, the plan of the Russians seems to have been to join up eventually with the French advancing from the south, as Chirol put it, to " squeeze out " Britain, whose centre of interest was in the Yangtze Valley.[52]

After the war with Japan the Chinese decided definitely upon a policy of railway development within the country. Of the utmost importance was the great trunk line from Peking south to Hankow and then on to Canton. The project was taken in hand vigorously, with the idea that only Chinese capital and material should be employed upon it. But it soon became clear that Chinese capitalists had too little confidence in the government to trust it with large funds. The necessary money being unobtainable, the Chinese opened negotiations with agents of American and Belgian interests, their thought being that only such countries as the United States and Belgium were above the suspicion of ulterior political aims. The Belgians, however, feared the wrath of the French who, harking back to a vague clause in a treaty of 1885, tried to set up a claim to first choice in the building of railways in China proper. Through the efforts of M. Gérard the French government was persuaded that it would be better to work with the Belgians than to try to uphold an impossible position. A French-Belgian syndicate was formed and the Russo-Chinese Bank was initiated into the scheme. Li Hung-chang used what influence he could behind the scenes and finally, after long and involved negotiations, conducted in great secrecy, the concession was awarded in May 1897 for the stretch from Peking to Hankow. The Hankow-Canton line went to the American Development Company, but in the event of its failing to meet the terms, the Belgian syndicate (really the Franco-Russian-Belgian combination) was to have the right to take it over. Once more Franco-Russian diplomacy had scored a great success and had managed to push its economic influence yet further into the body of China.[53]

---

    [51] Text of the statutes in MacMurray, op. cit., I, pp. 84–8; the financial arrangements are discussed at great length by Romanov, op. cit., pp. 117–26.

    [52] Chirol: *The Far Eastern Question*, p. 188.

    [53] The most important account is in Gérard: *Ma Mission en Chine*, pp. 169–84; see also Percy H. Kent: *Railway Enterprise in China* (London, 1907), pp. 91–7; René Pinon and Jean de Marcillière: *La Chine qui s'Ouvre* (Paris, 1900), pp. 53–4, 224 ff.

If there was to be a connexion between the Russian line in Manchuria and the Peking-Hankow trunk line, it was essential that some arrangement should be made to connect the Transmanchurian or Chinese Eastern Railway with the Tientsin-Shanhaikwan line. Witte's suggestion to Li at Moscow had led to no result, but now that the matter of the Transmanchurian line had been settled, Witte was prepared to take the question up anew. In May 1897 he sent his aide, Prince Ukhtomskii, on a mission to Peking. His secret instructions were to secure permission to run the line across Manchuria through Kirin, which was further south than the route finally decided on. In addition Ukhtomskii was to sound out the attitude of the Chinese government towards the proposal to run a Russian line to the south to join the Shanhaikwan route at Chingchow; and finally he was to see if the Chinese could be brought to agree to the construction of another branch to some Korean port. Ukhtomskii took with him a million rubles, representing the first installment of the bribe to Li Hung-chang and, incidentally, the only installment he ever received. But despite this persuader Li turned out to be as obdurate as he had been in Moscow. He objected to the junction of the Russian and Chinese lines, and did not even like the idea of a Russian road in the direction of Korea. All he would do was to give a promise that no concession for joining the Russian and Chinese lines would be given to any other power.[54]

Witte's failure to secure from the Chinese the right to construct a railroad to the Yellow Sea opened the way for the action of Muraviev in the occupation and lease of Port Arthur, a new policy which was inspired by the German occupation of Kiao-chow in November 1897. In other words, the evolution of the Far Eastern question took a distinct turn in the closing months of 1897. Thus far the key to the situation had been the weakness of China, so glaringly exposed in the war with Japan. France and Russia were fully determined to take advantage of this situation, and through their able representatives at Peking they were able to accomplish much. The British and the Germans played, on the whole, a secondary, defensive part while the Franco-Russian Alliance was on the offensive, putting forward a policy of so-called "peaceful penetration." Gérard, supported at home by Hanotaux, was in the fore, but Witte, the Russian finance minister, went far beyond any French schemes by the grandeur of his designs. Curiously enough, of the European great powers France and Russia were least in need of territorial expansion. In order to draw any good out of their acquisitions they had to make them practically a national preserve through the application of high tariffs. The British and the Germans, in violent but fair competition throughout the world, were almost more anxious to preserve open markets than to annex territory. It was only the action of France and Russia that drove them into a policy that was in some ways decidedly contrary to their interests.

However that may have been, the Franco-Russian Alliance reached its finest

[54] Romanov, op. cit., pp. 161–74; Gérard, op. cit., pp. 213 ff.

bloom in the Far East in the years 1896–1897. No other powers could hope to compete on even terms with it. The French found and gave support in all they did, while the Russians, through threats, bribery and intrigue all but succeeded in realizing the full program outlined by Witte. Under these circumstances both England and Germany saw salvation only in some sort of agreement with Russia. At any rate they did little to block the Russian schemes. Both governments encouraged the Russians by making clear their determination not to oppose the ultimate acquisition of a port on the Yellow Sea. There was more truth than poetry in Sir Cecil Spring Rice's remark in a letter to Theodore Roosevelt: " We all seem to be struggling for the honour of kissing the Czar's feet. Germany is as servile as France and (if it weren't so evidently useless) I shouldn't wonder if England would be as servile as Germany." Russia alone, he continued, was self-sufficient and invulnerable. Russia alone could bide her time. " The art of European diplomacy," wrote Henry Norman, " seems to have degenerated into the monotonous occupation of watching the progress of Russia." [55]

BIBLIOGRAPHICAL NOTE

DOCUMENTARY SOURCES

Documents Diplomatiques. Chine, 1894–1898. A thin collection of French documents, containing only the most obvious material.

Die Grosse Politik der Europäischen Kabinette, 1871–1914. Volume XIV, part I; chapter xc. Contains some material on Russian policy, but deals primarily with German aspirations in the Far East.

Treaties and Agreements with and concerning China, 1894–1919. Compiled by John V. A. MacMurray. New York, 1921. An admirably edited and remarkably complete collection of agreements. Indispensable for the student of Far Eastern problems.

Popov, A.: " Pervyie Shagi Russkogo Imperializma na Dal'nem Vostoke." (*Krasnyi Arkhiv*, LII, 1932, pp. 34–124). Contains the text of a number of important Russian documents used by Glinskii and Romanov.

MEMOIRS, AUTOBIOGRAPHIES, BIOGRAPHIES, AND LETTERS

Gérard, Auguste: *Ma Mission en Chine, 1894–1897.* Paris, 1918. Easily one of the most detailed and important sources, containing a minute account of French policy, but also much of interest on Chinese affairs and on the policy of Russia.

---

[55] *Letters and Friendships of Sir Cecil Spring Rice* (London, 1929), I, pp. 210 ff.; Henry Norman: " Russia and England " (*Contemporary Review*, February, 1897, pp. 153–71), p. 153.

Mémoires d'Auguste Gérard. Paris, 1928. Contains little or nothing on Far Eastern affairs that is not more fully given in the preceding.

The Memoirs of Count Witte. Edited by Abraham Yarmolinsky. New York, 1921. An important source, but one that must be used with caution. Witte's account must be checked by the researches of Romanov.

ROSEN, BARON: *Forty Years of Diplomacy.* Two volumes. New York, 1922. A valuable contribution, but deals chiefly with the later period.

SPECIAL STUDIES

NORMAN, HENRY: *The Peoples and Politics of the Far East.* New York, 1895. Still one of the best-informed and most interesting of contemporary works, written by a man widely travelled in the Far East.

CURZON, GEORGE N.: *Problems of the Far East.* Revised edition. London, 1896. Important because of Curzon's official position and because of his discussion of the Chinese problem after the war.

CHIROL, VALENTINE: *The Far Eastern Question.* London, 1896. One of the best and most illuminating contemporary studies. More outspokenly British in outlook than Norman's book.

COLQUHOUN, ARCHIBALD R.: *China in Transformation.* New York, 1898. Another admirable discussion of the problem as it appeared at the time. Good particularly for the discussion of the southern aspects of the penetration of China.

HENRI D'ORLEANS, PRINCE: *Around Tonkin.* London, 1894. A record of travel, interesting chiefly for its formulation of French aspirations in the Yunnan area.

BRANDT, MAX VON: *Drei Jahre Ostasiatischer Politik, 1894–1897.* Stuttgart, 1897. Written by a man who was for twenty years German minister to Japan and China. A detailed and well-informed discussion, especially of the Korean question.

BISHOP, ISABELLA L.: *Korea and her Neighbours.* Two volumes. London, 1898. One of the fullest and most interesting pictures of Korea during the years 1895–1898.

La Chine. Expansion des Grandes Puissances en Extrême-Orient, 1895–1898. Paris. 1899. The best contemporary French work on the events of the years named. Especially full on French accomplishments, and on economic aspects.

TRUBETZKOI, PRINCE G.: *Russland als Grossmacht.* Stuttgart, 1917. The author was an official of the Russian foreign office, and his book is still one of the best accounts of Russian policy after 1895.

WEIGH, KEN SHEN: *Russo-Chinese Diplomacy.* Shanghai, 1928. A dissertation of no great value.

CORDIER, HENRI: *Histoire des Relations de la Chine avec les Puissances Occidentales, 1860–1902.* Three volumes. Paris, 1901. The work of a great French scholar, this fundamental study is still very helpful, and astonishingly sound.

FRANKE, OTTO: *Die Grossmächte in Ostasien von 1894 bis 1914.* Hamburg, 1923. An excellent German account, now somewhat outdated.

ZÜHLKE, HERBERT: *Die Rolle des Fernen Ostens in den Politischen Beziehungen der Mächte. 1895–1905.* Berlin, 1929. A substantial but conventional account, based only on the more obvious material. Adds little to books like Franke's.

DAVID, HEINRICH: *Zur Politik der Grossmächte im Fernen Osten, 1894–1902.* Zurich, 1932. A brief survey.

McCORDOCK, R. STANLEY: *British Far Eastern Policy, 1894–1900.* New York, 1931. A doctoral dissertation, based on the more obvious materials and upon some study of contemporary newspaper and periodical literature. Adds relatively little to previous accounts.

JOSEPH, PHILIP: *Foreign Diplomacy in China, 1894–1900.* London, 1928. On the whole this is the best general modern account. It is based upon the contemporary and later documentary material. The viewpoint is, however, conventional, and the great weakness of the book is the author's complete neglect of Russian material.

STEINMANN, FRIEDRICH VON: *Russlands Politik im Fernen Osten und der Staatssekretär Bezobrazov.* Leipzig, 1931. Only the first part of this dissertation has been published. It promises to be the best general study of Russian policy available in a western language.

GLINSKII, B. B.: *Prolog Russko-Iaponskoi Voiny. Materialy iz Arkhiva Grafa S. I. Witte.* Petrograd, 1916. A source of the very first order. Based upon the Witte papers, this is the most detailed account of the finance minister's policy.

MARC, PIERRE: *Quelques Années de Politique Internationale; Antécédents de la Guerre Russo-Japonaise.* Leipzig, 1914. The name Marc is evidently a blind. This book is really a translation of the Glinskii volume, as it first appeared in installments in the *Istoricheski Viestnik* in 1914–1915. The later parts of it, however, are rather severely cut.

ROMANOV, B. A.: *Rossia v Manchzhurii, 1892–1906.* Leningrad, 1928. By far the most important single account of the Russian policy and a valuable supplement to the Glinskii volume. The author has made full and ruthless use of the Russian archive material and has thrown a great deal of light on almost every aspect of Russian policy. An indispensable book.

YAKHONTOFF, VICTOR A.: *Russia and the Soviet Union in the Far East.* New York, 1931. The author deals but briefly with the period here considered.

LOBANOV-ROSTOVSKY, PRINCE: *Russia and Asia.* New York, 1933. A general survey of Russian relations with the Asiatic countries, by the son of the former Russian foreign minister. Reliable, but contains no revelations.

WANG, CHIN CHUN: " The Chinese Eastern Railway." (*Annals of the American Academy of Political and Social Science,* CXXII, November, 1925, pp. 57–69). A good, accurate survey of the origins and history of the company, by one of its former presidents.

CHIA-PIN, LIANG: " History of the Chinese Eastern Railroad." (*Pacific Affairs,* III, February, 1930, pp. 188–211). Interesting as reflecting the Chinese viewpoint, but adds nothing factually.

LITERATURE SINCE 1935

(See also the Supplementary Bibliographical Note to Chapter VI.)

SUMNER, B. H.: *Tsardom and Imperialism in the Far East and Middle East, 1880–1914.* New York, 1942. 43 pp. An admirable summary review of Russian policy in Manchuria and Persia, by an outstanding authority.

WALSH, WARREN B.: " The Yunnan Myth " (*Far Eastern Quarterly,* II, May, 1943, pp. 272–286). A thorough, scholarly review, chiefly of contemporary writings.

ROMANOV, BORIS A.: *Ocherki Diplomaticheskoi Istorii Russko-Iaponskoi Voini, 1895–1907.* Moscow, 1947. 493 pp. A study of Russian-Japanese relations after 1895, based largely on the author's earlier monograph on Russian policy in Manchuria.

KRUPINSKI, KURT: *Russland und Japan; ihre Beziehungen bis zum Frieden von Portsmouth.* Königsberg, 1940. 126 pp. The best systematic study in a Western language. Makes full use of Russian and to some extent of Japanese materials.

POPOV, A.: " Dal'nevostochnaia Politika Tsarizma v 1894–1901 gg." (*Istorik Marksist,* XI, 1935, pp. 38–58). A valuable monograph, drawing heavily on contemporary writings and using also some Russian archive materials. Especially full on Russian economic penetration into China.

CRIST, DAVID S.: " Russia's Far Eastern Policy in the Making " (*Journal of Modern History,* XIV, September, 1942, pp. 317–342). A detailed analysis of the so-called " Korean clique " in Russian circles. Based on a large number of Russian publications.

TREUE, WILHELM: " Russland und die Eisenbahnen im Fernen Osten " (*Historische Zeitschrift,* CLVII, 1938, pp. 504–540). Relies chiefly on the published British and German documents. Slight on the period prior to 1904.

YERUSALIMSKII, A. S.: *Vneshniaia Politika i Diplomatiia Germanskogo Imperializma v Kontse XIX veka.* Moscow, 1948. 767 pp. Contains a very extended and heavily documented account of German Far Eastern policy.

ZUG, JOSEF: *Versuche der Wiederannäherung an Russland unter Fürst Chlodwig zu Hohenlohe-Schillingsfürst.* Rottenburg, 1934. 184 pp. A conventional treatment of German-Russian relations, with special emphasis on the Far East from 1895 to 1898.

SPINKS, CHARLES N.: " Origin of Japanese Interests in Manchuria " (*Far Eastern Quarterly,* II, May, 1943, pp. 259–272). Largely a study of the development of Japanese trade interests.

McCUNE, GEORGE M.: " Russian Policy in Korea, 1895–1898 " (*Far Eastern Survey,* September 26, 1945, pp. 272–274). A brief but well-informed summary, based on recent publications.

HARRINGTON, FRED H.: *God, Mammon and the Japanese.* Madison, 1944. 362 pp. The career of Dr. Horace N. Allen in Korea, 1884–1905. An interesting and valuable account of political and economic activity as seen by an American.

ZABRISKIE, EDWARD H.: *American-Russian Rivalry in the Far East: A Study in Diplomacy and Power Politics, 1895–1914.* Philadelphia, 1946. 226 pp. An excellent analysis of all phases of the subject, drawing heavily on Russian sources.

THE DIPLOMACY
OF IMPERIALISM

Part II

XIII

The New Navalism

∾

THE PROCESS OF " PEACEFUL PENETRATION " THROUGH THE EXTORTION OF concessions, as carried out by Russia and France in China during the years 1895–1897, was abruptly disturbed when the Germans occupied the harbor of Kiao-chow in November 1897 and thereby gave the evolution of the Far Eastern situation an entirely new turn.

The German action cannot be studied as an isolated episode. It must be viewed rather in the general setting of the German " Weltpolitik " which was the counterpart to the concurrent outburst of " Imperialism " in England. In France and Russia the movement for expansion was essentially an artificial one, resting upon considerations of national prestige, drawing its support from a group of statesmen who looked to the future, from a relatively small number of explorers and colonial enthusiasts, and from a syndicate of bankers and speculators who saw in the movement unusually good " diggings." With Britain and Germany the situation was quite different. England was the industrial and trading nation *par excellence,* dependent for her food supply upon importation and literally living upon her foreign trade. Her position in the world was, in the nineties, seriously threatened by the economic rise of Germany, a country rapidly becoming industrially top heavy and feeling ever more sharply the need for markets. Summed up in a few words, the story of European international relations in the 1890's is the story of the assault of Russia and France upon the territorial position of Britain in Asia and Africa, and the story of the great economic duel between England and her all-too-efficient German rival.

It has been argued, and with some brilliance, that it is incorrect to speak of Bismarck's policy as a " continental " policy, and to describe the policy of his successors as a " new world policy." Bismarck, it has been said, pursued a " world policy " in the sense that he took advantage of world events to gain his immediate aims. Not only that, he carried through a moderate colonial policy, and secured for Germany almost all the extra-European territory that she possessed before the World War. If Germany had devoted her whole attention to the development of her industry, to the employment of her people and to the production of ever higher and cheaper grades of goods, she would have been able to more than hold her own in the world, and she would have been able to do so without arousing the serious antagonism of England or any other power.[1]

This argument strikes one very much as an argument *ex post facto*. It leaves out of account the peculiar mentality of the last decade of the dying century. Anyone who has immersed himself in the contemporary writing will come away with the overwhelming impression of the almost panicky feeling which seized upon the European nations at that time. The phenomenal development of industry raised problems of which the solution could not be known. Even the most eminent economists, in Germany men like Adolf Wagner, Gustav Schmoller and Max Weber, believed in the absolute necessity for securing all that was possible of the world markets. They regarded the question of expansion as nothing less than a question of life and death. In a previous chapter something has been said of the reaction of these new problems upon the British mind. Attention has been called to the growth in England of a dogged determination not to be downed, and to the rapid spread of a ruthless and bellicose attitude in questions of international relations.

Much the same development took place in Germany. If the British came to dislike the Germans as uncomfortable competitors, the Germans came to resent British power and even British efforts to maintain their position unimpaired. The first colonial crisis of 1884–1885 had called forth a symptomatic outburst of hostility to England, which, to be sure, had died out somewhat in the last years of the Bismarckian period, when German interest was absorbed by continental tension. After Bismarck's fall, however, it revived and in a remarkably short time became a much deeper and more widespread feeling than it had ever been before. It was the sacrifice of German claims in Africa in the so-called Heligoland Treaty of 1890 that led to the foundation of the *General German League,* which was in 1894 reorganized as the *Pan-German League* (Alldeutscher Verband). Composed of professors and teachers, business men, officials and professional men, this group aimed to arouse

> " patriotic self-consciousness at home and to oppose vigorously any development of the German people along unpatriotic lines; to support and aid German endeavours in all lands where members of the German people must struggle to retain their individuality, and the union of all Germans on the earth for the furtherance of these aims; to promote an energetic German policy of might in Europe and oversea; above all to carry forward the German colonial movement to tangible results." [2]

The organization was avowedly anti-English, and combined its efforts with those of the Colonial Society and later with those of the Navy League to propagate the ideas of a world policy. Its leaders talked of establishing a central Euro-

---

[1] Otto Becker: " Bismarck und die Aufgaben Deutscher Weltpolitik " (in Hans Delbrück: *Am Webstuhl der Zeit,* Berlin, 1928, pp. 103–23).

[2] Mildred Wertheimer: *The Pan-German League* (New York, 1924), p. 37.

pean customs union and possibly an even closer connexion; Holland, Belgium and Switzerland, it was hoped, would somehow or other be brought into a greater German Empire. All this was, of course, to be effected through peaceful methods, through cultural propaganda, through the strengthening of the German " idea." But it could not be expected that other nations should take a naive view of this agitation. It is certainly true that the League never had an immense membership, that it never enjoyed heavy representation in the Reichstag, that it never succeeded in deluging the world with its pamphlets and other propaganda. But even Miss Wertheimer, who is apt to take a somewhat too indulgent view of the League's activity and to underrate its importance, is bound to admit that it " was doubtless one of the most strident jingo societies in the world and its noise was quite incommensurate with its size," that it " was a ringleader in the anti-English agitation in Germany," and that its " indirect influence was probably larger than its direct importance." [3] The fact is that the theories of the League, in one form or another, very soon found their way into much of the German political writing of the years 1895 to 1914, and that they raised apprehensions abroad which are reflected in the periodical literature at an early date. When, in 1899, the Germanized Englishman, Houston Stewart Chamberlain, published his *Foundations of the Nineteenth Century*, in which he declared that the whole present-day civilization and culture was the work of the Teutons and asserted that Germany was destined to become the heart of humanity, he was simply striking the loudest chords of the theme of race superiority. The idea no doubt went back to Count Gobineau's essay on *The Inequality of the Human Races*, which was first published in 1854, but the cult of this extravagant racialism and nationalism came only in the last lustrum of the nineteenth century. In England as in Germany it was carried to absurd heights. There is nothing in all the Bismarckian period to compare with this exaggeration of national egotism, with this hot passion for expansion. Whatever may have been the influence of the Pan-German League as such, there can be no question of the popularity and widespread influence of the new Pan-Germanic religion as expounded by Chamberlain and his enthusiastic followers.[4]

While theories of race superiority were being advanced in England and Germany to prove that one or the other of these great nations was the salt of

---

[3] Wertheimer, op. cit., pp. 210, 213, 217. On the history of the League see also Otto Bonhard: *Geschichte des Alldeutschen Verbandes* (Leipzig, 1920), pp. 1–17, 105 ff.; Anonymous: " Pan-Germanism " (*Quarterly Review*, July, 1902, pp. 152–75).

[4] It is worth noting that the Gobineau Vereinigung was founded at Freiburg in 1894. See Ludwig Schemann: *Gobineau, eine Biographie* (Strassburg, 1913–1916); Idem: *Fünfundzwanzig Jahre Gobineau-Vereinigung, 1894–1919* (Berlin, 1919); Idem: *Die Rasse in den Geisteswissenschaften* (Munich, 1928); Ernest Seillière: *Le Comte de Gobineau et l'Aryanisme Historique* (Paris, 1903); Idem; *Houston Stewart Chamberlain, le Plus Récent Philosophe du Pangermanisme Mystique* (Paris, 1917); Idem: *Introduction à la Philosophie de l'Impérialisme* (Second edition, Paris, 1911). Among the best critical studies are Frank H. Hankins: *The Racial Basis of Civilization* (New York, 1926), especially chapters iii and iv; Friedrich Hertz: *Race and Civilization* (New York, 1928), especially chapter viii.

the earth and preordained to ultimate victory over all competitors, another current of thought had sprung up which served in every way to fortify the teachings of the imperialists. In 1890 an American naval officer, Captain Alfred Thayer Mahan, published a book on *The Influence of Sea Power upon History*. This work was followed in 1892 by the same author's *Influence of Sea Power upon the French Revolution and Empire,* and in 1897 by his *Life of Nelson.* Of the first of these books thirty-two editions have been published to date. Of the other two seventeen and seven respectively. According to the publishers' figures almost twenty-three thousand copies of the first, almost twelve thousand of the second, and more than twenty thousand of the third have been disposed of in the United States alone.[5]

Mahan's books consisted of a general discussion of the elements of sea-power, followed, in the various volumes, by an analysis of the history of naval warfare, with special reference to the struggle of England with Holland and France in the seventeenth and eighteenth centuries, and down to the battle of Trafalgar and the death of Nelson. It has been objected by some writers that Mahan was a poor historian, that he used only a few secondary works, that his general ignorance of other aspects of history led him to exaggerate the importance of sea-power, and that he never realized that ideas similar to his own had been put forward by earlier writers. Bacon and Raleigh, not to speak of Leopold von Ranke, had had a very clear conception of sea-power, it was pointed out.[6]

Much of this is true, no doubt. It is also worth noting that at the very time when Mahan's first book appeared Admiral Philip H. Colomb of the British navy was publishing in the *Illustrated Naval and Military Magazine* a series of essays which appeared in book form in 1891 under the title *Naval War, its Ruling Principles and Practice Historically Treated,* in which he set forth much the same arguments and reached much the same conclusions arrived at independently by Mahan. But Colomb's book was verbose and heavy, while Mahan's was written with unusual charm, precision and breadth of view. Colomb's book was completely overshadowed by the American volumes, which literally took England by storm in the first years of the 1890's. Hardly had his first book appeared when the leading journals published extensive reviews. The second work, on the French Revolution and the Napoleonic Era, made an even deeper impression, in as much as it was less technical and of more immediate interest. One British officer declared that no book on a naval or military subject had attracted one tenth the notice given this study, and another, writing in 1893, remarked that Mahan's "discovery" of sea-power had been so widely discussed

---

[5] Letter of Little, Brown and Company to Dr. Gordon Benedict, one of my students, who has been kind enough to show me these figures.

[6] See especially the reviews of Mahan's books by Emil Daniels (*Preussische Jahrbücher,* March, 1898, pp. 567-9), and by Gustav Roloff (*Historische Zeitschrift,* LXXXVI, 1901, pp. 309-13); the very competent criticism of Fred T. Jane: *Heresies of Sea Power* (London, 1906); Vice-Admiral Alexander Meurer: *Seekriegsgeschichte in Umrissen* (Berlin, 1925), Introduction.

that its nature could no longer be unfamiliar to many people.[7] Admiral Sir Cyprian Bridge declared that "Mahan's opinions govern the naval thought of the world." "His volumes were inevitably accepted as final, and, in the true sense, were epoch-making," wrote another naval man. "I can remember no event in my time in the Navy so epoch-making as the publication of Mahan's first books," says Admiral Sir Reginald Bacon, looking backward.[8] When Mahan visited England in 1893 and 1894 as commander of the American cruiser *Chicago,* he was overwhelmed with attention. Earl Spencer, first lord of the admiralty, gave a great dinner for him. A public banquet was given by the lord mayor of London at St. James Hall. Over a hundred admirals and captains of the British navy received him at the Royal Navy Club. The Queen, the Prince of Wales, Lords Rosebery and Salisbury entertained and honored him. Both Oxford and Cambridge conferred honorary degrees. In short, Captain Mahan was lionized. Rarely if ever has a serious historical work produced on this side of the Atlantic been received with such favor and enthusiasm on the other side of the water. It may well be doubted if any historical work of the last few generations has had so great and profound an influence on the political development of the world.[9]

What was the secret of this great success, which Mahan himself was unable to understand? The answer is that the American officer first grasped, interpreted and made understandable the concept of "sea-power," which Admiral Colomb called "command of the sea." The popularity of his books in England was due further to the fact that they constituted a "scientific inquiry into the causes which have made England great."[10] Mahan was a pronounced Anglophil. He was filled with admiration for the accomplishments of British seamen, and he was convinced that British naval power had always been a boon to the world. The British therefore felt flattered, and rightly so.

But apart from these special aspects of Mahan's influence, it must be remembered that his thesis came as a revelation. If sea-power had been appreciated by earlier writers, it certainly had played no part in the thinking of the common man. Since the days of the Crimean War interest in the navy had waned in England. Great sums were spent upon the army and upon fortifications, but

---

[7] Captain F. N. Maude: "The Influence of Sea Power" (*National Review,* March, 1894, pp. 110–17); Nauticus (Laird Clowes): "Sea Power, its Past and Future" (*Fortnightly Review,* December, 1893, pp. 849–68); see also the important reviews of the first two books by Professor John Laughton in the *Edinburgh Review,* October, 1890, pp. 420–53; April, 1893, pp. 484–518.

[8] Charles C. Taylor: *The Life of Admiral Mahan* (London, 1920), p. 40; C. S. Alden and R. Earle: *Makers of Naval Tradition* (Boston, 1925), pp. 237 ff.; John Leyland: "Recent Naval Literature" (in *Brassey's Naval Annual,* 1897, p. 210); Admiral Sir Reginald Bacon: *A Naval Scrapbook* (London, n.d.), pp. 264–5. Similar opinions in Lord Fisher: *Records* (London, 1919), p. 135; Sir F. Maurice and Sir George Arthur: *Life of Lord Wolseley* (London, 1924), p. 285, and in many other books.

[9] For Mahan's reception in England see especially Taylor: *Life of Admiral Mahan,* pp. 61 ff.

[10] Review, "The Influence of Sea-Power upon History" (*Blackwood's Magazine,* October, 1890, pp. 576–84).

there was little faith in the navy. It was only in 1895–1896 that the expenditure for the navy once more came to equal that for the army. Many people had the idea that the advent of the steamship had nullified all the laws of naval warfare as they had been evolved in the days of sail. No new strategy had been worked out and no one had shown, as Mahan and Colomb did, that the fundamental principles of naval combat, as they could be derived from history, were still valid. The rapid changes in the design of steamships and ironclads reduced the world's navies to motley assemblages of craft of all types. The leading authorities were far from agreement on anything, and in the building programs ideas of coast defense, cruiser warfare and high-seas fleets were all entangled.

Mahan cleared the ground of all this confusion and misconception. Painting on a broad canvas he stressed not only the teachings of history, but the inter-relation of geographical factors, national character, commerce and colonial expansion in the determination of sea-power. From the standpoint of strategy his greatest contribution was the conclusive demonstration that commerce-destroying, much in vogue among naval theorists in 1890, had never been decisive in itself:

" Such a war cannot stand alone; it must be *supported,* to use the military phrase; unsubstantial and evanescent in itself, it cannot reach far from its base. That base must be either home ports, or else some solid outpost of the national power, on the shore or on the sea; a distant dependency or a powerful fleet. Failing such support, the cruiser can only dash out hurriedly a short distance from home, and its blows, though painful, cannot be fatal." " It is not the taking of individual ships or convoys, be they few or many, that strikes down the money power of a nation; it is the possession of that overbearing power on the sea which drives the enemy's flag from it, or allows it to appear only as a fugitive; and which, by con-trolling the great common, closes the highways by which commerce moves to and from the enemy's shores. This overbearing power can only be exercised by great navies, and by them (on the broad sea) less efficiently now than in the days when the neutral flag had not its present immunity." [11]

In other words, the ultimate, determining factor in sea-power is the possession of a strong battle-fleet, capable of overcoming the enemy and driving it from the sea.[12]

In France the theory of cruiser warfare had been most completely worked out by the writers of the so-called " Young School," of which Admiral Aube was the chief. Aube and his followers, Admirals Touchard, Jurien de la Gravière, Reveillère, and the journalists Étienne Lamy and Gabriel Charmes, argued that since the advent of the ironclad, which was independent of wind, sea battles of the old type had become impossible, for the weaker power would avoid combat and would seek to ruin its adversary by raiding and commerce destroying. The

---

[11] Mahan: *The Influence of Sea Power upon History, 1660–1783* (Boston, 1890), pp. 132, 138.
[12] The argument is well developed, along the lines of Mahan, by Spenser Wilkinson: *The Command of the Sea* (Westminster, 1894).

important thing, then, was to have a large number of fast cruisers and torpedoboats. For the price of one battleship one could build sixty torpedoboats. Besides, battleships were clumsy Goliaths, the expression of the megalomania of potentates and therefore unsuitable to a democratic republic. They were in contradiction to the principle of the division of labor. A swarm of little Davids would be much better.

This whole conception was well expressed by Aube in his many writings, one of which may be quoted:

> " To-morrow war breaks out; a torpedoboat has sighted one of these ocean steamers freighted with a cargo of greater value than that of the richest galleons of Spain; the torpedoboat will follow at a distance, keeping out of sight, and when night comes on will, unobserved, close with the steamer and send to the bottom cargo, crew and passengers, not only without remorse, but proud of the achievement. In every part of the ocean similar atrocities would be seen. Others may protest; for ourselves we accept in these new methods of destruction the developments of that law of progress in which we have a firm faith and the final result will be to put an end to war altogether."

It was an attractive theory and one which for twenty years profoundly influenced the course of French naval development. The French continued to build some battleships, of mixed types, but the emphasis until 1900 was upon cruisers and small craft of great speed.[13]

The British admiralty had never been won over to the theory of cruiser warfare to the extent of neglecting the battle-fleets. But naval authorities were much exercised by the great activity of the French in this branch of building, and they were particularly anxious when, in the late 1880's, the Russians began to devote large sums of money to naval construction. Like the French, the Russians put much emphasis on fast cruisers and devoted attention to the increase of the so-called volunteer fleet, consisting ostensibly of merchant ships plying between the Black Sea ports and the Far East, but composed in reality of convertible cruisers and commerce raiders, for which armaments were kept in readiness both at Odessa and at Vladivostok.[14] In 1887 there appeared in Russia the story of an imaginary war with England and of the exploits of a Russian cruiser which, equipped with the newest torpedo appliances and capable of developing great speed, was able to outsteam and capture British merchantmen while at the

---

[13] Admiral Aube, as quoted in the *Naval Annual*, 1890, p. iv. The texts of the Young School were the books of Commandant Z. and H. Montechant: *Les Guerres Navales de Demain* (Paris, 1892); and *Essai de Stratégie Navale* (Paris, 1893). Aube and his associates expounded their ideas in the *Revue des Deux Mondes*. See also Édouard Lockroy: *La Marine de Guerre* (Paris, 1897), especially pp. 30-1, 93. On the other side Admiral F. E. Tournier pleaded for a battle fleet in the sense of Mahan. See his books *La Flotte Nécessaire* (Paris, 1896) and *La Flotte de Combat* (Paris, 1899). A good general account may be found in René Jouan: *Histoire de la Marine Française* (Paris, 1932), II, pp. 260 ff.; and in Vice-Admiral Salaun: *La Marine Française* (Paris, 1934), pp. 16-40.

[14] A. Stroumillo: " The Russian Navy " (in *Brassey's Naval Annual*, 1898, chap. iv); Sir George S. Clarke: *Russia's Sea Power* (London, 1898), chaps. vii, viii; N. Monasterev and Serge Terestchenko: *Histoire de la Marine Russe* (Paris, 1932), chap. xi.

same time evading British warships. This story, which enjoyed great popularity, bore the significant title: " The ' Russia's Hope,' or Britannia no longer Rules the Waves." [15]

British alarm at the naval policy of Russia and France led in 1889 to the adoption of the principle of the two-power standard and the passage of the Naval Defence Act. The alliance of France and Russia, as symbolized in the great Toulon demonstration of October 1893, made the situation appear even more dangerous to British eyes. The Mediterranean was regarded as the chief route to the Far East, and England kept her newest and most formidable ships there. For this reason, and because of the growing naval power of Italy, the French did likewise. They had a splendid naval base at Toulon and in 1895 they built a second one at Bizerta, in Tunis. The establishment of the Russian Mediterranean squadron was so serious a threat to the British position that many experts advocated the abandonment of the Mediterranean entirely. So radical a solution met with considerable opposition, however, and in the end the situation was dealt with in other ways. It was decided to build new dockyards at Gibraltar and to modernize that base for the use of the Mediterranean fleet. The Channel, or Home fleet, was strengthened and kept off the Portuguese coast in order to be on hand to support the Mediterranean forces. At the same time a new naval program of large dimensions was introduced, after great popular pressure had been brought to bear upon the Gladstone government.[16] A number of leading naval and military authorities, Admiral Colomb, Colonel Maurice and others, collaborated in publishing one of those imaginary battle stories so dear to the British heart. In *The Great War of 189–* the avid public was treated to a thrilling account of a great European conflict in which British sea-power proved to be the decisive element. William Le Queux, popular teller of lively yarns, took the suggestion of Alfred Harmsworth (Lord Northcliffe), and outdid the naval men. In his novel *The Great War in England in 1897,* which went through edition after edition in 1894, he pictured a Franco-Russian invasion of England, the capture of Manchester and Birmingham, and the horrors of the attack on London. The preface of the book stated quite baldly: " The extraordinary preparations now going forward in France and Russia are being made in view of an attack upon England, and it is ominous that the downfall of our empire is a perpetual subject of discussion in the Paris press." Literature of this type may have no great artistic value, but it must be remembered that the man in the street read, not the long-winded, small-printed material in the *Times,* but just this sort of stuff, published in ephemeral journals like *Black and White,* or thrown on the book-stalls for a few pence.

From this time on there was little or no break in the rapid development of

---

[15] English translation, London, 1888.

[16] The naval situation in the early nineties is treated at some length in my *Franco-Russian Alliance,* pp. 336 ff., 359 ff.; since then there has appeared a solid, detailed though uninspired dissertation by Angela von Schönberg: *Um den Twopowerstandard* (Stuttgart, 1933).

the British navy. The English were irritated by the competition of France and Russia: "To all other Powers a strong navy is more or less of a luxury, useful for certain subordinate purposes, the chief of which is to act as a counterpoise to the maritime supremacy of England. To England alone it is from the very nature of the case an absolute and primordial necessity," wrote one of the leading authorities.[17] The clash of interests between Britain and France in Egypt and the Sudan, the advance of Russia in central Asia, and the developments in the Far East were all of them added arguments for greater and greater seapower. It may easily be imagined how well the teaching of Mahan fitted into this general international tension. We have the best contemporary evidence of his influence not only on the public, but on public men. " It would be impossible to overestimate the effect which his books have had on the practical tendencies of our politics," says one writer. " Mahan's books have done the country, and the Navy for that matter too, a world of good," wrote Lord Wolseley. " He had," according to another, " a distinct influence on the views of some of our public men in the direction of strengthening their conviction of the necessity of a large ship-building programme." Eminent merchants in the city confessed that he had awakened them to a realization that London depended on trade and that trade required adequate protection. At last it was clear to all that " every power in the world holds all its transmarine possessions merely as the caretaker of the ultimate Naval Power." [18]

From this time on British governments no longer had difficulty in persuading parliament of the need of increased appropriations. There was no subject so dear to the poets of imperialism as the greatness of England on the sea. In an unbroken line from Swinburne's *The Armada* (1888) to Kipling's *A Fleet in Being* (1898) there was an outpouring of verse, good, bad, and indifferent, but all of it serving to stimulate popular pride and arouse popular interest. The *Navy League,* founded in 1894, through lectures, meetings and the dissemination of thousands of leaflets and pamphlets, kept urging the needs of the navy and kept stressing England's dependence on sea-power for her daily bread, for her raw materials, for her trade outlets, for security against invasion and for " peace with honor." The chief object of the League was to prevent the cutting of appropriations for party purposes. There was hardly much need of that. When Lord Goschen in 1896 brought in estimates much larger than any preceding ones, he was criticized by the Liberal Sir Charles Dilke, who maintained that for safety's sake England required not a two-power standard but a three-power standard. The annual estimates, which were, roughly, thirteen million pounds for the year 1888–1889, rose to over seventeen and a half million for 1894–1895 and to more than twenty-six and a half million for 1899–1900. The

---

[17] James R. Thursfield: "Command of the Sea " (*Quarterly Review*, October, 1893), p. 123.
[18] " Balance of Power " (*National Review*, March, 1896), p. 24; Maurice and Arthur: *Life of Lord Wolseley*, p. 285; Admiral R. Vesey Hamilton: " Our Invasion Scares and Panics " (*Nineteenth Century*, March, 1896, pp. 399–415); John Leyland (in *Brassey's Naval Annual*, 1897, pp. 213 ff.).

expenditure for new construction, which had been twenty-four and a quarter million pounds for the eleven years from 1876 to 1887, amounted to forty-nine and a half million for the eleven years from 1887 to 1898. During these last eleven years England added to her fleet twenty-nine battleships, twenty-six first-class cruisers, forty-five second-class cruisers, thirty-one third-class cruisers, twenty-nine torpedoboats and fifty-five torpedoboat destroyers. By 1898 even the most insatiable navalists were obliged to admit that the fleet was big enough and that it was equal to all eventualities.[19]

Lord Goschen, in bringing in the estimates for the great expansion of the British fleet in the years 1895–1900 spoke of them as " estimates not of provocation, but of self-defence." The British navy was at that time on the two-power standard and was intended as a means of self-defense against France, the second naval power of the world, and Russia, the fourth. Both these powers, especially Russia, were greatly increasing their naval appropriations, while Italy, after the disaster at Adua, was obliged to retrench and give up the extensive program of earlier years. But the British were arming not only against the combination of France and Russia, which had been paraded before the world at Toulon and proclaimed from the rooftops in 1895–1896. The south African crisis of January 1896 had brought another factor into the situation. Theretofore the British had always counted on the assistance or at least on the benevolent neutrality of the Triple Alliance. After the Kruger telegram episode there was no further thought of such an alignment. Austria was of little moment as a naval power, and Italy was almost paralyzed after the collapse of her Abyssinian policy. The Germans were clearly hostile. Indeed, they were evidently drawing closer and closer to the Franco-Russian combination. The intervention at Shimonoseki had demonstrated the feasibility of co-operation in extra-European problems. In the Cretan and Greek crises of 1896–1897 the continental powers once again stood together and frustrated the British program.

The speech of Sir Charles Dilke on the naval estimates on March 5, 1897, reveals the preoccupation of British statesmen with this new alignment. Few politicians were so well versed in military and naval questions. Dilke's opinions carried weight, and are therefore worth quoting:

" What had occurred in Northern China in joint pressure by the three Powers — Russia, Germany and France — in the acceptance of the Russian loan as against our proffered loan, and in the dominance of Russia in Manchuria and Korea, recently secured by treaty, pointed to great risk of common action against ourselves by three great maritime Powers, and it seemed improbable that we could ourselves break up that Concert except by giving way upon points which were vital to our interests, such as our China trade. We had been told on the Naval

---

[19] Abundant figures may be found in the volumes of *Brassey's Naval Annual*, but see also Elliot: *Life of George J. Goschen*, II, pp. 207–19, and the splendid survey account written by the great British naval designer Sir William H. White: " The Latest Reconstruction of the Navy " (*Nineteenth Century*, April, 1898), pp. 534–48. On the origins of the Navy League see Harry Spenser Wilkinson: *Thirty-Five Years* (London, 1933), pp. 187–97.

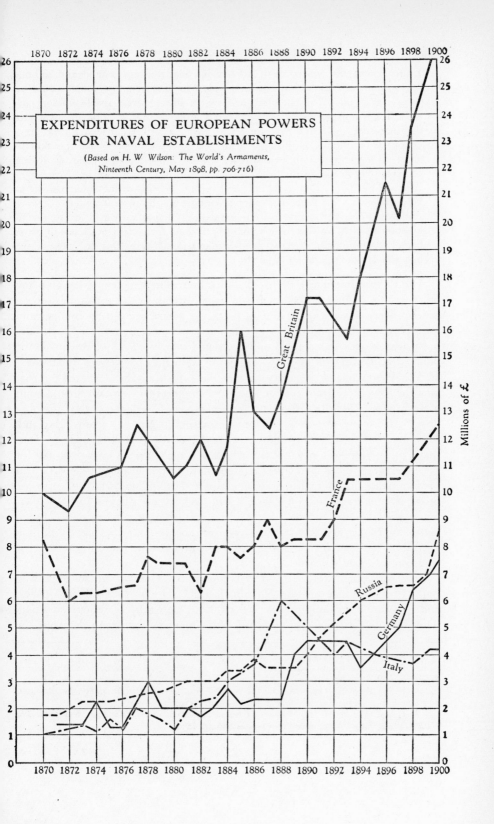

EXPENDITURES OF EUROPEAN POWERS
FOR NAVAL ESTABLISHMENTS

(Based on H. W. Wilson: The World's Armaments,
Ninteenth Century, May 1898, pp. 706-716)

Estimates last year, what was in fact obvious, that we were isolated, and he himself was all for isolation, as against a policy of alliances; for nothing could be weaker as a policy than one of sham alliances where there was no common purpose; but it must never be forgotten for a moment that isolation meant a predominant fleet. The risks were increasing. . . . The three great maritime Powers of the Northern Continent were, as their recent actions showed, able now to agree on a policy of Continental peace — joint support of the policy of Russia of expansion on the Pacific, of France in the Further East, and of Germany in Africa. This conjunction could only be faced by us being strong enough at sea to hold our own. . . . Peace was happily certain for the present, but in the long run would only be preserved if our naval strength was such as to cause a combination of three Powers, which could be formed for certain purposes, to pause before attacking us. . . . As Captain Mahan had put it, the British Navy was the best security for peace." [20]

Dilke's speech merely reflected the ideas that were being expressed by many other writers. A German officer, Baron von Lüttwitz, at this time published an article advocating a strong German fleet as a means for getting colonies and for coping with England. The essay was not very convincing nor very important, but it was at once seized upon and translated into English and was made the point of departure for many warnings of Germany's aggressive intentions.[21] H. W. Wilson, one of the most active of the British navalists, pointed out that after the Kruger telegram episode it was only logical that Germany should build a large navy. Lüttwitz' article was taken as official evidence of far-reaching designs. Germany was clearly planning a coalition directed against England. Had not the *Kreuzzeitung* said in so many words (March 9, 1897): "Germany must aspire to a naval power which will make her an important ally for the other great naval States if England should assume an attitude of selfish predominance in reckless disregard of all interest except her own." [22] George W. Steevens, another well-known writer, had declared even before this that Germany was the real enemy, and that the danger of a combination between Germany, France and Russia was a very real one. Professor Spenser Wilkinson harped on the same theme, and stressed the threat to the English position that was implied in such a coalition.[23]

It is sometimes argued that the extremely anti-German articles appearing in the British press at this time had no effect upon the conduct of British policy, and that they were simply hysterical effusions unworthy of serious attention. This view is certainly over-optimistic. We may not know much about the

---

[20] Hansard: *Parliamentary Debates*, Series IV, vol. XLVII, pp. 68–70.

[21] Baron von Lüttwitz: " German Naval Policy and Strategy " (*Journal of the Royal United Service Institution*, March, 1897).

[22] H. W. Wilson: " The Naval and Colonial Policy of Germany " (*Fortnightly Review*, June, 1897, pp. 923–935); see also the *Saturday Review*, March 13, 1897.

[23] George W. Steevens: *Naval Policy* (London, 1896), pp. 184, 190; Spenser Wilkinson: *The Nation's Awakening* (Westminster, 1897), especially pp. 125 ff.

deeper motives of British policy in these years, in as much as the documents have not been published and the memoir material is scant. But here and there may be found bits of evidence that illuminate the attitude of higher circles. Take for example a letter of Lord Salisbury to Lord Lansdowne, written in April 1897 when, for a short time, there was serious danger of renewed trouble in south Africa. Salisbury informed his colleague that he had warned Chamberlain of the inconvenience of war at that time, if only because of the unfavorable effect it would have upon relations with Holland:

> " I dread great unpopularity in the Netherlands. In the next year or two the young Queen of Holland will probably be married. If she marries anyone under the Emperor William's influence the Germans will get out of the Dutch some form of Kriegsverein which may enable them to man their fleet with Dutch sailors. His great ambition is to have a fleet, but until he gets a maritime population he cannot have a fleet. Some control over Holland is very necessary to him." [24]

These few remarks speak volumes. They show that Salisbury shared the expectation of H. W. Wilson that the Germans hoped " at no very distant date to win Holland to a voluntary union, or to annex her by force." It was an apprehension that had been widespread in the years just after 1870, an apprehension that was now growing strong once more, at a time when the writings of the Pan-Germans could only just have become known in England.[25]

It should be clear from the preceding discussion that German writers are in error when they assert that the British paid little or no attention to German naval power before 1904. It is perfectly true that the British did not fear the German navy, though they were quite aware of its high quality and general efficiency. What they did fear was that Germany might actually succeed in realizing the Emperor William's dream of a continental coalition against England, and that then a naval combination would result which Britain could not hope to combat on equal terms.

As a matter of fact there was some ground for the British uneasiness. We know of the Emperor's continuous efforts to effect a close understanding with France and Russia, and it can also be shown that the important German policy of naval construction which began with the first naval bill of 1898 hinged more or less upon this idea of a " continental combine."

William II, even before he had ascended the throne, had developed an almost abnormal interest in things maritime. When, in 1889, Queen Victoria named him admiral of the British fleet, it was her hope and Salisbury's hope that the appointment would put an end to the Russophil proclivities of the young ruler and would draw him over to the English side. This hope was entirely justified. In fact, the scheme worked only too well. William not only took a lively interest

---

[24] Lord Newton: *Lord Lansdowne* (London, 1928), pp. 144–5.
[25] *Die Alldeutsche Bewegung und die Niederlande,* by Fritz Bley, an active Pan-German, was published at Munich in 1897.

in the British fleet, but became more and more convinced of the necessity for a larger and more powerful German fleet. In 1894 his mother wrote to Queen Victoria in her usual extravagant fashion: "William's one idea is to have a Navy which shall be larger and stronger than the British Navy, but this is really pure madness and folly and he will see how impossible and needless it is." [26] Overdrawn though this statement was, so much was true, that the Emperor kept up a constant agitation about the fleet, referring to the matter in his speeches, bombarding the Reichstag deputies with charts and plans, and never failing to call the attention of his ministers to Germany's impotent position at sea when, as in the Far Eastern and Cretan affairs, the powers tried to reinforce their decisions by a demonstration of sea-power.

At first the country showed little interest in the naval problem. It was felt by many that Germany, which already maintained one of the largest military establishments, could not hope to pose as a first-class naval power. Besides, the fleet agitation was generally regarded as just one of the young Emperor's whims. Not even the ministers of marine had any use for far-reaching plans. Stosch had declared in a memorandum of 1883 that " naval battles alone seldom decide the destinies of States, and for immeasurable time the decision of every war will for Germany lie with her land army." [27] Stosch's successor, General von Caprivi (later chancellor) took the same military view. For him the fleet was simply a secondary factor in the operations of a future war against France and Russia. The important thing was a really adequate coast defense and if possible a fleet strong enough to prevent an effective blockade of the German coasts. Caprivi resigned in 1888 because he was unwilling to subscribe to or support the plans of the new ruler. Admirals Monts and then Hollmann, the first naval officers to hold the position of minister of marine, might have done something, but Monts died in a few months and Hollmann's efforts from 1890 to 1897 seem to have been devoted chiefly toward maintaining the good will of the Reichstag by avoiding unreasonable demands. He appears to have had no very clear conception of what was wanted, and pursued a mere hand-to-mouth policy. The result was that, while France and Russia were forging ahead, Germany sank from the position of third sea power to that of fifth in the decade from 1885 to 1895.[28]

By the middle of the 1890's this situation began to call forth anxiety in German circles that previously had not been impressed with the Emperor's attitude.

---

[26] *Letters of the Empress Frederick,* p. 447.

[27] Quoted by Archibald Hurd and Henry Castle: *German Sea-Power* (London, 1913), p. 94.

[28] Good general accounts in Ulrich von Hassell: *Tirpitz* (Stuttgart, 1920), chaps. i–iv; Admiral Hopmann: *Das Logbuch eines Deutschen Seeoffiziers* (Berlin, 1924), pp. 171–4; Hans Hallmann: *Krügerdepesche und Flottenfrage* (Stuttgart, 1927), pp. 15 ff.; Raimund Foerster: *Politische Geschichte der Preussischen und Deutschen Flotte* (Dresden, 1928), pp. 50 ff.; Eckart Kehr: *Schlachtflottenbau und Parteipolitik* (Berlin, 1930), pp. 25 ff.; and above all in the recent detailed study of Hans Hallmann: *Der Weg zum Deutschen Schlachtflottenbau* (Stuttgart, 1933), chaps. i, ii, iv.

The phenomenal development of German industry and trade was probably the decisive factor. The teachings of Mahan, directly or indirectly, began to affect the thinking of scholars and business men alike. German economic interests were forcing her into a " World Policy " whether she desired it or not. Colonies, sea-power, naval bases, all these things took on a new value. " A Navy does not make trade," wrote an English authority, " but trade either makes a navy that is strong enough to support it, or passes into the hands of more provident merchants." [29] Now the German merchant marine had increased in tonnage by almost 150% between 1873 and 1895, and the value of German maritime imports and exports had increased over 200% in the same period. Apart from the wealth thus entrusted to the sea there was the further consideration that Germany had become dependent on overseas countries for a not inconsiderable share of her food supply. Even English writers of a much later period were obliged to admit " that at this time (i.e. 1897–1898) the German fleet bore no reasonable relation to Germany's growing trade and oversea interests." [30] Germany was the second power in the world so far as foreign trade was concerned. Yet in sea-power she ranked not only behind England, France and Russia, but behind Italy.

There is something convincing, then, in the argument that dependence on food and the development of trade interests would have forced a fleet upon Germany irrespective of the efforts of individual statesmen.[31] From 1894 onward the Hamburg merchants, led by Woermann, began to agitate for more cruisers to protect German commerce. Karl Peters, the stormy petrel of German colonial policy, joined in the cry and before long carried with him the German Colonial Society with its twenty thousand members. The Pan-German League took its side by the sister society, and from the very beginning, in 1894, came out strongly for an increase in the navy. Eminent historians, like Dietrich Schäfer and Hans Delbrück, created popular interest in the German Hanse of the middle ages and argued that this great commercial league had fallen simply because it lacked sufficient naval power to compete successfully with the rising national states. For Germany, it was said, the question of an adequate fleet was a question of life and death. There was no example in history of a great commercial state that was able to maintain its position for any length of time without the support of sea-power. The teachings of biological determinism were used to buttress the same viewpoint. Gustav Schmoller, Adolf Wagner, Max Weber and other prominent economists were carried away by the problems arising from Germany's spectacular evolution. " With terrifying rapidity we are approaching the time when the provision of half-civilized Asiatic peoples will have reached its greatest expansion. Then nothing but might, nothing but

---

[29] Nauticus (Laird Clowes): " Sea-Power; its Past and Future " (*Fortnightly Review*, December, 1893, pp. 849–68); on Mahan's influence see Georg Wis(licenus): Reviews of Mahan's first two books in *Literarisches Zentralblatt*, May 29, 1897 and April 28, 1900.

[30] Hurd and Castle, op. cit., p. 118.

[31] See Hans Herzfeld: " Der Deutsche Flottenbau und die Englische Politik " (*Archiv für Politik und Geschichte*, VI, 1926, pp. 97–146), pp. 99–100.

naked force will decide the question of foreign markets," wrote Max Weber. "German sea-power," asserted Schmoller, "will moderate present-day trade hatred and hostile economic tension; it will keep open the door for a just international division of labor." Germany, it was argued on all sides, must face the situation squarely. Sir Charles Dilke had advanced the theory that in a relatively short time the world would be divided between three great empires, the British, the American and the Russian. Obviously it behooved the Germans to assure themselves of what Prince Bülow later called "a place in the sun." [32]

By 1895-1896 the members of the Reichstag had become less hostile than they had been to the appropriation of larger sums for the navy. The trouble was that they could not make out what it was that the minister of marine wanted. There seemed to be no rhyme or reason to the government's building program. It was impossible even to discover whether the object aimed at was a large fleet of cruisers to protect commerce, or the strengthening of the battle-fleet. Then, in January 1896, came the acute international tension resulting from the Jameson raid and the Kruger telegram. Emperor William was determined to make use of the popular excitement to present a supplementary program and to ask approval for a loan of one hundred million marks for this purpose. Even this program was intended to be merely the first installment of a larger plan running over a period of perhaps ten years. In order to prepare public opinion a beginning was made toward the mobilization of the newspapers and the enlistment of the aid of friendly organizations and individuals. On January 18, 1896, the twenty-fifth anniversary of the foundation of the Empire, William made his first great speech on world policy: "Colonial policy is only a branch of world policy which the German Empire must follow for the protection of its continental position. The time of Germany's philistinism is past, when she was oblivious to whatever went on in the world."

In the meanwhile, on January 8, the Emperor had been in conference with Hohenlohe, Hollmann and Admiral von Knorr, chief of the naval high command. William urged upon his advisers the need for striking while the iron was hot. So favorable an opportunity would not present itself again. The Reichstag would not dare refuse a demand for a loan for the purchase of cruisers abroad. But Hohenlohe was lukewarm and even Hollmann objected to the introduction of an extensive program at that time. Such a policy would only endanger the annual estimate, which had not yet been voted. Informally Hohenlohe consulted the party leaders. He reported them opposed to the scheme and finally the Emperor was persuaded that his plan was impracticable for the time being. In

---

[32] The contemporary pamphlet and periodical literature is simply immense. See the accounts of the early agitation in Foerster, op. cit., p. 80; Kehr, op. cit., pp. 40 ff., 55 ff. and pp. 390-422 (discussion of the writings and influence of the historians and economists). See also Heinrich Dietzel: "Die Theorie von den Drei Weltreichen" (Die Nation, XVII, 1899-1900, pp. 414-8, 431-5, 443-7, 456-9, 472-4), where a large number of economists are quoted. Contemporary statistical material is conveniently assembled in Die Seeinteressen des Deutschen Reiches, zusammengestellt auf Veranlassung des Reichs-Marine-Amts (Berlin, 1898).

March Baron Marschall denied in the Reichstag that the government was considering " boundless " (uferlose) plans for the navy.[33]

The Emperor now decided to replace Hollmann, and his choice fell upon Alfred von Tirpitz, chief of staff of the high command of the navy. Tirpitz was probably the ablest naval man produced by any country in modern times. In 1896 he already had behind him a long and distinguished career; during many years he had been chief of the torpedo service and had done much to perfect this new weapon of naval warfare. He had, furthermore, given much attention to strategy and tactics, and had, in contrast to the French, come to the same conclusions as Colomb and Mahan. In a memorandum of 1891 he had expressed his conviction " that the decision for our navy must be sought in open battle." As chief of the naval staff he organized the modern battle squadron and worked out battle-line tactics. Perhaps most interesting of all his writings was an important memorandum (Dienstschrift no. IX) of June 16, 1894, in which his views were expressed in concise form.

" The starting point for the development of a fleet must be the marine interests of the nation." " A state that has marine or world interests, must be able to represent them and must be able to make its power felt beyond its territorial waters. Rational world trade, world industry, to a certain extent deep-sea fishing, world communications and colonies are impossible without a fleet capable of assuming the offensive." " The natural purpose of a fleet is the strategic offensive." Or, as he says in his memoirs, " The navy never seemed to me to be an end in itself, but always a function of these maritime interests. Without sea-power Germany's position in the world resembled that of a mollusc without a shell." [34]

In this memorandum Tirpitz did not confine himself to generalities. He outlined a plan for a fleet of seventeen battleships (two squadrons of eight each and one flagship), six first-class cruisers, twelve third-class cruisers and six torpedoboat flotillas. The Emperor was much impressed with Tirpitz' views, but was evidently too uncertain in his own mind or too much under Hollmann's influence to make them wholly his own. Despite the fact that he knew Mahan's writings (he received Mahan on his yacht at Cowes in 1895), he still showed a pronounced partiality for the theories of cruiser warfare. In November 1895 the high command was urging the need of building battleships. It pointed out that by 1901 France and Russia would each have twice as many as Germany. At least twelve battleships should be constructed by 1908. The Emperor referred this document back to Tirpitz for an opinion, and the latter, on January 3, 1896,

---

[33] Hallmann: *Krügerdepesche, etc.*, pp. 34–53; Idem: *Deutscher Schlachtflottenbau*, pp. 171 ff.; Kehr, op. cit., pp. 51 ff. These accounts may be supplemented by Hohenlohe: *Denkwürdigkeiten der Reichskanzlerzeit*, pp. 151–8, 161, 164, 240–1.

[34] See Alfred von Tirpitz: *My Memoirs* (New York, 1919), I, p. 77; Ulrich von Hassell: *Tirpitz* (Stuttgart, 1921), pp. 88 ff.; Hopmann, op. cit., pp. 181 ff.; Hallmann: *Krügerdepesche*, pp. 25 ff.; Hallmann: *Deutscher Schlachtflottenbau*, chap. iii; Bernhard Michalik: *Probleme des Deutschen Flottenbaues* (Breslau, 1931), pp. 20 ff.

handed in a report running to twenty-nine folio pages. Tirpitz subscribed entirely to the view of Admiral von Knorr, and suggested only a few changes in the projected long-term program. The south African crisis put a new aspect on the whole problem, for it had now become clear that British friendship could not be counted on in the future as in the past. " Even the greatest sea power," said Tirpitz in his report, " would act more accommodatingly towards us if we were able to throw into the scales of international politics, or if necessary into the scales of conflict, two or three well-schooled squadrons. With cruisers nothing of this sort could be accomplished." Tirpitz disapproved of the Kruger telegram because it made Germany, weak as she was at sea, an easy butt for British ill humor. On the other hand he realized how much the Transvaal crisis helped to awaken popular interest in German sea-power.[35]

Despite the urgent and convincing arguments of Knorr and Tirpitz, the Emperor, in the discussions of January 8, 1896, seems to have talked only of more cruisers. Why he should have decided to appoint Tirpitz minister of marine when he was not ready to accept his program remains a mystery. It is at any rate not surprising that Tirpitz accepted the appointment without enthusiasm. He was probably glad when, after the Reichstag had accepted the ordinary annual estimates, the Emperor changed his mind, retained Hollmann and named Tirpitz commander of the squadron in the Far East.[36]

The admiral remained abroad for a full year. In the meantime Hollmann met his doom. The naval estimates for the year 1897–1898 were exceedingly modest, amounting only to seventy million marks. But they were so poorly managed by the minister that the Reichstag refused to accept them. In March 1897 parliament reduced the appropriation by twelve million marks, striking two cruisers from the list of projected ships. The Emperor was infuriated by this action, partly because the Catholic Centre party was chiefly responsible for the fiasco, but even more because he was already busily at work evolving a new long-term program. As time passed he had become more and more firmly convinced that trade rivalry was at the bottom of the Anglo-German tension, and that Germany's whole commerce was at the mercy of one hundred and thirty British cruisers, to which Germany herself could oppose only four. Hohenlohe shared this opinion entirely, though he appears to have had no sympathy with a huge program of battleship construction.[37]

So far as one can detect (the matter is not at all clear) the Emperor had decided, even before the failure of the estimates in the Reichstag, to embark upon an extensive program of construction. The German fleet, he declared, must be half as strong as the combined French Atlantic and Russian Baltic fleets. The

[35] Tirpitz: My Memoirs, I, pp. 84–6; Hallmann: Krügerdepesche, pp. 30–8; Idem: Deutscher Schlachtflottenbau, chaps. iv, v; Hassell, op. cit., pp. 105–15.

[36] Tirpitz: My Memoirs, chap. viii; Hallmann: Deutscher Schlachtflottenbau, pp. 183 ff.

[37] Die Grosse Politik, XIII. no. 3396; Hohenlohe: Denkwürdigkeiten, pp. 191–2, 193, 382–3; Hallmann: Deutscher Schlachtflottenbau, chap. vi.

high command of the navy was ordered to prepare proposals and details. In the meanwhile the Emperor decided to accept the resignation of Hollmann and to recall Tirpitz. Marschall, the foreign minister, whom the Emperor had disliked intensely for some time, was allowed to go. In his stead William appointed to the foreign office Count von Bülow, the ambassador at Rome, who was willing to devote himself to the realization of the Emperor's naval plans.

The high command reported on May 10, 1897. Its suggestions were a curious medley of the battleship proposals of Tirpitz and the cruiser plans so dear to Hollmann and the Emperor. But William, despite the fact that he had replaced Hollmann with Tirpitz, was still unprepared to accept the battleships. He struck several of them off the plans and very considerably increased the number of projected cruisers. The whole program, he decided, should be sanctioned by legislation, in order to avoid in future the annual wrangling about estimates. By 1910 the whole new fleet was to be ready.[38]

Tirpitz returned from the Far East in the middle of June. His first move was to induce the Emperor to scrap the scheme which had been so laboriously evolved. Tirpitz says himself that his stay in the Far East had shown him more clearly than before the keen commercial rivalry between British and Germans, and had made him realize all the more keenly what a disadvantage the lack of sea-power was from the German standpoint. Cruiser warfare, he argued to the Emperor, was of little importance to Germany because of her unfavorable geographical position and because of her lack of overseas bases for coaling, revictualling and repairs. The only decisive factor would be the battle-fleet in the North Sea. Curiously enough the Emperor made but slight objection. The admiral was surprised at the ease with which William was willing to change his mind and adopt the new views which he presented.

Having persuaded the sovereign, Tirpitz was able to apply himself to the elaboration of his own scheme. The plan was characterized throughout by moderation, precision and clarity. Nothing like it had been done before. Tirpitz knew what he wanted and why he wanted it. All the details were gone over meticulously, all the arguments *pro* and *con* were carefully weighed and considered. In August the whole matter was discussed at length by the Emperor, Bülow and Tirpitz in a series of conferences at Wilhelmshöhe. Bülow seems to have had no doubt that the plan could be gotten through the Reichstag, but he did doubt whether England would ever give Germany time to carry the program through. The political situation, he pointed out, would be easier " if, in our new building, we did not put battleships into the foreground and laid stress rather on cruisers, torpedoes and coast defences." It was the same objection that Tirpitz had had to meet so often before. But the Emperor, who had always been a cruiser advocate himself, would no longer tolerate what had come

---

[38] Hallmann: *Krügerdepesche*, pp. 57 ff.; Idem: *Deutscher Schlachtflottenbau*, pp. 239–47; Waldersee: *Denkwürdigkeiten*, II, pp. 392–5; Foerster, op. cit., pp. 98 ff.; Hohenlohe: *Denkwürdigkeiten*, pp. 295, 297, 311, 317, 319, 321, 326–7.

to sound like heresy. The Tirpitz program was accepted and put into final form in October 1897.[39]

The basic provision of the projected naval bill was the construction of eleven battleships, five first-class cruisers and seventeen smaller cruisers by 1905. This was regarded as a minimum, barely enough to raise the German fleet above the status of a *quantité négligeable*. With such a naval force Germany would be able, in a war against France or Russia or against both, to prevent a blockade of the German coasts and so keep open the lanes of commerce and food supply. But Tirpitz' thought no longer moved exclusively along the traditional lines of the war on two fronts. Since the Kruger telegram episode and since his observation of Anglo-German trade rivalry in the Far East, the problem of a possible conflict with England never left his mind. In his memoirs he admits his conviction that if Germany had not built a fleet the British would soon have called a halt to German economic expansion. Writing to the Emperor in 1898 he formulated his idea in a few direct sentences:

> "The imposing economic development of Germany in the last decade stands in direct relationship to the political power of the Empire. The essential connexion which exists, especially between sea-power and the development of economic interests, will in future become even more sharply delineated. In the economic struggle which the nations must wage in the coming century it will become ever more necessary to defend the maritime interests of Germany by armed force." [40]

But what prospect had Germany of protecting herself from a war of attrition waged by England? Tirpitz was bound to admit that in 1897 Britain, with her home fleet alone, could destroy the German fleet and blockade the German harbors within a few weeks. The German merchant marine would be captured and the colonies lost. The projected increase in the fleet would not put Germany in a position to fight England on even terms, not by any means. But it " would give us a maritime fighting force of such strength that it could not be overcome without much ado even by one of the larger naval forces." The geographical position of Germany would make the new fleet particularly dangerous for England. For safety's sake she would have to recall part of her Mediterranean and other squadrons. To avoid this Britain, he felt certain, would be more prepared to adjust her quarrels with Germany in an amicable way.[41]

Here is the whole " doctrine of risk " (Risiko-Gedanke) upon which the Tirpitz naval policy was built up in the succeeding years. There was no thought of attempting to build a fleet as large as the British. There was no need for so large a force, for the Germans always reckoned on the fact that the English would never be able to concentrate all their squadrons in the North Sea. What

---

[39] Tirpitz: *My Memoirs*, chap. ix; *Memoirs of Prince Bülow* (Boston, 1931), I, pp. 132 ff.; Hallmann: *Deutscher Schlachtflottenbau*, pp. 247 ff.; Foerster, op. cit., pp. 104 ff.

[40] Hohenlohe: *Denkwürdigkeiten*, pp. 441–3. The Emperor shared these ideas even before the Navy Law was passed (*Die Grosse Politik*, XIII, no. 3413).

[41] Tirpitz' draft for a speech to the Reichstag, March, 1896 (printed in Hallmann: *Krügerdepesche, etc.*, pp. 79 ff.).

Tirpitz aimed at, from the very beginning, was a fleet sufficiently powerful to make an attack by the British *home* fleet a risky undertaking for the aggressor. Once Germany had so strong a force he believed that the British, rather than run the risk of a collision, would be more accommodating in their relations with Germany. And this brings us to the third point: the alliance value of the fleet.

" Our policy," he complained in a letter of February 13, 1896, " does not understand that Germany's alliance-value, even from the point of view of European states, does not lie altogether in our army, but in our fleet." Or again: " German trade, the 'Open Door,' could no longer be protected by flying squadrons; we had to increase in general power all round, i.e. to qualify ourselves for an alliance with the Great Powers. But alliance-value could be achieved only by a battle-fleet." [42]

Whether Tirpitz envisaged an eventual alliance with England it is hard to say, but it seems doubtful. The point he made in his writings and speeches, especially in the years 1896–1898, deals rather with another aspect of the alliance-value of the fleet. Time and again he argued that in an age of world policy the interests of the great powers were bound to be extra-European. In such matters soldiers were of little aid. What was needed was sea-power. For example, the great antagonism of the later 1890's lay between France and Russia on the one side and Great Britain on the other. If this antagonism were to eventuate in an armed conflict, what would be the position of Germany? She would be of no value to Russia or France so long as she could furnish only soldiers. The French and the Russians had large enough armies of their own. But if she had a respectable fleet, then the combined sea-power of the three states might be of decisive value. France and Russia, as well as England, might therefore be expected to assume an entirely different attitude toward the Germans in world affairs once Germany had a fleet that was more than a *quantité négligeable*. There can be no doubt whatever that Tirpitz looked forward to closer relations with Russia and that he even hoped for an ultimate readjustment of the Franco-German problem. In other words, he shared the Emperor's enthusiasm for a continental league and believed it feasible. All this comes out clearly enough in his contemporary letters, and is borne out by his memoirs, where he says: " The object in view had to be the institution of a constellation of Powers at sea, which would remove the possibility of any injury to or attack upon our economic prosperity." " I must say that I did not myself regard the prospective battle-fleet as a panacea without an alliance with another secondary sea power." Tirpitz, says Bülow in his memoirs, lacked political sense and his lack of understanding for the finer nuances " led him to entertain occasional illusions about Russia and even about France, countries in which he sought support against England, the land he especially hated." [43]

---

[42] Tirpitz: *My Memoirs*, pp. 84, 120; Hallmann: *Deutscher Schlachtflottenbau*, pp. 248 ff.

[43] Tirpitz: *My Memoirs*, pp. 79, 121; Hopmann, op. cit., p. 242; Bülow: *Memoirs*, I, p. 127. See also Tirpitz' draft speech of March, 1896 (Hallmann: *Krügerdepesche, etc.*, pp. 79 ff.), and his

So much for Tirpitz' plans and the ideas that lay behind them. The admiral was not content, however, with a meticulous program and sound arguments. He understood that, if the scheme was to be realized, not only the Reichstag, but the nation at large would have to be convinced of its necessity and desirability. The Germans would have to be made sea-minded. So he threw into the work his extraordinary organizing abilities and set out on a campaign of propaganda such as Germany had never before seen. He himself visited many of the German princes and won their support, while the Emperor was persuaded to keep quiet in order not to give rise to the idea that the plan was a personal hobby: "You can understand that with such an advocate in prospect I naturally keep my mouth shut and use it only for eating, drinking and smoking," William wrote to Eulenburg.[44] Systematic agitation for a larger navy had already been initiated by the Pan-German League, with which Tirpitz secretly collaborated.[45] At the ministry of marine Tirpitz organized a publicity bureau, where newspaper men were cordially received and given information of which they could make good use. A great many journals were enlisted and a great many meetings arranged for. Through his assistants the admiral was able to secure the support of many scholars, historians like Schäfer and Delbrück, and especially economists, who, so Tirpitz says, showed more understanding than the historians. Hundreds of eloquent pamphlets were turned out and distributed by the thousand. Tirpitz himself arranged for the translation of Mahan's books. In order to get them before the public as quickly as possible they were issued in sections, beginning in the autumn of 1897. It will be readily seen that the American officer's arguments were exactly suited to Tirpitz' needs, and that the economists needed only to embroider upon the same themes. They showed that the expenditure on the fleet would be a productive outlay, they stressed the insecurity of Germany so long as she lacked sea-power, and they pointed out the danger that the superfluous population might become an intolerable burden instead of a source of wealth. Germany would be condemned to vegetate as a small nation unless she had the power to defend her interests and throw real might into the scales.[46]

In the fleet agitation which spread far and wide through Germany in the autumn of 1897 the theme of German maritime interests shared the honors with the theme of British trade hatred. On July 28 the English government had denounced the commercial treaty concluded with the German Zollverein in 1865. The reason for this action lay in the new tenderness for the colonies which was part of the Chamberlain program. The treaty in question contained a provision

---

letters to Stosch of February, 1896 (Hassell, op. cit., pp. 106–10). There is a good discussion of this whole problem in Michalik: *Probleme des Deutschen Flottenbaues*, pp. 20 ff., 31 ff.

44 Bülow: *Memoirs*, I, pp. 158 ff.

45 Bonhard: *Geschichte des Alldeutschen Verbandes*, pp. 105 ff.; Heinrich Class: *Wider den Strom* (Leipzig, 1932), p. 33.

46 Tirpitz: *My Memoirs*, chap. xi; Foerster, op. cit., pp. 109 ff. By far the most detailed and best account is that of Kehr: *Schlachtflottenbau und Parteipolitik*, pp. 93 ff.

that German imports into the colonies should pay no higher tariff than imports from the United Kingdom into the colonies. Henceforth, after the expiration of the Treaty a year later, the colonies would be free to charge German goods whatever rates they chose. It is perfectly clear that this action of the English government simply served to revive in Germany the fear of a commercial war and the banging of the colonial door in the face of German merchants. The British action, wrote Emperor William, means the beginning of war to the knife against our flourishing state.[47]

Worse yet was the determined and systematic German-baiting of part of the British press, especially of the *Saturday Review*. In an article of September 11, 1897 this violently anti-German paper established a new record for extravagance of language. The text of the sermon was an apocryphal interview with Prince Bismarck which was printed in the Paris *Gaulois* on September 7 and reproduced in the London *Times* on the following day. The old chancellor was there made to say that during the visits of Emperor William and President Faure to St. Petersburg the chief topic of conversation must have been England and the prospect of forming a continental league against her. He pointed out, it was reported, that in Ferry's time he himself had gotten along even with the French, and that he had assisted them in the foundation of their new colonial empire. To this the *Saturday Review* added that Bismarck's object had also been to divert Russia to southeastern Europe:

"France busy with her Tunis and her Tonkin, Russia quietly pushed to the east and the south, and there was left for Germany the simple task of sitting peacefully on her bulging coffers, while her merchants captured the trade of England and her diplomatists guided the diplomatists of England into perpetual bickerings with other countries. Prince Bismarck has long recognised what at length the people of England are beginning to understand — that in Europe there are two great, irreconcilable, opposing forces, two great nations who would make the whole world their province, and who would levy from it the tribute of commerce. England, with her long history of successful aggression, with her marvellous conviction that in pursuing her own interests she is spreading light among nations dwelling in darkness, and Germany, bone of the same bone, blood of the same blood, with a lesser will-force, but, perhaps, with a keener intelligence, compete in every corner of the globe. In the Transvaal, at the Cape, in Central Africa, in India and the East, in the islands of the Southern Sea, and in the far North-West, wherever — and where has it not? — the flag has followed the Bible and trade has followed the flag, there the German bagman is struggling with the English pedlar. Is there a mine to exploit, a railway to build, a native to convert from breadfruit to tinned meat, from temperance to trade gin, the German and the Englishman are struggling to be first. A million petty disputes build up the greatest cause of war the world has ever seen. If Germany were extinguished to-morrow, the day after to-morrow there is not an Englishman in the world who would not be the richer. Nations have fought for years over a city or a

---

[47] *Die Grosse Politik*, XIII, no. 3414.

right of succession; must they not fight for two hundred and fifty million pounds of yearly commerce? " The outrageous follies of William the Witless, the German schemes in the Transvaal and other transgressions have brought home the realization of the imminent probability of war. England is the only great power that could fight Germany " without tremendous risk and without doubt of the issue." " The growth of Germany's fleet has done no more than to make the blow of England fall on her more heavily. The ships would soon be at the bottom of the sea or in convoy to English ports; Hamburg and Bremen, the Kiel Canal and the Baltic ports would lie under the guns of England, waiting, until the indemnity were settled. Our work over, we need not even be at pains to alter Bismarck's words to Ferry, and to say to France and Russia ' Seek some compensation. Take inside Germany whatever you like: you can have it.' " " Germaniam esse delendam " was the fitting close of this extraordinary effusion.

No doubt this article was not representative of British opinion generally speaking. But it would be wrong to deny it all importance. It simply expressed in unpardonably strong language what a good many Englishmen unquestionably felt. And after all, the article was not a sporadic outburst. It was part of a systematic campaign carried on by the *Saturday Review,* and the *Review* was not an obscure or unimportant organ. In any case, whatever its significance from the British angle, no one could deny that this article had disastrous effects on Anglo-German relations. It may not have been widely read in England, but it certainly went the rounds in Germany. Just as the Kruger telegram furnished the British with a plausible excuse for giving vent to their trade hatred, so this article served the purpose of many a German extremist. Anyone who will take the trouble to read the contemporary material, and particularly the literature bearing on the projected naval law, will be impressed with this fact. One writer after another called attention to this specific article, pointing out that " it would be insane and criminal levity and neglect of all the teachings of history, not to take such discussion seriously." The article might be regarded as the sound of a few overloud notes from the war hymns that were being sung in England. If Britain had her way Germany would soon meet with the fate of Holland and France. The only adequate protection lay in a strong fleet.[48] Even Bismarck was not uninfluenced by this turn of events. He too believed that Germany required a larger navy, though he was still partial to cruisers and small ships " that could swarm like hornets around the big ships." There was no danger, he thought, of a British attack upon Germany: " If they came, we should slay them with the butt ends of our rifles," he told Tirpitz. But he realized that relations between England and Germany were getting worse and worse. Writing to a friend in

---

[48] Dietrich Schäfer: *Deutschland zur See* (Jena, 1897), pp. 53 ff.; Georg Wis(licenus): *Kernpunkte der Flottenfrage* (Berlin, 1898), pp. 44 ff.; *Eine Starke Flotte eine Lebensbedingung für Deutschland, von einem Vaterlandsfreunde* (Berlin, 1897), p. 37; B. Eckhorst: *Hermannschlacht* (Leipzig, 1898), pp. 17 ff.; R. A.: " England und Deutschland " (*Die Grenzboten,* 1897, IV. pp. 393–403). pp. 400–1. On the influence of the article see also Foerster, op. cit., pp. 114 ff.; Kehr, op. cit., pp. 89 ff.

April 1898, that is just before the old statesman's death, his son-in-law remarked: " Unfortunately he (Bismarck) does not know of any adequate remedy for this state of things, since the only one he is acquainted with — that we Germans should restrict our commercial industry — is not well applicable." [49]

When the naval bill was finally presented to the Reichstag on November 30, 1897, the government quite naturally said nothing about the English aspect of the naval problem. The stress was laid upon the need for adequate coast defense and commerce protection, and upon the indispensability of a fleet if Germany was to continue as a world power pursuing a world policy. Both the Emperor William and Hohenlohe flatly rejected any idea of competing with the greatest sea powers or of embarking upon a policy of adventure. But Germany, they claimed, had to have a fleet large enough to inspire respect and to serve as a factor in international relations. Tirpitz declared that the fleet was meant only as a protective measure: " When we have a fleet as strong as the one here proposed you will have provided Germany with a naval force which even a sea power of the first class would not attack on our coast without first thinking it over three times." [50]

The bill was, on the whole, well received by the Reichstag. Its moderation and clarity were in its favor, and Tirpitz' reasonable and accommodating attitude made it easier to discuss and to compromise. The National Liberals were strong in their support, and the Conservatives, while lukewarm, were prepared to vote for it. The Progressives were dead opposed, and so were the Socialists, while the decisive Centre party was rather unfriendly and uncertain. Several of the non-German groups were opposed to the government on principle. During the winter the bill went into committee. Objections centred on the long-term provision, which in a sense deprived parliament of control of expenditure. But the leader of the Centre, Herr Lieber, was willing to make an adjustment. Tirpitz agreed to the reduction of the time limit from seven to six years, and to a number of less important changes. In the final balloting two thirds of the Centre party voted for the bill, which was passed by the Reichstag on March 28, 1898 without a formal counting of votes.

There can be little doubt that the representatives of the people expressed the general wishes of the country on this occasion. The sentiment for a larger fleet had taken firm root in the country. According to the Emperor, Tirpitz had, single-handed and in the brief space of eight months, accomplished what everyone had regarded as impossible: he had succeeded in converting fifty million obstinate, ill-informed and ill-willed Germans.[51] Even though this be somewhat overdrawn, it cannot be denied that Tirpitz had done his work and done it well.

---

[49] Sidney Whitman: *Personal Reminiscences of Prince Bismarck* (New York, 1903), p. 288; see also Tirpitz' account of his visit to Bismarck (*My Memoirs,* chap. x); and Bismarck's remarks to Maximilian Harden (*Die Zukunft,* September 4, 1897).

[50] The speeches and debates are summarized and discussed by Foerster, op. cit., pp. 127 ff., and by Kehr, op. cit., pp. 122 ff.

[51] Hohenlohe: *Denkwürdigkeiten,* p. 437.

He had given the national feeling a direction and a program. His support came, naturally enough, from the munitions makers (especially the Krupps), and from the large trading interests (led by Woermann and the Hamburg merchants), who had done much to finance his extensive propaganda. These classes were, of course, those most interested in German expansion, those most conscious of the competition, those most hostile in their sentiments toward England. The Conservatives voted for the bill not because they had any love for colonial expansion and world policy, nor because they shared the viewpoint of the capitalist and industrial classes. They disliked England as the representative of liberalism and industrialism, but the real reason for their support of the bill seems to have lain in a more or less tacit gentlemen's agreement with the National Liberals. It was understood that if the Conservatives voted a fleet for the protection of industry and trade, the National Liberals would agree to the maintenance of a tariff on foodstuffs that would protect the agrarian interests. Both of these large and important groups shared in the common fear of the rise of socialism and the proletariat. In a letter written in 1895 Tirpitz pointed out that the fleet would serve as a palliative against socialism. It would give the country a new bond of union and would divert attention from domestic problems by focussing attention on a world policy. Perhaps it was in part the recognition of this purpose that made the socialists so uncompromisingly opposed.[52]

We are not here concerned, however, with the domestic aspect of the German naval problem. It is only the international side of the great programs of the dying century that we have to consider. It will be noticed that the tremendous increase in the British appropriations coincided with the acute tension in Anglo-German relations. By the Naval Defence Act of 1889 and the Spencer program of 1894 England had been put on the two-power standard. Ships were being constructed in reasonable number to meet the growing strength of Russia and France. But with the increasing certainty of an alliance between these two nations and the appearance of a strong Russian squadron in the Mediterranean the need for yet greater protection was felt. Still, at that time England was still reckoning on the aid of Italy and the benevolent neutrality, to say the least, of Germany. It was only after the Kruger telegram had opened the eyes of the public at large to the real state of affairs as between England and Germany that the great Goschen estimates were brought in. Not that England feared Germany in a maritime way, but that the loss of German neutrality or support in a possible war with Russia and France was acutely felt. To make matters worse

---

[52] Tirpitz: *My Memoirs,* pp. 88 ff. This theme is fully developed and discussed with great learning in several articles by Eckart Kehr: "Die Deutsche Flotte in den Neunziger Jahren und der Politisch-Militärische Dualismus des Kaiserreichs" (*Archiv für Politik und Geschichte,* IX, 1927, pp. 187–202); "England-Hass und Weltpolitik" (*Zeitschrift für Politik,* XVII, 1928, pp. 500–26); "Soziale und Finanzielle Grundlagen der Tirpitzschen Flottenpropaganda" (*Die Gesellschaft,* September, 1928, pp. 211–29), and particularly in his book *Schlachtflottenbau und Parteipolitik, 1894–1901,* more especially pp. 209 ff. I am disposed to agree with the criticism of this viewpoint advanced by Hallmann: *Deutscher Schlachtflottenbau,* chap. x.

there was, since the intervention against Japan in 1895, the prospect of Germany's joining with Russia and France in an anti-British policy. Hence the talk of a three-power standard, and the warning words of Dilke. The influence of Mahan's writings had been so considerable that the government had no difficulty in securing whatever sums it desired. The criticism levelled against it was rather that it did not ask enough.

British writers have often pointed out that Mahan's theories proved to be no unmixed blessing for England, for they justified not only the British navy, but sea-power in general. "The secret of our world power stood revealed, and there began, all over the world, and especially in Germany, a race for naval power which did not indeed deprive us of our supremacy at sea, but left us no longer in a position to confront all combinations with equanimity," writes Repington.[53] Germany was certainly deeply affected. Tirpitz saw the propaganda value of Mahan's books, while the Emperor found in them more than enough proof of his own theories. "I am just now not reading but devouring Captain Mahan's book," he wrote a friend in May 1894, "and am trying to learn it by heart." [54] It would certainly be wrong, however, to accept the argument of Mahan's biographer, that his books were primarily responsible for the change in German naval policy. Tirpitz, who may surely be described as the father of the modern German fleet, had reached his conclusions before Mahan could possibly have influenced him. Indeed, he reached his conclusions very largely through experiment and direct observation. Yet even Tirpitz could not possibly have succeeded with his program unless the spectacular development of German industry and trade had created a favorable atmosphere in Germany. Tirpitz stressed, and we must stress, the fact that the fleet was simply a function of maritime interests, that it was simply one of many manifestations of the new world policy.

To be sure, the first naval bill of 1898 did not provide Germany with a fleet comparable to those of France or England. Tirpitz himself spoke of it as only "a raiding fleet," and the London *Times* wrote (March 28, 1898) that Germany, situated between Russia and France, and committed to activity in the Far East, was justified in reconsidering her naval position, even if she was acting somewhat too ambitiously and under the influence of somewhat crude ideas. Later British writers have admitted that "in the light of the vast development of Germany's colonial and commercial interests the Navy Act of 1898 was of an unambitious character." [55] The British paid little attention to it in its own right. The *Saturday Review,* to be sure, thought that the Kaiser's naval schemes would "confirm the suspicions so widely entertained in England since the day of the famous letter to Kruger, that Germany is steadily preparing to measure her

---

[53] Charles à Court Repington: *Vestigia* (Boston, 1919), p. 277; similarly General· Sir George Aston: *Memories of a Marine* (London, 1919), p. 96.
[54] Charles C. Taylor: *Life of Admiral Mahan,* pp. 131 ff.
[55] Tirpitz: *My Memoirs,* p. 149; Hurd and Castle: *German Sea Power,* p. 115.

strength against England." But it was the alliance value of the German fleet that concerned the English more than anything else.

"Were Germany the real ally of France," wrote H. W. Wilson, "the neutrality of Holland and Belgium would not stand for a week. Germany might confidently be calculated to march her troops into Holland, where the Dutch would make little or no resistance. Belgium would as certainly fall to France. The Scheldt and the Texel might then, as in the days of the great Napoleon, harbour a flotilla, destined for the transport of an army of invasion. . . . Politically a coalition of Russia, France and Germany would be immensely strong. The allies would run little or no risk whilst they would impose the gravest risks upon us. At the best, supposing us successful, we could not effectually blockade their vast coast-line. . . . Nor should we stand favourably from the purely naval point of view. . . . The opinion of the best-instructed naval officers would not countenance the belief that in battleships we are equal to the three powers." [56]

These were the fears already expressed by Dilke a year before. As we have seen, they had a real foundation in fact. Tirpitz' writings show that he regarded co-operation with one and preferably with both of the members of the Dual Alliance as a *sine qua non*. The new German fleet would be large enough, he thought, to enhance Germany's alliance value, and strong enough to make the British hesitate before a commercial war like those of the 17th and 18th centuries. If one bears in mind the "great fear" of the 1890's and the desperate struggle for markets in a contracting world, one can easily understand the outburst of navalism which characterized the imperialism of that day; one can without difficulty explain and defend both the British and the German viewpoints. On the other hand, as we look back we cannot fail to note that this fundamental change was one of the most important factors making for the later alignment of the powers. It was one of the most dangerous of innovations. It helped tremendously to embitter Anglo-German relations, and thereby to set the stage for the ultimate conflict.

BIBLIOGRAPHICAL NOTE

MEMOIRS, AUTOBIOGRAPHIES, BIOGRAPHIES, AND LETTERS

ELLIOTT, ARTHUR D.: *Life of George J. Goschen*. Two volumes, London, 1911. The standard biography of the man who was first lord of the admiralty in the Salisbury cabinet. Not as full as it might be on the naval policy of the time.

LORD SYDENHAM OF COMBE: *My Working Life*. London, 1927. The autobiography of one of the most active naval propagandists, in the 1890's still known as Sir George S. Clarke.

---

[56] *Saturday Review*, December 11, 1897, p. 654; H. W. Wilson: "Our Navy against a Coalition" (*Fortnightly Review*, June, 1898, pp. 898–909), pp. 898–9.

TAYLOR, CHARLES C.: *The Life of Admiral Mahan.* London, 1920. The only full biography, based upon Mahan's papers. Leaves much to be desired.

TIRPITZ, ALFRED VON: *My Memoirs.* Two volumes. New York, 1919. Belongs with the most interesting and instructive of all memoirs of the pre-war period. Frank and outspoken, this book is indispensable to students of modern naval problems.

HASSELL, ULRICH VON: *Tirpitz, sein Leben und Wirken mit Berücksichtigung seiner Beziehungen zu Albrecht von Stosch.* Stuttgart, 1920. A very important supplement to the preceding, containing many new letters of great interest.

TROTHA, VICE ADMIRAL ADOLF VON: *Grossadmiral von Tirpitz.* Breslau, 1933. Primarily a character study and an attempt to put Tirpitz' policy in the larger national setting. Does not add much to Tirpitz' memoirs.

HOHENLOHE, FÜRST CHLODWIG ZU: *Denkwürdigkeiten der Reichskanzlerzeit.* Stuttgart, 1931. Contains a number of entries bearing on the fleet question at this time. An important contribution.

Memoirs of Prince von Bülow. Four volumes. Boston, 1931–1933. Bülow discusses the Tirpitz program, but what he adds to our knowledge is very meagre.

HOPMANN, ADMIRAL A.: *Das Logbuch eines deutschen Seeoffiziers.* Berlin, 1924. A fascinating volume of recollections covering the period of German naval expansion.

SPECIAL STUDIES

TRAMOND, JOANNÈS and REUSSNER, ANDRÉ: *Éléments d'Histoire Maritime et Coloniale Contemporaine.* Paris, 1924. One of the few attempts to survey European international relations from the colonial and naval viewpoint. Curiously enough the book is particularly weak on the period discussed in this chapter.

MEURER, VICE ADMIRAL: *Seekriegsgeschichte in Umrissen.* Berlin, 1925. This is perhaps the best brief account of modern naval policy and history.

SCHÖNBERG, ANGELA FREIIN VON: *Um den Twopowerstandard. Englische Flotten-politik 1880–1895.* Stuttgart, 1933. One of the few systematic, scholarly studies of British naval policy.

McHARDY, C. M.: *The British Navy for 100 Years.* London, 1897. One of the publications of the Navy League. A good survey of the situation, with statistics, quotations, etc.

STEEVENS, GEORGE W.: *Naval Policy.* London, 1896. Another excellent survey of the world's fleets in 1896, with a discussion of Britain's position and needs.

CLARKE, GEORGE S. and THURSFIELD, JAMES R.: *The Navy and the Nation.* London, 1897. A collection of essays contributed to the *Times* and to leading periodicals. The work of two prominent navalists.

CLARKE, GEORGE S.: *Russia's Sea-Power.* London, 1898. The best contemporary study of Russia's naval policy and its political implications.

MONASTEREV, N. and TERESTCHENKO, SERGE: *Histoire de la Marine Russe.* Paris, 1932. A well-informed account, unfortunately very brief.

JOUAN, RENÉ: *Histoire de la Marine Française.* Paris, 1932. The best brief account of the French navy in the 19th century.

SALAUN, VICE ADMIRAL: *La Marine Française.* Paris, 1934. The only systematic account of French naval policy and history devoted entirely to the Third Republic.

LOCKROY, ÉDOUARD: *La Marine de Guerre.* Paris, 1897. The author was for a short time French minister of marine and was regarded as a leading authority. The book describes his projected reforms, but also gives a good survey of the French navy at the time.

HURD, ARCHIBALD and CASTLE, HENRY: *German Sea-Power.* London, 1913. A general account, well-informed and generally fair. Now outdated, but still worth consulting.

GALSTER, VICE ADMIRAL KARL: *England, Deutsche Flotte und Weltkrieg.* Kiel, 1925. A general discussion, with little that is new on the earlier period.

THALHEIMER, SIEGFRIED: *Das Deutsche Flottengesetz von 1898.* Düsseldorf, 1926. A doctoral dissertation, containing nothing of great importance, though based upon newspaper material and other contemporary sources.

HERZFELD, HANS: " Der Deutsche Flottenbau und die Englische Politik." (*Archiv für Politik und Geschichte,* VI, 1926, pp. 97–146). A thorough and independent piece of work. Deals chiefly with the later period.

HALLMANN, HANS: *Krügerdepesche und Flottenfrage.* Stuttgart, 1927. Based upon the German marine archives. An important and interesting contribution. The book is by no means as poor as Kehr tries to make out.

—: *Der Weg zum Deutschen Schlachtflottenbau.* Stuttgart, 1933. An expansion of the previous title. Based on the Tirpitz papers and other materials, this is the best single study of the origins of the first naval bill.

ZIEBERT, ALEXANDER: *England und der Bau der Deutschen Schlachtflotte.* Endingen, 1927. Contains almost nothing of interest on the earlier period.

FOERSTER, RAIMUND: *Politische Geschichte der Preussischen und Deutschen Flotte.* Dresden, 1928. One of the best general accounts, dealing strictly with the political aspect of the question.

KEHR, ECKART: *Schlachtflottenbau und Parteipolitik, 1894–1901.* Berlin, 1930. This is certainly the most noteworthy contribution to the history of the German naval policy. The author has been through an immense amount of contemporary material of all kinds and shows an unusual grasp. He is concerned, however, chiefly with the social factors entering into the naval policy, and these, it seems to the present writer, he somewhat over-emphasizes.

MICHALIK, BERNHARD: *Probleme des Deutschen Flottenbaues.* Breslau, 1931. Chiefly an analysis of the political and strategical views of Tirpitz. A useful survey of the material which does not alter accepted notions in any important respect.

LITERATURE SINCE 1935

(See also the Supplementary Bibliographical Note to Chapter III.)

WESSELY, KURT: *Pangermanismus: Geschichte und Widerlegung eines Schlagwortes*. Linz, 1938. 208 pp. An interesting though biassed examination of the history and content of the Pan-German movement.

WERNER, LOTHAR: *Der Alldeutsche Verband, 1890–1918. Ein Beitrag zur Geschichte der öffentlichen Meinung in Deutschland*. Berlin, 1935. 294 pp. Easily one of the best works on the subject, stressing the deeper roots of the movement in German development.

JUNG, DIETRICH: *Der Alldeutsche Verband*. Wurzburg, 1936. 37 pp. Based on a few obvious sources, of no value.

HENDERSON, W. O.: "The Pan-German Movement" (*History*, December, 1941). An able, compact evaluation of the recent literature.

GURALSKII, A.: "Iz Istorii Pangermanizma" (*Istoricheski Zhurnal*, 1945, no. 5, pp. 22–33). A general review, which adds little.

BRODIE, BERNARD: *Sea Power in the Machine Age*. Princeton, 1941. 466 pp. An excellent study of the technical development of modern navies, with reference to the evolution of naval strategy.

PULESTON, W. D.: *Mahan: The Life and Work of Captain Alfred Thayer Mahan*. New Haven, 1939. 380 pp. Based upon the Mahan Papers and on oral testimony, this is a general account of Mahan's life and doctrine, with particular reference to his world influence.

LIVEZEY, WILLIAM E.: *Mahan on Sea Power*. Norman, 1947. 334 pp. A well-documented monograph, based on much unpublished material. Thorough, but in no sense revolutionary.

PRATT, JULIUS W.: "Alfred Thayer Mahan" (in William T. Hutchinson, ed.: *The Marcus W. Jernegan Essays in American Historiography*. Chicago, 1937, pp. 207–226). A competent brief analysis of Mahan's writings and influence.

PULESTON, W. D.: "A Re-Examination of Mahan's Concept of Sea Power" (*United States Naval Institute Proceedings*, LXVI, September, 1940, pp. 1229–1236). Stresses the fact that Mahan did not confound sea power and naval power, but that he fully realized modern changes.

SPROUT, MARGARET T.: "Mahan: Evangelist of Sea Power" (in Edward M. Earle, ed.: *Makers of Modern Strategy*. Princeton, 1943, pp. 446–457). By far the best brief digest of the Mahan teaching.

ROSINSKI, HERBERT: "Mahan and the Present War" (*Brassey's Naval Annual*, 1941, pp. 192–209). A brilliant critique of the concepts of both Mahan and Tirpitz.

CLINARD, OUTTEN J.: *Japan's Influence on American Sea Power, 1897–1917*. Berkeley, 1947. 235 pp. Really a thoroughly documented review of Japanese policy as it affected American imperialism and naval expansion.

KIRAFFY, ALEXANDER: "The Influence of Democracy upon Sea Power" (*United States Naval Institute Proceedings*, LXVII, June, 1941, pp. 767–779). Analysis of the background of Mahan's teaching — concludes that democratic politics tend to influence sea power adversely.

ROPP, THEODORE: "Continental Doctrines of Sea Power" (in Edward M. Earle, ed.: *Makers of Modern Strategy*. Princeton, 1943, pp. 446–457). By far the best brief account of this aspect of the problem.

MARDER, ARTHUR J.: *The Anatomy of British Sea Power*. New York, 1940. 580 pp. This is the fundamental treatment of the history of British sea power after 1880, based upon very extensive original research.

SCHÜDDEKOPF, OTTO E.: *Die britische Marinepolitik: Wehrgeographische und strategische Grundlagen, 1880–1918*. Hamburg, 1938. 221 pp. A good book, which attempts to intertwine naval and foreign policy. Brief on the earlier period and adds little that is new.

WOODWARD, E. L.: *Great Britain and the German Navy*. New York, 1935. 524 pp. Primarily a diplomatic study, based on the British and German published documents.

HALE, ORON J.: *Publicity and Diplomacy, with special reference to England and Germany, 1890–1914*. New York, 1940. 486 pp. Studies in detail the development of propaganda and public opinion. A valuable contribution.

LEHMENT, JOACHIM: *Kriegsmarine und politische Führung*. Berlin, 1937. 132 pp. A general review of the rise of German navalism.

SCHEIBE, ALBERT: *Tirpitz*. Lübeck, 1943. 63 pp. A well-informed, popular biography.

MÜLLER-EBERHART, WALDEMAR: *Tirpitz — Dollar und Völkertragödie*. Leipzig, 1936. 254 pp. Tirpitz glorified for Nazi purposes.

HASSELL, ULRICH VON: "Tirpitz' aussenpolitische Gedankenwelt" (*Berliner Monatshefte*, XVII, April, 1939, pp. 318–336). A reconsideration of the Tirpitz doctrine, by one of the Admiral's closest associates.

GRAHAM, GERALD S.: "Admiral von Tirpitz and the Origin of Anglo-German Naval Rivalry" (*Canadian Defence Quarterly*, April, 1938, pp. 305–312). A competent analysis of the trade and colonial rivalry as a background to Tirpitz' plans for coercing Britain.

ROSINSKI, HERBERT: "Strategy and Propaganda in German Naval Thought" (*Brassey's Naval Annual*, 1945, pp. 125–150). Deals chiefly with Tirpitz and with his methods of popularizing the German fleet.

OLDENHAGE, GUSTAV: *Die deutsche Flottenvorlage von 1897 und die öffentliche Meinung*. Gutersloh, 1935. 91 pp. A doctoral dissertation which supplies an excellent survey of German press opinion on naval expansion.

XIV

The Far Eastern Crisis
Kiao-chow and Port Arthur

∾

I N August 1897 Emperor William and President Faure of France
appeared in succession at St. Petersburg to pay their respects to the autocrat
of all the Russias. The German ruler arrived accompanied by his chancellor,
Prince Hohenlohe, and by the secretary for foreign affairs, Count Bülow. Between them there was no difference of opinion touching Germany's relations
with Russia. The Emperor declared that the English were behaving so dis-
gracefully toward him that it was necessary for him to cultivate good relations
with Russia all the more assiduously. Hohenlohe was determined that everything possible should be done to make amends for " the biggest piece of foolish-
ness in the whole of our last seven years' policy, namely, the termination of the
Re-insurance Treaty." Bülow himself was firmly convinced that so long as Germany maintained friendly relations with Russia, England would never attack.[1]
Cecil Spring Rice was quite correct when he reported, in the last days of July,
that German policy had veered definitely in the Muscovite direction, and that
the Russians had taken care to capitalize this German affection by borrowing
ten million pounds on the Berlin market.[2]

The visit of the German ruler and his counsellors was a complete success.
At the great banquet reference was made to the " traditional ties " that bound
the two countries. In private conversation the foreign minister, Count Muraviev,
repeatedly stated that at bottom he would have preferred an alliance with Germany to the alliance with France. This may have been a lie, for Muraviev was
not noted for his truthfulness. In any event it was too late for Russia to change,
as he himself took care to point out. But at the same time it was fairly clear that
the Russians had no intention of making the alliance with France an instrument
of aggression. Relations with Germany were, as Muraviev said, not only friendly
and cordial, but truly intimate.[3]

Hardly had the German party left the Russian capital when President Faure
and the French foreign minister, M. Hanotaux, arrived aboard the battleship

---

[1] Bülow: *Memoirs*, I, pp. 11, 19, 55.
[2] *Letters and Friendships of Sir Cecil Spring Rice*, I, p. 225.
[3] *Die Grosse Politik*, XIII, nos. 3438–44; Meyendorff: *Correspondance de M. de Staal*, II,
pp. 348–9.

Pothuau. There was another round of festivities, receptions and reviews, cul-minating on the last day with the famous *Pothuau* toasts in which the two nations were referred to as *amies et alliées.* It is said that the French had pressed for an announcement of the alliance and the use of the word *alliance,* to which the Russians objected. Hanotaux finally insisted that the French cabinet of M. Méline would undoubtedly fall unless some sop could be thrown to the im-patient public. And so the words *amies* and *alliées* were at last agreed to, the Russians adding the further phrase " equally resolved to contribute with all their power to the maintenance of the peace of the world." This phrase was not de-signed to appeal to the French patriots who saw in the alliance a promise of the reconquest of Alsace and Lorraine. Clemenceau, for example, protested against the maintenance of a peace that was the Peace of Frankfurt. Under the cir-cumstances, he declared, Nicholas and Faure might just as well have combined with the powers of the Triple Alliance.[4]

Even if the circumspection of the Russians displeased the French irreconcil-ables, it served the purpose of reassuring the Germans. The last thing the Rus-sians wished at the time was to become involved in war about Alsace-Lorraine or any other European issue. They were deeply committed to the Far Eastern policy, and needed security on their western frontier. At the same time they desired the support of the Germans against the British in Asia. " The time has come for a decision as to Germany's fate," wrote one influential paper; " either open rivalry with England, with the support of continental Europe, or impotent protests against English activity." " From day to day," declared another, " it be-comes clearer and clearer that the two continental alliances, acting in the same sense, are able to direct the destinies of the whole of civilised humanity, by pro-tecting it against the consequences of the ambition, the implacable egoism, and the avidity of England." [5] The same stress on the possibility and necessity for co-operation between the two alliance groups was to be found in most of the German and Austrian papers. The continental combine was in the air. " The whole sum of the tendency here is distinctly — organise a continental alliance against England," wrote Spring Rice from Berlin.[6]

In a vague and general way the Emperor William had been advocating such a policy for some time. Even after the disillusionment occasioned by the refusal of France and Russia to co-operate in the critical days after the Kruger telegram he had clung to the idea that the continental powers should stand shoulder to shoulder in order to frustrate the " designs " of England. In the Cretan-Greek

---

[4] Hohenlohe: *Denkwürdigkeiten der Reichskanzlerzeit,* p. 380; Bernhard Schwertfeger: *Amt-liche Aktenstücke zur Geschichte der Europäischen Politik, 1885–1914* (Berlin, 1925), II, no. 1; Georges Michon: *The Franco-Russian Alliance* (London, 1929), pp. 93 ff.; *Questions Diplomatiques et Coloniales,* September 1, 1897, pp. 172 ff., September 15, 1897, pp. 233 ff., for French and Euro-pean press comment.

[5] *Petersburgskaia Viedemosti and Novoie Vremiia,* quoted in *Questions Diplomatiques et Coloniales,* September 1, 1897, p. 178; October 15, 1897, p. 366.

[6] *Letters and Friendships of Sir Cecil Spring Rice,* p. 226.

crisis this policy had succeeded, much to William's delight. He was then already envisaging a broadening of the policy and a welding together of the continental powers for resistance against the tariff policies of the United States. During his visit to St. Petersburg he discussed the matter with General Obruchev, the chief of staff, and with Count Witte, the finance minister. These gentlemen seem to have been well impressed with the idea, though they were more interested in its anti-British than in its anti-American aspect. Tsar Nicholas asked the Emperor to send him a memorandum on the subject. William was so elated that he wrote his friend Eulenburg:

"The visit to Russia turned out far better than I expected, and in several exhaustive discussions I reached *complete agreement* with Nicky on all important political questions, so that together we have, so to say, disposed of the world. A restoration of Alsace and Lorraine to France by Russian aid is an *absolute and downright impossibility*. Thus a war between Gaul and us and Russia and us is, God willing, *no longer* to be feared. The *Continental blockade* against America, and, *it may be,* England has been *decided* upon. Russia has *pledged* herself to bring France over to the idea *bon gré mal gré.*" [7]

The Emperor's enthusiasm was distinctly premature and exaggerated. Witte was plainly unwilling to become involved in a policy of excluding American products, and it was more than doubtful whether the French could ever be won over either to the tariff scheme or to the league against England. Furthermore, it can be shown quite conclusively that the German foreign office did not share the Emperor's sanguine hopes. William was impulsive, but at bottom he was himself never prepared to go the limit of an anti-British policy. His advisers, from Hohenlohe to Holstein, were more than dubious about a continental league and were genuinely anxious not to antagonize England too much. They never went so far as to join France in challenging the British position in Egypt. All they wanted was to scare Britain into taking a more considerate attitude toward German aspirations in the field of world politics. When, in September 1897, General Obruchev suggested to Bülow the conclusion of a defensive and offensive alliance for three years between the continental powers, the Germans not only evaded, they actually empowered the ambassador at London to communicate this interesting item to Lord Salisbury! [8]

The upshot of it all was that in practice the continental "combine" was

---

[7] Bülow: *Memoirs*, I, pp. 160–1; see further *Die Grosse Politik*, XIII, nos. 3426, 3433, 3438; "Kuropatkin Diary" (*Krasnyi Arkhiv*, II, p. 10); *The Memoirs of Count Witte*, pp. 408–10; Claus Grimm: *Graf Witte und die Deutsche Politik* (Freiburg, 1930), pp. 16–7, 25. There is a good anonymous account and defense of the German policy under the title "Der Zusammenschluss der Kontinentalen Mächte" in *Die Grenzboten*, 1897 (III), pp. 577–94. See also the discerning analysis of the international situation by E. J. Dillon: "The New Political Era" (*Contemporary Review*, November, 1897, pp. 609–31). The study of Hilde Prowaseck: *Der Gedanke einer Kontinentalliga gegen England unter Wilhelm II* (Leipzig, 1928), is almost worthless.

[8] *Die Grosse Politik*, XIII, nos. 3451–2; Hohenlohe: *Denkwürdigkeiten*, pp. 261, 296–7, 393–4. The point is well discussed in Michalik: *Probleme des Deutschen Flottenbaues*, pp. 77 ff., and in Friedrich von Trotha: *Fritz von Holstein* (Berlin, 1931), pp. 177 ff.

little more than the pursuit of a common policy in the Near East and in the Far East. It had been born in the united action of Russia, Germany and France in intervening at Shimonoseki in 1895 and it continued to function best in the further development of the Chinese problem.

Since the intervention of the three powers against Japan in 1895 the policy of Germany in the Far East had been dominated by two ideas: to engage Russia in Asia and thus weaken the Franco-Russian Alliance as it touched Europe; and to secure, through Russian support, some sort of commercial and naval base in Chinese waters. Time and again in the years from 1895 to 1898 Emperor William wrote the Tsar that Germany would keep Europe quiet and guard her rear while she was busy in Manchuria. To Muraviev he said in January 1897: "Even if you had to send all your troops to the East, following political aims in accordance with your interests, I not only will not attack France, but will not allow anyone in Europe to stir; there, that is what I mean by my promise to guarantee your rear." [9] The Emperor may have been genuinely impressed by the so-called Yellow Peril. Many remarks of his would seem to testify to the fact. But at the same time he saw how useful an argument this cultural danger would be in discussion with so religious a person as the Tsar. In 1895 he had had the German artist, H. Knackfuss, draw an allegorical picture from an imperial design. The first copy of this was presented to the Tsar. In William's own words: "It shows the powers of Europe represented by their respective Genii called together by the Arch-Angel Michael, — sent from Heaven, — to *unite* in resisting the inroads of Buddhism, heathenism and barbarism for the Defence of the Cross. Stress is especially laid on the *united* resistance of *all* European Powers, which is just as necessary also against our common internal foes, anarchism, republicanism, nihilism." The picture was lurid enough to stir even the most immovable. On a high rock overlooking a rich and prosperous plain stood Michael, while the European powers in female personification (Germany, France and Russia in the lead, Austria taking reluctant England by the hand, Italy in the background) were gazing upon the distant menace. Behind them in the sky was a gleaming cross, while on the farther side of the plain, enveloped in flame and riding a dragon, was a figure of Buddha, not at all blood-curdling, but pensive and contemplative. [10]

So much for the general policy of Germany with regard to the Far Eastern situation. The special problem confronting the Berlin government was to find the necessary props for the world policy that was being initiated. Unlike England and France, Germany had no coaling stations or naval bases scattered over the world. In the years from 1895 to 1900 much of her world policy hinged upon this search for foreign establishments. The West Indies, the Brazilian coast, the

[9] F. V. Kelyin: "Zagranichnoe Puteshestvie M. N. Muraviева v 1897 g." (*Krasnyi Arkhiv*, XLVII, 1931, pp. 71–89), pp. 86 ff. See also *The Kaiser's Letters to the Tsar* (London, 1920), pp. 10, 11, 13, 27.

[10] *The Kaiser's Letters to the Tsar*, pp. 17 ff. The picture is reproduced and described in Arthur Diosy: *The New Far East* (London, 1898), pp. 326 ff.

Philippines and other Pacific islands, and especially the Chinese coast, were surveyed with this object in view. Here again the Emperor was the moving spirit. In the very midst of the war between China and Japan he was already urging that advantage be taken of the situation to secure what Germany needed. After all, German commerce in China was second only to the English. Yet Germany possessed no commercial base like Hongkong, no coaling station, no docking and repairing facilities, no fortified naval post. She was dependent almost entirely upon Hongkong, which meant that she was dependent on British good will.

The conclusion of peace between China and Japan and Germany's championing of the Chinese cause seemed to offer a rare opportunity for the realization of German desires. The prospect of a reward certainly had some bearing upon German policy in the spring of 1895. Unfortunately, however, the foreign office did not share the Emperor's eagerness in the matter, and — more unfortunately yet — there was no agreement as to the place to be demanded. Everyone who was consulted recommended a different locality. The arguments between the admiral on the spot, the naval high command, the ministry of marine and the foreign office were so interminable that years elapsed before a definite decision could be reached. Many years before this the German geographer, Baron von Richthofen, had recommended Kiao-chow, on the south side of the Shantung Peninsula, pointing out the value of the coal deposits in that region, the high quality of the inhabitants and the nearness of the north China market. But Kiao-chow made little appeal, since it was not on one of the main trade arteries, would require large expenditures for development, and, it was believed, was not entirely ice-free in winter. The naval authorities at first insisted on the acquisition of two bases, one in the north and one in the south. Their preference was for the Chusan Islands in the Bay of Hangchow, near the mouth of the Yangtze, and for Amoy, which lay opposite Formosa. Neither of these places, however, proved feasible, for in 1846 the Chinese government had promised the British government never to alienate Chusan, while Amoy, being a treaty port, could hardly be secured without conflict with other powers. The naval authorities kept coming back to these places, but in the meanwhile other possibilities were canvassed: the Montebello Islands, off the Korean coast; Weihaiwei on the north side of the Shantung Peninsula; Wusung at the mouth of the Yangtze; Samsah Bay, just north of Foochow; and Mirs Bay, near Hongkong. Occasionally Kiao-chow was mentioned, but no one seemed impressed with its possibilities. Despite the Emperor's constant prodding no great progress was made and the Chinese government, when the matter was first broached in the autumn of 1895, treated it evasively, pointing out that to abandon or even lease a port to the Germans would whet the appetite of the other powers and possibly result in a concerted attack upon China's territorial integrity.

In the summer of 1896 Tirpitz went to the Far East as commander of the German squadron stationed in Chinese waters. At the same time the easy-going

German minister at Peking, Schenck von Schweinsberg, was replaced by Baron von Heyking, who had made a reputation for energy as representative of his government in Cairo. These two men, it was hoped, would be able to accomplish something. But even they could not agree. Heyking continued to insist upon Amoy, though Tirpitz, after careful investigation, came to the conclusion that the easiest and most profitable acquisition, from almost every point of view, would be Kiao-chow. The Emperor was very eager to do something in the autumn of 1896, but the squadron was not in condition to act and differences of opinion paralyzed action. It was not until an expert in harbor construction, Georg Franzius, was sent out and reported favorably in the summer of 1897 that Kiao-chow Bay was definitely decided upon.[11]

In choosing a suitable location on the Chinese coast the German government had, from the start, tried to avoid collision with either British or Russian interests. Chusan, which was probably the most desirable of all the stations considered, was finally rejected because of the British interests and claims. With Kiao-chow it was long feared that the Russians had a lien on the place. Their Far Eastern squadron had wintered there in the season of 1895–1896 and in the newspaper reports of the Russian-Chinese Treaty (the so-called Cassini Convention) it was said that the Chinese had granted the Russians a lease of Kiao-chow for a period of fifteen years. It was considered necessary, therefore, to clear up this important point. On inquiry it turned out that the Chinese government refused to recognize any Russian rights to the place. Admiral Alexeiev, the commander of the Russian Far Eastern squadron, admitted to Tirpitz that the place had been considered by the admiralty, but said it had been rejected. At St. Petersburg the foreign office did not pretend that the Russians had rights in Kiao-chow, though the foreign minister, Count Muraviev, and the minister to China, Count Cassini, were evidently displeased by the prospect of a German occupation and tried to discourage the plan. Cassini, to be sure, egged on the Germans to help themselves, but he was very anxious to have them locate themselves in the south, where they would come into conflict with the English.[12]

In order to clarify the Russian attitude it was decided that Emperor William, during his visit to St. Petersburg in August 1897, should take up the matter directly with the Tsar. Nicholas replied to William's query that Russia was interested merely in assuring herself access to the bay until she had obtained a more northern harbor already selected, namely Ping-yang, on the northwest coast of Korea. There was no objection whatever, he said, to German ships anchoring at Kiao-chow in case of need, after securing the consent of the Rus-

---

11 The main sources are *Die Grosse Politik*, XIV, chap. xc (A); Tirpitz: *Memoirs*, chap. viii; Elisabeth von Heyking: *Tagebücher aus vier Weltteilen, 1886–1904* (Fourth edition, Leipzig, 1926), chap. v; Hohenlohe: *Denkwürdigkeiten*, pp. 279 ff.; George Franzius: *Kiautschou* (Seventh edition, Berlin, 1900); Gérard: *Ma Mission en Chine*, pp. 156, 207–10. All this material, together with some unpublished correspondence, is so well reviewed in Arthur J. Irmer: *Die Erwerbung von Kiautschou, 1894–1898* (Cologne, 1930), chaps. i–iv, that it has seemed unnecessary to go into greater detail or to give more specific references.   12 See especially Heyking, op. cit., pp. 192, 214.

sian naval authorities. On the German side the Tsar's declaration was taken to mean approval of Germany's desire to make use of the port. Toward the end of September the Chinese government was informed of Germany's intention, Baron Heyking making special reference to the approval of the Russian government. A few weeks later the St. Petersburg foreign office was officially notified. The news seems to have made a bad impression. Count Lamsdorff, chief assistant to the foreign minister, immediately pointed out that the Germans had agreed to secure the assent of the Russian naval authorities on the spot. Why the German government had ignored this point it is hard to say: possibly because there were no Russian ships at Kiao-chow. However that may have been, they did give the Russians an opening for opposition by not keeping to the strict letter of the St. Petersburg arrangement.[13]

On the German side the plan seems to have been to send the Far Eastern squadron to winter at Kiao-chow as a first move in extorting the concession of the port from the Chinese. In the discussions with the Russians mention had been made only of the right to use the harbor. But on November 1 (not November 4 as stated by Joseph and many other writers) two German Catholic missionaries in southern Shantung were killed by a Chinese gang in the course of an attempted robbery.[14] The incident came most conveniently. The news reached Germany on November 5 and was confirmed on November 7. Between these two dates the Emperor had already determined on a course of action. Thoroughly tired of procrastinating and absolutely convinced that nothing could ever be secured from the Chinese without a show of force, he suggested that the squadron be immediately sent to Kiao-chow, that it occupy the Chinese settlement and threaten heavy reprisals unless the Chinese authorities at once agreed to a heavy indemnity and to the punishment of the offenders: " I am firmly determined to give up our over-cautious policy which is regarded as weak throughout eastern Asia, and to demonstrate through the use of sternness and if necessary of the most brutal ruthlessness toward the Chinese, that the German Emperor cannot be trifled with."

Prince Hohenlohe was not so completely carried away by the incident. He warned the Emperor that an occupation of Kiao-chow would require the consent of the Russian government, according to the agreement made in August. With a sense of humiliation the Emperor therefore wired to the Tsar: " Chinese attacked German missions Shantung, inflicting loss of life and property. I trust you approve according to our conversation Peterhof my sending German squadron to Kiautschou, as it is the only port available to operate from as a base against maurauders. I am under obligations to catholic party in Germany to

---

[13] *Die Grosse Politik*, XIV, nos. 3679 ff.; Irmer, op. cit., chap. v. The account given by Dillon: *The Eclipse of Russia*, pp. 245 ff. and by Witte: *Memoirs*, pp. 98–9 is distinctly misleading.

[14] It is generally stated, on the basis of a report in the *North China Herald*, November 17, 1897, that the missionaries were killed by members of an anti-foreign organization. The Chinese sources do not bear this out, as I see from an unpublished dissertation by Benjamin M. Bee: *The Leasing of Kiaochow* (Cambridge, 1935), pp. 166 ff.

show that their missions are really safe under my protectorate." To which Nicholas replied promptly: "Cannot approve, nor disapprove Your sending German Squadron to Kiao-Chou, as I have lately learned that this harbour only had been temporarily ours in 1895–1896." This was enough for the Emperor. Orders were at once despatched to the admiral in command in Chinese waters, and William wrote to Bülow, who happened to be in Rome: "Thousands of German Christians will breathe easier, when they know that the German Emperor's ships are near; hundreds of German traders will revel in the knowledge that the German Empire has at last secured a firm footing in Asia; hundreds of thousands of Chinese will quiver when they feel the iron fist of Germany heavy on their necks; and the whole German nation will be delighted that its government has done a manly act." [15]

The Emperor was in a state of high elation: a sense of outraged national honor, religious sentiment and thirst for conquest all combined to call forth an almost abnormal emotional outburst. But within a day or two the Russians turned a cold douche on the Emperor's enthusiasm. On November 9 the Russian chargé d'affaires at Berlin handed in two telegrams from Count Muraviev in which the Russian foreign minister declared that Russia would do all that was possible to induce the Chinese to give satisfaction for the murder of the missionaries, but at the same time set forth a Russian claim to Kiao-chow. According to Muraviev Russia had received from China a right of first anchorage (droit de premier mouillage) which amounted to priority if ever the port were to be alienated to another power. Therefore the Russian admiral had been instructed to enter the port with his ships in the event that the Germans attempted to do so.

These telegrams came like a bombshell to the Germans. In the foreign office there was something akin to panic. The Emperor was not in Berlin; neither was the chancellor or the foreign minister. Holstein seems to have been convinced that the news from Russia put Germany before the alternatives of war or retraction. He had been opposed all along to the Emperor's Chinese policy and was deeply distrustful of the Russians. Now his feeling was that the Germans would have to withdraw and give up their plans. Both the Emperor and Hohenlohe, however, took a somewhat calmer attitude. William stood firmly by the Tsar's telegram and insisted that the admiral in the Far East should follow the instructions already sent him. Russia, he was convinced, would not start a war about Kiao-chow. Hohenlohe shared this conviction, adding that Muraviev was evidently attempting a game of intimidation and bluff.[16]

For ten days to two weeks the situation was really tense, with constant exchange of telegrams between Berlin and St. Petersburg. The Germans refused to recognize any earlier arrangements and insisted on the letter of the Tsar's

---

[15] *Die Grosse Politik*, XIV, nos. 3688–90.

[16] *Die Grosse Politik*, XIV, nos. 3693 ff.; Hohenlohe: *Denkwürdigkeiten der Reichskanzlerzeit*, pp. 409 ff.

telegram, which Muraviev attempted to explain away. At the same time they repulsed all efforts of the Russians to act as mediators in securing satisfaction for Germany. Both Hohenlohe and Bülow spoke very frankly to the Russian ambassador at Berlin, Count Osten-Sacken, pointing out that Russia should be glad to see Germany establish herself in the Far East and that the German occupation of Kiao-chow would not hinder the Russians from using the port. He encouraged the Russians to take a port of their own, meaning, presumably, Port Arthur. At the same time it was indicated to Osten-Sacken that if the Russians persisted in their stiff attitude, it might be necessary for the Germans to turn toward the west for support.[17]

The Germans did, in fact, sound out the British at the very height of the crisis. Hatzfeldt was empowered, if necessary, to offer the British compensation in the form of a free hand in south Africa and in the southern part of the Portuguese colony of Mozambique, including Delagoa Bay. He was to hint that in the event of British opposition to Germany's action it might be necessary for the Germans to get out of the scrape by paying a "high price," by which was probably meant the purchase of an alliance with Russia. On the other hand the ambassador was given permission to show Lord Salisbury the suggestions made by Obruchev for an offensive and defensive alliance between Russia, France and Germany against Britain. Whether the proposal was ever communicated to the English prime minister cannot be said. Hatzfeldt found the British statesman rather well disposed. Despite the fact that the English press was almost as rabid in its denunciations as the Russian, Salisbury appears to have thought that the German enterprise would lead to friction between Russia and Germany and that in any event the Germans at Kiao-chow would serve as a useful counterweight to the Russians in the north. At any rate he raised no objection to the German action and thus strengthened the Berlin government in its dealings with Russia.[18]

In the meanwhile the German admiral, Diederichs, had landed troops in Kiao-chow Bay on November 14. The Germans were working out their demands upon the Chinese government. They had now decided to establish themselves on the Bay in any case, and therefore aimed to make their terms so stiff that the Chinese could not accept them. At the same time arrangements were made to send more ships and troops to the Far East. But despite veiled threats it proved difficult to do much with the Chinese mandarins. Russia stood behind them and gave detailed advice. The Tsungli Yamen or foreign office therefore offered to meet all the German demands, provided the troops and ships were first withdrawn from Kiao-chow. The German minister replied that this was the one point which he was not authorized to discuss. Negotiations took a different turn when the Chinese suggested that Germany give up Kiao-chow and

---

[17] Hohenlohe, op. cit., p. 413; Bülow: *Memoirs*, I, pp. 214–5.
[18] *Die Grosse Politik*, XIV, nos. 3698, 3702–4, 3708–10; R. Stanley McCordock: *British Far Eastern Policy, 1894–1900* (New York, 1931), pp. 196–7.

take some other port farther south (evidently another Russian suggestion designed to enhance the antagonism between Germany and England). Nothing could be done under these conditions. But finally, toward the close of the year, the Russians gradually withdrew their support from the Chinese and made their peace with the Germans. Baron von Heyking, the German minister at Peking, took a stronger and stronger tone until, early in January 1898, the Yamen was obliged to yield. There were many details to be worked out, and it was only on March 6 that the agreement was formally signed. Germany secured the lease of Kiao-chow for ninety-nine years, with a neutral zone fifty kilometers wide surrounding the concession. Two railroad lines (from Kiao-chow by way of Wei-hsien to Tsinanfu on the Yellow River, and from Kiao-chow to Ichow and thence to Tsinanfu) were to be constructed by a Chinese-German company. In a zone fifteen kilometers wide on either side of these lines German subjects were to be allowed to hold and develop mining properties. German nationals were also given priority in furnishing the Chinese government with personal assistance, capital or materials " for any purpose whatever within the Province of Shantung." Clearly the Chinese-German agreement gave Germany not only a naval base in China, but also a strong and promising position in the development of the whole rich Shantung province.[19]

The outstanding development of the Far Eastern crisis in the last weeks of the year 1897 was the settlement of the German-Russian dispute and the reestablishment of co-operation between the two governments. The resurrection of the entente was due in part to Germany's inflexible attitude in the matter of Kiao-chow, but chiefly to the momentous decision taken by the Russian government to salve its disappointment by occupying Port Arthur. To understand this remarkable *volte face* one must have clearly in mind the peculiar circumstances of Tsarist policy in the Far East. Why did Muraviev object so strenuously to the German occupation of Kiao-chow? Evidently because the Russians sincerely feared that the German move would result in a general scramble for Chinese territory. They wanted China to remain intact, not from altruistic motives, but because the whole Russian plan of campaign as worked out by Witte envisaged a steady peaceful penetration of Russian influence, eventual undisputed control at Peking and so something in the nature of a protectorate over all China. To be sure, the Russians were determined to secure a port in Chinese waters themselves, for Vladivostok was frozen for four to five months in the year, and even though American ice-breakers had successfully kept it open in the winters from 1895 to 1897, the port was too far north to meet Russian needs. Evidently Kiao-chow had been considered in the winter of 1895–1896, but had been given up on advice from the naval authorities and out of consideration for China.

---

    [19] The final negotiations may be followed in *Die Grosse Politik*, XIV, chap. xc (B) passim, and in Heyking, op. cit., chap. vi, which adds considerably to the documents; an important account, making full use of the Chinese sources, is to be found in the unpublished thesis of B. M. Bee, mentioned above. There is a good summary in Irmer, op. cit., chap. vii.

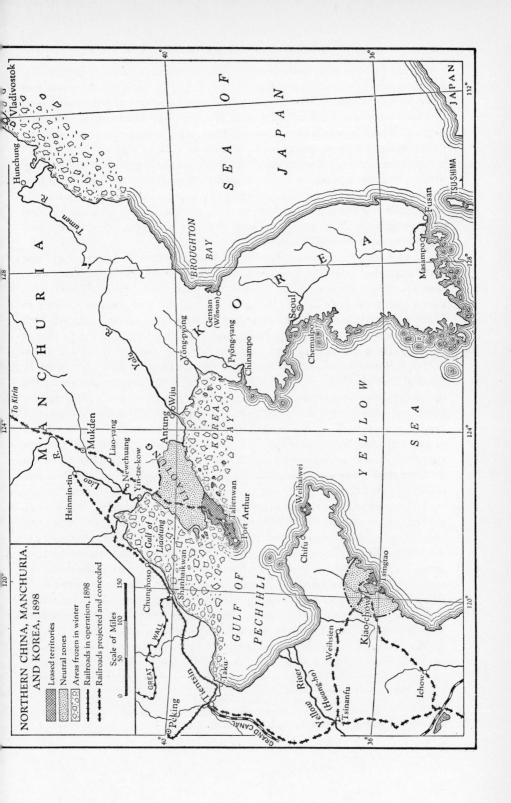

NORTHERN CHINA, MANCHURIA,
AND KOREA, 1898

Leased territories
Neutral zones
Areas frozen in winter
Railroads in operation, 1898
Railroads projected and conceded

Scale of Miles
0   50   100   150

But the problem of a Russian port in Chinese waters, which was so important from the standpoint of the naval authorities, could be easily solved without in any way compromising Russian policy in China. Good ports on the north coast of China were few. In Korea they were plentiful. Korea was supposedly independent. The Chinese government could not take umbrage at what went on there. In fact Li Hung-chang, when at Moscow in 1896, advised the Russian government to take a Korean port.[20] At that time the Tsar repudiated the suggestion. So far as one can detect, the Russians, like the Germans, had a hard time deciding what port they wanted. Naval men apparently favored Masampo, at the southern tip of the peninsula, while the Tsar, speaking to Emperor William in August 1897, indicated that Ping-yang (Phyöng-yang) on the northwest coast had all but been decided upon.[21]

The question then arises, why did the Russians not seize upon one of these ports, instead of attempting to block the action of the Germans? They were, after all, nearly all-powerful at Seoul at this time. Two factors evidently contributed to make them hesitate. In the first place the new Russian minister to Japan was convinced that a new arrangement with Japan about Korea was both possible and necessary. The Japanese armaments would be complete in 1902 or 1904, and there was always a good chance that England would support Japan and that Russia would find herself in a serious predicament. " It cannot be doubted," he reported home in September 1897, " that the immense armaments of the Japanese are directed against us and that Japan is eagerly preparing for an armed conflict with us. It is equally unquestionable that this conflict will break out over the Korean question." In his opinion the Japanese would attack as soon as Russia became involved in war in Europe or with England. Japanese statesmen desired an agreement with Russia and it would be a mistake for the St. Petersburg government to persist in its effort to establish an unofficial protectorate over Korea.[22]

This advice was not taken too seriously at first. On the contrary, the Russian government continued with the mission of officers to organize the Korean army and Witte lent his support to this policy by arranging for the establishment of the Russian-Korean Bank and by sending off his agent Kyril Alexeiev. Alexeiev arrived at Seoul early in October. On November 5 the Emperor of Korea signed with the Russian minister, M. Speyer, an agreement naming Alexeiev chief adviser to the treasury and chief superintendent of customs for an indefinite period, and specifying that in future this position should be held only by a Korean or a Russian. The move was a daring one, for the position was that of financial dictator. Since 1895 it had been held by Mr. M'Leavy Brown, formerly of the Chinese customs service, an extremely able and efficient person who had

---

[20] *Die Grosse Politik*, XIV, no. 3663.

[21] *Die Grosse Politik*, XIV, nos. 3663, 3695, 3697.

[22] G. Trubetzkoi: *Russland als Grossmacht* (Stuttgart, 1917), pp. 52–5; Baron Rosen: *Forty Years of Diplomacy* (New York, 1922), I, pp. 142–51.

in a few years straightened out the Korean finances and paid back a large part of the Japanese loan. Brown's term had not expired and he therefore refused to move. Alexeiev won over to his side the officials of the administration, whose salaries he doubled. But Brown could not be manoeuvred from his position. He was waiting for support from the British government. Before long this support was forthcoming. England had no great interests in Korea, but such as they were the government was not prepared to sacrifice them to Russia. Speaking in the house of commons in August 1897 Mr. Curzon said: " Our interests in Korea are commercial, and, first, to see that the independence of Korea is maintained, and that it is not territorially or administratively absorbed into the Empire of Russia; secondly, that Korean territory and Korean harbours are not made the base for schemes for territorial aggrandizement, so as to disturb the balance in the Far East and give to one Power a maritime supremacy in the Eastern seas." In pursuance of this policy the British government determined to act. We know nothing of the negotiations with Russia following Brown's dismissal. Perhaps there were none. But a strong British squadron composed of nine cruisers and accompanied by a few Japanese ships suddenly appeared late in December in the harbor of Chemulpo. The hint was enough for the Russians. After some talk Brown was reinstated, and in March 1898 Alexeiev was recalled.[23]

It must have been quite obvious to the Russian authorities that action in Korea would certainly lead to trouble. Both the British and the Japanese were opposed to the acquisition by Russia of territory in Korea. Under the circumstances Muraviev would have preferred blocking the German action at Kiao-chow. But he was unable to do so. The appeals of the Chinese for support could not be heeded for long. Orders to the Russian squadron to repair to Kiao-chow had to be countermanded. For not even Muraviev could explain away the Tsar's compromising telegram of November 7, which gave the Germans practically a free hand. Yet something had to be done, and so the Russian minister decided that the proper course of action would be to follow the example of Germany. On November 23 he presented to the Tsar a memorandum in which he pointed out that circumstances were favorable and that Russia should not allow the opportunity to slip by for occupying the Chinese port of Talien-wan at the southern tip of the Liaotung Peninsula. Russia had in years past considered Kiao-chow as a possible naval base, but it was now " inconvenient " to order the Far Eastern squadron to that port. Nicholas agreed that it was " inconvenient." On November 26 he presided over a council of ministers to discuss the Muraviev memorandum. Those present were Muraviev, Witte, Vannovsky (minister of war) and Tyrtov (minister of marine). The foreign minister repeated his argument: this was the time to secure both Talienwan and

[23] *Korean Repository,* January, 1898, pp. 35–6, September, 1897, pp. 353–4, November, 1897, pp. 434–5; Glinskii: *Prolog Russko-Iaponskoi Voiny,* pp. 64–5; F. A. McKenzie: *The Tragedy of Korea* (London, 1918), pp. 94–5; William F. Sands: *Undiplomatic Memories* (New York, 1930), p. 52.

Port Arthur, which was close by. But his proposal met with the bitterest opposition, especially from Witte. The finance minister insisted that such action would be contrary to the spirit of the Moscow Treaty of 1896. If Japan followed the example of Germany and took territory in China, Russia would be obliged to come to China's assistance. Yet now it was proposed that she should do the very thing that she had promised to prevent others from doing. The proper course of action would be not to imitate Germany, but to send the Russian squadron to Kiao-chow and do everything to force the Germans to withdraw.

To these arguments Muraviev replied that the treaty with China obliged Russia to aid only in resisting an attack upon China or Korea by Japan. As for Kiao-chow, " peculiar circumstances " made it impossible for Russia to prevent the German occupation. Witte remained unconvinced. The war minister threw the responsibility for choosing the proper naval base upon the minister of marine. Tyrtov was perfectly frank: the naval authorities had examined and considered Port Arthur and had found it not very suitable. The best thing would be to get along with Vladivostok for a few more years in the hope of ultimately getting a port in Korea.

Not a single minister supported the plan put forward by Muraviev. Witte redoubled his attack upon the scheme. Of course Russia needed a base in the Far East, he said. But that was a question of time, and could be settled by peaceful methods. Who would have believed a few years before that Russia would so easily secure the right to run the railroad through Manchuria? If Russia maintained her traditional policy and played her cards right she would get everything she needed without the use of force. These arguments evidently carried the day. For the time being the Muraviev plan was shelved.[24]

But Muraviev did not relinquish his scheme. The Tsar was with him, and the Germans were constantly assuring Russia that their presence at Kiao-chow would make it easier for them to support the Tsarist policy in the Far East. So Muraviev proceeded, carefully feeling his way. On December 14 the German government was informed that, with the consent of the Chinese government, a detachment of the Russian Far Eastern squadron would temporarily anchor at Port Arthur. The Tsar, persuaded " that Russia and Germany ought and could go hand in hand in the Far East," wished the German government to be informed of this fact. The Emperor William's delight can be better imagined than described. He summoned the Russian ambassador and assured him of Germany's support and good will: " Your enemies, whether they be called Japanese or English, now become my enemies, and every trouble maker, who-

---

[24] The best and most detailed accounts in Glinskii, op. cit., pp. 43 ff. and in Romanov: *Rossiia v Manchzhurii*, pp. 186 ff.; but see also Dillon: *The Eclipse of Russia*, p. 249; Witte: *Memoirs*, pp. 99 ff.; Rosen, op. cit., I, p. 156; Alexander Iswolski: *Memoirs of an Ambassador* (New York, 1921), pp. 119 ff. The Muraviev memorandum of November 23 has now been published by A. Popov: " Pervie Shagi Russkogo Imperializma na Dal'nem Vostoke " (*Krasnyi Arkhiv*, LII, 1932, pp. 34-124), pp. 103 ff.

ever he be, who wishes to hinder your intentions by force, will meet the German squadron side by side with your warships." [25] His brother, Prince Henry, was just about to leave for the Far East with additional ships and troops. On the evening of December 16 the Emperor gave him a farewell dinner in the castle at Kiel. He there made one of his most bombastic and extravagant speeches, talking as though his brother were embarking on a mission of the greatest danger:

> " Make it clear to every European there, to the German merchant, and, above all things, to the foreigner in whose country we are or with whom we have to deal, that the German Michael has set his shield, decorated with the imperial eagle, firmly upon the ground. Whoever asks him for protection will always receive it. . . . But if any one should undertake to insult us in our rights or wish to harm us, then drive in with the mailed fist and, as God wills, bind about your young brow the laurels which no one in the entire German Empire will begrudge you."

To which Henry replied that his sole purpose was " to declare abroad the gospel of your Majesty's anointed person; to preach it to everyone who will hear it, and also to those who will not hear it."

This high-flown language was undoubtedly due in part to the changed attitude of Russia. At any rate the German congratulations upon the Tsar's decision were hardly less remarkable. The Emperor applauded the energetic measure which Nicholas had taken and hailed the re-establishment of the Russian-German entente in the Far East. " Russia and Germany at the entrance of the Yellow Sea," he wired the Tsar, " may be taken as represented by St. George and St. Michael shielding the Holy Cross in the Far East and guarding the Gates to the Continent of Asia. May you be able fully to realise the plans you often unrolled to me; my sympathy and help shall not fail in case of need." [26]

Emperor William understood well enough that the mission of Russian ships to Port Arthur was simply the prelude to the acquisition of the place. Witte must have known it too, but it was hard for him to object so long as no definite move was made in that direction. Muraviev claimed that the Russian fleet was sent to forestall action by the British, and he asserted further that the Chinese government had " invited " the measure. This was certainly not the fact. The Russian representative at Peking knew nothing about the matter until he received a telegram from the Russian admiral. He then had to convince the Chinese that the ships were being sent for China's protection. [27]

For many weeks it was not clear what was to happen at Port Arthur. The Japanese were much excited by the appearance of the Russians in the very port

---

[25] L. Teleshev: " Vil'gel'm II o Zaniatii Tsarskoi Rossiei Port-Arthura " (Krasnyi Arkhiv, LVIII, 1933, pp. 150–5).

[26] Die Grosse Politik, XIV, nos. 3733, 3734, 3739; Bülow: Memoirs, I, pp. 236 ff.

[27] Glinskii, op. cit., p. 48; and especially B. Romanov: " Konzessia na Yalu " (Russkoie Proshloye, I, 1923, pp. 87–108), p. 93.

from which they themselves had been debarred in 1895 on the plea that the presence of a foreign power there would be a menace to the independence of China. The press, already much wrought up by Germany's occupation of Kiao-chow and by recent developments in Korea, became violent in its denunciations.[28] Some diplomats, like Hayashi and Kato, the minister at London, favored an arrangement with England and co-operation against the Far Eastern Triplice, but other influential figures, like Ito, Inouye, and the foreign minister Nishi, still hoped that an agreement could be come to with Russia. In December advances for an alliance with China were made to some of the most powerful governors in the Yangtze region. Chang Chih-tung, the influential viceroy of Liang-hu, strongly recommended the alliance with Japan and England to the Peking authorities, but the Tsungli Yamen was set on a policy of non-resistance, which was based on the fear that war might lead to the loss of all important coastal towns. At Peking the distrust of England was very great, and there was, in addition, a chronic sense of fear of China's " friend," Russia.[29] Whether Muraviev learned of the Japanese soundings we do not know, but he evidently saw the need of appeasing the indignation of the Japanese. In January 1898 he suggested an accommodation. The Tokyo government thereupon proposed that Russia accept a free hand in Manchuria in return for similar freedom of action for Japan in Korea. This was more than the Russian government was prepared to concede, but negotiations were under way and finally resulted, in April 1898, in the Rosen-Nishi agreement, which will have to be discussed later.[30]

Had the English taken a stronger stand the Japanese might have been less ready to compromise with the Russians. But in British government circles, as in the Japanese, there was divided opinion. Lord Salisbury appears to have favored a waiting game, and gave no encouragement to Kato. Chamberlain, on the other hand, favored at least an understanding with Japan, and Curzon, at that time undersecretary for foreign affairs, strongly urged the need for such an agreement: " If the European Powers are grouping themselves against us in the Far East, we shall probably be driven sooner or later to act with Japan. Ten years hence she will be the greatest naval Power in those seas, and the European Powers who now ignore or flout her will be then competing for her alliance. . . . I argue for a watching attitude, but for a determination to pounce the moment anyone else pounces." [31] Other influential members of the government, like Hicks Beach, insisted on continuing the policy of the last years and striving for an arrangement with Russia. Even Chamberlain, speaking to the Russian am-

---

[28] See H. W. Wilson: " England and Japan " (*Fortnightly Review*, March, 1898, pp. 503–12).

[29] This is all drawn from the Chinese sources, as reported in the manuscript thesis of B. M. Bee, pp. 315 ff. and appendix A.

[30] Rosen, op. cit., I, pp. 155–8; Trubetzkoi, op. cit., pp. 59 ff.; *The Secret Memoirs of Count Tadasu Hayashi* (New York, 1915), p. 93.

[31] Garvin: *Life of Chamberlain*, III, p. 249; Curzon to Salisbury, December 29, 1897 (Earl of Ronaldshay: *The Life of Lord Curzon*, London, 1928, I, pp. 278–9). For British press opinion in favor of an alliance with Japan see Chung-Fu Chang: *The Anglo-Japanese Alliance* (Baltimore, 1931), pp. 63 ff.

bassador, declared that in his view there was only one sane policy for England to follow: that of an entente with Russia and *par ricochet* with France.[32]

It is almost always stated by writers on the subject that British policy in the Far East at this time rested firmly upon the principle of Chinese integrity. Britain's interests were largely commercial; she wished to preserve the Chinese Empire because it was a huge market; if it were divided, large parts of it would be shut off by high tariff barriers.

The argument seems logical enough, and with certain qualifications it may be accepted. But it must be remembered that since 1895 many of the most competent writers on Chinese affairs entertained grave doubts whether the Empire could be kept intact. Henry Norman, for example, was convinced that before long it would be partitioned among the powers. Demetrius Boulger in 1895 predicted the course of Russian policy and insisted that, since dismemberment was certain, England should arrange to take over southern China. Holt Hallett declared the only solution to be a division of the spoils. England should take over the Yangtze Valley, Kuantung and Yunnan, and abandon the rest of southern China to France. Japan and Russia could settle the division of the north between them. Archibald Colquhoun agreed that China was no longer an effective buffer, and that Britain should therefore occupy the Yangtze region and southern China.[33]

So far as the British government was concerned, the evidence would seem to indicate the same doubt as to the endurance of the Celestial Kingdom or the possibility of preventing encroachment upon it by other powers. The materials on British policy are by no means adequate for a final judgment, but there are certain illuminating points. For example, in February 1896 a member of the government, Mr. Balfour, had in a public speech all but invited the Russians to secure for themselves an ice-free port, while immediately afterward Mr. Curzon had made it clear that this port should not be in Korea. It could, then, be only in China. In the same spirit England showed no great objection to the German action at Kiao-chow. It must be concluded then that the British, while desiring the integrity of China, were prepared to see this principle infringed to a certain extent by other powers in order to prevent its being discarded entirely. It seems that in the autumn of 1897 the British were ready to go even further in their anxiety to reach an agreement with Russia. The evidence may be found in the correspondence regarding the so-called Kinder incident. Mr. Kinder had for many years been in the employ of the Chinese government. He was a very able engineer who was in charge of the Chinese railways running north from Tientsin toward Manchuria. From October to December 1897 the Russian representative

[32] Meyendorff: *Correspondance de M. de Staal*, II, pp. 355–8. See also Victoria Hicks Beach: *Life of Sir Michael Hicks Beach* (London, 1932), II, pp. 58–9.

[33] Henry Norman: *The Peoples and Politics of the Far East* (New York, 1895), p. 593; Demetrius C. Boulger: "The New Situation in the Far East" (*Contemporary Review*, December, 1895, pp. 815–25); Holt S. Hallett: "The Partition of China" (*Nineteenth Century*, January, 1898, pp. 154–64); Archibald R. Colquhoun: *China in Transformation* (New York, 1898), p. 140.

at Peking, M. Pavlov, tried repeatedly to have him removed or transferred and to have a Russian engineer put in his place. In the course of discussion with the British minister, Sir Claude MacDonald, Pavlov said quite frankly " that the Russian Government intended that the provinces of China bordering on the Russian frontier must not come under the influence of any nation except Russia." To this pretension the British government, so far as the documents show, raised no objection, though it did insist on the retention of Kinder as it insisted on the retention of Brown in Korea.[34]

It would certainly be going too far to deduce from this that England was ready to abandon northern China to Russia. But British statesmen no longer had much confidence in their ability to uphold the principle of Chinese integrity. When it was learned that the Russian squadron had gone to Port Arthur, Chamberlain wrote to Salisbury to point out that English opinion would demand " some sensational action " on the part of the government. To this Salisbury replied with his usual amusing cynicism that he had no doubt that the public would require " some territorial or cartographic consolation in China." " It will not be useful," he added, " and it will be expensive; but as a matter of pure sentiment, we shall have to do it. I think it will be Chusan." [35] From which we may conclude that Salisbury was already more or less reconciled to a policy of grab. One gets the impression that the British government was interested above all things in the preservation not of China's territorial integrity but in the maintenance of the open door in the territories that were lost. In the Kiao-chow affair the London cabinet made its acquiescence in German action conditional on the principle of equal opportunity and no special privileges. The Germans refused to give a formal undertaking of this nature, but met the British desires in an informal way.[36]

What the fate of the territories coveted by Russia would be was still a matter of doubt. As between Russia and England the matter was fought out over the question of a loan to China and the conditions of such a loan. The Peking government required funds for the payment of the third and last installment of the indemnity to Japan. Negotiations had been opened with both British and Russian interests in June 1897, but the conditions, of which we know nothing much, appear to have been too hard and the matter was postponed. Now, on December 14, Li Hung-chang approached the Russians with renewed proposals. Witte on December 26 submitted his conditions, of which the most important were the following: only Russian subjects were to be permitted to build railroads and establish industrial enterprises in the three provinces of Manchuria and in Mongolia; China was to grant to the Chinese Eastern Railway Company a concession to construct a branch line to whatever port the company might choose

[34] China No. I (1898), nos. 13, 14, 19, 38, 44; Kent: Railway Enterprise in China, p. 51; McCordock: British Far Eastern Policy, pp. 176 ff.; A. Popov: " Anglo-Russkoe Soglashenie o Razdele Kitaiia " (Krasnyi Arkhiv, XXV, 1927, pp. 113-34), p. 113.

[35] Garvin: Life of Chamberlain, III, pp. 248-9.

[36] China No. I (1898), nos. 17, 21, 24, 39, etc.; Die Grosse Politik, XIV, nos. 3747, 3750.

on the Yellow Sea east of the town of Yin-tse (mouth of the Liao-ho and port for Newchuang); China was to allow Russia to construct a port in the harbor chosen, with the exclusive right for Russian ships to enter.[37]

The object of the Chinese was evidently to play off one side against the other in the matter of the loan, for even before the Russian conditions were known, advances had been made to the British minister, Sir Claude MacDonald. At the latter's suggestion the London government too laid down conditions which can in no sense be described as modest. The Chinese were to allow the necessary control of the revenue to ensure repayment; to sanction the building of a railway from the Burmese frontier to the Yangtze Valley; to guarantee not to cede any territory in the Yangtze Valley to any other power; to make Talienwan a treaty port; to permit greater freedom of internal trade, and to free foreign goods from likin (internal customs) in the treaty ports.[38]

We need not here enter upon a discussion of the long and involved negotiations which took place during January 1898 with respect to this loan. The Chinese wanted the money to pay off the indemnity and thus secure the evacuation of Weihaiwei by the Japanese. They took the opportunity to bring Russia and England on the scene to counterbalance each other. The Russians saw their chance to put forward the demand for a port on the Yellow Sea and a railway from the Transsiberian to this port. The English on the other hand did not want to let the chance slip by for checkmating the French designs in southwest China, for safeguarding the market of the great Yangtze Valley and for blocking the known designs of the Russians by demanding that Talienwan be made a treaty port. As for the Chinese, they miscalculated very seriously, for the conditions on both sides were very hard, and they soon found themselves sailing between Scylla and Charybdis. The Russian minister at Peking declared that refusal of the Russian terms would " entail an interruption of the friendly relations " between the two governments. His British colleague warned the Tsungli Yamen that any attempt to exclude Britain from the loan would " seriously imperil " relations between China and England. A suggestion by Li Hung-chang that the loan be divided between England and Russia was not taken up. The attempt to raise the money by a domestic loan failed completely. What were the Chinese to do?

As between the conditions set by the two opponents the demands of the British, hard as they were, represented the lesser evil. The one proposition that even Li Hung-chang had steadfastly refused to consider was the Russian plan for a harbor on the Yellow Sea and a railway from there to the Transsiberian. In vain Li tried to induce them to select a harbor in Korea near the mouth of the Yalu. In vain the Russian government authorized its agents to bribe Li and his associates to the tune of a million rubles and more. Nothing could move

---

[37] Glinskii, op. cit., p. 47 ff.; Romanov: *Rossiia v Manchzhurii*, pp. 191 ff.; the terms as given in *China No. 1 (1898)*, no. 26 are incorrect in several respects, and the argumentation of writers like Joseph and McCordock has suffered from their reliance exclusively upon this source.

[38] *China No. 1 (1898)*, nos. 30, 46.

the Tsungli Yamen. The Russian demand had confirmed its worst fears. The Russians were asked for a written promise to evacuate Port Arthur. Muraviev evaded, and said that the Russian ships would leave " when circumstances permitted." There could be no further doubt of the Russian designs. The Chinese thereupon all but invited the British to send a few ships to Port Arthur, where they arrived from Korea early in January 1898.

The Peking court was gradually turning toward England. The British demands were never met in connexion with the loan, but the Chinese government finally agreed to several important concessions. It had been rumored that the Russians were insisting that the position of inspector-general of the Chinese customs, a post long held by Sir Robert Hart, should be given to a Russian when it became vacant. The Chinese agreed that the post should remain in the hands of an Englishman so long as British trade with China exceeded that of any other nation. They further engaged never to cede territory in the Yangtze Basin to any other power. Once these concessions were secured the British did not press for the other points, and the Chinese government in February 1898 signed an agreement with the Hongkong and Shanghai Bank (an English concern) for a private loan. Therewith this difficult problem was gotten out of the way.[39]

The discussions of January caused acute tension in Anglo-Russian relations. It is hard to see what the British were driving at when they demanded the opening of Talienwan as a treaty port. Most of the English ministers seem to have been favorable to an understanding with Russia, and they had, after all, invited Russia to find a commercial outlet on the Yellow Sea. Now Talienwan was the only possible port for the purpose, as all the others were frozen during part of the winter. Why did the British open the door to the Russians and then slam it in their face? The only reasonable explanation seems to be that they hoped not so much to keep Russia out of Talienwan, as to secure from her a promise that the port should be a free port. If the Chinese could be brought to recognize it as a treaty port, then England and all other nations would secure treaty rights (most-favored-nation rights) which Russia would be bound to respect. The theory that the demand regarding Talienwan was meant chiefly as a bargaining point is borne out to some extent by the utterances of British statesmen during the month of January. Balfour, speaking at Manchester on January 10, expounded the British policy in detail. British interests, he said, were not territorial but commercial. In view of the fact that British trade in China was eighty per cent of the total foreign trade of that country, England had a special claim to see that Chinese policy was not directed to the discouragement of foreign

[39] The important source on the British side is *China No. 1 (1898)*, passim; on the Russian side the accounts of Glinskii, op. cit., pp. 47 ff. and Romanov, op. cit., pp. 195 ff. Detailed accounts based on the British Blue Book may be found in Joseph: *Foreign Diplomacy in China*, pp. 226 ff., and in McCordock: *British Far Eastern Policy*, pp. 164 ff., neither of whom make use of Russian material. The documents on the bribing of Li Hung-chang were published in the *Krasnyi Arkhiv*, II (1924), pp. 287–93: " Perepiska o Podkupe Kitaiiskikh Sanovnikov " and are translated in George N. Steiger: *China and the Occident* (New Haven, 1927), pp. 69 ff.

trade, either by setting up regulations in favor of particular countries or by allowing other powers to dot the coast with stations through which world trade could not freely permeate. England could and would resist such action. There was no objection to Russia's seeking an outlet for her commerce below the line of winter and ice, provided always that " we are not excluded from going there too." On January 17 Sir Michael Hicks Beach, in an address at Swansea, reiterated these principles, but went even further and attempted to set up what amounted to a Monroe doctrine for China: " We do not regard China as a place for conquest or acquisition by any European or other Power. We look upon it as the most hopeful place of the future for the commerce of our country and the commerce of the world at large, and the Government was absolutely determined, at whatever cost, even — and he wished to speak plainly — if necessary, at the cost of war, that the door should not be shut against us." [40]

These bellicose words caused something like an attack of war fever in England. The *Times* made them its own and declared that all parties stood together behind the government in support of this policy.[41] And yet it seems fairly clear that the strong language used by Balfour, Hicks Beach, and a little later in January by Chamberlain was meant to impress not the English public, but the Russian government. All these men were in favor of an agreement with Russia and anxious to secure one if possible. There was nothing especially new about this policy, which had been tried by the Rosebery cabinet in 1894–1895 and which had been taken up time and again by the Salisbury administration. In January 1898 the British government was faced with two alternatives: either to try to secure German and Japanese support against Russia, or to try to reach an adjustment with Russia. For co-operation with Japan there was a good deal of public sentiment, though there were still many people " to whom an alliance with a non-Christian power against Christians would seem something like treason to God." [42] But with Germany it was different. The occupation of Kiao-chow had called forth a storm of angry protest in England, where it was generally regarded as part of a French-Russian-German plot. In December opinion was so wrought up that the British military attaché at Berlin could write: " We must go for the Germans and that right soon or they will go for us later." The same apprehensions appear in Spring Rice's correspondence from Berlin:

> " The whole incident has been used as a sort of peg to hang their hatred of England on — which is so plain and evident that no one who is resident in this part of the world can doubt it. . . . It would be absurd to deny that both the

---

[40] Joseph, op. cit., pp. 234 ff.; Victoria Hicks Beach: *Life of Sir Michael Hicks Beach*, II, pp. 58–9; Diplomaticus: " A Monroe Doctrine for China " (*Fortnightly Review*, February, 1898, pp. 321–33).

[41] London *Times*, January 19 and 31, 1898; see also Meyendorff: *Correspondance de M. de Staal*, II, pp. 364–6, 369; *Die Grosse Politik*, XIV, no. 3751.

[42] H. W. Wilson: "England and Japan " (*Fortnightly Review*, March, 1898, pp. 503–12); Arthur Diosy: *The New Far East* (London, 1898), pp. 361 ff.; Chang: *The Anglo-Japanese Alliance* (Baltimore, 1931), pp. 63–4.

Emperor and his people are actuated by feelings of hostility against England which are only limited by the German regard for law and by the practical fear of reprisals. . . . The reason for this is quite simple. We stand in their way everywhere — we have most to take — and we are personally objectionable." " I should say that the desire here was to organize a common course of action against us — less perhaps for the sake of Asia than for Europe; to unite in China what Europe has disunited: to establish themselves in China, to have a point d'appui so as no longer to be treated as a negligible quantity by the two allied powers: but at the same time to avoid a direct conflict with us until they are ready — which will certainly not be yet." [43]

As a matter of fact the German policy at this time was marked by very great caution. Public opinion was certainly very hostile to England, and even a man like Delbrück declared that no amount of diplomatic courtesy, no political tactics could ever bridge the fundamental trade antagonism between the two countries.[44] Emperor William, too, was completely under the spell of the continental league. He blamed Muraviev, not the Tsar, for the unpleasantness regarding Kiao-chow, and was quite prepared to continue support of Russia in the Far East. Speaking to Grierson on January 15, 1898, he said that he had tried for eight years to be friendly with Britain and to gain her alliance, but had failed. The British would never have that chance again. What, he asked, was the British policy anyway? Grierson replied that England aimed to hold aloof from both continental groups. She was strong enough against either and it was unlikely that they could combine. To which the Emperor replied warmly: " You are mistaken. They can combine and they *shall* combine. Socialism and other causes will force the Monarchs of the Continent to combine for mutual assistance and the yellow races of the East are our greatest danger." [45]

But the German foreign office was much more circumspect. Bülow was ready to go a long way to meet the needs of Russia. When the Russians, in correspondence with Berlin, set up a claim to a sphere of " exclusive action " to include all of Manchuria, the province of Chihli and Chinese Turkestan, the Germans offered no objection. They thought the demand for Chihli a " rather big bite " but were interested chiefly in reserving Shantung and the valley of the Yellow River, to its bend northward, for their own sphere.[46] At the same time Bülow refused to commit the German government in advance to the support of Russian policy. He continued his efforts to take the edge off the Anglo-German tension and his policy was ably seconded by Hatzfeldt in London. German assurances that Kiao-chow would, at least for the present, be made an open and free port, helped to calm British opinion somewhat. Lord Salisbury himself seems to have been anxious to better relations. It was probably at his

[43] *Letters and Friendships of Sir Cecil Spring Rice*, I, pp. 243–4; Macdiarmid: *Life of Grierson*, p. 133.
[44] Hans Delbrück: " Politische Korrespondenz " (*Preussische Jahrbücher*, October, 1897, p. 176).
[45] Macdiarmid, op. cit., pp. 134 ff.; *British Documents on the Origins of the War*, I, nos. 62–3.
[46] *Die Grosse Politik*, XIV, nos. 3743 ff.

request that the Queen asked Sir Theodore Martin to see the important editors of English newspapers and induce them to adopt a better tone towards the German Emperor and people. This démarche had an almost instantaneous effect and the improvement in the tone of the newspapers was immediately noticeable. Later on Lord Salisbury hotly refuted the idea that he had been an obstacle to an agreement with Germany. That charge he declared to be " the very reverse of the truth." [47]

It appears, however, that Salisbury, if he was really desirous of an understanding with Germany, was obliged to yield to the opposition in the cabinet, that is, to Balfour, Chamberlain and Hicks Beach, who, while stirring up British opinion against Russia, were hoping to scare Russia into an agreement. At any rate, about the middle of January, at the height of the competition for the loan to China, the British government began to make approaches to Russia. M. de Staal, the Tsar's ambassador at London, had already complained of the presence of British ships at Port Arthur, and the same point had been taken up by Muraviev with the British ambassador at St. Petersburg. The presence of these ships, he said, was so unfriendly as to have set afloat rumors of war with Great Britain. Lord Salisbury, while stressing the fact that the ships had a perfect right to be there, declared that they had gone on orders of the British admiral in the Far East, not on orders of the government. Nevertheless instructions were soon sent out to withdraw the ships, whereupon the Russians began to start rumors that the ships had left on the demand of the Russian authorities.[48]

In the meanwhile Salisbury had sent instructions to Sir Nicholas O'Conor on January 17: " If practicable ask Monsieur Witte whether it is possible that England and Russia should work together in China. Our objects are not antagonistic in any serious degree: on the other hand we can both do each other a great deal of harm if we try. It is better therefore we should come to an understanding. We would go far to further Russian commercial objects in the north, if we could regard her as willing to work with us." [49]

This is a curious document which deserves some scrutiny. It must not be taken too seriously, because, in the first place, it was an instruction to sound out Witte, not to negotiate with the Russian foreign minister; in the second place it makes the strange statement that British and Russian objects are not antagonistic in any serious degree; in the third place it expresses willingness to make concessions only " to further Russian *commercial* objects in the North." Now what actually happened was that O'Conor, instead of approaching Witte, spoke to Muraviev; instead of sticking to his instructions and discussing China, he expressed the opinion that " any understanding, to be really effective and last-

---

[47] *Letters of Queen Victoria*, III, pp. 224–5, 259; see also *Die Grosse Politik*, XIII, no. 3423; XIV, 3747–53; Karl O. Herkenberg: *The Times und das Deutsch-Englische Verhältnis im Jahre 1898* (Berlin, 1925), pp. 44 ff.

[48] See *China No. I (1898)*, nos. 48, 61, 63, 67; Meyendorff, op. cit., II, p. 370.

[49] *British Documents*, I, no. 5.

ing ought to extend to the general area of our respective interests, and not to be confined to the important questions affecting the Far East." [50]

The material on these negotiations, both from the British and the Russian sides, is pretty incomplete, but it seems fairly clear that O'Conor distorted the affair from the start and gave Muraviev a wrong impression of the points at issue. The Russian minister said he would lay his cards on the table if Salisbury would do likewise. He went even further and revealed the fact that Russia claimed a sphere " which was practically all northern China from Tientsin to Peking and from Peking to Manchuria." Apparently he thought the British were inviting a discussion of spheres. Witte, when approached a few days later, evidently gained the same impression, for he spoke of Russia's willingness to recognize the Yangtze Valley as England's sphere, at the same time drawing from his desk a map of China and saying that sooner or later Russia would probably absorb the entire provinces of Chihli, Shansi, Shensi and Kansu.

The Russian ministers must have been more than a little astonished when Salisbury's proposal was laid before them in detail. The document, dated January 25, is a remarkable one, and worth quoting at some length:

" Our idea was this. The two Empires of China and Turkey are so weak that in all important matters they are constantly guided by the advice of Foreign Powers. In giving this advice Russia and England are constantly opposed, neutralizing each other's efforts much more frequently than the real antagonism of their interest would justify; and this condition of things is not likely to diminish, but to increase. It is to remove or lessen this evil that we have thought that an understanding with Russia might benefit both nations. We contemplate no infraction of existing rights. We would not admit the violation of any existing treaties, or impair the integrity of the present empires of either China or Turkey. These two conditions are vital. We aim at no partition of territory, but only a partition of preponderance. It is evident that both in respect to Turkey and China there are large portions which interest Russia more than England and *vice versa*. Merely as an illustration, and binding myself to nothing, I would say that the portion of Turkey which drains into the Black Sea, together with the drainage valley of the Euphrates as far as Bagdad, interest Russia much more than England: whereas Turkish Africa, Arabia and the Valley of the Euphrates below Bagdad interest England much more than Russia. A similar distinction exists in China between the Valley of the Hoango with the territory north of it and the Valley of the Yangtze. Would it be possible to arrange that where, in regard to these territories, our counsels differ, the Power least interested should give way to and assist the other? I do not disguise from myself that the difficulty would be great. Is it insuperable? I have designedly omitted to deal with large tracts in each Empire, because neither Power has shown any keen interest in them." [51]

Salisbury indicated his readiness to define " spheres of preponderance," but on the understanding that there should be no infraction of existing rights, no violation of existing treaties, no impairment of the integrity of China or Tur-

---

[50] Ibid., no. 6.   [51] *British Documents*, I, no. 9.

key, and that, furthermore, the agreement should extend to the Near as well as
to the Far East. All this ran counter to the Russian conception. What was
wanted in St. Petersburg was a definition of spheres in China and the right to
an absolutely free hand in those spheres. The Russians were distinctly averse to
a discussion of Turkey at this time. Even the Tsar, who seems to have favored an
understanding, insisted on its restriction to China. The Russians were prepared
to abandon the loan, but only on condition that England agree to a lease by
Russia, say for twenty years, of Talienwan and Port Arthur or any other port
in the north that might be considered more desirable. A railway was to be built
to this port. At first, making full use of the friendly discussions with London,
they felt out the ground very carefully. England, they pointed out, had recognised Russia's right to a commercial outlet. If Russia took Talienwan the port
would be " open to commerce of all the world." On the strength of this assurance the British seem to have given up the demand that Talienwan be made a
treaty port, as put forward in the loan discussions with China. Lord Salisbury
announced the happy news in the house of lords on February 8, only to learn
from Staal the next day that what the Russians meant was a treaty port (that is,
open to all nations), not a free port (that is, without special tariffs). Furthermore, the Russian assurance, he said, could not be looked upon as a formal
written one.[52]

Soon the Russians became more specific. Count Lamsdorff, Muraviev's aide,
bluntly told the British ambassador that the Russians intended to hold these
ports at any cost, though they were still open to a deal. By that was meant that
the Russians would agree to a loan by the British. When it became known that
the Chinese government had made arrangements for this loan with the Hongkong and Shanghai Bank, the St. Petersburg government took it as an excuse
to drop the entire negotiation and press its demands for Talienwan and Port
Arthur upon the Chinese government. And so ended the episode of the British
advances to Russia. On the British side they seem to have been carried on without confidence or enthusiasm from the very start. O'Conor pointed out in the
beginning how important it was " to take care that any understanding we may
come to gives no such headway that it cannot be set aside when it may seem to
Russia to have served its temporary purpose." Before the discussion had proceeded very far Salisbury wrote to the minister in China that the Russians were
insincere and their language ambiguous. When the whole affair came to an end
the British officials saw clearly what they had suspected all along: the Tsar had
performed an " acquit de conscience " towards his English relatives by showing
good will to the theoretical idea of a general understanding, but he could not run
counter to his ministers' designs.

All this is not to be wondered at, for the British proposals were fairly transparent. The London government was prepared to recognise the Russian sphere

---

[52] *China No. 1 (1898)*, nos. 72, 76, 82, 83, 87; Meyendorff, op. cit., II, p. 372.

in China if it could extort a recognition of treaty rights and the Open Door in this whole vast tract, and if the arrangement could be extended to the Near East. Chamberlain made no bones about saying this afterward. In his famous speech at Birmingham on May 13, he declared:

> " The present government did try to come to an understanding with Russia. We took care to inform her that we had no jealousy, no objection to what we understood to be her commercial objects, or to the development of her trade, or to the expansion of her legitimate authority, but we sought to induce her to give up the idea of political predominance and military occupation. We failed — that was not consistent with the ambition of her Government — we failed to persuade her."

The Russians had no difficulty in seeing through the English tactics. As the Tsar wrote later to his friend William, the British proposals " were of such a new character that I must say we were quite amazed and yet their very nature seemed suspicious to us; never before had England made such offers to Russia. That showed us clearly that England needed our friendship at that time to be able to check our development in a masked way in the Far East." [53] Taken all in all, then, one can hardly describe the British advances as a serious offer of an entente or agreement. They were hardly more than a half-hearted and none too adroit move to commit the Russians to a program which they had no intention of following. The Russians never took them very seriously, but merely debated until they had secured from England something like an unofficial and informal recognition of the great sphere which they had mapped out for themselves, and until their own preparations for further action were complete.[54]

Since the middle of February (that is, long before the discussions between Russia and England came to an end) a committee of high officials had been sitting in St. Petersburg engaged in the task of working out the demands to be presented to China. The new war minister, General Kuropatkin, had come out definitely in favor of the retention of Port Arthur, and even Witte had given up his opposition. He disliked the whole idea as much as ever, but he felt that it was better, now that the decision was all but irrevocable, to join in the action and serve as a moderating influence rather than lose all control of the situation. The committee finally decided to ask for the lease of the southern tip of the Liaotung Peninsula, with Port Arthur and Talienwan, and for the right to build the Railway via Kirin and Mukden south to Port Arthur, or, if necessary, to any other point on the Liaotung Peninsula. On March 3 these demands were laid before the Tsungli Yamen, buttressed by the argument that Russia, once in occupation of the Liaotung Peninsula, could the better defend China against her enemies. The Russian minister, Pavlov, asked for acceptance within five days.

---

[53] *Die Grosse Politik*, XIV, no. 3803.

[54] The chief documents, in *British Documents on the Origins of the War*, I, nos. 5-24, should be supplemented by the Russian documents published by A. Popov: " Anglo-Russkoe Soglashenie o Razdele Kitaiia " (*Krasnyi Arkhiv*, XXV, pp. 111-34), pp. 114 ff., and the discussion in Romanov: *Rossiia v Manchzhurri*, pp. 201 ff.

As a matter of fact the negotiations dragged out for more than three weeks, because the Chinese left no stone unturned to evade these demands. They appealed to England and Japan to give assurances that they had no designs on Manchuria or Liaotung. They tried to procrastinate by sending a special negotiator to St. Petersburg. They argued that the lease to Russia would inevitably lead to demands by other powers. Eventually they attempted to bribe England with the offer of a lease of Weihaiwei, in the hope that thus they might effect an alliance between England, Japan and China directed against Russia. But all these efforts proved to be of no avail. Whatever else may be said about the Russian policy in appropriating Port Arthur and Talienwan, it must be confessed that the affair was ably handled from the diplomatic standpoint. The French evidently disliked the whole business, but there was no chance of their openly opposing it.[55] The Germans made it clear that they would do nothing to increase Russia's difficulties.[56] There remained Japan, and the danger of action from Japan, supported by England, was, of course, always in the minds of the Russian statesmen. Muraviev, however, embarked boldly upon the only sound procedure. He decided to buy off the Japanese by making concessions in Korea. Ever since the middle of February the Japanese government had been pressing for an agreement based upon the idea that Japan should accord Russia a free hand in Manchuria in return for similar freedom for Japan in Korea. This was too much for the Russians, who were unwilling to abandon Korea entirely and equally unwilling to have Japan in sole control on the flank of Manchuria. They therefore temporized, putting off the Japanese with demonstrations of good will. The Russian military instructors and the financial adviser were withdrawn, and the Russian-Korean Bank, which had been established only three months before, suspended its operations. Eventually the negotiations were brought to a close after the Port Arthur matter had been disposed of. In the Nishi-Rosen Agreement of April 25, 1898 the two governments recognized the full independence of Korea and engaged to abstain from all interference in the domestic affairs of that country. They agreed further that if Korea appealed to either of them for counsel or support, they would take no steps to appoint military instructors or financial advisers without reaching an understanding first between themselves. In Article III it was specified that in view of the large industrial and commercial enterprises of Japan in Korea and the large number of Japanese resident in the country, Russia would not in any way hinder the development of these interests. The agreement, in short, put Russia and Japan on an equal footing of abstention, with the sole exception that Japan was given a free hand economically in Korea.[57]

From the information we have it is pretty clear that the Japanese govern-

---

[55] British Documents, I, no. 33.   [56] Die Grosse Politik, XIV, no. 3756.
[57] The fullest account in Glinskii, op. cit., pp. 65 ff.; see also Romanov, op. cit., pp. 206 ff.; Rosen: Forty Years of Diplomacy, I, pp. 156 ff.; Trubetzkoi: Russland als Grossmacht, pp. 59 ff. On the Japanese side see K. Asakawa: The Russo-Japanese Conflict (Boston, 1904), pp. 269 ff.

ment, particularly Marquis Ito, was at the time much opposed to antagonizing Russia. The Japanese political situation was uncertain, and the national finances in bad shape. Military and naval preparations would not be complete for some years, and there was, besides, the danger that Japan, if she antagonized Russia, might have to deal with France and Germany as well. So it was deemed advisable to postpone the struggle which was already regarded as inevitable.[58]

While the Japanese were patching up their differences with Russia, the English, having tried to square the Russians and having failed, could do little but nurse their mortification. For a man like Chamberlain that was a hard course to follow, and he did not accept Salisbury's laisser faire policy without question. In the early days of February he had written to Balfour warning that the government would meet with disaster if it did not follow a stronger line in China. He proposed that the British approach the American and German governments with a suggestion that all occupied ports be made treaty ports. If the Russians refused, they should be driven out of Port Arthur.[59]

We do not know what Balfour's reply to this proposal was, but at all events Chamberlain seems to have stuck by his idea. On March 8 the British ambassador at Washington submitted to the state department an unofficial memorandum asking whether the British government " could count on the co-operation of the United States in opposing action by foreign Powers which may tend to restrict freedom of commerce of all nations in China either by imposing preferential conditions or by obtaining actual cession of Chinese coast territory." The American government returned an evasive reply, something to the effect that it saw no immediate danger.[60]

The response was discouraging, but it did not prevent Chamberlain from approaching other governments, first the Japanese and later the German. On March 17, at the most critical moment of the Port Arthur affair, he had a long talk with the Japanese minister at a dinner party. With his usual bluntness Chamberlain asked Baron Kato what Japan proposed to do. The minister replied that he did not know. England's policy, he said, seemed to be based on purely commercial considerations, but how did England expect to keep her commercial position intact if she lost her political influence in China? How far would England be prepared to go to defend China's integrity? Chamberlain agreed with Kato in principle, but hinted that England lacked the land forces necessary to oppose Russia in Manchuria. How could the Russian advance be stopped? he inquired. To which Kato replied by asking whether the guns of the British ships would not reach to the Liaotung Peninsula? Chamberlain rejoined by asserting that such action would not stop Russia. Japan, he said, must desire Chinese integrity as much as England. Why should the two countries

[58] Ito Masanori: Kato Takaaki (Tokyo, 1929), I, pp. 280 ff.

[59] Garvin: Life of Chamberlain, III, p. 251.

[60] Alfred L. P. Dennis: Adventures in American Diplomacy, 1896–1906 (New York, 1928), pp. 170–1.

not act together? Why did Japan not make a proposition? Kato answered that
the Tokyo government might be wondering why the British did not make a
proposition, but Chamberlain deprecated the silence of the Japanese. The two
countries, he thought, should open their hearts and say what they meant. England would receive Japanese overtures with great good will and would give
full consideration.[61]

Kato forwarded a report of this interesting conversation to his government
and followed it up on March 26 with a memorandum of ten thousand words
urging the desirability and need of an alliance with England, which would
give the two powers undisputed naval control in the Far East and make them
all-powerful. But Ito was anxious to get out of the crisis without making larger
commitments. He preferred an arrangement with Russia about Korea, and was
prepared to be put off with very meagre concessions even in that matter. Kato
secured no support for his plan, and thereupon resigned his position.[62]

The British were left to settle their score with the Russians alone. What was
to be done? The Russian government insisted that there was no intention of
infringing the sovereign rights of China: the two ports were to be leased, not
taken. Furthermore, Russia was willing to promise that they should be open to
the trade of all nations and that the treaty rights of other powers should be respected. The British statesmen had no undue confidence in Russian assurances.
It was not Talienwan that they objected to, but the idea of Russia securing Port
Arthur. Everyone knew that this port could never be made a commercial centre.
It was a purely military stronghold, but as such was of tremendous importance,
commanding as it did the entire Gulf of Pechili and the approaches to Peking
by sea. From the time when the Russian demands on China became known the
English government considered the advisability of leasing Weihaiwei if the Russians could not be brought to give up the demand for Port Arthur. The place
was still occupied by the Japanese, under the terms of the Treaty of Shimonoseki,
but they were to withdraw in May 1898, when the final installment of the indemnity would have been paid by China. The Tsungli Yamen was quite prepared to have the British take it over as a counterweight to Russia, but the
British government hesitated to join in the scramble for territory, the more so
as parliament had passed a resolution on March 1 declaring " that it is of vital
importance for British commerce and influence that the independence of Chinese
territory should be maintained." The government had accepted the resolution,
though Curzon warned the House that he could conceive " of circumstances arising in the future, circumstances gravely affecting, and perhaps seriously imperil-
ling our interests in China, which might tempt us to depart from that attitude
of reserve."

---

[61] Such is the account given in Kato's memoirs: Ito Masanori: *Kato Takaaki* (Tokyo, 1929),
I, pp. 292 ff. These advances are mentioned also in *The Secret Memoirs of Count Hayashi*, p. 89, and
are vaguely referred to in *Die Grosse Politik*, XIV, nos. 3759, 3782.

[62] Masanori, op. cit., I, pp. 280 ff., 313 ff., 330 ff.; see also Atsushi Hiratsuka: *Ito Hirobumi
Hiroku* (Tokyo, 1929).

Curzon himself shared the opinion of the ambassador at St. Petersburg, namely that the Russian action could not be blocked and that it would be better to secure Weihaiwei before the Russian demands had been accepted by the Chinese. But the majority of the members of the cabinet seem to have been opposed. Lord Salisbury was ill and Balfour, who had taken his place at the foreign office, had a hard time convincing his colleagues. To allow Russia to lease Port Arthur and to have England take Weihaiwei as a makeweight would mean abandoning northern China, he argued, but after all that region was bound to fall to Russia sooner or later. To require the Russians to abstain from taking Port Arthur might lead to war, but it would prevent the partition of China, would check Russian influence at Peking and would save the balance of power in the Far East. Lord Salisbury from his sick-bed seems to have decided the cabinet's choice of these alternatives. He thought it would be best to secure from China a promise not to alienate Weihaiwei and to give England the first refusal of it. As for Russia's influence at Peking, this he thought would not be affected by her occupation of Port Arthur, since this influence rested on Russia's proximity to China by land and the existence of several thousand miles of common frontier. " The only thing to be done," concluded Salisbury, " is to object to the military occupation of Port Arthur in language sufficiently measured to allow Russia to find a way out."

In the meanwhile the Russians had been bringing greater and greater pressure to bear at Peking. Li Hung-chang and Chang Yin-huan were the two negotiators on the Chinese side. They were quite amenable to reason. On March 21 the Russian chargé d'affaires, Pavlov, and the Russian financial agent, Pokotilov, carried out instructions from St. Petersburg and offered the two Chinese a bribe of five hundred thousand taels each if the matter were arranged in the next few days. Li protested, but not too much. On March 24 the British minister at Peking could report that the Chinese were going to yield. They did. On March 27 the agreement between China and Russia was signed. The Russians secured all they wanted.[63]

The British cabinet had decided on March 25 that Port Arthur was not worth a war and that the best solution would be to secure a lease of Weihaiwei. They therefore notified the Russian government of their " grave objections " to its action and reserved to themselves liberty " to take what steps they think best to protect their own interests and to diminish the evil consequences which they anticipate." [64] As for Weihaiwei, this aspect of the problem was not serious. The

---

[63] Details of the negotiations in Glinskii, op. cit., pp. 53 ff.; *China No. I (1898)*, nos. 95 ff.; *British Documents on the Origins of the War*, I, nos. 23 ff. On the attitude of the British cabinet see especially *Letters of Queen Victoria*, III, pp. 237–8; Earl of Ronaldshay: *Life of Curzon*, I, pp. 283 ff. Witte: *Memoirs*, pp. 102–3, admits the bribery of Li Hung-chang. The documents on this subject are in the *Krasnyi Arkhiv*, II, pp. 290–3.

[64] *British Documents*, I, no. 41. Balfour told Staal that the occupation of Port Arthur was regarded as a matter " of immense gravity " (Meyendorff: *Correspondance de M. de Staal*, II, pp. 375–7).

Japanese were ready to evacuate when the indemnity was paid. They expected the Chinese to take it over, but if the Chinese were too weak they preferred to see it in the hands of Britain rather than in the hands of any other power. They therefore gave their assent, on the understanding that if Japan should later find it necessary to take similar measures to " strengthen her defences or to promote her interests " they might count on the " concurrence and support " of England.[65] The Germans were squared by being given assurances that England, in establishing herself at Weihaiwei, had " no intention of injuring or contesting the rights and interests of Germany in the province of Shantung or of creating difficulties for her in that province." " It is especially understood," continued the British note, " that England will not construct any railroad communication from Weihaiwei, and the district leased therewith, into the interior of the province." [66]

In the Chinese scramble of the winter 1897–1898 the French government played a subordinate rôle. M. Hanotaux assured the British ambassador that France desired " the maintenance as long as possible of the integrity of the Chinese Empire." The " attacks " on China by Germany and Russia he considered " premature and consequently regrettable." But, despite his dislike for the principle of spheres of influence, he insisted that " France must sustain her claims to consideration in the provinces contiguous to Tongking." [67] As a matter of fact the struggle between England and France in southwest China had been going on apace. When, in June 1897, the British secured from China the opening of the West River to commerce, the French regarded this as a direct blow at their interests. They therefore obliged the Chinese to agree to the eventual extension of the railroad from Langson to Longchow in the direction of Nanning and Pe-se. Furthermore, the Chinese government was to turn first to French engineers and contractors for all mining services in the three provinces of Kuangtung, Kuangsi and Yunnan. In the meanwhile the French, like the Germans, were carefully canvassing the possibilities of establishing a coaling and naval station on the Chinese coast. In 1896 a Frenchman, Claudius Madrolle, for the first time explored the interior of the island of Hainan, and presented to the Geographical Society a glowing report of its possibilities. In January 1897 the French induced the Chinese government to promise not to alienate this island to any other power. French naval vessels were busy throughout the year 1897 taking soundings around the island and about the Leichow Peninsula. In January 1898 it was reported that French ships had seized Hainan, and a British warship was hastily sent to investigate. The report proved unfounded, but the French had gone north to the harbor of Kuangchow. In the meanwhile the French representative at Peking loyally supported the Russian demands on China, while the Russian chargé d'affaires did the same for his colleague. The French desiderata were put forward immediately after the Russian, on March 7,

---

[65] *British Documents*, I, nos. 28, 30, 39 ff.

[66] *Die Grosse Politik*, XIV, no. 3770. For the negotiations see ibid., nos. 3760 ff.; *British Documents*, I, nos. 47 ff.   [67] *British Documents*, I, no. 33.

1898. France asked for a Chinese promise not to alienate the three provinces of Yunnan, Kuangtung and Kuangsi; the appointment of a Frenchman to the position of director of the posts; the definitive concession for a railroad to Yunnan-fu; the right to establish a coaling station on the south coast. On April 10 these demands were conceded, and on April 22 the French flag was raised at Kuangchowwan, leased by the French for ninety-nine years. Outrages against French nationals in southern China soon gave the Paris government a pretext for further demands. On May 28 the Chinese government agreed to the construction of a railroad from Pakhoi on the coast, to some point on the West River. By this method the French hoped to draw the commerce of the southern provinces away from Canton and Hongkong and bring it down to the Gulf of Tongking.[68]

So ended the first phase of the victimization of China after her defeat by Japan in 1895. The occupation of Kiao-chow by the Germans was a very important landmark. Thus far the Russians and the French, followed by the British, had been pursuing their policy of "peaceful penetration." Had this process been allowed to continue uninterrupted, Russia would, in a relatively short time, have established control over Manchuria and even over the province of Chihli and the capital, Peking. Of that there can be little doubt. Russia was the champion of Chinese integrity, for she saw endless possibilities in a policy of friendship and restraint. The British could not have frustrated these plans. That comes out clearly enough from the British documents. The London government was quite prepared to accept the inevitable and to allow northern China to fall under Russian influence. The great aim of the British was to preserve, if at all possible, the rights laid down in the treaties, to open as many Chinese ports as possible to foreign trade and to make sure that everywhere the open door and equality of opportunity should be the rule.

Prior to 1898 the Russians had done nothing to interfere with British interests, which were, as a matter of fact, rather slight in northern China. The British raised no objection to the Russian railroad schemes or to the project for a commercial terminus on the Yellow Sea. In fact, they took rather the attitude that a Russian railroad into Manchuria would open the way for the influx of British goods. In the years before 1898, then, the British were almost entirely concerned with French activity in the south. The duel for the control and exploitation of Yunnan and Szechuan has been less written about, but it was of tremendous importance and has been neglected simply because in the following years the Russian policy drew all the fire of objection. British interests in the Yangtze Valley and in the southwest were very great, and there can be no ques-

68 Documents Diplomatiques: *Chine, 1894-1898,* nos. 34 ff., 59 ff.; *China No. 1 (1899),* passim; Claudius Madrolle: "Kouang-Tchéou, Sancian, Hainan" (*Questions Diplomatiques et Coloniales,* May 1. 1898, pp. 6-12); J. Silvestre: "La France à Kouang-Tchéou-Ouan" (*Annales des Sciences Politiques,* July 15, 1902, pp. 473-93); Alfred Bonningue: *La France à Kouang-Tchéou-Wan* (Paris, 1931), pp. 7-8.

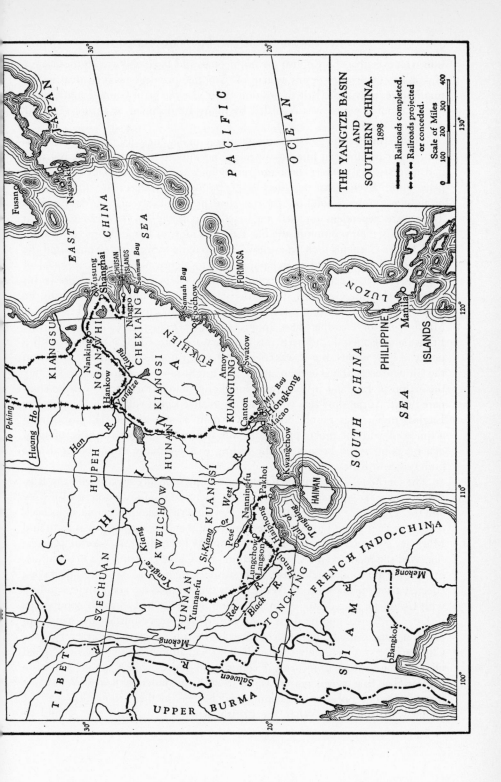

THE YANGTZE BASIN
AND
SOUTHERN CHINA.
1898

——————— Railroads completed.
∗∗∗∗∗∗∗ Railroads projected
or conceded.

Scale of Miles
0   100   200   300   400

tion whatever that the English government would have opposed to the utmost any cession of territory or any system of economic privilege in these areas which might have injured the British position. This was *the* great Chinese market, the preservation of which was regarded by many Englishmen as almost a matter of life and death.

The Germans were at a great disadvantage in dealing with the Chinese situation. Their commercial interests were second only to those of Britain, but they had no territorial contact, no base from which to operate a policy of peaceful penetration. Even when they decided to build up their fleet the problem was brought no nearer a solution, for they had no Far Eastern base for this fleet. They were dependent for coal and repairs upon the docks at Hongkong. In other words, their position in the Far East was more or less at the mercy of England. So the Germans took Kiao-chow, after having scrupulously considered the merits of other ports and after having tried to secure the friendly approval of the Russians. It is certainly an exaggeration to claim, as M. Witte does in his memoirs, that the Germans started the scramble for Chinese territory. On the other hand, it will not do to minimize the significance of Germany's action, as Mr. Joseph for example does, in his *Foreign Diplomacy in China*. Russia, France and England had been pushing forward into Chinese territory with a policy of concessions. But it was a very different thing to take or lease a port on the Chinese coast. The German attack, one might say, was a frontal attack. Only the action of England in securing Hongkong many years earlier can be compared to it. At the time this was generally realized, particularly in Britain. The English public was rabid about the German action, and if the government acquiesced without much protest, it was because of larger considerations of general politics and because of the feeling that Germany might be used as a buffer against Russia.

The German occupation of Kiao-chow unquestionably precipitated the Russian action at Talienwan and Port Arthur, the special contribution of Muraviev and the Tsar to the development of the Far Eastern situation. As one looks back on this move it is hard to escape the conviction that Witte's policy was right and Muraviev's was wrong. Had Russia continued her policy of peaceful penetration, had she made even a show of helping the Chinese against the German demands, her position would have been stronger than ever. As it was Muraviev effected a clear break with the Witte policy, he wrecked the good understanding with China, he placed himself in a position where he had to make concessions to Japan in Korea, and he drew upon himself the heavy burden of British opposition. One must be fair, of course. The British policy in the matter of the Chinese loan was incredibly clumsy. Balfour had announced that the British had no objection to Russia's securing a commercial outlet, while Curzon had made it clear that Russia was not to aspire to such an outlet in Korea. What was there left? The only ice-free commercial harbor on the Yellow Sea coast of China was Talienwan. When the British demanded that this port should be made a treaty port, they were, clearly, trying to secure treaty rights there before the Russians could establish themselves. The motive was correct enough, but from the tactical standpoint it was a challenge. A port with a wide open door and with equal opportunities for all may have been a British or a German ideal, but it wasn't a French ideal, much less a Russian, for these powers simply could not compete with Britain and Germany on equal terms. The Russians therefore fought the British demands tooth and nail. The French and the Germans stood behind them. The British would not fight. In fact their squadron in the Far East was barely superior to the Russian, to say nothing of the French and German contingents.[69] In the end they had to let the Russians win. Talienwan was leased, and Port Arthur too. The latter was the " helmet and shield " of the former, to quote the phrase of William T. Stead. The commercial port was unprotected without the naval fortress. Knowing as they did that the Russians were determined to have both, the English government made an obvious mistake in lodging more protests.

But the taking of Weihaiwei was perhaps an even greater mistake. The place was of little value. Its harbor was not deep enough for large ships, it was expensive to fortify, and it was cut off from the hinterland by a range of high hills.[70] The English had to commit themselves to support Japanese aspirations in order to get Weihaiwei, and they had to give the Germans assurances that they would never do anything with the place that was worth doing. In other words they assumed a liability instead of securing an asset. Not only that, they placed themselves opposite the Russians at Port Arthur, thus taking the vanguard in opposition to the Russian policy. The Germans were delighted to have the British act as a wedge between themselves and the Russians. Germany, Bülow told the Reichstag on April 29, had no objection if Russia and England watched the play of the waves in the Gulf of Pechili from their respective windows.

What was worse yet was the abandonment of Britain's traditional policy of respecting the integrity of the Chinese Empire, a policy which had just been reaffirmed by the resolution of the house of commons on March 1. If Germany, Russia and France were following a criminal policy, Britain, having protested, now decided to join the criminals. This did her position in China no good, while it weakened her in relation to other powers. Furthermore, every new concession extorted from China made the scramble more general. France joined, and it was merely a matter of time before Japan and other nations would put forward their demands. It is a mistake to call in Beelzebub to fight Satan. It was all well and good to talk, as all the powers did, of the need for preserving the integrity of the Chinese Empire. It was all well and good to maintain that the leases taken in the spring of 1898 left Chinese sovereignty untouched. This was mere camouflage

---

69 Brassey: *Naval Annual*, 1898, pp. 59–60; " Naval Squadrons in the Far East " (London *Times*, March 28, 1898).

70 See, e.g., Anonymous: " Wei-hai-wei: Its Value as a Naval Station " (*Blackwood's Magazine*, June, 1899).

and the statesmen knew it. Nothing is to be gained by cynicism of this kind. The plain facts were that in 1898 China, unless she could rouse herself, was doomed. Her break-up and partition among the powers had begun. It was a calamity for the British, who could find not a single power to stand by them. So they jumped from the frying pan into the fire.

BIBLIOGRAPHICAL NOTE

(SUPPLEMENTARY TO THE BIBLIOGRAPHY OF CHAPTER VIII)

DOCUMENTARY SOURCES

Accounts and Papers. 1898, volume CV: *China No. 1 (1898)*. An important and rather full collection of papers on the Kiao-chow and Port Arthur episodes.

British Documents on the Origins of the War, 1898–1914. Edited by G. P. Gooch and Harold Temperley. London, 1927—. Important chiefly for the documents bearing on Anglo-Russian negotiations. The documents on the Chinese situation do not add greatly to the material in *China No. 1.*

Die Grosse Politik der Europäischen Kabinette, 1871–1914. Volume XIV, part I. Contains a large number of documents on the background and negotiations concerning the German occupation of Kiao-chow.

TELESHEV, L.: " Vil'gel'm II o Zaniatii Tsarskoi Rossiei Port Artura." (*Krasnyi Arkhiv,* LVIII, 1933, pp. 150–5). Three reports by Osten-Sacken of conversations with William II in the winter of 1897–1898.

POPOV, A.: "Pervyie Shagi Russkogo Imperializma na Dal'nem Vostoke." (*Krasnyi Arkhiv,* LII, 1932, pp. 34-124). Contains the text of the famous Muraviev memorandum of November 23, 1897.

MEMOIRS, AUTOBIOGRAPHIES, BIOGRAPHIES, AND LETTERS

HOHENLOHE, FÜRST CHLODWIG ZU: *Denkwürdigkeiten der Reichskanzlerzeit.* Stuttgart, 1931. Contains a few notes of interest on German policy in the Far East and especially touching on Kiao-chow.

BÜLOW, PRINCE VON: *Memoirs.* Four volumes. Boston, 1931–1932. The first volume of Bülow's memoirs has some discussion of the Kiao-chow episode, but adds relatively little.

TIRPITZ, ALFRED VON: *My Memoirs.* Two volumes. New York, 1919. The admiral gives a detailed account of his command in the Far East in 1896–1897 and of the preparations for the occupation of Kiao-chow.

HEYKING, ELISABETH VON: *Tagebücher aus vier Weltteilen, 1886–1904.* Fourth edition. Leipzig, 1926. Fascinating and instructive diaries of the wife of the German minister at Peking. A valuable source.

GARVIN, J. L.: *The Life of Joseph Chamberlain.* Three volumes. London, 1933—. Not as valuable as one might expect.

RONALDSHAY, EARL OF: *The Life of Lord Curzon.* Three volumes. London, 1928. The authoritative biography of Curzon, who in 1898 was undersecretary for foreign affairs. Contains a few interesting letters and memoranda.

MEYENDORFF, ALEXANDRE: *Correspondance Diplomatique de M. de Staal, 1884–1900.* Two volumes. Paris, 1929. Very disappointing. Contains little of value.

MASANORI, ITO: *Kato Takaaki.* Two volumes. Tokyo, 1929. The biography and papers of the Japanese minister to England. Contains much on the problem of an Anglo-Japanese alliance.

HIRATSUKA, ATSUSHI: *Ito Hirobumi Hiroku.* Tokyo, 1931. Diplomatic papers of the Japanese premier. Valuable as a reflection of the views of the school of statesmen who favored an agreement with Pussia.

POOLEY, A. M.: *The Secret Memoirs of Count Tadasu Hayashi.* New York, 1915. Still one of the best sources from the Japanese side, but rather slight on this period.

SCHELKING, E. DE: *Recollections of a Russian Diplomat.* New York, 1918. The author was attached to the Russian embassy in Berlin. His book is sensational and unreliable. A source to be avoided.

SPECIAL STUDIES

IRMER, ARTHUR JULIUS: *Die Erwerbung von Kiautschou, 1894–1898.* Cologne, 1930. The best monograph on the subject, digesting not only the German documents, but also some unpublished correspondence of Tirpitz.

—: *Kiautschou. Die Diplomatische Vorbereitung der Erwerbung.* Cologne, 1932. This is the same as the preceding title, with a few minor changes. The documentation is omitted and some pictures added.

ROLOFF, GUSTAV: "Die Erwerbung von Kiautschou." (*Preussische Jahrbücher,* June, 1918, pp. 348–54). Now out of date. Primarily a summary of the revelations in Hayashi and a few other books.

BECKER, WILLY: "Die Deutsch-Russische Krise bei der Erwerbung von Kiautschou." (*Zeitschrift für Politik,* XV, 1925, pp. 58–71). A careful survey, based chiefly on the German documents. Now superseded by Irmer.

POPOV, A.: "Anglo-Russkoe Soglashenie o Razdele Kitaiia, 1899 g." (*Krasnyi Arkhiv,* XXV, 1927, pp. 110–34). Based upon Russian archive material. An important supplement to the British documents.

GRIMM, CLAUS: *Graf Witte und die Deutsche Politik.* Freiburg, 1930. A doctoral dissertation, based upon Russian material, but adding little to the German documents and the Witte memoirs.

PROWASECK, HILDE: *Der Gedanke einer Kontinentalliga gegen England unter Wilhelm II.* Leipzig, 1928. A doctoral thesis of very little value. Hardly more than a summary of the material in the German documents.

ASAKAWA, K.: *The Russo-Japanese Conflict.* Boston, 1904. Still the best account of these critical years as seen from the Japanese side. A careful, moderate and helpful book.

KLEIN, ALFRED: *Der Einfluss des Grafen Witte auf die Deutsch-Russischen Beziehungen.* Münster, 1931. Makes no use of Russian materials and adds very little.

HSIA, CHING-LIN: *Studies in Chinese Diplomatic History.* Shanghai, 1924. A collection of essays on concessions, leased territories, spheres of influence, etc., with reference to the international law of the subject.

CHANG, CHUNG-FU: *The Anglo-Japanese Alliance.* Baltimore, 1931. The best book on the subject, but has little to say on this period.

RICHTHOFEN, FERDINAND, FREIHERRR VON: "Kiautschou, seine Weltstellung und Voraussichtliche Bedeutung." (*Preussische Jahrbücher,* January, 1898, pp. 167–91). Written by the most eminent authority on the geography of China, this is a compact and in every way excellent study of the importance and prospects of the German acquisition.

FRANZIUS, GEORG: *Kiautschou.* Seventh edition. Berlin, 1900. The author, who investigated the Bay of Kiao-chow for the German government in 1897, gives a detailed general survey of the territory.

MADROLLE, CLAUDIUS: "Kouang-Tchéou, Sancian, Hainan." (*Questions Diplomatiques et Coloniales,* May 1, 1898, pp. 6–12). A concise account of the French activities and the taking of Kuang-chow; written by a prominent French explorer.

SILVESTRE, J.: "La France à Kouang-Tchéou-Ouan." (*Annales des Sciences Politiques,* July 15, 1902, pp. 473–93). Perhaps the best study of the French policy that led to the occupation.

BONNINGUE, ALFRED: *La France à Kouang-Tchéou-Wan.* Paris, 1931. Not of much account. Chiefly a survey of the station and a review of the administration.

HOYNINGEN GENANNT HUENE, HEINRICH, FREIHERR VON: *Untersuchungen zur Geschichte des Deutsch-Englischen Bündnisproblems, 1898–1901.* Breslau, 1934. The first part of this book is an analysis of the Far Eastern crisis of 1898, based upon the Romanov book and upon some of the other Russian material. It is one of the best accounts available.

BEE, BENJAMIN MING-CHU: *The Leasing of Kiaochow.* Cambridge, 1935. This is an unpublished doctoral dissertation submitted at Harvard, which the author has been kind enough to let me use. It goes over the western materials thoroughly and draws upon recently published Chinese sources. Of these latter the most important seem to be:

1. *Ching-chi wai-chiao shih-liao*. Edited by Wang T'ao-fu and Wang Hsi-yin. Peiping, 1932 ff. A collection of Decrees, Instructions, Reports, etc., for the years 1875–1911.
2. Chang Chih-tung: *Chang Wên-hsiang-kung chi*. Peking, 1919–1921. The works of the viceroy of Liang-hu.
3. Hsü Ching-ch'eng: *Hsü Wên-hsü-kung i-kao*. Peking, 1918. Valuable papers of the Chinese representative at St. Petersburg and Berlin.
4. Wêng T'ung-ho: *Wêng Wên-kung-kung jih-chi*. Shanghai, 1925. Important diaries of a member of the Tsungli Yamen.
5. *Ch'ing-shih-kao*. Edited by Chao Erh-sun. Peiping, 1929. A dynastic history of considerable source value.

LITERATURE SINCE 1935

(See also the Supplementary Bibliographical Notes to Chapters VI and XII.)

GROTE, GERHARD: *Untersuchungen zur deutschen Kolonialpolitik um die Jahrhundertwende*. Berlin, 1940. 112 pp. A solid monograph which, though adducing no new materials, provides a systematic review of the German acquisition of Samoa, Kiau-chow, the Carolines and other colonial possessions.

SCHÜDDEKOPF, OTTO E.: *Die Stüztpunktpolitik des deutschen Reiches, 1890–1914*. Berlin, 1941. 115 pp. A well-documented essay, based on good command of the English as well as the German literature. The author is critical of the failure of the Germans to appreciate the importance of bases.

NOREM, R. A.: *Kiauchow Leased Territory*. Berkeley, 1936. 150 pp. A thorough, analytical study.

ANONYMOUS: "Zakvat Germaniei Kiao-Chao v 1897 g." (*Krasny Arkhiv*, no. 87, 1938, pp. 19–63). A valuable collection of Russian documents on the German seizure of Kiau-chow.

KAWAI, KAZUO: "Anglo-German Rivalry in the Yangtze Region, 1895–1902" (*Pacific Historical Review*, VIII, September, 1939, pp. 413–434). An excellent analysis on the published materials on the subject.

TREAT, PAYSON J.: *Diplomatic Relations between the United States and Japan, 1895–1905*. Stanford, 1938. 291 pp. An important collection of American diplomatic documents, which throws a good deal of light on the development of international rivalries in the Far East.

YERUSALIMSKII, A. S.: *Vneshniaia Politika i Diplomatiia Germanskogo Imperializma v Kontse XIX veka*. Moscow, 1948. 767 pp. Exceedingly detailed study of German policy, especially in the Far East.

XV

The Anglo-German Negotiations

⁓

T HE EVENTS OF THE WINTER OF 1897–1898 IN THE FAR EAST CAUSED
something akin to panic in England, where public opinion had a keen
sense of the danger of losing part of the Chinese market. Rarely was the
political world so united behind the government as in January 1898 when Mr.
Balfour enunciated the guiding principles of the government's Chinese policy.
But two months later almost everyone was disillusioned. The Russians, so far as
one could determine, had been successful all along the line, while the British
government, despite its brave utterances, had yielded on all essentials and had
sacrificed even the fundamental principle of maintaining the independence and
integrity of the Celestial Empire. The press was almost unanimous in its criticism and condemnation of Salisbury's conduct of affairs, and when he went on
vacation in March it was generally assumed that he would never again take up
the dual burden of the premiership and the foreign office. Every sort of charge
was brought against him — accusations of vacillation, pusillanimity and loss of
nerve, together with cynical remarks about the famous policy of " amicable understanding " and " graceful concession." Even the supporters of the government, notably the Unionist element, joined in the general indignation. Salisbury
received the brunt of the attack, but his associates, " Port Arthur Balfour " and
" Cocksure Curzon," were not let off easily. It was the general opinion that the
British handling of the situation had been " a triumph of diplomatic incompe-
tency," and that there was not much to choose between the helplessness and
weakness of the Chinese and British governments. " A sadder and sorrier attempt to steer a ship of State through the waters of which every sandbank was
distinctly marked on the charts and every rocky headland clearly denoted by a
lighthouse it would be hard to find even in the histories of the States which
have already declined," wrote one of the ablest and sharpest of the government's
critics.[1]

According to the fault-finders the government had talked big and acted little.

---

[1] Anonymous: " The Failure of our Foreign Policy " (*Contemporary Review*, April, 1898, pp.
457–80), p. 462. See also Diplomaticus: " Where Lord Salisbury has Failed " (*Fortnightly Review*,
April, 1898, pp. 513–23); Idem: " The Breakdown of our Chinese Policy " (ibid., May, 1898,
pp. 844–54); Anonymous: " Lord Salisbury and the Far East " (ibid., June, 1898, pp. 1029–38);
A. Michie: " Our Future Policy in China " (*National Review*, July, 1898, pp. 654–70); W. T. Stead:
" Russia and Mr. Chamberlain's Long Spoon " (*Contemporary Review*, June, 1898, pp. 761–77).

It had withdrawn the British ships from Port Arthur at the " demand " of the Russian government, it had abandoned the proposal that Talienwan be made a treaty port because of the Russian " threats," it had dickered with Muraviev for assurances about Talienwan and Port Arthur and had allowed itself to be put off by equivocal and variable promises, and it had crowned the whole policy of ineptitude by taking Weihaiwei (renamed Woe! Woe! Woe!), thereby scrapping the sacred principle of Chinese integrity.

Balfour had a very hard time trying to answer these objections. Twice he rose in the house of commons to defend the government's policy, on April 5 and on April 29, that is, before and after publication of the Blue Book. He admitted the " considerable anxiety " not to say " irritable anxiety " of the country and tried to explain the situation by stressing the " entirely new political phenomena " that had resulted from the " extraordinary," almost " unaccountable weakness of China." But at the same time he insisted that the British ships had not been withdrawn from Port Arthur because of Russian pressure. He denied that he had ever " invited " the Russian government to take Port Arthur, or that the British cabinet had ever intended Russia to have more than a " commercial " port. The objection to the lease of Port Arthur was simply that it would constitute a perpetual threat at the Chinese capital, as the Russians had themselves pointed out to Japan in 1895. Russia had a great and inevitable influence at Peking because of her four thousand miles of land frontier. It was intolerable, therefore, that she should control the sea approaches as well. But Port Arthur was not worth a war and so the government had decided to re-establish the balance of power in the Gulf of Pechili by occupying Weihaiwei, which, to be sure, was not as strong as Port Arthur, but which would serve the purpose. As for the rest, there was no good ground for attacking the government. Russia's railroad policy in Manchuria was one to which England need take no exception, as it would help to open up the whole area to British trade, despite any special duties that might be levied. Furthermore, no British treaty rights had been violated. The Russian government had promised that they should not be in any way infringed. Besides, there were the concessions obtained by the British government, the opening of new treaty ports, the opening of the rivers to foreign trade, the promise that the director of the customs should be an Englishman as long as British trade exceeded that of other nations, and the promise not to alienate territory in the Yangtze Basin.[2]

The speech was admittedly a good one, but it did not satisfy the opposition. Eminent speakers like Harcourt, Dilke, Grey and Beresford upheld their previous criticisms. " The measures adopted were maladroit, and the retreat consequently has been undignified. Proposals of an irritating character were advanced, and they were withdrawn under menace." The action of the government had been a " record of continual failure at every point," declared Harcourt.[3] What-

---

[2] Hansard: *Parliamentary Debates,* Series IV, vol. LVI, pp. 224 ff., 1581 ff.
[3] Hansard, LVI, pp. 1560 ff., especially pp. 1569, 1579.

ever the government might say it was clear that the ships had been recalled from Port Arthur because of Russian protests. The whole Port Arthur occupation had been precipitated by the ill-timed demand for the opening of Talien-wan. Weihaiwei was of little value, and was certainly not worth the sacrifice of Britain's traditional policy. As for the assurances and concessions obtained, those of Russia were of little use, and would be thrown into the discard whenever convenient. "I would not believe in any assurances Russia might give to this country if they were twenty fathoms long," declared Beresford. The concessions granted by China were all right so far as they went. But there was always the objection that the assurance not to alienate territory in the Yangtze Basin might give the impression that England was reserving this as her sphere and was withdrawing from her rights in the rest of China. The bald fact was that Manchuria was lost to all intents and purposes. Already there had arisen the spectre of Russia training fifty to sixty thousand Manchus and using them to overrun northern and central China.[4]

Under the fire of strong criticism the British government, constantly prodded by the China Association, the London Chamber of Commerce and kindred organizations, began to take a stronger line in its dealings with China. In the months following the crisis it entered frankly upon the race for concessions. To counterbalance the French advance in south China, it secured from the Tsungli Yamen, on June 9, a ninety-nine year lease of the territory on the mainland opposite Hongkong, from Deep Bay to Mirs Bay, thus increasing about eight-fold its territorial holding at the mouth of the West River. At the same time efforts were made to open up more and more towns to foreign trade (notably Nanning-fu, to which the French planned to build a railway), to regulate internal navigation, and so on. The greatest activity of the powers during the year 1898 was, however, concentrated on the matter of railroad and mining concessions. The question of communications seemed to be the key to the whole future development of the Chinese situation. This is certainly not the place to go into the details of the many and complicated negotiations carried on by the British and other governments. The Blue Book contains nearly five hundred documents bearing almost exclusively on concessions of this kind in the period from April 1898 to January 1899. Suffice it to say that the British policy aimed directly at the recognition by the Chinese and other governments of the Yangtze Valley as a British sphere, in which British interests should be given the first opportunity in the construction of railroads and the exploitation of natural resources. Recapitulating what had been done, the English minister to Peking was able to write in November 1898: "Not a single *bona fide* or approximately practical scheme which has been brought to this Legation has failed to be put through. Every single *bona fide* complaint from the Treaty ports has been looked into and settled." Specifically this meant that the British had secured nine concessions for railroads, totalling twenty-eight hundred miles. Next came the Rus-

---

[4] Hansard, LVI, pp. 284, 1669, 1674.

sians with three concessions totalling fifteen hundred miles; the Germans, with two concessions of seven hundred and twenty miles; the Belgians, with one concession of six hundred and fifty miles; the French, with three concessions of four hundred and twenty miles; the Americans with one concession of three hundred miles. Together with German interests the Hongkong and Shanghai Bank was to construct the important Tientsin-Chinkiang line, which, it was hoped, would compete successfully with the Belgian Peking-Hankow line. Furthermore, British interests were to build the Shanghai-Nanking railway, and it was hoped that an arrangement could be made with the American concessionaires to share in the Hankow-Canton line. The extension of the Burma railroad system toward the upper Yangtze was also envisaged. Mining rights had been secured by the Peking Syndicate in the provinces of Shansi, Hunan and Chekiang. Sir Claude MacDonald was speaking the plain truth when he remarked that England had not come out second best.[5]

But a more vigorous policy in dealing with the Chinese situation did not entirely meet the needs of the moment. What impressed many critics of the government's policy was the inability of the British to enlist the aid of other nations in support of the policy of the status quo in China.

> " Never before in this century, at least, has the British Empire been in such serious danger as today, despite the frequent boast that our means of defence are most efficient and the absolute certainty that our Government not only disposes of an overwhelming majority in Parliament, but has a united people outside at its beck and call, ready and even anxious to lend it every conceivable assistance," wrote one of the ablest commentators. " Great Britain, the very essence of whose existence is foreign commerce, is being gradually ousted out of the neutral markets of the world; her political prestige has so completely disappeared that, whenever her Government ' puts its foot down,' foreigners laugh and tell us truly that the attitude is assumed the better to spring backwards; territory purchased with the life blood of her best men is being frittered away in ' graceful concessions ' leading to further losses, and now even the very conditions essential to commercial expansion are being deliberately and systematically destroyed by our pushing rivals . . ." " It is hardly too much to say that since the days of Charles II foreign states have never treated the rights and interests of Great Britain with less consideration and more studied disrespect." " There is not a serious politician on the Continent of Europe who believes that our present Government will risk a war, however great the provocation." [6]

As a matter of fact this aspect of the situation had occupied the government more than any outside contemporary could know. There is still but little material available to enlighten us about the discussions which took place in a series

---

[5] *China No. 1 (1899)*, nos. 295, 459. The details may be read in this voluminous collection of documents. Among the secondary accounts the reader may consult Joseph: *Foreign Diplomacy in China*, chaps. xii–xiv, passim; McCordock: *British Far Eastern Policy*, chap. iv, passim.

[6] Anonymous: "The Failure of our Foreign Policy" (*Contemporary Review*, April, 1898, pp. 457–80), especially pp. 457, 471, 477.

of important cabinet meetings during the last ten days of March. The British documents thus far published are silent on the matter, and of the authorized biographies not even Garvin's *Chamberlain* is of much help. All we can do, then, is to piece together what scraps of evidence may be gleaned from divers sources. This much we know, that various solutions were discussed. Balfour, speaking in the house of commons on April 29, lifted the curtain to a certain extent. Defending the occupation of Weihaiwei, he asked the question whether the Russians could have been prevented from taking Port Arthur. His answer was affirmative but qualified:

" It would have been, I believe, perfectly possible for us to do so," he maintained. " I believe it is extremely probable that if we had sent our Fleet to Port Arthur and occupied the port Russia would not have made it a *casus belli*. There is no certainty about it. It might have involved us and Russia, and by a not unnatural consequence the whole of the civilised world in arms, and, for my part, I would never consent to take part in a game of bluff, which may have consequences like that unless I am prepared to face those consequences. I do not think we should have been wise to engage, and I do not believe anybody in this House would have the courage to say we ought to have engaged in a European war in order to prevent the Russians from going to Port Arthur."

But, he continued, even if the Russians had not gone to war, where would England be? She would have had to hold Port Arthur with large forces and to fortify it to the hilt. Relations with Russia would have been strained to the breaking point. Russia would have employed all her efforts to get Britain involved in war elsewhere. In the meanwhile the Russian railroad would be creeping southward, and nothing would be able to stop it.[7]

This revelation of Balfour's is supported by the evidence contained in Curzon's biography and by statements which Chamberlain made to the German ambassador. We know that the suggestion to lease Weihaiwei was at first opposed by all influential members of the cabinet — Balfour, Chamberlain, Goschen, the Duke of Devonshire, Lansdowne and Hicks Beach, and that it was only after five cabinet meetings that the proposal was finally adopted. In the meanwhile the British fleet was ordered to leave Hongkong and steam north, probably with instructions to await further orders. According to Chamberlain it was discovered that there was a height near Talienwan from which Port Arthur could be completely dominated.[8]

But, in the end, the cabinet decided that Port Arthur was not worth the chance of war. Balfour went over to the Weihaiwei project and Salisbury approved the decision. Then there arose the further question, how could Russia be prevented from advancing yet further in the months or years to come? The British were convinced that before long the Russians would throw the mantle of

---

[7] Hansard, LVI, pp. 1592-4.

[8] Ronaldshay: *Life of Curzon*, I, pp. 284-5; *Letters of Queen Victoria*, III, p. 238; *Die Grosse Politik*, XIV, no. 3782.

their influence over the Peking government and gradually smother it. Anxiety on this point speaks out of all the critical writing and out of all the debates in parliament. After all, the negotiations with Russia had shown that the Tsar's government was unwilling to draw even an imaginary line to define the limits of its aspirations.

In the Near East the British had always been able to check Russian expansion by drawing upon the support of Austria and Italy. Who would perform the same service in the Far East? Chamberlain, who took the Far Eastern crisis more seriously than any of his colleagues and who had already become convinced that isolation was more dangerous than profitable, was very intent on developing a close friendship with the United States. He had harbored the phantastic notion that the great Republic might be induced to co-operate with England in the Near Eastern crisis, and it was therefore natural that he should have thought first of America in connexion with the Far East, where American interests were considerable and well recognized. It must be admitted that there was some ground for hoping that the Americans would play an active part. The occupation of Kiao-chow had called forth a storm of protest in the American press, which accused Germany of " land-grabbing propensities " and described the Kiao-chow episode as a " piratical seizure." In December 1897 the *New York Times* had gone so far as to declare: " Our interest in the cutting up of China is that the British lion shall get his share." The United States and Britain should collaborate in keeping the door open. Alfred Austin was apparently expressing a feeling widespread on both sides of the Atlantic when he published, on March 29, 1898, his poem, *A Voice from the West,* which read in part:

> " Yes, this is the voice of the bluff March gale;
>   We severed have been too long;
> But now we have done with a worn-out tale —
>   The tale of an ancient wrong —
>   And our friendship shall last as love doth last
>   And be stronger than death is strong."

To all appearances the blood-brothership of America and Britain was in the air.[9]

Chamberlain was by no means the only statesman of note who favored an Anglo-Saxon understanding. Leaders of both parties, from Salisbury and Balfour to Rosebery and the other Liberal Imperialists, were convinced protagonists of the idea. The American ambassador at London, John Hay, and his first secretary, Henry White, were hand in glove with these men. At home President McKinley, Senator Lodge, Richard Olney, Whitelaw Reid, Theodore Roosevelt, Admiral Mahan, Lyman Abbott and many other influential men expressed themselves favorably. The New York press threw its weight on the same side of the scales. On the side of Britain this unprecedented outburst of affection was

    [9] Bertha A. Reuter: *Anglo-American Relations during the Spanish-American War* (New York, 1924), pp. 74–6, 118 ff.; Clara E. Schieber: *American Sentiment toward Germany, 1870–1914* (Boston, 1923), chap. iii, passim.

due in part to the rapidly spreading cult of race solidarity, in part to the international exigencies of the moment. On the American side the approaching war with Spain was certainly a decisive factor. Henry White was surprised to find that even the most rabid English-baiters among the senators had suddenly become converted to the new gospel. American friendliness was, if we may adopt the phrase of White's biographer, " the friendliness of a country shivering a little to find herself out in the great arena of world affairs, feeling the chill hostility of all the continental nations, and glad for once to meet John Bull halfway." [10]

But all this " billing and cooing," which the hostile *Saturday Review* (April 30, 1898) condemned as " indecent humbug," never got far beyond the domain of sentiment. There was really little prospect that the United States would give up her freedom from " entangling alliances " and join forces with Britain. Even the most enthusiastic supporters of close relations were disposed to think that an alliance was impossible. They therefore declared it unnecessary. Only Chamberlain, whatever he may have said later, cherished hopes of real collaboration. In the preceding chapter mention has been made of his approaches to the American government in the early days of March, and of the evasion which was the only reply. At bottom the United States, which had generally maintained very cordial relations with Russia, had no idea of entering the lists against the Muscovite advance. The oncoming Spanish War was, in the crucial first months of 1898, absorbing all the public attention on this side of the ocean.[11]

Next to the United States Chamberlain would have preferred an understanding if not an alliance with Japan, which, after all, had the same interest as Britain in preventing China from becoming a Russian protectorate. There was, in England, a considerable body of opinion in favor of such a combination and there is no reason to suppose that if an understanding had been consummated it would have aroused much opposition. At any rate, Chamberlain does not seem to have had any apprehensions in the matter. He boldly approached Baron Kato, as we have seen. If Kato had had his way the proposal would have been followed up. In Tokyo a number of the younger statesmen, like Count Hayashi, were very well disposed. But Count Ito and the Elder Statesmen were circumspect. They felt that Japan would have to bear the brunt of the conflict and that she was not yet sufficiently prepared. No move was made to negotiate with the English. On the contrary every effort was bent to the attainment of a settlement

[10] Allan Nevins: *Henry White* (New York, 1930), pp. 129–35. See further William R. Thayer: *The Life and Letters of John Hay* (Boston, 1915), II, pp. 165 ff.; Tyler Dennett: *John Hay* (New York, 1933), pp. 188–9, etc.; Garvin: *Life of Chamberlain*, III, chaps. liii and lx. Of contemporary writings see especially Sir Charles Dilke: " The Future Relations of Great Britain and the United States " (*Forum*, January, 1898, pp. 521–8); Richard Olney: " The International Isolation of the United States " (*Atlantic Monthly*, May, 1898, pp. 577–88); and the very large body of opinion collected by the English *Review of Reviews*, June, 1898, pp. 602 ff.

[11] On Russian-American relations see P. Kelyin: " Severo-Amerikanskie Soedinennie Shtati i Tsarkaia Rossiia v 90 gg. XIX v." (*Krasnyi Arkhiv*, LII, pp. 124–42).

with Russia. Apparently even the inconclusive Nishi-Rosen agreement was preferred to the prospect of an alliance with Britain.[12]

Of the remaining powers directly interested in the Far East only Germany could be considered as a possible ally. Relations between England and Germany had not been good. In fact public opinion in both countries had rarely been so wrought up as in the autumn of 1897. There was friction, too, between the governments, for the Germans were constantly pressing for a favorable settlement of disputed questions in Togoland, Samoa and elsewhere.[13] The British government showed no disposition to make concessions, but was, nevertheless, very careful not to identify itself with the popular animosity. It was a time when England had enough troubles without incurring unnecessary hostility. Steps were taken to moderate the tone of the press, and the London editors who, it was always said, could not be influenced, responded most readily to the hint from high quarters.[14] On the German side there was the same desire not to push matters too far. A breach with England was a thing that the foreign office was most anxious to avoid. England's acceptance of the German occupation of Kiao-chow was a striking contrast to the desperate opposition of Muraviev. It helped to instill something like cordiality into the relations of the two countries and at the same time served to make the German Emperor realize the futility of the continental league. The Berlin government was bound to conclude that in the Far East Germany's interest and that of Britain were more nearly alike than the interests of Germany and Russia. During the winter the general tone of Anglo-German relations underwent a marked change for the better. Even the Emperor, while still complaining that all his advances had been rejected, was taking an attitude of aggrievement and regret rather than an attitude of anger and defiance.[15]

It was evidently this perceptible change in Anglo-German relations that decided the London cabinet to try for an agreement with Germany. The decision appears to have been reached in the crucial cabinet meeting on March 25, 1898, when the whole question of British action in reply to the occupation of Port Arthur was discussed. We know that on that day Balfour lunched with the German ambassador, after which he called upon Lord Salisbury, who was about to leave for the Continent the next day at eleven. The cabinet met at about three-thirty and remained in session until seven in the evening, all the leading members being present.[16]

It is quite important to bear these details in mind, for the impending negotia-

---

[12] In addition to what has been said in the preceding chapter, see Sir Ellis Ashmead Bartlett's account of his conversation with a Japanese statesman, evidently Baron Kato (Hansard, LVI, pp. 1672–3), and the statements of Chamberlain to the German ambassador (*Die Grosse Politik*, XIV, nos. 3782, 3789).   [13] Garvin: *Life of Chamberlain*, III, pp. 245–7.

[14] *Letters of Queen Victoria*, III, pp. 224–5.

[15] *British Documents*, I, no. 63; MacDiarmid: *Life of Grierson*, pp. 134–6.

[16] *Letters of Queen Victoria*, III, p. 238; *Die Grosse Politik*, XIV, no. 3781. The visit of Balfour to Salisbury is reported in the *Times*, March 26, 1898, p. 7. Salisbury was unable to leave London on account of a very severe storm. He departed for the Continent on March 28.

tions with Germany have been made the subject of an extraordinary amount of critical writing, and the question has been raised again and again whether Lord Salisbury was a party to the policy. It cannot be proved that Balfour and Salisbury discussed the projected understanding with Germany, or that the matter was taken up in the cabinet meeting of March 25, when it was decided not to go the limit in opposing the Russian action. But it would certainly be strange if the matter was not brought up. What evidence we possess would indicate that it was. When Balfour lunched with Hatzfeldt he clearly did not yet have a mandate from the cabinet, though he may have already gone over the question with Salisbury. His remarks were of a general nature. He expressed the desire for better relations between England and Germany, pointing out that the two nations had no great conflicting interests. Hatzfeldt, who had no instructions, made a cordial if evasive reply, taking the opportunity, however, to bring up once more the German grievances touching African affairs and German desires in Shantung. The whole conversation was obviously intended as a reconnaissance, and it ended with Balfour's expression of the hope that Hatzfeldt would soon look him up.[17]

Four days later the ambassador had a long, informal and very frank talk with Chamberlain, who acted as the chief British negotiator throughout the forthcoming discussions. This is in itself surprising, for Balfour, not Chamberlain, was acting foreign minister in Salisbury's absence. It has been thought by some German writers that the colonial secretary was working on his own and that his proposals were at best nothing more than personal advances. That there is no foundation for such a surmise has been conclusively shown by the recently published biography of Chamberlain. It is perfectly clear that not only Salisbury and Balfour, but other cabinet members, like the Duke of Devonshire, desired a closer connexion with Germany. They were, perhaps, less sanguine and less ready to go all the way to an alliance, but they sympathized with the effort. Chamberlain apparently carried on the conversations because he was, next to Salisbury, the most influential member of the government, because he was most impressed with the danger in the Far East and because his Unionist followers were most dissatisfied with the policy of Salisbury in the preceding few months. The Unionists had, in fact, formed a " Committee to Promote a Policy of Resistance to the Ascendency of Russia and other Foreign Powers in China," and this committee, composed of members of parliament, had passed a resolution on March 24 " that the doors through which our trade in China must pass should be kept open at the risk of war." [18] This helps to explain Chamberlain's strong line in the cabinet on March 25 and his determination to do something to prevent further gains by Russia. At the time there was much talk of a split in the cabinet. The *Saturday Review* went so far as to speak of a " fierce fight." [19] That

---

[17] *Die Grosse Politik*, XIV, nos. 3782, 3788.   [18] London *Times*, March 24, 25, 1898.
[19] *Saturday Review*, February 26, 1898; Gardiner: *Life of Harcourt*, II, pp. 450–1; Elliot: *Life of Goschen*, II, pp. 219 ff.

was overshooting the mark. Salisbury and Chamberlain did not see eye to eye, especially in the Far Eastern business. Weeks before the critical days of March the colonial secretary had confessed to a friend that he had had " a strong difference of opinion with Lord Salisbury." [20] But despite all this the two men were far more tolerant of each other than one would have thought possible. Hatzfeldt and other diplomats surely exaggerated the disagreement in the cabinet. We now know that Chamberlain informed Balfour and the cabinet promptly of what passed between him and Hatzfeldt, and that he laid the whole matter before Lord Salisbury immediately on the latter's return on April 29. It is senseless, then, to try to make out that Chamberlain was playing a lone hand. [21]

The colonial secretary was by nature a business man. He had no professional training as a diplomat and was apt to approach problems of international relations too directly, too bluntly, and rather with the idea that anything could be had for a price. German support was needed for a particular purpose. Bids were to be made, and if they were found satisfactory the " deal " could be closed. Unmindful of Talleyrand's famous saying that language was given men to enable them to conceal their thoughts, Chamberlain scorned circumlocutions and went straight to the point. [22]

For more than a decade after the publication of the German documents we had no other source than that for the story of the Chamberlain-Hatzfeldt conversations. Now at last we have, in Garvin's *Life*, the memoranda of the British statesman, which enable us to check more closely the aims and arguments of both sides. In the first meeting, on March 29, there was some skirmishing and some talk of the identity of British and German interests on larger issues of world affairs. Hatzfeldt reported Chamberlain as saying that the world situation had taken a turn which made it impossible for England to maintain any longer her traditional policy of isolation. According to the British account the proposition was not so bald. The ambassador had remarked that the former community of interest and feeling had been wrecked by the Jameson episode and that " there was a general impression on the Continent that the policy of the United Kingdom was to bring about a war between other powers but to take no part in it herself," which tended to produce irritation and distrust. It was this that led Chamberlain to remark: " It is possible that the policy of the United Kingdom may be changed by circumstances which are too strong for us to resist." Thereupon the conversation turned to the question of an alliance. Hatzfeldt's version was that Chamberlain suggested that if Germany would stand on the side of England, England would stand on Germany's side if she were attacked. This

---

[20] January 29, 1898 (*Journals and Letters of Reginald Viscount Esher*, [London, 1934], I, pp. 210–1).

[21] See especially Garvin: *Life of Chamberlain*, III, pp. 256 ff.

[22] There is a rather interesting anonymous estimate of this side of Chamberlain, entitled " Mr. Chamberlain as Foreign Minister " (*Fortnightly Review*, August, 1898, pp. 317–25). I need hardly say that my estimate does not agree entirely with that of Mr. Garvin, though the latter has undoubtedly done much to put matters in a clearer setting.

would be the equivalent of England's joining the Triple Alliance, and could be arranged through a formal treaty. A decision should be reached within the next days. In Chamberlain's own record of the discussion there is no mention of the Triple Alliance, and nothing to suggest the need of haste. The suggestions as they emerged from the conversation were these: " That an alliance might be established by Treaty or Agreement between Germany and Great Britain for a term of years. That it should be of a defensive character based upon a mutual understanding as to policy in China and elsewhere." [23]

These two accounts do not differ in any fundamental respect, but it is worth noting the difference of emphasis. Hatzfeldt, even though he rather disliked and distrusted Chamberlain, was undoubtedly very favorable to an agreement with England. He reported to his government as forcefully as possible, making Chamberlain appear more positive than he really was and bringing in the Triple Alliance to make the prospective arrangement more attractive. Evidently he feared that the Berlin foreign office was too pro-Russian and that the advantages of the British connexion would not be duly considered. As a matter of fact, however, the foreign office showed more than a slight interest in the English advances and promptly outlined the conditions of an agreement. First and foremost, wrote Bülow, the alliance would have to be sanctioned by parliament, so that all British governments would be bound by it. Germany, he admitted, had a great interest in the preservation of British power, for if England were ruined, Russia and France would turn on Germany unmolested. It was a mistake, he pointed out, for England to become embroiled with Russia and France at the same time. The wise course would be to settle with the Russians, so that they would no longer support the French. France, on the other hand, would always back Russia, no matter what concessions were made to her. Having squared the Russians, then, the British would have no need to fear France, for if war broke out Germany would remain neutral and Italy, too, would stand by England. French troops would be tied up on the frontiers, while the British ruled the seas.

The Bülow reflections smack strongly of the Holstein reasoning. They dealt less with the problem of an Anglo-German agreement than with the ways and means for England to get herself out of an unenviable situation. Certainly they do not betray a very ardent desire for an immediate agreement. But Hatzfeldt communicated Bülow's ideas to Chamberlain at once, in a second meeting of the two men on April 1. He made rather far-reaching assurances respecting Germany's position and policy: " As regards Germany, their interest was against any policy which would materially cripple the sea-power of England. They knew perfectly well that in such a case they would be attacked next. Therefore, in no case would they join a combination against us. Treaty or no Treaty, the worst we had to anticipate from them was that they would remain neutral." Chamberlain on his side tried to dissipate all ideas that England would not remain true to any obligations she undertook. What he wanted, he said, was a

---

[23] *Die Grosse Politik,* XIV, nos. 3782, 3789; Garvin: *Life of Chamberlain,* III, pp. 259–60.

treaty which would be approved by parliament and made public. Turning then to the concrete purposes of the proposed agreement he stressed the fact that there was no thought of trying to undo what Russia had done. " We object most strongly to what we think she (Russia) may and will obtain." That is, the purpose of the agreement would be to check Russian advance beyond Manchuria. " I said if we had a clear understanding with Germany and a joint policy we might adopt a much stronger attitude than if we were alone, and in this case we could lay down the bases of a settlement in China which neither France nor Russia would be likely to resist." Asked what kind of arrangement he proposed, he went on: " I said, speaking only for myself, that I thought we might say to Russia — 'You have got all you say you want. We are ready to recognise your position, but you must not go further. The rest of China is under our joint protection.'" Germany, he suggested, might act as protector of Shantung and the hinterland, assume a certain financial control, and use the money to train a native army under German officers. England could do the same in the central and southern provinces. Then, " if in the future Russia attempted further aggression, she would have to confront not only a war with two great European Powers but also the defensive forces of China organised and led by European officers." [24]

Chamberlain had certainly laid his cards on the table. While Bülow had suggested that Britain and Russia reach an agreement which would have left France isolated and helpless, the colonial secretary had put forward the suggestion for an agreement, a public alliance, unqualifiedly directed against Russian policy in China. The Celestial Empire was to be divided into Russian, German and British spheres, the British being the largest and most populous, while at the same time furthest removed from the Russian. The Germans, indeed, were to serve as buffers, as shock absorbers. No wonder that Hatzfeldt avoided reporting to his government the details of Chamberlain's suggestions. He toned it all down, emphasizing the fact that the English statesman was interested, not in opposing the Russian action at Port Arthur, but merely in checking any future advance. He indicated that Chamberlain might be willing to accord Germany an extension of her sphere of influence, but said nothing of what the British would demand for themselves.

If the Berlin government had known as much of Chamberlain's remarks as we can now learn from his memorandum, it is almost a certainty that it would have taken a stronger stand against the alliance project. Even on the basis of the somewhat misleading Hatzfeldt report the foreign office showed little enthusiasm and a good deal of incredulity. It seemed hardly believable that the British parliament would approve the alliance, for, as Bülow pointed out, the Kruger telegram had shown the depth of English animosity and not even Chamberlain could honestly believe that such feelings could be transformed overnight. If the treaty were submitted to parliament and rejected, Germany

---

[24] *Die Grosse Politik,* XIV, no. 3784; Garvin, op. cit., III, pp. 263–6.

would be left at the mercy of the greatly enhanced hostility of Russia and France. It would therefore be better to wait until England was still harder pressed — until she needed the alliance even more urgently. In the meanwhile German opinion could be brought around to the idea if England were more considerate in her dealings with Germany.[25]

At this stage in the discussion came the government's explanations to parliament, on April 5. These have already been touched upon, and it is necessary to note here only the fact that Balfour on this occasion sounded out the House on the question of alliances. The German assurances regarding Kiao-chow, he said,

" indicate what I believe to be the absolute truth, which is that within China — certainly in China — I do not limit the statement to that, but certainly in China — British interests and German interests are absolutely identical. Jealousy, I suppose, there may be between individual traders, individual concessionaires, and individual producers. But fundamentally the interests of the two countries are the same and must be the same, and I certainly believe that we shall be able without difficulty to work hand in hand towards carrying out these general commercial objects, which I believe approve themselves to the sense of this House." And towards the end of his statement he referred to the possibility of a time coming " when the great Powers primarily interested in the commerce of the world " might " feel that their interests draw them together, and require them to join an alliance which no man can resist for the purpose of seeing that China shall not fall a prey to any exclusive interest." [26]

Sir William Harcourt described this idea of a general alliance as a " Utopian dream," but Sir Edward Grey came to the support of Balfour. " There is," he said,

" a group of six Powers more likely to be interested in the Far East than any other — Russia, France, Germany, United States, Japan and ourselves; but surely it is for the interests of several of these Powers, as much as our own, that there should be an open door to China and a neutral market? We have heard much in recent years of the successful commercial competition of Germany, the United States as successful all over the world, and Japan as competing in that part of the world; and it becomes more and more to the interest of these nations that the policy of the open door should be maintained. It may be a paradox to say that out of successful commercial rivalry may come political agreement; but I do not see why in future years the interests of these Powers should not, through commercial rivalry, more and more make themselves felt, to help attain this. . . . Isolation is sometimes apt to be mistaken for indifference, and in future years, when it is required, is likely to become unsuccessful. We must not look to isolation. We must find a common ground of interest with other Powers."

---

[25] *Die Grosse Politik,* XIV, no. 3785.
[26] Hansard: *Parliamentary Debates,* Series IV, vol. LVI, pp. 232, 238.

Sir Charles Beresford went even further, and declared: " I believe that the time
for our ' splendid isolation ' is gone. It was very useful for Noah, but it is not
suitable for the present time, and I believe if the Government of this country
would try to make an alliance with Germany, that really would make for peace
for a very long period." [27]

On the very day of this debate Balfour had a second talk with the German
ambassador. He admitted that there was room for doubt whether an alliance
could be gotten through parliament (on this point Chamberlain was confident),
and agreed with Hatzfeldt that the immediate task was to prepare the ground
and improve public opinion in both countries. Balfour hinted quite broadly
that in his estimation Chamberlain was trying to go too fast. Hatzfeldt thought
Balfour would not be sorry if the colonial secretary failed in his efforts. This
was certainly an erroneous impression, the result, probably, of the ambassador's
dislike of Chamberlain. Still, Hatzfeldt reported home that he was convinced
of Chamberlain's sincerity and believed that the cabinet was behind the advances to Germany. Even the Liberal leaders, he thought, were well disposed
(which Grey's utterances in parliament would seem to bear out).[28]

The question of whether parliament and the country would have accepted
an alliance with Germany in the spring of 1898 is a really crucial one, for any
judgment of the negotiations must of necessity hinge upon it. So much, at least,
is clear: there was no widespread sentiment in the country for such a connexion.
In parliament, apart from Grey, only those two amusing and erratic members, Beresford and Ashmead Bartlett, spoke openly in favor of an alliance with
Germany. The major organs of the periodical press made no response, though
Henry M. Stanley declared isolation to be a " gaudy air-bladder " and recommended that England join the Triple Alliance, which would be backed by the
moral support of the United States and the material forces of Japan, if it came
to a question of blocking the Russians and French in China.[29] As against this
lone note of warning there sounded the strident calls of the vigorously anti-
German papers, like the *Saturday Review,* which asserted roundly that Germany was the chief enemy in the Far East: " It will be well for England when
our natural and inevitable hostility towards our greatest rival can have free
play." " It is natural for Germany to look to us; but she is our rival, our true
' natural enemy '; and it would be better for England to fight than be
' friendly.' " [30]

It may be conceded at once that the *Saturday Review* was not typical of the
press at large. But what do you find if you consult a newspaper like the *Times,*
which generally supported Chamberlain and which was almost rabid in its denunciations of Russian schemes in China? Editorially the *Times* hardly men-

---

[27] Ibid., pp. 280–1, 285–6.

[28] *Die Grosse Politik,* XIV, no. 3786.

[29] Henry M. Stanley: " ' Splendid Isolation ' or What? " (*Nineteenth Century,* June, 1898,
pp. 869–78).   [30] *Saturday Review,* March 26, April 16, 1898.

tioned the suggested rapprochement with Germany. When the Blue Book was published toward the end of April, the editor recognized that Germany's attitude in the Far Eastern crisis had shown anxiety not to antagonize England. Nevertheless the *Times* criticized sharply the government's assurances to Germany with respect to Weihaiwei, and the Berlin correspondent from the very outset warned his countrymen against cherishing hopes of German support. "It must be remembered," he wrote, "that it is far from likely that an understanding between Germany and England could assume other than a commercial aspect. Germany's position in the map of Europe dictates to her the necessity of maintaining her friendly relations with Russia." To which the editor of the *Times* added: "It seems difficult for Germans to comprehend that an identity of commercial interests does not imply that this country should or would make political concessions, either to Germany or her allies, in order to purchase co-operation in the sphere of trade." A month later the Berlin correspondent, summing up the discussion of the problem by the German press, wrote at some length:

"It is a matter of elementary knowledge to those who have followed the trend of German foreign policy for even a very few years that neither 'spontaneous' declarations nor far more material concessions have the slightest prospect of succeeding in placing Germany in the position of an ally of England against Russia, either in Europe or in Asia. The only conceivable result of such amiable and well-meant endeavours would be to facilitate for Germany the development of the essentially Bismarckian policy of grasping the tongue of the balance between England and Russia and reaping a handsome commission as 'honest broker' from both sides. It is equally to the interest of England and Russia to prevent the realization of such schemes, and this interest ought undoubtedly, amid many subjects of conflict, to be one of the considerations which from time to time may smooth the path for a good understanding and for loyal co-operation between the two greatest Asiatic Powers." [31]

What shall we conclude, then, with regard to the chances of an alliance being accepted by the English parliament and by the country? My personal impression is that in this matter Balfour, and perhaps most of those in the cabinet who were sympathetic, were nearer the right track than Chamberlain. Certainly the country would have been glad of an agreement with Germany which would have assured England support against Russian aggression in China. Through such an agreement England would have had everything to gain and very little, if anything, to lose. But there was, of course, almost no chance that the Germans would gratuitously enlist in a crusade against Russia, the more so as they were glad to see Russia deeply involved in China. They had no desire to stop her. Chamberlain was keen-witted enough to see that. He therefore suggested a defensive alliance as a makeweight. The real question is whether this alliance, not

[31] London *Times,* April 9, May 2, 1898. I have made no use of Karl O. Herkenberg: *The Times und das Deutsch-Englische Verhältnis im Jahre 1898* (Berlin, 1925), because it is incomplete and the dates are not always accurate.

the Far Eastern agreement, would have proved acceptable. The answer depends in part on the control of Chamberlain and Salisbury over their parliamentary majority. Let us assume that there was enough discipline to get the treaty through parliament. There would have still remained the opinion of the country. The view of Balfour seems to have been that there should be careful preparation of opinion before the treaty were brought forward. I think this was the sound approach to the problem. The yawning chasm between violent popular hostility and close political alliance was still too wide to be bridged without long and arduous labor. Even if the treaty had been made and put through parliament, its existence would not have been healthy until the popular attitude had changed or been changed.

On the German side there was no more popular enthusiasm than on the English. Many influential papers, like the *Vossische Zeitung,* the *National Zeitung,* the *Kölnische Zeitung* and the *Hamburgische Correspondent* spoke appreciatively of Balfour's references to the community of British and German interests in the Far East, and expressed the desire for friendlier relations. On the other hand they one and all rejected the idea of hostility to Russia, and took the stand that England must deal with Germany as an equal — she must be willing to pay the price. " Our answer to the voice of the charmer," said the Hamburg paper on April 9, " should be dictated exclusively by our own practical political interests, and these interests point to the necessity for holding on in the course we are at present following. . . . To give up for the sake of a few fine words, which every breeze may blow away, the principles of our east Asiatic policy, to let ourselves be elbowed out of our entente with Russia and France, these are things which are, of course, quite out of the question." " Our policy," wrote the *Vossische Zeitung* on April 13, " will continue to be guided solely by the dictates of German interests, which require the cultivation of friendly relations with Russia quite as much as with England." In a long and obviously inspired review of the international situation the *Kölnische Zeitung* on May 1 flatly denied that there had been any cooling off of German-Russian relations or any change in German policy respecting England: " German policy, in a word, will never be oblivious of the fact that its most essential interests lie in Europe and that its most important task is to maintain and to establish peace with honour for Germany in Europe." [32]

These newspapers gave a fair reflection of the attitude of the German foreign office toward the suggestions of Chamberlain. In all probability the papers were inspired by the press bureau of the Wilhelmstrasse. From the German documents the reaction of the Emperor and of Bülow is quite clear. " Chamberlain," noted the Emperor, " must not forget that in East Prussia I have one Prussian army corps against three Russian armies and nine cavalry divisions located close to the frontier; that no Chinese Wall separates me from them and no British warship can keep them away from me." " The Niger and the Gulf of Pechili

---

[32] I quote from the abstracts in the London *Times,* April 7, 8, 9, 11, 14, May 2, 1898.

concern us less than Alsace-Lorraine." Colonial concessions would not out-weigh the increased hostility of Russia and France resulting from an Anglo-German agreement on the Far East and Africa. If the British were willing later on to extend the entente to Europe that would be another story. In the mean-while England should be kept warm: " Through a well-disposed England we have one card more to play against Russia, and we have besides the prospect of securing from England concessions in the colonial field and in tariff nego-tiations." To all of which Bülow agreed: "We must remain independent be-tween the two powers (Russia and England); we must be the tongue of the balance, not the restlessly swinging pendulum." [33]

Whatever may be said of the Emperor and Bülow, their attitude in this question was clear and understandable. It is important to bear it in mind in order to understand a little interlude which occurred at this stage in the nego-tiations. Baron von Eckardstein, secretary of the German embassy at London, married to a wealthy English heiress and prominent in high financial and so-cial circles, was an almost fanatical adherent of the idea of an alliance and had had something to do with the initiation of the discussions. In mid-April, so he tells us in his memoirs, he went off to Germany ostensibly for private purposes, but in reality to visit the Emperor at Homburg, lay the facts before him and thus counteract the nefarious influence of Holstein and the foreign office. His interview with the Emperor fell in the very days (around April 10) when the correspondence between Homburg and Berlin, mentioned above, was taking place. Yet when Eckardstein was back in London he arranged for a confer-ence with Chamberlain, and gave him a very different picture of the Emperor's attitude.

" The Emperor," he said, " viewed such a possibility (of an alliance) with the greatest favour, and was most anxious that an agreement should be come to. He was very desirous that the matter should be dealt with immediately, as he feared, if there was any delay, that the pourparlers would leak out and would come to the knowledge of Russia. . . . The Emperor thought that at an early date Italy and Austria should be made acquainted with any proposals, and was confident that they would eagerly join in such an arrangement. The Russians were intriguing most actively to bring about a combination against England, but he recognised that the interests of Germany lay in the opposite direction. The prin-ciple of such an arrangement would be a guarantee by both Powers of the posses-sions of the other. Baron Eckardstein seemed to think that this guarantee might be against any attack by any other Power, or, if it were desired to limit it, against any attack by two Powers combined. In the event of such an agreement the Em-peror recognised that we ought to have a free hand in Egypt and the Transvaal. Baron Eckardstein again and again repeated that the Emperor was most anxious that the matter should be dealt with quickly." [34]

---

[33] *Die Grosse Politik*, XIV, nos. 3788–90.
[34] Garvin: *Life of Chamberlain*, III, pp. 2712; Hermann Freiherr von Eckardstein: *Leben-serinnerungen und Politische Denkwürdigkeiten* (Leipzig, 1919), I, pp. 294 ff.

Chamberlain, in making a memorandum of this conversation, noted that he told Eckardstein that the discussions were absolutely personal and unofficial (which had been agreed to from the beginning), and that Salisbury, being away, was not yet informed of what had taken place. He evidently and naturally took everything that had been told him to be true and important. But, having the materials on both sides, we can see that one of two things was true: either the Emperor entirely misled Eckardstein, or else Eckardstein misrepresented the Emperor and misled Chamberlain. There can, I think, be little if any doubt that Eckardstein was the culprit. We have here a first glaring example of the appalling and disastrous mystification which he practiced in 1901. Knowing the German foreign office to be lukewarm, he tried to go over the heads of Bülow and Holstein and enlist the aid of the Emperor. Finding William no more enthusiastic, he simply falsified the facts and gave a glowing account to Chamberlain. The constant emphasis on the need for haste was probably meant to stampede both sides into an agreement before there was time to think too much about it. The worst part of the situation was that the ambassador, Count Hatzfeldt, was not entirely innocent of this work of deception. We have seen that, from the very outset, he had tended, in his reports, to gloss over the difficulties and to magnify Chamberlain's " offers." Now in April he knew that the Emperor was not enthusiastic, as Eckardstein pictured him, for he had instructions from Berlin which made the German view perfectly clear. Yet he apparently did nothing to prevent Eckardstein from going to Chamberlain and arousing false hopes. Of course Eckardstein may have misled Hatzfeldt as he did others, though it would have been more difficult.

On April 25 the colonial secretary lunched with Hatzfeldt at the home of Eckardstein. (Hatzfeldt reported to Berlin that the meeting had been arranged at Chamberlain's request, though in reality it was Eckardstein's suggestion). The ambassador's report of the conversation makes a very long document. He maintained that Chamberlain once again " pressed " for an alliance and stuck to his guns even after all the familiar German arguments against it had been marshalled once more. Hatzfeldt indicated the possibility of reviving the Mediterranean Agreements of 1887, with the idea that a closer connexion between England on the one hand and Austria and Italy on the other would of necessity lead to closer Anglo-German relations. Chamberlain showed little interest in this approach and reiterated that Germany and the alliance with Germany were the crucial points. England needed the agreement to check the further advance of Russia in China. If Germany rejected the British offer, England might find it necessary to make separate agreements with Russia or France.[35]

Chamberlain's memorandum of the conversation is much briefer and much more to the point. He says nothing of having pressed for an alliance, but of course discretion may have kept him from recording his eagerness. He does, however, speak of the arguments which Hatzfeldt brought forward against

---

[35] *Die Grosse Politik*, XIV, no. 3793.

an immediate agreement and of the suggestion to revive the Mediterranean Agreements. But there is no mention of any hints on Chamberlain's part that England might seek an agreement with Russia or France. The colonial secretary's report ends thus: "I said that I gathered that he thought any attempt to secure a direct defensive alliance between Germany and England was premature. He assented, but said the opportunity might come later. I reminded him of the French proverb, ' le bonheur qui passe.' " [36]

It is most difficult to reconstruct an accurate account of this conversation from the reports of the two participants, for even if there is general agreement on the facts, the tone of the two records is quite different. It is likely that, after his conversation with Eckardstein, Chamberlain was more eager and enthusiastic than would appear from his memorandum, and it may well be that, when his eyes were opened to the real state of affairs, he spoke more sharply about the possibility of an arrangement with Russia and France than he was willing to admit in writing. At any rate, so much is beyond dispute: Hatzfeldt, following his instructions, had definitely deflated the idea of an alliance and admitted to Chamberlain in so many words that the Germans thought the project premature. In reporting to his government, however, Hatzfeldt still tried to provoke favorable action. He not only stressed the eagerness of Chamberlain, but also underlined the danger of agreements between England, Russia and France. But the warnings disturbed neither the Emperor nor Holstein, both of whom made heavy annotations on the Hatzfeldt report. Bülow made the marginal notes his own and wrote cold-bloodedly to London that Germany was not menaced by Russia and therefore could not take the risk of throwing herself in Russia's way. Chamberlain, he said, was evidently trying to play off Germany against France. Let him try to reach an agreement with France. He would find that France would never abandon Russia. When the British had learned this lesson, it would be easier to talk to them of a profitable alliance.[37]

To all intents and purposes the alliance discussions were over. Eckardstein, who hurried to the colonial office to smooth things over, tried to assure Chamberlain that the Emperor was really strongly in favor of the alliance, and suggested that Prince Hohenlohe must have interfered to spoil the whole thing. To which Chamberlain gave an unanswerable reply: "I said that I did not see that there was anything to be done. Either Count Hatzfeldt's language was that of the Emperor, in which case the matter was ended; or it was not, and in this case it was for the Emperor to make the next move." [38]

Lord Salisbury returned from the Continent on April 29 and was informed at once by Chamberlain of the discussions that had been going on. The letter of the colonial secretary shows that in spite of his disappointing experience he had not changed his mind about the dangers of England's position and the desirability of the alliance with Germany:

---

[36] Garvin, op. cit., III, pp. 273–4.
[38] Garvin, op. cit., III, pp. 276–7.
[37] *Die Grosse Politik*, XIV, no. 3794.

"Recent experience seems to show that we are powerless to resist the ultimate control of China by Russia, and that we are at a great disadvantage in negotiating with France, as long as we retain our present isolation, and I think the country would support us in a Treaty with Germany providing for reciprocal defence. I think such a Treaty would make for peace and might be negotiated at the present time. But it is for you to say whether the matter should be pressed or allowed to drop."

The prime minister, as Chamberlain's biographer says, "shared the wish but not the faith." Hatzfeldt came to see him on the afternoon of May 2 and spoke in a general way of the desirability of better relations. But he took care to add that nothing must be hurried and hinted that if England wished an alliance, it must be prepared for by amiability in other matters. "His business," wrote Salisbury to Chamberlain, "was evidently to throw cold water. . . . I quite agree with you that under the circumstances a closer relation with Germany would be very desirable; but can we get it?" There was some talk between the two men on May 3, after the cabinet, and Salisbury suggested that, if Eckardstein came again, Chamberlain might say that the Government was prepared to consider the idea favorably. It is clear from the record of these conversations that Chamberlain was still taken in by Eckardstein, and that he put considerable stock in the latter's story of the Emperor's being led astray by his advisers.[39]

Though Salisbury would have been as glad as any other Englishman to secure German support against Russia, he did not take the Far Eastern situation as seriously as Chamberlain and was not as deeply impressed with the dangers of isolation. This he revealed in the famous "Dying Nations Speech" which he delivered at the Albert Hall on May 4, and which may be taken as a classic example of the projection of Darwinian ideas into political calculations. As on previous occasions the prime minister spoke half lightly, half cynically about the international situation. The Chinese question, he thought, had perhaps received more attention than it deserved. It had been "a sort of diplomatic cracker that has produced a great many detonations, but I think the smoke of it has now floated into the distance." The government had been absolutely opposed to Russia's taking Port Arthur, and the Russians had probably made a mistake in going there. Since the British had leased Weihaiwei, however, the possession of Port Arthur could no longer enhance Russian influence at Peking. Weihaiwei could be defended from the sea, which Port Arthur could not. To be sure, similar crises might occur in the future:

"But we know that we shall maintain against all comers that which we possess, and we know, in spite of the jargon about isolation, that we are amply competent to do so."

---

[39] Garvin: *Life of Chamberlain*, III, pp. 278–80; there is no record of the Salisbury-Hatzfeldt conversation in the German sources.

But that in itself might not secure peace for the world, for there were living and dying nations, the ones growing ever stronger, the others ever weaker:

" For one reason or another — from the necessities of politics or under the pretext of philanthropy — the living nations will gradually encroach on the territory of the dying, and the seed and causes of conflict amongst civilised nations will speedily appear. Of course, it is not to be supposed that any one nation of the living nations will be allowed to have the profitable monopoly of curing or cutting up these unfortunate patients, and the controversy is as to who shall have the privilege of doing so, and in what measure he shall do it. . . . These are the dangers which, I think, threaten us in the period that is coming on. It is a period which will tax our resolution, our tenacity and imperial instincts, to the utmost. Undoubtedly we shall not allow England to be at a disadvantage in any rearrangement that may take place. On the other hand, we shall not be jealous if desolation and sterility are removed by the aggrandisement of a rival in regions to which our arms cannot extend."

This speech, coming as it did after much bitter criticism of the government, is of great interest. It shows beyond question that Salisbury took the Far Eastern situation less seriously than most people and that he was less upset by the Russian advance. It shows — and this is more important — that he felt no disposition to give up isolation. England was, he maintained, quite able to hold her own.[40] It was in this sense that the speech was read by his contemporaries. In a long letter to the *Times* a Tory member of parliament voiced his condemnation and insisted that Salisbury should give over the foreign office to Balfour. Everybody, he wrote, knows that Salisbury has handled foreign affairs by himself: " Neither the Cabinet nor the party exercise the slightest influence or control in that *mare clausum*." Therefore Salisbury alone must be held responsible for the turn events had taken. The nation was grateful that he had preserved peace, but wished he had been somewhat more solicitous to preserve honor as well. In a leading article the *Times* subscribed to these sentiments, which, it declared, were widely shared. With great bitterness it recalled Salisbury's remark of two years before to the effect that people were apt to " foreshorten distance " in dealing with the Chinese problem. It was time to put an end to the handling of vital national interests by the methods of " neatly-turned epigrams." [41]

In view of the expressed sentiments of Salisbury, it is no cause for wonder that Count Hatzfeldt found him sceptical about entering upon a discussion of the matter broached by Balfour and so frankly debated by Chamberlain. In a conversation of May 11 the prime minister recurred to the question, but only to remark irritably: " You ask too much for your friendship." Hatzfeldt urged

---

[40] This is, it seems to me, the only possible interpretation of the speech. It is incomprehensible to me how writers like Joseph: *Foreign Diplomacy in China*, p. 318, can read it as an invitation to the English people to give up isolation.

[41] London *Times*, May 5, 1898.

his government not to take this remark or, in fact, the general pessimism of Salisbury too seriously. He believed that most members of the cabinet still favored a rapprochement with Germany, though Chamberlain was said to be as disappointed as Salisbury was pessimistic.[42]

The German ambassador was a very experienced, a very well-informed and a very clever man. But he could not foresee the remarkable turn which the situation was to take in the next days. On May 13 Chamberlain addressed the Liberal Union Association in his Birmingham constituency. Even for Mr. Chamberlain the speech was an extraordinary utterance, remarkable throughout for its absolute frankness and strong language. After reviewing the history and domestic policies of Liberal Unionism he turned to a long disquisition upon foreign affairs, the importance of which he emphasized: " There is, and there has been for some time past, a combined assault by the nations of the world upon the commercial supremacy of this country, and if that assault were successful our existence would be menaced in a way in which it never has been threatened since the time . . . when the great Napoleon attempted to lay an interdict upon British trade." The situation was too serious a one to be dealt with along party lines and it was neither wise nor patriotic to do what some party leaders had done, namely to represent the foreign minister as " discredited and defeated," to " gloat over the alleged humiliation of the country," and to " say on every occasion that the Government as a whole is weak and vacillating." If such statements were believed in foreign countries those countries might make a great mistake. He personally intended to speak frankly to the people, whose judgment he would take as soon as that of the wisest diplomatist in the world.

" Now the first point I want to impress upon you is this. It is the crux of the situation. Since the Crimean War, nearly fifty years ago, the policy of this country has been a policy of strict isolation. We have had no allies, — I am afraid we have had no friends. That is not due altogether to the envy which is undoubtedly felt at our success; it is due in part to the suspicion that we are acting in our own selfish interests, and were willing that other people should draw the chestnuts out of the fire for us; that we would take no responsibilities, whilst we were glad enough to profit by the work of others. In this way we have avoided entangling alliances, we have escaped many dangers; but we must accept the disadvantages that go with such a policy. . . . A new situation has arisen, and it is right the people of this country should have it under their consideration. All the powerful states of Europe have made alliances, and as long as we keep outside these alliances, as long as we are envied by all, and as long as we have interests which at one time or another conflict with the interests of all, we are liable to be confronted at any moment with a combination of Great Powers so powerful that not even the most extreme, the most hotheaded politician would be able to contemplate it without a certain sense of uneasiness."

---

[42] *Die Grosse Politik*, XIV, no. 3796 footnote.

What was the duty of the government in these circumstances? First of all " to draw all parts of the Empire closer together, to infuse into them a spirit of united and Imperial patriotism." This had been done. The next duty was

" to establish and to maintain bonds of permanent amity with out kinsmen across the Atlantic. They are a powerful and a generous nation. They speak our language, they are bred of our race. Their laws, their literature, their standpoint upon every question are the same as ours; their feeling, their interest in the cause of humanity and the peaceful development of the world are identical with ours. I do not know what the future has in store for us. I do not know what arrangements may be possible with us, but this I know and feel, — that the closer, the more cordial, the fuller, and the more definite those arrangements are, with the consent of both peoples, the better it will be for both and for the world. And I even go so far as to say that, terrible as war may be, even war itself would be cheaply purchased if in a great and noble cause the Stars and Stripes and the Union Jack should wave together over an Anglo-Saxon Alliance."

Turning then to the Far East, Chamberlain recognized that it was on this score that the government was most commonly attacked. Again and again he insisted that " we are only at the beginning of great events," that the campaign was not yet over, and that therefore it was too early to condemn the government. That the " absolute corruption, the crass ignorance and the gross misgovernment " of the Chinese mandarins had reduced China to a state of impotence had become known when the previous government was in power, yet that government had taken no adequate measures to come to an understanding with Russia, at whose mercy China was.

" The expected happened, and Russia did go down to Port Arthur and to Talienwan. As to the way in which Russia secured that occupation, as to the representations which were made and repudiated as soon as they were made, as to the promises which were given and broken a fortnight afterwards, I had better perhaps say nothing except I have always thought that it was a very wise proverb, ' Who sups with the Devil must have a long spoon.' The present government did try to come to an understanding with Russia," but failed to persuade her, and had to fall back on the alternative policy of taking Weihaiwei. In the " preliminary skirmish " England had done pretty well, but the general situation was " far from satisfactory." An understanding with Russia had proved impossible. The only other alternative would be war. " I am one of those who think that for any country there are worse things than war; there is loss of honour; there is loss of those interests which are so vital to the security of the existence of the nation. But, in any case, I hope I am sensible enough never to give my voice for war unless I can see at the commencement of the war a fair probability that at the end of the war the objects of the war will have been obtained. Now, what does history show? It shows that unless we are allied to some great military power, as we were in the Crimean War . . . we cannot seriously injure Russia, although it may also be true that she cannot seriously injure us. If that is the case, it is a case which deserves the serious consideration of the people of this country. It is impossible to over-rate the gravity of the issue. It is not a question of a single port in China — that is a very small matter. It is not a question of a single province; it is a question of the whole fate of the Chinese Empire, and our interests in China are so great, our proportion of the trade is so enormous, and the potentialities of that trade are so gigantic that I feel that no more vital question has ever been presented for the decision of a Government and the decision of a nation, and for my part I have tried to-night to state clearly and without exaggeration the conditions of the problem that we have before us. I think you will see that it is complicated enough to preclude all hasty judgment. One thing appears to me to be certain. If the policy of isolation, which has hitherto been the policy of this country, is to be maintained in the future, then the fate of the Chinese Empire may be, probably will be, hereafter decided without reference to our wishes and in defiance of our interests. If, on the other hand, we are determined to enforce the policy of the open door, to preserve an equal opportunity for trade with all our rivals, then we must not allow jingoes to drive us into a quarrel with all the world at the same time, and we must not reject the idea of an alliance with those Powers whose interests most nearly approximate to our own."

Chamberlain's speech appeared to most readers to be a direct contradiction of Salisbury's address of May 4. The prime minister was optimistic about China and disdainful of the " jargon of isolation." The secretary for the colonies drew an alarming picture of the Far Eastern situation and seemed to indicate that England would be lost without the alliance of a strong military power. In many quarters his remarks were interpreted as a speech against Salisbury, as a " counter-manifesto," to borrow the phrase of Sir William Harcourt. While the chief of the government was administering " soothing syrup " his colleague was sounding " the tocsin of alarm." [43] When the opposition tried to draw out Lord Salisbury on the subject in the house of lords on May 17 the prime minister refused to discuss the question. But he did say: " Our general policy is not changed. We shall cultivate to the utmost of our ability the friendship of all the Powers with whom we come into contact." Which simply amounted to a reiteration of his earlier statements. [44]

What is the real explanation of the Chamberlain speech? Hatzfeldt thought that Salisbury must have known in advance about it, and that he had approved of it as a sounding out of public opinion in the matter of an alliance. [45] But from Chamberlain's later utterances and from other evidence it is plain that the prime minister at best knew only of the general tenor of his colleague's forthcoming speech. We know that he thoroughly disapproved of the strong expressions used, which he considered in bad taste. [46] But Chamberlain himself in a later debate in parliament hinted broadly that he had not written out the speech

---

[43] Hansard: *Parliamentary Debates*, Series IV, vol. LVIII, pp. 1412 ff.
[44] Hansard, op. cit., LVII, p. 1514.   [45] *Die Grosse Politik*, XIV, no. 3797.
[46] Meyendorff: *Correspondance de M. de Staal*, II, pp. 386–7; *Die Grosse Politik*, XIV, no. 3800; Elliot: *Life of Goschen*, II, pp. 219 ff.

beforehand and that therefore it could not have been approved by the cabinet. Besides, he said, the cabinet could not be held responsible for " every word, every phrase, every turn of expression " on the part of one member, but only for " every declaration of principle, every statement of important fact, every declaration of policy." If there was disagreement between the prime minister and a member of the cabinet, it was the duty of that member to resign. The fact that he himself had not resigned, had not been cast out by his colleagues, had not been rejected by the prime minister should be enough to explode all stories of a split in the cabinet.[47]

At bottom there was no fundamental difference of opinion between Salisbury and Chamberlain. Both men, so far as one can detect, would have preferred an understanding with Russia, which would have been welcomed by the country at large. But, the attempt having been made and having failed, they saw the necessity of strengthening relations with the United States, Japan and Germany. The only divergence between them was with respect to how fast and how far England should go. Salisbury and Balfour evidently thought there was no hurry, and envisaged a gradual rapprochement, for which the price would not be exorbitant. It seems more than doubtful whether they had much hope of a hard and fast alliance. Chamberlain, on the other hand, began by thinking of an immediate alliance agreement and did not shrink even at the idea of war to check the Russians. But by May 1898 he had certainly seen the futility of this idea. His language in the Birmingham speech was strong and tactless, but there is no reason to question his later explanation of it. Speaking in parliament on June 10 he declared that the object of the speech " was not to lay down a policy. . . . It was to state the facts." " We are the most powerful Empire in the world; but we are not all-powerful." He had aimed simply to point out what England could not do under the existing circumstances. " I neither spoke for nor against alliances . . . except in regard to one particular nation," by which he meant the United States. His chief point, he went on, was to stress the fact that if the country insisted on maintaining the policy of isolation, which had been the right one for a long time, it must take the consequences, it must not make impossible demands upon the government, it must not expect to exercise a controlling influence in China as it had in the past. " Nobody ever talked of a permanent alliance. All I said was that the policy of this country, hitherto well known to all nations of the world and declared again and again, was that we would not accept any alliance . . . but once it becomes known that we are willing to consider alliances, provided they are for mutual interests with reciprocal advantages, I do not think we shall find the difficulty right honourable Gentlemen suggest in getting offers well worth our consideration." To wait until war broke out, he said, might be to wait too long. Permanent alliances did not necessarily lead to trouble. The Triple Alliance was founded to keep the peace. To join such an alliance for such purposes

---

[47] Hansard, LVIII, p. 1426; Garvin: *Life of Chamberlain*, III, pp. 282 ff.

would not be a "jingo proceeding." England could defend her present possessions, but what about future interests, about "potentialities of trade and commerce"? As things were England would have to vote naval expenditures sufficient to enable her to meet not two, but three powers. "It seems to me that any assurance, I will not say of an alliance — I am not speaking of an alliance, but of a thorough and complete understanding — a mutual arrangement for particular interests — with any one of the great Powers would be one of the most economical things that this country could possibly undertake, because it would save at once one, at all events, of the great Powers from entering into a combination against us, and we should then be satisfied that the preparations we have made against all eventualities were absolutely sufficient." He then admitted that there was no great hurry. The Transsiberian Railroad would take three to five years to complete. Nevertheless the country should look forward to the problems of the next ten to twenty years, and it was with this idea that he had examined the situation.[48]

Whatever the truth may be with regard to the Salisbury-Chamberlain relationship, it is not surprising that the Birmingham speech should have come as a shock to public opinion both in England and on the Continent. At home some people objected to the "new" diplomacy which involved calling other nations and rulers by unpleasant and discourteous names. Even more people resented Chamberlain's "abject confession of weakness." "What have we done," demanded Asquith in parliament, "what have the people of Great Britain done or suffered, that, after bearing, as we have done for nearly fifty years, the ever-growing weight of empire on our own unaided shoulders, without finding the burden too heavy for the courage, the enterprise, the self-reliance of our people, what have we done or suffered that we are now to go touting for allies in the highways and byways of Europe?"[49]

Chamberlain's key suggestion, the possibility of England's concluding alliances, found no response in the country. Take the matter of an alliance with the United States. The American ambassador, John Hay, speaking at the Lord Mayor's banquet on April 21, 1898 went even further than Chamberlain when he asserted that "all who think cannot but see there is a sanction like that of religion which binds us in partnership in the serious work of the world. . . . We are joint ministers in the same sacred mission of freedom and progress." Hay claimed that Chamberlain's references to America were partly due to his (Hay's) warning that the opposition should not be allowed to have a monopoly of expressions of good will toward America. Yet despite the unusual cordiality on both sides of the Atlantic, serious writers and politicians had no faith in the possibility of a formal alliance: "Every man welcomes an alliance,

---

[48] Hansard, LVIII, pp. 1427–37. On Salisbury's attitude see also *Die Grosse Politik*, XIV. no. 3801; Meyendorff, op. cit., II, p. 387; and Salisbury's letter to the Queen repudiating the idea that he had been less friendly to Germany than Chamberlain (*Letters of Queen Victoria*, III, p. 259).

[49] Hansard, LVIII, pp. 1347 ff.; similarly Labouchere and Harcourt (ibid., pp. 1375, 1418).

if you like to call it so, of hearts between the two countries, but none of us, and
few Americans, think that it would be likely to produce what may be called a
war alliance," said Sir Charles Dilke. " Expressions of friendship with England are almost universal," reported the New York correspondent of the *Times,*
but it is remarked that Mr. Chamberlain made, and could make, no definite
proposal. The question of an alliance is for this Government and people novel.
We have not advanced to that point. . . . Most members of Congress continue
to decline to express other than general views. They are politicians bred in a
school of distrust. Distrust of England is with many of them traditional. They
distrust her no longer, but when the word ' alliance ' is pronounced, they ask
for time." [50]

Much the same attitude was taken toward the suggestion of an alliance
with " a strong military power." Everyone understood that this could mean
only Germany, and not a single speaker in the house of commons had anything
to say in favor of the idea. Sir Charles Dilke doubted whether Germany would
ever be willing to make such an alliance; Asquith thought German policy in
the Far East more reprehensible than the Russian, and pointed out that an
alliance with Germany would cost too much; Labouchere was dubious whether
Germany would be anxious to pull the chestnuts out of the Chinese fire for
England. " I am no particular friend of Germany," he said, " but I am bound
to say that the German people are all a great deal too intelligent to dance to
the piping of the Right Honourable Gentleman the Member for West Birmingham." England would have to guarantee Germany's possessions before an alliance could be made, and that would involve a guarantee of Alsace and Lorraine, to which he objected strongly. Harcourt joined the other opposition
speakers in declaring against the whole idea of permanent alliances. [51]

Let us turn now to the German side. The first reaction of the German press
was one of astonishment and shock at the bluntness of the Chamberlain statement. The *National Zeitung* declared that it amounted to " a declaration of
the bankruptcy, not only of past English policy, but, what is more, of the whole
power of England." This impression was shared by most of the other German
papers, until the London *Times,* which tried to correct the erroneous idea of
British weakness, warned the continental nations that England had no thought
of purchasing aid at an exorbitant price: The speech, it wrote, was " neither a
cry for foreign help nor necessarily a preparation for a new departure." If a
departure were made in British policy

" it will be the Foreign Secretary who will have to bring forward the subject. He
will do so with the utmost regard for the conventions of European and other
diplomacy, we may be sure, nor will the matter of ' concession ' be forgotten.
But when that delicate topic comes to be debated in connexion with a review of
the general balance of advantages to either side, we are not satisfied that they

<hr/>

[50] *Times,* May 17, 1898; Hansard, LVIII, pp. 1335 ff.; William R. Thayer: *Life of John Hay,*
II, p. 169.   [51] Hansard, op. cit., LVIII, pp. 1337 ff., 1348 ff., 1377-8, 1420.

will have to be made by us. After all, the British Fleet, a chain of coaling stations encircling the globe, the command of the seas will be considerable assets on our side of the account." [52]

On second thought the German press became more circumspect. The *Kölnische Zeitung,* often inspired by the government, was cordial but vague. Chamberlain, it said, seemed to take the attitude that Providence had assigned to other great powers the honorable mission of fighting England's battles. What the British minister evidently desired was a " continental sword." But in the German view alliances were concluded for peaceful purposes, not for war and conquest. It would be better to wait until the English proposition was made clearer. " As yet Mr. Chamberlain has only set continental politicians a riddle." The Berlin correspondent of the *Times* thought that in secret the German statesmen would probably endorse Chamberlain's reference to the long spoon required for supping with Russia, but they were unwilling to jeopardize their relations with the Tsar.[53]

This was a fairly accurate estimate of the situation. In the conversations between Salisbury and Hatzfeldt in the weeks following the Chamberlain speech it turned out that an alliance was still in the far and foggy future. The British prime minister was distinctly unenthusiastic and complained that England could not always be the giving party. He had little faith in alliances concluded far in advance. Hatzfeldt came away with the impression that, while the British statesmen all desired an agreement, they were unwilling to pay a high price. Under the circumstances it would be best to keep them hopeful. On the German side there was the same mixed feeling. Speaking to the English ambassador the Emperor said that he would welcome " a thoroughly good understanding with England .   . but it must be clearly understood that Germany did not intend to go to war with Russia for the purpose of driving her out of China." He did not share Chamberlain's fear of the Russian advance. It would take Russia generations to assimilate what she had already secured. Even if the Germans were prepared to fight England's battles, they would at once be attacked by Russia and France. What help could the British fleet give? [54]

For the Emperor the matter evidently reduced itself to a question of bargaining. On May 30, 1898 he despatched a most astonishing letter to his friend Nicky, telling him of the whole development of the Anglo-German problem, of Chamberlain's first approaches, of the German conditions and objections, etc.

" I thought the affair had ended. Now however the request has been renewed for the third time in such an unmistakable manner, putting a *certain short term* to my definite answer and accompanied by such enormous offers showing a wide

---

[52] London *Times,* May 16, 1898. For several days the *Times* published whole columns of extracts from the continental press. See also the extensive extracts from the newspaper press in *Questions Diplomatiques et Coloniales,* June, 1898, pp. 173–81.

[53] *Kölnische Zeitung,* May 18, 1898; London *Times,* May 18, 1898.

[54] *Die Grosse Politik,* XIV, nos. 3798–801; *British Documents,* I, no. 53.

and great future opening for my country, that I think it my duty to Germany duly to reflect before I answer. Now before I do, I frankly and openly come to you, my esteemed friend and cousin, to inform you, as I feel that it is a question so to say of life and death. We two have the same opinions, we want peace, and we have sustained and upheld it till now! What the tendence of the Alliance is, you will well understand, as I am informed that the Alliance is to be with the Triple Alliance and with the addition of Japan and America, with whom pourparlers have already been opened! What the chances are for us in refusing or accepting you may calculate yourself! Now as my old and trusted friend I beg you to tell me what you can offer me and will do if I refuse. Before I take my final decision and send my answer in this difficult position, I must be able to see clearly, and clear and open without any back-thoughts must your proposal be, so that I can judge and weigh in my mind before God, as I should, what is for the good of the Peace of my Fatherland and of the world. You need not fear for your Ally in any proposal you make should she be placed in a combination wished by you." [55]

The Emperor's apologists claim that this most unedifying letter was not only suggested but actually worked out by Bülow together with William.[56] There is no proof of this, and it seems on the whole hardly plausible. The letter was too tactless and too crude to have emanated from the German foreign office, though it is always possible that the idea of asking the Tsar what he would offer if Germany refused the British proposition may have come from Bülow. The outcome, in any case, was quite amusing, for the Tsar covered the Emperor's card with a trump. In his reply he told of the " tempting proposals " made to Russia by England three months before.

" That showed us clearly that England needed our friendship at that time, to be able to check our development, in a masked way, in the Far East. Without thinking twice over it, their proposals were refused. Two weeks later Port Arthur was our's. As you know we have arrived at an understanding with Japan upon Corea and we have been since a long time on the best of terms with North America. I really do not see any reason, why the latter should suddenly turn against old friends — only for the ' beaux yeux ' of England's? It is very difficult for me, if not quite impossible, to answer your question whether *it is* useful or *not* for Germany to accept these often repeated English proposals, as I have not got the slightest knowledge of their value. *You* must of course decide what is best and most necessary for your country." [57]

A neater turning of the tables could hardly be imagined. The Russians, far from making offers to the Germans, simply pricked the bubble of their pride by revealing to them the proposals of the British, the rejection of which had led to Chamberlain's approaches to Berlin. Germany was not the first love of the

[55] *The Kaiser's Letters to the Tsar*, pp. 50–5.
[56] For example Karl Friedrich Nowak: *Germany's Road to Ruin* (New York, 1932), p. 188.
[57] *Die Grosse Politik*, XIV, no. 3803.

British, but only a second choice. In communicating the Tsar's reply to Count Hatzfeldt, Bülow pointed out that the revelation of the British offers to Russia showed how unreliable the British were. To the British ambassador he recapitulated the German viewpoint: any agreement must be preceded by an assurance that the English public and parliament would accept it, by a British guarantee of reinsurance against Russia, and by a greater English generosity in colonial questions. The fundamental underlying principle must be that of *live and let live*.[58]

We need not pursue this subject farther. It has been necessary to enter into considerable detail and to enlarge upon the matter of public opinion, not only because of the intrinsic importance of the Anglo-German problem, but also because of the very extensive writing on the subject and the many aspects of the question to which attention has been called by other students. German critics are divided into two schools — those who believe that the German government was to blame for the failure of the negotiations, and those who maintain that there were, in reality, no British offers to be rejected. This much can be said with a reasonable degree of certainty: that Lord Salisbury had little use for a policy of permanent alliances and that he preferred to retain for England complete freedom of action; that, though he undoubtedly desired an improvement of Anglo-German relations and hoped for co-operation between the two powers to keep the door open in the Far East and elsewhere, his chief thought was to keep Germany from sinking entirely into the arms of Russia. Even so, he was unwilling to pay an extravagant price for German friendship and support. As he said to Hatzfeldt quite bluntly: "You ask too much for your friendship." To Queen Victoria he wrote: " The truth is that on questions of territorial cession the German Emperor and public opinion here take very opposite views. It would be impossible to do what the German Emperor desires without incurring the reproach of deserting British interests and making undue concessions." [59]

Salisbury and the foreign office never gave their unqualified *imprimatur* to the proposals and negotiations carried on by Chamberlain. The colonial secretary was no great friend of Germany, but he was infuriated by the conduct of Russia and wanted to stop her at all costs. Casting aside the traditions of diplomatic practice he threw his cards on the table and set about making a counting-house deal. But commendable though his frankness may have been in principle, it was hardly likely to make for practical success. The suggestion that the Germans throw over their friendly relations with Russia to aid the British in blocking the Muscovite advance in China was really somewhat naive. No doubt the British people would have welcomed such a combination. But it is more than doubtful whether parliament or public opinion would have countenanced a

---

[58] *Die Grosse Politik*, XIV, nos. 3804–5.

[59] *Letters of Queen Victoria*, III, p. 263; see also the illuminating letter of Hatzfeldt to Bülow. in Bülow: *Memoirs*, I, pp. 323–5.

suggestion that England join the Triple Alliance or enter upon any definite policy of permanent alliances. At all events, as the *Times* pointed out, if a departure became necessary it would have to come from the foreign minister through the regular channels. Salisbury and Balfour, as we know, had a much more modest goal in view. They did not approve of the methods of the " new diplomacy," neither did they have much faith in the policy put forward by their colleague. Salisbury made it perfectly plain to Hatzfeldt that he did not desire the discussions with Chamberlain to go on after he, the prime minister, had returned to the foreign office.[60]

Under the circumstances it is difficult to find fault with the policy of the German government, whether Bülow or Holstein was the moving spirit. Germany was not, at the time, seriously menaced by the Franco-Russian Alliance. It would have been foolhardy to break with Russia without very definite and binding agreements with England. Germany's position between the British on the one side and the French and Russians on the other side was a very strong one, which the foreign office was eager to make the most of. As Bülow said, any agreement generally or specifically eastern Asiatic would have a point against Russia, just as any agreement with Russia would have a point against England. The former would diminish the security of the German frontiers, the other would reduce the chances of gains in the colonial field. Tnings being what they were it would be better to retain a free hand, making special arrangements with one side or the other when that seemed desirable.[61] After all, this was the policy of Bismarck, who had never allowed himself to be made the tool of the anti-Russian policy pursued by the English in Asia. It is all well and good to maintain that the Iron Chancellor always desired close relations, not to say an alliance with England, but it must not be forgotten what a decisive rôle he assigned to Russia. It may be that the German statesmen were too much afraid that a fast agreement with England would lead to a European war on two fronts. It is probably true, as Professor Meinecke suggests, that the effect of the agreement would have been just the reverse, namely to make the Russians and the French more cautious than ever.[62] It is also likely that the Germans, especially Holstein, underestimated the possibility of an eventual agreement between England on the one hand and the Dual Alliance of Russia and France on the other. But, after all, one must not demand too much of human foresight. In 1898 an agreement between England and France was perhaps feasible, but only at the cost of great concessions by England, which the British public would hardly have agreed to make. But an understanding with Russia was practically impossible. It was tried in the first months of 1898 and

---

[60] Hatzfeldt to Bülow, June 27, 1898 (Bülow: *Memoirs*, I, pp. 324–5).

[61] *Die Grosse Politik*, XIV, no. 3802.

[62] Friedrich Meinecke: *Geschichte des Deutsch-Englischen Bündnisproblems, 1890–1901* (Munich, 1927), p. 92; similarly Konrad Lehmann: " Die Ablehnung des Englischen Bündnis antrags, 1898–1901 " (*Preussische Jahrbücher*, August, 1930, pp. 162–83), p. 169.

failed completely. The British and the Russians were at daggers drawn, and it took the complete defeat of Russian policy in the Far East in 1904–1905 to bring an entente within even the range of possibility. Bismarck said somewhere that one could not predict the course of events for more than three years. Judged by the master's standard Bülow and Holstein were quite right.

And after all there was this very great obstacle to an Anglo-German Alliance, even in 1898. For Germany the greatest question, the question of life and death, was always the safety of the frontiers. For England the problem was one of her general position in the world, a problem of world empire. For Germany, of necessity a European power rather than a world power, it was important to divert the other powers to the colonial field and avoid friction on the Continent. Far from desiring to check the Russian policy in Asia, the Germans were deeply interested in seeing Russia become involved in China, where England rather than Germany and Austria would feel the impact of the northern colossus. For that very reason the British policy was to erect a bulwark against Russia in China, so as to shift the burden back to the Continent. This idea was ex-pounded quite baldly by Lord Charles Beresford when he advocated the alliance with Germany in the house of commons on April 5, 1898: "If we have an alliance with Germany there must be 50,000 or 60,000 Russian troops kept on the frontier of Germany. At present there is not any army of Russia at all on the frontier of Germany(!), but there is a good number of troops in Man-churia, a large number in the Caucasus." [63] One could hardly blame the German government for not wanting to be used as a cat's-paw for the British. The American government, though warmly wooed, made even less of a move to follow the British suggestions. Chamberlain was not authorized to make a definite proposal. He never claimed to be speaking in anything more than an informal and unofficial way. The German government could, therefore, give nothing more than an academic answer. The terms it laid down for an eventual alliance were reasonable and necessary if the security of the country was to be safeguarded.[64]

A number of German historians have stressed the point that, in spite of the failure of Chamberlain's proposals, relations between England and Germany were not embittered; that, on the contrary, they remained on a distinctly better basis. This thesis can be accepted only with reservations. The difference was that the two governments talked more with each other than they had in the preceding two years. But the results were meagre enough. Take the case of China, for example. The Germans had refused the suggestion that they join in blocking the further advance of Russia, but they had expressed themselves as anxious for commercial co-operation. There was a good basis for such common action in

---

[63] Hansard: *Parliamentary Debates,* Series IV, vol. LVI, p. 286.

[64] I subscribe here almost unreservedly to the argumentation of Gerhard Ritter: *Die Legende von der Verschmähten Englischen Freundschaft, 1898–1901* (Freiburg, 1929), especially pp. 16–7.

the economic field, because the Hongkong and Shanghai Bank and the Deutsch-Ostasiatische Bank had joined in a loan to China soon after the war of 1894–1895 and had maintained close relations ever since. In the spring of 1898, however, a dispute arose with regard to the concession for the building of the important Shanghai-Nanking Railway. Into the very complicated details of the matter we need not go, the more so as the version of each side flatly contradicted that of the other. What interests us here is the larger aspect of the negotiation. The British government, having failed to secure in the discussions with Russia a demarcation of spheres in China, now tried to obtain from the German government a recognition of its special position in the Yangtze Valley as a set-off against the position secured by Germany in Shantung. The German foreign office, however, refused to regard these two areas as roughly equivalent and insisted that, despite its preferential position in Shantung, it still had a right to participate in railway building in the Yangtze Valley. The discussions at times took on a rather acrimonious tone and led to no satisfactory result, although in September 1898 the two banking groups made an agreement regarding the spheres of their activity.[65]

Within China the international struggle had become centred upon the definition of spheres of interest and upon the competition for railroad concessions. Outside China the great powers were engaged in the partition of the few remaining unappropriated parts of Africa and in the staking out of claims for the future in the territories of the " dying nations," as Lord Salisbury called them. The year 1898 was the year of the Spanish-American War, which thrust the United States quite suddenly into the ranks of the great imperial powers and threw open the question of the succession to Spain's colonial empire. In these questions the British and the Germans were again on opposite sides of the fence. The attention of the British was concentrated on the Far East and on Africa. There was no desire in London to secure any part of the Spanish spoils, but a very decided policy aiming to keep these territories out of the hands of other European powers, notably Germany. Lord Salisbury had, in 1897, consistently rejected German proposals for a protest against the projected American annexation of Hawaii.[66] After Dewey's naval victory over the Spanish squadron at Manila in May 1898 British statesmen and diplomats made it quite clear to the hesitant Washington government that they would like to see the United States take the Philippines. Men like Cecil Spring Rice fanned the flames of American suspicion of Germany. There was talk of England's having frustrated a German plan for a coalition against the Republic, and ever greater efforts were made during the summer of 1898 to popularize the idea of an Anglo-American alliance. An Anglo-American League was founded in London

---

[65] The documents in *Die Grosse Politik*, XIV, nos. 3771–7; *China No. 1 (1899)*, passim. They are well analyzed by Joseph: *Foreign Diplomacy in China*, chap. xiv, passim.

[66] *Die Grosse Politik*, XIII, nos. 3409 ff.

and an Anglo-American Committee in New York. There was hardly a respectable journal on either side of the Atlantic that did not do its bit in the good cause.[67]

The German attitude and policy certainly served as an effective cement for the entente between the Anglo-Saxon countries. Political circles in Berlin had been more or less swept away by the tide of navalism and imperialism, and there was a very general feeling that Germany, having entered the field of colonial activity too late, must not under any circumstances fail to make the most of what opportunities still presented themselves. The naval authorities were anxiously surveying the globe for possible coaling and naval stations and the revolution in the Philippines, followed by the destruction of the Spanish squadron, seemed to offer a rare chance. The Americans were by no means sure that they wanted the islands. The fact was well known and it was therefore quite natural that the Germans should cherish hopes of the succession, the more so as Andrew White, the American ambassador at Berlin, spoke encouragingly. Immediately after Dewey's victory the German admiral in command in the Far East was ordered to send ships to Manila, ostensibly to protect German commercial interests, which, incidentally, were impressively small.[68] Before long the Germans had a squadron at Manila as large as Dewey's, with more marines on board than there were Germans in the whole archipelago. Friction developed between the German commander, Admiral Diederichs, and his American colleague, and the American press before long was engaging in bitter attacks upon the Germans. It was felt that the German fleet, " unmannerly and provocative," was intended " not to protect existing German interests, but to find new interests to protect." By the summer of 1898 relations were so strained that John Hay, wholly under the influence of his English friends, could write to one of the most rabid of American imperialists, Senator Lodge, that the Germans were the enemy:

> " They want the Philippines, the Carolines and Samoa; they want to get into our markets and keep us out of theirs. They have been flirting and intriguing with Spain ever since the war began, and now they are trying to put the Devil into the head of Aguinaldo. I do not think they want to fight. In fact, they frankly tell us they can't. . . . But they want, by pressure, by threats, and by sulking and wheedling in turn to get something out of us and Spain. There is to the German mind something monstrous in the thought that a war should take place anywhere and they not profit by it." [69]

---

[67] See especially Thayer: *Life of John Hay*, II, chap. xxiii; Nevins: *Henry White*, chap. ix; *Letters and Friendships of Sir Cecil Spring Rice*, I, pp. 246–7, 248–53; and the excellent treatment of Bertha A. Reuter: *Anglo-American Relations during the Spanish-American War*, pp. 136, 157 ff.

[68] According to the British sources most of the " German " firms in Manila were Swiss. British interests handled 70% of the imports of the islands, and of the export of sugar, hemp and copra they controlled 80% (" Letter of the Manila Merchants," London *Times*, May 2, 1898).

[69] Alfred L. P. Dennis: *Adventures in American Diplomacy, 1896–1906* (New York, 1928), p. 98.

This letter is a flagrant example of gross exaggeration, and it is quoted merely as a reflection of feeling in high places. Anyone who reads over the documents and periodical literature of the time will be impressed by the tactlessness of German policy toward the hyper-sensitive American republic, but he will be impressed even more with the almost pathological suspicion of Germany which was prevalent in American political and diplomatic circles and with the obvious efforts of men like Spring Rice to fortify the Americans in their distrust. If dislike of Germany had anything to do with inducing the American government to retain the Philippines, then the British object was attained. British policy was successful, but the success was gained at the expense of Germany. It was a strange manifestation of the supposed rapprochement between the two countries.[70]

The German government had begun with the project of establishing a protectorate over the Philippines, and had then reduced its program to a scheme of neutralization or partition. The hostile attitude of the United States, supported by the British, had rendered these plans nugatory. In the late summer of 1898 the German government changed its policy and did everything possible to conciliate the Americans. The explanation for this change lay in the hope of the Germans to avoid American opposition to the purchase from Spain of the Caroline and other Pacific island groups. We need not pursue this matter into its minute details. Secret provisional arrangements were made with Spain on September 10 and December 10, 1898 which resulted eventually in the purchase by Germany of the Caroline, Pelew and Marianne Islands, excepting Guam. Hopes of the Germans for the Sulu Islands, the Canaries and Fernando Po had to be given up. The settlement of the Samoan question had to be left to a later date. The German acquisitions in the Pacific helped to meet the need for naval and coaling stations, the "maritime fulcra" as the Emperor called them, but from the larger viewpoint they could hardly be described as worth the hostility of the United States or the opposition of England.

In the meanwhile other possibilities opened up, possibilities of much greater promise. If Spain was defeated in war, her Iberian neighbor, Portugal, had also descended from her former high estate to the position of a " dying " nation. Since 1852 the little kingdom had been faced with a growing annual deficit which obliged the government to float no less than fourteen loans between 1856 and 1892. The public debt, which came to about twenty-eight million pounds in 1860 and to ninety-seven million in 1880, had risen to one hundred and sixty-

---

[70] On the whole subject of German-American relations at this time see *Die Grosse Politik*, XV, chaps. xcvii and xcviii; and the detailed treatments of Jeannette Keim: *Forty Years of German-American Relations* (Philadelphia, 1919), chap. vi; Clara E. Schieber: *American Sentiment toward Germany, 1870–1914* (Boston, 1923), pp. 110 ff.; Hermann Leusser: "Ein Jahrzehnt Deutsch-Amerikanischer Politik, 1897–1906 " (*Beiheft der Historischen Zeitschrift*, no. 13, 1928), pp. 18 ff.; Alfred L. P. Dennis: *Adventures in American Diplomacy*, chap. iii; and particularly Lester B. Shippee: "Germany and the Spanish-American War " (*American Historical Review*, July, 1925, pp. 754–77).

three million by 1898. Portuguese credit was exhausted and the government in 1893 felt obliged to resort to desperate measures. It arbitrarily reduced interest on government loans by two thirds, in gold. This measure led to strong protests from the foreign bondholders, and to the use of pretty strong language by the French and German governments, whose nationals, together with the British, held most of the government bonds. Negotiations began between the Lisbon government and the foreign investors, but these dragged on for years before they led to an even halfway satisfactory result.[71]

One of the reasons for Portugal's financial distress was the burden of her undeveloped colonies, of which Angola and Mozambique, in southwest and southeast Africa respectively, were the largest and most important. The English had been connected with Portugal by an alliance dating back to 1373 and often renewed, notably in 1703. It had been reaffirmed by Lord Granville in 1873. In the later part of the nineteenth century the development of the situation in south Africa led to close contact between the British and Portuguese colonies. Mozambique controlled the communications from the sea to the great British possessions in Rhodesia, and, what was more important, to the South African Republic. The English were anxious to secure, if possible, that part of Mozambique south of the Zambezi River, or at any rate to prevent any other power from establishing itself there. In a treaty of June 1891 Britain and Portugal had agreed that in the event of one of them proposing to part with any territories south of the Zambezi the other should be recognized as possessing a preferential right to the territories in question. The construction of the Transvaal-Delagoa Bay Railway, largely financed by German interests, made for greater and greater tension in south Africa. Between 1891 and 1897 Rhodes personally and the Cape Government officially tried on various occasions to buy the southern part of Mozambique or at least the Delagoa Bay area with Lorenzo Marques and the Portuguese part of the railway to the Transvaal. It was natural that banking interests affected by Portugal's financial collapse should try to connect the two problems by either writing off part of the debt in return for the cession of the desired territory or by offering a loan with the revenues of the colonies as security. Many efforts of this sort were made, but they were always rejected by the Portuguese government, because the Portuguese nation regarded the retention of the colonies, last remnant of former greatness, as a matter of national pride. The colonies, said the Portuguese, were their "only guarantee of national importance."[72]

---

[71] The Portuguese financial crisis is well discussed in Augusto Fuschini: *O Presente e o Futuro de Portugal* (Lisbon, 1899), chaps. v and vi. See also Angel Marvaud: *Le Portugal et ses Colonies* (Paris, 1912), pp. 80 ff.; and the excellent brief account in Herbert Feis: *Europe the World's Banker, 1870–1914* (New York, 1930), chap. xi.

[72] Marvaud, op. cit., pp. 274 ff.; Teixera de Sousa: *Para a Historia da Revolução* (Coimbra, 1912), I, pp. 239–40. The British efforts are recounted in detail in W. Basil Worsfold: *The Reconstruction of the New Colonies under Lord Milner* (London, 1913), I, pp. 114 ff.; Sir Lewis Michell: *Life and Times of Cecil John Rhodes* (New York, 1910), II, pp. 95–8; Garvin: *Life of Chamberlain*, III, p. 309.

Since the time of the Jameson raid the relations between Britain and the Transvaal had been growing steadily worse, until in April 1897 the two governments were on the verge of war. Under these circumstances the control of Delagoa Bay became of paramount importance. The British were afraid that Germans, who were acquiring land in the area, might eventually be able to establish themselves there. In any case it was of the utmost importance to England that the wide-open door to the Transvaal, through which Creusot and Krupp were shipping heavy guns for the fortification of Pretoria, should be brought under British surveillance and control. Early in May 1897 Chamberlain therefore proposed to the Portuguese representative in London that England should guarantee the African possessions of Portugal on condition that the latter open no other route from the sea to the Transvaal; Lorenzo Marques and the railway to the Transvaal frontier should be run by a Portuguese-British Company; within a specific area surrounding Lorenzo Marques the Portuguese government should grant no concessions without the consent of the British. Chamberlain also suggested that the Portuguese raise a loan in London, offering the African colonies as security. Such a loan, he thought, would justify the British guarantee suggested in the first proposal. But these proposals, which would have given Britain effective control of Delagoa Bay and the Railway, were rejected by the Lisbon government, as so many similar proposals had been rejected in the past.[73]

Rumors of impending British action in south Africa had aroused the apprehensions of the Germans in the spring of 1897. The foreign office had to make up its mind what attitude to take in the event of a British offensive against the Transvaal. Hatzfeldt, the ambassador at London, strongly urged his government not to contemplate intervention, but to try to come to an agreement with England on the basis of compensations. Seizure of Delagoa Bay by Britain would be a "serious provocation" and might be replied to by a German occupation of those parts of the Portuguese colonies adjacent to the German possessions. Salisbury, to be sure, denied any warlike intentions on the part of Her Majesty's government, but Hatzfeldt carried away the impression that the prime minister would be glad to reach an agreement with Germany regarding the Transvaal if the price were not too high. It seems to have been understood even then that an arrangement might be made with regard to the Portuguese colonies.[74]

The unwillingness of the Lisbon government to consider the British proposals and the temporary relaxation of the tension in England's relations with the Transvaal led to a postponement of the whole problem. The negotiations of 1897 are of importance only in so far as they illustrate the aims of the parties

---

[73] *British Documents*, I, no. 65; Garvin: *Life of Chamberlain*, III, p. 309; Fritz Schwarze: *Das Deutsch-Englische Abkommen über die Portugiesischen Kolonien vom 30 August 1898* (Göttingen, 1931), pp. 15-7.

[74] *Die Grosse Politik*, XIV, nos. 3403 ff.

chiefly concerned. But by May 1898 the situation was once more so acute that a
solution seemed imperative. In south Africa events had taken a turn that convinced even the British high commissioner, Sir Alfred Milner, that the Transvaal government was incorrigible and that matters would have to be brought to
a head.[75] At the same time affairs in Portugal had gone from bad to worse, until
revolution loomed on the horizon and the fall of the dynasty seemed not unlikely. All efforts of the government to make an adjustment with its creditors
had failed and there was imminent danger that far-reaching demands might
be made before long by the French and German governments. The Lisbon
cabinet therefore reopened negotiations with the British government in the hope
of securing financial aid. The British conditions were, roughly, the same conditions laid down in 1897: a loan with the revenues of the colonies as security;
Portugal to agree not to alienate in any way any part of Delagoa Bay or the
approaches to the Transvaal, or to grant any concessions in that area without
British consent. The Bay and Railway should be jointly managed. The British
aim, wrote Chamberlain to Milner, was to secure commercial control in time
of peace and right of occupation in time of war of Delagoa Bay and the
Railroad.[76]

While these negotiations were going on in London, news of them leaked out
and came into possession of the German and French governments. On June
14, 1898 Count Hatzfeldt interviewed Salisbury on the subject and protested
against separate action by the British in the matter of the Portuguese colonies.
Salisbury's attitude was not encouraging, for he took the stand that the British
government had the right to lend Portugal money. Despite the ambassador's
insistence that the security for a loan would necessarily involve the colonies,
the prime minister continued to maintain that the question was a financial one.[77]

The German government was, from the very beginning, prepared to make
far-reaching concessions in return for an agreement regarding the ultimate
disposition of these colonies. Bülow had no use for the anti-British policy of his
predecessor in the Transvaal question. He was ready to abandon the Boers
to their fate and he was prepared to give up whatever claims or hopes the
Germans might have had with regard to Delagoa Bay, if only the Germans
could succeed in ear-marking for themselves a fair share of the remaining
Portuguese possessions. When Salisbury refused to bargain with the Germans,
the Berlin foreign office decided to bring pressure. The French were as much
exercised by news of the Anglo-Portuguese negotiations as the Germans, and
began to put out feelers in Berlin as to what might be done. Bülow took

---

[75] The Milner Papers, edited by Cecil Headlam (London, 1931), chap. viii, passim; Eric A.
Walker: A History of South Africa (London, 1928), pp. 471 ff.

[76] Milner Papers, p. 266; Garvin, op. cit., III, p. 310 ff.

[77] The important sources are Die Grosse Politik, XIV, chap. xcii; British Documents, I, chap. ii.
They are analyzed and discussed by Fritz Schwarze: Das Deutsch-Englische Abkommen über die
Portugiesischen Kolonien, passim, and summarized in Raymond W. Bixler: Anglo-German Imperial-
ism in South Africa, pp. 114 ff.

advantage of the opportunity. On June 18 he instructed the ambassador at Paris to find out what the French government was prepared to do in the way of bringing pressure on Portugal, hinting at a threat to establish an international financial control. Münster was even to suggest the possibility of practical co-operation in all special questions arising at the time.[78]

Münster discussed this matter with Hanotaux on June 19, and found the French minister much interested and impressed. Unfortunately, however, the cabinet had already fallen and Hanotaux was carrying on at the foreign office only as interim minister. He did, nevertheless, send the suggestion to the embassies, and in the meanwhile lodged a vigorous protest in Lisbon. Nothing more was done in the matter, for Hanotaux' successor, M. Delcassé, did not take the suggestion very seriously and allowed it to drop.[79]

In his later writings Hanotaux took the stand that Delcassé's indifference spoiled the chance of an understanding which might have been of very great value to France on the eve of her great conflict with England over the Sudan. This is probably something of an exaggeration. The evidence would indicate that Bülow from the beginning desired an arrangement with England. The suggested action with France was simply intended to force the British into negotiations. In any event the move was a good one. The British were evidently uneasy about French territorial designs on the African coast opposite Madagascar, and they realized that any financial agreement they might make with Portugal would be apt to arouse opposition among other powers having a financial stake in the country and being therefore unwilling to see the national income in any way impaired or endangered. As a matter of fact the negotiations with Portugal were making no satisfactory progress. The Portuguese minister in London, Marquis de Soveral, was evidently willing to go to any lengths to secure the support of England, but the Lisbon government was in constant dread of public opinion if important sacrifices had to be made.[80]

Originally, when the Germans had made known in London their objection to a separate agreement between England and Portugal, the British statesmen seem to have planned to buy off German opposition by modest concessions. Chamberlain wrote to Milner that the colonial office was willing to offer Germany Walfisch Bay in return for her services as " honest broker " to induce Portugal to give England " the predominating influence in the region of the port of Delagoa." To which Milner replied that he feared the cession of Walfisch Bay would cause an outcry at the Cape unless some further compensation were secured.[81] At the very same time the British learned of the German and French

---

[78] *Die Grosse Politik*, XIV, nos. 3812, 3813.

[79] Hanotaux: *Fachoda*, p. 132; André Mevil: *De la Paix de Francfort à la Conférence d'Algésiras* (Paris, 1909), pp. 12–8, giving the Delcassé version. Delcassé in March 1902 denied that any propositions had been made by Germany to Hanotaux concerning " the Portuguese colonies," which was mere quibbling. See *Documents Diplomatiques Français, 1871–1914*, II, no. 157.

[80] These points are well discussed by Schwarze, op. cit., pp. 19 ff.

[81] *Milner Papers*, pp. 266–7.

protests and threats to Portugal. Taken together these developments practically forced a widening of the basis of negotiation. Discussions were begun between Salisbury and Hatzfeldt early in July and continued through August. This is not the place for a day by day record of the proposals and counter-proposals. We must content ourselves with the mention of the chief points in the negotiation. From the start it should be said that there was little enthusiasm on the British side. Foreign office officials, like Francis Bertie, argued in a number of memoranda that no concessions should be made, for England could get everything she wanted without German aid, and these sacrifices would not lead to any further entente in matters like the Far Eastern. These memoranda seem to have had no important effect on the negotiations, but Lord Salisbury apparently shared the feeling expressed in them, namely that the Germans asked too much (" you want the whole of Africa," he told Hatzfeldt on one occasion), and that they were intent on.securing the succession to a large part of the Portuguese colonial empire, which England would have liked to see kept intact under British influence. There was something in Hatzfeldt's remark that the British would rather make considerable concessions to other nations than to abandon any colonial territory to Germany, their chief rival.[82] Nevertheless the question had to be settled somehow. The British needed control of Delagoa Bay and the Railroad to the Transvaal. It was of key importance. " I look on possession of Delagoa Bay as the best chance we have of winning the great game between ourselves and the Transvaal for the mastery of South Africa without a war," wrote Milner. On other occasions he spoke of it as " politically invaluable," " a trump card." [83]

Realizing this, the Germans were determined to make the best of their opportunity. Their demands from the beginning were really high, and during the course of the negotiations they showed no compunction about using strong language. The English were given to understand that if they were obdurate the Germans would have to look elsewhere, that they would have to act with France and Russia, and that in African affairs they might have to seek an agreement with France that would extend even to Egypt. At other times they used the opposite tactics and dangled before the British the prospect of a larger entente, touching even the Far East, if the London government would only be reasonable.[84]

The Germans began by asking for participation in the projected loan to Portugal, security for the British part to be the revenues of Mozambique south of the Zambezi River, security for the German part to be the revenues of the northern part of Mozambique as well as of the whole of Angola. The British declared these demands to be exorbitant, but in a general way they eventually agreed to them. The arguments centered chiefly on the modalities of the loan,

---

[82] *Die Grosse Politik*, XIV, no. 3823; Garvin, op. cit., III, pp. 313 ff.
[83] *Milner Papers*, pp. 267–8.
[84] *Die Grosse Politik*, XIV, nos. 3818, 3854, 3865, etc.

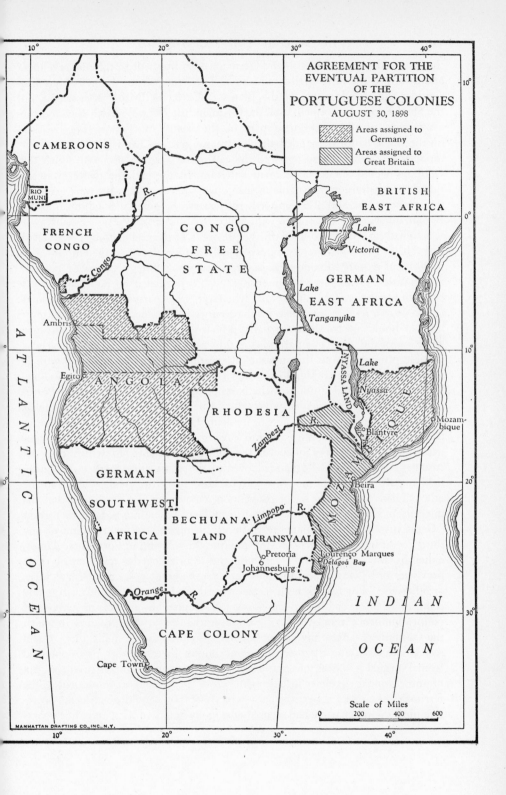

AGREEMENT FOR THE
EVENTUAL PARTITION
OF THE
PORTUGUESE COLONIES
AUGUST 30, 1898

Areas assigned to
Germany

Areas assigned to
Great Britain

CAMEROONS

RIO
MUNI

FRENCH
CONGO

CONGO
FREE
STATE

BRITISH
EAST AFRICA

Lake
Victoria

GERMAN
EAST AFRICA

Lake
Tanganyika

Congo R.

Ambris

Egito

ANGOLA

RHODESIA

Zambezi

Lake
Nyassa

NYASSA LAND

MOZAMBIQUE

Blantyre

Mozam-
bique

ATLANTIC OCEAN

GERMAN

SOUTHWEST

AFRICA

BECHUANA-
LAND

Limpopo R.

TRANSVAAL

Pretoria

Johannesburg

Orange R.

Beira

Lourenço Marques
Delagoa Bay

INDIAN

OCEAN

CAPE COLONY

Cape Town

Scale of Miles
0   200   400   600

MANHATTAN DRAFTING CO., INC., N.Y.

the time and extent of British and German control over these colonial revenues, and details of the territorial demarcation. The British from the first refused to consider the abandonment of the Blantyre district of British Nyassaland, on the Shiré River. As compensation the Germans asked for Walfisch Bay and the assignment of the Portuguese part of the island of Timor. The British, on the other hand, demanded that Germany give up her right of extraterritoriality in Zanzibar, and agree to the cession of Togo, a proposal which the Germans would not for a moment entertain. In the end the matter was adjusted by the division of Angola in such a way that the Germans were assigned the southern part and also the northern quarter, the remainder falling into the British sphere. For the rest it will suffice to summarize the agreement as it was signed on August 30, 1898. In the preamble of the convention it was stated that "in order to obviate the international complications" which might arise if Portugal required financial assistance from some foreign power or powers, and in order "to preserve her integrity and independence," it had been agreed between Germany and England that whenever either party believed it expedient to accede to a request for a loan on the security of the Portuguese colonial revenues, it should inform the other party, which should have the right to advance a portion of the loan. The part advanced by either party should be as nearly as possible proportional to the amounts of revenue respectively assigned as their security, and the loans should be on terms as favorable to Portugal as possible. Then followed the definition of the parts of Mozambique, Angola and Portuguese Timor, the revenues of which should be assigned to either Germany or England as security for their part of the loan. Delegates might be sent by either party to these areas, but they were to have no rights of administration or control unless Portugal defaulted on the interest payments, in which case the customs houses should be handed over to the contracting parties. In future neither party was to attempt to secure concessions in the areas assigned to the other. There followed a secret convention, envisaging the possibility that the integrity of the Portuguese possessions could not be maintained. In that event "Great Britain and Germany agree jointly to oppose the intervention of any third Power in the Provinces of Mozambique, Angola and in Portuguese Timor, either by way of loan to Portugal on the security of the revenues of those provinces, or by way of acquisition of territory, by grant, cession, purchase, lease, or otherwise." Henceforth both parties agreed to abstain "from advancing any claim of whatsoever kind to the possession, occupation, control, or exercise of political influence in or over those portions of the Portuguese provinces in which the Customs revenues have been assigned" to the other. Finally there was a secret note clarifying the preceding conventions. In case either party obtained from Portugal a cession of territory or the concession of special privileges not of an occasional character in its sphere before the general abandonment of the territories envisaged above, the cession or concession should not become operative until the other party had secured analogous grants in its sphere. Each party should inform the other of applications for privileges of an occasional character and should help the other get similar grants if it so desired.[85]

The course of the discussions in London was constantly disturbed by the intervention of the Emperor William. At his instigation his mother, the Empress Frederick, wrote a number of letters to Queen Victoria during the last days of July and the beginning of August, in which she seems to have stressed the eagerness of the Emperor and Bülow for an agreement with England, while hinting at the same time that Salisbury was an obstacle to a good understanding. The text of most of these letters has not been published, either in the *Letters of the Empress Frederick,* or in the *Letters of Queen Victoria.* It is clear from Salisbury's correspondence with the Queen, however, that the prime minister greatly resented the implications in the Berlin letters, that he denied having received the German proposals with " something between a joke and a snub," and that he simply felt that the German demands were so extravagant that British public opinion would never tolerate them.[86] He was probably glad when his physician ordered a vacation and he could turn over the conduct of the negotiations to Balfour.

The Emperor's conversations with the British ambassador were marked by the same querulousness. At a meeting at Friedrichshof on August 21, 1898, His Majesty spoke with great bitterness of British hesitation and close-fistedness. The English must realize, he asserted, that Germany had to have colonies and coaling stations and that she was going to get them. He much preferred to attain his object through understanding and co-operation with England, but if the London government forced him to it, he could and would succeed even against British opposition. His relations with Russia and France were excellent, and his relations with the United States government, despite British efforts to poison the American press, had also remained cordial.

Sir Frank Lascelles tried to assuage the Emperor's indignation by referring to the projected agreement between England and Germany. He understood perfectly that the Germans could not commit themselves to opposition of Russia, inasmuch as England could not help to protect the German frontier. He had told this to some of his friends during a recent visit to England. Indeed he had been at lunch with Chamberlain, Balfour, Goschen and other cabinet ministers when the whole subject was discussed. The colonial secretary had been greatly impressed with the argument that England could do nothing to defend Germany, and had finally suggested that a defensive alliance might be concluded between the two nations providing that if either were attacked by two powers, the other should come to its assistance: " One of us is strong enough to fight any *one* Power, who should attack him, but in case of *two*

---

[85] *Die Grosse Politik,* XIV, no. 3872; *British Documents,* I, nos. 90–2. By far the best digest of the negotiations is in Schwarze: *Das Deutsch-Englische Abkommen, etc.,* pp. 31–61; the summary in Bixler: *Anglo-German Imperialism in South Africa,* pp. 114–34 is dull and unenlightening.

[86] *Letters of Queen Victoria,* III, pp. 258–63; Lee: *Edward VII,* I, pp. 736–7.

Powers attacking, the issue is at least very doubtful; therefore: should Germany be assaulted by any *two Powers* at *once* England is ready to assist with every armament in her power to knock down one of her antagonists, whilst Germany is fighting the other one; the same England would wish Germany to do should the case be the reverse." The other ministers present, according to Lascelles, approved of this project. The Emperor was much taken with it and suggested that it might be a feasible basis for an agreement.[87]

So far as one can judge from the documents the Germans took Lascelles' remarks very much *au sérieux,* and immediately began to consider the advisability of a general agreement on this basis. The Emperor's remarks to Lascelles in December of the same year show that he regarded the reputed plan for a defensive alliance almost as an informal promise of assistance. German historians have, many of them, looked upon this conversation as almost crucial and have criticized the government for its hesitancy and failure to follow up the suggestion. To the present writer this all seems somewhat beside the point. Lascelles admitted later that he had had no instructions to touch upon the matter. He protested that the Emperor had made more of his remarks than had been intended. The whole scheme smacked strongly of Chamberlain's general line of thought, and there is nothing unlikely in the statement that Balfour and other members of the cabinet who desired a rapprochement with Germany approved the plan in principle. But Salisbury was not at the luncheon, and it may be doubted whether he would have approved so far-reaching a project. The whole discussion was of a purely academic character and no steps were ever taken from the British side to make the subject a matter of negotiation.

Indeed, when one looks even at the agreement respecting the Portuguese colonies it is hard to find in it any great contribution to a sound Anglo-German understanding. The two powers who concluded this agreement did not see eye to eye, they did not have the same objectives in view. England began with a burning desire to get control of Delagoa Bay and the railway to the Transvaal, or at any rate with the firm determination that no other powers should secure such control. Because of Portugal's desperate financial position, because of her financial obligations to Germany and France as well as to England, there was always the danger that the all-important Bay might be hypothecated by the Lisbon government. It was almost a certainty that any British effort to secure control of that area would meet with unyielding opposition from the continental powers. Yet the English never could shake off the feeling that they should have been allowed to make their own arrangements with Portugal without interference by other powers. Even Chamberlain had the feeling that the Germans were blackmailing the London government: " The only advantage to us," he wrote to Balfour, " is the assurance of Germany's abstention from further interference in Delagoa Bay and the Transvaal — in other words, we pay

---

[87] *Die Grosse Politik,* XIV, no. 3865; *British Documents,* I, nos. 87, 122; II, nos. 96, 97; Garvin, op. cit., III, pp. 290 ff.

Blackmail to Germany to induce her not to interfere where she has no right of interference. Well! it is worth while to pay Blackmail sometimes." [88] And so the idea of blackmail became firmly fixed in the minds of the men who conducted Britain's international affairs. The agreement did not by any means make for greater confidence or trust between the two nations, even though, as we see it now, it was of tremendous importance to England so far as the south African situation was concerned and there was every reason why the London government should have been satisfied with it. After all, it put an end not only to the pro-Boer policy of the Germans, but also shut out France from any share in the ultimate division of the south African spoils.[89]

What really lay at the bottom of British discontent was the idea that the Germans should get so large an increase in territory even prospectively. Chamberlain's thought originally was to make arrangements with Portugal and then settle with the Germans. If that plan had succeeded, we may rest assured that the Germans would have gotten very little, and *that* probably not in south Africa. For the British did not want to partition the Portuguese colonies with any other power. They wanted no other partner in south Africa and liked to think of the Portuguese colonies as a British preserve. Once the agreement with Germany was made, they did their utmost to prevent it from materializing. Within a month of the signature of the document Balfour seems to have informed the Portuguese minister, Soveral, of its general tenor, and the substance of the treaty was allowed to get into the press. The Lisbon government, possibly with English aid, managed to raise funds in Paris on the security of domestic revenues and was thus able to avoid a loan in London or Berlin with a pledge of the colonies. The satisfaction of the English, I think, still rings through the pages of Garvin's *Life of Chamberlain,* where there are gleeful references to the " imaginary repasts " which were spread before the Germans, to " imaginary reversions," to the " mirage " of which Germany was given a share, and to " the castle in the clouds " for which the Emperor William gave up his pro-Boer policy.[90]

Fortunately for Anglo-German relations and for the peace of the world, the Berlin government was not aware of British intentions. The Germans paid a high price for the agreement and they expected to realize upon it at an early date. It was to be some time before they understood that after weeks of acrimonious bargaining they had " waged and won a fight for shadows." During the autumn of 1898 they were still deluded, still hopeful. And so, for the time being, the relations between London and Berlin benefitted from the agreement.

---

[88] Garvin, op. cit., III, p. 315.

[89] Balfour and Milner, at least, appreciated these aspects of the agreement and therefore welcomed it. See *Milner Papers,* p. 299; *Letters of Queen Victoria,* III, p. 266.

[90] Garvin, op. cit., III, pp. 313–6; the substance of the agreement was published by Diplomaticus (probably Lucien Wolf): " The Anglo-German Agreement " (*Fortnightly Review,* October, 1898, pp. 627–34). On this whole aspect of the problem see the excellent discussion in Schwarze, op. cit., Part III, which obviates more detailed treatment here.

As we review the Anglo-German problem we can see that imperialism, as it spread to the continental nations, tended to put the British into a position where, in the opinion of some cabinet ministers at least, isolation had become dangerous and outside support indispensable. The historian, in discussing this situation, must guard against the unwarranted use of hindsight and against bootless sentimentality. Let us assume that if a close Anglo-German alliance had existed in 1914 the world cataclysm would have been impossible. Let us grant the great importance and desirability of this combination, which, as we look back, seems so logical, so sensible, so sweetly reasonable. But in 1898 affairs were such that the conclusion of such an agreement was practically impossible. In the first place there was the strong current of popular dislike on both sides. German press opinion may be discounted, since it was to a large degree inspired. But the British public saw in Germany its chief rival, the pushing parvenu whose efforts it was something of a pleasure to frustrate. It need not be assumed that this popular hostility was an insurmountable obstacle to an agreement. John Morley once spoke with some alarm of the "almost reckless vacillation of popular humour" with respect to foreign nations.[91] The government could undoubtedly have done much to change the general temper. In fact, the tone of the British press was improved as a result of the efforts of the Queen.

More important, then, than the popular hostility to Germany was the attitude of the directing statesmen. It is certain that since 1895 the British government had been trying first and foremost to effect an agreement with Russia. It was the logical policy to follow, for if successful it would have obviated many points of friction and would at the same time have undermined the Franco-Russian Alliance. This policy met with complete failure in the winter of 1897–1898. A policy of enlisting the aid of Japan and America proved illusory. The alliance with Germany was never anything more than a second or third choice. Chamberlain approached it cold-bloodedly. He really hoped to find in Germany a continental sword. Balfour appears more than any other British statesman to have seen the Anglo-German problem in its larger setting and to have worked for a gradual amelioration of the relationship between the two countries. Salisbury, however, had the deciding vote, and Salisbury had been soured by his past experiences with the Germans and especially with the Emperor. He took the Far Eastern situation more lightly and more stoically than Chamberlain, and he did not believe that the time had come to throw away the advantages of isolation, that is, the advantages of an absolutely free hand. What was more, he did not like the idea of making sacrifices to secure the support of the Germans, though he was prepared to throw half of Asia to the omnivorous Russian bear. Our material is still very inadequate, but it seems reasonably clear that Salisbury was never in favor of the Chamberlain policy and refused to assume responsibility for it. Since he was prime minister and foreign minister, it was his opinion, his policy that counted, not Chamberlain's.

---

[91] Speech of March 24, 1898 (London *Times,* March 25, 1898).

In considering the German attitude one must begin with the realization that no British offers were rejected, for the simple reason that no offers were made. The British *foreign office* never went beyond the modest expression of desires for better relations and for an agreement on special points, as put forward by Balfour in March 1898. The important point on the German side was the discussion and determination of a policy to be followed if offers were eventually made. There can be little question that both the Emperor and Bülow desired improved relations. They were, however, decidedly opposed to being made the cat's-paw against Russia. If it was to Britain's interest to check the Russian expansion in the Far East, it was to Germany's interest to see her eastern neighbor deeply involved in Asia. To block the Russians in China would have meant simply to throw them back on Europe. Even if war with Russia and France had not followed the conclusion of an Anglo-German alliance (and it is unlikely that war would have resulted) the fact remains that such an alliance would have diverted to the German frontier much of the pressure that was being exerted on the Celestial Empire. The Germans were therefore sceptical, and rightly sceptical, of any far-reaching alliance with England, the more so as there was every reason to believe that further developments would make the abandonment of isolation all the more imperative for England and that eventually even the Salisbury viewpoint would have to be modified.

In the meanwhile both sides had expressed their readiness to discuss special problems. The negotiations that took place during the year indicated, however, how difficult even minor agreements were in practice. The trouble was that the proper atmosphere was lacking. Suspicion, jealousy, recrimination prevailed on both sides. The British hated the idea of making extensive concessions to the Germans, while the Germans always felt that the British, already the possessors of a large part of the globe, begrudged their late-coming cousins even the most trivial acquisitions. Of course there was more than a little hysteria in this rampant imperialism and much sleep was lost over territories of no importance. But these psychological elements must be considered. People simply became panicky as they saw the world shrinking. Nothing seemed quite so important as to get everything possible before it was too late, and to allow as little as possible to pass into the hands of competitors. It must be confessed that the Germans made something of a nuisance of themselves by interjecting themselves into every problem and by demanding compensation everywhere and at all times. But it is equally true that the British took a negative stand to begin with and showed an extraordinary tendency to look with greater equanimity upon the voracious appetite of Russia and France than upon the relatively unimpressive nibblings of the Germans. The curious thing is that the British knew that what went to Russia and France would be pretty securely locked against competing traders, while the German territories were almost as wide open as the British. The only explanation is that the Russians and the French were not serious commercial rivals of the British. One could hold one's own against them despite their exclusive policy. With the Germans the reverse was true. They were getting the better of the British even in the markets of the Empire. That was where the shoe pinched. It was that which lay at the bottom of the suspicion and the jealousy. To be sure, rivalries of this type have a way of adjusting themselves with the passage of time. The commercial antagonism between England and Germany was probably less marked in 1912 than it was in 1898. But we are concerned here with the earlier period, and when one reviews the situation as it was in the last years of the dying century one can hardly avoid the conclusion that the general setting of affairs was such that a real reconciliation between England and Germany was a high fence to ride at.

BIBLIOGRAPHICAL NOTE

DOCUMENTARY SOURCES

Accounts and Papers. 1899, volume CIX. *China No. 1 (1899)*: *Correspondence respecting the Affairs of China*. Contains the material on the occupation of Weihaiwei, on the concessions secured by the French, on various railway problems, etc.

Die Grosse Politik der Europäischen Kabinette, 1871–1914. Volume XIV, chapters xci and xcii. The most important source for the history of the Anglo-German negotiations and the agreement on the Portuguese colonies.

British Documents on the Origins of the War, 1898–1914. Volume I, chapter ii. Though the British documents contain almost nothing on the Anglo-German alliance negotiations, they are quite full on the Portuguese affair and form an admirable supplement to the German publication.

TELESHEV, L.: " Anglo-Germanskoe Sblishenie v 1898 g." (*Krasnyi Arkhiv*, LVI, 1933, pp. 65–79). A series of reports from the Russian ambassador at Berlin, revealing his uneasiness about the Anglo-German rapprochement. These documents have been translated and published in the *Berliner Monatshefte*, XI, 1933, pp. 492–510.

MEMOIRS, AUTOBIOGRAPHIES, BIOGRAPHIES, AND LETTERS

GARVIN, J. L.: *The Life of Joseph Chamberlain*. Three volumes. London, 1933—. Volume three is by far the most important English source on the Anglo-German negotiations of 1898.

The Letters of Queen Victoria. Edited by George E. Buckle. Series III, volume III. London, 1932. In view of the paucity of British source material these letters are of great interest and value.

LEE, SIR SIDNEY: *King Edward VII, a Biography.* Two volumes. New York, 1925. Contains a discussion of the Anglo-German problem, but the account is very incomplete and remarkably biassed.

The Milner Papers. South Africa, 1897–1899. Edited by Cecil Headlam. London, 1931. Apart from their value for the study of the south African question these papers contain some illuminating bits on the Portuguese colonial problem.

Memoirs of Prince von Bülow. Four volumes. Boston, 1931–1932. Volume I deals with this period but contains extraordinarily little of importance.

ECKARDSTEIN, HERMANN FREIHERR VON: *Lebenserinnerungen und Politische Denkwürdigkeiten.* Two volumes. Leipzig, 1919. The recollections of the counsellor of the German embassy in London. Full of sensational revelations, elegantly written, but thoroughly unreliable and therefore of very little use.

SPECIAL STUDIES

MEINECKE, FRIEDRICH: *Geschichte des Deutsch-Englischen Bündnisproblems, 1890–1901.* Munich, 1927. Easily the most brilliant treatment of the whole question. Written with breadth of view and fairness. Based on the German documents, this is the classic formulation of the critical view of German policy in its relation to England.

RITTER, GERHARD: *Die Legende von der Verschmähten Englischen Freundschaft, 1898–1901.* Freiburg, 1929. Another brilliant piece of synthetic work, which, in the opinion of the present writer, comes nearer the truth than Meinecke's interpretation. Ritter has used the British as well as the German documents and argues that the British offers were never concrete enough to lead to anything.

PRIBRAM, ALFRED F.: *England and the International Policy of the European Great Powers, 1871–1914.* Oxford, 1931. A series of lectures, giving in brief scope an excellent factual and interpretive account.

FISCHER, EUGEN: *Holsteins Grosses Nein.* Berlin, 1925. One of the most extensive and one of the most critical and hostile accounts of the policy of Bülow and Holstein. Now rather out of date.

SALOMON, FELIX: " Die Englisch-Deutschen Bündnisverhandlungen von 1898–1901, im Weltpolitischen Zusammenhang." (*Die Grenzboten,* August 29, 1920, pp. 200–14). Though now out of date this essay is still worth reading.

ROLOFF, GUSTAV: " Die Bündnisverhandlungen zwischen Deutschland und England 1898–1901." (*Berliner Monatshefte,* December, 1929, pp. 1167–222). One of the best systematic accounts, based on both the British and German documents. Supersedes the author's earlier essay in the *Preussische Jahrbücher,* September, 1919, pp. 345–64. Critical of the Meinecke viewpoint.

HALLER, JOHANNES: *England und Deutschland um die Jahrhundertwende.* Leipzig, 1929. Written by one of Bülow's keenest and most merciless critics. Sticks by his condemnation of the German policy despite the British documents.

BECKER, WILLY: *Fürst Bülow und England, 1897–1909.* Greifswald, 1929. An extensive study of Bülow's English policy. Conventional and adds little. See also the same author's article " Englands Bündniswerben — eine Legende " (*Vergangenheit und Gegenwart,* XX, 1930, pp. 21–8), which is a reply to Ritter.

EHRINGHAUS, FRITZ: " Die Ergebnisse der Englischen Akten über die Deutsch-Englischen Bündnisverhandlungen 1899–1901." (*Vergangenheit und Gegenwart,* XIX, 1929, pp. 471–80). Goes even beyond Ritter in deflating the conventional German view.

ROTHFELS, HANS: " Zur Beurteilung der Englischen Vorkriegspolitik." (*Archiv für Politik und Geschichte,* 1926, no. 12, pp. 599–615). A brilliant discussion of the larger problem of general British policy.

LEHMANN, KONRAD: " Die Ablehnung des Englischen Bündnisantrags, 1898–1901." (*Preussische Jahrbücher,* August, 1930, pp. 162–83). An excellent recent presentation of the Meinecke viewpoint, with due consideration for the British documents.

KEHR, ECKART: " Das Deutsch-Englische Bündnisproblem der Jahrhundertwende." (*Die Gesellschaft,* July, 1928, pp. 24–31). Elaborates the idea tentatively put forward by Meinecke, that the fundamental reason for the failure of the negotiations was the objection of certain social classes in Germany to any connexion with England.

HOYNINGEN GENANNT HUENE, HEINRICH FREIHERR VON: *Untersuchungen zur Geschichte des Deutsch-Englischen Bündnisproblems, 1898–1901.* Breslau, 1934. Does not deal with the negotiations properly speaking, but gives a good analysis of the international background.

MECENSEFFY, GRETE: " Die Deutsch-Englischen Bündnisverhandlungen 1898–1901 im Lichte der Englischen Aktenpublikation." (*Vierteljahrschrift für Politik und Geschichte,* I, 1929, pp. 175–91). A conventional analysis of the British documents.

LÖDING, WALTER: *Die Deutsch-Englischen Bündnisverhandlungen 1898–1901.* Hamburg, 1929. A doctoral dissertation that adds very little, but gives one of the most complete factual digests of the material.

JOHNSON, EDGAR N., and BICKFORD, JOHN D.: " The Contemplated Anglo-German Alliance. 1890–1901." (*Political Science Quarterly,* March, 1927, pp. 1–57). A fairly pedestrian piece of work, of no great importance.

STAL'NYI, V.: " Popytka Anglo-Germanskogo Sblisheniia v 1898–1901 gg." (*Istorik Marksist,* X, 1928, pp. 89–120). A Marxian interpretation, based chiefly on Eckardstein and the German Documents.

GOOCH, GEORGE P.: " Baron von Holstein." In the author's *Studies in Modern History.* London, 1931. Easily the best scholarly study of the extraordinary figure who had so much to do with directing German policy in these years.

BECKER, OTTO: Review of the books by Meinecke and Ritter. (*Deutsche Literaturzeitung,* L, pp. 903–25). This extensive review of two conflicting interpretations is in itself an interesting contribution to the discussion of the problem.

PICK, FRITZ: "Das Deutsch-Englische Bündnis." (*Preussische Jahrbücher,* January, 1935, pp. 56–65). A discussion of the third volume of Garvin's *Chamberlain.*

ROSEN, FRIEDRICH: "Die Deutsch-Englischen Bündnisverhandlungen des Jahres 1898." (*Berliner Monatshefte,* March, 1935, pp. 192–207). Like the preceding, an evaluation of the new English material.

SCHWARZE, FRITZ: *Das Deutsch-Englische Abkommen über die Portugiesischen Kolonien vom 30 August 1898.* Göttingen, 1931. A doctoral dissertation that is far above the average. Combines good command of the material in the British and German documents with keen understanding of the broader issues involved.

BIXLER, RAYMOND W.: *Anglo-German Imperialism in South Africa.* Baltimore, 1932. Contains an extended digest of the British and German material on the Portuguese Treaty of 1898. Conventional, unilluminating and dull.

LOPES, ARTHUR RIBEIRO: *A Convenção Secreta entre a Alemanha e a Inglaterra sôbre a Partilha das Colónias Portuguesas.* Lisbon, 1933. Nothing more than a digest of the British Documents on the secret treaty of 1898.

LITERATURE SINCE 1935

(See also the Supplementary Bibliographical Note to Chapter II.)

DUGDALE, BLANCHE E. C.: *Arthur James Balfour.* New York, 1937. Two volumes. An important biography, with interesting material on Anglo-American and Anglo-German relations.

PENSON, LILLIAN M.: "The New Course in British Foreign Policy, 1892–1902" (*Transactions of the Royal Historical Society,* Series IV, Volume XXV, 1943, pp. 121–139). A discerning essay on the forces leading to Britain's realignment.

TARKOW-NAAMANI, ISRAEL: "The Abandonment of Splendid Isolation by Great Britain" (*Canadian Historical Review,* XXVII, June, 1946, pp. 163–188). A useful analysis of the evolution of English opinion on foreign commitments.

HEINDEL, RICHARD H.: *The American Impact on Great Britain, 1898–1914: A Study of the United States in World History.* Philadelphia, 1940. 439 pp. A unique analysis of the growth of British public opinion with regard to the United States. Deals not only with diplomacy, but with economic relations, naval strategy and cultural forces.

GELBER, LIONEL M.: *The Rise of Anglo-American Friendship: A Study in World Politics, 1898–1906.* New York, 1938. 278 pp. The best general account of the subject, based on all available materials.

PRATT, JULIUS W.: *Expansionists of 1898: The Acquisition of Hawaii and the Spanish Islands.* Baltimore, 1936. 376 pp. A series of lectures which constitute the best general study of the United States' role in the late nineteenth century scramble for territory. Makes use of unpublished American documents.

HARRINGTON, FRED H.: " The Anti-Imperialist Movement in the United States, 1898–1900 " (*Mississippi Valley Historical Review,* XXII, September, 1935, pp. 211–230). A concise, scholarly study of the subject.

BEAZLEY, RAYMOND: "Joseph Chamberlain und die englisch-deutschen Beziehungen im Jahre 1898 " (*Berliner Monatshefte,* XIII, December, 1935, pp. 1011–1032). Primarily a review of Garvin's biography of Chamberlain. Adds little.

WOLF, MARIE-LUISE: *Botschafter Graf Hatzfeldt: Seine Tätigkeit in London, 1885–1901.* Speyer, 1935. 79 pp. A conventional dissertation, based on obvious sources.

SCHÜSSLER, WILHELM: *Deutschland zwischen Russland und England: Studie zur Aussenpolitik des bismarckschen Reiches.* Third edition. Leipzig, 1940. 174 pp. Contains one of the most discerning and competent studies of the negotiations of 1898–1901.

ROLOFF, GUSTAV: " Die englisch-deutschen Bündnisverhandlungen im Jahre 1898 " (*Berliner Monatshefte,* XIII, October, 1935, pp. 849–876). A review of the problem in the light of the British documents and the Garvin biography of Chamberlain. Concludes that Salisbury was basically opposed to the Chamberlain policy.

VOEGTLE, ERICH: *Die englische Diplomatie und die deutsche Presse, 1898–1914.* Würzburg, 1936. 121 pp. Contains only a short chapter on the relation of the government and the press in Germany prior to 1905.

ANDERSON, PAULINE R.: *The Background of Anti-English Feeling in Germany, 1890–1902.* Washington, 1939. 382 pp. Essential for the study of the Anglo-German negotiations.

HALE, ORON J.: *Publicity and Diplomacy, with special reference to England and Germany, 1890–1914.* New York, 1940. 486 pp. One of the most illuminating studies of public opinion in Germany and Britain.

DITTMAR, GUSTAV H.: *Die deutsch-englischen Beziehungen in den Jahren 1898–1899. Die Vorbesprechungen zu den Bündnisverhandlungen von 1900–1901.* Stuttgart, 1938. 143 pp. A disappointing treatment of the subject, which adds nothing.

TÜMMLER, HANS: " Die deutsch-englischen Bündnisverhandlungen um die Jahrhundertwende, 1898–1901 " (*Vergangenheit und Gegenwart,* XXVIII, 1938, pp. 617–634). A Nazi re-interpretation of the subject, drawing on the Garvin biography to demonstrate the ruinous policy of Bülow and Holstein.

FRAUENDIENST, WERNER: " Deutschland und England an der Jahrhundertwende: mit unveröffentlichen Dokumenten aus dem Nachlass des Botschafters Grafen Paul von Hatzfeldt " (*Berliner Monatshefte,* XVII, December, 1939, pp. 970–985). Extracts from the Hatzfeldt papers with commentary designed to show the German readiness for an alliance.

JAENECKE, W. A.: *Britisches Bündnisspiel um die Jahrhundertwende.* Berlin, 1941. 67 pp. Retrospective Nazi commentary on the failure of the Anglo-German negotiations.

BITTNER, LUDWIG: "Oesterreich-Ungarn und die deutsch-englischen Bündnisverhandlungen im Frühjahr 1898" (*Festschrift für Heinrich Srbik*. Munich, 1938, pp. 372–380). Adduces Austrian diplomatic reports which tend to show that Salisbury favored the planned agreement with Germany and that the entire British Cabinet supported Chamberlain.

FERRARA, ORESTES: *The Last Spanish War: Revelations in 'Diplomacy.'* New York, 1937. 151 pp. A study of the international relations of the Spanish-American War, by a Cuban diplomat. Makes use of American and Spanish records, and to some extent of French and Italian documents.

WROWBLEWSKI, VIKTOR A.: "Der englisch-spanische Konflikt von 1898" (*Berliner Monatshefte*, XVI, April, 1938, pp. 341–360). Based on the Russian documents cited in the following title.

ANONYMOUS: "Ispano-britanskii Konflikt, 1898–1899" (*Krasny Arkhiv*, no. 60, 1933, pp. 3–60). Russian diplomatic correspondence to and from Madrid, revealing Spanish fears of an Anglo-American alliance to dismember the Spanish colonial empire.

KUNZ-LACK, ILSE: *Die deutsch-amerikanischen Beziehungen, 1890–1914.* Stuttgart, 1935. 242 pp. An excellent general review of the subject.

VAGTS, ALFRED: *Deutschland und die Vereinigten Staaten in der Weltpolitik.* New York, 1935. Two volumes. Based on German and American archive materials, this is a most exhaustive, sociological examination of German-American relations. A most important contribution.

SHIPPEE, LESTER B.: "German-American Relations, 1890–1914" (*Journal of Modern History*, VIII, December, 1936, pp. 479–488). Primarily a critical review of the two preceding titles.

BLAKE, NELSON M.: "England and the United States, 1897–1899" (in *Essays in History and International Relations, in honor of George Hubbard Blakeslee.* Worcester, 1949, pp. 257–284). Chiefly an analysis of the American and British press to show the development of closer relations during the Spanish-American War.

PETERS, EVELENE: *Roosevelt und der Kaiser. Ein Beitrag zur Geschichte der deutsch-amerikanischen Beziehungen, 1895–1906.* Leipzig, 1936. 163 pp. Views the problem against the background of American-British and American-Japanese relations. A useful study which draws upon the American literature.

BAILEY, THOMAS A.: "Dewey and the Germans at Manila Bay" (*American Historical Review*, XLV, 1939, pp. 59–81). A definitive study, based on German and British naval documents. Explodes the traditional story of German intervention.

EYRE, JAMES K., JR.: "Russia and the American Acquisition of the Philippines" (*Mississippi Valley Historical Review*, XXVIII, March, 1942, pp. 539–562).

QUINN, PEARLE E.: "The Diplomatic Struggle for the Carolines, 1898" (*Pacific Historical Review*, XIV, September, 1945, pp. 290–302). Based primarily on the German and British documents.

BEAZLEY, RAYMOND: " Britain, Germany and the Portuguese Colonies, 1898–1899 "
(*Berliner Monatshefte,* XIV, November, 1936, pp. 866–887). A digest of the German and British documents — adds little.

DUBOIS, PIERRE: " Le traité anglo-allemand du 30 aôut 1898 relatif aux colonies portugais " (*Revue d'histoire de la guerre mondiale,* XVII, July, 1939, pp. 232–246). A solid re-examination of the subject in the light of the German, British and French documents, as well as of contemporary literature.

XVI

The Struggle for the Nile
III. The Fashoda Conflict

I N THE SPRING OF 1898, DURING THE HEIGHT OF THE FAR EASTERN CRISIS AND at a time when the foreign policy of Lord Salisbury was being bitterly criticized, one of the under-secretaries of the foreign office is reputed to have said to a prominent journalist: " There are certain things we can do and certain things we cannot do. Believe me, we shall retrieve ourselves completely in the Soudan." [1] And, in very fact, when the great victory was won over the French in the autumn of 1898 the prime minister's reputation was completely re-established. Many people thought that his whole policy since 1895 had been pointed towards the great African crisis. Concessions had been made to both the Russians and the Germans, and the Far Eastern situation had not been brought to a climax, simply because the thought and determination of the foreign office had been concentrated upon the struggle for the Nile, a struggle that had been steadily developing for years and had entered upon the swelling act after the battle of Adua and the British advance to Dongola. [2]

The reader will recall the argument advanced in a previous chapter with respect to the motives that led to the first phase of the reconquest of the Sudan. The British decided to march upon Dongola not only in order to relieve the pressure upon the Italians, but also in order to anticipate action by the French upon the upper Nile. Dongola was occupied by the Egyptian forces in the autumn of 1896, but that settled nothing. From the beginning Lord Salisbury realized that the Egyptians, perhaps supported by British troops, would have to advance at least as far as Khartum. In June he told the house of lords: " We shall not have restored Egypt to the position in which we received her, and we shall not have placed Egypt in that position of safety in which she deserves to stand, until the Egyptian flag floats over Khartum." But there were great obstacles to the realization of this object. The Egyptian government did not have the one or two million pounds required for such an expedition, and could not borrow it. The British parliament almost certainly would have refused to finance the undertaking. Besides, Salisbury had always planned an advance from

---

[1] Diplomaticus: " Fashoda and Lord Salisbury's Vindication " (*Fortnightly Review*, December, 1898, pp. 1002–14), p. 1002.   [2] See supra, chapter IX.

the south to meet the push from the north. But operations from Uganda were impossible before the Railway was completed to Lake Victoria. For troops to march from the coast to the interior would have required ninety days alone. The Railway was indispensable, but another two years were needed to bring it to the Lake.[3]

Because of these considerations the military operations were suspended for some time, excepting for the construction of a railway from Wady Halfa across the desert that fills the great bend in the Nile below Abu Hamed. The latter place was occupied by Egyptian troops in August 1897. In the meanwhile developments were taking place which were to force the British government to hasten operations and to press on to Khartum before it really felt ready. We must turn now to an account of events in the interior of Africa and in Abyssinia, events which make an extraordinary and thrilling story.

For years the French government had been trying to effect the evacuation of Egypt by the British. Having failed to attain this object it had decided to make a thrust at the upper Nile and to force an agreement on the Egyptian question by threatening to interfere with the water supply of the regions along the lower river. It had frustrated the effort of the British to block the advance from the French Congo by setting up Leopold as lessee of the upper Nile territory as far north as Fashoda. After the agreement between France and the Congo State in August 1894 the French expedition under Monteil was, indeed, recalled, but his place was taken by M. Liotard, who was instructed to establish effective occupation in the regions along the M'Bomu River and on the other side of the Congo-Nile watershed. In February 1896 the French government, warmly harangued by Monteil's associate, Captain Marchand, had decided to resume its earlier plan and send an expedition to the upper Nile. When Marchand left France in May 1896 he was placed under the general direction of Liotard, was told to avoid hostilities, especially with the dervishes, and to remember that his force was too small to make actual conquest possible. In other words, the purpose of the Marchand mission, whatever may have been said of it later, was to get a footing on the upper Nile to serve as a pawn in later negotiations with the British about Egypt. To quote General Mangin, who was one of the members of the expedition, the object was " to remove all pretext for the occupation of Egypt by the English and to put an end to the dream of our dear friends, who wish to unite Egypt with the Cape and their possessions in East Africa with those of the Royal Niger Company." Hanotaux himself told Marchand as the latter left Paris: " Go to Fashoda. France is going to fire her pistol." [4]

---

[3] *Letters of Queen Victoria*, Series III, vol. III (New York, 1932), pp. 39, 50, 72, 85; Lord Cromer: *Modern Egypt* (New York, 1908), II, p. 94.

[4] Général Mangin: " Lettres de la Mission Marchand " (*Revue des Deux Mondes*, September 15, 1931, pp. 241–83), pp. 246–7, 277. See also Jules Cocheris: *La Situation Internationale de l'Égypte* (Paris, 1903), p. 492. These utterances hardly fortify the arguments of Hanotaux and Lebon (at that time foreign minister and colonial minister respectively) that they tried to tone down the earlier in-

Into the details of the Marchand mission we cannot enter here. At the very outset the expedition was delayed by a native rising on the lower Congo, so that it did not leave Brazzaville until March 1897. But by August 1897 the French force had crossed the watershed of the Nile and Congo and had joined Liotard in establishing posts in the Bahr-el-Ghazal area. A small steamboat, the *Faidherbe,* was demounted, thousands of natives were pressed into service, and in a remarkably short time the steamer was carried and dragged over the high ground to the nearest navigable stream of the Nile system. Unfortunately the season of low water made it impossible to navigate the shallow, sluggish streams until the spring of 1898. But then activity was immediately resumed. On July 10, 1898 Marchand, accompanied by half a dozen European officers and some hundred and twenty Senegalese troops, arrived at Fashoda on the Nile and raised the French flag on the ruins of the old Egyptian fort.[5]

The Marchand mission, in its advance up the Congo and the Ubanghi, had been given all possible assistance by the officials of the Congo government. Indeed, the expedition had been transported on one of the Congo ships, the *Ville de Bruges.* This co-operation was merely the outward manifestation of what amounted to an alliance between France and the Congo State. Leopold, having tried repeatedly to induce Lord Salisbury to make over to him on lease all the Sudan south of Khartum, simply reversed his tactics when the British turned a deaf ear to his suggestions. His mind was still working along large lines. It was not enough to assure himself of the upper Nile area known as the Lado Enclave. Leopold had dreams of extending the power of the Congo State even to the east side of the Nile. After the battle of Adua, when the Italian government was seriously thinking of abandoning its Red Sea possessions, one of Leopold's agents appeared in Rome and carried on long negotiations with General Dal Verme. An agreement was drafted under the terms of which Italy should keep Massaua, but should cede the rest of Eritrea and the whole Abyssinian sphere of influence as defined in the Anglo-Italian Treaty of 1891 to a *Société Congolaise de Colonisation et d'Exploitation.* Half of the officials of this company were to be Italians and the Italian government was to receive half of the revenues. It was evidently planned to initiate the German Emperor into this scheme and to use him to secure the approval of England and France. The Italian government seems to have considered the scheme with some care. In November 1896 General Dal Verme sounded out political opinion by making some veiled references to the scheme in parliament. Objections were raised and the foreign minister, Visconti Venosta, appears to

---

structions to Marchand and to avoid friction with England (see Gabriel Hanotaux: *Fachoda,* Paris, 1909, pp. 105–9; André Lebon: *La Politique de la France en Afrique, 1896–1898,* Paris, 1901, pp. 3–6, 15 ff.; Louis Gillet: *Gabriel Hanotaux,* Paris, 1933, p. 79).

[5] The best accounts are those of the participants: Albert E. Baratier: *À travers l'Afrique* (Paris, 1910); J. Émily: *Mission Marchand, Journal de Route* (Paris, 1913); Général Mangin: " Lettres de la Mission Marchand " (*Revue des Deux Mondes,* September 15, 1931, pp. 241–83).

have opposed further consideration. At any rate, nothing more was heard of the plan.[6]

The failure of Leopold's Abyssinian hopes, however, had nothing to do with his activities along the Nile. In 1896 two great expeditions were organized in the Congo, one under Baron Dhanis, with more than a thousand native troops, and another under an officer named Chaltin. Dhanis, the chief in command, was to advance down the Nile to Lado and beyond, possibly in order to support Marchand against a dervish attack, and to protect his rear. It is said that Dhanis had secret instructions, to be opened only when he reached Fashoda! As a matter of fact he never reached even Lado. In February 1897 his Batetela force mutinied and slaughtered its officers, whereupon it began to return to Stanleyville. A very serious and widespread native rising followed, which was not entirely suppressed until 1899. In the meantime, however, Chaltin with the advance guard pushed on to the Nile, which he reached near Rejaf in February 1897. There was some fighting with dervish detachments, in which the Belgians were victorious. Chaltin gradually made his way to Lado, fortifying various places and increasing the Nile garrisons as he went till they numbered almost three thousand men. By the time when Marchand reached Fashoda the Belgians were already firmly established on the left bank of the upper Nile.[7]

The Marchand mission was only the most spectacular and best-known aspect of French activity in Africa in the years 1897–1898. At the same time efforts were apparently made to get in touch with the Khalifa at Omdurman and to secure his good will in return for support against the British advance from the north. So far as one can detect nothing came of these advances, which, when they were made known by the French press in the autumn of 1898, were characterized by an English writer as being " so infamous, so diabolical " that not only chivalrous Frenchmen, but even circumcised Hottentots might reasonably be supposed incapable of lending a hand to realize them.[8]

In Abyssinia, on the other hand, the French met with no serious obstacle. From the very beginning their idea had been to match an expedition from the west with another from the east. They had secured Menelik's friendship by supporting him against the Italians. If the King of Kings could be induced to make good his claim to the whole right bank of the upper Nile, set forth in his circular to the powers in 1891, the British would find before them not

---

[6] Théophile Simar: " Léopold II et l'Érythrée " (*Congo*, October, 1924, pp. 319–26), based on Leopold's papers; Pierre Daye: *Léopold II* (Paris, 1934), pp. 411 ff.

[7] Colonel Chaltin: " Vers le Nil " (in Louis Franck: *Le Congo Belge*, [Brussels, (?) 1928], II, pp. 103–14); A. J. Wauters: *Histoire Politique du Congo Belge* (Brussels, 1911), chaps. xx, xxiii; Fritz Masoin: *Histoire de l'État Indépendant du Congo* (Namur, 1913), II, pp. 282 ff., and chap. v; Arthur B. Keith: *The Belgian Congo and the Berlin Act* (Oxford, 1919), pp. 99–100, 112; Demetrius C. Boulger: *The Reign of Leopold II* (London, 1925), II, pp. 25 ff., 34 ff.

[8] Anonymous: " France, Russia and the Nile " (*Contemporary Review*, December, 1898, pp. 761–78), p. 765; see also Morrison B. Giffen: *Fashoda* (Chicago, 1930), pp. 17–8.

a mere handful of men, but tens of thousands of well-armed and warlike Abyssinians. Obviously the thing to do was to exploit the Abyssinian opportunity to the full. In December 1896 the French government decided to send M. Lagarde, governor of French Somaliland, on a special mission to Adis Abeba. He was to take large sums of money to be used for strengthening French influence in Abyssinia. As a special present for Menelik he was given one hundred thousand Gras rifles and two million rounds of ammunition. The mission was to be on a grand scale, and did, in fact, cost six hundred thousand francs. Lagarde was instructed to do all he could to prepare the way for two expeditions to the Nile, one under M. Clochette, who was already in Abyssinia, and the other under M. Bonvalot, which was to follow soon afterward.[9]

The French representative reached the Abyssinian capital early in March 1897. It is said that his reception was a cool one because Menelik suspected him of having had dealings with the Italians in the period before Adua. However this may have been, Lagarde seems to have scored an unqualified success before he returned to the coast. He arranged for a renewal of the French-Abyssinian treaty of friendship of 1843 and for the delimitation of the frontier of French Somaliland. Political reasons, taken together with the handsome present of guns and the willingness of the French to accept Abyssinian terms in the territorial settlement — all these factors appear to have softened Menelik's heart. He made Lagarde Duke of Entoto. Alfred Ilg, Swiss adviser of the King of Kings, was made counsellor of state, and threw the weight of his influence on the French side. M. Camille Mondon, correspondent of the Paris *Temps* in Adis Abeba, was made counsellor for public instruction and posts. Léon Chefneux, moving spirit behind the project of an Abyssinian railway, was named counsellor of railways and consul-general of Ethiopia in Europe. The doors were set open for French commerce. Everything seemed to be going swimmingly.[10]

So far as the Nile country was concerned, Lagarde found Menelik eager to follow the suggestions made by the French. He was determined to uphold his claim to the right bank of the Nile between the 5th and the 14th degrees north latitude, that is, from the vicinity of Lado to a point roughly one hundred and fifty miles upstream from Khartum. He was quite willing to give the Clochette and Bonvalot missions freedom of passage and to support them in every way.[11]

As soon as Lagarde was back at Jibuti the Clochette and Bonvalot missions

---

[9] Lebon, op. cit., pp. 30 ff.; Hanotaux, op. cit., pp. 133 ff.; Charles Michel: *Vers Fachoda, à la Rencontre de la Mission Marchand à travers l'Éthiopie* (Paris, 1901), pp. 8–9, 31.

[10] The Lagarde Treaty of March 20, 1897 was not published until 1908 (*Revue Générale de Droit International Public,* XV, 1908, Documents, p. 1). Sylvain Vigneras: *Une Mission Française en Abyssinie* (Paris, 1897) is a record of the mission by an official of the ministry for colonies, but the author carefully abstains from discussion of political activities. One of the fullest discussions of the mission is in L. J. Morié: *Histoire de l'Éthiopie* (Paris, 1904), II, pp. 443 ff.

[11] Lebon, op. cit., pp. 33–4.

started for the Abyssinian capital. A third group, led by Prince Henri d'Orleans, took the same course. The great traveller had no official standing, inasmuch as the French government could never summon enough courage to employ a member of the fallen dynasty. But he was always prepared to work for the glory of France, and played no unimportant part in the events of the next years. Unfortunately the three French missions failed to collaborate, for reasons that have never been cleared up. The members of the Bonvalot group maintained that Lagarde, instead of aiding them, put obstacles in their way and never gave proper support. The French governor was accused of having favored Clochette at the expense of the other mission. In any event Clochette went on toward the west, while Bonvalot returned to the coast to get the boats needed for navigation of the rivers that led to the Nile. He never returned, but abandoned the leadership of his group to Bonchamps. Bonchamps tried to get away from the capital, but the Abyssinian guides led him in great detours, evidently having been instructed to procrastinate as much as possible. Finally Bonchamps and Clochette met at Goré, in western Abyssinia. There they were both detained until further permits could be secured from Adis Abeba. In the meanwhile Clochette died and Bonchamps had to return to the capital to put an end to the obstruction which had so long delayed him. He found Lagarde at Adis Abeba on a second mission from the coast. The governor had failed to bring up the necessary boat. There were recriminations and sharp words, but finally Lagarde ordered the union of the Clochette and Bonchamps groups. Bonchamps was to proceed along the left bank of the Sobat River to the Nile. There he was to erect an Abyssinian fort on the right bank, and a French fort on the left.[12]

At last Bonchamps was able to set out. During the winter he and his companions proceeded in the direction laid down by Lagarde, signing treaties with the native chiefs along the way, not in the name of France, but in the name of Menelik. The going was incredibly hard. Once the highlands of Abyssinia were left behind the travellers found themselves in the great flat plain of the Nile, sparsely inhabited by humans, but well supplied with elephants and crocodiles. Food was scarce, the heat terrific, and fever all too common. Without boats it was almost impossible to cross the great swamps and the sluggish rivers that flowed through the grass. The expedition reached the junction of the Sobat and the Ajuba, late in December 1897. It had no means of crossing the great rivers, and was almost reduced to starvation. There was nothing to do but turn back, though the expedition was hardly more than one hundred miles from Fashoda! [13]

On the frontiers of Abyssinia the expedition came upon a large force of

---

[12] Bonchamps openly accused Lagarde of obstruction; see Anon: "L'Abyssinie et la France après Fachoda " (*Le Correspondant,* February 25, 1899, pp. 675–87); see further Michel: *Vers Fachoda,* passim; Jules Cocheris: *Situation Internationale de l'Égypte et du Soudan* (Paris, 1903), pp. 457–8.   [13] I follow the excellent account of Michel, who was a member of the party.

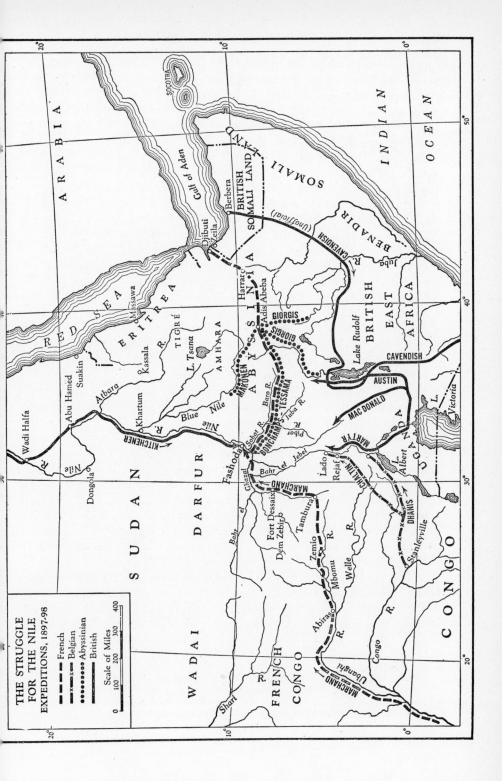

THE STRUGGLE
FOR THE NILE
EXPEDITIONS, 1897-98

French
Belgian
Abyssinian
British

Scale of Miles
0   100 200 300 400

Menelik's troops under the command of Dedjaz Tessama. This army comprised 10,000 men, and was accompanied by a Russian adventurer named Artamanov, who was attached to the Russian legation at Adis Abeba. Its purpose was to rescue the Bonchamps mission and to establish Abyssinian control of the whole Sobat valley to the Nile. Bonchamps did not retrace his steps, but two of his associates, the artist Potter and an officer named Faivre, went along. The army set out in March 1898 and advanced as far as it could. But the difficulties were very great. There was little food, and the Abyssinian troops showed once more that, accustomed as they were to a high altitude, they could not stand the humid heat of the plain. Fever took them off like flies. Nevertheless a detachment of some eight hundred men, including the Europeans, struggled on to the Nile, which was reached on June 22, 1898, that is, less than three weeks before Marchand reached Fashoda. The French and their Russian comrade therefore looked in vain for traces of the expedition from the west. They could not stay in the swamps, and simply had to turn back. But before going they wanted to plant the French flag on an island in the Nile. Unfortunately Faivre could not swim and Potter was deadly ill with fever. Finally one of the blacks agreed to take his chances with the crocodiles and take the flag out in return for a fancy reward. But when he was already in the water Artamanov saw the impropriety of the thing, dived into the dangerous flood and carried the tricolor to the island.[14]

Tessama's expedition down the Sobat was only one part of an extensive operation undertaken by Menelik to secure his claims to the frontiers enumerated in the circular of 1891. In the autumn and winter of 1897–1898 three other armies set out. The first, which left in June 1897, comprised 15,000 men under the command of Hapta Giorgis and was accompanied by a Frenchman, Léon Darragon. It reached and overran the entire country to the north of Lake Rudolf. On its return another expedition was sent out under the leadership of Ras Wedda Giorgis, who took along several Frenchmen with a force of Senegalese sharpshooters, and a Russian, named Bulatovič, with a few cossacks.[15] The fourth Abyssinian expedition, probably regarded as the most important, was sent out under the well-known commander, Ras Makonen. It advanced down the Blue Nile in the spring of 1898.[16]

A few words ought, perhaps, to be said of the mysterious activities of Prince Henri d'Orleans and Count Leontiev at this time. Orleans stayed at Adis Abeba throughout the spring of 1897 and left for Europe only in June. His intention was to return to Abyssinia at an early date. He had " a pile of big

---

[14] Michel, op. cit., pp. 412, 431; *Bulletin du Comité de l'Afrique Française,* November, 1898, p. 365; March, 1899, p. 95.

[15] See A. K. Bulatovič: *S Voiskami Menelika II* (St. Petersburg, 1900).

[16] The best accounts of these expeditions are those of L. J. Morié: *Histoire de l'Éthiopie,* II, pp. 450 ff. (which is closely followed by Leonard Woolf: *Empire and Commerce in Africa,* pp. 199 ff.), and of Conrad Keller: *Alfred Ilg* (Leipzig, 1918), pp. 163 ff.

projects " and was planning " something grand." No great secret was made of these projects. The King of Kings announced that Leontiev had been made " Governor of the Equatorial Provinces of Ethiopia " and that Prince Henri would be associated with him in the opening up of that territory. During the winter of 1897–1898 the Prince organized a syndicate, capitalized at 1,800,000 francs, for development purposes. This syndicate was a Belgian undertaking, in which King Leopold himself was heavily interested. There were very few colonial pies in which the wily King did not have a finger. This was simply another aspect of his plan to extend the Congo territory to Abyssinia and the Red Sea.

In the spring of 1898 Orleans was back at Jibuti, with a considerable force of Senegalese sharpshooters. He took, as a present to Menelik, a large shipment of rifles and ammunition. There was perfect understanding between him and the Abyssinian ruler, for it was arranged that Orleans and Leontiev should extend the frontier of Abyssinia to the Nile on the west and to Lake Victoria in the south. But in the end nothing came of the scheme. It was reported that Leontiev had been accidentally shot in both legs at Harrar, but there is also some evidence that his sharp and deceptive practices deprived him of Belgian financial support. No doubt Menelik too lost interest when the Fashoda crisis precipitated the withdrawal of the French.[17]

From the foregoing discussion it will be clear that the French, associated with the Belgians, were extremely active in Abyssinia during the years 1897–1898; that the Russians, too, were working toward the same end; and that the Franco-Russian influence was practically supreme at the court of Menelik. Unfortunately their efforts were not well co-ordinated. Lagarde's rôle is not at all clear, but there can be no doubt that he did not give the proper support to the Bonchamps mission. Bonchamps had previously been employed by King Leopold in the Congo, and seems to have gone to Abyssinia originally as an emissary of the King to enlist the help of Menelik against the dervishes. It is possible that Lagarde and the French government were suspicious of him and distrusted him. In any case, it is beyond dispute that Bonchamps got little official support. When he reached Jibuti on his way back to France, he found there the demounted boat which had been lying on the pier for some time and which might have changed the Nile expedition from failure into success. Nevertheless, it must not be forgotten that the French accomplished

---

[17] Prince Henri d'Orleans: *Une Visite à l'Empereur Ménélik* (Paris, 1898), passim, and the Prince's open letter to Delcassé, reprinted in the London *Times*, November 21, 1898; see also his statements to Henri Pensa in April, 1898 (*Revue Politique et Parlementaire*, XVI, May, 1898, pp. 171–5); and further Keller: *Alfred Ilg*, pp. 124–5, 207–8; Paul Bourdarie: " La Mission du Prince Henri d'Orléans en Abyssinie " (*Questions Diplomatiques et Coloniales*, August 15, 1897, pp. 68–71); G. de la Génardière: " Les Provinces Équatoriales d'Éthiopie " (ibid., May 1, 1898, pp. 12–9); Edmund D. Morel: " The Congo State and the Bahr-el-Ghazal " (*Nineteenth Century*, August, 1901, pp. 202–13); *Bulletin du Comité de l'Afrique Française*, September, 1897, p. 321; November, 1897, p. 404; August, 1898, p. 268.

at least this much: they stirred up Menelik and made him see the danger of the British advance against the dervishes. After all, they induced him to send out four sizable expeditions. Even if the nature of the territory in question was such that the Abyssinian troops could not stand it for any length of time, at least it had been made clear that the powerful King of Kings was to be reckoned with in any future settlement.

Now the important point about these French activities is that they were perfectly well known, almost without exception. Anyone who will take the trouble to look through the files of that excellent contemporary publication, the *Bulletin du Comité de l'Afrique Française,* will find abundant evidence of this fact, to say nothing of the voluminous quotations from the British, Belgian and French press indicating exactly the state of knowledge in these countries. The British papers followed the Belgian expeditions in detail, and from September 1897 onward there were periodic reports of the Marchand and Bonchamps groups. It was known that by the autumn of 1897 Marchand had reached the Bahr-el-Ghazal region. Some thought he was already at Fashoda, and it was reported that Bonchamps had joined hands with him there. Then, in December 1897, it was rumored that the mission had met with a tragic end. For two months the situation was widely discussed in the press on both sides of the Channel, and the leading English papers, like the *Times,* issued strong warnings to France as to what would be the outcome if their schemes were persisted in. All of the Abyssinian expeditions were reported, so that there was no lack of information. It is true that when Kitchener fought the battle of Omdurman on September 2, 1898 it was not certainly known in Europe whether Marchand had reached Fashoda or not; neither was it known whether the Abyssinian expedition had found its way to the Nile. But more than enough was known to cause elation in Paris and to call forth grave anxiety in London.[18]

The British government was not behind the public in close observation of the French enterprises, especially those that hinged on Abyssinia. At Menelik's court the British enjoyed no credit whatever, since their friendship with the Italians was known and it was thought that they had supported the Adua campaign with ample funds. It was therefore decided to send a mission to Adis Abeba early in 1897. Rennell Rodd, one of Lord Cromer's ablest assistants in

---

[18] See *Bulletin du Comité de l'Afrique Française,* September, 1897, pp. 316, 320; October, 1897, p. 350; December, 1897, p. 444; January, 1898, pp. 3 ff., 32–3; February, 1898, pp. 44–5, 62; August, 1898, pp. 263 ff.; September, 1898, pp. 278 ff., 286 ff.; October, 1898, pp. 325 ff. See also *Questions Diplomatiques et Coloniales,* September 15, 1897, pp. 237 ff.; October 15, 1897 (P. Vuillot: "La France dans le Haut-Nil"); January 15, 1898, pp. 99 ff., 109 ff.; February 15, 1898 (Paul Bourdarie: "Les Missions Liotard-Marchand-de Bonchamps et la Question du Nil"); October 1, 1898 (Henri Pensa: "La France au Bahr-el-Ghazal"). Further accounts in A. J. Wauters: "Autour de l'Abyssinie" (*Mouvement Géographique,* October 10, October 17 and October 31, 1897), in the *Geographical Journal,* February, 1898, pp. 169–71; and especially in Frederick A. Edwards: "The French on the Nile" (*Fortnightly Review,* March, 1898, pp. 362–77).

Egypt, was assigned to lead the mission, which was composed largely of British and Egyptian army officers who, it seems, were chosen partly for their size and physical impressiveness (*amiable giants,* Sir Charles Dilke called them). Rodd tells us in his memoirs that the British government was greatly worried by rumors of a combination between the Abyssinians and the dervishes, as well as by the reports of the projected Bonchamps mission. The object of his mission, therefore, was " to ensure if possible that there would be no co-operation with the Khalifa, and to obtain a more intimate knowledge of internal conditions." [19]

When the mission reached the end of the first stage it learned at Harrar that Lagarde and Bonvalot had a two months' start. On their arrival at Adis Abeba they found Prince Henri d'Orleans and Leontiev also upon the scene. The French made no bones about stating what their plans were. The general atmosphere was not a very friendly one. Nevertheless Rodd entered boldly upon negotiations. He seems to have convinced Menelik that the dervishes would be, in the future as in the past, dangerous adversaries of the Abyssinians as of the Egyptians. In any case the King of Kings promised not to allow shipments of arms to reach the dervishes through Abyssinia. He also agreed to certain commercial arrangements which put British goods on a par with imports from other countries. But what Menelik was most interested in was the question of territorial settlements. Rodd was willing enough to discuss the Somali frontier, and eventually an agreement was made by which the British abandoned almost 15,000 square miles of what they had claimed on that side. But so far as the all-important problem of the southern and western frontiers of Abyssinia was concerned, no progress was made. Menelik stuck by his claim to the Nile frontier and Rodd therefore decided that it would be better to let this matter go over until the British and Egyptians were at Khartum. Even after twenty-five years Rodd refused, when writing his memoirs, to reveal the course and the outcome of his discussions with Menelik on larger African problems. He was impressed with the Abyssinian ruler's quick and keen intelligence and claimed to have succeeded in establishing cordial relations by removing apprehensions. Whether or not he weakened the French position it is hard to say. Appearances are against it. After all, the treaty signed by Rodd on May 14, 1897 marked no progress toward the settlement of the frontier problem. Menelik's four expeditions, sent out after Rodd's departure, would not seem to indicate a very trustful relationship between the King of Kings and Her Majesty's government. Indeed, when Makonen returned from the Blue Nile in the spring of 1898 he brought dervish emissaries with him, who were given presents by Menelik. From this it would seem that the British had secured no guarantee even against an Abyssinian-Dervish combination. No wonder there was criticism of the Rodd Treaty in the British parliament.[20]

[19] Sir J. Rennell Rodd: *Social and Diplomatic Memories*, II, pp. 112–4.

[20] Rodd, op. cit., II, chaps. iv and v. A narrative of the mission by Count Albert E. W. Gleichen: *With the Mission to Menelik, 1897* (London, 1898). On Menelik's relations to the dervishes see

When Rodd returned to England in June 1897 he had a long talk with Salisbury. The prime minister made it clear that he did not care how much " light soil " in Somaliland had to be sacrificed to the Abyssinians. What he was most concerned about was the danger of the French reaching the Nile. Rodd confirmed him in his fears and urged that an expedition be pushed forward from Uganda along the Nile and to Fashoda, in the hope of anticipating Marchand. This idea was not new to Salisbury; the decision had already been made to send out a considerable force under Colonel James MacDonald, who had had much experience in Uganda. The colonel left England early in June 1897, with instructions " to explore the districts adjacent to the Italian sphere in which the River Juba is believed to rise, and to cultivate friendly relations with the tribes residing in that portion of the British sphere." [21]

MacDonald's expedition was no more fortunate than that of Baron Dhanis in the Congo. Hardly had he set out in September 1897 than his Sudanese troops mutinied. A dangerous rising followed among the Waganda in Uganda, with the result that MacDonald was obliged to spend most of the winter campaigning in country that was supposedly already under British control. By the time the expedition was ready to resume its original plans the secret of its destination had leaked out. Someone found in his instructions that the Uganda authorities were to supply MacDonald with a certain number of Dinkas and Shilluks. Now these people inhabit the Nile country about Fashoda, and it was hard to see why they should be wanted by an expedition headed for the sources of the Juba River. Sir Charles Dilke openly accused the government of having led the public astray. MacDonald's mission, he maintained, was to head off the Marchand mission. And so it was. Lord Salisbury later on admitted it in a general way (though Curzon had originally described the charge as *all imagination*). It seems that the sources of the Juba which MacDonald was to investigate were not the sources of the great Juba River which flows into the Indian Ocean, but the sources of another Juba River (also Jubba, Adjuba, etc.) which was a confluent of the Sobat and which, it was thought, would give a clear route from the vicinity of Lake Rudolf to the Nile at Fashoda. When MacDonald finally did make his journey in the summer of 1898 this was the course he took. While he did not reach the Nile, he came within one hundred miles of Lado. His subordinate, Lieutenant Austin, led another column to the northern end of Lake Rudolf. A French writer has asserted that the Abyssinians, coming from the north, met one or the other of these columns and that the British cleared out, leaving their baggage. This is probably an exaggeration. Neither MacDonald nor Austin say anything of meeting the Abyssinians, though they do say that the

---

Augustus B. Wylde: *Modern Abyssinia* (London, 1901), pp. 73–5. For criticism of the treaty in parliament see Hansard, Series IV, vol. LIII, pp. 489–90 (February 14, 1898), pp. 1527–8, 1579 ff. (February 24, 1898). See also *Bulletin . . . de l'Afrique Française*, July, 1897, pp. 238–9; August, 1897, pp. 276–7.

[21] *Africa No. 2 (1898)*, appendix.

country had been so thoroughly ravaged by them that their expeditions had to turn back for want of food.[22] It is conceivable that the Abyssinians met an expedition under Mr. Cavendish, which was non-official but attracted a great deal of attention in France.[23]

The serious rising in Uganda rendered MacDonald's mission impotent during the winter of 1897–1898, and the British government therefore had to make up its mind as to what else might be done to block the French schemes on the upper Nile. Lord Wolseley, commander in chief of the British forces, argued warmly in October 1897 that Kitchener's troops should advance from Abu Hamed upon Khartum, and that he should be given two British infantry brigades to help the Egyptian forces. In this way the Khalifa's army could be certainly destroyed and Khartum and the White Nile could be occupied before the French established posts there: " As far as I can learn," he wrote to Lansdowne, " the French are now working hard to forestall us on the upper Nile, and if they do so we may have to face serious complications with them when we attempt the job in the autumn of 1898." [24] Lansdowne, however, was opposed to the action suggested by the commander in chief. It was felt that a further advance would be too hard on the troops and that the financial aspects of the problem would be hard to settle. Lord Salisbury supported Lansdowne. He seems to have stressed the consideration that Britain, faced with a rather serious war on the Indian frontier and deeply involved in other parts of the world, would do well to avoid further complications. He appreciated the fact that the French might get to the Nile before the Egyptian troops reconquered Khartum, but, he wrote to Lansdowne: " I am not greatly impressed by this danger, because we shall have to meet it anyhow." If England tried to apply the Anglo-German Treaty of 1890, which defined her sphere on the upper Nile, it would mean a row with the French whether they reached the Nile or not. " It is to be remembered," he added, " that by destroying the dervish power we are killing the defender who is holding the valley for us now." To Lord Cromer he wrote in a similar vein: " If ever we get to Fashoda, the diplomatic crisis will be something to remember and the ' What next? ' will be a very interesting question." [25]

So the decision was made to let matters take their course. The advance on

---

[22] Morié: *Histoire de l'Éthiopie*, II, p. 452; J. R. L. MacDonald and H. H. Austin: " Journeys to the North of Uganda " (*Geographical Journal*, August, 1899, pp. 129–47); Herbert H. Austin: *With MacDonald in Uganda* (London, 1903). See further the discussion of the mission in parliament, in Hansard, LIV, pp. 528, 537, 544 ff., 557; LXIX, p. 9; LXVII, pp. 703 ff., 718 ff.; LXXV, pp. 1513–4; also H. R. Fox Bourne: " The Uganda Protectorate and its Relation to the Sudan " (*Asiatic Quarterly Review*, April, 1899, pp. 322–37); J. W. Gregory: *The Foundation of British East Africa* (London, 1901), pp. 244 ff.; Sir Harry Johnston: *The Nile Quest* (New York, 1903), p. 271.

[23] H. S. H. Cavendish: " Through Somali Land to Lake Rudolf " (*Geographical Journal*, April, 1898, pp. 372–96).

[24] Sir F. Maurice and Sir George Arthur: *The Life of Lord Wolseley* (London, 1924), p. 304. Similarly Wolseley's letter to the Queen (*Letters of Queen Victoria*, III, p. 206).

[25] Lord Newton: *Lord Lansdowne* (London, 1929), pp. 147–8; Marquess of Zetland: *Lord Cromer* (London, 1932), p. 259; *Letters of Queen Victoria*, III, p. 208.

Khartum was to be resumed only at the next high Nile, that is, in September 1898. During the winter, however, relations between England and France were strained to the breaking point as a result of the dispute which arose regarding the frontier of their respective possessions on the upper Niger. The details of this complicated problem may be omitted here, interesting though they are. Suffice it to say that there were good arguments on both sides and there were questionable proceedings on both sides. British and French alike attempted to send expeditions into the disputed area and to secure actual control of as much territory as possible while the negotiations were going on. On one occasion British and French actually clashed, through a misunderstanding. In February and March 1898 war seemed not far in the offing. But in the end the matter was settled by a compromise, and an agreement was duly signed in June 1898.[26]

During this whole Niger dispute British public opinion, as expressed in the newspapers and periodicals, was astonishingly rabid. From Queen Victoria's letters and Garvin's recent biography it appears that Chamberlain was no less determined to hold fast. Salisbury complained to the Queen that the colonial secretary was " a little too warlike, and hardly sees the other side of the question." Still, Salisbury himself found it necessary to assume a very firm stand and to refuse all concessions of importance.[27] The French government, on the other hand, was obviously anxious to avoid trouble and come to some agreement. In their apologies both Hanotaux and Lebon have stressed the hopes they entertained at the time that an agreement with regard to west Africa would lead to a similar compromise agreement with respect to the valley of the Nile. They bemoan the fact that the discussions of the Niger problem were drawn out so long that the Méline cabinet fell from power (June 1898) before the other problems could be raised. They accuse Delcassé (Hanotaux' successor at the foreign office) of having failed to open negotiations immediately and of having neglected to reach some settlement before Kitchener reconquered Khartum.[28]

It is rather difficult to understand how the French statesmen could have deluded themselves in this way. They themselves raised the question of a general settlement in their discussions with the British ambassador in December 1897 and were given a most unambiguous reply. England, said Sir Edmund Monson, " must not be understood to admit that any other European power than Great

---

[26] *British Documents on the Origins of the War*, I, chap. iv, part I; Accounts and Papers, *Treaty Series No. 15, 1899*, with map; Documents Diplomatiques: *Correspondance et Documents relatifs à la Convention Franco-Anglaise du 14 juin, 1898*. The best French accounts may be found in Darcy, op. cit.; *Bulletin . . . de l'Afrique Française*, December, 1897, pp. 410 ff.; P. Vuillot: "La France et l'Angleterre sur le Niger" (*Questions Diplomatiques et Coloniales*, April 1, 1898, pp. 404–30). On the British side see especially Garvin: *Life of Chamberlain*, III, chap. lv; Frederick A. Edwards: "The French on the Niger" (*Fortnightly Review*, April, 1898, pp. 576–91); J. Westlake: "England and France in West Africa" (*Contemporary Review*, April, 1898, pp. 582–92). An excellent critical examination of the question may be found in Heinz Kossatz: *Untersuchungen über den Französisch-Englischen Weltgegensatz im Fashodajahr* (Breslau, 1934), pp. 23 ff.   [27] *Letters of Queen Victoria*, III, pp. 209–12; Garvin, op. cit., III, pp. 212 ff.
[28] Hanotaux: *Fachoda*, pp. 118 ff., 144–5; Lebon: *La Politique Française en Afrique*, pp. 43 ff

Britain has any claim to occupy any part of the valley of the Nile." [29] It is perfectly true that M. Hanotaux immediately voiced reservations to the British claims, but it is nevertheless difficult to see how he could have deluded himself with the hope that England would be willing to negotiate on this question. As a matter of fact the British government decided almost at once to resume the advance up the Nile. It was said that the threat of a dervish attack on Berber forced this reversal of the decision made in October, but few people were taken in by this explanation.

There is not much more to be told about the Khartum campaign. Supported by several battalions of British troops, the Egyptian army pushed vigorously ahead. The dervishes under Emir Mahmud were swept aside on April 8, 1898 at the battle of the Atbara. On September 2 the decisive engagement was fought against the Khalifa himself on the plains of Kerreri, outside Omdurman and Khartum. Some twenty-two thousand Egyptian and British troops turned the Maxims on the valorous ranks of the advancing dervishes (some forty thousand in all). The slaughter might have been foreseen and probably was. While the Anglo-Egyptian forces had fifty men killed and a couple of hundred wounded, the dervishes left ten thousand dead on the field, and had another five thousand wounded. The Khalifa himself escaped from Omdurman, but his power was broken. The Egyptian and British flags were soon flying side by side from the old palace at Khartum.

Before the resumption of hostilities against the dervishes there had been an important cabinet meeting at London, at which Lord Cromer was present. It was there decided that when Khartum was reconquered, the British and Egyptian flags should fly side by side in the Sudan, and that Egypt should be expected to follow British advice with respect to the government of this region. Furthermore, it was decided to instruct Kitchener to send gunboat flotillas up the Blue Nile and to push on up the White Nile with a small force as far as Fashoda or beyond if possible. He was to acknowledge no French or Abyssinian claims to any part of the Valley, and was to avoid a collision with the troops of Menelik at all costs.[30]

Kitchener found it necessary to act upon these instructions almost at once after the defeat of the Khalifa, for on September 7 a Mahdist steamer, coming down the Nile, was stopped near Khartum. On being questioned the crew reported that the steamer had been sent up the White Nile some time before, but had been fired on by white men (" Turks ") at Fashoda and had been turned back. An examination of the bullets which still lodged in the woodwork of the steamer bore out the fact that there were Europeans at Fashoda. The authorities at Khartum hardly needed to guess who they were. Three days later Kitch-

---

[29] *Egypt No. 2 (1898),* no. 1; Documents Diplomatiques: *Affaires du Haut-Nil, 1897–1898,* no. 1.

[30] *Egypt No. 2 (1898),* no. 3; Sir George Arthur: *Life of Lord Kitchener* (London, 1920), I, p. 246; *Letters of Queen Victoria,* III, p. 260.

ener set out with five steamers and a force of Sudanese, supplemented with a
small number of British troops. As he approached Fashoda, on September 18,
he sent a letter to Marchand, to which the French commander replied saying
that he had occupied the territory since July 10 and that he could not leave without further instructions from his government. On the following day the two
men met. Marchand refused to retire, despite the protests of Kitchener. The
negotiations were carried on throughout as between gentlemen, Marchand behaving " with quiet dignity and soldierly bearing," while Kitchener and his
officers, who felt a " twinge of pity and not a little admiration " for their gallant
enemies, were " the pink of politeness." The matter was soon adjusted in an
amicable way, for Marchand made no objection to the raising of the Egyptian
flag at the southern end of the station and the establishment of a Sudanese
battalion. For the rest the settlement of the affair was left to the home governments and the discussions ended with Kitchener's proposing that they both take
a whiskey and soda.[31]

In England the victory at Omdurman called forth a remarkable outburst of
enthusiasm. Moved far beyond their wont, says Winston Churchill, the people
sat themselves down to give thanks to their God, their Government, and their
General. To judge by the press, the whole country had gone mad with the lust
of fighting glory.[32] Then, within a week, came rumors of the French " appari-
tion " on the upper Nile. Despite Kitchener's efforts to keep his moves secret,
his encounter with Marchand was reported home by the correspondents at Khartum, and before the end of September the incident was common property in
England. Churchill, again, gives a vivid picture of the popular reaction. The
Fashoda episode was a " discordant note " in the general rejoicing. The British
public was " confronted with the fact that a ' friendly power ' had, unprovoked,
endeavoured to rob them of the fruits of their victories. They now realised that
while they had been devoting themselves to great military operations, in broad
daylight and the eye of the world, and prosecuting an enterprise on which they
had set their hearts, other operations — covert, deceitful, behind-the-back — had
been in progress in the heart of the Dark Continent, designed solely for the
mischievous and spiteful object of depriving them of the produce of their labours. And they firmly set their faces against such behaviour." [33]

In almost complete unison the British press launched upon an attack against
the French. Here and there a liberal paper like the *Manchester Guardian* kept
its head, but many of the British journals were abusive and most of them un-

---

[31] *Egypt No. 3 (1898)*, no. 2; *British Documents on the Origins of the War*, I, no. 193; Gen-
eral Sir Horace Smith-Dorrien: *Memories of Forty-eight Years' Service* (London, 1925), chap. viii;
Letters of Queen Victoria, III, pp. 285 ff.; Arthur: *Life of Kitchener*, I, pp. 247 ff.; A. B. de Guerville:
New Egypt (London, 1905), pp. 330 ff.; Marchand's somewhat dramatized account in the *Figaro*,
August 26, 1904 (reprinted in London *Times*, August 27, 1904); see also General Mangin: " Lettres
de la Mission Marchand " (*Revue des Deux Mondes*, September 15, 1931, pp. 241-83), pp. 265 ff.;
Morrison B. Giffen: *Fashoda* (Chicago, 1930), pp. 7-11, 35-6.

[32] Winston Churchill: *The River War* (London, 1899), II, p. 311; Wilfrid S. Blunt: *My Diaries*
(London, 1919), I, p. 365.   [33] Churchill, op. cit., II, pp. 311-2.

compromising. Marchand's party was described as a band of "irregular marauders" and as the "scum of the desert." The newspapers were impatient of negotiation and wholly averse to elaborate arguments. In the British view the whole Marchand mission was a demonstration of "indubitable hostility" and of "conscious antagonism" to England. Marchand was an intruder, who would have to be ejected, even though it meant an ultimatum, mobilization and war.[34]

The unanimity of the press was matched by the unanimity of the politicians. Liberals vied with Unionists and Tories in putting themselves at the disposal of the government and in calling upon the cabinet to assume an unyielding attitude. Rosebery struck the keynote in his speech at Epsom on October 12. There followed a veritable flood of eloquence. Asquith, Grey and ultimately even Harcourt were among the Liberals who came out in support of a firm policy, while among the members of the government the hard-hitting Sir Michael Hicks Beach capped the movement in an address at North Shields on October 19, when he declared that "the country has put its foot down. If, unhappily, another view should be taken elsewhere, we, the Ministers of the Queen, know what our duty demands. It would be a great calamity. . . . But there are greater evils than war."

It may be questioned whether Lord Salisbury required all the encouragement and prodding which was given him by the press and by the politicians. Whatever may have been his own view of the merits of the case, he had long since come to see that in the question of the Nile the British public simply would not stand for a policy of "graceful concession." The French had been warned time and again that the British foreign office could not and would not consider or discuss claims to any part of the Nile Valley. After the battle of Omdurman Sir Edmund Monson, the ambassador at Paris, had been instructed to inform the French foreign office that "all territories which were subject to the Khalifa passed to the British and Egyptian Governments by right of conquest" and that this right was not open to discussion.[35] Throughout the debate which followed the news of the Marchand-Kitchener meeting Salisbury stuck to his guns. He refused to talk about French claims until Marchand should have been recalled.

We must turn now to a consideration of the situation as it presented itself in Paris. And above all we must remember that the autumn and winter of 1898–1899 was perhaps the most critical period in the whole domestic history of the Third Republic prior to the World War. The famous and dreadful Dreyfus case, which dated back to the autumn of 1894, had entered upon the crucial phase and France was already torn between Dreyfusards and Anti-Dreyfusards. It was in January 1898 that Zola published his astonishing letter: *J'Accuse*. He

---

[34] A good digest of the press in T. W. Riker: "A Survey of British Policy in the Fashoda Crisis" (*Political Science Quarterly*, March, 1929, pp. 54–78), pp. 65–6; see also the extracts in the *Bulletin . . . de l'Afrique Française*, October, 1898, pp. 334 ff., and in Jules Cocheris: *La Situation Internationale de l'Égypte*, pp. 452 ff., 461–2.   [35] *British Documents*, I, no. 189.

had been tried and condemned, but before the excitement had in any way subsided Colonel Henry, forger of the documents that had been used against Dreyfus, committed suicide on August 31. General Cavaignac, the minister of war,
resigned on September 3, 1898. On the same day Madame Dreyfus appealed to
the minister of justice for a revision of the trial of 1894. During the next weeks
and months the Dreyfus case reached the climactic phase and threatened to assume the character of a civil war. On both sides the forces had been marshalled.
The revisionists, still a minority but reinforced by a large group of intellectuals,
had closed their ranks. The socialist fractions joined hands. Committees of
vigilance were formed and innumerable meetings of protest were organized in
Paris and the provinces.

On the other side the Anti-Dreyfusard forces were rallying around the stand-
ards of patriotism, anti-Semitism and royalism. Déroulède came out of retirement, reopened his League of Patriots and began a campaign of heckling the
revisionists. Guérin, Buffet and others, financed by the Orleanists, came to the
assistance of the Jew-baiters, the clericals and the army. On September 13 there
began a strike in Paris which soon involved 20,000 men in the building trades.
Some 60,000 troops were concentrated in and near the capital, there was marching and countermarching, bivouacking of soldiers in the squares — everything
that might be taken to indicate action by the patriots. There was talk of a great
military plot and the whole capital was on edge for days on end. Even when the
strike was settled, the tension continued. October was filled with demonstrations
and conflicts, with rumors of all kinds, and with a general revival of the " great
fear." [36]

It may well be imagined that in the midst of the furor caused by the Dreyfus case the average Frenchman, never much interested in colonial affairs, had
little thought left for Egypt and the Sudan. The active proponents of expansion
did, of course, follow the progress of events with considerable attention. These
circles evidently believed that the reconquest of Khartum, by raising the whole
problem of the Sudan, would of necessity result in the resumption of discussions
between England and France regarding Egypt.[37]

Delcassé, the foreign minister, was evidently not suffering from such illusions. Just what his ideas of foreign policy were in these first months of office
has always been a matter of dispute. Various schemes were attributed to him
at the time, but to the foreign representatives in Paris he appeared as a contradictory character, an opportunist, a garrulous and yet secretive *arriviste*.[38]

[36] The most detailed and on the whole the best account is still Joseph Reinach: *Histoire de
l'Affaire Dreyfus* (Paris, 1904), IV, pp. 270 ff., 296 ff., 300 ff.; but see also Alexandre Zévaès:
L'Affaire Dreyfus (Paris, 1931), pp. 135 ff.

[37] See the abstracts from the press in *Questions Diplomatiques et Coloniales,* September 15,
1898, pp. 111 ff.

[38] *Die Grosse Politik,* XIII, no. 3555; *British Documents,* I, no. 183; Constantin Dumba:
Dreibund und Entente-Politik (Zürich, 1931), p. 100; E. Malcolm Carroll: *French Public Opinion,*
p. 171; Kossatz, op. cit., pp. 40 ff.

Hanotaux and Lebon accused him later of having failed to follow up the west African settlement with England, of June 1898, with further negotiations respecting eastern Africa and the Nile. This accusation can hardly be taken seriously, however. Hanotaux knew from his own discussions with the British foreign office that while the British were prepared to recognize French claims to the east of Lake Chad in return for recognition of British claims in the Nile Valley, they would not discuss French pretensions in the Nile Valley itself. Hanotaux also knew that he himself had rejected these offers " with no excess of courtesy." [39] It is hard to see on what basis Delcassé was to negotiate when the English claims were so well known and when the unwillingness of the London government to discuss these claims had been so often demonstrated.

There is probably more point in Hanotaux' charge that Delcassé failed to follow up the advances made by Germany with regard to the Portuguese colonies in June 1898. Delcassé was a political disciple of Gambetta. In Boulangist times he had been secretary-general of Déroulède's League of Patriots, and it is said that in 1898 he was taken into the Brisson cabinet because Déroulède promised to support the new government if Delcassé were made foreign minister.[40] Whether all this be true or not, it is clear that Delcassé's political antecedents and connexions were with the patriot party, and there is no inherent improbability in the story told of him: that he took office with the idea of grouping about France the largest number of European friends, in the hope of securing their support for an eventual war with Germany. It is said that he hoped to add England to the Franco-Russian grouping and that he declared that he did not want to leave office until he had re-established a friendly understanding with England.[41]

These stories of Delcassé's desire to reach an agreement with England gain some weight from the British documents on the crisis of the autmun of 1898. It is, of course, true that Delcassé, in 1893 and 1894 when he was at the colonial office, was one of the prime movers in organizing the expedition to the Nile. But that was in the days before the Congo Treaty of 1894, in the days before the Grey declaration, in the days before the Dongola expedition and the breakdown of the negotiations which had been carried on from time to time between London and Paris. There is no evidence of any kind to show that Delcassé continued to approve and support the scheme after 1894. Within a week of the British victory at Omdurman he spoke to the British ambassador and remarked that Marchand might be met with. The explorer, he continued, was " only an emissary of civilisation." He had no power to make decisions, and it was hoped

[39] *British Documents*, I, no. 175.

[40] André Mévil: *De la Paix de Francfort à la Conférence d'Algésiras* (Paris, 1909), p. 140; Charles Maurras: *Kiel et Tanger* (Third edition, Paris, 1921), p. 176; Auguste Gérard: *Mémoires* (Paris, 1928), p. 316.

[41] Victor Bérard: "Politique Française" (*Revue de Paris,* July 1, 1905, pp. 208–24); Georges Reynald: *La Diplomatie Française. L'Œuvre de M. Delcassé* (Paris, 1915), p. 22; René Pinon: *France et Allemagne* (Paris, 1913), pp 117–8.

that all differences might be " amicably arranged by the exercise of patience and conciliation." In other conversations with Monson in September the French foreign minister kept insisting that there was really no " Marchand mission " in the ordinary sense of the term. The French cabinet, he reiterated, was strongly desirous of avoiding serious difficulty with England. He personally would much prefer an understanding with England to the existing one between France and Russia.[42]

The British government does not seem to have questioned the good will of Delcassé, and there is no reason why we should. A conciliatory attitude was the only sensible one for the French government to take in 1898. The country was in the throes of a full-blown domestic crisis and was quite unprepared to wage war. Marchand's own position was most precarious. He himself and his associates always claimed that the position at Fashoda was strong. A dervish attack had been turned back and the neighboring Shilluk tribes were friendly. The expedition still had 130,000 cartridges and 18,000 kilograms of wheat. Gardens had been planted, so there was no threat of famine. Reinforcements and supplies were expected from the French Congo and from Abyssinia. According to General Mangin the French force could have given the British a great deal more trouble than had the dervishes at Omdurman, the more so as the Sudanese troops in the Sirdar's forces were disposed to side with the French. Kitchener, on the other hand, reported from the beginning that Marchand's position was " as impossible as it is absurd." Only the victory of Omdurman had saved him from annihilation by the Mahdists, and it was inconceivable that he could have held his position for long in the fever-ridden swamp area around Fashoda.[43]

Delcassé's readiness to negotiate and to reach an amicable settlement was not reciprocated in London. The British had always refused to define their own claims or discuss the claims of others. From the start Salisbury took the stand that the Sudan belonged to Great Britain and Egypt by right of conquest and that this right was not open to debate. " No offer of territorial concession on our part would be endured by public opinion here," he wrote to the Queen, who agreed.[44] It was this unwillingness of the British even to discuss the question, together with the uncompromising rabidness of the British press, that made it almost impossible for Delcassé to give in. He made it perfectly clear that Marchand could be and would be recalled if the London government would negotiate. To which Salisbury responded by a flat rejection of all debate until the French post had been evacuated.

Nothing would be drearier than to review here the detailed arguments ad-

---

[42] *British Documents,* I, nos. 188, 190, 191, 196, 198; *Letters of Queen Victoria,* III, p. 288.

[43] *British Documents,* I, no. 193; *Die Grosse Politik,* XIV, nos. 3890, 3894; General Mangin: " Lettres de la Mission Marchand " (*Revue des Deux Mondes,* September 15, 1931, pp. 241–83), p. 276; Cocheris, op. cit., p. 496; A. B. de Guerville: *New Egypt* (London, 1905), pp. 330 ff., reporting conversations with British and Egyptian officers; Bennet Burleigh: *Khartoum Campaign 1898* (London, 1899), p. 309; Giffen: *Fashoda,* pp. 45 ff.

[44] *Letters of Queen Victoria,* III, p. 290.

vanced in the following weeks to prove or disprove the French right to be at Fashoda. Since the days of the Crimean War no international dispute had been clouded with such contradictory and illogical argumentation. Wilfrid Blunt very wittily noted in his diary that, both sides being in the wrong, each saw the other's wickedness and so believed itself right. M. Cocheris, one of the ablest writers on the subject, pointedly remarked that at bottom the French and British arguments were the same. The trouble was that the same argument was never advanced by both sides at the same time. The Sudan had been evacuated by the Egyptians under protest and at the behest of the British. What was its international status after that? The opinion even of the most eminent French jurists, men like Despagnet and Bonfils, was that the Egyptian claims stood, and that the Sudan was neither *res nullius* nor *res derelicta*. On the other hand such competent people as Sir Samuel Baker and Sir Frederick Lugard took the view that the territory had been abandoned and that it would belong to the first power which could take it from the Mahdists. The British government itself had appropriated parts of the former Egyptian territory along the Red Sea and in Uganda and Unyoro. It had helped the Italians get other parts on the Red Sea and had leased sections to the King of the Belgians. In the agreement with Germany of 1890 the British had claimed a large part of the Equatorial region as a British sphere.

It was because of the freedom with which the British government took or signed away parts of the erstwhile Egyptian possessions that M. Hanotaux had, in 1894 and 1895, insisted upon rejecting the *res nullius* theory and stressing the rights of the Khedive and the Sultan. Despite this stand, Hanotaux had given his blessing to the Marchand mission, and the whole French policy in the years after 1895 was to secure part of the spoils. When the crisis arose in 1898 the positions of the two rivals were reversed. The French now claimed that the Sudan was *res nullius,* that they had as much right there as the Italians on the Red Sea, or the British in Uganda, or the Belgians in Lado. Marchand, despite his small force, had established effective occupation in the Bahr-el-Ghazal province. To which the British replied that the rights of the Khedive had never been more than dormant and that Britain was acting for Egypt, by what right was not clear. Not content with this line of argument the British struck another note: assuming that the territory was lost to Egypt and that it had belonged to the dervishes, it had now been conquered from them and belonged entirely to the Egyptian and British conquerors.[45]

It is perfectly clear now that these arguments and other subsidiary ones had

---

[45] See the correspondence in *Egypt No. 2 (1898)* and *Egypt No. 3 (1898); Affaires du Haut-Nil et du Bahr-el-Ghazal, 1897–1898; British Documents,* I, nos. 198 ff. Among the best secondary studies are Georges Blanchard: " L'Affaire de Fachoda et le Droit International " (*Revue Générale de Droit International Public,* VI, 1899, pp. 380–430); Cocheris: *Situation Internationale de l'Égypte, etc.,* pp. 472 ff.; Despagnet: *La Diplomatie de la Troisième République,* pp. 744 ff.; Fernand Vatin: *La Vérité sur Fachoda* (Chaumont, 1923), pp. 52 ff.; Riker, *op. cit.,* pp. 61–63; and the detailed review in Giffen: *Fashoda,* chap. iv.

very little if anything to do with the final disposition of the case. Briefly summarized the situation was simply this: The French, disappointed in their hopes
that the Gladstone government of 1892 would arrange for the evacuation of
Egypt, and inspired by the engineering report of M. Prompt of 1893, had sent
first Monteil and then Marchand to establish himself on the Nile at Fashoda,
where he was to be reinforced by an Abyssinian army. With the Abyssinians on
the one side and the French on the other the British Cape-to-Cairo schemes
would be wrecked. At the same time the threat to construct a barrage on the
lower Sobat and cut off the summer water supply of Egypt would force the
British to negotiate, to arrange for a reconsideration of the Egyptian problem.
All this can be proved to the hilt from what has been said in previous chapters
concerning the origins and instructions of the mission. It is equally clear from
what we know of the unpublished instructions sent to Cairo by Hanotaux on the
eve of his fall in June 1898.[46] Marchand's activities bear it out. French critics have
often accused Hanotaux of not having devoted enough men and supplies to the
mission, of having made of it " une aventure de condottiere " or an " hors d'œuvre
colonial." [47] But these criticisms are really unjustified; the conception of the Marchand mission was as grand as it was daring. The trouble was not with the plan
or with Marchand's part in it. The hitch came rather with the failure of the
Abyssinian contribution. Hardly had Marchand reached Fashoda than he sent
out his lieutenant, Baratier, to find the Abyssinians. Later Mangin was sent up
the Sobat. He actually met the Abyssinian Ras and together they began to march
back to Fashoda. But it was too late; the order to evacuate had already reached
Marchand.[48] To crown the disappointment of the French it turned out that M.
Prompt was quite in error with respect to the possibility of building a barrage
at the mouth of the Sobat. When Marchand came to Cairo early in November
1898, he had a long talk with the Belgian consul. He pointed out to him that
there was not a stone within miles of the position and that Prompt's idea was
therefore not realizable. The Nile at the mouths of the Sobat and the Bahr-el-
Ghazal ran in a number of lateral arms, all of which would have to be blocked.
And yet, he complained, it was a mistake to sacrifice the expedition. Failing the
Abyssinians, the French government could in a few weeks have put two hundred companies of Senegalese on foot and have swept the British out of western
Africa, thus relieving pressure on the Nile.[49]

The French government could not be blamed for the inability of the Abyssinians to hold out on the Nile until Marchand arrived. Neither could the government have predicted the errors in the calculations of M. Prompt. The French

---

[46] André Mévil: *De la Paix de Francfort à la Conférence d'Algésiras* (Paris, 1909), pp. 26–7.

[47] J. L. de Lanessan: " L'Évacuation de Fachoda " (*Questions Diplomatiques et Coloniales*,
November 15, 1898, pp. 321–9); Robert de Caix: " La Leçon de Fachoda " (*Bulletin . . . de
l'Afrique Française*, November, 1898, pp. 358 ff.).

[48] Mangin: *Regards sur la France d'Afrique* (Paris, 1924), p. 255.

[49] Report of the Belgian consul, printed in Th. Simar: " Léopold II et le Soudan " (*Congo*,
November, 1924, pp. 506–28), pp. 521–2.

schemes simply did not work out properly. But apart from this it must be remembered that when Marchand was despatched the Dongola expedition was only beginning. The British, warned by Sir Samuel Baker of the danger of another power's getting control of the upper Nile and constantly reminded by men like Lugard and Scott-Moncrieff of this menace, had had their attention called to the Prompt projects and had realized what the French were up to. This came out in the parliamentary debates at the time of the Grey declaration in 1895. Egypt depended upon the White Nile flow for her summer water, which was essential for the £10,000,000 cotton crop. By 1898 there was already a crying need for more summer water and for more storage reservoirs.[50] Sir Edward Grey enlarged upon the danger of diversion of Nile water by a hostile power in his speech at Huddersfield on October 28, 1898. In the house of commons the question was gone over in detail on February 24, 1899, when Grey said in so many words: " The possibility of danger to the interests of Egypt in the Nile Valley, rendered possible by engineering science, is such as has never existed before, and the conditions are entirely altered." [51]

It is not to be wondered at, then, that the British pushed forward the reconquest of the Sudan, even at their own financial expense, or that they decided to add British troops to the Egyptian forces. Once Kitchener had conquered the dervishes no time was lost in seeking out Marchand or in investigating the situation on the upper Nile. A gunboat was sent up the Bahr-el-Ghazal almost to the French post at Meshra-el-Rek, and another was despatched up the Bahr-el-Jebel, where it was blocked by sudd. Then the Bahr-el-Zeraf was reconnoitred and an expedition was sent up the Sobat and its confluent the Pibor (Juba). Forts were erected along the course of the Sobat River, presumably to meet any Abyssinian force which might try to reach the Nile again.[52]

A mere review of this evidence will show that the Marchand mission was not a " French picnic party that was outstaying its welcome," [53] and that the British government could not and did not regard it as such. Here was a question which involved the whole welfare of Egypt. Salisbury was determined not to yield, not to consider any concessions to the French view. That being the case, it became chiefly a problem of power. Marchand could easily have been swept aside by the forty thousand troops of Kitchener, but that would have meant a war between England and France. This was realized in London, but the government did not shrink from the prospect. Writing when the crisis was practically over, the *Times* pointed out that in 1878 the British had

---

[50] *Egypt No. 1 (1898): Reports on the Finances, Administration and Condition of Egypt,* pp. 19 ff.

[51] Hansard: *Parliamentary Debates,* Series IV, vol. LXVII, pp. 493 ff. See also the speeches of Brodrick, Durning-Lawrence and Balfour (ibid., pp. 475 ff., 487 ff., 518 ff.).

[52] *Egypt No. 3 (1899): Report on the Finances . . . of Egypt and the Soudan,* p. 7; *Egypt No. 5 (1899): Despatch . . . enclosing a Report on the Soudan by Sir William Garstin.* This was the first of the remarkable hydrographic reports of Garstin.

[53] William Stead, in the *Review of Reviews,* November 15, 1898, pp. 431 ff.

bravely sung "We've got the men, we've got the ships, we've got the money too." In 1898, said the great London journal, there was no singing. The British had no need to stimulate public confidence. It was the first time that England had faced a great crisis without a scare.[54]

This general confidence appears to have been wholly justified. The last years of ardent shipbuilding and general naval increases had put British supremacy at sea beyond discussion. There was no need of "flying squadrons" and other spectacular devices. Of battleships less than ten years old and having a speed of at least sixteen knots, England had thirty-four as against the thirteen of France and the seventeen of Russia. It was only in first-class cruisers and torpedoboats that she was inferior. So eminent an authority as Sir Thomas Brassey, writing on the eve of the crisis, thought that the British fleet was equal in battleships to the French, Russian and German fleets combined and pointed out that the British ships were assembled in much more homogeneous squadrons. A French critic expressed the opinion that, aside from ship-by-ship counts (which never mean much), the British fleet was four times as strong as the French and stronger than all the fleets of Europe put together.[55]

British naval preparations were pushed forward during the whole month of October. At Portsmouth all provisions were made to enable the less mobile part of the forces to take to sea at short notice. Of the details nothing has ever become known, as the deepest secrecy was observed. It appears, however, that the Channel squadrons cruised off the French coast, ready to blockade the French battleships at Brest. Another force watched the Straits of Gibraltar to prevent the French Mediterranean fleet from coming out. In the Mediterranean itself a large squadron was posted between Malta and Gibraltar, ready to blockade Toulon or to debark at Bizerta. Another force was despatched to Alexandria to guard the Suez Canal.[56]

The British felt that they were prepared for all eventualities. Among the French, on the other hand, there was something akin to a general panic. The French fleet was, by common consent, next to the British the strongest in the world. But the French naval staffs had been more or less paralyzed for years by the never-ending dispute between the advocates of capital ships and the proponents of cruisers and torpedoes. Politics may also have had something to do with the condition of French naval preparations. In any event there seems to be no room for doubt that the situation in 1898 was pathetic. French

---

[54] London *Times*, November 22, 1898.

[55] See especially T. A. Brassey: "Can we hold our own at Sea?" (*Fortnightly Review*, July, 1898, pp. 141–7); H. W. Wilson: "The Navies and Naval Construction Programmes of 1898" (*Engineering Magazine*, August, 1898); Lieutenant X: *La Guerre avec l'Angleterre* (Paris, 1900), pp. 22–3.

[56] J. L. de Lanessan: *Histoire de l'Entente Cordiale Franco-Anglaise* (Paris, 1916), p. 203. Lanessan was a former French minister of marine and had good sources of information. See also Sir Thomas Barclay: *Thirty Years* (Boston, 1914), p. 145. I find no evidence whatever for his story that the French Mediterranean fleet actually slipped by the British at Gibraltar with lights extinguished, and that it reached Cherbourg.

naval power, in relation to the English, was about on a par with the Spanish with respect to the American. The Channel fleet was composed of battleships built prior to 1885. The ships were of diverse design, and there was no definite plan of campaign. The naval ports, at home and in the colonies, were suffering from a serious lack of men, while the arsenals were inadequately equipped. At Brest, Cherbourg and Toulon only one third of the batteries could have been manned on the first day of mobilization.[57]

The Paris government was quite aware of the dangers of the situation. Having put the match to the Fashoda powder barrel, the French woke up astonished, frightened and impotent.[58] The tone of the British press was rightly taken as symptomatic of a bellicose spirit. There was certainly a widespread idea in England that the moment was favorable for settling accounts with France. In most circles war would have been popular. Within the cabinet itself voices were evidently raised in favor of this solution. Among several members of the cabinet, of whom Chamberlain was one, there was some apprehension lest Salisbury might yield. There is no evidence that he had any intention of doing so; in fact, he had been quite clear in his own mind for years that no " graceful concessions " could be made in this matter. But the prime minister was clearly anxious to avoid provocation as much as possible. On October 28 the cabinet decided that the fleet should be concentrated. Salisbury was worried by the decision, because, as Lord Esher noted at the time, " the others seemed to take the view that the row would have to come, and that it might as well come now as later." On the very same day Lord Rosebery told Esher that he was inclined " to think that a war with France now would simplify difficulties in the future." There can be no doubt whatever that there was considerable sentiment in governing circles for a preventive war.[59]

Reports of all this reached Paris all through October. At the ministry of marine there was general agreement that the British might provoke a war in order to dispose of the French fleet before the new German fleet had become too strong. The French officers were mostly of one mind, namely that France could not fight at sea, not even by commerce-destroying. Some thought that France's honor required her to fight even if defeat were certain, but these heroes were looked at askance. They were suspected of being in league with the general staff, which was in turn supposed to be not wholly averse to a war which would compromise only the navy, while it made way for a military dictatorship. At all events the minister of marine was convinced that a war would

---

[57] The revelations of the minister of marine, Édouard Lockroy, in the Chamber, March 17, 1899; see also Lockroy: *La Défense Navale* (Paris, 1900), pp. 4 ff.; Comm. H. Chassériaud: " Politique Navale " (*Nouvelle Revue*, January 15, 1899, pp. 216–31).

[58] Cocheris, op. cit., p. 466.

[59] *Journals and Letters of Reginald Viscount Esher* (London, 1934), I, pp. 221–2; Garvin: *Life of Chamberlain*, III, pp. 228, 231; Gardiner: *Life of Harcourt*, II, p. 468; Blunt: *My Diaries*, I, pp. 368, 372, 377 (quoting statements of George Wyndham, the undersecretary for war); *Die Grosse Politik*, XIV, nos. 3898, 3899.

be hopeless, and the prime minister, Brisson, as well as President Faure, agreed with him.[60]

Delcassé's strategy appears to have hinged on the desire to gain time enough to enable France to do two things: firstly, to make the most urgent naval preparations; secondly, to sound out Russia with regard to the chances of securing support. In the meanwhile he pleaded with the British for time until he should have received Marchand's report, and then for time to get an oral report from Captain Baratier, who was summoned to Paris. At the same time everything was done to put at least the coasts in a state of defense. Troops and ammunition were rushed to Brest and Cherbourg; the ships were hurriedly made ready for service. At Toulon the yards were working day and night, and all leave was cancelled. The whole Mediterranean squadron was revamped and put under the command of Admiral Fournier, one of the ablest sea officers. Ultimately President Faure induced the chairmen of the finance committees of the Senate and Chamber to sanction the expenditure of about one hundred million francs without the approval of parliament. An extensive naval reform program was then initiated.[61]

At the height of the crisis, in the midst of the domestic turmoil, the Russian foreign minister arrived in Paris on October 15, followed shortly by M. Witte and by General Kuropatkin, the minister of war. What transpired in the course of the conversations which extended over several days has never been revealed, though it is not hard to conjecture. Franco-Russian relations were not of the best at the time. Political groups in France, from the Right to the Left, were disappointed and disillusioned about the alliance with Russia, an alliance which appeared to be little more than an arrangement to maintain the status quo on the Continent and to draw France into the orbit of German policy. In August 1898 the Tsar had issued his famous peace rescript without consulting his allies. The French were pretty sure that they did not want to disarm, and the general reaction in political circles could be summed up in the phrase: *on nous lache*.[62]

On the Russian side the dissatisfaction was hardly less pronounced. What good was an ally who was paralyzed by so acute a disease as the Dreyfus Affair? What could one do anyway with a radical ministry like that of Brisson, which was supported by men like Clemenceau, Jaurès, Ranc and other well-known opponents of the Franco-Russian Alliance? The inspired Russian press made no secret of its dislike of the French government and of its determination to

---

[60] London *Times*, October 31, 1898 (quoting a high French official); Lockroy: *La Défense Navale*, pp. 19 ff., 187 ff.; de Lanessan: *Histoire de l'Entente Cordiale*, p. 202; Dumba: *Dreibund und Entente-Politik*, pp. 104–5; *National Review*, January, 1899, editorial; Reinach: op. cit., IV, p. 359.

[61] Lockroy, op. cit., pp. 130 ff., 298–310; *Times*, October 20, October 25, November 2, November 3, November 12, November 15, 1898; Barclay: *Thirty Years*, pp. 145–6; Charles Maurras: *Kiel et Tanger* (New edition, Paris, 1913), appendix iii; Ernest A. Vizetelly: *Republican France* (Boston, 1913), pp. 440–1.

[62] Sir Thomas Barclay: *Thirty Years*, p. 149. See also Michon: *The Franco-Russian Alliance*, pp. 99–102.

lend it no support. " When a man ceases to think his wife handsome he begins to think her dowry meagre," wrote the Paris correspondent of the *Times* on October 14, pointing out that on both sides there was nothing but discontent and recrimination.[63]

According to the newspaper reports the French government in October 1898 told M. Witte that he had better wait before trying to float another loan in Paris. This may or may not have been so; in any case it concerns us less than the outcome of the Muraviev-Delcassé conversations. So far as one can detect, the Russian foreign minister was convinced that his French colleague was loyal to the Alliance. For the rest he seems to have assured Delcassé that Russia would honor her obligations, but that her mobilization would take a long time, that her fleet would be frozen up for the winter, and that therefore it would be better for France to yield, the more so as the Fashoda swamps could not be regarded as a matter of vital interest. Later on Russia might help France to reopen the whole Egyptian question.[64]

Sir Edmund Monson, the British ambassador at Paris, was never quite certain whether, in the event of a rupture, the Russians might not give the French more than moral aid, but the government at London lost no sleep over this possibility. It is hard to understand how anyone could have been under any illusion after reading the articles in the French press. The *Soleil*, for example, wrote on November 13 as follows:

" We sent our sailors to Kiel on the occasion of the opening of the Baltic Canal in order to please Russia; we consented after the Chino-Japanese War to pull the chestnuts out of the fire for Russia, and she thereby gained Manchuria and obtained a preponderating position in the China Seas without spending a single rouble and without risking the bones of a single Cossack; we have given Russia several milliards of francs from our savings, which might perhaps better have been employed at home. In the Fashoda Affair Russia has not lifted a finger to defend us. She doubtless considers that the services we have rendered her are sufficiently repaid by some telegrams which have flattered the vanity of M. Félix Faure and some decorations which have pleased M. Hanotaux." [65]

The situation of France, then, was one of complete helplessness. In the throes of domestic unrest she found herself militarily unprepared and without the whole-hearted support of her ally. The British were determined to go the limit if necessary. There was therefore no other solution for the French but to yield. Naturally no one, least of all Delcassé, liked to be the agent of France's disgrace. One can understand his efforts to make capital out of the downfall of

---

[63] Reports in the *Times*, October 13, 15, 19, 1898; see also the press quotations in *Questions Diplomatiques et Coloniales*, November 1, 1898, pp. 270-3.

[64] *British Documents*, I, nos. 213, 215, 218, 221; *Letters of Queen Victoria*, III, pp. 299-300; London *Times*, October 20, 1898; *Die Grosse Politik*, XIII, no. 3558; XIV, nos. 3891 ff.; Barclay, op. cit., p. 150; Witte: *Memoirs*, p. 178; Reinach, op. cit., p. 315. Giffen, op. cit., chap. ix; and Kossatz, op. cit., pp. 61 µ. give a detailed discussion.

[65] Quoted in the London *Times*, November 14, 1898.

the Brisson cabinet on October 25 by threatening not to join the new ministry if England persisted in humiliating France. But Delcassé was too fond of power to relinquish it if he could avoid doing so. It is certain that by this time he had become convinced that Fashoda had to be evacuated. The British cabinet had met on October 28 and had showed no sign of yielding. On the contrary military and naval preparations were being pushed with more vigor than ever, and on many sides there was talk of an ultimatum that was to be presented to France. So in the end Delcassé retained his portfolio in the new Dupuy cabinet, fully resigned to the necessity of advising retreat from a position thus far so staunchly maintained. The new ministry was formed on October 29, and on that very day the Paris press began to talk of the impending decision. The matter was discussed by the French cabinet on November 3. On the following day the world knew that France had decided to draw back. Fashoda was to be unconditionally evacuated.[66]

Marchand, who had come down the Nile to Cairo, evidently without authorization from Paris, was ordered back to Fashoda to arrange for the departure of his force. He was to leave the disputed post and travel by way of the Sobat to Abyssinia and thence to the French possessions on the Red Sea. It was on December 11 that the French flag was finally hauled down and the valiant adventurers departed. After further trials and tribulations they ultimately reached the Abyssinian capital, and in the spring were back in Paris. It is said that Marchand was forbidden to publish any account of his experiences, and that Delcassé generally took a hostile attitude, indicating that Marchand should have left when Kitchener put in an appearance. No doubt this would have spared Delcassé a distasteful step, and would have supplied him with a convenient scapegoat.[67]

Unfortunately the French withdrawal from Fashoda by no means marked the end of the international crisis. There still remained the problem of French claims in the Bahr-el-Ghazal and the delimitation of the French and British possessions in the Sudan-Congo area. It was to be expected that these matters would be taken up at once, but such was not the case. For weeks on end the British showed no disposition to embark upon negotiations. On the contrary they continued their military and naval preparations. Ministers, notably Chamberlain, continued to make unkind, not to say threatening remarks about the French, until finally Sir Edmund Monson, speaking to the British chamber of commerce in Paris, went the limit and accused the government to which he was accredited of having deliberately pursued a " policy of pinpricks which, while it can only procure an ephemeral gratification to a short-lived ministry, must inevitably perpetuate across the channel an irritation which a high-spirited nation must eventually feel to be intolerable."

---

[66] *British Documents*, I, nos. 221 ff.; *Letters of Queen Victoria*, III, pp. 299–308; *Die Grosse Politik*, XIV, nos. 3901–7; London *Times*, October 31, November 1, 1898; Riker, loc. cit., pp. 71 ff.

[67] On this see especially C. Castellani: *Marchand l'Africain* (Paris, 1902), pp. 337 ff.

Sir Edmund was one of the most cautious and circumspect of diplomats. His utterance, it was felt in Paris, must have rested upon definite instructions from home. In actual fact this was not so, but the French took it to be symptomatic and became more firmly than ever convinced that the British were preparing to provoke a war. The German ambassador at Paris, Count Münster, thought this apprehension quite justified, and it was widely shared in the political circles of other European capitals.[68] In all probability the British activities are to be explained in another way. It was essential for the London government to settle the matter of *Egyptian* claims to the Sudan first of all. Not until January 19, 1899 was the agreement between the British and Egyptian governments signed which decided that the Sudan should be governed by a partnership of two, with England the predominant partner. The British claim to this position rested frankly upon the right of conquest. Other powers might question this right and query the validity of the agreement in international law, but it was more than unlikely that any one of them would be prepared to contest the arrangements made.[69]

While the British remained uncommunicative and the fear of war spread in Paris and on the Continent generally, it was natural that the French, unable to count for much upon their ally, should look elsewhere for support. We have to do here with fundamental problems of foreign policy. There was the Alliance with Russia, which, despite much disappointment and criticism, most Frenchmen regarded as the sheet-anchor of security and which few would have been prepared to give up. But this Alliance had proved of no value in the Anglo-French dispute, which had wide ramifications and which was, for the moment, the most important aspect of French foreign policy. Political circles in Paris were of different opinions regarding the methods for dealing with this situation. A considerable group of staunch republicans favored the conclusion of a general agreement and an entente with England, which, it was hoped, might eventually be extended into an English-French-Russian combination. In this group were a number of business men, who remembered that Britain was France's best customer and took one and a half milliards of francs' worth of French products each year. Under the leadership of J. L. de Lanessan, eminent scientist, colonial administrator and one-time minister of marine, an Entente Cordiale Society had been founded in France in April 1897. It had some enthusiastic supporters but found an early death because the French foreign office and the politicians, so Lanessan claims, were not well disposed towards the idea.[70]

---

[68] *British Documents*, I, nos. 237, 241; Garvin, op. cit., III, pp. 231–2; *Die Grosse Politik*, XIV, nos. 3908–13, 3921–3, 3927; Dumba: *Dreibund und Entente-Politik*, pp. 104–5; Hohenlohe: *Denkwürdigkeiten der Reichskanzlerzeit*, pp. 470, 475–6; *Lettres de la Princesse Radziwill au Général de Robilant* (Bologna, 1933), II, pp. 152, 155.

[69] See Cromer: *Modern Egypt*, II, pp. 155–9, and the very keen and elaborate criticism of the agreement in Cocheris, op. cit., chap. xiii.

[70] J. L. de Lanessan: *Histoire de l'Entente Cordiale Franco-Anglaise* (Paris, 1916), pp. 229–33.

This last statement was only partially true, for there always was a group of French diplomats and statesmen, mostly Gambettists, who favored such a rapprochement. The Comte de Chaudordy was perhaps the most eminent, but D'Estournelles de Constant was also an active protagonist of the idea. M. Ribot, one of the best-known French politicians, appears to have been favorably disposed, while M. Paul Cambon, the ambassador at Constantinople, had been working all through the Armenian crisis to effect an understanding with England. That Delcassé's inclinations were in the same direction has already been emphasized in another connexion. It was obviously in the hope of coming to some general agreement and entente that Delcassé sent Cambon to London as ambassador in the midst of the Fashoda crisis, and it is worth noting that Cambon accepted the post only on condition that efforts be made in that direction.[71]

In the autumn of 1898 this question of an entente with England became closely bound up with the domestic situation in France which arose from the Dreyfus agitation. The Radicals, men like Clemenceau, Zola, Ranc and others, were at one with the Socialists in their dislike of the Russian and German monarchical systems and in their desire to defend the Republic. They were the Dreyfusards, the anti-militarists, the champions of justice and of the common man. Jean Jaurès, the rising socialist leader, attributed the whole trouble to the Anglophobia of M. Hanotaux, and insisted that only British capitalism, not British labor, was bellicose. De Lanessan, after consulting with President Faure, published two articles in the *Rappel* on October 14 and 18, 1898, in which he urged the need for an adjustment. Later on, in January 1899, D'Estournelles de Constant, Denys Cochin, Ribot and Delcassé spoke in behalf of an entente in the Chamber, the first named demanding an end of *all* misunderstandings, and *at once*.[72]

Opposed to these forces of conciliation were the advocates of an arrangement with Germany. These were mostly the patriots, the army circles, the Anti-Dreyfusards, curious though it may seem. The most violent of them, men like Maurras, Déroulède, Cassagnac, Drumont, and Rochefort, maintained that the whole Dreyfus scandal was started and financed by England to weaken France.[73] " If Germany is an object of hatred," wrote Cassagnac, " it is for a definite past which can be effaced. . . . But England's hatred against us is inextinguishable, England is the enemy of yesterday, tomorrow and for ever." [74]

---

[71] Eugène Julien: " Notice sur la Vie et les Travaux de M. Paul Cambon " (*Séances et Travaux de l'Académie des Sciences Morales et Politiques*, March–April, 1929, pp. 177–217), pp. 187, 193–4; Schéfer: *D'Une Guerre à l'Autre*, p. 232; Theodor Wolff: *Das Vorspiel* (Munich, 1924), p. 140; *British Documents*, I, no. 238.

[72] *Œuvres de Jean Jaurès*, edited by Max Bonnafous (Paris, 1931), I, pp. 212–5; De Lanessan: " Les Relations de la France et de l'Angleterre " (*Questions Diplomatiques et Coloniales*, March 1, 1899, pp. 259–72); De Lanessan: *Histoire de l'Entente Cordiale*, pp. 236–7; *Journal Officiel*, January 23, 1899, pp. 107 ff., 109 ff., 114 ff., 118 ff.

[73] See Charles Maurras: *Au Signe de Flore* (Paris, 1931), pp. 58–9.

[74] Quoted in the London *Times*, November 14, 1898.

This *volte face* on the part of the reactionaries and partisans of the general staff would have been of little consequence if the unbending attitude of England had not obliged France to drink the cup of humiliation to the dregs. During November and December there was a steady growth of feeling in the direction of an entente with Germany. Apparently the Russian government exerted itself in behalf of this policy. Colonialists, disciples of Ferry and followers of Hanotaux, maintained then and afterward that Delcassé's predecessor had always envisaged some arrangement and that the Marchand mission without the proper diplomatic preparation was an act of insanity.[75] This group blamed Delcassé for his failure to follow the line marked out by Hanotaux. The moderate republican press began to strike the same note and to favor some rapprochement with Germany. M. Lemaitre of the Academy came out openly in this sense, and the eminent jurist, Paul Fauchille, argued that the Continent should unite economically and politically to put a check on England. France should learn to accept the consequences of her defeat. A government, he claimed, that had the courage to ignore the yelping of a few chauvinists would earn the gratitude of the whole country.[76]

There can be no doubt that the feeling of *revanche* receded considerably in France under the influence of the clash with England. The older generation and the Radicals like Clemenceau stood by their guns, but many of the younger intellectuals and even the younger officers were prepared to let bygones be bygones.[77]

Delcassé's stand in this whole matter is not entirely clear. As a Gambettist it seems hardly plausible that he should have seriously considered an agreement with Germany, though he may have wanted to keep a line out for the event of an actual war with England. There is some evidence that the Russians brought pressure to bear in favor of a rapprochement. The St. Petersburg government was profoundly moved by the news of the Anglo-German understanding regarding the Portuguese colonies, and feared that there might be some more far-reaching agreement between the two countries. From Russian documents we know how anxious Muraviev was to hold the Germans on the Russian side.[78] Whether it was this pressure or other considerations that moved Delcassé,

---

[75] See for example the articles by Robert de Caix in the *Bulletin . . . de l'Afrique Française*, September, 1898, pp. 278 ff.; November, 1898, pp. 358 ff. The same view is taken by Cocheris, op. cit., p. 469.

[76] Press comment in Carroll: *French Public Opinion*, etc., pp. 176 ff. See further Paul Fauchille: " L'Europe Nouvelle " (*Revue Générale de Droit International Public*, January 15, 1899, pp. 5-8); Anonymous: " Le Dilemme de notre Politique Extérieure " (*Revue de Paris*, May 1, 1899, pp. 224-32).

[77] See the numerous quotations from the French and Russian press in *Questions Diplomatiques et Coloniales*, January 15, 1899, pp. 43-5, March 1, 1899, pp. 300-4, and the enquête of the *New York Herald*, summarized in the London *Times*, December 12, 1898. Similarly Theodor Wolff: *Das Vorspiel*, pp. 114 ff.; Constantin Dumba: *Dreibund und Entente-Politik*, pp. 106 ff.; *Die Grosse Politik*, XIII, no. 3556.

[78] L. Teleshev: " Anglo-Germanskoe Sblishenie v 1899 g." (*Krasnyi Arkhiv*, LVI, 1933, pp. 65-79), especially pp. 77-9.

we do not know. But it is interesting to observe that in the last number of the *Revue Générale de Droit International Public* for 1898 there appeared an article by a high French official, who was commonly believed to be one of Delcassé's adherents. The author of this article pleaded for an understanding between France and Germany on the ground that they were both ruining themselves by armament expenditures while England and the United States were forging ahead. The question of Alsace-Lorraine, he maintained, was not insoluble. France should give up all ideas of retrocession, for no victorious nation could be expected to give up territory voluntarily and the German people would never allow the government to abandon the provinces, even if the government wished to do so. In the same way it was, he said, futile to talk of neutralization. That solution had been put forward in 1871 and had been rejected as impracticable. What the author thought really feasible was a plan put about by Admiral Reveillère: Alsace and Lorraine should remain with Germany and be in the complete military control of Germany, but they should be given full autonomy — a position like that of Jersey and Guernsey in the United Kingdom. This plan would satisfy the German desire for military security and the French desire that the faithful Alsatians and Lorrainers should have free opportunity to develop as they wished. Economically too they would remain in the German system, but possibly in the future they might serve as a bridge to a Franco-German tariff union.[79]

In keeping with this general attitude was Delcassé's behavior in the course of his conversations, early in December, with Arthur von Huhn of the *Kölnische Zeitung,* who had already, in 1896, been the intermediary in discussions of the possibility of a Franco-German rapprochement. Huhn noted in his reports how bitter was the feeling toward England among the members of the French foreign office. Delcassé personally assured him that the spirit of revenge was rapidly dying out and that he regarded a rapprochement with Germany as a highly desirable development.[80] A few days later the French foreign minister dined rather ostentatiously at the German embassy.

From the beginning the Germans accepted these advances cordially but sceptically. The hint was constantly being thrown out in Paris that Germany might take some French colony in return for a part or for the whole of Alsace-Lorraine, a suggestion which historians like Vandal and de Broglie declared from the start to be impracticable. Huhn's paper, the *Kölnische Zeitung,* on December 15 made this quite clear: " The possibility of a Franco-German rapprochement can only arise when the word Alsace-Lorraine shall have disappeared from the vocabulary of French statesmen and of the French press. . . .

---

[79] Anonymous: " La Question d'Alsace-Lorraine est-elle Insoluble? " (*Revue Générale de Droit International Public,* V, 1898, pp. 744–9).

[80] *Die Grosse Politik,* XIII, nos. 3558, 3559. The matter is discussed by Carroll, op. cit., p. 177, and by Giffen: *Fashoda,* pp. 195–6. See also Manfred Zapp: *Deutsch-Französische Annäherungsversuche* (Weida, 1929), pp. 137 ff.

Germany will persist in declining to enter upon any interchange of views so long as she has reason to apprehend that were any conversation opened it might by so much as a hint allude to a subject which for Germany is completely settled." [81] The German ambassador at Paris, Count Münster, was also pretty sceptical about the whole matter. The French would, he thought, try to get the Germans to pull the chestnuts out of the English fire for them, and in addition would demand some concession in the matter of Alsace-Lorraine, if a really sincere entente was to be effected. In this he was quite right. Delcassé, while avoiding official steps, did approach an influential Alsatian shipowner and asked whether he thought the Emperor William would consider an exchange of Alsace-Lorraine for a French colony. The answer, of course, was negative, and before long the whole idea disappeared from political discussion. The Emperor, to be sure, still liked to toy with the idea of a continental combine, a dyke against British pretensions, a naval league against the mistress of the seas. In February 1899 he was saying to the French naval attaché that the time had come for the Continent to unite. The French ambassador at Berlin was convinced that something could be done. But the obstacles to such a settlement were too great. On both sides the governments knew it, and the whole flirtation might be said to have come to a close when on March 2, 1899 the *Temps* remarked: "France has not yet reached the point of repudiating the fundamental principles of her public law by passing off to the account of profit and loss the sacrilegious mutilation which has taken from her the flesh of her flesh and the purest of her blood." [82]

While the question of Alsace-Lorraine still formed an insurmountable barrier in the way of a Franco-German reconciliation, the British were able to pursue their policy without serious misgivings regarding the German attitude. The agreement concerning the Portuguese colonies, which had been signed on the eve of the Fashoda crisis, came just in time to put the Berlin government in a friendly frame of mind. To be sure, the excitable Emperor William took the gloomiest view of the international situation and tried to exploit the occasion to strengthen his relations with the Tsar. In the drafts of the correspondence which passed at that time there is more evidence of jealousy and dislike for the British than of friendship. The Tsar did not react to the suggestions made to him, while the English, on their part, continued to make advances. Salisbury suggested to the Queen in mid-November that it would be well to invite the Emperor to visit England in the coming year. " The attitude of France," he wrote, " makes it desirable that the world should believe in an

[81] Quoted by the London *Times*, December 16, 1898.

[82] Quoted by Carroll, op. cit., p. 181. See also the summary of an inquiry among German deputies, made by *La Vie Illustrée*, as given in *Questions Diplomatiques et Coloniales*, February 15, 1899, pp. 240–5. Delcassé's advances in Hohenlohe: *Denkwürdigkeiten*, p. 483; there also, p. 470, a letter from Münster. The Emperor's advances in Bourgeois and Pagès: *Les Origines . . . de la Grande Guerre*, pp. 266, 277–8.

understanding between Germany and England." Victoria followed up the suggestion in December, and before the year was out the Emperor had accepted the invitation with his usual enthusiasm. In a speech at Wakefield on December 8 Chamberlain had underlined the British desire for co-operation and for an agreement with Germany based on common defense of common interests. The address had been very well received by the German press, and the German public no doubt shared the smug feeling that there were prophets on the right and prophets on the left, while Germany was the child of the world between them. It was both comfortable and flattering to be wooed by France and England at the same time, while relations with Russia were good.[83]

This brief review of the Franco-Russian, the Franco-German and the Anglo-German relationships will make it perfectly clear that when the British, having settled accounts with the Egyptians, were at last ready to talk with the French, the Paris government found itself all alone. Paul Cambon, who had taken up his work as ambassador at London, advised from the start that the French foreign office give up all claim to territory on the Nile. When the discussions at last got under way in February 1899 the French no longer pressed even the claim to the Bahr-el-Ghazal area. Cambon suggested a delimitation which would take the Nile-Congo watershed as a basis. The proposal was, of course, wholly satisfactory to the British, and the agreement which was finally signed on March 21, 1899, ran along these lines. France was excluded from the whole Nile Basin, but was left Wadai and the whole Sudan region from Darfur in the east to Lake Chad in the west.[84]

The agreement which disposed finally of the French claims in the Nile Valley did not, however, mark the end of the Sudan problem. We know how much Kitchener feared a possible clash with the Abyssinians.[85] That they had large armies on foot was perfectly well known when the Sirdar went to meet Marchand at Fashoda. After Omdurman, forces had been sent up the Blue Nile and up the Sobat, where garrisons were established. These precautions proved to be somewhat superfluous, for at the very time of the Fashoda crisis King Menelik was obliged to devote himself to a serious revolt led by Ras Mangasha, the turbulent governor of Tigré. By the time this rising was suppressed, in February 1899, Marchand had already reached Abyssinia on his way home. The Franco-Abyssinian campaign was no longer a matter of practical politics.

French writers have thought that the British meant to proceed militarily against Menelik, whose territorial claims extended to the Nile at Khartum. They believe that the outbreak of the Boer War in the autumn of 1899 alone

---

[83] London *Times*, December 10, 12, 1898. The Emperor's correspondence with Nicky in *Die Grosse Politik*, XIV, nos. 3900, 3905, 3913–9. For British policy see especially the *Letters of Queen Victoria*, III, pp. 312, 321–5.

[84] Documents Diplomatiques: *Correspondance Concernant la Déclaration Additionnelle du 21 mars, 1899; British Documents*, I, nos. 242–5; *Die Grosse Politik*, XIV, nos. 3931–3, 3941 ff.; Cocheris, op. cit., pp. 499 ff.; Giffen, op. cit., pp. 87 ff.

[85] *Letters of Queen Victoria*, III, p. 315.

saved the King of Kings from an attack. This is probably an exaggeration. The English were not looking for trouble. But it is likely that the Boer War postponed serious efforts to come to an arrangement with Menelik. We know next to nothing of what went on in the ensuing years. Colonel Harrington, the British minister at Adis Abeba, was a very able man, who seems to have succeeded in drawing Menelik away from the French influence. It is said that Menelik never could get along with M. Lagarde, who had become the regular French representative, and that the African ruler was much put out by the high-handed activity of the Ethiopian Railway Company, which was a French concern. However this may have been, all we know for certain is that on May 15, 1902 the British and the Abyssinians concluded a treaty which defined the eastern frontier of the Sudan. Menelik gave up his earlier claims and contented himself with a boundary which, in general, followed the line of the highlands. In view of what has been said previously of the Nile problem, it is interesting to note that Article III of this treaty engaged Menelik " not to construct, or allow to be constructed, any work across the Blue Nile, Lake Tsana, or the Sobat which would arrest the flow of their waters into the Nile except in agreement with His Britannic Majesty's Government and the Government of the Soudan." [86]

More difficult to deal with was the King of the Belgians, who had already made so much trouble for the French and the British. It will be recalled that in the Treaty of May 1894 the English government had leased to Leopold for the duration of his life a considerable strip of territory on the west bank of the Nile between Lake Albert and Fashoda, to say nothing of the lease to the Congo State of the rest of the Bahr-el-Ghazal region. Because of French opposition the King had been unable to take advantage of this lease in the area north of 5° 30′ north latitude. Now when the Marchand expedition reached Fashoda and the crisis between England and France ensued, Leopold came forward with his own solution. He suggested to the French that the Congo State be substituted for France in the conflict, inasmuch as the Congo had treaty rights in the area. The proposal was, however, at once rejected by the French government.[87]

By this time the Congo forces had effectively occupied the region along the upper Nile. They had posts at Rejaf, Lado, Kero, Dufilé and Wadelai. As soon as the French were ejected from Fashoda, the Congolese troops began to invade the more northern region. In May 1899 the British government protested against such action, pointing out the rights of Egypt and the rights which had accrued to England by conquest. There then followed years of argumentation between London and Brussels. Leopold insisted throughout that the treaty of

---

[86] Sir E. Hertslet: *The Map of Africa by Treaty* (Third edition, London, 1909), II, pp. 431 ff. On events in Abyssinia from 1899 to 1902 see Morié: *Histoire de l'Éthiopie*, II, pp. 461 ff.; Darcy: *France et Angleterre*, pp. 459 ff.; *Bulletin . . . de l'Afrique Française*, July, 1902, pp. 254-6; January, 1903, pp. 5-10. [87] Auguste Gérard: *Mémoires* (Paris, 1928), p. 348.

1894 was fully valid, and quoted a despatch of Lord Salisbury to Sir Edmund Monson of October 6, 1898 in which he said in so many words that this agreement was " in existence and full force still. It has never been cancelled and never been repudiated by this country." [88] The French, said the Belgian King, had obliged him to suspend the occupation of the leased area, but now that they had been forced to evacuate there was no reason why the operations of the Congo State should not be resumed. To which the British replied by claiming that Leopold had, in 1894, handed over the exploitation of these territories to the British Tropical Africa Company and the Anglo-Belgian Africa Company without taking guarantees for their treatment of the natives; that, in actual fact, nothing had been done to occupy or administer the region, inasmuch as the Congo State had given them up in the treaty signed with France in August 1894; that, indeed, the whole British-Congo Treaty of May 1894 had fallen flat when Leopold, at Germany's behest, had given up Article III (leasing the twenty-five kilometer strip between Lakes Tanganyika and Albert Edward to England), and had thus deprived England of the one gain she was to make in return for the lease of the Bahr-el-Ghazal.

In rebuttal of these arguments the Belgian King pointed out that the French-Congo Treaty of 1894 was, so far as Britain was concerned, a *res inter alios acta* and had no bearing on the dispute. Furthermore, he stressed the point that in the agreement of May 1894 what the British wanted most was not the twenty-five kilometer strip, but the recognition, by the Congo government, of the British sphere of influence, and this they had secured.

One can hardly resist the conviction, after reading the documents, that the logic and the right was on the side of Leopold. But it had been shown over and over again in the course of the struggle for the Nile that logic and right were of secondary importance. We need not pursue this subject in all its minute details. Leopold offered to submit the matter to arbitration, but the London government rejected the proposal. Instead it made the King a compromise offer in 1902. In return for the cancellation of the leases of 1894 the British government was prepared to cede to the Congo State in full sovereignty a block of territory bounded on the east by the Yei River, on the north by parallel 6° 30′ north latitude, and on the west by the Nile-Congo watershed. In order to make this scheme comprehensible it should be pointed out that the River Yei is a confluent of the Nile on the left side. It flows roughly south to north and is, at 6° 30′ north latitude, about ninety to one hundred miles west of the Nile. In other words, the point of the British suggestion was that Leopold should agree to the Congo State's being cut off from the Nile, with a frontier removed by a hundred miles from the great river.

Leopold rejected this proposal, and matters began to drift toward a crisis. The British had begun to re-occupy the French posts in the Bahr-el-Ghazal and

---

[88] *Egypt No. 3 (1898),* no. 1.

Belgian expeditions began to push up into the disputed area. There was every prospect that another Fashoda crisis would ensue, but ultimately an agreement was come to on May 9, 1906, after the British had cut Leopold's communications by way of the Nile. Leopold gave up his claims to the Bahr-el-Ghazal lease, but was given, for the duration of his life, the so-called Lado Enclave, that is, the area along the left bank of the Nile from Mahagi on Lake Albert northward to 5° 30′ and westward to the 30th meridian and the Nile-Congo watershed. In this treaty, too, one can find the inevitable water clause. Article III specifies that the government of the Congo State shall " not construct, or allow to be constructed any work on or near the Semliki or Isango River, which would diminish the volume of water entering Lake Albert, except in agreement with the Soudanese Government." [89]

With these concluding arrangements the great struggle for the Nile came to a close; the whole course of the river, from its sources in the central African lakes to the sea, was under British or Anglo-Egyptian control, and after the death of Leopold the territory of no other power extended to within a hundred miles of it. More than perhaps any other great international problem in the pre-war period this question of the control of the Nile had the quality of an epic. You have here issues of primary importance, you have grand conceptions, and you have a rivalry drawn out over more than a decade and marked at every stage by drama, daring and heroism.

Despite the immense literature on the subject and the undeniable excellence of much that has been written upon it, no study has yet treated it adequately in all its multitudinous aspects. Its complexity is simply baffling and the many contradictions on all sides only serve to enhance the confusion. Under the circumstances a brief résumé may not be taken amiss. The question as such has its beginning about the year 1889. At that time the situation was still essentially what it had been five years previously, when the British practically obliged the Egyptian government to evacuate the Sudan with the clearly expressed idea that it should be allowed to revert to the native chiefs. The Egyptians, who knew the significance of the Sudan for Egypt, never got over this move. In a memorandum of December 1888 Riaz Pasha wrote rather eloquently: " No one will deny, so clear and evident a proposition is it, that the Nile is the life of Egypt. Now the Nile means the Soudan, and nobody will doubt that the bonds and

[89] Text in Hertslet, Third edition, II, no. 165. The most important material on this dispute was published in the *Deutsches Kolonialblatt*, June 1, 1916, pp. 135–61: " Aus den Archiven des Belgischen Kolonialministeriums, III. Das Lado und Bahr-el-Ghazal-Pachtgebiet des Kongostaates," especially pp. 149–59. See also the highly interesting Belgian memorandum of 1899 published by Th. Simar: " Léopold II et le Soudan " (*Congo*, November, 1924, pp. 506–28), pp. 509–19. There is some discussion of the problem in A. J. Wauters: *Histoire Politique du Congo Belge* (Brussels, 1911), chap. xxix; in Fritz Masoin: *Histoire de l'État Indépendant du Congo* (Namur, 1913), II, pp. 285 ff.; and in Arthur B. Keith: *The Belgian Congo and the Berlin Act* (Oxford, 1919), pp. 112–3. See also Victor Collin: " La Question du Haut-Nil et le Point de Vue Belge " (*Bulletin de la Société de Géographie d'Anvers*, XXIII, 1899, pp. 149–223); and Edmund D. Morel: " The Congo State and the Bahr-el-Ghazal " (*Nineteenth Century*, August, 1901, pp. 202–13).

connections which unite Egypt to the Soudan are as inseparable as those which unite the soul to the body." [90] But the British officials had not changed their minds. Cromer stated emphatically: " There is not now and since the destruction of General Hicks' army there never has been, any serious idea of deliberately adopting a policy involving the reconquest of the Soudan by force of arms." Or again: " I have pointed out over and over again during the last five years that the true interests of Egypt are not to reconquer, but to trade with the Soudan." [91]

What, then, brought about the change? There were two distinct reasons. In the first place, the unusually low Nile of 1888 led to much talk of the possibility of interference with Nile water beyond the frontiers of Egypt. It was then that Sir Samuel Baker wrote his highly interesting letters to the *Times*. Their effect can hardly be doubted, as echoes of them can be found in most writings on the subject in the ensuing years. The growing need of summer water in Egypt raised, at the same time, the problem of further storage of water. The Aswan Dam came under discussion, but already engineers were beginning to talk of the possibility of storing water at Lake Tsana in Abyssinia or at Lake Albert or Victoria in central Africa. All this quite naturally resulted in a growing conviction that the upper Nile was of vital importance to Egypt and that, under no circumstances, could another power be permitted to secure control of these areas.

Now it was at this very time that the danger of such foreign interference in the Sudan became real. With the death of King John of Abyssinia in 1889 Menelik came to the throne. The Italians had concluded with him the Treaty of Uccialli and were preparing to establish a protectorate over a country which claimed and always had claimed territory extending to Khartum and the Nile. Everyone knew that the Mahdist power was on the down-grade and that, if it did not soon collapse, it could easily be defeated. There was no knowing, then, whether the Italians might not become a factor in the Sudan problem. But they were not the only ones. In east Africa the Germans were uncomfortably active and in this very same year, 1889, Peters was pushing inland to Lake Victoria. The hectic enterprises of the British East Africa Company and the hasty negotiations with the Germans in the spring of 1890 indicate plainly enough how seriously this aspect of the problem was viewed in London.

In the Anglo-German Treaty of 1890 and in the Anglo-Italian Treaty of 1891 the danger from Germany and Italy was removed. Neither power, henceforth, would extend its claims and activities into the Nile Basin. The British themselves then embarked on the work of establishing their own control over the upper Nile. For years the country was exercised by the Uganda problem, which in the end became the great test case of imperialism and led to the mortal split in the Liberal party and to the definitive victory of the Liberal Imperialists.

---

[90] *Egypt No. 1 (1889)*, no. 35, inclosure.
[91] Ibid., nos. 22, 35.

Uganda was retained and before long Unyoro was conquered. British officers appeared on the right bank of the upper Nile and stations were established.

In the meanwhile a serious menace had appeared on the left bank. King Leopold, sovereign of the Congo State, had really been the first to move. For the Emin Pasha Relief Expedition, sponsored by him, aimed primarily at the removal of the last Egyptian governor and the acquisition of his Equatorial Province by Leopold. Now in the years 1891–1894 Belgian forces were over-running the whole Equatorial Province, and before long the French were joining in the rush for the Nile. At Paris there had been high hopes that the Gladstone government, which came into power in 1892, would evacuate Egypt. Rosebery had blasted these hopes in no uncertain way. It was clear that not even the Liberals would fulfill the oft-repeated British promises. It was just at this moment that President Carnot became acquainted with the report of M. Prompt, who suggested that a power in command of the upper Nile could build barrages which, if opened, could drown out the whole of Egypt. It is perfectly obvious that the French had no idea of committing so monstrous an atrocity. But they did see that if they were in a position to make the threat, the British would be forced to reopen the question of evacuating Egypt. Whatever may have been said later of French objects in the Bahr-el-Ghazal, it is beyond dispute that the original plans were intended to secure for France an effective " talking point " with respect to the Egyptian question.

The British had protested against the activities of Leopold. When the French began to push into the Nile area the matter became more serious. Ultimately, in order to shut the door on the French, the British government leased the territory in question to Leopold. The French protested and, probably because of the German protests regarding another clause of the British-Congo Treaty, were able to force Leopold to eschew activity in the Bahr-el-Ghazal. The British did nothing to support their lessee. In the treaty of August 1894 the Belgian King was obliged to accept the French terms.

The rest of the story we need not repeat. French plans and the collapse of the Italian-Abyssinian front induced the British to decide on the reconquest of the Sudan from the north, though Salisbury had always hoped the matter could wait until the Mombasa Railway was finished to Lake Victoria and troops could be brought up from the south. So what happened in the end was that the British pushed up the Nile from Wady-Halfa and Dongola to Khartum while the French were advancing from the Atlantic through the French Congo and the Belgian Congo and at the same time organizing a complementary movement in conjunction with the Abyssinians. After the Battle of Omdurman a crisis was inevitable and the Fashoda affair ensued.

Knowing the deep significance of the problem and realizing all its ramifications, we can see now that the British could not yield. Their warnings to France had been absolutely sincere. The trouble was that the British position was legally weak. The levity with which one argument was discarded in favor of another is truly astounding. Unfortunately for the French their own policy and arguments also lacked continuity and consistency. But we can leave the debate to the jurists. From the standpoint of diplomacy so much is clear: that nothing further could be gained by argument. The time for the *ultima ratio* had come. The British were prepared to fight. Some, it seems, were rather anxious to fight, knowing full well the superiority of the British naval forces and the helplessness of France, wracked as she was by the domestic crisis of the Dreyfus affair. The outcome of the conflict was a foregone conclusion. France ended by recalling Marchand and by abandoning all claims to the whole Bahr-el-Ghazal region. After which the British proceeded to evict Leopold, who had an indubitable claim to a lease of the territory, a claim which the British themselves held up to the French in the course of the Fashoda debate. Here again the rights and wrongs did not play any rôle. Leopold was forced to give in by the stoppage of his communications on the Nile by the British. Once again it was a matter of *force majeure*. And it should not be forgotten that the British, through clever financial and military manipulation of the Sudan campaign, had established, or claimed to have established, an indubitable right to joint administration in the Sudan. So long as they remained there the Egyptian question was settled. Even in our own day the independence of Egypt is a mere illusion so long as the British continue in the Sudan.

From the angle of European international relations very little need be said about the Fashoda crisis. France was all alone, for the Russians, with their attention focussed on the Far East, had no stomach for African adventure. They felt that the French had deserted them in the Near Eastern crisis of the winter of 1896–1897 and they took their revenge. The Franco-Russian Alliance had reached its nadir. The Russians kept it up because of its financial value and because it more or less guaranteed them a well-behaved Germany. The French stood by it because for them it was the keystone of security in Europe and they could not dispense with it. But the illusions of the honeymoon period were all gone. Even in 1898 the Radicals and Socialists, who had little use for autocratic Russia, were talking of the need of a general understanding with England. The harsh tone of the British in the Fashoda crisis, and the uncompromising attitude of the British government made the *entente cordiale* for the time being a pious hope and little more. But the lines of the future were already being marked out.

The much discussed Franco-German reconciliation and the continental coalition against Britain were hardly more than extravagant fancies in 1898 and 1899. In France the whole idea was a counsel of despair. Hard-headed reactionaries and militarists, in general the Anti-Dreyfusards, championed a union with the strong military monarchies. No doubt the revenge feeling generally was gradually diminishing, but still the reconciliation between the two great nations was a long way off. Good Frenchmen would not have considered it without having been first given some satisfaction in the matter of Alsace-Lorraine. This fact in itself ruined all prospects of the scheme, for the Germans would not for a moment entertain the suggestion of returning even part of the conquered provinces. Why should they? Their position in international affairs was never better. With England they had come to some sort of *modus vivendi*. The London government much resented what was called the German policy of blackmail, but it had seen the need for accepting it. Germany had been admitted to a share in the future Portuguese colonial spoils. In other words, the Germans felt very smug, sitting in the middle, as they did, while the Anglo-Russian, Anglo-French antagonisms raged around. It was the ideal setting for the Holstein policy of having two irons in the fire, a policy which Bülow adopted in full. The foreign minister defined Germany's standpoint during the crisis as one of careful abstention. Germany would maintain friendly relations with all parties, but would pursue an independent policy, avoiding all attempts to enlist her on the one side or the other. So the Fashoda affair ended without any fundamental dislocation in the established international system. The Franco-Russian Alliance still existed, though relations had cooled. England still maintained her isolation, but the tension in Anglo-French relations had grown very great. In the succeeding years it was to be one of the prime factors in European diplomacy. The leading question came to be the question whether Germany could be brought to join the anti-British group without reservations.

BIBLIOGRAPHICAL NOTE

DOCUMENTARY SOURCES

Accounts and Papers. 1899, volume CXII. *Egypt No. 2 (1898)*; *Egypt No. 3 (1898)*. The original British Blue Books on the crisis, now largely superseded by the *British Documents on the Origins of the War.*

Documents Diplomatiques. Affaires du Haut-Nil et du Bahr-el-Ghazal, 1897–1898. Paris, 1898. *Correspondance Concernant la Déclaration Additionnelle du 21 mars 1899.* The French Yellow Books, less full than the British publications, but the most valuable material on the French side.

British Documents on the Origins of the War, 1898–1914. Edited by G. P. Gooch and Harold Temperley. London, 1927 ff. The first volume of this important series contains additional material on the Fashoda crisis.

Die Grosse Politik der Europäischen Kabinette, 1871–1914. Volume XIII, chapter lxxxix: Franco-German Relations in 1898–1899. Volume XIV, chapter xciii: The Fashoda Crisis. This last chapter contains documents of considerable importance, bearing especially upon the British side of the crisis.

"Aus den Archiven des Belgischen Kolonialministeriums. III. Das Lado und Bahr-el-Ghazal Pachtgebiet des Kongostaates." (*Deutsches Kolonialblatt,* June 1, 1916, pp. 135–61). Belgian documents, of prime importance for the Congolese aspect of the problem.

MEMOIRS, AUTOBIOGRAPHIES, BIOGRAPHIES, AND LETTERS

Letters of Queen Victoria. Third Series, volume III. New York, 1932. Easily one of the most important sources for the study of British policy.

GARVIN, J. L.: *The Life of Joseph Chamberlain.* London, 1933 ff. Contains but little material on the Fashoda crisis.

ARTHUR, SIR GEORGE: *Life of Lord Kitchener.* Three volumes. London, 1920. The official biography of the British commander.

SMITH-DORRIEN, GENERAL SIR HORACE: *Memories of Forty-Eight Years' Service.* London, 1925. Contains a detailed account of the Fashoda meeting, by one of the British officers present.

BLUNT, WILFRID S.: *My Diaries.* London, 1919. Contains some valuable sidelights on the Fashoda crisis.

BARCLAY, SIR THOMAS: *Thirty Years. Anglo-French Reminiscences.* New York, 1914. One of the best-known accounts, by an Englishman well acquainted with French affairs.

MANGIN, GENERAL: "Lettres de la Mission Marchand." (*Revue des Deux Mondes,* September 15, 1931, pp. 241–83). An interesting addition to the amount of eyewitness material. Mangin was one of Marchand's associates.

BARATIER, CAPTAIN ALBERT E.: *À travers l'Afrique.* Paris, 1910. The account of Marchand's chief aide. One of the best narratives of the expedition.

Mission Marchand. Journal de Route du Dr. J. Émily. Second edition, Paris, 1913. A detailed and beautifully illustrated narrative, but of little political importance.

MICHEL, CHARLES: *Vers Fachoda, à la Rencontre de la Mission Marchand à travers l'Éthiopie.* Paris, 1901. By far the most important account of the Abyssinian aspect of the French activity.

CASTELLANI, CHARLES: *Marchand l'Africain.* Paris, 1902. Probably the best biography of Marchand, though entirely uncritical.

WAUTERS, A. J.: *Souvenirs de Fashoda et de l'Expédition Dhanis.* Brussels, 1910. Important for the Belgian activities. This material is largely included in the author's *Histoire Politique du Congo Belge* (Brussels, 1911).

SPECIAL STUDIES

HANOTAUX, GABRIEL: *Fachoda*. Paris, 1909. The apology of Delcassé's predecessor. Deals chiefly with the period before the crisis.

LEBON, ANDRÉ: *La Politique de la France en Afrique, 1896–1898*. Paris, 1901. Written by a former minister for the colonies; also concerned chiefly with the earlier period.

DE CAIX, ROBERT: *Fachoda*. Paris, 1899. The best contemporary study. Very well informed and thoroughly critical.

COCHERIS, JULES; *La Situation Internationale de l'Égypte et du Soudan*. Paris, 1903. Even allowing for the French bias, this is still probably the best scholarly account of the whole question.

DARCY, JEAN: *France et Angleterre: Cent Années de Rivalité Colonial*. Paris, 1904. Another good book, though less scholarly and more highly colored than Cocheris'.

ANONYMOUS: "La Mission Marchand." (*Revue de Paris*, June 1, 1899, pp. 457–86). An excellent, well-informed, critical account.

DELONCLE, J. L.: "La Question de Fachoda." (*Revue Politique et Parlementaire*, November 1898, pp. 277–300). A good historical account, by a former French secretary for the colonies.

BLANCHARD, GEORGES: "L'Affaire de Fachoda." (*Revue Générale de Droit International Public*, VI, 1899, pp. 380–430). A sound, scholarly, legal study.

COLLIN, VICTOR: "La Question du Haut-Nil et le Point de Vue Belge." (*Bulletin de la Société de Géographie d'Anvers*, XXIII, pp. 149–223). A detailed historical review of the whole Sudan problem.

ANONYMOUS: "France, Russia and the Nile." (*Contemporary Review*, December, 1898, pp. 761–78). A rather sensational article, purporting to reveal the French-Mahdist conspiracy.

DIPLOMATICUS: "Fashoda and Lord Salisbury's Vindication." (*Fortnightly Review*, December, 1898, pp. 1002–14). A strong presentation of the case against France.

BOURDARIE, PAUL: *Fachoda. La Mission Marchand*. Paris, 1899. A general review of the incident.

GUÉTANT, LOUIS: *Marchand-Fashoda*. Paris, 1899. Another good popular survey of the origins and aspects of the problem.

VATIN, FERNAND: *La Vérité sur Fachoda*. Chaumont, 1923. Reviews the Egyptian problem and the Anglo-French relationship. Takes the view that England's claim in 1898 was good and that the French were in the wrong.

RIKER, T. W.: "A Survey of British Policy in the Fashoda Crisis." (*Political Science Quarterly*, March, 1929, pp. 54–78). The first study of the British and German documents on the subject. A very meaty article, valuable especially for the account it takes of the British press.

GIFFEN, MORRISON B.: *Fashoda, the Incident and its Diplomatic Setting*. Chicago, 1930. The best general treatment, based upon the newer documentary publications and containing most of the important information. There is little that is novel about the viewpoint, and the value of the monograph for the general reader is much diminished by the extraordinary arrangement of the material, which makes it impossible to get a systematic view of its historical development.

BATUT, GUY DE LA: *Fachoda, ou le Renversement des Alliances*. Fourth edition, Paris, 1932. A popular review of the Egyptian problem as an Anglo-French problem. Fairly well-informed, but in no sense a contribution.

KOSSATZ, HEINZ: *Untersuchungen über den Französisch-Englischen Weltgegensatz im Fashodajahr*. Breslau, 1934. In most respects a well-informed and well-balanced monographic study. Much broader in analysis and interpretation than most studies of the subject.

LITERATURE SINCE 1935

(See also the Supplementary Bibliographical Notes to Chapters IV and IX.)

GOOCH, GEORGE P.: *Before the War. Studies in Diplomacy*. Volume I: *The Grouping of the Powers*. London, 1936. 438 pp. Includes interesting critical essays on Delcassé, Lansdowne and Bülow.

ANONYMOUS: "Une négociation sécrète de Léopold II; ses efforts pour acquérir l'accès du Congo au Nil. Les pourparlers avec l'Italie au sujet de l'Erythrée" (*Le XXe siècle politique*, January 6, 1933).

—: "Léopold II et le Bahr el-Ghazal. Une négociation ardue du fondateur de notre empire africain" (*Le XXe siècle politique*, January 26, 1933). These two articles, based on unpublished materials, throw interesting light on Leopold's designs.

COOK, ARTHUR N.: *British Enterprise in Nigeria*. Philadelphia, 1943. 330 pp. The best treatment of the Anglo-French conflict in Nigeria, based on the Lugard Papers and on the records of the Royal Niger Company.

DELEBECQUE, JACQUES: *Vie du général Marchand*. Paris, 1936. 253 pp. A competent general biography, making use of private letters and papers.

MANGIN, GENERAL CHARLES M.: *Souvenirs d'Afrique*. Paris, 1936. 264 pp. The recollections of one of Marchand's companions.

BOBICHON, HENRI: "Vers Fachoda: le gouverneur General Victor Liotard" (*Revue des questions coloniales et maritimes*, November–December, 1935, pp. 97–162).

—: *Contribution à l'histoire de la mission Marchand*. Paris, 1937. 86 pp. These writings, by one of the members of the Marchand Mission, deal with that exploit rather than with the international crisis.

VERGNIOL, CAMILLE: "Les origines de la mission Marchand" (*Revue de France,* August 1, 1936, pp. 420–434; August 15, 1936, pp. 630–645; September 1, 1936, pp. 112–129). One of the most thorough studies of the problem, unfortunately uncompleted. These three installments cover the background, from 1885 to 1895.

RENOUVIN, PIERRE: "Les origines de l'expédition de Fachoda" (*Revue historique,* CC, October–December, 1948).

TRÈVES, PAOLO: *Il dramma di Fascioda: Francia e Inghilterra sull'alto Nilo.* Milan, 1937. 244 pp. A competent, systematic account, exploiting the British and French documents and also adducing some information derived from Marchand himself.

KENNEDY, A. L.: "Fashoda" (*Quarterly Review,* CCLXXXVI, April, 1948, pp. 145–161). A general review, of no great importance.

PORTER, CHARLES W.: *The Career of Theophile Delcassé.* Philadelphia, 1936. 356 pp. A scholarly treatment, comprehensive but conventional.

BERGER, ERNST E.: *Die grosse Politik Delcassés: Frankreichs Kampf um die Vorherrschaft in Europa.* Essen, 1939. 213 pp. A well-informed review of Delcassé's aims and policies, written with a certain wry admiration.

MAUROIS, ANDRÉ: *Edouard VII.* Paris, 1936. Quotes two rather important letters written by Delcassé at the time of the Fashoda crisis.

MANTOUX, PAUL: "The Debut of M. Paul Cambon in England, 1899–1903" (in Coville, Alfred and Temperley, Harold: *Studies in Anglo-French History.* Cambridge, 1935, pp. 143–159). The part of Cambon in effecting the Anglo-French settlement. Based chiefly on unpublished French documents.

ANONYMOUS: "Paul Cambon à Londres et les préliminaires de l'Entente Cordiale" (*Revue de Paris,* April 1, 1937, pp. 545–564). A chapter from the book listed in the next entry.

(CAMBON, HENRI): *Paul Cambon, ambassadeur de France, 1843–1924, par un diplomate.* Paris, 1937. 323 pp. A general biography of Cambon, based on family correspondence.

CATALUCCIO, FRANCESCO: "La politica di Marchese Visconti-Venosta" (*Rassegna di politica internazionale,* III [2], December, 1936, pp. 887–912). An important analysis of Italian policy after Crispi's fall, with special reference to relations with France.

BITTNER, LUDWIG: "Neue Beiträge zur Haltung Kaiser Wilhelms II in der Fashodafrage" (*Historische Zeitschrift,* CLXII, 1940, pp. 540–550). Quotes unpublished Austrian documents to show that the Emperor encouraged the British to expect German benevolence in the event of an Anglo-French conflict.

KAMPLADE, WALTHER: *Delcassé und Deutschland, 1898–1911*. Emsdetten, 1940. 106 pp.

LEAMAN, BERTHA R.: "The Influence of Domestic Policy on Foreign Affairs in France, 1898–1905" (*Journal of Modern History*, XIV, December, 1942, pp. 449–480). Stresses the lack of interest in the ruling group and analyzes the small but active colonial group supporting Delcassé.

HERZOG, WILHELM: *From Dreyfus to Pétain: 'The Struggle of a Republic.'* New York, 1947. 313 pp. Primarily a well-informed and interestingly written review of the Dreyfus affair, making full use of the German documentation.

CHARPENTIER, ARMAND: *Les côtes mystérieux de l'affaire Dreyfus*. Paris, 1937. 331 pp. A critical analysis, with much emphasis on the unsolved aspects of German complicity.

XVII

Peace Dreams and Political Realities

✑

DVOCATES OF PEACE AND PROPONENTS OF THE IDEA OF INTERNATIONAL
co-operation regard the year 1899 as marking the opening of a new
era in human history, for in May of that year the first peace conference
opened its sessions at The Hague. This Conference, they say, was " in germ the
true Parliament of Man." " The dream of the prophets and the songs of the
poets here found their first partial realization in plain prose." [1]

For the historian of European diplomacy it is no easy task to put it into the
proper setting. The last years of the century were marked by the great Fashoda
crisis, by the Spanish-American War, by the ruthless assault of the powers
upon China, and by the beginning of the Boer War. No doubt about it, the
atmosphere of Europe was a warlike atmosphere in which talk of peace and
disarmament was bound to sound like hypocrisy. How is one to integrate
the episode of the Hague conference with the manifestations of exuberant
imperialism?

Fortunately sufficient material is now available to enable us to speak with
reasonable authority about the political aspects of the First Hague Peace Conference. Its origins must be sought in the growing movements for peace and
disarmament which marked the last decade of the century. There had been,
especially in England and America, an impressive " peace crusade " in the years
of the mid-century, a movement typical of the humanitarian ideas of that period.
Less was heard of peace in the stormy decades from 1870 to 1890, but the tremendous development of armies and armaments in those years made a revival
of the movement almost inevitable. There was, on many sides, a feeling that,
apart from the horrors of war itself, the cost of preparation for war was so
enormous that sufficient funds could no longer be found for urgent social
reforms. With the organization of the Interparliamentary Union in 1889 the
demand for action, especially the demand for the extension of international
arbitration, became a regular thing. The modern movement for peace may be
said to date roughly from that time. [2]

---

[1] I quote from the preface of Andrew D. White: *The First Hague Conference* (Boston, 1912),
which is a reprint of part of White's *Autobiography,* issued by the World Peace Foundation.

[2] The literature on the history of the peace movement is still pathetically inadequate. The best
single treatment seems to me to be Christian L. Lange: " Histoire de la Doctrine Pacifique et de son
Influence sur le Développement du Droit International " (*Académie de Droit International, Recueil*

Considering the financial strain of modern armament, it is not to be wondered at that European statesmen turned their attention to the problem. One of the most cynical and disillusioned of them, Lord Salisbury, appears to have had the matter at heart for some time. He is said to have had a memorandum worked out in 1888, and on various occasions he warned Europe of the danger in his Guild Hall speeches, notably in November 1897. Lord Rosebery, who prided himself on the continuance of Salisbury's policies when the Liberals were in power, shared the convictions of the older statesman in this matter. In April 1894 a conference of the representatives of all the Free Churches in London drew up a memorial asking the government to take the initiative in bringing the matter before the powers. Many religious leaders and many heads of labor organizations signed the memorial, to say nothing of eighty members of parliament. When presented to Lord Rosebery, at that time prime minister, it bore no less than 35,000 signatures.[3]

Rosebery appears to have taken the matter up without delay, for he began conversations with the Russian ambassador, M. de Staal, suggesting that Alexander III, as the greatest guarantor of peace in Europe, should summon an international conference to discuss the question of limitation or reduction of armaments. The English army, he pointed out, was too small to allow England to speak authoritatively. We do not know what the Russian reply to these proposals was, but it is clear from the marginal notes of Alexander III that, much as he desired peace, he regarded the suggestion as somewhat utopian and suspected that the advances of Rosebery were designed to drive a wedge into the newly formed Franco-Russian Alliance. " Only England," he noted, " would benefit, for her army is insignificant while her navy is powerful, and England would never consider a reduction of her fleet." [4]

The question of limitation of armaments came up again in Russian official circles in the spring of 1898. On March 13 the minister of war, General Kuropatkin, spoke to the Tsar and wrote to the foreign minister, Count Muraviev, of the difficulties presented by the introduction of rapid-firing field artillery in the German army (the French had adopted the famous 75 mm. piece in 1896). The new German guns, Kuropatkin pointed out, could fire six shells per minute, compared with the single shell per minute fired by the Russian. This situation

des Cours, XIII, 1926, pp. 175–422), especially pp. 389 ff.; see also his *Die Interparlamentarische Union und die Entwicklung des Völkerrechts* (Kiel, 1927). Much may be learned, too, from G. Olphe-Galliard: *La Morale des Nations* (Paris, 1920); Alfred H. Fried: *Handbuch der Friedensbewegung* (Leipzig, 1911), and Hans Wehberg: *Die Internationale Beschränkung der Rüstungen* (Stuttgart, 1919), part A. A good general survey is Arthur C. F. Beales: *The History of Peace* (New York, 1931).

[3] William T. Stead, in the *Review of Reviews,* September 15, 1898, pp. 293–7; Frederic Whyte: *The Life of William T. Stead* (New York, n.d.), II, pp. 122 ff.

[4] Stead, loc. cit., discusses Rosebery's advances to Russia, and claims that the outbreak of war between China and Japan, followed by the death of Alexander, put an end to the discussion. The correspondence may now be found in A. Meyendorff: *Correspondance Diplomatique de M. de Staal* (Paris, 1929), II, pp. 241–9, and the Tsar's comments are given in L. Teleshev: " K Istorii Pervoi Gaagskoi Konferentsii " (*Krasnyi Arkhiv,* L–LI, 1932, pp. 64–96), pp. 74 ff.

led the general to point out that the race for armaments had reached an unprecedented and phantastic stage, which could end only in war or in a move for limitation. The moment seemed to him opportune for approaching the Austrian government, which was faced with the same problem and which, like the Russian, was hard up for funds. Each country saw before it the prospect of introducing a new weapon at the cost of some fifty million dollars, only to see it antiquated before many years had passed. He therefore suggested an agreement with Austria providing that for ten years neither would introduce a rapid-firing field piece.

It is said that Count Witte, the Russian finance minister, refused to assign the funds necessary for the introduction of the new weapon and that he was the driving force behind the idea of a general conference to check competitive armaments for a given period. Witte makes this claim himself and foreign diplomats at the time suspected that the real reason for the Tsar's generous gesture was to be found in the finance minister's inability to raise the money for further equipment.[5]

In any event, the foreign minister took up the idea with some enthusiasm. He thought of drawing all the continental powers together in a ten-year holiday, and contemplated with glee the resulting isolation of England. In a memorandum dated April 5 he recapitulated the arguments in favor of limitation of armaments and pointed out that Austria could not be expected to make a separate agreement without Germany. On the other hand it was fairly certain that a proposal for general international action would meet with the support of both Austria and Italy. England and France would probably be sympathetic. Muraviev therefore suggested a conference to discuss, not so much limitation of armaments, which would be difficult to control, but limitation of forces and of budgets, and furthermore an agreement to settle international disputes by arbitration rather than by war. The moment, he pointed out, was peculiarly favorable for Russia, inasmuch as she had just acquired her port in the Far East and an agreement not to increase forces would leave Russia her great preponderance.[6]

This memorandum, which appears to have been the work of M. Basily, an official of the foreign office who was genuinely interested in the cause of disarmament and peace, seems to have been approved by the Tsar, who gave instructions to draw up a suitable note for submission to the powers. But for unknown reasons there was considerable delay. It was only in July that the Tsar

[5] E. J. Dillon: *The Eclipse of Russia* (London, 1918), pp. 269 ff.; *The Memoirs of Count Witte* (New York, 1921), pp. 96–7; *Die Grosse Politik*, XV, nos. 4216, 4232, 4251; *British Documents on the Origins of the War*, I, nos. 263, 271. The whole matter is discussed in some detail in August Junk: *Die Mächte auf der Ersten Haager Friedenskonferenz* (Leipzig, 1928), pp. 2–13.

[6] Teleshev, op. cit., pp. 74 ff.; Idem: " Noviye Materialy o Gaagskoi Mirnoi Konferentsii 1899 g." (*Krasnyi Arkhiv*, LIV–V, 1932, pp. 49–79), pp. 55–6. This and other documents in the Teleshev articles have been translated into German and published in the *Berliner Monatshefte*, June, 1933, pp. 571–80; July, 1933, pp. 679–92; April, 1934, pp. 320–32.

showed Kuropatkin the draft of a note suggesting a conference, which had been worked out in the foreign office. There would seem to have been some opposition to the scheme in the foreign office itself.[7] It may be that Basily and one of his colleagues, Priklonsky, brought about a favorable decision. These two gentlemen had both been stationed at Budapest in 1896 during the meeting of the Interparliamentary Union, and the latter had at that time drawn up a memorandum which he exhumed in 1898 and which is said to have influenced Lamsdorff and Muraviev.[8] The better known story has it that the Tsar was so impressed by the great six-volume book on war by Ivan Bloch, which appeared at this time, that he took the initiative. Witte always denied quite stoutly that Bloch had anything to do with it, and I think we may assume that if he did have influence it must have been indirect and secondary. The Russian materials which we now have show conclusively that sentiment had very little to do with the formulation of the Russian policy.[9]

I should like to suggest that in the consideration of the origins of the peace manifesto of August 24, 1898 some thought should be given to the importance of the international situation at that time. Russia had become involved in a serious dispute with England regarding the control of certain Chinese railways. The whole matter will have to be discussed in greater detail later, in connexion with the development of the general Far Eastern problem, but it may be remarked here that the tension had reached such a point that on August 18 the British ambassador at St. Petersburg told Muraviev that refusal to yield might "lead to serious international complications." The Russians were distinctly frightened by the strong stand taken by the British, and obviously feared an attack in the Far East which might jeopardize all the gains made in past years. Muraviev therefore raised the question whether it would not be wiser to seek an agreement with the British, whereupon the Tsar commented: "Peace is more important than anything else, unless our honor is touched."[10]

It was probably to counteract the danger of a clash in the Far East that the Imperial communication was handed to the representatives of foreign powers

[7] W. T. Stead: *La Chronique de la Conférence de la Haye* (The Hague, 1899), p. 8, and the apparently trustworthy account of Komarov, one of the officials of the foreign office, as given in *Die Grosse Politik*, XV, no. 4350.

[8] M. Priklonsky: "Die Vorgeschichte der Ersten Haager Friedenskonferenz" (*Friedenswarte*, May, 1929, pp. 129 ff.); this is the explanation which Hans Wehberg says was given him by several high officials of the Russian foreign office; see his *Die Internationale Beschränkung der Rüstungen*, pp. 173 ff.; his statement in *Das Werk des Untersuchungsausschusses der Verfassunggebenden Deutschen Nationalversammlung*, Series I, vol. V (Berlin, 1929), pp. 5–6; and his most recent essay: "La Contribution des Conférences de la Paix de la Haye au Progrès du Droit International" (*Académie de Droit International, Recueil des Cours*, XXXVII, 1931, pp. 533–669), pp. 544–6.

[9] Bertha von Suttner: *Die Haager Friedenskonferenzen, Tagebuchblätter* (Leipzig, 1901), p. 19, and Alfred H. Fried: *Handbuch der Friedensbewegung*, II, pp. 134 ff., as well as Komarov (*Die Grosse Politik*, XV, no. 4350) asserted the importance of Bloch, who was said to have been received at this time by the Tsar. Witte's denial in *Die Grosse Politik*, XV, no. 4251, and in his *Memoirs*.

[10] Teleshev: "K Istorii Pervoi Gaagskoi Konferentsii" (loc. cit.), p. 67; A. Popov: "Anglo-Russkoe Soglashenie o Razdele Kitaiia, 1899 g." (*Krasnyi Arkhiv*, XXV, 1927, pp. 111–34), pp. 120–1.

at St. Petersburg on August 24, 1898. The document itself was couched in the most general terms. It reviewed the growth of the desire for peace and the military preparations that had been made to ensure it. Despite their great cost, armaments had not given the desired security:

> " Hundreds of millions are devoted to acquiring terrible engines of destruction which, though to-day regarded as the last word of science, are destined to-morrow to lose all value in consequence of some fresh discovery in the same field. . . . The economic crises, due in great part to the system of armaments *à outrance,* and the continual danger which lies in this massing of war material, are transforming the armed peace of our days into a crushing burden, which the peoples have more and more difficulty in bearing. It appears evident then that if this state of things were prolonged it would inevitably lead to the very cataclysm which it is desired to avert, and the horrors of which make every thinking man shudder in advance."

The Tsar therefore proposed the meeting of a conference to occupy itself with this grave problem.

Nicholas could not have devised a move better calculated to dumbfound the diplomatic and political circles of Europe. His manifesto struck his French allies like a thunderbolt. They had not been consulted in the matter and feared from the outset that a peace conference might end in a reaffirmation of the peace as fixed by the Treaty of Frankfurt. The stock of the Franco-Russian Alliance had already reached a very low point, and popular dissatisfaction was openly expressed in the newspapers. The *Temps,* generally regarded as the mouthpiece of the foreign office, wrote: " Until the injustice of 1871 has been rectified, until France has re-established the past at the risk of her very existence, until she has assured the future, the true heirs of the Revolution cannot subscribe to the principles of Count Muraviev." The *Autorité* was even more bitter: " The initiative of the Tsar leads to the saddest consequences for France and deprives her of the last hopes. We did not go to St. Petersburg to accept a policy of resignation. We do not need to go to that capital in order to lay down our arms. Berlin has for a long time desired nothing better than to do business with us on that basis." [11]

Delcassé himself made no secret of his disillusionment. He told the Russian ambassador that France would follow the Tsar's lead as soon as a definite program for the conference were submitted. France, he said, had carefully observed the Treaty of Frankfurt, despite her feelings about it. Thereby she had clearly shown her love of peace. To demand more of her would be unjust. France could not recognize anew or approve the theft of her territory, for which she still suffered. It was only after Muraviev had assured the French ambassador at St.

[11] Quoted by Junk, op. cit., p. 25. For the French attitude see further Nicolas Notovitch: *La Pacification de l'Europe* (Paris, 1899), especially chap. iii; Sir Thomas Barclay: *Thirty Years* (Boston, 1914), p. 149; *Die Grosse Politik,* XV, nos. 4227, 4230, 4231; *British Documents,* I, no. 262; and the Belgian reports in *Zur Europäischen Politik* (Berlin, 1919), I, pp. 35–6.

Petersburg that the Russians had no thought of disarming but only of limiting armaments, and that political questions would not be raised in any form at the conference that Delcassé declared himself satisfied.

Even then it appeared to the Russian authorities desirable to placate the Paris government. Kuropatkin and Muraviev as well as Witte visited the French capital in October, at the very height of the Fashoda crisis. The Russian war minister found military circles in Paris very dejected. After twenty-seven years of effort in armaments they saw themselves before the possibility of losing everything, even their hopes for the ultimate recovery of the lost provinces. Military men even began to doubt the permanence of the convention with Russia of 1893. It took no small effort to convince them that the French had not been consulted simply because that would have given the proposal the appearance of a Franco-Russian program, which the powers of the Triple Alliance would have rejected out of hand. Russia, insisted Kuropatkin, had no thought of jeopardizing the alliance with France, of reaffirming the Treaty of Frankfurt, or of interfering with French armaments past or present. The French were ultimately satisfied that the whole scheme was quite innocuous, but President Faure closed his conversation with the Russian war minister with the remark: "We French have our own problems and the conference will naturally not aim at disturbing us in the solution of these problems." [12]

It was perfectly clear from the outset that the Russian proposal would fall flat unless Germany, the most powerful continental state, agreed to participate in the work of the conference. The Tsar therefore appealed specially to his friend the Kaiser for support. William was quite ready to recognize the benevolent intentions of his younger colleague, but regarded the whole business as pure Utopia. For years, he noted, Russia had been piling armaments on armaments, and had been building railways for purely strategical purposes. Recently she had embarked upon a great naval construction program. And all this time the country had been suffering from crop failure, famine and disease. Now that Russia no longer found it possible to borrow money in Paris her finances were giving out and she was anxious to stop other powers from getting ahead of her in a military way.

This estimate was more accurate and more fair than perhaps even the Emperor realized. It did not, however, determine the German attitude. Both the Emperor and Bülow were eager not to estrange Russia. They did not want to serve as the shoal on which the Russian project should be wrecked, but hoped that the opposition of the English would serve that purpose. William therefore replied at once to Nicholas' appeal, complimenting the Tsar on his love of mankind, declaring that " honour will henceforth be lavished upon you by the whole world, even should the practical part fail through the difficulties of the detail,"

---

[12] The documents are printed by Teleshev: " K Istorii Pervoi Gaagskoi Konferentsii," pp. 80–9. On Muraviev's conversations there is no material beyond the account which he gave shortly afterward to the German ambassador at Vienna (*Die Grosse Politik*, XV, no. 4231).

and promising that the German government would give the matter its most serious attention.[13]

Of the official British response to the peace rescript little can be said. Balfour, who was acting as foreign minister in Salisbury's absence, gave vague assurances of sympathy, but it was not until late in October that the English government officially agreed to attend the conference. The foreign office first assured itself that no current political issues, like the Chinese or Egyptian questions, would be raised. Salisbury, indeed, made it clear to the German ambassador that he regarded the whole program as "not serious." Even if there were a limitation of armament it would be practically impossible to ensure its enforcement.[14]

English public opinion was distinctly divided. The tradition of humanitarianism and peace was strongly rooted in the country. Several churchmen, a number of prominent Liberal leaders, and the Trade Union Congress came out in favor of the peace program almost at once. William T. Stead, the well-known editor of the *Review of Reviews,* who incidentally might be described as the father of modern British naval programs because of his great agitation in 1884, at once championed the good cause. He was an almost fanatical Russophil as well as a lover of peace, and threw himself wholeheartedly into the organization of a great "peace crusade." In the autumn of 1898 he made a tour of the European capitals and was received by the Tsar at Livadia. Nothing much came of the Peace Crusade, as Stead himself had to admit that opinion on the Continent was not prepared for it. In England however a goodly number of town meetings were held. The churches and the labor organizations generally backed the movement.[15]

While Stead tried to mobilize British opinion through an elaborate campaign of agitation, a great many leaders of political thought remained aloof. There was in England a good deal of resentment and suspicion of Russia, especially over Far Eastern affairs. The Tsar's appeal was described in some of the leading journals as pure hypocrisy and as a rather thinly veiled ruse by which Russia hoped to gain time to prepare herself better. Some writers were not at all sure that armaments were ruining Europe (they pointed to the prosperity of Germany and France), and others were by no means convinced that war was necessarily or always an evil. It would be as wrong to ignore the strong militaristic streak in England as to attempt to deny the force of the pacifist current.[16]

[13] *Die Grosse Politik,* XV, nos. 4216–22.

[14] *Die Grosse Politik,* XV, nos. 4220, 4237.

[15] The story may be followed in the files of the *Review of Reviews* for the autumn of 1898 and the spring of 1899, but see further Whyte: *Life of Stead,* II, pp. 129–50.

[16] William E. H. Lecky, in his *Democracy and Liberty* (New edition, London, 1899) called attention to the growing popularity of conscription and the cult of the military virtues. See further the following articles: Sidney Low: "Should Europe Disarm?" (*Nineteenth Century,* October, 1898); Soldier: "The Tsar's Appeal for Peace" (*Contemporary Review,* October, 1898); Arnold White: "The Tsar's Manifesto" (*National Review,* October, 1898); Sir Henry Howorth: "Plain Words about the Tsar's New Gospel of Peace" (*Nineteenth Century,* February, 1899); Edward Markwick: "Is War an Unnecessary Evil?" (*New Century Review,* February, 1899); Diplomaticus:

Enough has been said, without going into further detail, to show that the idealism and love of mankind with which Nicholas II was credited played little if any part in the elaboration of the famous peace rescript. The document sprang from decidedly realistic and practical needs of the Russian government. It struck the world with amazement and bewilderment. There were, of course, plenty of people, including statesmen, who saw the dangers of the armed peace, but very few of them considered limitation of armaments feasible, and there was, from the very outset, widespread suspicion of Russia's motives — fear of a political ruse, dread of the raising of political issues and apprehension lest the conference might result in a general conflict rather than in the guarantee of peace.

The Russian statesmen themselves seem to have had little hope of realizing their plans. The great Fashoda crisis led to a violent outburst of bellicosity in England and to naval preparations on an unprecedented scale. It was generally assumed in Europe that war would break out before the end of the year. It was, indeed, an inauspicious moment to talk of limitation of armaments or of international action for peace. In view of this situation Muraviev all but decided to send out a circular asking whether the powers considered the time opportune for a conference, but a sympathetic reference in the German Emperor's speech from the throne in December made it seem desirable to reconsider the decision. The Russians were anxious lest the Germans go over entirely to the British side or join an English-American-Japanese coalition for Far Eastern action. Witte expatiated to the German ambassador on the folly of the continental states in arming against each other, while England was steadily enlarging her fleet, " the only important weapon for future world domination." The sensible thing to do, he argued, would be for Europe to suspend land armaments and save its money for naval construction. Muraviev therefore decided to arrange a conference of ambassadors at St. Petersburg to discuss the opportuneness of a larger meeting and the elaboration of a program. His memorandum shows how cynical was the Russian attitude in the whole matter. Muraviev expected a number of powers to refuse, and reckoned that such refusal would be of political advantage to Russia. England would be unwilling to consider limitation of naval armament, while the United States would insist on increasing its army. The exposure of this egotistic and dangerous policy of England and of America would make public opinion see where the shoe rubbed. It would, further, sharpen the feeling of solidarity among the continental powers in opposition to the naval supremacy of the Anglo-Saxons, and would create for Russia an enviable position between the two camps.[17]

" The Vanishing of Universal Peace " (*Fortnightly Review*, May, 1899); Sidney Low: " The Hypocrisies of the Peace Conference " (*Nineteenth Century*, May, 1899).

[17] Teleshev: " K Istorii Pervoi Gaagskoi Konferentsii," pp. 89–96; see also his article " Anglo-Germanskoe Sblishenie v 1898 g." (*Krasnyi Arkhiv*, LVI, 1933, pp. 65–79), pp. 77–9; Witte's conversation with Radolin in *Die Grosse Politik*, XV, no. 4232.

Muraviev's circular was presented to the representatives of the powers on January 11, 1899. It pointed out that "notwithstanding the strong current of opinion which exists in favor of the ideas of general pacification, the political horizon has recently undergone a change," and that "several powers have undertaken fresh armaments, striving to increase further their military forces." The question was asked whether the powers considered the time opportune for discussion. If so, they were invited to a preliminary exchange of views. The objects of the prospective conference were to be those of "seeking without delay means for putting a stop to the progressive increase of military and naval armaments, a question the solution of which becomes evidently more and more urgent in view of the fresh extension given to these armaments;" and of "preparing the way for the discussion of the questions relating to the possibility of preventing armed conflicts by the pacific means at the disposal of international diplomacy." There were other proposals for the humanizing of warfare, such as the prohibition of new and more deadly explosives and of the submarine, and the extension of the provisions of the Geneva Convention.

These proposals were, of course, purely tentative. The powers agreed to talk the situation over, and it was finally arranged to hold a conference at The Hague. The meeting opened on the Tsar's birthday, May 18, and remained in session until July 29. Representatives of twenty-six powers were present. They were a motley crew, composed almost exclusively of old and hardened diplomats, of decidedly realistic military and naval men, and of technical experts in international law. The head of the Russian delegation was M. de Staal, the ambassador at London, a suave and none too intelligent octogenarian who knew little of parliamentary procedure, but who was, nevertheless, named president of the meeting out of deference for the Tsar. M. de Martens, the Russian legal expert, was a man of world reputation who was undoubtedly devoted to the furtherance of international law. The Germans were represented by Count Münster, another octogenarian, who regarded the whole business with something akin to hatred and expected nothing good to come of it. The German military expert was Colonel Schwarzhoff, an able man with unbounded confidence in the strength of armies. The Germans sent also two international lawyers, of whom one, Freiherr von Stengel, had distinguished himself by publishing a pamphlet entitled *Perpetual Peace,* in which he pointed out that the Bible supported the idea that war is an integral part of the divine order, that war has immense cultural value, that armaments do not ruin a nation, and that eternal peace is impossible.[18]

Passing over the representatives of Austria and Italy, who played no prominent rôle at the Conference, a few words may be said of the delegates of France, England and the United States. The French government showed itself extremely clever in the selection of its men. At the head of the delegation was Léon Bourgeois, former prime minister and radical, who posed as a great and

---

[18] Freiherr Karl von Stengel: *Der Ewige Friede* (1898).

whole-hearted exponent of international co-operation, though later he was to show himself as uncompromising as any Frenchman in matters of security. The second representative was Baron d'Estournelles de Constant, brilliant young descendant of Benjamin Constant, outstanding advocate of an entente with England and genuinely devoted to the cause of international understanding. England sent Sir Julian Pauncefote, the ambassador at Washington, a man who had taken a leading part in the drafting of an arbitration treaty with the United States and who was one of the outstanding exponents of that method of settling international disputes. The experts were Sir John Ardagh, whose views did not differ substantially from those of Schwarzhoff, and Sir John Fisher, a fire-eating admiral who made no bones about declaring *urbe et orbe* that in his view might was right, arbitration or no arbitration. The United States was represented by Andrew D. White, ambassador at Berlin, like Sir Julian Pauncefote a believer in arbitration and a man anxious to make the best of the Conference. As naval expert the American government sent Captain Mahan, world-famous author of *The Influence of Sea Power*, a man with little if any sympathy with the aims of the Conference.[19]

It cannot be said that the meeting opened auspiciously. Some of the older diplomats felt outraged at being sent to what they regarded as a farce and at having to end their careers on a fruitless errand. "Probably, since the world began, never has so large a body come together in a spirit of more hopeless skepticism as to any good result," wrote Andrew White in his diary on May 17. It was perfectly obvious, even to the most optimistic, that reduction or even limitation of armaments was out of the question, and that the most one could hope for was some further regulation of the methods of warfare and perhaps some progress towards establishing a recognized system of arbitration.

As a matter of fact no serious move was made in the armaments question after the German military expert, Colonel Schwarzhoff, had set forth the difficulties of the subject. The other representatives joined in expressing a pious wish that eventually something might be done and therewith the problem was dismissed. Better results were obtained in the regulation of warfare — the prohibition for five years of the use of projectiles thrown from balloons, prohibition of gas warfare and dum-dum bullets, extension of the Red Cross convention to naval warfare, the definition of belligerency, provisions for the better treatment of war prisoners and of the sick and wounded, etc., etc. But ultimately the work of the Conference centred upon the discussion of a so-called permanent court of arbitration. In this matter Sir Julian Pauncefote took a leading part. Questions of national vital interest and honor were, by general consent, ex-

---

[19] The delegates to the Conference and their attitudes are reflected in *Die Grosse Politik*, passim, and in the writings of the participants, notably Andrew D. White: *The First Hague Conference* (Boston, 1912); *Heinrich Lammasch: Seine Aufzeichnungen, sein Wirken und seine Politik* (Vienna, 1922), and in the narratives of W. T. Stead: *La Chronique de la Conférence de la Haye* (The Hague, 1901), and Bertha von Suttner: *Die Haager Friedenskonferenz* (Leipzig, 1901). See further August Junk: *Die Mächte auf der Ersten Haager Friedenskonferenz* (Leipzig, 1928), pp. 37–43.

cluded from the application of the system, but it was proposed to make arbitration compulsory in certain disputes of minor importance. The Germans in particular opposed both compulsory arbitration and the erection of a permanent body of arbitrators. As Münster explained to White, arbitration would be injurious to Germany, for Germany was prepared as no other country could be. She could mobilize in ten days. Arbitration would simply give rival powers time to put themselves in readiness and would therefore be a great disadvantage to Germany.[20]

In the end the idea of compulsory arbitration was completely abandoned, but the German government was finally persuaded by Münster himself that the permanent court must be accepted if Germany wished to avoid blame for the failure of the Conference and the resentment of the Tsar. It is unnecessary to go into all the details, which have been thoroughly analyzed in many other works. Suffice it to say that Holstein was unalterably opposed to the whole arbitration program and handed in his resignation when Bülow and the Emperor finally decided to give in for political reasons.[21]

The importance of the first Hague Peace Conference lay not so much in *what* it actually accomplished as in the fact that that it accomplished *something* and that it set a precedent for future meetings. The greater part of its achievement dealt not with peace, but with war, and no one knew whether even the new regulations for warfare would be observed in the heat of conflict. The question of limitation of armaments had made no progress whatever and the permanent court of arbitration was as innocuous as one could imagine. Earlier opinions of the work done were not very enthusiastic, and it was only later, when the second Conference met in 1907, that the realization gradually spread that in 1899 the first step had been taken in the direction of international organization.[22]

Politically the Conference was of no importance. It had no bearing on current political problems and it did not in any way affect the relations of the powers to each other. It was, in fact, distinctly a side show. Only one power may be said to have suffered from it, and that power was Germany. The strong stand taken by the German delegation in the matter of limitation of armaments and the German opposition to the perfectly harmless permanent court was heavily underlined by unfriendly journalists like Stead and later supplied useful ammunition for the campaign of defamation waged in the immediate pre-war and world-war periods. As we see it now, the German attitude in 1899 did not

---

20 White, op. cit., p. 19.

21 *Friedrich von Holstein's Lebensbekenntnis in Briefen an eine Frau* (Berlin, 1932), pp. 194–5; on Holstein's attitude see further *Die Grosse Politik*, XV, nos. 4312; Philipp Zorn: " Zur Geschichte der Ersten Haager Friedenskonferenz " (*Archiv für Politik und Geschichte*, October, 1924, pp. 285–306), p. 298.

22 Early opinions are well summarized in Otfried Nippold: *Die Fortbildung des Verfahrens in Völkerrechtlichen Streitigkeiten* (Leipzig, 1907), pp. 94 ff.; see also Walther Schücking: *Der Staatenverband der Haager Konferenzen* (Munich, 1912), pp. 21 ff.

differ materially from the attitude of most of the other powers. It was tactless of the Germans to take the lead in disposing of the armaments question, and it was a serious political and psychological error to make a great issue of a board of arbitration which had no real power. The German attitude was a perfectly honorable one; the German objections were honest objections, and even though the Germans had no faith in the Conference or anything connected with it, they tried to play the game, if only to please the Tsar. One might almost say that they were too honest. They said what others thought, and thereby assumed the odium which other powers were only too eager to avoid. This is now generally recognized by German writers themselves.[23]

So far as European alignments were concerned, the situation remained as amorphous in 1899 as it had been in the previous years. Speaking to the German ambassador in the spring of the year Lord Salisbury remarked that the day of alliances was over. International relations had become a matter of agreements between states with common or at least non-contradictory interests. Count Hatzfeldt rejected this argumentation, but as one looks back on the situation it is clear that the British premier was the more nearly right.[24] The old alliances had pretty much disintegrated, and the day of business deals had arrived.

Take the Triple Alliance, for instance. If Austria had been attacked by Russia, there is no doubt that Germany would have supported her ally in 1899 as she would have done in 1879. Still, the Triple Alliance had been languishing for years. It was not really to be resuscitated until the days of Aehrenthal. In 1899 it lacked an immediate *raison d'être*. Russia, deeply engaged in the Far East, was not hostile to Austria. In fact the two powers had made an agreement in 1897 to preserve the status quo in the Balkans. Not only that: the Germans and the Austrians were by no means cordially friendly to each other, as they had been in the days of Bismarck and Andrássy. The Hapsburg Monarchy was racked by internal crises of the most dangerous sort. The Emperor Francis Joseph was getting old, and his demise was expected in the none-too-distant future. The Slavic elements in the empire had come to play an ever more decisive rôle and the Vienna government had fallen largely under Czech influences. The Czech nationalists, however, were outspokenly hostile to Germany and to the Triple Alliance. Kramarsch, one of the Czech leaders, declared in so many words that the famous alliance was a " played-out piano," and uttered the warning that if Pan-Germanism actually became a threat to Austria's national existence, it would have to be checked by other powers.[25] This article

[23] E.g. by Zorn, op. cit.; by most of the experts who testified before the post-war parliamentary commission of inquiry (*Das Werk des Untersuchungsausschusses der Verfassunggebenden Deutschen Nationalversammlung*, Series I, vol. V, Berlin, 1929, passim); by Junk, op. cit.; A Fonck: " Deutschlands Haltung zur Abrüstungsfrage auf der Friedenskonferenz im Haag 1899 " (*Berliner Monatshefte*, November, 1929, pp. 1091–5); Egon Gottschalk: " Deutschlands Haltung auf den Haager Friedenskonferenzen " (ibid., May, 1930, pp. 447–56).   [24] *Die Grosse Politik*, XIV, no. 4044.
[25] K. Kramarsch: " L'Avenir de l'Autriche " (*Revue de Paris*, February 1, 1899).

was regarded in Berlin as nothing less than a direct provocation. There had been a good deal of friction between the two allies in December 1898 and the tension continued until the fall of Count Thun's ministry in October 1899. During this period there was good reason to doubt not only the continuance of the German-Austrian Alliance, but of the Hapsburg monarchy itself.[26]

Italy, too, was no longer to be counted upon as in the days of Crispi. The disaster at Adua had ushered in a period of acute domestic unrest, which culminated in the famous May Days of Milan in 1898. By many observers it was thought that the Savoy monarchy was approaching its last days, and that the republican factions would soon be in the ascendant. It was widely felt that Germany was responsible for the crushing burden of Italian armaments, for the extravagant policy of Crispi, and for the disastrous hostility of France. The irredentism of the republicans was stimulated by the uncertainty of Austrian affairs and by the forward policy of the Slavic elements.[27] Furthermore, Pope Leo XIII was old and ill. His secretary of state, Cardinal Rampolla, was notoriously anti-German and pro-French. It was always feared at Rome that the French government, working with the Papacy, was encouraging the republican agitation and undermining the monarchy.[28]

Since Crispi's fall the Italian government had set itself definitely to effect a rapprochement with France. The estrangement of England and Germany after the Kruger telegram episode undoubtedly had much to do with this, for it was obvious that Italy, for geographical reasons, could not afford to join in an anti-British policy. This point has been made by practically all writers of pre-war diplomacy, but it does not cover the whole situation by any means. In the last years of the century the hostility between England and France was so great that for Italy to give up Germany to join France was like jumping from the frying-pan into the fire so far as relations with England were concerned. The Italians had to seek a rapprochement with France because they could not hope to stand out against French pressure, political and commercial. Their problem was to improve relations with France without antagonizing Germany and without estranging England.

The accomplishment of this difficult task was the work of Marchese di Rudini, the prime minister, and of Visconti-Venosta, the foreign minister. Signor Luzzatti, the minister of finance, was an able and determined assistant. The policy was embarked upon at once and bore its first fruits in the French-

---

[26] See especially the documents in *Die Grosse Politik,* XIII, chap. lxxxvii; Johannes Haller: *Philip Eulenburg* (New York, 1930), II, pp. 76–80; and the monographic study of Wolfgang Rudert: *Die Stellung des Deutschen Reiches zur Inner-Oesterreichischen Lage . . . 1890–1900* (Leipzig, 1931).

[27] See especially the letter of Monts to Holstein, in *Erinnerungen und Gedanken des Botschafters Anton Graf Monts* (Berlin, 1932), pp. 387 ff.

[28] There are some highly interesting letters on conditions at the Vatican in Hohenlohe: *Denkwürdigkeiten der Reichskanzlerzeit,* pp. 182 ff., 404 ff., 491 ff. See also G. M. Fiamingo: " Die Politik Leos XIII und seine Diplomatie " (*Deutsche Revue,* June, 1898, pp. 280–90).

Italian agreement regarding Tunis, which has already been discussed. It will be recalled that in this agreement the Italians made the concessions in order to win the good will of France. The next step was to be a commercial treaty to put an end to the disastrous tariff war which had been going on since 1886, and perhaps after that a political understanding. Of course, the whole policy presupposed a willingness on the part of the French to make up with the Italians. For years they had been devoting themselves to the task of forcing the Italians out of the Triple Alliance by economic and political pressure. Crispi claimed that as late as the end of 1895 Bourgeois told an Italian politician that no commercial agreement would be possible so long as Italy remained in the Triple Alliance.[29]

Crispi's fall undoubtedly helped to ease the situation, for he was the favorite aversion of the French. But the French ambassador at Rome, M. Albert Billot, had, so he says, been arguing for some time that it was futile to continue on the old tack, and that the wise thing would be to seek a rapprochement which would create new interests in Italy more favorable to France.[30] At any rate, the Italian government began to take soundings for a tariff treaty almost immediately after the conclusion of the Tunis Convention in 1896. Official pourparlers were opened in the summer of 1897, but it turned out that the French government, which was highly protectionist, was unwilling to consider concessions in the matter of silk or wine imports. The terms offered Italy were hard ones. Negotiations dragged on, and were finally postponed till after the French elections of May 1898. The fall of the Méline cabinet in June 1898 and the downfall of Rudini in the following month probably served to delay matters further, though the new governments in both countries were anxious to conclude an arrangement. Finally in October 1898 Luzzatti came to Paris and the details were worked out satisfactorily in a very short time. On November 21, 1898 the agreement was signed. The essential point was that it established most-favored-nation treatment on both sides, with some exceptions to protect French " silk and wine interests." [31]

The French-Italian commercial settlement of 1898 has been regarded quite rightly as the beginning of that change of Italian policy which ended in the agreements of 1900 and 1902 and ultimately in Italy's neutrality in 1914. It has often been described as the first great triumph of Delcassé and the first step in the progressive isolation of Germany. This is undoubtedly an exaggeration. Delcassé and the famous French ambassador at Rome, Barrère, had nothing to

---

[29] Francesco Crispi: " L'Accordo Franco-Italiano " (*Rivista d'Italia*, February 15, 1899, pp. 197–208).

[30] Albert Billot: " Le Rapprochement Commercial entre la France et l'Italie " (*Revue des Deux Mondes*, January 1, 1899, pp. 131–145). This article is much more revealing than the memoirs of Billot, published under the title *La France et l'Italie* (Paris, 1905).

[31] The fullest accounts are those given by Billot in the article mentioned and in his *France et l'Italie*, II, Book III, chap. iv. See also Maximilian Claar: " Die Abkehr Italiens vom Dreibund " (*Europäische Gespräche*, VIII, 1930, pp. 425–39).

do with the initiation of the policy, which was the work of Hanotaux and Billot. If we may believe the latter, substantial agreement had been reached by the end of 1897 when he (Billot) retired from his post and Barrère was appointed. Delcassé, to be sure, was warmly in sympathy with the policy, but there is no evidence that he regarded it at the time as a part of a larger plan. During the debates in the French chamber he carefully avoided any reference to the political implications of the agreement and confined himself to saying that the French should congratulate themselves on now having a friendly people on their frontier.

The Italians, it seems, were much more interested than the French in the political side of the question. Visconti-Venosta was no longer at the foreign office, but he wrote his friend Luzzatti that " political friendship will result from friendly economic relations, and the return of a fatal conflict is made impossible." [32] In the Italian senate, too, he emphasized the important political reactions which the commercial rapprochement was bound to have.[33] But Visconti went much further than authoritative government officials were prepared to go. Admiral Canevaro, the foreign minister, insisted in parliament that Italy remained loyal to the Triple Alliance, and told the British ambassador that he saw no reason why Italy should not take advantage of the advances (!) made by the French. Italy, he went on, was not deceived by them: " The Italian Government was perfectly aware that the object of France, if she could only detach Italy from her allies, would be to proceed, in combination with the Vatican, to bring about troubles in Italy with a view to upsetting the Monarchy and establishing a Republican form of government, which would be more subservient to French influence than the Monarchy." Italy " would under no circumstances make any change in her policy as regarded the Triple Alliance or England." [34]

It is impossible to judge of the sincerity of these utterances. It may be that Canevaro really wanted the agreement for purely economic reasons, but it seems more likely that, in the midst of the Fashoda crisis, he found it necessary to placate the British and avoid suspicion in London. But Anglo-Italian relations were soon exposed to another trial. The Anglo-French agreement on the Sudan of March 21, 1899 was taken in Rome as involving the abandonment of the hinterland of Tripoli to the French and as a disturbance of the status quo on the shores of the Mediterranean. The Italians had long before marked out Tripoli as a future possession, and they were greatly alarmed by what had happened. They tried to get the British government to make a declaration in the Italian sense, and attempted to enlist the assistance of Germany for this purpose. Nothing came of the negotiations, inasmuch as Salisbury refused to bind himself for the future. Delcassé, on the other hand, scored a point by

---

[32] The letter is quoted in Luigi Luzzatti: *God in Freedom* (New York, 1930), pp. 428–9.
[33] Billot: *La France et l'Italie*, II, pp. 450–1.
[34] *British Documents*, I, no. 347.

giving the Italians an unwritten assurance that they had no reason to fear finding France in their way if, eventually, they decided to put forth claims to Tripoli.[85] The upshot of this incident was that the Italians failed to get satisfaction from England and found the aid of the Triple Alliance of little value, while Delcassé could and did embark upon the course that was to lead to the Tripoli-Morocco bargains of the next years.

We have surveyed the relations of the members of the Triple Alliance to each other, and have seen how much altered was the famous international combination of the Bismarckian period. It is important to note that much the same process of disintegration had been taking place in the Franco-Russian Alliance. It will be recalled that the Fashoda crisis and the Tsar's peace rescript had thrown a deep shadow upon the relations of the Republic and the Empire of the Tsar. The French people had become disabused of their ideas of Russian help in recovering the lost provinces. They were frankly sore, and at this time were quite unwilling to sink further funds into Russian securities.

Naturally the French government was obliged to take into account other factors than the uncritical likes and dislikes of the population. The Military Convention with Russia had been concluded for very specific purposes, and the situation in Europe in 1898–1899 was not such that the French government felt free to dispense with the arrangement. The Triple Alliance, to be sure, was not as formidable as it had been, but there was a much sharper antagonism between France and England, and there was never any knowing whether Germany might not join England if it came to a clash. These military questions had been discussed between the French authorities and General Kuropatkin during the latter's visit to Paris in October 1898. It had been agreed on then that the Military Convention should continue as before, and that certain revisions should be made in the number of troops each ally was to contribute in the event of trouble.[36]

In the meanwhile a further problem arose from the crisis in Austria. There was, as aforesaid, general apprehension that the Dual Monarchy might fall to pieces and that, as a result, the Triple Alliance would come to an end. A conflict of nationalities would be inevitable, and it was to be feared that the Berlin government might attempt to annex the German provinces of Austria. In that event a general European war would almost certainly ensue, since Russia would never allow a semi-Slavic area like Bohemia to pass under German rule.[37] The Austrian question, as it developed between 1896 and 1899 had not been envisaged at the time of the conclusion of the Franco-Russian Alliance. In fact the Military Convention, which constituted the really important part of the Alliance, had been timed to last only as long as the Triple Alliance. If Austria were to fall

---

[85] *Die Grosse Politik*, XIV, nos. 3946–57; *British Documents*, I, nos. 246 ff.; see also James L. Glanville: *Italy's Relations with England, 1896–1905* (Baltimore, 1934), chap. vi.

[36] L. Teleshev: "K Istorii Pervoi Gaagskoi Konferentsii 1899 g." (*Krasnyi Arkhiv*, L–LI, 1932, pp. 81–8).   [37] See especially *Die Grosse Politik*, XIII, no. 3539.

apart, the Triple Alliance, and therewith the Franco-Russian Military Convention, would simply disappear. And yet it would be at just that crucial moment that war would be most likely and the Convention most needed. It was to meet this situation that Delcassé paid a sudden, unannounced visit to St. Petersburg early in August 1899. We know next to nothing of the inner history of this move. Who brought Delcassé to a realization of the dangers inherent in the Austrian situation? It is unlikely that men like Chéradame and Henry, who later became active agitators of the question, had anything to do with it, and it seems hardly credible that the Kramarsch article referred to above should have exerted enough influence to bring about an important change in French policy. The explanation is probably this, that the Russians, not the French, were primarily alarmed by the Austrian crisis, and that Delcassé was dragged into the St. Petersburg negotiation. There is at least one bit of evidence which would appear to support this interpretation. Just before his visit to Paris in October 1898 General Kuropatkin had a long talk with Tsar Nicholas. In his diary he noted:

" I developed the idea that we could not do much for the cause of peace until we had occupied the Bosporus. Then we shall have a firm position with relation to all other Slavic states and shall lay the foundation for a federation of the Slavic states between themselves and with us. Then we shall destroy the aim of William II: namely to draw Turkey into an alliance against us, to get control of our frontiers from Erzerum to Polangen, to influence Rumania and get her to join this alliance, and to influence the Slavic states — Serbia and Bulgaria — to preserve their neutrality at the least in the event of a war between the Triple Alliance and the powers of the Dual Alliance, France and Russia. Our appearance on the Bosporus would hasten the collapse of Austria. Then it would be possible to abandon the German territories to Germany and to oblige the latter to return Alsace and Lorraine to France. I explained that in my opinion Germany would not voluntarily do this. Germany's powers of defense are so strong that, even after the collapse of Austria and the formation of a league of the Slavic states which would go hand in hand with Russia and France, an attack on Germany might not be successful. In the last count everything would probably depend on the skill and genius of the commanders on both sides. The suitable moment for an attack will arrive when Germany becomes involved in war with England and America. Such a war is probable in view of the industrial over-production in Germany and the resulting necessity for her to seek new markets." [38]

These extraordinary speculations at least throw some light on what was being discussed in high circles of the Russian court. There is, in this whole period, a great blank in our knowledge. There are constant veiled references to Russian encouragement of a French entente with Germany and in the press no end of talk about the return of Alsace-Lorraine to France in exchange for the French Congo or some other colony. Were the Russians really planning some

[38] L. Teleshev: "Noviye Materialy o Gaagskoi Mirnoi Konferentsii 1899 g." (*Krasnyi Arkhiv*, LIV–LV, 1932, pp. 49–79).

such arrangement as that outlined by Kuropatkin for the event of Austria's collapse? Was Delcassé taken in by this mirage? It will be recalled that he actually took soundings to find out whether the Germans would consider an exchange of Alsace and Lorraine for a French colony.

We cannot answer these questions even now. At the time the diplomatic world was agog at the sudden departure of the foreign minister to the Russian capital. In Paris it was explained that he was merely making a courtesy call. Gallifet, the war minister, told the German ambassador that the whole business was the result of Delcassé's personal vanity: he desired recognition by the Tsar. Of course this kind of talk was not taken seriously. The Germans conjectured that Delcassé was intent on breathing new life into the nearly defunct Franco-Russian Alliance, and suspected that the visit might have some connection with the Dreyfus case or with the approaching crisis in south Africa. The British press, on the other hand, feared that the visit might be a step on the road to a reconciliation between France and Germany and therefore to the formation of a continental coalition.[39]

Nearly all we know for certain of Delcassé's visit has to do with the results. We know that on August 9 he and Muraviev exchanged letters reaffirming the Alliance and extending its scope. The agreement of 1891 had stated that the object of the two powers was the maintenance of peace. To this was now added the maintenance of the balance of power in Europe. At the same time the Military Convention was made coterminous in time with the general agreement, in other words, provision was made that it should be in full force when a crisis arose from the dissolution of the Austrian monarchy.[40]

Since we know nothing of the conversations which accompanied the drafting of these changes it is difficult to appraise them. Radical historians, like Albert Mathiez, felt that Delcassé herewith completed the betrayal of France. He put the forces of France at the disposal of Russia to secure for her a share in the spoils of the Hapsburg possessions, and furthermore put France in a position where she would be bound to oppose the right of self-determination of the Germans in Austria. Not only that: any dislocation of affairs in the Balkans might in future be described as a change in the balance of power in Europe and might therefore involve France in conflict.[41]

I see no reason for questioning this interpretation. Such evidence as we have would seem to show that Delcassé, despite the fact that Russia gave no support in the Fashoda crisis, was so eager to uphold the alliance with Russia that he committed France to a certain course of action in Near Eastern affairs which

---

[39] *Die Grosse Politik*, XIII, nos. 3577, 3578; *Questions Diplomatiques et Coloniales*, August 15, 1899, pp. 498–501, quoting at length from the British press.

[40] *Livre Jaune: L'Alliance Franco-Russe* (Paris, 1918), nos. 93–5.

[41] Mathiez, in the newspaper *L'Internationale*, August 2, 10, 26, 1921, as quoted by Georges Michon: *The Franco-Russian Alliance* (London, 1929), pp. 101–7. Michon's account is a reasonably full one, but see now also Pierre Renouvin: "Les Engagements de l'Alliance Franco-Russe" (*Revue d'Histoire de la Guerre Mondiale*, October, 1934, pp. 297–310), pp. 301 ff.

Hanotaux had always refused to adopt. It is true, of course, as M. Renouvin has pointed out, that the principle of maintaining the balance of power meant that Russia assumed obligations with respect to the Alsace-Lorraine question just as France shouldered certain responsibilities in Balkan affairs. But these obligations, so far as Russia was concerned, were inherent in the alliance from the outset and the French had already had ample opportunity to learn that the Russians did not take them very seriously. In the present state of our knowledge it is hard to see how the results of the St. Petersburg visit can be interpreted as a success for Delcassé's statesmanship. He proclaimed in the Chamber on November 24, 1899 that the alliance with Russia was complete and that " the union was never closer, that the dual alliance made possible far-reaching plans (longs desseins), and that, in order to realize them, there was need of patience, consistency and time."

All this sounded beautiful, but so far as one can see the Alliance continued to be after the visit what it had been before. The French were dissatisfied with it and disappointed. The radical régime, which came into power in France with the ministry of Waldeck-Rousseau in 1899, was not very favorably disposed towards Russia, and during the next years, as revolutionary movements began to develop in opposition to the Tsarist government, there was much agitation against the autocracy on the part of French radicals and socialists. The feeling was widespread at that time that the Alliance was an instrument which militated against the introduction of reform in France itself.[42] It is no exaggeration to say that between 1898 and the Russo-Japanese War the Franco-Russian Alliance reached its nadir. The best political minds in France at that time were already beginning to turn toward the idea of an entente with England. Not until the advent of Poincaré in 1912 was the Alliance to become once again an active and effective combination.

With both the Triple Alliance and the Franco-Russian Alliance more or less in eclipse there continued to be, during 1899, talk of the possibility of a reconciliation between France and Germany and of the ultimate combination of these two countries with Russia to form a counterweight to British naval preponderance. Witte, it will be recalled, expounded this idea at some length to the German ambassador, and used it as an argument for the reduction of expenditure on land armaments by the continental powers.[43] The Spanish government, which in February 1899 agreed to the sale of the Caroline and Mariane Islands to Germany, also tried to further the scheme.[44] There was, of course, something very intriguing about the whole idea, and in a sense all three of the great continental powers were bound together by a certain common antagonism to Great Britain. It appears from the German Emperor's comments on the report of Witte's suggestions, however, that he was no longer interested in the plan.

---

[42] See especially Michon, op. cit., chap. vi, where this argument is well worked out, and extensive quotations from the French press are given.

[43] Die Grosse Politik, XV, no. 4232. [44] Die Grosse Politik, XV, nos. 4205-14.

"Too late, too late!" this was the general sense of his reaction. A few years before, at the time of the Kruger telegram, he had proposed this combination and had been rebuffed by both France and Russia. Since then, German relations with England had improved very decidedly and the Germans had come to appreciate the attractions of the policy of the free hand, which enabled them to play off the British against the French and the Russians. "The powers which could become dangerous for us," wrote Holstein in January 1899, "are at present so taken up by foreign or domestic troubles or with both, that a coalition such as formerly worried Bismarck and Moltke, is no longer thinkable unless one assumes great errors on Germany's part." [45]

This does not mean that the Germans failed to make the most of the friendly advances from Paris and from St. Petersburg. The Emperor was eager to win the good will of the French and was evidently more sanguine on this score than his ministers. In July he paid a visit to the French school ship at Bergen, and then sent to President Loubet a telegram couched in the warmest terms. In August he dedicated a German monument on the battlefield of St. Privat, and took the occasion to honor the valiant French dead who had fought as bravely for their country as the Germans had for theirs. All this made a good impression in France, though naturally it did not wipe out the problem of the lost provinces. As one looks back upon the situation one can easily see that a real reconciliation was impossible so long as the Germans were not prepared to make at least a compromise with regard to Alsace-Lorraine. But there was, clearly, a détente in the relations of Germany and France. These relations were more cordial than they had ever been since the war of 1870. [46]

Relations between Germany and Russia were not so satisfactory. The Germans were anxious to keep on the good side of Russia, but they were suspicious of and nettled by the Tsar's peace move, and personal friction between the Emperor and the Tsar did not help to improve matters. Although the Emperor had visited Nicholas on several occasions during his stays at Darmstadt, the Tsar had never yet paid a visit to Berlin or Potsdam. William now insisted that he would no longer go running after his Russian brother like a satrap. The Tsar was finally persuaded to come to Berlin for half a day in November 1899. The visit went off quite successfully. Nicholas spoke approvingly of the German naval plans and once again emphasized the need for continental sea-power to keep England in check. But at the same time both he and Muraviev referred to German activities in the Near East, which, they felt, were an indirect threat at Russian interests. Efforts had, in fact, been made by the St. Petersburg government to reach some agreement with Germany regarding Russian interests in the Straits. Such an agreement, however, would have identified the Germans too much with Russian policy and would have jeopardized relations with Eng-

---

[45] Monts: *Erinnerungen und Gedanken*, pp. 357–8.

[46] On Franco-German relations see *Die Grosse Politik*, XIII, nos. 3569, 3571 ff., 3581; Bourgeois and Pagès: *Les Origines . . . de la Grande Guerre*, pp. 278–9.

land. The advances of Muraviev were rejected, and the result was a marked cooling in the Russian-German relationship. But this factor must not be over-emphasized. The Russians, so long as they were at daggers drawn with England in the Far East, could not afford to estrange Germany. There was a certain amount of friction and a good deal of mutual suspicion, but on the whole the Germans were successful in their efforts to keep intact the wires to both Paris and St. Petersburg.[47]

Without a clear conception of the status of the great European alliances it would be impossible to follow intelligently the course of diplomacy as the century drew to its close. The peace rescript had been a sort of bomb thrown into an already confused situation. It had no immediate effect on the general alignment of the powers, which was itself anything but clear. It might be said that the situation, so far as the Continent was concerned, was a fluid one. Extra-European activities had completely dislocated the accepted groupings of the powers, which were based upon consideration of European problems. Under these circumstances it would be futile to seek the key to European diplomacy in the history of the alliances. The really important development in the year 1899 had to do with British affairs. The clouds of the coming conflict in south Africa were beginning to cast their shadows over the international scene. England was on the verge of becoming involved in a struggle much more serious and prolonged than anyone could suspect. Her policy had to be shaped to meet this new situation, and the main theme must therefore concern itself with the safeguarding of the British position in Europe, and with the countermoves of Britain's chief rivals, Germany, France and Russia.

BIBLIOGRAPHICAL NOTE

(Account is here taken only of the First Hague Peace Conference, since the other matters dealt with in this chapter are illuminated by the German documents — *Die Grosse Politik der Europäischen Kabinette,* volume XIII and by the *British Documents on the Origins of the War,* volume I).

DOCUMENTARY SOURCES

The Hague Peace Conferences of 1899 and 1907. Edited by James Brown Scott. Two volumes. Baltimore, 1909. The best documentary collection, containing all the debates.

Documents Relating to the Program of the First Hague Peace Conference. Oxford, 1921.

---

[47] For general German-Russian relations see *Die Grosse Politik,* XIII, nos. 3540–8. The problem of the Near East as it affected these relations will be discussed in a later chapter.

Livre Jaune. Conférence Internationale de la Paix. Paris, 1900.

Die Grosse Politik der Europäischen Kabinette, 1871–1914. Volume XV, chapter c. One of the most important documentary sources.

British Documents on the Origins of the War, 1898–1914. Volume I, chapter **vi.** Adds relatively little.

Das Werk des Untersuchungsausschusses der Verfassunggebenden Deutschen Nationalversammlung und des Deutschen Reichstages, 1919–1930. Series I: *Die Vorgeschichte des Weltkrieges.* Volume V, part II: "Deutschland auf den Haager Friedenskonferenzen." Berlin, 1929. This volume contains the studies and opinions of German experts, those of Wehberg, Montgelas and Thimme being the most important. The volume does not include any material of importance that is not to be found in *Die Grosse Politik.*

TELESHEV, L.: "K Istorii Pervoi Gaagskoi Konferentsii 1899 g." (*Krasnyi Arkhiv,* L–LI, 1932, pp. 64–96). "Noviye Materialy o Gaagskoi Mirnoi Konferentsii 1899 g." (ibid., LIV–LV, 1932, pp. 49–79). An absolutely fundamental collection of Russian documents, which had not appeared when Wehberg and other experts wrote their accounts. Some of this material has been translated into German and published in the *Berliner Monatshefte,* June and July, 1933, and April, 1934.

MEMOIRS, AUTOBIOGRAPHIES, BIOGRAPHIES, AND LETTERS

WITTE, SERGIUS: *Memoirs.* Translated by A. Yarmolinsky. New York, 1921. An important, though brief account, in which there is a frank avowal of the Russian policy. Much the same material is given, with somewhat more detail, in the book of Witte's confidant, E. J. Dillon: *The Eclipse of Russia* (London, 1918).

WHITE, ANDREW D.: *The First Hague Conference.* Boston, 1912. This is merely a reprint of the chapters in White's *Autobiography.* Two volumes. New York, 1904. White's account is one of the best and most reliable left by participants.

HOLLS, FREDERICK W.: *The Peace Conference at The Hague.* Boston, 1900. Holls was one of the American representatives. His work is rather a critical study than a volume of personal reminiscences. It is one of the best systematic accounts.

FISHER, LORD: *Memories.* London, 1919. Fisher was the British naval expert. His memoirs contain little of importance.

Heinrich Lammasch. Seine Aufzeichnungen, sein Wirken und seine Politik. Edited by Marga Lammasch and Hans Sperl. Vienna, 1922. Lammasch was one of the Austrian delegates. His reminiscences throw an interesting light on the personalities and activities of the Conference.

SUTTNER, BERTA VON: *Die Haager Friedenskonferenz. Tagebuchblätter.* Dresden, 1901. The recollections of the leading German pacifist. A valuable and interesting account of the Conference.

STEAD, WILLIAM T.: *La Chronique de la Conférence de la Haye*. The Hague, 1901. A valuable account, written by the well-known British journalist and pacifist.

WHYTE, FREDERIC: *The Life of William T. Stead*. Two volumes. New York, n.d. Adds little to Stead's own account, but contains a few unpublished letters.

ZORN, PHILIPP: *Deutschland und die beiden Haager Friedenskonferenzen*. Berlin, 1920. "Zur Geschichte der Ersten Haager Friedenskonferenz." (*Archiv für Politik und Geschichte,* III, 1924, pp. 285–306). Careful studies of German policy, by one of the German delegates.

MOWAT, R. B.: *The Life of Lord Pauncefote*. Boston, 1929. Adds nothing.

SPECIAL STUDIES

HULL, WILLIAM I.: *The Two Hague Conferences, and their Contributions to International Law*. Boston, 1908.

CHOATE, JOSEPH H.: *The Two Hague Conferences*. Princeton, 1913. A series of lectures, of no great importance.

LAPRADELLE, A. DE: "La Question du Désarmement." (*Revue Générale de Droit International Public,* 1899, pp. 651–846). One of the best and most heavily documented contemporary studies.

STENGEL, KARL VON: "Die Haager Friedenskonferenz und das Völkerrecht." (*Archiv für Öffentliches Recht,* 1900, II, 139–201). A careful, but not very favorable review of the Conference's work, by one of the German delegates.

FRIED, ALFRED H.: *Handbuch der Friedensbewegung*. Leipzig, 1911. One of the best German accounts.

LAMMASCH, HEINRICH: *Die Beiden Haager Friedenskonferenzen von 1899 und 1907*. Berlin, 1915. Written by one of the Austrian representatives, this is primarily a study in international law.

MÉRIGNHAC, A.: *La Conférence Internationale de la Paix*. Paris, 1900. Primarily devoted to technical analysis of the proceedings.

MEURER, CHRISTIAN: *Die Haager Friedenskonferenz*. Two volumes. Munich, 1905. A substantial study, dealing chiefly with the development of arbitration.

NIPPOLD, OTFRIED: *Die Fortbildung des Verfahrens in Völkerrechtlichen Streitigkeiten*. Leipzig, 1907. A careful, scholarly treatment of the problem of arbitration.

SCHÜCKING, WALTHER: *Der Staatenverband der Haager Konferenzen*. Munich, 1912. The work of a leading German international jurist, who attempts to set the Conference in the general development of international organization.

KRAFFT, E.: *Die Ersten Internationalen Friedenskongresse und ihre Entstehung*. Frankfurt, 1922. A dissertation.

Junk, August: *Die Mächte auf der Ersten Haager Friedenskonferenz.* Leipzig, 1928. Far and away the best study of the political aspects of the Conference and of the policies of the powers. Now requires supplementing with the evidence presented to the German parliamentary commission, and by the Russian documents.

Gottschalk, Egon: "Deutschlands Haltung auf den Haager Friedenskonferenzen." (*Berliner Monatshefte,* May, 1930, pp. 447–56). A review of German policy, with special reference to the evidence of the German parliamentary commission.

Wehberg, Hans: *Die Internationale Beschränkung der Rüstungen.* Stuttgart, 1919. An excellent, thoroughly documented study. It really treats the whole problem of international co-operation and peace, and still remains one of the best historical accounts.

—: "La Contribution des Conférences de la Paix de la Haye au Progrès du Droit International." (*Académie de Droit International. Recueil des Cours,* XXXVII, 1931, pp. 533–669). The most recent and one of the best historical and analytical treatments of the Conference.

LITERATURE SINCE 1935

Hoffmann, Frieda: *Beiträge zur Vorgeschichte der ersten Haager Friedenskonferenz.* Hamburg, 1935. 78 pp.

Ford, Thomas K.: "The Genesis of the First Hague Peace Conference" (*Political Science Quarterly,* LI, 1936, no. 3). Essentially a digest of the Russian materials published in the *Krasnyi Arkhiv.*

Tate, Merze: *The Disarmament Illusion: The Movement for a Limitation of Armaments to 1907.* New York, 1942. 398 pp. A systematic, scholarly treatment, which takes full account of the movement of public opinion.

Abrams, Irwin: "The Austrian Question at the Turn of the Twentieth Century" (*Journal of Central European Affairs,* IV, July, 1944, pp. 186–201). An excellent analysis of the international effects of the Austrian crisis, utilizing all the recently published documents.

Schimpke, Friedrich: *Die deutsch-französischen Beziehungen von Fashoda bis zum Abschluss der Entente Cordiale.* Emsdetten, 1935, 71 pp. An exceptionally sound doctoral dissertation, based not only on the documents but on extensive study of the contemporary press.

Barrère, Camille: "Lettres à Delcassé" (*Revue de Paris,* April 15, 1937, pp. 721–763). A collection of letters of the French Ambassador to Rome, valuable for the study of the French-Italian reconciliation from 1899 to 1902.

Berger, Ernst E.: "Camille Barrère" (*Berliner Monatshefte,* XVIII, November, 1940, pp. 704–719). A competent and well-balanced review of Barrère's career.

XVIII

Origins of the Boer War

◡◠

T HE OUTCOME OF THE FASHODA EPISODE WAS A VERY GREAT VICTORY FOR the British and led to a veritable revolution in the popular attitude toward foreign affairs. The years of discouragement which followed upon the rise of Germany as a great commercial rival and upon the conclusion of the Franco-Russian Alliance had shaken the confidence of the country in its ability to hold its own against the demands of the great continental countries for a share of the unclaimed areas of the world. Fashoda had shown conclusively that Britain could still score a resounding success, that isolation after all did not necessarily mean impotence, and that Mahan was right — everything in matters of world policy depended upon sea-power. So long as Britain maintained her great fleets she was not only safe, but supreme. France, which had really been feared as a naval power, had proved herself helpless, and the Franco-Russian Alliance had been shown up as a fiction. In the eyes of the exuberant imperialists France no longer counted. George Wyndham, undersecretary for war, speaking to his friend Wilfrid Blunt in May 1899, expressed quite baldly what must have been the idea of many of the imperialists: " It is now simply a triangular battle between the Anglo-Saxon race, the German race, and the Russian, which shall have the hegemony of the whole world." France he considered gone as a great power, as much gone as Spain or Austria, but the Emperor William, he believed, meant to be supreme overlord. He was holding his hand for the moment till he could get an efficient navy, but as soon as that was ready there would be a coalition against England. He, Wyndham, and the young imperialists, however, were " going in for England's overlordship" and they wouldn't " stand half-measures or economy in pushing it on." [1]

The continental powers took due note of the great change that had been wrought in the international situation, and they were much more circumspect in their dealings with England. The Emperor William, as we have seen in the preceding chapter, was convinced that it was already too late to talk of a continental combine, and the Russians hastened to conclude with the British an agreement with regard to China, which we shall have to discuss at greater length later. The general outlook for England was extremely favorable when, in 1899, she became involved in a war in south Africa which tied up her forces almost before she was able to realize on the Fashoda victory.

---

[1] Wilfrid S. Blunt: *My Diaries* (New York, 1919), I, p. 397.

It is as difficult to discuss the origins of the Boer War as to analyze the causes of the Crimean War. Both conflicts were slow in coming to a head and both involved a host of factors which were hopelessly intertwined. Something has already been said in a previous chapter of the complications in south Africa which followed the discovery of gold in the Transvaal and the great influx of foreigners into Johannesburg, and also of the schemes of Rhodes and his associates which eventuated in the famous Jameson raid of December 1895. This abortive attempt to overthrow the government of Kruger must be taken as the starting point of the later clash. Its importance can hardly be overestimated. By common consent of all writers it left behind it a feeling of profound suspicion and resentment. Nothing could convince the Boers after the Raid that there was not a plot afoot to take their country from them and that the British were not seeking a pretext for a fight. This feeling was enhanced by the enthusiastic reception accorded Jameson in England, by the mild treatment meted out to the raiders, and by the conduct of the parliamentary committee, which in the spring of 1897 investigated the whole affair. It was common knowledge that no serious attempt was made to get at some of the important evidence. The world generally was shocked when, after the committee had roundly castigated Rhodes, Chamberlain got up in parliament and exonerated him of dishonorable action.[2]

The British position having been seriously compromised by Jameson's action, the government for a time seemed anxious to smooth matters over and reach some sort of adjustment of the questions at issue. Into the details we need not go. Suffice it to say that within a year the situation had again become critical. Legislation regulating immigration into the Transvaal and providing for the expulsion of undesirable foreigners created friction and caused something of a war scare in the spring of 1897.[3] This crisis passed when Chamberlain took a strong line and the Pretoria government decided it would be best to yield. The years 1897 and 1898 were on the whole fairly quiet. The British government was deeply involved in serious imperial problems in other parts of the world, while the Transvaal generally suffered from bad times and financial difficulties.

In the meanwhile Sir Alfred Milner was sent out as high commissioner. Milner was the author of the widely acclaimed book *England in Egypt,* and was generally regarded as one of the ablest of the young imperialist group. Since the time of the Boer War he has been generally held responsible for the outbreak of the conflict. The Boers regarded him as an agent of Chamberlain and Rhodes, sent out to pick a quarrel. Not a few English writers have felt and said the same thing.[4] We now have the illuminating papers of Milner himself, so

---

[2] See, among others, E. T. Cook: *Rights and Wrongs of the Transvaal War* (New edition, London, 1902), chap. viii: The "Committee of No Inquiry."

[3] The details may be read in such recent books as Eric A. Walker: *A History of South Africa* (London, 1928), pp. 463 ff.; Reginald I. Lovell: *The Struggle for South Africa* (Cambridge, 1934), pp. 387 ff.; Garvin: *Life of Chamberlain,* III, chap. lii, especially pp. 140 ff.

[4] E.g. J. A. Hobson: *The War in South Africa* (London, 1900), chap. xix; W. T. Stead: Leading article in the *Review of Reviews,* August 15, 1899, pp. 119–20; Blunt; *Diaries,* I, p. 401.

that it is possible to form an independent judgment.[5] From them it appears that after spending the first year in becoming acquainted with the questions at issue, the high commissioner came to the conclusion that the situation in the Transvaal offered little prospect of peaceful reform from within, and that there was no " way out of the political troubles of south Africa except reform in the Transvaal, or war." Kruger was re-elected president for five years in February 1898 and therewith all hope of a more liberal régime evaporated. In the " scandalous " abuses of the Transvaal administration Milner saw the root of all the trouble. Looking at the question from the purely south African viewpoint, Milner wrote to Chamberlain, he, the high commissioner, would be inclined " to work up a crisis." But naturally everything would depend on the imperial outlook as a whole.

Chamberlain's reply to these revelations was detailed and unambiguous. He reminded Milner of the bases of policy agreed upon when he was sent out. They were to maintain Britain's rights under the Convention of 1884 and to avoid public pressure in regard to less important grievances. The considerations upon which these bases rested were:

" (1) The conviction that a war with the Transvaal would certainly rouse antagonism in the Cape Colony, and leave behind it the most serious difficulties in the way of South African union. We felt that if a struggle was to come, it was most important that the Transvaal should be the aggressor, and that the Imperial Government should have the active sympathy of at all events a considerable section of the Dutch in the Colony. (2) We felt that the Raid has placed this country in a false position and has alienated the confidence of the Afrikander Party, and that it would be desirable that the irritation caused by this event should pass away before we resumed any pressure upon the Transvaal in regard to its internal policy. (3) We were of opinion that the waiting game was the best for this country as time must be on our side. The misgovernment in the Transvaal will in the long run produce opposition within its borders, and when the present rule of President Kruger comes to an end, as it must do before many years are over, we might confidently look for an improvement in the position. (4) A war with the Transvaal, unless upon the utmost and clearest provocation, would be extremely unpopular in this country. It would involve the despatch of a very large force and the expenditure of many millions." " Most of the grievances of which we have to complain are of a character which would not excite great sympathy in this country, and they would not be considered as sufficient to constitute a *casus belli*." The foreign situation was a further argument against war. " We have on hand difficulties of the most serious character with France, Russia and Germany. We are engaged in an important expedition in the Soudan, and it is uncertain as yet whether the war on the north-west frontier of India has been finally concluded. We may emerge from all these

---

Milner's policy is examined in great detail and favorably appraised by E. B. Iwan-Müller: *Lord Milner and South Africa* (London, 1902), and W. Basil Worsfold: *Lord Milner's Work in South Africa, 1897-1902* (London, 1906).

[5] Cecil Headlam: *The Milner Papers* (London, 1931).

troubles without a war, but I cannot conceal from myself that the prospect is more gloomy that it has ever been in my recollection. . . . Accordingly I wish to emphasize the fact that for the present at any rate our greatest interest in South Africa is peace, and that all our policy must be directed to this subject." [6]

This exchange of letters has been quoted at length because it touches almost every aspect of the situation. The British could not go to war to bring the Transvaal into a south African federation because of danger of estranging the Dutch population at the Cape, because of the unenviable position in which the Jameson raid had placed the British government, because the grievances of the Uitlanders were not such that they would arouse much sympathy in England. Public opinion in England was opposed to war, and the government had its hands full elsewhere. Thus warned, Milner was obliged to exercise patience. The year 1898 was generally a quiet one, as things went in south Africa.

A new chapter opened with the new year. Milner paid a visit home in November and worked hard on the politicians to convince them that England must secure genuine reforms from the Transvaal government.[7] The situation was now much more favorable, for the Germans had been bought off with the agreement regarding the Portuguese colonies, and France had received a decided setback in the Fashoda business. Kitchener had completed his work in the Sudan, and the Russians were negotiating for an agreement with respect to China. England was, for the moment, at the top of the pile and had no serious international complications to fear. But public opinion was still cool toward south Africa and the cabinet was sceptical of Milner's views. Chamberlain himself counselled caution and emphasized his desire not to hasten the crisis.[8]

Even though Milner received little or no encouragement in London, the situation after his return to south Africa played into his hands. In the last days of December a man named Edgar, an English miner at Johannesburg, had been shot and killed by a Boer policeman. The case itself need not detain us here. The important thing is that the affair led to a marked revival of Uitlander agitation against the Kruger system and to the presentation of the first petition to Queen Victoria, which General Butler, who acted as commissioner in Milner's absence, rejected because of a technicality. In the midst of the agitation some effort was made by Kruger to reach an agreement with the mine owners. His hope was evidently that many of the outstanding questions could be removed in this way and that the bottom could thereby be knocked out of the entire opposition movement. We need not enter upon the details of the pourparlers. The British looked upon them from the outset as a mere manoeuvre designed to split the ranks of the Uitlander population. When they consulted Chamberlain he discouraged them. Sir Percy Fitzpatrick has told us himself how he gave the

---

[6] *Milner Papers*, I, pp. 220–9, correspondence with Chamberlain of February and March, 1908; Garvin, op. cit., III, pp. 355 ff., 366 ff.

[7] *Milner Papers*, I, p. 298; Garvin, op. cit., III, pp. 377 ff.

[8] Garvin, op. cit., III, pp. 377 ff.

correspondent of the London *Times* at Pretoria the money with which to bribe a Boer official in order to get the text of Kruger's proposals. The premature publication of the offer was admittedly an important reason for the breakdown of the negotiations.[9] Whether Kruger was sincere or not it is hard to say, but it does seem that the old man had become convinced that some extension of the franchise was necessary, and that he was prepared to make concessions in this matter as fast as the opinion of his burghers would permit.

The question of the part played by the Rand capitalists in bringing about the war has always been a warmly debated one. It has been said that they were not interested in politics, and that they preferred to get along as best they could with the government rather than to start a row. Of course they were deeply involved in the conspiracy which ended in the Jameson raid, but that was an aberration. After the disaster Rhodes scrupulously kept out of the whole business. But this is certainly not the whole story. It would appear rather that the capitalists were against war so long as it was obvious that the British government would not play the game. Despite the low mining taxes in the Transvaal, they had grievances, of which the famous and obscure dynamite monopoly was the principal one, while maladministration, corruption, the liquor laws and the pass laws for laborers were others. Least talked about, however, was the most important question, that of labor supply. J. A. Hobson has shown pretty conclusively that the supply of native labor was a crucial matter on the Rand, and that in June 1899 there was a shortage of 12,000 men. He has shown further, on the basis of remarks made by the capitalists themselves, that they hoped, if they got control of the Transvaal government, to make a saving of two and a half million pounds sterling annually by securing for themselves an unrestricted labor supply and thus lowering the wage-rate.[10]

Now it is worth noting that the capitalists, who, according to Fitzpatrick, did not want to introduce the question of the franchise into the negotiations for the " Great Deal," did ask that the government assist the mines in getting labor, that it enforce the liquor laws, and that it admit to the executive council an " independent " financier like Rothschild to control future taxation. When the whole project fell flat through the unwillingness of the government to accept these terms, the financial interests began to take the lead in the great campaign of villification that followed. Rhodes may have stayed in the background, but the fact remains that he controlled the Johannesburg *Star* and the Transvaal *Leader*, the *Cape Times* and other south African newspapers, to say nothing of some of the London dailies. His friend Harmsworth's *Daily Mail* was one of the most violent enemies of the Boers; the Liberal *Daily News* was acquired by his friends and pressed into service; the London *Times* championed

---

[9] Percy Fitzpatrick: *The Transvaal from Within* (London, 1899), pp. 342–60; Idem: *South African Memories* (London, 1932), chaps. x and xi; see further *Milner Papers*, I, pp. 318 ff.; Garvin, op. cit., III, pp. 388–9; and among many secondary accounts E. T. Cook: *Rights and Wrongs of the Transvaal War*, chap. xxiv.   [10] J. A. Hobson: *The War in South Africa*, Book II, chap. iv.

the Uitlanders and demanded a forward policy, for reasons that are not clear.
Furthermore, in April 1899 Rhodes became president of the powerful South
African League, representing the British nationalists as against the Dutch
Afrikander Bond. The Outlanders' Council, founded in June 1899 at Johannesburg, was patently under the direction of the capitalists, who at this time healed
the split in their own ranks which had occurred after the Jameson raid and who
thenceforth pulled together.

In April 1899 the Uitlanders sent to the Queen a petition recounting their
grievances. There were more than 21,000 signatures attached, which according
to Milner were on the whole genuine and according to the Boers largely forged.
Milner followed up the petition with the famous " helot " despatch of May 4,
in which he reviewed the hardships of the Uitlanders, and declared that " the
true remedy is to strike at the root of all these injuries, the political impotence
of the injured. What diplomatic protests will never accomplish, a fair measure of Uitlander representation would gradually but surely bring about. . . .
The case for intervention is overwhelming." Then, to drive the point home, he
issued a significant warning:

> " The spectacle of thousands of British subjects kept permanently in the position
> of helots, constantly chafing under undoubted grievances, and calling vainly to
> Her Majesty's Government for redress, does steadily undermine the influence
> and reputation of Great Britain and the respect for the British Government within
> its own dominions. A certain section of the press, and not in the Transvaal
> only, preaches openly and constantly the doctrine of a Republic embracing all
> South Africa, and supports it by menacing references to the armaments of the
> Transvaal, its alliance with the Orange Free State, and the active sympathy
> which in case of war it would receive from a section of Her Majesty's subjects.
> I regret to say that this doctrine, supported as it is by a ceaseless stream of
> malignant lies about the intentions of the British Government, is producing a
> great effect upon a large number of our Dutch fellow-colonists. . . . I can see
> nothing which will put a stop to this mischievous propaganda but some striking
> proof of the intention, if it is the intention, of Her Majesty's Government not
> to be ousted from its position in South Africa." [12]

Before leaving this despatch a few words of comment will be in order. In
the first place, it ought to be pointed out that there has always been much difference of opinion as to the extent of the grievances of the Uitlanders. It is
impossible at this date to make any definite pronouncement, but the conscientious reader will want to consult the writings of men like Stead and Hobson
before accepting in full the statements of Fitzpatrick and E. T. Cook, to say
nothing of less responsible imperialists. Hobson was in the Transvaal in the
summer and autumn of 1899 and declared that he could secure little concrete
evidence of oppression, though the place was full of stock stories that could not

---

[11] See especially Hobson, op. cit., Book II, chap. iii; Walker: *History of South Africa*, p. 476.
[12] *Milner Papers*, I, pp. 348–53; Garvin, op. cit., III, pp. 394 ff.

be corroborated. " The notion that Englishmen or White British subjects have commonly been made the victims of oppression and terrorism is grotesquely and utterly false," he said. " So far as practical freedom of action, speech and publication are concerned, there was no place upon the continent of Europe which could for a moment compare with it (Johannesburg)." " There are liars and credulous folk in every land; but for a minute detailed mendacity and the wanton acceptance of the same, South Africa stands pre-eminent." There was, of course, corruption and maladministration, but corruption had been more or less fostered by the financial interests themselves, and if it had been as bad as it was made out to be, it might have been reasonably urged that the capitalists " would have found it cheaper and safer to buy the Boer Government than to enter a troublesome political campaign for its reformation or its overthrow." [13]

Hobson was convinced that reform would have come in the course of time and through the pressure of circumstances, and Professor Walker, in his *History of South Africa,* has shown that there was more than a merely negligible measure of reform between 1896 and 1899. Furthermore, by Milner's own admission only a percentage of the foreigners in Johannesburg desired the franchise. Most of them were transients, who had no desire to give up their citizenship, but were interested chiefly in making their pile and then clearing out. Finally, a word about the much-discussed Dutch conspiracy to oust the British from south Africa. Talk of this plot became prevalent in south African circles after the victory of the Afrikander Bond in the Cape elections of the autumn of 1898. In actual fact there was little justification for the imputation of disloyalty so far as the Cape Dutch were concerned. The Bond and its leader, Hofmeyr, had always been for the connexion with Britain and in 1899 did their utmost to effect a peaceful settlement. They had no use for Krugerism and certainly had no desire to spread that system to the whole of south Africa. That there were some hot-headed young bloods in the Transvaal there can be no doubt, but there is little evidence to support the idea of a general policy aimed at ejecting the British. In fact the idea is rather preposterous. " Of all the disreputable, contemptible and discreditable proceedings by which a nation has ever been jockeyed into war," wrote W. T. Stead, " this fighting for the paramountcy is about the worst." His opinion was echoed by an anonymous writer in the *Edinburgh Review,* who declared that " the notion that there is a formidable Dutch conspiracy ' to oust British influence . . . from South Africa ' is the strangest nightmare that ever afflicted the most nervous of ' Imperialist ' minds." [14]

The simple truth of the matter is that the franchise demand and the spectre of the Dutch conspiracy cannot be examined on their merits. Milner had come

[13] Hobson, op. cit., Book I, chaps. viii, x.

[14] W. T. Stead: Leading article, *Review of Reviews,* October 15, 1899, p. 333; Anonymous: " Great Britain and South Africa " (*Edinburgh Review,* October, 1899, pp. 530–52). The most is made of the argument by Cook, op. cit., chap. xxx; on the other side see Hobson, op. cit., Book I, chap. xiv. Garvin is circumspect in dealing with this question.

to the conclusion that the franchise would do better as a lever than a host of lesser questions which concerned the capitalists rather than the Uitlanders as a whole. The conspiracy alarm, too, was probably meant chiefly as an incentive to British public opinion. Milner was working for a crisis, though it should be carefully noted that this is not saying that he wanted war. He was ready for armed conflict if it proved unavoidable, but he undoubtedly hoped to get what he wanted by mere pressure. Rhodes told a British cabinet minister in the spring of 1899 that Kruger was " only bluffing." " If you were to employ your troops you could undoubtedly bring him to subjection." To his friend Beit he wrote: " Nothing will make Kruger fire a shot." [15] These same ideas recur in the Milner correspondence. Here are a few excerpts from his letters at the time: May 17, 1899: " I don't want war, but I admit I begin to think it may be the only way out." " Absolute downright determination plus a large temporary increase of force will assure a climb down. It is 20 to 1." May 24, 1899: " My view has been and still is, in spite of all these alarms and excursions, that if we are perfectly determined we shall win without a fight or with a mere apology for one." [16]

The great obstacle to the realization of Milner's policy was the negative attitude of British opinion and the resulting unwillingness of the cabinet to embark upon a policy that might lead to war. Milner's helot despatch was written with the idea that it should be published and that it would serve as an effective irritant. But for the time being it had to be held back and Milner was obliged to accept the mediation of President Steyn of the Orange Free State, who arranged a meeting with Kruger at Bloemfontein. There discussions took place between May 30 and June 5. From the outset they were doomed to failure. Milner had been instructed by Chamberlain to show a conciliatory spirit, but instead of doing so " he bombarded the president with dialectical artillery, bowling over in summary fashion his arguments, making debating scores off him, and eventually driving the old man to an attitude of obstinate despair." [17] It was certainly a mistake to try to deal with the old Vortrekker as though he were a polished European diplomat, but it was positively fatal to the Conference to do what Milner did, namely to demand a straight five-year retrospective franchise in place of the existing fourteen-year franchise, and to refuse to discuss other matters until this demand was accepted. Kruger seems to have come with the idea that all the " nasty questions " were to be discussed. Naturally he was not prepared to accept a measure which, he felt, would deliver his country into the hands of the Uitlanders, without some sort of guarantee of a *quid pro quo*. Even then it was Milner who broke off the conference, too hastily, as he himself acknowledged later.[18]

---

[15] Sir Lewis Michell: *The Life of Cecil John Rhodes* (London, 1910), II, p. 253.

[16] *Milner Papers*, I, pp. 384–5, 400–1.   [17] Hobson, op. cit., pp. 165–6.

[18] *Milner Papers*, I, pp. 404 ff.; Garvin, op. cit., III, pp. 392 ff., 400 ff.; *Correspondence relating to the Bloemfontein Conference*, 1899 (Command no. 9404).

Chamberlain was alarmed by Milner's uncompromising attitude and was not at all certain that Kruger had said his last word. It was essential, he wired Milner, that the Pretoria government be put clearly in the wrong. But the mistake had been made and in the succeeding weeks the colonial secretary gradually turned up the road marked out by Milner. He published the famous helot despatch and his own reply adopting the case of the Uitlanders. The despatch, says Walker, "clanged like a trumpet-call presaging war." Perhaps for this very reason it did not go over with the public nearly as well as had been hoped. Chamberlain attempted to secure the support of the Liberals for a forward policy. He told Campbell-Bannerman that he was, and always had been, striving for a peaceful settlement, "but he was afraid that a demonstration . . . would be necessary. It would, however, be a game of bluff, and it was impossible to play that game if the Opposition did not support the Government." But the Liberals were unwilling to support an "open military demonstration." Furthermore, the cabinet, convinced that a war would be very unpopular, refused to commit itself to anything beyond firm language and protests.[19]

While the British government was marking time, all sorts of pressure was being brought to bear on Kruger by the Dutch leaders at the Cape. The Dutch and German governments too sent strong advice to yield.[20] Such a course was not easy, for the burghers were filled with distrust. They hated that *verdomde Kimberlain,* who, they felt convinced, had been bought by Rhodes with a generous block of Consolidated Goldfields stock. Even reputed progressives, like Joubert, were opposed to concessions, and it was widely believed that the British were merely bluffing — that they would not fight.[21] Nevertheless, Kruger had offered a seven-year franchise during the Bloemfontein discussions, and on July 18 he got the Volksraad to accept such a scheme. Chamberlain was elated by this turn of events. He inspired a statement in the *Times* saying that the crisis was at an end, and he wired to Milner: " If . . . President South African Republic has really given seven years retroactive franchise and five seats (in the Volksraad to the Rand), I congratulate you on great victory. No one would dream of fighting over two years in qualification period and President South African Republic will have been driven by successive steps to almost exact position taken by you. We ought to make most of this and accept it as basis of settlement." [22]

Milner was horrified. The *Times* article, he telegraphed Chamberlain, had " created consternation among British party " in south Africa. The Transvaal offer, he declared, was far from satisfactory. At the same time the south African press and the Uitlanders raised a howl and reiterated their demand for the five-

[19] *Milner Papers,* I, pp. 444 ff.; Garvin, op. cit., III, pp. 411–5; J. A. Spender: *The Life of Sir Henry Campbell-Bannerman* (London, 1923), II, p. 234; *Letters of Queen Victoria,* III, pp. 382–4.
[20] *Die Grosse Politik,* XV, nos. 4357–4360, 4367, 4368.
[21] Hobson, op. cit., pp. 43–5.
[22] *Milner Papers,* I, p. 468; Garvin, op. cit., III, pp. 418 ff.

year franchise as a minimum. All this fuss made Chamberlain waver. He had, so his biographer points out, intended from the beginning to secure guarantees for the satisfactory working of the proposed franchise scheme, and secured cabinet approval for his next step. On July 27 he proposed a joint inquiry into the working of the new law. This idea was particularly distasteful to the Boers, who regarded it as interference in their domestic affairs. They therefore accepted the suggestion of President Steyn and, after consultation with the British agent at Pretoria, put forward (August 19) a five-year-franchise plan with the assignment of at least a quarter of the seats in the Raad to the mining areas, but all this on condition that the Imperial government drop the claim to suzerainty, interfere no more in the internal affairs of the Republic, and agree to refer minor points in dispute to arbitration.

No doubt something might have been done with this offer, if the British negotiators had been willing to make the most of it. The press of south Africa, controlled by the capitalists, was demanding nothing less than the whole hog, and Milner was constantly insisting that all that was needed was firmness: " There is at bottom a very great indisposition to fight on the part of the Boers, not only in the Colony and Orange Free State, but even in the Transvaal itself. . . . The larger our force, the smaller is likely to be theirs, and I think one good slap in the face may dissipate them " (August 2, 1899); " They will collapse if we don't weaken, or rather if we go on steadily turning the screw " (August 16, 1899).[23] With such assurances dinning in his ears Chamberlain was bound to take a cynical attitude toward the Boer offers. In a resounding speech at Highbury on August 26 he declared: " Mr. Kruger dribbles out reforms like water from a squeezed sponge, and he either accompanies his offers with conditions which he knows to be impossible, or he refuses to allow us to make a satisfactory investigation of the nature of these reforms. . . . The sands are running down in the glass. . . . The knot must be loosened . . . or else we shall have to find other ways of untying it."

A few days later the colonial secretary sent a despatch accepting the Boer proposals without the provisos, on the plea that the British government could not abandon its rights under the conventions or give up the substance of suzerainty. Chamberlain later maintained that this despatch was one of " qualified acceptance " and that he had agreed to nine tenths of the Boer proposals. This is absurd. The Chamberlain reply was what the Boers thought it was — a rejection of the terms offered.[24] They therefore withdrew the offer of the five-year franchise and fell back on the earlier British suggestion of a joint inquiry into the working of the seven-year franchise. It had been explicitly stated that the proposal of a five-year franchise did not involve a rejection of the joint inquiry on the part of the Boers, but Chamberlain now refused to entertain his

---

[23] *Milner Papers,* I, pp. 515–6.

[24] Garvin, op. cit., III, pp. 433 ff., discusses the negotiations without referring to the " qualified acceptance." For a good analysis of the problem see Lovell: *The Struggle for South Africa,* pp. 419 ff.

own earlier suggestion. He had evidently fixed on a line of action and had no intention of swerving. In a letter to Milner (September 2) he stated that he had asked for a cabinet to consider the terms of an ultimatum. The situation, he pointed out, was a difficult one, for " the technical *casus belli* is a very weak one and, thanks to past concessions and weaknesses, our hands are tied in regard to many matters which might otherwise be put forward to justify extreme action." Neither the Uitlanders nor the British at the Cape, he continued, were wholly without reproach, for the former were

" unfortunately identified with money-making — with the Raid — and are not supposed to be capable of much self-sacrifice even for a holy cause — and the latter are quite too ready to take all the profits of a war in the shape of Imperial expenditure while doing nothing themselves but shouting on every occasion that they will cut the painter if the Imperial Government does not do everything they want and do it as quickly as they consider possible and desirable."

There were other obstacles to a forward policy. Chamberlain confessed himself surprised that so much progress had been made:

" It is a great thing to say that the majority of the people have, as I believe, recognised that there is a greater issue than the franchise or the grievances of the Uitlanders at stake, and that our supremacy in South Africa and our existence as a great Power in the world are involved in the result of our present controversy. Three months ago we could not — that is, we should not have been allowed to — go to war on this issue. Now — although still most unwillingly and with a large minority against us, we shall be sufficiently supported." But " we must play out this game *selon les règles* and it seems to me to-day that we ought to exhaust the franchise proposals and get a clear refusal before . . . we ask for more. If and when we ask for more it means war, and therefore, before we do this, we must have a sufficient force in South Africa to defend ourselves during the time that will be required to get a full fighting force into the country. . . ." [25]

This letter would seem to indicate that by the beginning of September negotiation was simply a blind so far as Chamberlain was concerned. He had convinced himself that British opinion was sufficiently persuaded to make it possible to go on, but the whole situation was such that more time was needed to get troops to the scene. In order to gain time the franchise issue was to be wrung dry, but Kruger was not to escape even if he gave in, for in that event the British, like the French in 1870, would bring forward more demands, knowing full well that when they asked for more it would mean war. With this program Chamberlain went before the cabinet and carried his colleagues with him. It was decided to send 10,000 more men to south Africa and in the meanwhile to string out the discussions with Pretoria. In a despatch of the same date Chamberlain insisted on the five-year franchise without conditions and, failing that, reserved to the British government the right " to consider the situation *de novo,* and to formulate their own proposals for a final settlement."

---

[25] Garvin, op. cit., III, pp. 457-9.

There was, by this time, no turning back, for the government was committed. Salisbury, Balfour and other members of the cabinet gave in to the colonial secretary, but only reluctantly and with misgivings. The prime minister wrote to Lansdowne on August 30 that Milner's view was " too heated, if you consider the intrinsic significance and importance of the things which are in controversy." But, he went on, " it recks little to think of that now. What he has done cannot be effaced. We have to act upon a moral field prepared for us by him and his jingo supporters. And therefore I see before us the necessity for considerable military effort — and all for people whom we despise and for territory which will bring no profit and no power to England." [26] Almost to the very end Salisbury seems to have hoped that Milner would prove right in his contention that the Boers would back down before a show of force.[27]

But there was absolutely no chance of that. In south Africa the exodus of the Uitlanders from Johannesburg had already begun. The local press was full of atrocity stories which were assiduously copied in the English press. Popular excitement was rising high and matters had already been pushed to the very verge of war. Kruger rejected Chamberlain's proposal on September 17 and the cabinet had to decide on the next step. Salisbury favored a temporizing policy until the time when reinforcements should have reached the scene, but Chamberlain carried the cabinet with his suggestion for secret mobilization. On September 22 he wired triumphantly to Milner: " Cabinet unanimous and resolves to see matter through." [28] Another despatch was to be sent by steamer so as to gain another four weeks for preparation.

By this time even Salisbury seems to have become convinced, or, shall we say, seems to have convinced himself that more than Uitlander grievances were at issue and that there was a Dutch conspiracy to drive the British out of south Africa. It may be that the publication of Fitzpatrick's *The Transvaal from Within* had something to do with his conversion. Fitzpatrick was one of the capitalist group who had taken an active part in the revolutionary movement which eventuated in the Jameson raid. He had, in general, served as liaison officer between the mining interests and the Uitlander agitators. His book, while still in manuscript, had been read by Milner late in 1898, and is said to have confirmed him in the policy which led to war. It is said that the book made a deep impression also upon Salisbury when it was published in England in September 1899.[29] At any rate the prime minister seems to have swallowed the plot-story whole. He wrote to the Queen on September 23: " It is impossible to avoid believing that the Boers really aim at setting up a South African Republic, consisting of the Transvaal, the Orange Free State and Your

---

[26] Lord Newton: *Lord Lansdowne* (London, 1929), p. 157.

[27] *Letters of Queen Victoria*, III, p. 395; *Die Grosse Politik*, XV, nos. 4374, 4379, 4380.

[28] *Milner Papers*, I, p. 545; Garvin, op. cit., III, pp. 461–2.

[29] Sir Percy Fitzpatrick: *South African Memories*, chap. xii, and especially p. 188; W. T. Stead in the *Review of Reviews*, November 15, 1899, pp. 521 ff.

Majesty's Colony. It is impossible to account in any other manner for their rejection of our most moderate proposals." And on October 5 he declared in a letter to Lord Courtney that while he could not convict Kruger of conspiracy in a court of law, he had become convinced, from watching the course of negotiations " that Kruger was using the oppression of the Outlanders as a lever to exact from England a renunciation of suzerainty; and the conduct of President Steyn and Mr. Schreiner (prime minister at the Cape), of the Africanders generally and of their sympathisers in Europe, has brought home to me the belief that there is an understanding among the leaders of Dutch opinion, and their aspiration is the restoration of South Africa to the Dutch race." [30]

The British were now rushing troops to south Africa and were merely sparring for time in the hope of getting 70,000 men to the scene before the storm broke. Recognizing the futility of further discussion the Transvaal government, after asking for the British terms and being put off, drew up an ultimatum demanding that the troops be withdrawn from the frontiers, that all reinforcements sent out since June 1 be recalled within a reasonable period, and that the forces then on the sea should not be landed at any south African port. This ultimatum was presented on October 9, and simply forestalled a British one. The British government simply declared these " peremptory demands " impossible of discussion and therewith the war began.

It is hardly necessary to say much by way of recapitulation. No one would deny that the south African situation had for years been a most difficult one, complicated as it was by the peculiar race problem and by the troubles that were bound to arise from the establishment of great mining interests and the influx of thousands of foreigners into an essentially backward agrarian state. Things had really come to a head with the Jameson raid, which had set all these antagonisms in a lurid light and had left an atmosphere of distrust in which it was nearly impossible to negotiate in any cordial way. Both the capitalists and the workers in the Transvaal had undoubted grievances, though they were probably not as serious as Fitzpatrick, for example, made them out to be.[31] It seems unlikely that the Transvaal government could have maintained its exclusive policy for very much longer in the face of changing conditions. At any rate it was not given the chance. Rhodes and the other capitalists were set upon a federation of south Africa and that implied control of the Transvaal government. Having failed to get what they wanted from Kruger they made use of the Uitlander grievances, mobilized the press which they controlled and raised the hue and cry of the Dutch conspiracy. Milner's views suited them perfectly and those views were that England must intervene in the domestic affairs of the Transvaal, which she was hardly justified in doing,

---

[30] *Letters of Queen Victoria*, III, p. 400; G. P. Gooch: *Life of Lord Courtney* (London, 1920), pp. 377-8.

[31] This was also the opinion of an expert observer like James Bryce: " Historical Causes of the War " (*North American Review*, December, 1899, pp. 737-59).

no matter what opinion one may hold of the unhappy suzerainty issue. Milner finally convinced Chamberlain, who was at first hopeful and circumspect but came round after the Fashoda crisis. He wrote to the Queen retrospectively that he had "long felt that the differences between this country and the Transvaal could only be settled by force." [32]

Affairs might well have been brought to a head in the spring of 1898 excepting for the fact that British public opinion was so little interested in Uitlander grievances and the government was so deeply involved in serious questions of international politics that it was absolutely unwilling to follow Milner and Chamberlain. It was not until Germany had been squared by the agreement on the Portuguese colonies and France had been taken care of in the Fashoda crisis that the field became clear. Even then it required a long campaign of propaganda to bring the British public into line, and to convert Lord Salisbury, who disliked both capitalists and jingoes. In the meanwhile negotiations dragged on, marked throughout by a certain insincerity. The British consistently refused to submit their final terms and thereby gave the Transvaalers good reason to suppose that every concession would be followed by further demands and that the root of the whole business was the desire of the British to get control of the Transvaal and its great wealth. Whether Milner actually believed that the Boers would not fight it is hard to say. In any event his policy of bluff was a dangerous one, which, as he himself recognized, might lead to war. But he did not fear war. In his opinion only "an apology for a fight" would be necessary. A "slap in the face" would do the business. Had he appreciated the seriousness of the struggle on which England was embarked so light-heartedly, he would undoubtedly have made greater efforts to find another way out. Chamberlain showed himself throughout to be much better informed and statesmanlike and came only gradually to the conclusion that force was the only method that would bring a solution. Salisbury and other cabinet ministers, as we have seen, were even more sceptical and reluctant. They allowed Milner to push them into a crisis from which there was no decent escape except through war.

That Salisbury did not commit himself to a policy of war without carefully considering the international situation goes without saying. Writing to the Queen on August 12 he admitted that England's position was exceptionally strong, but that there was always uncertainty and anxiety regarding France and Germany, whose colonial aspirations crossed England's more frequently than before. But two weeks later he said to the German ambassador that he did not think France or Russia would attempt to take action. France was still submerged in the chaos of the Dreyfus affair and Russia was afflicted with famine and financial distress. [33]

As a matter of fact, the problem for England narrowed down pretty much

---

[32] *Letters of Queen Victoria*, III, pp. 406–7, letter of October 12, 1899.
[33] *Letters of Queen Victoria*, III, p. 392; *Die Grosse Politik*, XV, no. 4374.

to the problem of her relationship with Germany, for the French and Russians could hardly afford to become involved in a conflict with England if Germany stood on the other side. This aspect of the situation was of course recognized in London, and for that reason Chamberlain had worked eagerly for the agreement on the Portuguese colonies, which bought off the Germans so far as south Africa was concerned. Bülow admitted quite frankly that the convention " removed from discussion the question of Delagoa Bay, which threatened to embitter the relations between the two countries and to cause an estrangement which might take thirty or forty years to overcome." [34] From the English angle the agreement worked perfectly, for the Germans thenceforth showed no interest in the Boers. In fact, they repeatedly warned the Pretoria government to yield. Dr. Leyds, the Boer agent, who has often been accused of having encouraged Kruger by assurances of foreign aid, on the contrary warned his government repeatedly that no assistance was to be expected, least of all from Berlin.[35]

But the Germans, recognizing their importance to England, were determined to make the most of the situation. They were disappointed with the Portuguese agreement, for it soon became clear that the British had concluded it with reluctance and that they had no desire to hasten the partition of the Portuguese possessions.[36] Consequently the Germans were ever ready to cast about for further concessions which might be demanded of England. It was the policy later described so bitterly by Sir Eyre Crowe as that of the " professional blackmailer," which forced Britain into a " systematic policy of gratuitous concessions." [37]

A rare opportunity to capitalize the general situation presented itself in the winter of 1898–1899, when troubles once more broke out in the Samoan Islands. It might be said by way of preface that this little island group caused more international friction than it was worth. After prolonged troubles in the 1880's the situation had been settled in 1889 by the Berlin Act, which provided that the islands, though independent, should be under the collective supervision of the British, Germans and Americans. The United States had certain rights to the island of Tutuila and the excellent harbor of Pago-Pago under the terms of a treaty concluded in 1878, but the work of converting and educating the natives had been done almost entirely by British missionaries. In fact, British nationals outnumbered the Germans and Americans together in 1899. But the Germans had long taken an active interest in the group. The great Hamburg commercial

---

[34] *British Documents*, I, no. 127.

[35] W. J. Leyds: *Eenige Correspondentie uit 1899* (The Hague, 1919), especially nos. 47, 93, 95, 97, 101, 182, 183. See also Johannes A. Wüd: *Die Rolle der Burenrepubliken in der Auswärtigen und Kolonialen Politik des Deutschen Reiches in den Jahren 1883–1900* (Nürnberg, 1927), pp. 130 ff.

[36] *Die Grosse Politik*, XIV, nos. 3873 ff.; *British Documents*, I, nos. 94 ff.; Raymond W. Bixler: *Anglo-German Imperialism in South Africa, 1880–1900* (Baltimore, 1932), pp. 135 ff.; Fritz Schwarze: *Das Deutsch-Englische Abkommen über die Portugiesischen Kolonien* (Göttingen, 1931), part iii.

[37] *British Documents*, III, appendix A, pp. 416, 419.

firm of Goddefroy had organized the Deutsche Handels und Plantagengesell-
schaft der Süd-See Inseln zu Hamburg (The Long Handle Company, for short)
and had established several large cocoanut plantations on the island of Apia.
In all the Germans held some 75,000 acres of land, valued at well over $1,000,000.
They controlled the export trade in copra, though four fifths of the imports
were British.[38]

The history of Samoa under the Berlin Act was by no means a happy one.
The natives were constantly at war with each other and the European consuls
seem to have suffered from an aggravated form of what Bismarck described as
the *furor consularis*.[39] In August 1898 the Samoan king, Malietoa, died. His
traditional rival, Mataafa, returned to Apia in the middle of September and
was recognized by the great majority of the chiefs, as well as by the consuls. But
in December the chief justice, an American named Chambers, with whom the
decision rested in the event of a disputed succession, declared for Malietoa's
son, Malietoa Tanu. Civil war ensued, Mataafa easily defeated his opponents,
and the vanquished faction, including Chambers, took refuge on a British
warship. Early in January 1899 the consuls set up a provisional government
under Mataafa, pending instructions from their governments. Chambers refused to recognize it, whereupon the German head of the municipality of
Apia declared the supreme court closed on account of the flight of the chief
justice. But the British ship, with the consent of the American consul, landed
marines and reopened the court despite the protests of the Germans.

These events caused a storm in Europe and America. For a short time
relations between Berlin and Washington were extremely tense. The German
government, however, hoped to make good use of the whole business to secure a long-desired partition of the islands between the interested powers:
The Americans should have Tutuila and Manua, the Germans should receive
the two large islands of Upolu and Savaii (the latter of no value), while the
British should receive the Tonga Islands by way of compensation. This suggestion had been made in London as early as August 31, 1898, but it had met
with no encouragement whatever from the British statesmen, who urged the
objections of the New Zealand and Australian governments. Far from playing
the German game the British seem to have been intent on building up a strong
Anglo-American combination to frustrate the policy of Berlin. The recent
biographer of the American secretary of state, John Hay, tells us that the British ambassador at Washington " repeatedly approached the State Department
with suggestions which would have involved more aggressive measures than
Hay was prepared to approve." A high official of the British foreign office later

[38] J. F. Rose-Soley: "German and English Interests in Samoa" (*Westminster Review*, September, 1896, pp. 277-95).

[39] See especially the excellent account of the American chief justice, Henry C. Ide: "The Imbroglio in Samoa " (*North American Review*, June 1899, pp. 679-93); and Robert M. Watson:
History of Samoa (Wellington, 1918), chap. vii.

stated that his impression was that Lord Salisbury " did his best to rouse the opposition of the United States," to the German proposals.[40]

The American government, despite these efforts, showed itself not averse to a bargain.[41] But early in March 1899 the American cruiser *Philadelphia* arrived at Apia. The commander, Admiral Kautz, finding things in general confusion, declared both the provisional government and Mataafa deposed. The German consul protested and supported Mataafa. Factional strife broke out, and on March 15 British and American ships bombarded Apia, damaging the German consulate. For a month there was civil war in the islands, the Anglo-American forces occasionally taking part on the side of Malietoa Tanu, who was proclaimed King March 23.

During this critical period the German government renewed its efforts to draw the British into an agreement, but quite without success. Hatzfeldt was obliged to report from London that Salisbury would do nothing and that he was not disposed to make any sacrifices for German good will.[42] At this juncture a curious interlude took place in the relations of the two powers. Cecil Rhodes entered upon the scene. He had come to London in the interest of the Cape-to-Cairo telegraph and railway scheme, to which he was the more closely wedded since Kitchener had wired him from Khartum: " I have founded a post to the south of Fashoda. When are you coming up? "[43] Rhodes was trying to raise a loan of £2,000,000 to extend his railway from Bulawayo to Lake Tanganyika, and attempted, though in vain, to get a government guarantee, so that the money could be got at 3% rather than at 5%. At the same time he was confronted with the problem of running the telegraph and railway from the northern end of Lake Tanganyika to Uganda and the Sudan. This section would have to pass either through the Belgian Congo or through German East Africa. To make the necessary arrangements Rhodes went to Brussels. But Leopold was unwilling to make a deal, excepting on condition that the Bahr-el-Ghazal should be left to him as arranged in the Congo Treaty of 1894.[44]

In the meanwhile the German colonial office had been considering the possibility of enlisting the aid of Rhodes to settle the Samoan business. It was believed that he would be able to influence Chamberlain, who was as obdurate about Samoa as was Salisbury. Rhodes was invited to Berlin, where he was received by the Emperor on March 10. The audience was quite informal, and

    [40] Tyler Dennett: *John Hay* (New York, 1933), p. 281; *British Documents*, III, p. 423, opinion of Lord Sanderson. The documents on the subject are in *Die Grosse Politik*, XIV, nos. 4028 ff., and the *British Documents*, I, nos. 127 ff.

    [41] *Die Grosse Politik*, XIV, nos. 4041, 4042; Hermann Leusser: " Ein Jahrzehnt Deutsch-Amerikanischer Politik, 1897–1906 " (*Beiheft 13 der Historischen Zeitschrift*, Munich, 1928), p. 35.

    [42] *Die Grosse Politik*, XIV, no. 4044.

    [43] W. T. Stead, in the *Review of Reviews*, October 15, 1898, p. 332. Stead had the story from Rhodes himself.

    [44] W. T. Stead, in the *Review of Reviews*, April 15, 1899, p. 312; November 15, 1899, p. 442; Basil Williams: *Cecil Rhodes* (London, 1921), p. 310; *Letters of Queen Victoria*, III, pp. 349–51.

the two men made a most favorable impression upon each other. Within three days an agreement was reached to run the telegraph line through German East Africa. Negotiations for the railway transit were to be undertaken when the time came. Almost overnight Rhodes became an enthusiastic supporter of the Emperor and a warm advocate of Anglo-German co-operation. When told about the Samoan friction he was beside himself and promised to do his utmost to bring his government to reason.[45]

Apparently Rhodes was unable to accomplish much in London. The Germans were quite wrong in thinking that he could influence either Salisbury or Chamberlain. The colonial secretary distrusted him and had no intention of listening to him on matters touching south Africa or any other question.[46] During the second half of March and the first half of April relations between Germany and England were badly strained. At Berlin it was felt that the British were trying to use the Americans to help them get rid of the Germans in the Samoan business. An effort was therefore made to settle with the Americans. The United States government, as before, made no objection. It let fall a suggestion for a tripartite investigating commission and at once accepted the proposal when the German government put it forward. Salisbury, however, would agree to the proposal only on the understanding that decisions might be made by the commission by majority vote, which was contrary to the unanimity rule provided for in the Berlin Act. Acrimonious discussion followed. Bülow finally told the British ambassador that the whole affair threatened " to very seriously impair the good relations," between the two countries. The Germans had determined to break off diplomatic relations if the British remained obdurate. Some inkling of this was undoubtedly allowed to reach high circles in London, and finally Salisbury yielded. The commission was appointed and arrived at Apia on May 13.[47]

In the course of the negotiations the German ambassador reported that Salisbury no longer had any use for the Germans and that England was so cocksure since the Fashoda victory that she did not even fear a coalition organized against her.[48] On both sides there were recriminations. Queen Victoria wrote to her grandson complaining of the virulence of the German press, to which the Emperor replied by bitter accusations of inconsiderate treatment by Lord Salisbury. " He knew," he said to the British ambassador, " that England was powerful and Germany weak at sea, and therefore the former could

---

[45] See first of all Rhodes' account of the meeting in Vindex: *Cecil Rhodes* (London, 1900), pp. 707 ff.; also Michell: *Life of Rhodes*, II, p. 256; *Die Grosse Politik*, XIV, nos. 4045-7; Wilhelm II: *Ereignisse und Gestalten* (Leipzig, 1922), pp. 72-4; Bülow: *Memoirs*, I, pp. 338-9, 409; Hermann Freiherr von Eckardstein: *Lebenserinnerungen und Politische Denkwürdigkeiten* (Leipzig, 1919), I, pp. 314-6; Karl F. Nowak: *Germany's Road to Ruin* (New York, 1932), pp. 205 ff.

[46] Garvin, op. cit., III, pp. 329 ff.

[47] *Die Grosse Politik*, XIV, nos. 4049 ff.; *British Documents*, I, nos. 133 ff.; Eckardstein, op. cit., II, p. 15.

[48] *Die Grosse Politik*, XIV, nos. 4067, 4071.

act with impunity, but the time would come when even England would have to consider the German fleet as an important factor, and he only hoped that it would not then be too late, and that Germany would not by that time have formed other combinations which would certainly not be agreeable to England, but which she would have brought upon herself by the constant disregard and contempt with which she treated German interests." These veiled threats were not calculated to appease Salisbury. The Queen sent a reply in which she pointed out that no government had ever spoken to another as had the German to the British; she enclosed a memorandum in which the prime minister refuted the charges brought against him. By June 1899 Anglo-German relations were at low ebb. The Emperor's plan of coming to the races at Cowes was given up and the atmosphere was frigid.[49]

But forces were working on both sides to save the situation. Bülow was genuinely anxious to avoid hostility, while Balfour and Chamberlain also were eager to maintain good relations.[50] In mid-July the report of the Samoan commission was published, recommending, among other things, that the islands be placed under the direct rule of a single power. It was understood that Tutuila and Manua should go to the United States. The real question was how the other two islands, Upolu and Savaii (the latter being quite worthless) should be divided between England and Germany. The crisis in south Africa was now rapidly coming to a head, and it was to the interest of the British to cultivate the Germans as much as possible. The Emperor William was therefore invited to pay a visit to England in November, and discussions regarding Samoa were resumed. The Germans at first suggested that the possession of Upolu be decided by an impartial arbitrator, but it was impossible to agree on the terms of reference. Then a scheme was worked out by which the Germans should leave Upolu to Britain, taking in return for their rights either British New Guinea or the Solomon Islands, or Savaii, the Savage Islands and the Tongas. Salisbury kept temporizing and complaining that too much was being asked and in the end the plan failed because of Tirpitz' insistence that the Germans keep Upolu and the harbor of Apia.

It is hardly necessary to go into the details of these dreary negotiations or to examine the innumerable deals that were suggested now by one side, now by the other. The Germans throughout insisted that the negotiations be brought to a satisfactory conclusion before the Emperor visited England. Ultimately Salisbury withdrew entirely from the discussions, which were carried on by Chamberlain and Baron Eckardstein, who acted for the German ambassador. With the application of considerable pressure the matter was finally wound up on November 1, 1899. Under the terms of the agreement Germany was assigned Upolu and Savaii, while the British received the Tonga Islands, Savage

---

[49] *Die Grosse Politik*, XIV, nos. 4074, 4076; Sir Sidney Lee: *Edward VII*, I, pp. 743 ff.; *Letters of Queen Victoria*, III, pp. 357–9, 375 ff.; *British Documents*, I, no. 141.

[50] *Die Grosse Politik*, XIV, nos. 4072, 4075, 4079.

Islands, some of the lesser islands in the Solomon group and a disputed area in Togoland.[51]

" The whole of Samoa," said a high official of the German foreign office on one occasion, " was not worth the money spent upon telegrams to and from Apia." [52] It was most unfortunate that this relatively insignificant matter should have arisen to disturb the relations of two great European powers, the more so as there were particular difficulties inherent in it. The Germans had a sentimental attachment to the place, for it was one of the very first fields of German colonial enterprise and they had a real investment in the islands. On the British side there was the perpetual problem of dominion interest. The Australians and particularly the New Zealanders had long had their eyes on the archipelago and were dead opposed to Britain's abandoning it. But beyond these factors were others which embittered the whole transaction. The Germans, having entered late upon the colonial scene, were eager to get something almost anywhere. They had distinctly the feeling that Britain ought to recognize their strong position and ought to buy them off from any continental coalition. The British, on the other hand, were filled with self-assurance after their Fashoda victory. They resented the policy of blackmail and saw no reason for making concessions to Germany, especially as Germany was less dangerous as a sea power than France and Russia. " The policy of the German Empire since Bismarck," wrote Chamberlain to Salisbury in September, " has been always one of undisguised blackmail." [53] He had used the same word a year before in connexion with the Portuguese negotiations. It was now becoming a fixed idea in the foreign office. On the German side, at the same time, there grew up the idea of English malevolence. There was at least a grain of truth in the Emperor William's bitter remark to the British military attaché: " You make any concessions asked for by France and Russia, you cede half continents to them, but when Germany asks for an island, two-thirds of which has been planted over by her subjects, she is met by a refusal." [54] Add to all this the personal ill will and pique of Lord Salisbury and the situation was as unsatisfactory as it well could be. Had the Boer War not broken out in October 1899 the Samoan affair might have taken on an even more sinister aspect. As it was, Germany's friendship had suddenly become of first-rate importance, and even Salisbury felt obliged to accept a settlement against which he had fought for months.

Possibly Lord Salisbury found some inner satisfaction in concluding at this time another agreement which was a severe blow at German hopes, though at the time the Germans did not know it. This agreement was the so-called Windsor Treaty of October 14, 1899, between England and Portugal. The

---

[51] The negotiations may be followed in *Die Grosse Politik*, XIV, nos. 4081 ff.; *British Documents*, I, nos. 146 ff.; Eckardstein, op. cit., II, chaps. i and ii; Garvin, op. cit., III, pp. 334 ff.

[52] *British Documents*, I, no. 128.

[53] Garvin, op. cit., III, p. 334.   [54] *British Documents*, I, no. 154.

British had bought off German interests in Delagoa Bay by the agreement of August 1898, but this did not give them immediate control of the famous harbor. In fact, the Transvaal was importing large stocks of arms and munitions by way of Lorenzo Marques, and the Portuguese government replied to British protests in July 1899 that the Transvaal was entitled to do so under the terms of a convention signed in 1875. The truth was that the Portuguese were by no means well disposed toward the British. The fact of the Anglo-German agreement had been allowed to leak out in the press and it caused all sorts of apprehensions. It is fairly certain that the Portuguese minister in London, Marquis de Soveral, who was a close personal friend of the Prince of Wales, knew a good deal about the terms of the Treaty, if not all the details.[55] It was therefore to the interest of the Portuguese to avert the danger to their empire as best they might.

On September 13 Soveral suggested to Salisbury a close alliance for the event of war with the Transvaal. This, he pointed out, would enable Britain to use Delagoa Bay for her own purposes. The British prime minister agreed almost at once to an offensive and defensive alliance against the Transvaal, even on the understanding that Portugal should not actually declare war. There was some discussion as to the form of the agreement, but finally Salisbury's suggestion, that the words of earlier treaties be used, was adopted. The Anglo-Portuguese Secret Declaration (there is no justification for the name *Windsor Treaty*) was signed on October 14. It renewed the treaties of 1642 and 1661, which involved a mutual guarantee of territory, and included a Portuguese promise not to let arms pass through Lorenzo Marques to the Transvaal, or to declare neutrality, which would have made it impossible for British warships to coal in the port.[56]

Sir Arthur Nicolson once described the Portuguese policy of the British government in 1898 and 1899 as " the most cynical business that I have come across in my whole experience of diplomacy." He could not see how England could agree in 1898 to partition with Germany the possessions of a power which, under the terms of former treaties, Britain was obliged to defend and maintain intact.[57] This was one side of the story, which dealt with the agreement of 1898. Hardly less reprehensible was the British policy in 1899, for, having concluded the partition treaty with Germany, Salisbury then turned back to the old treaties of guarantee and subscribed to a new declaration which completely nullified the agreement of August 1898. The partition treaty was not in keeping with Britain's obligations to Portugal, and the declaration of 1899 was incompatible with *it*.[58] Of course it may be argued that Britain did not want to

---

[55] The evidence for this statement is well examined in Fritz Schwarze: *Das Deutsch-Englische Abkommen über die Portugiesischen Kolonien* (Göttingen, 1931), pp. 75-7.

[56] For the negotiations see *British Documents*, I, nos. 111–8; Schwarze, op. cit., pp. 77 ff.

[57] Harold Nicolson: *Portrait of a Diplomatist* (New York, 1930), p. 393.

[58] On this point see especially the keen analysis by Schwarze, op. cit., pp. 84 ff. Grey admitted in 1913 that there was a " crying contradiction " between them.

partition the Portuguese colonies, and that she was more or less forced into the agreement with Germany by the insistence of the Germans themselves. This is the line taken by Mr. Garvin in his recent biography of Chamberlain. It may also be argued that the declaration of 1899 was necessitated by the situation in south Africa. Delagoa Bay, according to Milner, had become " absolutely the decisive point." [59] But even these considerations do not exonerate the British foreign office of the charge that on two occasions it played a questionable game, first with Portugal, then with Germany. If the Germans made too much of their chance in the Samoan business, the British evened the account by emasculating an agreement on which the Germans had placed the highest hopes.

BIBLIOGRAPHICAL NOTE

DOCUMENTARY SOURCES

Die Grosse Politik der Europäischen Kabinette, 1871–1914. Volume XIV, chapter xcvi: The Samoan Question. Volume XV, chapter ci: The Origins of the Boer War.

British Documents on the Origins of the War, 1898–1914. Volume I, chapter ii: Great Britain, Germany and Portugal, 1898–1899; chapter iii: Great Britain, Germany and Samoa; chapter vii: The South African War.

Accounts and Papers. There is a large series of papers relating to south Africa, of which the chief ones, with the command numbers, are the following: 1898, vol. LX: C. 8721, *Further Correspondence relating to Affairs in the South Africa Republic.* 1899, vol. LXIV: C. 9317, *Correspondence relating to the Explosives Monopoly in the South African Republic;* C. 9345, *Papers relating to the Complaints of British Subjects in the South African Republic;* C. 9404, *Correspondence relating to the Bloemfontein Conference;* C. 9415, *Further Correspondence relating to Proposed Political Reforms in the South African Republic;* C. 9507, *Correspondence relating to the Status of the South African Republic;* C. 9518, *Further Correspondence relating to the Proposed Political Reforms in the South African Republic;* C. 9521, *Further Correspondence relating to Political Affairs in the South African Republic;* C. 9530, *Further Correspondence relating to Political Affairs in the South African Republic.* 1900, vol. LVI: C. 18, *Correspondence relating to the Despatch of Colonial Military Contingents to South Africa.*

MEMOIRS, AUTOBIOGRAPHIES, BIOGRAPHIES, AND LETTERS

The Milner Papers. South Africa, 1897–1899. Edited by Cecil Headlam. London, 1931. A most important collection of correspondence, containing many letters exchanged by Milner and Chamberlain.

---

[59] *Milner Papers,* II, p. 32.

GARVIN, J. L.: *The Life of Joseph Chamberlain*. London, 1933—. The third volume contains a long and eloquent defense of Chamberlain's policy, but adds relatively little of a factual nature. Not as important as the *Milner Papers*.

Letters of Queen Victoria. Edited by George E. Buckle. Series III, volume III. London, 1932. Valuable, especially for the light they throw on proceedings in the British cabinet.

KRUGER, PAUL: *The Memoirs of Paul Kruger*. New York, 1902. Gives the Boer side, without adding much of importance.

FITZPATRICK, SIR J. PERCY: *South African Memories*. London, 1932. The recollections of the famous author of *The Transvaal from Within,* who was one of the outstanding representatives of the Uitlanders.

BUTLER, SIR W.: *Autobiography of Sir William Butler*. London, 1911. The author was commander of the forces in south Africa during the years 1898 and 1899. He is very critical of the Uitlander agitation and has much to say for the Boer viewpoint.

COOK, E. T.: *Edmund Garrett, a Memoir*. London, 1909. An illuminating study of the editor of the *Cape Times,* with many sidelights on the development of the situation.

HOFMEYR, J. H.: *The Life of Jan Hendrik Hofmeyr*. Capetown, 1913. A valuable biography of the leader of the Afrikander Bond, and an outstanding contribution to the history of south African politics.

LEYDS, W. J.: *Eenige Correspondentie uit 1899*. The Hague, 1919. The reports of Leyds from Europe. Important for the international side of the crisis.

WALKER, ERIC A.: *Lord de Villiers and his Times*. London, 1925. Another important contribution, containing many letters by the chief actors in the south African drama.

VAN DER MERWE, N. J.: *Marthinus Theunis Steyn*. Two volumes. Capetown, 1921. The biography of the president of the Orange Free State, who played an important part as mediator.

ECKARDSTEIN, HERMANN FREIHERR VON: *Lebenserinnerungen und Politische Denkwürdigkeiten*. Two volumes. Leipzig, 1919–1920. The sensational memoirs of a German diplomat, to be used with great caution, but containing much material, especially on the Samoan negotiations.

SPECIAL STUDIES: THE AFRICAN SITUATION

COOK, E. T.: *Rights and Wrongs of the Transvaal War*. New edition, London, 1902. One of the best analyses from a viewpoint favorable to the government.

HOBSON, J. A.: *The War in South Africa*. London, 1900. Perhaps the ablest critique of the British policy, with special reference to the capitalists.

FITZPATRICK, J. PERCY: *The Transvaal from Within*. London, 1899. The best-known contemporary account of the Uitlander problem.

BRYCE, JAMES: *Impressions of South Africa.* London, 1899. A vivid and searching contemporary analysis.

BOTHA, P. R.: *Die Staatkundige Ontwikkeling van die Suid-Afrikaanse Republiek onder Krüger en Leyds.* Capetown, 1926. The best scholarly study from the Boer side.

WALKER, ERIC A.: *A History of South Africa.* London, 1928. A sound, well-balanced and scholarly book, but rather unreadable.

WÜD, JOHANNES A.: *Die Rolle der Burenrepubliken in der Auswärtigen und Kolonialen Politik des Deutschen Reiches in den Jahren 1883–1900.* Nürnberg, 1927. A dissertation which brings together most of the material on German policy.

LOVELL, REGINALD I.: *The Struggle for South Africa, 1875–1899.* New York, 1934. The most recent and on the whole the best critical scholarly account of the development of the crisis.

SCHWARZE, FRITZ: *Das Deutsch-Englische Abkommen über die Portugiesischen Kolonien vom 30 August 1898.* Göttingen, 1931. An unusually able and keenly analytical study of the Portuguese problem.

SPECIAL STUDIES: THE SAMOAN QUESTION

HENDERSON, JOHN B.: *American Diplomatic Questions.* New York, 1901. Contains a detailed discussion of the problem as seen from the American angle.

MARQUARDT, CARL: *Zur Lösung der Samoafrage.* Berlin, 1899. The account of one of the German officials in the islands.

LEUSSER, HERMANN: " Ein Jahrzehnt Deutsch-Amerikanischer Politik, 1897–1906." (*Beiheft no. 13 der Historischen Zeitschrift*). Munich, 1928. Contains a succinct account of the problem, with reference to the German-American relationship.

DENNIS, ALFRED L. P.: *Adventures in American Diplomacy, 1896–1906.* New York, 1928. Contains a brief discussion of the problem and makes use of some unpublished American material.

LITERATURE SINCE 1935

(See also the Supplementary Bibliographical Note to Chapter VIII.)

The Cambridge History of the British Empire. Volume VIII. *South Africa.* New York, 1936. An authoritative account, from the British viewpoint.

LUCKWALDT, FRIEDRICH: " Lord Milner und die englische Südafrikapolitik " (*Berliner Monatshefte*, XVIII, December, 1940, pp. 759–777). An extended critical review of the Milner Papers, the Garvin biography of Chamberlain and other recent materials.

WECK, ALFRED: *Deutschlands Politik in der Samoafrage.* Leipzig, 1933. 157 pp. A dissertation which covers the subject from 1876–1899 and analyzes the published sources.

BEAZLEY, RAYMOND: "Samoa: eine deutsch-englische Kolonialverständigung" (*Berliner Monatshefte,* XV, December, 1937, pp. 1040–1059). A detailed examination of the events of 1898–1899, as reflected in the German and British documents.

ELLISON, JOSEPH W.: "The Partition of Samoa" (*Pacific Historical Review,* VIII, September, 1939, pp. 259–288). A heavily documented monograph, utilizing not only the German and British sources, but also American consular reports and newspaper material.

XIX

The Bagdad Railway Project

HILE THE BRITISH WERE GIRDING THEMSELVES FOR THE CONFLICT IN south Africa, an important though little noticed event took place in the Near East. On November 25, 1899 the Sultan signed a preliminary concession granting a German company the right to construct a railway to Bagdad and Basra. This concession was the consummation of a policy that went back a full decade and that introduced an entirely new factor into European international relations. The development of German interests in the Ottoman Empire was to become a crucial issue of European politics; it was to influence profoundly the relations between Germany on the one hand and England and Russia on the other. It is therefore essential that some account of its earlier stages be given here, the more so as its implications were already recognized by the powers when the preliminary concession was awarded.

The story of the Bagdad Railway scheme may be said to go back to the time just before the Crimean War. The British, ever deeply interested in the problem of communications with India, had in the 1830's sent out a very capable officer, Colonel Chesney, to explore the Euphrates River and report on its navigability. His report was extremely favorable, and one of his party, Captain Lynch, opened up steamship traffic as far as Bagdad in the succeeding decade. It was the heyday of European railway building, and it is therefore not to be wondered at that phantastic schemes cropped up for opening up the whole east to British commerce. In 1842 Mr. William Pare, of the Seville Ironworks in Dublin, put forward a plan for a railway to run from Calais to Constantinople, and thence to Calcutta and Peking! The very next year Mr. Alexander Campbell proposed to the British East India Company a railway to run from Ostend by way of Vienna and Belgrade to Constantinople and thence across Asia Minor to Aleppo, along the Euphrates and the coast of Persia to Kurrachee and Calcutta. A similar scheme was put forward in 1851 by James B. Thomson, who spent many years collecting data and ultimately secured the favorable consideration of the Porte as well as the support of Lord Stratford de Redcliffe.[1]

---

[1] F. R. Chesney: *Narrative of the Euphrates Expedition* (London, 1868); William P. Andrew: *Memoir on the Euphrates Valley Route to India* (London, 1857), p. 6. Many of the early projects are catalogued and discussed in Noel Verney and George Dambmann: *Les Puissances Étrangères dans le Levant* (Paris, 1900), pp. 293 ff.; but by far the best critical account is that of Halford L. Hoskins: *British Routes to India* (Philadelphia, 1928), especially pp. 148 ff., 327 ff.

On the close of the Crimean War the project was taken up by William P. Andrew, chairman of the Sindh Railroad, who, together with Chesney, put forward a more modest plan for a railway from Suedia (Seleucia) on the Gulf of Alexandretta to Jaber Castle on the upper Euphrates, a distance of some eighty miles. This line was intended to connect with steamer service on the Euphrates, though it was planned to extend the road ultimately to Bagdad and Basra (Bussorah), where ocean-going ships could call. A Euphrates Valley Railway Company was formed, and Lord Stratford helped it secure a 6% guarantee from the Turkish government, which at that time was still enthusiastically encouraging foreign enterprise and capital investment. An active campaign was carried on in England, Andrew stressing the value to Turkey of developing the formerly rich territories of Mesopotamia, and the commercial and strategic value to England of a short route to India. Andrew's book is colored throughout by suspicion of Russian designs in Armenia and Persia and the need for frustrating them.[2] But the plan fell through because Lord Palmerston, probably out of consideration for Napoleon III, could not be brought to consent to a British government guarantee, which was regarded as indispensable.[3]

Nothing further was done with regard to Asiatic railways until after the Franco-Prussian War, though in 1856 and in 1863 British interests were granted concessions for lines from Smyrna to Aidin and Cassaba respectively. The whole idea of a railway from the Syrian coast was dealt a severe blow by the studies of the eminent Austrian engineer, Wilhelm von Pressel, who made careful surveys for the Sultan in the years 1872–1874. Pressel finally recommended a network of railways totalling 6000 kilometers. The trunk line was to run from Haidar Pasha (opposite Constantinople) through Angora, Diarbekr and Mosul to Bagdad and Basra, with branches to Eskishehr, Kutahia, Konia and other places. Pressel's opinion was that a line from Syria running through the desert and through the barren area along the middle Euphrates could never be made a paying proposition. A more northerly route through Anatolia would tap richer provinces, which should be colonized. He suggested the settlement of some two million Germans along the line in order to hasten the development of the country.[4]

We may assume from the attitude of the Sultan later that he was not much taken with the idea of a large-scale immigration, but for the rest the report of

---

[2] Andrew, op. cit., especially pp. 2, 18, 124; Hoskins, op. cit., pp. 330 ff.

[3] The address of the deputation to Palmerston is given in W. P. Andrew: *Euphrates Valley Route to India* (London, 1882), pp. 64 ff. In addition to the excellent account of Hoskins, op. cit., pp. 330 ff., some discussion of these projects may be found in the anonymously published article of Alwyn Parker: "The Bagdad Railway Negotiations" (*Quarterly Review*, October, 1917, pp. 487–528), p. 489, and in Edward M. Earle: *Turkey, the Great Powers and the Bagdad Railway* (New York, 1924), pp. 176 ff.

[4] Wilhelm von Pressel: *Les Chemins de Fer en Turquie d'Asie* (Zürich, 1902), passim. See also the excellent analytical account of A. von Schweiger-Lerchenfeld: "Die Euphrat-Thal Bahn und kein Ende" (*Oesterreichische Monatsschrift für den Orient*, IX, March 15, 1883, pp. 45–51), who analyzes the report of von Pressel.

von Pressel became the general guide of the Turkish government. Work was at once begun on the first section of the line, from Haidar Pasha to Ismid, and this section, when completed, was turned over to a British company for exploitation. Just before Pressel made his investigations, the English government had indicated a renewed interest in the problem of land communication with India. The Suez Canal was finished, but that was a French undertaking and many Englishmen felt that there ought to be some alternative route under British control. A select committee of the house of commons was therefore appointed to " examine and report upon the whole subject of railway communication between the Mediterranean, the Black Sea and the Persian Gulf." It heard much evidence and many suggestions and finally recommended a line from Alexandretta or Suedia to Bagdad, Basra and Kuwait. It was pointed out that the Euphrates route would secure speedier transportation of mail and would provide a second and safer route for the conveyance of troops to India. The line would serve further to block any Russian advance towards the Persian Gulf, to say nothing of the great commercial advantages it would confer on England and India. The Committee pointed out, however, that sufficient traffic could not be expected soon, and that a government guarantee would be necessary. This guarantee the government refused to give in 1872 as in 1857.[5]

The matter came once more to an active stage in the years following the Russian-Turkish War and the Treaty of Berlin. Abdul Hamid had seen for himself the tremendous value of railways for the transport of troops, and the need for better communications if the Empire was to be held together. There can be no doubt whatever that throughout the succeeding years his railroad policy was based almost entirely upon military and political considerations. The British government, too, was interested in maintaining the Ottoman Empire as a bulwark against Russia. The Cyprus Convention and the whole program of reform in Asia Minor were designed with this idea in mind. Disraeli seems to have chosen Cyprus with the thought that it would serve to protect a railroad terminus on the Gulf of Alexandretta. He is said to have told Bismarck as much during the Berlin Congress, and to have had a high military officer trace a possible route.[6] In any event the subject was much debated in England, and an influential association, the so-called Stafford House Committee, began to elaborate schemes for a line from Constantinople to Alexandretta and thence to the Persian Gulf. The Sultan was anxious for action, but the plan died a lingering death, for reasons that are not wholly clear. The British occupation of Egypt in 1882 led to a distinct cooling in English relations with the Porte, and this fact may have had something to do with the disappearance of the scheme.[7]

---

[5] The report of the Select Committee is given in Andrew: *Euphrates Valley Route,* pp. 75 ff. See further Parker, op. cit., p. 490; David Fraser: *The Short Cut to India* (London, 1909), pp. 32 ff.; and especially Hoskins, op. cit., pp. 428 ff.

[6] Andrew: *Euphrates Valley Route,* p. 45; Hoskins, op. cit., pp. 439 ff.; and the interesting observations of Parker, op. cit., p. 490.

[7] See especially Andrew, op. cit., passim; D. G. Hogarth: " The Bagdad Railway " (*National*

In the meanwhile the Germans were showing increasing interest in Turkey, more particularly in its possibilities as a field for economic penetration. In the days of Chesney's explorations von Moltke, who was then in Turkish service, had called attention to these possibilities, and his views had been echoed by later mid-century writers, like Rodbertus and Roscher. In the 1880's there was a considerable body of German writing calling attention to Anatolia as a suitable territory for German colonization.[8] Bismarck, however, was not prepared to favor any activity that might estrange Russia and he therefore never went beyond giving consent for the mission of von der Goltz as instructor for the Turkish army.[9]

In 1888 the European trunk line was completed to Constantinople and the first train from Vienna entered the Turkish capital. The Sultan was more eager than ever to develop the Anatolian network, and to knit up the outlying provinces of Mesopotamia and Syria with the rest of the Empire. He had tried, through Pressel, to interest German financiers in 1885, but without success. In 1886 he approached the British company which ran the Haidar Pasha-Ismid Railway with a proposal that it extend the line to Angora and ultimately to Bagdad. For unknown reasons nothing came of these advances.[10] Nevertheless concessions were granted in 1888 for the extension of the Smyrna-Aidin and Smyrna-Cassaba lines, and the question of a railroad to Bagdad was very much to the fore. The British showed little interest; political relations were bad and London bankers had no confidence in Turkish finances. Furthermore, they looked upon the project primarily from the business angle and saw but little chance of an Anatolian line paying a reasonable return. The best policy, they held, would be to extend gradually the existing lines as conditions warranted.[11] The French, on the other hand, were very much interested. They had an enormous investment in Turkey already, and they controlled the Ottoman Bank, on which the Turkish government had to rely for financial aid. So strong, indeed, was their financial position that it had become irksome to the Sultan. He was determined not only not to grant them further concessions, but if possible to

---

Review, May, 1902, pp. 462–73); Hoskins, op. cit., pp. 441 ff. All previous accounts of this phase of the problem are now superseded by the thorough and illuminating study of Dwight E. Lee: *Great Britain and the Cyprus Convention Policy of 1878* (Cambridge, 1934), pp. 66 ff., 76 ff., and especially pp. 125 ff.

[8] Paul Dehn: *Deutschland und die Orientbahnen* (Munich, 1883); K. A. Sprenger: *Babylonien, das Reichste Land in der Vorzeit und das Lohnendste Kolonisationsfeld für die Gegenwart* (Heidelberg, 1886); Loehnis: *Beiträge zur Kenntniss der Levante* (Leipzig, 1882); Karl Kaerger: *Kleinasien, ein Deutsches Kolonisationsfeld* (Berlin, 1892); Edmund Naumann: *Vom Goldenen Horn zu den Quellen des Euphrates* (Munich, 1893). See further André Chéradame: *Le Chemin de Fer de Bagdad* (Paris, 1903), pp. 2–5; Georges Gaulis: *La Ruine d'un Empire* (Paris, 1913), p. 127; Earle, op. cit., p. 123.

[9] His attitude is discussed at length by Hajo Holborn: *Deutschland und die Türkei, 1878–1890* (Berlin, 1926), pp. 83 ff.

[10] Earle, op. cit., p. 31; Karl von Helfferich: *Georg von Siemens* (Berlin, 1923), III, pp. 28 ff.

[11] *Turkey No. 4 (1896)*, *Report by Major Law on Railways in Asiatic Turkey*, passim; Parker, op. cit., p. 493.

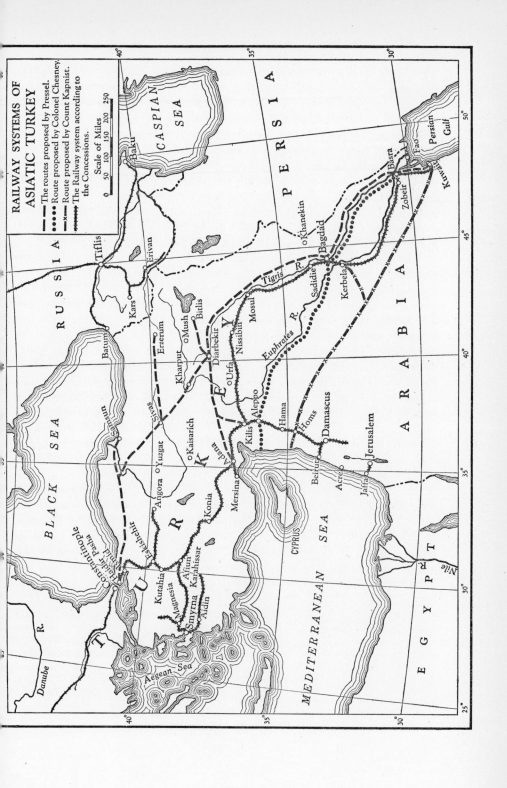

RAILWAY SYSTEMS OF
ASIATIC TURKEY

------ The routes proposed by Pressel.
•••••• Route proposed by Colonel Chesney.
××××× Route proposed by Count Kapnist.
━━━━━ The Railway system according to
the Concessions.

Scale of Miles
0   50   100 150 200 250

break their control. He therefore interested a German financier, Herr Kaulla, who was in Constantinople arranging for a large sale of munitions. Kaulla in turn managed to win over Georg von Siemens, head of the Deutsche Bank. The concession was applied for, and was vigorously supported by the " conspirators of Therapia," as the French called them, namely the ambassadors of England, Austria and Italy, the three powers united at that time in the Mediterranean Agreements. On October 4, 1888 the concession went to Kaulla and the Deutsche Bank, which paid six million pounds for rights in the Haidar Pasha line and agreed to build the railway to Angora, with the understanding that ultimately it should be continued to Bagdad. The government gave a kilometric guarantee to protect the Company against heavy loss. At the same time the German group made the Sultan a much-needed loan of some million and a half pounds.[12]

The Germans now went ahead full blast. An Anatolian Railway Company was formed, and in 1889 the Deutsche Bank and Wiener Bankverein purchased the controlling share in the Balkan railways. In 1890 a Bank for Oriental Railways was established at Zurich to serve as a holding company for both systems. The British were given three seats on the board of directors of the Anatolian company, and at first subscribed part of the capital. But in 1890 they sold out their shares. The Italians took no part, fearing French reprisals upon Italian securities.[13] For the Germans the Anatolian Railway was a good proposition, for they were now able to sell a good deal of construction material. In fact their exports to Turkey rose from about three million dollars in 1888 to about ten million in 1893. The Deutsche Levante Linie, which was opened in 1889, established direct communication by water and became an important part of the German commercial advance. A large number of German traders engaged in lively competition with the British and French, and before long captured a considerable part of the market.[14]

The line to Angora was completed by the autumn of 1892. But long before that time the struggle between rival concessionaires had been resumed. In the autumn of 1891 a French-Belgian group, probably backed by the Russians, brought forward a project for a line across Anatolia north and south, from Samsun on the Black Sea to Aleppo. The Sultan was greatly alarmed by this proposal and invited the German interests to apply for an extension of their line from Angora by way of Sivas to Bagdad. Engineers were sent out to survey the route, but Siemens and the Deutsche Bank showed little enthusiasm. They lacked money and the difficulties of the terrain indicated expensive construction

---

[12] The French interest in the scheme is reflected in such writings as Jean Blomdus: " La Lutte pour les Communications avec l'Asie " (*Journal des Sciences Militaires*, Series IX, vol. XVIII, 1885, pp. 65–93); Alexander Bérard: *La Route de l'Inde par la Vallée du Tigre et de l'Euphrate* (Lyon, 1887). The concession may be found in George Young: *Corps de Droit Ottoman* (Oxford, 1906), IV, pp. 120 ff. On the negotiations see Helfferich, op. cit., III, pp. 26 ff.; Earle, op. cit., pp. 31 ff.; Holborn: *Deutschland und die Türkei*, pp. 83 ff.

[13] Helfferich, op. cit., III, pp. 40–1, 51; Holborn, op. cit., p. 105.

[14] See especially Georges Gaulis: *La Ruine d'un Empire*, pp. 135 ff.

work. At best they were willing to consider a somewhat more southerly route, from Angora to Bagdad by way of Kaisarieh and Kharput, but they preferred building a long branch from the Angora line through Afiun Karahissar to the rich area around Konia.[15]

The matter dragged on. Abdul Hamid appealed to the Emperor William to support his scheme. William had paid an historic visit to the Sultan in 1889, and, unlike Bismarck, was profoundly interested in the Near East and its possibilities.[16] But even his approval failed to move the German bankers, who looked upon the whole affair from the business standpoint and saw little profit in a line which, after all, was designed for strategic rather than for economic purposes.

Negotiations took a new turn when, in the last months of 1892, the French-Belgian interests, who were arranging the purchase of the Smyrna-Cassaba line from the British, applied for an extension of this line to Konia. The Germans, in alarm, now pressed their own project for a line to Konia, and expressed readiness to build the Angora-Sivas-Bagdad route also. Abdul Hamid was much pleased and the bargain would undoubtedly have been closed at once, excepting for the fact that the British ambassador, Sir Clare Ford, quite unexpectedly registered a vigorous protest. The German Konia line, he argued, would injure the British Smyrna-Aidin line, which was the natural outlet for the products of the Konia region. This British opposition created quite a flurry for a time. The German government intervened and used strong language in London. Ultimately it even threatened to withdraw its support of British policy in Egypt. The moment was a critical one in Egypt and Lord Cromer used all his influence to induce the government to give in. Rosebery disclaimed any knowledge of the affair or any desire to antagonize the Germans. " Her Majesty's government," he wrote, " have no desire to take any step inimical to German influence or interest at Constantinople." Ford was obliged to desist from his protests, and on February 15, 1893 the Germans secured their concession.[17]

The concession of February 1893 provided for the construction of two lines: one from Eskishehr to Konia, which was to be built at once, and another from Angora to Kaisarieh. This second line was to be extended from Kaisarieh to Sivas as soon as the Haidar Pasha-Angora line showed receipts of 15,000 francs per kilometer for three consecutive years. It was to continue to Diarbekr and Bagdad as soon as the other German lines showed receipts large enough to enable them to dispense with the government guarantee. But the Turkish government reserved the right to demand at any time the prolongation of the line from Kaisarieh to Bagdad, making the necessary arrangements for guarantee.[18]

---

[15] *Die Grosse Politik*, XIV, nos. 3939 ff.; Helfferich, op. cit., III, pp. 58 ff.

[16] See especially Josef Maria von Radowitz: *Aufzeichnungen und Erinnerungen* (Berlin, 1925), II, pp. 249, 287, 288, 300–7.

[17] Helfferich, op. cit., III, pp. 62–9; *The Memoirs of Ismail Kemal Bey* (London, 1920), pp. 239 ff.; *Die Grosse Politik*, VIII, nos. 1816 ff.; XIV, nos. 3963 ff.; Parker, op. cit., pp. 499–500.

[18] Young: *Corps de Droit Ottoman*, IV, p. 147.

For some reason, however, only the Eskishehr-Konia line was built. The Sultan was chiefly interested in the Angora-Sivas-Bagdad scheme, but the terrain was difficult and the Germans did not promise themselves much profit from it. It has been said by many writers that this northern route was abandoned because of Russian protests, but there is no evidence of this. That the Russians were un-favorable to German enterprise in Anatolia even in 1893 is borne out by the German documents, but their opposition seems to have been to the general strengthening of Turkey by the development of communications, rather than to any particular line. It is perfectly obvious, of course, that they could not ap-prove of a line which would have facilitated Turkish mobilization in the Erzerum area, but no material at present available shows any actual protest in 1893, and it seems more likely that the Kaisarieh-Sivas-Bagdad route was not constructed because the Germans were not interested in it.[19]

The railroad from Eskishehr to Konia was completed in 1896, but in the years from 1894 to 1898 little interest was shown in Europe in any scheme of Turkish development. It was the time of the great Armenian massacres. Abdul Hamid was generally hated and the European public, far from wishing to strengthen his position, hoped for his deposition and expected the collapse of his empire. Furthermore, these were years of poor crops in Anatolia. The exist-ing railroads were not paying and with money tight in London, Paris and Berlin there was no prospect of further construction. The Sultan kept urging his Angora-Bagdad project upon the German bankers, but they lacked both interest and money. With British co-operation they might have been able to do some-thing, but apart from political considerations the British looked upon the Bag-dad railway scheme as a thing of the past. Lord Curzon wrote in 1892 that the idea, which had been so popular during the 1870's, had become " almost ex-tinct." " It does not, for the present at least, lie within the domain of practical politics." British interests would be best served by keeping a firm hold on Egypt and a safe watch on the Suez Canal, and in cheapening and quickening the maritime service between England and India.[20] Even Major Law, the British financial expert, who made a survey of the Anatolian railroads in 1895, con-sidered that there was no immediate prospect of the construction of a Euphrates line. As a route to India it would be 200 miles shorter than the Suez route, but would require two transshipments. He doubted if forty-eight hours could be saved by the overland route, and thought the whole matter had become less urgent since steamships had made travel by sea better and faster.[21]

---

[19] There is nothing in the elaborate and plausible argumentation of Hermann Schmidt: *Das Eisenbahnwesen in der Asiatischen Türkei* (Berlin, 1914), p. 7. On the Russian attitude in 1893 see *Die Grosse Politik*, XIV, no. 3970, and Helfferich, op. cit., III, pp. 69, 81. Helfferich does not repeat the statement he made in his earlier book, *Deutsche Türkenpolitik* (Berlin, 1921), p. 17, that Russian objections in 1893 led to the abandonment of the Angora-Bagdad route.

[20] George N. Curzon: *Persia and the Persian Question* (London, 1892), I, pp. 631 ff., espe-cially pp. 633, 635.

[21] *Turkey No. 4 (1896), Report by Major Law on Railways in Asiatic Turkey;* Theodore

After the victory of the Turks over the Greeks in 1897 had shown once again the value of railways and had demonstrated the vitality of the empire, there was renewed interest in Anatolia as a field for economic enterprise. The Pan-German League put out a pamphlet expounding extravagant hopes for the future, and a number of other German books emphasized the importance of the question.[22] The new German ambassador at Constantinople, Baron von Marschall, was enthusiastically in favor of pushing German influence almost from the moment of his arrival in 1897. But the German bankers held back, partly because the Sultan and the military men were still insisting on the Angora-Kaisarieh route. Finally, however, the German group was goaded into action by the projects of rival interests. M. Cotard, representing the Smyrna-Cassaba line, applied for a concession for a line from Konia to Bagdad, while a Russian and an English promoter both put forward plans for a line from the Syrian coast to Bagdad. Siemens and his friends regarded it as essential that competitors should be kept out. They considered an understanding with British financial interests, but this was frowned upon by the German ambassador at Constantinople. They then applied to the Berlin government for a guarantee, but this was refused after some delay. By the autumn of 1898 matters stood where they were before.[23]

In the interval the Emperor William embarked upon a second visit to the Near East. Apparently he had for some time been determined to make a pilgrimage to the Holy Land, largely from a genuine religious sentiment. But the plan undoubtedly had political implications, too. For many years the French had claimed a rather hazy right of protectorate over the Roman Catholics in both the Near and the Far East. The claim was naturally distasteful to national feeling in both Italy and Germany, and had led to an ever more insistent counter-claim on the part of the Italian and German governments not to a general protectorate over Catholics, but to a protectorate over their own Catholic subjects abroad.[24] These counter-claims found some support in the fact that France, since the conclusion of the Franco-Russian Alliance, did little or nothing to counteract the advance of Russian influence in Palestine and Syria. The influential Russian Imperial Palestine Society was doing its utmost to replace the Greek Orthodox clergy with Arab members of the Orthodox Church. It was organizing Russian pilgrimages on a large scale, opening training schools for missionaries, and generally spreading its influence in all directions. French writers themselves complained bitterly that their government was doing nothing to make good its claims to a protectorate, that it was giving the Russians a free

Monson and George T. Hutchinson: *The Life of Edward Fitzgerald Law* (London, 1911), pp. 149 ff. I do not see that the excellent report of Major Law has been used by other writers.

[22] Pan-German League: *Deutschlands Ansprüche an das Türkische Erbe* (Munich, 1896); Karl Kannenberg: *Kleinasiens Naturschätze* (Berlin, 1897); Ernst Friedrich: *Handels- und Produktenkarte von Kleinasien* (Halle, 1898).

[23] Helfferich, op. cit., III, pp. 85–7; *Die Grosse Politik*, XIV, nos. 3975–77; Earle, op. cit., p. 58.

[24] Theodore Aube: *Italie et Levant* (Paris, 1884); Anonymous: " La Politique Allemande et le Protectorat des Missions Catholiques " (*Revue des Deux Mondes*, September 1, 1898, pp. 5–41); Étienne Lamy: *La France du Levant* (Paris, 1900), pp. 217 ff.

hand, that the Alliance was undermining the French position in the Levant, and that the Russians were earmarking Syria as their base on the Mediterranean.[25]

The Germans decided to capitalize this situation, to undermine the French position in the east and to strengthen their own standing both with the Sultan, who disliked the French pretensions, and with the German Catholics, whose political support was always needed. In the spring of 1898 the German government encouraged the Sultan and the Pope to establish direct diplomatic relations. At the Vatican there was undoubtedly an active German party, of which Cardinals Hohenlohe, Galimberti and Ledochowski were the leaders. But ultimately the French minister, Lefevre de Béhaine, backed by the Papal secretary of state, Cardinal Rampolla, frustrated the scheme.[26]

The French regarded the Emperor's forthcoming visit with the most profound distrust. It was said, quite rightly, that German religious activity was a new thing and did not amount to much. Some claimed that the real object of the pilgrimage was to enlist the missionaries as agents for German influence and trade. Others noised it about that the Germans were planning to colonize in Palestine and Syria, and that they were out to get some harbor like Haifa, St. Jean d'Acre or even Rhodes.[27] Even in the midst of the Fashoda crisis the Paris press did not lose sight of the Levant. *Le Rire* published a special number on November 26, 1898 entitled *Tournée Guillaume II — Quinze Jours en Turquie, Palestine, Jérusalem et les Lieux Saints,* which was filled with unbelievably scandalous cartoons, one showing the Emperor off on an Armenian hunt with his friend the Bloody Sultan.[28]

As a matter of fact the whole business need not have been taken so seriously. Before the Emperor set out, in October 1898, the French had secured from the Pope a reaffirmation of their claims to the protectorate, and the trip itself was more amusing than important. *Simplicissimus* struck the right note with a cartoon for which the editor was condemned to a prison term. It showed Godfrey of Bouillon saying to Barbarossa: " Don't laugh so hard, Barbarossa, — our crusades, too, were really pointless."

---

[25] P. Pisani: " Les Russes en Syrie " (*Le Correspondant,* March 10, 1898, pp. 879–902); " La Propagande Russe en Palestine " (*Échos d'Orient, Chronique, février,* 1898, pp. 153–4); Lamy, op. cit., chap. iii; Alphonse d'Alonzo: *La Russie en Palestine* (Paris, 1901), passim. A detailed survey of Russian activities at this time may be found in Noel Verney and George Dambmann: *Les Puissances Étrangères dans le Levant, en Syrie et en Palestine* (Paris, 1900), pp. 131 ff.; Gaulis, op. cit., pp. 223 ff.

[26] *Die Grosse Politik,* XII, nos. 3351 ff., especially nos. 3357, 3358, 3359, 3361–5; Anonymous: " La Politique Allemande et le Protectorat des Missions Catholiques " (*Revue des Deux Mondes,* September 1, 1898, pp. 5–41); G. M. Fiamingo: " Die Politik Leos XIII und seine Diplomatie " (*Deutsche Revue,* June, 1898, pp. 280–90).

[27] " La Politique Allemande," loc. cit.; Pisani: " Les Allemands en Palestine " (*Le Correspondant,* September 10, 1898, pp. 895–920), p. 899; Étienne Lamy, op. cit., pp. 185 ff. The same fears were expressed in an English journal: Anonymous: " The German Emperor and Palestine " (*Fortnightly Review,* October, 1898), where it was said that the Germans were planning to settle ten to fourteen million colonists in Syria and Palestine!

[28] This was republished in translation in 1917: *The All-Highest Goes to Jerusalem* (New York, 1917).

The Emperor and Empress started out with a grand entourage. They visited the Sultan at Constantinople from October 18–22, and then went on to Palestine. The Turks had undertaken a grand housecleaning before the arrival of Their Majesties, and the Sultan had hurriedly bought from the Arab owner a holy place at Jerusalem, the *Dormition de la Vièrge,* which was only a cabbage patch worth a few hundred francs, but for which the Germans paid 120,000 francs in order that the Emperor might present it to the German Catholics. The pilgrimage was hot and uncomfortable, but it gave William a rare opportunity to indulge his love for theatricals and grandiloquence.[29]

The Imperial journey ended with a visit to Damascus, where William made his most resounding speech, proclaiming the fact that the three hundred million Mohammedans in the world could count upon him as a friend. This unfortunate utterance, which Bülow says he tried to excise before publication, pleased Abdul Hamid immensely, but did the Emperor no end of harm. It was quoted against him and against the Germans almost *ad nauseam* in the years before and during the World War, as evidence of German efforts to raise the Islamic world against England and France and Russia. As a matter of fact it created little stir at the time. The British, in the midst of the Fashoda crisis, took a rather benevolent view of the Emperor's motives, and indeed of the whole question of German influence in Turkey.[30]

The Emperor's pilgrimage had no direct bearing on the Bagdad Railway scheme. Siemens was at Constantinople at the time of William's visit to Abdul Hamid, and he was received by the Sultan in audience. But the Turks were still determined to have the road from Angora to Diarbekr and the German bankers had no heart for it. Siemens had little confidence in the future of Turkey so long as Abdul Hamid ruled, and his general attitude was to do nothing unless driven to it by pressure from competitors.[31] So for the time being the Germans concentrated their efforts on securing a concession for the construction of harbor works at Haidar Pasha, which was the terminus for the Anatolian line. In the last days of January 1899 they secured what they wanted and at once began work on the new development.

This Haidar Pasha concession proved to be a crucial step in the evolution of the Bagdad Railway policy. The French interests, which had a monopoly of harbor works at Constantinople, claimed that their rights extended to the Asiatic side and raised a grand protest against the German concession. Legally their protest appears to have had little basis, and nothing came of it, in fact. But it drove the French bankers to face squarely the whole problem of German

---

[29] One of the best accounts of the trip is in Gaulis: *La Ruine d'un Empire,* pp. 156–242, but see also the amusing account of Prince von Bülow, in his *Memoirs,* I, pp. 281 ff.

[30] London *Times,* October 28, 1898; *Morning Post,* October 12, 1898; see further *Die Grosse Politik,* XII, nos. 3345–7, 3366–83.

[31] See his conversation with Spring Rice (Sir Cecil Spring Rice: *Letters and Friendships,* I, p. 264), and Helfferich, op. cit., III, pp. 87 ff.; *Die Grosse Politik,* XIV, no. 3992.

enterprise. The new French ambassador, M. Constans, was anxious to restore French influence at the Porte. Where his predecessor, M. Cambon, had put himself in the front line of protesters at the time of the Armenian massacres, Constans tried to win back the confidence of the Sultan. At the same time he recognized that the Franco-Russian Alliance was not likely to inspire the Turks with friendly feelings and that the best course to pursue would be that of an entente with Germany. Delcassé seems to have approved this policy and the German government gave it its blessing. In April discussions were opened in Berlin which resulted in an agreement between the German and French bankers. The rivalry between the Anatolian and Smyrna-Cassaba lines was to be given up and each company was to appoint a number of directors to the board of the other. The French were to abandon their Bagdad Railway scheme and co-operate with the Germans in return for a 40% interest in the new line.[32]

Even more serious than the French protests were the objections of the Russian government. Whether these were at first inspired from Paris it is hard to say, but the Russians no doubt felt directly interested in the new turn of events at Constantinople. Count Osten-Sacken, the ambassador at Berlin, expressed to Bülow the uneasiness of his government. Constantinople, he said, was for Russia a *noli me tangere*. German economic interests in Turkey might easily develop into political hegemony and ultimately into a conflict of interests between Germany and Russia. Bülow stoutly denied this construction. Germany, he said, needed markets. Her aims were purely commercial and she had no idea of opposing Russian political aims. Russia, after all, could not claim the whole of Turkey as her own preserve.

These arguments did not satisfy the Russians. Osten soon returned to the charge. The Russians, he maintained, did not desire the collapse of the Ottoman Empire, but this collapse was bound to come before very long. Russia then could not tolerate the presence of another power at Constantinople. She would have to be sure of securing the Straits. If Germany could give her assurance on this point, then Russia might leave Germany a free hand for the furtherance of her projects in Anatolia.[33]

The Russian proposals were much more far-reaching than might at first appear. What Osten-Sacken was asking for was roughly what the Russians had secured from Bismarck under the terms of the famous Reinsurance Treaty. Consequently the Germans had to consider, as they had considered in 1890, whether they were prepared to orientate their policy towards the east and identify themselves with the Franco-Russian group. They argued the question in their inner councils and decided as they had decided nine years before, namely

---

[32] Helfferich, op. cit., III, pp. 92–7; Earle, op. cit., pp. 59–60; *Die Grosse Politik*, XII, no. 3349, XIV, nos. 3983–6; Louis Rambert: *Notes et Impressions de Turquie* (Paris, n.d.), pp. 62 ff. Delcassé later denied that French diplomacy had had a hand in the business, but the truth was well known. See the detailed discussion in André Chéradame: *Le Chemin de Fer de Bagdad* (Paris, 1903), pp. 266–75.

[33] These negotiations took place in April 1899 (*Die Grosse Politik*, XIV, nos. 3982, 4015–8).

that such an agreement would undermine and ruin the Triple Alliance and would mean turning their backs upon England. In return for such far-reaching sacrifices Russia was offering only commercial concessions. The game would not be worth the candle unless France could be gotten to join on the basis of a tripartite guarantee of territory, or at least unless Russia could be brought to promise friendly neutrality in the event of a Franco-German conflict. This proposal was made to Osten, but found little response. The ambassador maintained that Russia favored a combination with Germany and France to oppose England, but France could not officially abandon her claims to Alsace and Lorraine. To which Bülow replied that until France was willing to give up the idea of revenge Germany could not afford to turn her back on England. As long as Russia refrained from encouraging the French hopes, Germany would not antagonize Russia.

Although the Germans had quite definitely rejected the Russian advances, Count Muraviev came back to the question in the last days of June, using rather strong language and threatening quite clearly that if the Germans persisted in their refusal he would seek an agreement with England. But the Germans, who were on reasonably good terms with the French, stood by their earlier decision. The Emperor, in fact, was more than a little irritated by the high tone of the Russian foreign minister.[34]

Some German historians have made much of these discussions, and have interpreted them as something of a turning point in German policy. This is certainly a mistaken line. The Russians offered very little in return for the extensive concessions they demanded of the Germans, and it was impossible in 1899 to revive the situation as it had existed prior to the conclusion of the Russian alliance with France. The Germans, on the other hand, did not seriously consider the abandonment of the policy of the two irons. They were doing very well in playing off the Russians against the English, and they looked forward confidently to the time when both parties would be in even greater need of German support and would be prepared to pay an even higher price. As a matter of fact they had already made their peace with French financial interests, so that Russian displeasure did not seem very formidable.[35]

The immediate result of the rejection of the Russian advances was the systematic opposition of St. Petersburg to any further concessions being granted to the Germans. The Russian press was full of recriminations, claiming that the German scheme would hurt the Transsiberian Railway (!) and that it would make Anatolia and Mesopotamia a great granary competing with Russian agriculture. Furthermore, it would be a blow to Russian political preponderance in central Asia. Russia, said the *Novoie Vremia,* must tell the Germans to keep

---

[34] *Die Grosse Politik,* XIV, nos. 4019–25.

[35] Even Friedrich Meinecke: *Geschichte des Deutsch-Englischen Bündnisproblems, 1890–1901* (Munich, 1927), who discusses the matter at great length on pp. 118 ff., admits that there were almost insuperable obstacles to a German agreement with Russia.

hands off: " Our dear neighbors must know that Russia will never tolerate any infringement of the status quo in Asia Minor or Mesopotamia." [36]

The Germans were not greatly moved by Russian opposition, because, in 1899, they had the support not only of the French, but of the British. Feelings in London were rather mixed so far as the Bagdad Railway scheme was concerned. Or perhaps it would be more correct to say that the British cared little about a railway that would end at Bagdad or even Basra. " We may safely disregard croakings concerning the strategic danger offered to India by a railway which will set troops down at a point over 500 miles up a river navigated with difficulty by small sternwheelers and unfortified," wrote an English expert on the Near East in 1902.[37] From the very outset the British were interested in the control of the Persian Gulf, which they had policed for over a hundred years and where they claimed and maintained a special position.

In the autumn of 1898 Lord Curzon had been appointed viceroy of India. He went out filled with suspicion of Russian activity in Persia and central Asia, and determined to uphold the British position at all costs. In his book on Persia he had written years before: " I should regard the concession of a port upon the Persian Gulf to Russia by any power as a deliberate insult to Great Britain, as a wanton rupture of the status quo, and as an intentional provocation to war." [38] Curzon was very suspicious of Russian designs. He recognized the fact that any Bagdad railway scheme, to be successful, would have to envisage a terminus on the Gulf, and he saw that Kuwait (Grane), a wonderful harbor on the northwest end of the Gulf, would in all probability be the terminus chosen. In most of the earlier Euphrates Valley projects Kuwait had been regarded as the obvious terminal. The scheme for a railway from Syria to Kuwait, put forward by the Russian, Count Kapnist, in 1898, only served to confirm Curzon's fears. Kuwait formed part of the Turkish vilayet of Basra and paid tribute to the Turks, but its sheikh was little interfered with in the management of local affairs. He was very well disposed to the British and evidently hoped to secure from them support against eventual encroachments by the Turks. Curzon therefore arranged with him an agreement which was signed on January 23, 1899 by which the sheikh promised to cede no territory and to receive no agent of a foreign power without the sanction of the British government.[39]

The secret Kuwait agreement was directed squarely at Russian plans, though as a matter of fact it was to become much more important in the history of Anglo-German relations. At the very time of the conclusion of the agreement the Germans were turning over in their minds the possibility of acquiring a

[36] Quoted in *Questions Diplomatiques et Coloniales,* July 1, 1899, p. 313. On the Russian attitude see also Earle, op. cit., pp. 147–9.

[37] D. G. Hogarth: ' The Bagdad Railway " (*National Review,* May, 1902, pp. 462–73), p. 473.

[38] G. N. Curzon: *Persia and the Persian Question* (London, 1892), II, p. 465.

[39] Curzon: *Persia and the Persian Question,* II, pp. 462 ff., 597 ff.; Earl of Ronaldshay: *Life of Lord Curzon* (London, 1928), II, p. 50; *Peace Handbooks,* no. 76, pp. 51 ff.; Sir Arnold T Wilson: *The Persian Gulf* (Oxford, 1928), pp. 251–3; *British Documents,* I, p. 333.

footing at Muscat or Kuwait, but they were scared off by the harsh treatment meted out by the British to the French, when the latter secured the lease of a coal depot from the Sultan of Oman in February 1899. The British had a secret agreement with the Sultan, made in March 1891, by which he promised never to cede, sell, mortgage or otherwise give for occupation, save to the British government, the dominions of Muscat and Oman. This treaty was not wholly in consonance with earlier agreements by which England and France had engaged to respect the independence of Oman, but in 1899 the British consul at once assembled all available naval forces, went to Muscat and submitted an ultimatum. Under threat of bombardment he forced the Sultan to cancel the concession. Salisbury was greatly irritated by the affront offered to France at the very moment when the agreement about the upper Nile was being negotiated, but Curzon took a strong stand and the action was over before anything could be done to stop it. In any event, the French scheme was frustrated, and the Germans were too wise to repeat the experiment.[40]

From even this sketchy reference to the question of the Persian Gulf it should become clear that the British were intent on blocking any designs of the Russians and the French. The Germans as yet had not entered upon the scene. So long as they brought forward no plans to bring a railway to the Gulf they had no need to fear British opposition. British interests were represented on the board of directors of the Anatolian Railway Company, and they supported the idea of buying out the British-owned Smyrna-Aidin line as well as the idea of co-operation in the project of a line from Constantinople to Bagdad or even the Gulf.[41] Anonymous writers in the British press pointed out that it would be better to have the Germans in Anatolia and Mesopotamia than to have the Russians secure a footing there and then bang the door in the face of British commerce. German investment would give Germany an interest in bolstering up and reforming Turkey: " Germany thus becomes a sentinel, watchful against attack from without and an organiser of internal improvements." [42] Even the British ambassador to the Porte, Sir Nicholas O'Conor, favored support of the Germans on the basis of British participation.[43]

It was in general keeping with this attitude that Rhodes, during his visit to

---

[40] On German aspirations see *Die Grosse Politik*, XIV, nos. 3996–4006. The Muscat affair is dealt with in *British Documents*, I, nos. 255–60; see also *Die Grosse Politik*, XIV, nos. 3934 ff.; Ronaldshay, op. cit., II, pp. 45 ff.; Wilson, op. cit., pp. 239–40. There is a good account of French enterprise in the Gulf at this time in R. Vadala: *Le Golfe Persique* (Paris, 1920), pp. 26 ff. and a full discussion of the French case in the anonymous articles " L'Incident de Mascate " and " La Question de Mascate " (*Questions Diplomatiques et Coloniales*, March 1, 1899, pp. 281–6; March 15, 1899, pp. 367–9). See also Brunet-Millon: *Les Boutriers de la Mer des Indes* (Paris, 1910), pp. 209 ff., and Firouz Kajare: *Le Sultanat d'Oman* (Paris, 1914), pp. 196 ff.

[41] Monson and Hutchinson: *Life of Sir Edward Fitzgerald Law*, pp. 234 ff.

[42] Anonymous: " Asia Minor " (*Edinburgh Review*, April, 1899, pp. 515–42), pp. 530, 542; Anonymous: " Germany's Influence at Constantinople " (*Blackwood's Magazine*, May, 1899, pp. 921–4).

[43] *British Documents*, II, no. 202.

Berlin in March 1899, encouraged the Germans to proceed with their scheme. It was Germany's mission, he said, to open up Asia Minor and irrigate Mesopotamia, just as it was England's mission to develop Africa.[44] Bülow thereupon encouraged Siemens to embark upon the project. Siemens was not sanguine, but finally, in May 1899, he applied for a concession to extend the line from Konia to Bagdad. This route was chosen because the more northern Angora-Diarbekr-Bagdad line was longer and more difficult to construct. It may well be that the northern variant, which the Sultan had had so much at heart and which he abandoned only with great regret, was given up also out of consideration for Russia. So it has been claimed by many writers, though there is no direct evidence of Russian protest against any specific route.[45]

The negotiations with the Porte ran the usual course of intrigue and counterintrigue. " To complicate simple affairs," wrote the German ambassador when it was all over, " is regarded here as service to the state." There was no serious danger of the project falling through, though in the summer there was something of a flurry when an Englishman named Rechnitzer came forward with an offer to build a line from Alexandretta to the Persian Gulf without a government guarantee. The proposal was supported by the Ottoman ministry of public works, perhaps chiefly in the hope of being bought off by the German group. As a matter of fact the Rechnitzer project lacked adequate financial backing, and it is more than unlikely that the Sultan would ever have accepted a scheme for a railway from Syria to the Gulf, especially when no secret was made of the fact that the line was intended to strengthen the British position. Even O'Conor regarded it as counterfeit and wrote home that no one would undertake the work without a solid guarantee of some sort. Nevertheless, the Germans feared for a time that the project was being officially backed by the British embassy, and were uneasy about their own prospects. It was only after more disheartening intrigue that the Rechnitzer proposal was put aside. On November 27, 1899 the Sultan issued an *iradé* announcing the award of a preliminary concession to the Anatolian Railway Company. All the details were left to future decision, but in general the company undertook to build a line within eight years from Konia to Bagdad and Basra. The crucial step had been taken and the great Bagdad Railway project, so much discussed and so long hoped for, was definitely launched on the road to fulfilment.[46]

The story of the Bagdad Railway belongs to this narrative only in so far as it fits into the general picture of international relations in 1899 and in so far as it touches on the relations between Germany on the one hand and England,

---

[44] Wilhelm II: *Ereignisse und Gestalten*, pp. 73–4; Karl F. Nowak: *Germany's Road to Ruin* (New York, 1932), pp. 205 ff.; Bülow: *Memoirs*, I, pp. 338–9, 409.

[45] *Die Grosse Politik*, XIV, nos. 3980, 3987; Helfferich, op. cit., III, p. 98; Parker, op. cit., p. 503; Earle, op. cit., p. 34.

[46] For the last discussions see Helfferich, op. cit., III, pp. 99 ff.; Earle, op. cit., pp. 60–2; *Die Grosse Politik*, XIV, no. 3992; and *British Documents*, II, no. 202.

Russia and France on the other. Its great significance in the history of European diplomacy began several years later, when, after endless negotiations, the German bankers failed to interest British finance and when, after the transformation of the preliminary concession into a definitive concession in 1903, the Germans proceeded to build the line themselves in the teeth of opposition from England and Russia. Nevertheless it is quite legitimate and quite important to say a few words about the implications of the scheme and its larger bearings.

In the first place it should be noted that German enterprise was at first of a purely economic nature. Siemens, in fact, stuck to this view until his death. He was anxious not to antagonize other groups and always envisaged co-operation with the British. When the German plans collided with the powerful interests of the French, he was quite ready to strike a bargain and to give a fair share of the spoils to those who were willing to come into the scheme. This attitude resulted quite naturally from the magnitude of the project and the tremendous amount of capital it required. It must be remembered further that Siemens and the Deutsche Bank did not care much for the Bagdad scheme in itself. They wanted to open up the economically promising parts of Anatolia and cared nothing about the Sultan's strategic needs. In the end they undertook the construction of the line primarily in order to prevent other interests from cutting them out. But their activities underwent a profound change of character during the 1890's from the very force of circumstances. The mounting investment of German capital just naturally created a certain political interest in the strengthening and preservation of the Ottoman Empire, and the German government took a growing interest in this new field of endeavor. It was not to be wondered at, then, that the vision of a great German route from Berlin by way of Vienna and Belgrade to Constantinople and from Haidar Pasha to Konia, Bagdad, Basra and possibly the Gulf should seize upon the German imagination and conjure up hopes of a great economic dependency in the east.

But the emergence of a political interest in Turkey was bound to make the Bagdad Railway plan an important factor in the relations of Germany with the other European powers interested in the Near East. The French were most reasonable. They fought the growth of German influence tooth and nail until they saw that it was impossible to stop it. Then they consoled themselves with the reaffirmation of their protectorate claims in religious matters, with minor concessions for railway lines in Syria and Palestine and with participation in the German project. After all, for the French the matter was relatively simple. Their financial investment in the Ottoman Empire far exceeded that of any other European country. In government bonds and in economic enterprises they had sunk about two and a half billion francs. It followed, then, that they too had a tremendous interest in the maintenance of the Empire and the safeguarding of their investment. Failing to run the show themselves, the sensible thing for them to do was to join the Germans, whose interest at bottom was the same. In this matter the French stood more closely related to the Germans than to the Russians.[47]

The government of the Tsar was notoriously interested in preventing the strengthening of the Ottoman Empire, and for that reason it objected to any enterprise likely to benefit the Porte. But, as Bülow said, the Russians could not expect to put a fence around the Turkish Empire and let it gradually die. They were therefore obliged to restrict themselves to general protests against the political implications of the German enterprise. They tried, as we have seen, to safeguard their political position at Constantinople and to reserve the Straits for themselves. In this they failed, whereupon they fell back upon the policy of protesting against the construction of railways in the area adjacent to the Russian frontier. In April 1900 they extracted from the Sultan an agreement that no railways should be built in the Black Sea areas of Anatolia excepting by Russian interests. This agreement, of which but few of the details are known, secured the immediate needs of the Russians, though it left the larger problem of the growing German activity in Turkey unsolved.[48]

In the later period the German policy in the Near East was confronted with the joint opposition of the Russians and the English. The English attitude was the most important factor, for Russian objections might have been met or ignored had it not been for the fact that the British took the lead. It is therefore worth remembering that English policy was originally not hostile to the progress of German influence. The British had, to be sure, a great interest in all questions touching the communications with India, but they also had an interest in bolstering up the Ottoman Empire to serve as a bulwark against Russia and in preventing the Porte from becoming wholly dependent upon Russia's ally, France, in a financial way. For that reason Sir William White had encouraged the Germans and had helped them in 1888. Leaving aside the peculiar interlude of Sir Clare Ford's opposition in 1893 (and this seems really to have had no larger implications) the British attitude remained generally favorable throughout the rest of the century and there was every reason to suppose that the British would collaborate in the financing of the German scheme, as many English representatives advocated. It has been pointed out in the course of this chapter that they had pretty much lost interest in the Euphrates Valley route to the Gulf and India because the improvement of steam shipping through Suez and the avoidance of transshipments by that route had made it the more attractive as it was the cheaper. They no longer cared for the Bagdad route and it meant nothing to them so long as it did not reach the Gulf. All they needed do, therefore, was to safeguard their position in the Gulf, which they did by blocking French plans to establish a coaling station near Muscat and by concluding a

[47] Figures on the French investment about 1900 may be found in Chéradame, op. cit., pp. 261 ff., and in Herbert Feis: *Europe, the World's Banker* (New York, 1930), pp. 51, 320 ff.

[48] On these negotiations see especially *Die Grosse Politik*, XVII, nos. 5211, footnote, 5217, 5218, 5221.

non-alienation agreement with the Sheikh of Kuwait. The Agreement was secret, but in 1900 it became generally known when the British first warned the Germans of their special position at Kuwait and then openly deterred the Sultan from sending an expedition to reassert his authority over the dominions of the Sheikh.[49] There was no reason, then, for British opposition to the German enterprise, and it is greatly to be regretted, from the standpoint of general European politics, that British financiers did not at once take an active part in the construction and control of the line. It is fairly clear that the Germans were ready to strike a reasonable bargain which would have secured British interests in the Gulf.

Discussion of these factors is necessary because the charge has often been brought against German policy in the east that it was a great mistake because it involved the hostility of England and Russia and helped to bring these two antagonists together in common opposition to Germany.[50] The point need not be entered upon in detail here because, in the first place, it is ridiculous to argue that a state should abstain from all activity which may involve friction with another state. Under such conditions almost no activity abroad would be possible. It is the business of diplomacy to smoothe out such friction as inevitably arises. No one can deny that in the economic sense the German expansion in Anatolia was the most natural thing in the world. The growth of political interest flowed just as naturally from the economic. The Germans were willing from the start to avoid treading on the toes of others and it was hardly their fault if the British did not choose to follow the example of the French. At the same time it should be noted that the Bagdad Railway itself was never an insuperable obstacle in the way of good German-Russian or German-English relations. A multitude of other factors entered in, and ultimately the Bagdad difficulty was overcome by the Potsdam agreements with Russia of 1910 and 1911, and by the understanding with England which was concluded on the very eve of the Great War.

BIBLIOGRAPHICAL NOTE

DOCUMENTARY SOURCES

Die Grosse Politik der Europäischen Kabinette. Volume XII, chapter lxxxiii: The Question of the Protectorate of German Catholics and the Emperor's Journey to the East. Volume XIV, chapter xciv: The Bagdad Railway; chapter xcv; Russian Proposals for an Agreement regarding the Straits and Anatolia.

[49] Helfferich, op. cit., III, pp. 109 ff.; *Die Grosse Politik,* XVII, nos. 5278–86; Earle, op. cit., pp. 197–8.

[50] The question is discussed at great length in such books as Friedrich Meinecke: *Geschichte des Deutsch-Englischen Bündnisproblems* (Munich, 1927), pp. 122 ff.; Rudolf Ibbeken: *Das Aussenpolitische Problem Staat und Wirtschaft in der Deutschen Reichspolitik, 1880–1914* (Schleswig, 1928), chap. iv; Willy Becker: *Fürst Bülow und England* (Greifswald, 1929), pp. 50 ff.

British Documents on the Origins of the War. For some reason the Bagdad Railway negotiations were omitted from this collection. There is merely a short précis of documents in Volume II, no. 202.

Accounts and Papers. 1896, volume XCVI: *Turkey No. 4 (1896), Report by Major Law on Railways in Asiatic Turkey.* This is an excellent review of the history and general problem of Anatolian railways, which seems to have been little used by writers on the Bagdad Railway.

YOUNG, GEORGE: *Corps de Droit Ottoman.* Seven volumes. Oxford, 1906. Volume IV contains many of the texts of concessions for railway construction.

MEMOIRS, AUTOBIOGRAPHIES, BIOGRAPHIES, AND LETTERS

HELFFERICH, KARL: *Georg von Siemens.* Three volumes. Berlin, 1923. This is the authorized biography of the great German banker. Volume III contains what is probably the best single account of the Bagdad Railway project in the first phase.

BÜLOW, PRINCE VON: *Memoirs.* Four volumes. Boston, 1931. Volume I contains an entertaining but not very informative account of the Emperor's journey to the east.

RONALDSHAY, EARL OF: *Life of Lord Curzon.* Three volumes. London, 1928. Important for Curzon's views and for his action with regard to the Persian Gulf.

RAMBERT, LOUIS: *Notes et Impressions de Turquie.* Paris, n.d. Gives an interesting view of the political alignment at Constantinople in these years, with some sidelights on the activity of French finance.

MORISON, THEODORE, and HUTCHINSON, GEORGE T.: *The Life of Sir Edward Fitzgerald Law.* London, 1911. Law was president of the Ottoman Public Debt Administration in 1899 and was a director of the Anatolian Railway Company.

SPECIAL STUDIES

EARLE, EDWARD M.: *Turkey, the Great Powers and the Bagdad Railway.* New York, 1924. This is still the best general study of the diplomacy of the Bagdad Railway scheme, though its arrangement is such that one does not get a clear picture of the development of the problem. The book is based upon a considerable amount of new material, but now requires revision in the light of the German documents and other sources.

HOSKINS, HALFORD L.: *British Routes to India.* Philadelphia, 1928. An indispensable historical study of the communications problem. By far the best account of early railway schemes.

IBBEKEN, RUDOLF: *Das Aussenpolitische Problem Staat und Wirtschaft in der Deutschen Reichspolitik, 1880–1914* (Schleswig, 1928). Contains a detailed discussion of the political aspects of the enterprise, without adding much.

BECKER, WILLY: *Fürst Bülow und England*. Greifswald, 1929. A careful study of Bülow's general policy, with a detailed treatment of the Bagdad Railway. Based upon the obvious sources.

CHÉRADAME, ANDRÉ: *Le Chemin de Fer de Bagdad*. Paris, 1903. The work of a well-known propagandist. Contains much interesting contemporary material, and should not be neglected.

JASTROW, MORRIS: *The War and the Bagdad Railway*. Philadelphia, 1917. Of no value.

FRASER, DAVID: *The Short Cut to India*. London, 1909. Primarily a book of travel along the route, but contains a fair account of the early schemes for railway connexion.

HOLBORN, HAJO: *Deutschland und die Türkei, 1878–1890*. Berlin, 1926. A most important essay, based in large measure on unpublished German archive material. The best account of German policy prior to 1890.

SCHMIDT, HERMANN: *Das Eisenbahnwesen in der Asiatischen Türkei*. Berlin, 1914. Deals almost exclusively with the later period.

GÉRAUD, ANDRÉ: "The Story of the Bagdad Railway." (*Nineteenth Century*, May, 1914, pp. 958–72). A good general account, which, however, adds little.

(PARKER, ALWYN): "The Bagdad Railway Negotiations." (*Quarterly Review*, October, 1917, pp. 487–528). This is an inspired British account and is probably the best single treatment of British policy.

SCHÄFER, CARL A.: *Deutsch-Türkische Freundschaft*. Berlin, 1914. Deals chiefly with general German interest in Turkey and contains some good statistical material.

MORAWITZ, CHARLES: *Die Türkei im Spiegel ihrer Finanzen*. Berlin, 1903. A study of the Turkish financial system, with a good history of Turkish railway problems.

DU VELAY, A.: *Essai sur l'Histoire Financière de la Turquie*. Paris, 1903. Like the preceding title. Contains one of the best accounts of Turkish railway history in its financial aspects.

BENNETT, T. J.: "The Past and Present Connection of England with the Persian Gulf." (*Journal of the Society of Arts*, June 13, 1902). A good systematic review, now superseded by more detailed studies.

VADALA, R.: *Le Golfe Persique*. Paris, 1920. The work of a former French consul at Bushire. The book is devoted largely to trade problems, but contains much of interest on French activities and interests.

WILSON, SIR ARNOLD T.: *The Persian Gulf*. Oxford, 1928. A standard account, by a man who served for many years as a British official in the Gulf and in Mesopotamia.

VERNEY, NOËL, and DAMBMANN, GEORGE: *Les Puissances Étrangères dans le Levant.* Paris, 1900. An encyclopedic work based on very extensive research into contemporary material. Contains detailed statistics on foreign interests in Turkey as well as on Turkish railways and their history.

GAULIS, GEORGES: *La Ruine d'un Empire.* Paris, 1913. A collection of articles written in 1898 and later years. One of the best accounts of the Emperor's trip to Palestine and of the growth of German influence in Turkey.

LAMY, ÉTIENNE: *La France du Levant.* Paris, 1900. Another collection of periodical articles. Particularly valuable for the discussion of the protectorate issue.

REY, F.: *La Protection Diplomatique et Consulaire dans les Échelles du Levant et de Barbarie.* Paris, 1899. A sound systematic study of the protectorate problem.

LINDOW, ERICH: *Freiherr Marschall von Bieberstein als Botschafter in Konstantinopel, 1897–1912.* Danzig, 1934. This is a conscientious review of Marschall's ambassadorship. It is based on the more obvious sources and adds relatively little, though it brings much material together in convenient form.

BUTTERFIELD, PAUL K.: *The Diplomacy of the Bagdad Railway, 1890–1914.* Göttingen, 1932. A German dissertation, based on a narrow range of material. Of no value as a contribution to the subject.

LITERATURE SINCE 1935

(See also the Supplementary Bibliographical Notes to Chapters VII, X, XI.)

RAGEY, LOUIS: *La question du chemin de fer de Bagdad.* Paris, 1935. 212 pp. An excellent, clear review of the entire problem.

SITKI, BEKIR: *Das Bagdadbahn-Problem, 1890–1905.* Freiburg, 1935. 171 pp. Another solid piece of work, which makes some use of Turkish books. Especially strong on the period prior to 1901.

WOLF, JOHN B.: *The Diplomatic History of the Bagdad Railroad.* Columbia, 1936. 107 pp. The best systematic account in English, making use of all the recent documents.

HÜBER, REINHARD: *Die Bagdadbahn.* Berlin, 1943. 126 pp. Written by a German authority, this essay covers the entire story, including some of the technical aspects.

CHAPMAN, MAYBELLE K.: *Great Britain and the Bagdad Railway, 1888–1914.* (Smith College Studies in History, XXXI). Northampton, 1948. 248 pp. An exhaustive study of the British policy and the only monograph making use of the later volumes of the British documents.

XX

Europe and the Boer War

✺

W HEN BRITAIN EMBARKED UPON WAR WITH THE TWO BOER REPUB- lics, both the statesmen and the soldiers were convinced that what was before them was just another " sporting war," as Bismarck called England's colonial conflicts. All that was necessary was a " slap in the face" for Kruger and the thing would be over. Yet the most serious dis- illusionment was in store for them. It soon turned out that they had mis- calculated on almost every count. They underestimated the forces of the Boers, who could put about 50,000 burghers in the field, and they greatly underrated the number of troops required to overcome their opponents. The Boers showed little knowledge of strategy, but they were experienced fighters, they had a better rifle than the English and they completely baffled the enemy by their open fighting. At the outset the British had only about 25,000 men available. The rest had to be sent from England, 6000 miles away, or from India and the dominions. Before the end of the war in 1902 the British had no less than 300,000 men in south Africa.

Under these circumstances it was almost inevitable that the struggle should start with a series of setbacks for the British. General Sir Redvers Buller, who was in command, showed himself quite incompetent. Abandoning his original plan of keeping his forces together and pressing on to Bloemfontein and Pre- toria, he divided his army into three parts, hoping thereby to block the Boers at Kimberley in the west, at Colesberg in the centre and at Ladysmith in the east. But his hopes were everywhere disappointed. The Boers defeated the Brit- ish in three important engagements during the famous Black Week (Decem- ber 9–15, 1899) and shut up their forces in Kimberley and Ladysmith. The situation continued black for several months, despite the hurrying out of re- inforcements and the mission of Lords Roberts and Kitchener to command the operations. It was not until the second half of February 1900 that Kimberley and Ladysmith were finally relieved and Roberts was able to proceed slowly to the invasion of the Republics. The first, regular phase of the war closed with the annexation of the Transvaal in September 1900, but there followed almost two more years of desultory guerrilla warfare before the resistance of the Boers was finally broken.

The seriousness of Britain's problem and the magnitude of the army she was obliged to send to Africa naturally placed her in a most delicate international situation. In a hundred years she had never been so entirely without friends. Continental opinion was violently hostile and roundly declared the whole business a predatory enterprise plain and simple. The great, greedy British Empire was making no bones about attacking two valiant little republics simply in order to seize their gold mines. It was high time, said the press in more than one continental country, to put an end to British aggression and to deal the empire a telling blow. Everywhere there was talk of a continental coalition, of a union between Russia, France and Germany which would prove irresistible.

Few points in recent diplomatic history have been made the subject of so much recrimination as the question of intervention against England in the winter of 1899–1900. The French have accused the Germans of having made suggestions to this end, while the Germans have pointed to the Russian foreign minister, Count Muraviev, as the real culprit. It is therefore essential to review the evidence and to make some attempt to determine the true course of events.

Even before the outbreak of the war the British ambassador at Paris reported home on the hostility of the French press and noted that the favorite subject of discussion was the prospect of a combination of the continental powers against England.[1] The British newspapers were decidedly uneasy about the possibility of such action, the more so as Muraviev was at this very time paying a visit to the Spanish foreign minister at San Sebastian and to Delcassé at Paris. Almost nothing is known of the discussions that took place during these visits. The English ambassador at Paris, Sir Edmund Monson, learned that Muraviev had told the Spanish foreign minister that " the time had arrived when it became necessary for the Powers of Europe to take common action against the ever-increasing aggressions and expansion of England," and that he had dangled before the Spaniards prospects of acquisitions in Morocco. Monson learned further that the Russian minister had tried to bring Delcassé to adopt a hostile policy, but that the French statesman had resisted. Evidently the French attitude put an end to the scheme, if there was one, for nothing was said to the Germans by Muraviev when he and the Tsar visited Berlin in the first week of November. In any event there is no evidence to substantiate the later claim of French writers that Muraviev's proposal had been inspired by the German government.[2]

The French, including Delcassé, have always maintained that at the very time of Muraviev's démarche advances were made by the German Emperor

---

[1] *British Documents*, I, no. 285. It should be noted that the better French papers doubted the possibility of action. See the summaries of the press in *Questions Diplomatiques et Coloniales*, November 1, 1899, p. 301 and November 15, 1899, pp. 366–7.

[2] *British Documents*, I, nos. 286, 287, 294; VI, no. 129. The story was told in detail by Diplomaticus: " Count Muraviev's ' Indiscretion ' " (*Fortnightly Review*, December, 1899, pp. 1036–45) and is recounted by Delcassé's apologist André Mévil: " Delcassé and the Entente Cordiale " (*National Review*, July, 1908, pp. 712–9), and in his book *De la Paix de Francfort à la Conférence d'Algésiras* (Paris, 1909), p. 55. See also E. J. Dillon: *The Eclipse of Russia* (London, 1918), p. 318. Dillon drew his information from Witte.

to the French ambassador. In 1905 Delcassé told a British diplomat that the Emperor called on Noailles and spoke violently about England. The war, he is reputed to have said, offered " a unique opportunity which would not recur in a century for putting an end to the arrogance and aggression of England." A few days later Bülow is reported to have shown Noailles a map, from which he tried to prove that French and German interests clashed nowhere while Britain stood in the path of both. All they needed do was to combine their efforts.[3] Now there is nothing in the German archives bearing on this conversation. The French have published Noailles' despatch (October 18, 1899) but from the text it would appear that the talk was much more innocent than Delcassé made it out to be. The Emperor merely spoke of the community of French and German interests, especially in Africa. Ten days later he had another talk with the ambassador, the record of which has been published by the Germans but not by the French. From the Emperor's version it seems that Noailles began by expressing his uneasiness about the south African situation and by asking whether those powers interested should not eventually do something to check British expansion. To which the Emperor claims to have replied that it was already too late for such action. England would throw those who interfered into the sea. In 1896 she was still unprepared and surprised. If at that time other powers had joined Germany something might have been done. But now Germany had no fleet. In twenty years she would talk differently, but for the present she would have to remain neutral.[4]

What is one to make of this episode? So much, I think, is clear, that at this particular time, in the second half of October, the Emperor was exceedingly wrought up about the Samoan affair and the apparent unwillingness of Salisbury to make concessions. He may very well have spoken indiscreetly to Noailles about the possibility of co-operation with France in colonial matters. But even so the German suggestions were very vague. Delcassé seems to have been willing to follow up the lead. He wrote Noailles that the German proposition was worth considering in concert with Russia, and the ambassador did try to get Bülow to make a concrete suggestion. But the foreign minister evaded, and nothing came of the feelers, which were clearly not very seriously intended from the German side.[5] As for any combination against England, it is now obvious from the German documents that no proposition of that nature would have been entertained in Berlin. In mid-October Holstein wrote to Eckardstein that so long as German foreign policy remained in the same hands a rapprochement with France and Russia would hardly take place.[6]

In the autumn of 1899 German military men were generally of the opinion

[3] *British Documents*, III, pp. 432–3.

[4] Émile Bourgeois and Georges Pagès: *Les Origines . . . de la Grande Guerre* (Paris, 1921), pp. 281 ff.; *Die Grosse Politik*, XV, no. 4394.

[5] Bourgeois an. Pagès, op. cit., pp. 281–2.

[6] H. Freiherr von Eckardstein: *Lebenserinnerungen und Politische Denkwürdigkeiten* (Leipzig, 1919), II, p. 61.

that the British army would be beaten in south Africa.[7] Bülow claims that he did not share this belief, and neither did the Emperor. William, whatever his opinion of the British army, was immensely impressed with the British fleet, which he took at the English valuation and which, he was certain, would give short shrift to any power that interfered.[8] For that very reason he had long since grown into a feeling of helplessness with regard to England, and had made himself the champion of a large German navy. The Samoan business in particular proved once more that a continental state had to expect cavalier treatment from Britain if it had no fleet to inspire respect.

When the first naval law was passed in the spring of 1898 it was thought of by the Emperor and Tirpitz as only a first step in the right direction. It was designed to give Germany battleship power, but the size of the battle-fleet was such that it could hardly be classed as more than a mobile coast-defense. Its offensive possibilities were small and Tirpitz intended to ask for much more when the first program was completed in 1904. By the summer of 1899 he had convinced himself that a new program must be brought in at least a couple of years sooner. The Spanish-American War, the Fashoda crisis, the Philippine and Samoan episodes had, he felt, created a new world situation which made an increase of the fleet much more urgent.[9]

But Tirpitz meant to proceed carefully and methodically and not to shock the German public and Reichstag into opposition. His hand was forced by the Emperor, who on October 18, 1899 made a speech at Hamburg at the launching of the steamer *Karl der Grosse* in which he declared: "Bitter need have we of a strong German fleet." The speech called forth downright consternation in the ministry of marine. Tirpitz as well as Hohenlohe hesitated long whether to follow up the Emperor's precipitate lead. Finally it was decided to take advantage of the Boer War to bring in a second naval bill. Bülow made a great speech in the Reichstag on December 11, 1899, in which he first enunciated officially the idea of a risk-fleet, that is, the idea that Germany must have a fleet so powerful that even the strongest naval power could not attack it without serious risk.

The government had a much easier time than it had anticipated. Since 1898 German opinion had been educated to the idea of naval power. The Colonial Society had carried on a large-scale agitation, but even this was overshadowed by the work of the Navy League. This organization had been founded in April 1898 and was heavily financed by the Krupps and other steel interests, which were deeply interested in the guns and armor required for the ships. The League had 100,000 members in the middle of 1899 and the figure grew rapidly to 250,000. Its publication, *Die Flotte,* had a circulation of 250,000, while its

---

[7] *Die Grosse Politik*, XV, no. 4408, footnote; Prince von Bülow: *Memoirs* (Boston, 1931), pp. 341-2.   [8] His marginal note in *Die Grosse Politik*, XVIII, no. 5861.
[9] Alfred von Tirpitz: *Erinnerungen* (Leipzig, 1919), pp. 103 ff.: Bernhard Michalik: *Probleme des Deutschen Flottenbaues* (Breslau, 1931), pp. 68 ff.

lecturers made no less than three thousand speeches in the winter of 1899–1900.[10]
There was undoubtedly great popular interest in the fleet and in world policy.
German writers have pointed out that in the voluminous literature of the time
it is impossible to find any consensus of opinion as to the purpose of the projected fleet. There was less talk of its value for the protection of commerce
and colonies and more talk of its political value as an instrument of world policy,
but generally speaking the conception of the problem was nebulous. By some
writers this is taken as proof that the naval bill was not the result of an urgent
foreign situation, but rather the result of a bargain between industrial and
agrarian interests: the former were to have their fleet and world policy, the
latter protection for agriculture and a continuance of their social predominance.[11]
No doubt there is more than a grain of truth in this interpretation, though it
seems to me to lay too little stress on the imponderables. The new generation in
Germany did not, like its fathers, feel saturated. It felt cramped within the
continental horizon and yearned for a world policy. The fleet was for it an
aspiration, a symbol of added power, and for that reason the government project
found such wide support.[12]

We need not enter upon the detailed history of the Second Naval Bill. It
provided for a German fleet comprising thirty-eight battleships, to be completed in twenty years. It went through the successive readings in the Reichstag
in the spring of 1900 and was passed on June 12 with a vote of 201–103. Only the
Socialists, a small part of the Centre and a part of the Progressives voted against
it. The rest of the deputies accepted the government explanations, that if Germany were stronger at sea the other powers would respect her more highly,
and that for German purposes nothing less than a fleet strong enough to impress
even the strongest naval power would be sufficient. Parliament voted the government program without tying financial strings to it. The fleet was to be
built whatever the cost.

As we look back on the passage of the great German naval law, which was,
in a short space, to lift Germany from the position of fifth sea power to that
of second, we cannot help but feel that the Emperor, Bülow and Tirpitz were
laying the foundations of serious conflict with England. It seems fairly clear
that they did not realize how far the question of sea-power would lead. The
accusation may be justly brought against them that they worked on the sub-
conscious assumption that things would remain as they were in 1900. Of course
they did not envisage a fleet as strong as the British. What they aimed at was
simply this: a fleet large enough to proceed offensively against the British
Home fleet (at that time about thirty-two ships) and at the same time a fleet

---

10 Eckart Kehr: *Schlachtflottenbau und Parteipolitik, 1894–1901* (Berlin, 1930), pp. 98 ff.,
169 ff.; Archibald Hurd and Henry Castle: *German Sea-Power* (London, 1913), pp. 208 ff., 321;
Tirpitz, op. cit., pp. 95–6.
11 This is the general burden of Kehr's very interesting book.
12 The point is well argued in Michalik, op. cit., pp. 103 ff.

that would give Germany an alliance value, a fleet so strong that England would respect it and ultimately seek an agreement with Germany, or, failing that, a fleet so strong that Germany would become an attractive ally for France and Russia. What they did not foresee was that the British would put their own interpretation on German policy and that they would reply by building an ever more powerful navy. What they did not foresee was further this, that the English, instead of seeking an agreement with Germany, would ultimately find it cheaper to strike a bargain with Germany's potential allies at sea, France and Russia.

All this is clear as we look back, but it will not do to make too much use of hindsight. The European world in 1900 was obsessed with the ideas of imperialism and world policy and the idea of sea-power was an integral part of the larger imperial idea. Even sane people were victims of the obsession. Prince Hohenlohe, the octogenarian German chancellor, who was deeply rooted in the ideas of the Bismarckian age, wanted the naval bill passed. " We must not," he wrote, " expose ourselves to the danger of suffering the fate from England that Spain suffered from the United States. That the English are merely waiting for a chance to fall upon us is clear." Count Münster, the ambassador at Paris, who was also a left-over of an earlier period, shared the desire for sea-power, though his train of thought was more nearly that of Bülow and Tirpitz: If Germany had a strong fleet England would have to cultivate German friendship in order to prevent a naval coalition being formed against her: " The civilization of the world depends upon a naval agreement between England and ourselves, and therefore England must regard us not as an enemy, but as an equal; this she will do only if we are strong enough, even on the sea." [18]

But the introduction of the bill for a greatly increased navy in no sense reflected hostility to Britain at the time. In fact Anglo-German relations were distinctly good in the critical first months of the Boer War. Once the Samoan business had been disposed of in a way satisfactory to the Germans the Emperor was ready to start off on his long-discussed visit to England, the first he was to pay since the ill-fated visit to Cowes in 1895. The German public was as violently hateful of England and as favorable to the Boers as the public of any European country, so the Emperor's journey to England at a time when it appeared like an endorsement of British policy called forth no end of criticism. For that reason the private nature of the visit had to be underlined and William from first to last resisted all attempts that were made to have him visit London. He visited his grandmother at Windsor and spent some days with the Prince of Wales at Sandringham; in all he spent less than ten days in England (November 20–28).

Bülow accompanied the Emperor during the visit, and arrangements had been made for conferences between the German statesmen on the one hand and Salisbury, Chamberlain and Balfour on the other. As it happened, Lady Salisbury died just as the Imperial party arrived and the prime minister there-

---

[18] Hohenlohe: *Denkwürdigkeiten der Reichskanzlerzeit,* pp. 554, 575.

fore excused himself. In all probability he was not anxious to be drawn into the conversations. After the Emperor's attacks upon him in the summer he had less use than ever for the German connexion. It is quite clear that if Chamberlain had not taken the Samoan negotiations out of his hands a settlement would not have been reached in time. The Germans were under no illusions about Salisbury's feelings. Hatzfeldt had written home discussing the peculiar relationship between the prime minister and Chamberlain and pointing out that German hopes could be realized only through the latter. But Chamberlain would require careful and discreet handling.[14] Bülow, indeed, claims that after his arrival in England he received, through Sir Frank Lascelles, a letter from Salisbury warning him that Chamberlain would be speaking only for himself, not for the cabinet.[15] There is no trace of the letter in the German documentary publication and Bülow merely summarizes it in his memoirs. Its authenticity seems very doubtful, for it is rather hard to believe that one British statesman should write such a letter about another. Certainly it would have been contrary to all the accepted etiquette of English politics.

We may assume, I think, that the conversations at Windsor were frank and aboveboard. Chamberlain told both the Emperor and Bülow that what he wanted was an understanding between England, Germany and the United States. Britain, he said, was uneasy about Russian progress in China and needed Germany and America to help check it. He admitted that Salisbury was opposed to a formal alliance because he disliked being definitely bound in any direction. But an understanding would be possible, in Chamberlain's opinion. Britain, he said, would rather see the Germans than the Russians in Anatolia and he therefore favored English co-operation with Germany in the Bagdad Railway enterprise. He hinted further that England and Germany might work together in Morocco, England marking off for herself Tangiers and leaving to Germany part of the Atlantic coast area. To all of which the Emperor and Bülow replied by stressing England's aversion to binding alliances and pointing out that German relations with Russia and even with France were good and that Germany could not afford to compromise her relations with Russia. The Germans favored separate agreements on special points, but displayed no great interest in more extensive commitments.

The conversations between the visitors and Balfour were of a more general nature. Balfour, too, favored an agreement between England, Germany and the United States, though he was not as insistent as Chamberlain. He spoke at some length of the Anglo-German trade rivalry, which he attempted to minimize. There was no jealousy on the British side, he asserted, for both nations were pursuing much the same policy of the open door and both were making progress. On the other hand he complained bitterly of the violence of the German press. Bülow countered with complaints of Mr. Saunders, the *Times* correspondent in Berlin, who, he said, collected the worst utterances from obscure

---

[14] Bülow: *Memoirs*, I, pp. 362-3.   [15] Ibid., p. 367.

papers and sent them on to London. Parenthetically it might be said that Bülow returned from his visit much impressed with England and convinced that the British were much less hostile to Germany than the Germans were toward the British. For that reason, he noted, men like Saunders and Chirol, who really knew German opinion, were a menace to good relations.[16]

The Windsor visit was undoubtedly a great success, having been marred by no personal or other friction. It was welcomed by the British government and by the public as a mark of good will in a very dark hour and it demonstrated to the world that Germany could not be counted on for any hostile action. This was the interpretation current at the time. The Emperor, wrote the French ambassador at Berlin on November 26, was ill-disposed toward any long-term combination: " He does not want to bind himself definitely on any side, intends not to become involved with anyone, but to be on good terms with everybody, to keep abreast of opportunities, perhaps he even seeks to create them, and in any event profits by them." [17] This is a succinct and correct estimate of the German position. The Windsor conversations went no further than those that had taken place in 1898. The Germans were on their guard from the outset. They wanted to keep Chamberlain friendly, because they thought that through him alone they would be able to secure concessions in special questions. The colonial secretary, as usual, laid his cards on the table. He admitted that Salisbury was opposed to a formal alliance, yet advocated a triple grouping to block the Russian advance in the east. If Germany co-operated she would be rewarded with British support in Anatolia and Morocco.

German emphasis upon the necessity of maintaining good relations with Russia should have showed Chamberlain that his scheme had little prospect of success, for the very crux of the business was common action against Russia. He claimed later that Bülow had expressed the wish that he say something publicly of the mutual interests which bound the United States to an understanding with Germany and England.[18] But even if that was the case, the suggestion certainly could not have been reasonably interpreted as an invitation to say what Chamberlain said in his famous Leicester speech, delivered on November 30, just after the imperial party had left. He prefaced his remarks with a warning to the French press that if its attacks upon Her Majesty did not stop there might be " serious consequences." He then went on to pay a tribute to the friendly attitude of the United States, and finally came to the question of relations with Germany:

> " There is something more which I think any far-seeing English statesman must
> have long desired, and that is that we should not remain permanently isolated
> on the Continent of Europe; and I think that the moment that aspiration is

---

[16] On the Windsor visit see *Die Grosse Politik*, XV, nos. 4396 ff.; Bülow: *Memoirs*, I, pp. 369 ff.; Eckardstein: *Lebenserinnerungen*, II, chaps. iii and iv; Garvin: *Life of Chamberlain*, III, pp. 496 ff.; Sir Sidney Lee: *Edward VII* (New York, 1925), I, pp. 745 ff.

[17] Bourgeois and Pagès, op. cit., pp. 283–4.　　[18] Eckardstein, op. cit., II, p. 107.

formed it must have appeared evident to everybody that the natural alliance is between ourselves and the great German Empire. We have had our differences, our quarrels, misunderstandings, but at the root of things there has always been a force which has necessarily brought us together. What interest have we which is contrary to the interest of Germany? I can foresee many things which must be a cause of anxiety to the statesmen of Europe, but in which our interests are clearly the same, and in which that understanding of which I have spoken in the case of America might, if extended to Germany, do more perhaps than any combination of arms to preserve the peace of the world. At bottom the character of the Teutonic race differs very slightly indeed from the character of the Anglo-Saxon race. If the union between England and America is a powerful factor in the cause of peace, a new Triple Alliance between the Teutonic race and the two great branches of the Anglo-Saxon race will be a still more potent influence in the future of the world. I have used the word alliance, but it matters little whether you have an alliance which is committed to paper or whether you have an understanding which exists in the minds of the statesmen of the respective countries. An understanding is perhaps better than an alliance."

This remarkable speech created something of a furor even in England, where it found very little favor. The *Times* declared that relations with Germany could never be as close as those with the United States, and Stead wrote in the *Review of Reviews* that England wanted no alliance and was thoroughly sick of concessions, the newest of which were Samoa and Anatolia. As a matter of fact Stead and others were already suspicious of the German naval program, which was regarded as " a direct challenge addressed to Great Britain, intimating that Germany is going into training to snatch from us that sea-power upon the maintenance of which our Empire depends." In the same tone the *National Review* denounced the idea of friendship with Germany because the Emperor was obviously making use of German Anglophobia to build up a fleet with the hardly concealed object of threatening British naval supremacy.[19]

The Americans showed no more interest in the projected alliance. Public opinion beyond the Atlantic was cooling off in its affection for Britain since the Spanish War was at an end, and the Irish and German elements were loud in their attacks upon British policy in south Africa.[20] But what was more important was the violently negative attitude of German opinion, which was nothing less than brutal in its denunciations. Chamberlain was accused of exploiting the Emperor's visit in order to compromise German relations with other powers. Bülow could not resist this hostile pressure. On December 11 he

[19] *Review of Reviews*, November 15, 1899, p. 435; December 15, 1899, pp. 547 ff.; *National Review*, December, 1899 pp. 481–3. There is a good review of British opinion on the Leicester speech in the *Economist*, December 10, 1899, and in *Questions Diplomatiques et Coloniales*, December 15, 1899, pp. 504 ff. Garvin, op. cit., III, pp. 506 ff., recognizes that the Leicester speech was a *faux pas*.

[20] A. M. Low: " American Affairs " (*National Review*, April, 1900, pp. 276–88); Alfred L. P. Dennis: *Adventures in American Diplomacy* (New York, 1928), pp. 127 ff.; Tyler Dennett: *John Hay* (New York, 1933), chap. xx.

delivered a great speech in the Reichstag in which he reviewed Germany's relations with all the powers. He pointed out that Germany had always been able to work in harmony with France in colonial questions, and that he had always found Russia friendly and reasonable in such matters. Relations with the United States were good, and the same was true of relations even with Japan.

" As for England, we are quite ready to live in peace and harmony with her on the basis of full reciprocity and mutual consideration. But just because our foreign position is now a favorable one, we must use it in order to secure ourselves for the future. I wish, we all wish, that this future may be a peaceful one. Whether it will be a peaceful one, no one can tell. We must be secured against surprises not only on land, but on the sea. We must build a fleet strong enough to prevent an attack — I underline the word *attack,* for with the absolutely pacific nature of our policy there can be no talk of anything but defense — from any power."

To which he added veiled references to past disputes with England which had shown conclusively the urgent need of a German fleet.

Chamberlain's Leicester speech was surely a *gaucherie,* as Bülow claimed, but the German foreign minister's reply, too, was inexcusable. Not only did he definitely reject all ideas of more than bargainings between the two powers, but he seized the opportunity to inject the naval question and to put forward officially the thought of building a fleet strong enough to resist English attack. It was no wonder that Chamberlain felt that, after being invited to say something friendly, he had been given a smart slap in the face.[21]

But the friction engendered by the " new " diplomacy had no effect on the actual policies of the two countries. The British simply could not afford to estrange Germany at so critical a moment and the Germans had no intention of giving up their policy of the free hand or their hopes for reward for good behavior. Bülow gave assurances that Germany would abstain from any continental grouping or collective action against Britain and told the English ambassador that " any diminution of the authority and prestige of Great Britain would be little short of a calamity for Germany." [22] On the other hand, when General Buller urged a blockade of Delagoa Bay in order to prevent supplies going up to the Boers, the Germans made no secret of the fact that British action would necessitate some sort of compensation to Germany, and that Walfisch Bay would not be sufficient. Nothing less than Zanzibar would do. In the end the British government gave up the idea for fear of complications with Germany and France.[23]

---

[21] On Bülow's reply see Eckardstein, op. cit., II, pp. 123 ff.; Garvin, op. cit., III, pp. 511 ff.; Willy Becker: *Fürst Bülow und England* (Greifswald, 1929), pp. 141 ff.; *Die Grosse Politik,* XV, nos. 4401, 4456.

[22] Eckardstein, op. cit., II, pp. 126–7; *British Documents,* I, no. 302.

[23] *Die Grosse Politik,* XV, nos. 4404–11; Eckardstein, op. cit., II, pp. 128 ff.; *Letters of Queen Victoria,* III, pp. 428, 431; *British Documents,* I, no. 301; Garvin, op. cit., III, pp. 492 ff.

Yet the importation of arms and goods by way of Delagoa Bay was a matter of prime importance for the British. Efforts had to be made to stop it and Salisbury hoped to obtain the effects of a blockade " by carefully searching every vessel that comes in for contraband of war." [24] The immediate application of this decision was the stopping of the German mail steamer *Bundesrath* during the last days of December. Other German ships were stopped on suspicion soon afterward. It was believed later that the Boer representative in Europe had indirectly spread rumors that the German ships were carrying volunteers and armaments. However that may have been, the German ships were stopped on the basis of very inadequate evidence and they were taken into port for examination despite the protests of the Berlin government. During the first weeks of January the incident threatened to reach the proportions of a first-rate crisis, for German opinion was violently outraged and freely attacked the government for its weak policy toward England. The British, it was said, were making up for their reverses in the war by striking a blow at German commerce. Bülow pressed for the release of the steamer, but got little satisfaction. Finally he felt obliged to go so far as to suggest that if this was the reward for neutrality Germany would be obliged to seek some other combination. In London it was thought, evidently quite erroneously, that a German admiral was to be sent over to demand satisfaction and to break off relations if satisfaction were refused.[25] On January 16, 1900 the British government backed down. It admitted that no contraband had been found and promised that the *Bundesrath* should be released at once. It agreed further to pay an indemnity, not to stop other ships at a great distance from the scene of action and not to detain mail-steamers on mere suspicion.

The disposal of the matter came just in the nick of time so far as Bülow was concerned, for he had postponed as long as he could interpellations in the Reichstag. On January 19 he spoke on the subject in parliament and in order to appease German opinion underlined the fact that England had given in on every point to the strong representations of the German government. This speech in turn called forth so much dissatisfaction and criticism in England that the government felt constrained to publish a Blue Book in which the strong German notes were reproduced.[26] The English statesmen, to be sure, had at first thanked Bülow for his considerate handling of the matter, but after the Reichstag speech Chamberlain complained bitterly of the sharp telegrams from Berlin and declared that so long as such a tone were struck, better relations would be impossible.[27]

---

[24] *Letters of Queen Victoria*, III, p. 431.

[25] *Die Grosse Politik*, XV, nos. 4425, 4429; Eckardstein, op. cit., II, pp. 144 ff.

[26] *Africa No. 1 (1900), Correspondence respecting the Action of H. M.'s Naval Authorities with regard to Certain Foreign Vessels.*

[27] *Die Grosse Politik*, XV, no. 4456. The whole matter is dealt with in great detail in *Die Grosse Politik*, XV, chap. cii, but see also the Blue Book mentioned above and *British Documents*, I, nos. 304, 306; Eckardstein, op. cit., II, pp. 144 ff. and the analysis of the documents in Ray-

The *Bundesrath* affair was a most unfortunate interlude. Salisbury admitted in a letter to the Queen that the ship had been stopped " on very inadequate evidence " and that the mistake might prove a costly one.[28] A costly one it certainly was, for it not only interjected a further element of irritation into Anglo-German relations, but greatly facilitated the German government's task of passing the naval bill. When Tirpitz heard of the incident he is reported to have been delighted and to have exclaimed: " Now we have the wind we need to bring our ship into the harbor; the naval law will pass." [29]

In a sense it may be said that the stopping of the German ships revived also the question of possible international action against Britain. Since Chamberlain's Leicester speech the Paris press had been more rabid than ever. The whole country, wrote the British ambassador, " appears to have gone mad with jealousy, spite and resentment." [30] Everywhere the demand for intervention cropped out. Delcassé and the government were undoubtedly opposed to any policy of adventure, but the government was weak and the nationalist tide was strong. The German ambassador reported in January 1900 that French hatred of the English was almost deeper than it ever had been against Germany. The French public counted on the good will of the Germans.[31] On some sides it was felt that this was the moment to take revenge for Fashoda, and that if France failed to act England would ultimately make good her losses in south Africa by an attack on France or by the seizure of French colonies. France therefore needed a navy strong enough not only to defend herself but to make possible an eventual descent upon England. This was the burden of countless articles and books that appeared during the winter.[32]

In the hour of trial the British government relied upon the firm support of public opinion and upon the power of the fleet. " I am not in the least anxious about foreign complications," wrote Chamberlain on October 11. " It is a pleasant habit of our friends on the Continent to show their teeth when we are engaged with another dog. But in certain tempers of the British public these demonstrations are dangerous, and if I were ' a Frenchman or a Roosian or a Proosian ' I should be inclined not to twist the lion's tail at this precise juncture." [33] Nevertheless precautions were taken. It was reported to London at the very beginning of the war that the French were moving a large fleet into the Mediterranean. Thereupon Salisbury had a flying squadron organized at Port-

mond W. Bixler: *Anglo-German Imperialism in South Africa, 1880–1900* (Baltimore, 1932), pp. 152 ff.

[28] *Letters of Queen Victoria*, III, p. 462.

[29] Wilhelm II: *Ereignisse und Gestalten*, p. 197. See also Hurd and Castle, op. cit., p. 119 on the Bundesrath blunder and its effect on the German naval program.

[32] E.g. J. Legrand: *La Leçon de Fachoda* (Paris, 1899); Général de la Rocque: " Esquisse

[30] *British Documents*, I, no. 300.   [31] *Die Grosse Politik*, XVIII, nos. 5860, 5862.

d'un Programme Naval " (*Revue des Deux Mondes*, February 15, 1900, pp. 758–92); Anonymous: " Considérations sur une Guerre entre la France et l'Angleterre " (*Questions Diplomatiques et Coloniales*, March 15, 1900, pp. 352–7); Lieutenant X: *La Guerre avec l'Angleterre* (Paris, 1900).

[33] *Journals and Letters of Reginald Viscount Esher* (London, 1934), I, p. 240.

land and ordered the Channel fleet to Gibraltar and the Mediterranean, a very unusual step. For weeks the French movements were watched with eagle eye; when the fleet went through the Suez Canal to proceed to Madagascar, Lord Curzon telegraphed from India that he feared some intrigue on the Persian Gulf and that he thought the French should be shadowed. Salisbury refused to act provocatively, but he did warn the French that on account of the war they must not expect to find coaling and other facilities in south Africa.[34]

The government thus showed itself to be constantly on the alert. It was generally felt in England that the navy was strong enough to deter France and Russia, and that so long as Germany remained favorably neutral there was no real danger.[35] But the British public was distinctly worried. William T. Stead in the *Review of Reviews* organized a veritable invasion scare. Nothing, he maintained, could prevent the French from seizing the opportunity while the Channel fleet was at Gibraltar to transport 50,000 troops to England, destroy the only British arsenal at Woolwich and attack London. "The Empire, stripped of its armour, has its hands tied behind its back and its bare throat exposed to the keen knife of its bitterest enemies." "No fleet in the world can guarantee our shores against a sudden descent." Responsible people might not want war, but "the men in the street both in France and in England at this moment are rolling drunk with the heady wine of Nationalism and Jingoism. They regard each other with intense suspicion and deep-rooted dislike. Both are armed to the teeth. In their promenade up and down the international thoroughfare no one can say how soon or how violently they may reel up against each other in some narrow alley where one or the other must back down and out. And there is only one opinion everywhere: that if that should occur France will fight. Never again will she submit to a Fashoda humiliation." Since there were practically no troops left in England there was imminent danger of a raid.[36]

This scare must not be taken as a mere extravaganza or as a mere product of the journalistic imagination. Lord Rosebery on February 15 warned the house of lords of the danger and urged the introduction of conscription, and Lord Salisbury himself, in a speech delivered to the Primrose League on May 9, dilated upon the hostility of other countries and the consequent danger to England. London itself, he confessed, was in peril, and, he reminded his hearers, maritime powers had always perished by a blow struck at their heart.

The key to the whole situation lay in Berlin. It was more than unlikely that France would dare move unless she were secured on her eastern frontier.

---

[34] *Journals and Letters of Viscount Esher*, I, pp. 240–1; *Letters of Queen Victoria*, III, p. 475; Meyendorff: *Correspondance Diplomatique de M. de Staal*, II, pp. 424–7.

[35] Letter of Hatzfeldt, December 26, 1899 (Bülow: *Memoirs*, I, pp. 485 ff.).

[36] *Review of Reviews*, January 15, pp. 3, 32 ff.; February 15, pp. 123 ff.; April 15, p. 315. Similarly the *National Review*, January, 1900, p. 646; March, 1900, pp. 3–4, and W. S. Lilly: "The Parlous Position of England" (*Nineteenth Century*, April, 1900, pp. 580–93); H. W. Wilson: "Are we Misled about the Fleet" (*Nineteenth Century*, April, 1900, pp. 568–80); Edmund Robertson: "The Question of the Submarine Boats" (ibid., May, 1900, pp. 713–23).

For that reason the *Bundesrath* crisis of January was so fraught with danger. It will be recalled that at the height of that crisis Bülow had suggested the possibility of Germany's joining a combination hostile to England. In those very days some rather interesting conversations took place between Bülow, the Emperor, and the Russian ambassador at Berlin, Count Osten-Sacken. On January 13 the Russian representative spoke to the Emperor about the general situation and hazarded the opinion that the British fleet was probably not what it was supposed to be. Three smaller fleets, he thought, could probably handle it. The Emperor suggested whimsically that the Greek, Portuguese and Danish fleets might do for the purpose. Osten then touched upon the British violation of sea-law in stopping neutral ships, but the Emperor evaded by suggesting that the Tsar call a conference to settle the matter. The Emperor claimed, in his report of the conversation, that he rejected the idea of joining a coalition unless actually driven to it by the inconsiderateness of the English, but he renewed his former assurances that he would never attack Russia if she engaged in any enterprise in Asia.[37]

Now we have Osten's report of this same conversation. The ambassador said nothing of his own remarks concerning the naval situation and British violations of international law, but recounted the Emperor's assurances about not attacking Russia: "He would stand guard on our frontiers," William was reported as saying. Osten then wrote: "If my impressions do not deceive me . . . the Emperor is still somewhat irritated with the English and, circumstances being favorable, he might be brought to make common cause with England's enemies, always on the sole condition that we be a party to it." Osten hinted that he, personally, thought the time was ripe.[38]

If one compares these two accounts it becomes clear that the ambassador, anxious to start the ball rolling, reported only the half of the conversation which suited his purposes. Here again the Emperor may have been indiscreet, but judging from what we know of his general policy toward England at this time, there is every likelihood that his rejection of the coalition against England was actually made. Yet Osten felt, from what the Emperor said and from what Bülow had remarked some days before regarding the possibility of joint action to block any British action at Delagoa Bay, that there was some prospect of Germany's entering a coalition if the opportunity offered. There was some room for misunderstanding, for the German attitude was veiled in uncertainty.

What we have to consider now is the effect of the report of this conversation upon the Russian foreign office. Russian public opinion, which, according to the

---

[37] *Die Grosse Politik*, XV, no. 4465.

[38] Meyendorff: *Correspondance de M. de Staal*, II, pp. 447 ff. Sir Sidney Lee (*Edward VII*, I, pp. 762–3) saw the copy of this despatch in the Russian embassy archives in London. By using the old style date, January 1, he antedates the document and completely distorts the situation. His account should be left entirely aside, as it is extremely partial and hopelessly biassed. There is an account of this conversation, given to Spring Rice by a high Russian official in 1905, in *British Documents*, VI, no. 129.

German ambassador, had become a much more potent force than it had ever been before, was as hostile to England as the French or the German.[39] From the very beginning of the war there had been a pronounced demand for action against England and against British interests in Asia. But the London government relied upon the friendly disposition of Tsar Nicholas. He was supposed to be much attached to his English relatives and to be deeply moved by the ideas of international peace. He did, in fact, write to Queen Victoria that "nothing was further from his thoughts than to take advantage of our difficulties or to countenance any step likely to increase them" (December 17). A month later the English ambassador at St. Petersburg reported that the Tsar had "forbidden anything being done to embarrass us in our present difficulties." [40] But a recently published letter shows that these assurances were pure cant. Writing to his sister at the very beginning of the war (October 21) Nicholas revealed his real sentiments:

"You know, my dear, that I am not proud, but it is, nevertheless, pleasant to think that it is entirely up to me to decide the ultimate course of the war in South Africa. The reason is very simple: all I need do is to telegraph orders to all the troops in Turkestan to mobilize and advance to the border. That is all! No fleet in the world, however strong, can prevent us from striking at England at her most vulnerable point. But the time for this is not yet ripe: we are not yet sufficiently prepared for serious action, chiefly because Turkestan is not yet connected with the interior of Russia by an unbroken railway line. I have let myself go, but you will understand that there are times when one's innermost yearnings thrust themselves into the light of day and when one cannot resist putting them into words." [41]

This letter is significant not only because it reveals a side of the Tsar's character to which the English, for the most part, always remained blind, but because it supplies the key to the understanding of Russian policy. Muraviev, it will be remembered, made suggestions for action in October. They may have been sincerely intended, and they may have been meant simply to show up the Germans or to frighten the English. By January 1900, at any rate, even Muraviev had come to the conclusion that intervention was not practicable, even for Russian policy. We have a long memorandum of his, dated January 25 / February 7, in which the whole question of policy was gone over in great detail and examined from every angle. In this document Muraviev pointed out the demands of Russian opinion that some advantage be taken of England's temporary impotence. The idea of joining a coalition he put aside at the outset, for the following reasons: 1) the United States could not be induced

---

[39] *Die Grosse Politik*, XV, no. 4395.

[40] *Letters of Queen Victoria*, III, pp. 439, 461.

[41] " Nikolai Romanov ob Anglo-Burskoi Voine " (*Krasnyi Arkhiv*, LXIII, 1934, pp. 124-6). This letter has been published in German translation in the *Berliner Monatshefte*, December, 1934, pp. 1005-8.

to join; 2) the French government was too much involved in domestic difficulties and too much taken up with the coming world exposition at Paris; 3) the Italian government seemed to have some agreement with England; 4) Austria was completely immersed in a serious constitutional crisis; 5) the German Emperor had demonstrated his intention of maintaining neutrality and was obviously aiming at an agreement with England. He had already secured Samoa and the Bagdad Railway concession as a price of his good will.

A coalition being out of the question, there remained the possibility of Russia's scoring a few peaceful victories at England's expense. People talked of taking Ceuta, or Burgas, or some points in the Mediterranean, the Black Sea or the Persian Gulf. The answer to this demand, said Muraviev, was that all naval bases, however valuable, were expensive to fortify and difficult to hold in war. Then there was the question of Russia's seizing the Bosporus. The foreign minister admitted that such a step was necessary and inevitable sooner or later, and that Russia must be prepared to anticipate all competitors. For the moment, however, such action would precipitate war. Russia should, for the time being, content herself with an agreement with Turkey by which the Sultan should promise not to let other interests than Russian build railways in northern Anatolia and by which he should agree further not to fortify the Bosporus. As for Persia, Russia had neither the money nor the political need for building railways in the northern part. If she made such a demand, England would reply by securing concessions for railways in southern Persia. Russia had therefore induced the Shah to renew for ten years his promise of 1890 not to build railways without consulting the Russian government. There was, said Muraviev, no point in Russia's trying to conclude with England a treaty partitioning Persia into spheres of influence, for the Russian position in northern Persia was already unassailable and she could not hope to get more by an agreement with England. Afghanistan was another point of great importance. People talked of the seizure of Herat, but such a move would only call forth the hostility of the Amir and weaken Russia's reputation in central Asia.

This memorandum was submitted to the ministries of finance, war and navy, and we have the replies of the various ministers, which were handed in between February 23 and February 29. Witte in his comments made much of Russia's financial troubles and generally took a stand adverse to any further advance or expensive project. Operations in central Asia would require a great many troops and would call forth further armaments by Britain, so that the costly competition would become greater than ever. As for the Bosporus it would be difficult to make plans in advance. It was unlikely that Russia would ever get possession of it except through a general war or through making far-reaching concessions elsewhere. The minister of marine, on the other hand, regretted that Russia was to get nothing from the favorable situation that existed at the time. He stressed the urgent need of a port in southern Korea, and agreed that all possible preparations should be made for action against the

Bosporus. It was this last point that interested the war minister, General Kuro-patkin, more than any other. The occupation of the Bosporus he declared to be Russia's most important problem. He too favored all possible preparations and an agreement with Germany to this end.

Taking this series of documents together it is significant to note that the Russian foreign ministry excluded the possibility of a coalition against England. All the ministries consulted saw, too, the hopelessness of any expensive military or naval action. Whatever was to be gained would have to be gained by diplomacy. For the rest they agreed that the occupation of the Bosporus was more important than any other question.[42]

Muraviev, in his summary of the discussion, pointed out that Russia had already made a number of peaceful gains, and that was the fact. The British, in their usual businesslike way, had foreseen the possibilities and had made up their minds to some sacrifices. While Chamberlain, for example, was appre-hensive of French designs in Morocco and talked to the Germans about an eventual agreement to frustrate these designs, Salisbury had made up his mind from the start that England would take Tangiers if trouble arose, and that there would be no point in opposing the French advance from Algiers. Nothing was done to stop the French encroachment on the important oasis of Tuat and the Germans suspected, probably with justice, that Salisbury would be ready for a bargain with France if the matter came to a head.[43]

The same attitude was taken in London with respect to Russian designs. When the war broke out Salisbury told the German ambassador that England would do nothing if Russia attempted to open the Straits for her warships, but in actual fact the powerful Mediterranean fleet was at once concentrated at Saloniki as a warning. The Germans were probably right in their conjecture that England would oppose Russia in the Near East if Austria and other powers joined, and that an understanding with Russia would be made only if England got no support from Germany. After all, Russia would hardly dare move unless she were certain of not being attacked on her German and Austrian frontiers. It would be more sensible on the part of the Muscovites, thought the Germans, to advance in areas where other powers were not interested. The Russians thought so, too. In fact they realized that common sense dictated action in regions where the British fleet would be of no avail.[44]

One such area was Persia. The story of Anglo-Russian rivalry is a long and important one, but the question became a burning one only in a later period and we shall have to content ourselves here with only casual references.

---

[42] M. Pokrovski: "Tsarskaia Diplomatiia o Zadachaiakh Rossii na Vostoke v 1900 g." (*Krasnyi Arkhiv*, XVIII, 1926, pp. 3–29). These documents have been translated into German and published in full under the title "Die Zaristische Diplomatie über Russlands Aufgaben im Orient im Jahre 1900" (*Berliner Monatshefte*, July, 1928, pp. 638–69).

[43] *Die Grosse Politik*, XVII, nos. 5152–68; *British Documents*, II, nos. 304, 307; Augustin Bernard: "Touat et Maroc" (*Questions Diplomatiques et Coloniales*, June 1, 1900, pp. 653–64).

[44] *Die Grosse Politik*, XVIII, nos. 5640–4.

By the end of the nineteenth century the Russian influence had made very great strides. It had, in fact, become the dominant influence at the Persian court, so there was a real prospect of the whole country's falling within the Russian sphere. Muraviev, as we have seen, pointed out in his memorandum that the Russian position in northern Persia was unshakeable, but that there was not much hope of advancing in the center and south excepting at the expense of large troop concentrations and possible conflict with England. This estimate, we now know, was substantially correct. No serious Englishman had any idea of being able to stem the Russian tide in northern Persia. Even the central areas were regarded as practically lost. Lord Curzon, as viceroy of India, contemplated the situation with more than a little apprehension. It was on September 21, 1899 that he wrote his great memorandum on the Persian question, indicating the urgent need of a well-defined British policy. England, he thought, should openly oppose the Russian advance or else seek an understanding with Russia. In any event it was imperative that Russia should be kept from reaching the Persian Gulf. It was only in July 1900 that he received a reply, and an evasive one at that, to his communication. Salisbury was above all things anxious not to force the issue, and almost nothing was done to prevent the Russians from arranging with Persia the great loan of January 1900, which was secured by the revenues of all Persia excepting the southern areas. The London government was determined not to stand on anything but the question of southern Persia and the Gulf. Encroachment there, to be sure, " would be a very serious matter indeed," but the danger of Russian aggression did not seem a pressing one for the moment. In other words, Salisbury was prepared to let the Russians spread themselves in northern and central Persia just as he was willing to see the French help themselves to a large part of Morocco. In both places there was a limit for which England would fight, but France and Russia both had a long way to go before that limit was reached.[45]

Finally there was the Afghan question, so often a bone of contention between England and Russia. In January 1900 the Russians sent a force of men from the Caucasus to the Afghan frontier opposite Herat. It was reported that 30,000 men were being concentrated there and that an attack upon the key position, Herat, was imminent.[46] The Russians announced that the expedition was simply a trial mobilization and Kuropatkin told the German ambassador that only about 2500 men had been sent. Russia, he said, had no designs on Herat. All she wanted was a couple of forts at the entrance of the Bosporus, and

---

[45] The unpublished parts of the Curzon memorandum and the reply may now be found in the *British Documents*, IV, nos. 319–20. See also *Die Grosse Politik*, XVII, nos. 5212, 5335, 5336; General Sir Thomas Gordon: " The Problem of the Middle East " (*Nineteenth Century*, March, 1900, pp. 413–25). Details on Russian policy and the developments in Persia may be found in General Krahmer: *Die Beziehungen Russlands zu Persien* (Leipzig, 1903) and in Sir Percy Sykes: *A History of Persia* (Second edition, London, 1921), II, chap. lxxx.

[46] *Questions Diplomatiques et Coloniales*, January 15, 1900, p. 116; March 1, 1900, p. 307: *Review of Reviews*, February 15, 1900, p. 107; Demetrius C. Boulger: " Cabul and Herat " (*Contemporary Review*, January, 1900, pp. 40–50).

these she would get sooner or later. Salisbury himself put little stock in the rumors of an attack on Afghanistan, but he must have been very disagreeably surprised when, on February 6, 1900, the Russians handed in a memorandum pointing out that, while observing earlier declarations that Afghanistan lay outside the sphere of Russian influence, trade relations had made it necessary for them to establish direct relations with Cabul in order to settle frontier matters. It was well recognized in London that this was simply the opening wedge to the establishment of political relations between Russia and Afghanistan. The British did not like the move at all, but they abstained from making an issue of it at the time.[47]

After this long digression we must return to the European scene. The second half of February marked the turning of the tide in a military sense, for with the relief of Kimberley and Ladysmith and the surrender of General Cronje at Paardeberg the British could look forward to the ultimate conquest of the two republics. This situation induced Muraviev to make a suggestion that came nearer than any other to being a proposal for intervention against England. On February 28 he suggested to Delcassé that the German government might be brought to take sides as between England and the Franco-Russian Alliance by an invitation that she join in a démarche to bring about peace. Delcassé, it is said, was dubious about the proposal, but agreed to take part in order not to estrange Russia. France, he said, would join if Russia carried on the negotiations with Berlin and if Germany would agree to take the initiative.[48]

The Russian proposition was laid before the German government on March 3. The three powers were to join in " amicable pressure " to prevent the complete crushing of the Boers. Bülow's reply was definite: Such a step would be a long-term affair and Germany could not think of joining in it unless the three powers first agreed to a mutual guarantee of their territory for a certain number of years. To which Muraviev replied that all Russia wanted was to act in the interests of humanity. The negotiation of such a guarantee agreement would take a long time. Furthermore it would nullify the chief purpose for the action, namely the early termination of the war. The Germans were asking too much. No cabinet could stand for twenty-four hours in France if it proposed what amounted to a recognition of the Treaty of Frankfurt. So the whole business fell flat. Shortly afterward the Boers themselves appealed to the powers for mediation on the basis of the independence of the republics, whereupon Salisbury declared publicly that Britain would not accept mediation on that basis. This firm stand put an end to suggestions for intervention, for it was then perfectly obvious that England would fight first.[49]

---

[47] *Die Grosse Politik*, XVII, nos. 5212, 5334, 5336; *British Documents*, I, nos. 376, 377.

[48] Mévil: *De la Paix de Francfort, etc.,* p. 57; Bourgeois and Pagès, op. cit., pp. 286 ff.

[49] The fundamental documents and accounts of the Muraviev démarche are in *Die Grosse Politik,* XV, nos. 4472 ff. and in Bourgeois and Pagès, op. cit., pp. 286 ff. See further the misleading account given by Delcassé to Mallet in 1905 (*British Documents*, III, pp. 432–3); the inspired ac-

There has been no end of speculation as to the origin and purpose of the Muraviev proposal. It seems the more mysterious since we know of the February memorandum in which he excluded a combination against England as not feasible. Later on he tried to make out that he had been led to take the step by the hints made by Bülow and the Emperor in January! The obvious explanation is probably the correct one. Muraviev told Delcassé that his démarche would oblige the Germans to show their colors. He must have known that the Germans would reject the proposal. Certainly everything possible was done to misrepresent their position. The English were informed indirectly that the Germans had made suggestions for action against England, and when the Prince of Wales visited his relatives in Denmark in April he was given a long Russian memorandum recounting the sins of the Berlin government. Russia was to be rewarded in Asia, and France in Africa, if they would join Germany in common action against England.[50]

This was, of course, a complete reversal of the facts. There was never any possibility of Germany's joining with Russia and France in any project for intervention, and there is no reason to doubt the sincerity of Bülow's argument that the guarantee formula was intended only to show up France and to crawl out of an embarrassing situation with some grace.[51] This is perfectly clear from the contemporary documents. The Emperor William, in conversation with the British ambassador on February 6, had shown himself very friendly, even though he complained of the " kicks in the shins " which the British occasionally gave him. At the same time he sent his grandmother further " aphorisms " on the conduct of the war, which, whatever else may be said of them, appear to have been well-intentioned. When the Emperor learned of the advances of Muraviev he noted: " If the Russians are itching for intervention, let Muraviev do it himself, or with France." [52] Throughout the remainder of the war the German attitude continued to be perfectly correct. Neither the Boer delegation nor Kruger himself was received in Berlin.

The Germans were quick, however, in making capital of Muraviev's *faux pas*. William at once informed Queen Victoria and the Prince of Wales. The Queen thought Muraviev's conduct " really too monstrous " and noted: " William, I am sure, wishes to be our true friend, and he indeed deserves our thanks and confidence." Lord Salisbury, too, found the Russian minister's action " very inexplicable," while the Prince of Wales wrote to his nephew: " What you tell me about Mouraviev's conduct does not surprise me, as I believe there is nothing he would not do in conjunction with France to annoy us in every possible

count of André Mévil: " Delcassé and the Entente Cordiale " (*National Review*, July, 1908, pp. 712–9); the inspired anonymous account written by Fritz Heilbron: " Deutsche Intrigen gegen England im Burenkriege, von einem Wissenden " (*Deutsche Revue*, September, 1908, pp. 257–63); and the strongly biassed account of Sir Sidney Lee: *Edward VII*, I, pp. 765 ff.

[50] *Die Grosse Politik*, XV, no. 4493; Eckardstein: *Lebenserinnerungen*, II, pp. 167 ff.
[51] *Die Grosse Politik*, XV, no. 4496.
[52] *Die Grosse Politik*, XV, nos. 4479, 4507; *British Documents*, I, no. 311.

way. . . . You have no idea, my dear William, how all of us in England appreciate the loyal friendship which you manifest towards us on every possible occasion." To which William replied in a letter to the Queen: " I am most thankful to Providence that I was granted such an opportunity of saving your country from a most dangerous situation in warding off a combination aiming a blow at England in a moment which was vital to her." [58]

The history of European diplomacy during the Boer War is a chronicle of distrust, intrigue and innuendo. Few chapters in the history of modern Europe are more disgusting. It was indeed a long call from the diplomacy on the grand scale of the days of Bismarck. The gist of the whole problem was, of course, that the advent of colonial expansion and imperialism had created a new and serious set of antagonisms which was superimposed upon the old continental rivalries. England, having the lion's share of empire and the instrument *par excellence* for the carrying out of a policy of colonial expansion, was of necessity looked upon askance by all the others, and was soon put down as the dog in the manger who had all he needed, who wanted more and who snarled at everyone who looked for a few scraps. There can be no doubt that the " new diplomacy " of Chamberlain had a good deal to do with exciting public opinion in other countries. Speeches like the " Long Spoon Speech " and the Leicester Speech were not soon forgotten, and the whole diplomacy that led to the Boer War looked suspiciously like a flagrant attack upon two small states which were wanted for their mineral wealth.

With hatred of England rife on all sides, it was inevitable that the moment of her trial and tribulation should tempt other powers. No subject was more discussed in the winter of 1899–1900 than the possibility of a coalition against England. The scheme was bound to fail, for the Germans had definitely made up their minds that France and Russia, however well-disposed, were not safe company. It would be better for Germany to stand by England and put in her claims for reward afterward. So long as the Germans took this attitude (and there is no satisfactory evidence that they thought seriously of departing from it) action by France or Russia was out of the question. The mistake of German policy was that Bülow and the Emperor were clumsy in their manipulation of it. They kept on harping upon their good will, but at the same time kept stressing the need for payment. Not only that, they kept toying with the idea of co-operation with France or Russia in colonial matters in the event of the British not showing due recognition. In this way they laid themselves open to compromising interpretations in London.

As for the French, their stand is by no means clear. The public, to be sure, was ready for almost anything and was literally thirsting for revenge for Fashoda. But the government does not appear to have shared this enthusiasm. The great world exposition, for which long preparations had been made, was

---

[58] *Letters of Queen Victoria*, III, pp. 499–500, 503, 507–8, 519; *Die Grosse Politik*, XV, nos. 4480, 4484, 4485; Eckardstein, op. cit., II, pp. 167 ff.

about to open in April 1900, and its success depended on peace and quiet. Delcassé gave the British ambassador the distinct impression that the government was opposed to any action against England. On the other hand he was willing to make what he could out of the situation. There was the French advance on the frontier of Morocco, for example. Further yet, he seems to have been quite ready to listen to German hints for common action in colonial affairs, and the Russian ambassador reported him deeply disappointed that the German advances in October 1899 had not been followed up by concrete proposals.[54] From all of which one is led to believe that Delcassé would not have hung back if Russia had actually succeeded in drawing the Germans into a common action. He was certainly more discreet and circumspect than were the Germans or the Russians.

Both the Tsar and Muraviev, it may be taken for granted, would have been glad to deal England a telling blow. The latter certainly made advances in October and again in March, but these were chiefly manoeuvrings. The Russians wanted to act, but they weren't ready. They had no money, and so they had to eschew all policies that would entail heavy expenditure. They made some gains at Britain's expense, but the gains were nothing compared to what the public and Muraviev would have liked. The only chance of getting more was through action with other powers, and that chance faded completely after the German rejection of Russian advances.

So far as England was concerned there is only this to be remarked: That the British government fully understood the value of German neutrality and good will. Chamberlain, Balfour and others were, in fact, ready to go beyond mere co-operation and were prepared to pay a price for a close understanding, a price which would probably have taken the shape of a Moroccan agreement. Salisbury, on the other hand, had become by this time opposed to buying the support of the Germans. He disliked them intensely and resented their constant demands for the pound of flesh. He had held out to the end on the Samoan affair and he showed no readiness whatever to discuss questions like the Moroccan. His policy was rather to take what he could and leave what he must. If France could be kept quiet by the abandonment of part of Morocco, well and good. If the Russians really made a move to seize the Bosporus, either England could join with Austria and Italy in opposing her, or England could strike a bargain and get adequate compensation. An advance in Persia was permissible so long as the Russians stayed away from the south and from the Persian Gulf. Northern Persia was already theirs so far as Salisbury was concerned. In fact he stomached a rather serious setback in Afghanistan rather than provoke a conflict. In all this one sees already the broad outlines of the future ententes with France and Russia. The dawn of the new century was already casting over Europe the rays of future developments.

---

[54] Meyendorff: *Correspondance de M. de Staal*, II, p. 453.

BIBLIOGRAPHICAL NOTE

DOCUMENTARY SOURCES

Die Grosse Politik der Europäischen Kabinette, 1871–1914. Volume XV, chapter cii: The seizure of German ships; chapter ciii: The question of intervention during the Boer War. Volume XVII, chapter cxiii: The Moroccan Question Volume XVIII, chapter cxix: The Dardanelles Question; chapter ccxxvi: German-French relations.

British Documents on the Origins of the War, 1898–1914. Volume I, chapter vii: The Boer War. Volume II, chapter xiv: France, Spain and Morocco.

Accounts and Papers. 1900, volume LVI. *Africa No. 1 (1900), Correspondence respecting the action of H. Mj's Naval Authorities with regard to certain Foreign Vessels.*

" Tsarskaia Diplomatiia o Zadachaiakh Rossii na Vostoke v 1900 g." (*Krasnyi Arkhiv*, XVIII, 1926, pp. 3–29). Edited by M. Pokrovski. The important Muraviev memorandum of February 1900. These documents have been translated and published in full under the title: " Die Zaristische Diplomatie über Russlands Aufgaben im Orient im Jahre 1900 " (*Berliner Monatshefte*, July, 1928, pp. 638–69).

" Nikolai Romanov ob Anglo-Burskoi Voine " (*Krasnyi Arkhiv*, LXIII, 1934, pp. 124–6). A most illuminating letter of the Tsar to his sister. A German translation has been published in the *Berliner Monatshefte*, December, 1934, pp. 1005–8.

MEMOIRS, AUTOBIOGRAPHIES, BIOGRAPHIES, ANL LETTERS

LEE, SIR SIDNEY: *King Edward VII, a Biography.* Two volumes. New York, 1925. Discusses in detail the Emperor's visit to England and the question of intervention during the war. Contains a number of interesting documents, but for the rest is biassed and misleading.

GARVIN, J. L.: *The Life of Joseph Chamberlain.* Three volumes. London, 1933—. Contains very little on European diplomacy during the war, and that chiefly from the German Documents.

BÜLOW, PRINCE VON: *Memoirs.* Four volumes. Boston, 1931. Discusses in detail the Anglo-German relationship, but adds very little to what may be learned from the documents.

ECKARDSTEIN, HERMANN FREIHERR VON: *Lebenserinnerungen und Politische Denkwürdigkeiten.* Two volumes. Leipzig, 1919. Interesting but not always reliable. The period dealt with in this chapter forms the most instructive part of Eckardstein's book.

MEYENDORFF, BARON A.: *Correspondance de M. de Staal.* Two volumes. Paris, 1929. Valuable chiefly because it gives the text of important reports from Berlin in January 1900.

Letters of Queen Victoria. Edited by George E. Buckle. Third series, volume III. London, 1932. Of interest chiefly for the correspondence of the English and German ruling families.

TIRPITZ, ALFRED VON: *Erinnerungen.* Leipzig, 1919. One of the chief sources for the history of the German naval policy.

HOHENLOHE, PRINCE CHLODWIG ZU: *Denkwürdigkeiten der Reichskanzlerzeit.* Stuttgart, 1931. Contains some interesting notes on the evolution of the second German naval bill.

SPECIAL STUDIES

BOURGEOIS, ÉMILE, and PAGÈS, GEORGES: *Les Origines et les Responsabilités de la Grande Guerre.* Paris, 1921. Contains the French documents bearing on the question of intervention. Incomplete, but of considerable importance.

DIPLOMATICUS (?LUCIEN WOLF): " Count Muravieff's ' Indiscretion.' " (*Fortnightly Review,* December, 1899, pp. 1036–45). A remarkable article, revealing pretty accurately the démarches of Muraviev in October 1899.

MÉVIL, ANDRÉ: " Delcassé and the Entente Cordiale." (*National Review,* July, 1908, pp. 712–9). An inspired article, giving Delcassé's version of the intervention projects.

—: *De la Paix de Francfort à la Conférence d'Algésiras.* Paris, 1909. Practically repeats what is said in Mévil's article.

ANONYMOUS (FRITZ HEILBRON): " Deutsche Intrigen gegen England während des Burenkrieges." (*Deutsche Revue,* September, 1908, pp. 257–63). A reply to Mévil's article. This article was written from the German documents and published anonymously by the foreign office. It says substantially what the Emperor said at the same time in his famous *Daily Telegraph* interview on October 28, 1908.

TREUE, WILHELM: " Presse und Politik in Deutschland und England während des Burenkrieges." (*Berliner Monatshefte,* August, 1933, pp. 786–803). A quite inadequate article, dealing chiefly with the unsuccessful efforts made during the war to influence the press. Based almost entirely upon the German and British documents and the obvious memoir material.

HURD, ARCHIBALD, and CASTLE, HENRY: *German Sea-Power.* London, 1913. Still one of the best general accounts of the German naval policy. Contains the essential documents.

KEHR, ECKART: *Schlachtflottenbau und Parteipolitik, 1894–1901.* Berlin, 1930. The most detailed study of the German naval policy, extremely useful despite the fact that it deals very largely with the domestic aspects.

MICHALIK, BERNHARD: *Probleme des Deutschen Flottenbaues.* Breslau, 1931. A good antidote to Kehr's book, and an interesting discussion of the international aspects of the German naval policy.

BECKER, WILLY: *Fürst Bülow und England.* Greifswald, 1929. One of the most detailed studies of German policy with respect to England. Not particularly instructive.

MEINECKE, FRIEDRICH: *Geschichte des Deutsch-Englischen Bündnisproblems, 1890–1901.* Munich, 1927. Another detailed analysis of the period, with conclusions which seem to me frequently unsound.

LÖDING, WALTHER: *Die Deutsch-Englischen Bündnisverhandlungen 1898 bis 1901.* Hamburg, 1929. One of the best factual accounts of Anglo-German negotiations during this period.

LITERATURE SINCE 1935

(See also the Supplementary Bibliographical Notes to Chapters II, VIII, XIII, XV, XVIII.)

FERGUSON, JOHN H.: *American Diplomacy and the Boer War.* Philadelphia, 1939. 240 pp. A thorough and valuable study, making use of State Department and American private papers.

PÜCKLER, KARL GRAF VON: *Aus meinem Diplomatenleben.* Schweidnitz, 1934. 232 pp. Contains some interesting information on the Anglo-German relations of 1900.

BAUERMANN, WERNER: *Die Times und die Abwendung Englands von Deutschland um 1900.* Cologne, 1939. 78 pp. A dissertation.

HALLMANN, HANS: *Spanien und die französisch-englische Mittelmeer-Rivalität, 1898–1907.* Stuttgart, 1937. 143 pp. A careful, systematic examination of one aspect of the Anglo-French relationship. Makes no use of Spanish materials.

WILLIAMSON, FRANCIS T.: *Germany and Morocco before 1905.* Baltimore, 1937. 210 pp. A fundamental work, investigating German commercial activities as well as German policy.

DIEDRICH, HEINRICH: *Frankreich und Marokko, 1890–1905.* Hamburg, 1939. 93 pp. A dissertation.

BROCKWAY, THOMAS P.: " Britain and the Persian Bubble, 1888–1892 " (*Journal of Modern History,* XIII, March, 1941, pp. 36–48). A scholarly monograph devoted largely to British efforts at economic exploitation.

HANNEKUM, WILHELM: *Persien im Spiel der Mächte, 1900–1907.* Berlin, 1938. 203 pp. Perhaps the best, systematic treatment, based on the German and British documents.

TAILLARDAT, F.: " La rivalité anglo-russe en Asie centrale. Les états tampons, 1860–1914 " (*Asie française,* August–September, 1935, pp. 214–220). A well-informed summary review.

TERENZIO, PIO C.: *La rivalité anglo-russe en Perse et en Afghanistan jusqu'aux accords de 1907.* Paris, 1947. 178 pp. A convenient survey of the problem from earliest times, based on obvious sources.

XXI

The Boxer Rising

∽

O F ALL THE ISSUES WHICH CONFRONTED THE EUROPEAN GOVERNMENTS in the period between Bismarck's fall and the conclusion of the Anglo-French Entente in 1904 the Far Eastern question was the most serious and the most complex. To be sure, it lacked the high drama and color of the African problems. There was no Menelik, no Mahdi, no Marchand and there was no Paul Kruger, no Cecil Rhodes, in fact no spectacular clash of personalities whatever. If you except Li Hung-chang and the old Empress Dowager, of whose innermost thoughts we know little or nothing, there were no great figures to captivate the imagination. But the conflict of interests was of infinitely greater importance. In the Far East the powers were dealing with the fate of an empire of upward of three hundred million souls and no less than five major states were disputing the spoils.

We left the Far Eastern situation as it was in the spring of 1898, after the spectacular occupation of Kiao-chow, Port Arthur, Weihaiwei and Kuang-chow and after the great scramble for concessions. Needless to say, these thrilling events made an even deeper impression upon the Chinese than upon the Europeans. The utter helplessness of the Empire was patent to all, the days of the state were obviously numbered and the partition of China was discussed among high and low. Even the Emperor, Kuang-hsü, could no longer shut his eyes to the imminence of collapse. Kang Yu-wei, the great Chinese reformer, had appealed to him in a great memorial of December 1895, urging the need of a thoroughgoing reorganization of the Empire on western lines if the situation was to be saved. No attention was paid to the prophets of disaster at that time, and Kang's Reform Club was reduced to impotence. But now that the catastrophe had happened and the hated foreigner sat in the most desirable ports along the coast, Kang renewed his efforts with more success. In a memorial to the Emperor in the spring of 1898 he warned in no vague terms: " If Your Majesty will not decide, or will prefer to remain in the old grooves of the Conservatives, then your territories will be swallowed up, your limbs will be bound, your viscera will be cut up, and Your Majesty will scarcely manage to retain your throne or to rule over more than a fragment of your ancient Empire."

This time the Emperor listened. He saw his country, says Kang, " about to sink in the earth, about to be buried in ruins, about to burst like an egg, about to be divided up, about to mortify, about to be torn in shreds, about to become like India or Annam, or Burmah — a dependent of another Power! . . . If one had but the lightest knowledge of this, at every thought of it one would get so anxious as to burst into perspiration, and be so angry as to make one's hair stand on end, one's eyes stare out of their sockets, and not be able to endure it for a single day."[1] He therefore called Kang to Peking, and in the summer of 1898 embarked upon the remarkable Hundred Days of Reform. Day after day during this short period decrees were issued aiming at the modernization of the educational system, the administration, the finances, the army and navy and the economic life of the country. There was hardly a phase of government activity that was not touched. If the policy had been carried through it would undoubtedly have transformed and greatly strengthened China. But authoritative writers are generally agreed that the reform policy, however well-intentioned, never had much chance of success. Kang was immensely impressed with the story of Peter the Great and would have wished the Emperor to play the part of the ruthless Russian iconoclast. But Kuang-hsü was anything but a Peter. He meant well, but he lacked understanding and he lacked force of character. Kang himself failed to appreciate the difficulties of the problem. He had only a general knowledge of European affairs and thought China could follow the path of Japan much more easily than was the case. He tried to do too much in too short a time and took far too little account of the forces of opposition. The Chinese Emperor was far from all-powerful; reforms meant nothing unless they were carried through by the provincial authorities. And then there was the canny old Empress Dowager and her following of Manchu conservatives to be taken into account. The opposition of the local authorities to any attempt at greater centralization and the dislike of the conservatives for any radical westernization sealed the fate of the reform experiment. When, in September, Kang and his associates planned to remove the old Empress from the scene, the plot was revealed to her by Jung-lu, the military chief. On September 21 the old lady, with her usual decision, turned the tables upon the Emperor, carried through a coup d'état and brought the work of the reformers to an abrupt close.[2]

The reform movement in China in 1898 remained an interlude, interesting as a reflection of the Chinese reaction to the aggression of the European powers but devoid of any direct bearing upon international relations. It has been aptly

[1] Kang Yu-wei: " The Reform of China " (*Contemporary Review*, August, 1899, pp. 180–98).

[2] There are many good accounts of the reform interlude, among which may be mentioned Kang Yu-wei's " The Reform of China," loc. cit.; George S. Owen: " The Reform Policy of the Chinese Emperor " (*National Review*, September, 1899, pp. 119–32); Charles Johnston: " The Struggle for Reform in China " (in *The Crisis in China*, New York, 1900); J. O. P. Bland and E. Backhouse: *China under the Empress Dowager* (Philadelphia, 1910), pp. 178–200; Hosea B. Morse: *The International Relations of the Chinese Empire* (New York, 1918), III, chap. vi; George N. Steiger: *China and the Occident* (New Haven, 1927), pp. 81 ff.; Borton Butcher: " The Emperor's Attempt to Reform the Chinese Government in the Summer of 1898 " (*Political Science Quarterly*, XLIII, 1928, pp. 544–66); and, most recently, Meribeth E. Cameron: *The Reform Movement in China, 1898–1912* (Stanford, 1931), chap. ii.

pointed out that the efforts of the Emperor met with no support from European governments, that, in fact, the battle for concessions reached its apogee during the summer of 1898.[3] It was this complete misunderstanding of the Chinese mentality that was to cost the European powers dearly in the not far distant future, but for the moment we must neglect Chinese domestic affairs and return to the problems of European policy.

The Far Eastern crisis of the winter of 1897–1898 had left the two chief rivals, England and Russia, at daggers drawn. Both powers had joined in the scramble for leases and concessions, but no compromise had been reached between them and the British had been unable to find allies to assist them in blocking the Russian advance. It was not enough that the Russians had planted themselves firmly in Manchuria, to the horror of British business interests at Tientsin and New-chuang.[4] They were also invading central China, using Belgian and French interests as spearpoints. On June 27, 1898 the Franco-Belgian syndicate, backed by the Russo-Chinese Bank, secured the definitive concession for the all-important Peking-Hankow line, which, when completed, would bring Russian influence and interests to the banks of the Yangtze Kiang. The British protested vigorously against the award of the concession, pointing out that " a concession of this nature is no longer a commercial or industrial enterprise, and becomes a political movement against British interests in the region of the Yangtze." But despite these protests the Chinese government, insisting that the Russians had nothing to do with it, granted the application of the syndicate and ratified it in August 1898.[5]

The advance of Russia and her friends led to continued criticism of British policy by the press. In a strongly-worded article published on July 30, 1898, the *Times* declared:

" While we are lulled to sleep for months by parliamentary statements of a more or less disingenuous character, other nations are acting with indefatigable energy. While we go talking about a policy of open doors, other nations are consolidating and extending their spheres of exclusive influence at such a rate that there will soon be no door to open. . . . Are we to go on forever, trying to keep out the ocean with a mop or are we going to take the world as we find it, and to secure at least some area of Chinese territory where British enterprise may have a chance? "[6]

The British government was, as a matter of fact, doing its best. It gave the utmost support to a project advanced by the Hongkong and Shanghai Bank which would serve as an effective reply to the Russian invasion of central China.

---

[3] Steiger, op. cit., pp. 81 ff.

[4] Cf. Lord Charles Beresford's observations, recorded in his *The Break-up of China* (New York, 1899), pp. 14 ff., 32 ff.

[5] Jean de Marcillac: " Les Chemins de Fer en Chine " (*Questions Diplomatiques et Coloniales*, July 1, 1899, pp. 265–74); Percy H. Kent: *Railway Enterprise in China* (London, 1907), pp. 93–101; Philip Joseph: *Foreign Diplomacy in China* (London, 1928), p. 337.

[6] Quoted by Chung-fu Chang: *The Anglo-Japanese Alliance* (Baltimore, 1931), p. 59.

Since before the war with Japan the Peking government had planned to build a railroad from Tientsin along the coast of the Gulf of Pechili to Shanhaikwan and thence into Manchuria. Part of the road had already been built by the English engineer, Mr. Kinder, and in 1898 the line was open to beyond the great wall, to the little town of Chunghuso. Now, on June 7, 1898, the Peking authorities concluded a preliminary agreement with the Hongkong and Shanghai Bank by which the latter was to furnish a loan of sixteen million taels for the extension of the line from Chunghuso to Sinminting (some fifty miles to the northwest of Mukden), with a branch line to Ying-k'ou and Newchuang, the busiest port on the Manchurian coast. The permanent way, the rolling stock, the earnings of the entire line from Peking to Tientsin and thence to Sinminting, and various coal and iron mining rights were to serve as security for this loan. In other words, the all-important railway from Peking and Tientsin into Manchuria was to be built by the Chinese, but it was to be mortgaged to the British.

The Russian minister protested at once against this arrangement. He claimed that the Chinese government had promised Russia on December 8, 1897 that only Russians should be allowed to participate in the construction of railways to the north of Shanhaikwan, and recalled warnings he had made against the award of the loan to British interests in the early months of 1898.[7] As usual, the Chinese authorities were between the devil and the deep sea. Pavlov threatened while Sir Claude MacDonald insisted. The British government was determined not to back down, but to make an issue of the question. " You may inform Yamen that Her Majesty's Government will support them against any Power which commits an act of aggression on China because China has granted to a British subject permission to make or support any railway or similar public work," Lord Salisbury wired to the British minister on July 22, 1898.[8] But even this offer of support did not lessen the fright of the Chinese. On July 31 Pavlov extracted from the Yamen a promise not to use the projected railway beyond the great wall (that is, Shanhaikwan) as security for a loan and not to allow foreign control of the operation of the line.[9]

But the Russian government was by no means prepared to force a crisis in its relations with England. Lessar, the chargé d'affaires at London, was instructed to approach the British foreign office in a spirit of conciliation. On this same July 31 he had an excited talk with Balfour, in the course of which Lessar suggested the possibility of an agreement. Balfour, in turn, proposed a general discussion between all interested powers regarding their spheres of influence in China, a proposal to which Muraviev was unwilling to give any support.[10] In the end the British government accepted the Russian suggestion

---

[7] B. B. Glinskii: *Prolog Russko-Iaponskoi Voiny* (Petrograd, 1916), pp. 78 ff.

[8] *British Documents,* I, no. 55.

[9] Glinskii, op. cit., pp. 81–2; A. Popov: " Anglo-Russkoe Soglashenie o Razdele Kitaiia " (*Krasnyi Arkhiv,* XXV, 1927, pp. 111–34), p. 119.

[10] Popov, op. cit., pp. 119–20.

for negotiations à *deux*. From the great speech delivered by Balfour in the house of commons on August 10 it is clear that English hopes of maintaining the Open Door were rapidly vanishing. " A concession must be given to someone," he remarked, " and when the someone has got it, other people must be excluded. . . . That is not inequality of treatment." In other words, the British were practically giving up the Open Door policy so far as concessions were concerned. Their aim henceforth was to use the Manchurian railway project as a bargaining point, and to secure in return for the recognition of Manchuria as a Russian sphere a similar recognition by Russia of the Yangtze Valley as a British sphere. The award of the Peking-Hankow line to the Franco-Belgian syndicate was ratified in mid-August and served to bring matters to a head. In a sharp note of August 17 Balfour informed the Russian government that England could not " acquiesce in an arrangement which while excluding England from her share in the railway enterprises of Manchuria leaves all China open to the railway enterprise of Russia. Such a pretension, if persisted in, must inevitably produce the most serious international difficulties." [11]

But even this strong stand did not help much. The Chinese refused to ratify the preliminary arrangement with the Hongkong and Shanghai Bank, though they were forced by British threats and by the concentration of British naval forces to grant new concessions to counterbalance the award of the Peking-Hankow line. In rapid succession English interests, associated to some extent with German and Italian interests, secured concessions for railroads from Kowloon to Canton, from Soochow to Hangchow, from Pukow to Sinyang and from Chinkiang to Tientsin, most of them lines designed to consolidate the British position in the Yangtze Valley.[12] At the same time the London government suggested to Russia an arrangement regarding the Manchurian line: the Hongkong and Shanghai Bank should be allowed to make the loan to China, but as security it was to accept the Peking-Tientsin-Shanhaikwan line and only the profits of the line beyond Shanhaikwan. This solution the Russians were glad to accept, since they regarded the line as far as the great wall as already under British control. The British, however, wanted to tie up this arrangement with a larger agreement regarding spheres of influence, their object being always to secure, if possible, the recognition of the Yangtze Valley as the British sphere, and also a guarantee of the Open Door for trade in the spheres of Russia and other powers. Chamberlain declared quite frankly in a speech delivered on November 16, 1898 that it was not to England's interest " to give anything like a guarantee of the integrity and independence of an empire which appeared to be decaying." Neither was it her business, he continued, to impede the ambitions of others or to appear as the champion of China, providing only that the others observed the principle " that no acquisition of territory by any foreign power should alter the existing state

---

[11] *British Documents*, I, no. 57.
[12] The best discussion may be found in Joseph, op. cit., pp. 345–63.

of things in this respect, that the markets of China should be open to fair and even competition to all through the open door." This Open Door, he admitted, did not apply to concessions. In other words, Britain would not defend the independence and integrity of China or oppose the establishment of spheres of exclusive influence so far as concessions were concerned. But she would insist on a fair field and no favor in the matter of trade, even within the spheres of the other powers.[18]

In another speech, on December 8, 1898, Chamberlain pleaded for an agreement with Russia, which was, he said, necessary if very serious complications were to be avoided. It was quite possible, he maintained, " to conciliate what we may call the reasonable ambition of Russia with the fixed and settled policy of this country to maintain equal opportunities in trade for all nations." But the Russians were not much interested in British attempts to secure promises of equal trade opportunities in the Russian sphere and they were not much impressed with the suggestion that they recognize the Yangtze Valley as a British sphere in return for recognition of Russia's special position in Manchuria. Witte, in particular, objected to an agreement along such lines. The British proposals, he pointed out, would give Russia no rights in Manchuria which she did not already possess. Furthermore, Manchuria had an area only half that of the Yangtze Basin as defined by the British (the provinces adjacent to the Yangtze River and in addition the provinces of Hunan and Chekiang), and Manchuria was much less populous. Besides, the British proposal would restrict the field of activity of the Russo-Chinese Bank, which had the right to undertake affairs anywhere in China. The French, who had put up most of the money for the bank, would resent any such arrangement. In the large, said Witte, the British suggestions were " impossible and disastrous." [14]

The Russian foreign minister and the minister of war, however, felt the urgent need of some agreement with England, and deprecated the necessity of defending Russian enterprises as far south as the Yangtze River. After months of wrangling between the Russian ministries it was finally decided to return to the original proposal of an agreement on spheres of influence for railroad concessions, leaving aside all reference to the Open Door for trade. Negotiations with England were initiated in February 1899 and finally led to the exchange of notes of April 28, 1899. By the terms of these notes Russia engaged " not to seek for her own account or for Russian subjects any railway concessions in the basin of the Yangtze, nor to obstruct, directly or indirectly, in that region any applications for railway concessions supported by the British Government." England undertook similar obligations with regard to the area " north of the great wall." The agreement included further the arrangements made with regard to the Shanhaikwan-Sinminting Railway, but contained the further

---

[18] Quoted by Joseph, op. cit., pp. 378–9.
[14] Glinskii, op. cit., pp. 84 ff.; B. A. Romanov: *Rossiia v Manchzhurii* (Leningrad, 1928), pp. 212–2; Popov, op. cit., pp. 122–5.

clause stating that it did not " interfere in any way with the right of the Russian government, if it think fit, to support applications of Russian subjects or establishments for concessions for railways which, starting from the main Manchurian line in a south-western direction, would traverse the region in which the Chinese line, terminating at Sinminting and Newchwang, is to be constructed." [15]

This agreement was much less extensive than the British had hoped for. To be sure, it secured Russian recognition of the Yangtze Basin as a British railroad sphere, but no other power had officially recognized it as such, and the Russian acceptance was therefore of qualified value. In return the British had recognized as a Russian railroad sphere not only Manchuria, but all China north of the great wall. No guarantee whatever had been secured for equal trade opportunities in the Russian sphere, and in return for recognition of British interests in the Peking-Tientsin-Sinminting railway line the English government had been obliged to admit the Russian right to a concession for a line to Peking itself, which, if built, would have been a serious competitor of the Chinese-British line and would have constituted the all-important link between Peking and Europe. The Russo-Chinese Bank, to the surprise of the British, applied at once for the concession, but the Chinese government, which had announced in December 1898 that it would not grant further railway concessions for the present, resisted the demand and was supported by the British. The Russians, who had enough to do already in Manchuria, therefore contented themselves with a promise that if foreigners should ever be asked to build the line, the Russians would be given the preference (June 1899). [16]

The Chinese government had definitely set its face against further demands from the foreigners, as the Italians learned to their disappointment in March 1899, when they put forward a request for the lease of San Mun Bay and the recognition of the larger part of Chekiang as a sphere of influence. The demand was supported by the British, but was flatly rejected by the Yamen. There was talk of an ultimatum, but in the end the Italian minister was recalled on the plea that he had exceeded his instructions. Although the demand was pressed again on various occasions during the spring and summer of 1899, it was clear that nothing would come of it, and finally even the Italian government dropped it.[17]

The rejection of the Italian demands did not impress the European powers as deeply as it should have done. To be sure, there were no further attempts to

[15] *British Documents*, I, no. 61. The negotiations are well summarized in Kent, op. cit., p. 55; Mongton Chih Hsu: *Railway Problems in China* (New York, 1915), pp. 48 ff., 65 ff.; Popov, op. cit., pp. 125–8; Joseph, op. cit., chap. xvii; R. S. McCordock: *British Far Eastern Policy, 1894–1900* (New York, 1931), pp. 277–88.

[16] Glinskii, op. cit., pp. 88 ff.; Popov, op. cit., pp. 128–9; Joseph, op. cit., pp. 391 ff.

[17] Guido Cora: " La Baia di San Mun " (*Nuova Antologia*, March 16, 1899, pp. 341–53); Anonymous: " L'Italia in Cina " (ibid., April 16, 1899, pp. 746–58); A. A. Fauvel: " L'Italie au Tché-kiang " (*Le Correspondant*, August 10, 1899, pp. 505–26).

secure concessions during the year 1899 and the first half of 1900, but the situation remained ominous and there was a latent feeling that the definitive partition of China was just round the corner. As between the powers, the antagonism between England and Russia was still the dominant factor. " Nine out of ten persons in the United Kingdom believe that Russia wants to take possession of the whole of China, or at least of Peking and all North China," wrote one observer.[18] Lord Charles Beresford, who made an extensive tour of China in the autumn of 1898 as the representative of the Associated Chambers of Commerce, came back to England through the United States in the spring of 1899. He was immensely impressed with the dominant position of Russia in the Far East and reported the conviction of the Chinese that England was afraid of Russia. British business interests, he found, were entirely demoralized by the Russian advance and by the uncertainty and weakness of British policy. There was no hope, he believed, of saving the situation unless England, Germany, the United States and Japan could arrange to undertake the reform of China, especially the reform of the Chinese army. As an alternative to this policy, England's only hope would be the setting aside of a sphere for herself in the Yangtze Valley.[19]

The same feeling of dissatisfaction and hopelessness with regard to British policy was frequently voiced in the English press and parliament. Sir Charles Dilke accused the government of having tried to ride two horses: " The muddle between the policy of the ' open door ' and that of the Yangtze sphere has led to confusion which seems to have caused failure." Beresford shared the same feeling: " From what I can gather from Her Majesty's Government," he said in parliament, " they have been bellowing for the open door, but they have been working all the time for the spheres of influence." He was sick, he said, of the " pipe down " policy.[20]

The government's reply was not very promising. England was still for the Open Door and was still reluctant about staking off a sphere. " We cannot make the Yangtze Valley a province like Shantung or Manchuria, first, because it is infinitely larger, and secondly, we are not prepared to undertake the immense responsibility of governing what is practically a third of China." [21] Which was another way of saying that the government was determined to continue the attempt to ride two horses, despite the fact that it was impossible to preserve the Open Door (which the British government had itself given up so far as con-

---

[18] Gilbert Reid: " The Powers and the Partition of China " (reprinted from the *North American Review* in *The Crisis in China*, New York, 1900).

[19] Charles Beresford: *The Break-up of China* (New York, 1899) and similarly his article " China and the Powers " (in *The Crisis in China*).

[20] Debates of June 9, 1899 (Hansard, Series IV, vol. LXXII, pp. 778 ff., 785 ff.). Much the same stand was taken by writers in the periodical press, for example Senex: " The White Man's Burden in China " (*Contemporary Review*, September, 1899, pp. 318–32); R. S. Gundry: " The Yangtse Region " (*Fortnightly Review*, September, 1899, pp. 448–64).

[21] Statement by Mr. Brodrick, June 9, 1899 (Hansard, LXXII, pp. 803 ff.).

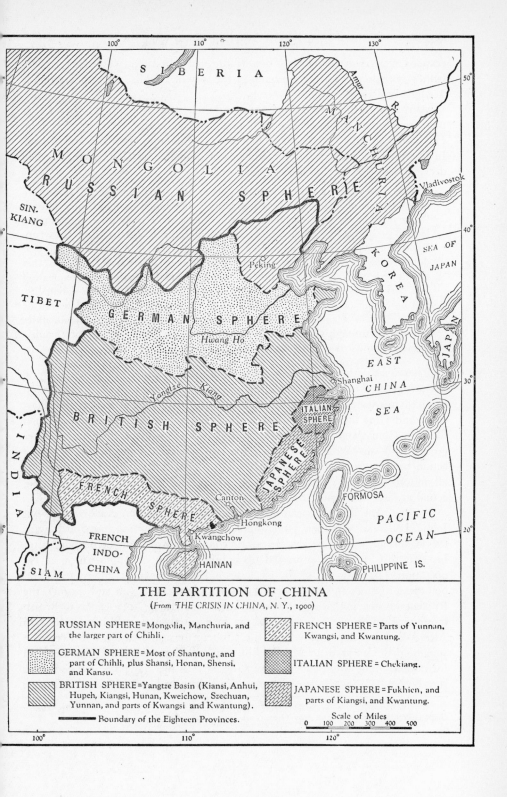

THE PARTITION OF CHINA
(*From THE CRISIS IN CHINA, N. Y., 1900*)

RUSSIAN SPHERE = Mongolia, Manchuria, and the larger part of Chihli.

GERMAN SPHERE = Most of Shantung, and part of Chihli, plus Shansi, Honan, Shensi, and Kansu.

BRITISH SPHERE = Yangtze Basin (Kiansi, Anhui, Hupeh, Kiangsi, Hunan, Kweichow, Szechuan, Yunnan, and parts of Kwangsi and Kwantung).

FRENCH SPHERE = Parts of Yunnan, Kwangsi, and Kwantung.

ITALIAN SPHERE = Chekiang.

JAPANESE SPHERE = Fukhien, and parts of Kiangsi, and Kwantung.

Boundary of the Eighteen Provinces.

Scale of Miles
0   100   200   300   400   500

cessions were concerned), and despite the fact that there were obvious difficulties, both local and international, in the way of establishing a sphere in the
Yangtze Valley.

At this point the British suddenly found their efforts supported from a rather
unexpected quarter. On September 6, 1899 the American secretary of state, John
Hay, sent out his famous Open Door note to England, Germany and Russia.
In this note the powers claiming spheres of influence in China were asked to
declare: first, that they would

> "in no wise interfere with any treaty port or any vested interest within any so-
> called 'sphere of interest' or leased territory " they might have in China; second,
> "that the Chinese treaty tariff of the time being shall apply to all merchandise
> landed or shipped to all such ports as are within said 'sphere of interest' (un-
> less they be 'free ports'), no matter to what nationality it may belong, and that
> duties so leviable shall be collected by the Chinese Government "; third, "that
> it will levy no higher harbor dues on vessels of another nationality frequenting
> any port in such 'sphere' than shall be levied on vessels of its own nationality,
> and no higher railroad charges over lines built, controlled, or operated within its
> 'sphere' on merchandise belonging to citizens or subjects of other nationalities
> transported through such 'sphere' than shall be levied on similar merchandise
> belonging to its own nationals transported over equal distances."

There was nothing new or original about these proposals; they were nothing
but a re-edition of the British policy as it had been put forward for years. In
the parliamentary debates of March and April 1898 Liberal leaders like Harcourt and Grey had suggested an international agreement to secure the Open
Door in China, and the government itself had proposed to the United States
government on March 8, 1898 that the two powers co-operate "in opposing
action by foreign powers which may tend to restrict freedom of commerce of
all nations in China either by imposing preferential conditions or by obtaining
actual cession of Chinese coast territory." [22]

At that time the American government had returned an evasive reply, but
John Hay, who was then ambassador to London, was in close touch with
the leaders of British policy. Beresford consulted with him before and after
his visit to China, and impressed upon him the idea of Anglo-American co-
operation. The trade of the United States in China was increasing by leaps and
bounds, and, since this trade was largely with Manchuria (oil and cotton), the
Russian advance in that region was as much a menace to American as to British
interests. Even so, the inspiration of the Hay note was British. It went back to
Alfred E. Hippisley, formerly of the Chinese maritime customs service, who
suggested the program to Mr. Rockhill, one of Hay's assistants. The Rockhill
memorandum of August 28, 1899 was the basis of the Hay note. It stated quite
simply that "if the (Chinese) Empire is in a disturbed condition, and if foreign

---

[22] Alfred L. P. Dennis: *Adventures in American Diplomacy, 1896–1906* (New York, 1928),
chap. viii; Tyler Dennett: *John Hay* (New York, 1933), pp. 284–5.

interests suffer thereby, this is entirely due to the unseemly haste of some of the treaty powers in their scramble for commercial advantages and acquisition of territory." But, Rockhill went on to say, the spheres of influence " have now been recognized by Great Britain as well as by France, Germany and Russia, and *they must be accepted as existing facts.*" " We should insist on absolute equality of treatment in the various zones, for equality of opportunity with the citizens of the favored powers we can not hope to have." [23]

In other words, the American position was exactly that of Britain. The spheres were there, and there was no hope of preventing preferential treatment in the spheres so far as concessions were concerned. All that could be hoped for was respect for treaty rights and equal trade opportunities within the spheres. The Hay note was decidedly not an attempt to proclaim the principles of Chinese independence and integrity. The question was whether even the limited program of the Open Door for trade could be carried through. The British and German governments accepted it, and so did the Italian, French and Japanese governments when it was presented to them somewhat later. But the crux of the whole problem lay in the Russian policy.

It will be recalled that the assurances asked by Hay had been demanded by England in her negotiations with Russia in the winter of 1898–1899, and that they had been rejected. The Russians had agreed to a restricted railway sphere arrangement rather than bind themselves not to levy preferential rates and differential tariffs in their sphere. It was unlikely that they would change their attitude to please Hay. As a matter of fact we know that Muraviev was enraged by the American démarche and that at first the Russians were determined to make no reply whatever. Then they made their policy dependent on that of France, their conviction being that France would not give a favorable reply. When the French deserted them and went their own way, the Russians were obliged to crawl out as best they could. Their reply was a masterpiece of equivocation: " In so far as the territory leased by China to Russia is concerned, the Imperial Government has already demonstrated its firm intention to follow the policy of the ' open door ' by creating Dalny (Talienwan) a free port; and if at some future time that port, although remaining free itself, should be separated by a customs limit from other portions of the territory in question, the customs duties would be levied, in the zone subject to the tariff, upon all foreign merchandise without distinction as to nationality." No mention was made of Russia's sphere of influence in Manchuria, and no mention was made of navigation dues or preferential railway rates. Russia rejected the proposals of Hay as she had rejected those of Lord Salisbury, and since all the powers had made their acceptance of the Open Door policy conditional on the acceptance of the other governments, the whole program really fell to the ground.

Hay understood this perfectly well, but for practical purposes he chose to regard the Russian reply as an acceptance and notified the powers that the

---

[23] Dennis, op. cit., pp. 208 ff.

United States considered the assent of the various powers to be final and definitive. The whole move greatly enhanced Hay's reputation in his own country, though, as his most recent biographer remarks, " it would have taken more than a lawyer to define what new rights had been recognized, or acquired, or even what had actually been said." [24]

The efforts of Hay, then, had no practical bearing on the situation as it was at the turn of the century. The powers were all busy consolidating their past gains, the Russians in particular pushing forward their construction program, developing the new commercial port of Dalny, refortifying Port Arthur and building the southern branch of the Manchurian Railway. The only immediate international danger lay in a possible clash between Russia and Japan.

Since the seizure of Port Arthur Japanese influence had, to a large extent, replaced that of Russia at Peking. The Chinese reformers looked to Japan as a model and an inspiration. They planned to send students to Tokyo and even talked of calling in Count Ito to direct the work of reorganization. This same policy was pursued by the Empress Dowager after the coup d'état of September 1898. Ito urged upon the Peking government the need for reform if China was to be saved from the Europeans. He paid a visit to Peking himself, and was reported to have offered China an alliance. In the autumn of 1899 a Chinese mission was sent to Tokyo asking for support, and soon afterward some forty Japanese officers were sent to China. The Japanese League of Culture and Education aimed directly at the spread of Japanese influence and the development of Chinese-Japanese solidarity against Europe. It opened schools in China and in general unfolded an extensive program of propaganda.[25]

For this development the Russians had only themselves to blame, though there was nothing they could do about it. But with Korea the situation was somewhat different. Since the Rosen-Nissi Agreement of April 1898 the Japanese had been spreading themselves in Korea, establishing commercial settlements and securing concessions. The Korean Independence Club, which worked for reform along western lines, was well known to be under Japanese influence. Here, as in China, the Japanese were intent on building up resistance to the encroachments of the Europeans.[26] The question was whether the Russians were

[24] Dennett: *John Hay*, p. 295. The most important account is that of Dennis, op. cit., chap. viii, which is based on unpublished American documents, but see also Paul S. Reinsch: *World Politics* (New York, 1900), pp. 176 ff.; Shutaro Tomimas: *The Open Door Policy and the Territorial Integrity of China* (New York, 1919), chap. iii and iv; M. J. Bau: *The Open Door Doctrine* (New York, 1923), chap. i; Joseph: *Foreign Diplomacy in China*, chap. xviii; R. S. McCordock: *British Far Eastern Policy, 1894–1900* (New York, 1931), pp. 291 ff.; Paul H. Clyde: " The Open Door Policy of John Hay " (*Historical Outlook*, May, 1931, pp. 210–14).

[25] Glinskii: *Prolog Russko-Iaponskoi Voiny*, pp. 90–103; Charles Johnston: " The Struggle for Reform in China " (in *The Crisis in China*, New York, 1900); O. Franke: " Japans Asiatische Bestrebungen " (*Deutsche Rundschau*, August, 1903, pp. 256–74); C. E. Maitre, in *Bulletin de l'École Française d'Extrême Orient*, IV, 1904, pp. 499–522.

[26] Arthur D. Brown: *The Mastery of the Far East* (New York, 1919), pp. 150 ff.; André Chéradame: *Le Monde et la Guerre Russo-Japonaise* (Paris, 1906), pp. 104 ff.

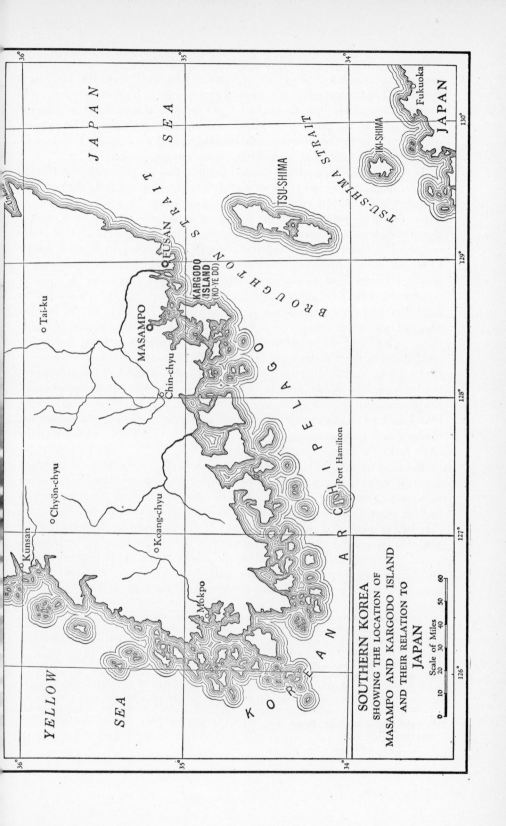

SOUTHERN KOREA

SHOWING THE LOCATION OF
MASAMPO AND KARGODO ISLAND
AND THEIR RELATION TO

JAPAN

Scale of Miles

0   10   20   30   40   50   60

prepared to abandon their original designs in Korea and leave the Japanese a free field. The foreign office, as well as Witte, appears to have made up its mind to that policy, and to have decided once and for all to throw all energy into the consolidation of the position in Manchuria and northern China. This appears quite clearly from the government's attitude toward the famous Yalu concession, which was to become so important in the ensuing period.

In 1896 a Russian merchant named Brinner had secured from the Korean ruler a concession for the exploitation of the timber preserves along the northern boundary of Korea. In view of Russian commitments he had been unable to develop this concession, which in 1897 he turned over to a group composed of Russian diplomats, bankers and developers. In the spring of 1898 this group succeeded in interesting the imperial court in the scheme. An Eastern Asiatic Company was to be formed, which should serve as a cloak for the absorption of northern Korea. Some 20,000 troops were to be smuggled in under the guise of woodsmen. The Tsar approved the scheme and supplied the 250,000 rubles needed to send out an expedition of reconnaissance. The party set out in June 1898 and made extensive surveys as well as a description of the country. Not only that, the leader of the expedition, who was disappointed with the lumbering possibilities of the Yalu area, secured from the Korean King a concession for the exploitation of all the mines in Korea on condition that he arrange a much-needed loan. The whole story is an exceedingly complicated one, which need not be recounted here in all its details. Suffice it to say that Witte, who had not been informed of the expedition, refused absolutely to furnish the money for the loan, or to have anything to do with the Yalu project. In November 1899 the affair had to be dropped for the time being.[27]

But even though Witte was able to frustrate the Korean schemes with which the Tsar himself sympathized, it was harder for him to counteract another policy which was dangerous to his own designs. The Russian naval authorities had for years set their hearts on the acquisition of a base in Korea. Since 1895 they had concentrated their attention on Masampo and the near-by island of Kargodo (Ko-ye-do) at the southeastern tip of Korea, just opposite the Japanese island of Tsushima and commanding the all-important straits between Korea and Japan. The Tsar had been completely converted to the idea that Russia must secure such a port.[28] Masampo was certainly a most desirable place. By

[27] The main account of the project was published by one of its leading spirits (V. M. Vonliarliarski): "Why Russia Went to War with Japan, the Story of the Yalu Concession" (*Fortnightly Review*, May and June, 1910, pp. 817-31, 1031-44). Since then there have appeared two important studies based on Russian archive material: B. A. Romanov: "Kontzessia na Yalu" (*Russkoe Proshloye*, I, 1923, pp. 87-108) and Friedrich von Steinmann: *Russlands Politik im Fernen Osten und der Staatssekretär Bezobrazov* (Leipzig, 1931). Curiously enough neither of these writers seems to be aware of Vonliarliarski's published account. See further W. L. Langer: "Der Russisch-Japanische Krieg" (*Europäische Gespräche*, June, 1926, pp. 279-322), pp. 290-3.

[28] A. Popov: "Pervie Shagi Russkogo Imperializma na Dal'nem Vostoke" (*Krasnyi Arkiv*, LII, 1932, pp. 34-124), pp. 67 ff., 76-7, 103 ff.; Baron Rosen: *Forty Years of Diplomacy* (New York, 1922), II, p. 141.

many writers it was considered the best harbor in the whole Far East. The French had surveyed it carefully in 1895 and had hopes all along of securing it at some favorable opportunity.[29]

During 1899 the Russian ministry of marine made several attempts to obtain a concession of land at Masampo, but in every case they seem to have been anticipated by Japan. The Russians threatened reprisals at Seoul, but the Koreans were supported by the Japanese representative. By the autumn of 1899 war between the two powers seemed not at all unlikely, and English writers were already calling for an alliance between England and Japan to block the Russian advance.[30] But Japan was not ready for a conflict at that time, and the Russians too were anxious to postpone the clash which they regarded as inevitable until the Transsiberian Railway should have been finished.[31] The whole question was gone over in the great memorandum drawn up by Muraviev in January 1900. He there pointed out that Japan would oppose Russian action even if England did not. Only when the railroad to Port Arthur was completed could Russia proceed with the scheme.[32]

This argumentation, however, did not satisfy the naval authorities. In reply to Muraviev's memorandum Admiral Tyrtov pointed out that Russia's position in the Far East could not be regarded as secure until she had a base in southern Korea. Port Arthur would be of no use against Japan. In fact, if Japan seized the Korean harbors she could cut off all communication between Port Arthur and Vladivostok. On the other hand, if Russia could get control of Masampo and Kargodo she would have in hand an effective weapon with which to threaten Japan. This would force the latter power to consider carefully before challenging Russia in the Far East.[33]

The argument was reinforced by renewed efforts on the part of the naval authorities to secure an establishment at Masampo. On March 16, 1900 a Russian squadron anchored at Chemulpo. The admiral went up to Seoul, where, together with Pavlov, the Russian minister, he was received in audience by the King. Two days later the Russians secured a lease of land at Masampo for a coal depot and naval hospital, as well as a promise of the non-alienation of Kargodo. News of this success caused great excitement in Japan and England. " This establishment, unimportant in the beginning, might later on assume a more formidable character constituting a permanent menace to Japan," re-

---

[29] This interesting fact is revealed in the anonymous article " L'Occupation de Cargodo par la Russie " (*Questions Diplomatiques et Coloniales*, November 1, 1899, pp. 276–9).

[30] Holt S. Hallett: " The War Cloud in the Far East " (*Nineteenth Century*, December, 1899, pp. 988–95); Ignotus: " The Coming Storm in the Far East " (*National Review*, December, 1899, pp. 494–505). By far the best account of the whole matter is that of K. Asakawa: *The Russo-Japanese Conflict* (Boston, 1904), pp. 274–8, based on Japanese sources. But see also Rosen, op. cit., II, p. 161; Brown, op. cit., pp. 142 ff.

[31] *Die Grosse Politik*, XVII, no. 5336; Hatzfeldt to Bülow, November, 19, 1899 (Bülow: *Memoirs*, I, p. 363).

[32] " Tsarskaia Diplomatiia o Zadachaiakh Rossii na Vostoke " (*Krasnyi Arkhiv*, XVIII, 1926, pp. 3–29).   [33] Ibid.

ported the British minister at Tokyo. For a short time the situation was very tense. Practically the whole Japanese navy was mobilized and part of the army was put in a state of readiness. The details are not known, but it seems that the Japanese accepted the situation only when they learned late in April that the Russians had been obliged, in return for the lease, to bind themselves never to apply for their own use or for the use of Russian subjects for any land on the island of Kargodo or on the opposite mainland or on any of the surrounding islands.[84]

With the atmosphere of Far Eastern affairs heavily charged, the storm broke in May 1900 in what is commonly called the Boxer Rebellion. There has always been a good deal of uncertainty and not a little misunderstanding with respect to the anti-foreign outbreaks in China in 1900, but recent researches have helped considerably to clarify the problem. Hatred of the " foreign devils " was nothing new in China, but it came to a head chiefly after the crisis of 1897-1898. The Emperor Kuang-hsü had tried to meet the emergency by a program of strengthening the Empire through reform along western lines. The effort was frustrated by the Empress Dowager, supported by the conservative Manchu party at court. But it would be a mistake to suppose that the Empress did not share the apprehensions of the reform party. She too was alarmed by the encroachments of the foreigners and she too was determined to offer resistance. Not all the reforms of the Hundred Days were cancelled, but the policy of the government after September 1898 became concentrated more and more upon the problem of military reorganization. Decrees of November and December 1898 ordered the increase and strengthening and drilling of local militia companies, which were the traditional organization used against bandits. The Chinese name of this militia was the I-ho T'uan, which, translated, means The Righteous and Harmonious Band. The fact that the young men who enrolled for this service engaged in elaborate gymnastic exercises and mystic rites gave rise to misinterpretation on the part of missionaries and diplomats, who believed the organization to be part of one of the great secret societies. The name was translated as The Society of Harmonious Fists, hence the popular name Boxers. References to them have been found in missionary correspondence as early as January 1899.[85]

The Boxer groups were unquestionably intended for purposes of defense against foreigners, and their organization was decreed first in the provinces of Chi-li, Shantung, Shansi and Fengtien (Manchuria), which were the provinces at the same time most loyal to the dynasty and most exposed to European encroachments. There were some outbreaks and demonstrations against foreigners in the autumn of 1898, when extra guards were brought up to Peking to pro-

---

[84] *British Documents*, II, nos. 39, 40; Hansard: *Parliamentary Debates*, Series IV, vol. LCCCIII, pp. 730-1, 1503-4; Ignotus: " Britain's Debt to Japan " (*National Review*, May, 1900, pp. 378-88), pp. 382-3; Asakawa, op. cit., p. 276.

[85] I follow here the interesting argumentation of George N. Steiger: *China and the Occident* (New Haven, 1927), chaps. vii and viii, which is sound so far as I can tell.

tect the legations. But serious trouble began in Shantung in the autumn of 1899, when popular feeling against the "foreign devils" assumed alarming proportions. European commerce in China had almost doubled since 1891 and everywhere telegraphs and railroads were penetrating the countryside. Considering the popular opposition to the first railways in Europe it is not surprising that the Chinese disliked the innovation, the more so as the railroads often interfered with the sacred burial places and threw out of work large numbers of porters, boatmen and other transport workers. Add to this the fact that northern China was suffering from two successive years of drought and bad crops, to say nothing of a disastrous flood of the Yellow River, and it is not hard to understand that a superstitious people should have held the outsiders responsible for all their woes. Hatred of the European became widespread and violent and, quite naturally, took the form of attacks upon Chinese converts to Christianity and their protectors, the missionaries, who were generally put down as the agents of foreign business.[36]

From November 1899 the European ministers at Peking began to protest against the activities of the Boxers and to demand their abolition as an illegal organization. They got little satisfaction from the government, partly because the organization was not illegal and could not be proceeded against without outraging Chinese opinion, partly because the Empress sympathized with its aims and felt the need of its support. This is clear from the secret edict of November 21, 1899 sent to all the viceroys. In this paper it is said:

" The various powers cast upon us looks of tiger-like voracity, hustling each other in their endeavors to be the first to seize upon our innermost territories. They think that China, having neither money nor troops, would never venture to go to war with them. They fail to understand, however, that there are certain things which this Empire can never consent to, and that, if hardly pressed upon, we have no alternative but to rely upon the justice of our cause, the knowledge of which in our breasts strengthens our resolves and steels us to present a united front against our aggressors." The viceroys were urged " to fight for the preservation of their homes and native soil from the encroaching footsteps of the foreign aggressor." [37]

Although this document became known to the foreign ministers in January 1900 they persisted in regarding the Boxer movement as a rebellion and continued to press restrictive measures upon the government. Some concessions were made and orders were issued prohibiting violence, but yielding on the

---

[36] Steiger, loc. cit. Among other accounts of the rise of the movement see the very fair study of George B. Smyth: "Causes of Anti-Foreign Feeling in China" (in *The Crisis in China*, New York, 1900); A. de Pourvoirville: "À Propos des Boxers" (*Nouvelle Revue*, July 1, 1900, pp. 115–27); Arthur H. Smith: *China in Convulsion* (New York, 1901), chaps. x, xi; Bland and Backhouse: *China under the Empress Dowager*, chap. xvi; Henri Cordier: *Histoire des Relations de la Chine avec les Puissances Occidentales* (Paris, 1902), III, chap. xxiv; Paul H. Clements: *The Boxer Rebellion* (New York, 1915), pp. 70 ff.

[37] *United States Foreign Relations 1900*, pp. 85–6, quoted by Clements, op. cit., pp. 105–6.

part of the government was accompanied by rising indignation on the part of the population. By the end of May the situation was getting out of hand. On May 28 an attack was made on the foreigners working on the Peking-Hankow railway, and therewith the critical phase of the Boxer rising may be said to have begun.

The story of the Chinese crisis of 1900 and the siege of the legations has been so often told that no good purpose could be served in recounting it here. The ministers at Peking at once called up additional guards, but these amounted to only a few hundred men. When disorders began to break out along the Tientsin-Peking railway there was obvious danger that the foreigners in the capital would be cut off. General panic seized the Europeans. On June 10 Admiral Seymour, with a small force of 2,000 men from the ships at Taku, set out from Tientsin. He met with serious opposition and was obliged to turn back after a week of fighting without having reached the capital. Prince Tuan, patron of the Boxers and leader of the anti-foreign faction at court, was made head of the Yamen on June 10 and from that time on the government openly identified itself with the movement. The Boxers appeared in Peking on June 13. Two days later telegraphic communication with the outside world was cut off. Thereupon the admirals demanded the surrender of the forts at Taku. The demand remaining unanswered they bombarded and took the forts on June 17. Technically the powers were at war with China, and so the Chinese evidently regarded the situation. Imperial troops began to take part in the fighting along with the Boxers. On June 19 the German minister, von Ketteler, was assassinated on the streets of Peking and the attacks on the legations began. Most of the foreigners took refuge in the British legation, which was valiantly defended until a relief force reached Peking on August 14. In the interval the rising spread to Shansi and Manchuria. Considerable numbers of Chinese converts and European missionaries were killed, and it was reported that the ministers at Peking themselves had been murdered. During June and July 1900 Europe had little thought for anything but the catastrophe in the Far East.

In the early stages of the crisis the European powers had been obliged to act together from force of circumstances. There was little discussion about the Seymour expedition. But this did not imply that the European governments had in any way overcome their earlier rivalries and traditional suspicions. In order to prevent the spread of the movement to central and southern China they adopted the fiction that there was no war, that the Boxer rising was a " rebellion," and that their purpose was simply to relieve the legations and secure guarantees for the future. Beyond that they continued to regard themselves with the deepest distrust. The British government, sadly incapacitated by the South African War, was unable to take as active a part as it might otherwise have done. It did send a considerable force from India, but for the rest devoted itself to the conclusion of arrangements with the viceroys of the Yangtze region to prevent disturbances in what the British regarded as their sphere. Determined efforts were made to induce the Japanese to send a strong force to relieve the legations and to secure for the Japanese something akin to a European mandate. Suggestions of this sort were, however, rejected by the German and Russian governments, for fear that the Japanese and their English friends might be planning to feather their own nests.[38]

England, then, was obliged to fall back on her own resources and to rely upon the benevolent support of Japan and the United States, while trying throughout to maintain contact with Germany and prevent that power from following the lead of Russia. "Russia, not China, seems to me the greatest danger at the moment," wrote Lord Salisbury on June 10.[39] Everywhere in England it was feared that Russia stood behind the Empress and that the outcome of the whole business would be the establishment of Russia in Chi-li and at Peking. The press during July and August called for revenge for the supposed murder of the ministers, pointed out that the conquest or partition of China was inevitable and demanded that England secure her share.[40]

The Russian policy, however, was not as single-minded as the British supposed. Ever since 1895 there had been different opinions in official Russian circles with respect to the policy to be pursued in China. Witte had been opposed to the seizure of Port Arthur and had always favored the policy of an alliance with China, which would serve as a cloak for Russian penetration and ultimate control of a large part of the Empire. The military and naval men, and to some extent the foreign office, had taken the opposite view and had advocated taking whatever could be taken whenever the opportunity presented itself. This same divergence of view cropped up at once when the Boxer disturbances began, with this important difference, that the foreign office now sided with Witte. Muraviev had died suddenly in the last days of June and was succeeded by the much more conservative and circumspect Lamsdorff. On the other hand, Witte's influence upon the Tsar was not what it had been. Kuropatkin, the war minister, was now Nicholas' favorite, and it was therefore a very debatable question whether Witte and Lamsdorff would be able to counteract the demands of the forward party.

Witte tells us in his *Memoirs* that when news of the Boxer rising reached St. Petersburg Kuropatkin exclaimed: "I am very glad. This will give us an excuse for seizing Manchuria. . . . We will turn Manchuria into a second

---

[38] *Die Grosse Politik*, XVI, nos. 4527 ff. These questions have been so thoroughly gone over by various writers that I eschew specific references to the voluminous contemporary and later documentary sources, except when definite references seem desirable. On this point see especially McCordock: *British Far Eastern Policy*, pp. 336 ff.

[39] *Letters of Queen Victoria*, III, p. 561.

[40] Demetrius Boulger: "The Scramble for China" (*Contemporary Review*, July, 1900, pp. 1–10); Idem: "Peking — and After" (*Fortnightly Review*, August, 1900, pp. 198–208); Anonymous: "Distracted China" (*Blackwood's Magazine*, August, 1900, part II, pp. 287–94); Diplomaticus: "Have We a Policy in China?" (*Fortnightly Review*, August, 1900, pp. 327–37); Emerson Bainbridge: "China and the Powers" (*Contemporary Review*, August, 1900, pp. 172–82), etc.

Bokhara." [41] This is in keeping with what we know generally of the war minister's attitude. In a memorandum of March 1900 he had expressed the opinion that Manchuria should, preferably, remain a part of China, but that Russia should secure " absolute commercial control " and generally consolidate her position.[42] During June and July he made it perfectly clear in conversations with German diplomats that Russia was much more interested in Manchuria than in the Peking legations, and that Russia demanded for herself a free hand in Manchuria.[43]

Witte, too, favored leaving Manchuria in the hands of the Chinese and confining Russian activity to a policy of peaceful penetration. But he objected to Kuropatkin's idea of seizing the opportunity for establishing control of the Manchurian provinces. He was very anxious to avoid attacks on the Railway and tried to arrange with Li Hung-chang for protection of the Russian enterprise.[44] Nothing came of these efforts, for in the middle of July Chinese bands began to attack the Railway. The Russians had only about 6000 men in Manchuria and were unable to hold their own. They were obliged to evacuate Mukden, Kirin and Tsitsihar, while the Chinese besieged their forces in Harbin and at Blagovestchensk. There was nothing for it but to send in considerable numbers of troops. A regular campaign was undertaken from the north, south and east, and by mid-October the Russians were in complete military control of the three Manchurian provinces.[45]

In the meanwhile the question of an international expedition to relieve the legations had become a burning one. Witte and Lamsdorff were flatly opposed to Russian participation, on the plea that China's friendship could be regained by a tolerant attitude. Kuropatkin, however, saw in the expedition a chance to extend Russian influence over Chi-li. He convinced the Tsar and in the end Russia contributed 4000 men to the relief forces. The Russian commander was ordered, however, not to advance beyond Yang-tsun. The fact that he entered Peking in the van of the other troops on August 14 was due entirely to accident — the order did not reach him until it was too late to obey it.[46] But hardly had the legations been relieved when the Russian foreign office surprised the world by an invitation to withdraw the ministers and forces to Tientsin, since it was clear that the Empress and the court, which had fled to Sian-fu, would not return and negotiate so long as the capital was occupied by the foreigners. In a circular to the powers on August 25 the Russian government declared that its

---

[41] *The Memoirs of Count Witte* (New York, 1921), p. 107.

[42] Kuropatkin: *The Russian Army and the Japanese War* (New York, 1909), p. 70.

[43] *Die Grosse Politik,* XVI, nos. 4537, 4548, 4552.

[44] Glinskii: *Prolog,* etc., pp. 106 ff.; Romanov: *Rossiia v Manchzhurii,* pp. 250 ff.

[45] The German translation of the official Russian account: *Die Kämpfe der Russischen Truppen in der Mandschurei im Jahre 1900* (Leipzig, 1901); Glinskii, op. cit., pp. 118 ff.; Clive Bigham: *A Year in China* (London, 1901), chap. xiv.

[46] Glinskii, op. cit., pp. 116–8; Witte: *Memoirs,* p. 108; *Die Grosse Politik,* XVI, nos. 4558, 4573.

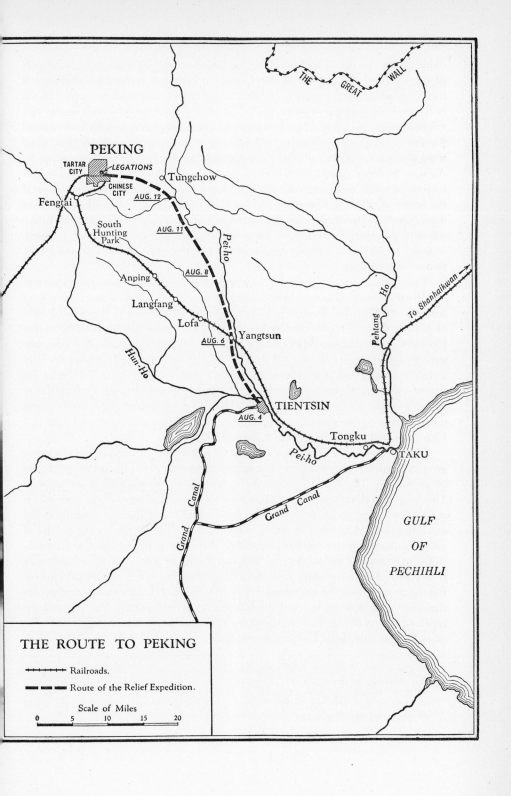

THE ROUTE TO PEKING

Railroads.

Route of the Relief Expedition.

Scale of Miles

0   5   10   15   20

objects from the outset had been the protection of the legations and the support of the Chinese government in the repression of the disturbances. Therefore it had favored the maintenance of the Concert of Powers and the preservation of the existing political order in China, and had been opposed to everything that might conduce to the partition of the Empire. Unforeseen attacks had obliged Russia to occupy Newchuang and to send troops into Manchuria, but these were provisional measures which did not indicate any change in Russian policy. As soon as order should have been re-established in Manchuria and the necessary steps taken to protect the railway, Russia would withdraw her troops, if the action of other powers were no obstacle to that course. The relief of Peking meant the accomplishment of the first object of the Russian program, and Russia now proposed to withdraw her representative and her forces to Tientsin, in order to make possible the return of the Chinese government and the initiation of negotiations.[47]

This famous circular was the outward expression of a temporary victory of the Witte-Lamsdorff group over Kuropatkin and the military men. In a long report to the Tsar on August 24 Witte had pointed out that if Russia took part of China, the other powers would do likewise. Japan would probably seize Korea. Then Russia would no longer have weak neighbors in the Far East, but strong powers on her flanks. All this would call for huge expenditures for protective measures and would weaken Russia's position in Europe. To one of his fellow ministers Witte wrote bitterly of the advance to Peking and of Kuropatkin's whole policy in Manchuria: " There is no definite policy, no firmness, no adherence to one's word, — and Kuropatkin is in a state of chronic rage. . . . I have done all I could to prevent a disaster." [48]

The Russian circular did not make a very favorable impression on the other governments, which were generally agreed that withdrawal from Peking would be premature. The French government alone gave the suggestion its support. The American government gave an evasive and equivocal answer in a note which meant something different every time one looked at it.[49] Russian assurances did not impress the American secretary, who declared that " her vows are as false as dicers' oaths when treachery is profitable." As a matter of fact the Far East was full of rumors of Russian designs, and the Shanghai press propagated the story that Russia had bargained with Li Hung-chang to effect the evacuation of Peking in return for the abandonment of Manchuria.[50] Under the circumstances the other governments rejected the Russian proposals, as they also rejected the repeated efforts of the St. Petersburg foreign office to have Li recognized as the official negotiator of the Chinese government.

---

[47] China No. 1 (1901), p. 113; Affaires de Chine (1900), no. 258; Die Grosse Politik, XVI, no. 4621; Glinskii, op. cit., p. 121.

[48] Witte: Memoirs, pp. 113-4; Glinskii, op. cit., pp. 119-20.

[49] Dennett: John Hay, pp. 311 ff.; Dennis: Adventures in American Diplomacy, pp. 230 ff.

[50] Morse, op. cit., III, p. 305.

The German cabinet felt itself more directly touched than any other by what was regarded as Russian perfidy. From the very outset the Emperor William, who suffered severely from the Yellow Peril idea, had taken a vigorous and bold initiative in the move against the Boxers. He had sent out troops on his own responsibility and had bidden them farewell in that most unfortunate of all his utterances, the speech of July 27, in which he instructed his men to give no quarter and take no prisoners: " Let all who fall into your hands be at your mercy. Just as the Huns a thousand years ago, under the leadership of Attila, gained a reputation by virtue of which they still live in historical tradition, so may the name of Germany become known in such a manner in China, that no Chinese will ever again even dare to look askance at a German." This hysterical attitude was no doubt due in a measure to the murder of the German minister, which, in a sense, gave the Germans some claim to leadership in the crusade of Europe. William therefore had much at heart the appointment of a German general as commander in chief of the associated forces. He tried in vain to get the British to put forward the suggestion, and then induced the Tsar to agree to the appointment of Field Marshal von Waldersee. The Tsar's assent was then communicated to the French as a Russian proposal, and before the middle of August Bülow had the more or less grudging approval of all the European powers.[51]

Waldersee was made the object of prolonged and somewhat ridiculous ovations in Germany before his departure for the Far East on August 22. The German imperialists were greatly flattered by the idea of leadership and celebrated Waldersee's victories in advance. At the time it was generally agreed that no expedition could start for Peking before the middle of September, and it was therefore taken for granted that the Germans would play a very prominent part. Great, therefore, was the Emperor's disappointment to learn of the sudden and successful relief of the legations, in which the Russian general, Linevich, took the leading part and German troops were wholly absent.[52] Coming so close upon the expedition to Peking the Russian proposal to withdraw seemed to William a direct slap in the face for himself. The whole business would be over before the much-fêted Waldersee could appear. And to think that the Russian object was simply to win the friendship of the Chinese in order to secure Manchuria as a present. In bitter marginal notes on the diplomatic correspondence the Emperor castigated the whole Russian policy, from its initial indifference to the fate of the legations to its willingness to bargain with the arch-rascal Li and even the chief of the murderers, Prince Tuan.[53]

Fortunately for the Emperor's pride the other powers were not ready to fol-

[51] *Die Grosse Politik*, XVI, nos. 4598 ff.; Bourgeois and Pagès: *Les Origines de la Grande Guerre*, p. 289; *Letters of Queen Victoria*, III, p. 573. The whole matter is discussed at length in Willy Becker: *Fürst Bülow und England* (Greifswald, 1929), pp. 166 ff. and in many other older books.

[52] *Die Grosse Politik*, XVI, no. 4614.   [53] *Die Grosse Politik*, XVI, no. 4614.

low the Russian lead. But the whole Russian policy was so suspect that the Berlin government began to sound out the British with a view to co-operation. On August 22 the Emperor met the Prince of Wales at Wilhelmshöhe and discussed the Chinese situation. It was generally agreed that negotiations with Li Hung-chang should not yet be initiated. In fact, the Emperor was determined to do all he could to obstruct Russian attempts to conclude a " rotten " peace. The conversation then turned to the Yangtze problem, William pointing out that " German commercial interests were second and not far inferior to those of England in the valley of the Yangtze, and if Her Majesty's Government could see their way to give assurances that they would maintain the policy of the open door, they would find the German Government on their side." [54]

As usual Lord Salisbury did not react favorably to the idea of an agreement with Germany. Indeed there was little popular sentiment in England for such a policy. Since the passage of the second German naval law there had grown up a distinct feeling that the Berlin government harbored dangerous designs. From that time may be dated the beginning of a regular anti-German campaign in the English periodical press, a campaign in which the *National Review* was to play a prominent part. The point is worth noting, because Mr. Maxse, the editor of the review, was known to be a friend of Lord Salisbury. But other writers also took an alarmist tone. William Stead declared that the doubling of the German fleet was " a menace to the very foundation of our Empire a thousand times more alarming than all the armaments of the Boers," and an anonymous writer in the *Quarterly Review* asserted that in view of German naval ambitions it was now necessary " for this country to be prepared to meet and crush the allied navies of the three strongest and richest Powers in the Continent of Europe." [55] In the *National Review* Mr. Maxse revealed how, in the autumn of 1899, Bülow had invited Chamberlain to speak for an agreement and had then disavowed him. He accused Germany openly of the determination to smash England: " The German fleet is admittedly not yet strong enough for this task, therefore other European fleets must be requisitioned for the service of the Kaiser. That is the true meaning of his constant grovelling to Russia. Through Russia he hopes to get control of French policy and French ships. We shall certainly court a naval Sedan unless we pull ourselves together." [56] The same theme was developed by other contributors to the *Review,* who accused Germany of ulterior and sinister motives in the Far East. " It is certain that in the case of the disruption of China, Germany would claim the whole region from the Yellow River up to the north bank of the Yangtze. She supports the open door as long as possible, but when partition comes she will join France and Russia against England." It would be a mistake for England to rely on Germany to help her get control of

[54] *British Documents,* II, no. 8; *Die Grosse Politik,* XVI, nos. 4617, 4712.

[55] W. T. Stead: editorial in *Review of Reviews,* April 15; 1900, p. 314; Anonymous: "Domestic Parties and Imperial Government" (*Quarterly Review,* July, 1900, pp. 241–69).

[56] Review of current events, *National Review,* September, 1900, pp. 1–6.

the Yangtze basin or to oppose Russia.[57] " At present the greatest external danger to England arises from Germany. . . . The Kaiser is a reincarnation of Napoleon. In Europe he represents a Continental coalition against what is still the greatest maritime power of the world. He intends to displace us, with or without a struggle, and for that end is rapidly forging the means. . . . If, for any reason, Germany should decide to precipitate the contest, and should succeed in forming a coalition with Russia and France, nothing could now arrest our fall." [58]

These citations are significant, because we learn from the British documents that the fears they expressed were shared at least in part by the foreign office. In a memorandum drawn up in connexion with the German suggestion regarding the Yangtze, Mr. Bertie pointed out that the German stand was that they had a special position in Shantung, but that they also had equal rights with Britain in the Yangtze basin:

" What Germany will claim as her special field will probably be Shantung and the valley of the Yellow River. . . . Germany will further claim that between the Yellow River Valley and the north bank of the Yangtzse River the division of good things between British and Germans must be absolutely equal, viz., that every concession granted to an Englishman must be counterpoised by one to a German. On these conditions the German Government may be willing to recognise to Great Britain the same rights in the Yangtzse region *south* of that river as Germany claims in Shantung and the Yellow River Valley. We should then have to fight out with the French and other Governments, who have not recognised our Yangtzse sphere of interest, any claims which we desire to support in the special sphere conceded to us by Germany. As to making use of Germany to come between the Russians and ourselves in China, we are not likely to have much success." [59]

Despite these suspicions Salisbury finally yielded to the prodding of the German ambassador. It was agreed that the two powers should draw up an arrangement the object of which should be to keep China open to the trade of all nations, to renounce for themselves all attempts to take advantage of the crisis for purposes of further acquisitions, and to oppose other powers in making any similar attempt. The Germans tried to restrict the application of the agreement to the Yangtze Valley, but the point was finally compromised and the maintenance of the Open Door was made to apply to " the ports of the rivers and littoral of China." Thereupon Hatzfeldt made it clear that Germany would not agree to anything that might appear directed against Russia. He suggested that the ports of the Amur River and Port Arthur be specifically excluded.

[57] X.: " The German Danger in the Far East " (*National Review*, October, 1900, pp. 178-96). See also the very unfriendly article of Sir Rowland Blennerhassett: " The Foreign Policy of the German Empire " (ibid., September, 1900, pp. 37-52).

[58] An Englishman: " Reconstruction or Catastrophe? " (*National Review*, November, 1900, pp. 330-41).

[59] *British Documents*, II, no. 12.

There was talk on the English side of confining the Open Door agreement to the region south of 38° N.L., which would have left out not only Manchuria but Chi-li. In the end a vague wording was chosen: the principle of the Open Door should be upheld in all Chinese territory "so far as they (England and Germany) could exercise influence."

Salisbury was not much pleased with the course of the discussion. To the German ambassador he wrote frankly: "I confess that since you have altered it to make it agreeable to Russia I am not much in love with this agreement. It is liable to so much misunderstanding." [60] This feeling was undoubtedly strengthened by the German refusal to accept the phrase "will oppose" with respect to efforts of other powers to take advantage of the situation to make acquisitions at China's expense. This part, too, was finally toned down to read that the two powers should "direct their policy towards maintaining undiminished the territorial condition of the Chinese Empire."

It is fairly clear that the British government consented to the agreement only because of the growing threat of Russian action in northern China, a matter to which we shall have to recur later. In any event the document that was signed on October 16, 1900 was diluted and innocuous enough. The essential three clauses read:

1) It is a matter of joint and permanent international interest that the ports on the rivers and littoral of China should remain free and open to trade and to every other legitimate form of economic activity for the nationals of all countries without distinction; and the two governments agree on their part to uphold the same for all Chinese territory as far as they can exercise influence.

2) The Imperial German Government and Her Britannic Majesty's Government will not, on their part, make use of the present complication to obtain for themselves any territorial advantages in Chinese dominions, and will direct their policy towards maintaining undiminished the territorial condition of the Chinese Empire.

3) In case of another Power making use of the complications in China in order to obtain under any form whatever such territorial advantages, the two contracting Parties reserve to themselves to come to a preliminary understanding as to the eventual steps to be taken for the protection of their own interests in China.

Clause 4 simply provided for the communication of this agreement to the other powers and for an invitation to them to accept the principles recorded in it.

When the agreement was made public, John Hay wrote to one of his close friends: "My heart is heavy about John Bull. Do you twig his attitude to Germany? When the Anglo-German pact came out, I took a day or two to find out what it meant. I soon learned from Berlin that it meant a horrible practical joke on England. From London I found out what I had suspected, but what it astounded me after all to be assured of — *That they did not know!* When

[60] *Die Grosse Politik*, XVI, no. 4732; *British Documents*, II, no. 38.

Japan joined the pact, I asked them why. They said, ' We don't know, only if there is any fun going on, we want to be in.' " [61]

Even though Hay's jocularity need not be taken too seriously, there was much truth in what he said. The agreement was so vague that it was bound to cause misunderstanding later. Taking it at face value one can hardly refrain from asking: If the two powers meant what they said, what was the use of saying it? The English ministers were almost unanimous in their dissatisfaction with the agreement. It would not, they felt, prevent Russia from doing what she wished in China, and by no means assured England that Germany would take a firm attitude against Russia. The Duke of Devonshire, one of Germany's best friends, declared that he could not understand how Salisbury could have consented to the exclusion of Manchuria: " In view of this restriction the whole treaty becomes a document which is not worth the paper it is written on." [62] Whatever gains there may have been were undoubtedly on Germany's side. She had succeeded in forestalling any attempt by the British to establish themselves in the Yangtze and had secured British assurances of the continuance of the Open Door in that important area, all without in any way committing herself to opposition to the Russian designs. [63]

British fears that the agreement would prove ineffectual in stopping Russia were only too well founded. The reply from St. Petersburg was a cleverly worded evasion: " The first point of this Agreement, stipulating ' that the ports on the rivers and littoral of China, wherever the two Governments exercise their influence, should *remain* free and open to commerce,' can be favourably entertained by Russia, this stipulation not prejudicing in any way the *status quo* established in China by existing treaties." This was tantamount to restricting the principle of the Open Door to those areas where England and Germany had special interests. Salisbury protested against this wilful distortion of Article I and pointed out that the intention was to extend the principle " to the whole of the Chinese Empire so far as the two Powers can exercise influence." Apparently the Russians refused to enter upon further debate of the matter, which was certainly open to a variety of interpretations. [64]

In the interval the powers had come to an understanding with regard to negotiations with China. The basis for discussion was a note sent out on October 4 by Delcassé, which provided for punishment of guilty officials, reparation for losses suffered, and guarantees for the future. There was more than enough wrangling before the details were settled, for the Germans, more or less supported by the British, favored the stiffest possible terms, while the Russians, and to a certain extent the Americans and the Japanese, advocated gentler treatment, for reasons of their own. It is quite unnecessary to follow the dreary course of

---

[61] William R. Thayer: *Life and Letters of John Hay* (Boston, 1915), II, p. 248; Dennett: *John Hay*, p. 320.

[62] Eckardstein: *Lebenserinnerungen*, II, p. 202; *Die Grosse Politik*, XVI, no. 4745.

[63] *Die Grosse Politik*, XVI, no. 4766.

[64] *British Documents*, II, nos. 20, 21; *Die Grosse Politik*, XVI, no. 4747.

the negotiations here, the more so as they have been well summarized by many writers on Far Eastern diplomacy.[65] Suffice it to say that a joint note was presented to the Chinese plenipotentiaries, Li Hung-chang and Prince Ching, on December 24, 1900. Discussion of details was then begun. The negotiations, which dragged on through the winter and spring, became at times very heated, and it was only in September 1901 that the final agreements were signed.

European diplomats as a whole had no ground for priding themselves on the handling of the Boxer movement and its aftermath. Europe's treatment of China in the whole period from 1895 to 1900 had been devoid of all consideration and of all understanding. The Celestial Empire to them was simply a great market to be exploited to the full, a rich territory to be carved up like a sirloin steak. Hardly anywhere in the diplomatic correspondence does one find any appreciation for the feelings of the Oriental or any sympathy for the crude efforts made at reform. The dominant note was always that force is the father of peace and that the only method of treating successfully with China is the method of the mailed fist. The Boxers were considered to be simply so many ruffians, who deserved no better treatment than that ordinarily meted out to common criminals. When the trouble began legation guards were rushed to Peking, where they evidently took the initiative by shooting at Chinese troops. The American minister thought these " exhibitions of skill and courage " would serve as " good object lessons." [66] In their negotiations with the Yamen the foreign ministers rarely bothered with the facts. Indeed, a careful student of the problem has put on record his opinion that " each of the decisive steps taken by the diplomats at Peking, or by their naval commanders at Taku, was taken on the strength of rumors which have never been substantiated; each has been justified only by appealing to subsequent events as evidence of the wisdom and necessity of the act." [67] It is well known that the Chinese government tried to prevent an assault on the foreigners and that it spared the legations, which could easily have been taken. Against this you have to place the merciless looting of Peking by the associated forces after the relief of the legations. It was a chapter of European activity which the Oriental cannot be expected to forget for a long time to come.

So far as the relationship of the powers to each other was concerned there was little occasion for compliments. The governments worked together in the heat of the crisis, but there was no real heart for a European concert. From the outset each power regarded every other with distrust and suspicion. Russia's willingness to sacrifice the legations in order to win the friendship of the Chinese government only served to confirm British and German suspicions of ulterior motives. In the last count the Russian military men were determined to seize not only Man-

---

[65] E.g. Morse: *International Relations of the Chinese Empire*, III, chap. xii; Clements: *The Boxer Rebellion*, part iii; Steiger: *China and the Occident*, chap. xii; recent material may be found in *Die Grosse Politik*, XVI, chap. civ, and in Alfred Graf von Waldersee: *Denkwürdigkeiten* (Stuttgart, 1923), III, chap. xii.

[66] Steiger: *China and the Occident*, pp. 221–2.

[67] Ibid., pp. 232 ff.

churia, but Chi-li as part of the spoils. Britain, still paralyzed by the South African War, was unable to do much and found it advisable to quiet German fears of British designs in the Yangtze Basin by concluding the ill-fated Agreement of October 16, 1900. Salisbury regarded the thing as " unnecessary but innocuous," [68] and must have realized that it left matters just where they were. But he accepted it — accepted the German wording, chiefly in order to keep Germany from joining Russia in a general scramble when England was not in a position to get her full share.

In a sense the German policy was decisive throughout the crisis, not so much because of her leadership in the operations in China and her constant advocacy of the stiffest possible demands upon the Chinese government, but because of her careful navigation between the rocks of British and Russian policy. This delicate balancing of German policy was more or less a reflection of the division of opinion in the government with respect to Far Eastern affairs. The Emperor was positively outraged by the Russian policy and was, no doubt, extremely jealous of the gains he expected his cousin Nicky to make. His general feeling was for co-operation with England. Bülow, on the other hand, was intent on preserving close relations with Russia. He yielded to the Emperor only so far as he had to, in order to maintain his own position (he became chancellor in October 1900). The result was that while the Germans were encouraging the British to hope for support in upholding the integrity of China, they were telling the Russians that they might do what they liked in Manchuria without fear of German opposition. It was not to be expected, under these conditions, that either side would be satisfied in the long run. The time would come — the time had to come — when the Germans would be forced into the open. Friction of one kind or the other was inevitable.

BIBLIOGRAPHICAL NOTE

DOCUMENTARY SOURCES

Accounts and Papers. There is a long list of Blue Books on the affairs of China, which have been thoroughly exploited by other writers. It seems unnecessary to do more than list them here: 1899, volume CIX. *China No. 1 (1899), Correspondence respecting the Affairs of China. China No. 2 (1899), Correspondence between Her Majesty's Government and the Russian Government with regard to their respective Railway Interests in China.* 1900, volume CV. *China No. 1 (1900), Further Correspondence respecting the Affairs of China. China No. 2 (1900), Correspondence with the United States' Government respecting Foreign Trade in China. China No. 3 (1900), Correspondence respecting the Insurrectionary Move-*

---

[68] Sanderson Memorandum, 1907 (*British Documents* II, no. 1).

ment in China. China No. 4 (1900), Reports from Her Majesty's Minister in China respecting Events at Peking. China No. 5 (1900), Correspondence respecting the Anglo-German Agreement of October 16, 1900, relating to China. 1901, volume XCI. *China No. 1 (1901), Correspondence respecting the Disturbances in China. China No. 2 (1901), Despatch from His Majesty's Ambassador at St. Petersburgh respecting the Russo-Chinese Agreement as to Manchuria. China No. 3 (1901), Further Correspondence respecting Events at Peking. China No. 4 (1901), Plans referred to in China No. 3. China No. 5 (1901), Further Correspondence respecting the Disturbances in China. China No. 6 (1901), same. China No. 7 (1901), Correspondence respecting the Imperial Railway of North China.* 1902, volume CXXX. *China No. 1 (1902), Correspondence respecting the Affairs of China.*

British Documents on the Origins of the War, 1898–1914. Volume II, chapter ix contains some material to supplement the Blue Books.

United States Foreign Relations. The volumes for the years 1899–1901 contain much important documentary material on the Chinese situation, and are unusually full.

Documents Diplomatiques. Chine, 1898–1899 (Paris, 1900). *Chine, 1899–1900* (Paris, 1900). These French Yellow Books are less valuable than the Blue Books but are important for the study of French policy.

Die Grosse Politik der Europäischen Kabinette, 1871–1914. Volume XVI of this great publication is devoted entirely to Far Eastern affairs in 1900 and 1901 and is of prime importance for the study not only of German policy, but of general European diplomacy.

Popov, A., editor: "Bokserskoe Vosstanie." (*Krasnyi Arkhiv*, XIV, 1926, pp. 1–48). A collection of important Russian documents on the Boxer affair. I have not quoted these specifically, because the material they contain has been incorporated in the work of Romanov.

MEMOIRS, AUTOBIOGRAPHIES, BIOGRAPHIES, AND LETTERS

The Memoirs of Count Witte. Edited by Abraham Yarmolinsky. New York, 1921. Contains some things of interest, but is now overshadowed by later Russian studies.

Dennett, Tyler: *John Hay.* New York, 1933. The most recent and most understanding biography of the American secretary of state, based in part on unpublished material.

Waldersee, Alfred Graf von: *Denkwürdigkeiten.* Edited by Heinrich O. Meisner. Volume III. Stuttgart, 1923. The diary of the German commander in chief in China. A most important source.

SPECIAL STUDIES

The Anglo-Russian Railway Problem:

KENT, PERCY H.: *Railway Enterprise in China.* London, 1907. In general this is still the best single account of the railway problem.

MARCILLAC, JEAN DE: " Les Chemins de Fer en Chine." (*Questions Diplomatiques et Coloniales,* July 1, 1899, pp. 265–74; July 15, 1899, pp. 321–31). An unusually well-informed contemporary analysis.

HSU, MONGTON CHIH: *Railway Problems in China.* New York, 1915. A straightforward conventional account which, for the period here treated, does not go beyond Kent.

POPOV, A.: "Anglo-Russkoe Soglashenie o Razdele Kitaiia, 1899 g." (*Krasnyi Arkhiv,* XXV, pp. 111–34, 1927). A most important publication, consisting primarily of the Russian documents on the agreement of 1899. An abstract of this article has been published in German translation by I. Lewin: " Neue Russische Dokumente zum Russisch-Englischen Chinavertrag 1899 " (*Zeitschrift für Politik,* XIX, September, 1929, pp. 339–48).

FAUVEL, A. A.: " Le Transsinien et les Chemins de Fer Chinois." (*Revue Politique et Parlementaire,* September, 1899, pp. 453–92). Another reliable and careful contemporary study of the railway problem.

General treatments:

CORDIER, HENRI: *Histoire des Relations de la Chine avec les Puissances Occidentales.* Three volumes. Paris, 1902. Though based entirely upon contemporary material this is still one of the most illuminating accounts, because of the author's unrivalled knowledge of Chinese affairs.

MORSE, HOSEA B.: *The International Relations of the Chinese Empire.* Three volumes. New York, 1918. Based very largely upon published British and American documents, but useful also for its references to the European press in China.

FRANKE, OTTO: *Die Grossmächte in Ostasien von 1894 bis 1914.* Hamburg, 1923. The work of an eminent sinologue, based in part on German archive material. Distinctly anti-English bias.

ZÜHLKE, HERBERT: *Die Rolle des Fernen Ostens in den Politischen Beziehungen der Mächte, 1895–1905.* Berlin, 1929. A substantial though rather conventional account, based chiefly on the British and German documents. Suffers from inadequate knowledge of Russian materials.

JOSEPH, PHILIP: *Foreign Diplomacy in China, 1894–1900.* London, 1928. Comparable to the preceding. A careful, conscientious study, but decidedly weak on the Russian side.

McCORDOCK, R. STANLEY: *British Far Eastern Policy, 1894–1900.* New York, 1931. A minute re-examination of the more obvious sources. Adds relatively little.

GLINSKII, B. B.: *Prolog Russko-Iaponskoi Voiny. Materialy iz Arkhiva Grafa S. I. Witte.* Petrograd, 1916. A fundamental Russian treatment, based chiefly on the Witte papers.

MARC, PIERRE: *Quelques Années de Politique Internationale. Antécédents de la Guerre Russo-Japonaise.* Leipzig, 1914. This is a translation of the preceding, the name *Marc* being a pseudonym.

ROMANOV, B. A.: *Rossiia v Manchzhurii, 1892–1906.* Leningrad, 1928. By far the most important Russian treatment, based on extensive archive material and counteracting the account of Glinskii.

STEINMANN, FRIEDRICH VON: *Russlands Politik im Fernen Osten und der Staatssekretär Bezobrazov.* Leipzig, 1931. A most valuable account of the Russian Korean policy. Based almost entirely on Russian archive material.

ASAKAWA, K.: *The Russo-Japanese Conflict.* Boston, 1904. An old book that can be highly recommended as a careful piece of work. Especially valuable because of its use of Japanese newspaper and other material.

DENNIS, ALFRED L. P.: *Adventures in American Diplomacy, 1896–1906.* New York, 1928. Based in large part on unpublished material, this is about the best account of American policy in this period.

The Boxer Rising:

CLEMENTS, PAUL H.: *The Boxer Rebellion.* New York, 1915. An orthodox treatment of the diplomatic side. Based almost entirely on British and American documents.

STEIGER, GEORGE N.: *China and the Occident.* New Haven, 1927. This is by far the best critical study of the Boxer movement as a domestic and international problem. Thoroughly well informed, it is distinguished from many other books by the originality of its interpretation.

CAMERON, MERIBETH E.: *The Reform Movement in China, 1898–1912.* Stanford, 1931. The most recent monographic treatment, employing most of the older material.

BLAND, J. O. P., and BACKHOUSE, E.: *China under the Empress Dowager.* London, 1910. An interesting and well-informed though somewhat colored narrative of modern China.

SERGEANT, P. W.: *The Great Empress Dowager of China.* London, 1910. A rather more scholarly and broad-minded volume on the same period.

SMITH, ARTHUR H.: *China in Convulsion.* Two volumes. New York, 1901. The best general contemporary account of the rising, and particularly of its origins.

ANTHOUARD, BARON D': *La Chine contre l'Étranger.* Paris, 1902, A narrative written by a French diplomat in China.

ALLEN, ROLAND: *The Siege of the Peking Legations.* London, 1901. Still one of the best accounts of what took place at Peking.

BIGHAM, CLIVE: *A Year in China*. London, 1901. A travel book by an English journalist. Contains an interesting account of the Seymour expedition and of conditions in Manchuria and Korea.

MARTIN, W. A. P.: *The Siege in Peking*. London, 1900. A narrative marked by violent hatred of the Empress Dowager.

PUTNAM WEALE, B. L.: *Indiscreet Letters from Peking*. London, 1907. A well-known and highly dramatized pseudonymous account of the siege.

THOMSON, H. C.: *China and the Powers*. London, 1902. A reprint of articles from the *Monthly Review,* by a very able observer. Distinctly favorable to China.

HART, SIR ROBERT: *These from the Land of Sinim*. London, 1901. A reprint of articles originally published in the *Fortnightly Review* by the famous head of the Chinese maritime customs service.

The Crisis in China. New York, 1900. A collection of interesting articles on various aspects of the crisis, originally published in the *North American Review* in 1899 and 1900.

DUYVENDAK, J. J. L.: *The Diary of His Excellency Ching-shan*. Leiden, 1924. The most important Chinese source. Evidently requires to be used with some caution.

LITERATURE SINCE 1935

(See also the Supplementary Bibliographical Notes to Chapters VI, XII, XIV, XV.)

FAIRBANK, JOHN K., and KWANG-CHING LIU: *Bibliographical Guide to Modern China*. Cambridge, 1950. Lists a considerable number of Chinese sources and writings on the Boxer Rebellion, not itemized here.

PELCOVITS, NATHAN A.: *Old China Hands and the Foreign Office*. New York, 1948. 349 pp. An interesting study, based on British commercial records. It demonstrates the divergence between mercantile demands and official policy.

VARG, PAUL A.: " The Foreign Policy of Japan and the Boxer Revolt " (*Pacific Historical Review,* XV, September, 1946, pp. 279–285). A sound study, exploiting chiefly the published American sources.

GRINEVICH, P.: " Bokserskoe Vosstanie " (*Problemy Kitaia,* XIII, 1934, pp. 242–275).

CHANG FENG-CHEN: *The Diplomatic Relations between China and Germany since 1898*. Shanghai, 1937. 281 pp. Noteworthy chiefly for the use of the Chinese publications.

GRISWOLD, ALFRED W.: *The Far Eastern Policy of the United States*. New York, 1938. 530 pp. Important for its account of the Open Door policy, which is based on the Rockhill and Hippsley Papers.

PRITCHARD, EARL H.: " The Origin of the Most-Favored-Nation and the Open Door Policies in China " (*Far Eastern Quarterly,* February, 1942).

XXII

The Anglo-German Negotiations

〜

D URING THE AUTUMN AND WINTER OF 1900–1901 INTEREST IN FAR EAST-
ern affairs became more and more focussed upon the activities of the
Russians. It was generally suspected that the military men had made up
their minds to establish Russian power not only in Manchuria, but in Chi-li.[1]
They had some fifty thousand troops in Manchuria, they had occupied Newchuang and taken over the customs house, they had pushed their forces to the
westward as far as the line of the projected railway to Sinminting, and they had
seized the all-important line from Peking to Tientsin and from there to the
north. Early in November it was announced that the Russians had obtained from
the Chinese government a concession of land at Tientsin, on the left bank of the
Peiho, where the railway station was located. The news led to an immediate
scramble for similar concessions on the part of the French, Germans, Belgians,
Austrians and Japanese. For all one could tell, the partition of China was about
to begin in earnest.[2]

Russian activity created such serious international tension in November that
eventually the government was obliged to draw back. The Peking-Tientsin Railway was handed over to the control of the powers and the concession at Tientsin
was explained away as having nothing whatever to do with sovereignty. But
there remained the crucial line from Tientsin to Shanhaikwan, in which British
capital was invested and which the British had so long defended against Muscovite encroachments. The English hoped, at first, to secure German support
against Russia, under the terms of the October Agreement. But Bülow declared
openly in the Reichstag: " we shall take good care not to do other people's business in China. We have no thought of serving as a lightning rod for any other
power." [3] This unaccommodating attitude was very disappointing to the British,
but the question was too nearly a decisive one to permit of half measures. The
English government therefore took a firm stand, and ultimately the Russian
military authorities decided that it would be better to restrict their ambitions to
the region north of the great wall. Still, it was only in February 1901 that the
Tientsin-Shanhaikwan line finally came into the hands of the British.[4]

---

[1] *Die Grosse Politik*, XVI, no. 4735; Waldersee: *Denkwürdigkeiten*, III, pp. 25–6.

[2] Morse, op. cit., III, pp. 321 ff.; Asakawa, op. cit., pp. 147 ff., 156 ff.; and many others.

[3] *Die Grosse Politik*, XVI, nos. 4755 ff., 4781 ff.

[4] Morse, op. cit., III, p. 323; Waldersee, op. cit., III, passim, where all the details of the dispute
may be followed.

It remained for the Russians to regularize their position in Manchuria. Ever since September 1900 secret negotiations had been carried on between Li Hung-chang and Prince Ukhtomskii, the special agent of Count Witte. They had led to nothing because of Witte's unwillingness to pay a huge bribe until it was clear that Li would be able and willing to do something worth-while.[5] In the interval the commanders on the spot made their own arrangements with the Tartar General at Mukden, Tseng-chi. The so-called Alexeiev-Tseng Agreement, signed on November 9, provided that the civil administration of Manchuria should be restored to the Chinese, but that Russian troops should be stationed at Mukden and other points along the railroad. All Chinese troops were to be disarmed and disbanded. All weapons, arsenals and military supplies were to be handed over to the Russian authorities, and the local Chinese officials were to organize only police guards.[6]

This separate agreement met with the disapproval of both Li Hung-chang and Witte, of the former probably because he wanted to do the negotiating himself and receive an adequate bribe, of the latter because he was as firmly as ever opposed to the permanent occupation of Manchuria. Russia had given assurances, he argued, that the country would be evacuated as soon as possible. She should live up to these promises in order to retain the confidence of both China and the European powers. After all, why should troops be kept in Manchuria, at great expense? There was no real danger, now that the Boxer disturbances had been put down. If further trouble arose, Russia could always send in the necessary troops by the Railway.

This viewpoint was generally shared by the foreign office, but it did not appeal to the military men, many of whom favored the outright annexation of northern Manchuria. Long discussions ensued between the ministries of foreign affairs, finance and war, the victory resting, ultimately, with Kuropatkin. Witte, having failed to get his way, determined to get satisfaction (or perhaps to ruin the agreement) by having written into the Russian terms a goodly number of economic concessions. Further arguments followed, and in the end only a few of Witte's demands were incorporated in the draft agreement which was submitted to the Chinese minister at St. Petersburg on February 8, 1901.[7]

The further development of the Far Eastern question depended so much

---

[5] Romanov: *Rossiia v Manchzhurii*, pp. 263 ff.

[6] Romanov, op. cit., p. 267; Glinskii, op. cit., pp. 137 ff.; Witte: *La Guerre avec le Japon*, pp. 42–5; this agreement was reported by Dr. Morrison, the London *Times* correspondent at Peking, and published in the *Times* on January 3, 1901. The terms there given, reprinted in a number of English books, are not accurate.

[7] It is curious that early in February, before the draft was handed to the Chinese, Witte himself passed on to the Japanese minister at St. Petersburg the text of certain articles which, far from being the actual agreement or any part of it, appear to have been rather those clauses which Witte wanted inserted and which his colleagues threw out. Is it possible that the finance minister, enraged by the failure of his own schemes, determined to wreck the convention by putting about a draft much more extreme than that actually submitted to the Chinese? The clauses in question may be found in *Die Grosse Politik*, XVI, no. 4809.

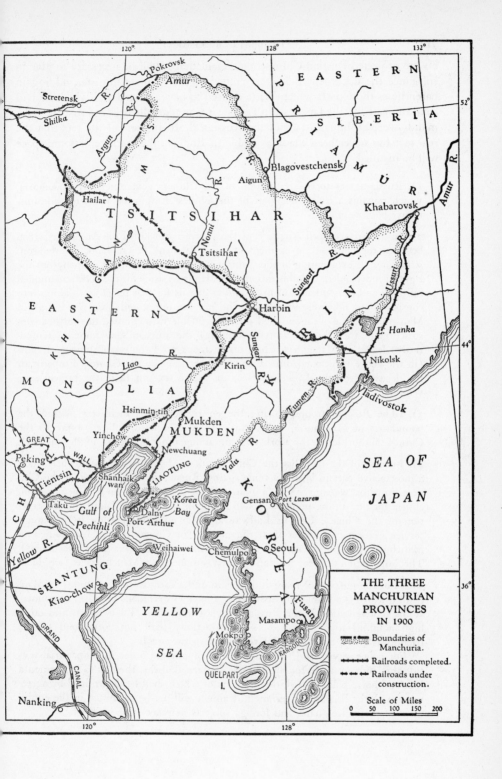

THE THREE
MANCHURIAN
PROVINCES
IN 1900

━━━ ▲━━━ Boundaries of
Manchuria.

┼┼┼┼┼┼ Railroads completed.

╍╍ ╍╍ ╍╍ Railroads under
construction.

Scale of Miles
0   50   100   150   200

on the projected Russian-Chinese agreement that it will be necessary to give in substance the document that was handed to the Chinese minister, adding in parentheses those parts which Witte desired to have inserted and which he had communicated to the Japanese. In Europe it was generally believed that these demands were an integral part of the Russian draft. In view of the fact that the real text has never been made available in English, the sacrifice of some space will be justified.

1). Russia agrees to the restoration of the Chinese government in Manchuria, which remains a constituent part of the Chinese Empire on the same administrative basis as of old.

2). In accordance with Article 6 of the contract concluded on August 27, 1896 between the Chinese Government and the Russian-Chinese Bank for the construction and exploitation of the Chinese Eastern Railway, the Company has the right of independent administration of the lands set aside for the above-mentioned railroad, and consequently of maintaining guards for that purpose. (Taking into consideration, however, that under the present unrestored order of things in Manchuria, the above-mentioned guard is unable to guarantee the further construction of the Chinese Eastern Railway) the Russian Government (temporarily) leaves in Manchuria a part of its troops until the establishment of calm (in the above mentioned district and the execution by the Chinese Emperor of the decisions contained in Articles 9, 10, 11, 12, 13 and 14 of the present convention).

3). (The Russian troops, during the entire period of their stay within the boundaries of Manchuria, will furnish, in case of need, full assistance to the Chinese authorities in the work of maintaining order and calm in the district).

4). In view of the fact that the Chinese troops, distributed in Manchuria, took a most active part in hostile actions against Russia, the Government of the Chinese Emperor, wishing to give a guarantee for the preservation of peace in Manchuria for the future, promises not to maintain troops there (until the construction of the Chinese Eastern Railway and the establishment on it of regular service is completed. After that, the number of Chinese troops maintained in Manchuria will be determined by agreement with the Russian Government). The importation of weapons and military supplies into Manchuria is forbidden.

5). (For the purpose of maintaining calm and a correct order of things in Manchuria, which is adjacent to Russia, the Chinese Government promises to remove, at the representation of the Russian Government, those Tsian-Tsiuns and other high administrative officials . . . whose activity shall not correspond to the friendly relations established between the two Empires).

For police service and the maintenance of internal order in Manchuria, outside the lands set aside for the Chinese Eastern Railway, there is to be formed a foot and horse police guard, the numbers of which shall be determined by agreement with the Russian Government. Cannon will not be permitted in the equipment of the police guard, and foreign subjects may not serve in it.

6). (In accordance with the solemn promises given by it more than once, the Chinese Government promises not to admit foreign instructors either into the ranks of the army or of the fleet of Northern China).

7). (For the purpose of guaranteeing firmer order and calm in the neutral zone, established by Article 5 of the Convention of March 15, 1898, both contracting powers allow their local authorities to come to an agreement on this question. For the same reason the right of autonomous administration granted . . . to the city of Tsing-chow is abolished).

8). The Chinese Government will not grant on all the area of the districts adjacent to Russia, namely Manchuria and Mongolia, Tarbagatai, Ili, Kashgar, Yarkand, Khotan and Keri, any concessions for the construction of railroads, working of mineral deposits, or any industrial enterprises whatsoever to foreign powers or to their subjects without the consent of the Russian Government. On all the territory of the above-mentioned districts the Chinese Government will not build railways and will not grant parcels of land for the use of foreigners without the consent of the Russian Government, except in the free port of Newchuang.

9). The Government of the Chinese Empire will compensate the Russian Government for expenditures made in consequence of the disturbances in China, to an amount relative to the actual expenditure of the Russian Government and the compensation given to other powers. The amount of this compensation as well as the terms of payment may be determined by joint discussion with the other powers interested.

10). The Chinese Government will enter into agreement with the administration of the Chinese Eastern Railway regarding compensation for damages caused by the destruction of a considerable part of the railway, the plundering of the property of the company and its officials and the delay in the construction of the road.

11). The compensation mentioned in the preceding article may, by agreement between the Chinese Government and the Company, be paid in whole or in part by granting to the Company certain privileges, by changing the existing concession (or by granting new concessions).

12). The Chinese Government promises to grant to the Chinese Eastern Railway Company a concession for the construction and exploitation of a railway line from one of the points of the Chinese Eastern Railway or its South Manchurian branch to the Chinese Wall, in the direction of Peking, on conditions similar to those granted the Chinese Eastern Railway itself. The agreement in principle to this demand was given by the Chinese Government in 1899.

13). The Chinese Government will enter into agreement with the Russian-Chinese Bank concerning indemnification for the losses of the Bank, caused by the destruction of its property and the stoppage of its operations.

14). The claims of Russian subjects and Russian private institutions and enterprises for compensation for damages caused by the disturbances in China, the

Chinese Government promises to pay as soon as they are reviewed by the Russian mission in Peking and transmitted to the Chinese Government.[8]

The Russian government depended on Li Hung-chang to get this draft accepted. At this very time it refused to join the other foreign representatives in the demand for the punishment of guilty Chinese officials. But even the promise of a million rubles could not prevent the canny old Chinaman from playing a double game. While he put up a show of advocating the signature of the Convention, he also appealed to the powers to save his country. He suggested to the British representative that the European governments demand the communication of the Russian terms and added that " China would be delighted to communicate them and place itself in the hands of the powers for protection against Russia, whose demands it could not deny and whose constant threats terrified it." [9]

Ever since the publication of the Alexeiev-Tseng Agreement in the London Times on January 3, 1901 the Russian dealings with China had called forth excitement in Europe, as in Japan and in America. The Tokyo government felt more alarmed than any other, possibly because of the apprehension caused by Russian proposals that the two powers should agree on the neutralization of Korea under a guarantee of the powers.[10] The cabinet of Prince Ito (September 1900 to June 1901) was not at all ill-disposed towards an arrangement with Russia, but the foreign minister, Baron Kato, who had resigned his position as minister to London in 1898 because of the government's unwillingness to follow up his suggestions for an agreement with England against Russia, was as uncompromisingly opposed to a yielding policy as ever. His view was that " a peaceful agreement with Russia will mean a defeat for Japan. A firm attitude on our part, even a resort to arms if necessary, is the only policy left to us." On January 17 he rejected the Russian suggestion regarding Korea in rather sharp terms. Indeed, he went further and kept pressing the Russians on the matter of the evacuation of Manchuria. He realized that the proposals touching Korea were meant merely as a blind to divert the attention of the Tokyo government from Manchuria. As his biographer says, " he focussed his eyes on Manchuria; instead of being attracted by a kite in the sky, he looked for the man on the ground who was holding it." [11]

Before the middle of January 1901, that is, long before the Russian terms were actually submitted to the Chinese, the Japanese cabinet, following in this the lead of Kato, attempted to enlist the support of the British for an inquiry at St.

---

[8] Text in Romanov, op. cit., pp. 297 ff. The text hitherto known is in China No. 2 (1904), no. 42. On the negotiations see Romanov, pp. 278 ff.; Glinskii, op. cit., pp. 142 ff.

[9] Rockhill to Hay, January 29, 1901 (published by Dennis: Adventures in American Diplomacy, p. 242); on Li's attitude and action see further Romanov, op. cit., pp. 300–4.

[10] British Documents, II, no. 42.

[11] Kato Takaaki (Tokyo, 1929), I, pp. 402 ff. The correspondence between St. Petersburg and Tokyo has now been published under the title " Nakanunie Russko-Iaponskoi Voiny " (Krasnyi Arkhiv, LXIII, 1934, pp. 3–54); see especially pp. 8–9.

Petersburg. Evidently the English government did not follow up the suggestion, for the Japanese seem to have approached the Russians alone. They were told by Lamsdorff on January 29 that the reputed Manchurian agreement was fictitious, but that reply did not, of course, satisfy them. There were some heated discussions between Kato and the Russian minister, Alexander Izvolski, of later fame. The result of these first exchanges was that the relations between Russia and Japan were exceedingly strained by the beginning of February.[12]

On February 5 the Japanese minister at London, Count Hayashi, again approached the British foreign office. The Japanese, he said, were going to warn China against concluding an agreement with Russia about Manchuria and would like to have the British join in this warning. The suggestion raised a serious problem, for no one could predict what might follow. The British government, however, felt that if the Japanese advances were rejected the Tokyo government might be driven into the arms of Russia. Once Russia and Japan had joined hands in the Far East, there would be little hope for British interests. But in order to fortify its own position the English cabinet decided to try to associate Germany in the action.

The official relations between England and Germany were at this time more cordial than they had been for some time. Since the Agreement of October 16, 1900 the two powers were supposedly pursuing the same policy in China. Lord Lansdowne, the new British foreign minister, was ready to make every effort to strengthen the friendly relations between the two countries,[13] a policy which enjoyed the cordial support of other cabinet members, like Chamberlain and the Duke of Devonshire. Indeed, if we may believe Baron Eckardstein, the first secretary of the German embassy at London, Chamberlain told him quite frankly that he favored strongly an alliance with Germany and the Triple Alliance. The days of splendid isolation were over, and the basis for the new order could be laid by an agreement concerning Morocco. But if this failed, England would have to reach an understanding with France and Russia, even at the cost of far-reaching concessions. There were already some voices being raised in the cabinet and in the press in favor of such a policy.[14]

It is remarkable that Chamberlain should have talked so freely to Eckardstein, though there is no reason to question his outlook as revealed in this conversation. At any rate, the German foreign office took Eckardstein's report at face value and, in characteristically German fashion, embarked upon a course of elaborate speculation regarding the Anglo-German problem. It was generally agreed by those who controlled German policy (and of these Baron von Holstein was the most authoritative) that the threat of an agreement between England and Russia or France was " pure humbug." England would never be able to

[12] *Kato Takaaki*, pp. 421 ff.; "Nakanunie Russko-Iaponskoi Voiny," pp. 9–12; *China No. 2 (1904)*, no. 6; *British Documents*, II, no. 42; *Documents Diplomatiques Français*, I, no. 63.

[13] Lord Newton: *Lord Lansdowne* (London, 1929), pp. 196–7.

[14] Eckardstein: *Lebenserinnerungen*, II, p. 238; *Die Grosse Politik*, XVII, no. 4979.

afford the price these powers would ask, and concessions on her part would only accentuate the appetite of her antagonists. The British were beginning to realize the absolute need of German friendship and support. Time was on the side of the Germans and ultimately the London government would be prepared to pay a high price. Only the Germans must know how to wait. Separate agreements, like the Agreement of 1898 in regard to the Portuguese Colonies, were not very profitable and nothing could be realized from them for some time. What Germany must get was a general alliance, the British paying for it at the high price of concessions in Asia and Africa and at the same time giving Germany every needed security against Russia. For the time being, however, it was essential to stand off and wait until the British had softened. In the interval they must not be discouraged by Germany but, at the same time, Germany must avoid becoming estranged from Russia.[15]

It was just at this point that the mortal illness of Queen Victoria became known. The Emperor William thereupon hurried to her bedside. He was with her when she died and stayed in England for a full two weeks afterward. This demonstration of filial piety made a deep and favorable impression upon British court circles and upon the public. Never before or after was the Emperor so popular. Even the new King, Edward VII, who had more difficulty than almost any one else in getting on with William, was apparently converted to the idea of close Anglo-German co-operation. The Emperor had a long discussion with Lord Lansdowne, which seems to have come to something like an imperial lecture. The foreign minister was warned of the danger of staking too much upon the friendship of the United States, a power which would, in the end, follow its own selfish interests. Indeed, according to the Emperor the American Republic was already flirting with Russia in the Far East. Ultimately they would divide the political and commercial hegemony between them. It was urgently necessary that England and Germany and the rest of Europe should stand together against the common danger. France, which had paid dearly in loans to Russia for the revenge which she had not secured, must be brought back into the European family. The French spirit was as necessary for Europe as the pepper on the beefsteak.

It was in keeping with this attitude that the Emperor showed his best side to the French ambassador. He even assured him that he desired a strong France, and that he would help France when she was in trouble.[16] We need not pursue this particular idea of the Emperor any further. The important thing is that William's visit to England created an atmosphere of friendliness such as had not existed since the days preceding the Kruger telegram.

---

[15] This is the burden of many letters and memoranda written between January 18 and 21, 1901 (*Die Grosse Politik*, XVII, nos. 4979–85; Eckardstein, op. cit., II, pp. 239, 260 ff.).

[16] *Documents Diplomatiques Français*, I, nos. 54, 60, 67, 69, 114; on the Emperor's visit see further *Die Grosse Politik*, XVII, nos. 4986 ff.; Bülow: *Memoirs*, I, pp. 578 ff.; Eckardstein, op. cit., II, pp. 252 ff.; Newton: *Lord Lansdowne*, pp. 197–9.

There was every reason, then, for the British government to hope for German support in backing the Japanese on the Manchurian question. These hopes were not disappointed. The matter was considered with great care at Berlin, where the officials of the foreign office viewed it against the background of the general Anglo-German problem. They saw clearly enough that support of England would arouse unfavorable criticism in the press and parliament, and they had their own compunctions about coming out definitely against Russia in the Manchurian question, which itself was of little interest to Germany. On the other hand, they thought it important not to drive either Japan or England into an agreement with Russia, and they weighed the whole question with reference to the larger prospect of an alliance with England. Now, they thought, the English are beginning to feel the pinch. They will have to appeal to Germany more and more frequently. As yet it is too early to come forward with a full catalogue of demands and conditions. But England must not be scared off. When she has been baited a little longer, Germany will be in a better position to get her own terms accepted. Germany does not need England, and therefore she can ask in return for her alliance full guarantees against complications with Russia and very extensive concessions in Africa as well as in Asia. And so the Germans formulated a very cautious program. They agreed to warn the Chinese government against concluding an agreement with any one power while the obligations of the Peking government to the other powers had not yet been definitely fixed. They hinted, furthermore, that in a war between Russia and Japan or Russia and England their neutrality could be counted upon. It was made clear to the Japanese minister at London that there was no agreement between Russia and Germany with reference to the Far East.[17]

The British foreign office was much gratified with the readiness of the Germans to join in the action at Peking. To be sure, the German note was milder than the Japanese or the British, but that was intentional, and Lord Lansdowne reckoned quite correctly that something was better than nothing. The Japanese and British representatives warned the Peking government in the middle of February that the reputed Manchurian agreement would be " a source of danger to the Chinese government and that no arrangement affecting territorial rights in the Chinese Empire ought to be concluded between the Chinese government and any one of the Powers." At the same time the German government issued its own warning.[18]

So far as one can deduce from the documents the warnings of the powers in Peking were of little avail. The Russian government consistently took the stand that the matter did not concern other governments, and that it was simply trying to arrange with the Chinese for the evacuation of Manchuria, of course with adequate guarantees for the protection of Russian interests. In the last days of

---

[17] *Die Grosse Politik*, XVI, nos. 4810–7; XVII, nos. 4988–91. It is most unfortunate that these documents, so closely related, should have been placed in separate volumes, so that the connexion is not obvious.   [18] *China No. 2 (1904)*, no. 12; *Die Grosse Politik*, XVI, nos. 4815–6.

February it was reported from the Chinese capital that the Russians were renewing their pressure to force the Yamen to sign. On March 1 the Peking government again appealed to the powers for " mediation." At the same time it communicated a text in twelve articles, which seems to have been a rather seriously garbled version of the Russian draft.[19]

This further development called forth a terrific storm of indignation in Japan. From the reports of the Russian and French ministers at Tokyo we learn that Japanese naval circles in particular were eager to take up the cudgels against Russia. So serious was the situation that Izvolski advised his government to double the troops along the frontier of Manchuria. The Russian minister firmly believed that war was inevitable and he therefore prepared to leave the Japanese capital at short notice.[20] Fortunately for the peace of the Far East the Japanese premier, Prince Ito, was determined not to overreach himself. It is clear that the great statesman, mindful of what had happened to Japan in 1895, was ready to strike a bargain with Russia if possible, and, failing that, to go to war only if assured that the international alignment was favorable.[21]

Before resorting to the arbitrament of war it was essential for Japan to know exactly what the odds were. She was certain of her ability to defeat the Russians on land, and fairly certain of being able to take care of them also by sea. The question was whether France would join her ally, and whether Japan could count on the support of the British fleet to restore the balance at sea. If England could be brought to do something to hold the French in check, then nothing more would be necessary, for Japan had been assured that the Germans had no agreements with Russia, and the French would presumably not dare enter the conflict if England stood behind Japan.

And so there ensued, during the first half of March 1901, long and crucial discussions in London. The Japanese minister, Baron Hayashi, long one of the most vigorous proponents of an alliance with England, left no doubt of the fact that the Japanese were in dead earnest. He asked directly whether England would agree to hold France in check. Japan, he pointed out, would fight for Korea single-handed and under any conditions, but she would not go the limit with respect to Manchuria unless she had some assurances that she would not have to face both Russia and France. The whole problem placed the British foreign office in a serious dilemma. Cabinet meetings followed each other in rapid succession, frequently lasting for hours at a time. It was understood in London that the Japanese were rather anxious to fight, even on the Manchurian issue, because it was obvious that Russia, once she had control of Manchuria, would begin operations in Korea. From the Japanese standpoint it would be better to fight

---

[19] *China No. 2 (1904)*, nos. 11, 14, 17, 18, 25; *British Documents*, II, no. 47; *Die Grosse Politik*, XVI, nos. 4819–23, passim.

[20] " Nakanunie Russko-Iaponskoi Voiny," pp. 13 ff.; *Documents Diplomatiques Français*, I, nos. 133, 181, 202.

[21] *Kato Takaaki*, I, pp. 421–47; *Documents Diplomatiques Français*, I, nos. 133, 181; *Die Grosse Politik*, XVI, no. 4825.

the inevitable duel before the Transsiberian Railway was complete. In other words, there was every possibility that England might become involved in a large-scale conflict. On the other hand, if no support were given Japan she would probably turn about and make some sort of agreement with Russia, to the serious detriment of British interests in China. Possibly such a development could be checked by England's trying herself to strike a bargain with the Muscovite. The Germans strongly suspected that Lord Salisbury was the great obstacle to a definite arrangement between the British and the Japanese, and that he favored direct agreement with Russia. Whether this was the fact or not (it seems likely that it was), the British government seemed unable to come to a decision.

The Berlin government was most disgusted by the "knuckling-down" policy. No one who reads the documents can escape the feeling that the German statesmen were eager to have the British take a strong stand, support Japan to the limit and, if necessary, stop Russia by force of arms. The reason for this attitude was not to be sought so much in the desire to see Russia checked or humiliated as in the hope that Britain, in the moment of crisis, would be brought to the point of really wanting an alliance with Germany and being willing to pay a high price for it. From the very outset the German ambassador at London made it clear that in the event of a conflict his government would remain benevolently neutral. Despatches from Berlin argued that Russia, already in financial difficulties, would surely not fight; that this was the grand opportunity for England to settle the score; that with Japan in the vanguard, victory would be certain, and that, if England backed down again, she would get nothing but the briefest respite from Russian encroachment. Similar encouragement was given the Japanese. Once again the German foreign office made it clear that there was no agreement between Germany and Russia, that Germany would remain benevolently neutral, and that this neutrality would have the effect of preventing France from taking any active part in operations.

Finding it most difficult to reach a decision, the British government followed an evasive policy. Inquiries were made in St. Petersburg, followed by efforts to induce the Russians to communicate their terms, a course which Lamsdorff indignantly refused to consider. At the same time the ambassador at Paris was instructed to find out whether France was under obligations to Russia to take part in a Far Eastern conflict. Sir Edmund Monson was unable to learn anything of value, but he reported that there was in France very little interest in the Far East and that "enthusiasm for the Russian Alliance has so cooled down in France that it appears to flame up only when the occasion serves to accentuate the animosity against England." [22] In the meanwhile Lord Lansdowne, after repeated encouragements from the German embassy, asked the Berlin government whether, in a crisis, it would be willing to join England in a declaration to France that the two powers wished the localization of the conflict in the Far East and would themselves maintain strict neutrality.

[22] *British Documents*, II, no. 56.

Bülow at once rejected this suggestion. Germany, he argued, had assured England and Japan of her neutrality, but she could not make a declaration of this sort at Paris, at least not until the first shot had been fired. As a matter of fact, France would not dare move as long as Germany remained neutral. It might be interjected here that the Germans had no thought of estranging France at this time. In fact, they, especially the Emperor, were hoping to draw France away from Russia and bring her back to the " European " family of nations.[23]

Of course the German reply could not satisfy Lansdowne. It was obvious that the Germans were intent on keeping their hands free, and that they wished, if possible, not to become embroiled with Russia. The Russian ambassador had already made it clear that Germany's warning to the Chinese had not been much appreciated in St. Petersburg. At any rate the Berlin foreign office refused to go further than the promise of benevolent neutrality, which, at the request of the British ambassador, it defined as " correct and strict neutrality." This chapter of the story may be said to have come to an end when Bülow got up in the Reichstag on March 15 to explain Germany's obligations under the terms of the agreement with England of October 1900. He referred to this agreement as the *Yangtze Agreement,* thus making it clear that for the Germans its purpose was primarily to secure a share in the Yangtze Basin. The Agreement, he went on to explain, " was in no sense concerned with Manchuria; it contained no secret clauses, but had been communicated to the public *in extenso.* There were no German interests of importance in Manchuria, and the fate of that province was a matter of absolute indifference to Germany. On the other hand, it was of importance to her that at the present moment, while China's obligations towards the Powers were as yet unsettled, her estate should not be unduly reduced, and that she should not dispose of her assets *in fraudem creditorum* while the claims of the latter remained unsatisfied."

Bülow's explanations caused something akin to consternation in England. There were some confused statements made in parliament, and some discussion between London and Berlin. Eventually the British government was obliged to admit that the Germans had, in connexion with the negotiation of the Agreement, made it clear that they excepted Manchuria from the application of the Open Door policy, but the English continuel to insist that Article II, dealing with the maintenance of the integrity of China, applied to the whole of the Empire, of which, they maintained, Manchuria was an integral part. There the matter rested, each side holding its own view, with the result that the Agreement was completely emasculated and valueless. The incident served at the time to break down the negotiations with regard to the future action of the two powers in the Far East, and it left a permanent scar on Anglo-German relations. Years later we find Sir Eyre Crowe making cutting remarks about it, and even Lord San-

---

[23] See the Emperor's talk with the Duc de Noailles, March 1, 1901 (*Documents Diplomatiques Français,* I, no. 114).

derson, who was much more favorably disposed towards Germany, speaking of the proceeding as " no doubt shifty and not over creditable." [24]

While the English and the Germans were wrangling about the interpretation of the Yangtze Agreement, the Japanese government, too, was wrestling with the larger problems of policy. Baron Kato was more insistent than ever on taking a strong line with Russia. On March 12 he handed a memorandum running to thousands of words to Prince Ito, and thereby precipitated a heated argument that lasted for weeks. Ito and the rest of the cabinet still favored some sort of compromise, but Kato stood by his guns and finally secured permission to send a protest to St. Petersburg (March 24). The note, though couched in courteous terms, was unequivocal. Kato suggested that the Russian-Chinese agreement be referred to the conference of diplomats at Peking which was engaged in settling the Boxer indemnity and kindred questions. The Russian reply, which came promptly, was purely negative. Lamsdorff refused to diverge from the position that the whole question was one between Russia and China, and that there was no excuse for outside interference.

The attitude of Russia left the Japanese cabinet exactly where it was to begin with. Kato favored even stronger action. There were long conferences between him and Ito on March 30 and 31, in which the foreign minister advocated sending a note expressing " general dissatisfaction " with the Russian reply. After several days of crisis Kato was finally persuaded to tone down this phrase, but the cabinet agreed to a note which was sent on April 6 and which read: " The Imperial (Japanese) Government is unable to accept the answer of Count Lamsdorff of March 25, and reserves its opinion under the present circumstances." [25]

The soundness of Kato's policy was proved by the results. The Russians, despite their brave declarations, recognized the seriousness of the situation and began to back down. After the first protests they scaled down their demands on China: the Peking government was to be permitted to keep some troops in Manchuria and to arrange for indemnities in accordance with the general methods applied in negotiation with the other powers. Russian demands for concessions were restricted to Manchuria.[26] But the Chinese refused to sign even on these terms. Li Hung-chang may have been willing to do so, and he was expected to do so by the representatives of the other powers, who looked upon him as nothing less than a paid agent of Russia. But the powerful Yangtze viceroys, vigorously backed by England, offered such sturdy opposition that not even Li

---

[24] *British Documents,* II, nos. 32–5; III, pp. 412–3, 426 ff.; Hansard: *Parliamentary Debates,* Series IV, vol. XCVIII, debates of July 26, 1901. All the material on the March crisis may be found in *China No. 2 (1904),* nos. 14 ff.; *British Documents,* II, nos. 33, 45, 47, 50–6; *Die Grosse Politik,* XVI, nos. 4819–32. Individual references have seemed unnecessary.

[25] *Kato Takaaki,* I, pp. 421–47; the correspondence may be found in the recent publication " Nakanunie Russko-Iaponskoi Voiny " (loc. cit., pp. 21 ff.).

[26] The details in Glinskii, op. cit., pp. 158 ff.

could act in the face of it. The Yamen therefore appealed to the powers for aid. The English joined Japan in a new warning to Peking, but the Germans refused to have anything more to do with the matter.

The language of the Japanese warning to China appears to have been pretty strong: the Yamen was told that the acceptance of the Russian terms would mean the partition of China and that Japan intended to ask for extensive concessions if the Russian demands were granted. There the matter stood when Kato sent his note of April 6 to Russia. The St. Petersburg authorities evidently thought the game was up. They announced that the draft convention with China had been withdrawn. Since the Chinese government was unwilling to make an arrangement and since the foreign powers did not appreciate Russia's efforts to evacuate Manchuria, things should remain as they were. The whole thing, explained Lamsdorff, was intended merely as a provisional arrangement, which in no way involved any infringement of Chinese sovereignty or integrity. The reports of the Agreement had been completely garbled. There had never been a draft in twelve articles, but only a program, used by various departments of the government in the course of the negotiations. Needless to say, these explanations severely taxed the credulity of the other powers; they were regarded with pronounced scepticism in all the European chancelleries. " Really the Russians are occasionally, to use their own term, colossal," wrote Lord Sanderson to the British minister at Peking.[27]

The German Emperor found it absolutely impossible to conceal his disappointment with the course of British policy in the Far East. " Was it likely," he asked the English ambassador, " that so favorable an opportunity for resisting the encroachments of Russia would occur again? " In a letter to King Edward he went even further, and called the English ministers " unmitigated noodles " for their policy in China.[28] The members of the foreign office did not much appreciate this language, but they were too level-headed to be much moved by it. They saw through the German game easily enough. " The German Emperor," wrote Lord Sanderson, " is apparently furious with us for not having got into a quarrel with Russia over the business, and obviously that would have suited the Germans very well." [29]

It was perfectly true that the Germans were consumed with the hope of seeing Britain ever more deeply embarrassed, not from any feeling of spite, but simply in order to force her to seek Germany's alliance and accept it on German terms. As viewed from Berlin the situation of England was such that only one little jog would be needed. The war in south Africa kept dragging on. With 250,000 men in the field the British seemed unable to force a decision. The policy of de-

---

[27] *British Documents*, II, no. 73. See further ibid., nos. 60, 61, 65; *China No. 2 (1904)*, nos. 36-9; *Documents Diplomatiques Français*, I, nos. 154, 162, 174; *Die Grosse Politik*, XVI, nos. 4833 ff.

[28] *British Documents*, II, nos. 72, 73; Eckardstein, op. cit., II, pp. 297-9; Lee: *Edward VII*, II, p. 119.   [29] *British Documents*, II, p. 58, footnote.

vastating the Boer farms and of concentrating Boer women and children in unhealthy concentration camps was causing a storm of indignation throughout Europe. Never in modern times was England so intensely hated and never, one might add, was she so generally underrated. The army was looked upon as an ineffectual and yet ruthless band of mercenaries, led by officers wholly unfitted for their jobs. As a military power England was regarded on the Continent as a veritable farce. Surely, with Russia threatening in Asia and France becoming stronger and more active in the Mediterranean, England would, before long, have to come touting for the alliance of the Germans. If only she could have been induced to come out strongly in support of Japan against Russia, the trick would have been turned.

It was probably for that very reason that the British pursued so circumspect a policy, even at the risk of estranging Japan. They scented the German aims and had no intention of being roped in. As a matter of fact the English were not nearly as dejected as the Germans thought they ought to be. They knew that they would carry the South African War to a successful conclusion, and they relied on their fleet to continue to stave off any hostile demonstration. So far as China was concerned they hoped to muddle along. From what few indications one can glean from the documents it is clear that Salisbury was opposed to making an issue of the Manchurian question. If anything, he, and probably a considerable part of the cabinet, desired an agreement with Russia. " We shall certainly not reject an overture, if one is made to us," wrote Lansdowne to the ambassador at St. Petersburg on April 23; " You cannot do wrong in repeating that we wish to be friends, and that we recognise the special interests which Russia possesses in Manchuria." [30]

It is true, of course, that British opinion was, on the whole, suspicious of Russia and hostile to any Russian advance. But at this very time there began a systematic campaign of education in favor of an understanding. The *Spectator,* commenting on this aspect of the problem, wrote:

" Why assume that public opinion is a great, immoveable fact? Examine it, and realize that it is a hap-hazard creation which can be modified if it is only dealt with in a proper spirit. If Lord Salisbury even now were to take the trouble to instruct and guide public opinion in regard to our relations with Russia, he would very soon have behind him a public opinion that would correspond to the true and reasonable view, and not a public opinion which, as he imagines, he must partly obey and partly get round by oblique methods." [31]

Other writers came out vigorously for an entente with the Tsarist government. So influential a journalist as E. J. Dillon criticized the British policy in Manchuria and stressed the fact that nothing was to be gained from opposition

---

[30] Newton: *Lord Lansdowne*, pp. 215 ff.; similarly Sanderson to Satow, April 12 (*British Documents*, II, no. 73): an understanding with Russia " would be much the best plan if it could be managed." On Salisbury's attitude see further his letter to Canon MacColl, in Russell: *Malcolm MacColl*, p. 282.   [31] *Spectator*, April 6, 1901, p. 487.

to Russia. Sir Rowland Blennerhassett, who was to become one of the most un-relenting German-baiters, began a long series of articles in favor of an agreement with Russia.[82] Anonymous writers were, naturally, even more outspoken. *Calchas* sounded the notes of the German peril, and declared: " To settle with Russia . . . would relieve to an extraordinary extent the sense of diplo-matic pressure under which the nation and the Foreign Office live now. It would advance Russia's economic development by several generations, and it would make a Continental coalition against us impossible, and it ought to be the grand aim of British policy." " The interests of Germany clash with ours everywhere," said *Ignotus;* " those of Russia hardly anywhere beyond the reach of a friendly understanding." [83]

Now as a matter of fact there is some evidence that certain Russian statesmen, notably Witte, were ready to consider some sort of adjustment. Russia was in dire financial straits, and the finance minister apparently hoped and tried to secure a loan in London. The details are not known, but it is probably safe to assume that not only the hostility of British bankers (notably Rothschild), but also the opposition of Russian court and military circles made a rapprochement difficult at the time.[84]

It is important to note that while, in the spring of 1901, not a few voices were being raised in England on behalf of a settlement with Russia, hardly anything was said in favor of Germany or of an agreement with Germany. Apropos of the article by *Ignotus,* mentioned above, William T. Stead, who had advocated an agreement with Russia for twenty years, wrote in the *Review of Reviews:* " It is a very unfortunate habit of the English people that they never seem to be happy unless in international politics they have fashioned a devil after their own heart. The working devil of the English cosmogony for years past has been Russia; but now those who have been most active in propagating the theory of the diabolism of Russia are displaying an inclination to transfer this evil rôle from Russia to Germany." [85] And yet Stead was one of those who first and most insistently called attention to the German naval menace, and it was on this theme that all the anti-German, pro-Russian writers most particularly harped. " The broad issue for the twentieth century," according to *Calchas,* " is whether Great Britain or the German Empire at the end of the next two or three generations will possess the relative ascendancy in trade and its inseparable attribute of sea-power." England, he went on, required a three-power naval standard, in view of Germany's determination to fight, not alone, but at the head of a coalition. And

---

[82] E. J. Dillon: " Micawberism in Manchuria " (*Contemporary Review,* May 1901, pp. 649–63); Sir Rowland Blennerhassett: " England and Russia " (*National Review,* March 1901, pp. 21–33).

[83] Calchas: " Will England Last the Century? " (*Fortnightly Review,* January, 1901, pp. 20–34), p. 31; Calchas: " Will Germany Fail? " (ibid., April, 1901, pp. 575–90); Ignotus: " Germany and England " (*Fortnightly Review,* April, 1901, pp. 663–74), pp. 672–4.

[84] Eckardstein, op. cit., II, pp. 277–8, tells of the Russian advances in mid-March.

[85] *Review of Reviews,* April 15, 1901, p. 372.

Ignotus, after a most hostile and distorted review of German policy since 1870, appealed to the country thus: " Let it be clearly understood that Germany is the one country in Europe with which it is quite impossible for England to arrive at a working understanding beneficial to each; and this, not from national antipathy, but from economic necessity." Germany had a growing population, which made necessary a constant expansion of trade and colonial dominion. " But Great Britain crosses her path in every direction as a formidable commercial and colonial rival, and it has been the dream of the German Foreign Office ever since Bismarck began to shape its policy, to destroy our commercial and naval supremacy."

Events in the Far East had done little to foster the idea of Anglo-German co-operation. On the contrary, the German policy, with its constant trimming between England and Russia, had caused real bitterness. Bülow's stand with regard to the so-called Yangtze Agreement had put the finishing touch on the disillusionment of the London government and of the English people. But — this must be reiterated and re-emphasized — the German government was quite blind to most of this. The reason for the misapprehension that prevailed in Berlin was two-fold. In part it was due to plain, ordinary, political miscalculation — underrating of England's position and overrating of her need for support, too great optimism with respect to Germany's alliance value, and a naive incredulity with regard to the possibility of an Anglo-Russian or Anglo-French settlement. It must be confessed that the German ambassador at London, Count Hatzfeldt, was in part responsible for this viewpoint. He was a really eminent diplomat, but in the period since 1898 he too had become convinced that England would come to Germany and be glad of the German alliance, even though the price were high. As it happened, Hatzfeldt was a very sick man in 1901. It was only rarely that he was able to leave his bed. For the Germans this was a great misfortune, for the old ambassador knew how to maintain proper relations with a foreign government, and he had been trained under Bismarck to report and report correctly.

During Hatzfeldt's illness the affairs of the embassy were conducted by the first secretary, Freiherr von Eckardstein, who, after some years of residence in the United States and England, had married the heiress of the millionaire furniture manufacturer, Sir Blundell Maple, and had then retired from the diplomatic service. In view of his excellent social connexions with the Rothschilds, the Duke of Devonshire, Joseph Chamberlain and other statesmen and financiers, he was a valuable aid to the embassy, so that in November 1899 Bülow appointed him first secretary. Bülow admits in his memoirs that he had been warned about Eckardstein. Count Metternich, Hatzfeldt's successor at the embassy in London, had pointed out that the Baron's utterances were to be taken " not *cum grano sed cum copia salis.*" The appointment, Bülow confesses, " was not a fortunate stroke." [36]

---

[36] Bülow: *Memoirs,* I, pp. 400–1.

Eckardstein was moved by the wholly commendable desire to promote the understanding between England and Germany, but it is perfectly obvious that personal vanity and the ambitious hope that he might be the instrument chosen to effect an epoch-making alliance played a leading rôle in his conduct. The famous memoirs which he published just after the war were designed to show that only the utter stupidity of the German foreign office was responsible for the frustration of his efforts. Germany, he claimed, rejected the British offer of an alliance in 1901, and therewith sealed her own fate.

These ideas dominated the minds of German historians for a decade after the war, despite the fact that the publication of the German documents showed that Eckardstein did not hesitate to alter words or phrases when printing diplomatic correspondence, if that was necessary to support his argument. Only since the publication of the British documents on this subject in 1927 has the truth finally emerged. German and English historians are now fairly well agreed as to what took place. Since it has become evident that the Anglo-German alliance project was not nearly so serious in 1901 as was formerly supposed, it will not be necessary to enter into minute detail; a general review of the main lines will suffice.[37]

On March 18, while the tension over the Manchurian question was still at its height, Eckardstein reported a conversation with Lansdowne, who raised the question whether there was still any prospect of Germany's acting to hold France in check in the event of a Russian-Japanese War. According to his own account, Eckardstein replied that there was no chance of this so long as Germany had no assurances of support from England. Thereupon, he claims, Lansdowne raised the question of a general defensive agreement, which, so he is reputed to have said, was favored by some of the most influential members of the cabinet. Naturally no official advances could be made until it was known in London that the German government would be favorably disposed towards such a proposition.[38]

Now we have Lansdowne's own account of this interview, as he reported it to Sir Frank Lascelles, the ambassador at Berlin. From this it appears that the English minister said he thought there was no prospect of England and Germany combining to " keep the ring " for Russia and Japan, since it had been made clear that the Germans would remain strictly neutral and since Bülow had repudiated

---

[37] On the English side perhaps the best account is now G. P. Gooch: " Baron von Holstein " (in *Studies in Modern History*, London, 1931); of the very extensive German literature on the subject I should mention as among the best recent studies Gerhard Ritter: *Die Legende von der Verschmähten Englischen Freundschaft* (Freiburg, 1929); the keen and critical account of Gustav Roloff: " Die Bündnisverhandlungen zwischen Deutschland und England, 1898–1901 " (*Berliner Monatshefte*, December, 1929, pp. 1167–222); Heinrich Walther: " Die Deutsch-Englischen Bündnisverhandlungen von 1901 und ihre Ergebnisse " (*Historische Vierteljahrschrift*, XXV, 1931, pp. 602–35); Johannes Dreyer: *Deutschland und England in ihrer Politik und Presse im Jahre 1901* (Berlin, 1934); Heinrich Freiherr von Hoyningen genannt Huene: *Untersuchungen zur Geschichte des Deutsch-Englischen Bündnisproblems, 1898–1901* (Breslau, 1934).

[38] *Die Grosse Politik*, XVII, no. 4994. Eckardstein indicates that there were two conversations, but this is certainly not the fact.

all responsibility for what happened in Manchuria. It was Eckardstein who then raised the question of a defensive agreement directed solely against France and Russia. This would require the two allies to come to each other's aid only in the event of either one of them being attacked by those two powers. Lansdowne at once raised objections. Such an arrangement seemed to entail the adoption of an identic foreign policy by the two powers in *all* their external relations. There was the further difficulty of defining *defensive* action. In any case the matter would have to be carefully considered by his colleagues.[39]

These two accounts of the same conversation are wholly divergent. Which is to be accepted? Obviously Lansdowne's, for his narrative fits much more accurately into the general setting of the situation and reflects the attitude which we know to have been that of the British foreign office. Not only that: it would be hard to find any reason why the foreign minister should have wanted to mislead the ambassador at Berlin. Time and again, in later documents, Lansdowne referred to the initiative which Eckardstein had taken in this matter. Even German scholars are now practically agreed that only the Lansdowne account is worthy of credence.

Then Eckardstein's story is little short of a fabrication. Unbelievable as it may seem, this appears to be a shocking instance of a diplomat knowingly leading his government astray. The Baron knew perfectly well that his government hoped for an alliance with England, but wanted to wait until the British needed the Germans badly enough to be willing to pay their price. He had been instructed not to take the initiative on any account. On March 17 Holstein had written him " not to breathe a syllable about an alliance." Whether this letter had reached London by the time of the Eckardstein-Lansdowne conversation cannot be determined, but previous instructions, which Eckardstein must have had, were of the same tenor.[40] Furthermore, Eckardstein gives himself away in his own memoirs when he confesses that, contrary to instructions, he had, on March 16, given Lansdowne a very broad hint that he ought to make an alliance offer.[41] From another source we know that he was very busy at this time prodding the Japanese minister, Count Hayashi, to take the initiative in proposing an Anglo-German-Japanese alliance. Lansdowne, Balfour, Chamberlain and Devonshire, he asserted, favored the scheme, and Salisbury had accepted the suggestion.[42]

To cover up the violation of his instructions Eckardstein therefore attributed the first move in the alliance negotiations to Lansdowne. The Berlin government was led to believe that the British had at last come to the point where they felt the urgent need of German support, and that they would, in the near future, come forward with concrete proposals. Although Holstein continued to be sceptical of Salisbury's approval of an agreement with Germany, instructions were at once

---

[39] *British Documents*, II, no. 77.
[40] Eckardstein: *Lebenserinnerungen*, II, p. 314, 316.
[41] Eckardstein, op. cit., II, p. 280.
[42] A. M. Pooley: *The Secret Memoirs of Count Tadasu Hayashi* (New York, 1915), pp. 119 ff.

sent to Eckardstein. From these it is clear that the Berlin foreign office considered the moment decisive: both England and Germany were at the parting of the ways. The Germans were favorable to a defensive alliance and thought that possibly Japan might be brought into it. Not only that, they felt that the other powers of the Triple Alliance should be associated, and wished the British to open discussions with Vienna. In view of the none-too-cordial relations between the German and Austrian capitals it was felt that this would be a striking demonstration of Germany's confidence in her ally.[48]

Hardly had these instructions reached London when Eckardstein sat down to report on another conversation he had had with Lansdowne on March 22. The foreign minister, so the German diplomat claimed, had worked out a memorandum on the question and had submitted it to some of his colleagues. Even Salisbury had declared in favor of a strictly defensive pact, though he wanted all possible eventualities to be carefully weighed. Lansdowne, wrote Eckardstein, then asked a number of questions touching on the probable obligations of the contracting powers, the problem of a public as against a secret treaty, the advisability of including Japan, etc. Eckardstein, on his part, took care not to raise the question of drawing Austria and Italy into the arrangement. The time, he wrote home, had not come for this.[44]

There is no direct English report of this conversation, but there can be little doubt that Eckardstein's account of it, like his earlier report, was badly distorted. It has been pointed out by German critics that much of what he attributed to Lansdowne on this occasion had already been said on March 18, and it is, of course, clear from later documents that Lansdowne could not have said what he is reported by Eckardstein to have said. His attitude, as we see it in the despatch to Lascelles mentioned above, is not at all what Eckardstein attributed to him. Furthermore, it is absolutely certain that Salisbury was never as favorably disposed as Eckardstein reported Lansdowne as saying that he was, and it is therefore more than unlikely that the foreign minister would have misrepresented the views of his chief.[45]

It is not necessary to follow the further course of the discussions in minute detail. Eckardstein averred that he had another talk with Lansdowne on March 25 and that they practically reached an agreement at that time on the essential points. It is morally certain, however, that this conversation never took place. There is no mention of it either in the British or in the German documents. Neither is there the slightest trace of any agreement.[46] All we know is that in the last days of March the German government sent a special emissary to Lon-

---

[48] *Die Grosse Politik*, XVII, nos. 4996, 5001, 5003.

[44] *Die Grosse Politik*, XVII, no. 4997.

[45] There is a good critique of this report in Walter Löding: *Die Deutsch-Englischen Bündnisverhandlungen 1898–1901* (Hamburg, 1929), pp. 83 ff.; Roloff, loc. cit., pp. 1185 ff. seems to me to confuse this conversation with a later one.

[46] Eckardstein, op. cit., II, pp. 286 ff. On this point see Ritter, op. cit., p. 34; Löding, op. cit., pp. 86–7; Dreyer, op. cit., pp. 70–1.

don to try to bring the English to give up their opposition to German policy in the matter of the Boxer indemnity negotiations and the increase of the Chinese customs. Thinking that the British were anxious for an alliance, the Germans clearly expected to realize on the situation. As a matter of fact the English, having been approached through Eckardstein, saw the situation in a very different light. The special negotiator had no success whatever. On the contrary, his mission caused some friction. On March 29 Lansdowne told Eckardstein that Salisbury's illness made it impossible to go on with the discussions for the time being. The premier, he said, took a cautious attitude towards the proposal, and the other ministers, while they desired a good and well-assured understanding with Germany, " regarded with a certain amount of apprehension the idea of an international arrangement of the somewhat indefinite but very far-reaching character " which had been suggested. Thereupon, according to Lansdowne, Eckardstein said that he did not think the moment propitious for pursuing the subject further. There was a certain amount of anti-British feeling in Berlin at the moment, and it might be better to let the thing rest for the time being. Eckardstein on his part reported home that the British minister had suddenly shown himself reticent about the whole business. The implication was that the injection of the Chinese indemnity problem had spoiled the Baron's efforts. The reality probably was that Eckardstein, seeing that he had gone too far, was trying to get out of a tight place. Indeed, he went so far as to offer his resignation, which was not accepted.[47]

Lord Salisbury left for the Riviera early in April and did not return to London until May 10. In the interval Eckardstein continued his game. He tried to reopen the question on April 9, but found Lansdowne unwilling to do anything in Salisbury's absence. This did not prevent the Baron from encouraging his own government. On April 13 he reported that Lansdowne was considering the matter with Devonshire and Chamberlain, both of whom favored the scheme. The foreign minister, he went on, had no doubt that even Salisbury would be brought to agree to it. In actual fact we learn from Lansdowne's reports to Lascelles that he had some doubt about Eckardstein's communications and was trying to find out whether the Berlin government stood behind him. Furthermore, Lansdowne had grave questions about the feasibility of the whole plan: " I doubt whether much will come of the project. In principle the idea is good enough. But when each side comes, if it ever does, to formulate its terms, we shall break down; and I know Lord Salisbury regards the scheme with, to say the least, suspicion." [48]

While awaiting the return of the prime minister, Eckardstein bestirred himself on another tack. He attempted to get the Japanese minister to press upon Lansdowne the advantages of an English-German-Japanese combination. Hayashi, so far as we know, did open discussions, but only with regard to a possible Anglo-Japanese agreement. When the German government learned by way of

---

[47] *British Documents*, II, no. 79; Eckardstein, op. cit., II, p. 326.
[48] *British Documents*, II, no. 81; Eckardstein, op. cit., II, pp. 334 ff.

Tokyo of Eckardstein's talks with Hayashi, it demanded some explanation. The Baron evaded responsibility for his unauthorized action by maintaining that it was Hayashi who had made the suggestion. By this time everything was thoroughly mixed up. Lansdowne had not only refused to discuss an alliance with Germany until the prime minister's return, but had also evaded the advances of Hayashi. On April 23 he wrote to the ambassador at St. Petersburg saying that England would not reject overtures from Russia, and that she was ready to recognize Russia's special interest in Manchuria.[49]

It must be remembered that the German government was completely in the dark with regard to the real situation. Early in May, in expectation of Salisbury's return, long instructions were sent to London reiterating the views of the Berlin foreign office. What was desired was an agreement between England, the Triple Alliance and Japan. This would be sufficient to block any Russian-French action in China. To which Eckardstein replied on May 15 that Lansdowne had reopened the discussion, and had restated his conviction that Salisbury could be brought round. But, the foreign minister is said to have argued, there were certain difficulties connected with an alliance between England and the whole Triple Alliance. The English did not object so much to a union with a vigorous and on the whole liberal and progressive state like Germany, but they had some doubts about a relationship with a moribund state like Austria-Hungary and a Latin state like Italy. Still, Lansdowne hoped to overcome these obstacles, and thought the time had now come to sit down and try to set terms on paper, so that some agreement could be come to.[50]

With regard to this report of Eckardstein it may be said that it appears that he now for the first time raised the question of England's making an agreement with the whole Triple Alliance. There is no reliable evidence that he had broached the problem before, though he knew that his government regarded this as a *conditio sine qua non*. Of course, after Salisbury's return there was no longer any possibility of dodging the issue. As for Lansdowne's proposal that they sit down and try to work out the lines of an agreement on paper, there is every reason to believe that this suggestion came from Eckardstein, who was anxious to get along with the project. In any event, it appears from the British documents that Eckardstein promised Lansdowne a memorandum setting forth the German view. All this was contrary to instructions from Berlin and the question of the memorandum was to cause a good deal of embarrassment in the sequel.

The comedy of errors was now approaching the dénouement. Count Hatzfeldt, the sick ambassador, had returned to London in mid-April. Now that the discussions were coming to a head, he asked Lansdowne to come to the embassy to talk the situation over. The crucial conversation took place on May 23. We

---

[49] Newton: *Lord Lansdowne*, pp. 215 ff.; for the rest see Hayashi: *Secret Memoirs*, pp. 121 ff.; Eckardstein, op. cit., II, pp. 339 ff.; *British Documents*, II, no. 99.

[50] *Die Grosse Politik*, XVII, nos. 5003 ff.; Eckardstein, op. cit., II, pp. 344 ff.

have the reports of both Hatzfeldt and Lansdowne, and in this case there is no divergence worth mentioning. In the two reports there is some difference of emphasis on minor points, but they agree in laying the main stress on the discussion of an alliance between England on the one hand and the Triple Alliance on the other. Lansdowne pointed out what difficulties this arrangement would cause, while Hatzfeldt insisted that Germany could not enter a pact on any other terms. After all, he remarked, there never had been an alliance with only advantages and no risks. Could England really afford to continue her isolation? She might, of course, try an agreement with Russia, but that would cost her dearly. An alliance with Germany, Austria and Italy would be of immense benefit and would protect the British Empire against attack by any two opponents. Lansdowne did little of the talking, but promised to think the matter over and discuss it again in a week or so.[51]

In the course of his conversation with Hatzfeldt the foreign minister made it clear that he would like to get down to concrete terms, even though the discussions, like the entire negotiation thus far, should be regarded as unofficial and academic. Hatzfeldt, on the other hand, shared the view of the Berlin foreign office, that details could be discussed only after there were agreement on the general principle of an alliance between England and the Triple Alliance. Still, Eckardstein had promised Lansdowne a written memorandum, and during the days following Lansdowne tried hard to get it. The ambassador had the very greatest difficulty in explaining away the rash promise of his subordinate. Eckardstein himself found it advisable to leave town for some days.[52]

That Lansdowne was prepared to take the matter up in serious fashion is indicated by the fact that he asked one of the undersecretaries, Lord Sanderson, to outline the possible terms of the projected alliance. The Sanderson draft envisaged an alliance only between England and Germany, but tried to take into account the obligations of Germany to Austria. For the rest it is interesting more particularly for Sanderson's own opinion of the project. Qualifications, he remarked, would be necessary, in order to prevent either party from being dragged into a quarrel of which it disapproved and for which it would not have popular support. At the same time these qualifications would be likely to cause serious dispute between the contracting parties, " and the Germans will be much less scrupulous in making use of them to throw us over than we can be in leaving them in the lurch. Our public opinion would not allow it — theirs would." And further: " However the Convention may be worded, it seems to me that it will practically amount to a guarantee to Germany of the provinces conquered from France, and that is the way in which the French will look at it. I do not see exactly what Germany will guarantee us." [53]

---

[51] *Die Grosse Politik,* XVII, no. 5010; *British Documents,* II, no. 82.

[52] *Die Grosse Politik,* XVII, nos. 5011–7; *British Documents,* II, no. 87. There is a good discussion of this point in Walther, op. cit., pp 614 ff.

[53] *British Documents,* II, no. 85.

The remarks of Sanderson are interesting as the reflection of the viewpoint of an intelligent and by no means ill-willed official. Far more important, however, was the memorandum on the subject drawn up by Salisbury himself on May 29. In it he questioned the advantages of an agreement for England: " The liability of having to defend the German and Austrian frontiers against Russia is heavier than that of *having to defend the British Isles against France.* Even, therefore, in its most naked aspect the bargain would be a bad one for this country. Count Hatzfeldt speaks of our ' *isolation* ' as constituting a serious danger for us. *Have we ever felt that danger practically?* " In the wars against Napoleon England had many allies, but they could not have saved her if Napoleon had been able to command the Channel. Excepting during that period England had not been in danger and it was therefore impossible to judge whether or not isolation involved any peril. " It would hardly be wise to incur novel and most onerous obligations, in order to guard against *a danger in whose existence we have no historical reason for believing.*" But there were even weightier objections to the projected agreement: " The fatal circumstance is that *neither we nor the Germans are competent to make the suggested promises.*" The British government could make war only if the country approved. If it did not approve, then any promises that had been given would be repudiated and the cabinet turned out. " I do not see how, in common honesty, we could invite other nations to rely upon our aid in a struggle, which must be formidable and probably supreme, when we have no means of knowing what may be the humour of our people in circumstances which cannot be foreseen." The problem might be solved by laying the agreement with the Triple Alliance before parliament, but there were " very grave objections " to such a course. The whole argument about public opinion applied, though in less measure, to the German side. " *A promise of defensive alliance with England would excite bitter murmurs in every rank of German society.*" [54]

This is one of the few documents we have which throws light on Salisbury's general ideas on foreign policy during his later years. It bears out completely the indications that may be found here and there in the sources. The old statesman was still wedded to the idea of splendid isolation. Presumably the fact that no serious attempt had been made to intervene against England during the Boer War had fortified him in the feeling that the much-discussed continental coalition was a chimaera and that England was safe so long as she commanded the Channel. For the rest it is worth noting how highly Salisbury appraised the force of public opinion. The old aristocrat had never liked the appeal to the man in the street. He did not understand, as did Chamberlain and other politicians, the technique of influencing the masses. He simply felt the dead weight of popular opinion; he feared and distrusted it; he did not know how malleable it is, for he had rarely tried to mold it. It is the indisputable fact, however, that in 1901 the project of an alliance was, in Lansdowne's words, " a very stiff fence

---

[54] *British Documents,* II, no. 86.

to ride at." German opinion was violently, rabidly prejudiced against England. The press could find no words to express its scorn and its delight at Britain's discomfiture. From the quotations given earlier in this chapter from the British press it is quite obvious that much the same feeling was being developed in England. Under such circumstances the alliance project was, in a sense, something of the nature of a pipe dream. Much would yet have had to be done to educate public opinion on both sides before the agreement could have been made a reality.

The Salisbury memorandum, together with Lansdowne's failure to get the promised German draft, rang the death knell of the proposed alliance. Eckardstein, who, incidentally, had reported to his government three days before Salisbury drew up his memorandum that Lansdowne, Devonshire and Chamberlain were firmly determined to see the alliance through and that even the prime minister now saw that England could not continue isolated but would have to do something, saw himself before a complete debacle.[55] Whether or not he went to Berlin in these days it is impossible to say. But it is fairly certain that he got himself out of the scrape by blacking the eye of Hatzfeldt and convincing the Berlin foreign office that the ambassador had bungled the affair by going too fast! In the same way he told Lansdowne that Hatzfeldt had represented his conversation with the foreign minister " as indicating much more alacrity on our part than we have actually exhibited." [56] The result was that the ambassador was recalled almost at once. He died in November of the same year, the last of the really great diplomats of the Bismarckian school.[57]

Despite Lansdowne's promise to the ambassador, he did not come back to the subject. Apparently he felt that the next move, now that nothing had come of the Eckardstein memorandum, was up to the Germans. In the same way the Berlin foreign office continued to expect further advances from London. Naturally nothing was known there of Eckardstein's misrepresentations. Though Holstein in particular had his doubts from the beginning about Salisbury's readiness to make an alliance and questioned whether England was yet ready to realize her need, the foreign office continued to labor under the misapprehension that the English had raised the question and that, sooner or later, probably after Salisbury's retirement, the project would mature. Memoranda drawn up by Count Metternich and by Holstein himself in the first half of June show that the Germans were still hoping for an alliance and were only too ready to receive English proposals. The English, on the other hand, were waiting for the Germans to move, though they were evidently quite content to let the whole question rest for the time being.[58]

The problem of a defensive agreement between the two countries never

---

[55] Eckardstein, op. cit., II, pp. 351–2.   [56] *British Documents*, II, no. 89.

[57] The whole matter of Eckardstein's intrigue against Hatzfeldt is admirably treated by von Hoyningen, op. cit., pp. 128 ff., footnote.

[58] *Die Grosse Politik*, XVII, nos. 5018, 5019; *British Documents*, II, no. 89.

came to the stage of serious official discussion, but there was an interesting post-lude, which demands some attention. The English foreign minister was plainly interested, and for obvious reasons, in keeping the Germans friendly and in co-operating with them so far as possible. He was quite ready to make agree-ments with them on special points. Indeed, it should be remembered that the whole discussion in the spring of 1901 arose from the Far Eastern crisis and the efforts of the English and Japanese to draw the Germans into common action against the Russian advance in Manchuria. Nothing had come of this project, but there was another matter of crucial importance to Britain on which an understanding might have been reached, and that was the question of Morocco.

The Moroccan problem turned out later to be as complicated and dangerous a question as any which confronted European diplomacy in the pre-war period. Because of its complexity, and because of the fact that only its beginnings fall within the scope of this volume, there would be no point in making it the sub-ject of a minute review. That work has, in fact, been excellently done by other writers. We need here recall merely a few of the essential features of the prob-lem. The French occupation of the Tuat oasis in the spring of 1900 has already been mentioned in a preceding chapter. It was quite clear at that time that Morocco would, in the near future, become a focal point of European politics, for the dominions of the Sultan were most attractive, the government was weak and ineffectual and the state generally was in European eyes one of the " de-caying nations " of which Salisbury spoke in a famous address.[59]

The interests of the French in this region were too obvious to require much analysis. Their African possessions practically surrounded Morocco and unrest in the territory of their neighbor was bound to react upon Algeria. Apart from these political, strategic considerations there were larger interests in the balance of power in the Mediterranean, and to some extent economic interests, though it must be confessed that the French rarely made the most of the development of their colonies. It is rather surprising that the French did not do more to take advantage of Britain's preoccupation with south Africa to strengthen their posi-tion in Morocco. Possibly the explanation lies in fear of a repetition of Fashoda, possibly in the realization that Italy and Spain, to say nothing of Germany, would have to be squared first. At all events, Delcassé seems to have decided upon a very circumspect policy. He scored a first great success when, with the aid of the ambassador at Rome, M. Barrère, he induced the Italians to sign the Agreement of December 14, 1900, which gave France a free hand in Morocco in return for a free hand in Tripoli. The Italians, who looked with great alarm upon the French advance in north Africa, had appealed to both Germany and England for support. They had found encouragement on neither side, and had

[59] Conditions in Morocco at this time are interestingly depicted in such books as Walter B. Harris: *Morocco that Was* (London, 1921) and Eugène Aubin: *Morocco of To-day* (London, 1906); René Pinon's *L'Empire de la Méditerranée* (Paris, 1904) is still a useful discussion of the problem as it presented itself early in the century.

therefore taken a further step along the road to the entente with France. The way was now clear for the crowning effort of Barrère. It took him eighteen months to effect the Morocco-Tripoli agreement and it was to take him just about as long again to secure from the Italians the famous statements of 1902 which rendered Italy's membership in the Triple Alliance quite innocuous.[60]

The French had much less success in their attempts to strike a bargain with the Spaniards, though their position in Spain was at the time stronger than it had been for years past. Weakened by the war with the United States, the Spanish apparently did not feel equal to taking an active part in the Moroccan question at that time. Their interest was to maintain the status quo for some years at least, and for that reason they rather attempted to obstruct than to aid the French plans. They made repeated efforts to effect a French-German understanding which would include Spain and safeguard Spanish interests in Morocco, but these efforts proved futile and ultimately the Madrid government was obliged to reopen negotiations directly with Paris.[61]

Important though Italy and Spain were for any solution of the Moroccan problem, the chief rivals of the French were the British, with their tremendous interest in the control of the Straits of Gibraltar and in the balance of power in the Mediterranean. It has been pointed out in a previous chapter that Lord Salisbury was prepared, if it came to a crisis, to strike a bargain with the French, reserving for England Tangiers and some of the other port towns and leaving the remainder for the others. Count Hatzfeldt at the time warned his government of this possibility, and Bülow agreed that it would be a departure of positively crucial importance for Germany. Whereas, a few years before, the Germans had shown very little interest in the problem and had viewed it chiefly as one element in European international relations — as a question in which Italy was concerned — they now took a very real interest in the matter. Hatzfeldt, who seems to have foreseen its future significance, made it clear to the British in 1899 that in any eventual partition the Germans would require a share on the Atlantic coast.[62]

The German demand for consideration seems to have displeased Salisbury, who thereafter showed no readiness to discuss the question with the ambassador. But Chamberlain, at that time still the exponent of the idea of the German alliance, appears to have envisaged a Moroccan agreement as the first stage in the evolution of the future alliance. The matter was discussed at various times

---

[60] The Morocco-Tripoli agreement was really signed on January 4, 1901, though it was antedated to December 15, 1900 (*Documents Diplomatiques Français*, I, nos. 1, 17, 59, 88; Abel Combarieu: *Sept Ans à l'Élysée*, Paris, 1932, pp. 106-7). This whole problem is most admirably dealt with in Pinon, op. cit., introduction, and in the well-documented books of Eugene N. Anderson: *The First Moroccan Crisis* (Chicago, 1930), chap. ii; Herbert E. Brenning: *Die Grossen Mächte und Marokko, 1898-1904* (Berlin, 1934), chap. iv; James L. Glanville: *Italy's Relations with England, 1896-1905* (Baltimore, 1934), pp. 80 ff.

[61] See Anderson, op. cit., chap. iii, and the literature there cited.

[62] *Die Grosse Politik*, XVII, nos. 5152 ff.; Anderson, op. cit., pp. 63 ff.; Brenning, op. cit., pp. 44 ff.

between him and Eckardstein, but the Samoan dispute reacted unfavorably upon general relations and caused some postponement, rather to the disappointment of the Germans, who in 1899 and 1900 were quite anxious to strike bargains on special questions, though unwilling to consider a definite alliance that would involve hostility to Russia.

The Moroccan problem hung fire, therefore, while the British were busy in south Africa. Appeals from the Sultan Abdel Aziz for support against the encroachments of the French were allowed to go unheeded. The object of the British was, if possible, to avoid complications.[63] But by the summer of 1901 it was becoming almost impossible to stay by this policy. Friction had developed very rapidly between France and Morocco in the spring. Tribal raids along the Algerian frontier resulted in a great French naval demonstration in May and a widespread fear that the Paris government would at last resort to extreme measures. The Sultan once again called upon the British for help, and in June sent his minister of war, El Menebhi, on a mission to London and Berlin, evidently in the hope that an English-German combination, backed by Spain and Italy, could be brought about to check the threat from France. Apparently the mission to London caused a good deal of uneasiness in Paris, although the Sultan had at the same time despatched his foreign minister, Abdel Krim, to Paris to negotiate a demarcation of the Algerian frontier. We need not enter upon all the details. The essential point is that on both sides, British and French, a cautious policy was pursued. The war minister got little beyond kind words in London, while Delcassé confined himself to warnings. On both sides of the Channel it was stated that nothing was to be done to raise the dangerous Moroccan issue at that time.[64]

The reason why neither the French nor the British government was ready to press the matter in the summer of 1901 was probably the uncertainty as to Germany's attitude. The two chief rivals both knew that the Germans expected to be consulted, and they both knew that, with German support, their chances of success would be greatly enhanced. They therefore both made efforts to draw the Berlin government to their side. Early in June the French foreign minister approached the German ambassador through his friend Leon y Castillo, the Spanish representative in Paris. He suggested that if the German government would take the initiative, he would be glad to discuss various matters with a view to reaching an entente. He admitted that no French minister could agree to the abandonment of claims to Alsace and Lorraine, but he suggested that a rapprochement could be sought along other lines. At the same time the inspired French press pointed out that now the opportunity had come for Germany to

---

[63] See especially Harold Nicolson: *Portrait of a Diplomatist* (Boston, 1930), chap. v.

[64] Nicolson, loc. cit.; G. Saint-René Taillandier: *Les Origines du Maroc Français* (Paris, 1930), chap. i; Anderson, op. cit., pp. 12 ff.; Brenning, op. cit., pp. 70 ff., who has used not only the German and British documents, but also the recently published French documents. There is an excellent review of French policy from January 1900 to August 1901 in *Documents Diplomatiques Français*, I, no. 372.

show in the Moroccan question that her good will went beyond words. But nothing came of these advances. The German government replied that it could not enter upon an agreement with France which would incur the hostility of another power unless the French were prepared to accept a mutual guarantee of territory. As on previous occasions the conquered provinces proved an insurmountable obstacle to understanding.[65]

At the time the German government was certainly much more interested in bargaining with the British. The foreign office would have been glad to make an agreement with respect to Morocco, but only as part of a larger defensive alliance. In other words, the German attitude had changed completely since 1899–1900. At that time what was wanted was a series of special agreements of the Samoa or Yangtze type, without the obligations of a broader alliance. Now no special arrangements would be considered excepting in the framework of a general agreement. The reason for this reversal was simply the disappointment of the Germans with the Agreement of 1898 regarding the Portuguese colonies. In December 1900 the whole British Channel squadron paid a visit to Lisbon, where the admiral, Sir Harry Rawson, was fêted and welcomed. In a speech made on this occasion King Carlos celebrated the alliance of Portugal and Britain in such a way that there could be no doubt in the minds of the Germans that all was not right with the Treaty of 1898. Prince Bülow says in his memoirs that he learned, at about this time, the story of the so-called Windsor Treaty of 1899. It is not entirely unlikely that some indications of the truth reached Berlin from Paris, since the British government seems at this time to have warned the importunate French creditors of Portugal not to go too far in their schemes for bringing pressure.[66] In any case it is clear from the German documents that the German statesmen were most unfavorably impressed with the Lisbon demonstrations, despite the assurances that were given them in London.[67] To this disappointment must be added the feeling that had grown up in Berlin that special agreements, whether they applied to Morocco or to Asia, would involve the same risk as a larger agreement while they would net a much smaller return, and also the fear that a special agreement with England would diminish the desire of the British for a general alliance. Taken all together these factors explain quite fully the attitude of the Berlin government in the summer of 1901.[68]

Eckardstein claims in his memoirs that early in July he was approached by Sir Arthur Nicolson, the British minister at Tangiers, who was in London

---

[65] *Die Grosse Politik,* XVIII, nos. 5868 ff.; Anderson, op. cit., pp. 13–4; Brenning, op. cit., pp. 73–4.

[66] Texeira de Sousa: *Responsibilidades Historicas* (Coimbra, 1917), II, pp. 49–53; Geoffrey Rawson: *Life of Admiral Sir Harry Rawson* (London, 1914), pp. 201–3. On Bülow's knowledge of the Windsor Treaty see his *Memoirs,* I, p. 321; Maximilian von Hagen: "Hat Fürst Bülow den Windsorvertrag Gekannt?" (*Berliner Monatshefte,* February 1931, pp. 183–6).

[67] *Die Grosse Politik,* XVII, no. 4981; Eckardstein, op. cit., II, pp. 207 ff.

[68] *Die Grosse Politik,* XVII, nos. 4993, 5174; Eckardstein, op. cit., II, pp. 314–5.

with the mission of El Menebhi. Nicolson, he says, told him that Lansdowne desired to co-operate with Germany in maintaining the status quo in Morocco, and Nicolson further suggested the possibility of collaboration for the economic exploitation of the country. Eckardstein asserts that he immediately sent a long telegram to Berlin supporting the suggestion, but never received a reply. Nothing of all this appears in either the German or the British documents, while Nicolson's biographer has shown that the English diplomat, though he favored co-operation with Germany, was probably not authorized to make such advances and in all likelihood did not make them. No doubt we have here simply another instance of Eckardstein's untrustworthiness.[69]

The British seem to have made no concrete proposals to the Germans for common action in opposition to France in the Moroccan question, even when, on his return home, El Menebhi fell into disfavor and both the London and Berlin governments used their influence to save him. Evidently the English foreign office realized that the prospects of German support were too slight to make advances worthwhile. On the German side the documents indicate that it was hoped that the English would become more deeply involved with the French and that, as a consequence, the London government would be more ready to reopen the alliance question. Eckardstein encouraged his government in this idea, and the foreign office therefore made no secret of the fact that it would not regard an attack upon Morocco as being in itself a sufficient cause for war against France. " In this matter we must for the time being maintain complete reserve and act the part of the sphinx," wrote Bülow. In a memorandum which was shown the British in August 1901 it was stated unequivocally: " The Morocco Question by itself is not sufficiently important for us to justify a policy by which Germany might incur the risk of serious international complications." [70]

With the German evasion of all advances regarding Morocco the famous negotiations for an alliance may be said to have come to a close. The problem was touched upon again later in the year and we shall therefore have to refer to it again in another connexion. But by July 1901 the important phase was over — the British had put aside the suggestion made and discussed unofficially by Eckardstein, and the Germans had made it clear that they were not interested in anything but a general defensive alliance.

Many, many books and articles have been written on these negotiations and there has been no end of wrangling over the question whether or no this was the crucial point in the whole history of pre-war diplomacy. Considerable space has been devoted to the problem here — more space really than the subject warrants. For, since the publication of the British documents, there is relatively little ground left for divergent opinions. We can now see (and the most

---

[69] Eckardstein, op. cit., II, pp. 357–8; Nicolson: *Portrait of a Diplomatist*, pp. 103–4.

[70] *Die Grosse Politik*, XVII, no. 5177 and pp. 119 ff. For details see Anderson, op. cit., pp. 73–4; Brenning, op. cit., pp. 81–5; Hoyningen, op. cit., pp. 136 ff.

recent writers are generally agreed on this point) that the Germans were never in the position to reject an alliance offer because none was ever made to them. It is now beyond dispute that the German foreign office was at the time only too ready to consider an alliance with England, even though it had rather distorted ideas regarding the need and desire of England for an alliance and regarding the price that could be gotten for German friendship. The complete misapprehension of the German foreign office was, of course, due very largely to the reporting of Baron von Eckardstein. Without the documentary evidence it would be almost impossible to believe that in a diplomatic service so rigorously trained in the Bismarckian tradition anything like the misrepresentations of Eckardstein could have been possible. Certainly his whole action, though undoubtedly well-intentioned, was in flagrant contradiction to everything that good diplomacy stands for. It is unthinkable that anything worthwhile could be accomplished by the methods he employed.

Eckardstein systematically misled his government into thinking that the British were making advances for an alliance and that even Lord Salisbury was favorable to the idea. Now we know that Salisbury himself was as much an isolationist as ever. If pressed to the limit he would have made an agreement with Russia or even with France in preference to one with the Germans, whom he distrusted and had come to dislike. It is certainly true that Lord Salisbury, now an old and infirm man, was not the only influential person in the British government. Chamberlain was hardly less powerful in the cabinet than the prime minister himself, and Chamberlain had always been the chief exponent of an agreement with Germany. It should be noted, however, that Chamberlain's idea from 1898 onward had been to draft the support of the Germans to oppose the Russians in the Far East. This policy was tried again in February and March 1901, and it failed then as it had failed before. Even he who ran could read that the Germans would not allow themselves to become involved in war with Russia, and consequently with France, either for the sake of the British or for the sake of anything the Far Eastern situation could offer. It is interesting to note that after March 1901 there is relatively little reference even in Eckardstein's correspondence to the views of Chamberlain. In all likelihood he had definitely given up the idea of enlisting the Germans. For him the alliance idea died as soon as he saw that he could not get what he wanted.

There remained Lord Lansdowne, the influential foreign minister. Obviously Lansdowne was not wedded to the idea of isolation as was Salisbury. Indeed, like Chamberlain he saw the dangers of Britain's position, at least the dangers to her interests in Asia and Africa at a time when she was too deeply involved in the South African War to play her rôle fully. But it seems probable that he, like the colonial secretary, despaired of the German connexion when it became clear that Germany would not compromise her relations with Russia. It would be most interesting to know how much there was behind the suggestion of an agreement with Russia which we find in Lansdowne's letter of April

1901. The present writer is convinced that the British statesmen generally would have preferred an arrangement with Russia to any other settlement. Failing to interest the St. Petersburg government, they were driven back upon some other solution. Lansdowne may have — probably did — contemplate a special agreement with Germany on the Moroccan question, though he was not given the opportunity to make concrete advances.

In the view of some recent writers this Moroccan aspect of the negotiations was the really crucial aspect. There is some force in this argument, for while one can understand the unwillingness of the Germans to risk a war with Russia, which would have meant a war with France, this same risk would not have existed in a Moroccan agreement with England. The Russians, we may assume, would not have backed France to the extent of war in the Moroccan affair any more than they did in the Fashoda affair. Of course, if the Moroccan question led to war between France and Germany, it would have been to the interest of Russia not to allow France to be defeated again by her neighbor. But it would still have been doubtful whether, if Germany were backed by England, the Russians would have been willing to face both. Surely one cannot escape the feeling that in the Moroccan problem, from the very outset, the Germans failed to understand the ultimate implications. They lost the loyalty of the Italians largely through their unwillingness to take the matter seriously enough. They failed to capitalize the opportunity for an agreement with England on the subject in 1901 and thereby contributed indirectly at least to the formation of the Entente between England and France. By 1904–1905 the German claims could receive a hearing only at the expense of a great international crisis. It is hard to avoid the feeling that an agreement between Germany and England on Morocco in 1901 might have led to a closer connexion later, just as the Anglo-French Entente evolved into something more than a mere colonial settlement.

But all this brings us back again to the misrepresentations of Eckardstein. It was not good will but understanding that was lacking in Berlin, and Eckardstein's distortion of the facts meant simply that the discussions came to an end leaving both sides distrustful and suspicious. The Berlin government believed that the British had made the first overtures and had then dropped them unceremoniously. It felt justified in thinking that England, having been obliged to take the first step, would soon be impelled to take the second. In London, on the other hand, it was thought that the Germans wanted the alliance and had offered it, only to follow up the offer with what seemed like impossible conditions. The result was naturally that the conviction became fixed that the Germans were playing a slippery game. From 1901 onward one notes among the members of the foreign office a steady growth of the dislike which had already become fixed in the popular mind. For psychological reasons, if for no other, an alliance was rapidly becoming impossible.

BIBLIOGRAPHICAL NOTE

DOCUMENTARY SOURCES

Die Grosse Politik der Europäischen Kabinette, 1871–1914. Volume XVI, chapter cvi: The Manchurian Agreement. Volume XVII, chapter cix: The Anglo-German Alliance Discussions; chapter cxiii: The Moroccan Question. Volume XVIII, chapter cxxv: Italy and the Triple Alliance.

British Documents on the Origins of the War. Volume II, chapter ix: The Far East, 1900–1901; chapter x: The Anglo-German Negotiations; chapter xiv: France and Morocco.

Documents Diplomatiques Français, 1871–1914. Published by the Commission de Publication des Documents Relatifs aux Origines de la Guerre de 1914. Series II, volume I, January 2–December 31, 1901. Paris, 1930. Part of the important French publication. This volume is rich particularly in documents on French relations with Italy and on the Moroccan question.

Accounts and Papers. 1904, volume CX. *China No. 2 (1904), Correspondence respecting the Russian Occupation of Manchuria and Newchwang.* A useful collection, which should be read in connexion with the *British Documents*.

Documents Diplomatiques. Affaires du Maroc, 1901–1905. Paris, 1905. This collection must now be supplemented with the material in the collection mentioned above.

Documents Diplomatiques. Les Accords Franco-Italiens de 1900–1902. Paris, 1920. Important.

" Nakanunie Russko-Iaponskoi Voiny." (*Krasnyi Arkhiv,* LXIII, 1934, pp. 3–54). A most important collection of correspondence, chiefly between St. Petersburg and Tokyo, covering the year 1901. Much of this material has, to be sure, been used by Romanov.

MEMOIRS, AUTOBIOGRAPHIES, BIOGRAPHIES, AND LETTERS

Kato Takaaki. Two volumes. Tokyo, 1929. The papers of the foreign minister in the Ito cabinet and a most important source for the study of Japanese policy.

ECKARDSTEIN, HERMANN FREIHERR VON: *Lebenserinnerungen und Politische Denkwürdigkeiten.* Two volumes. Leipzig, 1920. These memoirs must, of course, be used with much caution, but they are important because they contain a number of private telegrams and letters that cannot be found in the German documentary collection.

NEWTON, LORD: *Lord Lansdowne.* London, 1929. A good but rather brief biography. It contains some letters and information not to be found elsewhere.

743

LEE, SIR SIDNEY: *Edward VII, a Biography*. Two volumes. New York, 1925–1927. Volume II contains some material on the relations between Edward and the Emperor William in 1901.

NICOLSON, HAROLD: *Portrait of a Diplomatist*. Boston, 1930. A most interesting biography of Sir Arthur Nicolson (Lord Carnock). Valuable for the discussion of affairs in Morocco between 1895 and 1904.

BÜLOW, PRINCE: *Memoirs*. Four volumes. Boston, 1931–1932. Contains almost nothing of importance on the Anglo-German negotiations.

SAINT-RENÉ TAILLANDIER, G.: *Les Origines du Maroc Français*. Paris, 1930. The French minister's account of his mission to Morocco, 1901–1906. An important source.

SPECIAL STUDIES

MEINECKE, FRIEDRICH: *Geschichte des Deutsch-Englischen Bündnisproblems, 1890–1901*. Munich, 1927. The best-known study, being the work of an eminent German historian. Published before the appearance of the British documents, it is no longer reliable on the factual side, though still stimulating.

RITTER, GERHARD: *Die Legende von der Verschmähten Englischen Freundschaft*. Freiburg, 1929. One of the keenest and most discerning discussions of the problem as it emerged after the publication of the *British Documents*.

ROLOFF, GUSTAV: " Die Bündnisverhandlungen zwischen Deutschland und England, 1898–1901." (*Berliner Monatshefte,* December, 1929, pp. 1167–1222). A detailed, careful criticism of the texts; constitutes perhaps the most effective indictment of Eckardstein.

WALTHER, HEINRICH: " Die Deutsch-Englischen Bündnisverhandlungen von 1901 und ihre Ergebnisse." (*Historische Vierteljahrschrift,* XXV, 1931, pp. 602–35). A study along the lines of Roloff's, with some additional points.

MECENSEFFY, GRETE: " Die Deutsch-Englischen Bündnisverhandlungen 1898–1901, im Lichte der Englischen Aktenpublikation." (*Vierteljahrschrift für Politik und Geschichte,* 1929, pp. 175–91). A perfectly conventional analysis of the British materials.

LÖDING, WALTER: *Die Deutsch-Englischen Bündnisverhandlungen 1898–1901. Ihr Verlauf auf Grund der Deutschen und Englischen Akten*. Hamburg, 1929. One of the best narratives of the negotiations, though unimportant from the critical standpoint.

DREYER, JOHANNES: *Deutschland und England in ihrer Politik und Presse im Jahre 1901*. Berlin, 1934. One of the few studies that takes account of public opinion. It is thorough and reliable. One of the best works on the Anglo-German problem in 1901.

HOYNINGEN GENANNT HUENE, HEINRICH FREIHERR VON: *Untersuchungen zur Geschichte des Deutsch-Englischen Bündnisproblems, 1898–1901*. Breslau, 1934. Another careful and generally excellent study. Noteworthy chiefly for the emphasis placed upon the Moroccan aspect of the problem.

BECKER, WILLY: *Fürst Bülow und England, 1897–1909*. Greifswald, 1929. Very critical of the German policy, but not entirely abreast of the recent material and critical writing.

FISCHER, EUGEN: *Holsteins Grosses Nein. Berlin, 1925*. An able and keen critique of German policy, following largely along the lines of Eckardstein's memoirs. No longer of much use.

HALLER, JOHANNES: *England und Deutschland um die Jahrhundertwende*. Leipzig, 1929. The work of one of Bülow's most consistent critics. The author stands by his condemnation of the German policy despite the evidence of the *British Documents*.

EHRINGHAUS, FRITZ: " Die Ergebnisse der Englischen Akten über die Deutsch-Englischen Bündnisverhandlungen 1899–1901." (*Vergangenheit und Gegenwart,* XIX, 1929, pp. 471–80). A brief analysis of the *British Documents,* the author going even beyond Ritter in his revisionary tendencies.

LEHMANN, KONRAD: " Die Ablehnung des Englischen Bündnisantrags, 1898–1901." (*Preussische Jahrbücher,* August, 1930, pp. 162–83). Perhaps the best recent presentation of the Meinecke viewpoint.

JOHNSON, EDGAR N., and BICKFORD, JOHN D.: " The Contemplated Anglo-German Alliance, 1890–1901." (*Political Science Quarterly,* March, 1927, pp. 1–57). A solid but conventional review of Anglo-German relations.

MOWAT, R. B.: " Great Britain and Germany in the Early Twentieth Century." (*English Historical Review,* XLVI, July, 1931, pp. 423–41). A general survey of the whole period 1898–1914. Adds nothing.

GOOCH, GEORGE P.: " Baron von Holstein." In his *Studies in Modern History.* London, 1931. An admirable and exceptionally well-informed study of Holstein, containing perhaps the best account in English of the Anglo-German negotiations.

BECKER, OTTO: Review of the books of Meinecke and Ritter. (*Deutsche Literaturzeitung,* L, pp. 903–25). A penetrating and illuminating discussion of the two conflicting views with regard to the alliance negotiations.

STALNIJ, V.: " Popitka Anglo-Germanskogo Sblisheniia v 1898–1901 gg." (*Istorik Marksist,* X, 1928, pp. 89–120). An interesting Marxian interpretation, covering only the period from 1898–1900. Adds nothing in the way of factual material, since it is based almost exclusively on the Eckardstein memoirs and the German documents.

OSTWALD, PAUL: " Das Deutsch-Englische Abkommen über China vom 16 Oktober, 1900." (*Berliner Monatshefte,* December, 1933, pp. 1192–1204). A keen and thorough analysis of the German and British documents on the Yangtze Agreement.

THE EARLY PHASES OF THE MOROCCAN QUESTION

HARRIS, WALTER B.: *Morocco that Was*. London, 1921. Few people knew Morocco more intimately than Harris. This is a vivid picture of conditions in the period around 1900.

AUBIN, EUGÈNE: *Morocco of To-day*. London, 1906. Another excellent discussion of conditions before the storm.

PINON, RENÉ: *L'Empire de la Méditerranée*. Paris, 1904. One of the best contemporary discussions of the political problems of the Mediterranean and north Africa.

PEYRONNET, RAYMOND: *Le Problème Nord-Africain*. Paris, 1924. The first volume of a thorough and valuable French history.

ANDERSON, EUGENE N.: *The First Moroccan Crisis, 1904–1906*. Chicago, 1930. One of the best studies of the Moroccan question, full use being made of both the German and British documents. The book contains an extended discussion of the background and developments from 1900–1904.

BRENNING, HERBERT E.: *Die Grossen Mächte und Marokko, 1898–1904*. Berlin, 1934. Another thorough, systematic study, particularly valuable because based in part upon the recently published *Documents Diplomatiques Français*.

LITERATURE SINCE 1935

(See also the Supplementary Bibliographical Notes to Chapters VI, XII, XIV, XV, XX, XXI.)

THIMME, FRIEDRICH: "Der Ausklang der deutsch-englischen Bündnisverhandlungen 1901, nach Briefen des Botschafters Graf Wolff Metternich" (*Berliner Monatshefte*, XVI, June, 1938, pp. 540–557). Based essentially on Metternich's comments on the published British documents, as communicated to the author in 1929.

PENNER, C. D.: "The Buelow-Chamberlain Recriminations of 1901–1902" (*The Historian*, V, 1943, pp. 97–109). Chiefly a study of newspaper polemics on both sides.

The History of the "Times." Volume III: *The Twentieth Century Test, 1882–1912*. New York, 1947. 862 pp. A valuable contribution to the study of British foreign policy.

MATHEWS, JOSEPH J.: *Egypt and the Formation of the Anglo-French Entente of 1904*. Philadelphia, 1939. 151 pp. A thorough monograph on the origins of the Anglo-French rapprochement.

XXIII

The Anglo-Japanese Alliance

᷿

T HE MOROCCAN QUESTION MIGHT CONCEIVABLY HAVE SERVED THE PUR-
pose of bridging the widening chasm between England and Germany.
But the problem was not, in 1901, entirely ripe. It was not yet the crucial
issue in international relations which it became a few years later. On the contrary, the dominant questions of European diplomacy still lay in Asia. It is to
Far Eastern affairs that we must return in order to trace the epochal change
in British policy that resulted in the conclusion of the alliance with Japan.

Russia's withdrawal of the draft agreement with China concerning Manchuria settled nothing, for the Russians remained in occupation and the European powers were still confronted with the problem of inducing them to evacuate. It will be recalled that during the crisis of February and March there had
been some talk of a possible English-German-Japanese Alliance to regulate the
Far Eastern situation. Whether or not this idea sprang from the fertile brain
of Baron von Eckardstein is a matter of slight consequence. The important
thing is that it received the warm support of Count Hayashi, the Japanese
minister at London, who was one of the earliest and most persistent advocates
of an alliance between Britain and Japan. Hayashi had been authorized by his
government in mid-April to discuss the project with Lansdowne in an unofficial
way. There had been some conversation about it in May, but Lansdowne, while
he showed himself sympathetic, indicated that there would be difficulties when
it came to the discussion of details. He stressed the fact that the agreement, if
it were ever come to, would not need to be restricted to two powers, from which
we may conclude that he envisaged the association of Germany. Very little is
known of these pourparlers, which should probably be viewed as part of the
Anglo-German conversations. Lansdowne was presumably holding back until
he had some idea of what the Germans were prepared to do.[1]

The situation continued to be unsatisfactory. In June the Japanese cabinet of
Marquis Ito was replaced by a ministry headed by Count Katsura. In Russian
circles this change was regarded as a change for the worse, for Ito was looked
upon as a man of compromise and peace, while Katsura was thought to be the

---

[1] The only important source is A. M. Pooley: *The Secret Memoirs of Count Tadasu Hayashi*
(New York, 1915), pp. 119–25; but see also Eckardstein: *Lebenserinnerungen*, II, pp. 339, 342;
Die Grosse Politik, XVII, nos. 5037, 5038.

747

leader of the war party. Waldersee, who visited Tokyo in June on his return to Europe, found the capital much excited and noted the prevalence of a feeling that Japan was on the threshold of a great decision. The Japanese were convinced that once the Transsiberian Railway was completed it would be too late to stop Russia. They were confident that they could deal with Russia single-handed, but they were worried by Delcassé's visit to St. Petersburg in April and feared that France would stand by Russia in a Far Eastern conflict. In any event, they were determined to reply with a declaration of war to any Russian attempt to acquire a footing in southern Korea.[2]

The Japanese were certainly mistaken when they feared that the Russian government was contemplating a forward move in the summer of 1901. It is perfectly true that the military men, fed by disparaging reports on the Japanese army, lost no sleep over the Japanese threat. The military attaché at Tokyo reported that it would take many years, perhaps hundreds of years, before the army could acquire the moral basis on which the organization of European armies was built up, and before it could stand on an equal footing with even the weakest European force. A strong cavalry regiment supplied with artillery, he thought, could win a decisive victory over this army if it acted reasonably promptly and energetically. An army of sucklings, was the verdict of General Ivanov after watching the Japanese forces. Not to be compared with any major European army, least of all with the Russian, reported General Jilinski.[3]

Kuropatkin, who was sick of exaggerated accounts of Japanese prowess, accepted these reports at face value. In the summer of 1901 he was still pressing for the retention of northern Manchuria as far as the line of the Transman-churian Railway.[4] But the diplomats did not share the optimism of the war office. Izvolski appreciated the danger from Japan to the full, and both Lams-dorff and Witte understood the necessity for the early evacuation of Manchuria. The occupation, wrote Witte in June and again in July, would amount to the creation, on Russia's frontier, of a new province which would bring in nothing but would entail enormous expenditures, thus increasing the burden which already rested on the Russian people. The great task for Russia was to avoid war with Japan.[5] He therefore urged the resumption of negotiations for the withdrawal of the Russian forces. At the same time he approached the Japanese minister at St. Petersburg and suggested, unofficially, an arrangement regarding

    [2] *Die Grosse Politik*, XVII, no. 5039; Waldersee: *Denkwürdigkeiten*, III, pp. 153 ff.; see also Izvolski's report of April 5, 1901, in the collection " Nakanunie Russko-Iaponskoi Voiny " (*Krasnyi Arkhiv*, LXIII, 1934, pp. 3–54), pp. 24–7; *Documents Diplomatiques Français*, I, no. 310.
    [3] *Der Russisch-Japanische Krieg. Amtliche Darstellung des Russischen Generalstabs*. Deutsche Übersetzung von Freiherr von Tettau (Berlin, 1911–1912), I, pp. 163–6. The reports here quoted were all made in 1901.
    [4] Kuropatkin: *The Russian Army*, etc., I, p. 163; Witte: *La Guerre avec le Japon*, pp. 47–9; Romanov: *Rossiia v Manchzhurii*, p. 315; " Nakanunie Russko-Iaponskoi Voiny " (loc. cit.), pp. 28–9, 32–5.
    [5] Glinskii: *Prolog Russko-Iaponskoi Voiny*, p. 174; Romanov, op. cit., pp. 312 ff.; " Nakanunie Russko-Iaponskoi Voiny " (loc. cit.), pp. 29–35.

the crucial Korean problem. Russia, he said, would agree to a settlement making Korea a neutral area, but giving Japan the right to supply the Korean government with administrative and financial advisers as well as with a chief of police. In return Japan should officially recognize Russia's preponderance in Manchuria.[6]

Almost nothing is known of these Russian approaches to Japan. Neither can we say whether information of these moves reached the British government. All we do know is that about the middle of July rumors were put about in the British press that Russia and France were going to supply Japan with a much-needed loan. Eckardstein admits having worried the British government with warnings of a possible Russian-Japanese agreement and having inserted alarmist notices in the British press.[7] On the other hand Hayashi confesses that at this time he advised his government to hint to the British the possibility of an arrangement respecting Korea.[8] We are probably safe in assuming that these two gentlemen, both of them enthusiasts for an Anglo-Japanese alliance, made the most of the situation, for on July 15 Sir Claude MacDonald, the British minister to Japan, who was home on leave, told Hayashi that King Edward felt that an alliance was necessary and that Salisbury shared the feeling. The prime minister, he went on, realized that the matter would take time, and he rather feared that in the interval Japan and Russia might make up their differences. To this Hayashi replied: " As you know, the feelings of Japan are not friendly to Russia, but are friendly to England. Of course sentiment should be subordinated to considerations of actual profit, and without doubt if Russia should see her way to make substantial concessions to Japan, then certainly our feelings of enmity to that country would disappear." [9]

The ruse must have been completely successful, for on July 31 Lansdowne himself broached the subject in conversation with Hayashi. We have both Lansdowne's and Hayashi's account of what transpired. According to Lansdowne, Hayashi said that Japan had " a strong sentimental dislike " to the retention of Manchuria by Russia, seeing that they themselves had once been expelled from it. " But Japan's real concern was Corea. Corea could not possibly stand alone, its people were far too unintelligent, and sooner or later it would have to be decided whether the Country was to fall to Russia or not. The Japanese Government could not possibly accept the former of these alternatives. They would certainly fight in order to prevent it, and it must be the object of their diplomacy to isolate Russia, with which Power, if it stood alone, they were prepared to deal." To which Lansdowne replied that Korea was further from England than from Japan, but that, considering its geographical position, England could no more than Japan regard its fate with indifference. There was obviously much similarity between the Japanese and British policy; both de-

---

[6] *Die Grosse Politik*, XVII, no. 5041, Eckardstein's report of a conversation with Hayashi July 26, 1901.   [7] Eckardstein, op. cit., II, p. 370; *Die Grosse Politik*, XVII, no. 5040.   [8] Hayashi: *Memoirs*, p. 128.   [9] Hayashi: *Memoirs*, pp. 126–9.

sired the status quo. He, Lansdowne, would be ready to discuss the possibility of an understanding if Japan so desired.[10]

Hayashi's report is much fuller. In his memoirs he states that Lansdowne declared: " We think that the time has come to discuss seriously the question of making a permanent treaty with Japan." This remark does not, however, appear in the original despatch to Tokyo, which reported only Lansdowne's hope for the continuance of consideration of measures that might be taken to protect the interests of the two countries. It is clear, though, that Hayashi explained that Japan wanted to keep Russia out of Manchuria because " if Russia should one day occupy a part of Manchuria and extend her influence in those parts, then she would be able to absorb Korea, against which Japan would be obliged to protest. What Japan wants is to prevent Russia from coming into Manchuria, and if to do this she should be involved in war with Russia she wants to prevent a third party coming to the help of Russia." [11]

The Japanese minister relates in his memoirs that the Tokyo government approved entirely of his statements to Lansdowne and asked him to get further details. From the official correspondence it appears, however, that the government was somewhat doubtful of British intentions, and noted that MacDonald had spoken more enthusiastically than Lansdowne. Hayashi was told to continue his discussions with MacDonald, stressing the fact that Japanese policy aimed to block the expansion of any other power in Korea. If Russia went beyond existing treaties regarding Manchuria, the Japanese government would regard that as a threat to the independence of Korea. But at all events Hayashi was to continue to speak unofficially.[12]

Lansdowne spoke once more to the Japanese minister before leaving for a protracted vacation in Ireland. Hayashi told him that he felt no doubt that his government would be glad to come to an understanding, and asked for the British terms. But the foreign secretary, who in this matter as in the case of the Anglo-German discussions was not as forward as he was reported to be, pointed out that the issue concerned Japan more than England and that it was therefore up to the Tokyo government to state its requirements. He suggested further that Hayashi secure definite instructions. The Japanese minister had to explain to his government that MacDonald would not return to London before sailing for Japan, and that Lansdowne, though his language was restrained, had actually used the word *alliance* and had shown that he was really in accord with MacDonald. What party spoke first, he argued, was a matter of small import. In fact, he who took the initiative would probably have a certain advantage.[13]

---

[10] *British Documents*, II, no. 102.

[11] Hayashi, op. cit., pp. 129–31. Hayashi's original report of August 1, 1901 has now been published by Atsushi Hiratsuka: *Ito Hirobumi Hiroku (Personal Documents on and of Hirobumi Ito*, Tokyo, 1929), appendix, pp. 9–10 (in Japanese).

[12] Hayashi: *Memoirs*, p. 132; Hiratsuka, op. cit., appendix, pp. 10–1.

[13] *British Documents*, II, no. 103; Hayashi: *Memoirs*, p. 132; Hiratsuka, op. cit., appendix, pp. 11–2.

Despite this auspicious beginning, nothing further was done for almost two months. We have no documents from either side which would explain the reasons for this delay, and we are therefore obliged to fall back upon pure speculation. So far as Chinese affairs were concerned the outstanding development of these two months was the resumption of negotiations between Russia and China. Discussion was opened at the request of Li Hung-chang, who evidently feared that the longer the Russians remained in Manchuria, the more expensive it would be to get them out. The Russians on their side accepted the invitation with pleasure, for they dreaded lest the other powers might bring greater pressure to bear as soon as the Boxer settlement had been arrived at. The St. Petersburg government, indeed, proceeded with the greatest circumspection. The draft submitted to Li provided that Manchuria should be turned over to China, and that the Russian troops should be withdrawn, mostly in 1902. The Chinese Eastern Railway was to be restored to its Chinese owners and China was to be allowed to keep troops in Manchuria.

These terms were so mild and attractive that an agreement was practically reached by the end of October. But then the Russians showed their hand. Li was told that in addition to the convention for the evacuation of Manchuria China should sign a " private " agreement with the Russo-Chinese Bank, promising not to award railway or other concessions in Manchuria to foreigners other than Russians. This agreement was to be signed before the Russians would accept the Manchurian evacuation arrangements. Li was offered 300,000 rubles if he would go through with it. He objected vigorously, but ultimately intimated that he would sign the two agreements together. Then, at the crucial moment, on November 4, the aged Chinese statesman died and the whole negotiation had to be postponed.[14]

The question now arises: how much did the other powers, especially England and Japan, know of these negotiations, and did the Russian policy react in any way upon the discussion of the Anglo-Japanese alliance project? The question is a hard one to answer. All we can conclude from the British material is that the London cabinet knew that the negotiations were going on and that it did what had been done in February and March — it enlisted the aid of the powerful Yangtze viceroys to block any unfavorable settlement.[15] All this was perfectly natural. What we should like to know is whether any conversations took place between London and St. Petersburg on this subject. If so, that fact would do much to explain the suspension of Anglo-Japanese negotiations during this period.

From the contemporary material we may conclude with some assurance that the British government would have been glad at this time to come to an agreement with Russia. Quite apart from the Far Eastern situation there was much

---

[14] Glinskii, op. cit., pp. 177 ff.; *Der Russisch-Japanische Krieg. Amtliche Darstellung,* I, pp. 14–5; Romanov, op. cit., pp. 317 ff.; *China No. 2 (1904),* nos. 40, 41, 42.

[15] *China No. 2 (1904),* no. 41; *British Documents,* II, nos. 75, 76.

uneasiness in London, and especially in Calcutta, occasioned by the striking growth of Russian influence in Persia. Sir Mortimer Durand had for years been pressing upon the foreign office the danger of a policy of laisser faire and the urgent need of fixing upon a definite course of action to prevent Muscovite influence from controlling the whole country.[16] Lord Curzon, when he went out to India as viceroy, took up the cry and developed the ideas of Durand in a classic despatch reviewing the entire situation and recommending that an effort be made to come to an agreement with Russia based on the principle of the partition of Persia into a northern (Russian) and a southern (British) sphere. Curzon himself saw the objections to such an arrangement and was by no means optimistic about its possibility. The London government, while it saw the advantages, feared that proposals made to Russia might be used at Teheran to discredit the English, and that therefore it would be better, for the time being, to do nothing.[17]

In the meanwhile Russian activity was steadily increasing and Russian pretensions growing. In the years from 1899 to 1901 there were endless rumors of Russian plans to secure from the Persian government a lease of the town of Bunder Abbas and the near-by islands. Russian writers talked freely of building a railway from the Russian-Persian frontier to Teheran and thence to Bunder Abbas. In the spring of 1901 the St. Petersburg government established consulates at Bagdad, and at Bushire and Bunder Abbas on the Persian Gulf. A heavily subsidized merchant line was opened from Odessa to the Gulf Ports, while every now and then a splendid Russian cruiser would appear, give the natives an impressive display of searchlights and completely put to shame the couple of obsolete gunboats which represented the predominance of Britain. Needless to say, these developments caused no little excitement in England. By some it was thought that the French efforts to establish themselves in Muscat in 1899 were directly connected with Russian aspirations. When, in the spring of 1901, the Turks attempted to send a force to re-establish their authority over the Sheikh of Kuwait, it was suspected that the Russians had put them up to it in order to undermine the British position at that crucial point. The London government took a strong line, going so far as to threaten the Turks with bombardment if they refused to withdraw.[18]

---

[16] There is nothing of all this in Sir Percy Sykes: *Sir Mortimer Durand* (London, 1926), chaps. xvii and xviii, a book which is of no political value whatever.

[17] The famous Curzon despatch of September 21, 1899 seems to have been based on an unpublished despatch of Durand of February 12, 1899. It was printed in part in *Persia No. 1 (1908)*, where many of the essential passages are given. The text in *British Documents*, IV, no. 319 does not add much, but no. 320 gives the reply of Lord George Hamilton, dated July 6, 1900. No. 321 is a memorandum of October 31, 1905 which gives a succinct review of the whole problem.

[18] *Die Grosse Politik*, XVII, nos. 5292–7, 5304 ff., 5339 ff.; on Russian activities and aspirations there is an extensive literature; see, among others, *Documents Diplomatiques Français*, I, nos. 225, 396; the excellent special article in the London *Times*, December 21, 1901; the anonymous article "Persia and the Persian Gulf" (*Quarterly Review*, January, 1902, pp. 245–73); Paul Rohrbach's review of Hermann Brunnhofer's *Russlands Hand über Asien* (*Preussische Jahrbücher*, June, 1899, pp.

The British representatives at Teheran felt quite helpless and useless in the face of the Russian advance. One declared that he felt like a jellyfish in a whirlpool and another wrote home that he could do nothing but give virtuous advice to dissipated Persians.[19] Curzon appealed once more, this time to Lansdowne, who had himself been viceroy in India. In a long letter of April 5, 1901 he declared that the situation had changed decidedly for the worse since 1899 and that British prestige and influence stood lower than they had in the previous twenty-five years. The Shah and the grand vizir were both disgusted with the British:

> " The Russian Bank at Teheran is rapidly cutting out the Imperial Bank. Russian Consulates are being established in all parts of the country. The Persian Cossacks under Russian officers have been greatly raised in numbers. Their advanced guard is already at Ispahan, and we shall presently see detachments at Shiraz, Mohammerah, and Bushire. We affect to have prohibited Persia from making railways in Southern Persia without our consent, but bodies of Russian engineers perambulate the entire country and push their surveys unhindered. We have large claims for damage done to British persons and interests in the South, but we are unable to obtain compensation. Meanwhile, subsidized Russian steamers are making their way into the Persian Gulf, and the artificial creation of trade will assuredly be followed by the still more artificial generation of political rights and claims."

Curzon urged that the government make up its mind as to how far Russian encroachment to the south should be permitted, and then resist any effort to go beyond that. " We are at present drifting merrily towards another Port Arthur and a second Manchurian Convention," he concluded.[20]

In the preceding chapter some attention was paid to the violently anti-German articles which began to appear in the English press in 1901. It will be recalled that the authors of these articles all recommended that England seek an agreement with Russia. As the months slipped by this campaign increased in intensity. " Maintenance of an unfriendly attitude to Russia," wrote one critic in June, " is simply to play into the hands of Germany, a country which hates England with a fanatical hatred, and which is longing for the hour when she can strike at her with comparative safety." [21] Russophobism, declared *Calchas,* is " a game in which England consistently paid forfeits and German diplomacy drew the stakes." " Democracy would never fight to keep Russia out of Con-

---

531–7); H. Vambéry: " Russland am Persischen Meerbusen " (*Deutsche Revue,* December, 1901, pp. 316–29); Donald Stuart: *The Struggle for Persia* (London, 1902), chaps. xviii–xx; General Krahmer: *Die Beziehungen Russlands zu Persien* (Leipzig, 1903), especially pp. 79 ff., 101 ff.; M. Grulew: *Das Ringen Russlands und Englands in Mittel-Asien* (Berlin, 1909), pp. 97–108. There is nothing of importance in Sir Arthur Hardinge's *A Diplomatist in the East* (London, 1929), chap. ix.

[19] Newton: *Lord Lansdowne,* p. 232; *Letters and Friendships of Sir Cecil Spring Rice,* I, p. 327.

[20] Newton: *Lord Lansdowne,* pp. 230–2. This letter is not in the *British Documents,* as Lord Newton suggests in his footnote.

[21] An Old Parliamentary Hand: " The Causes of Unionist Discontent " (*National Review,* June, 1901, pp. 512–24).

stantinople, were all controversies between the two Empires adjusted." Of these, he continued, Persia was the crucial one. The Russian press had made it clear that while there was no desire on Russia's part to threaten India, the Russians simply had to get down to the Persian Gulf. Well and good, said *Calchas,* let them. Let them have Bunder Abbas. The whole idea of a Russian invasion of India is a ridiculous bogey. Opposition to Russia's establishing herself on the Gulf is out of date, now that the Germans have appeared as rivals of England in the Near East. " Politically, once the second great outlet had been secured, all the dangerous energies of Russia would turn once more to the Near East." India would thereby be relieved and England would no longer have to fear that Russia might join Germany and France in a naval coalition.[22]

Did the British government in any way share the views of this group, or did it make any effort to follow up the suggestions advanced by it? There is some pretty conclusive evidence to show that it did, though we know next to nothing as to the details. It has already been pointed out in the preceding chapter that in April 1901 Lansdowne was ready to consider an agreement with Russia. On July 26, 1901 Sir Edward Grey, speaking for the opposition, declared in the house of commons that an understanding with Russia was " really vital to any satisfactory condition of affairs." [23] From this we may assume that there was agreement between the government and the opposition with respect to the desirability of an understanding with Russia. Another question is whether advances were actually made. After the conclusion of the Anglo-Japanese Alliance, M. Cambon discussed the situation with Lansdowne and remarked that it was a pity that there was so much distrust between England and Russia. " I replied," wrote the foreign minister to the ambassador at Paris, " that I quite agreed as to this, and that I had always desired to see the establishment of more cordial relations between the two governments. I had, indeed, myself made overtures with this object, and endeavoured to bring about a better understanding as to our interests both in China and in Persia, but had not been successful." According to Cambon's report, Lansdowne said of the agreement with Japan: " We would have been very glad to make other arrangements, but we always found the Russian door closed." [24]

This conversation leaves no doubt that Russia was actually approached. When the advances were made, however, it is hard to say. In November 1901 the Russian ambassador at London, M. de Staal, told his French colleague that Lansdowne had several times hinted at the possibility of an agreement respecting China. I suspect that the discussions must have taken place in August or thereabouts, for a letter written by Lord Salisbury on September 6 already re-

---

[22] Calchas: " Russia and her Problem " (*Fortnightly Review,* June, 1901, pp. 1031–44; July, 1901, pp. 124–58), pp. 1031, 131, 135–8.

[23] Newton: *Lord Lansdowne,* pp. 215 ff.; Hansard: *Parliamentary Debates,* Series IV, vol. XCVIII, pp. 286 ff.; other members spoke in the same vein.

[24] *British Documents,* II, no. 131; *Documents Diplomatiques Français,* I, no. 493; II, no. 81.

flects the disappointment of the London cabinet. This letter is worth quoting at some length, for it is very revealing:

> "I agree, and have long agreed, in the expediency of a closer friendship with Russia. . . . But the possibility of improving our relations is constantly growing more questionable. Other statesmen are acutely watching the Chess-Board of Europe: and they perfectly know that a real sympathy between Russia and England would place the other Great Powers in a very inferior position. Therefore they will lose no opportunity of hindering such a consummation: and unfortunately they have too many opportunities of doing so, for they can offer enlargement of Russian territory on the Chinese, the Persian, and the Turkish frontier, and we cannot do so. Another insuperable difficulty lies in the attitude of what is called public opinion here. The diplomacy of nations is now conducted quite as much in the letters of special correspondents as in the despatches of the Foreign Office. The result is that there is a raw state of irritation between the upper classes in the two countries, which makes any advance on the part of either government quite impracticable. If a letter could be made to give room for further reasons, my catalogue is far from being exhausted. I wish it were otherwise: but wishing is no good." [25]

Though we know nothing specific about Anglo-Russian discussions in the autumn of 1901, we can easily see why an understanding was not effected. Although the discussion will take us beyond the resumption of Anglo-Japanese negotiations in mid-October, it will be well to dispose of the subject, the more so as it will serve as a useful background for what has to be said later.

In November 1901 the *National Review,* chief exponent of the anti-German policy, published an important article on "British Foreign Policy," by A.B.C. The editor pointed out that it was written by a number of persons and represented a consensus of opinion. It was hoped that it would find a large audience on the Continent, its chief purpose being to disabuse Englishmen about Germany: "Germany may be regarded as our most formidable political rival, and eventually, enemy." [26] The article itself began with a long review of the naval situation and the need for a three-power standard. German naval policy would require England to have a strong North Sea fleet. But the German menace necessitated also an entire revision of British foreign policy. Germany had achieved greatness "by trampling on her neighbours." Her object now was "to deprive us of our position on the ocean." It would therefore be best for England and Russia to get together and put an end to German exploitation of their rivalry. Furthermore, England should stand by Japan and use her influence to effect a Russian-Japanese understanding on Manchuria and Korea. But the most important thing would be the Anglo-Russian entente, which might be based on the idea of a free hand in the Balkans in return for a free hand in Egypt; a commercial outlet on the Persian Gulf in return for a promise to observe the status

---

[25] George W. E. Russell: *Malcolm MacColl* (London, 1914), pp. 282–3.
[26] *National Review:* "Episodes of the Month," November, 1901, pp. 317 ff.

quo in that area; a Far Eastern settlement which would give Korea to Japan, Manchuria and Mongolia to Russia, and the Yangtze Basin to England. Germany could then be given to understand that if she tried to disturb the peace her sea-borne food-supply would be cut off.[27]

This article immediately caused a sensation. The *Times,* which received advanced copy, commented at length upon it and expressed general agreement, though it thought the authors were offering Russia too much for too little. The idea of an English-Russian-Japanese agreement struck it as splendid.[28] The *Spectator,* also, was warm in its approval, but went even further than A.B.C. Russia, it declared, should have as free a hand in Persia as England in Egypt. " For a half-hearted agreement with Russia we feel no enthusiasm. . . . If we are to have an understanding, it must be on the boldest possible lines. . . . An understanding with Russia should approach very nearly, as far as we and Russia are concerned, a partition of Asia into ' spheres of influence.' " [29]

On the other hand the response from the Continent was not very encouraging. Some of the French papers expressed their warm approval of an Anglo-Russian rapprochement, while the German press showed itself pretty sceptical. The main thing, of course, was the reaction in Russia, and that was disappointing. The St. Petersburg newspapers replied in cool language, which provoked a reversal of feeling in London. The *Times* on November 16 published a letter from a correspondent protesting against concessions to Russia in the Persian Gulf. Such concessions would be a menace to India, in the opinion of the leading experts. Thereupon the *Times* remarked editorially that there was no evidence that Russia wanted an agreement on any terms which England could accept. Furthermore, no agreement could be made without the approval of the Indian government and there was no reason to suppose that Lord Curzon would consent to any diminution of British influence in south Persia or the Gulf. On November 22 the *Novoie Vremia* asserted that the agreement was neither desirable nor valuable for Russia. Britain was no longer the great power she once had been, and her approaches to Russia were merely a demonstration of weakness.[30]

The German ambassador watched the development of this debate with the utmost care. He learned that the A.B.C. article had been written by Mr. Maxse, the editor of the *National Review,* by Sir Rowland Blennerhassett and by M. Tatistchev, a Russian financial agent in London. It had been shown to the Russian ambassador, and also to Count Lamsdorff and Count Witte. Witte, it was said, favored an agreement with England, if only in the hope of raising a much-needed loan in London, but for the rest no enthusiasm was shown. Staal, the Russian ambassador at London, told his Austrian colleague that Russia did not need England and would attain her objectives without an arrange-

---

[27] A.B.C.: " British Foreign Policy " (*National Review,* November, 1901, pp. 343–58).

[28] *Times,* October 29, 1901.

[29] *Spectator,* November 2, 1901.

[30] *Times,* November 1, 4, 16, 21, 23, 1901.

ment with the English. The price Russia would ask for an alliance would be greater than England would be willing to pay.[31]

The sum total of this first offensive, then, was that the Russians showed themselves cool and that in England itself objections were raised to a policy which would allow Russia to advance to the Persian Gulf. But this did not discourage the *National Review*. In the December number the editor returned to the attack: " Great Britain has too long been the political satellite of Germany, who has treated her accordingly. This unnatural relationship has enabled the Berlin Government, on the one hand, to exploit Europe at the expense of England, and on the other England at the expense of Europe, by threatening each in turn with the hostility of the other." Russia and France should see the wisdom of cultivating English friendship: " If the Dual Alliance will only stand aside, the present *furor Teutonicus* will cause a complete revision of British foreign policy." If they join in Anglophobia, they will simply drive England back into the arms of Germany. " For although our public men are accused of pursuing Machiavellian policies abroad, they have ever since the days of Bismarck shown themselves to be simple as little children in dealing with their German confrères, who in every transaction between the two countries succeed in taking something either without giving anything in return or else something which is not theirs to give." [32]

The same number carried a second article by A.B.C., in which the writers claimed that their proposal had the support of some of the wisest Englishmen. They repeated, in general, the argument as at first advanced, stressing the fact that an Anglo-Russian agreement need not in any way conflict either with the Franco-Russian Alliance or with Anglo-Japanese friendship. " What we demand of Russian and British statesmen is that they shall dismiss the honest broker in Berlin and have direct dealings with one another. Let not friendly relations be compromised by unfriendly intrigues; let not any unavoidable difficulties bear the additional burden of a heavy German commission." [33]

This time *Calchas* came to the rescue. In a strong article in the *Fortnightly Review* he recalled all his past efforts for an agreement with Russia and then complained that the trouble with A.B.C. was that they did not go far enough. A mere commercial port on the Persian Gulf would do Russia little good. She would not want a port she could not fortify. She ought to be given a free hand without reservation in Persia and on the Gulf.[34] The *Spectator* in turn approved entirely the stand taken by *Calchas*. It was perfectly clear, said this weekly, that England could not block both Russia and Germany in the Persian Gulf. The Germans certainly would not help to stop the Russians. They might, in fact,

---

[31] *Die Grosse Politik*, XVII, nos. 5343, 5345.

[32] *National Review*: " Episodes of the Month," December, 1901, pp. 478–87.

[33] A.B.C.: " Some Consequences of an Anglo-Russian Understanding " (*National Review*, December, 1901, pp. 513–25).

[34] Calchas: " The Crisis with Germany — and its Results " (*Fortnightly Review*, December, 1901, pp. 934–48).

join the Russians against the English. It would therefore be much better to give the Russians their port, which would not be a menace to England as long as she retained the command of the sea.[35]

These suggestions were debated on and off throughout December and January by the Russian press, which showed itself not over-enthusiastic and came to the general conclusion that in any event Russia must have a port on the Gulf. This was a *sine qua non* for an understanding.[36] But it was exactly this concession that even British opinion balked at. In the *National Review* itself an anonymous writer, who was described by the editor as a " distinguished contributor " with wide experience of foreign affairs, while expatiating on the fact that the German nation was " saturated with hatred " for England, and while urging an entente with Russia, nevertheless questioned the advisability of letting Russia have a port which might become another Port Arthur.[37] So well-known a writer as A. R. Colquhoun took the same line,[38] while the *Quarterly Review,* in an excellent survey of the whole problem, also warned against the repetition of the Kiao-chow or Port Arthur policy in the Persian Gulf: " Possibly enlightened Russian statesmen and generals have no design of invading India; but deep down in the sub-conscious aspirations of the Russian people lies the Tartar impulse of rolling down upon the prizes of Asia." Let England by all means seek an agreement with Russia, but not by merely asking what Russia wants. Let England say what she intends to keep. She must remain supreme not only in the Gulf, but in the whole zone of mountains which lie between the sea and the salt desert.[39]

It seems likely that some tentative advances were made to Russia in December by Sir Arthur Hardinge, the British minister at Teheran, who was strongly in favor of the policy put forward by the *National Review*. The offers were probably very modest, and if made, were rejected.[40] At all events the British government had made up its mind to a policy by January 6, when instructions were sent to Hardinge: England had no designs on the independence and integrity of Persia; she recognized the superior interest of Russia in northern Persia; she had no objection to a Russian commercial outlet on the Gulf, but she " could not consent to the acquisition by Russia of a military or naval station in the Persian Gulf, for the reason that such a station must be regarded as a challenge to Great Britain and a menace to her Indian Empire "; nor could she agree to Russia's having any preferential political or commercial privileges in southern

[35] *Spectator,* December 7, 1901, pp. 888–9.

[36] London *Times,* December 25, 1901, January 4, 17, 1902; A Russian Diplomatist: " Russia and England " (*National Review,* January, 1902, pp. 677–90); *National Review:* " Episodes," February, 1902, p. 820; *Die Grosse Politik,* XVII, no. 5350.

[37] A Free Lance: " A Plea for the Isolation of Germany " (*National Review,* January, 1902, pp. 703–15).

[38] A. R. Colquhoun: " Our German Ally " (*Monthly Review,* January, 1902, pp. 73–87).

[39] Anonymous: " Persia and the Persian Gulf " (*Quarterly Review,* January, 1902, pp. 245–73), especially pp. 258 ff.

[40] *Die Grosse Politik,* XVII, nos. 5348, 5349; Newton: *Lord Lansdowne,* pp. 234–5.

or southeastern Persia; if necessary she would take "such measures as might appear . . . best calculated to protect the interest so endangered, even though in the adoption of such measures it might no longer be possible to make the integrity and independence of Persia their first object as hitherto." [41]

Much the same statement of policy was made publicly in the House on January 22. At that time Joseph Walton, Sir Henry Norman and Sir Edward Grey all spoke warmly in favor of a far-reaching agreement with Russia extending over all Asia. Lord Cranborne, the undersecretary for foreign affairs, thereupon replied that the government desired friendly relations, but that "these friendly relations are not to be sought at the cost of any of the rights which by treaty we possess. Whether to Russia or to any other country, it does not become us and it is not our interest to go cap in hand for an understanding." England, he concluded, could not abandon her rights in Persia and on the Gulf.[42]

While the question of an Anglo-Russian accord was a live subject of discussion in England, the members of the Japanese government were also wrestling with the problem of policy. Before the Hayashi-Lansdowne conversations were approved in August, there appears to have been a conference held at the villa of Count Katsura, the prime minister. At this meeting were present Prince Ito, Marquis Yamagata, Count Inouye and Count Matsukata. Those present, including Prince Ito, agreed in principle to an alliance with England, and therefore approved Hayashi's conversations with Lansdowne. But even then Ito, the most authoritative of Japanese statesmen, seems to have had little hope that the alliance would be concluded. It was so contrary to Britain's policy of isolation that it seemed unlikely that much would come of it. At the suggestion of his friend, Count Inouye, he therefore proposed that an effort be made to reach an agreement with Russia regarding Korea. The two countries, he argued, could not go on looking at each other with "cross eyes." If an agreement were too long postponed, war would result inevitably. Katsura and the others apparently assented to this viewpoint in a general way.[43]

Ito, who was out of office at the time, was planning to take a trip to America to recover his health. Inouye and Yamagata urged him to take this opportunity of going on to Europe, visiting St. Petersburg and attempting to come to some arrangement with Russia. There seems to have been another conference on September 11, at which Katsura also requested that the eminent statesman go on to Russia. Later on the friends of Ito claimed that Katsura was set on an alliance with England and that he spoke as he did only for politeness' sake. Kurino, who was to go to St. Petersburg as the new minister, and who was to assist in work-

---

[41] British Documents, IV, no. 321 a.

[42] Hansard: Parliamentary Debates, CI, pp. 574 ff., 599 ff., 609 ff., and especially 615 ff.

[43] Hayashi: Memoirs, pp. 142 ff. (Ito's own account to Hayashi); pp. 207 ff. (revelations made later in Count Okuma's paper). Hayashi never could convince himself that Ito had approved the idea of an alliance with England, but Ito's statements are completely borne out by other Japanese sources, e.g. the memorandum of Viscount Kurino (Hiratsuka: Ito Hirobumi Hiroku, pp. 349–54), and The Memoirs of Kikujiro Ishii on Diplomatic Affairs (Tokyo, 1930), pp. 52–60 (in Japanese).

ing out an agreement, complained later that Katsura regarded Ito as something of an eyesore, because of his great influence with the Emperor. He urged him to take a long trip in order to get rid of him for the time being.[44]

At any rate the Japanese government was preparing a hard bed for itself. Hardly had Ito left for America than Count Komura was appointed foreign minister and negotiations with England were resumed on the initiative of the Japanese. On October 8 Hayashi was given authorization to discuss the matter with Lansdowne. The two statesmen opened the subject on October 16, Hayashi going once more over the familiar ground. He stated that his government was above all interested in Korea and that it was a matter of life and death for Japan to keep Russia out of Korea. Manchuria was of importance chiefly because of the fact that it might become a base for encroachments on Korea. In China, Japan stood for the principles of integrity and independence, as well as of the Open Door. The alliance desired would assure either Japan or England of the support of her ally in the event of having to go to war with more than one power in defense of her interests in the Far East.

So far the reports of Hayashi and Lansdowne agree. But there are some rather significant discrepancies, which almost suggest that Hayashi, like his friend Eckardstein, did not always report with complete accuracy. Lord Lansdowne stated in his report that Hayashi suggested that the understanding " should be made to extend even to the action of the two Powers in regard to Siam." This idea was to cause some trouble later. Hayashi says nothing of the suggestion in his report to his government. Even more serious is another discrepancy. Hayashi had, since the spring of 1901, favored the idea of including Germany in the agreement. Lansdowne noted that at the very outset of the conversation of October 16 the Japanese minister asked whether Germany should be made a party to the understanding, which, he thought, would " look much more formidable " if Germany were included. Hayashi reported that he brought up this matter not at the outset, but just before his departure. He explains in his memoirs that he asked about Germany because he was uncertain about the relationship between England and Germany and desired, as instructed by his government, " to find out whether or not there was a definite arrangement between England and Germany that the latter country would have to be invited to join in the treaty." Lansdowne's account seems more trustworthy, because it fits in better with what went before. In any case the reports on both sides agree with respect to his reply. He said that Anglo-German relations were friendly and intimate, but that Germany's interests in the Far East were smaller than the British and Japanese and that it would be better to come to an agreement à deux before considering whether Germany should be invited to join.

There is one more point of difference, which is of some importance in connexion with what followed. Hayashi says nothing of the remark of Lansdowne

---

[44] Hayashi, op. cit., pp. 140–6; the accounts of Kurino (Hiratsuka, op. cit., pp. 349–54) and of Ishii (op. cit., pp. 52–60) support Ito's own account to Hayashi.

that he presumed " that the two Powers would, in the event of such an under-standing being arrived at, agree that neither should, without consulting the other, make separate arrangements, or come to separate understandings with another Power as to Chinese or Corean affairs." Hayashi should certainly have reported this to the home government, the more so as he must have known from personal experience that there was an influential group in Tokyo that for years had favored an agreement with Russia.[45]

Matters now moved more quickly. The Japanese government approved of Hayashi's formulation of the case, and Komura showed real anxiety to get along with the business. On November 6 Lansdowne handed the Japanese minister a draft treaty based upon their previous conversations. He pointed out that this had been submitted to the cabinet, and that the only point that had been raised in connexion with it was the extent of the projected treaty. Some members felt that " what after all was of importance to both Great Britain and Japan was that neither of them should be overwhelmed by a combination of foreign powers. The disappearance of Great Britain as a sea Power in the Far East would be a calamity to Japan, and it would make no matter to her whether such a calamity were to be brought about by a quarrel originating in the Far East or by com-plications in some other part of the World." Hayashi recognized the force of the argument and recommended to his government that the agreement be extended to include India. At the same time he tried hard to get the first clause of the draft re-written. In Lansdowne's draft this clause spoke of the two powers being interested " in preventing the absorption of Corea by any Foreign Power." Hayashi therefore urged the need for some statement by which Britain should recognize Japan's paramount interests in Korea, and should give an assurance that Great Britain would not interfere with Japan in any action she might feel called upon to take to protect her interests in the peninsula.[46]

Before any decision was come to by either side with respect to these details, Hayashi received a telegram on November 13 instructing him to wait for final instructions: " You are now advised to go immediately to Paris, or wherever Prince Ito may be staying, to show him all the cablegrams pertaining to the present question, and to make an effort to obtain his endorsement of the essen-tials of the British draft." [47]

Before the eminent Japanese statesman arrived in Paris, careful preparation was made. Delcassé had for some time been watching the Far Eastern situation with some uneasiness, and was evidently more than a little worried by the evi-dences of English-German-Japanese collaboration in the spring of 1901. In April he paid another visit to St. Petersburg. We know nothing of the conversations

---

[45] The conversation is reported by Lansdowne in *British Documents*, II, no. 105; by Hayashi to Komura, October 16 (Hiratsuka, op. cit., appendix, pp. 12-3); see also Hayashi: *Memoirs*, pp. 133-6.

[46] *British Documents*, II, nos. 107-10; Hayashi: *Memoirs*, pp. 137-9; Newton: *Lord Lans-downe*, p. 222; Hiratsuka, op. cit., appendix, pp. 13-4 (Komura to Hayashi, October 19; Hayashi to Komura, November 6; Hayashi to Komura, November 7, 1901).

[47] Hiratsuka, op. cit., appendix, pp. 14-5; Hayashi: *Memoirs*, p. 139.

that went on there, but there are some indications that the main subject of discussion was the course of action to be followed in the event of war with England or with England supported by the Triple Alliance. The French general staff had worked out certain arrangements for such an eventuality and these dispositions were approved by the Tsar and by the French foreign office in May 1901. It appears, from these plans, that the French decided to concentrate their main naval strength in the Mediterranean, leaving in the Channel only second-class ships and coast-guard craft. The threat of an invasion of England was to be kept alive in order to force the British to keep part of their fleet in the north. The Russian plans evidently called for a defensive in the Baltic. Eight battleships were to be kept ready in the Black Sea and three more in the Mediterranean. The plan of holding an army corps in readiness to proceed to the Bosporus was maintained. But the Russians hoped to build up their Far Eastern force till it numbered sixteen battleships. The idea was that Russia should relieve France of the need of keeping a large squadron in the Far East and should be prepared to aid France in the Mediterranean by sending the Black Sea fleet through the Dardanelles to help the French against the British.[48]

These arrangements throw a bright light on the tension between England on the one hand and France and Russia on the other. Delcassé evidently felt the need of further Russian promises. In return for them he did his best to aid the Russians in the Far East and to prevent the outbreak of hostilities between Russia and Japan. " We must apply ourselves to the job of avoiding a clash between Russia and Japan as long as possible," he wrote in July; " we must prevent England from finding in Japan the soldier she needs in the Far East." [49] What he hoped for was an agreement between Russia, Japan and France.[50] It was known in Paris that Ito was favorable to an understanding, and it was hoped that the Japanese need of money would pave the way to an agreement through a loan. Russia, reported the chargé d'affaires at St. Petersburg, would probably never give up Korea entirely, but she needed a few more years for preparation and hoped that Ito would come to arrange a compromise. Delcassé undertook to open the discussions with Ito. The Russian foreign office gave him a memorandum stating that Russia did not envisage the annexation of Korea or any exceptional position for herself. The Russian government recognized the commercial and industrial expansion of Japan in Korea as natural, but could not admit that Korea should be made a strategic centre to the detriment of Russian interests. Russia would not annex Manchuria, but would evacuate the country as soon as she had adequate guarantees.[51]

Ito had several interviews with Delcassé during his stay in Paris. Both sides

---

[48] *Documents Diplomatiques Français*, III, annexes, pp. 601 ff., nos. I, II.
[49] *Documents Diplomatiques Français*, I, no. 310.
[50] Combarieu: *Sept Ans à l'Élysée*, pp. 144 ff., reporting a statement by Loubet.
[51] *Documents Diplomatiques Français*, I, nos. 399, 435, 447, 500; " Nakanunie Russko-Iaponskoi Voiny " (*Krasnyi Arkhiv*, LXIII, 1934, pp. 3–54), pp. 41–3.

agreed that there was no question of conflict of interests between them, and that between Russia and Japan the only crucial issue was Korea. Ito expressed the hope that an arrangement would be made and promised to appeal to French mediation if necessary.[52] The great difficulty was that Ito said nothing about a loan, so that the French foreign minister more or less lost the wind he needed for his sails.

On November 14 Hayashi reached Paris from London, bringing with him the Lansdowne draft. Ito was completely surprised to find that the negotiations with England had progressed so far. He told Hayashi how he had been asked to visit Russia and seek an agreement. He was entirely at a loss as to what to do, and apparently thought for a moment of returning to Japan. In the end he decided that it would be best to go on to Russia, where he was expected. In the meanwhile he cabled to Katsura that he had no objection to the general idea of the alliance with England, though he thought the question of inviting Germany ought to be settled before it was too late, that the government ought to decide whether the agreement should be limited to China proper or extended to the whole of the Chinese Empire, and that the clause relating to Korea should be broadened in Japan's interest. He urged the government to postpone action on the British draft until he could see what was to be done with the Russians. He and Hayashi agreed to keep each other informed. Hayashi was to temporize in London until he heard the outcome of Ito's Russian mission. Ito on the other hand was to confine his conversation in the Russian capital to " harmless gossiping." [53]

Passing through Berlin on his way to Russia, Ito received cables from his government pointing out that the negotiations with England were so far advanced that Japan could not step back without impugning her honor. Ito was urged to go to St. Petersburg as quickly as possible, but to restrict himself to " harmless gossiping " as suggested by Hayashi.[54] In the meanwhile Hayashi returned to London on November 19. Lansdowne and Bertie, who harbored strong suspicions about Ito's peregrinations, used pretty plain language in speaking to Hayashi about the delay, and all the minister could do was to make excuses. The British government was assured that Ito's visit to Russia was unofficial and that he had no power to negotiate. But the British government was obviously unimpressed with the excuses. Hayashi was warned against the danger of an agreement with Russia.[55]

Under the circumstances the Japanese government simply could not wait. On November 30 Hayashi was able to submit the proposed amendments to the

---

[52] Hiratsuka, op. cit., appendix, pp. 3–9 (Katsura to Ito, November 11; November 12; Ito's notes on conversations with Delcassé and Loubet on November 13, 14, 1901); *Documents Diplomatiques Français*, I, no. 527; " Nakanunie Russko-Iaponskoi Voiny " (loc. cit.), pp. 53–4.

[53] Hiratsuka, op. cit., appendix, pp. 15–6 (Ito to Katsura, November 15; Ito to Hayashi, November 24; Katsura to Ito, November 22; Ito to Katsura, November 26; Katsura to Ito, November 27, 1901); Hayashi: *Memoirs*, pp. 142 ff., which appear to be absolutely reliable.

[54] See preceding footnote.

[55] Hayashi: *Memoirs*, pp. 149–50; *British Documents*, II, nos. 112–3; Hiratsuka, op. cit., appendix, pp. 15–6 (Hayashi to Komura, November 23, 1901).

draft which the British had had ready on November 6. But the minister at London was at the same time instructed to send a special messenger to St. Petersburg to submit these amendments to Ito for approval. Why the amendments could not have been sent directly from Tokyo to St. Petersburg is not clear. It seems that the Japanese government was still trying to gain time.[56]

M. Matsui, who was sent from London, did not arrive at St. Petersburg until December 3, not long before Ito was to depart. Much had happened in the interval. The Japanese statesman had arrived on November 25 and had been given a splendid reception. The Tsar decorated him with a very high Russian order, and Count Lamsdorff gave a dinner in his honor at which Witte, Kuropatkin, Pobiedonostsev and other high officials were present.[57] Yet Ito was in St. Petersburg for a full wěek before he began his conversations with Lamsdorff and Witte. During this time several cables passed between him and his friend Count Inouye in Tokyo. Inouye wrote that he could not understand England's intentions, in view of her traditional attachment to the principle of isolation. Was she not trying to use Japan for selfish ends? It was clear that Germany would not join the alliance. Would not the conclusion of the treaty with England induce Russia, France and Germany to re-form the Triplice of 1895? Inouye thought it would be wise to sound out the Russian government with regard to Korea before going on with the negotiations at London.

To this cable Ito replied approvingly. Contrary to original plans he had been instructed not to touch on the question of an agreement with Russia, but it seemed to him that Russia desired an agreement and in his opinion it would be wise to find out how far she would go. He asked that the matter be referred to the premier and that a reply be sent to him at once. Apparently no direct reply was ever received.[58]

Ito evidently decided to proceed on his own responsibility. The Russian press spoke very warmly in favor of an accord, not to say an alliance.[59] We know further that both Lamsdorff and Witte were eager to reach some sort of understanding. They had been warned by Izvolski from Tokyo that it would be their last chance and they understood quite well that a breakdown in the negotiations might have grave consequences. Relations with Japan must be cleared up, wrote Witte on November 28. A war might be successful, but it would be very expensive and might prove disastrous for the government. " It may be advisable to give up Korea altogether. . . . Between the two evils, an armed conflict with Japan and the complete cession of Korea, I would unhesitatingly choose the

---

[56] Hayashi: *Memoirs*, pp. 153–6; Hiratsuka, op. cit., appendix, pp. 28–9 (Katsura to Ito, by way of London; Komura to Hayashi, November 30, 1901).

[57] London *Times*, November 26, 30, 1901.

[58] Hiratsuka, op. cit., appendix, pp. 18–9 (Inouye to Ito, received November 28; Ito to Inouye, November 28; Ito to Inouye, November 30).

[59] London *Times*, December 3 (St. Petersburg, December 1); December 5 (St. Petersburg, December 2).

second." [60] Witte does not quote in his memoirs the rest of the letter, in which he argued that Japan would be much enfeebled by the expenditures she would make in Korea and that she would be much more susceptible to Russian pressure, especially when the Transsiberian Railroad should have been completed. All of which would make it easier for Russia to take possession of Korea later, if circumstances required.[61]

In other words, Witte was simply searching for a *modus vivendi* until Russian preparations were complete.[62] But Lamsdorff was not willing to go so far as that. He would give Japan a free hand in Korea in the economic sense, but he refused to renounce *all* Russian interest in the peninsula. All this came out when the foreign minister had his first extended talk with Ito on December 2. The Japanese statesman pointed out that he had no official mission and was therefore ready to speak frankly. Korea, he said, was a matter of life and death for Japan. The country was still undeveloped and the government unable to maintain order or protect foreign rights. It was therefore necessary that Korea have advice and assistance. But if both Russia and Japan gave this advice and assistance, the result would probably be a clash between them. To which Lamsdorff replied that an agreement between Russia and Japan in advance would obviate any conflict. Just what did Ito mean by "assistance"? The Japanese statesman admitted that he had in mind military assistance to quell disorders.

The admission led Lamsdorff to say that Russia had no designs on Korea, but that she could not allow the country to be used by any other power for military purposes. How could Japan guarantee that troops sent to restore order would not be used for other purposes? Ito suggested a promise, but this seemed inadequate. Lamsdorff proposed instead that Russia be given a small section on the southern coast of Korea, leaving the rest to Japan. Ito objected that the southern part of the country was the most important for Japan, but the Russian minister argued that the apprehension which would be felt in Japan at the presence of the Russians in a small part of southern Korea would be as nothing compared to the apprehension of the Russians in having the Japanese control the whole of Korea. Ito refused to accept this viewpoint and suggested that if Russia were willing to give the Japanese people a sense of security by leaving them Korea, Russia might do as she liked in China without needing to fear Japanese intervention. The conversation ended with Lamsdorff's request that Ito put on paper what his ideas were with regard to Korea.[63]

On the following day Ito had an even franker discussion with Witte. The

---

[60] Witte: *Memoirs*, p. 117; *Documents Diplomatiques Français*, I, no. 545; see also the accurate account in Prince G. Trubetzkoi: *Russland als Grossmacht* (Stuttgart, 1913), p. 69.

[61] The letter in full as printed by Glinskii, op. cit., pp. 187 ff.; Romanov, op. cit., p. 338.

[62] The same thing comes out in the remarks of the Tsar to Prince Henry of Prussia early in November (*Die Grosse Politik*, XVIII, no. 5399).

[63] Hiratsuka, op. cit., appendix, pp. 19–23 (Ito's own memorandum). The Russian accounts tally exactly with Ito's (Trubetzkoi, op. cit., pp. 68–9; Glinskii, op. cit., pp. 187–9; Romanov, op. cit., pp. 333 ff.; *Documents Diplomatiques Français*, I, no. 548).

finance minister admitted that it was Japan, not Russia, that had a vital interest in Korea, but he insisted that Russia had to think of the protection of her railway interests in the Far East, which represented an investment of three hundred million rubles. Ito then went over his arguments as he had expounded them to Lamsdorff: Japan would be willing to agree to a guarantee of Korean independence and a guarantee that she would construct no fortifications on the coasts that might menace Russian communications by sea between Port Arthur and Vladivostok. Witte declared himself completely satisfied: " If you can guarantee these things, you can do what you like in Korea." [64]

On December 4 Ito had a second discussion with Lamsdorff, which was to be the last. He brought with him an itemized plan setting forth the Japanese desire for a free hand in Korea commercially, industrially, politically and militarily, and offering a guarantee that the country should not be used for military purposes against Russia. But Lamsdorff thought this too one-sided. What concession would Japan make to Russia? Would she give Russia a free hand in China? This, again, was too much for Ito, who maintained that all he had suggested was that if Russia squared Japan with regard to Korea, she would be able to take a decided stand in Chinese affairs without having to reckon with Japanese hostility. Lamsdorff then suggested a free hand in northern China, by which he said he meant the sections adjoining the Russian frontier. This Ito was willing to accept, at least tentatively. It was agreed that the Russians should set down their ideas, and that negotiations should be continued with Ito in Berlin or Paris, or directly with Tokyo, provided there was a reasonable basis for agreement.[65]

The Prince left St. Petersburg the same night, evidently very well satisfied. M. Matsui, the emissary from London, came just before he departed, bringing the news that the Japanese government felt committed to the negotiation with England, and bringing also the modified Japanese draft for the alliance. Matsui followed the Prince to Berlin, and there heard from Ito his objections, general and special, to the projected alliance.

" In both the British draft, and also in the Japanese amendments to it, there are words to the effect that the absorption of Korea by a foreign country shall be prevented. But in Korea only Japan and Russia have interests of any importance. England has no interests there. In regard to Korea the proper thing to do is to make a convention with Russia, and settle the problem of that country. Even if we make an alliance with England it is not certain that we shall reap much benefit from it. Besides this, according to the draft, England will attain the same position in Korea as Japan has already. It really means giving to England a position in that country which she has not now got. From this point of view I consider that

---

[64] Hiratsuka, op. cit., appendix, pp. 23–7. There appears to be no Russian record of this conversation.

[65] Hiratsuka, op. cit., appendix, pp. 28–31, giving the full text of Ito's draft; this is given also in Lamsdorff's report to Nicholas II, December 5, 1901, in " Nakanunie Russko-Iaponskoi Voiny " (loc. cit.), p. 44–6.

the proposal is unreasonable. Again, even if we have another country joining in the alliance, as Germany, we shall only be giving to that country the same as we are giving to England. That country also will obtain a new position in Korea which she had not got before. Consequently the proposed instrument would be doubly bad. The Japanese Government certainly ought to make some proper amendments with regard to all that touches Korea. . . . We ought also to study carefully the whole question of the international relations between the European nations. Count Inouye's telegram shows that whilst all the members of the Cabinet have agreed, he himself has not hastily thrown himself on the side of the proposed alliance. According to his opinion, it is difficult to understand why England has broken her record in foreign politics and has decided to enter into an alliance with us; secondly, the mere fact that England has adopted this attitude shows that she is in dire need, and she therefore wants to use us in order to make us bear some of her burdens; thirdly, Germany in Count Inouye's view may not enter the alliance. It is for these reasons that the Count has telegraphed me to reconsider the relations between the European Powers and only then to form my opinions. . . .

" Now what we ought to pay special attention to in connexion with this problem is, in my opinion, the attitude of Russia. I think that all negotiations for an Anglo-Japanese Alliance ought to be suspended until we are quite sure that it is hopeless to attempt to conclude a convention with Russia. I am convinced from what I have seen and heard in the Russian capital that the attitude of that country is at least rather conciliatory towards Japan, and it appears to me that she is sincerely desirous of co-operating with us to settle the Korean question. . . . As the result of my informal negotiations in St. Petersburg we are in a position to commence formal negotiations with the Russian Government through the Japanese Minister at St. Petersburg, and this we can now do at any time. That is the situation in regard to Russia at this moment, and in my opinion the prospects of our being able to make a satisfactory convention with Russia are very favourable." [66]

At the same time Ito telegraphed to Katsura reporting his success and advising strongly that the effort be made to come to an agreement. A convention with Russia would not be possible after the conclusion of the alliance with England. The Japanese draft of the alliance with England was open to various objections, which Ito communicated to his government. But before his comments could reach Japan, the Elder Statesmen, in a council before the throne, had decided unanimously on December 7 to go on with the alliance and to drop all further negotiations with Russia. Count Inouye seems to have held out against this course until the Emperor had documents brought out to show that Ito, while still premier, favored an alliance with England. Inouye explained in a telegram to Ito that the discovery that Japan had made the first advances to England had induced him to vote with the others. [67]

---

[66] Hayashi: *Memoirs*, pp. 157–62.

[67] Hayashi: *Memoirs*, p. 165; Hiratsuka, op. cit., appendix, pp. 34–6 (Inouye to Ito, received December 5; Ito to Katsura, December 6; Ito to Inouye, December 6; Hayashi to Ito, December 8; Inouye to Ito, n.d.); also the account in the *Memoirs of Kikujiro Ishii*, pp. 52–60.

The die was cast. The Japanese cabinet did not even allow itself to be influenced by Ito's objections to the draft. It simply felt that further delay would lose Japan the sympathies of England as well as of Russia. On December 10 Hayashi was instructed to go on with the negotiations.[68] But before turning to this subject a few words must be said about the end of the discussions with Russia. On December 17 Ito received, through the Russian embassy in Berlin, Lamsdorff's draft of an agreement. The foreign minister had set down his objections to the Ito draft on the very day following his last talk with his Japanese guest. But Kuropatkin had insisted on some stiffening of the Russian terms. He demanded that Japan alone assume the obligation not to make any preparations in Korea for operations against Russia or any other dispositions which might interfere with the freedom of the Korean Straits. Lamsdorff refused to accept these emendations and was evidently supported by the Tsar, but Kuropatkin succeeded in having a provision written into the Russian proposals permitting Japan to introduce her troops into Korea only after previous agreement with Russia. Just as Lamsdorff was about to despatch the Russian draft to Ito, the minister of marine came forward with a blanket condemnation of the whole thing, but Lamsdorff managed to have the objections of the naval authorities overruled. The Russian proposals went off pretty much in the form worked out by Lamsdorff, with the one significant modification by Kuropatkin, mentioned above.[69]

To clarify the situation it will be well to put the Russian proposals in juxtaposition to the draft submitted by Ito.

Japanese Draft	*Russian Draft*
1. Mutual guarantee of the independence of Korea.	1. Same.
2. Mutual obligation not to make use of any part of Korean territory for strategic purposes.	2. Mutual obligation (or Japan promises) . . .
3. Mutual obligation not to make, on Korean coasts, any military preparations menacing the free passage of the Korean Straits.	3. Mutual obligation (or Japan promises) . . .
4. Recognition by Russia of Japan's freedom of action in Korea in political, industrial and commercial respects, as well as exclusive right of Japan to come	4. Recognition by Russia of Japan's freedom of action in Korea in industrial and commercial respects, as well as preferential right of Japan to come,

[68] Hayashi: *Memoirs*, pp. 165–7; Hiratsuka, op. cit., appendix, pp. 36–9 (Ito to Inouye, December 10; Hayashi to Ito, December 12; Ito to Katsura, December 12; Katsura to Ito, December 13).
[69] "Nakanunie Russko-Iaponskoi Voiny" (loc. cit.), pp. 48–53 (Lamsdorff to Nicholas II, December 13; Kuropatkin to Lamsdorff, December 10; Lamsdorff to Nicholas II, December 14, 1901).

Japanese Draft	*Russian Draft*
to Korea's assistance with advice and action directed to helping her fulfill the obligations incurred by every well-ordered government, including military assistance in so far as necessary for suppressing revolts and every kind of disorder likely to endanger the peaceful relations between Japan and Korea.	in agreement with Russia, but alone, to Korea's assistance with advice directed to helping her fulfill the obligations incurred by every well-ordered government, including military assistance in so far as it may prove necessary for suppressing revolts and every kind of disorder likely to endanger the peaceful relations between Japan and Korea.
5.	5. In the case provided for in the preceding article, Japan promises to send to Korea only the number of troops absolutely necessary, and to recall her troops as soon as their purpose has been fulfilled. It is agreed, at the same time, that Japanese troops shall never cross the boundary of a district to be defined exactly in the future and situated along and close to the Russian border.
6.	6. On her part Japan recognizes Russia's preferential rights in the districts of the Chinese Empire adjacent to the Russian border, and promises in no way to hinder Russia's liberty of action in these districts.
7. The present agreement replaces all the previous agreements.	7. The present agreement replaces previous agreements.[70]

It will be seen at a glance that the Russians accepted the Japanese demands with respect to Korea with only minor qualifications: Japan was to send troops to Korea only after consultation with Russia, and to withdraw them as soon as possible. In return Russia was to be left a free hand in Manchuria and the other regions bordering on the Siberian frontier. Ito was evidently very favorably impressed with the draft. He was still urging his government not to drop the negotiation. He was not opposed to the alliance with England, he wired to Katsura, and did not suggest an alliance with Russia. All he envisaged was an agreement with Russia on Korea. It was therefore urgently necessary to reserve freedom of action in this matter.[71] Now that he had the Russian terms he renewed his plea. In my opinion, he cabled, we can succeed in concluding

---

[70] " Nakanunie Russko-Iaponskoi Voiny " (loc. cit.), pp. 51–2; Romanov, op. cit., pp. 335–6; Hiratsuka, op. cit., appendix, pp. 42–4 (text); *Documents Diplomatiques Français*, II, no. 4; *Der Russisch-Japanische Krieg. Amtliche Darstellung*, I, p. 16.

[71] Hiratsuka, op. cit., appendix, pp. 39–40 (Ito to Katsura, December 13).

an agreement with Russia, if we start the negotiation at once. Article IV will have to be modified and Article VI clarified, but this will probably be possible. It is a question of " Now, or never." But Katsura refused to accept this argumentation. He did not show Ito's telegram to the cabinet or to the Elder Statesmen, but replied saying that the whole proposal was not in keeping with Japan's dignity. Japan had declared time and again that she favored the territorial integrity of China and equal opportunity for all nations. If she now conceded Russian freedom of action in Manchuria, she would lose the confidence of other powers.[72]

Ito wired an immediate reply to Tokyo, pointing out that the Korean business was of prime importance. If Russia were to accept Japan's views on this question, Japan should be ready to leave Russia a free hand in Manchuria. What he intended to do was to concede Russia as much freedom there as she had had before the occupation of the country in 1900, and such privileges as were beyond the power of Japan to control. Once again he reiterated his conviction that an agreement with Russia was possible, while he pointed out that an agreement with England regarding Korea would be worthless unless Russia was also won over.[73]

On the day after sending this telegram Ito replied to Lamsdorff stating that the question would have to be considered further, but at the same time expressing doubt regarding the feasibility of a permanent agreement. He criticized the Russian draft for its vagueness in Article VI, and objected that in Article IV the Russian demand that she be consulted before troops were sent to Korea was the very negation of the freedom of action which Japan had asked for. At any rate, he asked for more time to think the matter over.[74]

The Russians did not take this to mean a rupture of negotiations. On the contrary, they wanted the agreement and they still hoped it would materialize. Ito, too, cherished the hope that something might still be done. The curious thing is that at the last minute he convinced Katsura. On December 28 and 29 the prime minister cabled to Ito (who was at that time in London) saying that he now realized that the proposal to make concessions to Russia in Manchuria did not go so far as to compromise Japan, and that he hoped Ito could persuade the Russians of his standpoint. He made objection to some of the details of the Russian draft, but expressed readiness to enter upon official negotiations if Russia accepted the Japanese standpoint in the essentials. In any event, however, he hoped to conclude the alliance with England before opening official discussions with St. Petersburg.[75]

---

[72] Hiratsuka, op. cit., appendix, pp. 44–7 (Ito to Katsura, December 17; Katsura to Ito, December 21).

[73] Hiratsuka, op. cit., appendix, p. 47 (Ito to Katsura, December 22, 1901).

[74] Hiratsuka, op. cit., appendix, pp. 47–9 (Ito to Lamsdorff, December 23); Romanov, op. cit., pp. 338–9.

[75] Hiratsuka, op. cit., appendix, pp. 49–51 (Katsura to Ito, December 28 and 29, 1901); see also Hayashi, op. cit., p. 167 on Ito's hope of still coming to an agreement.

It was too late for Ito to continue negotiations before his return to Japan. But early in January he stopped at Paris on his way to Rome and the east. There he found his ardent supporter, Viscount Kurino, newly appointed minister to St. Petersburg. Kurino was very anxious for a pact between Russia, France and Japan, and had accepted the post only on condition that he be allowed to do something toward its consummation. He was horrified to learn from Ito that the Anglo-Japanese Alliance negotiations were already so far advanced, and decided not to go on to St. Petersburg. Ito finally induced him not to give up the ship, and indeed he received a cablegram from home on January 20, 1902 saying that the government favored an agreement with Russia and desired him to discuss the matter with the Russian foreign office. In other words, there can be no shadow of doubt that the Japanese government planned and hoped to make an agreement with Russia right down to the time of the signature of the alliance with England, and that the Russian government had the same expectation.[76]

How the Japanese government could have come to think that the British cabinet would accept an agreement between Japan and Russia collaterally with the Anglo-Japanese Alliance is a mystery hard to solve. From the very outset Lansdowne had made it clear that neither side should make separate agreements regarding China or Korea without consulting the other, and the British draft of November 6 had specifically provided against such agreements.[77] When Ito visited Lord Lansdowne in England early in January he tried to sound him out on this question. Lansdowne then restated the British view. It would depend on what kind of agreement Japan contemplated: " It would obviously be improper that Japan should enter into a bargain with us affecting our common interests in the Far East, and should then enter into another bargain of a conflicting character with a third power." Ito of course repudiated any idea of a " double-handed arrangement," but it is difficult to see how the Korean agreement, as it emerged from the discussions of Ito and Lamsdorff, could possibly have been made to conform with the Anglo-Japanese Alliance. Russia would certainly not have made concessions in Korea excepting in return for concessions in Manchuria, and that would have been in contradiction with the aims of England, as Katsura had pointed out in his correspondence with Ito.[78]

The British had been obliged to wait from November 6 until December 12 for a reply to the draft which was handed to Hayashi on the former date. We know that during these weeks there was much uneasiness in London on account of Ito's peregrinations. But whether the delay in the negotiations with Japan had anything to do with the final phase of the Anglo-German discussions it is impossible to say. All we know is that on November 9 one of the under-

---

[76] Kurino's memorandum on the alliance with England (Hiratsuka, op. cit., p. 58; also Kurino to Ito, January 20, 1902 [ibid., appendix, p. 58]); Hayashi: *Memoirs,* pp. 200 ff. On the Russian expectation see especially *Documents Diplomatiques Français,* II, no. 4.

[77] *British Documents,* II, nos. 105, 125.

[78] Ito's conversation with Lansdowne in *British Documents,* II, no. 120.

secretaries, Mr. Bertie, wrote a long memorandum reviewing the whole Anglo-German problem. Bertie, like Salisbury earlier, discounted the dangers of isolation and noted the fact that Germany in Bismarck's time had made a treaty with Russia behind the back of Austria, so that Germany could not be entirely trusted. The whole memorandum was a reflection of dislike and hostility. Bertie accused the Germans of coveting the seaboard of Holland and also the Belgian Congo. The Germans, he thought, wanted an alliance with England chiefly in order to protect themselves against the danger of an agreement between England on the one hand and France and Russia on the other. The events of the spring had shown that Germany was not to be counted upon for support against Russia in the Far East. At best it might be possible to reach an agreement defining the interests that England and Germany would defend in Europe and the Mediterranean:

> " If once we bind ourselves by a formal defensive alliance and practically join the Triplice we shall never be on decent terms with France, our neighbour in Europe, or with Russia, whose frontiers are coterminous with ours or nearly so over a large portion of Asia. In our present position we hold the balance of power between the Triple and Dual Alliances. There is but little chance of a combination between them against us. . . . Treaty or no Treaty if ever there were danger of our destruction or even defeat by Russia and France Germany would be bound in order to avoid a like fate for herself to come to our assistance. She might ask a high price for such aid, but could it be higher than what we should lose by the sacrifice of our liberty to pursue a British world policy, which would be the result of a formal defensive alliance with the German Empire." [79]

Lansdowne himself made a survey of the negotiations of the spring, emphasizing the fact that the time had come when some sort of answer would have to be given the Germans. He thought that perhaps too much could be made of the safety of isolation: " I think that we may push too far the argument that, because we have in the past survived in spite of our isolation, we need have no misgivings as to the effect of that isolation in the future. In approaching the Japanese we have, indeed, virtually admitted that we do not wish to continue to stand alone." But Lansdowne, too, felt that there were great difficulties in the way of a full-blown defensive alliance, and that these were, at the moment, " virtually insuperable." He enumerated these obstacles, with which we are already familiar from the discussions of the spring. Therefore he, too, rejected the idea of an alliance, though he favored an understanding of a limited nature with regard to certain interests common to both countries. This might be applied to the Mediterranean and possibly the Persian Gulf, and might take a form like that of the Mediterranean Agreements of 1887. In a further memorandum the foreign secretary, at the request of Lord Salisbury, specified the details of such an agreement, which would aim at the maintenance of the status quo in the Mediterranean, Adriatic, Aegean and Black Seas and

---

[79] *British Documents*, II, no. 91.

prevent territorial acquisitions on the shores of the Persian Gulf. It would amount " to little more than a declaration of common policy and of a desire to maintain close diplomatic relations," though it would be to England's advantage to have the status quo upheld and also " to exclude Russia and Germany from establishing themselves strategically on the shores of the Persian Gulf." Lansdowne thought the German government would probably want more and that it would refuse such an overture, but " should they do so, no great harm will have been done, and we shall have put it out of their power to accuse us of having ' dropped ' them." [80]

Salisbury seems to have been dubious about the advisability of this course, but probably gave his consent, for on December 19 Lansdowne had a decisive interview with Count Metternich, the new German ambassador. He once again recapitulated the history of the negotiations. The British government, he said, had thought the alliance proposal over carefully and saw its advantages. But it seemed doubtful whether the government could go before parliament with such a scheme. Metternich remarked that an agreement would probably have ensured peace for half a century and expressed his surprise that England did not " jump at " the opportunity. Her isolation, he thought, was becoming ever more dangerous. To which Lansdowne replied by reiterating his desire for good and close relations, and by suggesting the possibility of special agreements. " His Excellency unhesitatingly replied that no such minor proposal was likely to find favour with the German Government. It was a case of ' the whole or none.' " [81]

Therewith ended the discussion of an Anglo-German Alliance. There was, throughout this final phase, a certain amount of unofficial side play. In the last days of October 1901 Sir Valentine Chirol, foreign editor of the *Times,* paid a visit to Berlin and had a long talk with his former friend, Baron von Holstein. The history of the Anglo-German relationship since 1895 was gone over and the German standpoint set out in detail. Bülow, too, received Chirol, and, so it appears, suggested the possibility of an agreement to uphold the status quo in Europe, Africa, America and the Pacific, leaving Asia to be provided for by the Anglo-Japanese Alliance. It may well be that this was what led to the reopening of the whole subject in the bosom of the British government and what induced Lansdowne to put forward the idea of such an agreement. We know that a report of the Bülow-Chirol conversation was presented to the foreign office. But at all events nothing came of the suggestion and nothing was gained by the later correspondence of Holstein with Chirol. It is of interest chiefly as a reflection of the misapprehension caused by Eckardstein's reports and of the distrust and soreness that remained when the whole matter was finally closed.[82]

---

[80] *British Documents,* II, nos. 92, 93.

[81] *British Documents,* II, no. 94; *Die Grosse Politik,* XVII, no. 5030.

[82] Valentine Chirol: *Fifty Years in a Changing World* (London, 1927), pp. 288–97; Friedrich Rosen: *Oriental Memories of a German Diplomatist* (London, 1930), pp. 179–80, contradicts some points in Chirol's narrative. See further the Holstein-Chirol correspondence and the comments of the foreign office in *British Documents,* II, nos. 96–8.

By this time public opinion on both sides of the North Sea had risen almost to the boiling point, so that the project of an alliance strikes one as something of an incongruity. It was on October 25 that Chamberlain made his famous Edinburgh speech replying to criticisms of British warfare in south Africa. He pointed out that if necessary the English would have to resort to even stiffer measures to make the Boers give in, but that even if they did, they would still be within the precedents set by other nations in war. Among these other nations he mentioned the Germans in the war of 1870. It has been suggested by some writers that Chamberlain's purpose was to notify the Germans that he was through with them, and that he must have known that his remarks would cause offense. This seems more than unlikely, because the colonial secretary included France and other nations in his list and his language, if rightly read, was not insulting, even if it was indiscreet. However that may be, the speech raised a perfect storm in Germany and brought pretty strong complaints from the Berlin government.[83] Immense crowds of students and war veterans heard speakers tell of the " robber raids " in south Africa, the purpose of which was to steal the gold of the Transvaal. Six hundred and eighty German pastors signed a document recounting the legend that the British troops in south Africa fired at the enemy while standing behind Boer women. Reputable newspapers like the *Berliner Neueste Nachrichten* declared that any comparison between the British army, " recruited from the scum of the street," and the German nation in arms was an " insult " to the latter. Here and there efforts were made to stem the tide, notably by the *Frankfurter Zeitung,* the *Kölnische Zeitung* and the Berlin *Post,* but on the other hand eminent writers and artists lent themselves to the agitation. The wave of Anglophobia, which had been steadily rising since the beginning of the Boer War, now reached its crest.[84]

The violent protests and denunciations of the German press were the counterpart of the campaign being waged in England against Germany and in favor of an agreement with Russia. The *Times* defended Chamberlain to the limit, and took care to stress the significance of German hatred:

"It denotes the rancour pent up for years, which has been gradually growing throughout the country, which has become intensified by the war, and which has at last found an outlet in the spontaneous national demonstrations aimed at Mr. Chamberlain directly, but indirectly against the British nation and the policy of Great Britain. No greater mistake could be made than to regard these demonstrations as artificial or to think they are not genuine. They reflect the feeling of the Germans towards the British, a feeling growing in power and capable of becoming one day a serious menace to peace between the two peoples." Or again: "The storm of vituperation . . . represents no passing emotion, but a deep-

---

[83] *British Documents,* I, nos. 324 ff.; *Die Grosse Politik,* XVII, nos. 5073 ff.; Bülow: *Memoirs,* I, pp. 635 ff.

[84] *Times,* November 5, 22, 23, 26, 1901; there is some discussion of this press campaign in Johannes Dreyer: *Deutschland und England in ihrer Politik und Presse im Jahre 1901* (Berlin, 1934), chap. ii.

seated and apparently incurable popular disease of animosity towards the British Empire." [85]

We need not pursue this disheartening and unedifying subject much further. Perhaps the worst part of it was the fact that the governments did not keep clear. The British foreign office quite rightly rejected the idea of giving any explanation or apology. Chamberlain himself became understandably sore. In a speech at Birmingham on January 6 he practically bade adieu to any idea of co-operation with Germany. England, he said, must count on herself alone: "I say alone, yes, in a splendid isolation, surrounded and supported by our kinsfolk." Two days later Bülow declared in the Reichstag that German excitement was quite comprehensible and suggested that ministers would do well, in defending their own domestic policies, to leave foreign nations alone. Not even this was enough for the extremists. On January 10 a rabid Pan-German deputy in the Reichstag called Chamberlain "the most accursed scoundrel on God's earth" (den verruchtetsten Buben den Gottes Erdboden trägt) and characterized the British army as "a pack of thieves and brigands" (Diebe und Raubgesindel). Bülow protested, but not too much. "Seldom, if ever," wrote the *Times*, "has a friendly nation been so grossly insulted in a foreign Parliament, and never within our memory has the insult met with such a mild rebuke." The influential London paper thereupon published two long articles on *The Literature of German Anglophobia*, in which once again the German desire for sea-power and the hope of whipping England were duly underlined. The whole episode may be said to have been closed by a new speech delivered by Chamberlain at Birmingham on January 11, in which he declared: "What I have said, I have said. I withdraw nothing, I qualify nothing, I defend nothing. . . . I do not want to give lessons to a foreign Minister, and I will not accept any at his hands. I am responsible only to my own Sovereign and to my own Countrymen." [86]

The Chamberlain-Bülow debate and the mutual recriminations of the British and German press make a most peculiar setting for the discussion of an Anglo-German alliance. Whether or not the German press campaign was inspired, as Sir Valentine Chirol thought, by the German foreign office in revenge for the refusal of the London government to conclude an alliance, it is unthinkable that a coalition between the two nations, even if worked out and approved by the governments, could have found any real response in the hearts of the peoples. German opinion was undoubtedly a more artificial thing than British opinion, and the alliance project would certainly have met with more effective opposition in the house of commons than in the Reichstag. Lansdowne knew what he was saying when he spoke of the parliamentary handling of the problem as "a stiff fence to ride at." Indeed, we may say that by the end of 1901 British opinion was

---

[85] *Times*, November 23, 26, 1901.
[86] *Times*, January 7, 9, 11, 13; Bülow: *Memoirs*, I, pp. 636–7; Lee: *Edward VII*, II, pp. 137–9, etc.

an insurmountable obstacle to the realization of the project. After the Chamberlain episode the government capitulated entirely and became as suspicious and unfriendly as the press. Cecil Spring Rice, visiting London in April 1902, was astounded at the change of official attitude toward Germany: "Everyone in the (foreign) office and out talks as if we had but one enemy in the world, and that Germany. . . . The change in Chamberlain's mind is most remarkable."[87]

This has been perhaps too long a digression, but it seems justified in view of the great significance of the Anglo-German problem and because of the fact that the position of Germany was an important aspect of the Anglo-Japanese Alliance negotiation. To this we must now return. It will be recalled that Hayashi handed the Japanese draft to Lansdowne on December 12. The main point in the Japanese amendments involved the rejection of the proposal for a general defensive alliance. The Tokyo government felt that the agreement, if extended to India, the Straits Settlements and Siam, would involve a liability which the Japanese could not assume. England was asked further to accept a secret article to this effect: "Great Britain recognises that Japan may take such suitable measures as she deems necessary to safeguard and promote the preponderating interests which she actually possesses in Corea." Further secret articles were to provide that the naval forces of the two powers should act in concert so far as possible, and that either might use the docks and coaling stations of the other; that each of the contracting powers should endeavor to maintain in the Far East at all times naval forces superior in efficacy to the naval strength of any other power which had the largest naval forces in the Far East.[88]

Lansdowne at once pointed out the difficulties inherent in the Korean question. What Japan wanted was virtually a free hand there, and that would mean friction with Russia and possibly war between all the powers. At the same time he objected to any arrangement which would bind England to maintain a certain naval force in any one part of the world. We need not follow the negotiations of December and January in detail, the more so as they have been well analyzed by other writers. Suffice it to say that the naval question was ultimately dealt with separately and in general terms in a diplomatic note. The turning point in the whole negotiation came on December 19, when the British cabinet discussed the alliance question and Lansdowne afterward went over the Japanese draft with Hayashi. Salisbury evidently was not at all enthusiastic about the projected alliance, and Chamberlain thought it was too narrow.[89] The foreign minister was therefore obliged to be firm with respect to the scope of the agreement: "It seemed . . . scarcely reasonable that, while we were to face the possibility of war with two great European Powers in consequence of a dispute between Japan and Russia in regard to Corea, we were not to have any assistance from Japan should we find ourselves involved with the same two Powers

[87] Letters and Friendships of Sir Cecil Spring Rice (London, 1929), I, p. 350.
[88] British Documents, II, no. 115.
[89] Newton: Lord Lansdowne, p. 228; Hayashi Memoirs, pp. 186 ff.

in regard to a dispute as to India." But Hayashi was adamant on this point, asserting that Japan was doing enough in supporting Britain's interests in the Yangtze Valley. In the end the British accomplished nothing in this direction. The treaty remained restricted to what the Japanese called the " Extreme East."

The crucial point in the whole discussion dealt with Korea. The English objected to any separate or secret article on the subject and wanted it embodied in the Treaty itself. Furthermore (and this was the decisive consideration) they did not want to give Japan a free hand in Korea, for fear that she would make use of such freedom to provoke a conflict with Russia. Hayashi, of course, gave assurances that Japan would not lightly engage in war. But he rejected the idea that Japan and Britain should consult first before resorting to action. This would cause delay and frustrate effective operations. And so the debate continued between Lansdowne on the one hand and Hayashi and Ito on the other. The Japanese would accept nothing but recognition of their freedom of action in Korea, but they showed little inclination to entertain a proposal for strengthening the clauses regarding Chinese independence and integrity. Amendment followed amendment and proposal succeeded proposal over a period of weeks, until a wording could be found which gave Japan what she wanted, while at the same time making the concession so unnoticeable that it would not rouse strong opposition in the English parliament. The Treaty as finally signed on January 30, 1902 stated in the preamble that the two governments were actuated solely by a desire to maintain the status quo and general peace in the extreme east and were interested especially in maintaining the independence and integrity of the Empire of China and the Empire of Korea, and in securing equal opportunities in those countries for the commerce and industry of all nations. The all-important Article I was a masterpiece of careful wording. It read as follows:

" The High Contracting Parties, having mutually recognised the independence of China and Corea, declare themselves to be entirely uninfluenced by any aggressive tendencies in either country. Having in view, however, their special interests, of which those of Great Britain relate principally to China, while Japan, in addition to the interests which she possesses in China, is interested in a peculiar degree politically as well as commercially and industrially in Corea, the High Contracting Parties recognise that it will be admissible for either of them to safeguard those interests if threatened either by the aggressive action of any other Power, or by disturbance arising in China or Corea, and necessitating the intervention of either of the High Contracting Parties for the protection of the lives and property of its subjects."

Article II provided that if either party, in defense of its interests as above defined, should become involved in war with a third power, the other party should remain strictly neutral. But if (Article III) any other power or powers should join in hostilities against the ally, the other contracting party should make war in common and make peace in mutual agreement with its ally. The fourth Article provided that neither would, without consulting the other, enter into separate arrangements with another power to the prejudice of the interests above described. Article V stated that if either party thought the above-mentioned interests to be in jeopardy, the two governments should communicate with each other fully and frankly. The final article fixed the term of the Alliance at five years, or longer unless denounced one year in advance by either party. If, at the time of expiration, either party should be involved in war, the Alliance was to continue automatically until peace had been concluded.[90]

The treaty was sent to the British minister at Tokyo with a covering letter which was published with the actual text. This letter reviewed the genesis of the Alliance and its terms, but contained also an explanatory paragraph of some significance:

" His Majesty's Government have been largely influenced in their decision to enter into this important contract by the conviction that it contains no provisions which can be regarded as an indication of aggressive or self-seeking tendencies in the regions to which it applies. It has been concluded purely as a measure of precaution, to be invoked, should occasion arise, in the defence of important British interests. It in no way threatens the present position or the legitimate interests of other Powers. On the contrary, that part of it which renders either of the High Contracting Parties liable to be called upon by the other for assistance can operate only when one of the allies has found himself obliged to go to war in defence of interests which are common to both, when the circumstances in which he has taken this step are such as to establish that the quarrel has not been of his own seeking, and when, being engaged in his own defence, he finds himself threatened, not by a single Power, but by a hostile coalition." [91]

Throughout the course of the negotiations both powers had kept in mind the question of Germany's relationship to the projected pact. The Japanese were clearly anxious to have the Germans associated. They were never able to free themselves from the spectre of a new Russian-German-French combination, and it is very possible that the ostentatious visits of the Tsar to the Emperor William at Danzig and to France in September 1901 helped to revive sad memories of the coalition of 1895. But the Japanese from the outset deferred to the British in this matter, and Lansdowne took the stand that it would be wiser to settle first and consider Germany afterward. By December, that is after the violent press campaign between England and Germany was well under way, there was no further talk of inviting Germany to join, but simply of taking the Berlin government into confidence when the time came. Lansdowne had no hope that the Germans would accede, and probably no longer desired any such thing. He had constantly in mind the problem of bringing the Alliance with Japan through parliament and certainly did not want to complicate

---

[90] *British Documents*, II, no. 125; details of the negotiations may be followed in the *British Documents*, II, nos. 115 ff. and in Hayashi: *Memoirs*, pp. 168–95, where the various amendments are discussed at great length. [91] *British Documents*, II, no. 124.

matters by adding an unpopular agreement with Germany. Furthermore, he felt certain that the Berlin government would approve an alliance which it had itself recommended. Under the circumstances there was no need for more than advance notice. This was the course agreed upon and carried through. The Germans were notified of the terms of the Alliance a full week before the Treaty was published.[92]

The text of the Alliance was laid before parliament on February 11 and was made known in Tokyo on the following day. The news took the British public by surprise and caused no little bewilderment. There had been no audible demand in the press for an agreement with Japan. In fact, the possibility of such a combination was much less discussed in 1901 than in 1898. The British public had come to look with some favor upon the idea of an agreement with Russia, yet here was an alliance which was clearly directed against Russia. It is interesting to note that the *Times,* in a leading article on February 12, while welcoming the agreement as a benefit to China, tried to make out that it was no obstacle to an arrangement with Russia. In the house of lords Lansdowne attempted to anticipate criticism of Britain's abandonment of isolation just after Chamberlain had declared that England must rely upon herself and her colonies in " splendid isolation." The foreign minister insisted that the government could not be deterred by a mere tradition. The old arguments would no longer hold good. The nations were now joined in groups and were heavily armed. War might break out very suddenly, and England therefore had to be prepared. He hoped that the House would not allow itself to be swayed " by any musty formulas or old-fashioned superstitions." Fortunately the government had the support of Lord Rosebery, who declared at once that his first impressions were favorable.[93]

Things were not quite so easy in the house of commons, where Sir Henry Norman, famous expert on Far Eastern affairs, spoke very thoughtfully of the new departure. The Treaty, he pointed out, might bring England into war with Russia and France at Japan's choosing. And for what? " Our only interest in Korea is that it is of very great importance to Japan, whose welfare is always a matter of consideration to us." But Korea was a " worthless country," and it would be horrible to become involved in war on account of it. He had always, said Sir Henry, been in favor of an agreement with Japan, but the question was whether British interests were sufficiently safeguarded in this treaty. It was quite useless to deny that it was aimed at Russia. And yet the most serious political writers and thinkers, from Lord Salisbury down, had come to favor better relations with Russia. Russia had, after all, behaved well towards England during the Boer War. Had the government tried to come to an agreement with her about Manchuria?

---

[92] *Die Grosse Politik,* XVIII, no. 5043 (February 3, 1902); *British Documents,* II, nos. 118, 120, 126, 127; Hayashi: *Memoirs,* pp. 190–5.

[93] Hansard: *Parliamentary Debates,* Series IV, vol. CII, pp. 1174 ff.

To this Lord Cranborne, the undersecretary for foreign affairs, rejoined that "the real origin of this treaty was our anxiety to maintain the status quo in China. . . . This agreement merely follows on principles which have already been accepted by almost every other Power." Thereupon the question was raised by Sir Henry Campbell-Bannerman why, if most powers had agreed to the principle, the alliance was necessary? Balfour defended it by saying that it would make for peace. He agreed that England should have friendly and cordial relations with Russia: "There is no wish dearer to the heart of His Majesty's Government." [94]

The press generally took the Alliance in good grace. In fact, one may take this as a striking instance of the political instinct that leads the British people to recognize their deeper interests. While there had been no agitation for an alliance, there had been a growing feeling of community of interest, a feeling that could have been overcome only by a much more attractive arrangement with Russia. There was, of course, some criticism. William T. Stead thought the text entirely too vague, and pointed out that the statements of ministers in parliament did not agree entirely with the exact wording of the text.[95] Others complained that Lansdowne had exchanged splendid isolation for splendid complication and that he was simply driving Russia and France into the arms of Germany. Russia would take her revenge in Persia, Afghanistan and India, while Japan would play a dazzling game with limited liability. Even if Russia were defeated by Japan, others would suffer by a new explosion on the Bosporus, while Japan would make herself mistress of China and the Far East.[96]

In Japan the Treaty was given a rousing reception. Opinion was practically unanimous in approving it, and for some time there were entertainments and demonstrations to celebrate the new connexion.[97] The German government, too, was quite content: "The noodles seem to have had a lucid interval," remarked the Emperor to Sir Frank Lascelles in expressing his surprise that the British government had not made the agreement earlier.[98]

All this was to be expected. The real question was what the reaction to the agreement would be in Russia and France. The Paris government, which was certainly cherishing hopes of some kind of understanding with England with respect to Morocco, was most disagreeably surprised. Cambon spoke pretty frankly to Lansdowne about the danger of England's being dragged into war with Russia by Japan. The foreign minister tried to soothe him, and pointed

---

[94] Hansard, op. cit., pp. 1273 ff., 1281 ff., 1288 ff., 1295 ff.

[95] William T. Stead: "The Anglo-Japanese Treaty" (Review of Reviews, March 15, 1902, pp. 253-5).

[96] Zeta: "The Anglo-Japanese Alliance — and After" (Fortnightly Review, March, 1902, pp. 365-80); China Station: "A Russo-Japanese War" (Contemporary Review, March, 1902, pp. 424-36); Sir Wemyss Reid: "Last Month" (Nineteenth Century, March, 1902, pp. 506 ff.); Stafford Ransome: "Japan's Imperial Policy" (Fortnightly Review, April, 1902, pp. 565-74).

[97] Times, February 14, 15, 1901; Alfred Stead: "The Anglo-Japanese Alliance from the Japanese Point of View" (Contemporary Review, March, 1902, pp. 437-45).

[98] British Documents, II, no. 128; Newton: Lord Lansdowne, p. 247.

out that England had tried to reach an understanding with Russia but had always found the door closed. In the end Cambon consoled himself with the idea that the British government had concluded this "useless" convention simply to show the public that it had not gone to sleep about Far Eastern affairs.[99]

Most disagreeably surprised was the Russian foreign minister, Count Lamsdorff, who was still hoping for an agreement with Japan. He simply could not understand an alliance which envisaged war at a time when no one was thinking of it, and concluded that the British must have aimed chiefly at the prevention of an understanding between Russia and Japan. His first reaction was to propose a counterblast, and he approached both Germany and France with the the suggestion that they join in a declaration. The Germans declined and the French evidently attempted to evade. It was only in mid-March that the two allies, after prolonged negotiations, agreed to the note of March 20, 1902, in which they declared that they too favored the principles enunciated in the preamble of the Anglo-Japanese Alliance, and then went on to say that, being obliged to consider the possibility of aggressive action by third powers or renewed troubles in China which might jeopardize the integrity and free development of the country, they reserved to themselves the right to take counsel as to the means to be used to safeguard their interests.[100]

This declaration is sometimes spoken of as an extension of the Franco-Russian Alliance to the Far East. This is almost certainly an exaggeration. The document was probably meant only as a demonstration. At any rate, the Russians were not as calm as they pretended to be. Since November they had been negotiating once more with the Chinese and towards the end of January they had come to some sort of compromise regarding the evacuation of Manchuria. In return the Chinese were to sign a separate agreement with the Russo-Chinese Bank which would secure for Russia the concessions she wanted. But in the first days of February the United States government lodged a protest which so stiffened the back of the Chinese that on February 11 they rejected the idea of an agreement with the Bank. There matters stood when the Anglo-Japanese Alliance was published. In the debate in the house of commons on February 13 the British government spokesman stated unequivocally that "Manchuria is no more excluded from the scope of the agreement than any other province of the Chinese Empire." [101] In other words, the Manchurian affair might well lead to a clash between Russia and the new allies. Witte and Lamsdorff therefore decided not to press matters too far. In the face of opposition from Kuropatkin

---

[99] *Documents Diplomatiques Français*, II, no. 81; Combarieu: *Sept Ans à l'Élysée*, p. 178; *British Documents*, II, no. 131.

[100] *British Documents*, II, no. 145, enclosure; *Documents Diplomatiques Français*, II, nos. **97**, 103, 110, 117, 129, 138, 145. On the Russian attitude see further London *Times*, February 15, **17**, 1902; *British Documents*, II, nos. 130, 140, 141, 147; *Die Grosse Politik*, XVII, nos. 5047, 5049, 5050, 5051 ff.

[101] Hansard, op. cit., CII, p. 1247.

they gave up the projected bank agreement, and on April 8 signed an evacuation arrangement which was to take the Russians out of Manchuria within eighteen months. It was the first fruit of the Anglo-Japanese Alliance.[102]

The Far Eastern theme was not, of course, brought to a close by the Alliance of England and Japan. It continued unbroken to February 1904, to the outbreak of war between Russia and Japan over Korea.[103] It would be a mistake, however, to base a judgment of the Anglo-Japanese Alliance upon the later course of events. It is not entirely true that England, finding herself unable to check the advance of Russia in China by an agreement with Germany, thereupon turned to the avowed enemy of Russia, Japan, and sacrificed her highly-prized isolation in order to use the Japanese army to drive out the Muscovite. In the first place one has to face the problem presented by Manchuria. The British had practically recognized the special position of Russia in the three provinces in the agreement of April 1899, and, whatever may have been said later, they acquiesced in the exclusion of Manchuria from the Anglo-German Convention of October 1900 when that instrument was in process of negotiation. In the course of the discussions which led to the Alliance with Japan Count Hayashi said in so many words that Japan was not sufficiently interested in Manchuria to go to war about it, while Lansdowne admitted to Ito that England had never concealed from herself that Russia had special interests there. Though England objected to the terms of the agreement Russia was trying to make for the evacuation of the country, he did not think it probable that these terms would be so objectionable as to force England into war with Russia.[104] In other words, Manchuria really had nothing to do with the Alliance. Neither Japan nor England would fight to keep the Russians out of those provinces. The statements in parliament to the effect that the Alliance extended to Manchuria were probably made chiefly to nip opposition to the agreement.

Why then did the British make the Treaty? Surely it could not have been on account of Korea, where England had very small interests and where Japan could be counted upon in any event to oppose the Russians. Indeed, the great preoccupation of the British in making the Alliance was the chance that the Japanese might utilize it to force the pace in the Korean question and so bring on a war in which England might become involved. A careful study of the documents brings one almost of necessity to the conclusion that the Alliance, which turned out to be a great landmark in British policy, was in itself less impressive in 1901 than it seems to us today. Briefly stated there was a real clash of interests between England and Russia, but not so much in Manchuria as

---

102 The details are given in Glinskii, op. cit., pp. 178–83; Romanov, op. cit., pp. 340–5; Asakawa: *The Russo-Japanese Conflict*, pp. 190 ff.; *British Documents*, II, nos. 135, 136, 143, 144; *Documents Diplomatiques Français*, II, nos. 115, 137.

103 The later stage I have dealt with in some detail in an article " Der Russisch-Japanische Krieg " (*Europäische Gespräche*, 1926, no vi, pp. 279–322).

104 *British Documents*, II, nos. 117, 120.

in China generally, in Tibet, in Persia, in Turkey. Salisbury had for years tried to overcome this antagonism by striking a bargain and there is every indication that in the autumn of 1901 further advances were made to Russia by Lansdowne, who was more convinced than Salisbury that the days of profitable isolation were past. The Russians then as before turned a cold shoulder, for the simple reason that they thought they could get all they wanted without England — that there was little to gain and much to lose. They might well have proved themselves right. They were not far from an agreement with Ito with respect to the main bone of contention — Korea, but the negotiations with Ito were frustrated by the willingness of England to consider an alliance with Japan, an arrangement which struck most Japanese statesmen as more reliable and less costly than a bargain with Russia. What it comes to, then, is that the English made the agreement with Japan in order to prevent an understanding between Russia and Japan, which would have rendered the British position in the Far East almost hopeless. If one looks at the Alliance from this viewpoint there will be less difficulty in seeing why the British gave the Japanese the free hand in Korea and avoided pressing too far their demand for an extension of the Alliance to India. The important thing for England was not what was in *the* Alliance, but the fact that there was *an* Alliance.

Throughout the discussions a distinct note of distrust could be heard. The Japanese were not certain how much England could be depended upon to do, and the British on their side were more than a little suspicious of the use Japan might make of the treaty once she had got it. As a matter of fact there was no ground for this suspicion on either side. War was not nearly as close as many people thought. Russia could not afford it and was anxious to avoid it. France was even more eager to prevent friction, and would have been only too glad to see England brought into an agreement with Russia, or, failing that, to have the Russians and the Japanese make up their differences. But even the Japanese and the British were still hoping to make arrangements with Russia that would obviate the need of war. The Anglo-Japanese Alliance forbade either member making separate arrangements with another power to the prejudice of the interests mentioned in the pact, without consulting its ally. But we have seen that in parliament Balfour spoke of the desirability of better relations with Russia. The English ambassador at St. Petersburg, Sir Charles Scott, explained to Lamsdorff that the Alliance did not diminish the hope of the English government for a frank and friendly understanding with Russia.[105] The leaders of the famous campaign for an agreement with Russia also took this interpretation.[106] All of which forces us to the conclusion that the British did not mean to mobilize Japan against Russia, but still cherished hope that Russia would make an arrangement. And, after all, the efforts of the English to approach the St. Petersburg government did not end in February 1902. They went on and they became

---

[105] *British Documents*, II, no. 140.
[106] A.B.C.: " The Japanese Alliance " (*National Review*, March, 1902).

accentuated in the next years, and they were taken up again just as soon as the Russian-Japanese War drew to its end.[107]

Exactly the same thing was true of Japan. Like the English, the statesmen at Tokyo interpreted Article IV of the Alliance to mean that a separate agreement was permissible provided only that it did not prejudice the interests of the other party. In February Ito at least still expected to come to an agreement with Russia and Lamsdorff still hoped that the discussions opened in St. Petersburg would bear fruit. The plain truth is that in the years 1902–1903 the Japanese did make efforts to reach an understanding with Russia. With the material we have at our disposal now no other conclusion is possible than this: that the Tokyo government went as far as it could to settle the Korean question pacifically. The Russians had only themselves to blame for the war of 1904–1905, and when we say the Russians we need not include either Witte, who fell from power in 1903, or Lamsdorff, who favored conciliation from the outset. We refer simply to the military and naval cliques and the Korean adventurers who captured the imagination of Nicholas II and light-heartedly took up the struggle with Japan. No statesmanship can reckon with the ignorance and blindness of groups like these, and certainly the negotiators of the Anglo-Japanese Alliance did not do so. Taken in the large, then, it is really necessary to reduce the Alliance to its proper proportions and to see it in the perspective of its own time.

BIBLIOGRAPHICAL NOTE

DOCUMENTARY SOURCES

British Documents on the Origins of the War, 1898–1914. London, 1927. Volume II, chapter ix: The Far East, 1900–1901; chapter x: The Anglo-German Negotiations of 1901; chapter xi: The Anglo-Japanese Alliance. One of the most important sources for the history of the Anglo-Japanese Alliance, but not as informing as might have been expected.

Accounts and Papers. 1904, volume CX. *China No. 2 (1904), Correspondence respecting the Russian Occupation of Manchuria and Newchwang.* Contains most of the material on the British side dealing with the Manchurian situation.

Documents Diplomatiques Français, 1871–1914. Series II, volumes I and II. Paris, 1930—. These first two volumes of the great official French publication cover the years 1901 and 1902. They contain some interesting material, though little of prime importance.

---

[107] See my article "Russia, the Straits Question, and the European Powers, 1904–1908" (*English Historical Review*, January, 1929, pp. 59–85).

Die Grosse Politik der Europäischen Kabinette, 1871–1914. Volume XVI, chapter cvi: The Russian-Chinese Agreement of 1901. Volume XVII, chapter cix: The Anglo-German negotiations; chapter cx: The Anglo-Japanese Alliance; chapter cxi: German opinion during the Boer War; chapter cxiv: Near Eastern Questions, including Persia and the Persian Gulf Problems.

ATSUSHI HIRATSUKA: *Ito Hirobumi Hiroku.* Tokyo, 1929. (In Japanese). A source of absolutely first-rate importance, containing over seventy cablegrams that passed between Ito and the government during the crucial months of the Alliance negotiations.

" Nakanunie Russko-Iaponskoi Voiny." (*Krasnyi Arkhiv,* LXIII, 1934, pp. 3–54). Important correspondence between St. Petersburg and Tokyo, together with some of the vital documents relative to the Ito negotiations.

MEMOIRS, AUTOBIOGRAPHIES, BIOGRAPHIES, AND LETTERS

The Secret Memoirs of Count Tadasu Hayashi. Edited by A. M. Pooley. New York, 1915. The material in the Ito documents shows that this remarkable volume of memoirs is entirely reliable. It remains the most important single source in English on the making of the Anglo-Japanese Alliance.

NEWTON, LORD: *Lord Lansdowne.* London, 1929. Useful as a supplement to the *British Documents.*

LEE, SIR SIDNEY: *Edward VII, a Biography.* Two volumes, New York, 1925–1927. Of importance chiefly for the study of the personal factor in the Anglo-German problem.

CHIROL, VALENTINE: *Fifty Years in a Changing World.* London, 1927. Contains some account of the discussions with Holstein and Bülow in the autumn of 1901.

GOOCH, G. P.: " Baron von Holstein." (In his *Studies in Modern History,* New York, 1931). Easily the best study of Holstein in English, and at the same time a compact and reliable review of the Anglo-German problem.

SPECIAL STUDIES: THE ANGLO–JAPANESE ALLIANCE

DENNIS, ALFRED L. P.: *The Anglo-Japanese Alliance.* Berkeley, 1923. A succinct and competent monograph, though now out of date.

ROMANOV, B. A.: *Rossiia v Manchzhurii, 1892–1906.* Leningrad, 1928. For this, as for the earlier period, Romanov is the best Russian account.

GLINSKII, B. B.: *Prolog Russko-Iaponskoi Voiny.* Petrograd, 1916. Based on material from the Witte archives, and reflecting the standpoint of the ministry of finance.

TRUBETZKOI, GREGORY: *Russland als Grossmacht.* Stuttgart, 1913. Written by an official of the Russian foreign office, this book contains much that is of interest, among other things an accurate account of the negotiations with Ito.

CHANG, CHANG-FU: *The Anglo-Japanese Alliance.* Baltimore, 1931. A good book, but remarkably slight and conventional on the making of the Alliance.

OSTWALD, PAUL: "Das Englisch-Japanische Bündnis." (*Berliner Monatshefte,* November, 1931, pp. 1081–98). A thorough analytical study, making use of the British Documents.

LANGER, WILLIAM L.: "Der Russisch-Japanische Krieg." (*Europäische Gespräche,* 1926, pp. 279–322). A detailed study of the background of the war.

MINRATH, PAUL: *Das Englisch-Japanische Bündnis von 1902.* Stuttgart, 1933. The most recent and most detailed treatment, giving a reliable account of the negotiations but indulging in somewhat too much geopolitical speculation. The author, like other writers, has made no use of Japanese materials.

LITERATURE SINCE 1935

(See also the Supplementary Bibliographical Notes to Chapters XIX to XXII.)

HAMADA, KENGI: *Prince Ito.* London, 1937. 240 pp. Based on Ito's works and official papers, this is an important contribution to the story of the Russian-Japanese negotiations of 1901.

ISHII, VISCOUNT KIKUJIRO: *Diplomatic Commentaries.* Baltimore, 1936. 351 pp. These reflections of an eminent Japanese diplomat throw much light on Japanese policy after 1895 and especially on the Anglo-Japanese Alliance.

CRAMER, ANNELIESE: *Die Beziehungen zwischen England und Japan von 1894 bis 1902.* Zeulenroda, 1935. 78 pp. A doctoral dissertation.

SPINKS, CHARLES N.: "The Background of the Anglo-Japanese Alliance" (*Pacific Historical Review,* VIII, September, 1939, pp. 317–340). One of the best and most up-to-date treatments of the subject.

WENIGER, J. M.: *Die historischen Hintergründe des englisch-japanischen Bündnisses von 1902.* Halle, 1943. 450 pp. (typed). A dissertation.

GALPERIN, A.: *Anglo-iaponskii Soiuz, 1902–1921 gg.* Moscow, 1947. 448 pp. An impressive study, despite the Marxian approach. The author examines the development of the alliance from 1898 onward, using all available materials in western languages, as well as some unpublished Russian sources.

XXIV

Reflections

～

The conclusion of the Anglo-Japanese Alliance and the abandonment of British isolation have generally been taken as marking a turning point in the history of pre-war diplomacy. There is something to be said for this traditional interpretation, though it must not be carried too far. At the time of the negotiation of the treaty neither side regarded it as crucial, for both parties still hoped to make some sort of arrangement with Russia. The great problem upon which the new combination hinged was by no means settled, neither was there any way of knowing how, ultimately, it would be settled. In 1902 the war between Russia and Japan was not at all a foregone conclusion. The Russians could have made their peace with Japan on attractive terms. They probably would have done so, had the foreign office not been overridden by the military and naval authorities. To arrive at an accurate estimate of the importance of the alliance between Britain and Japan, it would be necessary to carry the story to its logical conclusion, the defeat of Russia in 1905. But to trace the course of European diplomacy to that year would have obvious disadvantages: it would require full treatment of such entirely new problems and international alignments as the Moroccan question and the Anglo-French Entente of 1904. The temporary settlement of the Far Eastern question overlaps these new developments in a way that admits no logical dividing point. I have, therefore, followed tradition and broken the narrative at the change of British policy.

There is even further justification for this division. The year 1902 marks the end of a generally recognizable period. The Victorian age had drawn to its close and the great tide of imperialism had begun to break on the resistance of the Boers. Imperial problems continued to agitate the international relations of Europe, but disillusionment was setting in and a few years later, after Russia's reverses in the Far East, interest definitely shifted to the old familiar channels of continental politics. It will not be entirely out of place, then, to review the decade following the dismissal of Bismarck and attempt some general estimate of its importance in the history of European diplomacy.

The most striking thing about international relations in this period is the extraordinary complexity. There is not, as in the Bismarckian era, any straightforward development or any understandable system. Everything and everybody seems to be at odds, and the historian finds himself confronted at every turn by almost insuperable problems of presentation. This complexity was the direct result of two factors: one was the breach made in the Bismarckian system by the abandonment of the Reinsurance Treaty, which brought in its wake the Franco-Russian Alliance and the division of the Continent between two alliance systems; the other was the tremendous expansion of the field of possible conflict. Diplomacy had to deal not only with the accepted problems of European politics but with a multitude of world problems. The old questions continue to be of great importance, as a study of the Near Eastern crisis of 1894–1897 will show. But they come to be regarded almost as irritating distractions. The interests of the governments and to some extent of the peoples are focussed upon the ends of the world, upon the Nile, upon the jungles of central Africa, upon the mines of south Africa, upon Mesopotamia, Persia and the whole Far East. The great problems of the period, therefore, were not only the readjustment of international relations necessitated by the break-up of the Bismarckian system and the emergence of a new alignment, not only the continued unrest in southeastern Europe, but also the surge of imperialism, the criss-crossing of colonial aspirations, the development of new and dangerous antagonisms which reacted upon Europe and conditioned the policies of the powers in questions which themselves had nothing to do with extra-European expansion.

Three of the most eminent German historians, Meinecke, Brandenburg and Oncken, together with many other competent scholars, have studied in whole or in part the development of German policy during this period. But German policy was no longer crucial in the nineties. Germany was at the head of a group of allied powers, but the coalition of the central powers was counterbalanced by a new combination. The interplay of these competing systems was important as it was interesting, but the outstanding characteristic of the alliances in these years was their failure to function properly. The Triple Alliance was in process of disintegration and the Franco-Russian Alliance was more or less paralyzed by Russia's unwillingness to act in the matter of Alsace and Lorraine, and by the refusal of France to underwrite the aspirations of her ally in the Near East. In continental problems the powers were deadlocked. There was as much or more occasion and danger of a clash in the Near East in 1894–1897 as in 1875–1878, but there was no general war because the various powers and groups of powers checkmated each other, leaving Abdul Hamid to settle the question in his own way, through massacre and war.

To understand the diplomacy of these years I think attention must be concentrated upon British policy, for two reasons: firstly, because neither the Triple Alliance nor the Franco-Russian Alliance could upset the balance of power on the Continent in its own favor without the accession and support of England; secondly, because the European nations when they turned to world affairs were confronted with a situation in which England easily played the most prominent rôle. She had the empire which the others coveted. They met her at every turn and found her everywhere blocking the road. Even more im-

portant was England's command of the seas. Imperialism and sea-power —
these concepts were inseparable. So long as Britain had her fleets and could
challenge any other power to build beyond her, the continental powers had
their choice between backing down or pooling their forces. In the last years of
the century the British Empire really formed a third grouping in European
international relations. Whether her great power could be drafted in the interests of either of the other two combinations or whether they could coalesce
to overwhelm Britain, was still a question.

It has been the traditional policy of England, according to most historians,
to stand aloof from European affairs, so that in a crisis she might throw herself on the weaker side and prevent the hegemony of any one power or group of
powers. This is the famous theory of the balance of power, a theory which I
think should be discarded with reference to recent history, for the story of
European diplomacy in the past fifty years or more completely contradicts it.
During the Bismarckian period England was associated with the Triple Alliance, a combination which, under German leadership, dominated the Continent as it had rarely been dominated before. France was then the helpless, isolated power and England aided and abetted that isolation. Obviously England
was, in the last half of the nineteenth century, interested less in the balance of
power than in the maintenance of peace. In the heyday of her economic prosperity she had nothing to gain by war and had a good deal to lose even from
war between other powers. England, too, was satiated; in fact, the phrase which
Bismarck applied to Germany was much more appropriate for describing England.

By the balance of power theory England should have welcomed the conclusion of the Franco-Russian Alliance, which divided the continental nations
into two groups of roughly equal strength and theoretically left Britain at the
fulcrum of the balance. Of course we know that such was not the case. The
Alliance was on paper directed against Germany and her allies, but actually
England felt its first and most powerful impact. All historians may not realize
or appreciate this fact, but the British statesmen did. From the very moment
of the Toulon demonstrations and the conclusion of the alliance Downing
Street saw that a crucial decision would have to be made. England could not
hold the balance between the two continental groups because they would not
allow her to do so. With the shift of interest to world affairs there was, from
the very outset, danger of collaboration between the two alliance groups against
their common rival, England. The idea of a continental league was somewhat
nebulous and, as it proved, there were insurmountable obstacles in the way of
its realization. But that does not mean that it did not on occasion function informally or that England did not sense the threat. Co-operation between the
continental powers always implied the possibility of a pooling of naval forces,
which would have created for England a danger of the first magnitude.

Rosebery met this situation in 1894 by an attempt to revive the old connexion with the Triple Alliance. Having failed in that he tried for an agreement with Russia. Salisbury, when he came into power in 1895, followed exactly the same course: he approached Germany with his scheme for the partition of the Otto-man Empire and, having met with a rebuff, set himself to reach an arrange-ment with the members of the other group. Repeated efforts were made to settle outstanding disputes with France, efforts which invariably failed because of England's unwillingness to compromise on the Egyptian question. In much the same way attempts were made to reach a *modus vivendi* with Russia. These have been dealt with in detail in the preceding chapters, but it is worth em-phasizing the fact, which has been very imperfectly understood, that in the en-tire period from 1894 to 1902 the greatest desire of the British government was to come to an agreement with Russia. The most attractive terms were offered, but they were regularly refused, partly because the Russians, with their favor-able geographical position, had little reason to fear the British fleet, partly be-cause their field of expansion was not overseas and they were consequently less exposed to the pressure of sea-power, and partly because the Russians had the feeling that they could get what they wanted without paying England a price. It took the defeat at the hands of Japan in 1904–1905 to bring the Russians to the point of bargaining with England. During the last decade of the century all the European powers still found it more profitable to shelve their own particular antagonisms and work against England, and for that reason the posi-tion of England was the key to the whole problem. England did not go down simply because the continental league never developed to the point where it could strike at her in any matter of vital interest, but especially because she managed to maintain her predominance on the sea. If there was no intervention during the Boer War, it was because the fleet stood between the continental nations and the island empire.

One of the remarkable things about the history of modern England is the singleness of purpose of all parties in the conduct of foreign affairs. There was a veritable cult of the principle of continuity, and it is consequently useless to look for fundamental divergences on matters of major importance. It is true that in 1893–1894 Gladstone and Harcourt were still opposing a policy of ex-pansion and naval increases, but they were overruled by the younger men in their own party. Rosebery and Grey saw eye to eye with their political oppo-nents in questions of foreign policy and national defense. One might even say that Rosebery plotted the policy which was followed by the Conservative-Unionist government after 1895. Rosebery was, in fact, a remarkably able man, with a keen feeling for the movement of interest and opinion. But he was hampered from the start by the drag of mid-century liberal thought and by the tremendous prestige and authority of Gladstone. Furthermore, he lacked the absorbing personal interest in politics which is the mark of the great statesman. Even as a young man he was world-weary, unhappy, and apathetic. He never came up to the expectations of his followers, and never gave them the sure and consistent lead they had a right to hope for from a man of his natural endowment.

The dominant figure in British foreign policy during this period was, of course, Lord Salisbury, who was at the helm during all but three years of it. In many respects Salisbury was the commanding figure of the nineties, as Bismarck was of the eighties. He alone of all European diplomats had the experience, the understanding and the poise of a really great statesman. And yet, Salisbury's accomplishment is bound to strike one as disappointing. The great, bold conceptions were there (consider the Turkish partition scheme, the suggestions to Russia in January 1898, etc.), but the driving energy was absent. We need to know much more of Salisbury's inner thoughts, but even now we can see, from what few personal letters we have, that he was half a generation behind his times. He felt himself out of place, for he realized that international relations were no longer a question merely of political and military power, but were coming more and more to be decided by economic pressures. Furthermore, he was so much the great aristocrat that he never managed to adjust himself to the new democratic conditions. The untutored, emotional crowd was for him a disturbing factor, which he did not know how to handle. It made him feel helpless and embittered, and he resented it. In his later years he tended to drift, to put off vital problems with good epigrams. To the very end he stood firm by the ideas with which he had grown up, and remained proud of British sea-power, sceptical of the dangers of isolation, confident of England's ability to take care of herself, even against heavy odds. He had a keen understanding of the continental peoples, but he did not like them. In the years of tension which closed his career he became cynical and irritable, until purely personal rancor clouded his outlook. He always disliked the German Emperor, whom he considered an ill-bred young whelp and a dangerous man because of his instability. He ended with a strong antipathy toward the whole German people, because of their dislike of England and because of their naval ambitions, the importance of which he was one of the first to recognize. Nevertheless, there was something immensely impressive in the great calm of Lord Salisbury, as there was something sad, almost tragic in his inability to keep up with the times.

Salisbury worked in harness with Joseph Chamberlain, which was remarkable in view of the difference in talent and temperament of the two men. Chamberlain was the true representative of the bourgeois capitalist class that rose to power on the tide of the industrial revolution and liberalism. He was a successful business man who had a keen appreciation of the new world forces and an incomparable understanding of the democratic psychology. Leaving aside his idealism — his social programs, his imperialism, his cult of race solidarity — his views on international relations, I think, were fundamentally sound. Being unhampered by the prejudices and traditions of the foreign office, he could see diplomatic problems in perspective against economic conflict and popular feeling and could approach them without prejudice. For him diplomacy was a business, not an art. At an early date he became convinced that under the new world conditions England could not afford isolation. He sought salvation in the German connexion until trade competition and German interference in south Africa made it seem hopeless. In the years from 1896–1898 he was as much in favor of an agreement with Russia as was Salisbury. He would, indeed, have made any arrangement with anyone so long as England profited. When the Russians turned him down he approached the Japanese, and when they turned a cold shoulder he reverted to the idea of an agreement with Germany. He made them a business proposition which they rejected. He warned them of possible consequences, but they did not heed him. It was a mistake on their part, for Chamberlain found no difficulty in reversing himself once more. After 1901 he set out to reach an agreement with France as the stepping stone to an agreement with Russia. The price was high, but it was paid. With all Chamberlain's keenness, however, with all his directness and energy, he lacked the moderation and finesse which is indispensable for success in diplomacy. His speeches carried the country, but almost invariably estranged foreign powers. With one hand he destroyed what he built up with the other until his name was anathema to the Continent. Rightly or wrongly he came to represent in continental eyes all that was least attractive in the British temperament and policy.

One will look in vain among the European nations for the singleness of policy so characteristic of the British. To be sure, the bases of the foreign policy of all nations rest upon certain conditions and traditions, but within the larger framework remains wide scope for different policies. German policy, for example, was more than anything else a function of her geographic position. The military problem of the war on two fronts dominated German diplomacy after 1870. With almost superhuman astuteness Bismarck managed to build up a central European bloc to meet possible assaults from either east or west. He succeeded, moreover, in maintaining some connexion with Russia and thereby staved off an alliance between that country and France. His management of this situation without estranging England was probably the greatest diplomatic accomplishment of modern times.

In contrast, the "new course" started out by jilting Russia and courting England. At that time the British saw no advantage in a closer relationship with Germany and stood off, while the Russians felt obliged (one can hardly describe it otherwise) to conclude a distasteful alliance with France. This Alliance was directed against Germany and undoubtedly held the threat of a joint attack on two fronts. With the Hapsburg Empire sinking into the morass of domestic discord and the Italians reeling after the Adua disaster, Germany might have found herself in acute danger. As a matter of fact, the Germans were in no serious peril in the ten or twelve years after Bismarck's fall. On the contrary, they actually came to hold the balance of power in Europe, because the Russians had no desire to fight them for France's lost provinces, but even more because both France and Russia were deeply involved in colonial affairs and were so nearly at daggers drawn with England that the line of demarcation in European international relations was not between the Triple Alliance and the Franco-Russian Alliance, but between England and this latter combination. For a time at least Germany could afford the weakening of her allies, and could pursue a free-hand policy, a policy of having two irons in the fire. She could team with France and Russia, or with England, whichever seemed profitable.

Actually, the Germans flirted with the Russians and French, but tried to collaborate with the English. The intervention of Shimonoseki taught them what to expect from the Russians. The English, who were in a tight place, should and probably would offer more, and their good will was of greater importance and value in the field of overseas expansion. Besides, the whole cast of mind of the German statesmen made them incline toward England. The Emperor's impulse in 1890 was to dish the Russians and ally with the English, an impulse so deeply rooted that it was bound to crop out again and again. He was often furious with the English, but the feeling was one of envy and jealousy rather than of dislike or hatred. Neither Caprivi nor Marschall had enough experience to formulate a policy and Baron von Holstein, the soul of the foreign office, was distinctly a man of the English orientation. Whatever else may be said of Holstein, he had nothing to do with either the Kruger telegram or the German naval policy. His political ideas were substantially sound. His chief weakness was that he, like Salisbury, was unable to keep pace with the times. He continued to think in terms of purely continental policy long after other factors had transformed the basis of international relations. There is no indication that he ever really grasped the import of economic changes or that he understood the strong current of imperialism. Besides, Holstein had too much of what Chamberlain lacked — the exaggerated calculation and the too great finesse. His deep-rooted suspiciousness, his rancor, his proclivities for intrigue helped to confuse matters that were already complicated and ended by clouding many issues.

But even if Holstein had not been Holstein, the German foreign office would still have had to reckon with the personality of the Emperor who, if he was brilliant and energetic, was also erratic and unaccountable. Hohenlohe, as we know from his memoirs, regarded it as his chief duty to guide the Emperor and save him from himself. Bülow followed another line. He humored and flattered him and accentuated his worst traits. Bülow's reputation as a statesman has been pretty thoroughly exploded by the publication of his own memoirs. His was a charming, adroit and elusive personality, but he had no deeper seriousness, in fact no depth at all. So far as one can detect he shared the general predilection for the English connexion, but he did nothing to check the naval policy of Tirpitz and offered no resistance to the rising force of popular hatred toward England. Bülow never did anything that was unpleasant or that might injure his own position.

Quite apart from personalities, however, we can see that the connexion between Germany and England was a difficult one to maintain or develop, simply because of the forces already referred to so often. If there was any *one* revolutionary change in Europe in this period it was the spectacular rise of Germany as a great industrial power and as a formidable competitor in the field of foreign trade. Under the circumstances it is hard to see how Germany could have avoided colliding with England. The shock might have been eased here and there, but the collision of economic interests was inevitable. Germany was virtually driven into colonial expansion and consequently into a big navy policy. Commercial pressure and naval rivalry quite naturally disturbed the English and gave rise to a popular dislike of Germany which is hard to measure but not to be underestimated. The French and the Russians were also competitors of the British in the colonial field, but they were not serious trade rivals, so it was easier for the British government to get popular support for concessions to Russia or France than for concessions to Germany. On the other hand, the niggardliness of the English enraged the Germans, who with some justice felt that John Bull, already bloated with colonial spoils, wanted the whole world for his private preserve. He would, if he had to, give up substantial chunks to the Russians or French, but he begrudged the German every trivial bit. It would be hopeless to try to understand the Anglo-German problem in these years without taking due account of this clash of economic forces and of the resulting embitterment on both sides of the Channel.

The Emperor William cherished the illusion that he could influence and guide his cousin, Tsar Nicholas. Looking back on their correspondence we are apt to remember the danger of condescension in personal relationships. Nicholas certainly disliked and distrusted William for his patronizing ways. But the Tsar's likes and dislikes played a relatively unimportant part in the formulation of Russian policy, for Nicholas had such a pathetically weak character that he was little more than the puppet of his ministers. His father was stolid, obtuse and bigotted, but he was firm, even to the point of stuffing the Franco-Russian Alliance down the throat of his objecting foreign office. The foreign minister, Giers, was a decent bureaucrat who believed in a moderate, peaceful policy and in the connexion with Germany. When Berlin refused to renew the Reinsurance Treaty in 1890 it cut off Giers completely. There was no alternative to the French alliance and in the end the Russians felt obliged to capitulate. Giers died in 1895 and was succeeded by Lobanov — grand seigneur, diplomat by profession and man of ideas. His chief idea was to deal England a telling blow, for he hated England and would have liked to see the Continent united against her. It was a stroke of luck for Britain that he died after a year of office, for Lobanov saw things enough in the large to make substantial sacrifices to get what he wanted. His successor, Muraviev, was something of a fool or at any rate a bull in a china-shop. It was he who got Russia so deeply involved in the Far East by the lease of Port Arthur. His strength lay in tickling the vanity of Nicholas. The Tsar, like many weaklings, was constantly dreaming of great achievements. Apparently he always supported suggestions for expansion and conquest. That accounts for the fact that from 1897 onward the influence of Witte began to decline steadily, while the military and naval authorities, notably Kuropatkin, came nearer and nearer to complete dominance. When Lamsdorff, the former assistant of Giers, came into control of the foreign office in 1900, it was already too late to check the forward party. Even when Lamsdorff and Witte stood together they accomplished little. Russian policy was being made by the soldiers who had won over the Tsar and who were, before long, to march him straight into the disastrous conflict with Japan.

Russia was, in these years, the main element of uncertainty. That the Russians did not put the Near East so completely on ice as many have supposed, has been shown in the body of this work. But there was no knowing when or where the Russians would turn. The threat of their advance stretched from the Balkans to Korea and kept Europe generally on tenterhooks. This Far Eastern policy was in most respects indefensible, and was marked throughout by a certain grandiose indifference to the rights and interests of others, by an appalling amount of wrangling within the Russian government and by a reckless levity that could end only in disaster.

We cannot discuss in detail the policy of Austria or Italy. The Austrians were obliged, in this period, to pursue a strictly defensive course. Goluchowski, who was foreign minister after 1895, lacked repose. His policy estranged the Germans and amused the English. It culminated in the status quo agreement with Russia of the spring of 1897, the arrangement which appealed to him least. In Italy there was, naturally, a sharp dividing line between the policy of Crispi and that of his successors. Crispi was the great champion of colonial expansion, for which he tried, rather unsuccessfully, to enlist the support of his allies and of England. This policy, pursued with a kind of cranky excitability, brought Italy into conflict with France, just as the expansion of Germany created friction with England. It all ended at Adua, and for that catastrophe Crispi must be held chiefly responsible. Rudini and Visconti-Venosta, the leading figures after Crispi's fall, were obliged to retrench. They withdrew so far as they could from the extravagant colonial program of their predecessor and tried to make their peace with France. It has often been argued that the estrangement of Germany and England made it necessary for the Italians to loosen the ties of the Triple Alliance. But that is a misleading interpretation of the rapprochement with France, for at that time Anglo-French relations were more tense than the Anglo-German, and the Italians consequently would have been jumping from the frying-pan into the fire. Italy bargained with France not because she wished to, but because she had to. The Anglo-French Entente of 1904 saved her from a difficult situation and enabled her to revive the friendship with England which she had had to sacrifice in the years following Adua. If England and France had not come together the Italians would hardly have thrown in their lot entirely with that of France.

We know less about the inner springs of French policy than of almost any other. We cannot even say why French statesmen like Freycinet and Ribot should have been so anxious to conclude the alliance with Russia. There was, at the time, no danger — real or apparent — of attack by Germany, yet the French leaders were prepared to buy the alliance with milliards of francs of the savings of the parsimonious French peasantry and at the price of tying themselves to the apron-strings of the reckless Russian autocracy. No doubt the Parisian populace dreamed of reconquering the lost provinces with Russian help. But it is inconceivable that French statesmen should have deluded themselves with such expectations. At any rate, the honeymoon of the alliance was short enough. The French got little beyond the satisfaction of irritating England and a few gains in the Far East. In Africa they were left to their own devices. The Russians had no stomach for African adventure.

In matters of foreign policy two men stand out from the endless ranks of French politicians; one is Hanotaux, the other Delcassé. Too little is known of either to form anything like a final estimate. Hanotaux, historian and student of Richelieu, was undoubtedly the more significant. He dominated French policy from 1894 to 1898. A disciple of Jules Ferry, he was immensely impressed with the need for empire. Since under existing circumstances he had to reckon with the hostility of England, he tried to use the Franco-Russian Alliance for imperial purposes. Indeed, he went further and attempted to ease the tension between France and Germany sufficiently to make co-operation in colonial affairs possible. There was a time, in 1896 after the Kruger telegram episode, when Hanotaux and Lobanov might very well have built up something like an effective continental combination against England. Lobanov's death put an end to that possibility, but Hanotaux, right down to his fall, attempted to maintain respectable relations with Germany and to develop collaboration between the two countries. These were the days of the decline in the revenge feeling in France. Personally I think that an agreement between Germany and France was impossible so long as the Alsace-Lorraine question could not be satisfactorily disposed of, but it is not inconceivable that a better feeling might have been established.

Delcassé, who directed French policy after 1898, put an end to all this. From his antecedents we may conclude that he had no use for co-operation with Germany. He should have had but little sympathy for autocratic Russia. His preference probably was, from the very outset, for England and for a revival of the *entente cordiale* of earlier days. But he came into office on the eve of the Fashoda crisis. His preferences could play no part. The English made him drink the cup to the bitter dregs and he was therefore obliged to pursue a protective policy during the next couple of years. His approaches to Germany were hardly meant very seriously, but were intended to forestall German hostility. The Russians had deserted the French in their hour of tribulation, and Delcassé repaid them by throwing himself into their arms. In the years after 1899 the Russians had the French completely in tow. Delcassé could not stop them from rushing into disaster in the Far East. He was lucky to be able to buy off the English in the entente of 1904, even at the price of French claims in Egypt.

We have spoken much in these last pages about personalities. That there was no Bismarck among them is clear. It would be too much to expect a Bismarck in every generation. But in this period a statesman of the highest calibre was needed perhaps more than ever, for it must not be forgotten that international relations were developing to a state of chronic tension. The European territorial settlement was by no means complete. Nationalism was still advancing in southeastern Europe and was threatening the Ottoman Empire with disruption; it was already undermining central Europe and foreshadowing the disintegration of the Hapsburg Monarchy. But for a time many of these currents ran underground. Most impressive was the rising economic pressure on the Continent, the breaking over of European energies into Africa and Asia. I have tried to show, in a separate chapter, how closely this imperialism was bound up with the spread of popular education and the wider application of the principles of democracy. I have tried to show, too, how important a part was played by current sociological interpretations of international relations and by the cramping of human energy by the industrial system. One cannot study this period without marvelling at the exuberance and optimism which went hand in hand with recklessness and confidence in the conduct of foreign affairs. It was taken for granted that the world was marked out by Providence for exploitation by the European white man and that the principle of every man for himself and the devil take the hindmost was natural law. In the writings of the statesmen and in the writings of journalists there is very little trace of deeper understanding. The rise of Japan, the Adua disaster, the Boxer rising, none of these epoch-making events really opened the eyes of Europe. Even Lord Salisbury could see in the world nothing but a few virile nations and a large number of dying nations. The basic problem of international relations was who should cut up the victims. In our own day we have learned otherwise and all this now seems long ago.

Index

i

PRINTER'S NOTE

This book is set on the Linotype in GRANJON, *a type named in compliment to Robert Granjon, type-cutter and printer — 1523–1590, Antwerp, Lyons, Rome, Paris. Granjon, the boldest and most original designer of his time, was one of the first to practice the trade of type-founder apart from that of printer.*

Linotype GRANJON *was designed by George W. Jones, who based his drawings upon a face used by Claude Garamond (1510–1561) in his beautiful French books.* GRANJON *more closely resembles Garamond's own type than do any of the various modern faces that bear his name.*

The book was composed, printed, and bound by The Plimpton Press, Norwood, Massachusetts.